KEITH WILLIAMS

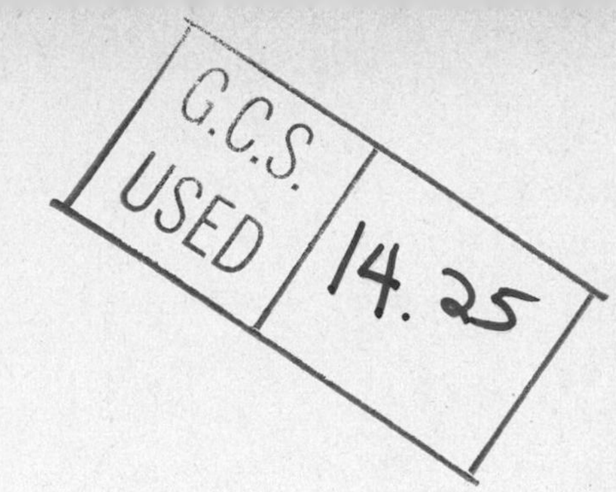

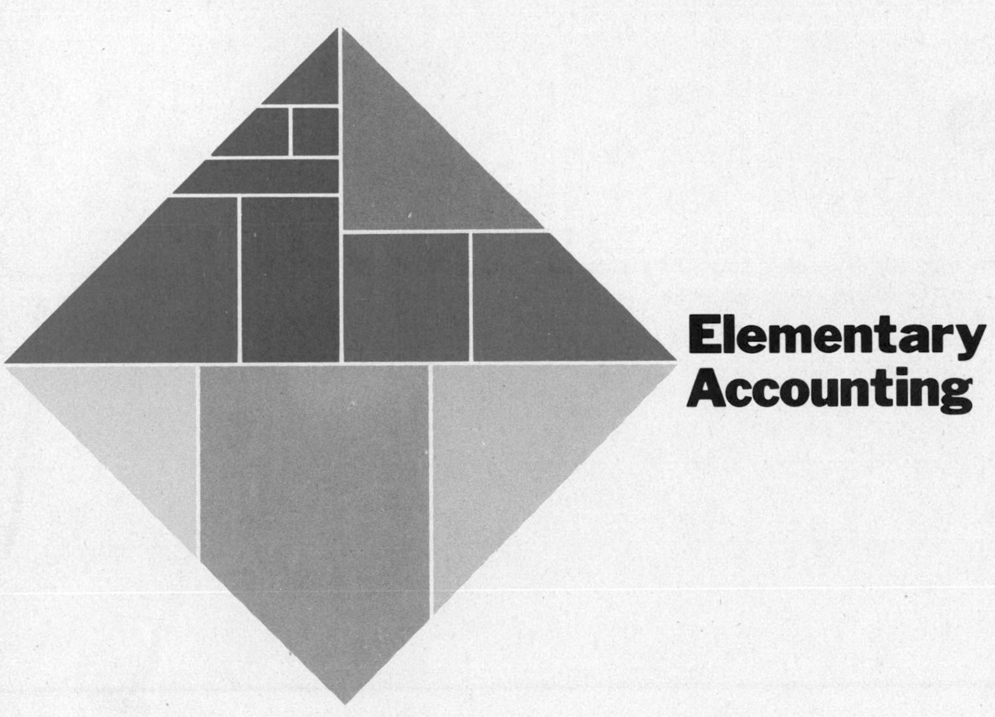

Elementary Accounting

Isaac N. Reynolds, Ph.D.
Professor of Accounting
University of North Carolina at Chapel Hill

Albert Slavin, Ed.M., CPA
Professor of Accounting Emeritus
Northeastern University

Allen B. Sanders, Ph.D., CMA
Professor of Accounting
Elon College

Elementary Accounting

The Dryden Press
Hinsdale, Illinois

A division of Holt, Rinehart and Winston, Publishers

Library of Congress Catalog Card Number: 77-81248
ISBN: 0-03-018021-X
Printed in the United States of America
9 039 9876543

To our wives
Dorothy, Beatrice, Maple
for their patience, understanding,
and inspiration

Preface

From the beginning of this project, it has been our intent to develop a book that students can read and understand. We realize there are many complex issues that beginning students have difficulty understanding. We have attempted to minimize these difficulties by using careful explanations, simple language, and familiar illustrations. The emphasis in every chapter is on teaching accounting fundamentals.

Thus, *Elementary Accounting* is a completely new book written with the student in mind. It is the result of a three year effort by the authors and a team of more than 35 reviewers to develop a teachable, easy-to-understand, first year accounting text. It is designed for a two-semester or three-quarter sequence. Strong points of the book include its readability, the thoroughness of topical development, and chapter organization. The book makes maximum use of comprehensive illustrations so that students are not constantly jumping from one set of names and numbers to another.

Organization of this book

The book is divided into seven parts:

1. The accounting model
2. Accounting systems
3. Income measurement and asset valuation issues
4. Accounting objectives and standards

5. Organizational forms and reporting issues
6. Cost accumulation and control
7. Income taxes

Part 1 (Chapters 1–7) develops step-by-step the elementary accounting model. Using the single proprietorship form, the first six chapters explain and illustrate the concepts and techniques of the steps in the accounting cycle. Chapter 7 covers accounting for a merchandising firm.

Part 2 (Chapters 8–10) continues to use single proprietorships to introduce various accounting systems or sub-systems. Chapter 8 uses special journals to illustrate overall accounting systems. Chapter 9 explains payroll systems and Chapter 10 discusses both cash control systems and the voucher system.

Part 3 (Chapters 11–14) deals with income measurement and valuation issues relating to various assets. These chapters also use the single proprietorship to illustrate and explain basic concepts in more depth.

Part 4 (Chapter 15) begins the second half of the book with a discussion of authoritative bodies who make or influence the rules in accounting. Also covered in this chapter are the generally accepted accounting standards (principles) discussed and then illustrated in a model set of financial statements complete with footnotes for a large single proprietorship, the Tarrant Trading Company.

Part 5 (Chapters 16–22) opens with a description of the various business organizational forms. Chapters 16, 17, and 18 develop the accounting ideas related to partnerships and corporations. Then the accounting for the issuance of bonds and accounting for investment in bonds and stocks is discussed. Chapter 21 illustrates the statement of changes in financial position using the T-account method. It is felt that the T-account method is easy for the student to understand. It gives students a basic understanding of the content of this fourth major financial statement. Chapter 22 has an extensive coverage of financial statement analysis and interpretation.

Part 6 (Chapters 23–27) describes cost accumulation and control for general manufacturing operations, job order, process cost, and standard cost systems. Job order and process systems are covered in two separate chapters followed by chapters on budgeting and the use of cost information in management decisions.

Part 7 (Chapter 28) is a one-chapter part which explains basic concepts, the formula for computation and tax planning for federal income taxes.

An end-of-book Appendix contains a short discussion of business combinations accompanied by a set of consolidated financial statements from an actual corporation. These statements are complete but short and simple enough to be understood by students whose only exposure to accounting has been this text.

Special teaching features of the book

Elementary Accounting contains many features that will enhance the teaching of accounting to students who have had no business experience.

1. Learning goals at the beginning of each chapter are listed. The student is told what major concepts he or she is expected to understand.
2. Key terms the reader should understand after reading a chapter are listed at the beginning of each chapter. Every key term is defined in the chapter and in the glossary.
3. A glossary at the end of each chapter defines each key term for that chapter, as well as other terms used in the chapter.
4. The debit-credit-balance form of ledger account is emphasized throughout the book starting with Chapter 3.
5. The totality of accounting is emphasized in the early chapters. This should enable the student to see the big picture while learning specific techniques and relationships.
6. Many of the key concepts are highlighted for easy recognition.
7. The book's first fourteen chapters deal with the single proprietorship form. The second fourteen chapters introduce the more complex corporate entity.
8. A wealth of teaching diagrams and flow charts are contained in the book.
9. A number of optional topics are placed as appendices to chapters. Any one or all of the appendices may be omitted with no loss of continuity; or they all may be taught with the chapters. Examples are reversing entries (appendix to Chapter 6) and valuation concepts (appendix to Chapter 14). This organizational feature gives the instructor much flexibility.
10. Each chapter contains one or more class exercises. These enable the instructor to illustrate an application of each major chapter concept. They may be used also in classroom laboratory situations or as homework.
11. Other end-of-chapter material includes questions, exercises and problems for in-class or out-of-class assignments. The exercises and problems are of three kinds: (a) brief single concept problems; (b) integrative problems which integrate in one problem most of the concepts discussed in the chapter; and (c) minicases—short, people-oriented type problems requiring decisions by men and women acting as administrators, owners, and investors.
12. There is a sizeable section on cost accumulation and control of which all students should have some knowledge. It opens with a simple chapter on accounting for a manufacturing firm. Some instructors may want to use only this chapter while others may find it desirable to continue with the material in Chapters 24–27.
13. Chapter 26 describes and illustrates a complete budgeting structure for a manufacturing concern. In this comprehensive illustration, the ultimate emphasis is on profit planning. A natural follow-up to this theme of profit planning is a consideration of standard cost accounting which is discussed in the latter part of Chapter 26.
14. Chapter 28 incorporates the changes in income tax laws made by the Tax

Reduction and Simplification Act of 1977 which made sweeping changes to the basic tax structure.

15. For convenience, the Check List of Key Figures is included at the end of the text.

The teaching package

In addition to the text, this package includes the instructor's manual, solutions manual, two test banks, transparency acetates, two practice sets, a study guide, and working papers.

For the instructor

1. *Instructor's Manual.* This manual is unlike any other manual that accompanies an elementary textbook in accounting. Separate from the Solutions Manual, it contains six sections as follows:

I. Guide to the use of the Instructor's Manual
II. List and description of elements in the learning package
III. Suggested assignments
IV. Guide to the appendices
V. Chapter organizers for each chapter
   A. Summary of major concepts
   B. Behavioral objectives
   C. Lecture notes
   D. Content analysis of problems and exercises
VI. References to authoritative sources (including a brief summary of each FASB pronouncement up to October 1977)

2. *Solutions Manual.* Contained in this manual are answers to all end-of-chapter questions, solutions to class exercises, and solutions to exercises and problems.
3. *Transparency Acetates.* Two sets of transparencies are included: (a) solutions to class exercises and to exercises and problems, and (b) teaching transparencies illustrating important figures and illustrations in the text.
4. *Test Banks.* Each of the test banks contains two parts: (a) a set of 25 true-false and multiple-choice questions for each chapter (these are suitable for computer scoring), and (b) a set of achievement tests for each semester consisting of (1) periodic tests for logical chapter groupings, (2) a mid-term examination, and (3) a comprehensive final examination. Test banks A and B include the same depth of coverage and level of difficulty. Solutions are included with the test banks. Achievement tests are provided on spirit masters for ease of duplication.

For the student

1. *Study Guide* by Allen B. Sanders. This learning aid is different from the usual workbook of exercises found with most accounting texts. In programmed format, the *Study Guide* is keyed directly to this textbook; it literally leads the student through some of the more difficult concepts in the book.
2. *Working Papers* (two volumes). In a volume for each half of the textbook, there is a working paper designed for each class exercise and for each exercise and problem. Some of the working papers for earlier chapters are partially completed; in later chapters, the working papers contain less help for the student.
3. *Practice Sets*. This learning package includes two practice sets:
   a. *Ronald Gilbert, CPA* by J. Allan Lander is a service business using a general journal, a general ledger, an accounts receivable ledger, and an accounts payable ledger. It is designed to be used after the student has completed Chapter 6.
   b. *Inland Boat Distributors* by Donald A. Nelson is a merchandising practice set. It uses special journals, a general ledger, subsidiary ledgers, and perpetual inventory cards. A single proprietorship, it is designed to be used after the student has completed Chapter 13.

Unlike most practice sets accompanying introductory texts, these are designed to be of practicable length for the average student.

Acknowledgement to members of the team

The development of this book and its supplementary materials has been underway for more than three years. Dozens of instructors from community colleges, technical institutes, four-year colleges and universities made up the team that reviewed and helped reshape the original manuscript into its present form. Although we are forever in the debt of those who reviewed the manuscript and gave other assistance, we take complete responsibility for any errors which may still be present in the book. Some of these dedicated teachers, practicing accountants, and students whose suggestions have made this work possible are listed below.

C. E. Belinn
Golden West College

Donald H. Clement
Essex County College

Ronald Copeland
University of South Carolina

R. B. McCosh
Colorado State University

Bill J. Mehrens
San Jacinto College

Buster Miller
Amarillo College

Janie E. Council
Elon College

Sherman H. Dearth
Mesa Community College

Thomas P. Dent
St. Louis Community College at Florissant Valley

L. E. Dreyfous
West Valley Joint Community College

John P. Farmer
Orange Coast Community College

Alan Gilman
New York City Community College

Anthony W. Jackson
Loyola University of Chicago

Dan R. Johnson
Richland Community College

B. D. Kalinski
New Hampshire College

George A. Katz, Jr.
San Antonio College

Frederick D. Kenamond
University of Southern Mississippi

William L. Kimball
Eastern Michigan University

Duncan Kretovich
Michigan State University

J. Allan Lander
Montgomery County Community College

Robert Leshin
Miami-Dade Community College

R. W. Magers
Tarrant County Junior College District

John Mathias
Mercer County Community College

Frances Murray
Peat, Marwick and Mitchell

Lynn Murray
Florida Junior College

Don Nelson
Merrimack College

Vincent Pelletier
College of DuPage

W. T. Pickle
California State University-Long Beach

Earl Purkhiser
Mt. San Antonio College

Michael Scanlon
Peat, Marwick and Mitchell

A. J. Schneider
University of Illinois-Circle Campus

Barry Smith
DeAnza College

Bonnie Slager
Santa Ana College

Jeffrey Slater
North Shore Community College

Lanny Solomon
University of Toledo

Charles E. Thompson
El Camino Community College

Rose Trunk
Harper Community College

James W. Walden
Sinclair Community College

John R. Ward
Pace University

In addition to the foregoing group, we would like to thank our colleagues at our respective schools who gave us encouragement through various discussions about the project and who read parts of the manuscript and made suggestions to us. We would like to thank especially the 1977 summer school students at Elon College who class tested the entire text and made many suggestions to us.

Chapel Hill, North Carolina	Isaac N. Reynolds
Boston, Massachusetts	Albert Slavin
Elon College, North Carolina	Allen B. Sanders

Table of contents

The accounting model

part one

chapter one

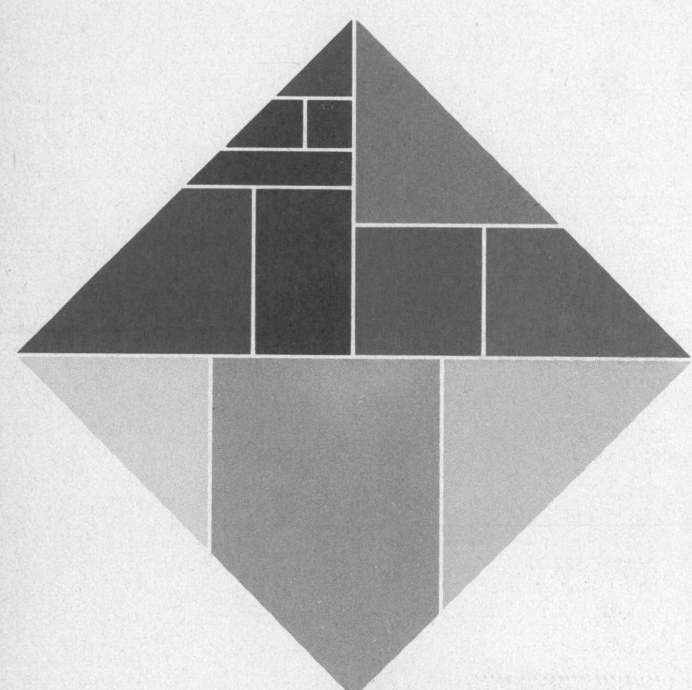

Introduction

Chapter 1 explains what accounting is and traces the history of accounting back to about 5000 B.C. It explains who uses accounting information and describes some ways in which this information serves as the essential basis for the decision-making process. It discusses the profession of accounting and the types of work that accountants perform.

With knowledge of uses and users of accounting, the methods and techniques in this book take on more meaning. Chapter 1, then, begins the development of the basic structure of accounting.

The environment and basic structure of accounting

Learning goals

To appreciate the reasons for the study of accounting.
To be able to define accounting.
To identify the various users of accounting information.
To compare some ways users make decisions with accounting information.
To have an idea of the nature of accounting as a profession.
To acquire a brief knowledge of the history of accounting.
To relate accounting to other fields of study.
To describe the entity concept.
To know and understand the basic accounting equation.
To recognize assets, liabilities, and owner's equity.
To be able to read a balance sheet and to know its classifications.

Key terms

accounting
accrued
asset
attest function
audit
balance sheet
bonds
budget
capital budgeting
CIA
CMA
controlling
CPA
creditors
current assets
current liabilities
entity
external users
internal users
liabilities
long-term liabilities
notes
owner's equity
planning
statement classification

Accounting information is used in making decisions about how wealth is to be distributed all over the world. How many loaves of bread to put on a supermarket shelf in New York or in Paris is decided by looking at records that show how many are usually sold in that store each day. The price of a loaf of bread in Los Angeles depends upon the costs of making the dough, baking it, the wrapper and transportation to get it on the shelf of a store. To know these costs every group in the chain from the farmer to the merchant needs accounting information. What people buy depends upon the amount of income they have. Salaries and wages, unemployment benefits, social security payments, interest on savings and their many other sources of income are all based on accounting records. The same is true of large companies; management decides to build new buildings or purchase new equipment if their accounting information indicates money can be made available and that these actions would be profitable. The term *profit* is used to describe the reward to an organization for bringing together men and resources to render services, to make and sell products, or to accomplish another objective. Because accounting is so important to society, this book is intended to provide a basic understanding of how accounting information is developed and how it is used. Decision making will be shown to be the primary reason for accounting records and reports.

Definition of accounting

Accounting consists of the gathering of financial and other economic data. In the metric system the basic physical unit of measure is the meter. In accounting in the United States and Canada the basic financial unit of measure is the dollar. Just as physical measurements are provided by the metric system, economic measurements are provided by the accounting system and are stated in financial terms. These economic measurements are put together in reports that carry the information essential for planning the activities, for control of the operations, and for decision making by managers of business units.

Accounting also provides financial reports that are needed by outside persons who invest in business units, lend money to them, or extend credit to them. Accounting also furnishes reports to be used by government agencies who regulate business and by tax authorities such as the Internal Revenue Service who must determine that the correct amount of tax is collected. When the unit accounted for is a not-for-profit organization (such as a school, hospital, church or other charitable group) its members and those who contribute to it need to know for what purposes and in what proportions their money is being used. Accounting reports tell them.

Definition of accounting

In summary,* accounting *is the set of rules and methods by which financial and economic data are collected, processed and summarized into reports that can be used in making decisions.

The next few sections of this chapter add to the picture of what accounting is all about. They provide some history of accounting, present a discussion of the uses of accounting in decision making, and describe the types of work that accountants do.

History of accounting

Some of the world's first documents came into existence as early as 5000 B.C., because the need to account for holdings of wealth prompted the development of a form of writing referred to as script.[1] The temple priests of Sumer operated a tax system that brought under their control vast stocks of grain, animals and estates. It was necessary for these priests to develop accounting methods to (1) maintain managerial control of collections, loans, repayments and other transactions and (2) give an account of their management over these holdings. Another writer has described in detail some of these accounting records.[2] He notes that: "Daily summaries were then collected into weekly summaries, and so on to yearly and even multiyearly summaries."

The Egyptian civilization, covering a broad span from about 5000 B.C. to 525 B.C., is described as one in which great construction projects were completed involving the labor of thousands of people, the operation of large stone quarries, and the large-scale transportation of building materials. Out of these operations arose a need for an information system to keep details of transactions both in business and government affairs. In Babylonian textile mills in existence about 600 B.C., production control records were kept and women workers were paid based upon the amount of their production. In 1494 an Italian monk named Luca Pacioli included a section on bookkeeping in a mathematics

Figure 1–1 An early accounting record

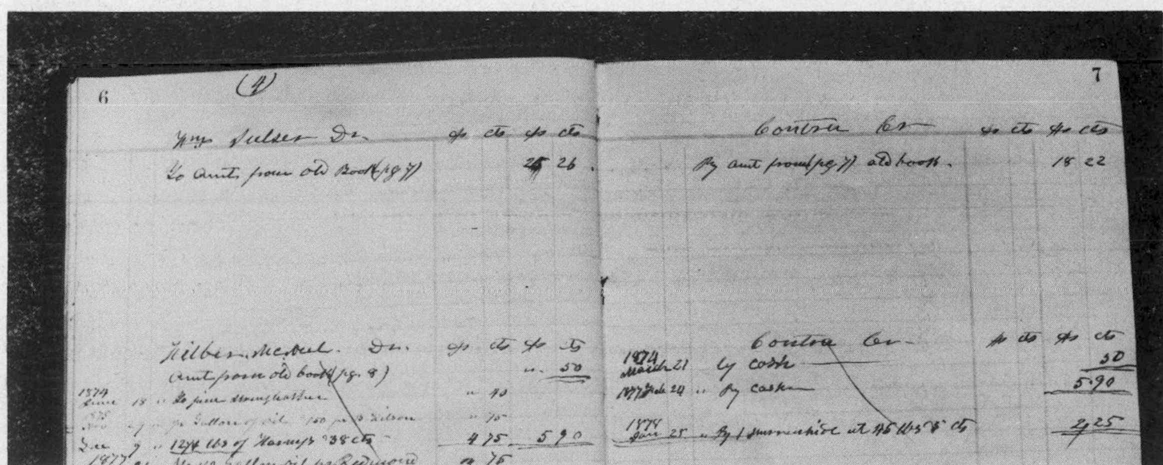

1 Claude S. George, *The History of Management Thought,* (Englewood Cliffs, N.J.: Prentice-Hall, 1968).

2 Blan McBride, "Accounting for Management in Early Mesopotamia," an unpublished paper prepared at the University of Illinois at Urbana-Champaign.

Figure 1–2
An annual report

textbook. This was the first known printed description of double entry bookkeeping.

In early America, accounting generally served to maintain records of business dealings of a firm with its customers. Figure 1-1 shows how a dealer in leather goods kept such accounting records.

As the United States moved toward an industrial economy, the appearance of large companies created requirements for more accounting information. New inventions brought forth new products and rapid population growth helped create a demand for them. Accounting methods and techniques had to be developed to meet those changes. Today almost every large commercial firm renders an annual report such as the one illustrated in Figure 1-2. Annual reports in booklet form contain financial information useful to a great variety of readers.

Why study accounting?

A group of accounting educators joined together in 1971 to study the approach to teaching the introductory college course in accounting. This group was sponsored by a national accounting firm, Price Waterhouse and Company. Its report said that "The purpose of accounting is to provide information that is useful in decision making affecting resource allocation. . . at all levels in society. . . ."[3] Each of us must make financial decisions daily. Those decisions

3 *A New Introduction to Accounting: Report of the Study Group on Introductory Accounting* (New York: Price Waterhouse and Company, 1971) p. 11.

will be much better if the person who makes them understands how the information upon which he or she relies was developed. In business and in personal transactions the person with a knowledge of accounting will have a distinct advantage.

Another reason to study accounting is that many persons work directly in the field of accounting. They may record purchases and sales, compute payrolls, or obtain cost and expense information in business firms. Others may work in not-for-profit organizations or in government. Some work as accountants; others in tasks involving sales, production management, personnel, and many other functions. They all need record systems to show how money of the organization was used and they need to be able to read and understand financial reports.

Many persons work in public accounting. Some keep records for organizations that are too small to afford their own accounting departments. Others perform a function known as *auditing;* this involves an independent review of the financial records of an organization. Public accountants also perform management services such as the design of accounting systems or help businesses with preparation of their tax returns. No matter what job a person holds in the accounting field, he or she will want to become an *expert in the field* of accounting.

Perhaps the most important reason of all to study accounting is that practically everybody must use accounting information in their personal and business lives. In the next section are some examples of people not in accounting jobs who depend upon accounting information. These persons need to know how to interpret the information that is available to them. If they understand accounting, their interpretations will be more likely to lead to sound choices among the many possible courses of action that may be open to them.

Who uses accounting information?

External users

External users are persons or groups outside an organization who need and use accounting information about that organization. Following are some examples of such external users.

Investors seek information that will allow them to study and compare the financial health and earning ability of business firms. Investors are individuals and groups who provide money that allows business firms to operate and to grow. Sometimes they lend money to a business firm, thus becoming *creditors*. A bank, for instance, may become a creditor of a firm by lending money in exchange for a formal written promise to repay called a *note*. Individuals or institutions (for example, large insurance companies) with excess funds on hand lend those funds to large corporations by buying *bonds*. Bonds are another form of formal written promise to repay a loan. In either case, the lenders (or creditors) receive interest in payment for the use of their money.

Sometimes investors would rather invest as owners. These investors who are owners—not creditors—receive payment for the use of their money when the company in which they invested distributes to them a portion of the profits. Most large companies mail checks for a share of the profits to owners four times per year. Owner investors may be individuals, insurance companies, large universities, or any other organizations that have accumulated more cash than they need for day-to-day expenditures.

As a basis for their investment decisions, all investors are dependent upon accounting information included in financial reports. In deciding whether or not to invest in a particular company, investors ask questions such as: Does this company have a history of profitable operations? How does its rate of profit compare with other companies? Does this company already owe an unreasonably large amount of money to banks or to other creditors? What amount of profits can be expected on an investment? How does that amount compare with expected returns from other possible uses of available cash?

Contributors to not-for-profit organizations such as community funds, churches, colleges, service clubs, and similar organizations need accounting reports. They want to know how their funds are being used so they can determine whether or not the organization deserves continued support and what the amount of such support should be. Persons who make charitable contributions obviously cannot give to all causes that appear to be worthy. They ask questions such as: What percentage of each contributed dollar actually reaches earthquake victims? What percentage of it is used for administrative expenses? For further fund raising? Does the organization already have a large amount of unused funds on hand? They look to accounting reports for the answers.

Taxing authorities, regulatory agencies, and other governmental institutions use accounting information. Income tax returns are financial reports to governmental agencies prepared with information taken directly from accounting records of individuals and businesses. The reports accompanying payment of taxes to fund federal social security programs or to fund unemployment compensation payments are based upon payroll records. Reports of collection of sales taxes as well as federal excise taxes must be based on accurate records of sales.

Important to consumers is the use of accounting reports by governmental regulatory commissions. Some of these commissions have the legal authority to set the rates that may be charged for services to the public. Rates that public utilities such as gas or electric producers are allowed to charge usually are based on the concept of allowing those companies to earn a fair, but not excessive, profit. It is not surprising, therefore, that the law establishing most such regulatory agencies allows them to prescribe accounting systems for and to require accounting reports from the firms subject to their regulation.

Internal users

Internal users of accounting are those users in an organization who must make management decisions regarding operations. Functions of management include planning, controlling, and a multitude of daily decisions regarding costs of operation.

Planning is the management function that defines the goals and objectives of the operation; a major portion of the planning is financial. Budget preparation is an important part of the planning function. A *budget* is simply a financial plan for a future period. Usually a budget covers one year and is developed in organizational detail. The starting point in preparing a budget is the accounting records of the current and prior years.

Controlling is the management function of checking on the day-to-day operations of an enterprise and taking action when necessary to redirect operations toward accomplishment of plans. The primary element of the controlling process is a group of special reports provided by the accounting system to each responsible manager. These periodic reports contain information that compares planned performance with actual performance, enabling the manager to exercise control. Typical is a report to the sales manager. It would show planned sales of merchandise to date compared with actual sales to date.

Cost determination is another management function. Many internal decisions require information about costs of operation. The setting of prices is an example. A firm may have to bid competitively against other firms for a specific job; if the price it bids exceeds cost plus a reasonable profit, it probably will not be awarded the contract. On the other hand, if the firm bids less than its cost to perform the job, it may be awarded the contract but will also incur a loss.

A federal law, the Robinson-Patman Act, prohibits discrimination in prices quoted to different buyers except where it can be demonstrated that actual cost differences were incurred while supplying different customers. Accurate accounting records are critical if the firm is asked to defend itself against criminal charges of price discrimination.

Other decisions that managers often face are *capital budgeting* decisions. These decisions involve the commitment of large amounts of funds to buy, to overhaul, to replace or to repair machinery, buildings, and equipment. Many businesses invest substantial sums in inventory, the merchandise items they intend to resell. For each inventory item carried in stock, decisions must continually be made about the best quantity to buy on the next order. Sometimes the basic question is: Shall the company make or buy the product it sells? In production operations, choices must be made between hiring and training additional workers or using the present work force on an overtime basis. In decisions such as these, managers use cost information provided by the accounting system. The expected costs of different courses of action are compared and management will decide upon the most profitable course of action.

What accountants do

About 150,000 accountants in the United States have passed a uniform national examination and are designated by state laws as *Certified Public Accountants* (CPAs). One of the major jobs of a CPA is independent review of the financial records of an organization (auditing). After the review, the CPA issues an audit report, which contains an opinion as to the fairness with which the organization's accounting reports reflect its financial condition and operating results. This professional role is referred to as the *attest function* of accounting. CPAs perform other types of work besides auditing. They do tax work for clients, they help design accounting systems, and they render other management services.

More than 800,000 other accountants work in every type of institution in society. Unlike the CPAs, who are licensed under state laws to perform public accounting, they work at various levels in business, government, government-related, and not-for-profit organizations. Some of them hold certificates attesting to their professional competence. The *Certificate in Management Accounting* (CMA) is granted to persons who demonstrate ability in management accounting by passing a national examination. Other accountants hold a *Certificate in Internal Auditing* (CIA). These internal auditors perform a review function, but solely of the records of the firm by which they are employed. Although much of accounting work is highly specialized and is performed in many types of organizations, the greatest number of accountants work at keeping the records of commercial enterprises. For this reason, the illustrations and problems in this book will focus mostly upon private business.

The entity concept

To understand accounting one must first clearly understand the meaning of an *accounting entity*. Suppose that Wesley Alexander owns a grocery store, a hardware store, and a service station. Suppose that he also has a car, a residence, some stocks and bonds and some other personal items of value. These are shown in graphic form as follows:

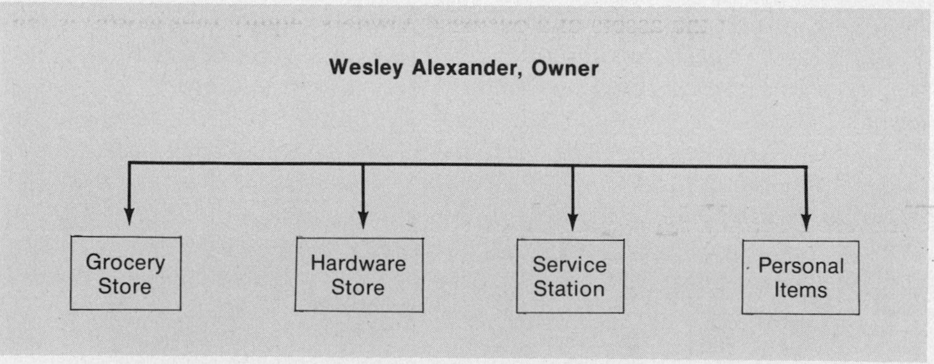

If total attention is focused on Wesley Alexander, the accountant may lose sight of the individual business and economic units. The accounting information for all of Alexander's activities lumped together is useless in making decisions for any single unit. A set of records must be provided for *each* of the individual business and economic units. The focal point of attention must be the individual unit rather than the owner. Each such unit is an accounting entity.

An **accounting entity** *is any organizational unit for which financial and economic data are gathered and processed.*

Accounting entity

Assets

The *assets* of a business are everything of value found in the business. The word value is used here in the sense of future usefulness to a continuing business enterprise. Cash, notes and accounts receivable (amounts owed to the business through transactions on credit), land, buildings, and high-grade, readily marketable stocks or bonds of other companies (marketable securities) are examples of assets in a business.[4] An asset is recorded on the books of the acquiring entity at its full cost even though it has not been fully paid for in cash; the amount of any debt or claim against the asset is shown as a liability.

Equities: liabilities and owner's equity

Equities are claims against the assets of a business. The two major classifications of individuals who have equities in a business are the *creditors* (liability holders) and the *owners*.

The *liabilities* of a business are owed to the creditors. Liabilities are claims of the creditors against the assets of the business unit. Accounts payable and notes payable, amounts owed by the business through purchases on credit, are some liabilities that a business may have. Wages owed to employees is another example.

Owners' equity (capital and proprietorship are alternative terms) are ownership claims against the assets of a business. Owners' equity (net worth) is the excess of total assets over total liabilities. Because creditor claims have priority over claims of the owner or owners, another name for owners' equity is residual claims.

The accounting equation

Because equities represent the total claims against assets, assets must equal equities. This relationship is shown on the next page.

4 Some items—for example, the loyalty of a work force—cannot be stated in dollar terms. Such items are not currently listed in the accounting records. Much research in this area is underway now; it is usually referred to as *human resources accounting*.

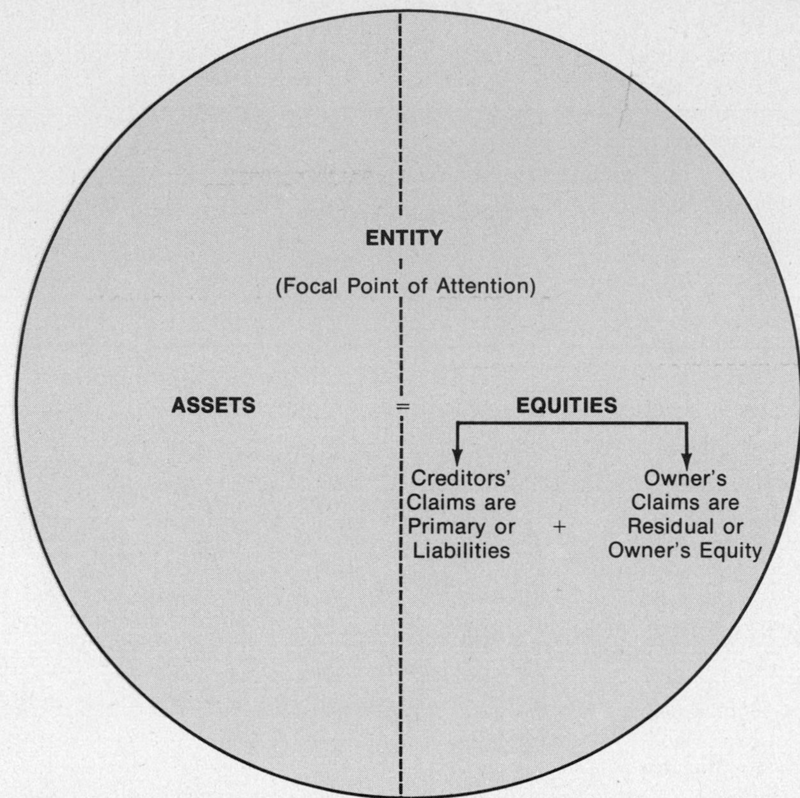

As illustrated, the equities of the unit are broken down into the primary claims—those of the creditors—and the residual claims—those of the owner(s).[5] Since assets are derived from these two sources, the following is true.

$$\text{Assets} = \text{Liabilities} + \text{Owner's Equity}$$

This is the *basic accounting equation,* which expresses the financial position of any business entity at all times. The term *net assets* often is used in business. It may be expressed as follows:

$$\text{Assets} - \text{Liabilities} = \text{Net Assets}$$

The balance sheet

The *balance sheet* is an expanded expression of the accounting equation. It summarizes the assets, liabilities, and owner's equity of a business entity as of

5 Note that owners may be singular or plural. There may be a single owner, two owners or several owners of any individual business entity.

Assets = Liabilities + Owner's Equity

MODERN CLOTHING STORE
Balance Sheet
December 31, 1979

Assets			Liabilities and Owner's Equity		
Current Assets			Current Liabilities		
Cash	$ 325.00		Accounts Payable	$12,060.00	
Marketable Securities . .	1,900.00		Notes Payable	2,060.00	
Accounts Receivable . . .	11,025.00		Accrued Wages Payable .	970.00	
Notes Receivable	2,520.00		Total Current Liabilities		$15,090.00
Merchandise Inventory . .	14,750.00				
Prepaid Insurance . . .	275.00				
Office Supplies	26.00		Long-Term Liabilities		
Store Supplies	89.00		Bank Loan Payable		
Total Current Assets .		$30,910.00	(due June 1, 1982) . .	$ 4,000.00	
			Mortgage Payable	10,000.00	
Plant and Equipment			Total Long-Term Liabilities		14,000.00
Land	$ 3,000.00				
Building	10,000.00		Total Liabilities . .		$29,090.00
Store Equipment	2,500.00				
Delivery Equipment . . .	3,250.00		Owner's Equity		
Total Plant and Equipment		18,750.00	Thomas Parker, Capital .		20,570.00
Total Assets		$49,660.00	Total Liabilities and Owner's Equity		$49,660.00

Figure 1–3
Balance sheet

a specific point in time. This statement is also called a statement of financial position. A common form of balance sheet with the accounting equation superimposed is shown in Figure 1–3. Another form of the same statement is shown in Figure 1–4. Both are acceptable forms. They simply express the basic accounting equation in greater detail by showing amounts of specific asset, liability and owner's equity items.

The balance sheet is a snapshot of the status of assets, liabilities, and owner's equity at any moment. Operations that take place later will make changes, but the basic equation is always true.

The heading of any financial statement usually contains three lines of information.

1. Name of the business.
2. Name of the statement.
3. Date of the statement or period of time covered.

The date given in the balance sheet shows that it presents the financial position of the firm as of the close of business on December 31, 1979.

Dollar signs are used on formal typed or printed statements at the top of each column of figures. A new column is created whenever a line is drawn for addition, subtraction, or other reasons. A double line is drawn under any amount that is the final result of a series of calculations.

Figure 1–4
Balance sheet

MODERN CLOTHING STORE Balance Sheet December 31, 1979		
Assets		
Current Assets		
Cash	$ 325.00	
Marketable Securities	1,900.00	
Accounts Receivable	11,025.00	
Notes Receivable	2,520.00	
Merchandise Inventory	14,750.00	
Prepaid Insurance	275.00	
Office Supplies	26.00	
Store Supplies	89.00	
Total Current Assets		$30,910.00
Plant and Equipment		
Land	$ 3,000.00	
Building	10,000.00	
Store Equipment	2,500.00	
Delivery Equipment	3,250.00	
Total Plant and Equipment		18,750.00
Total Assets		$49,660.00
Liabilities and Owner's Equity		
Current Liabilities		
Accounts Payable	$12,060.00	
Notes Payable	2,060.00	
Accrued Wages Payable	970.00	
Total Current Liabilities		$15,090.00
Long-Term Liabilities		
Bank Loan Payable (due June 1, 1982)	$ 4,000.00	
Mortgage Payable	10,000.00	
Total Long-Term Liabilities		14,000.00
Total Liabilities		$29,090.00
Owner's Equity		
Thomas Parker, Capital		20,570.00
Total Liabilities and Owner's Equity		$49,660.00

Need for classification in a financial statement

Statement classification

Classification *is the arrangement of financial statement items into groupings that have some common basis of similarity.*

A financial statement should be classified if it is to be of maximum value to an analyst, banker, creditor, employee or other interested person. It can be made more easily understandable by the manner in which the terms are arranged. The kind of classification and the order of arrangement to be shown in the statement depend on tradition, the nature of the business activity, and the expected use of the statement. In the example the assets and liabilities of the Modern Clothing Store are classified as to their nature.

Classification of assets—current assets

Current assets consist of cash and other assets that are expected to be converted into cash or to be used in the operation of the business within one year. Current assets are usually listed in descending order of their probable liquidity (expected conversion into cash). The current assets of the Modern Clothing Store in order of liquidity are the following:

Cash Cash is any item that a bank will accept as a deposit and that is immediately available and acceptable as a means of payment. Cash includes coins, currency, checks, money orders, and the amount on deposit in the entity's checking account.

Marketable securities Businesses that have a temporary excess of cash on hand and want to earn interest on it may buy promises to pay issued by other companies (usually referred to as commercial paper) or by governmental agencies or institutions (notes or bonds). Since these can readily be resold whenever cash is needed, they are called marketable securities.

Accounts receivable Accounts receivable represent the amounts due from customers for services rendered, for merchandise, or for any asset sold on credit (open account). Figure 1–5 shows a simple sales ticket for a piece of merchandise sold on credit resulting in an account receivable.

CHARGE SALE

7996052

Modern Clothing Store

Account Number 123-4567-89

Name Marcia Pulaski

Date	Sold by	Store No.	Dept.
12/19/79	132	2	4422

Qty	Description	Price	Amount
1	Gloves		12.50
2	Ties	7.50	15.00
		Tax	1.10
		Total	28.60

Credit Authorized JP.

Marcia Pulaski

Customer's Signature

Figure 1–5
Sales ticket

Notes receivable Notes receivable are formal written promises to pay a fixed amount of money on a future date. Most notes can usually be exchanged for cash at a bank.

Merchandise inventory Businesses that offer products for sale must have them readily available. All the merchandise on hand at any given time is called merchandise inventory. Merchandise inventories are found on retail store shelves and in stockrooms or warehouses.

Prepaid items Prepaid items are unconsumed current assets that have been acquired for the purpose of consumption during the next twelve months. Some common prepaid items are:

Prepaid insurance Every business must protect itself against hazards. Consequently, businesses take out insurance policies for protection. The cost of this type of protection is called an insurance premium and is paid in advance. Insurance policies commonly are issued against such hazards as fire, burglary, personal injury, business interruption, and injury to employees (workmen's compensation). The unexpired portion is an asset.

Office supplies Supplies such as stamps, stationery and business forms required in an office are grouped under the title Office Supplies and are current assets of the business.

Store supplies Store supplies include wrapping paper, twine, paper bags, and similar items used in a store. They are also classified as current assets. Office supplies and store supplies to be used in the general operation of the business should not be included in the merchandise inventory.

Classification of assets—plant and equipment

Plant and equipment comprises assets used over a long period in the operation of the business. These assets are customarily listed on the balance sheet according to the degree of permanency; the most permanent item is listed first. Some typical plant and equipment assets are:

Land Land is shown separately. Although land and the buildings on the land are usually sold together, they are classified separately because the buildings will deteriorate through usage, whereas the land will not. Land is considered to be the most permanent asset.

Buildings Buildings owned by the business appear on the balance sheet. Rented buildings are not owned and are, therefore, not assets.

Store equipment Showcases, counters, and shelves are typical permanent items of store equipment used in selling the merchandise inventory.

Delivery equipment Delivery equipment consists of trucks, cars, and other types of equipment owned that are used for the delivery of products to the customer.

Classification of liabilities—current liabilities

The term *current liabilities* is used principally to designate obligations whose liquidation (payment or settlement) is reasonably expected to require the use of current assets or the creation (substitution) of other current liabilities. All liabilities to be paid within a one-year period are classified as current. In general, current liabilities are listed in their probable order of liquidation; those that are expected to be paid first are shown first, those to be paid next are next, and so on. Some typical current liabilities are:

Accounts payable Accounts payable result from purchases on credit. They are the unpaid amounts owed to creditors from purchases on an open account arrangement. They are usually due to be paid within thirty days.

Notes payable Notes payable are the opposite of notes receivable. They are formal written promises by the entity to pay money to creditors. Trade notes payable arise from the purchases of merchandise or services used in the course of business. Notes payable to a bank arise when a company borrows money for business use. Notes payable are classified as current liabilities unless the date for payment is more than one year in the future. Figure 1–6 illustrates a sample note payable.

Accrued liabilities *Accrue* means to increase by growth or to accumulate in a uniform manner. Accrued wages payable and accrued interest payable are typical accrued liabilities. These are debts that have accumulated because of

Figure 1–6
Notes payable

Courtesy: North Carolina National Bank

$2,060.00 November 21, 1979

3 months ---------after date, for value received and with interest payable at maturity

at 8 % per annum, the undersigned promise(s) to pay

to **NORTH CAROLINA NATIONAL BANK** or Order

Two thousand sixty and No/100 ----------------------------------Dollars
payable at any office of the North Carolina National Bank in North Carolina. Interest shall be computed on the basis of a 360 day year for the actual number of days in the interest period and interest shall accrue after maturity or demand, until paid, at the rate stated above.

The holder of this note may accelerate the due date hereof or require the pledging of collateral as security herefor, or both, at any time the holder deems itself insecure. In the event the indebtedness evidenced hereby be collected by or through an attorney at law after maturity, the holder shall be entitled to collect reasonable attorneys' fees. The Bank is hereby authorized at any time to charge against any deposit accounts of any parties hereto any and all liabilities hereunder whether due or not.

All persons bound on this obligation, whether primarily or secondarily liable as principals, sureties, guarantors, endorsers or otherwise, hereby waive the benefits of all provisions of law for stay or delay of execution or sale of property or other satisfaction of judgement against any of them on account of liability hereon until judgment be obtained and execution issued against any other of them and returned unsatisfied or until it can be shown that the maker or any other party hereto has no property available for the satisfaction of the debt evidenced by this instrument, or until any other proceedings can be had against any of them; also their right, if any, to require said Bank to hold as security for this note any collateral deposited by any of said persons as security for this demand, or any other demands. Demand, presentment, protest, notice of protest and notice of dishonor waived by all parties bound hereon. Witness my/our hand(s) and seal(s).

Address 123 Front Street, Anywhere, USA Modern Clothing Store (Seal)

Due February 21, 1980 No. 07286 Owner (Seal)

NCNB 2151 REV. 5-73

the passage of time but are not yet due for payment. These items are customarily placed last among the current liabilities.

Classification of liabilities—long term liabilities

Debts that are not due for at least a year are called *long-term* (or fixed) *liabilities*. There is no particular sequence in which long-term liabilities should appear in the balance sheet.

Mortgage payable A mortgage payable is a debt owed by the business for which specific assets are pledged as security. The legal document by which the debt is secured and in which the pledge of assets is made is called a mortgage. A business may arrange a long-term loan with a bank, for example, and give to the bank as security a mortgage on its land and building. If the business fails to meet the terms of payment of the mortgage, the bank can take necessary legal action to assume possession of the assets, or to sell them and pay the mortgage claim from the proceeds of the sale. Any balance remaining from the sale of the asset reverts to the business.

Bonds payable As a means of raising funds, some businesses borrow money by issuing bonds. Bonds are long-term promises to repay funds that are borrowed; they usually extend over a period of ten to thirty years.

Classification of ownership claims—owner's equity

The form of a business organization determines the manner of reporting the owner's equity on the balance sheet. Many businesses are owned by individuals; they are referred to as *single proprietorships*. The Modern Clothing Store is a single proprietorship owned by Thomas Parker. His equity is shown on the balance sheet as follows (See Figure 1–3)

```
Owner's Equity
  Thomas Parker, Capital . . . . $20,570.00
```

The owner's equity for the single proprietorship is listed with the name of the proprietor, followed by the word "Capital." The total owner's equity is shown as one item, because there are no legal restrictions on withdrawals by a single proprietor. The early parts of this book will deal only with accounting for single proprietorships. Two other forms of business, partnerships and corporations, will be described in Chapter 16.

Making accounting data more useful

An organization experiences hundreds of individual economic events in a typical business day. For example, there may be sales, purchases, collections, payments, borrowing, and a variety of other happenings. Each of these makes some change in elements within the basic accounting equation. Methods and procedures are needed for recording each of these changes and summarizing them into an updated balance sheet. Such procedures are explained and illustrated in Chapter 2.

A real-life example

> BUSINESS OPPORTUNITIES
> Chance of a lifetime! Owner must sell now. Dry cleaning shop and laundromat. Buyer take over building, equipment, receivables, and payables. Own your own business for $12,000! Call Mr. Webb—555-6071.

John Smith had wanted to go into business for himself for some time. This looked as if it may be his chance to become his own boss. Things looked even better after he called Mr. Webb and went to look at the business. The building was new and the equipment appeared to be in good condition. Only a few customers showed up while John was there, but Mr. Webb explained that it was the off-season. Mr. Webb also told John that the total value of the building and equipment was $25,000.

John asked an accountant for advice and was told, "Ask to see the latest balance sheet." The next day, upon looking at the business balance sheet, John saw that total assets were $25,000 just as Mr. Webb had told him. But he also noticed that current liabilities added to $7,200 and that there was an item entitled Mortgage Payable of $12,500 under long-term liabilities. Remembering that the ad said the buyer must take over payables, John computed the owner's equity that he would really be buying. Total assets of $25,000 minus total liabilities of $19,700 equals a net asset value of $5,300. John Smith realized that he would be paying $12,000 for an owner's equity of less than half of that! Thinking to himself that it had been a good move to ask the accountant for advice, John politely told Mr. Webb that he would continue to look for a while before investing in his own business.

Glossary

Accounting The discipline that provides information which is useful for the making of economic decisions.

Accrued Accumulated or grown over a period of time.

Asset A thing of value owned by an entity.

Attest function The independent review of an entity's accounting reports accompanied by an opinion as to fairness of presentation.

Auditor An accountant who makes an independent review of an entity's accounting reports.

Balance sheet An expanded expression of the accounting equation which summarizes the assets, liabilities and owner's equity of an entity as of a specific date.

Bonds Long-term written promises to repay a specified amount and to pay interest.

Budget A financial plan for a future period developed in organizational detail.

Capital budgeting Decisions to make major expenditures on plant and equipment.

CIA Holder of the Certificate in Internal Auditing.

Classification (*See* Statement classification.)

CMA Holder of the Certificate in Management Accounting.

Controlling The management function which consists of monitoring actual versus planned activity, and taking corrective action where appropriate.

CPA A certified public accountant.

Creditors Persons or groups to whom debts are owed.

Current assets Cash and other assets that will be consumed or converted into cash within one year.

Current liabilities Liabilities to be paid within one year.

Entity The focal point of attention of accounting records; an organization such as a business.

External users Individuals, groups or organizations outside the enterprise.

Internal users Individuals within the firm who need accounting information.

Liabilities Everything owed to creditors; creditor claims against assets of the entity.

Notes Short-term or long-term written promises to repay borrowed money.

Owner's equity Residual claims of owner(s) against the assets of an entity.

Planning Setting the goals and objectives for a future period.

Statement classification Grouping of similar elements of the accounting equation in a financial statement.

Questions

Q1–1 What is the distinction between external users and internal users of accounting information? Give two examples of each.

Q1–2 What are some of the types of organizations in which accountants work?

Q1–3 What is the work of a CPA? How does one become a CPA? Explain the significance to our present-day economy of the attest function.

Q1–4 What is an accounting entity?

Q1–5 How would you define an asset? A liability? An owner's equity item?

Q1–6 What determines when an asset is classified as a current asset?

Q1–7 What is the basic accounting equation? Explain the nature of a balance sheet in terms of the elements of the accounting equation.

Q1–8 What are five examples of current assets?

Q1–9 What are three examples of current liabilities?

Q1–10 What are three examples of plant and equipment?

Class exercises

CE1–1 Harold Weaver has a checking account, a savings account, and ownership of a general merchandising store and a wholesale distribution center. How many accounting entities are involved?

CE1–2 On each line below, provide the missing amount:

	Total Assets	*Total Liabilities*	*Owner's Equity*
1.	$10,000.00	$ 3,000.00	$?
2.	?	16,000.00	3,000.00
3.	27,000.00	?	18,000.00

CE1–3 On each line below provide the missing amount.

	Current Assets	*Plant and Equipment*	*Current Liabilities*	*Long-term Liabilities*	*Owner's Equity*
1.	$ 6,000.00	$19,000.00	$5,000.00	$10,000.00	$?
2.	17,000.00	23,000.00	?	18,000.00	12,000.00
3.	?	30,000.00	8,000.00	25,000.00	10,000.00
4.	6,000.00	?	3,000.00	20,000.00	5,000.00
5.	10,000.00	36,000.00	5,000.00	?	21,000.00

CE1–4 Identify each of the following as (1) a current asset, (2) a plant and equipment item, (3) a current liability, (4) a long-term liability, or (5) an owner's equity item:

a. Accounts Payable
b. Accounts Receivable
c. Bonds Payable
d. Buildings
e. Cash
f. Delivery Equipment
g. Frances Caroll, Capital
h. Land
i. Notes Payable (due June 17, 1984)
j. Notes Receivable (due 60 days from date)
k. Office Supplies
l. Prepaid Insurance
m. Store Equipment

CE1–5 On December 31, 1979, the following captions and amounts appeared on the balance sheet of Paul McLaughlin, Electronics Consultant:

Accounts Payable	$ 9,500.00
Accounts Receivable	39,200.00
Accrued Wages Payable	2,120.00
Bank Loan Payable (due June 1, 1983)	10,000.00
Bank Loan Payable (due June 1, 1980)	5,000.00
Office Supplies	1,500.00
Prepaid Insurance	3,140.00
Shop Equipment	12,000.00

Required:

1. Compute the amount of the current assets.
2. Compute the amount of the current liabilities.

CE1–6 Neutroma Oxygen Supply Service is owned and operated by George Neutroma. He has the following assets and liabilities on June 30, 1979:

Cash	$ 5,000.00
Accounts Receivable	11,198.00
Repair Parts	2,160.00
Building	40,000.00
Repair, Cleaning and Refilling Equipment	12,000.00
Accounts Payable	6,824.00
Accrued Wages Payable	1,600.00
Mortgage Payable	28,000.00
Long-Term Notes Payable	10,000.00
Land	5,000.00

Required: Prepare, with a proper heading, a classified balance sheet. (Hint: You will need to compute his owner's equity.)

Exercises and problems

P1–1 The loan officer of a bank is considering a request from Miller's Pet Shop for a 60-day loan. She obtained the following balance sheet figures from Miller's accountant by telephone:

Cash	$ 2,000.00
Accounts Receivable	26,000.00
Merchandise Inventory	32,500.00
Land, Building and Equipment	46,000.00
Accounts Payable	7,500.00
Notes Payable	?
Mortgage Payable	20,000.00
John Miller, Capital	58,000.00

After hanging up the phone, she realized she had failed to write down the amount of notes payable.

Required:
1. Compute the amount of total assets.
2. Compute the amount of total liabilities.
3. Supply the missing figure that represents the amount of notes payable.

P1–2 The following items appear in the accounting records of the Campus Shop. Identify each of them as (1) a current asset, (2) a plant and equipment asset, (3) a current liability, (4) a long-term liability, or (5) an owner's equity item.

a. A group of glass display cases carried under the title "Store Equipment."
b. An amount due to a book publisher for a shipment of textbooks that have been received for sale to the students.
c. A van used for pickup and delivery of merchandise.
d. Cash in the cash register.
e. A fire insurance policy that has been paid one year in advance covering the stock of merchandise.
f. A note payable to the local bank that is not due for three years.
g. An item entitled "Buck Bayliff, Capital."
h. An amount owed to the Campus Shop for raquetball equipment purchased on a 30-day charge account.
i. Paper bags with the Campus Shop emblem that are used to package customer purchases.
j. A 60-day note due from a student who was unable to pay her account on time and asked for an extension.

P1–3 Each of the following describes a balance sheet item:
1. Money on deposit in the business checking account.
2. A fire insurance policy for the year 1979 with premiums paid on January 15, 1979.
3. Unpaid amounts owed to suppliers.
4. Marie Miller's residual claim against the total assets of her hat shop.
5. Stamps and boxes of blank forms used to send out bills to customers monthly.
6. Unpaid amounts owed to the business by customers.
7. An amount due to be paid to a bank in sixty days that is covered by a formal written promise to make the payment.
8. The unpaid amount due on the building. It is to be paid in ten years with the building pledged as security in a legal document.

Required: What title (or caption) should be given on the balance sheet to each of the foregoing items?

P1–4 All the following are current assets. They are listed in alphabetical order:

Accounts Receivable	Notes Receivable
Cash	Office Supplies
Marketable Securities	Prepaid Insurance
Merchandise Inventory	Store Supplies

Required: Rearrange this list to place the items in the proper sequence for a balance sheet.

P1–5 Following, in alphabetical order, are some of the items found in the balance sheet of Marsha Company on December 31, 1979:

Accounts Payable	$20,000.00
Accounts Receivable	8,000.00
Building	40,000.00
Cash	2,100.00
Delivery Equipment	17,500.00
Land	10,000.00
Notes Payable (due March 1, 1980)	6,000.00
Notes Receivable (due April 15, 1985)	10,000.00

Required:
1. Compute total current assets.
2. Compute total current liabilities.
3. Comment on the ability of Marsha Company to pay its current debts.

P1–6 Halfpenny Flying Service has used an inexperienced bookkeeper who prepared this balance sheet on December 31, 1979. Although no items are omitted, there are some errors in the statement.

HALFPENNY FLYING SERVICE
Balance Sheet
December 31, 1979

Assets

Current Assets		
Cash in Business Bank Account	$12,100.00	
Cash in Mary Halfpenny's Personal Checking Account	1,020.00	
Aircraft and Equipment less unpaid balance due of $9,020.00	90,980.00	
Accounts Receivable	7,000.00	
Total Current Assets		$111,100.00
Plant and Equipment		
Land	$18,000.00	
Hangar and Maintenance Equipment	49,500.00	
Rent Payable on Office Building	4,000.00	
Total Plant and Equipment		71,500.00
Total Assets		$182,600.00

Liabilities and Owner's Equity

Current Liabilities		
Notes Payable (due June, 1984)	$40,000.00	
Accounts Payable	3,800.00	
Accrued Salaries Payable	2,100.00	
Total Current Liabilities		$ 45,900.00
Long-Term Liabilities		
Mortgage Payable (due in 1989)	$12,000.00	
Estimated Amount of Mary Halfpenny's 1979 Income Taxes Payable	11,100.00	
Total Long-Term Liabilities		23,100.00
Total Liabilities		$69,000.00
Owner's Equity		
Mary Halfpenny, Capital		113,600.00
Total Liabilities and Owner's Equity		$182,600.00

Required:

1. List the errors in the foregoing statement and explain how each erroneous item should have been handled.
2. Ms. Halfpenny's equity in the business is obviously incorrect. Compute the correct amount for Mary Halfpenny, Capital.

P1–7 (Integrative) Jake's Amusement Center has the following items as of June 30, 1979:

Cash	$ 7,650.00
Accounts Receivable	16,797.00
Prepaid Insurance	3,240.00
Land	6,000.00
Building	60,000.00
Equipment	18,000.00
Accounts Payable	10,236.00
Wages Payable	2,200.00
City Property Tax Payable	200.00
Long-Term Notes Payable	15,000.00
Mortgage Payable (due 1986)	42,000.00
Jake Smith, Capital	?

Required:

1. Compute the owner's equity.
2. Prepare a classified balance sheet as of June 30, 1979.

P1–8 (Minicase) Student A argues that accounting is a recently developed art that is only for commercial firms required to make government reports. Student B agrees that accounting is a newly developed art but feels that all commercial businesses should prepare accounting reports even if not required by government. Do you agree with Student A, Student B, or neither? What is your view with regard to (1) whether accounting is a new or an old art, (2) which entities should prepare accounting reports, and (3) the uses of accounting information?

chapter two

Introduction

To obtain the data needed to prepare a balance sheet and other financial statements, a rational accounting system must be developed. This chapter starts with the evidence by which the accountant learns that a business activity has occurred. It then describes several possible accounting systems, or means for recording transactions accurately. This introduction leads to a discussion of the system in general use in modern business, the double entry system. Only those transactions affecting the balance sheet are used in the chapter.

In this chapter and in the following four chapters, service businesses (such as real estate offices, accounting firms and doctor's offices), which sell services rather than merchandise, are used to illustrate the operation of an accounting system.

The development of the accounting model using balance sheet accounts

Learning goals

To be able to make practical application of the accounting equation.
To understand the transactions approach to recording accounting information.
To know the function of the basic accounting records (journal and ledger).
To apply a basic method of processing data: the journalizing of simple transactions and posting to ledger accounts.
To prepare end-of-period trial balance and balance sheet.

Key terms

account
account form of balance sheet
asset
balance
balance sheet
business forms
compound entry
credit
debit
folio
footing
invoice
journal
journalizing
ledger
liability
merchandising business
owner's equity
plant and equipment
posting
report form of balance sheet
T account
transaction
trial balance

Objective evidence — the business document

Business firms are initially created by investments by owners. These firms buy assets, sell assets, collect receivables, pay debts, and engage in other operating activities. In accounting, these activities or events are referred to as *transactions*. Before an accountant can record or process a transaction, he or she must be made aware that the transaction has taken place. In other words, there must be some objective evidence of the transaction. This evidence will usually be in the form of a business document. For example, an accountant can learn that cash has been paid out of the firm by viewing either a copy of a check, the check stub of a checkbook, or a receipt for payment of cash. A copy of the supplier's invoice (the description of the item shipped in terms of quantity and price) could be used to indicate that supplies or merchandise had been purchased. Other appropriate accounting forms will indicate that transactions have occurred.

These business documents will flow across the accountant's desk. They will be used in developing the accounting information described in the chapter. These documents are then filed for future reference and for review by the independent certified public accountant.

Transactions of the Ubuy Realty Company

All businesses go through a cycle in which the owner makes an investment and acquires various assets prior to opening the doors to start regular operations. The transactions involved in the organization of the Ubuy Realty Company, a single proprietorship, owned and operated by John F. Ubuy, illustrate this cycle.

1979

July 3 The Ubuy Realty Company was organized by John F. Ubuy. Ubuy opened a bank account under the name of Ubuy Realty Company and made a deposit, taken from his savings account, of $50,000 to start the new business.

5 Purchased land and building for $30,000 in cash. The land was valued at $5,000; the building at $25,000. Issued check No. 1.

10 Received furniture purchased on open charge account from the Jones Company for $8,000; supplier's invoice dated July 8, 1979.

20 Paid the Jones Company $5,000 on amount owed to it. Issued check No. 2.

25 The company found that some of the furniture was not what it wanted, so it sold the furniture, which had cost $1,800, to James Hill for $1,800 on account. Hill promised to pay this amount in 30 days; issued invoice No. 1.

31 Collected $1,000 from James Hill on amount he owed to the Ubuy Company.

The following discussion is based on these transactions.

Preparation of a balance sheet after each transaction

Since the balance sheet is an expanded variation of the accounting equation, it stands to reason that the total of the separate sides should always be equal. A possible solution to the problem of accumulating data is the preparation of a balance sheet immediately after each transaction.

Transaction 1 *Initial Investment of $50,000 by Owner.* Using the basic accounting equation of

$$\text{Assets} = \text{Liabilities} + \text{Owner's Equity}$$

the *balance sheet* shown in Figure 2–1 can be prepared after John F. Ubuy invests $50,000 in the business. (In this chapter, the traditional or *account form* of the balance sheet is used to show the effect of each transaction on each side of the accounting equation.[1])

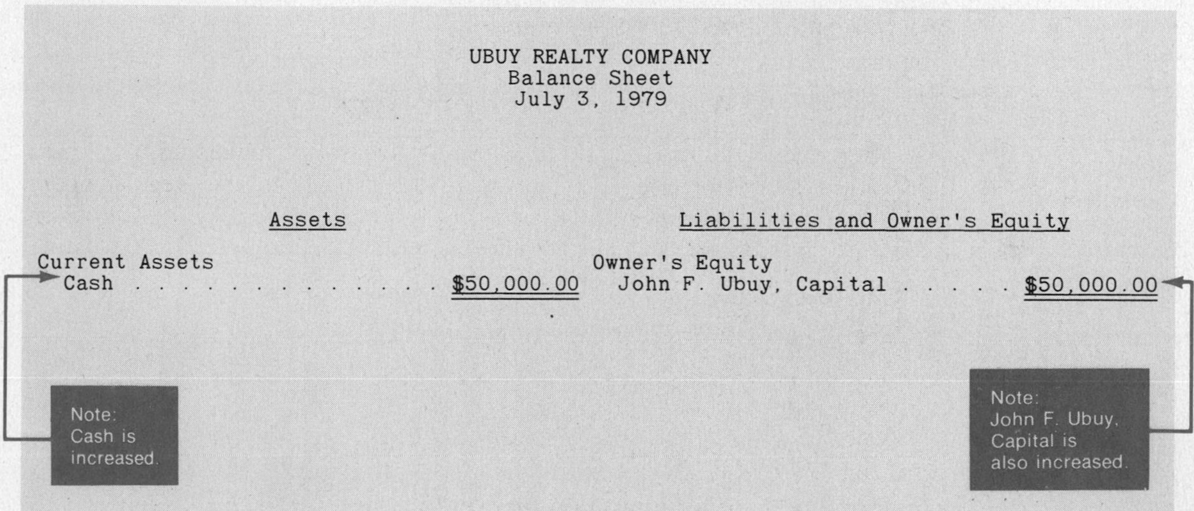
UBUY REALTY COMPANY
Balance Sheet
July 3, 1979

Assets		Liabilities and Owner's Equity	
Current Assets		Owner's Equity	
Cash	$50,000.00	John F. Ubuy, Capital	$50,000.00

Figure 2–1
After original investment

This transaction involves an increase of an asset, Cash, accompanied by an increase in an owner's equity item, John F. Ubuy, Capital.

Transaction 2 *Purchase of Land and Building for $30,000.* A balance sheet prepared after the land and building are purchased appears in Figure 2–2. This transaction involves increases of assets, Land and Building, accompanied by a

1 See page 41 for the definition of an account.

Note: Cash is decreased.

UBUY REALTY COMPANY
Balance Sheet
July 5, 1979

Assets			Liabilities and Owner's Equity	
Current Assets			Owner's Equity	
Cash		$20,000.00	John F. Ubuy, Capital	$50,000.00
Plant and Equipment				
Land	$ 5,000.00			
Building	25,000.00			
Total Plant and Equipment		30,000.00		
Total Assets		$50,000.00	Total Owner's Equity	$50,000.00

Note: Both Land and Building are increased.

Figure 2–2 After purchase of land and building

decrease of an asset, Cash, with no change occurring in the owner's equity.

Transaction 3 *Purchase of Furniture on Account for $8,000.* The balance sheet prepared after the business purchased furniture on account, that is, for credit, from the Jones Company is shown in Figure 2–3. This transaction involves an increase of an asset, Furniture, accompanied by an increase of a liability, Accounts Payable, with no change occurring in the owner's equity and no change in any other assets.

Figure 2–3 After purchase of furniture on account

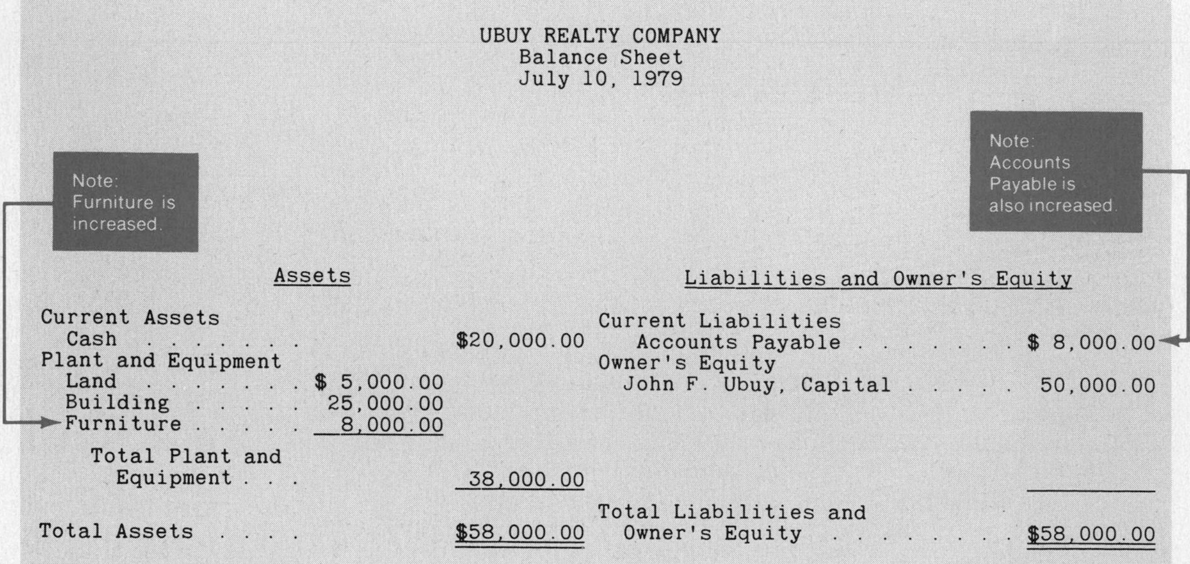

UBUY REALTY COMPANY
Balance Sheet
July 10, 1979

Note: Furniture is increased.

Note: Accounts Payable is also increased.

Assets			Liabilities and Owner's Equity	
Current Assets			Current Liabilities	
Cash		$20,000.00	Accounts Payable	$ 8,000.00
Plant and Equipment			Owner's Equity	
Land	$ 5,000.00		John F. Ubuy, Capital	50,000.00
Building	25,000.00			
Furniture	8,000.00			
Total Plant and Equipment . . .		38,000.00		
Total Assets		$58,000.00	Total Liabilities and Owner's Equity	$58,000.00

UBUY REALTY COMPANY
Balance Sheet
July 20, 1979

Note: Cash is decreased.

Note: Accounts Payable is also decreased.

Assets			Liabilities and Owner's Equity	
Current Assets			Current Liabilities	
Cash		$15,000.00	Accounts Payable	$ 3,000.00
Plant and Equipment			Owner's Equity	
Land	$ 5,000.00		John F. Ubuy, Capital	50,000.00
Building	25,000.00			
Furniture	8,000.00			
Total Plant and Equipment . . .		38,000.00		
Total Assets		$53,000.00	Total Liabilities and Owner's Equity	$53,000.00

Figure 2–4
After partial payment of accounts payable

Transaction 4 *Payment of Accounts Payable of $5,000.* The balance sheet appearing in Figure 2–4 is prepared after the business pays to the Jones Company on account $5,000 in cash. The transaction reflected in this balance sheet involves a decrease of a liability, Accounts Payable, accompanied by a decrease of an asset, Cash.

Transaction 5 *Sale of Furniture on Account for $1,800.* After the proprietor sells some of the furniture to James Hill on account, the balance sheet shown in

Figure 2–5
After sale of furniture on account

UBUY REALTY COMPANY
Balance Sheet
July 25, 1979

Note: Furniture is decreased

Note: Accounts Receivable is increased.

Assets			Liabilities and Owner's Equity	
Current Assets			Current Liabilities	
Cash	$15,000.00		Accounts Payable	$ 3,000.00
Accounts Receivable	1,800.00		Owner's Equity	
Total Current Assets		$16,800.00	John F. Ubuy, Capital	50,000.00
Plant and Equipment				
Land	$ 5,000.00			
Building	25,000.00			
Furniture	6,200.00			
Total Plant and Equipment . .		36,200.00		
Total Assets		$53,000.00	Total Liabilities and Owner's Equity	$53,000.00

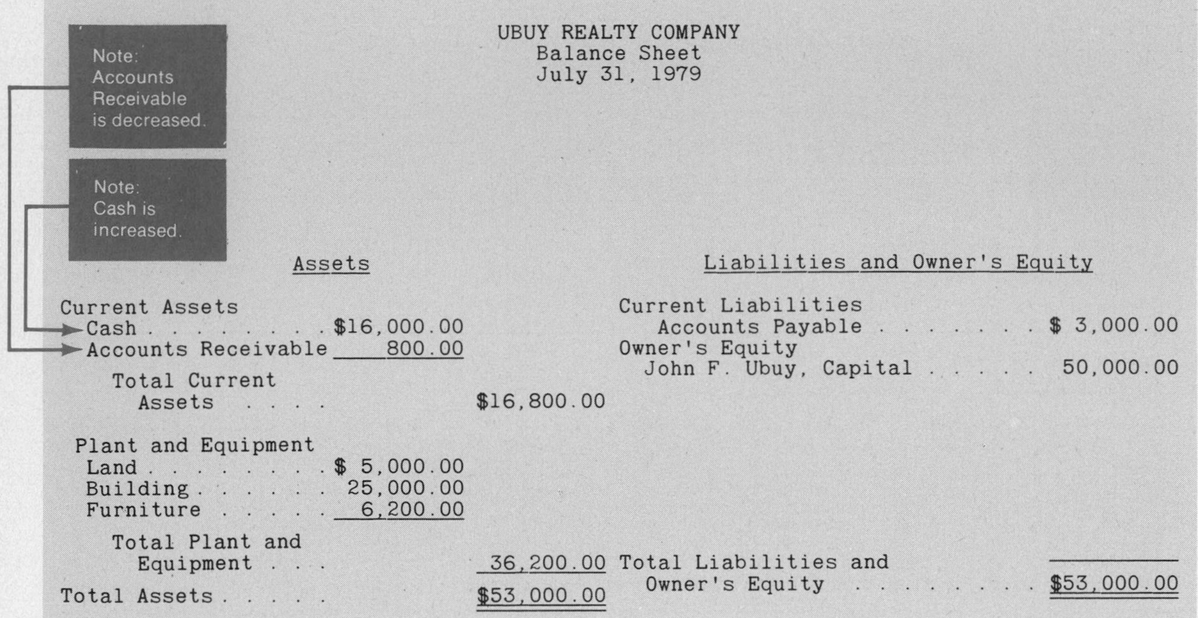

UBUY REALTY COMPANY
Balance Sheet
July 31, 1979

Assets			Liabilities and Owner's Equity	
Current Assets			Current Liabilities	
Cash	$16,000.00		Accounts Payable	$ 3,000.00
Accounts Receivable	800.00		Owner's Equity	
Total Current Assets		$16,800.00	John F. Ubuy, Capital	50,000.00
Plant and Equipment				
Land	$ 5,000.00			
Building	25,000.00			
Furniture	6,200.00			
Total Plant and Equipment		36,200.00	Total Liabilities and Owner's Equity	$53,000.00
Total Assets		$53,000.00		

Figure 2–6
After collection of accounts receivable

Figure 2–5 is prepared. Three points should be noted.

1. The amount of money yet to be received from James Hill is reflected as an asset, Accounts Receivable. It is a current asset because it is expected to be collected within a year.
2. This transaction involves an increase of an asset, Accounts Receivable, accompanied by a decrease of an asset, Furniture. It is similar to the transaction of July 5 in that it consists of an exchange of one asset for another (Figure 2–2.)
3. The furniture was sold at cost. If it had been sold at a price above its cost, the owner's equity item, John F. Ubuy Capital, would have been increased by the amount of the gain.

Transaction 6 *Collection of Accounts Receivable of $1,000.* After James Hill makes a payment of $1,000, the balance sheet shown in Figure 2–6 is prepared. As in Figure 2–5, this transaction involves an increase of an asset, Cash, accompanied by a decrease of an asset, Accounts Receivable.

Expansion of the accounting equation

The method of accumulating accounting data illustrated thus far in most instances is time consuming and costly. Moreover, those who use accounting information do not need a balance sheet prepared after each transaction. Using the basic accounting equation, it is possible to show how each transaction will

UBUY REALTY COMPANY
Expanded Accounting Equation Revealing Financial Position
For Month Ended July 31, 1979

Date	Business Transaction	Assets					=	Liabilities +	Owner's Equity
		Cash +	Accounts Receivable +	Land +	Building +	Furniture	=	Accounts Payable +	John F. Ubuy Capital
1979 July 3	Investment of $50,000 in cash to start business	+$50,000.00					=		+$50,000.00
5	Purchased land and building for $30,000 in cash. Land is appraised at $5,000; building, at $25,000	-30,000.00		+$5,000.00	+$25,000.00				
	Balances . .	$20,000.00 +		$5,000.00 +	$25,000.00		=		$50,000.00
10	Purchased furniture on account from the Jones Company for $8,000					+$8,000.00		+$8,000.00	
	Balances . .	$20,000.00 +		$5,000.00 +	$25,000.00 +	$8,000.00	=	$8,000.00 +	$50,000.00
20	Paid the Jones Company $5,000 on account . .	-5,000.00						-5,000.00	
	Balances . .	$15,000.00 +		$5,000.00 +	$25,000.00 +	$8,000.00	=	$3,000.00 +	$50,000.00
25	Sold furniture at cost to James Hill for $1,800 on account		+$1,800.00			-1,800.00			
	Balances . .	$15,000.00 +	$1,800.00 +	$5,000.00 +	$25,000.00 +	$6,200.00	=	$3,000.00 +	$50,000.00
31	Collected $1,000 from James Hill on account	+1,000.00	-1,000.00						
	Balances . .	$16,000.00 +	$ 800.00 +	$5,000.00 +	$25,000.00 +	$6,200.00	=	$3,000.00 +	$50,000.00

Figure 2–7 Expanded accounting equation

affect the balance sheet and yet have all six transactions combined in one end-of-month statement. In Figure 2–7 the balances are brought down after each transaction and form an equation from which a formal statement similar to Figure 2–6 could be prepared.

After each transaction, the total of the Assets columns equals the total of the Liabilities plus Owner's Equity columns. For example, after the July 25 transaction, the assets total of $53,000 = ($15,000 + $1,800 + $5,000 + $25,000 + $6,200) equals the liabilities plus owner's equity total of $53,000 = ($3,000 + $50,000). A classified balance sheet could be prepared from Figure 2–7 after the July 31 transaction by simply arranging the various assets, liabilities, and owner's equity items in the form illustrated in Figure 2–6.

Although this method tends to shorten the accounting process, it is unsuitable for most companies because it cannot easily be expanded to provide for a large number of asset and liability items. For example, it would be virtually impossible to use this procedure in a business that has fifty assets and twenty-five liabilities.

A separate page for each item

Another solution to the problem of data accumulation for an expanded number of assets and liabilities is to designate a separate page for each asset, liability, and owner's equity item. Using the six transactions of the Ubuy Realty Company, this method may be illustrated:

ASSET PAGES

	CASH	Page 101
1979		
Jul. 3	Investment by owner	+$50,000.00
5	Purchase of land and building	− 30,000.00
20	Payment to Jones Company on account	− 5,000.00
31	Collection from James Hill	+ 1,000.00
	(Cash on hand $16,000.00)	

	Accounts Receivable	Page 111
1979		
Jul. 25	Sale of furniture on account	+$1,800.00
31	Collection on account	− 1,000.00
	(Balance receivable $800.00)	

	Land	Page 151
1979		
Jul. 5	Purchase of land	+$5,000.00

	Building	Page 152
1979		
Jul. 5	Purchase of building	+$25,000.00

	Furniture	Page 157
1979		
Jul. 10	Purchase of furniture on account	+$8,000.00
25	Sale of furniture at cost	− 1,800.00
	(Furniture on hand $6,200.00)	

LIABILITY PAGES

	Accounts Payable	Page 201
1979		
Jul. 10	Purchase of furniture on account	+$8,000.00
20	Payment on account	− 5,000.00
	(Balance payable $3,000.00)	

OWNER'S EQUITY PAGES

John F. Ubuy, Capital — Page 251

1979		
Jul.	3 Investment by owner	+$50,000.00

A comment about the accounting page numbering system should be made. The pages could be numbered 1, 2, 3, 4, 5, 6, 7; but the numbers used should have a specific meaning—for example, 100–199 for assets, 200–249 for liabilities, and 250–299 for owner's equity items—especially if expansion is expected.

At the end of a designated period, the *balance,* or final amount, of each page may be obtained by adding the plus items and the minus items and subtracting the total of the minus items from the total of the plus items. These balances can then be arranged as a classified balance sheet as shown in Figure 2–6.

Although this procedure permits unlimited expansion, it is still inadequate. Use of the plus and minus signs contributes to arithmetic errors, and there is no economical way to run a mathematical check on the accuracy of the items contained in the accounting equation. Something else needs to be done to the system.

Division of each accounting page into columns—creation of accounts

A possible solution is to divide each page, referred to in accounting as an *account,* into two sections by drawing a line down the middle of the page and using both sides to record financial information. The accounting equation

Assets = Liabilities + Owner's Equity

suggests the following possible arrangement: Assets appear on the left side of the equation; therefore, the left side of the account is used to record increases of assets, and the opposite side, the right side, is used to record decreases. Similarly, since liabilities and the owner's equity appear on the right side of the accounting equation, the right side of the account is used to record increases in liability and owner's equity accounts, and the opposite side, the left side, is used to record decreases. An account number replaces the page number. An example of this kind of account is shown here.

Account Title — **Account Number**

Date	Explanation	Amount	Date	Explanation	Amount
	Use this side to record increases in assets and decreases in liability and owner's equity items.			Use this side to record decreases in assets and increases in liability and owner's equity items.	

Again using the same six transactions of the Ubuy Realty Company, the "account" feature of the accounting system is demonstrated. Before information is recorded in the accounts, each transaction is analyzed in the light of the foregoing rules for recording the information.

1979

July 3 The Ubuy Realty Company was organized and the proprietor, John F. Ubuy, invested cash of $50,000 to start the business. Cash, an asset, is increased by $50,000, and John F. Ubuy, Capital, an owner's equity item, is likewise increased. The $50,000 is placed on the left side of the asset account, Cash, to indicate that it has been increased, and the same figure is placed on the right side of the Owner's Equity account to indicate that it also has been increased.

5 Purchased land and building for $30,000 in cash. The cost of the land was determined to be $5,000; the building, $25,000. Both land and building are assets; thus, the $5,000 and the $25,000 are placed on the left sides of the Land and Building accounts, respectively, to reflect increases. The Cash account is decreased by $30,000; thus, this amount is placed on the right side of the Cash account.

10 Purchased furniture on account from the Jones Company for $8,000. The asset, Furniture, is increased by $8,000; this amount is placed on the left side of the Furniture account. A liability account, Accounts Payable, is increased by the amount due the Jones Company; $8,000 is placed on the right side of the Accounts Payable account to indicate that it has been increased.

20 Paid the Jones Company $5,000 on account. The liability, Accounts Payable, is decreased and the asset Cash is also decreased. The $5,000 is placed on the left side of the Accounts Payable account to record the decrease; the same figure is placed on the right side of the asset account, Cash, to reflect the decrease.

25 Sold furniture that cost $1,800 to James Hill for $1,800 on account. The asset, Accounts Receivable, is increased by $1,800 and the asset, Furniture, is decreased by $1,800. The increase in the asset, Accounts Receivable, is shown by placing the amount on the left side of the Accounts Receivable account; and the decrease in the asset, Furniture, is shown by placing the amount on the right side of the Furniture account.

31 Collected $1,000 from James Hill on account. The asset, Cash, is increased by $1,000; the asset, Accounts Receivable, is decreased by $1,000. The increase of the asset, Cash, is shown by placing the $1,000 on the left side of the Cash account; the decrease of the asset, Accounts Receivable, is shown by placing the $1,000 on the right side of the Accounts Receivable account.

These transactions would appear in the accounts as shown here.

Cash — Acct. No. 101

Date		Explanation	F	Debit		Date		Explanation	F	Credit	
1979						1979					
Jul.	3	Investment by proprietor*		50,000	00	Jul.	5	Purchased land and building		30,000	00
	31	Collection from Hill		1,000	00		20	Payment to Jones Co		5,000	00
		16,000.00		51,000	.00					35,000	.00

Accounts Receivable — Acct. No. 111

Date		Explanation	F	Debit		Date		Explanation	F	Credit	
1979						1979					
Jul.	25	Sold furniture on account		1,800	00	Jul.	31	Collection on account		1,000	00
		800.00									

Land — Acct. No. 151

Date		Explanation	F	Debit		Date		Explanation	F	Credit	
1979											
Jul.	5	Purchased land		5,000	00						

Building — Acct. No. 152

Date		Explanation	F	Debit		Date		Explanation	F	Credit	
1979											
Jul.	5	Purchased building		25,000	00						

Furniture — Acct. No. 157

Date		Explanation	F	Debit		Date		Explanation	F	Credit	
1979						1979					
Jul.	10	Purchased furniture on account		8,000	00	Jul.	25	Sold furniture on account		1,800	00
		6,200.00									

Accounts Payable — Acct. No. 201

Date		Explanation	F	Debit		Date		Explanation	F	Credit	
1979						1979					
Jul.	20	Paid on account		5,000	00	Jul.	10	Purchased furniture on account		8,000	00
								3,000.00			

John F. Ubuy, Capital — Acct. No. 251

Date		Explanation	F	Debit		Date		Explanation	F	Credit	
						1979					
						Jul.	3	Investment by owner		50,000	00

*After the journal is introduced, it will be evident that explanations in the accounts are rarely needed.

Figure 2–8
Trial balance

UBUY REALTY COMPANY
Trial Balance
July 31, 1979

Acct. No.	Account Title	Left-Side Balances	Right-Side Balances
101	Cash	$16,000.00	
111	Accounts Receivable	800.00	
151	Land	5,000.00	
152	Building	25,000.00	
157	Furniture	6,200.00	
201	Accounts Payable		$ 3,000.00
251	John F. Ubuy, Capital		50,000.00
	Totals	$53,000.00	$53,000.00

After all transactions are recorded the accounts are *footed;* that is, each amount column containing more than one entry is totaled in small figures (in practice this is usually done in pencil) under the last amount on each side (see the Cash account, for example). Then the balance of each account is determined by subtracting the smaller amount from the larger. The balance is placed in the Explanation column of the side with the larger amount. As a check on the accuracy of the work, the total of the *balances* on the left sides of the accounts is compared to the total of the balances on the right sides. Since the left-hand balances represent the left side of the accounting equation items and the right-hand balances represent the right side of the accounting equation items, their totals should be equal. If the totals agree, it is presumed that the accounting is correct up to this point. This presumption may not be correct, for the equality only shows that Assets = Liabilities + Owner's Equity. Yet the accountant, acting as if the accounting is correct, proceeds to complete the remaining steps in the accounting process. The listing of account balances is called a *trial balance* (see Figure 2–8). After the trial balance is prepared, a classified balance sheet similar to Figure 2–6 can be prepared from it.

Tools of accounting

Before the final stage of the basic accounting model is discussed, the following accounting tools are considered:

The T account
Debits and credits
The formal account.

The T account

A "T account" is so named because of its shape. Owing to its simplicity, this form makes it easy to understand the effects of transactions on a given account.

Each T account consists of a left side and a right side, with the title of the account written across the top.

Account Title	
Left Side (the debit side)	Right Side (the credit side)

Debits and credits

Debits and credits

The left side of an account is called the* debit *side, and the right side of an account is called the* credit *side.

Although originally the terms "debit" and "credit" had a specific meaning related to *debtor* and *creditor* accounts, today they are used as nouns, verbs, or adjectives depending on whether one is talking about an amount on the left side *(a debit)* or the right side *(a credit),* or the process of placing an amount on the left side *(to debit)* or the right side *(to credit),* or the characteristics of information on the left side *(a debit entry)* or the right side *(a credit entry).*

Substituting the terms "debit" and "credit" for the longer description above, the following rules may be stated:

Debit an account to record:	*Credit an account to record:*
An increase of an asset	A decrease of an asset
A decrease of a liability	An increase of a liability
A decrease in the owner's equity	An increase in the owner's equity

The relationship of the rules of debit and credit to the balance sheet and to the accounting equation may be illustrated as follows:

Assets (Property Owned by a Business)		=	Liabilities (Creditors' Claims to Assets)		+	Owner's Equity (Owner's Claims to Assets)	
Debit Increase	Credit Decrease		Debit Decrease	Credit Increase		Debit Decrease	Credit Increase

The abbreviation for credit is *Cr.;* for debit, *Dr.* For any account in the above illustration the side marked "increase" is the normal balance side.

The formal account

In actual business practice, the T account is expanded to a formal account. An *account* is a recording device used for sorting accounting information into similar groupings. It often consists of two sides, with four columns on each side: the date, an explanation, the page number of the source from which the amount was transferred (called the *folio column* or *posting reference*), and the amount. A standard form of the account for Cash is shown on the next page. Note that the folio column is indicated by an F.

Cash — Acct. No. 101

Date	Explanation	F	Amount	Date	Explanation	F	Amount

A variation of the T form is the three-amount-column form, with Debit, Credit, and Balance columns. After each entry, the balance of the account may be computed and entered in the Balance column. This form is useful when frequent reference is made to the balance of an account, as, for example, in the individual separate customers and creditors accounts; it is extremely popular in the general practice of accounting.

A three-amount-column account form is shown below.

Cash — Acct. No. 101

Date	Explanation	F	Debit	Credit	Balance

Other variations of accounts are found in practice. For example, one of these variations is a four-column-account where the last two columns are for the balance to indicate whether it is a debit or credit. The collection of all the accounts is called the *ledger*. It may be a book or other storage medium. Larger businesses that have electric or electronic data processing would use punched cards, magnetic tapes, or some other form of record for an account. In all cases, the basic concepts are the same as in the handwritten model.

A simple accounting system

In the preceding sections of this chapter, the six transactions of the Ubuy Realty Company were analyzed in terms of their effect on asset, liability, and owner's equity accounts, and the information was entered directly into the accounts. Records can be kept in this manner; most businesses, however, need more detailed information as well as a means of ensuring a properly functioning and systematic procedure for the recording of transactions. These businesses need a chronological record of transactions and a complete history of all transactions recorded *in one place*. It is often necessary to view a transaction in its entirety in terms of the specific business unit. Since every transaction consists of at least one debit and one credit, the entry is necessarily recorded on different ledger pages. If the ledger contains many accounts, it may be difficult to reconstruct the debit and credit for any single transaction.

To provide this needed detailed information, the recording process is commonly divided into two parts:

1. Journalizing
2. Posting

1. **Journalizing,** *or recording transactions in a book called a* **journal,** *a book of original entry. The record of a transaction in the journal is called a journal entry.*
2. **Posting,** *or transferring amounts in the journal to the correct accounts in the ledger, a book of final entry.*

A fully developed, but simple, accounting system can now be presented in pictorial form as shown by the following flow diagram:

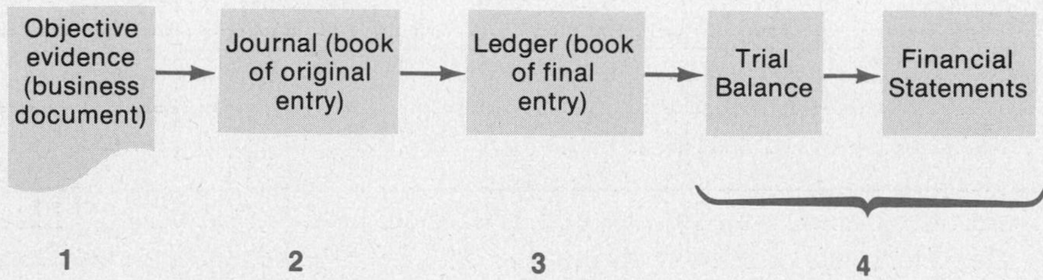

Explanation of numbered items:

1 Every entry made in an accounting system must have objective evidence, usually a business document, to justify the entry.
2 All entries are *first* recorded in a *journal,* a book of original entry.
3 All journal entries must be *posted* to the ledger. Absolutely no entries are made in a ledger except those posted from a journal. There is no other source for ledger entries.
4 A test check is made of the accounting system in the form of a trial balance. Financial statements (the balance sheet only in this chapter) are then prepared from the information presented in the trial balance.

Recording in the general journal

The accounting system just described is developed in more detail in the remaining sections of this chapter. The following example, in the basic form of a journal usually referred to as the *general journal,* shows the July 3 transaction of the Ubuy Realty Company.

GENERAL JOURNAL

Page 1

	Date	Debit-Credit-Account Titles: Explanation	F	Debit	Credit	
1	1979					
2	Jul 3	Cash		50000 00		5
3		John F. Ubuy, Capital			50000 00	7
4		To record the investment of				
6		$50,000.00 by the proprietor to				
8		start a business to be called				
		Ubuy Realty Company.				

Explanation of numbered items follows.

1 The year is written in small figures at the top of the Date column. It should be written in that position on every page of the journal.
2 The month of the first transaction recorded on this page is entered. It is not necessary to write the month again on this page unless it changes.
3 The date of each transaction is entered.
4 The title of the account debited is placed in the Debit-Credit-Account Titles-Explanation column against the date line. In order to eliminate confusion, it is important that the account title written in the journal entry should be the exact title of the account as it appears in the ledger.
5 The amount of the debit is entered in the Debit amount column.
6 The title of the account credited in practice should be indented approximately one inch from the Date column.
7 The amount of the credit is entered in the Credit column.
8 The explanation is entered on the next line, indented an additional one inch. The explanation should contain all the essential information as well as a reference to the relevant source document from which the information was obtained—check number, cash receipt date or number, and so on.

In journals, ledger accounts, and trial balances, the use of two zeros or a dash in the cents column to indicate that the cents are zero is a matter of choice. Thus, an amount may be written 2,357.00 or 2,375.—. In a balance sheet and other statements it is preferable, for sake of appearance, to use zeros. Dollar signs should *not* be written in journals and ledger accounts. They should be used in the balance sheet and other formal statements.

Posting from the general journal

It should be emphasized that the journal does not *replace* the ledger account. The journal is called a book of *original entry*. It is necessary first to journalize the transaction and then to post to the proper accounts in the ledger.

Figure 2–9 Posting flow chart

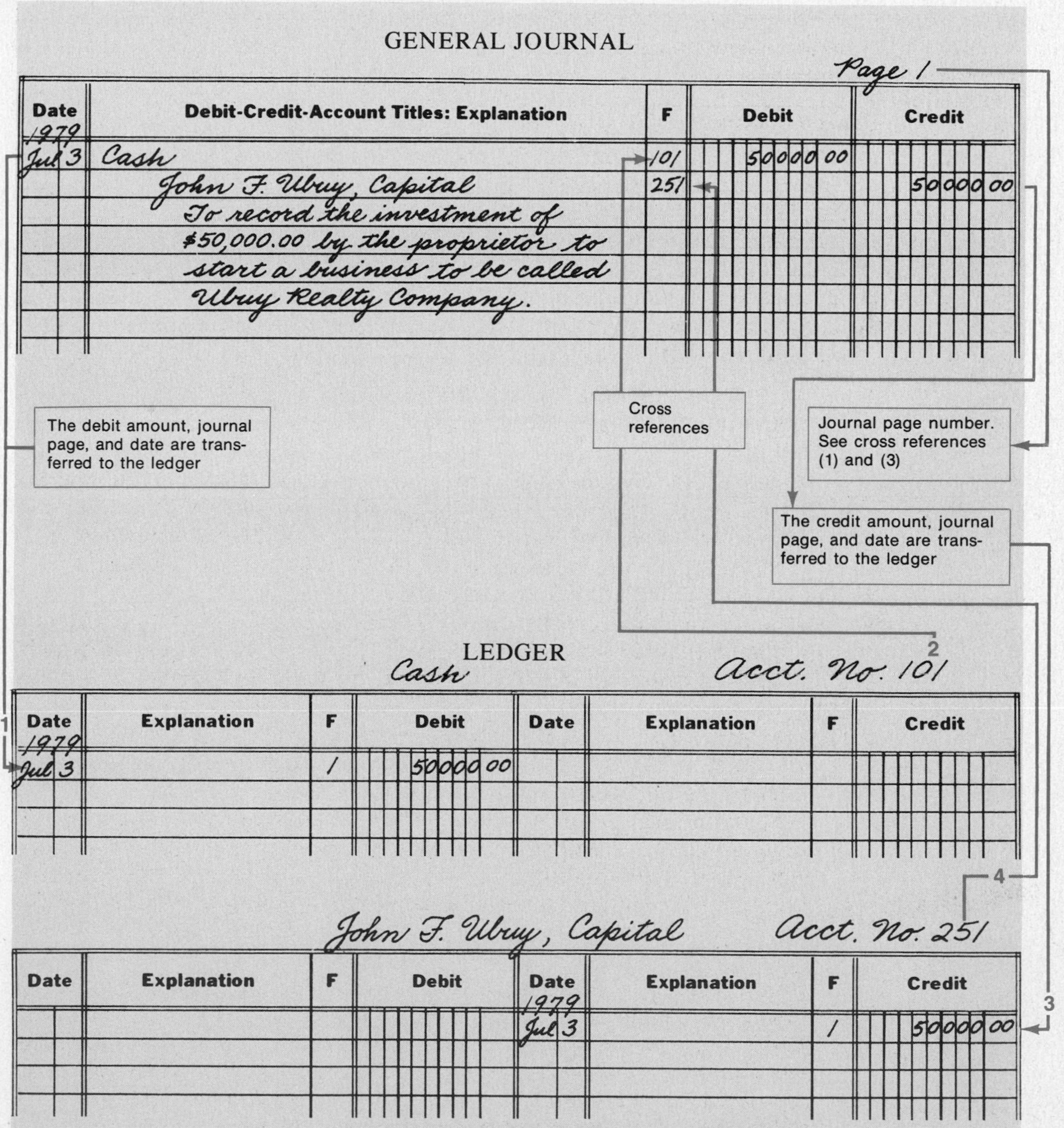

Figure 2–9 illustrates the posting of the July 3 entry from the general journal of the company to its ledger. Posting normally should be done daily. Explanations of numbered items in Figure 2–9 follow.

1 The debit amount, \$50,000, the journal page, 1, and the date, July 3, are entered on the debit side of the Cash account in the ledger. The year, 1979, is written at the top of the Date column. Remember that dollar signs are not used in journals or ledgers.

2 The ledger account number for the debit entry, 101, is entered in the folio (F) column of the journal to cross-reference the journal and the ledger. The presence of the account number here indicates that the item has been posted; so it must *not* be inserted until after the posting has been made.

3 The credit amount, \$50,000, the journal page, 1, and the date, July 3, are entered on the credit side of the John F. Ubuy, Capital account in the ledger. The year, 1979, is written at the top of the Date column.

4 The ledger account number for the credit entry, 251, is entered in the folio column of the journal to complete the cross referencing. It follows again that the cross reference in the journal indicates that the posting to the ledger has been completed.

It should be observed that explanations are not usually used in the Explanation columns of the ledger accounts. The cross reference to the journal page from which the information was recorded permits any interested person quickly to find a complete story of the transaction. Short explanations are used in the ledger accounts only when it is deemed that they will be especially useful in particular transactions.

The accounting sequence for the Ubuy Realty Company

The accounting model used in actual practice is illustrated with the six transactions of the Ubuy Realty Company. To review, the steps in the accounting sequence are:

1. Journalizing
2. Posting
3. Preparing a trial balance
4. Preparing a balance sheet

Journalizing and posting

The six transactions of the Ubuy Realty Company appear in the following general journal. Although cross reference figures are shown in the folio column, they would not be entered until after posting to the ledger. Note also that a blank line is left to separate each journal entry.

The transactions are posted from page 1 of the general journal to the ledger accounts shown. The cross references are entered in both the journal and the accounts.

After all the journal entries are posted, the accountant foots each account as shown in the ledger on page 39.

This accounting system is called *double-entry accounting,* because it requires that each record of a transaction have debits and credits of equal amount. Every transaction does not necessarily have a single debit and a single credit. For example, the July 5 entry of the business involves two debits totaling $30,000 and one credit of $30,000. A journal entry that has more than one debit or more than one credit is called a *compound entry*. Regardless of the number of accounts debited and credited in a single transaction, the total amount of all the debits and the total amount of all the credits in each transaction must be equal. It follows that the total of the debit balances and the total of the credit balances in the ledger of all the accounts must also be equal.

GENERAL JOURNAL

Page 1

Date 1979		Debit-Credit-Account Titles: Explanation	F	Debit	Credit
Jul	3	Cash	101	50000 00	
		John F. Ubuy, Capital	251		50000 00
		To record the investment of			
		$50,000.00 by the proprietor to			
		start a business to be called			
		Ubuy Realty Company.			
	5	Land	151	5000 00	
		Building	152	25000 00	
		Cash	101		30000 00
		To record purchase of land			
		and building for cash; issued			
		check No. 1.			
	10	Furniture	157	8000 00	
		Accounts Payable - Jones Company	201		8000 00
		To record purchase of			
		furniture on account;			
		supplier's invoice is dated			
		July 8, 1979.			
	20	Accounts Payable - Jones Company	201	5000 00	
		Cash	101		5000 00
		To record payment on account;			
		issued check No. 2.			

Page 1 continued

Date		Debit-Credit-Account Titles: Explanation	F	Debit	Credit
1979					
Jul.	25	Accounts Receivable – James Hill	111	1800 00	
		Furniture	157		1800 00
		To record credit sale of			
		furniture at cost; invoice No. 1.			
	31	Cash	101	1000 00	
		Accounts Receivable – James Hill	111		1000 00
		To record collection on account.			

LEDGER

Cash — Acct. No. 101

Date		Explanation	F	Debit	Date		Explanation	F	Credit
1979					1979				
Jul.	3		1	50000 00	Jul.	5		1	30000 00
	31	$16,000.00	1	1000 00		20		1	5000 00
				51000 00					35000 00

Accounts Receivable — Acct. No. 111

Date		Explanation	F	Debit	Date		Explanation	F	Credit
1979					1979				
Jul.	25	James Hill $800.00	1	1800 00	Jul.	31		1	1000 00

Land   Acct. No. 151

Date		Explanation	F	Debit	Date		Explanation	F	Credit
1979									
Jul.	5		1	5000 00					

Building   Acct. No. 152

Date		Explanation	F	Debit	Date		Explanation	F	Credit
1979									
Jul.	5		1	25000 00					

Furniture   Acct. No. 157

Date		Explanation	F	Debit	Date		Explanation	F	Credit
1979					1979				
Jul.	10	$6,2000.00	1	8000	Jul.	25		1	1800 00

Accounts Payable   Acct. No. 201

Date		Explanation	F	Debit	Date		Explanation	F	Credit
1979					1979				
Jul.	20		1	5000 00	Jul.	10	$3,000.00	1	8000 00

John F. Ubuy, Capital — Acct. No. 251

Date	Explanation	F	Debit	Date	Explanation	F	Credit
				1979 Jul. 3		1	50000 00

Trial balance

As stated previously, it is customary to prepare a trial balance to test the equality of the debit and credit balances in the ledger before a formal balance sheet is prepared. The July 31, 1979, trial balance of the Ubuy Realty Company follows:

UBUY REALTY COMPANY
Trial Balance
July 31, 1979

Acct. No.	Account Title	Debits	Credits
101	Cash	$16,000.00	
111	Accounts Receivable	800.00	
151	Land	5,000.00	
152	Building	25,000.00	
157	Furniture	6,200.00	
201	Accounts Payable		$ 3,000.00
251	John F. Ubuy, Capital		50,000.00
	Totals	$53,000.00	$53,000.00

The trial balance proves the equality of debits and credits but does not prove the accuracy of the accounts; for example, an entire transaction could be omitted, the debit and credit amounts of an entry could be identically incorrect, a wrong account could be debited or credited, or both the debit and credit amounts for a given transaction could be posted twice. If the trial balance is in balance, however, the accountant considers this strong presumptive evidence of accuracy and proceeds from that point.

The trial balance is useful to the accountant in preparing periodic financial statements. The accountant could prepare a balance sheet directly from the accounts, but the trial balance furnishes a convenient summary of the information for the preparation of the balance sheet.

If a trial balance does not balance, the following steps should be followed in sequence to locate the error:

1. Find the difference between the trial balance totals.

2. Examine the trial balance for balances that may be in the wrong column.
3. Re-add the trial balance columns.
4. Check the trial balance figures against those appearing in the ledger to see whether the amounts correspond and whether they have been entered in the proper columns.
5. Check the additions on each side of each ledger account and recompute the balances.
6. Check postings from journal to ledger.

The trial balance may not balance because of a single error. Time and effort may be saved by applying the following special tests after step 1:

1. Errors in the amount of $0.01, $0.10, $1, $10, $100, and so on, may be due to errors in addition or subtraction.
2. If the trial balance difference is divisible by 2, the error may be due to a debit amount entered as a credit amount, or vice versa.
3. If the trial balance difference is divisible by 9 or 99, the error may be due to a transposition of figures (a transposition occurs when two figures are reversed, for example $83.41 is posted as $38.41) or a slide (a slide occurs when a decimal is misplaced, for example, $1.05 is posted as $105.00).

Balance sheet

The next step in the accounting sequence is the preparation of the formal balance sheet for the Ubuy Realty Company (Figure 2–10). Note that Figure 2–10 is the same as Figure 2–6. Also keep in mind that this form of the balance sheet is referred to as the *account form* because information is placed on the left and right side of the statement as accounting information is placed in the

Figure 2–10 The account form of the balance sheet

UBUY REALTY COMPANY
Balance Sheet
July 31, 1979

Assets			Liabilities and Owner's Equity	
Current Assets			Current Liabilities	
Cash	$16,000.00		Accounts Payable	$ 3,000.00
Accounts Receivable	800.00		Owner's Equity	
Total Current Assets		$16,800.00	John F. Ubuy, Capital	50,000.00
Plant and Equipment				
Land	$ 5,000.00			
Building	25,000.00			
Furniture	6,200.00			
Total Plant and Equipment . . .		36,200.00		
Total Assets		$53,000.00	Total Liabilities and Owner's Equity	$53,000.00

traditional account (the T form).[2]

As indicated previously, dollar signs are used on formal statements. In placing dollar signs on statements, they should be put at the beginning of each column of figures. Note, however, as can be seen in Figure 2–10, a new column of figures is started whenever a line is drawn for addition or subtraction.

In the preceding illustration, the transactions of the Ubuy Realty Company were journalized. The information in the journal was posted to appropriate accounts. Account balances were determined and a trial balance was prepared. A balance sheet was prepared from the information summarized in the trial balance. Only balance sheet accounts, referred to as real accounts, were used in these illustrations. The accounting process now fully established is adapted to include information about revenues and expenses in Chapter 3.

Glossary

Account A recording device used for sorting accounting information into similar groupings.

Account form of balance sheet A form of the balance sheet that shows the assets on the left side of the statement and the liabilities and owner's equity on right side.

Asset A thing of value held by an economic enterprise.

Balance The difference between the total of the debit amount in an account and the total of the credit amount in an account.

Balance sheet The statement that summarizes the assets, liabilities, and owner's (or owners') equity of a business unit as of a specific date.

Business forms Documents that describe business activities of a firm.

Compound entry A journal entry with more than one debit account or more than one credit account.

Credit The right-hand side of an account, the amount shown on the right side of an account, or the process of placing an amount on the right side of an account.

Folio The cross-reference column in a journal or a ledger; also referred to as posting reference.

Footing The totaling of a column of figures and showing of the total in small pencil figures under the last amount in the column (also used as a noun).

Invoice A business form that describes the quantity and price of items shipped.

Journal The book(s) of original entry for all transactions.

Journalizing The process of recording a transaction, analyzed in terms of its debits and credits, in a record of original entry referred to as a journal.

2 The alternative form of the balance sheet described in Chapter 1 is called the *report form* since it is prepared in the same manner as a typical report.

Ledger The book that contains all the ledger accounts; or a collection of ledger accounts in any form.

Liability An obligation of a business, or a creditor's claim against the assets of a business.

Merchandising business A business that sells products or merchandise.

Owner's equity The owner's or owners' claims against assets of a business. As used in this text, owner's equity implies that the business is a single proprietorship and, therefore, represents the proprietor's claims against assets of the single proprietorship.

Plant and equipment The long-lived assets of a firm that are used in the operations of the firm and are not held for resale.

Posting The process of transferring an amount recorded in the journal to the indicated account in the ledger.

Report form of balance sheet A form of the balance sheet that shows the assets at the top of the statement with the liabilities and owner's equity appearing immediately below the assets.

Transaction A business activity or event which has taken place.

T account A simple form of ledger account in the shape of a T, used for analyzing transactions and for teaching purposes.

Trial balance A statement that shows the name and balance of all ledger accounts arranged according to whether they are debits or credits. The total of the debits must equal the total of the credits in this statement.

Questions

Q2–1 What is a business transaction? Give eight examples.

Q2–2 In practice, why is a balance sheet not prepared after each transaction?

Q2–3 What is the difference between the terms *debit* and *credit?*

Q2–4 What is the function of (a) the general journal? (b) the ledger?

Q2–5 Why is a trial balance prepared? If it does not balance, how do you locate the errors?

Q2–6 A balanced trial balance is a correct trial balance. Discuss.

Q2–7 John Johnson purchased furniture on account from the Hinton Company. Johnson debited the Furniture account for $800, and erroneously credited the Accounts Receivable account for $800.

a. What effect would the error have on the debit and credit total of the trial balance taken at the end of the period?
b. What accounts in the trial balance would be incorrectly stated?

Q2–8 What does the term *ledger account* mean? Indicate two forms of the account. State the reasons and circumstances for using each form.

Q2–9 Why are balance sheets classified as to assets and liabilities?

Q2–10 Give an example of transaction that would result in:

a. An increase of an asset accompanied by an increase in the owner's equity.
b. An increase of an asset accompanied by an increase of a liability.
c. An increase of an asset accompanied by a decrease of an asset.
d. A decrease of an asset accompanied by a decrease of a liability.

Class exercises

CE2–1 (Development of an accounting system) The following transactions occurred at the Eagle Grocery Store during its first month of operations:

1979

Mar. 1 Robert Eagle decided to start a grocery store; he opened a bank account under the name of Eagle Grocery Store and deposited $75,000 in cash.

2 Purchased land and building for $40,000. The Company paid $10,000 in cash and issued a 20-year mortgage payable for the balance. The land was valued at $12,000 and the building at $28,000.

3 Purchased furniture from the Garwood Company for $7,500 on account.

15 Paid the Garwood Company $2,500 on account.

20 Sold a portion of the land purchased on March 2 at its approximate cost of $4,500 to the Hill Realty Company on account.

31 Received $2,000 in cash and a 90-day note for $2,500 from the Hill Realty Company.

Using these six transactions, illustrate the five stages discussed in the text:

1. Prepare a balance sheet after each transaction.
2. Record the transactions in an expanded accounting equation.
3. Record the transactions on separate pages, not divided.
4. Record the transactions on separate pages, divided into Debit and Credit columns.
5. Journalize the transactions, post to formal ledger accounts, take a trial balance, and prepare a balance sheet.

CE2–2 (Account form of balance sheet) The following alphabetical list of accounts is taken from the records of The Joseph Jenkins Store for December 31, 1979.

Accounts Payable	$125,000
Accounts Receivable	138,000
Building	400,000
Cash	250,000
Delivery Equipment	140,000
Joseph Jenkins, Capital	614,000
Land	115,000
Merchandise Inventory	70,000
Mortgage Payable (due July 1, 1996)	280,000
Notes Payable (due April 1, 1980)	110,000
Notes Receivable	18,000
Prepaid Insurance	12,000
Wages Payable	14,000

Required: Prepare a balance sheet.

Exercises and problems

P2–1 The following information is available for the Macys Drug Store as of December 31, 1979.

Marketable Securities	$ 20,000
Accounts Receivable	80,000
Wages Payable	120,000
Buildings	100,000
Prepaid Insurance	2,000
Inventories	90,000
Douglas Macy, Capital	?
Accounts Payable	65,000
Cash on Hand	4,500
Cash in Bank	210,000
Land	40,000
Bonds Payable	200,000

Required: Prepare a balance sheet for the Macys Drug Store as of December 31, 1979.

P2–2 The following balance sheet was prepared by the bookkeeper of the Durham Company:

DURHAM RETAIL STORE
Balance Sheet
For the Year Ended December 31, 1979

Assets

Current Assets		
Cash	$ 4,000	
Accounts Receivable	12,000	
Building	24,000	
Merchandise Inventory	6,000	
Total Current Assets		$46,000
Plant and Equipment		
Marketable Securities	$ 6,000	
Store Equipment	3,000	
Office Supplies	200	
Delivery Equipment	2,700	
Total Plant and Equipment		11,900
Total Assets		$57,900

Liabilities and Owner's Equity

Current Liabilities		
Accounts Payable	$13,200	
Notes Payable (due June 1, 1980)	4,000	
Notes Payable (due July 1, 2000)	2,000	
Total Current Liabilities		$19,200
Long-Term Liabilities		
Mortgage Payable (due May 1, 1999)	$16,000	
Accrued Wages and Salaries Payable	500	
Total Long-Term Liabilities		16,500
Total Liabilities		$35,700
Owner's Equity		
Woody Durham, Capital		22,200
Total Liabilities and Equity		$57,900

Required: List the errors in this statement.

P2–3 Edward Baker engaged in the following transactions during the first week of operations:

1979

May 1 Invested $100,000 in cash.

3 Purchased office equipment from White and Sons for $4,000 on account.

5 Purchased land for a future building site at a cost of $20,000; paid $5,000 down and issued a mortgage note payable in 10 years for the balance.

Required: Prepare a balance sheet after each transaction.

P2–4 The following transactions were engaged in by the Fast Food Service Store owned by Mamie Smith during the month of February 1979:

1979

Feb. 1 Mamie Smith invested $120,000 in cash to create Fast Food Service Store.

2 Purchased land and buildings for $10,000 in cash and a 20-year mortgage payable for $50,000. The land was appraised at $8,000 and the building at $52,000.

3 Purchased service supplies from the Belk Company for $4,000 on account.

28 Sold a portion of the lot purchased on February 2 for its approximate cost of $3,500. The buyer, the Gulf Sands Company, paid $1,200 in cash and issued a 90-day note for $2,300.

Required:

1. Journalize the transactions.
2. Post to formal ledger accounts. (Assign appropriate numbers to accounts.)
3. Take a trial balance.
4. Prepare a balance sheet.

P2–5 The Carson Garage was started on March 20, 1979. During the first several days of operations, its part-time bookkeeper (a high school student who had a few months' instruction in bookkeeping) recorded the transactions and rendered the following unbalanced trial balance as of March 31, 1979:

CARSON GARAGE
Trial Balance
March 31, 1979

Account Title	*Debit*	*Credit*
Accounts Payable	$ 8,550	
Accounts Receivable		$10,000
Building	50,000	
Joseph Carson, Capital	75,000	
Cash	15,500	
Furniture	6,000	
Land		12,000
Marketable Securities		9,600
Mortgage Payable		20,000
Notes Payable	10,350	
Notes Receivable		8,000
Service Supplies	2,800	
Totals	$168,200	$59,600

Required:

1. Assuming that the amounts are correct but that the bookkeeper did not understand the proper debit-credit position of some accounts, prepare a trial balance showing the accounts in correct balance sheet order.
2. Prepare a balance sheet.

P2–6 The Turned-on-Transistor Company has been owned and operated by James Evans, Jr., for a period of years. In September, 1979, the accountant of the company disappeared, taking the records with him. You are hired to reconstruct the accounting records, and with this in mind you make an inventory of all company assets. By checking with banks, counting the materials on hand, investigating the ownership of buildings and equipment, and so on, you develop the following information as of October 31, 1979:

Account Title	*Balance*
Land	$15,000
Equipment	25,000
Buildings	20,000
Accounts Receivable	10,000
Marketable Securities	5,000
Inventories	14,000
Cash on Hand	3,000
Cash in Banks	53,000

Statements from creditors and unpaid invoices found in the office indicate that $40,000 is owed to trade creditors. There is a $10,000 long-term mortgage (30 years) outstanding.

Interviews with the board of directors of banks and a check of the daily diary records indicate that James Evans, Jr., had invested $30,000 in cash in the business. The remaining investment of the proprietor results from retention of past earnings.

Required: Prepare a trial balance and a balance sheet as of October 31, 1979.

P2–7 The following balance sheets were prepared immediately following each of three transactions engaged in by the Catz Company:

CATZ COMPANY
Balance Sheet
July 1, 1979

Assets			*Owner's Equity*	
Current Assets			Owner's Equity	
Cash		$45,000	John Catz, Capital	$45,000

CATZ COMPANY
Balance Sheet
July 3, 1979

Assets			*Liabilities and Owner's Equity*	
Current Assets			Long-Term Liabilities	
Cash		$39,000	Mortgage Payable	$49,000
Plant and Equipment			Owner's Equity	
Land	$ 5,000		John Catz, Capital	45,000
Building	50,000			
Total Plant and Equipment		55,000		
Total Assets		$94,000	Total Liabilities and Owner's Equity	$94,000

CATZ COMPANY
Balance Sheet
July 5, 1979

Assets			*Liabilities and Owner's Equity*		
Current Assets			Current Liabilities		
Cash	$39,000		Accounts Payable		$ 1,000
Office Supplies	1,000				
Total Current Assets		$40,000	Long-Term Liabilities		
			Mortgage Payable		49,000
Plant and Equipment					
Land	$ 5,000		Total Liabilities		$50,000
Building	50,000				
Total Plant and Equipment		55,000	Owner's Equity		
			John Catz, Capital		45,000
Total Assets		$95,000	Total Liabilities and Owner's Equity		$95,000

Required: Date and describe each transaction.

P2–8 The following account numbers and titles were designed for the Hilton Car Rental System, a single proprietorship:

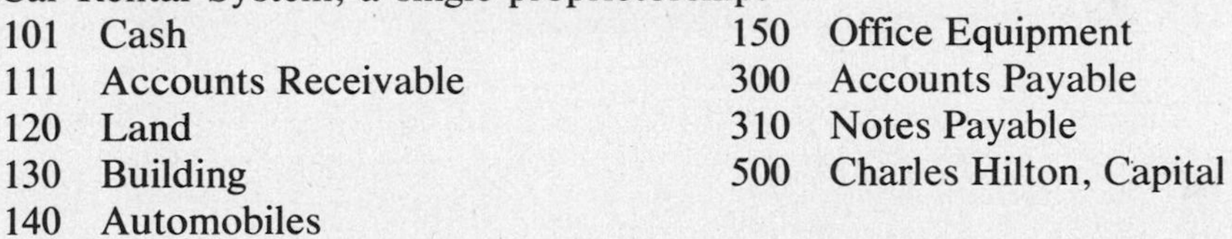

No.	Account	No.	Account
101	Cash	150	Office Equipment
111	Accounts Receivable	300	Accounts Payable
120	Land	310	Notes Payable
130	Building	500	Charles Hilton, Capital
140	Automobiles		

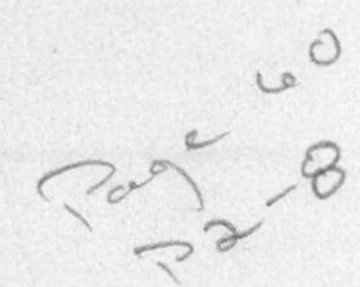

During the first month of operation the following transactions occurred:

1979

Jan. 1 Hilton deposited $95,000 in cash in a bank account in the name of the business, Hilton Car Rental System, a single proprietorship.

3 Purchased land for $5,000 and a building on the lot for $30,000. A cash payment of $15,000 was made, and a promissory note was issued for the balance.

4 Purchased 15 new automobiles at $2,300 each from the Allied Motor Company. A down payment of $20,000 in cash was made; the balance was promised to be paid in 30 days.

5 Sold one automobile to one of the company's employees at cost. The employee paid $1,000 in cash and agreed to pay the balance within 30 days.

6 One automobile proved to be defective and was returned to the Allied Motor Company. The amount due was reduced by $2,300.

1979

Jan. 11 Purchased a cash rcgister and office desks for $1,850 in cash.

31 Paid $6,000 in cash to the Allied Motor Company on account.

Required:

1. Journalize the transactions.
2. Post to ledger accounts (use account numbers).
3. Prepare a trial balance.

P2–9 The following lists show selected statement totals for four different firms: A, B, C, and D. In each case, the amount for one total is omitted.

	A	*B*	*C*	*D*
Current Assets	$200,000	$ 70,000	$?	$ 35,000
Plant and Equipment	400,000	120,000	100,000	180,000
Current Liabilities	?	20,000	10,000	15,000
Long-Term Liabilities	150,000	?	26,000	60,000
Owner's Equity	350,000	70,000	114,000	?

Required: Compute the missing figure for each firm.

P2–10 The following T accounts were taken from the ledger of Arthur Rawson Company.

Cash

Debit	Credit
65,000	53,200
	1,500
	450
	1,050
	300
	125

Land

Debit	Credit
10,000	

Office Supplies

Debit	Credit
100	
450	

Accounts Payable

Debit	Credit
125	435
110	110

Maintenance Supplies

Debit	Credit
500	
435	

Mortgage Payable

Debit	Credit
	50,000

Prepaid Insurance

Debit	Credit
1,500	

Arthur Rawson, Capital

Debit	Credit
	64,700

Machine	
20,000	

Delivery Equipment	
1,050	

Building	
72,000	

Office Equipment	
600	

Required:

1. Determine the account balances and prepare a trial balance as of October 31, 1979, in the proper order.
2. Prepare a balance sheet.

P2–11 (Integrative) Accounts included in the trial balance of the William Agustian Company as of September 30, 1979, were as follows:

Acct. No.	*Account Title*	*Balance*
101	Cash	$24,215
111	Accounts Receivable	11,785
150	Office Supplies	1,220
200	Land	?
250	Building	?
300	Furniture and Fixtures	8,000
350	Machines	60,000
400	Delivery Equipment	3,210
600	Accounts Payable	3,750
650	Notes Payable	25,000
700	Taxes Payable	103
800	William Agustian, Capital	?

Land and building were acquired at a cost of $30,000. It was determined that one third of the total cost should be applied to the cost of land.

The following transactions were completed during the month of October:

1979

Oct. 2 Paid in full a liability of $110 to the Doozier Company.

3 Collected in full an account receivable of $670 from the Parkside Mills Company.

4 Purchased office supplies from the Baxter Company for $400 on account.

8 Agustian made an additional investment of $16,000 in cash in the business.

10 Collected $1,000 from the Johnson Company on account.

1979

Oct. 11 Purchased a machine from the National Business Machine Company for $22,000; a cash payment of $2,000 was made, the balance to be paid within 30 days.

15 Paid in full a liability of $400 to the Pace Company.

20 Paid $10,000 in cash to the National Business Machine Company in partial settlement of the liability of October 11. Issued a note payable for the balance.

31 Collected in full an account receivable of $300 from the Durham Company.

Required:

1. Journalize these transactions.
2. Enter the balances of September 30, 1979, in ledger accounts, post the October entries, and determine the new balances.
3. Prepare a trial balance as of October 31, 1979.
4. Prepare a balance sheet.

P2–12 (Integrative) William Jackson has completed the arrangements for opening a new business, Precision Recordkeepers, an electronic data processing (EDP) center. Since Jackson decided to open the center he has been required to make numerous business decisions and to spend much time and money on the arrangements. However, Jackson is very pleased that everything has proceeded smoothly and that tomorrow morning at 9 o'clock (May 1) the business will officially open as scheduled.

Jackson is now reviewing the records with Wallace Jones, the company treasurer, and they are trying to determine how the firm stands just before operations begin. The business checkbook contains the following entries:

Deposits to account of Precision Recordkeepers,

April 27	Jackson invested $10,800 in cash in the business	$10,800	
29	Received from Thomas Taylor on loan	3,300	
30	Received from bank on loan (issued a note)	1,800	
	Total deposits		$15,900

Checks issued on the Gibraltar Bank & Trust Company:

April 27	Rental deposit paid to landlord	$ 150	
27	Payment of rent on office space for the month of May	150	
28	Insurance for one year beginning April 30	350	
28	Payment for purchase of office furniture	1,350	
29	Payment for office supplies	1,200	
30	Deposit paid to lessor of EDP equipment	3,000	
30	Payment for rental of EDP equipment for the month of May	1,500	
	Total payments		7,700
Balance on deposit, April 30	....		$8,200

They are pleased that the firm has this much cash, but they do not know how long it will last. They are aware of the following unpaid bills:

Balance due on purchase of office furniture (due in two equal payments on June 1 and July 1)	$ 650
Amount due as one month's rental on EDP leased equipment (due May 30)	1,500
Unpaid invoices on supplies purchases (due in three equal payments on June 1, July 1, and August 1)	400
Payment of second month's office rental (due May 27)	150
Amount owed to Taylor (due whenever the company can repay at a 5% annual interest rate)	3,300
Amounts owed to bank (due November 1 at a 6% annual interest rate)	1,800

While they are computing the firm's status, they make the following notes:

1. The deposit paid to the landlord will be returned in 10 years if the lease is not renewed at that time.
2. The leased equipment can be used as long as the rental is paid each month. The deposit is forfeited unless the equipment is used (and the rental is paid) for at least 24 months.
3. The insurance is for fire and public liability coverage from April 30 through the following April 29 (one year).
4. All employees begin working tomorrow. The total weekly payroll should be about $500.

Required:

1. Prepare a properly classified balance sheet for Precision Recordkeepers as of April 30.
2. Give your reasons for including or excluding each item of information presented in the problem.
3. Explain what a balance sheet is and what function it serves.
4. Explain why you arranged the items on the balance sheet as you did.
5. Jackson also wishes to know what the items "on the left" have in common since they do not appear to be closely related. Answer this question for items "on the left" and also for items "on the right."

P2–13 (Minicase) Many years ago when double-entry bookkeeping was new to her, a woman by the name of Eleanor McConnell lived in a small town in the Rockies. Eleanor, a woman of simple tastes, thought of opening a small store on Elkhorn Highway. She decided to call the store "The Backpacker." Eleanor sold 70 different types of packs in the store; and to keep an account of all the transactions she hired Miles Zimmerman as her accountant. In order to keep Miles alert in his work, she decided to pay him an additional $1 for every account he stated correctly and to deduct from his salary $2 for every account he stated incorrectly.

The following is a trial balance that Zimmerman submitted to McConnell on August 31, Year A:

THE BACKPACKER
Trial Balance
August 31, Year A

Account Title	*Debits*	*Credits*
Accounts Payable	$18,550	
Accounts Receivable		$ 10,000
Building	50,000	
Eleanor McConnell, Capital	75,000	
Cash	15,500	
Furniture	6,000	
Land		12,000
Merchandise Inventory		9,600
Mortgage Payable		20,000
Notes Payable	10,350	
Notes Receivable		18,000
Service Supplies	2,800	
Totals	$178,200	$69,600

Required:

Analyze the foregoing information and answer the following. Assume that the amounts are correct.

1. Is the trial balance in balance? If not, what is wrong?
2. Prepare a correct trial balance, showing the accounts in proper balance sheet order.
3. Prepare a classified balance sheet.
4. Taking into account the bonus and penalty system installed by McConnell, if Miles worked 33 hours in total and was getting paid $3 per hour, what net amount will he receive from McConnell? (Show all calculations.)

chapter three

Introduction

In the previous chapter, changes in the owner's equity of a single proprietorship caused by the proprietor's investments were discussed. Other changes in owner's equity are caused by: (1) revenues, (2) expenses, and (3) withdrawals by the owner. These changes, and the statements on which they are reflected, are explained in Chapters 3 and 4. In this chapter the basic fundamentals are introduced. Then an extended illustration is started where the normal recurring transactions are journalized. The remaining steps in the accounting sequence for this illustration are completed in Chapter 4.

Extension of the accounting model using income statement accounts—fundamentals and journalizing

Learning goals

To use the three-amount-column form of ledger account.
To identify changes in owner's equity brought about by operations (net income and net loss).
To understand the nature and use of nominal accounts (revenue, expense, and proprietor's drawing).
To know the rules for use of debit and credit for all types of accounts.
To recognize the need for and the method of using subsidiary ledgers and their relationship to controlling accounts.
To describe the preparation of and use of a chart of accounts.
To journalize the normal recurring transactions of service organizations.

Key terms

chart of accounts
controlling account
cost
expense
income statement
income statement accounts
loss
matching concept
net income
net loss
revenue
subsidiary ledger

Two forms of ledger accounts were introduced in Chapter 2. The T-form is an excellent device for teaching many concepts and will be used for this purpose throughout this book. The three-amount-column form of ledger account has good theoretical and practical reasons for its use. It is widely used in practice. Because the form will be used for illustration later in this chapter, we will review its use before proceeding.

The three-amount-column, or the debit-credit-balance, form of ledger account is easy to prepare and is extremely useful when frequent reference has to be made to the balance of an account. Its use also aids the preparation of the trial balance since the balance of each individual account is already determined.

The Cash account of the Ubuy Realty Company (see page 48 in Chapter 2) is illustrated here in the debit-credit-balance ledger account.

Cash — Acct. No. 101

Date		Explanation	F	Debit	Credit	Balance
1979						
Jul.	3		1	50000 00		50000 00
	5		1		30000 00	20000 00
	20		1		5000 00	15000 00
	31		1	1000 00		16000 00

Balance is a debit

It should be pointed out that the preparer *must* know the type of balance (debit or credit) of each account. The Cash account, for instance, normally has a *debit* balance; this fact is stated in the illustration. In this chapter and in a few illustrations in the next three chapters, the debit-credit characteristic will be indicated by a notation similar to that indicated in the foregoing Cash account of the Ubuy Realty Company.

Recording changes in owner's equity

Revenues

The term *revenue* describes the source of inflows of assets received in exchange for (1) services rendered, (2) sales of merchandise, (3) gains from sales or exchanges of assets other than merchandise, and (4) earnings from investments in stocks and bonds. It does not include increases arising from owner's contributions or from borrowed funds. For revenue to be earned, it does not have to be collected immediately in cash; it is sufficient that claims for cash on customers or clients exist. Although, revenue items are first recorded in separate accounts, they ultimately increase the proprietor's capital account balance. The method of accounting for this is discussed later in this chapter.

Revenue accounts are created to accumulate the amounts earned during a specified period. This typical accounting period is usually one year; for teaching purposes, however, a shorter period of one month will often be used. Progressive monthly statements are frequently prepared for the information of the management. The title of a revenue account should indicate the nature of the source of revenue; examples are Commissions Earned, Sales, Interest Earned, Dividends Earned, Accounting Fees Earned, and Shop Repair Revenue.

Since revenues are essentially parts of the proprietor's capital, the rules for increasing and decreasing proprietor's capital apply. Revenue accounts, therefore, are *credited when they are increased;* the particular asset that is received is *debited.* Revenue accounts are debited to reflect decreases. To illustrate the journalizing of revenue transactions, several companies that earned different kinds of revenue are considered.

First, suppose that on August 2, 1979, the Ubuy Realty Company sells a house and lot and receives a commission of $500 in cash; this can be recorded in the Ubuy journal as follows:

GENERAL JOURNAL

Date		Debit-Credit-Account Titles: Explanation	F	Debit	Credit
1979					
Aug.	2	Cash		500 00	
		Commissions Earned			500 00
		To record receipt of commission			
		on sale of house and lot.			

Next, assume that on July 31, 1979, A. N. Sanders, CPA,[1] bills the Anderson Company for $1,000 for an annual audit. The Sanders journal entry would look like this:

1 In Canada and other United Kingdom commonwealths, this practitioner would be designated chartered accountant, or CA.

GENERAL JOURNAL

Page 1

Date	Debit-Credit-Account Titles: Explanation	F	Debit	Credit
1979				
Jul. 31	Accounts Receivable		1000 00	
	Accounting Fees Earned			1000 00
	To record billing of following client for audit:			
	Anderson Company $1000.00			

Suppose that on January 2, 1979, the Ho-down Rental Agency receives $750 in cash for January rent. Ho-down shows this journal entry:

GENERAL JOURNAL

Page 1

Date	Debit-Credit-Account Titles: Explanation	F	Debit	Credit
1979				
Jan. 2	Cash		750 00	
	Rent Earned			750 00
	To record rental receipts for month of January, 1979.			

Expenses

Expenses are expired costs of the materials consumed and services received during a specified period. To be an expense the materials and services must have been used in the production of revenue during that same period. A *loss* is an expired cost that does not produce revenue. At this stage of the learning process emphasis will be placed on expenses only; thus, the accounting for losses will be postponed until later chapters. Examples of expense accounts are Salaries Expense, Rent Expense, and Office Supplies Expense.

Expenses are recorded by a debit to the appropriate expense account and a credit to the Cash account, to a liability account, or to some other type of account. Although they are recorded in separate accounts, it should be noticed that expenses decrease the proprietor's capital balance. The specific way that this decrease is reflected in the Capital account is discussed later in this chapter. The recording process for expenses is illustrated by the following transactions that took place at the Hoagie Company.

1979
Jan. 2 Paid $400 in rent for the month of January.
10 Purchased an advertisement in the local newspaper for $75 in cash.
16 Paid semimonthly salaries of $600.
20 Had some office machinery repaired at a cost of $45.

These transactions are recorded in the Hoagie Company general journal as follows:

GENERAL JOURNAL

Page 1

Date		Debit-Credit-Account Titles: Explanation	F	Debit	Credit
1979 Jan	2	Rent Expense		400 00	
		Cash			400 00
		To record payment of rent for month of January 1979, issued Check No. 101.			
	10	Advertising Expense		75 00	
		Cash			75 00
		To record payment for advertising, issued Check No. 102.			
	16	Salaries Expense		600 00	
		Cash			600 00
		To record payment of semi-monthly salaries, issued Checks No. 103–105.			
	20	Repairs Expense – Office Equipment		45 00	
		Cash			45 00
		To record payment of repairs to office equipment, issued Check No. 106.			

Operating results

The accountant compares revenues and expenses to determine operating results. Depending upon whether the expenses or the revenues are greater, a business may have a net income or a net loss for the period. *Net income* for any period is measured by deducting total expenses for that period from total revenues for the same period. The net income, or profit, shows the change in owner's equity resulting from business operations. The statement showing the calculation of net income is called the *income statement*.

An increase in owner's equity resulting from business operations may be expressed in equation form as

Total revenues − Total expenses = Net income

If revenues exceed expenses, the right-hand figure is *net income*. If the total expenses for a period exceed the revenues for that period, however, a *net loss* results, and the owner's equity is decreased. The equation now becomes

Total expenses − Total revenues = Net loss

Costs and expenses

Cost, ***the amount paid to purchase an asset, becomes an*** **expense** ***when the purchased item is no longer an asset; that is, when it can no longer produce future revenue.***

It is necessary to distinguish between an expense and a cost. A *cost* is the amount paid or payable in either cash or the equivalent, for goods, services, or other assets purchased. When a cost no longer has asset status—that is, when its potential to produce future revenue is lost—it is said to be expired and thus to have become typically an *expense*. From this statement the following conclusions are warranted:

Expenses = Expired costs (used up in *producing* this period's revenue)

Assets = Unexpired costs (to be used to produce future revenue)

For example, rent paid in advance for three months is an asset, Prepaid Rent. As time passes, this becomes Rent Expense. The required adjusting process is discussed in detail in Chapter 5.

A disbursement is a payment in cash or by check. Hence, a machine may be acquired at a cost of $10,000; the transaction is completed by a disbursement in the form of a check for $10,000. As the machine is used in operations, it loses part of its service value, or depreciates. The original purchase is not an expense. However, the expiration of service value is an element of expense, Depreciation Expense.

The basic objective of operating a business is to produce a net income. This results from receiving more from customers for services rendered than the total expense to the business of producing the services. A net loss is incurred when the expense of the services to the enterprise is more than the income received from customers for the services rendered.

Most businesses cannot keep the detailed records necessary to indicate the expense of each service rendered and therefore cannot determine the net income or net loss from each transaction. Even when it is possible, the clerical costs involved in getting the information would not justify the end result. For example, a lawyer bills his client for $1,000 for services performed. How much did it cost the lawyer to perform the service and how much net income did he make on this *one* transaction? The lawyer might total the number of hours he devoted to the case and arrive at an expense in terms of time spent. But how about the rent for his office? the secretary's salary? the telephone bill? the electricity bill?

Since the determination of the exact expense involved in rendering service for a particular client would require a considerable amount of record keeping, accounting has evolved another and easier method for accomplishing an acceptable result. No attempt is made to determine the cost of each service; instead, records of revenue and expense are kept for a period, a year or perhaps a shorter period of time.

Matching concept

At the end of the period, the period's expenses are* matched *against the period's revenue to determine the net income or net loss for that period. This information is contained in a financial statement called an* income statement, *discussed and illustrated later in Chapter 4.

Withdrawals by proprietor

Distributions of income (whether it is earned in the current period or in past periods) in the form of withdrawals are debited to a special account called the proprietor's drawing account. The reasons for this accounting are: (1) the earnings of a single proprietorship belong to the owner, (2) it is beneficial for the owner to have a record of periodic withdrawals, and (3) there are no legal restrictions on the withdrawal of earnings by a proprietor. Therefore, the owner of a single proprietorship may withdraw cash or any other asset in expectation of income. Suppose, for example, John F. Ubuy, owner of the Ubuy Realty Company, withdrew cash of $500 on September 2, 1979. This transaction would be recorded in the general journal of the company as follows:

GENERAL JOURNAL

Page 3

Date		Debit-Credit-Account Titles: Explanation	F	Debit	Credit
1979					
Sep.	2	John F. Ubuy, Drawing		500 00	
		Cash			500 00
		To record withdrawal by owner			
		in expectation of income.			

The amount of the proprietor's drawing decreases owner's equity and is shown on the statement of owner's equity, which will be illustrated later in this chapter.

Expanded rules for debits and credits

Since new types of accounts have been introduced, the rules for debiting and crediting accounts are expanded and restated:

Debit to record:	*Credit to record:*
1. An increase of an asset account	1. A decrease of an asset account
2. An increase of an expense account	2. A decrease of an expense account
3. An increase of proprietor's drawing account	3. A decrease of proprietor's drawing account
4. A decrease of a liability account	4. An increase of a liability account
5. A decrease in an owner's equity account	5. An increase in an owner's equity account
6. A decrease in a revenue account	6. An increase in a revenue account

The relationship of the rules of debits and credits to the accounting equation may be diagramed in T-account form as follows:

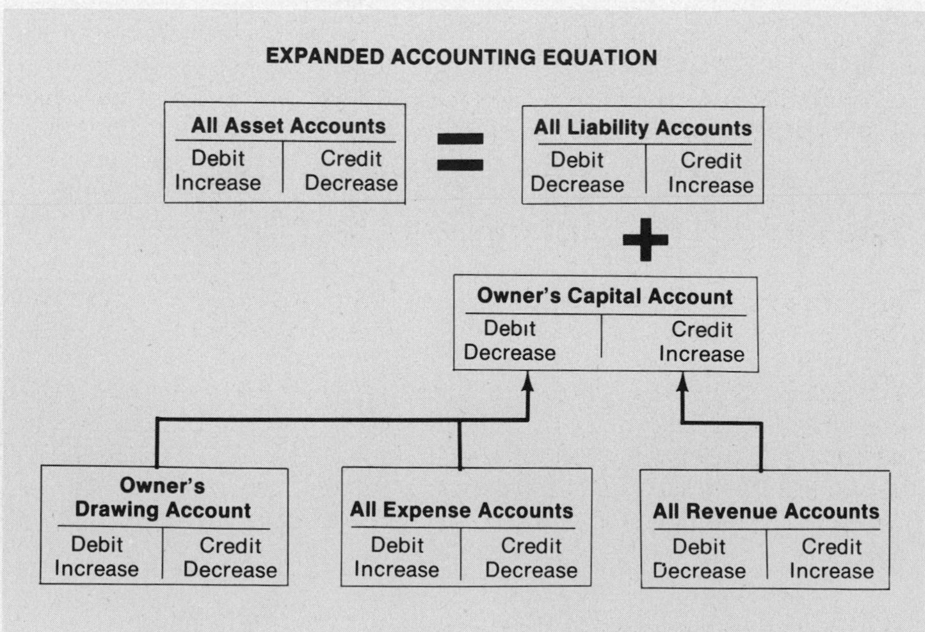

Although the debit-credit processing rules for expenses and the owner's drawing are the same, it should be emphasized that the owner's drawing account is *not* an expense account. The payment made to the owner in the form of a withdrawal *does not* produce revenue.

In earlier rules for debit and credit it was noted that use of a credit to show an increase in owner's equity is consistent with the fact that owner's equity is on the right-hand side of the accounting equation. Since revenues, in fact, increase owner's equity, it is logical as shown in the diagram that an increase in a revenue account would also be a credit. Expenses have an opposite effect. They are working to decrease owner's equity. Accordingly, as expenses are incurred (increased) they are recorded as debits. This specific relationship between expenses and owner's equity accounts is further illustrated as follows:

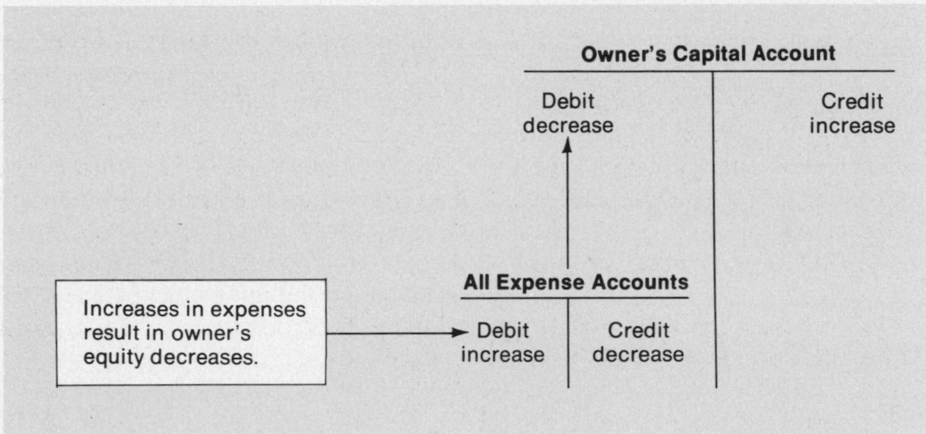

It naturally follows that withdrawals by the proprietor reduce owner's equity. As they occur (increase) they are also recorded as debits.

The general ledger and subsidiary ledgers

General ledger

***Accounts that are incorporated in the balance sheet and the income statement are kept in a separate book or collection, called the* general ledger.**

The general ledger may actually be a loose-leaf binder, a bound book, cards in open trays, punched cards, or one of the several types of computer data storage devices. Accounts are usually arranged in the sequence in which they will appear in the financial statements—that is, assets, liabilities, owner's equity, revenue, and expenses. These accounts are referred to as general ledger accounts.

Accounts receivable ledger

Many businesses have a large number of customers, and detailed information must be kept of transactions with each one. A separate account thus is required for each customer. If the general ledger were to include each customer's account, it would become too large and unwieldy. Consequently, a summary account, Accounts Receivable, is maintained in the general ledger. This account shows the combined increases and decreases in the amounts due from all customers. The individual customer accounts are kept in a separate, or *subsidiary,* ledger called the accounts receivable ledger. The Accounts Receivable account, referred to as a controlling account, summarizes those individual customers' accounts that are assigned to the subsidiary ledger. After all the transactions for the period have been entered, the balance of the Accounts Receivable account in the general ledger should be equal to the sum of the individual account balances in the subsidiary ledger.

Accounts payable ledger

Many businesses have a large number of individual creditors. Consequently, a summary account, Accounts Payable, is kept in the general ledger. This account shows total increases and decreases in amounts due to creditors. The individual creditors' accounts are kept in a subsidiary ledger called the accounts payable ledger. Accounts Payable, another controlling account, summarizes those individual creditors' accounts which are assigned to the subsidiary ledger. After all the transactions for the period have been entered, the balance of the Accounts Payable account in the general ledger should be equal to the sum of the individual account balances in the subsidiary ledger.

Controlling accounts

As mentioned above, the Accounts Receivable and Accounts Payable accounts appearing in the general ledger are referred to as *controlling accounts*. These accounts contain summary totals of many transactions, the details of which appear in subsidiary ledgers. The accounts receivable ledger is sometimes referred to as the *customers ledger;* the accounts payable ledger, as the *creditors ledger*. Other controlling accounts and their appropriate subsidiary ledgers may be established when enough similar general ledger accounts are created to make it more efficient to assign these accounts to a separate ledger.

Controlling account

A **controlling account** ***is any account in the general ledger that controls or is supported by a number of other accounts in a separate ledger.***

Posting to the general ledger and subsidiary ledgers

To illustrate the method of posting from the general journal to the general and subsidiary ledgers, the following transaction is considered.

On August 3, 1979, Ace Bookkeeping Services billed the following clients for professional services performed:

Jay Jones	$550
O. M. Owens	120
C. W. Ransom	230

This information is recorded and posted as indicated in Figure 3–1.

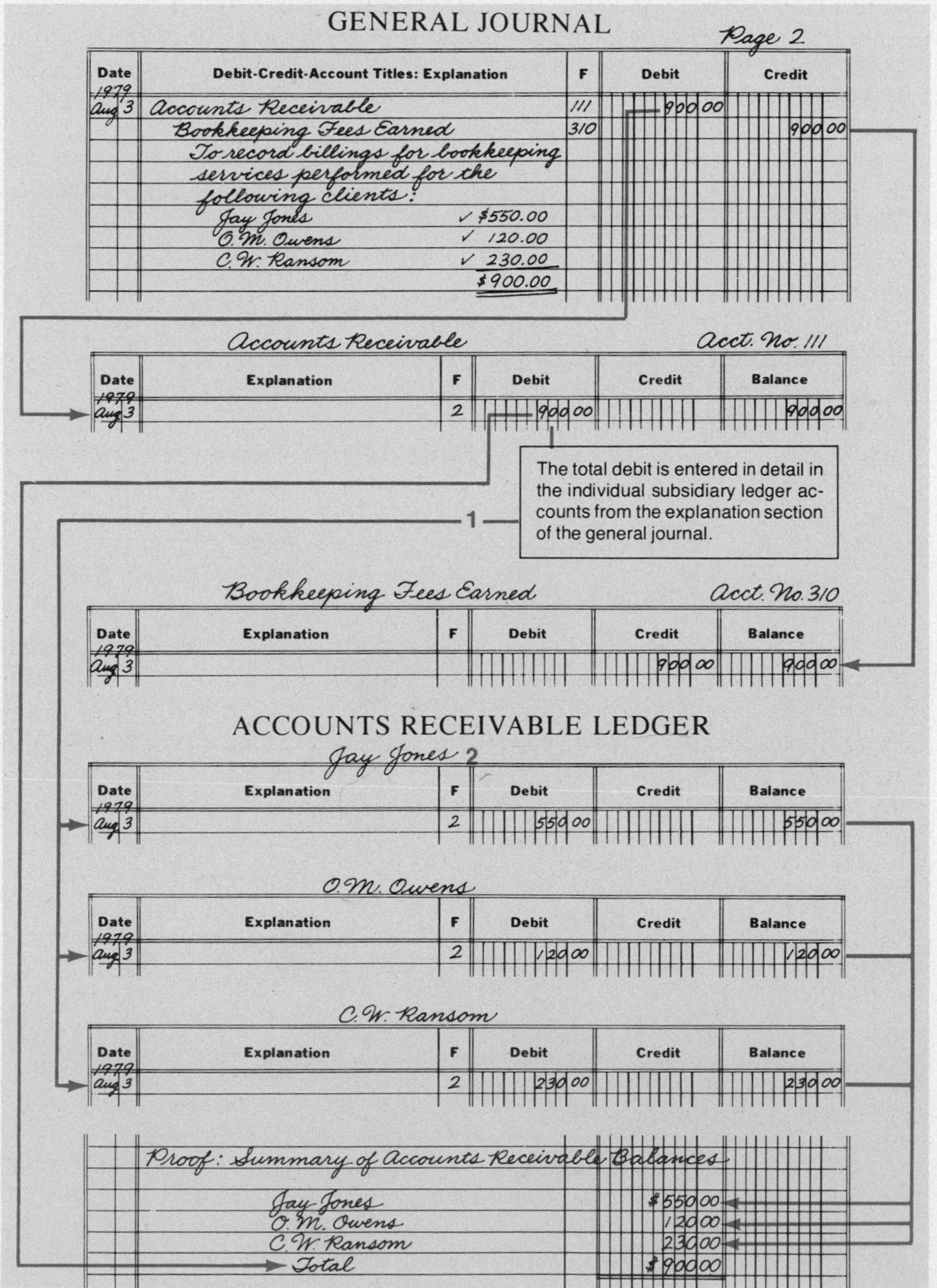

GENERAL JOURNAL

Page 2

Date	Debit-Credit-Account Titles: Explanation	F	Debit	Credit
1979 Aug 3	Accounts Receivable	111	900 00	
	Bookkeeping Fees Earned	310		900 00
	To record billings for bookkeeping services performed for the following clients:			
	Jay Jones ✓ $550.00			
	O. M. Owens ✓ 120.00			
	C. W. Ransom ✓ 230.00			
	$900.00			

Accounts Receivable — Acct. No. 111

Date	Explanation	F	Debit	Credit	Balance
1979 Aug 3		2	900 00		900 00

Bookkeeping Fees Earned — Acct. No. 310

Date	Explanation	F	Debit	Credit	Balance
1979 Aug 3				900 00	900 00

ACCOUNTS RECEIVABLE LEDGER

Jay Jones

Date	Explanation	F	Debit	Credit	Balance
1979 Aug 3		2	550 00		550 00

O. M. Owens

Date	Explanation	F	Debit	Credit	Balance
1979 Aug 3		2	120 00		120 00

C. W. Ransom

Date	Explanation	F	Debit	Credit	Balance
1979 Aug 3		2	230 00		230 00

Proof: Summary of Accounts Receivable Balances

Jay Jones	$550 00
O. M. Owens	120 00
C. W. Ransom	230 00
Total	$900 00

Figure 3–1 Posting to control and subsidiary accounts

An explanation of the figures in Figure 3–1 follows:

1 Figure 3–1 shows the total posting of the $900 debit to the Accounts Receivable account in the general ledger and detailed posting to the subsidiary ledger accounts. Each customer is debited for the amount shown in the explanation of the general journal entry; the balance is extended to the Balance column; the journal page number is entered in the folio (F) column; and the date is entered. After each posting has been completed, a check mark (√) is entered to the left of each amount in the Explanation column of the general journal to indicate that the amount has been posted to the proper subsidiary ledger account. A check mark is used rather than a page number because subsidiary accounts in the illustration may not be numbered but may be kept in alphabetical order.

2 The three-amount-column form of ledger account is also used for the accounts receivable ledger. This form is used in subsidiary ledgers for two reasons: The balances have to be referred to quite often and the form is adaptable to machine accounting, which is frequently employed for subsidiary ledger accounting.

It will be obvious to the reader that a business such as a department store that makes hundreds of credit sales daily does not list each one in the journal entry explanation; instead, postings to the subsidiary ledger accounts are made from the copies of the sales tickets. The principle, however, is the same as illustrated in Figure 3–1.

At first it may *seem* that this dual accounting for accounts receivable would result in double debits that will be incorrectly reflected in the trial balance. Note carefully, however, that only one debit goes into the Accounts Receivable controlling account for later use in the trial balance. The amounts entered in the accounts receivable ledger will *not* go in the trial balance, but the total of the uncollected balances at the end of a period will be compared with the single balance of the Accounts Receviable controlling account as a check on the accuracy of both the accounts receivable ledger and the Accounts Receivable controlling account in the general ledger.

Entries to the Accounts Payable controlling account and the Accounts Payable ledger are handled similarly.

The accounting sequence illustrated

In the remaining part of this chapter and in Chapter 4 nine steps in the accounting sequence are illustrated through the example of a newly formed proprietorship called the Good Times Wheels Repair Shop owned and operated by Thomas Toy. These steps are: (1) selecting a chart of accounts, (2) analyzing and journalizing the transactions, (3) posting to the general and subsidiary ledgers, (4) preparing a trial balance, (5) preparing a schedule of accounts receivable, (6) preparing a schedule of accounts payable, (7) preparing the financial statements, (8) closing the revenue, expense, and owner's drawing accounts, and (9) taking a postclosing trial balance. An explanation of each step in the sequence is presented along with the accounting procedure for that step.

Selecting a chart of accounts

The first step in establishing an efficient accounting system that will satisfy the needs of management, government agencies, and other interested groups is the construction of a *chart of accounts*.

Chart of accounts

A separate account should be set up for each item that appears in the financial statements to make the statements easier to prepare. The* chart of accounts *is the complete listing of account titles to be used in the entity.

The classification and the order of the items in the chart of accounts corresponds to those in the statements.

GOOD TIMES WHEELS REPAIR SHOP
Chart of Accounts

Asset Accounts (100–199)

Current Assets (100–150)
101 Cash
121 Accounts Receivable
131 Repair Parts and Supplies
141 Prepaid Insurance

Plant and Equipment (151–199)
151 Land
161 Automotive Tools and Equipment

Liability and Owner's Equity Accounts (200–399)

Current Liabilities (200–250)
201 Accounts Payable
202 Notes Payable

Long-Term Liabilities (251–299)

Owner's Equity (300–399)
301 Thomas Toy, Capital
311 Thomas Toy, Drawing

Income Statement Accounts (400–699)

Revenue (400–499)
401 Shop Repair Revenue

Expenses (500–599)
501 Rent Expense—Shop Building
502 Rent Expense—Automotive Tools and Equipment
504 Salaries Expense
508 Electricity and Water Expense
509 Repair Parts and Supplies Used

Clearing and Summary Accounts (600–699)
601 Income Summary

Account titles should be carefully selected to suit the needs of the business, and should indicate clearly and precisely the nature of the accounts to ensure proper recording of transactions. However, titles are not standardized; for example, one business may use Unexpired Insurance and another Prepaid Insurance to describe the same asset.

In our example, a three-digit system is used to number the accounts; a larger business with a number of departments or branches may use four or more digits. Notice that in this illustration accounts 100–199 represent assets; accounts 200–399 represent liabilities and owner's equity; and accounts 400–699 represent *income statement* accounts (revenue and expense accounts that are incorporated in the income statement). The more detailed breakdown for current assets, plant and equipment, and current liabilities, for example, can be seen in the chart. As stated previously, the gaps between the assigned account numbers allow for additional accounts as they are needed by the business.

Analyzing transactions and journalizing

The transactions of the Good Times Wheels Repair Shop that occurred during January, 1979, are given. Before making entries in the journal, the accountant must analyze each transaction in terms of increases and decreases in the accounting equation and must apply the basic system of debits and credits that has already been outlined. For the first five transactions listed we have described the analytical thinking that must precede journalizing. These analyses may be studied as a guide to future action.

1979

Jan. 2 Thomas Toy opened a bank account under the name of his new business, Good Times Wheels Repair Shop. He deposited $30,000 in cash to start the new business. An asset, cash, is received by the Good Times Wheels Repair Shop. To record an increase of an asset, it must be debited; therefore, the Cash account is debited for $30,000. The increase in the owner's account, Thomas Toy, Capital, is shown by a credit to that account.

3 Rented a temporary shop and paid $300 for the January rent; issued check No. 1. Since all the rent will have expired by the time the financial statements are prepared, it is considered an expense of the month of January. An increase of an expense account is recorded by a debit; therefore, the Rent Expense—Shop Building account is debited. The decrease of the asset, cash, is recorded by a credit to Cash. A single rent account may be sufficient for all rented buildings and equipment. In this case, the accountant felt that managerial analyses required a separate rent expense account for the shop building.

5 Rented automotive tools and equipment until the firm could purchase its own. Rent in the amount of $80 was paid for January; issued check No. 2. As in the preceding transaction, all this rent will have expired before the financial statements are prepared; therefore, it is considered

an expense of January. An increase of an expense account is recorded by a debit, in this casc to Rent Expense—Automotive Tools and Equipment. The decrease of the asset, cash, is recorded by a credit to Cash. Again, a single rent expense account may have been sufficient.

1979

Jan. 5 Purchased repair parts and supplies described on invoice No. 306 from the Southern Supply Company for $400 on account. The Repair Parts and Supplies account is an asset and is increased by the transaction; the increase in the asset is shown by a debit to Repair Parts and Supplies. Since the purchase was on credit, a liability is created. To record the increase in the liability, the Accounts Payable account is credited. The amount payable to the particular creditor, the Southern Supply Company, must be shown in the books. A note should be made in the Explanation column of the journal to the effect that the creditor is the Southern Supply Company, so that the amount can be posted to the accounts payable ledger.

6 Performed repairs for several cash customers; received $1,000 in cash. Cash, an asset, is received; to record the increase of the asset, the Cash account must be debited. The particular source of this asset is a revenue. To record an increase in the revenue, Shop Repair Revenue is credited.

10 Purchased land as a prospective building site for $10,000. Paid $4,000 in cash (check No. 3) and issued a one-year note for the balance.

12 Made repairs on George Shipman's motorcycle for $40. Shipman asked that a charge account be opened in his name; he promises to settle the account within 30 days. This arrangement was authorized by the service manager.

15 Paid $800 in salaries for first half of month (check No. 4 issued to obtain payroll cash).

20 Performed repairs for cash customers for $2,000.

26 Made repairs on Jay Munson's motorcycle for $60. A charge account was opened in his name.

28 Made repairs on Robert Batson's motorcycle for $120. A charge account was opened in his name.

29 Purchased repair parts and supplies from the Delco Supply House for $250 on account (invoice No. 1004).

30 Paid the Southern Supply Company $300 on account (check No. 5).

31 Paid electricity and water bills for January, $80 (check No. 6).

31 Made shop repairs for cash customers for $1,800.

31 Paid $900 in salaries for last half of month (check No. 7 issued to obtain payroll cash).

1979

Jan. 31 Thomas Toy withdrew $300 in cash in anticipation that at least that much income had been earned (check No. 8).

31 Purchased automotive tools and equipment for cash, $4,000 (check No. 9). The list price was $5,000.

31 Paid a premium of $600 (check No. 10) on a 12-month comprehensive insurance policy; the policy becomes effective on February 1, 1979.

31 Received a check for $10 from George Shipman as part payment of his account.

31 Took a physical inventory of repair parts and supplies; it showed that parts and supplies costing $375 were on hand, thus indicating that $275 (January 5 purchase of $400, plus January 29 purchase of $250, minus inventory of $375) worth of repair parts and supplies had been used, becoming an expense. Originally, as repair parts and supplies were purchased, they were debited to an asset account. Now, as the amount used becomes known, an entry is made debiting an expense account, Repair Parts and Supplies Used, to show that the expense account has been increased, and crediting an asset account, Repair Parts and Supplies, to show that the asset account has been decreased. (This type of transaction is normally recorded in an *adjusting entry,* explained in Chapter 5. It is presented here to broaden the scope of this illustration.)

The results of this analytical reasoning are presented in the following general journal. Note that space is left between entries to ensure that they are separate and distinct.

GENERAL JOURNAL

Page 1

Date		Debit-Credit-Account Titles: Explanation	F	Debit	Credit
1979					
Jan	2	Cash		30000 00	
		Thomas Toy, Capital			30000 00
		To record investment by			
		proprietor to start a business			
		to be called Good Times Wheels			
		Repair Shop.			
	3	Rent Expense - Shop Building		300 00	
		Cash			300 00
		To record payment of rent on			
		shop building for month of			
		January, 1979; issued check No. 1.			

GENERAL JOURNAL

Page 1 (continued)

Date		Debit-Credit-Account Titles: Explanation	F	Debit	Credit
1979 Jan	5	Rent Expense – Automotive Tools and			
		Equipment		80 00	
		Cash			80 00
		To record payment of rent for automotive tools and equipment for month of January, 1979; issued check No. 2.			
	5	Repair Parts and Supplies		400 00	
		Accounts Payable			400 00
		To record purchase of parts and supplies on account on invoice No. 306:			
		Southern Supply Company. √$400.00			
	6	Cash		1000 00	
		Shop Repair Revenue			1000 00
		To record the rendering of repair services to cash customers.			
	10	Land		10000 00	
		Cash			4000 00
		Notes Payable			6000 00
		To record purchase of land; issued check No. 3 and gave a one-year note for the balance.			
	12	Accounts Receivable		40 00	
		Shop Repair Revenue			40 00
		To record billings for repairs rendered to:			
		George Shipman √$40.00			
	15	Salaries Expense		800 00	
		Cash			800 00
		To record payment of semi-monthly salaries; issued check No. 4 to obtain payroll cash.			

GENERAL JOURNAL

Page 2

Date	Debit-Credit-Account Titles: Explanation	F	Debit	Credit
1979 Jan 20	Cash		2000 00	
	Shop Repair Revenue			2000 00
	To record the rendering of repair services to cash customers.			
26	Accounts Receivable		60 00	
	Shop Repair Revenue			60 00
	To record billing for repair services rendered to:			
	Jay Munson ✓ $60.00			
28	Accounts Receivable		120 00	
	Shop Repair Revenue			120 00
	To record billing for repair services rendered to:			
	Robert Batson ✓ $120.00			
29	Repair Parts and Supplies		250 00	
	Accounts Payable			250 00
	To record purchase of parts and supplies on account on invoice No. 1004:			
	Delco Supply House ✓ $250.00			
30	Accounts Payable		300 00	
	Cash			300 00
	To record payment; issued Check No. 5 to:			
	Southern Supply Company ✓ $300.00			
31	Electricity and Water Expense		80 00	
	Cash			80 00
	To record payment of electricity and water bills for month of January; issued check No. 6.			

GENERAL JOURNAL

Page 2 (continued)

Date		Debit-Credit-Account Titles: Explanation	F	Debit	Credit
1979 Jan	31	Cash		1800 00	
		Shop Repair Revenue			1800 00
		To record the rendering of repair services to cash customers.			
	31	Salaries Expense		900 00	
		Cash			900 00
		To record payment of salaries for last half of January; issued check No. 7 to obtain payroll cash.			
	31	Thomas Toy, Drawing		300 00	
		Cash			300 00
		To record withdrawal by owner in anticipation of income earned; issued check No. 8.			

GENERAL JOURNAL

Page 3

Date		Debit-Credit-Account Titles: Explanation	F	Debit	Credit
1979 Jan	31	Automotive Tools and Equipment		4000 00	
		Cash			4000 00
		To record purchase of tools and equipment at a cost of $4,000.00 (list price, $5,000.00); issued check No. 9.			
	31	Prepaid Insurance		600 00	
		Cash			600 00
		To record payment of insurance premium for 12 months; insurance is effective February 1, 1979; issued check No. 10.			

GENERAL JOURNAL — Page 3 (continued)

Date		Debit-Credit-Account Titles: Explanation	F	Debit	Credit
1979					
Jan	31	Cash		10 00	
		Accounts Receivable			10 00
		To record collection to			
		apply on account of:			
		George Shipman ✓ $10.00			
	31	Repair Parts and Supplies Used		275 00	
		Repair Parts and Supplies			275 00
		To record cost of parts and			
		supplies used during			
		month of January.			

The basic accounting model has now been developed into a full-fledged system. This chapter has expanded the basic tools of accounting to include revenue, expense and the proprietor's drawing accounts. The concept of controlling and subsidiary accounts was introduced, so that the reader will know how to use these devices when he or she first encounters receivables or payables to several customers or creditors. An illustration of the basic, full-fledged system was started in this chapter. The transactions of the Good Times Wheels Repair Shop were presented; these are analyzed and journalized. A chart of accounts has been created for this firm. The remaining seven steps in this illustration will be completed in Chapter 4.

Glossary

Chart of accounts A list of all accounts in the general ledger which are anticipated to be used. Their numbering system indicates the types of accounts by subgroups.

Controlling account One account in the general ledger that controls, and is supported by, a group of accounts in a separate subsidiary ledger.

Cost The amount paid or payable in either cash or its equivalent for goods, services, or other assets purchased.

Expense Expired costs; the materials used and services utilized in the production of revenue during a specific period.

Income statement The statement showing the calculation of net income.

Income statement accounts Revenue and expense accounts that are incorporated in the income statement.

Loss Expired costs; the materials used and services utilized which did not produce any revenue.

Matching concept The identification of incurred expenses to a given time period, and matching them against earned revenue identified to the same time period, to determine net income for that period.

Net income Excess of revenue over expenses for given period.

Net loss Excess of expenses over revenue for a given period.

Revenue A term describing the source of inflows of assets received in exchange for services rendered, sales of products or merchandise, gains from sales or exchange of assets other than stock in trade, and earnings from interest and dividends on investments.

Subsidiary ledger A group of accounts in a separate ledger that provides information in detail about one controlling account in the general ledger.

Questions

Q3–1 Define the term *revenue*. Does the receipt of cash by a business indicate that revenue has been earned? Explain.

Q3–2 List ten small businesses and professions, and name the major source of revenue for each.

Q3–3 Define the term *expense*. Distinguish between expense and cost. Does the payment of cash by a business indicate that an expense has been incurred? Explain.

Q3–4 Define the matching concept. Why is it very important in determination of periodic income?

Q3–5 The accountant for J. A. Williams, owner of a parking-lot business, listed the parking lot at a cost of $10,000 on the balance sheet. Williams argues that this amount should be $18,000 because he has recently been offered $18,000 for the lot. Discuss.

Q3–6 List the advantages to management of a division of the general and subsidiary ledgers and the use of controlling accounts. Is it equally advantageous to exclude the schedules of accounts receivable and accounts payable from the general ledger trial balance? Explain.

Q3–7 The following transaction occurred on June 15, 1979:

Received bills representing charges for truck maintenance and repairs as follows: Beacon Hill Garage, $150; Uptown Garage, $225.

Showing the proper general journal and general and subsidiary ledger accounts, prepare flow charts as shown in Figure 3–1 to illustrate posting from the general journal to the general ledger and the accounts payable ledger.

Q3–8 Diagram and discuss the various parts of a simple accounting system.

Q3–9 Why are transactions first recorded in a journal?

Q3–10 Is the excess of cash received by a business over the cash paid out net income? Discuss.

Class exercises

CE3–1 (Journalizing) The chart of accounts of the Whitefield Laundry includes the following accounts and identifying numbers: Cash, 101; Accounts Receivable, 111; Cleaning Supplies, 135; Store Equipment, 164; Franklin Whitefield, Capital, 251; Cleaning Revenue, 301; Miscellaneous General Expense, 712; Wages Expense, 714.

1979

Dec. 1 Franklin Whitefield invested $6,000 in cash to start a cleaning business.

3 Purchased store equipment for $1,600 in cash.

10 Paid $100 in cash for cleaning supplies.

15 Billed the following customers for cleaning work for the first half of month:

G. Jamieson	$60
W. Nixon	50
J. Zarba	40

15 Paid $300 in salaries.

21 Paid $100 for miscellaneous general expenses.

26 Received cash from the following customers to apply on account:

G. Jamieson	$200
W. Nixon	120
J. Zarba	50

31 Paid $310 in salaries.

31 Billed the following customers for cleaning work for the second half of the month:

G. Jamieson	$210
J. Zarba	100

31 Received $560 from cash customers for the month.

Required: Journalize the foregoing transactions.

Exercises and problems

P3–1 A new accountant began work on January 2, 1979. Unfortunately, he made several errors that were discovered by the auditor (the outside independent accountant who is hired to review the year's work) during the year-end review. For each error described below, indicate the effect of the error by completing the following solution form. Treat each error separately; do not attempt to relate the errors to one another.

Suggested Solution Form					
Error	Would the December 31, 1979 Trial Balance Be Out of Balance?		If Yes, by How Much?	Which Would Be Larger?	
	YES	NO		Debit Total	Credit Total
a b etc.					

Required:

1. A typewriter was purchased for $450 and cash was paid and credited. The debit was entered twice in the asset account.
2. A debit to the Cash account of $1,192 was posted as $1,129.
3. Cash collections of $925 from customers in settlement of their accounts were not posted to the Accounts Receivable account, but were posted correctly to the Cash account.
4. A purchase of office supplies of $250 was recorded as a credit to Cash and also as a credit to Office Supplies.

P3–2 Some of the possible effects of a transaction are listed:

(1) an asset increase accompanied by an asset decrease
(2) an asset increase accompanied by an owner's equity increase
(3) an asset increase accompanied by a liability increase
(4) an asset increase accompanied by a revenue increase
(5) an asset decrease accompanied by a liability decrease
(6) an asset decrease accompanied by an owner's equity decrease
(7) an asset decrease accompanied by an expense increase
(8) an expense increase accompanied by a liability increase

Required: Using the identifying numbers to the left of the listed combinations, indicate the effect of each of the following transactions:
Example: Invested cash in the business. Answer: (2)

(a) Paid an account payable.
(b) Borrowed money from a bank and issued a note.
(c) Collected an account receivable.
(d) Collected a commission on a sale made today.
(e) Paid for an ad in a newspaper.

P3–3 The following cash receipt transactions occurred at the Ababa Realty Company during the month of July, 1979:

1979
July 1 Invested $50,000 in cash in the business.
7 Received a commission of $1,200 from the sale of a house and lot.
8 Received $2,500 in cash from the issuance of a note payable to a bank.
13 Received $750 in interest from U.S. government bonds.
20 Received $250 in cash for rent of part of a building for July, 1979.

Required: Journalize the revenue transactions only.

P3–4 The following were among the cash payment transactions at the Ballow Garage during the month of September, 1979:

1979
Sept. 3 Paid $3,000 for a truck.
7 Paid $760 for salaries for the month.
9 Paid $2,000 in settlement of an account.
12 Paid $350 for a typewriter.
16 Ballow drew $1,000 from business in expectation of income.
22 Paid $175 for rent of the office for September.

Required: Journalize the expense transactions only.

P3–5 The Cash account in the general ledger of Grossman's Repair Shop is given:

Cash — Acct. No. 101

(1)	1,000	(3)	600
(2)	400	(5)	500
(4)	500		

Item 1 is Grossman's original investment on June 1. Items 2 and 4 are cash receipts, and items 3 and 5 are cash payments made during June.

Required:

1. What is the balance of the account to be shown in the trial balance as of the end of June?
2. Will Grossman's income statement for the month of June reflect a net loss of $200—the excess of payments ($1,100) over receipts ($900) other than the original investment? Explain.

P3–6 (Integrative) The October, 1979, transactions of the Biltmore Travel Service are given:

1979

Oct. 1 Paid $150 for an advertisement in the Travel section of *The New York Times*.

2 Arranged a round-the-world trip for Mr. and Mrs. Hooker J. Sander. A commission of $175 in cash was collected from the steamship company.

3 Arranged fly-now, pay-later European trips for several clients. The Transatlantic Airway System agreed to a commission of $600 for services rendered, payment to be made at the end of month.

4 Another advertisement was placed in *The New York Times* for $250, payment to be made in 10 days.

16 Benjamin B. Biltmore, owner of the Biltmore Travel Service, withdrew $400 from the business for his personal use.

19 Collected $600 from the Transatlantic Airway System.

Required: Following the example given for the October 1 transaction, analyze each transaction and prepare the necessary journal entry.

Example:

Oct. 1 a. Advertising is an operating expense. Expenses are recorded by debits. Debit Advertising Expense for $150.

b. The asset Cash was decreased. Decreases of assets are recorded by credits. Credit cash for $150.

c. Journal entry:

Advertising Expense	150	
Cash		150

P3–7 (Integrative) The following transactions occurred at the Braskni Tax Service:

1979

Apr. 1 Billed the following customers for $450 for tax work:

Charles Allen	$100
Mason Dean	150
Mildred Schultz	200
Total	$450

30 Received $300 on account from the following customers:

Charles Allen	$ 75
Mason Dean	100
Mildred Schultz	125
Total	$300

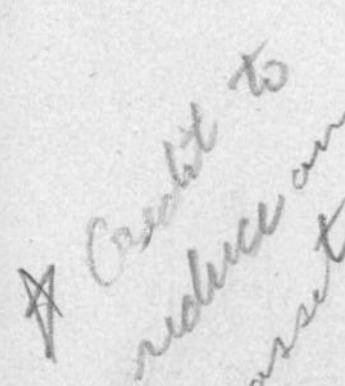

Required:

1. Prepare general journal entries to record the transactions.
2. Post to general ledger and accounts receivable ledger accounts. (Assign appropriate numbers to general ledger accounts.)
3. Prepare a schedule of accounts receivable.

P3–8 (Integrative) On August 1, 1979, the Office Machinery Repair Company purchased supplies on account as follows:

Aldan Company	$200
Jetson Company	80
Weston Company	520
Total	$800

On August 15, 1979, the Office Machinery Repair Company paid its creditors on account as follows:

Aldan Company	$150
Jetson Company	50
Weston Company	420
Total	$620

Required:

1. Prepare general journal entries to record the transactions.
2. Post to general ledger and accounts payable ledger accounts. (Assign appropriate numbers to general ledger accounts.)
3. Prepare a schedule of accounts payable.

P3–9 (Minicase) For the year 1979 the Jones Shoe Repair Shop showed: Shoe Repair Revenue, $20,000; Expenses, $12,000; Fire Loss, $18,000. Richard Jones, the owner, stated that he felt that his net income should be reported as $8,000 since the fire loss did not recur every year. He argues that the fire loss should be shown as a direct reduction of his capital and not be considered in the calculation of his net income.

Required:

1. Is Jones correct in his statement?
2. Discuss the concept of net income and the purpose of net income calculation.

chapter four

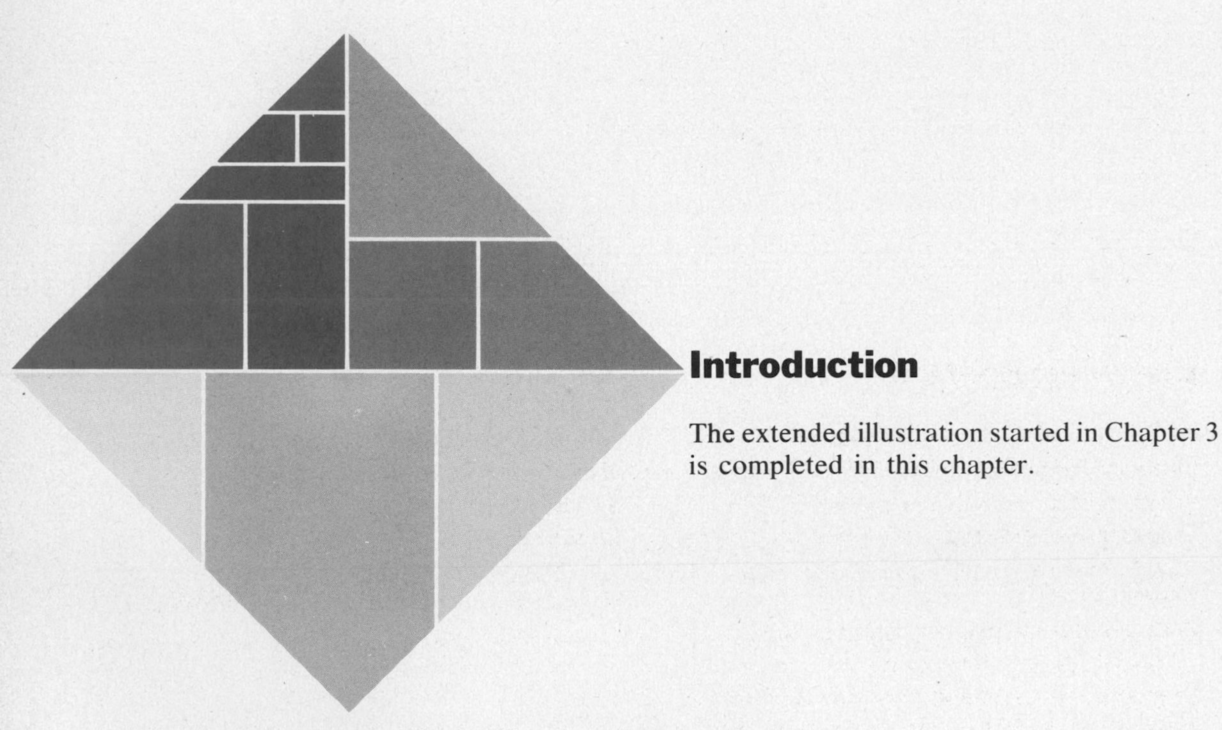

Introduction

The extended illustration started in Chapter 3 is completed in this chapter.

Extension of the accounting model using income statement accounts—completion of the basic accounting sequence

Learning goals

To explain the nature of an extended simple accounting system.

To prepare an income statement, statement of owner's equity, balance sheet, closing entries, and postclosing trial balance.

To know how to rule and balance the T-form ledger real accounts.

To prepare a statement of owner's equity when there is a beginning balance in the proprietor's capital account.

To state the interrelationship of financial statements of a single proprietorship.

Key terms

central processing
closing the books (accounts)
financial statements
  balance sheet
  income statement
  statement of owner's equity
inputs
outputs
nominal accounts
postclosing trial balance
real accounts
schedule of accounts payable
schedule of accounts receivable

Recall that there are nine steps in the accounting sequence we have defined. The first two steps were completed in Chapter 3. The journal entries recorded there are posted in this chapter (step 3) and a trial balance is prepared (step 4). A schedule of accounts receivable and accounts payable is prepared (steps 5, 6); the financial statements including income statement, statement of owner's equity, and balance sheet are prepared (step 7); and revenue, expense, and owner's drawing accounts are closed (step 8). Finally, a postclosing trial balance is taken (step 9).

Before we again pick up this illustration, let us take another look at the overall accounting system we are developing. The way the various parts are related to each other is graphically presented in Figure 4–1.

Figure 4–1
The accounting system

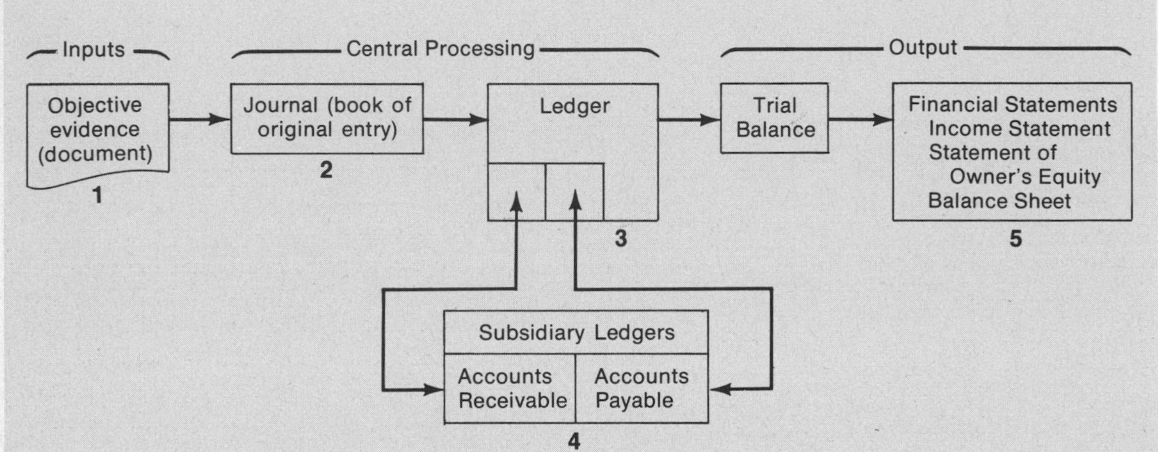

Explanation to numbered items follows:

1 Every entry in an accounting system must have objective evidence, usually a document such as a receipt for payment of cash, to justify the entry. These business documents are referred to as *inputs* into the accounting system because they are the method by which data are introduced into the accounting system.

2 All transactions are analyzed and recorded first in a journal, a book of original entry. The journalizing and posting process is referred to as *central processing*.

3 All journal entries must be posted to the ledger. Absolutely no transaction entries can be made in a ledger except those posted from a journal. There is no other source for ledger entries.

4 Various subsidiary ledgers—represented here by Accounts Receivable and Accounts Payable—are used to present a detailed breakdown of a larger account in the general ledger. This larger account is referred to as a controlling account.

5 As a test check of the equality of debits and credits a trial balance is taken. The final *output* of central processing is the financial statements. These are prepared from the information taken from the ledgers.

An illustration—the Good Times Wheels Repair Shop

Journalizing

The transactions of the Good Times Wheels Repair Shop for the month of January, 1979, were analyzed and journalized in Chapter 3. The journal entries showing the posting references are repeated here for your convenience.

GENERAL JOURNAL

Page 1

Date		Debit-Credit-Account Titles: Explanation	F	Debit	Credit
1979					
Jan	2	Cash	101	30000 00	
		Thomas Toy, Capital	301		30000 00
		To record investment by proprietor to start a business to be called Good Times Wheels Repair Shop.			
	3	Rent Expense – Shop Building	501	300 00	
		Cash	101		300 00
		To record payment of rent on shop building for month of January, 1979; issued check No. 1.			
	5	Rent Expense – Automotive Tools and Equipment	502	80 00	
		Cash	101		80 00
		To record payment of rent for automotive tools and equipment for month of January, 1979; issued check No. 2.			
	5	Repair Parts and Supplies	131	400 00	
		Accounts Payable	201		400 00
		To record purchase of parts and supplies on account on invoice No. 306:			
		Southern Supply Co. ✓ $400.00			

GENERAL JOURNAL

Page 1 (continued)

Date		Debit-Credit-Account Titles: Explanation	F	Debit	Credit
1979					
Jan	6	Cash	101	1000 00	
		Shop Repair Revenue	401		1000 00
		To record the rendering of repair services to cash customers.			
	10	Land	151	10000 00	
		Cash	101		4000 00
		Notes Payable	202		6000 00
		To record purchase of land; issued check No. 3 and gave a one-year note for the balance.			
	12	Accounts Receivable	121	40 00	
		Shop Repair Revenue	401		40 00
		To record billings for repairs rendered to:			
		George Shipman √ $40.00			
	15	Salaries Expense	504	800 00	
		Cash	101		800 00
		To record payment of semi-monthly salaries; issued check No. 4 to obtain payroll cash.			

GENERAL JOURNAL

Page 2

Date		Debit-Credit-Account Titles: Explanation	F	Debit	Credit
1979					
Jan	20	Cash	101	2000 00	
		Shop Repair Revenue	401		2000 00
		To record the rendering of repair services to cash customers.			

GENERAL JOURNAL

Page 2 (continued)

Date	Debit-Credit-Account Titles: Explanation	F	Debit	Credit
1979				
Jan 26	Accounts Receivable	121	60 00	
	Shop Repair Revenue	401		60 00
	To record billing for repair			
	services rendered to:			
	Jay Munson ✓ $60.00			
28	Accounts Receivable	121	120 00	
	Shop Repair Revenue	401		120 00
	To record billing for repair			
	services rendered to:			
	Robert Batson ✓ $120.00			
29	Repair Parts and Supplies	131	250 00	
	Accounts Payable	201		250 00
	To record purchase of parts			
	and supplies on account on			
	invoice No. 1004:			
	Delco Supply House ✓ $250.00			
30	Accounts Payable	201	300 00	
	Cash	101		300 00
	To record payment; issued			
	check No. 5 to:			
	Southern Supply Co. ✓ $300.00			
31	Electricity and Water Expense	508	80 00	
	Cash	101		80 00
	To record payment of			
	electricity and water bills			
	for month of January;			
	issued check No. 6.			
31	Cash	101	1800 00	
	Shop Repair Revenue	401		1800 00
	To record the rendering of			
	repair services to cash			
	customers.			

GENERAL JOURNAL Page 2 (continued)

Date	Debit-Credit-Account Titles: Explanation	F	Debit	Credit
1979				
Jan 31	Salaries Expense	504	900 00	
	Cash	101		900 00
	To record payment of salaries for last half of January; issued check No. 7 to obtain payroll cash.			
31	Thomas Toy, Drawing	311	300 00	
	Cash	101		300 00
	To record withdrawal by owner in anticipation of income earned; issued check No. 8.			

GENERAL JOURNAL Page 3

Date	Debit-Credit-Account Titles: Explanation	F	Debit	Credit
1979				
Jan 31	Automotive Tools and Equipment	161	4000 00	
	Cash	101		4000 00
	To record purchase of tools and equipment at a cost of $4000.00 (list price, $5000.00); issued check No. 9.			
31	Prepaid Insurance	141	600 00	
	Cash	101		600 00
	To record payment of insurance premium for 12 months; insurance is effective February 1, 1979; issued check No. 10.			
31	Cash	101	10 00	
	Accounts Receivable	121		10 00
	To record collection to apply on account of: George Shipman ✓ $10.00			
31	Repair Parts and Supplies Used	509	275 00	
	Repair Parts and Supplies	131		275 00
	To record cost of parts and supplies used during month of January.			

Posting to the ledgers

As the transactions are posted to the ledger, the account numbers are entered in the general journal folio (F) column. At the same time, the number of the journal page from which the entry is posted is entered in the folio (F) column of the ledger account.

The timing of the posting process is a matter of personal preference and expediency, but all postings must be completed before financial statements can be prepared. It is advisable to keep accounts with customers and creditors up to date so that the account balances are readily available. Because of this, it is probably best to post from the journal to the ledgers on a daily basis. (Note to student: If you are somewhat ''rusty'' on posting procedure, please turn back to page 45, Chapter 2, for a review.)

The posting of the transactions of the Good Times Wheels Repair Shop for the month of January, 1979 is shown in the general ledger below:

GENERAL LEDGER

Cash *Acct. No. 101*

Date		Explanation	F	Debit	Credit	Balance
1979						
Jan	2		1	30000.00		30000.00
	3		1		300.00	29700.00
	5		1		80.00	29620.00
	6		1	1000.00		30620.00
	10		1		4000.00	26620.00
	15		1		800.00	25820.00
	20		2	2000.00		27820.00
	30		2		300.00	27520.00
	31		2		80.00	27440.00
	31		2	1800.00		29240.00
	31		2		900.00	28340.00
	31		2		300.00	28040.00
	31		3		4000.00	24040.00
	31		3		600.00	23440.00
	31		3	10.00		23450.00

Balance is a debit

Accounts Receivable *Acct. No. 121*

Date		Explanation	F	Debit	Credit	Balance
1979						
Jan	12		1	40.00		40.00
	26		2	60.00		100.00
	28		2	120.00		220.00
	31		3		10.00	210.00

Balance is a debit

GENERAL LEDGER *(Continued)*

Repair Parts and Supplies — Acct. No. 131

Date		Explanation	F	Debit	Credit	Balance
1979						
Jan	5		1	400 00		400 00
	29		2	250 00		650 00
	31		3		275 00	375 00

Balance is a debit

Prepaid Insurance — Acct. No. 141

Date		Explanation	F	Debit	Credit	Balance
1979						
Jan	31		3	600 00		600 00

Balance is a debit

Land — Acct. No. 151

Date		Explanation	F	Debit	Credit	Balance
1979						
Jan	10		1	10000 00		10000 00

Balance is a debit

Automotive Tools and Equipment — Acct. No. 161

Date		Explanation	F	Debit	Credit	Balance
1979						
Jan	31		3	4000 00		4000 00

Balance is a debit

Accounts Payable — Acct. No. 201

Date		Explanation	F	Debit	Credit	Balance
1979						
Jan	5		1		400 00	400 00
	29		2		250 00	650 00
	30		2	300 00		350 00

Balance is a credit

GENERAL LEDGER *(Continued)*

Notes Payable — Acct. No: 202

Date		Explanation	F	Debit	Credit	Balance
1979						
Jan	10		1		6000 00	6000 00

Balance is a credit

Thomas Toy, Capital — Acct. No: 301

Date		Explanation	F	Debit	Credit	Balance
1979						
Jan	2		1		30000 00	30000 00

Balance is a credit

Thomas Toy, Drawing — Acct. No: 311

Date		Explanation	F	Debit	Credit	Balance
1979						
Jan	31		2	300 00		300 00

Balance is a debit

Shop Repair Revenue — Acct. No: 401

Date		Explanation	F	Debit	Credit	Balance
1979						
Jan	6		1		1000 00	1000 00
	12		1		40 00	1040 00
	20		2		2000 00	3040 00
	26		2		60 00	3100 00
	28		2		120 00	3220 00
	31		2		1800 00	5020 00

Balance is a credit

Rent Expense - Shop Building — Acct. No: 501

Date		Explanation	F	Debit	Credit	Balance
1979						
Jan	3		1	300 00		300 00

Balance is a debit

GENERAL LEDGER *(Continued)*

Rent Expense—Automotive Tools and Equipment — Acct. No. 502

Date		Explanation	F	Debit	Credit	Balance
1979						
Jan	5		1	80 00		80 00

Balance is a debit

Salaries Expense — Acct. No. 504

Date		Explanation	F	Debit	Credit	Balance
1979						
Jan	15		1	800 00		800 00
	31		2	900 00		1700 00

Balance is a debit

Electricity and Water Expense — Acct. No. 508

Date		Explanation	F	Debit	Credit	Balance
1979						
Jan	31		2	80 00		80 00

Balance is a debit

Repair Parts and Supplies Used — Acct. No. 509

Date		Explanation	F	Debit	Credit	Balance
1979						
Jan	31		3	275 00		275 00

Balance is a debit

Income Summary — Acct. No. 601

Date	Explanation	F	Debit	Credit	Balance

ACCOUNTS RECEIVABLE LEDGER

Robert Batson

Date		Explanation	F	Debit	Credit	Balance
1979						
Jan	28		2	120 00		120 00

Balance is a debit

Jay Munson

Date		Explanation	F	Debit	Credit	Balance
1979						
Jan	26		2	60 00		60 00

Balance is a debit

George Shipman

Date		Explanation	F	Debit	Credit	Balance
1979						
Jan	2		1	40 00		40 00
	31		3		10 00	30 00

Balance is a debit

ACCOUNTS PAYABLE LEDGER

Delco Supply House

Date		Explanation	F	Debit	Credit	Balance
1979						
Jan	29		2		250 00	250 00

Balance is a credit

Southern Supply Company

Date		Explanation	F	Debit	Credit	Balance
1979						
Jan	5		1		400 00	400 00
	30		2	300 00		100 00

Balance is a credit

Preparing a trial balance

After the accounts in the general ledger are posted up to date and the January 31 balances are obtained, the following trial balance is taken:

GOOD TIMES WHEELS REPAIR SHOP
Trial Balance
January 31, 1979

Acct. No.	Account Title	Debits	Credits
101	Cash	$23,450.00	
121	Accounts Receivable	210.00	
131	Repair Parts and Supplies	375.00	
141	Prepaid Insurance	600.00	
151	Land	10,000.00	
161	Automotive Tools and Equipment	4,000.00	
201	Accounts Payable		$ 350.00
202	Notes Payable		6,000.00
301	Thomas Toy, Capital		30,000.00
311	Thomas Toy, Drawing	300.00	
401	Shop Repair Revenue		5,020.00
501	Rent Expense—Shop Building	300.00	
502	Rent Expense—Automotive Tools and Equipment	80.00	
504	Salaries Expense	1,700.00	
508	Electricity and Water Expense	80.00	
509	Repair Parts and Supplies Used	275.00	
	Totals	$41,370.00	$41,370.00

Preparing a schedule of accounts receivable

The fact that the trial balance is in balance is one bit of evidence of the accuracy of the accounting up to this point; the accountant, therefore, takes the next step, that of preparing a *schedule of accounts receivable*.

At the end of a designated accounting period (one month in this example) the total of all the balances of customers' accounts should agree with the balance of the Accounts Receivable controlling account in the general ledger. A schedule of accounts receivable usually is prepared to check this agreement. The schedule of accounts receivable taken from the Good Times Wheels Repair Shop's accounts receivable ledger shows that the total of all customers' accounts is $210, which agrees with the balance of the Accounts Receivable controlling account.

GOOD TIMES WHEELS REPAIR SHOP
Schedule of Accounts Receivable
January 31, 1979

Robert Batson	$120.00
Jay Munson	60.00
George Shipman	30.00
Total Accounts Receivable	$210.00

Preparing a schedule of accounts payable

The next step is similar to the one before; it involves the preparation of a *schedule of accounts payable*.

At the end of the accounting period, the total of the balances of the individual creditors' accounts payable should equal the balance of the Accounts Payable controlling account. The schedule of accounts payable taken from the Good Times Wheels Repair Shop's accounts payable ledger shows that the total of the creditors' accounts is $350, which agrees with the balance of the Accounts Payable controlling account.

GOOD TIMES WHEELS REPAIR SHOP
Schedule of Accounts Payable
January 31, 1979

Delco Supply House	$250.00
Southern Supply Company	100.00
Total Accounts Payable	$350.00

Preparing the financial statements from the trial balance

The income statement, the statement of owner's equity and the balance sheet are usually prepared at the end of an accounting period. The first two have not yet been illustrated.

The income statement

The income statement shown in Figure 4–2 was prepared from the trial balance of the Good Times Wheels Repair Shop.

The heading of the income statement shows the following:

1. Name of the business
2. Name of the statement
3. Period covered by the statement

It is important that the period covered be specified clearly. The date January 31, 1979, is not sufficient; it, alone, does not indicate whether the net income of $2,585 was earned in one day, one month, or one year ended January 31, 1979. The analyst must know how long a period it took for the firm to earn the $2,585.

For a simple service-type firm, there is no standard order for listing accounts in the income statement. Size of each revenue and expense item may be one criterion; or the sequence of the accounts in the general ledger may be used as the basis for establishing the order used in listing the accounts in the income statement. The latter criterion is followed in Figure 4–2.

Figure 4–2
Income statement

GOOD TIMES WHEELS REPAIR SHOP
Income Statement
For the Month Ended January 31, 1979

Revenue		
Shop Repair Revenue		$5,020.00
Expenses		
Rent Expense—Shop Building	$ 300.00	
Rent Expense—Automotive Tools and Equipment	80.00	
Salaries Expense	1,700.00	
Electricity and Water Expense	80.00	
Repair Parts and Supplies Used	275.00	
Total Expenses		2,435.00
Net Income		$2,585.00

Statement of owner's equity

This statement shows the changes that take place in the proprietor's capital over a given period of time; it should cover the same period as the income statement. Net income, withdrawals by the owner, and additional investments by the owner are reflected in the statement. The *statement of owner's equity* of the Good Times Wheels Repair Shop for the first month of its operation is shown in Figure 4–3. The heading of the statement of owner's equity is similar to that of the income statement.

Figure 4–3
Statement of owner's equity for new business

GOOD TIMES WHEELS REPAIR SHOP
Statement Of Owner's Equity
For the Month Ended January 31, 1979

Original Investment, January 2, 1979	$30,000.00
Add Net Income for January, 1979	2,585.00
Total	$32,585.00
Less Withdrawals	300.00
Thomas Toy, Capital, January 31, 1979	$32,285.00

Statement of owner's equity where there is a beginning balance in the proprietor's capital account. For a business that has been in existence prior to the current period, there would be one change in the statement of owner's equity; the beginning-of-period balance of capital would be shown on the statement. For example, the statement of the Nancy Wooten Management Services is shown in Figure 4–4.

Figure 4-4 Complete statement of owner's equity

NANCY WOOTEN MANAGEMENT SERVICES
Statement Of Owner's Equity
For the Month Ended January 31, 1979

Nancy Wooten, Capital, January 1, 1979	$500,000.00
Add Net Income for January, 1979	100,000.00
Additional Investment	200,000.00
Total	$800,000.00
Deduct Withdrawals	50,000.00
Nancy Wooten, Capital, January 31, 1979	$750,000.00

The balance sheet

Since the January 31, 1979, capital balance of the Good Times Wheels Repair Shop has now been determined (Figure 4–3), it is possible to prepare the classified balance sheet, as shown in Figure 4–5. Remember that this form of the balance sheet is referred to as the account form.

Note that the heading of the balance sheet contains the single date *January 31, 1979*. This statement reveals the financial position as of the close of business on January 31. It is similar to a still photograph, whereas the income statement and statement of owner's equity are like moving pictures—they show the changes that have taken place during a specific period.

Figure 4-5 Account form of balance sheet

GOOD TIMES WHEELS REPAIR SHOP
Balance Sheet
January 31, 1979

Assets			Liabilities and Owner's Equity		
Current Assets			Current Liabilities		
Cash	$23,450.00		Accounts Payable . .	$ 350.00	
Accounts Receivable . . .	210.00		Notes Payable	6,000.00	
Repair Parts and Supplies	375.00		Total Current Liabilities . . .		$ 6,350.00
Prepaid Insurance .	600.00		Owner's Equity		
Total Current Assets		$24,635.00	Thomas Toy, Capital .		32,285.00
Plant and Equipment					
Land	$10,000.00				
Automotive Tools and Equipment . .	4,000.00				
Total Plant and Equipment		14,000.00			
Total Assets		$38,635.00	Total Liabilities and Owner's Equity		$38,635.00

Closing the revenue, expense, and proprietor's drawing accounts

Temporary or nominal accounts

The revenue, expense, and proprietor's drawing accounts are used to measure part of the changes that take place in the proprietor's capital account during a specified period. For this reason, these accounts are often called **temporary** *owner's equity accounts, or* **nominal accounts.**

At the end of an accounting period, the temporary or *nominal accounts* are emptied—or closed—so that they may be used to accumulate changes in owner's equity for the next period. Therefore, closing entries are made to transfer the final effects of the temporary owner's equity accounts to the proprietor's capital account. This is a permanent or *real account*.

Permanent or real accounts

The term **real** *is applied to the accounts that appear in the balance sheet; these accounts are not closed at the end of a period.*

The closing procedure

To facilitate the transfer of revenue and expense account balances, an intermediate summary account, called Income Summary, is used. The balances of all revenue and expense accounts are transferred to this account. The Income Summary account, the balance of which reveals the net income or net loss for the period, is then closed by transferring its balance to the proprietor's capital account. This action is justified because net income or net loss accrues to the owner. Since the proprietor's drawing account is not an expense account, it is not closed to Income Summary; rather, it is closed directly to the proprietor's capital account. After the revenue and expense accounts are closed, they have zero balances and are now available to accumulate information for measuring the changes in the proprietor's capital account in the next accounting period.

Using the T-form of the ledger accounts, the closing procedure is illustrated in Figure 4–6. The caption *Closing Entries* is written in the middle of the first unused line in the general journal under the transactions of the period, and the closing entries are begun directly under that.[1] They are posted immediately to the general ledger. As indicated in Figure 4–6, the closing entries are made in the following sequence:

1 All revenue accounts are debited in a compound entry, and the sum of the revenue items is credited to the Income Summary account.
2 All expense accounts are credited in a second compound entry, and the sum of the expense items is debited to the Income Summary account.
3 After entries 1 and 2 are posted, a credit balance in the Income Summary account represents net income; a debit balance, net loss. The balance of the account is transferred to the proprietor's capital account.

1 Later a group of entries called *adjusting entries* will be introduced; they will be entered between the transactions and closing entries.

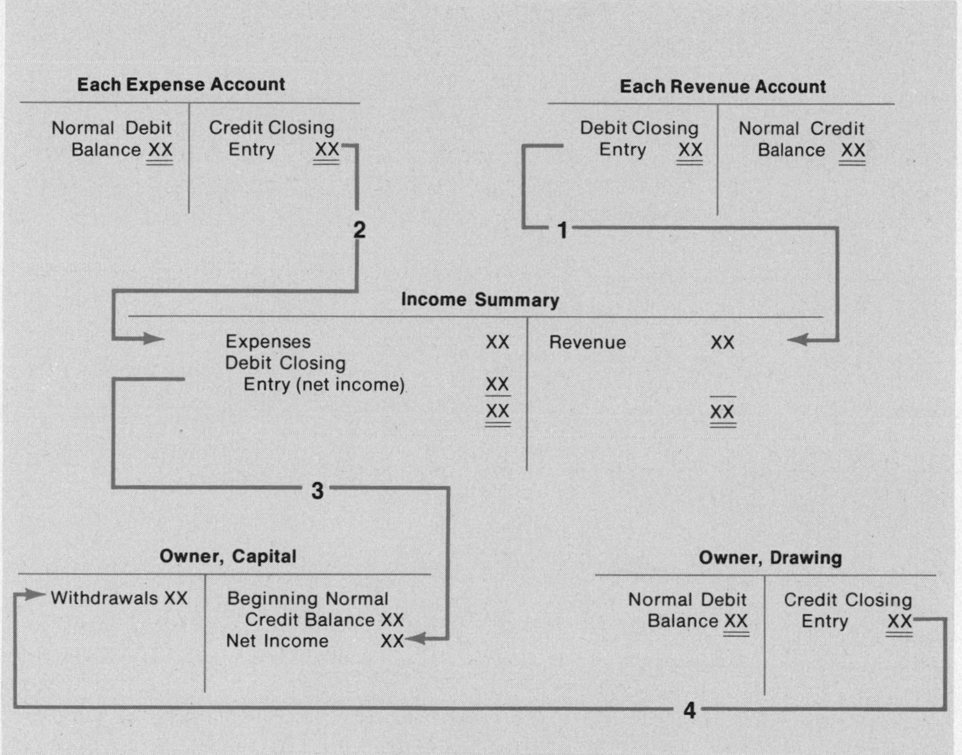

Figure 4–6 The closing procedure

4 The owner's drawing account is closed directly to the capital account by a debit to the capital account and a credit to the drawing account.

Unlike regular transaction entries, which require analysis and judgment, the closing process is purely mechanical and involves only the shifting and summarizing of previously determined amounts. The closing journal entries of the Good Times Wheels Repair Shop on January 31, 1979, are shown in Figure 4–7.

The presence of account numbers in the folio column of the journal indicates that the closing journal entries have been posted to the ledger accounts indicated in the journal (see Figure 4–8). Closing may be indicated by the words

Figure 4–7 Closing entries

GENERAL JOURNAL

Page 4

Date		Debit-Credit-Account Titles: Explanation	F	Debit	Credit
1979					
		Closing Entries			
Jan	31	Shop Repair Revenue	401	5020 00	
		Income Summary	601		5020 00
		To close revenue to summary account.			

GENERAL JOURNAL — Page 4 (continued)

Date		Debit-Credit-Account Titles: Explanation	F	Debit	Credit
1979					
Jan	31	Income Summary	601	2435 00	
		Rent Expense – Shop Building	501		300 00
		Rent Expense – Automotive			
		Tools and Equipment	502		80 00
		Salaries Expense	504		1700 00
		Electricity and Water Expense	508		80 00
		Repair Parts and Supplies Used	509		275 00
		To close expenses to summary			
		account.			
	31	Income Summary	601	2585 00	
		Thomas Toy, Capital	301		2585 00
		To transfer net income to			
		the Capital account.			
	31	Thomas Toy, Capital	301	300 00	
		Thomas Toy, Drawing	311		300 00
		To close the amount			
		withdrawn by the proprietor			
		to the capital account.			

Closing entry in the Explanation columns of the nominal accounts, as shown in Figure 4–8.

The condition of the closed nominal accounts

After the closing entries have been posted, the temporary owner's equity accounts have zero balances. Figure 4–8 shows the nominal accounts after the closing entries have been posted. Note that each of these accounts has a zero balance. As stated before, they can now be used to accumulate relevant information about revenues, expenses, and drawing for February, 1979, in the case of the Good Times Wheels Repair Shop.

Figure 4–8 The nominal accounts are closed

GENERAL LEDGER

Thomas Toy Drawing — Acct. No. 311

Date		Explanation	F	Debit	Credit	Balance
1979						
Jan	31		2	300 00		300 00
	31	Closing entry	4		300 00	–0–

GENERAL LEDGER *(Continued)*

Shop Repair Revenue — Acct. No. 401

Date		Explanation	F	Debit	Credit	Balance
1979						
Jan	6		1		1000 00	1000 00
	12		1		40 00	1040 00
	20		2		2000 00	3040 00
	26		2		60 00	3100 00
	28		2		120 00	3220 00
	31		2		1800 00	5020 00
	31	Closing entry	4	5020 00		—0—

Rent Expense - Shop Building — Acct. No. 501

Date		Explanation	F	Debit	Credit	Balance
1979						
Jan	3		1	300 00		300 00
	31	Closing entry	4		300 00	—0—

Rent Expense - Automotive Tools and Equipment — Acct. No. 502

Date		Explanation	F	Debit	Credit	Balance
1979						
Jan	5		1	80 00		80 00
	31	Closing entry	4		80 00	—0—

Salaries Expense — Acct. No. 504

Date		Explanation	F	Debit	Credit	Balance
1979						
Jan	15		1	800 00		800 00
	31		2	900 00		1700 00
	31	Closing entry	4		1700 00	—0—

Electricity and Water Expense — Acct. No. 508

Date		Explanation	F	Debit	Credit	Balance
1979						
Jan	31		2	80 00		80 00
	31	Closing Entry	4		80 00	—0—

GENERAL LEDGER *(Continued)*

Repair Parts and Supplies Used — Acct. No. 509

Date		Explanation	F	Debit	Credit	Balance
1979						
Jan	31		3	275 00		275 00
	31	Closing entry	4		275 00	-0-

Income Summary — Acct. No. 601

Date		Explanation	F	Debit	Credit	Balance
1979						
Jan	31	Revenue	4		5020 00	5020 00
	31	Expenses	4	2435 00		2585 00
	31	Closing to capital	4	2585 00		-0-

How the Thomas Toy, Capital account looks after closing

Figure 4–9 shows how the Thomas Toy, Capital account will look after the closing entries have been posted. Notice that the balance is $32,285, the amount that was shown on the balance sheet in Figure 4–5. The other real accounts are not affected by the closing entries. Their account balances will remain the same as shown in these accounts in pages 103–105.

Figure 4–9 The proprietor's capital account after closing

GENERAL LEDGER

Thomas Toy, Capital — Acct. No. 301

Date		Explanation	F	Debit	Credit	Balance
1979						
Jan	2	Original investment	1		30000 00	30000 00
	31	Net income	4		2585 00	32585 00
	31	Withdrawal by proprietor	4	300 00		32285 00

Figure 4-10
The postclosing trial balance

GOOD TIMES WHEELS REPAIR SHOP
Postclosing Trial Balance
January 31, 1979

Acct. No.	Account Title	Debits	Credits
101	Cash	$23,450.00	
121	Accounts Receivable	210.00	
131	Repair Parts and Supplies	375.00	
141	Prepaid Insurance	600.00	
151	Land	10,000.00	
161	Automotive Tools and Equipment	4,000.00	
201	Accounts Payable		$ 350.00
202	Notes Payable		6,000.00
301	Thomas Toy, Capital		32,285.00
	Totals	$38,635.00	$38,635.00

Taking a postclosing trial balance

After the closing entries have been posted, a *postclosing trial balance* is taken from the general ledger. Since the only accounts with open balances are the real accounts, the accounts and amounts in the postclosing trial balance are the same as those in the balance sheet. The postclosing trial balance tests the debit and credit equality of the general ledger before the accounts receive postings of the next accounting period. Its use, however, is optional, and a comparison of the general ledger account balances with the Balance Sheet will serve the same purpose. In any case, it is absolutely essential to start a new period with the accounts in proper balance. To show why: Suppose an error were made in the closing process for January, 1979. The capital account would reflect the error. If no postclosing trial balance were taken, no accounting procedure would reveal the error until the end of the next accounting period when the trial balance was prepared. The accountant would not think to look back at the preceding closing process for the error. He or she would spend precious time looking for errors in the current period data before examining the previous accounting period. The postclosing trial balance of the Good Times Wheels Repair Shop is shown in Figure 4-10.

Interrelationships of the financial statements

There is a significant interrelationship between the balance sheet, the statement of owner's equity, and the income statement, as illustrated in Figure 4-11. The income statement shows the net amount remaining after revenues have been matched with expenses for a given period. This amount, the net income, is transferred to the statement of owner's equity, which shows the changes that have taken place in owner's equity as a result of the operations of a period. The statement of owner's equity shows additional changes that have taken place in owner's equity—in this particular case, the withdrawals by the owner. The end-of-period balance of capital is transferred to the end-of-period balance sheet, which presents information as of a moment of time—that is, at the end of the accounting period. The income statement and the statement of owner's equity help to account for the changes in the owner's equity during the interval between balance sheets. Though it is not absolutely necessary, it is helpful if the statements are prepared in this sequence: income statement, statement of owner's equity, and balance sheet.

Figure 4–11 The interrelationship of financial statements

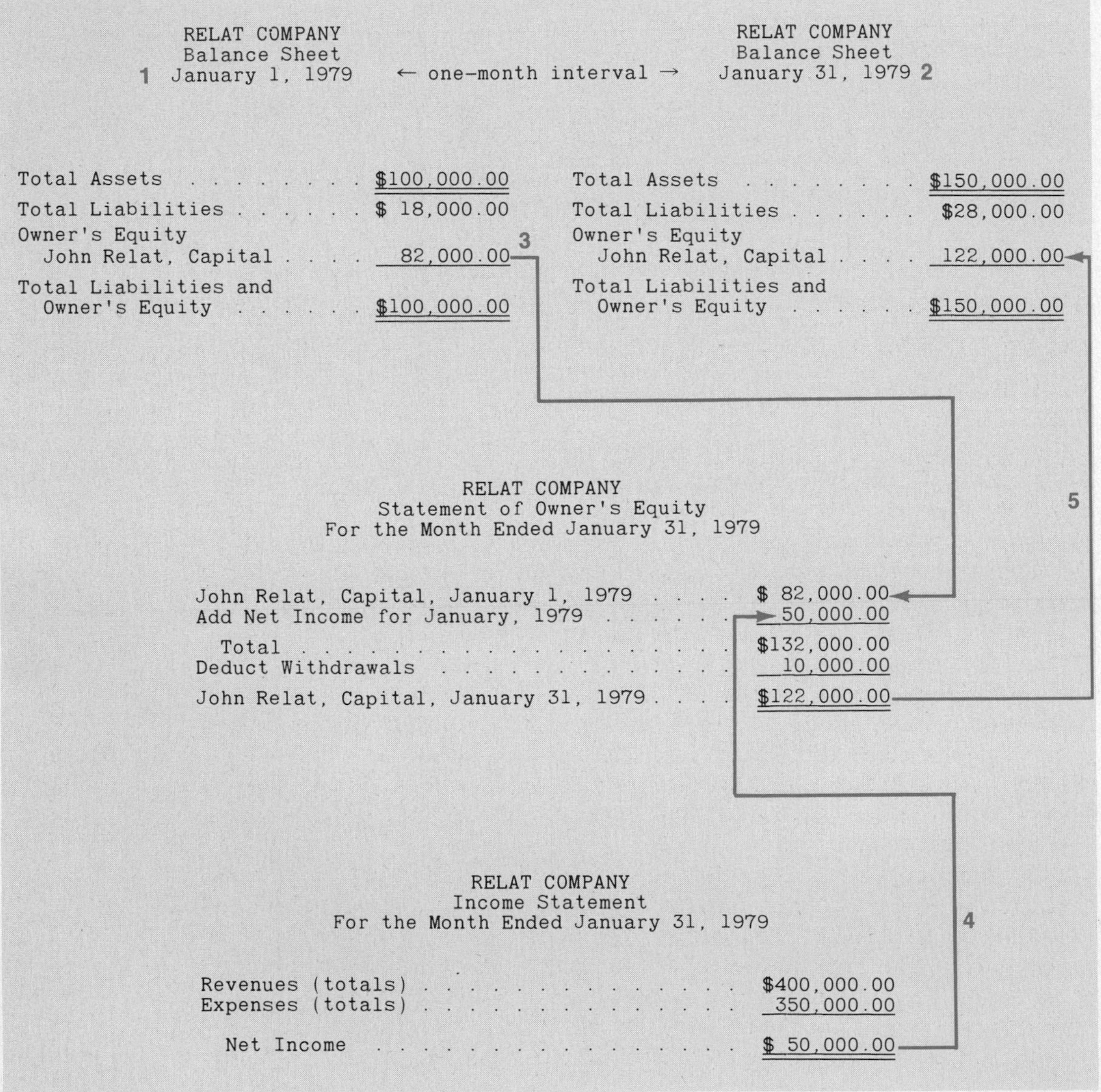

1 RELAT COMPANY
Balance Sheet
January 1, 1979

← one-month interval →

2 RELAT COMPANY
Balance Sheet
January 31, 1979

January 1, 1979		January 31, 1979	
Total Assets	$100,000.00	Total Assets	$150,000.00
Total Liabilities	$ 18,000.00	Total Liabilities	$28,000.00
Owner's Equity		Owner's Equity	
John Relat, Capital	82,000.00 (3)	John Relat, Capital	122,000.00
Total Liabilities and Owner's Equity	$100,000.00	Total Liabilities and Owner's Equity	$150,000.00

RELAT COMPANY
Statement of Owner's Equity
For the Month Ended January 31, 1979

John Relat, Capital, January 1, 1979	$ 82,000.00
Add Net Income for January, 1979	50,000.00
Total	$132,000.00
Deduct Withdrawals	10,000.00
John Relat, Capital, January 31, 1979	$122,000.00 (5)

RELAT COMPANY
Income Statement
For the Month Ended January 31, 1979

Revenues (totals)	$400,000.00
Expenses (totals)	350,000.00
Net Income	$ 50,000.00 (4)

Summary totals are used so that the statements can be presented on one page. This procedure is not acceptable for solving the end-of-chapter material; details should be given on all statements.

1 The date of the first balance sheet is also the beginning date of the statement of owner's equity and the income statement. (*For the Month Ended January 31, 1979,* means the period beginning January 1.)
2 The date of the second balance sheet (January 31, 1979) is also the ending date of the statement of owner's equity and the income statement.
3 The capital balance in the first balance sheet ($82,000) is the same as the beginning amount in the statement of owner's equity.
4 The net income ($50,000) is transferred from the income statement to the statement of owner's equity.
5 The end-of-period capital balance ($122,000) is transferred from the statement of owner's equity to the balance sheet dated January 31, 1979.

Balancing and ruling open real accounts

appendix

For the T-form of ledger account

When the T-form of ledger accounts is used in the general ledger, it is customary to balance and rule the real accounts. This procedure is followed to simplify the computations in the real accounts and to set apart the amounts from each accounting period. The steps in this procedure are:

1. The balance of the account is computed. The amount is transferred to the money column on the opposite side, dated as of the last day of the accounting period. The word *Balance* is entered in the Explanation column, and a check mark is placed in the folio (F) column.
2. The equal debit and credit footings are entered on the next unused full line.
3. Double lines are drawn across all the columns, except the Explanation columns.
4. The balance is written under the double lines on the appropriate side, dated as of the last day of the current accounting period. The word *Balance* is written in the Explanation column, and a check mark is placed in the folio (F) column. It is not necessary to balance and rule an account that contains only one amount. Balancing an account, unlike adjusting and closing, *does not* involve journalizing or posting, because the balance of the account does not change. That is to say, no new transaction information is recorded in the accounts.

The Cash account of the Good Times Wheels Repair Shop shown below illustrates balancing and ruling of T-form accounts.

GENERAL LEDGER

Cash — Acct. No. 101

Date	Explanation	F	Debit	Date	Explanation	F	Credit
1979				1979			
Jan 2		1	30000 00	Jan 3		1	300 00
6		1	1000 00	5		1	80 00
20		2	2000 00	10		1	4000 00
31		2	1800 00	15		1	800 00
31	$23,450.00	3	10 00	30		2	300 00
			34810 00	31		2	80 00
				31		2	900 00
				31		2	300 00
				31		3	4000 00
				31		3	600 00
							11360 00
				31	Balance	✓	23450 00
			34810 00				34810 00
1979 Jan 31	Balance	✓	23450 00				

For the three-amount-column form of ledger account

When the three-amount-column form of account is used, the balance of the real account is always currently maintained. For this reason, there is not as much of a compelling reason to rule the real accounts as there is when the T-form is used. Where it is deemed necessary, the debit-credit-balance form of accounts could be reduced to zero and then ruled in a manner very similar to that described above for the T-form. For example, to balance and rule the Cash debit-credit-balance form of account, it would be necessary to place the balance of $23,450 in the credit column, thus reducing the Cash account to a zero balance. The account could then be double ruled across the date, folio and the three amount columns. The balance then would be entered after the double rules.

Glossary

Central processing A method of sorting and analyzing data in terms of their effect on accounts; here central processing is done through a journal and various ledgers.

Closing the books The process of clearing the temporary or the nominal accounts at the end of a period; this process requires preparation of closing journal entries and posting of these entries to the nominal accounts that are closed.

Inputs The introduction of data in the accounting system through various objective evidence, such as business documents.

Income statement A statement showing all revenue and expense items for a given period, arranged so that the total of the expenses are subtracted from the total of the revenues, thus revealing the net income earned during that period.

Outputs The various statements, schedules, and reports produced by an accounting system.

Nominal accounts Temporary accounts to collect and to measure part of the change that takes place in applicable owner's equity account(s). They are closed out at the end of each accounting period.

Postclosing trial balance A trial balance taken of the ledger accounts that have any balances in them—the real accounts—after closing entries have been recorded and posted.

Real accounts The accounts that are not closed and that are incorporated in the balance sheet.

Schedule of accounts payable A listing of the individual creditors with amount owed to each and the total owed to all creditors at a given moment in time.

Schedule of accounts receivable A listing of the individual customers (debtors) with the amount owed by each and the total amounts receivable from all customers.

Statement of owner's equity A statement showing the changes that occurred in the proprietor's capital during a given period.

Questions

Q4–1 Assume that your store has 1,000 charge customers.
- a. Why would you want to keep your posting up to date?
- b. Is it true that posting depends on previous journalizing?
- c. Does journalizing, in turn, depend on earlier procedures in the complete accounting system? Explain.

Q4–2 What is the purpose of closing the books? Using T accounts for Revenue, Expenses, Income Summary, and Owner's Capital, diagram the closing process.

Q4–3 Draw a diagram showing the interrelationship of the balance sheet, statement of owner's equity, and the income statement.

Q4–4 The balance of Robert Taylor, Capital account in the Taylor's Grocery Store on December 31, 1979 was $1,000 less than on December 31, 1978. Give two possible reasons for the decrease.

Q4–5 What item is common to each of the following pairs: (1) The income statement and the statement of owner's equity? (2) The statement of owner's equity and the balance sheet as of the beginning of an accounting period? (3) The statement of owner's equity and the balance sheet as of the end of an accounting period?

Q4–6 Robert Hanion purchased electrical supplies on account from the Wilson Company for $350, and from Jackson, Inc., for $100. Hanion debited Electrical Supplies, $450, and erroneously credited Accounts Receivable for $450 in the general ledger. The credit postings to the accounts payable ledger were properly made.

a. What effect would the error have on the debit and credit totals of the trial balance taken at the end of the month?
b. What accounts in the trial balance would be incorrectly stated?
c. Would the error be discovered? How?

Q4–7 Define the following terms relating to an accounting system: (a) inputs, (b) central processing, (c) outputs.

Q4–8 Describe the relationship of subsidiary ledgers to the general ledger and the total accounting system.

Q4–9 What is the purpose of the postclosing trial balance?

Q4–10 List and discuss briefly the various steps in the accounting sequence presented in Chapters 3 and 4.

Class exercises

CE4–1 (Journalizing, posting, trial balance, and schedule of accounts receivable) The chart of accounts of the White Laundramat includes the following accounts and identifying numbers: Cash, 101; Accounts Receivable, 111, Cleaning Supplies, 135; Store Equipment, 164; Robert White, Capital, 251; Cleaning Revenue, 301; Miscellaneous General Expense, 712; Wages Expense, 714.

1979

Dec. 1 Robert White invested $3,000 in cash to start a cleaning business.

3 Purchased store equipment for $800 in cash.

10 Paid $50 in cash for cleaning supplies.

15 Billed the following customers for cleaning work for the first half of month:

G. Jamieson	$125
W. Nixon	100
J. Zarba	50

Dec. 15 Paid $200 in salaries.

21 Paid $90 for miscellaneous general expenses.

26 Received cash from the following customers to apply on account:

G. Jamieson	$100
W. Nixon	60
J. Zarba	25

31 Paid $250 in salaries.

31 Billed the following customers for cleaning work for the second half of the month:

G. Jamieson	$190
J. Zarba	80

31 Received $420 from cash customers for the month.

Required:

1. Journalize the transactions.
2. Open accounts and post from the journal to the appropriate ledgers. (Use appropriate numbers in general ledger accounts.)
3. Take a trial balance.
4. Prepare a schedule of accounts receivable.

CE4–2 (Journalizing, posting, and statements) Dr. Richard T. Kiley opened an office for the general practice of dentistry. During the month of October, 1979, the following transactions occurred.

1979

Oct. 1 Invested $2,000 in the business.

3 Purchased dental supplies on account, as follows:

Safety Dental Supply Company	$350
Sanitary Supply Company	400

3 Paid $300 for the October rent.

7 Paid $200 for miscellaneous general expenses.

8 Purchased office equipment from Dental Equipment Company for $5,000 on account.

10 Received $1,200 in cash for professional services rendered.

15 Paid $200 to the Safety Dental Supply Company on account, and $300 to the Sanitary Supply Company.

26 Mailed statements to the following clients for services rendered:

R. Beale	$45
P. Witty	75

31 Paid $1,000 in cash and issued a note payable for $4,000 to the Dental Equipment Company.

31 Received $20 in cash from R. Beale and $50 from P. Witty.

Required:
1. Journalize the transactions.
2. Post to the general ledger, accounts receivable ledger, and accounts payable ledger. (Assign numbers to the general ledger accounts).
3. Take a trial balance.
4. Prepare schedules of accounts receivable and accounts payable as of October 31, 1979.
5. Prepare an income statement, a statement of owner's equity, and a balance sheet.
6. Journalize the closing entries and post them.
7. Prepare a postclosing trial balance.

CE4–3 (Closing entries and postclosing trial balance) The trial balance of the Carter's Pizza Palace on December 31, 1979, is given:

CARTER'S PIZZA PALACE
Trial Balance
December 31, 1979

Acct. No.	*Account Title*	*Debits*	*Credits*
101	Cash	$50,000	
111	Accounts Receivable	4,000	
121	Supplies	1,800	
221	Equipment	20,000	
301	Accounts Payable		$ 4,000
401	Richard Carter, Capital		64,850
421	Richard Carter, Drawing	2,000	
501	Commissions Earned		15,000
511	Rent Earned		5,000
601	Salaries Expense	6,700	
602	Advertising Expense	1,000	
603	Supplies Used	1,600	
604	Miscellaneous Expense	1,750	
	Totals	$88,850	$88,850

Required:
1. Set up ledger accounts for Richard Carter, Capital; Richard Carter, Drawing, and each revenue and expense account listed in the trial balance. Enter the account balances.
2. Journalize the closing entries and post to ledger accounts.
3. Prepare a postclosing trial balance.

Exercises and problems

P4–1 The following transactions occurred at the Adden Rug Cleaning Company:

1979

Sept. 1 Billed customers for $285 for rug cleaning work, as follows:

Charles Abbot	$ 75
Morgan Hooley	120
Arthur Rogers	90
Total	$285

30 Received $135 on account from the following customers:

Charles Abbott	$ 25
Morgan Hooley	60
Arthur Rogers	50
Total	$135

Required:

1. Prepare general journal entries to record the transactions.
2. Post to general ledger and accounts receivable ledger accounts. (Assign appropriate numbers to general ledger accounts.)
3. Prepare a schedule of accounts receivable.

P4–2 On July 1, 1979, the Alden Plumbing Company purchased plumbing supplies on account, as follows:

Allan Company	$ 300
Jackson Company	100
Warren, Inc.	600
Total	$1,000

On July 15, 1979, the Alden Plumbing Company paid its creditors, as follows:

Allan Company	$200
Jackson Company	40
Warren, Inc.	150
Total	$390

Required:

1. Prepare general journal entries to record the transactions.
2. Post to general ledger and accounts payable ledger accounts. (Assign appropriate numbers to general ledger accounts.)
3. Prepare a schedule of accounts payable.

P4–3 As of December 31, 1979, the ledger of the Duncan Company contained the following accounts and account balances, among others: Cash, $60,000; Accounts Receivable, $20,000; John Duncan, Capital, $62,500; Commissions Earned, $50,000; Rent Earned, $6,000; Salaries Expense, $35,000; Office Expense, $5,000; Miscellaneous Expense, $12,000; John Duncan, Drawing, $6,000. (All the nominal accounts that are to be closed are included.)

Required: Journalize the closing entries.

P4–4 Financial information for three different single proprietorships is given:

a. Net income for 1979	$50,000
Owner's equity at the beginning of year	?
Owner's equity at the end of year	95,000
Withdrawals by owner during 1979	8,500
b. Net income for 1979	$?
Owner's equity at beginning of year	70,000
Owner's equity at end of year	68,000
Withdrawals by owner during 1979	6,200
c. Net loss sustained in 1979	$ 7,800
Owner's equity at beginning of year	30,000
Owner's equity at end of year	19,800
Withdrawals by owner during 1979	?

Required: Supply the missing figures. (Assume that no additional investments were made during 1979.)

P4–5 The following statements have been prepared for the H. Hobson Company:

H. HOBSON COMPANY
Income Statement
For the Month Ended January 31, 1979

Revenue		
Storage Fees		$2,485
Expenses		
Office Rent Expense	$ 300	
Salaries Expense	1,000	
Miscellaneous Expenses	335	1,635
Net Income		$ 850

H. HOBSON COMPANY
Balance Sheet
January 31, 1979

Assets			*Liabilities and Owner's Equity*	
Current Assets			Current Liabilities	
Cash	$1,000		Accounts Payable	$ 300
Repair Parts	500			
Total Current Assets		$1,500	Owner's Equity	
			H. Hobson, Capital	$4,700
Plant and Equipment				
Land	$1,000			
Building	2,500			
Total Plant & Equipment		3,500		
Total Assets		$5,000	Total Liabilities and Owner's Equity	$5,000

During January, Hobson withdrew $100 for his personal use.

Required: Prepare a statement of owner's equity for the H. Hobson Company for the month of January, and the closing entries as of January 31, 1979.

P4–6 The following information is taken from the books of the Gunn Company:

GUNN COMPANY
Statement of Owner's Equity
For the Year Ended December 31, 1979

Earl Gunn, Capital, January 1, 1979	$ 50,000
Net Income for 1979	100,000
Total	$150,000
Deduct Withdrawals	35,000
Earl Gunn, Capital, December 31, 1979	$115,000

The expenses for 1979 were: Salaries, $50,500; Advertising Expense, $10,000; Office Expense, $8,000; and Miscellaneous Expense, $18,000. The revenue came from only one source, Commissions Earned.

Required: Prepare a formal income statement for the Gunn Company. Show your computations of the amounts that are not given.

P4–7 (Integrative) The following transactions occurred during January, 1979, at the Dodd Roof Repair Company.

1979

Jan. 1 Tim Dodd invested $12,000 in cash and opened an account in the name of business, Dodd Roof Repair Company.

5 Paid $200 for two days' rental of a derrick and pulley assembly used on a repair job.

9 Purchased U.S. government bonds for $5,000 in cash.

11 Collected $1,300 on completion of roofing repair work.

20 Signed an agreement with Hampton College to repair dormitory roofs for $3,000. The work is to be completed during February and March.

25 Dodd drew $250 to spend on his vacation at Miami Beach.

28 Paid $450 for repair materials used on jobs during the month.

30 Paid $1,800 in salaries and wages.

31 Completed roofing repair work for Willard J. Evans in the amount of $1,600. Evans promised to pay for the work on February 10.

Use the following account titles and numbers:

11	Cash	41	Repair Service Revenue
15	Marketable Securities	51	Salaries and Wages Expense
18	Accounts Receivable	53	Repair Materials Expense
31	Tim Dodd, Capital	55	Rental Expense
33	Tim Dodd, Drawing	61	Income Summary

Required:

1. Journalize the transactions.
2. Post to general ledger accounts.
3. Take a trial balance.
4. Prepare an income statement, a statement of owner's equity and a balance sheet.
5. Prepare and post the closing entries.
6. Take a postclosing trial balance.

P4–8 (Integrative) The Sevran Service and Repair Tool Shop was started on September 1, 1979, and Bill Sevran invested $20,000 in cash in the business. During the month of September, the Tool Shop completed the following transactions:

1979

Sept. 1 Paid a $300 premium on a one-year comprehensive insurance policy, effective September 1, 1979.

1 Paid $450 for the September rent.

2 Purchased store equipment for $2,000 in cash.

1979

Sept. 2 Purchased shop supplies on account as follows:

Alex Supply Company	$1,200
Cambridge Supply House	600
Mystic Tool Company	400

5 Purchased an automobile for $3,100 from Hoamer's Motor Company, giving $800 in cash and a note payable for the balance.

9 Received $600 in cash for servicing and repairing tools.

10 Paid $50 in cash for advertising space in the *Cambridge Weekly*.

15 Paid cash for gas, oil, and other automobile expenses for two weeks, $68.

15 Paid $1,700 to the following creditors:

Alex Supply Company	$900
Cambridge Supply House	500
Mystic Tool Company	300

18 Received $800 in cash for repairing tools.

20 Paid $500 in cash on the note given for the purchase of the automobile.

21 Sevran drew $250 to pay to United Airlines for a personal trip he made to New York in August.

22 Paid $35 for telephone service.

23 Paid $18 for a new battery for the automobile. (Debit Automobile Expense).

24 Billed customers $500 for service and repair work, as follows:

Harris Jones	$225
William Meserve	175
Patrick Robinson	100

25 Paid $15 for cleaning the shop.

25 Received $450 in cash for servicing tools.

26 Purchased additional shop supplies on account, as follows:

Alex Supply Company	$225
Cambridge Supply House	150

27 Paid $58 for electric service.

28 Purchased a typewriter and an adding machine for $450.

29 Received $325 on account from the following customers:

Harris Jones	$100
William Meserve	150
Patrick Robinson	75

Sept. 30 Paid $55 for gas, oil, and other automobile expenses for two weeks.

30 Received $350 from customers for repair work not previously billed.

30 Paid $100 in cash for advertising space in a local magazine.

30 Received a promissory note from Harris Jones for the balance due on his account.

Required:

1. Open the following accounts in the general ledger: Cash, 101; Accounts Receivable, 111; Notes Receivable, 115; Shop Supplies, 136; Prepaid Insurance, 140; Automobile, 162; Store Equipment, 164; Office Equipment, 165; Accounts Payable, 201; Notes Payable, 204; Bill Sevran, Capital, 250; Bill Sevran, Drawing, 252; Repair Service Revenue, 301; Advertising Expense, 618; Rent Expense, 703; Heat and Light Expense, 705; Telephone and Telegraph Expense, 709; Automobile Expense, 710; Miscellaneous General Expense, 712.
2. Open customers' accounts in the accounts receivable ledger.
3. Open creditors' accounts in the accounts payable ledger.
4. Record all the transactions in the general journal.
5. Post to the appropriate ledgers.
6. Prepare a trial balance.
7. Prepare a schedule of accounts receivable.
8. Prepare a schedule of accounts payable.

P4–9. (Minicase) On December 1, In Evanston, USA, Chipper Garnella opened the Figure Eight Health Spa. Garnella decided to invest $5,000 in cash in the business. He opened an account in the First National Bank in the name of the business and deposited the cash. The rates in the Health Spa are as follows:

$15	Weight Reduction Program
$25	Deluxe Exercise Routine

Supplies acquired for the business were $1,200. Expenses incurred during the first month are:

Rent expense	$3,600
Wages—Sally Wagner	8,000
Wages—Thomas Griffin ...	9,000
Heat, light and water	1,100
Maintenance expense	500

The following were the advertising expenses incurred, but are *not payable* until the following month:

Local newspaper	$ 700
Local radio station	900
Local magazine	1,000

All the supplies were used during the first month. Revenues for the first month were from the following customers.

1,000 customers for the Weight Reduction Program
350 customers for Deluxe Exercise Routine

Required:

1. Prepare an income statement.
2. Prepare a statement of owner's equity.
3. How can the business incur a loss, when there is so much cash in the bank?

chapter five

Introduction

A complete but simple service company illustration, the transactions of the Good Times Wheels Repair Shop, was used in Chapters 3 and 4. A similar but more complex illustration is used in Chapters 5 and 6 to introduce five types of adjustments that are recorded at the end of the period and to complete the accounting process. Specifically in Chapter 5, the adjustment process is discussed in detail through an illustration called the Wheelo Trucking Company. The remaining steps in the end-of-period process for the Wheelo Trucking Company are completed in Chapter 6. Two accounting methods are compared in this chapter: the cash basis and the accrual basis.

End-of-period adjusting entries

Learning goals

To describe the accrual basis of accounting.
To identify the cash basis of accounting.
To understand the need for adjusting entries and the specific point in the accounting cycle that adjusting entries are made.
To explain the reasons for the different types of adjusting entries.
To know meaning of the broad classification of adjustments into accruals and deferrals.
To prepare and journalize adjusting entries.

Key terms

- *accrue, accrued*
- *accrued liability*
- *accounting methods*
  - *accrual basis*
  - *cash basis*
- *adjusting entries*
  - *accrued expenses*
  - *accrued revenue*
  - *long-term cost apportionment*
  - *short-term cost apportionment*
  - *short-term revenue apportionment*
- *adjustments*
  - *accruals*
  - *deferrals*
- *apportionment*
- *closing, closing entries*
- *contra account*
  - *contra asset*
  - *contra liability*
- *earned revenue*
- *incurred expenses*
- *matching revenue and expenses*
- *materiality*
- *maturity date (of a note)*
- *prepaid items*
- *salvage value*
- *straight-line method*
- *unearned items*

Cash basis

Under the cash basis of accounting, revenue is recognized and recorded only when the cash is received. Expenses are recognized in the period and time of payment. Recording of revenue and expenses during an accounting period is based on an inflow and outflow of cash—a matching of cash receipts and cash disbursements to determine operating results during an accounting period. This method of accounting is simple in application; but in most cases it *does not* properly measure net income. For example, it does not recognize uncollected revenue items as being earned and unpaid expense items as being incurred until actual payment is made. Hence, it matches only some of the revenues and some of the expenses for a given period. Recall that from a theoretical viewpoint an expense is incurred when the effort is expended (the asset status is lost) in attempting to create revenue. Revenue is said to be earned in a given period when all the efforts (except cash collection) are made to bring the revenue into being. There are instances, particularly in small professional and service businesses, in which the cash basis of accounting is used with acceptable results. For example, if a firm has few or no receivables and few or no payables, it could use the cash basis of accounting and still get an adequate matching of expired costs (expenses) against earned revenue of a given period. Mixed systems, or combinations of the cash basis and the accrual basis, are often found in practice.

The accrual basis

The accrual basis of accounting is based on the principle that to determine accurate net income all revenue earned during a period and all the related expenses of earning that income assignable to the period must be considered. Revenues are recognized at the time of sale of the services or merchandise and expenses are usually recognized at the time the services are received and used in the production of revenue. This is the concept, discussed earlier, of *matching revenue and expenses* for a given period.

Matching revenue and expenses

The central goal of the accrual basis of accounting is this process of* matching *the revenue of a period with the expenses of that period, regardless of when, whether, or how much cash has been received or paid. This feature underlies all the discussions in this text.

Each method produces a different net income figure, as the following example will show. The Jane Dough Company, which does landscape gardening, performed work during August for which it charged $1,000. It received $600 on August 15 and $400 on September 11. Wages (the only expense) of $550 were paid on August 31. No work was performed during September.

	CASH BASIS		ACCRUAL BASIS	
	August	September	August	September
Revenue	$600.00	$400.00	$1,000.00	$-0-
Expense	550.00	-0-	550.00	-0-
Net Income	$ 50.00	$400.00	$ 450.00	$-0-

Obviously the accrual basis of accounting presents a more useful picture of operating results, because revenue is reflected in the period to which it properly belongs; that is, the period in which it was earned. Net income is the difference between revenue earned and expenses incurred during the accounting period—the difference between the results achieved and the efforts expended. The accrual method, by matching expenses incurred with revenue earned for the period, presents the better measurement of net income. Since the accrual basis of accounting results in more useful financial statements, most businesses keep their books on that basis.

During the accounting period, regular business transactions are recorded as they occur. At the end of a period the accountant may find that the ledger accounts are incomplete: some new accounts must be brought into the books and other accounts must be brought up to date. The journal entries necessary to accomplish this are referred to as *adjusting entries*.

Periodic adjustment of the ledger accounts is required if the financial statements are to reflect the realistic position of the company—its assets and equities—as of the end of the period, and the results of its operations—revenue earned and expenses incurred—during the period.

Adjusting entries

At the end of each period the accountant must make* adjusting entries *to bring up to date such accounts as revenues and expenses in order to measure income for the period accurately; and also assets, liabilities, and owner's equity in order to measure financial position accurately at a given point in time.

Five types of adjustments—an illustration

It is impractical and sometimes impossible to record the day-to-day changes in certain accounts. For example, when the premium payment is made on an insurance policy, the asset, Prepaid Insurance, is usually debited. At the end of the accounting period, however, only part of the balance of the Prepaid Insurance account represents an asset. The amount that has expired with the passage of time is an expense; it represents the cost of insurance protection which has been received. At the end of the accounting period, therefore, Prepaid Insurance contains both an asset and an expense element. A *short-term cost apportionment adjustment* is necessary to record the correct amount of Insurance Expense and to reduce Prepaid Insurance. As used here as well as in other adjustments, the word *apportionment* simply means the dividing of a cost, or a revenue, among two or more periods.

An adjusting entry may be required to record previously unrecorded data. Assume, for example, that a company paid wages on March 28 for the two-week period that ended on that date. However, the employees worked on March 29, 30, and 31. If March 31 is the end of the accounting period, recognition must be given to this unrecorded but incurred expense as well as to the corresponding increase in liabilities. An *accrued expense adjustment* is needed so that the financial statements may show the liability and the proper assignment of the expense to the period. Note that, in this context, the term *accrued* simply means accumulated or built up.

A distinction is usually made between adjusting entries and entries that record regular business transactions. Regular business transactions start and complete their cycles within an accounting period. Adjusting entries deal with those transactions that may be termed *continuous transactions*. The adjusting entry for wages, for example, records a change that has already taken place—the increase in a liability incurred—but is unrecorded. The adjusting entry for Insurance Expense, on the other hand, recognizes the partial consumption of an item that was recorded in an asset account at the time of acquisition.

Five kinds of continuous transactions, or adjustments, discussed in this chapter are summarized in the following five groups:[1]

Short-term cost apportionments: recorded cost that must be apportioned between current and later accounting periods, which could be a month, a quarter, but usually a year. Examples: supplies, prepaid insurance, and prepaid rent.

Short-term revenue apportionments: recorded revenue that must be apportioned between current and later accounting periods. Examples: rent collected in advance and magazine subscriptions collected in advance.

Long-term cost apportionments: a type of adjustment similar to short-term cost apportionment except that the recorded cost will usually be apportioned between three or more accounting periods. Example: the cost of a building.

Accrued expenses: unrecorded accumulated expenses incurred in the current period. Example: wages earned by employees after the last pay day in an accounting period.

Accrued revenues: unrecorded accumulated revenues earned in the current period. Example: interest earned on a note receivable held for thirty days in the current period but not due until sometime in the next period.

These five adjustments are often classified into two broad groups called *deferrals* and *accruals*. The cost- and revenue-apportionment adjustments are referred to as *deferrals* and the accrued expense and accrued revenue adjustments are referred to as *accruals*. These concepts are emphasized in a more detailed form in an appendix to Chapter 6.

Before we start our illustration of the end-of-the-period process that includes adjusting entries, let us emphasize that as a usual rule an adjusting entry will affect both the balance sheet and income statement. Thus the adjusting entry will sharpen income measurement and update balance sheet accounts.

1 A sixth adjustment for bad debts is discussed in Chapter 12.

In this chapter the adjusting process is illustrated through an example of the Wheelo Trucking Company. Assume that the Wheelo Trucking Company started business on June 1, 1979. As a convenience in illustration of the end-of-period procedures, also assume that the books are closed on June 30 (books are customarily closed annually). The trial balance taken from the Wheelo Trucking Company's general ledger is shown in Figure 5–1.

The adjusting entries must be journalized and posted to ledger accounts. The end-of-period financial statements that are prepared—income statement, balance sheet, and statement of owner's equity—must reflect the regular transactions data as well as the adjustment data for the period.

Short-term cost apportionments

At the end of the period certain types of accounts contain mixtures of asset and expense elements; other types may contain mixtures of liability and revenue elements. In the Wheelo Trucking Company example there are three short-term cost apportionment adjustments. In these adjustments the accountant follows three steps in adjusting the mixed accounts involving a short-term cost apportionment between asset and expense elements:

1. Determines the balance of each account to be adjusted.
2. Determines the amount of the asset and expense elements in each account.
3. Records the adjusting entries.

Figure 5–1
Trial balance

WHEELO TRUCKING COMPANY
Trial Balance
June 30, 1979

Acct. No.	Account Title	Debits	Credits
101	Cash	$ 5,250.00	
111	Accounts Receivable	550.00	
112	Notes Receivable	1,440.00	
131	Office Supplies	230.00	
141	Prepaid Insurance	2,160.00	
142	Prepaid Rent	1,500.00	
201	Office Equipment	1,400.00	
211	Trucks	13,000.00	
301	Accounts Payable		$ 200.00
302	Notes Payable		8,000.00
321	Unearned Rent		600.00
401	John Wheelo, Capital		12,000.00
404	John Wheelo, Drawing	500.00	
501	Trucking Revenue		7,465.00
601	Heat and Light Expense	40.00	
602	Maintenance and Repairs Expense	375.00	
603	Telephone and Telegraph Expense	95.00	
604	Gas and Oil Expense	525.00	
605	Wages Expense	1,200.00	
	Totals	$28,265.00	$28,265.00

Adjustment of prepaid rent

On June 1, the Wheelo Trucking Company paid $1,500 in cash for three months' rent.

Step 1. The general ledger shows the following balance in the account:

Prepaid Rent (asset) Acct. No. 142

Date		Explanation	F	Debit		Credit		Balance	
1979 Jun.	1		1	1,500	00			1,500	00

The information in the foregoing ledger account (and other similar illustrations in this chapter) is reproduced from the original ledger and includes folio references for the original data.

Step 2. The amount of expense applicable to June is $500 = ($1,500 ÷ 3 months). On June 30, therefore, Prepaid Rent is a mixed account consisting of an expense element and an asset element.

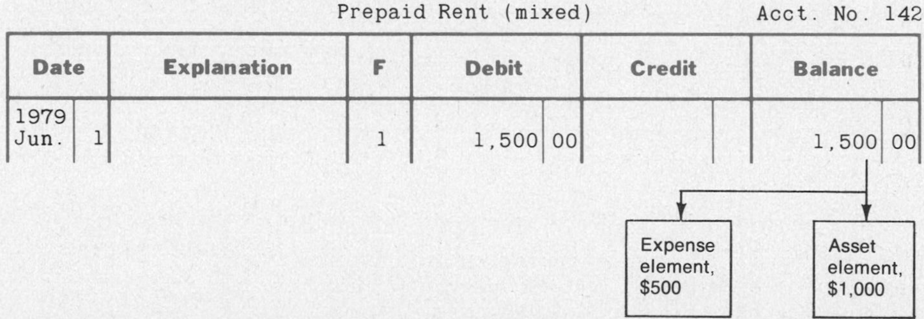

Prepaid Rent (mixed) Acct. No. 142

Date		Explanation	F	Debit		Credit		Balance	
1979 Jun.	1		1	1,500	00			1,500	00

Step 3. The timing of journalizing the adjustments is optional; it may be delayed until the formal financial statements are prepared and presented to management for its use. For teaching purposes the adjusting entries for the Wheelo Trucking Company are made and posted as each adjustment is explained.

The requiring adjusting entry is:

GENERAL JOURNAL

Page 4

Date		Debit-Credit-Account Titles: Explanation	F	Debit		Credit	
1979 Jun.	30	Rent Expense	606	500	00		
		Prepaid Rent	142			500	00
		To record rent expense for June.					

The expense element is thus removed from the mixed account, as shown by the following posting in the ledger accounts.

Prepaid Rent (asset) Acct. No. 142

Date		Explanation	F	Debit		Credit		Balance	
1979									
Jun.	1		1	1,500	00			1,500	00
	30	Adjustment	4			500	00	1,000	00

Rent Expense (expense) Acct. No. 606

Date		Explanation	F	Debit		Credit		Balance	
1979									
Jun.	30	Adjustment	4	500	00			500	00

Prepaid Rent ($1,000) is classified in the balance sheet as a current asset, and Rent Expense ($500) appears in the income statement as an expense.

Adjustment of prepaid insurance

The Wheelo Trucking Company paid a premium of $2,160 for a comprehensive three-year insurance policy, effective June 1, 1979.

Step 1. Prepaid insurance, before adjustment, shows a balance of $2,160. The title, Prepaid Insurance, classifies it as basically an asset account, but at June 30, 1979, it is in fact a mixed account; it is a mixture of an asset element and an expense element.

Step 2. An analysis of the account shows that the expense element for the month of June is $60 = ($2,160 ÷ 36 months), and that the unused portion of $2,100 is the asset prepayment benefiting future periods.

Step 3. The following adjusting entry is made:

GENERAL JOURNAL

Page 4

Date		Debit-Credit-Account Titles: Explanation	F	Debit		Credit	
1979							
Jun.	30	Insurance Expense.	607	60	00		
		Prepaid Insurance.	141			60	00
		To record insurance expense for June.					

The information is shown in the following ledger accounts:

Prepaid Insurance (asset) Acct. No. 141

Date		Explanation	F	Debit		Credit		Balance	
1979									
Jun.	1		1	2,160	00			2,160	00
	30	Adjustment	4			60	00	2,100	00

Insurance Expense (expense) Acct. No. 607

Date		Explanation	F	Debit		Credit		Balance	
1979 Jun.	30	Adjustment	4	60	00			60	00

Prepaid insurance ($2,100) is classified in the balance sheet as a current asset, and Insurance Expense ($60) appears in the income statement as an expense.

Adjustment of office supplies

Step 1. On the trial balance (Figure 5–1), Office Supplies has a debit balance of $230, representing a purchase made on June 6. Again, the title, Office Supplies, indicates that the account is an asset; but at June 30, 1979, it is a mixed account. It contains a mixture of asset and expense elements.

Step 2. The inventory taken on June 30 showed $60 worth of unused supplies; therefore, the expense element is $170 = ($230 − $60).

Step 3. The expense of $170 needs to be removed from the mixed account by the following adjusting entry, and the adjustment information is posted to the accounts shown below the journal entry:

GENERAL JOURNAL

Page 4

Date		Debit-Credit-Account Titles: Explanation	F	Debit		Credit	
1979 Jun.	30	Office Supplies Expense.	608	170	00		
		Office Supplies.	131			170	00
		To record supplies used during June.					

Office Supplies (asset) Acct. No. 131

Date		Explanation	F	Debit		Credit		Balance	
1979 Jun.	6		1	230	00			230	00
	30	Adjustment	4			170	00	60	00

Office Supplies Expense (expense) Acct. No. 608

Date		Explanation	F	Debit		Credit		Balance	
1979 Jun.	30	Adjustment	4	170	00			170	00

Office Supplies ($60) is classified in the balance sheet as a current asset and Office Supplies Expense ($170) appears in the income statement as an expense.

Short-term revenue apportionment—adjustment of unearned rent

The same three steps are followed in making short-term revenue apportionments of amounts originally recorded in mixed liability accounts. The Wheelo Trucking Company had only one such adjustment. On June 1, the Wheelo Trucking Company signed a contract for the use of its trucks on a part-time basis and received an advance payment of $600 for six months' rent. At that time, Cash was debited and a liability account, Unearned Rent, was credited for $600. By June 30, 1979, the Unearned Rent account has become a mixed account containing a mixture of liability and revenue elements. Therefore, on June 30, the portion earned in the month of June must be transferred from the liability account, Unearned Rent, to the revenue account, Rent Earned. The unearned portion must remain in Unearned Rent as a liability because the Wheelo Trucking Company must provide the use of its trucks on a part-time basis for another five months.

Step 1. The amount of the unearned rent liability as of June 1, 1979, in the ledger account is shown below:

Unearned Rent (liability) Acct. No. 321

Date		Explanation	F	Debit	Credit	Balance
1979 Jun.	1		1		600 00	600 00

Step 2. The rent actually earned in June is $100 = ($600 ÷ 6 mos.); on June 30, the mixed Unearned Rent account consists of a revenue element and a liability element.

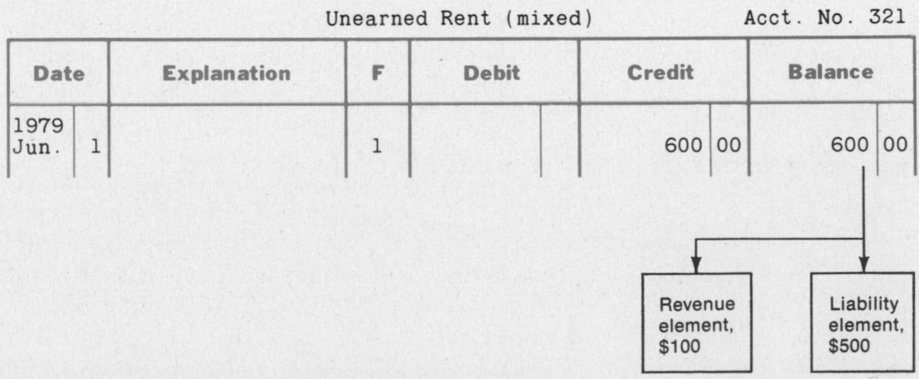

Unearned Rent (mixed) Acct. No. 321

Date		Explanation	F	Debit	Credit	Balance
1979 Jun.	1		1		600 00	600 00

Step 3. The following adjusting entry is made:

GENERAL JOURNAL

Page 4

Date		Debit-Credit-Account Titles: Explanation	F	Debit	Credit
1979					
Jun.	30	Unearned Rent	321	100 00	
		Rent Earned	511		100 00
		To record revènue earned from rental of trucks during June.			

The revenue element is removed from the liability account, Unearned Rent, and recorded in a revenue account as shown below:

Unearned Rent (liability) Acct. No. 321

Date		Explanation	F	Debit	Credit	Balance
1979						
Jun.	1		1		600 00	600 00
	30	Adjustment	4	100 00		500 00

Rent Earned (revenue) Acct. No. 511

Date		Explanation	F	Debit	Credit	Balance
1979						
Jun.	30	Adjustment	4		100 00	100 00

Rent Earned ($100) appears in the income statement as a revenue item, and Unearned Rent ($500) appears in the balance sheet as a current liability.

Long-term cost apportionments

Two of Wheelo's adjusting entries involve the recording of long-term asset cost expiration. Three steps similar to the short-term cost apportionments are followed.

Adjustment for depreciation of office equipment

Step 1. The trial balance, Figure 5–1 (see page 137), shows a balance of $1,400 in the Office Equipment account.

Step 2. The equipment, acquired on June 1, is estimated to have a useful life of ten years, or 120 months, and a *salvage value* of $200 at the end of that period. Salvage, or *residual,* value is the estimated price for which an asset may be sold when it is no longer serviceable to the business. In effect, the use of office equipment for ten years has been purchased at a net cost of $1,200 = ($1,400 – $200). A portion of this cost expires in each accounting period during the useful life of the equipment.

This periodic expired cost, called depreciation expense, requires no periodic cash outlay, but nevertheless is a continuous expense of operating the business.

Depreciation

***The portion of the cost of a plant and equipment asset assigned to the accounting period is called* depreciation.**

A number of methods may be used in calculating the periodic depreciation charge. Depreciation for the month of June is computed in this case by using the *straight-line method,* in which a uniform portion of the cost is assigned to each period. Other depreciation methods used in practice are discussed in Chapter 14. The straight-line method is the most popular method mainly because of its simplicity of calculation:

$$\frac{\text{Cost} - \text{Salvage value}}{\text{Estimated months of useful life}} = \text{Depreciation for month}$$

The depreciation expense for the office equipment in June is computed as $10.

$$\frac{\$1{,}400 - \$200}{120} = \$10$$

Step 3. The following adjusting entry is made:

GENERAL JOURNAL

Page 4

Date		Debit-Credit-Account Titles: Explanation	F	Debit		Credit	
1979							
Jun.	30	Depreciation Expense—Office Equipment.	609	10	00		
		Accumulated Depreciation—Office Equipment . .	201A			10	00
		To record depreciation for month of June.					

Both of the foregoing accounts are new accounts. The second is called a *contra-asset* account, because its balance is deducted from Office Equipment to show the book value, or carrying value, of the asset. Other negative-type accounts are established to measure separately specific deductions from parent-type accounts whose amounts are needed to be preserved. For instance, contra-liability, contra-revenue, or even contra-expense accounts are used; but none of these is used as frequently as the contra-asset accounts described here. Office Equipment could be credited directly, because the depreciation represents a decrease in the asset; but this procedure is undesirable because it fails to disclose information that is useful to management. Depreciation is an estimate; it is informative to keep asset cost separate from estimated reductions in cost. When separate accounts are used, the original cost and the accumulated depreciation can be determined readily. The June 30 adjusting information is shown in the following ledger accounts.

Depreciation Expense—
Office Equipment (expense) Acct. No. 609

Date		Explanation	F	Debit		Credit		Balance	
1979 Jun.	30	Adjustment	4	10	00			10	00

Accumulated Depreciation—
Office Equipment (asset valuation) Acct. No. 201A

Date		Explanation	F	Debit		Credit		Balance	
1979 Jun.	30	Adjustment	4			10	00	10	00

In the balance sheet (see Figure 6–8, Chapter 6), the asset valuation account, Accumulated Depreciation—Office Equipment, is deducted from Office Equipment; the remainder is the *undepreciated cost,* that is, the portion of the cost of the asset that is not yet charged to expense. Depreciation Expense-Office Equipment ($10) is shown in the income statement as an expense.

Adjustment for depreciation of trucks

Step 1. On June 1, the Wheelo Trucking Company purchased two trucks for business use, each costing $6,500. Because the useful life of the trucks is limited, a portion of the cost is allocable to the month of June. It is estimated that their useful life is five years, or 60 months, at the end of which time each truck will have a salvage value of $500.

Step 2. The computation and recording of the depreciation expense for the trucks is similar to that for the office equipment. The depreciation expense for June for the two trucks is calculated by the straight-line method as follows:

$$\frac{\text{Cost of \$6,500} - \text{Salvage value of \$500}}{\text{60 months}} = \text{\$100 depreciation per month for each truck, or \$200 for two trucks}$$

Step 3. The following adjusting entry is made on June 30 and posted to the accounts shown below the journal entry:

GENERAL JOURNAL

Page 4

Date		Debit-Credit-Account Titles: Explanation	F	Debit		Credit	
1979 Jun.	30	Depreciation Expense—Trucks	610	200	00		
		Accumulated Depreciation—Trucks	211A			200	00
		To record depreciation for June.					

Depreciation Expense—Trucks (expense) Acct. No. 610

Date		Explanation	F	Debit		Credit		Balance	
1979 Jun.	30	Adjustment	4	200	00			200	00

Accumulated Depreciation—
Trucks (asset valuation) Acct. No. 211A

Date		Explanation	F	Debit		Credit		Balance	
1979 Jun.	30	Adjustment	4			200	00	200	00

The Depreciation Expense—Trucks and Accumulated Depreciation—Trucks are classified in the financial statements in the same manner as was Depreciation Expense—Office Equipment and Accumulated Depreciation—Office Equipment; Depreciation Expense—Trucks is shown on the income statement as an expense and the Accumulated Depreciation—Trucks is deducted from the Trucks account on the balance sheet (see Figures 6–6 and 6–8, Chapter 6).

The Accumulated Depreciation accounts are used to accumulate the periodic charges made to expense and to set up in one account the amount of the deduction for the asset valuation. Depreciation Expense shows the expired cost for the accounting period and is closed along with the other expense accounts in an entry that transfers the total expense to Income Summary. Assume that the same adjusting entry for trucks is made on July 31. After it is posted, the general ledger accounts for Trucks, Depreciation Expense—Trucks, and Accumulated Depreciation—Trucks appear as follows:

Trucks Acct. No. 211

Date		Explanation	F	Debit		Credit		Balance	
1979 Jun.	1		1	13,000	00			13,000	00

Accumulated Depreciation—Trucks Acct. No. 211A

Date		Explanation	F	Debit		Credit		Balance	
1979									
Jun.	30	Adjustment	4			200	00	200	00
Jul.	31	Adjustment	8			200	00	400	00

Depreciation Expense—Trucks Acct. No. 610

Date		Explanation	F	Debit		Credit		Balance	
1979									
Jun.	30	Adjusting entry	4	200	00			200	00
	30	Closing entry	5			200	00	-0-	—
Jul.	31	Adjusting entry	8	200	00			200	00

Balance before the July closing is a debit.

The cost of the trucks and the accumulated depreciation are shown on the balance sheet at July 31 as follows:

Plant and Equipment		
Trucks	$13,000.00	
Deduct Accumulated Depreciation—Trucks . . .	400.00	$12,600.00

The $12,600 figure is referred to as the *book value* or book amount of the trucks.

Accrued expenses

Accrued expenses are expenses that have been incurred or accumulated in a given period but have not yet been paid. An expense is said to be *incurred* in the period when the effort to produce revenue is made. At the end of the accounting period the accountant must record the expense in the proper period of incurrence and must record the accompanying liability. The accrued expense adjustment described here involves unrecorded wages expense of $150.

Adjustment for unrecorded wages expense

Step 1. Wages Expense contains two debits of $600 each, representing wages paid every two weeks to employees through June 27.

Step 2. The employees earned wages of $150 for work on June 28, 29, and 30, the last three days of the accounting period. Although the company will not pay the employees again until July 11, it has nevertheless incurred $150 of wages expense for these three days, and a $150 liability exists as of June 30.

Step 3. The following adjusting entry is made on June 30 and posted to the accounts shown below the journal entry:

GENERAL JOURNAL

Page 4

Date		Debit-Credit-Account Titles: Explanation	F	Debit		Credit	
1979							
Jun.	30	Wages Expense	605	150	00		
		Accrued Wages Payable	311			150	00
		To record wages expense accrued during June 28–30, 1979.					

Wages Expense (expense) — Acct. No. 605

Date		Explanation	F	Debit		Credit		Balance	
1979									
Jun.	13	From cash payment	2	600	00			600	00
	27	From cash payment	3	600	00			1,200	00
	30	Adjustment	4	150	00			1,350	00

Accrued Wages Payable (liability) — Acct. No. 311

Date		Explanation	F	Debit		Credit		Balance	
1979									
Jun.	30	Adjustment	4			150	00	150	00

Wages Expense ($1,350) is shown in the income statement as an expense; Accrued Wages Payable ($150) is shown in the balance sheet as a current liability (see Figures 6–6 and 6–8, Chapter 6).

Adjustment for unrecorded interest expense

Step 1. On June 12, the Wheelo Trucking Company borrowed $8,000 from the bank and signed a 45-day, 6-percent interest-bearing note payable. This transaction was recorded in the general journal by debiting Cash and crediting Notes Payable for $8,000.

Step 2. The cost of the use of the $8,000—interest expense—continues throughout the 45 days because interest expense accumulates with the passage of time. The total interest expense plus the $8,000 principal amount will be paid to the bank on July 27, the *maturity,* or due, date. However, unpaid interest expense on an interest-bearing note payable for the 18-day period from June 12 through June 30 must be recognized by an adjusting entry debiting Interest Expense and crediting Accrued Interest Payable for $24.

The formula for computing interest is shown in Figure 5–2.[2]

Figure 5–2
Interest formula

$$\textbf{Interest} = \textbf{Principal} \times \textbf{Interest rate} \times \frac{\textbf{Elapsed time in days}}{\textbf{360}}$$

The unpaid interest expense accrued on June 30 is computed as follows:

$$\text{Interest} = \$8{,}000 \times 0.06 \times \frac{18}{360} = \$24$$

The principal multiplied by the interest rate equals the total interest for one year ($8,000 × 0.06 = $480); the interest for a *year* ($480) multiplied by the elapsed fraction of a year (18/360 or 1/20) is the interest expense for 18 days ($480 × 1/20), or $24. The use of 360 days in the formula is consistent with commercial practice, the primary reason being simplicity of calculation.

Step 3. The formal adjusting entry is made on June 30 and posted to the accounts indicated below.

GENERAL JOURNAL

Page 5

Date		Debit-Credit-Account Titles: Explanation	F	Debit		Credit	
1979							
Jun.	30	Interest Expense	611	24	00		
		Accrued Interest Payable.	303			24	00
		To record interest expense accrued during June 12–30, 1979.					

Interest Expense (expense) Acct. No. 611

Date		Explanation	F	Debit		Credit		Balance	
1979									
Jun.	30	Adjustment	5	24	00			24	00

Accrued Interest Payable (liability) Acct. No. 303

Date		Explanation	F	Debit		Credit		Balance	
1979									
Jun.	30	Adjustment	5			24	00	24	00

Interest Expense ($24) is reported as an expense in the income statement;

2 A more detailed presentation of the calculation of interest is found in Chapter 11.

Accrued Interest Payable ($24) appears as a current liability in the balance sheet. This entry gives rise to an *accrued liability*. This term refers to the liability for an expense accumulated and said to be incurred during one accounting period but payable in a future accounting period. Expenses incurred for which invoices have not yet been received—telephone, heat, light, water, and so on—are also in this category. These may be recorded by debits to appropriate expense accounts and a credit to Accrued Accounts Payable, or similarly named accounts.

Accrued revenues

Accrued revenue items are items that have been accumulated and earned in a given period but for which cash collections have not yet been received. The accountant's job at the end of the accounting period is to record the revenue in the proper period in which it is earned and also to record the accompanying receivable, an asset. The accrued revenue adjustment described is that of unrecorded earned interest of $4.

Adjustment for unrecorded interest revenue

Step 1. The Wheelo Trucking Company made a loan of $1,440 to one of its suppliers, who signed a 30-day, 5 percent interest-bearing note dated June 10. An entry was made debiting Notes Receivable and crediting Cash for $1,440.

Step 2. The company earned interest on the loan for 20 days in June (June 11 through June 30); it will be received on the maturity date, July 10, when the amount due (principal plus total interest) is paid by the supplier. Interest earned, like interest expense, accrues with the passage of time. The 20 days' interest earned by June 30 is recorded by an adjusting entry debiting Accrued Interest Receivable and crediting Interest Earned for $4. Using the formula shown in Figure 5–2, the computation of the interest is

$$\text{Interest} = \$1{,}440 \times 0.05 \times \frac{20}{360} = \$4$$

Step 3. The formal adjusting entry is made on June 30 and posted to the accounts indicated below.

GENERAL JOURNAL

Page 5

Date		Debit-Credit-Account Titles: Explanation	F	Debit	Credit
1979 Jun.	30	Accrued Interest Receivable	113	4 00	
		Interest Earned	521		4 00
		To record interest revenue accrued during June 10–30, 1979.			

Accrued Interest Receivable (asset) Acct. No. 113

Date		Explanation	F	Debit		Credit		Balance	
1979 Jun.	30	Adjustment	5	4	00			4	00

Interest Earned (revenue) Acct. No. 521

Date		Explanation	F	Debit		Credit		Balance	
1979 Jun.	30	Adjustment	5			4	00	4	00

Accrued Interest Receivable ($4) is a current asset in the balance sheet. Interest Earned is a revenue in the income statement.

The materiality concept

The adjustments described here have been made so as to update the assets, liabilities, expenses, and revenues of the Wheelo Trucking Company. After the adjustments are made, a correctly-stated income statement and a correctly-stated balance sheet can be prepared. No exceptions were mentioned to the general rule that all adjustments should be made.

One exception (usually referred to as the materiality concept) generally accepted in practice is that adjustments do not have to be made for insignificant, immaterial, or trivial items. For example, the box of paper clips in the bookkeeper's desk as of the balance sheet date is an asset of the company, although its cost has been charged to expense. It is possible but not practical to make an adjusting entry for the asset value of the unused clips. Because of the small cost of the unused paper clips, failure to make the adjustment will have no material effect on the financial statements and cannot mislead the user of such statements. A similar situation exists with respect to other minor items of supply or services.

The accountant is faced with the problem of determining what is material and what is immaterial. For instance, an item costing $100 may be material in a small business; whereas an item costing $1,000 may be insignificant and thus immaterial in a multimillion-dollar business. The decision hinges on whether the failure to disclose separately a given item will affect the decision of an informed statement user. For example, it may not be misleading to combine several insignificant items of expense or revenue into one account. It may be very misleading to combine a significant loss from a lawsuit with a regular expense account. Regardless of the amount, it may be necessary to disclose separately an item because it may be an essential component in a business decision or because of its very nature. For example, even a small bribe to an official of a foreign government may have far reaching implications.

Glossary

Accruals A classification of adjustments that includes accrued revenues and accrued expenses.

Accrual basis The accrual accounting basis assumes that revenue is realized at the time of the sale of goods or services irrespective of when the cash is received; and expenses are recognized at the time the services are received and utilized in the production of revenue irrespective of when payment for these services is made.

Accrued Accumulated or built onto.

Accrued expenses Expenses that have been incurred—for example, services received and used—in a given period but have not yet been paid or recorded.

Accrued liability The liability that has accumulated for an expense that has been incurred but not yet paid or recorded.

Accrued revenue Revenues that have been earned in a given period but have not yet been collected or recorded.

Accumulated depreciation The Accumulated Depreciation account reveals all past depreciation which has been taken on a depreciable plant and equipment item and charged against revenue; it is in essence a postponed credit to the applicable plant and equipment account.

Adjusting entries Regular continuous entries postponed to the end of an accounting period, for the convenience of the accountant, and made to update revenue, expense, asset, liability, and owner's equity accounts as required by the accrual basis of accounting.

Apportionment The dividing of a cost or revenue among two or more periods.

Cash basis. The cash basis of accounting reflects the recognition of revenue at the time that cash is received for the sale of goods and services and the recognition of expenses in the period of the payment for the receipt of a service.

Contra account A negative element of another account that is shown in a separate account; the contra account should always be shown in the ledger immediately following the account of which it is a reduction. Both assets and liabilities may have contra accounts.

Deferrals A classification of adjustments that includes short-term revenue apportionments, short-term cost apportionments, and long-term cost apportionments.

Depreciation (accounting depreciation) Accounting depreciation is the system of allocation of a part of the cost of a plant and equipment item (that has a limited useful life) over the estimated useful life in a systematic and rational manner.

Earned revenue Revenue is said to be earned when substantially all efforts to bring it into existence have been expended except the collection of the revenue in the form of cash.

Incurred expense An expense is incurred when the efforts are expended in an attempt to produce revenue; that is when the cost is expired and thus loses its asset status.

Long-term cost apportionment adjustment An adjustment requiring the apportioning of the cost of a long-lived asset between the current period and a future span of time of three or more years.

Materiality An accounting concept that requires an item that is large enough and significant enough so as to influence decisions by statement users to receive separate and identified accounting treatment.

Maturity date (of a note) The date that a note comes due and payment or settlement is required.

Salvage value The estimated scrap value or resale value that a plant and equipment item has at the end of the estimated life of the asset.

Short-term cost apportionment adjustment An adjustment that requires that a previously recorded prepaid item be apportioned between the current period and a future short period (usually a year). The prepayment may be originally debited to an asset.

Short-term revenue apportionment adjustment An adjustment that requires that a previously recorded advance collection of a revenue be apportioned between the current period and a future short period (usually one year). The advance collection may be originally credited to a liability or to a revenue account.

Straight-line method of depreciation A method that allocates the cost of a depreciable asset over the estimated useful life of the asset in equal amounts for each time period.

Unearned items Revenue payments received in advance of the earning process.

Questions

Q5–1 (a) What are the essential differences between the cash basis and the accrual basis of accounting? (b) Under what conditions is it appropriate to use the cash basis? (c) Under what conditions is it inappropriate to use the cash basis?

Q5–2 (a) What purpose is served by adjusting entries? (b) What events make them necessary?

Q5–3 (a) How do adjusting entries affect the work of the accountant? (b) How does the time period covered by the income statement affect the adjusting entries?

Q5–4 (a) How do adjusting entries differ from other entries? (b) What is a mixed account? (c) What are the results of the adjusting entries?

Q5–5 Does the need to make adjusting entries at the end of the period mean that errors were made in the accounts during the period? Discuss.

Q5–6 (a) Do you agree with the statement that "Items of little or no consequence may be dealt with as expediency may suggest"? (b) Do you agree with the statement that "Problems of materiality are easily resolved and, in any case, are not very important"?

Q5–7 (a) What is a contra account? (b) Name one contra account involved in adjusting entries. (c) What is the specific purpose served by the contra account named?

Q5–8 On the balance sheet, where do you classify (a) Accrued Interest Receivable? (b) Prepaid Insurance? (c) Accrued Wages Payable? (d) Unearned Rent?

Q5–9 Define the terms: (a) accrued revenues, (b) accrued expenses, (c) short-term cost apportionments, and (d) short-term revenue apportionments.

Q5–10 Most adjustments are said to be grouped into two categories: accruals and deferrals. Discuss these terms and indicate what kinds of adjustments would fall in each group.

Q5–11 From time to time during a given year, a company makes prepayments of premiums on one-year, two-year and three-year property insurance policies. The company records these in an account which it calls Prepaid Property Insurance.
(a) At the close of this given year will there be a deferral or an accrual? (b) Which of the following types of accounts will be affected by the related adjusting entry at the end of the year? (1) asset. (2) liability. (3) revenue. (4) expense.

Q5–12 On January 2, a company receives $6,000 from a tenant as rent for the current calendar year. The fiscal year of the company is July 1 to June 30. (a) Will the adjusting entry for the rent as of June 30 of the current year be a deferral or an accrual? (b) Which of the following types of accounts will be affected by the adjusting entry as of June 30? (1) asset. (2) liability. (3) revenue. (4) expense. (c) How much of the $6,000 should be allocated to the current fiscal year ending June 30?

Q5–13 On September 30, the end of its fiscal year, a company owes salaries of $1,000 for an incomplete payroll period. On the first payday in October, salaries of $3,000 are paid. (a) Is the $1,000 a deferral or an accrual as of September 30? (b) Which of the following types of accounts will be affected by the related adjusting entry: (1) asset, (2) liability, (3) revenue, (4) expense? (c) How much of the $3,000 salary payment should be allocated to October?

Q5–14 At the end of the fiscal year, a company has one 120-day interest-bearing note payable that had been issued to a supplier thirty days earlier. (a) Will the interest on the note as of the end of the current year represent a deferral or an accrual? (b) Which of the following types of accounts will be affected by the related adjusting entry at the end of the current year? (1) asset. (2) liability. (3) revenue. (4) expense. (c) Assuming that the note is not paid until maturity, what fraction of the total interest should be allocated to the year in which the note is paid?

Q5–15 The following accounts each have a balance after adjusting entries have been made and posted. State whether each is (a) an asset, (b) a liability, (c) a revenue or (d) an expense:

(1) Rent Expense
(2) Accrued Interest Payable
(3) Accrued Interest Receivable
(4) Rent Earned
(5) Prepaid Insurance
(6) Office Supplies
(7) Insurance Expense
(8) Unearned Rent
(9) Interest Expense
(10) Interest Earned

Class exercises

CE5–1 (Adjusting entries) Certain unadjusted account balances from the trial balance of Jim Foley's consulting firm, for year ended December 31, 1979, are given:

Account Title	*Debits*	*Credits*
Accounts Receivable	$20,000	
Notes Receivable	9,000	
Prepaid Insurance	1,080	
Office Supplies	620	
Automobiles	10,000	
Accumulated Depreciation—Automobiles		$ 2,000
Notes Payable		3,000
Revenue—Consulting Fees		240,000
Advertising Expense	900	
Rent Expense	20,000	
Salaries Expense	24,500	
Property Taxes Expense	1,675	
Heat and Light Expense	1,200	
Interest Earned		300
Rent Earned		1,200

Adjustment data on December 31 are as follows:

1. Office supplies on hand totaled $50.
2. Depreciation for the year was $1,000.
3. Estimated heat and light expense not recorded was $125.
4. Of the amount shown for Interest Earned, $100 was unearned as of December 31, 1979.
5. The balance of the Prepaid Insurance account consists of $360 for the premium on a three-year policy dated July 1, 1979, and $720 for premiums on a three-year policy dated January 1, 1979.
6. Advertising supplies on hand were $70.
7. The balance of the Notes Payable account represents a 6-percent interest-bearing note dated January 1, 1979, due July 1, 1980.
8. The rent expense is $2,000 a month.
9. Salaries earned by employees but not paid were $650.

10. Property taxes accrued were $95.
11. On January 1, 1979, the Foley Company subleased a section of its rented space. The lease with the tenant specifies a minimum yearly rental of $1,200 payable in 12 installments at the beginning of each month. The maximum annual rental is 5 percent of sales. The amount of the adjustment, in rent, if there is any adjustment, is due on January 15. The tenant reported sales of $26,500 for 1979.
12. Included in Revenue—Consulting Fees are advance payments of $7,500 by clients for services to be rendered early in 1980.

Required:
1. Record the adjusting entries.
2. Indicate the financial statement classification of each account in each entry.
3. Show the amount reported on the financial statements. Present the data in schedule form as shown (item 1 is done as an example):

Item No.	Adjusting Journal Entries December 31, 1979	Dr.	Cr.	Financial Statement Classification	Amount Reported on Financial Statement
1	Office Supplies Exp. Office Supplies	570	 570	Expenses Current Assets	$570 50

Exercises and problems

P5–1 Joseph De Roche, an electrician, prepares monthly financial statements. The following transactions occurred during December, 1979:

1979
Dec. 15 Billed customers $900 for services rendered this month.
17 Purchased $550 worth of electrical supplies on account.
31 Received $410 in cash from customers billed on December 15.
31 Paid $300 on account for electrical supplies purchased on December 17.
The electrical supplies inventory on December 31 was $90.

Required: Journalize the transactions, assuming that De Roche keeps his books (a) on the cash basis; (b) on the accrual basis. (c) What is the net income on the cash basis? on the accrual basis? (d) Which method should De Roche use? why?

P5–2 The Ajax Company purchased a new truck on January 1, 1979, for $5,200. It had an estimated useful life of four years and a trade-in value at the end of that time of $400.

Required:

1. What is the depreciation expense for 1979?
2. What is the balance in the Accumulated Depreciation—Delivery Equipment account at the end of 1979? 1980?
3. What will the book value of the truck be in the balance sheet of December 31, 1979? December 31, 1980?
4. Why is depreciation expense credited to Accumulated Depreciation—Delivery Equipment rather than directly to Delivery Equipment?

P5–3 The trial balance of the Bell Company on December 31, 1979, included the following account balances before adjustments:

Prepaid Insurance	$ 600
Prepaid Advertising Supplies	800
Prepaid Rent	1,200
Office Supplies	1,500
Office Equipment	3,300

Data for adjustments on December 31, 1979, were:

a. On November 1, 1979, the Company purchased a two-year comprehensive insurance policy for $600.
b. Advertising supplies on hand totaled $300.
c. On September 1, 1979, the Company paid one year's rent in advance.
d. The office supplies inventory was $720.
e. The office equipment was purchased on July 1, 1979, and has an estimated useful life of 10 years and a salvage value of $300.

Required: Make the adjusting entries.

P5–4 The Wilson Company employs three sales clerks at a weekly salary of $100 each. They are paid on Friday, the last day of a five-day workweek.

Required: Make the adjusting entry, assuming that the accounting period ended on Tuesday.

P5–5 (a) The balance sheet of the Durning Company as of December 31, 1979 and 1980, showed Office Supplies at $1,350 and $1,500, respectively. During 1980, office supplies totaling $2,200 were purchased.

Required: What was the Office Supplies Expense for the year 1980?

(b) The balances of the Prepaid Insurance account of the Barth Company were:

December 31, 1979	$930
December 31, 1980	520

The income statement for 1980 showed insurance expense of $1,100.

Required: What were the expenditures for insurance premiums during 1980?

P5–6 Make the end-of-year adjusting entries for the Rex Hall Company for the following items:

a. The debit balance of the Prepaid Insurance account is $720. Of this amount, $600 is expired.
b. Accrued salaries and wages payable total $150.
c. The Office Supplies account has a debit balance of $180; $30 worth is on hand.
d. Depreciation on store equipment is $200, on office equipment, $175.
e. Accrued interest receivable is $95.
f. Accrued interest payable is $60.
g. Unearned Rent has a credit balance of $2,600, of which, $2,400 was earned during the past year.

P5–7 The bookkeeper for the Ronson Company prepared the following condensed income statement for the year ended December 31, 1979, and the condensed balance sheet as of that date.

Income Statement

Revenue from Services		$31,500
Operating Expenses		
Insurance Expense	$ 1,050	
Miscellaneous Expense	3,800	
Office Supplies Expense	350	
Wages Expense	12,000	17,200
Net Income		$14,300

Balance Sheet

Assets

Cash	$ 3,500
Accounts Receivable	8,400
Equipment	30,500
Total Assets	$42,400

Liabilities and Owner's Equity

Accounts Payable	$ 8,400
Stanley Ronson, Capital	34,000
Total Liabilities and Owner's Equity	$42,400

The following items were overlooked entirely by the bookkeeper in the preparation of the statements:

a. The depreciation of equipment (acquired January 1, 1979): estimated life, 10 years; no salvage value.
b. Wages earned but unpaid, $600.

c. Office supplies on hand, $125 (purchases during 1979 were debited to Office Supplies Expense)

d. Unexpired insurance premiums, $425.

Required: What adjustments are needed?

P5–8 (Integrative) On August 1, 1979, Isaac Bostain opened a repair shop. During August, the following transactions were completed:

1979

Aug. 1 Transferred $1,000 from his personal savings account to a checking account under the name of Bostain Fixery.

2 Paid $50 for office supplies.

3 Purchased second-hand office equipment for $150 in cash.

4 Issued a check for $50 for August rent.

5 Paid a premium of $24 for an insurance policy on the equipment, effective August 1.

6 Purchased supplies on account to be used in repair work, as follows:

Andrews Supply Company	$ 35
Bonica's, Inc.	30
Fixit Supply Company	60
House of Berezin	20
Total	$145

17 Received $950 for repair work completed.

20 Additional repair work was completed, and bills were sent out, as follows:

Leo Bonner and Company	$105
William Curtis	35
Arnold Johnson	28
Peter Kent	60
Total	$228

22 Paid $20 for the telephone service for the month.

25 Paid the following creditors:

Andrews Supply Company	$20
Bonica's, Inc.	10
Fixit Supply Company	30
House of Berezin	10
Total	$ 70

1979

Aug. 27 Received cash from customers to apply on account, as follows:

Leo Bonner and Company	$ 50
William Curtis	10
Arnold Johnson	10
Peter Kent	20
Total	$ 90

30 Bostain withdrew $300 in cash for his personal use.

Supplementary adjustment data as of August 31, 1979 were:

a. The insurance premium paid on August 5 is for one year.

b. A physical count shows that (1) office supplies on hand total $25, and (2) repair supplies on hand are $65.

c. The office equipment has an estimated useful life of five years with no salvage value.

Required:

1. Open the following accounts in the general ledger: Cash, 101; Accounts Receivable, 111; Office Supplies, 136; Repair Supplies, 137; Prepaid Insurance, 140; Office Equipment, 163; Accumulated Depreciation—Office Equipment, 163A; Accounts Payable, 201; Isaac Bostain, Capital, 251; Isaac Bostain, Drawing, 252; Repair Revenue, 301; Insurance Expense, 702; Rent Expense, 703; Office Supplies Expense, 708; Telephone and Telegraph Expense, 709; Repair Supplies Expense, 712; Depreciation Expense—Office Equipment, 717.
2. Open accounts in the accounts receivable ledger for Leo Bonner and Company, William Curtis, Arnold Johnson, and Peter Kent.
3. Open accounts in the accounts payable ledger for the Andrews Supply Company; Bonica's Inc.; the Fixit Supply Company; and the House of Berezin.
4. Record all the transactions in the general journal; post to the appropriate ledgers. Prepare adjusting entries in the general journal and post to the ledger accounts.
5. Prepare a trial balance after the adjusting entries have been posted.

P5–9 (Minicase) You have been the accountant for John H. Fox since your graduation in June. At the end of each month you have used the cash basis of accounting and have ignored a number of small accruals of expenses and revenue. Fox says that these are too small to worry about. Yet when you consider them in the aggregate, they are sizeable.

Required: Write a report to Fox stating why you should or should not consider these accruals.

chapter six

Introduction

An illustration of the accounting for the end-of-the-period process of the Wheelo Trucking Company was started in Chapter 5, where detailed consideration was given to the adjustment process. The accounting for this illustration will be continued in this chapter and the remaining steps in the accounting cycle will be completed.

Completion of the accounting cycle

Learning goals[1]

To explain the steps in the accounting cycle.
To know how to prepare a work sheet.
To prepare from the work sheet an income statement, a statement of owner's equity, and a balance sheet.
To journalize adjusting and closing entries in the general journal using data from the work sheet and to post those entries.
To be capable of preparing a postclosing trial balance.
To journalize, in the period following adjustments, transactions that are related to those adjustments.

Key terms

accruals
adjusted trial balance
closing entries
deferrals
interim statements
keying (of adjustments)
nonreversing procedure
reversing entries
reversing procedure
work sheet

1 Since the appendix to this chapter is equivalent to an optional chapter, separate learning goals are provided on page 187 for the appendix.

Before we return to the Wheelo Trucking Company, let us review the "big picture" of the accounting process: (1) to see where we have been and (2) to see where we must go with our example. Figure 6–1 shows the individual phases of the accounting process. In Chapters 2–4, there were illustrated the various steps that must be taken during the accounting period: (1) collecting business information through the use of business documents, (2) selecting a proper chart of accounts, analyzing transactions and journalizing, and (3) posting the journal entries to the appropriate ledgers.

In this chapter we will reinforce certain steps that have been previously illustrated (in Chapters 3, 4, and 5) and will add some new dimensions to the accounting process through our example of the Wheelo Trucking Company. As can be seen from Figure 6–1, the accounting phases that must be accomplished at the end of the accounting period are: (1) preparing the unadjusted trial balance, (2) collecting the adjustment information, placing these on the work sheet and

Figure 6–1 Diagram of the accounting process

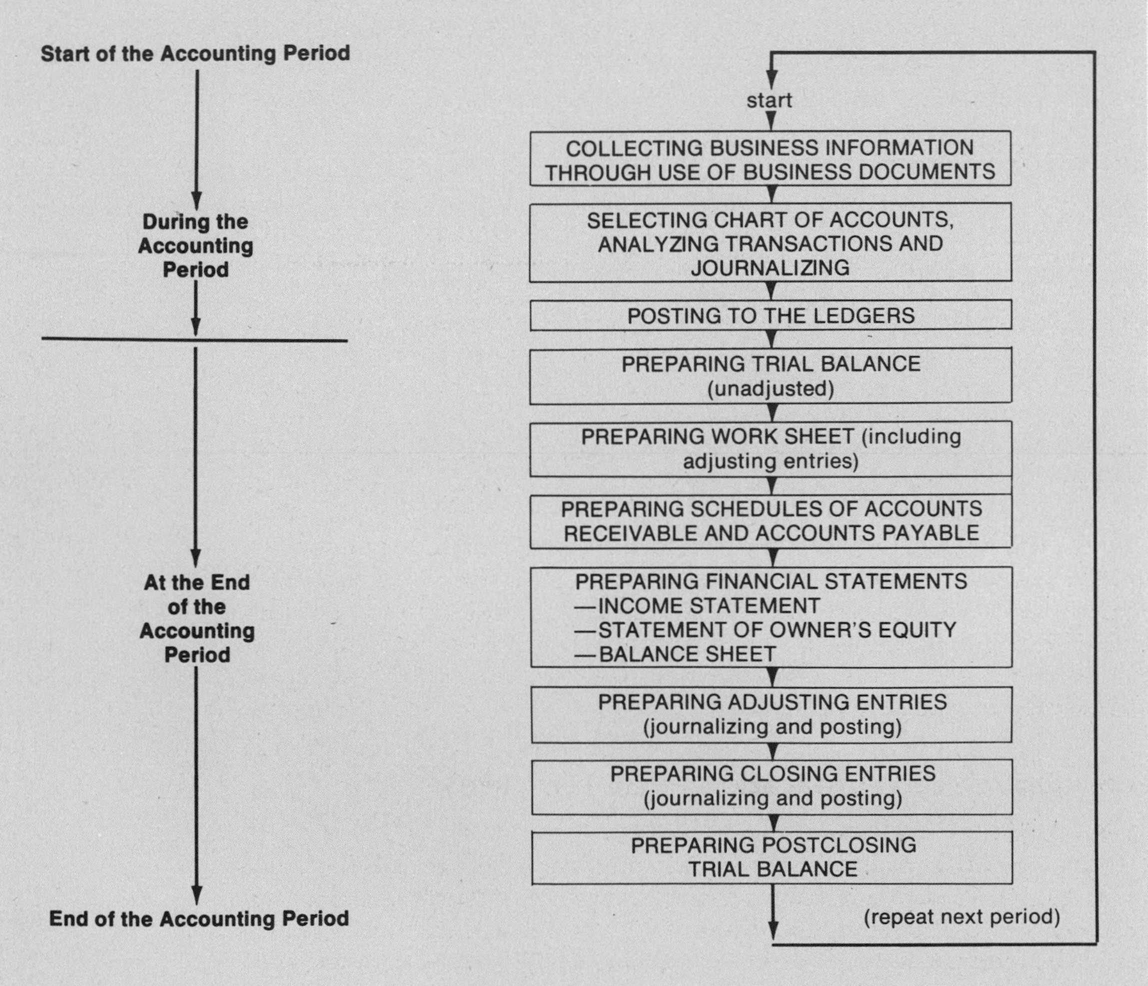

completing the work sheet, (3) preparing the schedules of accounts receivable and accounts payable, (4) preparing the financial statements, (5) journalizing and posting the adjustments, (6) journalizing and posting the closing entries, and (7) preparing a postclosing trial balance.

In the appendix to this chapter two different ways that an accountant may approach adjusting entries are discussed: (1) the method presented in Chapter 5 is reviewed and (2) the alternative approach involving accruals and deferrals is presented.

An accounting illustration— the Wheelo Trucking Company (continued)

We now pick up again with our illustration of the Wheelo Trucking Company. The reader should turn back to pages 137–151 (Chapter 5) to review the initial information presented in reference to this example. The next phase of the accounting process is that of preparing a work sheet.

The work sheet

The work sheet is a tool used by the accountant to bring together information necessary in the preparation of the formal financial statements; it is not a substitute for the financial statements. Although the work sheet is not absolutely essential, it would be difficult in most instances to prepare the statements directly from the journals and ledgers, since that approach would often require consolidating material from books, cards, and other documents. The work sheet bridges the gap between the accounting records and the formal statements and serves as a convenient device to calculate the effect of the adjustments and to determine the net income, or net loss, before the adjustments are formally journalized and posted to the ledger. The work sheet furnishes the accountant with a preview of the final statements. Most businesses formally close their books only once each year, yet they often prepare financial statements on a monthly or quarterly basis. When these monthly statements, referred to as *interim statements,* are prepared, the work sheet can substitute for the more formal procedure of recording and posting the usual adjusting and closing entries for the purpose of preparing these statements.

Four steps in the preparation of the work sheet

Preparation of the work sheet consists of four steps.

Step 1. The work sheet is headed to show the name of the company, the name of the statement, and the accounting period; the column headings are entered; the trial balance account titles and amounts are entered either directly from the general ledger or from a prepared listing, if available. The account titles are entered in the space provided and the amounts are entered in the first pair of money columns. The work sheet of the Wheelo Trucking Company after completion of step 1 appears in Figure 6–2.

Step 2. The adjustments are entered on the work sheet generally before they are formally journalized. This procedure helps speed up preparation of the formal financial statements—income statement, statement of owner's equity, and balance sheet. Nine adjustments for the Wheelo Trucking Company were discussed in detail in Chapter 5. Now they are entered on the work sheet:

Adjustment (a): To adjust for expired rent.
Adjustment (b): To adjust for expired insurance.
Adjustment (c): To adjust for office supplies used.
Adjustment (d): To adjust for the rent that is earned.
Adjustment (e): To adjust for depreciation of the office equipment.
Adjustment (f): To adjust for depreciation of the trucks.
Adjustment (g): To adjust for the accrued wages expense.
Adjustment (h): To adjust for the accrued interest expense.
Adjustment (i): To adjust for the accrued interest revenue.

The adjustments are *keyed* by letter for identification (cross referencing) as they are entered in the Adjustments columns. Any additional accounts required by the adjusting entries are written in below the trial balance. (Another way would be to list them in sequence with the other accounts without amounts in the Trial Balance columns.) In entry (a), for example, Rent Expense is debited for $500. Since this account does not appear in the trial balance, the title is written on the line immediately below the trial balance totals and the amount is entered directly in the Adjustments Debit column on the same line; the $500 is also entered in the Adjustments Credit column opposite Prepaid Rent. In this adjustment, only one of the accounts involved had to be written in below the trial balance. In entry (e), however, both the debited and the credited accounts had to be written in. After all the adjustments are entered, the Adjustments columns are added as a proof of their equality. The work sheet following the completion of step 2 is shown in Figure 6–3.

Step 3. Computations in this step result in the *adjusted trial balance* figure. The amounts extended to the Adjusted Trial Balance columns result from combining the amounts in the Trial Balance columns with the amounts in the Adjustments columns as follows:

If there are no adjustments to an account, extend a debit trial balance amount to the debit column of the adjusted trial balance, and extend a credit trial balance amount to the credit column of the adjusted trial balance.

If the account in the trial balance has a debit balance, add its debit adjustments and subtract its credit adjustments. The result, if a debit, is extended to the Adjusted Trial Balance Debit column; if a credit, it is extended to the credit column.

If the account in the trial balance has a credit balance, add its credit adjustments and subtract its debit adjustments. The adjusted balance is extended to the proper Adjusted Trial Balance column.

For the accounts listed below the trial balance totals, extend the adjustment amount directly to the appropriate Adjusted Trial Balance column.

Figure 6–2 Work sheet, step 1: trial balances entered

Wheelo Trucking Company
Work Sheet
For the month ended June 30, 1979

Acct. No.	Account Title	Trial Balance Dr.	Trial Balance Cr.	Adjustments Dr.	Adjustments Cr.	Adjusted Trial Balance Dr.	Adjusted Trial Balance Cr.	Income Statement Dr.	Income Statement Cr.	Balance Sheet Dr.	Balance Sheet Cr.
101	Cash	5250 00									
111	Accounts Receivable	550 00									
112	Notes Receivable	1440 00									
131	Office Supplies	230 00									
141	Prepaid Insurance	2160 00									
142	Prepaid Rent	1500 00									
201	Office Equipment	1400 00									
211	Trucks	13000 00									
301	Accounts Payable		200 00								
302	Notes Payable		8000 00								
321	Unearned Rent		600 00								
401	John Wheelo, Capital		12000 00								
404	John Wheelo, Drawing	500 00									
501	Trucking Revenue		7465 00								
601	Heat and Light Expense	40 00									
602	Maintenance and Repair Expense	375 00									
603	Telephone and Telegraph Expense	95 00									
604	Gas and Oil Expense	525 00									
605	Wages Expense	1200 00									
	Totals	28265 00	28265 00								

Trial balance before adjustments

Figure 6–3 Work sheet, step 2: adjustments entered

Wheelo Trucking Company
Work Sheet
For the month ended June 30, 1979

Acct. No.	Account Title	Trial Balance Dr.	Trial Balance Cr.	Adjustments Dr.	Adjustments Cr.	Adjusted Trial Balance Dr.	Adjusted Trial Balance Cr.	Income Statement Dr.	Income Statement Cr.	Balance Sheet Dr.	Balance Sheet Cr.
101	Cash	5250.00									
111	Accounts Receivable	550.00									
112	Notes Receivable	1440.00									
131	Office Supplies	230.00			(c) 170.00						
141	Prepaid Insurance	2160.00			(b) 60.00						
142	Prepaid Rent	1500.00			(a) 500.00						
201	Office Equipment	1400.00									
211	Trucks	13000.00									
301	Accounts Payable		200.00								
302	Notes Payable		8000.00								
321	Unearned Rent		600.00	(d) 100.00							
401	John Wheelo, Capital		12000.00								
404	John Wheelo, Drawing	500.00									
501	Trucking Revenue		7465.00								
601	Heat and Light Expense	40.00									
602	Maintenance and Repair Expense	375.00									
603	Telephone and Telegraph Expense	95.00									
604	Gas and Oil Expense	525.00									
605	Wages Expense	1200.00		(g) 150.00							
	Totals	28265.00	28265.00								
606	Rent Expense			(a) 500.00							
607	Insurance Expense			(b) 60.00							
608	Office Supplies Expense			(c) 170.00							
511	Rent Earned				(d) 100.00						
609	Depreciation Expense - Office Equipment			(e) 10.00							
201A	Accumulated Depreciation - Office Equipment				(e) 10.00						
610	Depreciation Expense - Trucks			(f) 200.00							
211A	Accumulated Depreciation - Trucks				(f) 200.00						
311	Accrued Wages Payable				(g) 150.00						
611	Interest Expense			(h) 24.00							
303	Accrued Interest Payable				(h) 24.00						
113	Accrued Interest Receivable			(i) 4.00							
521	Interest Earned				(i) 4.00						
				1218.00	1218.00						

Letters are used to cross reference the debit and credit adjustments.

Additional accounts are added for the adjustments.

Adjustments are entered in these columns.

On completion of step 3, the adjusted trial balance figures will be the same as the balances of the accounts in the general ledger after the adjusting entries have been journalized and posted. Each line on the work sheet essentially represents a general ledger account and functions in the same manner as to the debit and credit position. For example, after the adjusting entries are journalized and posted, the Prepaid Rent account appears in the general ledger as shown below:

Prepaid Rent — Acct. No. 142

Date		Explanation	F	Debit		Credit		Balance	
1979									
Jun.	1		1	1,500	00			1,500	00
	30	Adjustment	4			500	00	1,000	00

The new balance is a debit of $1,000, which is the amount shown opposite Prepaid Rent in the Adjusted Trial Balance Debit column of the work sheet. The work sheet following the completion of step 3 is shown in Figure 6–4.

Step 4. The amounts in the Adjusted Trial Balance columns are extended either to the Income Statement columns or to the Balance Sheet columns, depending on their statement classification. Expense and revenue accounts are entered in the Income Statement columns; asset, liability, and owner's equity accounts are entered in the Balance Sheet columns. The four columns are then totaled. The difference between the totals of the Income Statement columns is the net income or net loss for the period; a net income is indicated if the total of the credit column exceeds the total of the debit column. The excess is entered in the Income Statement Debit column and in the Balance Sheet Credit column just below the column totals. This procedure records on the work sheet the increase in the owner's equity resulting from an excess of revenue over expenses during the period. A net loss is indicated if the total of the Income Statement Debit column exceeds that of the Income Statement Credit column. A loss is shown on the work sheet in the Income Statement Credit column and the Balance Sheet Debit column just below the column totals. The designation Net Income, or Net Loss, for the Month, whichever is pertinent, is entered in the Account Title column on the same line. The work sheet following the completion of step 4 is illustrated in Figure 6–5.

If the difference between the Income Statement Debit and Credit columns (net income) and the Balance Sheet Debit and Credit columns are not the same, an error has been made. The totaling and ruling of the last four columns of the work sheet (step 4) is illustrated in Figure 6-5. Note that balancing the last four columns provides only a limited proof of the accuracy of the work sheet—proof that the equality of debits and credits has been maintained throughout its preparation. The extension of the Cash account debit into the Income Statement Debit column, for example, would not destroy the debit-credit relationship of the work sheet, although statements prepared from that work sheet would be inaccurate. Note also that the total of the Balance Sheet Debit column need not correspond with the total assets reported in the statement. Accumulated Depreciation—

Wheelo Trucking Company
Work Sheet
For the month ended June 30, 1979

Acct. No.	Account Title	Trial Balance Dr.	Trial Balance Cr.	Adjustments Dr.	Adjustments Cr.	Adjusted Trial Balance Dr.	Adjusted Trial Balance Cr.	Income Statement Dr.	Income Statement Cr.	Balance Sheet Dr.	Balance Sheet Cr.
101	Cash	5250.00				5250.00					
111	Accounts Receivable	550.00				550.00					
112	Notes Receivable	1440.00				1440.00					
131	Office Supplies	230.00			(c) 170.00	60.00					
141	Prepaid Insurance	2160.00			(b) 60.00	2100.00					
142	Prepaid Rent	1500.00			(a) 500.00	1000.00					
201	Office Equipment	1400.00				1400.00					
211	Trucks	13000.00				13000.00					
301	Accounts Payable		200.00				200.00				
302	Notes Payable		8000.00				8000.00				
321	Unearned Rent		600.00	(d) 100.00			500.00				
401	John Wheelo, Capital		12000.00				12000.00				
404	John Wheelo, Drawing	500.00				500.00					
501	Trucking Revenue		7465.00				7465.00				
601	Heat and Light Expense	40.00				40.00					
602	Maintenance and Repairs Expense	375.00				375.00					
603	Telephone and Telegraph Expense	95.00				95.00					
604	Gas and Oil Expense	525.00				525.00					
605	Wages Expense	1200.00		(g) 150.00		1350.00					
	Totals	28265.00	28265.00								
606	Rent Expense			(a) 500.00		500.00					
607	Insurance Expense			(b) 60.00		60.00					
608	Office Supplies Expense			(c) 170.00		170.00					
511	Rent Earned				(d) 100.00		100.00				
609	Depreciation Expense-Office Equipment			(e) 10.00		10.00					
201A	Accumulated Depreciation-Office Equipment				(e) 10.00		10.00				
610	Depreciation Expense-Trucks			(f) 200.00		200.00					
211A	Accumulated Depreciation-Trucks				(f) 200.00		200.00				
311	Accrued Wages Payable				(g) 150.00		150.00				
611	Interest Expense			(h) 24.00		24.00					
303	Accrued Interest Payable				(h) 24.00		24.00				
113	Accrued Interest Receivable			(i) 4.00		4.00					
521	Interest Earned				(i) 4.00		4.00				
	Totals			1218.00	1218.00	28653.00	28653.00				

Balances from the trial balance adjusted by the amounts in Adjustments Columns are extended here.

Figure 6–4 Work sheet, step 3: adjusted trial balance entered

Wheelo Trucking Company
Work Sheet
For the month ended June 30, 1979

Acct. No.	Account Title	Trial Balance Dr.	Trial Balance Cr.	Adjustments Dr.	Adjustments Cr.	Adjusted Trial Balance Dr.	Adjusted Trial Balance Cr.	Income Statement Dr.	Income Statement Cr.	Balance Sheet Dr.	Balance Sheet Cr.
101	Cash	5250.00				5250.00				5250.00	
111	Accounts Receivable	550.00				550.00				550.00	
112	Notes Receivable	1440.00				1440.00				1440.00	
131	Office Supplies	230.00			(c) 170.00	60.00				60.00	
141	Prepaid Insurance	2160.00			(b) 60.00	2100.00				2100.00	
142	Prepaid Rent	1500.00			(a) 500.00	1000.00				1000.00	
201	Office Equipment	1400.00				1400.00				1400.00	
211	Trucks	13000.00				13000.00				13000.00	
301	Accounts Payable		200.00				200.00				200.00
302	Notes Payable		8000.00				8000.00				8000.00
321	Unearned Rent		600.00	(d) 100.00			500.00				500.00
401	John Wheelo, Capital		12000.00				12000.00				12000.00
404	John Wheelo, Drawing	500.00				500.00				500.00	
501	Trucking Revenue		7465.00				7465.00		7465.00		
601	Heat and Light Expense	40.00				40.00		40.00			
602	Maintenance and Repairs Expense	375.00				375.00		375.00			
603	Telephone and Telegraph Expense	95.00				95.00		95.00			
604	Gas and Oil Expense	525.00				525.00		525.00			
605	Wages Expense	1200.00		(g) 150.00		1350.00		1350.00			
	Totals	28265.00	28265.00								
606	Rent Expense			(a) 500.00		500.00		500.00			
607	Insurance Expense			(b) 60.00		60.00		60.00			
608	Office Supplies Expense			(c) 170.00		170.00		170.00			
511	Rent Earned				(d) 100.00		100.00		100.00		
609	Depreciation Expense - Office Equipment			(e) 10.00		10.00		10.00			
201A	Accumulated Depreciation - Office Equipment				(e) 10.00		10.00				10.00
610	Depreciation Expense - Trucks			(f) 200.00		200.00		200.00			
211A	Accumulated Depreciation - Trucks				(f) 200.00		200.00				200.00
311	Accrued Wages Payable				(g) 150.00		150.00				150.00
611	Interest Expense			(h) 24.00		24.00		24.00			
303	Accrued Interest Payable				(h) 24.00		24.00				24.00
113	Accrued Interest Receivable			(i) 4.00		4.00				4.00	
521	Interest Earned				(i) 4.00		4.00		4.00		
	Totals			1218.00	1218.00	28653.00	28653.00	3347.00	7569.00	25304.00	21084.00
	Net Income for the month							4222.00			4222.00
								7569.00	7569.00	25304.00	25304.00

The difference between the Income Statement Columns is net income

Net income is transferred to the Balance Sheet Credit Column

Figure 6–5 Work sheet, step 4: complete

Trucks, for example, is extended to the Balance Sheet Credit column because it represents a balance sheet account with a credit balance. It is neither an asset nor a liability, but rather a deduction from Trucks, and is referred to as a contra asset. Since plus and minus symbols are not used on the work sheet, a deduction from an amount in a Debit column is effected by positioning the item to be deducted in the Credit column.

The work sheet may be varied in form—particularly with respect to the number of columns—to meet specific needs of the user. In Figure 7–3, for example, the columns for the adjusted trial balance are omitted.

Preparation of financial statements from the work sheet

The income statement is prepared from the amounts in the Income Statement columns of the work sheet; the statement of owner's equity and the balance sheet are prepared from the amounts in the Balance Sheet columns of the work sheet. In the preparation of financial statements, care should be taken to use each amount just once and in its proper debit and credit relation. The debit-credit relationship is not emphasized by the statements, but it is present. In the balance sheet, for example, Accumulated Depreciation—Trucks, with a credit balance of $200, is deducted from Trucks, which has a debit balance. Net Income (or loss) appears in both the income statement and the statement of owner's equity.

The financial statements of the Wheelo Trucking Company for June are shown in Figures 6–6, 6–7, and 6–8. Some form of designation should be used to identify

Figure 6–6
Income statement

WHEELO TRUCKING COMPANY
Income Statement
For the Month Ended June 30, 1979

Exhibit A

Revenues		
Trucking Revenue		$7,465.00
Interest Earned		4.00
Rent Earned		100.00
Total Revenues		$7,569.00
Expenses		
Heat and Light Expense	$ 40.00	
Maintenance and Repairs Expense	375.00	
Telephone and Telegraph Expense	95.00	
Gas and Oil Expense	525.00	
Wages Expense	1,350.00	
Rent Expense	500.00	
Insurance Expense	60.00	
Office Supplies Expense	170.00	
Depreciation Expense—Office Equipment	10.00	
Depreciation Expense—Trucks	200.00	
Interest Expense	24.00	
Total Expenses		3,349.00
Net Income—To Exhibit B		$4,220.00

and cross-reference the financial statements. The following is one possibility:

Exhibit A for the income statement
Exhibit B for the statement of owner's equity
Exhibit C for the balance sheet

Figure 6–7
Statement of owner's equity

WHEELO TRUCKING COMPANY — Exhibit B
Statement of Owner's Equity
For the Month Ended June 30, 1979

John Wheelo, Original Investment June 1, 1979	$12,000.00
Add: Net Income for Month of June, 1979—Exhibit A	4,220.00
Total	$16,220.00
Deduct: Withdrawals	500.00
John Wheelo, Capital, June 30, 1979 (To Exhibit C)	$15,720.00

Figure 6–8
Balance sheet

WHEELO TRUCKING COMPANY — Exhibit C
Balance Sheet
June 30, 1979

Assets

Current Assets			
Cash		$ 5,250.00	
Accounts Receivable		550.00	
Notes Receivable		1,440.00	
Accrued Interest Receivable		4.00	
Office Supplies		60.00	
Prepaid Insurance		2,100.00	
Prepaid Rent		1,000.00	
Total Current Assets			$10,404.00
Equipment			
Office Equipment	$ 1,400.00		
Deduct Accumulated Depreciation	10.00	$ 1,390.00	
Trucks	$13,000.00		
Deduct Accumulated Depreciation	200.00	12,800.00	
Total Equipment			14,190.00
Total Assets			$24,594.00

Liabilities and Owner's Equity

Current Liabilities		
Accounts Payable	$ 200.00	
Notes Payable	8,000.00	
Accrued Interest Payable	24.00	
Accrued Wages Payable	150.00	
Unearned Rent	500.00	
Total Current Liabilities		$ 8,874.00
Owner's Equity		
John Wheelo, Capital (Exhibit B)		15,720.00
Total Liabilities and Owner's Equity		$24,594.00

Since the company was organized on June 1, 1979, it had no beginning capital balance; the first amount shown in the statement of owner's equity is the initial investment of $12,000 by the owner, John Wheelo. The remaining items on this statement are the usual ones; net income earned and the withdrawals made by the owner.

Updating of accounts after preparation of work sheet

Recording adjustments in the general journal

As a practical matter, formal adjusting entries are usually not recorded in the general journal until after the financial statements have been prepared. The adjusting entries then may be taken directly from the Adjustments columns of the work sheet and dated as of the last day of the accounting period. The caption "Adjusting Entries" then is written in the general journal on the line following the last regular general journal entry. After the adjusting entries have been posted, the general ledger account balances will correspond with the amounts in the Adjusted Trial Balance columns of the work sheet. Although the adjusting journal entries for the Wheelo Trucking Company have already been made as they were introduced (see Chapter 5), to add realism to the accounting job, they are collected and repeated in Figure 6–9 in order to emphasize the recommended timing of the recording process. The account numbers in the folio column indicate that they have been posted.

Figure 6–9 Adjusting entries

GENERAL JOURNAL

Page 4

Date		Debit-Credit-Account Titles: Explanation	F	Debit		Credit	
1979		Adjusting Entries					
Jun.	30	Rent Expense	606	500	00		
		Prepaid Rent	142			500	00
		To record rent expense for June.					
	30	Insurance Expense	607	60	00		
		Prepaid Insurance	141			60	00
		To record insurance expense for June.					
	30	Office Supplies Expense	608	170	00		
		Office Supplies	131			170	00
		To record office supplies used during June.					
	30	Unearned Rent	321	100	00		
		Rent Earned	511			100	00
		To record revenue earned from rental of trucks during June.					

GENERAL JOURNAL

Page 4 (cont.)

Date		Debit-Credit-Account Titles: Explanation	F	Debit		Credit	
1979							
Jun.	30	Depreciation Expense—Office Equipment	609	10	00		
		Accumulated Depreciation—Office Equipment . .	201A			10	00
		To record depreciation for June.					
	30	Depreciation Expense—Trucks	610	200	00		
		Accumulated Depreciation—Trucks	211A			200	00
		To record the depreciation of trucks for June.					
	30	Wages Expense	605	150	00		
		Accrued Wages Payable	311			150	00
		To record wages expense accrued for last three days of June.					

GENERAL JOURNAL

Page 5

Date		Debit-Credit-Account Titles: Explanation	F	Debit		Credit	
1979							
Jun.	30	Interest Expense	611	24	00		
		Accrued Interest Payable	303			24	00
		To record interest expense accrued during June.					
	30	Accrued Interest Receivable	113	4	00		
		Interest Earned	521			4	00
		To record interest revenue accrued during June.					

The result of adjusting entries

When all the adjusting entries are recorded in the journal and posted to the general ledger, the mixed elements in the accounts will have been eliminated. Accounts consisting of asset and expense elements and accounts containing liability and revenue elements now have been apportioned so that each element is recorded in a separate account; advance payments for goods and services to be consumed in the future are shown in the appropriate asset accounts; advance receipts for future revenue are shown in liability accounts; and all other supplementary data not previously recorded but necessary for the preparation of financial statements are available in the ledger. The general ledger should contain all the accounts and amounts—expense, revenue, asset, liability, and owner's equity—necessary for the presentation of the financial position of the company as of the end of the accounting period and the results of its operations for the period then ended. Failure to adjust any mixed asset or liability account results in incorrect financial statements; failure to disclose all information may result in misleading financial statements.

Materiality

The need for adjustment and the need for full disclosure do not apply to insignificant, immaterial, or trivial matters.

Closing entries may be recorded directly from the work sheet

The caption "Closing Entries" is written in the middle of the first unused line on the journal page under the adjusting entries. The closing entries are recorded (Figure 6–10) and are then posted to the general ledger. The reader should recall (see Chapter 4, pages 112–116) that *closing entries* are made to empty (close, reduce balance to zero) those *temporary accounts* (nominal) that are set up to measure some of the changes in the owner's capital account during a given period of time. In the closing process, the net effect reflected in these temporary accounts is transferred to the owner's Capital account. The closing entries can be made directly from the work sheet in the following sequence.

Entry 1. Each account in the Income Statement Credit column is debited, and the sum of the debits is credited to the Income Summary account.

Entry 2. Each account in the Income Statement Debit column is credited, and the sum of the credits is debited to the Income Summary account.

Entry 3. The balance of Income Summary, which, after posting entries 1 and 2,

Figure 6–10
Closing entries

GENERAL JOURNAL

Page 5 (cont.)

Date		Debit-Credit-Account Titles: Explanation	F	Debit		Credit	
1979		Closing Entries					
Jun.	30	Trucking Revenue	501	7,465	00		
		Rent Earned	511	100	00		
		Interest Earned	521	4	00		
		Income Summary	902			7,569	00
		To close revenue accounts.					
	30	Income Summary	902	3,349	00		
		Heat and Light Expense	601			40	00
		Maintenance and Repairs Expense	602			375	00
		Telephone and Telegraph Expense	603			95	00
		Gas and Oil Expense	604			525	00
		Wages Expense	605			1,350	00
		Rent Expense	606			500	00
		Insurance Expense	607			60	00
		Office Supplies Expense	608			170	00
		Depreciation Expense—Office Equipment . .	609			10	00
		Depreciation Expense—Trucks	610			200	00
		Interest Expense	611			24	00
		To close expense accounts.					
	30	Income Summary	902	4,220	00		
		John Wheelo, Capital	401			4,220	00
		To transfer net income to the owner's capital account.					
	30	John Wheelo, Capital	401	500	00		
		John Wheelo, Drawing	404			500	00
		To close the drawing account to the owner's capital account.					

represents the net income or the net loss as shown on the work sheet, is transferred to John Wheelo, Capital.

Entry 4. The balance of John Wheelo, Drawing is closed into John Wheelo, Capital; the amount of this entry is the amount on the John Wheelo, Drawing account line in the Balance Sheet Debit column of the work sheet. It should be emphasized that John Wheelo, Drawing is *never* closed to the Income Summary. The amount in the Drawing account represents a distribution of income. It is *not* an expense; it has nothing to do with income determination.

The general ledger after closing

The general ledger of the Wheelo Trucking Company is reproduced after the adjusting entries and the closing entries have been posted. In reproducing the general ledger, exact dates are used when the information is given in the previous discussion. Otherwise the date of June 30 and the balance of the account as taken from the trial balance in Figure 5–1 (Chapter 5) are inserted because the detailed transactions were omitted from this example. It should be noted that when a balance is brought forward from another ledger page or ledger, the information is recorded in only the Balance column of the ledger account. A check mark is placed in the folio column to indicate that the particular amount was not posted at this time from a journal. The original amounts represented by the balance, however, were posted from journals and such procedure was reflected in the preceding ledgers and journals. The notations *Balance, Adjustment,* and *Closing Entry* are shown in the Explanation column as an aid in tracing the amounts to their sources. Since the full information about the ledger account balances is not shown in this illustration, the debit-credit nature of each account balance is again shown (as it was in Chapters 3 and 4). It should be noted, however, that it is *only a teaching aid;* it is not a part of the accounting procedure.

GENERAL LEDGER

Cash — Acct. No. 101

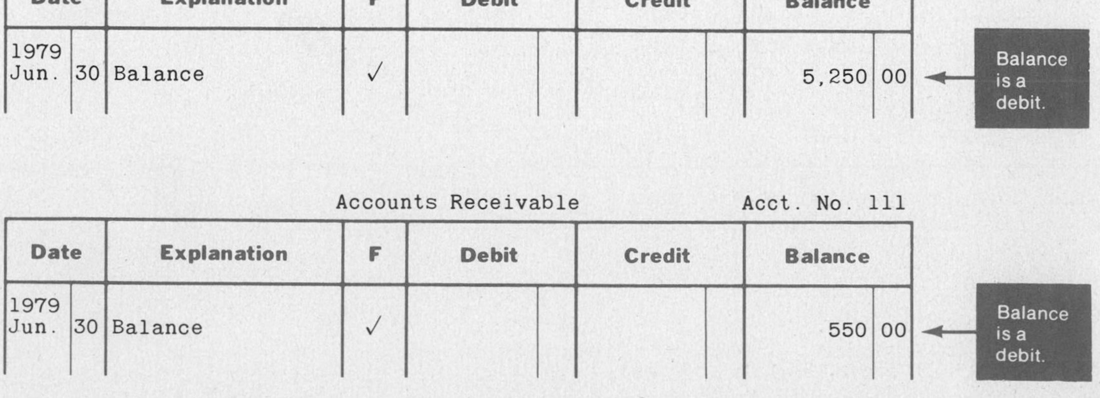

Date		Explanation	F	Debit		Credit		Balance	
1979 Jun.	30	Balance	✓					5,250	00

Accounts Receivable — Acct. No. 111

Date		Explanation	F	Debit		Credit		Balance	
1979 Jun.	30	Balance	✓					550	00

Notes Receivable Acct. No. 112

Date		Explanation	F	Debit		Credit		Balance	
1979 Jun.	30	Balance	✓					1,440	00

Balance is a debit.

Accrued Interest Receivable Acct. No. 113

Date		Explanation	F	Debit		Credit		Balance	
1979 Jun.	30	Adjustment	5	4	00			4	00

Balance is a debit.

Office Supplies Acct. No. 131

Date		Explanation	F	Debit		Credit		Balance	
1979 Jun.	6		1	230	00			230	00
	30	Adjustment	4			170	00	60	00

Balance is a debit.

Prepaid Insurance Acct. No. 141

Date		Explanation	F	Debit		Credit		Balance	
1979 Jun.	1		1	2,160	00			2,160	00
	30	Adjustment	4			60	00	2,100	00

Balance is a debit.

Prepaid Rent Acct. No. 142

Date		Explanation	F	Debit		Credit		Balance	
1979 Jun.	1		1	1,500	00			1,500	00
	30	Adjustment	4			500	00	1,000	00

Balance is a debit.

Office Equipment — Acct. No. 201

Date		Explanation	F	Debit		Credit		Balance	
1979 Jun.	1		1	1,400	00			1,400	00

Balance is a debit.

Accumulated Depreciation—Office Equipment — Acct. No. 201A

Date		Explanation	F	Debit		Credit		Balance	
1979 Jun.	30	Adjustment	4			10	00	10	00

Balance is a credit.

Trucks — Acct. No. 211

Date		Explanation	F	Debit		Credit		Balance	
1979 Jun.	1		1	13,000	00			13,000	00

Balance is a debit.

Accumulated Depreciation—Trucks — Acct. No. 211A

Date		Explanation	F	Debit		Credit		Balance	
1979 Jun.	30	Adjustment	4			200	00	200	00

Balance is a credit.

Accounts Payable — Acct. No. 301

Date		Explanation	F	Debit		Credit		Balance	
1979 Jun.	30	Balance	✓					200	00

Balance is a credit.

Notes Payable — Acct. No. 302

Date		Explanation	F	Debit		Credit		Balance	
1979									
Jun.	12		2			8,000	00	8,000	00

Balance is a credit.

Accrued Interest Payable — Acct. No. 303

Date		Explanation	F	Debit		Credit		Balance	
1979									
Jun.	30	Adjustment	5			24	00	24	00

Balance is a credit.

Accrued Wages Payable — Acct No. 311

Date		Explanation	F	Debit		Credit		Balance	
1979									
Jun.	30	Adjustment	4			150	00	150	00

Balance is a credit.

Unearned Rent — Acct. No. 321

Date		Explanation	F	Debit		Credit		Balance	
1979									
Jun.	1		1			600	00	600	00
	30	Adjustment	4	100	00			500	00

Balance is a credit.

John Wheelo, Capital — Acct. No. 401

Date		Explanation	F	Debit		Credit		Balance	
1979									
Jun.	1		1			12,000	00	12,000	00
	30	Net Income, closing entry	5			4,220	00	16,220	00
	30	Drawing, closing entry	5	500	00			15,720	00

Balance is a credit.

John Wheelo, Drawing — Acct. No. 404

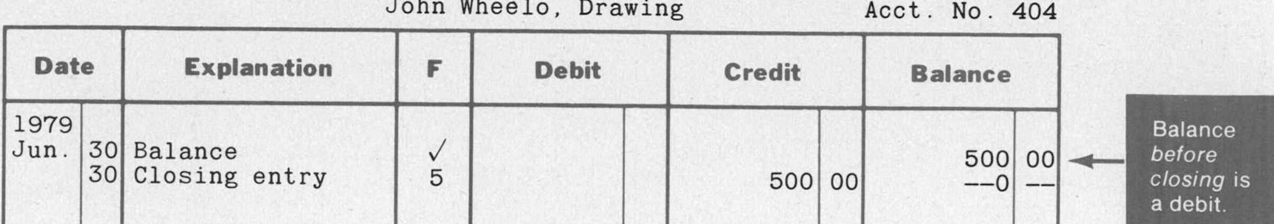

Date		Explanation	F	Debit		Credit		Balance	
1979									
Jun.	30	Balance	✓					500	00
	30	Closing entry	5			500	00	—0	—

Balance *before closing* is a debit.

Trucking Revenue — Acct. No. 501

Date		Explanation	F	Debit		Credit		Balance	
1979									
Jun.	30	Balance	✓					7,465	00
	30	Closing entry	5	7,465	00			—0	—

Balance *before closing* is a credit.

Rent Earned — Acct. No. 511

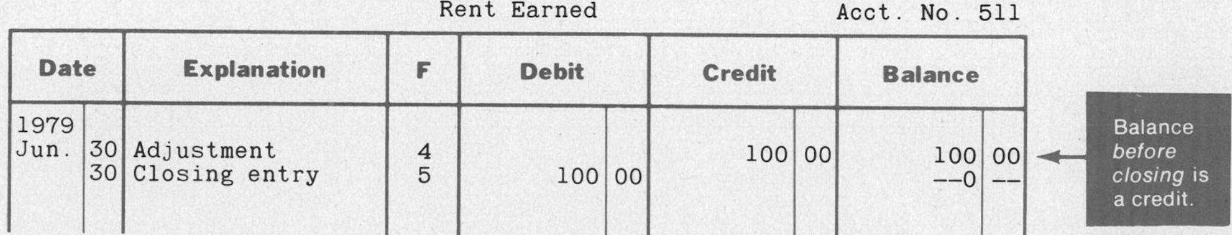

Date		Explanation	F	Debit		Credit		Balance	
1979									
Jun.	30	Adjustment	4			100	00	100	00
	30	Closing entry	5	100	00			—0	—

Balance *before closing* is a credit.

Interest Earned — Acct. No. 521

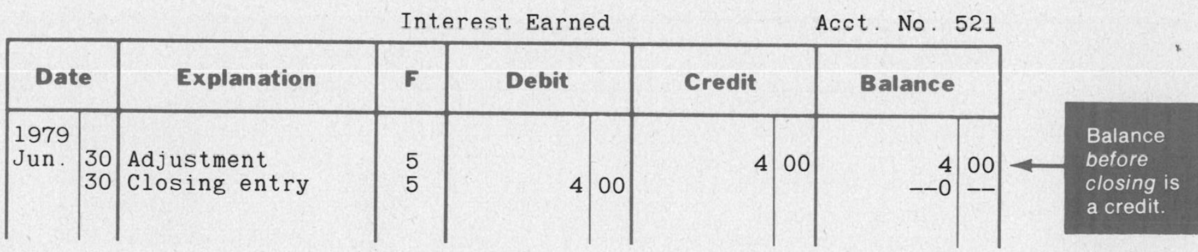

Date		Explanation	F	Debit		Credit		Balance	
1979									
Jun.	30	Adjustment	5			4	00	4	00
	30	Closing entry	5	4	00			—0	—

Balance *before closing* is a credit.

Heat and Light Expense — Acct. No. 601

Date		Explanation	F	Debit		Credit		Balance	
1979									
Jun.	30	Balance	✓					40	00
	30	Closing entry	5			40	00	—0	—

Balance *before closing* is a debit.

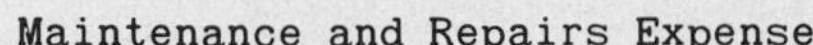

Maintenance and Repairs Expense — Acct. No. 602

Date		Explanation	F	Debit		Credit		Balance	
1979									
Jun.	30	Balance	✓					375	00
	30	Closing entry	5			375	00	—0	—

Balance *before closing* is a debit.

Telephone and Telegraph Expense — Acct. No. 603

Date		Explanation	F	Debit		Credit		Balance	
1979									
Jun.	30	Balance	✓					95	00
	30	Closing entry	5			95	00	—0	—

Balance *before closing* is a debit.

Gas and Oil Expense — Acct. No. 604

Date		Explanation	F	Debit		Credit		Balance	
1979									
Jun.	30	Balance	✓					525	00
	30	Closing entry	5			525	00	—0	—

Balance *before closing* is a debit.

Wages Expense — Acct. No. 605

Date		Explanation	F	Debit		Credit		Balance	
1979									
Jun.	13		2	600	00			600	00
	27		3	600	00			1,200	00
	30	Adjustment	4	150	00			1,350	00
	30	Closing entry	5			1,350	00	—0	—

Balance *before closing* is a debit.

Rent Expense — Acct. No. 606

Date		Explanation	F	Debit		Credit		Balance	
1979									
Jun.	30	Adjustment	4	500	00			500	00
	30	Closing entry	5			500	00	—0	—

Balance *before closing* is a debit.

Insurance Expense — Acct. No. 607

Date		Explanation	F	Debit		Credit		Balance	
1979									
Jun.	30	Adjustment	4	60	00			60	00
	30	Closing entry	5			60	00	--0	--

Balance *before closing* is a debit.

Office Supplies Expense — Acct. No. 608

Date		Explanation	F	Debit		Credit		Balance	
1979									
Jun.	30	Adjustment	4	170	00			170	00
	30	Closing entry	5			170	00	--0	--

Balance *before closing* is a debit.

Depreciation Expense—Office Equipment — Acct. No. 609

Date		Explanation	F	Debit		Credit		Balance	
1979									
Jun.	30	Adjustment	4	10	00			10	00
	30	Closing entry	5			10	00	--0	--

Balance *before closing* is a debit.

Depreciation Expense—Trucks — Acct. No. 610

Date		Explanation	F	Debit		Credit		Balance	
1979									
Jun.	30	Adjustment	4	200	00			200	00
	30	Closing entry	5			200	00	--0	--

Balance *before closing* is a debit.

Interest Expense — Acct. No. 611

Date		Explanation	F	Debit		Credit		Balance	
1979									
Jun.	30	Adjustment	5	24	00			24	00
	30	Closing entry	5			24	00	--0	--

Balance *before closing* is a debit.

Income Summary — Acct. No. 902

Date		Explanation	F	Debit	Credit	Balance
1979						
Jun.	30	Closing—for revenue items	5		7,569 00	7,569 00
	30	Closing—for expense items	5	3,349 00		4,220 00
	30	Closing—transfer of net income to capital	5	4,220 00		--0 --

Balance *before closing* is a credit.

The postclosing trial balance

The postclosing trial balance of the Wheelo Trucking Company, taken from the general ledger, is shown in Figure 6–11.

Figure 6–11
Postclosing trial balance

WHEELO TRUCKING COMPANY
Postclosing Trial Balance
June 30, 1979

Acct. No.	Account Title	Debits	Credits
101	Cash	$ 5,250.00	
111	Accounts Receivable	550.00	
112	Notes Receivable	1,440.00	
113	Accrued Interest Receivable	4.00	
131	Office Supplies	60.00	
141	Prepaid Insurance	2,100.00	
142	Prepaid Rent	1,000.00	
201	Office Equipment	1,400.00	
201A	Accumulated Depreciation—Office Equipment		$ 10.00
211	Trucks	13,000.00	
211A	Accumulated Depreciation-Trucks		200.00
301	Accounts Payable		200.00
302	Notes Payable		8,000.00
303	Accrued Interest Payable		24.00
311	Accrued Wages Payable		150.00
321	Unearned Rent		500.00
401	John Wheelo, Capital		15,720.00
	Totals	$24,804.00	$24,804.00

Subsequent period entries related to accruals

The adjusting entries are recorded in the general journal and posted to the general ledger. Three of the adjusting entries—g, h, and i (see Figure 6–3)—are *accruals;* they involve accrual of previously unrecorded revenue or expense items assignable to June. Thus the receipt or payment of cash in July must be analyzed to determine the respective effect of the transaction on June and on July accounts.

Paying the accrued wages payable

The next regular pay day at the Wheelo Trucking Company is on July 11. On July 1, Wages Expense had a zero balance as a result of the closing entries on June 30 but the Accrued Wages Payable account had a credit balance of $150 as a result of the adjusting entries. Assuming that the biweekly wages again amounted to $600, the entry on July 11 to record this payment is:

GENERAL JOURNAL

Page 5

Date		Debit-Credit-Account Titles: Explanation	F	Debit		Credit	
1979							
Jul.	11	Accrued Wages Payable	311	150	00		
		Wages Expense	605	450	00		
		Cash	101			600	00
		To record the payment of biweekly wages.					

Observe that in the Accrued Wages Payable and Wages Expense accounts, reproduced below, these results have been achieved: the biweekly wages of $600 is divided so that $150, which was recognized as a June expense, is debited to Accrued Wages Payable and $450 is recorded as an expense in July. Accrued Wages Payable now has a zero balance.

GENERAL LEDGER

Accrued Wages Payable — Acct. No. 311

Date		Explanation	F	Debit		Credit		Balance	
1979									
Jun.	30	Adjustment	4			150	00	150	00
Jul.	11		5	150	00			--0	--

Wages Expense — Acct. No. 605

Date		Explanation	F	Debit		Credit		Balance	
1979									
Jun.	13		2	600	00			600	00
	27		3	600	00			1,200	00
	30	Adjustment	4	150	00			1,350	00
	30	Closing	5			1,350	00	--0	--
Jul.	11		5	450	00			450	00

Paying the accrued interest payable

On the maturity date of the note payable, July 27 (45 days, including 18 days accrued in June), the Wheelo Trucking Company pays the bank $8,060, the maturity value. The amount consists of $8,000 principal plus $60, which is 45 days' interest at 6 percent on $8,000, calculated as follows:

$$\text{Interest} = \$8{,}000 \times 0.06 \times \frac{45}{360} = \$60$$

The entry to record the payment to the bank is

GENERAL JOURNAL

Page 5

Date		Debit-Credit-Account Titles: Explanation	F	Debit		Credit	
1979							
Jul.	27	Notes Payable	302	8,000	00		
		Accrued Interest Payable	303	24	00		
		Interest Expense	611	36	00		
		Cash	101			8,060	00
		To record the payment of a note payable and interest.					

The adjusting entry on June 30 allocated 18 days' interest expense ($24) on the note to the month of June. As may be seen from the Accrued Interest Payable and Interest Expense accounts presented below the July entry allocates the total interest of $60 in such a way so that the $24 liability applicable to June is canceled (reduced to zero) and the remaining $36 = ($60 − $24) is recorded as interest expense for 27 days in July.

GENERAL LEDGER

Accrued Interest Payable — Acct. No. 303

Date		Explanation	F	Debit		Credit		Balance	
1979									
Jun.	30	Adjustment	4			24	00	24	00
Jul.	27		5	24	00			--0	--

Interest Expense — Acct. No. 611

Date		Explanation	F	Debit		Credit		Balance	
1979									
Jun.	30	Adjustment	5	24	00			24	00
	30	Closing	5			24	00	--0	--
Jul.	27		5	36	00			36	00

Receiving the accrued interest receivable

On the maturity date of the note receivable, July 10 (30 days, including 20 days accrued in June), the Wheelo Trucking Company receives the maturity value, \$1,446. The maturity value is determined by adding to the principal of \$1,440, 30 days' interest at 5 percent, or \$6, computed as follows:

$$\text{Interest} = \$1{,}440 \times 0.05 \times \frac{30}{360} = \$6$$

The entry to record the receipt from the supplier is

GENERAL JOURNAL

Page 5

Date		Debit-Credit-Account Titles: Explanation	F	Debit		Credit	
1979							
Jul.	10	Cash	101	1,446	00		
		Notes Receivable	112			1,440	00
		Accrued Interest Receivable .	113			4	00
		Interest Earned	521			2	00
		To record the collection of a note and interest.					

On June 30, the adjusting entry accrued 20 days interest earned on the note, or \$4, in June. The Accrued Interest Receivable and Interest Earned accounts again show that the total interest earned of \$6 is split by the July entry in such a way so that the \$4 asset, Accrued Interest Receivable, is canceled (reduced to zero) and the balance of \$2 = (\$6 – \$4) is entered as interest earned in July.

GENERAL LEDGER

Accrued Interest Receivable — Acct. No. 113

Date		Explanation	F	Debit		Credit		Balance	
1979									
Jun.	30	Adjustment	5	4	00			4	00
Jul.	10		5			4	00	--0	--

Interest Earned — Acct. No. 521

Date		Explanation	F	Debit		Credit		Balance	
1979									
Jun.	30	Adjustment	5			4	00	4	00
	30	Closing entry	5	4	00			--0	--
Jul.	10		5			2	00	2	00

The accounting cycle–review

In this chapter and the preceding ones, the complete *accounting cycle* of a service business concern has been presented. The cycle consists of 11 steps, which are reviewed below.

1. *Selecting an appropriate chart of accounts,* which consists of selecting the accounts that are likely to be needed for financial statements and designating a numerical index system for these accounts. It should be noted that once this step has been taken, in subsequent periods all that is necessary is to use the correct accounts that are contained in the original chart of accounts or to add any new accounts that may be created by expansion or shifts of business for a given firm.
2. *Journalizing,* which consists of analyzing and recording transactions in chronological order in the journal.
3. *Posting,* which consists of transferring debits and credits to the appropriate ledgers and to the proper accounts in the ledgers.
4. *Preparing a trial balance,* or summarizing the general ledger accounts to test the equality of debits and credits; this can be prepared as a part of the work sheet.
5. *Preparing a schedule of accounts receivable,* which is summarizing the accounts receivable ledger accounts and reconciling the total with the balance of the Accounts Receivable controlling account in the general ledger.
6. *Preparing a schedule of accounts payable,* which is summarizing the accounts payable ledger accounts and reconciling the total with the balance of the Accounts Payable controlling account in the general ledger.
7. *Preparing the work sheet,* or assembling and classifying information in columnar form to facilitate the preparation of financial statements.
8. *Preparing the financial statements* from the work sheet; these are the income statement, statement of owner's equity, and balance sheet.
9. *Adjusting* the books, or recording and posting the adjusting entries from the work sheet.
10. *Closing the books,* which consists of recording and posting the closing entries from the Income Statement columns of the work sheet.
11. *Taking a postclosing trial balance,* or totaling the open-account balances to prove the equality of the debits and credits in the general ledger.

Alternative adjustment methods: accruals and deferrals

appendix

The exact point in an elementary course for this appendix to be taught is optional with the instructor. It may be omitted entirely. It may be taught after Chapter 6. It may be taught after Chapter 11, or after Chapter 14.)

Learning goals

To understand the recording of accrued revenues and accrued expenses by the nonreversing or the reversing approach.
To explain the relationship of the reversing entries to the adjustments and to the accounting cycle.
To illustrate why final figures appearing on the income statement and the balance sheet will be identical using either the nonreversing or the reversing approach
To understand the recording of deferrals by the nonreversing or the reversing approach.
To identify adjusting entries that are never reversed.
To identify adjusting entries that are reversed.

Introduction

There are two different ways that an accountant may approach adjusting entries. One way is discussed in Chapter 5. In this appendix a second general approach is presented. In this optional approach reversing entries are made for accrued revenues and expenses and for the short-term cost and revenue apportionments. Reversing entries are never made, however, for long-term cost apportionments.

The *reversing procedure* is so named because entries made on the first day of the next accounting period result in a reversal of the preceding period's adjusting entries. This appendix illustrates the alternative adjustments and indicates *how and under what circumstances* reversing entries may be made. To help the reader to learn the new alternative procedures, this appendix reviews the nonreversing procedures discussed in Chapter 5 and summarizes the optional procedures requiring reversing entries. The appendix also answers the question whether or not a given type of adjusting entry should be reversed. The adjustment procedures in Chapter 5 are then compared and contrasted with the optional alternative procedures presented here. Refer to Figure A6–1 as you encounter the examples in the text.

Summary of accruals and deferrals

To review, adjustments are broadly classified into two groups: *accruals* and *deferrals*. *Accruals* are certain expenses and revenues that accrue that is – they grow, increase, or accumulate – during an accounting period, but they do not need to be systematically journalized during the period. The incurrence of the expense or the earning of revenue precedes the cash transaction. Adjustments broadly classified as *deferrals* are those adjusting entries required when the cash transaction occurs before the revenue is realized, or the expense is incurred. The term *deferrals* includes those adjustments for short- and long-term cost apportionments and the short-term revenue apportionments. (See Figure A6–1.) The adjusting entries for accruals and deferrals discussed in Chapter 5 and in this ap-

Figure A6–1 Summary of accruals and deferrals.

Broad Classification	No.	Kind of Adjustment	Brief Definition	Pro Forma Adjusting Entry	Do you reverse?
Accruals	1	Accrued revenue	Revenue earned in a given period but not yet collected or recorded.	Dr. Accrued ______ Receivable (A) Cr. Appropriate Revenue (R)	Reversing is optional.
	2	Accrued Expense	Expense incurred in a given period but not yet paid or recorded.	Dr. Appropriate Expense (E) Cr. Accrued ______ Payable (L)	Reversing is optional.
Deferrals	3A	Short-term cost apportionment. Assumption A: The original debit is made to an asset account.	A prepaid item that benefits two or more periods; if the original amount is debited to an asset, it is necessary to apportion expense to appropriate periods.	Dr. Appropriate Expense (E) Cr. Prepaid Asset (A)	No, reversing is never done.
	3B	Short-term cost apportionment. Assumption B: The original debt is made to an expense account.	A prepaid item that benefits two or more periods; if for convenience the original amount is debited to an expense account, the unexpired portion at the adjustment date must be removed from the expense account and set up as an asset.	Dr. Prepaid Asset (A) Cr. Appropriate Expense (E)	Yes, it is necessary to reverse this kind of adjusting entries.
	4A	Short-term revenue apportionment. Assumption A: The original credit is made to a liability account.	A revenue item that is collected in advance of the period(s) earned; if the amount is credited to a liability account, it is necessary to apportion the revenue to the appropriate period in which it is earned.	Dr. Unearned ______ (L) Cr. Appropriate Revenue (R)	No, reversing is never done.
	4B	Short-term revenue apportionment Assumption B: The original credit is made to a revenue account.	A revenue item collected in advance of the period(s) earned; if for convenience the original amount is credited to a revenue account, the unearned portion at the adjustment date must be removed from the revenue account and set up as a liability.	Dr. Appropriate Revenue (R) Cr. Unearned ______ (L)	Yes, it is necessary to reverse this kind of adjusting entries.
	5	Long-term cost apportionment. (Note: this is always originally debited to an asset.)	A prepaid item that benefits the present and several future periods, the amount must be apportioned to the periods benefited by the prepayment.	For a depreciable plant and equipment item: Dr. Depreciation Expense (E) Cr. Accumulated Depreciation (Contra A)	No, reversing is never done.

Codes used:
A–asset; R–revenue; E–expense; L–liability; Contra A–contra asset or valuation account

pendix, with indicated alternative accounting procedures, are summarized in Figure A6–1.

Two methods of accrued revenue adjustments

The primary difference between the nonreversing method of accounting for accrued revenues, discussed in Chapter 5, and the method introduced here is that reversing is optional in most cases. In our development of the accounting for accrued revenue adjustment (and also the other accruals and deferrals) the nonreversing procedure is first reviewed. This accounting is followed by a discussion of the purpose and timing of the alternative procedure requiring reversing entries.

An excellent example to illustrate the accrued revenue adjustment is the interest accruing on a note receivable. Suppose, for example, that the Pop-Art Store, owned and operated by Johnson Goody, accepted on December 1, 1979, a 9 percent, 90-day, $2,000 note from Robert Newart in settlement of an open account. This transaction is recorded in the journal by a debit to Notes Receivable and a credit to Accounts Receivable. Goody closes his books *annually* each December 31. Two illustrations are presented: the case where accrued revenue adjustments are *not* reversed, and the case where they *are* reversed.

Assumption 1—Accrued Revenue Adjustments Are not Reversed. The procedure here is exactly the same as the adjustment for unrecorded interest revenue in the Wheelo Trucking Company illustration (see Chapter 5). So that the results of this approach can be compared with those in Assumption 2, the adjusting entry and closing entry, made on December 31, 1979, and the collection entry, made on March 1, 1980, are shown:

GENERAL JOURNAL

Page 10

Date		Debit-Credit-Account Titles: Explanation	F	Debit		Credit	
		Adjusting Entry					
1979 Dec.	31	Accrued Interest Receivable	113	15	00		
		Interest Earned	521			15	00
		To record accrued interest for 30 days on the Newart note.					
		Closing Entry					
	31	Interest Earned	521	15	00		
		Income Summary	902			15	00
		To close.					
		Regular Collection for 1980					
1980 Mar.	1	Cash	101	2,045	00		
		Notes Receivable	112			2,000	00
		Accrued Interest Receivable	113			15	00
		Interest Earned	521			30	00
		To record collection of note and interest from Robert Newart.					

When the journalized information is posted, the Accrued Interest Receivable and Interest Earned accounts appear as follows in the ledger:

GENERAL LEDGER

Accrued Interest Receivable — Acct. No. 113

Date		Explanation	F	Debit		Credit		Balance	
1979									
Dec.	31	Adjustment.	10	15	00			15	00
1980									
Mar.	1	Regular collection entry.	10			15	00	--0	--

Interest Earned — Acct. No. 521

Date		Explanation	F	Debit		Credit		Balance	
1979									
Dec.	31	Adjustment.	10			15	00	15	00
	31	Closing entry	10	15	00			--0	--
1980									
Mar.	1	Regular collection entry.	10			30	00	30	00

Observe that Interest Earned of $15 would appear on the 1979 income statement and that Interest Earned of $30 would appear on the 1980 income statement. The Accrued Interest Receivable of $15 would be shown on the December 31, 1979, balance sheet. After the collection of the note receivable and interest, the balance of the Accrued Interest Receivable is zero.

Assumption 2—Accrued Revenue Adjustments Are Reversed. Under this assumption, the adjusting and closing entries will be (and must always be) the same as under Assumption 1. The reversing entry is not made until January 1, 1980—after the income statement is prepared for 1979, which shows Interest Earned of $15, and after the balance sheet is prepared on December 31, 1979, which shows a current asset, Accrued Interest Receivable, of $15. The end-of-period adjusting, closing, and reversing entries and the collection entry on March 1, 1980, are presented below:

GENERAL JOURNAL

Page 10

Date		Debit-Credit-Account Titles: Explanation	F	Debit		Credit	
1979		Adjusting Entry					
Dec.	31	Accrued Interest Receivable.	113	15	00		
		Interest Earned.	521			15	00
		To record accrued interest for 30 days on the Newart note.					

GENERAL JOURNAL | Page 10 (continued)

Date		Debit-Credit-Account Titles: Explanation	F	Debit	Credit
1979		Closing Entry			
Dec.	31	Interest Earned	521	15 00	
		Income Summary	902		15 00
		To close.			
1980		Reversing Entry			
Jan.	1	Interest Earned	521	15 00	
		Accrued Interest Receivable	113		15 00
		To reverse.			
		Regular Collection for 1980			
Mar.	1	Cash	101	2,045 00	
		Notes Receivable	112		2,000 00
		Interest Earned	521		45 00
		To record collection of note and interest from Robert Newart.			

When the information presented above is posted, the Accrued Interest Receivable and Interest Earned accounts will show the respective balances over the period of the note:

Accrued Interest Receivable | Acct. No. 113

Date		Explanation	F	Debit	Credit	Balance
1979						
Dec.	31	Adjustment	10	15 00		15 00
1980						
Jan.	1	Reversing entry	10		15 00	—0 —

Interest Earned | Acct. No. 521

Date		Explanation	F	Debit	Credit	Balance
1979						
Dec.	31	Adjustment	10		15 00	15 00
	31	Closing entry	10	15 00		—0 —
1980						
Jan.	1	Reversing entry	10	15 00		(15 00)
Mar.	31	Regular collection entry	10		45 00	30 00

Observe that:

1. The 1979 income statement will show Interest Earned of $15, the same as under Assumption 1 (a must).
2. The balance sheet prepared at December 31, 1979, will show a current asset, Accrued Interest Receivable, of $15 (also a must); be sure to note that the reversing entry is *not* made until *after* the regular end-of-year statements are prepared.

3. The 1980 income statement will show Interest Earned of $30, the same as under Assumption 1 (another must).
4. The Interest Earned has a debit balance of $15 after the reversing entry is made. Notice how this debit or opposite-from-normal balance is shown in the Interest Earned account. It is circled; this means that if the normal balance is a credit, the circled balance is a debit.

Why are entries reversed?

What is the purpose of reversing entries? Reversing entries are mechanical devices that permit the normal or usual accounting to be done at some future date. The term of most short-term notes falls entirely within an accounting or fiscal year, thus all the interest on these notes is credited to Interest Earned. Under Assumption 1 above, the accountant had to analyze how much of the interest received on March 1, 1980, applied to the year 1979 and how much applied to the year 1980. The interest earned in 1979 had to be credited to the Accrued Interest Receivable account. Observe closely, however, that under Assumption 2, the accountant on March 1, 1980, credited the *entire* interest collected of $45 to the Interest Earned account. It was not necessary for the accountant to make an analysis of how much was earned in 1979 and how much in 1980. Why? The reversing entry that was made on January 1, 1980, reversed out the Accrued Interest Receivable and put a *debit* balance into the Interest Earned account. This $15 debit amount is the interest that was earned during the year 1979. When the note and interest were collected on March 1, 1980, the interest for the entire 90-day period could be credited to Interest Earned. The balance in the Interest Earned account of $30 is the *correct* amount earned in 1980 on the Newart note.

When are entries reversed?

Under what conditions does one choose the optional adjusting procedure requiring reversing? A company that accepts hundreds of notes from customers, the term of many of which cuts across two accounting periods, would surely find the reversing procedure very beneficial. The reversing approach would certainly save time for the accountant in that he or she would not have to analyze and compute the amount of interest applicable to each of the two accounting periods. *It should be used where it is beneficial; it should not be used when it is not helpful.*

Reversal of accrued expense is also optional

Procedures applicable to the recording and later possible reversing of accrued interest payable, accrued wages payable, and other accrued expenses are exactly the same as for accrued revenue adjustments. These adjustments *may be reversed* or *not,* depending on circumstances. If reversal would be beneficial to the accountant, he or she should use this procedure; if it would not be helpful, then the nonreversing procedure should be used. If a company issued 50 or 60 notes, the term of which cuts across two accounting periods, it would be beneficial to use the reversing procedure for the accrued interest adjustment. Since the reversing procedure is the same as that described above in connection with accrued revenue adjustment, only a brief illustration of the reversing of accrued expense adjustments is presented.

Suppose the following two accrued expenses were recorded:

GENERAL JOURNAL

Page 25

Date		Debit-Credit-Account Titles: Explanation	F	Debit		Credit	
1979 Dec.	31	Interest Expense		400	00		
		Accrued Interest Payable				400	00
		To record accrued interest on notes payable.					
	31	Wages Expense		5,000	00		
		Accrued Wages Payable				5,000	00
		To record accrued wages for 1979.					

The foregoing expenses and liabilities would be presented on the end-of-year income statement and balance sheet. The two expense accounts would be closed to the Income Summary. Observe that on January 1, 1980, the two accrued expense adjusting entries would be reversed, as shown below:

GENERAL JOURNAL

Page 26

Date		Debit-Credit-Account Titles: Explanation	F	Debit		Credit	
1980 Jan.	1	Accrued Interest Payable		400	00		
		Interest Expense				400	00
		To reverse.					
	1	Accrued Wages Payable		5,000	00		
		Wages Expense				5,000	00
		To reverse.					

Later, in 1980, when both the interest and wages are paid, the entire amount paid would be debited to Interest Expense and Wages Expense. The credits in the two expense accounts resulting from the reversing entries would subtract out the amount of the payment in 1980 which is applicable to 1979 expenses, thus leaving the two expense accounts with balances reflecting the expenses incurred in 1980.

Two methods for short-term cost and revenue apportionment adjustments: deferrals

A traveler to a distant city chooses one of two or more possible highways to arrive at the destination. One road may be slightly better than the other. When traffic is heavy the alternative route may be better. The goal is to get to a specific location regardless of route.

This analogy holds true in the case of recording items involving short-term revenue and cost apportionments. The diagram shown in Figure A6–2 illustrates the possible routes that could be taken.

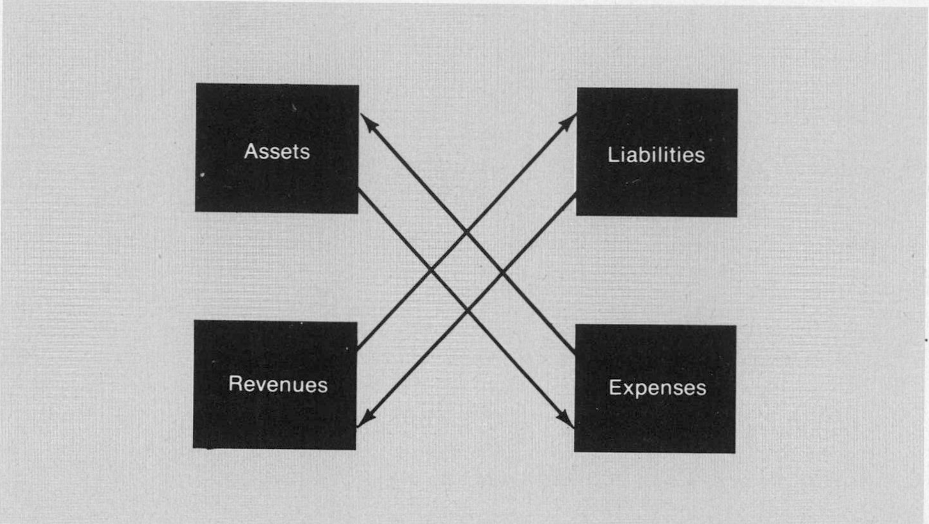

Figure A6–2 Possible routes for short-term cost and revenue apportionments

As shown in Figure A6–2 a prepaid item could be originally recorded in an asset account when it is prepaid; at the end of the period the expired portion could be removed and recorded as an expense. Under certain circumstances the prepaid item could be originally recorded in an expense account; at the end of the period the unexpired portion could be removed and recorded as an asset. A similar pattern could be followed with revenue collected in advance. The advance collection could be originally credited to a liability account; at the end of the period the earned portion of the revenue could be removed and recorded in a revenue account. Or the advance receipt of revenue could be originally credited to a revenue account; then at the end of the period, the unearned portion could be removed and recorded in a liability account. These optional procedures with the indicated reversing are discussed below.

Nonreversal for short-term cost apportionment

As indicated in the first three adjustments of the Wheelo Trucking Company (see Chapter 5), when a prepaid item is originally debited to an asset account, the adjusting entry at the end of the period removes the *expired* portion from the asset account and records it in an expense account. The flow diagram presented below illustrates the procedure for prepaid insurance:

Prepaid Insurance (asset)			Insurance Expense (expense)	
Original prepayment XX	End-of-period expired amount XX	Expired portion →	Expired amount is recorded as an expense XX	

The adjusting entry to record the expired or used amount of a prepaid item is *never* reversed. The nonreversing procedure is reviewed here with a specific example so that the results can be compared with that of the reversing approach.

Suppose that the Pop-Art Store on July 1, 1979, prepaid insurance for eighteen months in the amount of $3,600. The adjusting entries for both 1979 and 1980 and the closing entry for only 1979 are presented below:

GENERAL JOURNAL

Page 25

Date		Debit-Credit-Account Titles: Explanation	F	Debit		Credit	
1979		Adjusting Entry					
Dec.	31	Insurance Expense.	607	1,200	00		
		Prepaid Insurance.	141			1,200	00
		To record expired insurance					
		for six months.					
		Closing Entry					
	31	Income Summary	902	1,200	00		
		Insurance Expense.	607			1,200	00
		To close.					
						Page	40
1980		Adjusting Entry					
Dec.	31	Insurance Expense.	607	2,400	00		
		Prepaid Insurance.	141			2,400	00
		To record expired insurance					
		for 12 months.					

This information will be posted to the Insurance Expense and Prepaid Insurance accounts; if this is the only insurance item these two accounts will reveal the following:

GENERAL LEDGER

Prepaid Insurance — Acct. No. 141

Date		Explanation	F	Debit		Credit		Balance	
1979									
Jul.	1	Regular prepayment entry	22	3,600	00			3,600	00
Dec.	31	Adjustment	25			1,200	00	2,400	00
1980									
Dec.	31	Adjustment	40			2,400	00	--0	--

Insurance Expense Acct. No. 607

Date		Explanation	F	Debit	Credit	Balance
1979						
Dec.	31	Adjustment	25	1,200 00		1,200 00
	31	Closing	25		1,200 00	—0—
1980						
Dec.	31	Adjustment	40	2,400 00		2,400 00

Note the following:

1. Insurance Expense of $1,200 will be shown on the 1979 income statement.
2. Prepaid Insurance of $2,400 will be disclosed as a current asset on the December 31, 1979 balance sheet.
3. Insurance Expense of $2,400 will be shown on the 1980 income statement.

Reversal for short-term cost apportionment

The optional procedure that may be helpful under some circumstances is illustrated in the following flow diagram:

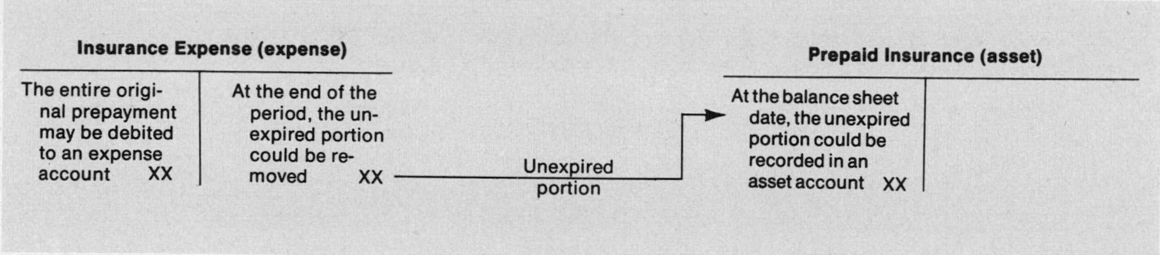

Depending upon who is doing the accounting (for example, a high school graduate who has had a year of bookkeeping), it may be easier for an owner to tell the bookkeeper to record all current year's payments and prepayments of insurance in an expense account. Then the auditor at the end of the period could suggest the correct adjusting procedure.

The entry to record the prepaid insurance as of July 1, 1979, in the books of the Pop-Art Store in the Insurance Expense account is made below.

GENERAL JOURNAL

Page 22

Date		Debit-Credit-Account Titles: Explanation	F	Debit	Credit
1979					
Jul.	1	Insurance Expense.	607	3,600 00	
		Cash	101		3,600 00
		To record payment of insurance for 18 months.			

These amounts would be posted, and then the auditor would have to make the adjusting, closing, and reversing entries indicated below.

GENERAL JOURNAL

Page 25

Date		Debit-Credit-Account Titles: Explanation	F	Debit		Credit	
1979		Adjusting Entry					
Dec.	31	Prepaid Insurance.	141	2,400	00		
		Insurance Expense.	607			2,400	00
		To remove the unexpired portion of insurance from the expense account.					
		Closing Entry					
	31	Income Summary	902	1,200	00		
		Insurance Expense.	607			1,200	00
		To close.					
		Reversing Entry					
1980							
Jan.	1	Insurance Expense.	607	2,400	00		
		Prepaid Insurance.	141			2,400	00
		To reverse.					

When the information on the general journal pages 22 and 25 are posted, the Prepaid Insurance and Insurance Expense accounts would look like this:

GENERAL LEDGER

Prepaid Insurance — Acct. No. 141

Date		Explanation	F	Debit		Credit		Balance	
1979									
Dec.	31	Adjustment	25	2,400	00			2,400	00
1980									
Jan.	1	Reversing entry	25			2,400	00	—0	—

Insurance Expense — Acct. No. 607

Date		Explanation	F	Debit		Credit		Balance	
1979									
Jul.	1	Regular prepayment entry	22	3,600	00			3,600	00
Dec.	31	Adjustment	25			2,400	00	1,200	00
	31	Closing entry	25			1,200	00	—0	—
1980									
Jan.	1	Reversing entry	25	2,400	00			2,400	00

Observe the following:

1. Insurance Expense of $1,200 will be shown on the 1979 income statement; this is the same as under the nonreversing procedure (a must).

Figure A6–3 Nonreversing and reversing approaches

Date		Nonreversing Approach: Original Credit is made to a Liability — Explanation	F	Debit	Credit	Reversing Approach: Original Credit is made to Revenue — Explanation	F	Debit	Credit
1979		Regular Entry				Regular Entry			
Jul.	1	Cash		7,200 00		Cash		7,200 00	
		Unearned Rent			7,200 00	Rent Earned			7,200 00
		To record advance collection of rent for 18 months.				To record advance receipt of rent for 18 months.			
		Adjusting Entry				Adjusting Entry			
Dec.	31	Unearned Rent		2,400 00		Rent Earned		4,800 00	
		Rent Earned			2,400 00	Unearned Rent			4,800 00
		To record the rent that is earned for six months.				To record the unearned portion of rent.			
		Closing Entry				Closing Entry			
	31	Rent Earned		2,400 00		Rent Earned		2,400 00	
		Income Summary			2,400 00	Income Summary			2,400 00
		To close.				To close.			
1980						Reversing Entry			
Jan.	1	No reversing entry is ever made under this assumption.				Unearned Rent		4,800 00	
						Rent Earned			4,800 00
						To reverse.			
		Adjusting Entry				Adjusting Entry			
Dec.	31	Unearned Rent		4,800 00		No adjusting entry is necessary in this particular case. If the advance collection had extended beyond Dec.31, 1979 an adjusting entry would be required.			
		Rent Earned			4,800 00				
		To record the rent that is earned for 12 months.							

2. Prepaid Insurance of $2,400 will be shown on the December 31, 1979, balance sheet as a current asset; this is also the same as under the nonreversing approach (also a must).
3. In this particular case, no adjusting entry is required as of December 31, 1980. Insurance Expense of $2,400, the amount in the Insurance Expense account, will be shown on the 1980 income statement (another must).

In the opening section of this Appendix it was stated that when prepaid items were originally debited to expense accounts, the adjustment that had to be made must be reversed. This statement is true unless the accountant decides to change back to the nonreversing procedure. The adjusting entries defer the prepaid amount to an asset account. If a consistent pattern is to be followed; that is, showing all prepaid items in expense accounts, the Prepaid Insurance amount must be reversed and thrown into the Insurance Expense account. The reversing entry accomplishes this fact.

The optional recording procedure of carrying prepaid items in expense accounts can have a distinct advantage at times. For example, suppose that a firm has 30 insurance policies and further suppose that it pays some of the premiums for just the current period while it prepays others for two or more periods. It may be easier for an inexperienced bookkeeper to record all these insurance premium payments in the Insurance Expense account. A more experienced accountant or the auditor could make the necessary end-of-period entries. Again, the principle should be obvious: If the optional adjustment procedure requiring reversing entries is beneficial, it should be used. Certainly, the procedure would be beneficial if it would be easier to record and if time could be saved in the recording stage. If it is not, then the nonreversing approach should be followed. These two approaches are simply different paths that lead to the same objective: *both must produce the same information for the income statement and the balance sheet.*

Two methods for short-term revenue apportionment

The two methods of recording and adjusting for short-term revenue apportionment are the mirror image of the methods of recording short-term cost apportionment. Suppose, for example, that the Pop-Art Store rented part of its building to the Musico Store for 18 months beginning July 1, 1979 and that Musico paid the Pop-Art Store $7,200 rent in advance for this period. The Pop-Art Store could record this collection by either the nonreversing or the reversing approach. Both methods are illustrated in the parallel journal entries shown in Figure A6–3.

Note that both methods do (and must) produce the identical information for the financial statements prepared for the two years:

1. Rent Earned of $2,400 would be shown on the 1979 income statement.
2. Unearned Rent of $4,800 must be disclosed on the December 31, 1979, balance sheet.
3. Rent Earned of $4,800 would be shown on the 1980 income statement.

Again, reversing entries are devices which can be helpful under some circumstances. They should be used *only* when they are beneficial to the accountant.

Guideline for reversal

If a particular optional adjustment procedure requiring reversing entries is helpful in some way to a firm, it should be used. If some beneficial results—ease of recording or saving in time and effort—are not achieved, it should not be used. Adjustments for deferrals originally set up as assets and liabilities are never reversed. Adjustments for long-term cost apportionments are never reversed.

Glossary

Accruals A classification of adjustments that includes accrued revenues and accrued expenses.

Adjusted trial balance A trial balance prepared after the adjusting entries are made.

Closing entries Those journal entries that accomplish the clearing of the temporary or nominal accounts at the end of a period; the process of reducing these accounts to a zero balance. (Also known as closing the books.)

Deferrals A classification of adjustments which includes short-term revenue apportionments and long-term cost apportionment.

Interim statements Any statements that are made during the period but *not* including those statements made at the end of the period.

Keying of adjustments The method of cross referencing the debit amount(s) of an adjustment to the credit amount(s); letters a, b, c, etc. are often used for the keying of adjustments.

Nonreversing procedure An adjustment procedure that does not require reversing entries to be made; those deferrals originally set up as assets and liabilities do not require reversing entries.

Reversing entry An entry made on the first day of a new fiscal period that is a reversal of an adjusting entry.

Reversing procedure An adjustment procedure that requires reversing entries; those deferrals originally set up in expense accounts or revenue accounts require reversing entries.

Work sheet An orderly and systematic method of collecting information needed for the preparation of financial statements.

Questions

Q6–1 (a) What is the purpose and function of the work sheet? (b) Can the work of the accountant be completed without the use of the work sheet?

Q6–2 (a) Where do the amounts on the work sheet come from? (b) What determines the number of columns to be used in the preparation of a work sheet?

Q6–3 (a) Why are the parts of each entry in the Adjustments columns cross-referenced with either numbers or letters? (b) How is the amount to be extended into another column determined?

Q6–4 (a) What determines the column into which an amount is to be extended? (b) Is the work sheet foolproof?

Q6–5 (a) Does the work sheet eliminate the need for formal financial statements? (b) Does the work sheet eliminate the need for recording the adjusting entries on the books?

Q6–6 (a) What is meant by the accounting cycle? (b) What are the steps in the complete cycle? (c) Is it possible for the bookkeeper to vary the sequence in which he or she performs the steps of the cycle?

Q6–7 Is it possible to prepare the formal financial statements from a four-column work sheet consisting of the trial balance amounts and all the necessary adjustments?

Q6–8 (a) When would the amounts for Depreciation Expense and for Accumulated Depreciation in the adjusted trial balance be the same? (b) When would these amounts be different?

Q6–9 (a) On the balance sheet, where do you classify Accrued Interest Receivable? (b) Prepaid Insurance? (c) Accrued Wages Payable? (d) Unearned Rent?

Q6–10 (Appendix) Assume that you rent an apartment on December 1, 1979. In addition to signing a 10-month lease, you must pay two-months' rent totaling $400. Accordingly, you debit Prepaid Rent for $400 and credit Cash for $400. (a) What will be your adjusting entry on December 31, 1979? (b) Will there be a reversing entry on January 1, 1980?

Q6–11 (Appendix) When earned but uncollected revenue is not recorded until the end of the year, for example, interest earned, the reversing entry on January 1 of the next year is optional. Explain what account is affected when the revenue is collected depending on whether a reversing entry is made or not.

Q6–12 (Appendix) The adjusting entry of December 31, 1979, consists of a debit to Rent Earned and a credit to Unearned Rent. (a) What was the original entry? (b) What is the closing entry and what will be the reversing entry on January 1, 1980, if necessary.

Q6–13 (Appendix) (a) Define long-term cost apportionment and give an example of a transaction that would require such an apportionment? (b) Would the adjustment for long-term cost apportionment ever be reversed?

Q6–14 (Appendix) (a) List two kinds of adjustments in which the reversing entry is optional. (b) Give an example of the reversing entry for each type of adjustment.

Q6–15 (Appendix) On July 1, 1979, the accountant for the Kaye Company debited Rent Expense for the prepayment of rent of $20,000 for two years. The proper adjusting entry was made on December 31, 1979; but no reversing entry was made on January 1, 1980. What problems will arise when adjustments are made on December 31, 1980?

Q6–16 (Appendix) How is it possible to determine from an unadjusted trial balance whether a particular type of prepaid expense item has been recorded initially as an asset or as an expense?

Q6–17 (Appendix) (a) State a general rule that may be applied in determining what adjustments should be reversed. (b) Give examples for both accrued revenue and accrued expenses where exceptions to the rule can be supported, i.e., situations where these items would not be reversed.

Q6–18 (Appendix) Payment of insurance in advance may be recorded in either (a) an expense account or (b) an asset account. Which method would you recommend? Why?

Class exercises

CE6–1 (Work sheet) The general ledger of Carter's Bowling Palace showed the following balances at December 31, 1979. The books are closed annually on December 31. The Palace obtains revenue from its bowling alleys and from a refreshment stand that is leased on a concession basis.

Cash	$19,000	Jim Carter, Drawing	$ 7,200
Bowling Supplies	7,200	Bowling Revenue	45,600
Prepaid Insurance	6,000	Concession Revenue	5,750
Prepaid Rent	6,500	Wages Expense	13,000
Bowling Equipment	50,000	Repair Expense	2,625
Accumulated Depreciation	12,250	Heat and Light Expense	2,100
Mortage Payable	28,000	Telephone and Telegraph Expense	275
Jim Carter, Capital	23,220	Miscellaneous Expense	920

Supplementary data:

a. Bowling supplies on hand based on physical count totaled $525.
b. The balance of the Prepaid Insurance account represents the premium on a three-year insurance policy, effective January 1, 1979.
c. Rent expense for the year was $6,000.
d. The bowling equipment has an expected useful life of 10 years and salvage value of $1,000. No equipment was acquired during the year.
e. Salaries earned by employees but unpaid on December 31 were $125.

Required:

1. Record the trial balance on a work sheet.
2. Complete the work sheet.
3. Why is the difference between the totals of the Income Statement columns and the totals of the Balance Sheet columns the same amount?

CE6–2 (Financial statements, closing entries) Boerner Decorators' adjusted trial balance, taken from the work sheet for the month ended July 31, 1979, was as follows:

Cash	$ 600	
Accounts Receivable	900	
Decorating Supplies	2,000	
Prepaid Insurance	1,200	
Building	10,000	
Accumulated Depreciation—Building		$ 5,700
Land	3,000	
Accounts Payable		2,000
Note Payable		1,200
Bank Loan Payable (due June 1, 1981)		3,600
Loren Boerner, Capital		2,190
Loren Boerner, Drawing	475	
Service Revenue		7,950
Heat and Light Expense	120	
Telephone and Telegraph Expense	40	
Wages Expense	800	
Decorating Supplies Expense	3,200	
Insurance Expense	160	
Depreciation Expense—Building	240	
Property Tax Expense	750	
Accrued Wages Payable		70
Interest Expense	25	
Accrued Interest Payable		50
Property Taxes Payable		750
Totals	$23,510	$23,510

Required:

1. An income statement.
2. A balance sheet.
3. A statement of owner's equity.
4. Closing entries.
5. The company needs additional cash to increase its volume of business. Suggest alternative means of raising money and the advantages and disadvantages of each alternative.

CE6–3 (Appendix) The following transactions and events took place in the Johnson Company during 1979:

(a) The office supplies inventory as of January 1 was $500, purchases of office supplies during the year totaled $1,600 and the December 31 inventory was $400.

(b) The accrued wages payable as of December 31, 1978, were $2,000. The gross payroll paid during 1979 up to December 20, 1979 was $79,000. The accrued wages payable as of December 31, 1979, were $2,500.

Required:

1. Prepare all entries for 1979 assuming that the nonreversing procedure is used.
2. Prepare all entries for 1979 assuming that the reversing procedure is used.

CE6–4 (Appendix) During 1979, the first year of its operations, the Chapel Hill Publishing Company received $105,000 from advertising contracts and $210,000 from magazine subscriptions respectively. At the end of 1979, the unearned advertising fees amounted to $54,375 and the unearned magazine subscriptions amounted to $69,750.

Required:

1. If no adjustments are made at the end of 1979, will net income for 1979 be overstated or understated and by what amount?
2. Prepare the adjusting entries that should be made at the end of 1979.
3. Prepare the entry(ies) to close the two revenue accounts.
4. Prepare the reversing entries as of January 1, 1980, if appropriate.

CE6–5 (Appendix) The following transactions took place in the Raye Company involving the receipt of an interest-bearing note from a customer:

1979

Dec. 1 Received a 9 percent, 90-day, $10,000 note in settlement of an open account from John Adams.

31 Recorded the accrued interest of $75 on the Adams note.

1980

Mar. 31 Collected the note and interest from John Adams.

Required:

1. Assuming that the Raye Company does not reverse accruals, prepare *all* the 1979 and 1980 entries to record the above including the *adjusting* and the *closing* entries.
2. Assuming that the Raye Company *does* reverse accruals, prepare all the 1979 and 1980 entries to record the above including the adjusting, the closing and reversing entries.

Exercises and problems

P6–1 The Jernigan Company's adjusted trial balance, taken from the work sheet for the year ended December 31, 1979, was as follows:

Cash	$ 15,700	
Accounts Receivable	11,400	
Machinery and Equipment	32,900	
Accumulated Depreciation		$ 12,000
Accounts Payable		3,040
Notes Payable		7,600
William Jernigan, Capital		32,360
William Jernigan, Drawing	5,000	
Service Revenue		50,000
Heat and Light Expense	1,000	
Wages Expense	35,000	
Depreciation Expense	4,000	
Totals	$105,000	$105,000

Required:

1. Enter the adjusted trial balance on a work sheet.
2. Complete the work sheet.
3. Prepare an income statement, a balance sheet, a statement of owner's equity, and the closing entries.

P6–2 Following is the trial balance on the SirPark Equipment Repair for the month of May, the first month of operations.

SIRPARK EQUIPMENT REPAIR
Trial Balance
May 31, 1979

Cash	$2,500	
Accounts Receivable	800	
Garage Supplies	450	
Prepaid Insurance	325	
Accounts Payable		$ 85
James SirPark, Capital		3,600
James SirPark, Drawing	350	
Garage Revenue		1,300
Advertising Expense	125	
Miscellaneous Expenses	230	
Telephone and Telegraph Expense	75	
Wages Expense	130	
Totals	$4,985	$4,985

Supplementary data on May 31 were:

a. Garage supplies on hand were $300.
b. Expired insurance was $250.
c. Wages earned by employees but not paid were $70.

Required:

1. Record the trial balance on a work sheet.
2. Complete the work sheet for the month of May.
3. Determine the net income for the month on the cash basis of accounting.

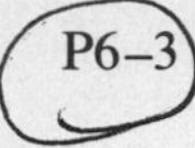

P6–3 Listed below are the account balances taken from the Trial Balance and Adjusted Trial Balance columns of the work sheet of the Fontaine Company for the 12-month period ended June 30, 1979, the first year of operation.

Account Title	*Trial Balance*	*Adjusted Trial Balance*
Cash	$ 1,200	$ 1,200
Accounts Receivable	2,000	2,000
Office Supplies	1,750	500
Store Supplies	1,500	100
Prepaid Insurance	1,800	600
Prepaid Rent	2,400	600
Equipment	20,600	20,600
Accounts Payable	7,000	7,000
James Fontaine, Capital	19,650	19,650
James Fontaine, Drawing	3,500	3,500
Service Revenue	15,500	15,500
Wages Expense	5,500	5,570
Miscellaneous Expense	1,900	1,900
Office Supplies Expense		1,250
Store Supplies Expense		1,400
Insurance Expense		1,200
Rent Expense		1,800
Depreciation Expense—Equipment		2,000
Accumulated Depreciation—Equipment		2,000
Accrued Wages Payable		70

Required: Reconstruct the Trial Balance, Adjustments, and Adjusted Trial Balance columns of the work sheet.

P6–4 The bookkeeper for the Davidson Company prepared the following condensed income statement for the year ended December 31, 1979, and the condensed balance sheet as of that date.

Income Statement

Revenue from Services		$94,500
Operating Expenses		
Insurance Expense	$ 3,150	
Miscellaneous Expense	11,400	
Office Supplies Expense	1,050	
Wages Expense	36,000	51,600
Net Income		$42,900

Balance Sheet
Assets

Cash	$ 10,500
Accounts Receivable	25,200
Equipment	91,500
Total Assets	$127,200

Liabilities and Owner's Equity

Accounts Payable	$ 25,200
Langley Davidson, Capital	102,000
Total Liabilities and Owner's Equity	$127,200

The following items were overlooked entirely by the bookkeeper in the preparation of the statements:

a. The depreciation of equipment (acquired January 1, 1979): estimated life, 10 years; no salvage value.
b. Wages earned but unpaid, $1,800.
c. Office supplies on hand, $375 (purchases during 1979 were debited to Office Supplies Expense).
d. Unexpired insurance premiums, $1,275.

Required:

1. What adjustments are needed?
2. Prepare revised financial statements.
3. Prepare a schedule reconciling the revised amount of owner's equity with the amount shown in the original statement.

P6–5 The closing entries and postclosing trial balance of the Fulton Realty Company, as of December 31, 1979, are given below. A yearly accounting period is used. Tyson Fulton, the proprietor, had a capital balance of $15,000 on January 1, 1979; he made one additional investment during the year.

General Journal
Closing Entries

Date	Account	Debit	Credit
1979			
Dec. 31	Rental Revenue	5,500	
	Commission Revenue	21,600	
	Income Summary		27,100
31	Income Summary	20,050	
	Rent Expense		1,800
	Insurance Expense		400
	Supplies Expense		150
	Commission Expense		16,500
	Depreciation Expense—Office Equipment		1,000
	Miscellaneous Expense		200
31	Income Summary	7,050	
	Tyson Fulton, Capital		7,050
31	Tyson Fulton, Capital	5,000	
	Tyson Fulton, Drawing		5,000

FULTON REALTY COMPANY
Postclosing Trial Balance
December 31, 1979

Account	Debit	Credit
Cash	$ 5,300	
Office Supplies	150	
Prepaid Insurance	1,600	
Office Equipment	16,000	
Accumulated Depreciation—Office Equipment		$ 2,000
Bank Loans Payable		1,000
Tyson Fulton, Capital		20,050
	$23,050	$23,050

Required:

1. An income statement for 1979.
2. A statement of owner's equity for 1979.
3. Fulton believes that the income statement should show a deduction of a reasonable amount for his services to the business. Comment.

P6– 6 (Integrative) On August 1, 1979, Paul Hoffman opened a repair shop. During August the following transactions were completed:

1979

Aug. 1 Transferred $4,000 from his personal savings account to a checking account under the name of Hoffman Fixery.

2 Paid $100 for office supplies.

3 Purchased second-hand office equipment for $300 in cash.

4 Issued a check for $100 for August rent.

5 Paid a premium of $48 for an insurance policy on the equipment, effective August 1.

6 Purchased supplies on account to be used in repair work, as follows:

Anson Supply Company	$140
Baker, Inc.	120
Fitch Supply Company	240
Hazel Company	80
Total	$580

17 Received $2,400 for repair work completed.

20 Additional repair work was completed, and bills were sent out, as follows:

Lawson and Company	$420
Donald Melsom	140
Nelson Nelson	112
Peter Younts	240
Total	$912

22 Paid $80 for the telephone service for the month.

25 Paid the following creditors.

Anson Supply Company	$ 80
Baker, Inc.	40
Fitch Supply Company	120
Hazel Company	40
Total	$280

27 Received cash from customers to apply on account, as follows:

Lawson Company	$100
Donald Melsom	20
Nelson Nelson	20
Peter Younts	40
Total	$180

30 Hoffman withdrew $600 in cash for his personal use.

Supplementary adjustment data as of August 31, 1979, were:

a. The insurance premium paid on August 5 is for one year.
b. A physical count shows that (1) office supplies on hand total $50, and (2) repair supplies on hand are $130.
c. The office equipment has an estimated useful life of six years with no salvage value.

Required:

1. Open the following accounts in the general ledger: Cash, 101; Accounts Receivable, 111; Office Supplies, 136; Repair Supplies, 137; Prepaid Insurance, 140; Office Equipment, 163; Accumulated Depreciation—Office Equipment, 163A; Accounts Payable, 201; Paul Hoffmann, Capital, 251; Paul Hoffman, Drawing, 252; Repair Revenue, 301; Insurance Expense, 702; Rent Expense, 703; Office Supplies Expense, 708; Telephone and Telegraph Expense, 709; Repair Supplies Expense, 712; Depreciation Expense—Office Equipment, 717; Income Summary, 902.
2. Open accounts in the accounts receivable ledger for the Lawson Company, Donald Melsom, Nelson Nelson, and Peter Younts.
3. Open accounts in the accounts payable ledger for the Anson Supply Company; Baker, Inc.; the Fitch Supply Company; and the Hazel Company.
4. Record all the transactions in the general journal, post to the appropriate ledgers and enter the general ledger account balances directly in the Trial Balance columns of the work sheet.
5. Enter the adjustment data in the Adjustments columns of the work sheet.
6. Complete the work sheet.
7. Prepare an income statement, a balance sheet, and a statement of owner's equity.
8. Prepare a schedule of accounts receivable.
9. Prepare a schedule of accounts payable.
10. Prepare adjusting journal entries in the general journal.
11. Post the adjusting journal entries from the general journal to the general ledger.
12. Prepare closing entries in the general journal and post to the general ledger.
13. Prepare a postclosing trial balance.

P6–7 (Integrative) The Newtown Reporter, a small-town triweekly newspaper, was founded by Barry Wright and began operations on September 1, 1979. The date is now August 31, 1980, and the Company bookkeeper wishes to adjust and close the books in order to prepare an income statement and a balance sheet. As a local certified public accountant, you have been asked to offer recommendations as to what adjusting and closing entries are necessary.

After talking with Wright about your very limited responsibilities, you ask the bookkeeper to let you see the Company balance sheet as of September 1, 1979 (the opening day), and the (unadjusted) trial balance as of today (August 31, 1980, the end of the first year's operations). He shows you the balance sheet given below and the trial balance given on page 212.

THE NEWTOWN REPORTER
Balance Sheet
September 1, 1979

Assets			*Liabilities and Owner's Equity*		
Current Assets			Current Liabilities		
Cash	$ 6,000		Accounts Payable	$2,000	
Accounts Receivable— Advertisers	1,200		Notes Payable	2,400	
Accounts Receivable— Subscribers	800		Unearned Advertising ..	1,200	
Supplies Inventory	2,500		Unearned Subscriptions	800	
			Total Current Liabilities		$ 6,400
Total Current Assets		$ 10,500	Long-Term Liabilities		
			Mortgage Payable		50,000
Land and Depreciable Assets					
Land	$15,000		Owner's Equity		
Building	60,000		Barry Wright, Capital ..		52,100
Printing Equipment ...	20,000				
Office Equipment	3,000				
Total Land and Depreciable Assets		98,000			
Total Assets		$108,500	Total Liabilities and Owner's Equity		$108,500

When the firm started operations, you suggested what general ledger account titles would be desirable, and you notice that the bookkeeper has placed all these titles on the trial balance, including those with zero balances.

During a discussion period with Wright and his bookkeeper, you make the following notes:

a. The supplies inventory consists of items that cost $2,850.
b. The building has an estimated useful life of 50 years.
c. The printing equipment has an estimated useful life of 11 years and an estimated salvage value of $2,400.
d. The office equipment has an estimated useful life of 10 years and an estimated salvage value of $300.
e. Interest of $9 on the 6 percent note payable for the month of August, 1980, will be paid on September 1, 1980, when the regular $50 installment payment will be made.
f. Unearned advertising as of August 31 is determined to be $450.
g. Unearned subscriptions as of August 31 are determined to be $2,800.
h. Salaries and wages that have been earned by employees but are not

due to be paid to them until the next payday (in September) amount to $325.

i. Interest of $199 on the 5 percent mortgage payable for the month of August will be paid on September 1, when the regular $200 payment is made.

j. The Company's insurance coverage is provided by a single comprehensive 24-month policy that began on last September 1, 1979.

THE NEWTOWN REPORTER
Trial Balance
August 31, 1980

Cash	$ 12,000	
Accounts Receivable—Advertisers	2,500	
Accounts Receivable—Subscribers	1,100	
Unexpired Insurance	–0–	
Supplies Inventory	2,500	
Land	15,000	
Building	60,000	
Accumulated Depreciation—Building		$ –0–
Printing Equipment	20,000	
Accumulated Depreciation—Printing Equipment		–0–
Office Equipment	3,000	
Accumulated Depreciation—Office Equipment		–0–
Accounts Payable		2,600
Notes Payable, 6 percent		1,800
Unearned Advertising		1,200
Unearned Subscriptions		800
Accrued Salaries and Wages Payable		–0–
Accrued Interest Payable		–0–
Mortgage Payable, 5 percent		47,600
Barry Wright, Capital		52,100
Income Summary	–0–	–0–
Advertising Revenue		37,900
Subscriptions Revenue		32,700
Depreciation Expense—Building	–0–	
Depreciation Expense—Printing Equipment	–0–	
Depreciation Expense—Office Equipment	–0–	
Interest Expense	2,365	
Insurance Expense	1,800	
Promotional Expense	4,300	
Salaries and Wages Expense	33,475	
Supplies Expense	15,800	
Utilities Expense	2,860	
Total	$176,700	$176,700

Required:

1. Prepare the adjusting journal entries that you would recommend.
2. Prepare the closing journal entries that you would recommend.
3. Explain to Wright and his bookkeeper the function of each journal entry that you recommend. (Note: Be sure to justify your inclusion of each part of each entry.)
4. Explain to Wright the difference between cash and owner's equity.
5. Explain to Wright what is meant by:
   a. Accumulated Depreciation.
   b. Unearned Subscriptions.
   c. Accrued Accounts Payable.
   d. Income Summary.

P6–8 (Minicase) You have been the accountant for Williams and Ireland since your graduation in June. At the end of each month you have prepared work sheets as a basis for monthly statements and then discarded them, because they were not part of the formal accounting record. As you are about to scrap November's work sheet, you wonder if it would be of any use at this time next month.

Required: Do you think some benefits could be had by keeping these monthly work sheets for later reference? List them.

P6–9 (Appendix) Leah McCall, DDS, has just graduated from dental school. She is in the process of setting up her own practice and has ordered subscriptions to some of the popular magazines, such as *Sports Illustrated, Time, Better Homes and Gardens,* and *Reader's Digest,* to put in her waiting room. She must pay for the 18-months subscriptions in advance. On November 1, 1979, she sends off checks totaling $127.80 to the various publishers. The part-time bookkeeper she has hired to manage her billings has the option of making thc cntry on November 1, 1979, as indicated in Case I or as indicated in Case II.

Case I:

Prepaid Subscriptions	127.80	
Cash		127.80
To record payment for magazine subscriptions for 18 months.		

Required:

1. Make the adjusting and closing entry as of December 31, 1979 and December 31, 1980.

2. Also make any reversing entries if necessary for January 1, 1980 and January 1, 1981.

Case II:

Subscriptions Expense	127.80	
Cash		127.80
To record payment for magazine subscriptions for 18 months.		

Required:

1. Make the adjusting and closing entry as of December 31, 1979 and December 31, 1980.
2. Where necessary, also make any reversing entries for January 1, 1980 and January 1, 1981.

P6–10 (Appendix) Joyce Fitzpatrick had borrowed $4,000 at 3 percent interest from the federal government over the past 4 years to help pay for her tuition at her state university. She did not have to start paying the 3 percent interest until she graduated on December 1, 1979. The first interest payment was not due until June 1, 1980, 6 months after graduation. At this time one-fourth of her loan was to be repaid. Fitzpatrick, an accounting major, liked to keep a record of her transactions. She made the necessary adjusting and closing entry on December 31, 1979, concerning the interest due on her note. She also realized she had an option to reverse or not to reverse the entry as of January 1, 1980.

Required:

1. Record both the adjusting entry and closing entry that Fitzpatrick would make on December 31, 1979.
2. Make the reversing entry on January 1, 1980 and the payment entry on June 1, 1980.
3. Do not make a reversing entry on January 1, 1980; but do make the necessary entry on June 1, 1980.
4. In Fitzpatrick's case which option would be best to follow? 2 or 3? Explain why.

P6–11 (Appendix) List which adjusting entries below would have a reversing entry. (If optional, specify.)

1. Salaries Expense	1,800.00	
Accrued Salaries Payable		1,800.00
2. Depreciation Expense—Building	4,000.00	
Accumulated Depreciation—Building		4,000.00
3. Accrued Interest Receivable	30.00	
Interest Earned		30.00
4. Life Insurance Expense	1,050.00	
Prepaid Life Insurance		1,050.00
5. Subscriptions Earned	8,200.00	
Unearned subscriptions		8,200.00
6. Prepaid Rent	2,050.00	
Rent Expense		2,050.00
7. Unearned Rent	620.00	
Rent Earned		620.00

P6–12 (Appendix) On February 28, 1979, Charles Goodby paid insurance for a three-year period beginning March 1. He recorded the payment as follows:

Prepaid Insurance	3,000	
Cash		3,000

Required:

1. What adjustment is required on December 31?
2. What reversing entry, if any, would you make?
3. What nominal account could be debited instead of Prepaid Insurance?
4. What adjustment would then be necessary?
5. What reversing entry, if any, would you make?

P6–13 (Appendix) Jack Evans received rent of $1,200 for one year beginning February 1. He recorded the transaction as follows:

Cash	1,200	
Unearned Rent		1,200

Required:

1. What adjustment is required on December 31?
2. What reversing entry, if any, would you make?
3. What nominal account could have been credited instead of Unearned Rent?
4. What adjustment would then be necessary?
5. What reversing entry, if any, would you make?

P6–14 (Appendix) The Hill Real Estate Rental Company had the following accounts in its adjusted trial balance as of December 31, 1979:

Accrued Rent Receivable
Unearned Rent
Rent Earned

The details of the Rent Earned account for 1979 with the entries related to the summarizing process identified by letters are given below.

Rent Earned — Acct. No. 531

Date		Explanation	F	Debit		Credit		Balance	
1979 Jan.	1	(a)	76	3,000	00			3,000	00
	1	(b)	76			4,500	00	1,500	00
Jan. 1 to Dec. 31		Transactions during 1979	—			100,000	00	101,500	00
Dec.	31	(c)	102			5,000	00	106,500	00
	31	(d)	103	4,000	00			102,500	00
	31	(e)	104	102,500	00			-0-	
1980 Jan.	1	(f)	106	5,000	00			5,000	00
	1	(g)	106			4,000	00	1,000	00

Required:

1. Identify each of the lettered entries as adjusting, closing, or reversing.
2. Reconstruct the adjusting, closing and reversing entries that were made by the accountant.

P6–15 (Appendix, integrative) The unadjusted trial balance of the Davido Company contained the following accounts as of December 31, 1979.

DAVIDO COMPANY
Partial Trial Balance
December 31, 1979

Acct. No.		*Debits*	*Credits*
121	Accrued Interest Receivable	$ –0–	
131	Office Supplies	425	
132	Prepaid Insurance	1,460	
133	Prepaid Advertising	–0–	
203A	Discount on Note Payable	–0–	
205	Accrued Wages Payable		$ –0–
212	Unearned Rent		–0–
406	Rent Earned		110,500
503	Wages Expense	25,000	
504	Advertising Expense	4,000	
505	Insurance Expense	–0–	
506	Office Supplies Expense	–0–	
601	Interest Earned		475
602	Interest Expense	260	
701	Income Summary	–0–	

Additional Information:

a. Interest that had accrued on notes receivable at December 31, 1979 amounted to $110.
b. The inventory of office supplies at December 31, 1979 was $150.
c. The insurance records shows that $500 of insurance has expired during 1979.
d. Included in advertising expense is a prepayment of a contract of $600 for advertising space in a regional magazine; 60 percent of this contract has been used and the remainder will be used in the following year.
e. A 90-day noninterest-bearing note payable was discounted at a bank in November. The amount of the total discount of $300 applicable to 1979 is $140. (Hint: Debit Discount on Notes Payable, a real account, for the amount of the entry applicable to 1980.)
f. Wages due to employees of $800 had accrued as of December 31, 1979.
g. Rent collected in advance that will not be earned until 1980 amounted to $4,000.

Required:

1. Open the accounts listed in the trial balance and record the balance in the Balance column as of December 31, 1979.
2. Journalize the adjusting entries and post to the appropriate account. In the accounts, identify the postings by writing "adjusting" in the explanation columns.
3. Journalize the closing entries.
4. Post the closing entries. In the accounts identify the postings by writing "closing" in the explanation columns.
5. On January 1, 1980, journalize the necessary reversing entries (including the optional ones). Post to the appropriate accounts. In the accounts, identify the postings by writing "reversing" in the explanation columns.

P6–16 (Appendix, integrative) The additional information given below was obtained from the records of the Bowen Company as of December 31, 1979.

a. Notes Receivable has a debit balance of $12,000 at December 31, 1979. The two interest-bearing notes, both of which were accepted at face value, are as follows:

Date	*Face*	*Term*	*Interest Rate*
Dec. 1	$8,000	120 days	9%
Dec. 16	4,000	60 days	10%

b. As advance premiums have been paid on insurance policies during 1979, they have been debited to Prepaid Insurance, which has a balance of $405.50 at December 31, 1979. Details of premium expirations are as follows:

Policy No.	*Premium Cost per Month*	*Period in Effect During 1979*
262Q	$7.50	Jan. 1–May 31
714R	8.00	Mar. 1–Oct. 31
4012Z	5.00	Jan. 1–Dec. 31

c. Prepaid Advertising has a debit balance of $1,430 at December 31, 1979, which represents the advance payment on May 1, 1979, of a yearly contract for a uniform amount of space in 52 consecutive weekly issues of a regional magazine. As of December 31, 1979, advertising had appeared in 43 issues of this magazine.
d. As office supplies have been purchased during 1979, they have been debited to Office Supplies Expense, which has a balance of $560 at December 31, 1979. The inventory of office supplies on hand at that date amounted to $205.
e. Rent Expense has a debit balance of $26,000 on December 31, 1979, which includes rent of $2,000 for January, 1980, paid on December 31, 1979.

f. Mortgage Payable has a credit balance of $50,000 at December 31, 1979. Interest at the rate of 9 percent is payable semiannually on April 1 and October 1. No entry has been made for the interest that has accrued since the last semiannual payment on October 1, 1979.
g. Rent Earned has a credit balance of $4,500. Of this amount $2,400 represents an advance payment for twelve months' rent at $200 a month, beginning with May 1, 1979.

Required:
1. Calculate the amount of each adjustment and journalize the adjusting entries as of December 31, 1979, identifying each entry by letter.
2. Journalize the reversing entries (including any that may be optional) that should be made as of January 1, 1980, identifying each entry by the corresponding letter used in (1).

P6–17 (Appendix, integrative) The partial work sheet of the Blocher Company given below shows the balances of the selected accounts before and after adjustments as of December 31, 1979.

BLOCHER COMPANY
Partial Working Papers
For the Year Ended December 31, 1979

	Trial Balance (before Adjustments)		*Trial Balance (after Adjustments)*	
Accrued Interest Receivable	–0–		200	
Office Supplies	1,400		600	
Prepaid Insurance	1,600		400	
Prepaid Property Tax	400		–0–	
Accrued Wages Payable		–0–		700
Accrued Interest Payable		–0–		260
Unearned Rent		–0–		450
Rent Earned		12,800		12,350
Office Supplies Expense	–0–		800	
Wage Expense	24,000		24,700	
Property Tax Expense	3,200		3,600	
Insurance Expense	–0–		1,200	
Interest Earned		800		1,000
Interest Expense	600		860	

Required:
1. Journalize the adjusting entries that were posted to the ledger at the close of 1979.
2. Insert the letter "R" in the date column opposite each adjusting entry that should be reversed (including the optional ones) as of January 1, 1980.

P6–18 (Appendix) The bookkeeper for the Ikerd Company prepared the following condensed income statement for the year ended December 31, 1979, and the condensed balance sheet as of that date:

Income Statement

Revenue from Services		$34,500
Operating Expenses		
Insurance Expense	$ 1,050	
Miscellaneous Expense	3,800	
Office Supplies Expense	350	
Wages Expense	14,000	19,200
Net Income		$15,300

Balance Sheet

Assets

Cash	$ 4,500
Accounts Receivable	8,400
Equipment	30,500
Total Assets	$43,400

Liabilities and Owner's Equity

Accounts Payable	$ 8,400
Newton Ikerd, Capital	35,000
Total Liabilities and Owner's Equity	$43,400

The following items were overlooked entirely by the bookkeeper in the preparation of the statements:

1. The depreciation of equipment (acquired January 1, 1979): estimated life, 10 years; no salvage value.
2. Wages earned by employees but unpaid, $600.
3. Office supplies on hand, $125 (purchases during 1979 were debited to Office Supplies Expense).
4. Unexpired insurance premiums, $425.
5. Heat and light invoices for December, $225.

Required:

1. What adjustments are needed? Journalize these adjustments.
2. Prepare revised financial statements.
3. Prepare a schedule reconciling the revised amount of owner's equity with the amount shown in the original statement.
4. Journalize reversing entries (including the optional ones) as of January 1, 1980.

P6–19 (Appendix; minicase) Lewis Stickney has recently started a new business to be called the Stickney Company. He anticipates that his business will receive approximately 400 notes receivable from various customers. These notes will be interest bearing. Stickney believes that there will be at least 50 of these notes outstanding at the end of each year. He has hired as his bookkeeper John Sloop who has recently been graduated from high school. Sloop had one semester of bookkeeping while he was in school. Sloop tells Stickney that he has read somewhere that it might be advantageous to reverse accruals under certain circumstances. Sloop asks Stickney for permission to engage a consultant to suggest the procedure that should be used at the end of a period in regard to the accounting for accrued interest on the notes.

Required: Suppose that you are the consultant. Write a report to the Stickney Company suggesting the kind of system that should be used. Indicate the advantages and disadvantages of the reversal procedure. Be very precise in the statements you make.

chapter seven

Introduction

Accounting for businesses that buy and sell merchandise differs from accounting for the service business we have studied. This chapter examines the functions and the financial statement classifications of the accounts needed for a merchandising business. The procedures for completing the work sheet and the preparation of financial statements for a merchandising business are illustrated. The chapter closes with a discussion of the management control principle of "management by exception," especially as it relates to the accounting for cash discounts.

Accounting for a merchandising firm

Learning goals

To understand the accounts needed for a merchandising business.
To identify the functions and financial statement classifications of merchandising accounts.
To compute cost of goods sold.
To prepare and complete a work sheet for a merchandising business.
To explain the difference between the income statements for nonmerchandising and merchandising businesses.
To journalize and post to the merchandising accounts in the closing process.
To use the concept of management by exception in recording cash discounts.
To distinguish between cash discounts and trade discounts and to compute both.
To journalize transactions involving cash discounts.

Key terms

allowance
cost of goods sold
discount
  cash discount
  chain discount
  trade discount
F.O.B. destination
F.O.B. shipping point
gross margin on sales
gross price methods
interim statements
inventory
  beginning
  ending
management by exception,
merchandising accounts
  merchandise inventory
  purchases
  purchases discounts
  purchases returns and allowances
  sales
  sales discounts
  sales returns and allowances
  transportation in
net cost of purchases
net price methods
other revenue and expenses
operating expenses
  general and administrative expenses
  selling expenses

The principal difference in the accounts of a merchandising business from those of a service business is that a merchandising business has to account for the cost of goods it has sold as well as for operating expenses. The income statement for a merchandising business, therefore, shows an operating income only if the goods are sold for more than their cost plus all other expenses of operating the business. Since a merchandising business is involved in the purchase of goods, their handling, and their sale, additional accounts are needed to report the financial position and operating results of the enterprise. The functions of the merchandising accounts and their classifications in the financial statements are discussed and illustrated in this chapter.

Net sales revenue

The sales account

A sale is a transaction involving the transfer of goods or services in exchange for cash or a promise to pay at a later date. A sale of merchandise is recorded by a credit to the revenue account, Sales. Suppose, for example, that the King Furniture Store sold merchandise on credit to John Roundtree. This transaction would be recorded as shown below.

1979						
Dec.	6	Accounts Receivable—John Roundtree .	200	00		
		Sales			200	00
		Sold merchandise on account.				

The debit to Accounts Receivable (or to Cash if the sale is for cash) records an increase in an asset. The credit to Sales, a revenue account, records the gross increase in the owner's equity. This credit constitutes a recovery of the cost of the merchandise sold as well as a profit. However, many businesses would find it next to impossible to divide each sale into a return of cost and a profit. Therefore, the entire sale price of the goods is recorded as revenue. The entire cost of goods sold becomes a deduction from revenue in the income statement. The result is called *gross margin*.

Gross margin

In the income statement, **gross margin** *is the figure that results when cost of goods sold is deducted from net sales revenue.*

The sales returns and allowances account

A customer may return merchandise because it is not exactly as ordered, or the customer may be entitled to an *allowance,* or a reduction of the price, for defective or broken goods that he or she retains. The effect of the entry to record a return or allowance is the opposite of a sale. However, when Cash or the customer's account is credited, an account entitled Sales Returns and Allowances, a contra account to Sales, is debited. This contra account is used, rather than Sales, so that a record may be available of the amount of returns and allowances.

			Debit	Credit
1979				
Dec.	8	Sales Returns and Allowances	10 00	
		Accounts Receivable—		
		John Roundtree		10 00
		Customer returned defective merchandise.		

The sales discounts account

The customer may be allowed a *discount,* or reduction in price, if he or she pays within a limited period. The purpose of the discount is to encourage the buyer to make payment within the discount period. The seller has the cash available sooner for reinvestment in the business and has also reduced the balance in the uncollected accounts receivable sooner.

Since the effect of a discount is to reduce the amount actually received from the sale, Sales Discounts is debited for the amount of the discount. Sales Discounts, or Cash Discounts, is a contra account to Sales and is also used to supply management with valuable information about the business. When discounts are offered, the customer is in fact being offered the choice of paying (1) the full amount of the invoice or, (2) the full amount reduced by the amount of the discount. The seller does not know at the time of the sale whether the customer is going to use the discount, so the customer is charged with the full amount of the sale. If payment is made within the discount period it is recorded under the *gross price method* as shown below.

			Debit	Credit
1979				
Dec.	14	Cash	186 20	
		Sales Discounts	3 80	
		Accounts Receivable—		
		John Roundtree		190 00
		Received payment for the sale of December 6 less the 2% discount:		
		Gross sale price . . $200.00		
		Merchandise returned . . . 10.00		
		Accounts receivable balance $190.00		
		2% discount 3.80		
		Cash received . . . $186.20		

An alternative procedure is discussed later in this chapter.

The following partial income statement of the King Furniture Store, whose accounts are used for illustrative purposes throughout this chapter, shows the classification of the Sales and contra Sales accounts to derive Net Sales Revenue.

KING FURNITURE STORE
Income Statement
For the Year Ended December 31, 1979 — Exhibit A

Sales Revenue		
Sales		$124,200.00
Deduct: Sales Returns and Allowances	$2,400.00	
Sales Discounts	1,800.00	4,200.00
Net Sales Revenue		$120,000.00

Cost of goods sold

The total cost of goods sold during the period may be calculated by several methods. One way, by reference to the invoices or other records showing the cost of the units sold, may be convenient and useful for some businesses, especially those that sell relatively few items such as large appliances, machinery and equipment, automobiles, diamonds, and so on. It is not sufficient, however, for businesses that sell large quantities of a large number of items—supermarkets, hardware stores, drug stores, and the like. Tracing each item sold to the supporting documents would be difficult, time consuming, and not very useful. A more practical approach is to add the balances of the group of accounts whose total is the cost of goods available for sale, and deduct the cost of the unsold goods on hand at the end of the period. Thus, when the periodic inventory method is in use, the term cost of goods sold does not identify an active account for the recording of transactions. It is the result of adding and subtracting the balances of several accounts. The computation is summarized as:

Cost of goods sold = Beginning inventory + Net cost of purchases − Ending inventory

The cost of goods sold for the King Furniture Store is determined as follows:

Goods on hand at the beginning of the year	$15,400.00
Net cost of goods purchased during the year	63,280.00
Total cost of goods available for sale during the year	$78,680.00
Goods on hand at the end of the year	11,480.00
Cost of goods sold during the year	$67,200.00

Merchandise inventory account

The system of accounting for merchandise inventory described in this chapter is called the *periodic inventory method.* (A different method, which yields a continuously updated inventory balance, is called the *perpetual inventory system;* it is described in Chapter 13.)

Merchandise purchased is recorded at *cost* in Purchases; merchandise sold is recorded at *selling price* in Sales. Therefore, an account, called Merchandise Inventory, is needed to show the merchandise actually on hand at the end of the accounting period. The amount is determined by making a list of the goods on hand, usually based on an actual count showing physical quantities and their cost. This *ending inventory* is entered in the books and becomes the beginning inventory of the next period. The amount in the ledger account will not be changed until the end of the next accounting period, because the Merchandise Inventory account is not used during the period. Since the account remains open, its balance—the beginning inventory—appears in the trial balance at the end of the period and is transferred to Income Summary when the books are closed.

Concurrently, the new ending merchandise inventory is entered as a debit to Merchandise Inventory and a credit to Income Summary, as follows:

Date		Account	Debit		Credit	
1979						
Dec.	31	Income Summary	15,400	00		
		Merchandise Inventory			15,400	00
		To close the beginning inventory.				
	31	Merchandise Inventory	11,480	00		
		Income Summary			11,480	00
		To record the ending inventory.				

Thus, the amount of the beginning inventory has been eliminated and replaced by the amount of the ending inventory. After the closing entries are posted, the Merchandise Inventory account in the general ledger of the King Furniture Store appears as shown below.

Merchandise Inventory — Acct. No. 121

Date		Explanation	F	Debit		Credit		Balance	
1978									
Dec.	31	**1**	12	15,400	00			15,400	00
1979									
Dec.	31	**2**	20			15,400	00	--0	--
	31	**3**	20	11,480	00			11,480	00

1 The debit amount of $15,400 is the cost of the merchandise inventory on hand at December 31, 1978 (the beginning inventory).

2 The credit posting of $15,400 closes the account temporarily and transfers the balance to Income Summary.

3 The debit posting of $11,480 is the cost of the merchandise inventory on hand at December 31, 1979 (the ending inventory); this amount will remain unchanged in the account until the books are closed again on December 31, 1980.

Net cost of purchases

The purchases account It is customary in many merchandising businesses to use a separate Purchases account for all merchandise bought for resale. The account is *not* used for the purchase of operating supplies, for example, or for store equipment used in operations. The Purchases account is debited for the cost of the goods bought as shown on the seller's *invoice*. It therefore provides a record of the cost of the goods purchased during the period—not a record of the goods on hand. During the year, Purchases will always have a debit balance; the credits to the account are to close the account or to correct errors requiring offsetting debits to some other account(s).

1979				
Dec.	5	Purchases	800 00	
		Accounts Payable—Jay Stores . . .		800 00
		Purchased merchandise on account.		

The transportation in account The invoice price of goods may include the cost of transporting the goods from the seller's place of business to that of the buyer. If so, no separation is made, and the entire purchase price is debited to Purchases. If the cost of transportation is not included, the carrier is paid directly by the buyer, who debits the amount to Transportation In or Freight In. This account is added to Purchases in the income statement to determine the delivered cost of merchandise.

The following terms are used in connection with the transporation of merchandise:

Transportation terms

1. **F.O.B.** *(free on board)* **destination** ***means that the seller bears the freight cost to the buyer's location. (Sometimes the buyer pays the cost and deducts the amount from his payment to the seller.)***
2. **F.O.B. shipping point** ***means that the buyer bears the freight cost from the point of shipment to the destination.***

1979				
Dec.	7	Transportation In	50 00	
		Cash		50 00
		Paid freight charges on merchandise purchased F.O.B. shipping point.		

The purchases returns and allowances account Goods bought for resale may be defective, broken, or not of the quality or quantity ordered. Either they may be returned for credit, or the seller may make an adjustment by reducing the original price.

1979				
Dec.	8	Accounts Payable—Jay Stores	100 00	
		Purchases Returns and Allowances		100 00
		Returned defective merchandise to vendor.		

Purchases Returns and Allowances is a contra account to Purchases. The same result could be accomplished by crediting Purchases, but it is useful to management to have the books show total Purchases as well as total Purchases Returns and Allowances. Analysis of the Purchases Returns and Allowances account may indicate the need for changes in the procedures of ordering and handling merchandise.

The purchases discounts account The Purchases Discounts account is a contra account to Purchases and is used to record cash discounts on the purchase price of goods for payment made within the discount period specified by the seller.

1979				
Dec.	13	Accounts Payable—Jay Stores	700 00	
		Cash		693 00
		Purchases Discounts		7 00
		Paid for merchandise purchased on December 5 less discount: Gross purchase . . . . $800.00 Merchandise returned . 100.00 Accounts payable balance . . . . . . $700.00 1% discount . . . . . 7.00 Cash paid $693.00		

The net cost of purchases, then, is the total cost of purchases plus transportation in, minus purchases returns and allowances and purchases discounts. The amounts for the King Furniture Store are as follows:

Purchases		$63,580.00
Transportation In		4,800.00
Gross Delivered Cost of Purchases		$68,380.00
Deduct: Purchases Returns and Allowances	$1,500.00	
Purchases Discounts	3,600.00	5,100.00
Net Cost of Purchases		$63,280.00

Gross margin on sales

The *gross margin on sales* is what is left after the cost of goods sold is deducted from the net sales revenue. The term gross indicates that the expenses necessary to operate the business must still be deducted to arrive at the net operating margin. If the gross margin on sales is less than the operating expenses, the difference is a net operating loss for the period. The amounts for the King Furniture Store are as follows (the detailed computations of net sales revenue and cost of goods sold have already been illustrated and are not repeated here):

Net Sales Revenue	$120,000.00
Cost of Goods Sold	67,200.00
Gross Margin on Sales	$ 52,800.00

Functions of the merchandise accounts

The following T accounts summarize the functions of the merchandise accounts described in this chapter and their locations in the financial statements. The accounts are presented in their income statement sequence. The description *Balance* in each account refers to the balance before the closing entries have been posted. After the closing entries are posted, all the merchandise accounts, except Merchandise Inventory, are closed.

Sales

Debited	Credited
At the end of the accounting period to close the account.	During the accounting period for the sales price of goods sold.
	Balance Before Closing A credit representing cumulative sales for the period to date.
	Statement Classification In the income statement, the first item under sales revenue.

Sales Returns and Allowances

Debited	Credited
During the accounting period for unwanted merchandise returned by customers and allowances granted for defective or broken goods.	At the end of the accounting period to close the account.
Balance Before Closing A debit representing cumulative sales returns and allowances for the period to date.	
Statement Classification In the income statement, a deduction from sales revenue.	

Sales Discounts

Debited	Credited
During the accounting period for the amounts that the customers deduct from the gross sales price when payment is made within the period established by the seller.	At the end of the accounting period to close the account.
Balance Before Closing A debit representing cumulative sales discounts taken by customers for the period to date.	
Statement Classification In the income statement, a deduction from sales revenue.	

Merchandise Inventory

Beginning Balance A debit representing the cost of goods on hand at the beginning of the period. This was the ending balance of the previous period. *Debited* At the end of each accounting period for the merchandise actually on hand (the *Ending Balance* of the account). *Statement Classification* 1. In the balance sheet the ending inventory under current assets. 2. In the income statement, in the cost of goods sold section, the beginning inventory is added to purchases and the ending inventory is deducted from the cost of merchandise available for sale.	*Credited* At the end of each accounting period to remove the beginning inventory from the account.

Purchases

Debited During the accounting period for the purchase price of goods bought for resale. *Balance Before Closing* A debit representing cumulative purchases for the period to date. *Statement Classification* In the income statement, added to the beginning inventory under cost of goods sold.	*Credited* At the end of the accounting period to close the account.

Transportation In

Debited During the accounting period for delivery costs—freight or cartage—on merchandise purchases. *Balance Before Closing* A debit representing cumulative costs for the period to date incurred by the buyer for the delivery of merchandise. *Statement Classification* In the income statement, in the cost of goods sold section, added to purchases.	*Credited* At the end of the accounting period to close the account.

Purchases Returns and Allowances

Debited	Credited
At the end of the accounting period to close the account.	During the accounting period for unwanted merchandise returned to the vendor or allowances received for defective or broken merchandise.
	Balance Before Closing A credit representing cumulative purchases returns and allowances for the period to date.
	Statement Classification In the income statement, in the cost of goods sold section, as a deduction from the gross cost of merchandise purchased.

Purchases Discounts

Debited	Credited
At the end of the accounting period to close the account.	During the accounting period for the amounts of discount from the gross purchase price of merchandise when payment was made within the period established by the seller.
	Balance Before Closing A credit representing cumulative purchases discounts taken for the period to date.
	Statement Classification In the income statement, in the cost of goods sold section, as a deduction from the gross cost of merchandise purchased.

The operating expense accounts

Operating expenses include salaries, postage, telephone and telegraph, heat and light, insurance, advertising, and any other costs incurred for goods or services used in operating the business. The breakdown of operating expenses into a number of detailed accounts facilitates analyses and comparisons that aid in the management of the business. The amount of detail shown depends on the size and type of the business and on the needs and wishes of the management.

The operating expenses are often classified into *selling* and *general and administrative*. The expenses incurred in packaging the product, advertising it, making the sale, and delivering the product are classified as selling expenses. Salesmen's salaries, commissions, and supplies used in the sales department are examples of expenses incurred in making the sale. Expenses of delivering the product include freight paid by the seller (transportation out—not to be confused with transportation in) and the expense of operating delivery vehicles. Expenses such as rent, taxes, and insurance, to the extent that they are incurred in selling the product, are also classified as selling expenses. All other operating expenses are classified as general and administrative, including office expenses, executive salaries, and the portion of rent, taxes, and insurance applicable to the administrative function of the business. The expenses that are common to both selling and administrative functions may be apportioned on some equitable basis. If an apportionment is not practicable, the account should be classified under the function it serves most. In Figure 7–1, the operating expense accounts that are entirely related to selling are classified as such; all the others are classified as general and administrative. The total operating expenses of $47,225 are deducted from the gross margin on sales of $52,800 to arrive at the net operating margin of $5,575.

If the operating expense accounts in the general ledger are too numerous, it is advisable to remove them to subsidiary selling expense and general and administrative expense ledgers. Two controlling accounts are substituted in the general ledger—Selling Expense Control and General and Administrative Expense Control—in place of the accounts that have been removed. The function of controlling accounts is explained in Chapter 3.

Other revenue and other expenses

The Other Revenue and Other Expenses sections of the income statement serve a valuable function; they permit calculation of the net operating margin without it being distorted by nonoperating items and link the net operating margin for the period with the net income for that period.

Other revenue

Some common examples of items classified as other revenue are gains from the sale of securities, dividends on shares of stock owned, and gains from the sale of plant and equipment. In Figure 7–1, the King Furniture Store shows $125 in interest earned and $300 in rent earned under Other Revenue. These are additional examples; they are included under Other Revenue because they arose from a source other than the basic business purpose of King Furniture Store.

Other expenses

Nonoperating expenses such as interest on money borrowed from the bank or on notes given to creditors for the purchase of merchandise, or losses from the sale of plant and equipment are shown under Other Expenses. In Figure 7–1, the King Furniture Store shows $75 in interest expense and $100 from a loss on a sale of equipment under this heading.

The King Furniture Store added $250, the excess of other revenue over other expenses, to the net operating margin. If other expenses exceed other revenue, the expenses are listed first and the excess is deducted from the net operating margin.

In the absence of other revenue or other expenses, net operating margin becomes net income and net operating loss becomes net loss.

The complete income statement for the King Furniture Store for the year ended December 31, 1979 is shown in Figure 7–1 below. It was prepared from the work sheet shown in Figure 7–3.

Figure 7–1
Income statement

Exhibit A

KING FURNITURE STORE
Income Statement
For the Year Ended December 31, 1979

Gross Sales Revenue				$124,200.00
Deduct: Sales Returns and Allowances			$ 2,400.00	
Sales Discounts			1,800.00	4,200.00
Net Sales Revenue				$120,000.00
Cost of Goods Sold				
Merchandise Inventory, January 1, 1979			$15,400.00	
Purchases		$63,580.00		
Transportation In		4,800.00		
Gross Delivered Cost of Purchases		$68,380.00		
Deduct: Purchases Returns and Allowances	$1,500.00			
Purchases Discounts	3,600.00	5,100.00		
Net Cost of Purchases			63,280.00	
Cost of Merchandise Available for Sale			$78,680.00	
Deduct Merchandise Inventory, December 31, 1979			11,480.00	
Cost of Goods Sold				67,200.00
Gross Margin on Sales				$ 52,800.00
Deduct Operating Expenses				
Selling Expenses				
Salesmen's Salaries Expense		$12,000.00		
Transportation Out Expense		2,400.00		
Advertising Expense		8,825.00		
Total Selling Expenses			$23,225.00	
General and Administrative Expenses				
Rent Expense		$ 6,000.00		
Property Tax Expense		7,800.00		
Heat and Light Expense		2,160.00		
Miscellaneous General Expense		480.00		
Insurance Expense		1,920.00		
Supplies Expense		2,040.00		
Depreciation Expense—Machinery and Equipment		3,600.00		
Total General and Administrative Expenses			24,000.00	
Total Operating Expenses				47,225.00
Net Operating Margin				$ 5,575.00
Other Revenue				
Interest Earned		$ 125.00		
Rent Earned		300.00	$ 425.00	
Other Expenses				
Interest Expense		$ 75.00		
Loss on Sale of Equipment		100.00	175.00	250.00
Net Income				$ 5,825.00

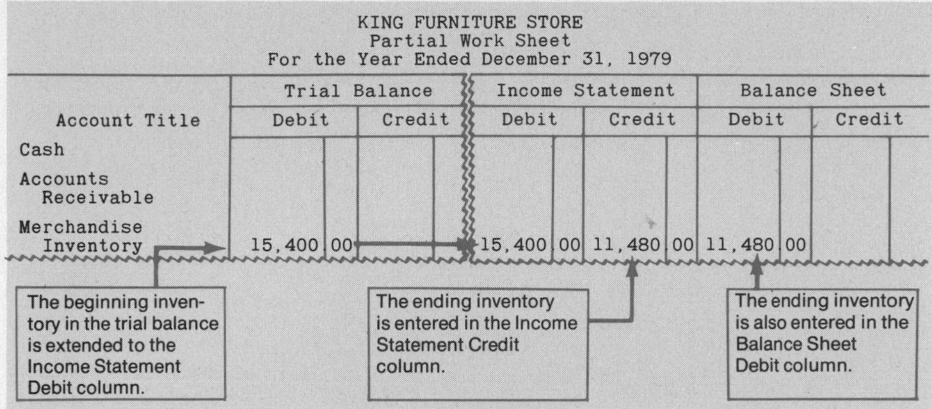

Figure 7–2
Partial work sheet

Work sheet for a merchandising business

The procedure for completing the work sheet of a merchandising business is similar to that of a service business, with the exception of the account for merchandise inventory.

At the end of the period, the balance of the Merchandise Inventory account, the beginning inventory of $15,400 is extended to the Income Statement Debit column of the work sheet because it is part of the cost of merchandise available for sale. The ending inventory, $11,480, is entered in the Income Statement Credit column because it is an offset or deduction from the accounts comprising the total cost of goods available for sale that will have been extended into the income statement debit column. The ending inventory amount is also entered in the Balance Sheet Debit column because it is a balance sheet asset. Entering a balance sheet debit and an income statement credit maintains the essential debit/credit equality of the work sheet as illustrated in Figure 7–2.

The work sheet of the King Furniture Store is shown in Figure 7–3. There are a number of possible variations in the form; for instance, the Adjusted Trial Balance columns are omitted in this example. The combined Trial Balance and Adjustment column amounts are extended directly to the proper Income Statement or Balance Sheet columns.

Trial balance columns

The account balances in the trial balance are taken from the general ledger of the King Furniture Store as of December 31, 1979.

Income statement columns

All the account balances that enter into the measurement of net income are extended to the Income Statement columns. The income statement accounts that enter into the determination of gross margin on sales are shown in Figure 7–4.

KING FURNITURE STORE
Work Sheet
For the Year Ended December 31, 1979

Acct. No.	Account Title	Trial Balance		Adjustments		Income Statement		Balance Sheet	
		Dr.	Cr.	Dr.	Cr.	Dr.	Cr.	Dr.	Cr.
101	Cash	7,200						7,200	
111	Accounts Receivable	39,800						39,800	
121	Merchandise Inventory	15,400				15,400	11,480	11,480	
131	Office Supplies	3,240			(b) 2,040			1,200	
141	Prepaid Insurance	3,740			(a) 1,920			1,820	
151	Machinery and Equipment	70,100						70,100	
151A	Accumulated Depreciation—Machinery and Equipment		7,200		(c) 3,600				10,800
201	Accounts Payable		23,525						23,525
202	Notes Payable		7,300						7,300
221	Mortgage Payable		20,000						20,000
301	J. King, Capital		65,150						65,150
302	J. King, Drawing	1,000						1,000	
401	Sales		124,200				124,200		
402	Sales Returns and Allowances	2,400				2,400			
403	Sales Discounts	1,800				1,800			
501	Purchases	63,580				63,580			
502	Transportation In	4,800				4,800			
503	Purchases Returns and Allowances		1,500				1,500		
504	Purchases Discounts		3,600				3,600		
601	Salesmen's Salaries Expense	12,000				12,000			
602	Transportation Out Expense	2,400				2,400			
603	Advertising Expense	8,825				8,825			
701	Rent Expense	6,000				6,000			
702	Property Tax Expense	7,800				7,800			
703	Heat and Light Expense	2,160				2,160			
704	Miscellaneous General Expense	480				480			
801	Interest Earned		125				125		
802	Rent Earned		300				300		
821	Interest Expense	75				75			
822	Loss on Sale of Equipment	100				100			
	Total	252,900	252,900						
705	Insurance Expense			(a) 1,920		1,920			
706	Office Supplies Expense			(b) 2,040		2,040			
707	Depreciation Expense—Machinery and Equipment			(c) 3,600		3,600			
	Totals			7,560	7,560	135,380	141,205	132,600	126,775
	Net Income for the Year					5,825			5,825
						141,205	141,205	132,600	132,600

Figure 7–3
Work sheet

The difference between the column totals in Figure 7–4 ($140,780 – $87,980 = $52,800) is the same as the gross margin on sales in the formal income statement (Figure 7–1), because all the accounts that enter into the determination of the gross margin are presented. Similar examples could be shown using all the other sections of the income statement and balance sheet.

Acct. No.	Account Title	Income Statement Dr.	Income Statement Cr.
121	Merchandise Inventory	15,400	11,480
401	Sales		124,200
402	Sales Returns and Allowances	2,400	
403	Sales Discounts	1,800	
501	Purchases	63,580	
502	Transportation In	4,800	
503	Purchases Returns and Allowances		1,500
504	Purchases Discounts		3,600
	Totals of the foregoing items	87,980	140,780

Figure 7-4 Abstract from the work sheet

Exhibit B

KING FURNITURE STORE
Statement of Owner's Equity
For the Year Ended December 31, 1979

Jay King, Capital, January 1, 1979	$65,150.00
Add Net Income for the Year–Exhibit A	5,825.00
Total	$70,975,00
Less Withdrawals	1,000.00
Jay King, Capital, December 31, 1979	$69,975.00

Figure 7-5 Statement of owner's equity

Balance sheet columns

All the amounts used to prepare the balance sheet and statement of owner's equity are extended to the Balance Sheet columns.

Completed financial statements

Figure 7–5 shows the statement of owner's equity and Figure 7–6 shows the classified balance sheet. These statements and the income statement (Figure 7–1) were prepared after the completion of the work sheet.

Closing entries

The procedure for recording the closing entries in a merchandising business is essentially the same as that in a service business (illustrated on pages 114–118). The only difference involves the accounts introduced in this chapter. The closing entries, including the closing of the beginning merchandise inventory and the recording of the ending inventory, are shown in Figure 7–7. After the closing entries are posted, all the revenue and expense accounts have zero balances. The remaining accounts—the open balance sheet accounts—are used to prepare a postclosing trial balance.

Figure 7-6
Balance sheet

		Exhibit C
KING FURNITURE STORE Balance Sheet December 31, 1979		
Assets		
Current Assets		
Cash	$ 7,200.00	
Accounts Receivable	39,800.00	
Merchandise Inventory	11,480.00	
Office Supplies	1,200.00	
Prepaid Insurance	1,820.00	
Total Current Assets		$ 61,500.00
Plant and Equipment		
Machinery and Equipment	$70,100.00	
Deduct Accumulated Depreciation	10,800.00	
Total Plant and Equipment		59,300.00
Total Assets		$120,800.00
Liabilities and Owner's Equity		
Current Liabilities		
Accounts Payable	$23,525.00	
Notes Payable	7,300.00	
Total Current Liabilities		$ 30,825.00
Long-Term Liabilities		
Mortgage Payable		20,000.00
Total Liabilities		$ 50,825.00
Owner's Equity		
Jay King, Capital		69,975.00
Total Liabilities and Owner's Equity		$120,800.00

Cash discounts—implications to management

Cash discounts—sales discounts and purchases discounts—are computed on the net sales price; the conditions of payment are stated on the invoice. Typical cash discount terms are 2/10, n/30 and 1/10, n/60; the term n/30 means that the invoice must be paid without discount within 30 days (or 45 days if the term is n/45). The term of 2/10, n/30 means that if the buyer of merchandise pays within 10 days from the date shown on the invoice, he or she may deduct 2 percent from the invoice price, or may take an additional 20 days, or 30 days in all, before paying the gross amount. It is important to recognize the magnitude of the discount offered. This can be done best if the discount is converted into its equivalent annual interest rate. Assuming terms of 2/10, n/30, the cost of the additional 20 days is high, because the loss of the 2 percent discount amounts to one-tenth of 1 percent per day (2% ÷ 20), or 36 percent per 360-day year (0.1% × 360). The prudent manager should therefore take all cash discounts, even if he or she has to borrow the money to do so.

Figure 7–7
Closing entries

GENERAL JOURNAL — Page 12

Date		Debit-Credit-Account Titles: Explanation	F	Debit		Credit	
		Closing Entries					
1979							
Dec.	31	Merchandise Inventory	121	11,480	00		
		Sales	401	124,200	00		
		Purchases Returns and Allowances	503	1,500	00		
		Purchases Discounts	504	3,600	00		
		Interest Earned	801	125	00		
		Rent Earned	802	300	00		
		Income Summary	901			141,205	00
		To record the ending inventory and to close the revenue accounts					
	31	Income Summary	901	135,380	00		
		Merchandise Inventory	121			15,400	00
		Sales Returns and Allowances	402			2,400	00
		Sales Discounts	403			1,800	00
		Purchases	501			63,580	00
		Transportation In	502			4,800	00
		Salesmen's Salaries Expense .	601			12,000	00
		Transportation Out Expense .	602			2,400	00
		Advertising Expense	603			8,825	00
		Rent Expense	701			6,000	00
		Property Tax Expense	702			7,800	00
		Heat and Light Expense . . .	703			2,160	00
		Miscellaneous General Expense	704			480	00
		Interest Expense	821			75	00
		Loss on Sale of Equipment . .	822			100	00
		Insurance Expense	705			1,920	00
		Office Supplies Expense . . .	706			2,040	00
		Depreciation Expense—Machinery and Equipment	707			3,600	00
		To close the beginning inventory and the expense accounts.					
	31	Income Summary	901	5,825	00		
		Jay King, Capital	301			5,825	00
		To transfer net income to capital account.					
	31	Jay King, Capital	301	1,000	00		
		Jay King, Drawing	302			1,000	00
		To close drawing account.					

Management control—the exception principle

The control principle of *management by exception* involves isolating those amounts or accounts which indicate operating inefficiencies, and focusing attention on the areas that might require corrective action. Since only exceptions from the norm require such corrective action, management's task is simplified and expedited by separating from the mass of data the exceptional items for further study.

The alternative method for recording cash discounts, the *discounts not taken method,* illustrates the principle of management by exception. Under the *gross price method* discussed earlier in this chapter, the volume of discounts granted or taken is accumulated in the Sales Discounts and Purchases Discounts accounts. Management is interested primarily, however, not in the amount of discounts taken, since it assumes that all available discounts should be taken, but rather in the exceptions—that is, the discounts not taken.

Purchases discounts lost method

The alternative procedure for recording purchase discounts is called the purchases discounts lost method or the *net price* method. Purchases are recorded at invoice price minus discount and discounts lost are entered in a special account. The Purchases Discounts account is not used.

To illustrate the accounting for discounts lost, assume that a purchase of $5,000 in merchandise is received on July 5, with terms of 2/10, n/30, and that the invoice is paid on July 14. Purchases and Accounts Payable recorded net of discount are:

Date		Account	Debit		Credit	
1979						
Jul.	5	Purchases	4,900	00		
		Accounts Payable—Ace Company . .			4,900	00
		Purchased merchandise on account.				
	14	Accounts Payable—Ace Company . . .	4,900	00		
		Cash			4,900	00
		Paid for merchandise purchased on July 5.				

If the invoice were not paid until July 19, the entries would be:

Date		Account	Debit		Credit	
1979						
Jul.	5	Purchases	4,900	00		
		Accounts Payable—Ace Company . .			4,900	00
		Purchased merchandise on account.				
	19	Accounts Payable—Ace Company . . .	4,900	00		
		Purchases Discounts Lost	100	00		
		Cash			5,000	00
		Paid for merchandise purchased on July 5.				

Under the discounts lost procedure, the debit to Purchases is $4,900 whether or not the discount is lost, and the loss of $100 appears in a separate account, isolating the amount for the detection of possible laxities in procedures. The loss of available discounts may indicate a weakness in the organization, such as lack of bank credit or slowness in processing invoices for payment. Although some believe that the cost of goods purchased is increased when discounts are lost, it is simpler to treat the Purchases Discounts Lost account as an expense classified under Other Expenses. The amount involved is not likely to be material in relation to the total cost of goods.

There are some disadvantages to recording purchases at the net price: (1) the amount of discounts taken is not reported separately in the income statement; (2) statements from creditors do not agree with the net amounts recorded in the accounts payable ledger; (3) the amounts entered on individual inventory record cards may not agree with the net amounts entered as purchases, since the inventory may be carried at invoice price; (4) the additional information may not justify the increased clerical costs and inconveniences; (5) an adjusting entry is needed at the end of the period to record lapsed discounts by debiting Purchases Discounts Lost and crediting Accounts Payable.

Sales discounts not taken

The rationale for the alternative method of recording and reporting sales discounts not taken is the same as for recording purchases discounts. Sales are recorded net of discount and sales discounts not taken are entered in a special Sales Discounts Not Taken account classified as Other Revenue in the income statement. The Sales Discounts account is not used. The accounting entries for sales discounts not taken are a mirror image of the entries for purchases discounts lost and are, therefore, not illustrated here.

Trade discounts

Another class of discount is the *trade discount,* which, unlike the cash discount, is not related to the prompt payment of the invoice and the list price is not recorded in the accounts. A trade discount is a percentage reduction from a list price. The seller prints a catalog in which the prices of the various articles are shown. The actual price charged may differ from the list price because of the class of buyer (wholesalers, retailers, and so on), the quantity ordered, or changes in the catalog. The granting of trade discounts eliminates the need for frequent reprinting of catalogs or printing different lists for different classes of buyers. If more than one discount is given—a so-called *chain discount*—each discount is applied successively to the declining balance to arrive at the invoice price. Thus, the actual price of an item listed at $300 less trade discounts of 20 percent, 10 percent, and 5 percent is $205.20, computed as follows:

List price	$300.00
Less 20% discount	60.00
Remainder	$240.00
Less 10% discount	24.00
Remainder	$216.00
Less 5% discount	10.80
Selling price	$205.20

Another way to compute the actual price is to multiply the list price by the complements of the discounts: for example, $\$300 \times 0.80 \times 0.90 \times 0.95 = \$205.20$. The journal entry on the buyer's books is:

1979						
Nov.	1	Purchases	205	20		
		Accounts Payable			205	20
		To record merchandise purchased.				

Interim financial statements

Financial statements are prepared at least once a year, at which time the adjusting and closing entries are recorded and posted to the general ledger. The closing of the books at intervals of less than one year is not customary but has been assumed in this text as a convenience in illustrating the periodic summary. Financial statements, however, may be prepared at frequent intervals—monthly or quarterly—without the formal recording and posting of the adjusting and closing entries.

Financial statements may be produced at regular or intermittent intervals during the accounting period for external reasons, such as the establishment of credit for a bank loan, or for the internal use of managers and stockholders. They are referred to as *interim statements* and are prepared with the aid of the work sheet. The general ledger account balances as of the end of the interim period are entered on the work sheet, the adjustments are listed, the adjusted balances are extended to the appropriate Income Statement and Balance Sheet columns, and formal statements are prepared.

The amounts in the Trial Balance columns of the work sheet represent the cumulative general ledger totals for the year to date and the adjustments are for the same interval; hence, the amounts in the interim income statement are for the year to date. However, if monthly income statements are desired, the amounts on the statements for the previous months are deducted from the amounts on the current statement, thereby providing year-to-date figures as well as results of the current period. The amounts in the Balance Sheet columns of the work sheet are the correct amounts for the Balance Sheet as of the close of the current period.

The preparation of interim statements requires a determination of the cost of the merchandise on hand. Taking a detailed physical inventory, however, is costly and time-consuming and may not be necessary. Alternative methods of determining the ending inventory, such as the gross margin method of inventory valuation and the perpetual inventory system, are discussed in Chapter 13.

Glossary

Cash discount A reduction in price offered by terms of sale or purchase to encourage payment within the discount period.

Cost of goods sold A computation that appears on the income statement in a separate section. It is calculated by adding net purchases to the beginning inventory to derive the cost of goods available for sale and then deducting from this sum the ending inventory.

Exception principle A principle of management that involves isolating amounts or accounts that indicate operating inefficiencies to focus attention on the areas that may require corrective action.

F.O.B. destination The seller of merchandise bears the transportation cost to the buyer's location.

F.O.B. shipping point The buyer of merchandise bears the transportation cost from the point of shipment to the destination.

General and administrative expenses Amounts paid for goods or services generally reflecting the cost of operating expenses other than the direct marketing cost.

Gross margin The amount obtained by deducting the cost of goods sold from the net sales revenue.

Gross price method Accounting for cash discounts by accumulating the amount of the discount in Sales Discounts and in Purchases Discounts accounts.

Interim statements Financial statements produced at regular or intermittent intervals during the accounting period.

Merchandise inventory Merchandise on hand (at cost price) at the end of the accounting period.

Net cost of purchases The cost of all merchandise bought for sale including transportation in but reduced by purchases returns and allowances and purchases discounts.

Net price method A procedure illustrative of the principle of management by exception by requiring that purchases and sales be recorded at net of discount prices in anticipation of qualifying for the discount.

Operating expenses Past or present expenditures for goods or services used or expired in operating the business, excluding cost of goods sold.

Other revenue and other expenses Nonoperating items of ordinary revenue and expense that arise from a source other than the basic business purpose of the company.

Purchases An account which is debited for the cost of goods bought for resale.

Purchases discounts An account credited with amounts of deductions from invoice price that are allowed for payment within the stated discount period.

Purchases returns and allowances An account credited for cost of merchandise returned to vendor or for allowances for defective merchandise.

Sales An account credited for the selling price of merchandise sold.

Sales discounts An account debited for the amounts that customers deduct from the invoice price when payment is made within the stated discount period.

Sales returns and allowances An account debited for selling price of merchandise returned by customers or allowances for defective merchandise.

Selling expenses Direct expenses incurred in marketing the product.

Trade discount A percentage reduction in a list price that, unlike the cash discount, is not recorded in the accounts.

Transportation in An account debited for various delivery costs of merchandise purchases.

Questions

Q7–1 What is the principal difference between the accounts of a merchandising business and those of a service business?

Q7–2 What is the procedure for entering and extending the merchandise inventory accounts on the work sheet of a merchandising business?

Q7–3 (a) What is the function of the Sales account? (b) the Sales Returns and Allowances account? (c) the Sales Discounts account?

Q7–4 (a) What is the function of the Purchases account? (b) the Purchases Returns and Allowances account? (c) the Purchases Discounts account? (d) the Transportation In account?

Q7–5 (a) What is the function of the Merchandise Inventory account? (b) How is its amount determined? In which columns of the work sheet is (c) the beginning inventory shown? (d) the ending inventory?

Q7–6 (a) How is the cost of goods sold determined? (b) Why is the cost of goods sold not recorded at the time of the sale? (c) What is the relationship between the cost of goods sold and the gross margin on sales?

Q7–7 Why is it desirable to show the following items separately on the income statement: (a) operating expenses and other expenses? (b) net operating margin and other revenue?

Q7–8 (a) How does the procedure of closing the books of a merchandising business differ from that of closing the books of a service business? (b) What advantage is gained by including merchandise inventory, beginning and ending, in the closing entries rather than in the adjusting entries? (c) List the various uses an accountant can make of the work sheet.

Q7–9 (a) What is the purpose of interim statements? (b) For whom are they prepared? (c) How are they prepared? (d) What special problems do they create?

Q7–10 Is it true (a) that management need not concern itself with the normal results but only with the exceptions? (b) that only the big exceptions require corrective action? (c) The alternative method for recording cash discounts illustrates the principle of management by exception. Can you think of any other alternative recording methods that further illustrate this principle? (d) What are the disadvantages of recording purchases at the net price?

Q7–11 (a) Distinguish between a cash discount and a trade discount. (b) Why are trade discounts used in quoting prices? (c) What are the advantages, if any, of recording purchases of merchandise at the invoice amount less cash discount, or net, over recording the full, or gross, invoice amount? (d) Explain the term *2/10, n/30*. (e) Discuss and illustrate alternative income statement presentations of Purchases Discounts and Sales Discounts.

Class exercises

CE7–1 (Cash discounts; gross and net price procedures) The following transactions were completed by the McGee Company during June, 1979.

1979

June 1 Sold merchandise on account to the Platt Company for $900; terms, 2/10, n/30.

5 Purchased merchandise from the Kravitz Company for $1,000; terms, 1½/10, n/30.

7 Purchased merchandise on account from the Jones Company for $850; terms, 1/10, n/30, F.O.B. shipping point.

7 Sold merchandise to the Harmes Corporation for $1,200; terms, 1/10, n/30.

9 Paid freight charges of $20 on the merchandise purchased from the Jones Company.

9 Received payment from the Platt Company, less the cash discount.

12 Received a $100 credit (gross amount) for defective merchandise returned to the Jones Company.

15 Paid the Jones Company.

26 Paid the Kravitz Company.

26 Received payment from the Harmes Corporation.

Required:

1a. Journalize the transactions, using the gross price method.

b. Prepare the cost of goods sold section of the income statement. Assume the following inventories: June 1, $500; June 30, $850.

2a. Journalize the transactions, using the net price procedure.

b. Prepare the cost of goods sold section of the income statement. Assume inventories as in 1b.

3. Under the net price procedure, how are Purchases Discounts Lost and Sales Discounts Not Taken classified in the income statement?

CE7–2 (Work sheet and financial statements) The trial balance of the Higbee Company for the year 1979 is shown below.

HIGBEE COMPANY
Trial Balance
December 31, 1979

Account Title	*Debits*	*Credits*
Cash	$ 84,200	
Accounts Receivable	366,300	
Merchandise Inventory	110,000	
Office Supplies	46,200	
Prepaid Insurance	50,900	
Store Equipment	479,100	
Accumulated Depreciation— Store Equipment		$ 77,500
Accounts Payable		125,000
Notes Payable		69,300
Tom Higbee, Capital		702,500
Tom Higbee, Drawing	44,000	
Sales		1,098,300
Sales Returns and Allowances	22,000	
Sales Discounts	20,300	
Purchases	649,000	
Transportation In	33,000	
Purchases Returns and Allowances		13,200
Purchases Discounts		19,800
Salesmen's Salaries Expense	84,500	
Transportation Out Expense	10,600	
Advertising Expense	31,700	
Rent Expense	42,300	
Heat and Light Expense	15,900	
Miscellaneous Expense	15,600	
Totals	$2,105,600	$2,105,600

Supplementary data on December 31, 1979
a. Merchandise inventory, $92,400
b. Unexpired insurance, $30,800
c. Office supplies on hand, $17,600
d. Depreciation on store equipment, $10,600

Required:
1. Enter the trial balance on and complete the work sheet.
2. Prepare an income statement.
3. Prepare a statement of owner's equity.
4. Prepare a balance sheet.

CE7–3 (Closing entries) The following account balances were taken from the Income Statement columns of Noah Sexton's work sheet for the year ended December 31, 1979.

Account Title	*Income Statement Debit*	*Income Statement Credit*
Merchandise Inventory	23,760	25,650
Sales		62,370
Sales Returns and Allowances	745	
Sales Discounts	1,215	
Purchases	19,210	
Transportation In	1,015	
Purchases Returns and Allowances		610
Purchases Discounts		1,730
Selling Expenses	4,590	
General Expenses	9,720	
Totals	60,255	90,360
Net Income	30,105	
	90,360	90,360

The Balance Sheet Debit column showed a balance of $3,500 in Noah Sexton's Drawing account.

Required: Prepare closing journal entries.

1. close revenues
2. close expenses
3. close income summary
4. close drawing

I close revenues

	Debit	credit
Sales	62,370.00	
Purchase Ret & All	610.00	
Purchase disc	1,730.00	
Merchandise Inv	25,650.00	
Income Summary		90,360.00

II close expenses

	Debit	credit
Income Summary		
Sales Ret. & All		745.00
sales disc		1215.00
Purchases		19,210.00
Trans In		1015.00
sell exp		4590.00
Gen exp		9720.00
Merch Inv		23,760.00

III Income Summary 30,105
capital 30,105

IV CAPITAL 3,500
WITHDRAWALS 3,500

CE7–4 (Partial income statements) The following financial data pertain to Companies Allen, Bache and Cord. Fill in the missing amounts for each company.

	Company Allen	*Company Bache*	*Company Cord*
Sales	$?	$31,640	$?
Merchandise Inventory, beginning	?	4,620	6,930
Purchases	31,790	?	28,611
Transportation In	2,400	1,440	?
Gross Delivered Cost of Purchases	34,190	20,514	?
Purchases Returns and Allowances	750	450	450
Purchases Discounts	1,800	?	1,620
Net Cost of Purchases	?	18,984	?
Cost of Merchandise Available for Sale	39,340	23,604	?
Merchandise Inventory, ending	11,480	?	10,557
Cost of Goods Sold	?	16,716	25,074
Gross Margin on Sales	22,240	?	24,676
Total Operating Expenses	?	7,650	14,625
Net Operating Margin	10,090	?	?
Other Revenue	?	-0-	650
Other Expenses	50	300	?
Net Income	10,190	?	9,951

Exercises and problems

P7–1 During the year 1979 the Chukiu Sales Company purchased merchandise costing $10,900. In each of the following cases, calculate (a) the total merchandise available for sale and (b) the cost of goods sold for the year.

Case	*Beginning Inventory*	*Ending Inventory*
1	None	None
2	$ 9,000	None
3	12,000	$15,000
4	None	3,000

P7–2 From the following information taken from the books of the Stuart Company, prepare a partial income statement through gross margin on sales:

Merchandise Inventory, January 1, 1979	$ 1,800
Merchandise Inventory, January 31, 1979	1,300
Sales	12,900
Transportation In	400
Purchases Discounts	330
Sales Returns and Allowances	210
Purchases	5,600
Sales Discounts	120
Purchases Returns and Allowances	100

P7–3 Prepare general journal entries to record the following transactions (a) on the books of the Damore Company, (b) on the books of the Kell Company, and (c) on the books of each company, assuming that the terms were F.O.B. shipping point.

July 3 Sold merchandise to the Kell Company for $4,800, terms 2/10, n/30; F.O.B. destination.
5 The Kell Company paid $275 freight on receipt of the shipment.
7 The Kell Company returned some unsatisfactory merchandise and received credit for $150.
12 The Kell Company mailed a check to the Damore Company for the net amount due.

P7–4 On June 5, Thomas Garvey, who uses the net price procedure, purchased merchandise for $5,000; terms 2/10, n/30. The invoice was paid on July 1. (a) Record on Garvey's books the purchase and the payment of the invoice. (b) Is the net cost of merchandise the same under both the gross and the net procedures? Show your computations. (c) Assume that Garvey takes advantage of all purchases discounts. Is there any advantage in his using the gross price method of recording the purchase of merchandise?

P7–5 A section of the work sheet of the Lily Lee Company is presented below. Enter the beginning and the ending inventory amounts in the appropriate columns.

Account Title	*Trial Balance*		*Income Statement*		*Balance Sheet*	
	Dr.	*Cr.*	*Dr.*	*Cr.*	*Dr.*	*Cr.*
Cash	4,000				4,000	
Accounts Receivable	11,000				11,000	
Merchandise Inventory						

Beginning inventory	$ 9,000
Ending inventory	13,000

P7–6 The accounts and balances in the Income Statement columns of David Ellsworth's work sheet for the year ended December 31, 1979, are given below.

Account Title	*Income Statement*	
	Dr.	*Cr.*
Merchandise Inventory	11,400	12,350
Sales		29,070
Sales Returns and Allowances	95	
Sales Discounts	665	
Purchases	13,300	
Transportation In	380	
Purchases Returns and Allowances		190
Purchases Discounts		950
Selling Expenses	3,420	
General Expenses	5,700	
Totals	34,960	42,560
Net Income	7,600	
	42,560	42,560

The Balance Sheet Debit column of the work sheet showed $1,900 for David Ellsworth, Drawing.

Required:

1. Prepare an income statement for 1979.
2. Journalize the closing entries.
3. Show the Merchandise Inventory and the Income Summary accounts after the closing entries have been posted.
4. Explain the difference, if any, between the closing entries of a merchandising business and those of a nonmerchandising business.

P7–7 The Key Company grants customer discounts on partial payments made within the discount period. On May 5, the company sold merchandise to Helen DeGrazia for $5,000; terms 3/10, n/30. On May 15, the company received $2,500 to apply on account; on June 4, it received a check for the balance of the invoice. (a) Record the transactions for the Key Company using (1) the net price procedure and (2) the gross price procedure. (b) Make the corresponding journal entries for Helen DeGrazia.

P7–8 (Integrative) The following balances, arranged in alphabetical order, were taken from the Adjusted Trial Balance columns of the work sheet of the Condon Company for the fiscal year ended June 30, 1979. The inventory on that date was $27,100.

Account Title	*Amount*
Accounts Payable	$ 9,775
Accounts Receivable	13,650
Accumulated Depreciation—Delivery Equipment	4,550
Advertising Expense	1,425
Cash	3,900
Delivery Equipment	17,760
Delivery Expense	2,850
Depreciation Expense—Delivery Equipment	2,150
Heat and Light Expense	1,160
Insurance Expense	2,240
Interest Earned	325
Interest Expense	210
John Condon, Capital	66,700
John Condon, Drawing	3,900
Marketable Securities	28,380
Merchandise Inventory, July 1, 1978	29,100
Notes Payable	2,600
Office Supplies	920
Prepaid Advertising	1,170
Prepaid Insurance	1,850
Purchases	77,600
Purchases Discounts	940
Purchases Returns and Allowances	1,600
Rent Earned	2,350
Rent Expense	3,250
Sales	120,250
Sales Discounts	2,100
Sales Returns and Allowances	5,600
Salesmen's Salaries Expense	8,175
Transportation In	1,700

Required:

1. Enter the amounts directly into the Adjusted Trial Balance columns and complete the work sheet.
2. Prepare an income statement for the year ended June 30, 1979.
3. Prepare a statement of owner's equity for the year ended June 30, 1979.
4. Prepare a balance sheet as of June 30, 1979.

P7–9 (Integrative) The following information was taken from the general ledger of the Barbara Company on December 31, 1979.

Account Title	*Amount*
Cash	$ 18,200
Marketable Securities	48,400
Accounts Receivable	106,600
Notes Receivable	18,200
Accrued Interest Receivable	–0–
Merchandise Inventory, January 1, 1979	130,000
Store Supplies	–0–
Advertising Supplies	–0–
Prepaid Insurance	6,500
Store Equipment	105,300
Accumulated Depreciation—Store Equipment	26,000
Accounts Payable	57,200
Notes Payable	59,800
Accrued Interest Payable	–0–
Accrued Wages Payable	–0–
Accrued Mortgage Interest Payable	–0–
Unearned Rent	–0–
Mortgage Payable (due 1982)	39,000
Joan Barbara, Capital	169,000
Joan Barbara, Drawing	14,300
Sales	650,000
Purchases	367,900
Transportation In	6,500
Advertising Expense	12,700
Miscellaneous Selling Expense	19,500
Depreciation Expense—Store Equipment	–0–
Heat, Light, and Power Expense	13,000
Insurance Expense	–0–
Miscellaneous General Expense	22,900
Rent Expense	12,500
Wages Expense	98,800
Interest Expense	3,900
Interest Earned	1,000
Rent Earned	3,200
Income Summary	–0–

Data for the end-of-period adjustments are as follows:

a. The Prepaid Insurance account consists of the following policies:

Policy Number	*Date of Policy*	*Life of Policy*	*Premiums*
A648	January 1, 1979	3 years	$3,900
P832	July 1, 1979	2 years	2,600

b. The Notes Receivable account consists of a 60-day, 9 percent note dated December 1, 1979.
c. The Notes Payable account consists of a 90-day, 9 percent note dated December 1, 1979.
d. Purchases of store equipment were as follows:

Purchase Date	*Cost*	*Useful Life*	*Salvage Value*
January 1, 1974	$57,200	10 years	$5,200
April 1, 1979	26,000	20 years	–0–
July 1, 1979	22,100	8 years	1,300

e. Wages earned by employees but unpaid as of December 31, 1979 totaled $1,000.
f. On August 1, 1979, the Barbara Company rented some store equipment to the Derby Company for 12 months and received a check for $3,200 representing the entire year's rental fee.
g. Interest on the mortgage payable is $2,100 a year, paid in semiannual installments on May 1 and November 1, 1979.
h. Inventories on December 31, 1979.

Merchandise	$93,000
Advertising Supplies	3,100
Store Supplies (the original debit was made to Miscellaneous General Expense)	800

Required:
1. Prepare a work sheet for the year ended December 31, 1979.
2. Prepare (a) an income statement, (b) a statement of owner's equity, and (c) a balance sheet.
3. Prepare the closing entries.

P7–10 (Minicase) John Burton, president of Burton Company, is dissatisfied with the results of operations of his company for the past year. He notes especially the failure to take full advantage of the cash discount terms of 2/10, n/30 that are offered by suppliers. He attributes this failure to (1) inadequate cash on hand and (2) the absence of internal accounting and invoice processing controls. His local bank is willing to arrange for a revolving line of credit to help the company pay its suppliers within the discount period at a borrowing rate of 10 percent. (Note: A revolving line of credit is a type of bank loan that may be drawn upon as needed; when the amount expended is repaid by the borrower, the bank automatically renews the loan and replenishes the fund.)

Required: Write a report indicating in specific terms (a) whether money should be borrowed for the purpose indicated and (b) the controls you would recommend to insure that available purchase discounts are not lost.

Accounting systems

part two

chapter eight

Introduction

The system of recording, classifying, summarizing, and reporting accounting information discussed in the preceding chapters has been satisfactory for teaching the fundamentals of the accounting process. As a business grows in size it usually becomes necessary to modify the method of capturing the flow of accounting data. This chapter describes briefly how an accounting system is designed for a business. After a brief discussion of record systems design, a simple manual system is illustrated. A clothing store, The New Generation Shop owned and operated by June Cox, is used throughout this entire illustration. The concepts used in manual accounting systems are the same as those used in mechanized and automated systems. A brief discussion of the use of bookkeeping machines and automated data processing in accounting concludes the chapter.

An introduction to accounting systems: special journals

Learning goals

To understand how financial statements and accounting reports depend upon a transaction-based record system.
To trace the flow of data from source documents into the system and the flow of useful information out.
To make journal entries in a manual system with four specialized journals and a general journal.
To know when to post column totals when posting from specialized journals into the ledger.
To understand that posting column totals from specialized journals to the ledger produces the same result as posting individual entries.

Key terms

accounting system
cashbook
general journal
invoice
processing
receiving report
source document
special journals
- *cash payments journal*
- *cash receipts journal*
- *purchases journal*
- *sales journal*

Design of a record system

The transaction is the basic source of accounting information; it is central to the data collection process. Before data processing by any system can begin, some evidence must exist that a transaction has occurred. A set of procedures and standard forms must require employees to make a record each time a transaction occurs. A general name for these business papers is *source documents*. Source documents are often purchased in sets of multicopy one-time carbon sheets. An example of a source document called a sales invoice is shown in Figure 8–1. Figure 8–1 is evidence that four items of chemicals have been sold and shipped to a customer. The original copy will be mailed to the customer as a request for payment. Other copies will go to the accounting department to be used to record the accounts receivable increase in a journal and in the customer's account in the subsidiary ledger. Figure 8–2, another source document, evidences receipt of three items of equipment by the shipping (combined with receiving) department. The initials BS verify receipt on October 21, 1979.

In the histology department, where the order originated, J. Murray has indicated its receipt. Accordingly, this document is evidence that an account payable exists. A copy of it must be sent to the accounting department for posting to a journal and to the accounts payable ledger.

Figure 8–1
Invoice

Biomedical Laboratories, Inc.
P. O. BOX 2230
1308 RAINEY ST.
BURLINGTON, N. C. 27215

INVOICE S 2653

SOLD TO
Sharon R. Scarlett Biological Supply Co.
1913 Pineville Road
Bristol, TN 37620

SHIPPED TO Same

ACCOUNT NO.	YOUR ORDER NO.	INVOICE DATE	TERMS	SHIPPED VIA	SALESMAN	PPD. OR COLL.
32300300	35347	9/4/79	2/10 NET 30 DAYS	Your truck	W. Irwin	

ORDERED	SHIPPED	ITEM NO.	DESCRIPTION	UNIT PRICE	AMOUNT
6x100ml	6x100 ml	680-5	Phosphotungstate	$ 2.00	$12.00
6x150ml	6x150 ml	680-4	Sodium Carbonate Soln.	1.54	9.24
3x300ml	3x300 ml	800-1	Sigama Lipase Substrate	12.54	37.62
1x5 g	1x5 g	P 3627	Phosphatase Acid Type I	26.80	26.80
					$85.66

INVOICE

Courtesy of Graphic Business Forms, Inc., Greensboro, N. C.

Biomedical Laboratories, Inc. RECEIVING REPORT

RECEIVED FROM	DATE RECEIVED
Cheek and Thompson Pharmaceutical Supply Co.	10/21/79
ADDRESS	PURCHASE ORDER NO.
894 N. Elm Street, Greensboro, NC 27401	14058

VIA	PRO. NUMBER	PREPAID	COLLECT	RECEIVED IN DEPT. BY
UPS		X		J. Murray JM
REC'D IN SHIPPING BY	WEIGHT	CHARGES		FOR DEPT.
BS BS		$		Histology

PCS. RECEIVED	PCS. PER FREIGHT BILL	BREAKAGE OR SHORTAGE
13		None

	QUANTITY REC'D.	QUANTITY BACK/O.	CATALOG NUMBER	DESCRIPTION
1	3	0	R 5330-3	Tubing Latex
2	9	0	B 7585-2	BTL Aspirator
3	1	0	S1803-35A	Standard Potassium Mixer
4				
5				
6				
7				
8				
9				
10				

COMMENTS:

ACCOUNTING COPY

Courtesy of Graphic Business Forms, Inc., Greensboro, NC

Figure 8–2 Receiving report

These are but two examples of the many source documents on which details of each transaction are recorded. Now the data must be introduced into the system. Data can be processed from these documents by handwritten procedures, by accounting machines, punched-card equipment, electronic equipment, or by a combination of these methods. Figure 8–3 shows that these concepts of data collection all lead to the same results. As volume and variety of the information becomes larger, the accounting system must become more sophisticated, detailed and elaborate. The information flow is from input to output. Source documents provide input data describing and measuring (in dollars) each transaction. Processing consists of a series of steps such as classifying or summarizing. The basic reason for these steps is to change the original data to useful form. The output is in the form of reports.

Development of the system will generally be in four stages: (1) *study and design,* (2) *implementation,* (3) *operation,* and *(4) audit as to efficiency*. The company's work is studied and a method of data collection is proposed for adoption. Once adopted it is put into operation for verification, for review for improvements and redesign, and for testing for effectiveness of the controls. The flow of information from the source of input to the disposition of the output is examined with the following considerations.

Figure 8–3
Information flow chart

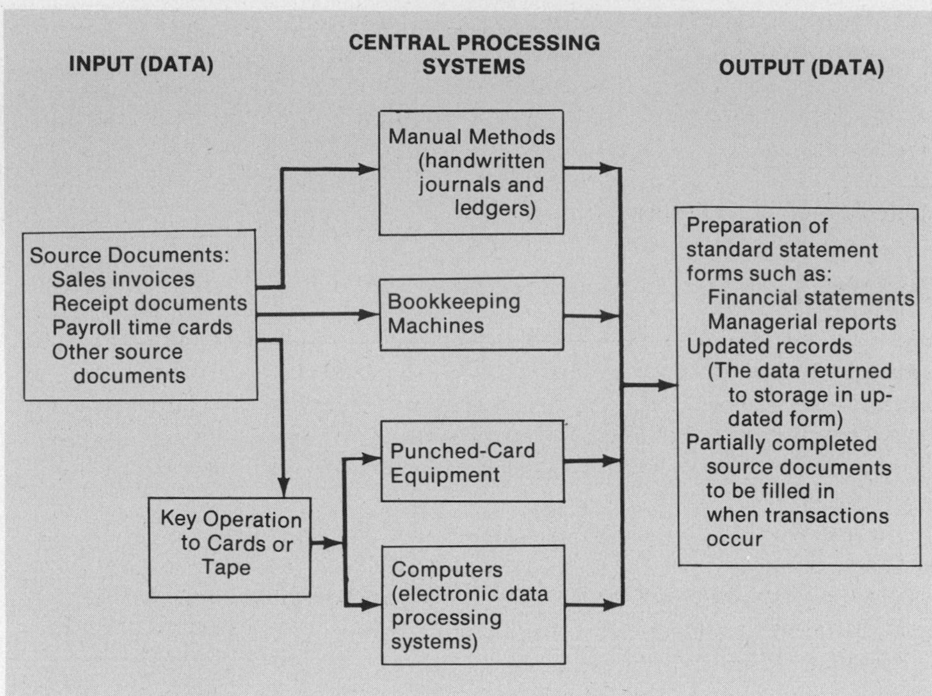

Where will the information be found and stored?
Who will use the information?
How will the information be used?
When will the information be needed?

Thus, setting up a system for collecting and processing data in a business requires a total examination of the business and its environment. In view of all this, we can now trace the evolution of a simple manual system by expanding the general journal and the ledgers.

Expansion of general journal: evolution of a simple manual system

As the frequency of similar transactions increases, a means of processing the resulting data must be devised that is more efficient than the two-column general journal illustrated in the preceding chapters. Time and effort must be saved. With use of the two-column journal each entry must be posted individually to its general ledger accounts, and in subsidiary ledger accounts each entry must be posted a second time. In essence, the data in the journal are repeated in detail in the ledger. In a large business thousands of transactions occur each day. Some means of streamlining the method and accelerating the processing of these data must be developed.

Accounting records and procedures should meet the needs of the individual business firm. For example, for a small firm where one accountant records all the transactions, additional columns (each representing an account that receives repeated entries) may be added to the general journal. As the number of transactions increases and the processing becomes too much for one accountant, similar transactions can be grouped into classes with a special journal used to record each class of transactions.

Special journals

The manual system illustrated in the following pages saves time in recording the transactions and in posting. This system also enables a business to divide the work among several employees. Small businesses, or those with limited transactions, find this type of system or an adaptation of it useful. Modifying some of the journals and subsidiary ledgers for use with mechanical equipment makes it even more useful.

The procedures in the preceding chapters can be modified by creating several journals, each of which carries a special class of transactions. They are called *special journals*. The number and kinds of journals used are influenced by the type of business and the information desired. The model used in this text is shown in the following chart:

Journal	*Class of Transaction*	*Symbol*
Sales Journal	Sale of *merchandise* on account	S
Purchases Journal	Purchase of *merchandise* on account	P
Cash Receipts Journal	Receipt of cash from *all* sources	CR
Cash Payments Journal	Payment of cash for *all* purposes	CP
General Journal	All other transactions that are not grouped in the four classes above—for example, closing or adjusting entries or purchase of equipment or supplies on credit	J

Special journals offer the following advantages:

1. Similar transactions are grouped in chronological order in one place. All credit sales of merchandise, for example, are entered in the sales journal.
2. The repeated writing of each account title—Sales, Purchases, Cash and so on—is eliminated.
3. Postings are made from column footings in total—rather than item by item—thereby reducing the volume of work. The general ledger is relieved of unnecessary detail, since fewer postings are made. This makes it more compact and easier to use, reducing the probability of error.

4. Bookkeeping duties may be divided by function. For example, one person may enter information regarding credit sales (taken from copies of sales invoices) in the sales journal; a second person may post either from the sales journal or directly from the sales slips to the accounts receivable ledger daily; and a third person may enter amounts of collections from credit customers in the cash receipts journal and post to the accounts receivable ledger daily. This division of responsibilities not only speeds up the work flow but also creates some protection against errors and the misappropriation of assets. This strengthens internal control.

This chapter emphasizes the sales/cash receipts cycle and the purchases/cash payments cycle. The information in these two cycles flows through the special journals into both the general ledger and the subsidiary ledger accounts. Figure 8–4 diagrams this flow. The individual journals for The New Generation Shop are illustrated throughout this chapter. They should be studied in the context of this overall relationship shown in Figure 8–4.

Figure 8–4 Special journals information flow

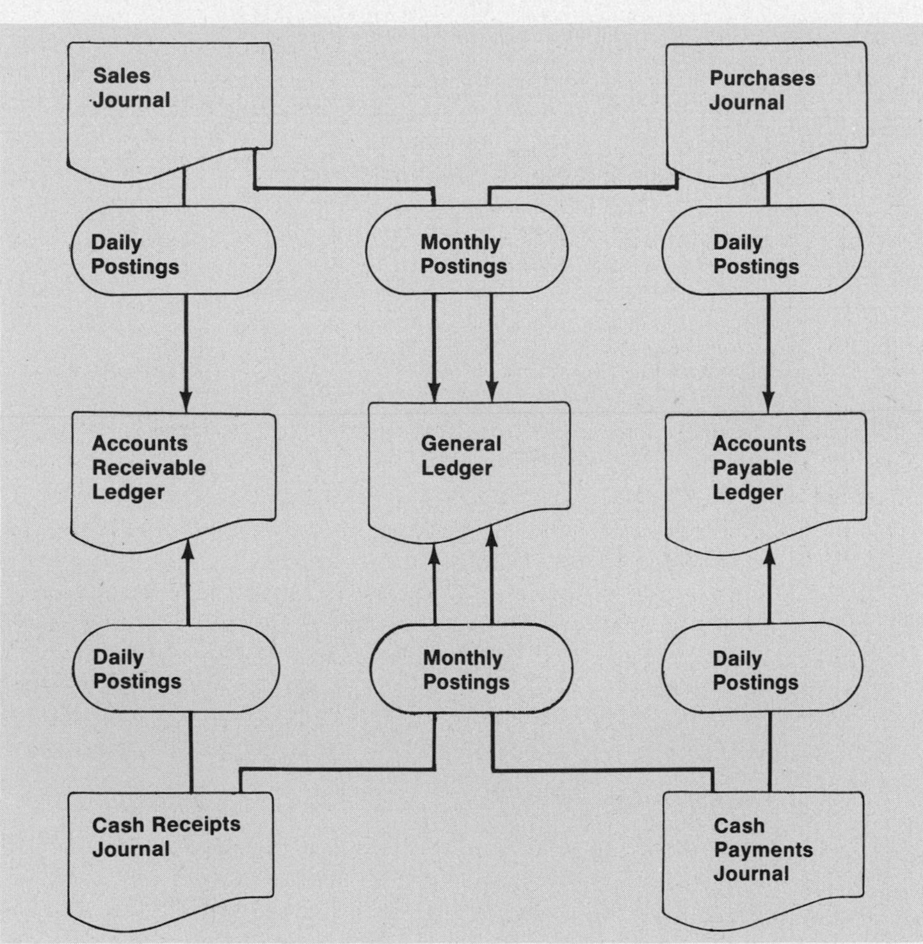

Sales journal

All sales of merchandise on account are recorded in the sales journal. To illustrate the use of the sales journal, assume that the following transactions took place at The New Generation Shop during June 1979.

June 3 Sold merchandise to Shirley Lloyd, $400; terms 1/15, n/60, invoice no. 1.

5 Sold merchandise to Frank P. Allen, $600; terms 2/10, n/30, invoice no. 2.

5 Sold merchandise to Linda Weavil, $300; terms 1/5, n/30, invoice no. 3.

30 Sold merchandise to Earl Sanders, $800; terms 2/10, n/30, invoice no. 4.

When merchandise is sold on account, the transaction is recorded in the sales journal (Figure 8–5) as follows:

1. Date of the transaction is entered in the Date column.
2. Sales invoices (See Figure 8–1) are numbered in sequence; the numbers are entered in the Sales Invoice No. column.
3. Name of the customer to whom the sale was made is entered in the Account Debited column.
4. Terms of the sale are listed in the Terms column.
5. If the subsidiary ledger account has a customer number, that number is entered in the folio (F) column when posting is complete; otherwise, a check mark is entered.
6. Amount of the sale is entered in the Amount column.

The sales journal illustrated in Figure 8–5 shows the entries for the transactions of The New Generation Shop.

Each entry in the sales journal is a debit to the Accounts Receivable account and to the customer's account in the accounts receivable ledger, and a credit to the Sales account. It has exactly the same effect as if it were entered in a two-column general journal. These transactions are *not* actually recorded in both the general journal and the sales journal.

Each amount is posted separately as a debit to the accounts receivable ledger, supporting the single debit that is posted at the end of the month to the Accounts Receivable controlling account in the general ledger. Posting to the subsidiary ledger accounts is usually done daily. It is important to have the up-to-date balance of each customer's account readily available so that requests for this information from the customer, the credit department, or others may be readily fulfilled.

Daily postings The daily posting in the subsidiary ledger is usually done in the following sequence:

1. The amount of the sale is posted to the Debit column of the customer's account and is added to the balance, if any, in the Balance column.

Figure 8-5
Sales journal

SALES JOURNAL Page 1

Date		Sales Invoice No.	Account Debited	Terms	F	Amount	
1979							
Jun.	3	1	Shirley Lloyd	1/15, n/60	✓	400	00
	5	2	Frank P. Allen	2/10, n/30	✓	600	00
	5	3	Linda Weavil	1/5, n/30	✓	300	00
	30	4	Earl Sanders	2/10, n/30	✓	800	00
	30		Total			2,100	00

2. The journal symbol and page number (in this case, S1) is written in the folio (F) column.
3. The date of the sale is recorded in the Date column.
4. A check mark (or the customer account number) is placed in the folio (F) column of the sales journal to indicate that the entry has been posted.

Monthly postings At the end of the month, the Amount column of the sales journal is totaled. The total, the date of the posting, and the sales journal page number are then posted as a debit in the Accounts Receivable controlling account and as a credit in the Sales account in the general ledger. The general ledger account numbers are recorded in the sales journal immediately below the footing. To minimize errors, a systematic procedure should be followed in posting. The following sequence is suggested:

Debit posting:

1. The amount is posted to the Debit money column of the Accounts Receivable account in the general ledger.
2. The journal symbol (S1) is written in the folio (F) column of the account.
3. The end-of-month date is recorded in the Date column; in this case it is June 30, 1979.
4. The Accounts Receivable account number is written in parentheses below and to the left of the double rule in the Amount column of the sales journal.

Credit posting:

5. The same amount as the debit posting is posted to the Credit money column of the Sales account in the general ledger.
6. The journal symbol (S1) is written in the folio (F) column of the account.
7. The date is recorded in the Date column.
8. The sales account number is written in parenthesis below the double rule in the Amount column of the journal, to the right of the debit posting reference number.

Postings from the sales journal of The New Generation Shop for June 1979 are shown in Figure 8–6.

Purchases journal

The relationship of the purchases journal and the accounts payable ledger is similar to that of the sales journal and the accounts receivable ledger. All purchases of merchandise on account are recorded in the purchases journal. The transactions of The New Generation Shop during June 1979 illustrate the use of this journal.

June 3 Purchased merchandise on account from Comfort Knit Company, \$900; terms 2/10, n/20.

8 Purchased merchandise on account from Denim Moderns, \$400; terms 2/10, n/60.

16 Purchased merchandise on account from Casual Clothiers, \$500; terms 3/5, n/30.

28 Purchased merchandise on account from the Baxter Tailors, \$700; terms 1/20, n/60.

Figure 8–6
Posting flow from the sales journal

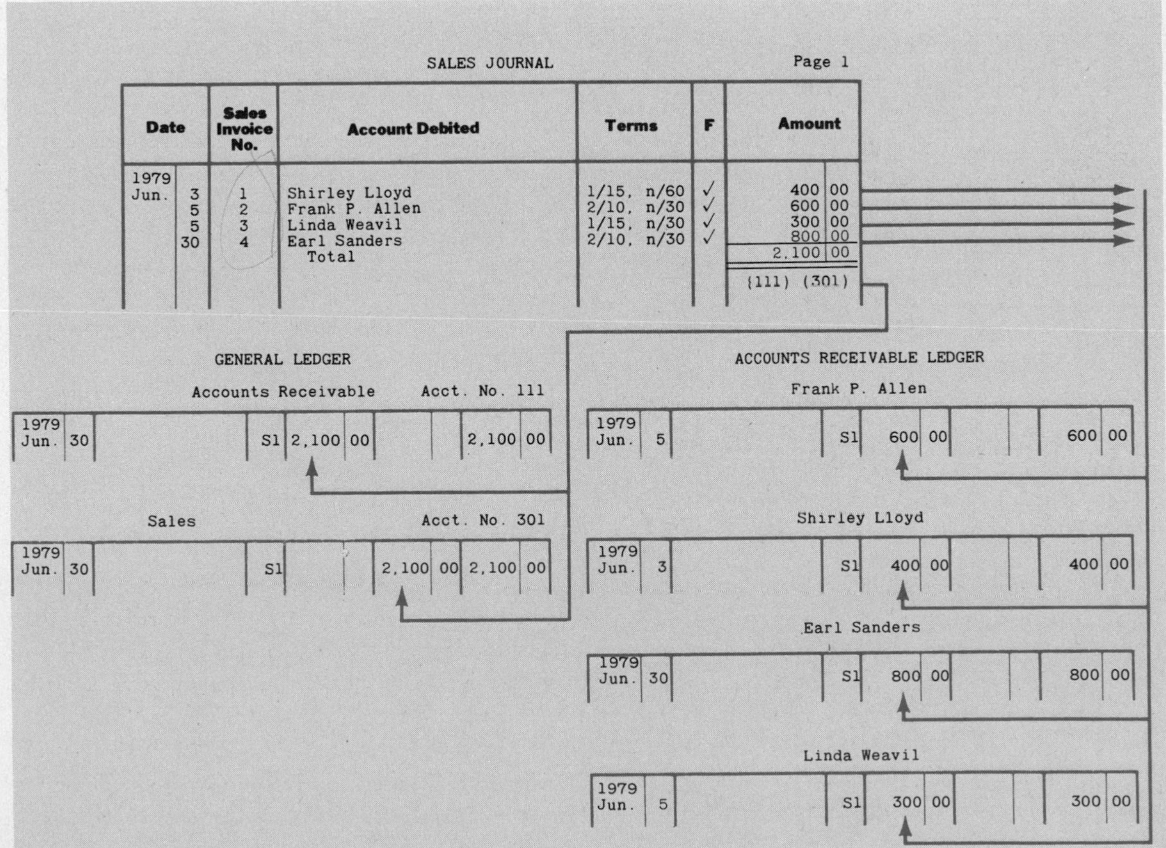

SALES JOURNAL Page 1

Date		Sales Invoice No.	Account Debited	Terms	F	Amount
1979 Jun.	3	1	Shirley Lloyd	1/15, n/60	✓	400 00
	5	2	Frank P. Allen	2/10, n/30	✓	600 00
	5	3	Linda Weavil	1/15, n/30	✓	300 00
	30	4	Earl Sanders	2/10, n/30	✓	800 00
			Total			2,100 00
						(111) (301)

GENERAL LEDGER

Accounts Receivable Acct. No. 111

Date			Ref.	Debit	Credit	Balance
1979 Jun.	30		S1	2,100 00		2,100 00

Sales Acct. No. 301

Date			Ref.	Debit	Credit	Balance
1979 Jun.	30		S1		2,100 00	2,100 00

ACCOUNTS RECEIVABLE LEDGER

Frank P. Allen

Date			Ref.	Debit	Credit	Balance
1979 Jun.	5		S1	600 00		600 00

Shirley Lloyd

Date			Ref.	Debit	Credit	Balance
1979 Jun.	3		S1	400 00		400 00

Earl Sanders

Date			Ref.	Debit	Credit	Balance
1979 Jun.	30		S1	800 00		800 00

Linda Weavil

Date			Ref.	Debit	Credit	Balance
1979 Jun.	5		S1	300 00		300 00

Figure 8–7 shows how these transactions are recorded in the purchases journal and posted to the general and subsidiary ledger accounts. Each transaction is posted separately as a credit to the accounts payable ledger to support the credit posted at the end of the month to the Accounts Payable controlling account in the general ledger. Transactions are usually posted to the subsidiary ledger daily. The date of the entry in the subsidiary ledger account is the invoice date, which is significant in determining if a discount may be taken. At the end of the month, the Amount column of the purchases journal is footed. This total is posted to the Purchases account in the general ledger as a debit. The same total is posted to the Accounts Payable controlling account in the general ledger as a credit.

Figure 8–7 Posting flow from the purchases journal

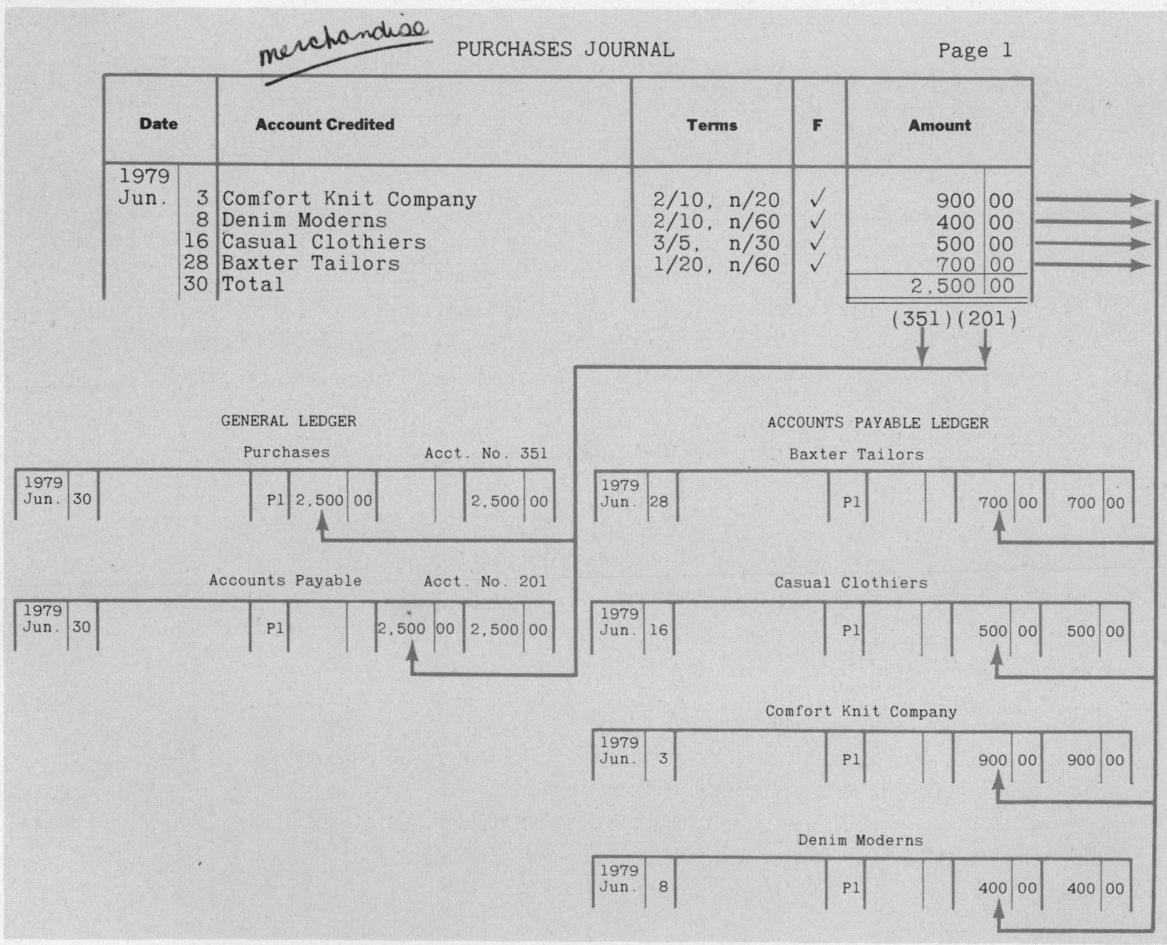

PURCHASES JOURNAL — Page 1

Date		Account Credited	Terms	F	Amount	
1979						
Jun.	3	Comfort Knit Company	2/10, n/20	✓	900	00
	8	Denim Moderns	2/10, n/60	✓	400	00
	16	Casual Clothiers	3/5, n/30	✓	500	00
	28	Baxter Tailors	1/20, n/60	✓	700	00
	30	Total			2,500	00
					(351)(201)	

GENERAL LEDGER

Purchases — Acct. No. 351

Date			F	Debit		Credit		Balance	
1979 Jun.	30		P1	2,500	00			2,500	00

Accounts Payable — Acct. No. 201

Date			F	Debit		Credit		Balance	
1979 Jun.	30		P1			2,500	00	2,500	00

ACCOUNTS PAYABLE LEDGER

Baxter Tailors

Date			F	Debit		Credit		Balance	
1979 Jun.	28		P1			700	00	700	00

Casual Clothiers

Date			F	Debit		Credit		Balance	
1979 Jun.	16		P1			500	00	500	00

Comfort Knit Company

Date			F	Debit		Credit		Balance	
1979 Jun.	3		P1			900	00	900	00

Denim Moderns

Date			F	Debit		Credit		Balance	
1979 Jun.	8		P1			400	00	400	00

Cash receipts journal

All transactions involving the receipt of cash are entered in the cash receipts journal. The column headings typically provide the flexibility necessary to record cash receipts from customers or any other source and to record sales discounts. The form may be varied, particularly in the number and headings of the columns, to meet the needs of the individual business. Using the cash receipts of The New Generation Shop, an explanation of the various columns in the cash receipts journal follows. It is illustrated in Figure 8–8.

Figure 8–8
Cash receipts journal

CASH RECEIPTS JOURNAL													
			Debits					Credits					
Date		Explanation	Cash	Sales Discount	Other Accounts			Account Credited	√	Accounts Receivable	Sales	Other Accounts	
					Account Title	F	Amount			Amount		F	Amount
1979 Jun.	1	Invested in business	2,500 00					J. Cox, capital					2,500 00
	10	Payment in full	588 00	12 00				F. P. Allen	√	600 00			
	15	Cash sales	1,000 00					Sales			1,000 00		
	17	Payment in full	396 00	4 00				S. Lloyd	√	400 00			
	22	Borrowed from bank	600 00					Notes Payable	√				600 00
	30	Cash sales	950 00					Sales			950 00		
	30	Payment on account	100 00		Notes Receivable		200	Linda Weavil	√	300 00			
	30	Totals	6,134 00	16 00			200 00			1,300 00	1,950 00		3,100 00

1. The date of the transaction is entered in the Date column.
2. The explanation of the transaction is written in the Explanation column. Every transaction entered in this journal includes a debit to Cash.
3. There are three Debit columns. Cash debits are entered in the first Debit column.
4. The Sales Discount Debit column is used for recording discounts granted to customers for paying within the discount period. (Throughout this chapter the gross price method will be used.)
5. The Other Accounts Debit column is for debits to general ledger accounts for which no special columns have been provided.
6. There are three folio columns, two labeled (F), one (√); a posting symbol indicating that the amount has been posted to the general ledger or to the accounts receivable ledger is placed in the folio columns.
7. The name of the general ledger or subsidiary ledger account to be credited is written in the Account Credited column.
8. When a charge customer makes a payment on account, an entry is made in the Accounts Receivable Credit column, the first of three Credit columns. The amount entered is the actual amount of cash received plus any sales discounts properly taken by the customer.
9. Sales of *merchandise* for cash are entered in the Sales Credit column.
10. The Other Accounts Credit column is for credits to general ledger accounts for which no special columns have been provided.

In previous chapters, transactions involving the receipt of cash were recorded in a simple two-column general journal. Similar transactions are recorded in the cash receipts journal in Figure 8–8. Although transactions may be entered on a single line, the equality of debits and credits is still maintained through the use of multiple columns. The following is an analysis of the debit-credit relationship of the entries in Figure 8–8 to indicate their effect on the accounts. These transactions, however, are actually recorded *only* in the cash receipts journal; *not* the general journal.

Transaction:

```
Jun.  1 June Cox, the owner, invested $2,500
        in The New Generation Shop.
```

In the cash receipts journal, Cash is debited by entering the amount in the Cash Debit column. Since there is no special column for J. Cox, Capital, the account title is written in and amount is entered in the Other Accounts Credit column.

Transaction:

```
Jun. 10 Received payment in full from Frank P. Allen.
```

The sales journal shows that on June 5, merchandise with an invoice price of $600 was sold to Frank P. Allen; terms 2/10, n/30. Since payment was made within 10 days, Allen deducted $12 from the invoice price and paid $588. Entering the three amounts in the special columns as shown has the same effect on the general ledger as entering them in a general journal entry. The customer's name is entered in the Account Credited column for posting to the accounts receivable ledger. If cash receipts from charge customers are numerous, a daily total may be entered from an adding machine tape; in that event posting to the subsidiary ledger is done from supporting documents.

Transaction:

```
Jun. 15 Cash sales for the first half of the month were $1,000.
```

The word *Sales* is written in the Account Credited column to fill the space. However, it could be omitted, since both the debit and credit amounts are entered in the special columns. Although a one-half month summary amount is used to simplify the illustration, cash sales should be recorded during each business day.

Transaction:

```
Jun. 17 Received full payment from Shirley Lloyd.
```

The sales journal shows that on June 3, merchandise with an invoice price of $400 was sold to Shirley Lloyd, terms 1/15, n/60. Since payment was made within 15 days, she deducted $4 from the invoice amount and paid $396.

Transaction:

```
Jun. 22 Borrowed $600 from the bank on a note payable.
```

Since there is no special column for the Notes Payable account, the amount is entered in the Other Accounts Credit column and the name of the account is written in the Account Credited column.

Transaction:

```
Jun. 30 Cash sales for the last half of the month were $950.
```

This transaction is recorded in the same manner as the June 15 cash sales.

Transaction:

```
Jun. 30 Received $100 from Linda Weavil on account and a promissory
        note payable in 30 days for the balance in her account.
```

The sales journal shows that on June 5 merchandise with an invoice price of $300 was sold to Linda Weavil, terms 1/5, n/30. The Sales Discounts account is not involved in this partial payment because the discount period has expired.

At the end of the month, the columns in the cash receipts journal are footed. Since each entry contains equal debits and credits, it follows that the total of the Debit column footings should equal the total of the Credit column footings. This equality should be proved for each special journal before the column totals are posted to the general ledger; otherwise, errors in the special journals may not be detected, the ledger will not have equal total debit and credit balances, and the trial balance will not balance. Moreover, the controlling accounts may not agree with their corresponding subsidiary ledgers. The cash receipts journal of The New Generation Shop is proved as shown below.

	Debits		Credits
Cash	$6,134.00	Accounts Receivable	$1,300.00
Sales Discounts	16.00	Sales	1,950.00
Other Accounts	200.00	Other Accounts	3,100.00
Total	$6,350.00	Total	$6,350.00

Postings from the cash receipts journal are shown in Figure 8–9. Individual credit postings are made to the accounts receivable ledger to support the $1,300 credit posting to the Accounts Receivable controlling account in the general ledger. A check mark is entered in the folio (√) column of the cash receipts journal on the line of the entry to indicate that the item has been posted to the customer's account in the subsidiary ledger. Any positive balance in an account would normally be a debit. Transactions have already been posted to these accounts from the sales journal.[1]

The totals of the Cash Debit column ($6,134) and the Sales Discounts Debit column ($16) are posted to the respective general ledger accounts. The regular sequence for transferring an amount from a journal to a ledger is followed. The general ledger account number entered in parentheses below the double rule in each column shows that the total has been posted to that account.

The (X) below the Other Accounts Debit column means that the individual amounts contained in the column total have already been posted to the general ledger. The $200 debit to Notes Receivable was posted individually during the month. The account number of Notes Receivable (112) was entered in the folio (F) column of the journal at the time the posting was done.

The Accounts Receivable account is credited for $1,300 and the Sales account is credited for $1,950. These postings are also dated June 30. No posting symbol

1 Earl Sanders' account is shown out of sequence to make the illustration of posting flow simpler. His unpaid balance of $800 is a debit and is equal to the balance in the Accounts Receivable account in the general ledger.

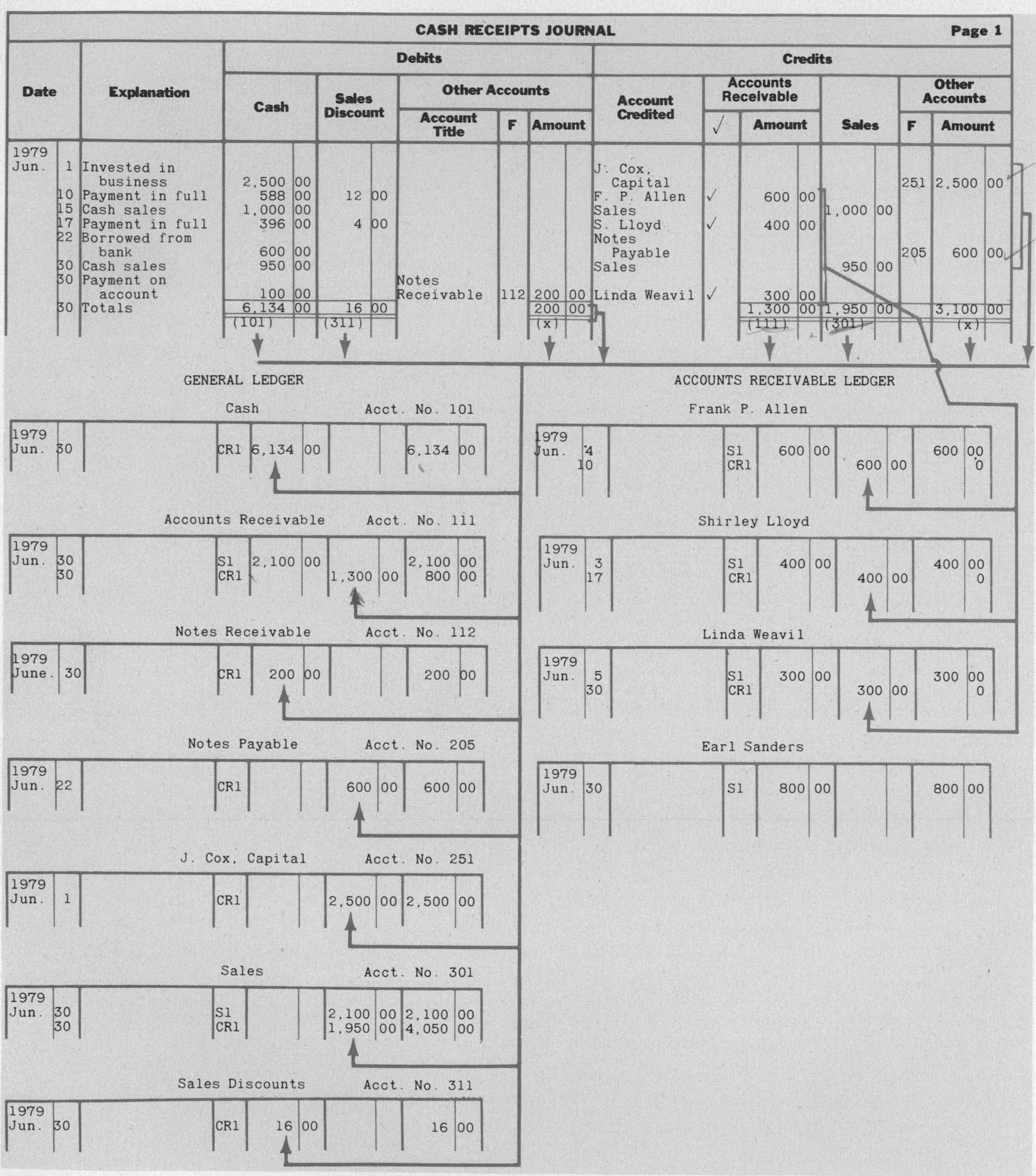

CASH RECEIPTS JOURNAL — Page 1

Date		Explanation	Debits: Cash	Debits: Sales Discount	Debits: Other Accounts – Account Title	F	Amount	Credits: Account Credited	Accounts Receivable ✓	Accounts Receivable Amount	Sales	Other Accounts F	Other Accounts Amount
1979 Jun.	1	Invested in business	2,500 00					J. Cox, Capital				251	2,500 00
	10	Payment in full	588 00	12 00				F. P. Allen	✓	600 00			
	15	Cash sales	1,000 00					Sales			1,000 00		
	17	Payment in full	396 00	4 00				S. Lloyd	✓	400 00			
	22	Borrowed from bank	600 00					Notes Payable				205	600 00
	30	Cash sales	950 00					Sales			950 00		
	30	Payment on account	100 00		Notes Receivable	112	200 00	Linda Weavil	✓	300 00			
	30	Totals	6,134 00	16 00			200 00			1,300 00	1,950 00		3,100 00
			(101)	(311)			(x)			(111)	(301)		(x)

GENERAL LEDGER

Cash — Acct. No. 101

Date		Explanation	F	Debit	Credit	Balance
1979 Jun.	30		CR1	6,134 00		6,134 00

Accounts Receivable — Acct. No. 111

Date		Explanation	F	Debit	Credit	Balance
1979 Jun.	30		S1	2,100 00		2,100 00
	30		CR1		1,300 00	800 00

Notes Receivable — Acct. No. 112

Date		Explanation	F	Debit	Credit	Balance
1979 June.	30		CR1	200 00		200 00

Notes Payable — Acct. No. 205

Date		Explanation	F	Debit	Credit	Balance
1979 Jun.	22		CR1		600 00	600 00

J. Cox, Capital — Acct. No. 251

Date		Explanation	F	Debit	Credit	Balance
1979 Jun.	1		CR1		2,500 00	2,500 00

Sales — Acct. No. 301

Date		Explanation	F	Debit	Credit	Balance
1979 Jun.	30		S1		2,100 00	2,100 00
	30		CR1		1,950 00	4,050 00

Sales Discounts — Acct. No. 311

Date		Explanation	F	Debit	Credit	Balance
1979 Jun.	30		CR1	16 00		16 00

ACCOUNTS RECEIVABLE LEDGER

Frank P. Allen

Date		Explanation	F	Debit	Credit	Balance
1979 Jun.	4		S1	600 00		600 00
	10		CR1		600 00	0

Shirley Lloyd

Date		Explanation	F	Debit	Credit	Balance
1979 Jun.	3		S1	400 00		400 00
	17		CR1		400 00	0

Linda Weavil

Date		Explanation	F	Debit	Credit	Balance
1979 Jun.	5		S1	300 00		300 00
	30		CR1		300 00	0

Earl Sanders

Date		Explanation	F	Debit	Credit	Balance
1979 Jun.	30		S1	800 00		800 00

Figure 8–9 Posting flow from the cash receipts journal

is used in the folio (F) column on the line of the entry for a cash sale because the item does not require individual posting.

The (X) below the double rule in the Other Accounts Credit column indicates that the column total is not to be posted to the general ledger. The total is not posted because the $2,500 credit to J. Cox, Capital, and the $600 credit to Notes Payable were posted separately during the month. The ledger page numbers of these accounts were entered in the folio (F) column of the journal when the posting was done. Note that account numbers 251 and 205 are written in the folio column of the cash receipts journal in Figure 8–9. Postings from the Other Accounts Credit column are dated as of the date of the entry.

Cash payments journal

All transactions involving the payment of cash are entered in the cash payments journal. Most cash payments should be made by check. When currency is required, payment may be made from a petty cash fund, for which procedures are discussed in Chapter 10.

A typical cash payments journal is illustrated in Figure 8–10. The columns provide for recording cash payments, either to creditors or for any other purpose, and for recording purchases discounts.

Explanation of the various columns follows.

1. The date of the disbursement of cash is entered in the Date column.
2. Detailed information is initially recorded on the check stub, which bears the same number as the check. Entries in the cash payments journal are then made from the check stub, and the check number is listed in the Check No. column.
3. An explanation of the transaction is entered in the Explanation column.
4. There are three Credit columns; they are located to the left of the Debit columns. In a special journal the sequence of columns need not follow the traditional placement. Cash is the first credit and will be used in each transaction entered in this journal.
5. The Purchases Discounts Credit column is used for recording discounts taken on invoices paid within the discount period.
6. Credits to general ledger accounts other than Cash and Purchases Discounts are recorded in the Other Accounts Credit column.

Figure 8–10
Cash payments journal

CASH PAYMENTS JOURNAL

Date	Check No.	Explanation	Credits					Account Debited	Debits				
			Cash	Purchases Discounts	Other Accounts				Accounts Payable		Purchases	Other Accounts	
					Account Title	F	Amount		✓	Amount		F	Amount
1979 Jun. 1	1	June rent	150 00					Rent Expense					150 00
10	2	Payment in Full	882 00	18 00				Comfort Knit Co.	✓	900 00			
14	3	Payment in Full	392 00	8 00				Denim Moderns	✓	400 00			
15	4	Cash Purchases	200 00					Purchases			200 00		
30	5	Partial Payment	300 00		Notes Payable		200 00	Casual Clothiers	✓	500 00			
30	6	Withdrawal of cash	400 00					J. Cox Drawing					400 00
30	7	Various Items	100 00					Misc. General Expense					100 00
30		Totals	2,424 00	26 00			200 00			1800 00	200 00		650 00

7. There are three folio columns, two labeled (F), one, (√); a posting symbol indicating that the amount has been posted to the general ledger or to the accounts payable ledger is placed in the folio column.
8. The name of the general ledger or subsidiary ledger account to be debited is written in the Account Debited column.
9. When a creditor is paid, the amount is entered in the Accounts Payable Debit column. The amount entered is the actual amount of the check plus any purchases discounts taken.
10. The purchase of merchandise for cash is entered in the Purchases Debit column.
11. The Other Accounts Debit column is used for entries to general ledger accounts that have no special column.

Although each transaction may be entered on a single line, this practice is not an absolute requirement. Each new transaction entry should begin on a vacant line. The equality of debits and credits is maintained through the use of multiple columns. The transactions in Figures 8–10 are analyzed in terms of debits and credits to indicate their effect on the accounts. They represent cash payments made by The New Generation Shop in June 1979.

Transaction:

Jun. 1 Issued check no. 1 in the amount of $150 for the June rent.

The $150 decrease in cash is entered in the Cash column on the same line as the explanation. Since there is not a special debit column for Rent Expense, the account title is written in the Account Debited column and the $150 debit amount to Rent Expense is shown in the Other Accounts column.

Transaction:

Jun. 10 Paid Comfort Knit Co., in full; check no. 2.

The Purchases journal shows that on June 3, merchandise with an invoice price of $900 was purchased from Comfort Knit Company; terms 2/10, n/20. Since payment was made within 10 days, a 2 percent discount of $18 is taken and a check for $882 is issued. Entering the three amounts in the special columns has the same effect on the general ledger as recording them in a general journal entry. The creditor's name is entered in the Account Debited column for posting to the accounts payable ledger.

Transaction:

Jun. 14 Paid Denim Moderns in full; check no. 3.

The explanation for this entry is similar to that for the entry of June 10.

Transaction:

Jun. 15 Purchased merchandise and issued a check for the full amount of the invoice; check no. 4.

Purchases of merchandise *on account* are entered in the purchases journal. A company may occasionally purchase merchandise for cash, probably from another company with which no credit relationship exists. These cash purchases are recorded directly in the cash payments journal. If cash purchases of merchandise occur frequently, a special Purchases Debit column may be provided in the cash payments journal.

Transaction:

```
Jun. 30 Paid Casual Clothiers $300 on account (check no. 5)
        and issued a promissory note for the balance, to be
        paid in 30 additional days.
```

Reference to the purchases journal shows that on June 16 merchandise with an invoice price of $500 was purchased from the Casual Clothiers, terms 3/5, n/30. Since the discount period has expired, no discount is taken.

Transaction:

```
Jun. 30 J. Cox, the owner, withdrew $400 (check no. 6) for her
        personal use in anticipation of earned income.
```

Since there is no special column for personal withdrawals, the cash withdrawal is entered in the Other Accounts Debit column. If such withdrawals are numerous, a special debit column with the heading J. Cox, Drawing could be provided.

Transaction:

```
Jun. 30 Issued check no. 7 in the amount of $100 for miscellaneous
        general expenses.
```

The expense account is debited for various items purchased and consumed during the month.

Before the end-of-the-month postings are made, the columns of the cash payments journal should be footed, and the equality of debits and credits proved as follows:

	Debits		Credits
Accounts Payable	$1,800.00	Cash	$2,424.00
Purchases	200.00	Purchases Discounts . .	26.00
Other Accounts	650.00	Notes Payable	200.00
Total	$2,650.00	Total	$2,650.00

The total debit and total credit postings from this journal to the general ledger are equal.

Posting from the cash payments journal of The New Generation Shop is shown in Figure 8–11.

The individual debit postings to the accounts payable ledger support the $1,800 debit posting to the Accounts Payable controlling account in the general ledger.

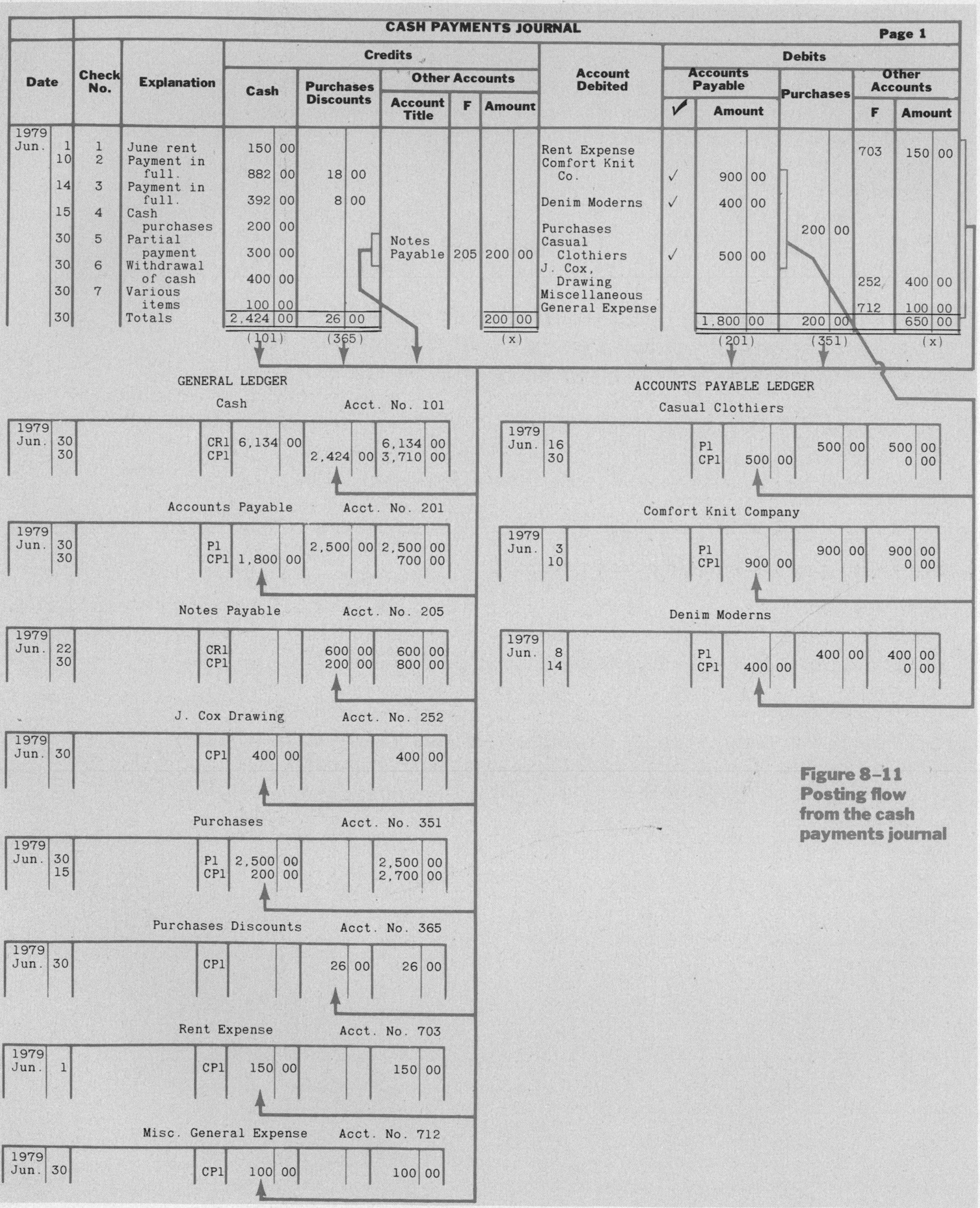

CASH PAYMENTS JOURNAL — Page 1

Date		Check No.	Explanation	Credits: Cash	Credits: Purchases Discounts	Credits: Other Accounts: Account Title	F	Amount	Account Debited	Debits: Accounts Payable ✓	Accounts Payable Amount	Debits: Purchases	Debits: Other Accounts F	Other Accounts Amount
1979 Jun.	1	1	June rent	150 00					Rent Expense				703	150 00
	10	2	Payment in full.	882 00	18 00				Comfort Knit Co.	✓	900 00			
	14	3	Payment in full.	392 00	8 00				Denim Moderns	✓	400 00			
	15	4	Cash purchases	200 00					Purchases			200 00		
	30	5	Partial payment	300 00		Notes Payable	205	200 00	Casual Clothiers	✓	500 00			
	30	6	Withdrawal of cash	400 00					J. Cox, Drawing				252	400 00
	30	7	Various items	100 00					Miscellaneous General Expense				712	100 00
	30		Totals	2,424 00	26 00			200 00			1,800 00	200 00		650 00
				(101)	(365)			(x)			(201)	(351)		(x)

GENERAL LEDGER

Cash — Acct. No. 101

Date			F	Debit	Credit	Balance
1979 Jun.	30		CR1	6,134 00		6,134 00
	30		CP1		2,424 00	3,710 00

Accounts Payable — Acct. No. 201

Date			F	Debit	Credit	Balance
1979 Jun.	30		P1		2,500 00	2,500 00
	30		CP1	1,800 00		700 00

Notes Payable — Acct. No. 205

Date			F	Debit	Credit	Balance
1979 Jun.	22		CR1		600 00	600 00
	30		CP1		200 00	800 00

J. Cox Drawing — Acct. No. 252

Date			F	Debit	Credit	Balance
1979 Jun.	30		CP1	400 00		400 00

Purchases — Acct. No. 351

Date			F	Debit	Credit	Balance
1979 Jun.	30		P1	2,500 00		2,500 00
	15		CP1	200 00		2,700 00

Purchases Discounts — Acct. No. 365

Date			F	Debit	Credit	Balance
1979 Jun.	30		CP1		26 00	26 00

Rent Expense — Acct. No. 703

Date			F	Debit	Credit	Balance
1979 Jun.	1		CP1	150 00		150 00

Misc. General Expense — Acct. No. 712

Date			F	Debit	Credit	Balance
1979 Jun.	30		CP1	100 00		100 00

ACCOUNTS PAYABLE LEDGER

Casual Clothiers

Date			F	Debit	Credit	Balance
1979 Jun.	16		P1		500 00	500 00
	30		CP1	500 00		0 00

Comfort Knit Company

Date			F	Debit	Credit	Balance
1979 Jun.	3		P1		900 00	900 00
	10		CP1	900 00		0 00

Denim Moderns

Date			F	Debit	Credit	Balance
1979 Jun.	8		P1		400 00	400 00
	14		CP1	400 00		0 00

Figure 8–11 Posting flow from the cash payments journal

Each check mark in the folio (√) column of the cash payments journal indicates that a posting has been made to the supplier's account in the subsidiary ledger. Note that the balance of each account is either a credit or zero.

The Accounts Payable account is debited for $1,800 as of June 30. The total of the Purchases Debit column, $200, is posted to the Purchases account in the general ledger.

The total of the Other Accounts Debit column is not posted, because it is used to record debits to accounts for which no special columns have been provided; each amount must be posted separately. The numbers of these accounts—703, 252, and 712—are entered in the folio (F) column. The (X) below the double rule in the Other Accounts Debit column indicates that the column total is not posted to the general ledger.

The totals of the Cash Credit column ($2,424) and the Purchases Discounts Credit column ($26) are posted to the general ledger. The basic posting steps are followed. The general ledger account numbers are placed in parentheses below the double rules in the columns to indicate that the postings have been done.

The total of the Other Accounts Credit column is not posted, since each entry in the column has been individually posted at the time the entry is made in the journal. The folio (F) column indicates the account to which the entry was posted.

Combined cash receipts and payments journal

Many small entities use a combined cash receipts and cash payments journal sometimes called a *cashbook*. This journal is simply a combination of the cash receipts journal and the cash payments journal described earlier. The specialized debit and credit columns (except for cash) would be unique to the needs of the particular entity using it. In addition to small commercial enterprises, such a journal is appropriate to many not-for-profit organizations such as fraternities and sororities and civic clubs, and to professional service organizations.

An outline of a simple combined cash receipts and payments journal is presented below.

Combined Cash Receipts and Payments Journal

Date	Explanation	Debits			Credits					Other Accounts			
		Cash	Purchases	Sales Discounts	Cash		Accounts Receivable	Sales	Purchases Discounts	Title	F	Debit	Credit
					Check Number	Amount							

Other special journals

Other special journals may be adopted as need becomes apparent. Such a need is indicated if labor may be saved or if the special journal provides an element of flexibility in the accounting system. Examples of other special journals are sales returns and allowances journal, purchases returns and allowances journal, notes receivable register, notes payable register, and voucher register.

Continuing need for general journal

Although special journals provide for recording frequently recurring transactions, there is still a need for recording unusual current transactions, correcting entries and adjusting and closing entries. For these purposes, a two-column general journal is used in conjunction with the special journals. All the transactions that cannot be entered in the special journals are recorded in the general journal. Sales returns and allowances and purchases returns and allowances, for example, are entered in the general journal if special journals for these transactions are not maintained. Other typical current transactions recorded in the general journal include credit purchases of assets other than merchandise inventory, the incurrence of liabilities for services, notes received from customers to apply toward accounts receivable, and notes issued to creditors to apply toward accounts payable.

If it is discovered that an error has been made in the process of journalizing and posting, it may be corrected by a general journal entry. Erasures should be avoided, because they may create doubt in the minds of persons who examine the records regarding the reason for the erasure. This becomes particularly important when the records are audited, and in cases of litigation when the records may be offered as evidence.

Assume that the following entry, recording the payment of an invoice for repairs to machinery, has been posted (actually journalized in the cash payments journal but for simplicity is shown here in general journal form):

1979						
Jul.	19	Machinery and Equipment	15	00		
		Cash			15	00
		Repairs to machinery.				

The debit should have been to an expense account; the error may be corrected by the following entry in the general journal:

GENERAL JOURNAL

Page 40

Date		Debit-Credit-Account Titles: Explanation	F	Debit		Credit	
1979							
Jul.	26	Maintenance and Repairs Expense		15	00		
		Machinery and Equipment				15	00
		To correct entry of July 19 in cash payments journal.					

If an error in a journal entry is discovered before it is posted, it may be corrected by drawing a line through the incorrect account or amount and entering the correction immediately above it.

Direct posting from business documents

In many business firms, data can be processed more efficiently and rapidly by posting from the original documents—sales invoices, sales slips, purchase invoices, and so on—directly to the subsidiary ledgers instead of first copying the information in special journals and then posting to the accounts. For example, if sales slips are serially numbered, a binder file of duplicate slips arranged in numerical order could take the place of a more formal sales journal. Amounts from the individual slips could be posted daily to the accounts receivable ledger; at the end of a designated period—a week or a month—the sales slips in the binder file are totaled and the following general journal entry is made:

GENERAL JOURNAL

Page 80

Date		Debit-Credit-Account Titles: Explanation	F	Debit		Credit	
1979							
Aug.	31	Accounts Receivable		120,000	00		
		Sales				120,000	00
		To record charge sales for the month of August, 1979					

A similar procedure may be used to record purchases on account.

If postings are made from sales slips to the accounts receivable ledger, and if for any reason a special sales journal is still desired, a streamlined journal can be constructed by simply eliminating the Account Debited, Terms, and folio (F) columns, as shown below.

SALES JOURNAL

Date	Sales Invoice Numbers	Amount

Entries to such a sales journal may be made in batches; for example, a single line may read:

Aug. 12 13,500–13,599 18,329.21

A batch could represent a day's credit sales, or simply a predetermined quantity of invoices or sales slips. The use of *batch totals* is one means of checking the accuracy of posting to subsidiary ledgers.

These changes in procedure and the increasing use of direct posting from original documents are discussed here to add emphasis to a statement made earlier in this chapter. Accounting records and procedures should be designed to meet the needs of the particular business firm.

Bookkeeping machine processing

The simple *posting machine* and similar electromechanical equipment can perform the two basic operations involved in the distribution of business transaction information to appropriate accounts: (1) *listing*—that is, writing such information as cross-reference, date, and amount, and (2) *adding* or *subtracting* amounts. Depending on the complexity of the machine—whether it has one or more *registers,* which allow it to accumulate amounts for further computation, and whether it has a built-in *program* (set of instructions for performing manipulations of data)—it may perform many additional tasks.

In a growing business, as the number of customers and credit transactions increases, the cost of hand posting to the accounts receivable ledger becomes excessive. It may be economical for such a company to buy or rent a simple posting machine that has a *horizontal register* (cross-footer) which can compute the difference between debits and credits on a single line. This type of machine can be used to post debits from sales invoices and credits from payments to each customer's account in the subsidiary ledger. The operator punches into the machine the beginning balance and both debits and credits, if applicable, to the account, and the machine records this information and prints out a new balance automatically.

Many firms have accounting systems that permit posting by bookkeeping equipment to all ledgers, including the general ledger. Economies can be achieved by machine accounting when the volume of similar accounting routines is large enough to enable the bookkeeper to gain speed through repetitive motions that can eventually become habitual. Accuracy and legibility of accounting records are attained by the use of electromechanical and electronic equipment. These machines facilitate proofs of the accuracy of journalizing and posting. The more complex machines perform several stages of accounting—the preparation of specialized reports, journal entries, and ledger posting—in one operation.

Other accounting systems

As a business engages in a larger number of transactions of similar nature, it may be economical to acquire punched-card equipment. This equipment rapidly, accurately, and automatically completes the three basic stages of distributing the details of accounting transactions to the appropriate accounts and reports: (1) recording information on an input medium; (2) classifying the information according to the accounts affected; and (3) summarizing the resulting account balances. Punched-card equipment is also useful for recording, classifying, and summarizing nonfinancial statistical data that help management to make decisions.

Further expansion of the accounting system would lead to the development of electronic data processing (EDP) systems. These offer the greatest speed, volume, and reliability, and consist of combinations of electronic equipment centered around digital computers. These machines are designed to receive a large mass of input data, perform basic arithmetic operations on the data, make comparison decisions regarding the data, update the previously stored data, almost immediately supply the information (reports) resulting from these operations, and then store the data for later use. Although they are used extensively in accounting, a complete discussion of EDP systems is beyond the scope of this text.

Glossary

Accounting system The various processing steps that change original data to useful form.

Cashbook A simplified combination of the cash receipts journal and the cash payments journal.

Cash payments journal A special journal in which *all* cash payments are recorded.

Cash receipts journal A special journal in which *all* cash receipts are recorded.

General journal The book of original entry in which all transactions that do not fit into special journals are recorded.

Invoice A form that provides evidence of sale and delivery of merchandise; it indicates that an account receivable exists.

Processing A series of activities that make data useful. Classifying and summarizing are examples.

Purchases journal A special journal in which purchases of merchandise on credit are recorded.

Receiving report A form that provides information on materials received; it indicates that an account payable exists.

Sales journal A special journal in which sales of merchandise on credit are recorded.

Source document A business paper on which each individual transaction is recorded. It provides objective evidence of the transaction.

Special journals Books of original entry that have been modified so that each carries a special class of transactions.

Questions

Q8–1 (a) What are the stages of systems development? (b) What are the considerations of the analyst in systems design? (c) In selecting the method or combination of methods of data collection, what criteria are used?

Q8–2 (a) What is the function of special journals? (b) What determines the types of special journals to be used? (c) How do special journals save time and labor? (d) Are there other advantages in using special journals?

Q8–3 Do the special journals eliminate the need for a general journal? Explain.

Q8–4 What is the rule for entering a transaction (a) in the sales journal? (b) in the purchases journal? (c) in the cash receipts journal? (d) in the cash payments journal? (e) in the general journal?

Q8–5 What is the purpose of an Other Accounts section in a special journal? Describe the posting procedure for items recorded in the Other Accounts section.

Q8–6 The Kuykendal Company uses sales, purchases, cash receipts, cash payments and general journals. State the journal in which each of the following transactions and events should be recorded:

1. Sale of merchandise on account.
2. Purchase of store supplies on account.
3. Return by a customer of a cash sale item for which the customer was given a refund check.
4. Purchase of delivery equipment on account.
5. Payment to a creditor.
6. Sale of merchandise for cash.
7. Adjusting entries.
8. Purchase of merchandise on account.
9. Note receivable issued by a customer in full settlement of his account.
10. Return of a credit purchase causing the customer's account to be credited.
11. Withdrawal of cash by owner for his own personal use.
12. Closing entries.
13. Payment of rent.
14. Purchase of merchandise for cash.
15. Note payable given to a creditor to apply on account.
16. Withdrawal of merchandise by the owner for personal use.

Q8–7 (a) When are postings made from the purchases journal (1) to the general ledger and (2) to the accounts payable ledger? (b) What is the relationship of the amounts posted?

Q8–8 (a) How is it possible to trace postings from the journals to the ledgers? (b) What is the significance of the check mark in the folio (F) column of the purchases journal? (c) Would it be advisable to use code numbers as posting references for creditors accounts rather than check marks?

Q8–9 The following questions relate to the cash receipts journal illustrated in this chapter: (a) What are the special columns? (b) Why is the journal cross-footed at the end of each month? (c) Explain the postings from this journal (1) to the general ledger and (2) to the accounts receivable ledger.

Q8–10 The column headings listed below might appear in one or more special journals.

1. Other Accounts—Debit
2. Purchases—Debit
3. Accounts Payable—Debit
4. Accounts Receivable—Credit
5. Office Supplies—Debit
6. Other Accounts—Credit
7. Accounts Payable—Credit
8. Cash—Credit
9. Accounts Receivable—Debit
10. Cash—Debit

The company maintains subsidiary ledgers for accounts receivable and accounts payable.

For each of the headings, state the special journal or journals in which it would be found and whether or not the amounts entered in the column would be posted as a total, or separately, or both as a total and separately.

Q8–11 What changes in the relationships shown in Figure 8–4 would be required if (a) bookkeeping machines were used? (b) if EDP equipment were installed?

Q8–12 What are at least three types of entries that would always be made in the general journal?

Class exercises

CE8–1 (Special journals) John Fletcher Ware has been in business for five years, selling merchandise for cash only. Beginning in January 1979 he plans to start making sales on account. The general ledger of the company shows the following account balances on January 1, 1979.

101	Cash	$ 40,000
121	Accounts Receivable	–0–
122	Notes Receivable	–0–
131	Merchandise Inventory	60,000
141	Prepaid Insurance	–0–
201	Store Equipment	20,000
201A	Accumulated Depreciation—Store Equipment	8,000
301	Accounts Payable	–0–
302	Notes Payable	–0–
401	J. F. Ware, Capital	112,000
501	Sales	–0–

502	Sales Returns and Allowances	–0–
503	Sales Discounts	–0–
601	Purchases	–0–
602	Purchases Returns and Allowances	–0–
603	Purchases Discounts	–0–
701	Salesmen's Salaries Expense	–0–

Transactions during the month of January

1979

Jan. 2 Sold merchandise to Edward Taylor on account, $900; terms 2/10, n/30.

4 Sold merchandise to James Gamble on account, $300; terms, 2/10, n/30.

6 Sold merchandise to Mary Hollerback on account, $600; terms 2/10, n/30.

7 Sold merchandise to Mayberry Goheen on account, $400; terms 2/10, n/30.

9 Purchased merchandise from the Woodworth Company on account, $2,000; terms 1/10, n/30.

9 Purchased merchandise from the Buford Company on account, $2,600; terms 1/10, n/30.

10 Purchased merchandise from the Seretha Company on account, $750; terms, n/45.

11 Purchased merchandise from the Three Rivers Company on account, $1,200; terms, n/60.

12 Received a check from Edward Taylor for the amount due from the sale of January 2.

14 Cash sales of $9,000 were made.

16 Received a check from James Gamble for $100 and a 60-day, 10 percent promissory note for the balance.

17 Received a check for $392 from Mary Hollerback in partial settlement of account—$400 invoice price less $8 discount. Because the check was mailed before the expiration of the discount period, the discount was allowed.

18 Cash sales of $5,000 were made.

18 Purchased store equipment, $4,000, making a down payment of $1,000 and issuing a 120-day, 9 percent note payable for the balance.

18 Paid $480 for a comprehensive 2-year insurance policy, dating from January 1, 1979.

18 Paid the amount due the Woodworth Company for the purchases made on January 9.

19 Paid $1,485 in partial settlement of the amount due the Buford Company; $1,500 invoice price less $15 discount.

20 Paid salesmen's salaries of $1,000.

20 Cash purchases of merchandise totaled $4,760.

28 Issued a 90-day, 9 percent note to the Buford Company in settlement of balance of account.

30 Returned merchandise to the Seretha Company and received credit $160.

31 Credited Mayberry Goheen for $120 for merchandise returned.

Required:

1. Open the necessary general and subsidiary ledgers.
2. Journalize all the charge sales in a sales journal and post them to the accounts receivable ledger. Provide invoice numbers starting with 001. Summarize the sales journal and make the January 31 postings to the general ledger.
3. Journalize all the charge purchases in a purchases journal and post them to the accounts payable ledger. Summarize the purchases journal and make January 31 postings to the general ledger.
4. Journalize all the cash receipts in a cash receipts journal and post them to the accounts receivable ledger. Summarize and cross-foot the journal and make January 31 postings to the general ledger.
5. Journalize all the cash payments in a cash payments journal and post them to the accounts payable ledger. Provide check numbers starting with 4062. Summarize and cross-foot the journal and make January 31 postings to the general ledger.
6. Journalize any other transactions in a two-column general journal.
7. Prove the balances of the Accounts Receivable and Accounts Payable accounts by preparing a schedule of accounts receivable and a schedule of accounts payable.

CE8–2 (Complex examples of cash receipts and cash payments) The following cash receipts and cash payments requiring multiple debits and/or credits occurred at the Kanawha Company during May 1979:

1979

May 1 Paid $39,500 in cash to Hugh Bierkamp for the net assets of his single proprietorship.

Assets received:

Accounts Receivable	$ 9,500
Merchandise Inventory	15,000
Land	20,000

Liability assumed:
Mortgage Payable 5,000

2 Purchased office equipment for $5,000 and office supplies for $800; paid $4,200 in cash and issued a 90-day, 9 percent note for the balance.

3 Sold for $9,000 part of the land acquired on May 1 at a cost of $7,000 (Credit: Gain on Sale of Land, $2,000.)

4 Received a partial payment of $2,970 (1 percent cash discount allowed) and a 30-day note in settlement of a $7,000 account receivable.

Required: Record the transactions in a cash receipts journal and a cash payments journal as illustrated in this chapter.

Exercises and problems

P8–1 The Obispo Company made the following merchandise sales on account during May 1979:

1979
May 2 To Mary Barr, $170.
3 To Edgar Leigh, $150.
4 To Jane Chambers, $300.
5 To William Ashby, $420.
6 To Mary Barr, $185.
12 To Edgar Leigh, $90.
20 To Jane Chambers, $65.
31 To William Ashby, $175.

Required:

1. Record the transactions in a sales journal similar to the one illustrated in this chapter. The terms on credit sales are 2/10, n/30. Number the sales invoices, starting with 101.
2. Open accounts in the accounts receivable ledger for the customers.
3. Open the following accounts in the general ledger: Accounts Receivable 111 and Sales 301.
4. Post from the sales journal to the accounts receivable ledger and the general ledger.
5. Prepare a schedule of accounts receivable.

P8–2 The Lopez Fishing Equipment Shop made the following merchandise purchases during December 1979.

1979

Dec. 1 From the Pismo Beach Company on account, $500.

2 From the Orcutt Company on account, $200.

5 From the San Ardo Company on account, $400.

13 From the Nipomo Supply Company on account, $360.

18 From the Morro Bay Company on account, $240.

19 From the Pismo Beach Company on account, $280.

22 From the Orcutt Company on account, $210.

26 From the Pismo Beach Company on account, $180.

30 From the Nipomo Supply Company on account, $215.

Required: Record the transactions in a purchases journal similar to the one illustrated in this chapter. The terms on all purchases of merchandise on account are 2/10, n/30.

P8–3 The Lincoln Company was formed on March 1, 1979. During the month of March, it completed the following cash receipt transactions:

1979

Mar. 1 J. Lincoln invested $40,000 cash in his business.

8 Received a check for $196 from White Oaks Company in settlement of a $200 sales invoice.

15 Cash sales for March 1 through 15 were $2,600.

17 Received $120 in cash from Rio Hondo Sales (no discount).

23 Borrowed $2,000 in cash from the Capitan National Bank and gave a note payable due April 23, 1979.

25 Received a check for $388 from Arroyo Company in settlement of a $400 sales invoice.

31 Cash sales for March 16 through 31 were $3,400.

31 Sold at cost a parcel of land purchased on March 1 for $5,500, receiving $2,500 in cash and a note receivable for the balance.

Required:

1. Record the transactions in a cash receipts journal similar to the one illustrated in this chapter.
2. Open the following general ledger accounts:
   Cash 101
   Accounts Receivable 111
   Notes Receivable 115
   Land 121
   Notes Payable 205
   J. Lincoln, Capital 275
   Sales 301
   Sales Discounts 311
   Post a debit of $890 to Accounts Receivable; date the posting March 31. This amount is from the sales journal.
3. Open the following accounts in the accounts receivable ledger and record the amounts given in the Debit and Balance columns (these are summary totals posted from the sales journal): Arroyo Company, $400; Rio Hondo Sales, $280; White Oaks Company, $210.
4. Post from the cash receipts journal to the accounts receivable ledger and the general ledger.
5. Prepare a schedule of accounts receivable.

P8–4 The Oak Park Company was organized on May 1, 1979; the following cash payments were made during the month:

1979

May 1 Purchased land and building for $50,000. Paid $20,000 in cash and a note for $30,000. Land is appraised at $10,000; building, at $40,000.

10 Paid the Melrose Park Company $980 in settlement of a purchase made on May 2; the invoice price was $1,000.

15 Cash purchases for May 1 through 15 were $8,000.

17 Paid the Berwyn Company $2,000 on account (no discount).

20 Purchased office equipment for $3,000 in cash.

31 Paid the Cicero Company $700 on account (no discount).

31 Paid a 9 percent, 30-day note due this date. Face value of the note was $6,000; interest was $45.

31 Cash purchases for May 16 through 31 were $12,000.

Required:

1. Record the transactions in a cash payments journal similar to the one illustrated in this chapter.
2. Open the following general ledger accounts.
   Cash 101
   Land 201
   Building 202
   Office Equipment 203
   Accounts Payable 301
   Notes Payable 302
   Purchases 401
   Purchases Discounts 402
   Interest Expense 501
   Enter the following account balances:
   a. Cash debit, $150,000—posted from the cash receipts journal.
   b. Accounts Payable credit, $5,700—posted from the purchases journal.
   c. Notes Payable credit, $6,000—posted from the cash receipts journal.
3. Open the following accounts in the accounts payable ledger and record the amounts given in the Credit and Balance columns (these are summary totals posted from the purchases journal): Berwyn Company, $2,400; Cicero Company, $1,800; Melrose Park Company, $1,500.
4. Post from the cash payments journal to the accounts payable ledger and the general ledger.
5. Prepare a schedule of accounts payable.

P8–5 The Elvers Company uses sales, purchases, cash receipts, cash payments and general journals. On December 31, 1979 it had the following amounts in its general ledger after journals had been posted:

Cash

F	Debit		Credit		Balance	
1	58,000	00			58,000	00
2			38,000	00	20,000	00

Accounts Receivable

F	Debit		Credit		Balance	
3	60,000	00			60,000	00
4			20,000	00	40,000	00

Accounts Payable

F	Debit		Credit		Balance	
5			19,500	00	19,500	00
6	8,000	00			11,500	00

Sales

F	Debit		Credit		Balance	
7			60,000	00	60,000	00
8			18,000	00	78,000	00
9	78,000	00			-0-	

Purchases

F	Debit		Credit		Balance	
10	19,500	00			19,500	00
11	6,000	00			25,500	00
12			25,500	00	-0-	

Purchases Returns and Allowances

F	Debit		Credit		Balance	
13			1,800	00	1,800	00
14	1,800	00			-0-	

Required: On a sheet of paper, opposite numbers 1 through 14 corresponding to the numbers that appear in the folio columns of the accounts, indicate the most probable journal source for each posting using the symbols for journals used in this chapter.

P8–6 During June 1979, the Madison Hardware Supply Company completed the transactions listed below.

1979		
June	1	Sold merchandise on account to Etta Heatwole, $2,300.
	3	Sold merchandise on account to John Bethalto, $920.
	10	Sold merchandise on account to Glen Carbon, $560.
	12	Sold merchandise on account to Easton Alton, $710.
	13	Received a check from John Bethalto for the amount due.
	15	Cash sales to date, $4,650.
	19	Sold merchandise on account to Troy Nameoki, $380.
	20	Borrowed $600 in cash from First State Bank and gave a 30-day, 9 percent note for that amount.
	23	Received a $200 check from Glen Carbon to apply on account.
	24	Received a check from Troy Nameoki for the amount due.
	26	Sold merchandise on account to National Stock Yards $520.
	27	Received a check from Etta Heatwole for the amount due.
	28	Sold merchandise on account to Glen Carbon, $200.
	29	Received a check from National Stock Yards for the amount due.
	30	Cash sales from June 16 through 30 were $4,060.
	30	Received $200 in rent on land for June.

Required:
1. Record the transactions in a sales journal and a cash receipts journal similar to the ones illustrated in this chapter. Terms of 2/10, n/30 apply to all sales on account. (Number the sales invoices, starting with 51.)
2. Open the following accounts in the general ledger: Cash, 101; Accounts Receivable, 111; Notes Payable, 205; Sales, 301; Sales Discounts, 311; Rent Earned, 351.
3. Open the customers' accounts in the accounts receivable ledger.
4. Post from the two journals to the accounts receivable ledger and general ledger.
5. Prepare a schedule of accounts receivable.

P8–7 (Integrative) The Montreal Company started operations on August 1, 1979. During August, the company used the following accounts:

Cash 101	H. Dauderis, Capital 301
Accounts Receivable 111	Sales 401
Notes Receivable 115	Sales Discounts 402
Prepaid Insurance 117	Sales Returns and Allowances 403
Office Supplies 118	Purchases 501
Land 151	Purchases Discounts 502
Store Building 154	Purchases Returns and Allowances 503
Store Fixtures 156	Transportation In 504
Office Equipment 158	Salaries Expense 601
Accounts Payable 201	Delivery Expense 611
Notes Payable 202	Office Expense 621
Mortgage Payable 251	Utilities Expense 631

The following transactions occurred during August:

1979

Aug. 1 Henry Dauderis invested $30,000 in his new business.

1 Purchased a store building and site for $60,000 of which $15,000 is considered land cost. Paid $10,000 in cash and issued a mortgage for the balance.

1 Purchased store fixtures from the Chelsea Company for $6,800 on account, terms, n/60.

2 Purchased merchandise from Templeton Company, on account, $4,000; invoice date August 1; terms, 2/10, n/60.

2 Purchased merchandise from John Hull on account, $8,000; invoice date, August 2; terms, 2/10, n/60.

7 Purchased a 3-year fire insurance policy for $720 in cash.

8 Purchased merchandise for $5,000 in cash.

9 Returned unsatisfactory merchandise to Templeton Company and received credit for $800.

13 Sold merchandise to Bailey Myers on account, $8,200; invoice no. 1; terms, 1/10, n/30.

14 Paid Templeton Company and John Hull the amounts due.

15 Cash sales from August 1 through 15 were $3,400.

16 Sold merchandise to Marie Owens on account, $4,700; invoice no. 2; terms 1/10, n/30.

16 Sold merchandise to Jay Wakefield on account, $6,300; invoice no. 3, terms, 1/10, n/30.

16 Paid salaries for August 1 through 15 totaling $2,650.

19 Sold merchandise to Glen Almond on account, $8,000; invoice no. 4; terms, 1/10, n/30.

21 Purchased merchandise from the Rockland Company on account, $4,900; invoice date, August 21, terms, 1/10, n/30.

21 Received bill for $130 from the Masson Supply Company for items chargeable to Office Expense; terms n/30.

23 Received merchandise returned by Glen Almond; issued credit memo no. 1 for $2,000.

23 Received cash from Bailey Myers for invoice no. 1, less discount.

26 Received cash from Marie Owens for invoice no. 2, less discount.

26 Purchased merchandise from Aylmer Company on account, $9,100; invoice date, August 24; terms, 3/10, n/30. Paid transportation charges of $90. The goods were shipped F.O.B. shipping point.

28 Received $1,300 cash from Jay Wakefield and a 9 percent 60-day note for the balance.

29 Sold merchandise to Walter Rockingham on account, $4,000; invoice no. 5; terms, 1/10, n/30.

29 Paid $215 in cash for electricity.

29 Paid the Rockland Company for the invoice of August 21, less discount.

29 Received cash from Glen Almond for the balance of invoice no. 4, less discount.

31 Cash sales from August 16 through 31 were $1,950.

31 Paid salaries for August 16 through 31 totaling $2,850.

31 Received a bill for $96 from the Delivu Company for delivery service for the month.

31 Purchased two filing cabinets and a typewriter at a cost of $750 and various office supplies at a cost of $300; paid $350 in cash and issued a $700 note payable for the balance.

Required:

1. Record the transactions in a general journal, a cash receipts journal, a cash payments journal, a sales journal, and a purchases journal.
2. Indicate how the posting would be made from the journals by entering the appropriate posting references.

P8–8 (Minicase) Dexter Distributors, owned by Harry Dexter, is a petroleum products dealership. They operate several trucks that are constantly on the road filling fuel tanks of customers who use fuel oil for home heating. For each such delivery a sales ticket is prepared. A meter on the truck automatically stamps the number of gallons delivered at each stop. These sales tickets are returned to the accounting department at the end of each day where they are priced so that invoices can be mailed to customers. Customers are allowed a discount of one cent per gallon if they pay within ten days of billing date.

Fuel oil is stored in a large tank that is refilled about twice a week by tankers from the area distributor. Each time the area distributor's tanker delivers a load, a receiver's report is prepared and sent to the accounting department. The distributor requires payment monthly, and does not offer a discount.

The business has 32 employees. They are paid on the 15th and last day of each month. Supplies and other expenses are billed to Dexter Distributors with almost all suppliers offering terms of 2/10, n/30.

You have been asked for your opinion on an accounting system for Dexter Distributors. Mr. Dexter has posed these questions:

1. Should he use a sales journal? Why or why not? If he should, what procedure should be used to record entries to it and get invoices mailed to customers as soon as possible after deliveries?
2. Does he need a purchases journal or could all purchases be recorded in the general journal? Explain.
3. Would a cash receipts journal be a good idea? (About 75–100 checks are received by mail per day). If so, what special columns should be included?
4. Is there any advantage to use of a cash payments journal? Explain your answer.

chapter nine

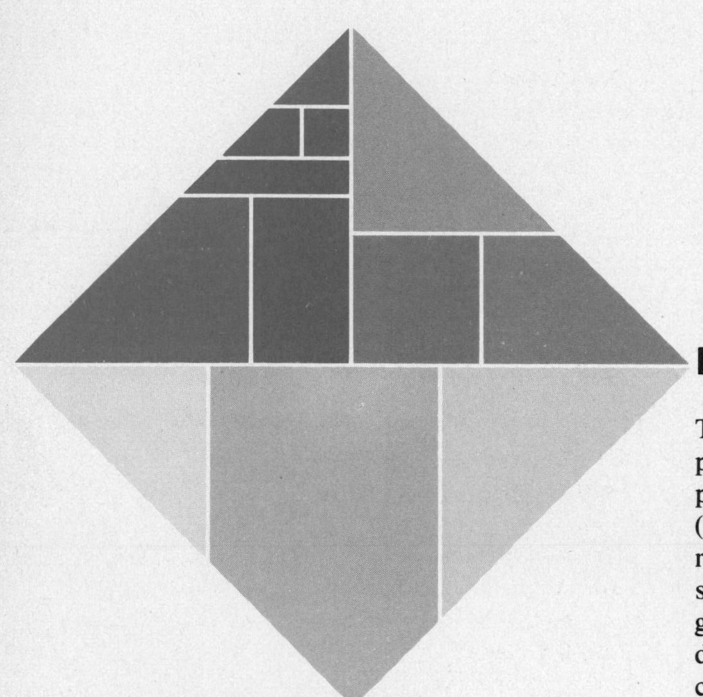

Introduction

This chapter describes the accounting for payrolls. It covers computation of gross pay, payroll deductions, and net pay (take-home pay). The recording and reporting of income taxes and social security taxes withheld from employees' gross pay is explained along with other deductions. Also discussed is the calculation, recording, and reporting of employers' social security tax and unemployment compensation taxes.

Payroll system

Learning goals

To identify and calculate the various payroll deductions and payroll taxes that apply to business.
To list major provisions of the Social Security Act.
To record a periodic payroll and the employer's payroll taxes.
To understand the requirements for reporting and remittance of payroll taxes.
To describe effective managerial control of payroll.

Key terms

FICA tax
federal income tax withholding
Federal Unemployment Tax Act
gross pay
internal control
net pay (take-home pay)
payroll deductions
Social Security Act
state unemployment compensation

Payroll deductions

It is highly unusual for an employee to receive *gross pay,* the full (gross) amount of his or her salary or wages. Amounts deducted from the pay check are illustrated in Figure 9–1. The amount remaining after deductions is *net pay.* The source and nature of these deductions will be discussed before proceeding to a discussion and illustrations of payroll accounting.

Deductions required by law that must be *withheld* by the employer from the employees' regular pay include the following:

1. Federal, state, and local income taxes of the employee
2. Old-Age, Survivors, and Disability Insurance (OASDI) and Hospitalization Insurance Tax (both often referred to as FICA for Federal Insurance Contributions Act, or the Social Security tax)
3. State unemployment tax (in some states).

Other deductions are optional with the employee, such as for the purchase of U.S. savings bonds or corporate stock; group life, accident, and hospitalization insurance; and savings clubs. Deductions may also be required under union agreements or to settle other claims. The deductions are paid to the federal and state governments and other designated agencies. Adequate records must be maintained to account for the deductions and their related liabilities and to prepare the required reports to the agencies involved.

Figure 9–1
Payroll check stub

PERIOD ENDING			HOURS	RATE	EMP. NO.	CURRENT EARNINGS			
MO.	DAY	YEAR				EARNINGS	N.C. W/H TAX	F.I.C.A.	FED. W/H TAX
8	31	79	-	-	153	2,000 00	107 08	121 00	357 70

OTHER DEDUCTIONS							
CONTRIBUTIONS	UNIFORM	CAMPAIGN	RETIREMENT	INSURANCE	UNITED FUND	MISCL.	TOTAL DEDUCT.
50 00	-	-	80 00	20 00	25 00	-	175 00

YEAR TO DATE EARNINGS					
GROSS	RETIREMENT	N.C. W/H	F.I.C.A.	FED. W/H	AMOUNT OF CHECK
16,000 00	640 00	856 64	968 00	2,861 60	1,239 22

NON NEGOTIABLE

Social Security Act and payroll deductions

The Social Security Act (approved on August 14, 1935) is a federal law creating a program that is operated in part by the states with assistance from the federal government. The act includes programs to provide benefits to retired workers, their families, and their survivors, as well as health insurance for the aged (Medicare).

Funds to finance these programs are provided by the tax and withholding provisions of the Federal Insurance Contributions Act (including the financing provisions for Medicare), and the tax under the Federal Unemployment Tax Act.

Federal Insurance Contributions Act

Under the Federal Insurance Contributions Act, both employers and employees contribute equally based on a stated percentage of taxable wages paid. The employee portion must be withheld by the employer from each payment of taxable wages until the currently designated amount of taxable wages has been reached. No further amounts are withheld during the remainder of that year. Each employer is required to continue to withhold the employees' share of the tax during each calendar year until the currently prevailing maximum amount has been withheld. An employee who works for more than one employer during the year may, as a result, pay more than the annual maximum. The excess may be recovered or offset against the income tax when the employee files the annual federal income tax return (Form 1040).

Federal medicare program

A federal medicare program was adopted in 1965 to provide hospital insurance for those 65 and over. Although this is a separate program of benefits, its funding is a part of the withholding provisions of the Federal Insurance Contributions Act. The FICA rate is a combined rate covering both OASDI and hospital insurance. Only one computation is made for the amount to be withheld.

Federal Unemployment Tax Act

Under the Federal Unemployment Tax Act a tax is levied on employers only. There is no withholding for this purpose. The current tax rate is applied to taxable wages until the wages reach the current taxable wage base. There is no further tax liability on the employer for wages paid beyond the maximum taxable base during the remainder of that year.

State unemployment compensation tax

All the states have laws requiring the payment of unemployment compensation taxes. The state unemployment compensation systems must be approved by and tied in to the federal unemployment system, which pays part of the administration costs of the state systems. Funds are provided by a payroll tax levy on the employer and, in several states, on both employer and employees. Unemployed persons who qualify for benefits are paid by a state agency from funds acquired through the tax.

State unemployment tax laws vary in their detail and application. There are maximum rates which may be reduced on a merit basis if the employer's annual contributions are sufficiently in excess of withdrawals for unemployment payments made to discharged employees. The merit-rating plan provides an incentive to employers to maintain steady employment. Employers who maintain a stable work force and whose employees experience relatively little unemployment will pay a lower rate than employers with a less favorable unemployment experience and unemployment expenditures. In Massachusetts, the range of rates (1976) was from a low of 3.9 percent to a high of 5.1 percent levied on employers only. Unemployed persons who met the eligibility requirement in regard to base period wages received compensation for 52 weeks up to a maximum of $101 weekly.

Federal income tax withholding

Employers must withhold from each employee's taxable earnings amounts required by the laws and regulations of the Internal Revenue Service. The amount that the employer is required to withhold (certain classes of wage payments are exempt) depends on the amount of earnings, the total number of exemptions claimed, and the frequency of the payroll period. Each new employee fills out an Employee's Withholding Allowance Certificate, Form W-4, (Figure 9–2) indicating the number of exemptions claimed. The employee files a new form when the number of exemptions changes. The employee may claim exemptions (1) for himself or herself, (2) for his or her spouse (unless the spouse is employed and claims his or her own exemption), and (3) for each qualified dependent. Additional exemptions may be claimed for old age (65 years or older) and blindness of the claimant or spouse. Some groups are exempt from the FICA withholding requirement, and some who are exempted from the federal income tax withholding requirements are subject to FICA tax withholding. Since tax rates are subject to change, persons responsible for payrolls should be acquainted with the latest tax rates and regulations, both federal and state and, in some cases, municipal. The Internal Revenue Service furnishes withholding tables (Figure 9–3) for different payroll periods in its *Circular E, Employer's Withholding Tax Guide*.

Other deductions

In some states, employees as well as employers are taxed under the state unemployment insurance programs. A number of states and some cities levy income taxes on the gross earnings of the employee. In some states, employees are taxed to provide funds for the cost of disability benefits. Such additional tax assessments are generally deducted from gross earnings by the employer and remitted to the designated agencies.

Form **W-4**
(Rev. May 1977)
Department of the Treasury
Internal Revenue Service

Employee's Withholding Allowance Certificate

(Use for Wages Paid After May 31, 1977)

This certificate is for income tax withholding purposes only. It will remain in effect until you change it. If you claim exemption from withholding, you will have to file a new certificate on or before April 30 of next year.

Type or print your full name	Your social security number
William H. Henry	123-45-6789

Home address (number and street or rural route)	Marital Status	☐ Single ☒ Married
50 Central Street		☐ Married, but withhold at higher Single rate
City or town, State, and ZIP code		**Note:** *If married, but legally separated, or spouse is a nonresident alien, check the single block.*
Boston, Massachusetts 02100		

1 Total number of allowances you are claiming	2
2 Additional amount, if any, you want deducted from each pay (if your employer agrees)	$
3 I claim exemption from withholding (see instructions). Enter "Exempt"	

Under the penalties of perjury, I certify that the number of withholding exemptions and allowances claimed on this certificate does not exceed the number to which I am entitled. If claiming exemption from withholding, I certify that I incurred no liability for Federal income tax for last year and that I anticipate that I will incur no liability for Federal income tax for this year.

Signature ▶ William H. Henry Date ▶ January 2, 19 79

Figure 9–2 Withholding allowance certificate

Wage bases and tax rates

The FICA and the FUTA wage bases and tax rates may be changed by Congress at any time. They have been increased steadily over the years. *To simplify the computations in all illustrations and problems in this textbook (except for illustrations of actual forms), the following assumed wage bases and tax rates are used* (the accounting principles and recording procedures are the same regardless of the rates used).

Figure 9–3 Wage bracket withholding table

MARRIED Persons — **WEEKLY** Payroll Period

And the wages are—		And the number of withholding allowances claimed is—										
At least	But less than	0	1	2	3	4	5	6	7	8	9	10 or more
		The amount of income tax to be withheld shall be—										
$440	$450	$85.00	$80.40	$76.40	$72.40	$68.30	$64.30	$60.30	$56.50	$52.90	$49.30	$45.70
450	460	88.20	83.60	79.20	75.20	71.10	67.10	63.10	59.00	55.40	51.80	48.20
460	470	91.40	86.80	82.20	78.00	73.90	69.90	65.90	61.80	57.90	54.30	50.70
470	480	94.60	90.00	85.40	80.80	76.70	72.70	68.70	64.60	60.60	56.80	53.20
480	490	97.80	93.20	88.60	84.00	79.50	75.50	71.50	67.40	63.40	59.30	55.70
490	500	101.00	96.40	91.80	87.20	82.60	78.30	74.30	70.20	66.20	62.10	58.20
500	510	104.20	99.60	95.00	90.40	85.80	81.10	77.10	73.00	69.00	64.90	60.90
510	520	107.70	102.80	98.20	93.60	89.00	84.30	79.90	75.80	71.80	67.70	63.70
520	530	111.30	106.10	101.40	96.80	92.20	87.50	82.90	78.60	74.60	70.50	66.50
530	540	114.90	109.70	104.60	100.00	95.40	90.70	86.10	81.50	77.40	73.30	69.30
540	550	118.50	113.30	108.10	103.20	98.60	93.90	89.30	84.70	80.20	76.10	72.10
550	560	122.10	116.90	111.70	106.50	101.80	97.10	92.50	87.90	83.30	78.90	74.90
560	570	125.70	120.50	115.30	110.10	105.00	100.30	95.70	91.10	86.50	81.90	77.70
570	580	129.30	124.10	118.90	113.70	108.50	103.50	98.90	94.30	89.70	85.10	80.50
580	590	132.90	127.70	122.50	117.30	112.10	106.90	102.10	97.50	92.90	88.30	83.70
590	600	136.50	131.30	126.10	120.90	115.70	110.50	105.30	100.70	96.10	91.50	86.90
600	610	140.10	134.90	129.70	124.50	119.30	114.10	108.90	103.90	99.30	94.70	90.10
610	620	143.70	138.50	133.30	128.10	122.90	117.70	112.50	107.30	102.50	97.90	93.30
[illegible]	[illegible]	147.30	142.10	136.90	131.70	126.50		116.10	110.90	105.70	101.10	

1. For FICA computations—a tax rate of 12 percent—6 percent each on employer and on employee—limited to a taxable wage base of $20,000 during a calendar year.
2. For FUTA computations—a tax rate on employers only of 5 percent limited to a taxable wage base of $10,000 with a maximum of 4 percent payable to the state and 1 percent payable to the federal government.

The taxable wage base is the same for all employees and applies to each employee. The amount of wages in any year subject to payroll taxes is limited to a taxable wage base. Therefore, earnings of those employees who have reached the taxable wage base for the current year will be excluded when calculating the employee and employer payroll tax liabilities.

Recording the payroll

Accurate payroll records are necessary to determine operating expenses and to report earnings information to employees and to federal, state, and other agencies. The records must show the names, earnings, and payroll deductions of all employees for each pay period (see Figure 9–4). An individual record for each employee showing his or her earnings and deductions must also be kept (Figure 9–5). A general journal entry is made to record the payroll for the pay period. Assume that the Burns Company payroll entry for the week ended January 27, 1979, was as follows:

			Debit	Credit
1979				
Jan.	27	Salesmen's Salaries Expense	1,018 00	
		Executive Salaries Expense	750 00	
		Office Salaries Expense	320 00	
		FICA Taxes Payable (assumed rate of 6%)		125 28
		Federal Income Tax Withholdings Payable		218 80
		Bond Deductions Payable		47 50
		Salaries and Wages Payable		1,696 42
		To record the payroll for the week ended January 27.		

Figure 9–4
Payroll register

PAYROLL REGISTER		BURNS COMPANY				
					Earnings	
Dept	Name of Employee	Rate or Salary	Total Hours Worked	Over-Time Hours	Regular	Overtime Premium
S	James B. Skinner	8.00	44.0	4.0	352 00	16 00
S	Paul Burke	8.00	42.0	2.0	336 00	8 00
S	John T. Howard	7.65	40.0	----	306 00	-- --
E	Richard E. Aldrich	750.00	40.0		750 00	-- --
O	William S. Ford	8.00	40.0	----	320 00	-- --
			206.0	6.0	2,064 00	24 00

YEARLY INDIVIDUAL COMPENSATION RECORD

Employee No. 141

FOR YEAR ENDING DECEMBER 1979

Soc. Sec. No. 103-05-7914

NAME William S. Ford

HOURS FULL WEEK

ADDRESS 50 Joy St., Boston, Mass. 02115

EARNINGS FULL WEEK $320.00

	TIME			EARNINGS RECORD					DEDUCTIONS					
					Other Compensation									
Period Ending	Days	Hrs	Rate	Salary or Wages	Detail	Amount	Total	Total To Date	S.S. Federal Old Age	Federal Income Tax	State Income Tax			Net Paid
FW'D														
	1/6	40.0	8.00	320 00			320. 00		19.20	47.00				253.80
	1/13	40.0	8.00	320 00			320. 00		19.20	47.00				253.80
	1/20	40.0	8.00	320 00			320. 00		19.20	47.00				253.80
	1/27	40.0	8.00	320 00			320. 00		19.20	47.00				253.80
Jan. Total		1600		1,280 00			1,280 00		76.80	188.00				1,015.20

Figure 9–5 Individual earnings record

The debits are to a selling expense account for $1,018 and to two general and administrative expense accounts for $1,070 or a total payroll of $2,088 of which the employees' take-home pay is $1,696.42 (Figure 9–4). The credits are to the accounts representing liabilities for the required amounts withheld by the employer for the employees' share of FICA taxes, employee federal income taxes, and the liability for employee optional U.S. bonds purchased.

Recording the employer's payroll tax expense

The employer's payroll tax expense may be recorded at the end of each payroll period or at the end of each month. Assume that the Burns Company records the

Week Ending 1/27/79

	Deductions						
Total	FICA	Federal w/h Tax	Savings Bonds	Other Deds.	Total	Net Pay	Check Number
368 00	22 08	42 60	7 50		72 18	295 82	141
344 00	20 64	38 10			58 74	285 26	142
306 00	18 36	30 10	10 00		58 46	247 54	143
750 00	45 00	61 00	30 00		136 00	614 00	144
320 00	19 20	47 00	—— ——		66 20	253 80	145
2,088 00	125 28	218 80	47 50	----	391 58	1,696 42	

payroll tax expense for each payroll and that, because of its merit-rating record, it is subject to a state unemployment tax rate of only 2 percent (reduced for merit from assumed 4 percent maximum). The general journal entry to record the payroll tax expense and the payroll tax liability for the week ended January 27 is:

1979						
Jan.	27	Payroll Tax Expense		187 92		
		FICA Taxes Payable				125 28
		State Unemployment Taxes Payable .				41 76
		Federal Unemployment Taxes Payable				20 88
		To record payroll taxes for week ended January 27.*				
		27 computed as follows:				
		*FICA tax ($2,088 x 0.06)	$125.28			
		State unemployment compensation tax ($2,088 x 0.02)	41.76			
		Federal unemployment compensation tax ($2,088 x 0.01)	20.88			
		Total	$187.92			

The debit is to the Payroll Tax Expense account; the three credits are the liabilities to the federal and state agencies. The liability for FICA taxes ($125.28) matches the amount deducted from the employee's wages. It is assumed that all the earnings were subject to payroll taxes. Earnings of any employee in excess of current maximums are not subject to payroll taxes for the remainder of the year. Assume, for example, that the Burns Company payroll for the week ended October 27 was $3,050, including $1,200 of nontaxable FICA earnings and $2,000 of nontaxable unemployment compensation earnings. The payroll tax liability is computed as follows:

	FICA Tax	Unemployment Taxes
Total payroll	$3,050.00	$3,050.00
Payroll (in excess of maximum) not subject to FICA tax	(1,200.00)	
Payroll (in excess of maximum) not subject to unemployment taxes		(2,000.00)
Payroll subject to taxes	$1,850.00	$1,050.00

Payroll taxes	
FICA tax ($1,850 x 0.06)	$111.00
State unemployment compensation tax ($1,050 x 0.02)	21.00
Federal unemployment compensation tax ($1,050 x 0.01)	10.50
Total tax liability	$142.50

The entry to record the employer's payroll taxes is:

1979				
Oct.	27	Payroll Tax Expense	142 50	
		FICA Taxes Payable		111 00
		State Unemployment Taxes Payable .		21 00
		Federal Unemployment Taxes Payable		10 50
		To record payroll taxes for week ended October 27.		

Figure 9–6 Employer's quarterly federal tax return*

Form 941 (Rev. Jan. 1977) Department of the Treasury Internal Revenue Service

Employer's Quarterly Federal Tax Return

Schedule A—Quarterly Report of Wages Taxable under the Federal Insurance Contributions Act—FOR SOCIAL SECURITY

List for each nonagricultural employee the WAGES taxable under the FICA which were paid during the quarter. If you pay an employee more than $16,500 in a calendar year, report only the first $16,500 of such wages. In the case of "Tip Income," see instructions on page 4. IF WAGES WERE NOT TAXABLE UNDER THE FICA, MAKE NO ENTRIES IN ITEMS 1 THROUGH 9 AND 14 THROUGH 18.

SSA Use Only

F ☐ 2 ☐ U ☐ E ☐
S ☐ 1 ☐ L ☐ T ☐
X ☐ 0 ☐ V ☐ A ☐

1. Total pages of this return including this page and any pages of Form 941a ▶ 1
2. Total number of employees listed ▶ 3
3. (First quarter only) Number of employees (except household) employed in the pay period including March 12th ▶ 3

4. EMPLOYEE'S SOCIAL SECURITY NUMBER 000 00 0000	5. NAME OF EMPLOYEE (Please type or print)	6. TAXABLE FICA WAGES Paid to Employee in Quarter (Before Deductions) Dollars Cents	7. TAXABLE TIPS REPORTED (See page 4) Dollars Cents

If you need more space for listing employees, use Schedule A continuation sheets, Form 941a.

Totals for this page—Wage total in column 6 and tip total in column 7 ⟶

8. TOTAL WAGES TAXABLE UNDER FICA PAID DURING QUARTER. $ 4,000.00
(Total of column 6 on this page and continuation sheets.) Enter here and in item 14 below.

9. TOTAL TAXABLE TIPS REPORTED UNDER FICA DURING QUARTER. $ 273.00
(Total of column 7 on this page and continuation sheets.) Enter here and in item 15 below. (If no tips reported, write "None.")

T	FP
FF	I
FD	TOT

Item	Dollars	Cents
10. Total Wages And Tips Subject to Withholding Plus Other Compensation ⟶	4,273	00
11. Total Income Tax Withheld From Wages, Tips, Annuities, Gambling, etc. (See instructions)	435	85
12. Adjustment For Preceding Quarters Of Calendar Year		
13. Adjusted Total Of Income Tax Withheld ⟶	435	85
14. Taxable FICA Wages Paid (Item 8) . . $ 4,000.00 multiplied by 11.7% = TAX	468	00
15. Taxable Tips Reported (Item 9) . . $ 273.00 multiplied by 5.85% = TAX	15	97
16. Total FICA Taxes (Item 14 plus Item 15) ⟶	483	97
17. Adjustment (See instructions)		
18. Adjusted Total Of FICA Taxes ⟶	483	97
19. Total Taxes (Item 13 plus Item 18)	919	82
20. TOTAL DEPOSITS FOR QUARTER (INCLUDING FINAL DEPOSIT MADE FOR QUARTER) AND OVERPAYMENT FROM PREVIOUS QUARTER LISTED IN SCHEDULE B (See instructions on page 4)	919	82
Note: If undeposited taxes at the end of the quarter are $200 or more, the full amount must be deposited with an authorized commercial bank or a Federal Reserve bank in accordance with instructions on the reverse of the Federal tax deposit form. This deposit must be entered in Schedule B and included in item 20.		
21. Undeposited Taxes Due (Item 19 Less Item 20—This Should Be Less Than $200). Pay To Internal Revenue Service And Enter Here ⟶	-0-	

EE and ER rate.

22. If Item 20 is More Than Item 19, Enter Excess Here ▶ $ And Check If You Want It ☐ Applied to Next Return, Or ☐ Refunded.

23. If not liable for returns in the future, write "FINAL" (See instructions) ▶ Date final wages paid ▶

Under penalties of perjury, I declare that I have examined this return, including accompanying schedules and statements, and to the best of my knowledge and belief it is true, correct, and complete.

Date 4/29/79 Signature John J. Jones Title (Owner, etc.) OWNER

218-245-1

* For tax periods beginning after December 31, 1977, a new Form 941 (Employer's Quarterly Federal Tax Return) should be used. This form was not available when this book was printed.

Reporting and payment of payroll taxes

The report forms and the payment schedules for the amounts withheld from employees' earnings and the employer's payroll taxes are explained in *Circular E, Employer's Withholding Tax Guide* published by the Internal Revenue Service. Employers who owe less than \$200 during a calendar quarter pay the amount due directly to the IRS at the time of filing their quarterly tax return. If the amount due is \$200 or more but less than \$2,000 a month, the employer must deposit the amounts due with an authorized depositary (usually a commercial bank) on or before the 15th day of the following month. If the amount due is over \$2,000 in a quarter-monthly period, the employer must pay the amounts due within 3 banking days after the end of the quarter-monthly period (the 7th, 15th, 22nd, and last day of any month).

On or before the last day of the month following the close of each quarter, the employer files a quarterly tax return (Figure 9–6) on which he reports the federal income taxes withheld and the amounts due on the taxable wages paid during the quarter.

Annually the employer must furnish a form W-2 (Figure 9–7) to each employee. The form shows, among other items, the amount of taxable wages paid the employee during the year, the amount of federal income taxes withheld, the amount of FICA taxes withheld, and the amount of state income taxes withheld (if applicable).

Deposits of federal unemployment taxes are required on or before the last day of the month following the close of the calendar quarter if the liability for the current quarter (and prior quarters during the year) is over \$100. Otherwise, the amount due is sent directly to the IRS with the annual FUTA return on Form 940 (Figure 9–8) due on or before January 31 of the following year.

Figure 9–7
Wage and tax statement

For Official Use Only

Wage and Tax Statement 1977

John Jones
50 Main Street
Boston, Massachusetts 02100
04-0000000

Type or print EMPLOYER'S name, address, ZIP code and Federal identifying number.

Copy A
For Internal Revenue Service Center

21 ☐

Employee's social security number	1 Federal income tax withheld	2 Wages, tips, and other compensation	3 FICA employee tax withheld	4 Total FICA wages
123-45-6789	524.00	6,000.00	351.00	6,000.00

Type or print Employee's name, address, and ZIP code below. (Name must aline with arrow)

5 Was employee covered by a qualified pension plan, etc.?	6 *	7 *
No		

Name ▶ William H. Henry
50 Central Street
Boston, Massachusetts 02100

* See instructions on back of Copy D.

Form **W–2** See instructions on Form W–3 and back of Copy D. Department of the Treasury—Internal Revenue Service

Form **940**
Department of the Treasury
Internal Revenue Service

Employer's Annual Federal Unemployment Tax Return

Name of State 1	State reporting number as shown on employer's State contribution returns 2	Taxable payroll (As defined in State act) 3	Experience rate period 4 From—	To—	Experience rate 5	Contributions had rate been 2.7% (col. 3 × 2.7%) 6	Contributions payable at experience rate (col. 3 × col. 5) 7	Additional credit (col. 6 minus col. 7) 8	Contributions actually paid to State 9
Mass.	704-00000	12,600.00	1/1/76	12/31/77	4.0	340.20	504.00	-0-	504.00
	Totals ▶	12,600.00						-0-	504.00

Line	Description	Approximate number of employees involved	Amount paid	
10	Total tentative credit (Column 8 plus column 9)			504 00
11	Total remuneration (including exempt remuneration) PAID during the calendar year for services of employees			18,705 00
	Exempt Remuneration			
12	Exempt remuneration. (Explain each exemption shown, attaching additional sheet if necessary):			
13	Remuneration in excess of $4,200. (Enter only the excess over the first $4,200 paid to individual employees exclusive of exempt amounts entered on line 12)	3	6,105.00	
14	Total exempt remuneration (line 12 plus line 13)			6,105 00
15	Total taxable wages (line 11 less line 14)			12,600 00
16	Gross Federal tax (3.2% of line 15)			403 20
17	Enter 2.7% of the amount of wages shown on line 15		340.20	
18	Line 10 or line 17 whichever is smaller		340.20	
19	Amount, if any, of wages on line 15 attributable to the following States:			
	(a) Vermont $ ______ × .003			
	(b) Washington $ ______ × .003			
	(c) Total (add lines 19(a) and (b))			
20	Credit allowable (line 18 less line 19(c))			340 20
21	Net Federal tax (line 16 less line 20)			63 00

Record of Federal Tax Deposits for Unemployment Tax (Form 508)

Quarter	Liability by period	Date of deposit	Amount of deposit
First			
Second			
Third			
Fourth			

22	Total Federal tax deposited	-0-
23	Balance due (line 21 less line 22—this should not exceed $100). Pay to "Internal Revenue Service" ▶	63 00
24	If no longer in business at end of year, write "FINAL" here ▶	

Under penalties of perjury, I declare that I have examined this return, including accompanying schedules and statements, and to the best of my knowledge and belief it is true, correct, and complete, and that no part of any payment made to a State unemployment fund, which is claimed as a credit on line 20 above, was or is to be deducted from the remuneration of employees.

Date ▶ 1/31/79 Signature ▶ John J. Jones Title (Owner, etc.) ▶ Owner

Figure 9–8 Employer's annual federal unemployment tax return

Accrual of salaries and wages

If the end of the payroll period does not coincide with the end of the accounting period, an adjusting entry is made for salaries and wages earned but not paid. The several salary and expense accounts are debited and Accrued Salaries and Wages Payable is credited. The employer's payroll tax expense on the accrued payroll for the partial pay period should be recognized although there is no legal liability for the tax until the wages are actually paid. An employer is liable for payroll taxes in the calendar year in which the payment for services was made. The time of payment, rather than the time the services were performed, establishes the legal existence of the liability.

Fair Labor Standards Act

The Fair Labor Standards Act, popularly known as the Federal Wage and Hour Law, establishes federal minimum wages, requires overtime pay, and regulates child labor. The law relates to those employed in interstate commerce and in the production of goods for interstate commerce. It currently requires that workers not specifically exempted be paid a minimum hourly rate and an overtime wage of *time and one-half,* or one and one-half times the hourly rate, for time worked over 40 hours a week. If no more than 40 hours are worked in a week, no overtime compensation need be paid regardless of the number of hours worked in any one day. Employers and employees may, of course, agree to more favorable terms, such as time and one-half for all work over eight hours in any day and double time for Sunday or holiday work. The act does not place a limitation on total working time; it fixes the 40-hour work week as the basis for overtime pay.

Managerial control of payroll

The payroll of a firm is a significant part of total expense, making continuous management control essential. The availability of machines and high-speed electronic equipment has facilitated the processing of payroll data and the establishment of effective controls at a reasonable cost. But the use of an electronic data-processing system for the payroll does not lessen the need for built-in self-policing control devices and procedures as part of the payroll system. Computer programs and data-processing systems can be manipulated to defraud the firm.

Effective managerial control of payroll requires that:

1. Management has properly authorized the payroll payment.
2. Wages paid be correct and have been received by authorized employees; that is, for example, that no fictitious names or names of persons no longer employed have been listed on the payroll.
3. The numerous reports based on payroll information that are made to governmental agencies, union organizations, and employees be reliable.

Glossary

FICA Tax A tax levied on employees and employers to help finance the Federal Insurance Contributions Act provisions of the Social Security program.

Federal income tax withholding An amount deducted from gross pay by employer and remitted to Internal Revenue Service.

Fair Labor Standards Act The Federal Wage and Hour Law that fixes minimum hourly and overtime rates for workers in industries engaged directly in the production of goods for interstate commerce.

Federal Unemployment Compensation Tax A tax levied on the employer at a specified rate up to a limited amount of wages paid.

Gross pay Total wages before any deductions; this amount is the Salaries and Wages Expense.

Internal control A built-in system of self-policing for the effective control and safeguarding of cash and other assets.

Net pay Wages after all deductions; this is referred to as take-home pay.

Payroll deductions Amounts withheld from gross pay by the employer; these include federal and state taxes, union dues, and savings bonds.

Social Security Act A federal law that includes programs to provide benefits to retired workers, their families, and their survivors, financed by taxes on wages at rates and base levels revised from time to time by Congress.

Questions

Q9–1 (a) What are three common payroll taxes levied on an employer? (b) What is the rate of each tax? (c) When and in what manner does the employer pay the tax?

Q9–2 (a) What classes of employees are subject to the federal unemployment compensation tax? (b) What is the tax rate? (c) When is a federal unemployment tax liability incurred? (d) When is the liability paid to the proper government agency?

Q9–3 (a) What is a state unemployment merit-rating plan? (b) Why are merit ratings assigned by the several states? (c) What are the maximum state unemployment tax rates? (d) How was the maximum rate initially established in the Federal Unemployment Tax Act? (e) When does the employer become subject to a state unemployment tax liability? (f) When and to whom is the liability paid?

Q9–4 (a) What two types of federal taxes are most employers required to withhold from their employees' wages? (b) When do taxes withheld become liabilities to the employer? (c) When and in what manner is the employer required to pay to the responsible federal agency the amounts withheld?

Q9–5 What are some requirements of effective managerial control of payroll?

Q9–6 What deductions are required by law? What are some other deductions that may be withheld by the employer?

Q9–7 Who fixes the FICA tax rate and the maximum earnings base?

Q9–8 What are the requirements for recognizing salaries and wages earned but not paid at the end of the accounting period?

Class exercises

Note: Unless indicated otherwise, the following rates and amounts are to be used in solving the payroll exercises and problems in this chapter:

a. *FICA tax:* 6 percent each on employer and employee, applicable to the first $20,000 paid to an employee during a calendar year.
b. *Federal unemployment compensation tax:* A maximum of 5 percent on the first $10,000 paid to each covered employee during each calendar year, with 4 percent payable to the state and 1 percent to the federal government.

CE9–1 (Payroll register) The partially completed payroll register of Leeds Company for the week ended December 15 is given below.

PAYROLL REGISTER

	Earnings		Deductions			Distribution		
Name	*Week Ending December 15*	*Cumulative Through December 8*	*FICA Tax*	*Federal Income Tax*	*Net Amount*	*Salesmen's Salaries*	*Executive Salaries*	*Office Salaries*
Cates, John	425	19,800		75.50		425		
Hill, Maxine	220	11,000		30.00		220		
Pyle, Herbert	400	14,950		75.00			400	
Soames, Leo	180	4,995		21.60				180
Totals								

Required:

1. Prepare a payroll register similar to the one shown, filling in all the blank columns.
2. Record the Leeds Company's payroll for the week in general journal form.
3. Record the Leeds Company's payroll tax expense in general journal form.

CE9–2 (Payroll tax expense calculations) Each of the ten employees of the Clover Company earned more than $10,000 during the calendar year 1979. (a) What was the state unemployment tax expense for 1979? (b) Compute the tax expense based on a tax reduced by a merit rating to 0.5 percent. (c) Compute the federal unemployment tax expense for 1979.

CE9–3 (Payroll tax liability) The following information is obtained from the payroll records of the Helen Yanow Company for the week ended July 7:

Total earnings	$3,600
Earnings subject to unemployment compensation tax	1,250
Earnings subject to FICA tax	3,000
Deductions	
FICA tax	180
Federal income tax	540
Accounts receivable	100

Required: Record (a) the payroll and (b) the employer's payroll tax expense.

Exercises and problems

P9–1 The payroll records of the Wyatt Company for the week ended February 24 showed the following:

Total wages earned		$5,500
Deductions		
FICA tax	$330	
Federal income tax	825	
Accounts receivable	100	1,255
Net amount paid		$4,245

Required: Record in general journal form: (a) total payroll, (b) payment of the payroll, (c) employer's payroll tax expense. Indicate the journal in which each entry would be properly reported. No employee has earned $10,000 in the year to date.

P9–2 The following payroll data for the year 1979 were taken from the records of the Krest Company:

Total wages expense	$85,000
Amount of wages to employees with earnings in excess of $10,000	35,000
Amount of wages to employees with earnings in excess of $20,000	20,000

Required: Calculate the employer's payroll tax expense for the year.

P9–3 The Lux Company had 15 employees who worked during an entire calendar year. One of them, Peter Webb, earned $21,000. What was the total expenditure for Webb's services for the year?

P9–4 M. Seth pays his five employees weekly. The payroll summary for the week ended January 13 follows:

Total earnings		$2,100
Deductions		
FICA tax	$126	
Federal income tax	460	
Union dues	30	
Total deductions		616
Net amount paid		$1,484

Required: Journalize (a) the recording of the payroll and (b) the employer's payroll tax expense.

P9–5 The Rock Company pays its salespeople monthly. On November 30, 1979, the following information was available:

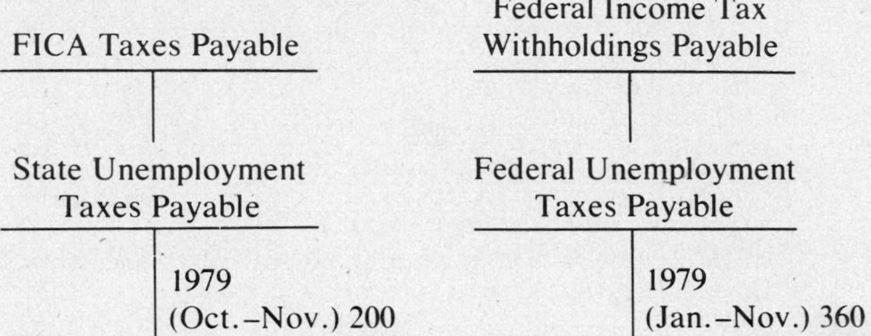

The December payroll was:

Total earnings		$14,250
Deductions		
FICA taxes	$ 450	
Federal income taxes	1,650	2,100
Net amount due		$12,150

Required: Copy the T accounts with the November 30 balances and enter the following:

1. The December payroll.
2. The December employer's payroll tax expense. The taxable portion of the December payroll for state and federal unemployment taxes is $3,000.
3. Checks and appropriate report forms mailed on January 31, 1980, as follows:
   a. To the Internal Revenue Service: a check for December and depositary receipts for October and November.
   b. To the Internal Revenue Service: a check for the federal unemployment tax liability for 1979.
   c. To the State Division of Employment Security: a check for the state unemployment tax liability for the fourth quarter of 1979.

P9–6 The following payroll information was taken from the records of the Haynes Company for the weekly pay period ending December 22, 1979.

	John Cole	*Stella Dole*	*Frank Slowe*	*Tom Yates*
Hours worked:				
Total hours	44	40	42	40
Overtime hours	4	0	2	0
Basic hourly rate	$10.00	$8.00	$7.50	$8.25
Income tax exemptions/ withholdings	4	$47.60	$47.60	$47.40
Medical insurance	$8.00	$8.00	$6.00	$6.00
Union dues	$3.00	$3.00	$2.50	$2.50
U.S. Savings Bonds deduction	$15.00	- - -	$9.00	- - -
Cumulative earnings through week ending 12/15/79	$19,800.00	$9,950.00	$7,650.00	$7,400.00

Required:

1. Prepare the payroll register for the Haynes Company for the week. For this purpose, refer to Figures 9–3 and 9–4. All employees are married.
2. Record the payroll for the week in general journal form using the payroll register totals. John Cole is the general manager; Stella Dole works in the office; Slowe and Yates are salesmen.
3. Record the Haynes Company payroll tax expense in general journal form. The Company is subject to the Fair Labor Standards Act.

P9–7 (Integrative) The following information regarding the payroll of the Brewster Company for the week ended July 21, 1979, is given:

Employee	*Type of Work*	*Cumulative Gross Wages to July 14*	*Gross Wages for Week Ended July 21*	*Federal Income Taxes Withheld*	*State Income Taxes Withheld*	*Group Life Insurance Premiums Withheld*
John Frank	Salesman	$14,800	$400	$55	$12	$15
James Toy	Salesman	8,500	350	33	8	8
Mary Cinque	Office Clerk	3,200	150	15	3	8
Paul Mayor	Office Clerk	4,900	150	25	7	10

Required:

1. Prepare a journal entry on July 21, 1979, to record and classify the payroll expense.
2. Prepare a journal entry on July 21, 1979, to record the employer's payroll taxes.
3. Prepare a journal entry on July 24, 1979, to record the payment of the payroll.

P9–8 (Minicase) As a product of its payroll system, the Xton Company receives a weekly report of year-to-date hours worked and year-to-date total labor cost subdivided by department.

Required: Describe some possible uses of this report (including other reports to be used at the same time):

1. by the plant superintendent
2. by the foremen of production departments
3. by the accounting department.

chapter ten

Introduction

This chapter is about the management and control of cash and about a system of internal control—the voucher system. The chapter examines the concepts of internal control, the operation of a petty cash fund, the use of a checking account, and the procedures for the monthly bank reconciliation. The discussion of the voucher system includes the design and use of the voucher, the voucher register, and the check register to control cash payments made by a business.

Cash and voucher system

Learning goals

To know the concepts of internal control.
To record entries using an imprest petty cash system.
To prepare a bank reconciliation.
To understand the use of vouchers to achieve internal control of disbursements.
To record transactions in the voucher register and the check register.
To know whether to post individual transaction entries or column totals from the voucher register to ledger accounts.
To describe the relationship between the voucher files and the voucher register.

Key terms

Bank reconciliation
Bank statement
Certified check
Deposits in transit
Internal control
NSF check
Outstanding checks
Petty cash
Voucher
Voucher register
Voucher system

Cash includes any item that a bank customarily accepts for deposit. Coins, *currency* (paper money), bank drafts, cashier's checks, money orders, and bank balances are included in the Cash account. Postdated checks and IOUs are receivables, not cash; postage stamps are prepaid expenses.

Effective management and control of cash is of the greatest importance to a firm, because cash represents instantly available purchasing power and because nearly every transaction ultimately involves the exchange of cash. The problems of good cash management are twofold: (1) a proper cash balance must be maintained at all times and (2) adequate safeguards must be established to prevent theft or misappropriation.

This chapter is about the management and control of cash and about a system of internal control—the voucher system. The chapter examines the concepts of internal control, the operation of a petty cash fund, the use of a checking account, and the procedures for the monthly bank reconciliation. The discussion of the voucher system includes the design and use of the voucher, the voucher register, and the check register to control cash payments made by a business.

Internal control

One of the primary functions of management is to protect the assets of a business against avoidable loss. As a business grows in size and complexity, it becomes increasingly important to organize the supervision of the bookkeeping and accounting records in a way that will (1) control the receipt of cash, (2) minimize or prevent the unauthorized payment of cash, and (3) eliminate errors. Employees must be carefully selected and trained and their duties, responsibilities, and authority clearly defined. Adequate organization also requires separation of duties, so that no one person is in complete charge of any business transaction. An error—whether intentional or not—is more likely to be discovered if a transaction is handled by two or more persons, so that, as far as possible, the work of each employee who records property is checked automatically by some other employee. It is customary business practice, for example, for one person to make the sale and prepare a sales slip and for another person to receive the cash or record the charge to the customer's account; one person may prepare the payroll and another person make the actual payments to employees; one employee may prepare the check for payment to a creditor, another employee or an officer may sign the check, and a third employee may post the debit to the creditor's account. Adequate organization also provides for periodic inspections to see how well the accounting work is being done. The system of self-policing is referred to as *internal control*. The reliability of the financial statements depends on the adequacy of the internal controls. Consequently, the independent auditor whose task is to render his or her opinion on the fairness of the statements must first evaluate the adequacy of the internal controls. Based on this evaluation, the auditor determines the nature and extent of the audit procedures.

Cash control

Cash is naturally vulnerable to theft or misuse. If cash is handled and controlled properly, both the employer and the employee benefit—the employer safeguards the asset and the employee avoids suspicion of inaccuracy or dishonesty. Embezzlers often begin their criminal careers by temporarily borrowing funds from the company, intending to replace the cash. The intention usually falters. It is to the advantage of both employer and employee to institute such safeguards as will deter employees from misappropriating funds. The safeguards must be designed to prevent the following:

1. Theft of cash receipts covered by failure to record the transaction in the cash receipts journal. For example, scrap and waste material may be sold by an employee for cash and not reported.
2. Delay in recording the receipt of cash (the cash being withheld during the interval), or recording false entries. For example, cash may be pocketed on receipt of a payment from a customer and his or her account credited. The debit, however, may be made to an account such as Sales Returns and Allowances.
3. The recording of false debits to expense accounts or other accounts to cover fraudulent cash withdrawals. For example, a branch supervisor may carry a terminated employee's name on the payroll for several additional pay periods, forging the endorsement of the former employee on payroll checks that continue to be issued.

Certain basic controls must be instituted to prevent the misuse of funds. The individual responsibility for each step in the flow of cash must be clearly established. An entry to record the receipt of cash must be made promptly. On receipt, all checks should be endorsed and rubber-stamped *For deposit only* to prevent their misuse. All cash receipts should be deposited intact daily; payments should be made by company check and not out of cash receipts. Automated accounting control devices should be used wherever possible.

The protection of cash against losses through fraud, error, and carelessness requires certain fundamental steps, including:

1. Clear segregation of duties and responsibilities.
2. Provision of the necessary facilities, such as cash registers.
3. Definite written instructions concerning authorization for and payment of cash.
4. Organization of the flow and recording of documents so that, whenever possible, the work of one employee is subject to automatic verification by another. The handling of cash should be separated from the record keeping so that no one person both receives or disburses cash and records it in the cash journals.
5. Periodic testing to see if internal controls are operating effectively. For example, at unannounced times, recorded cash receipts should be compared with cash on hand and deposits that have been made.

Petty cash For adequate internal control, total cash receipts should be deposited intact daily and all disbursements should be made by check. There are occasions, however, when payment by check is impractical, such as for postage, small contributions, express charges, carfare, and minor supplies. A special fund, called the *petty cash fund,* should be set up for these purposes. The fund is placed in charge of one person, and each payment should be supported by a signed receipt, called a *petty cash voucher,* that shows the purpose of the expenditure, the date, and the amount (Figure 10–1).

To set up the petty cash fund, a check is drawn to the order of the fund custodian and cashed by the custodian for the amount to be placed in the fund. The journal entry is:

1979						
Aug.	2	Petty Cash	50	00		
		Cash			50	00
		Established petty cash fund.				

Safekeeping of the money and the signed vouchers is the responsibility of the custodian, who should be provided with a secure petty cash box or cash register.

When the cash in the fund approaches a stated minimum, or at the end of each month, the fund is replenished; the signed petty cash vouchers serve as evidence of the disbursements. A typical entry[1] to record a check for $43.00 issued to replenish the petty cash fund for certain expenditures made is:

1979						
Aug.	31	Postage Expense	12	00		
		Telephone and Telegraph Expense . .	4	00		
		Miscellaneous Selling Expense . . .	14	50		
		Miscellaneous General Expense . . .	3	75		
		Transportation In	8	25		
		Cash Over and Short		50		
		Cash			43	00
		Replenished petty cash fund.				

The Petty Cash account in the general ledger remains at its original balance of $50. It is for this reason that the method described here is called the *imprest* (or fixed) petty cash system. The balance of the account remains unchanged unless the amount of the fund itself is either increased or decreased. The entry to increase the amount of the fund is a debit to Petty Cash and a credit to Cash. The fund should be replenished at the end of each accounting period, even when it is above its stated minimum cash balance, to record all the expenses incurred during the period and to bring the amount of currency and coins on hand in the fund up to the balance of the Petty Cash account in the general ledger.

Cash over and short In the foregoing illustration, a cash shortage of fifty cents was found when the petty cash fund was replenished. The daily count of cash in the cash registers may differ from the cash register readings. If the

1 Although shown in general journal form to illustrate ideas presented here, these entries would usually be made in the cash payments journal.

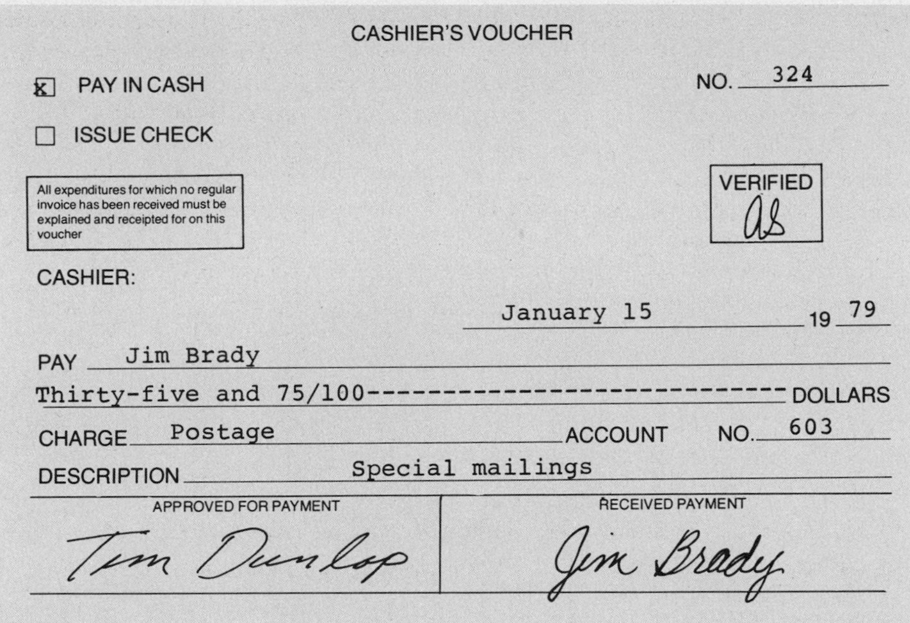
CASHIER'S VOUCHER

[x] PAY IN CASH

[ ] ISSUE CHECK

NO. 324

All expenditures for which no regular invoice has been received must be explained and receipted for on this voucher

VERIFIED
AS

CASHIER:

January 15 19 79

PAY Jim Brady

Thirty-five and 75/100-------------------------------- DOLLARS

CHARGE Postage ACCOUNT NO. 603

DESCRIPTION Special mailings

APPROVED FOR PAYMENT Tim Dunlop

RECEIVED PAYMENT Jim Brady

Figure 10–1
Petty cash voucher

records do not disclose a clerical error, it may be assumed that the overage or the shortage was caused by an error in making change. The discrepancy may be entered in the books as a debit or a credit to Cash Over and Short. To illustrate, assume that the cash register tape shows cash sales for the day of $100 but the count shows the cash on hand to be $101.50. The journal entry[2] to record the cash sales and the cash overage is:

Date		Account	Debit		Credit	
1979						
Nov.	30	Cash	101	50		
		Sales			100	00
		Cash Over and Short			1	50
		To record cash sales and cash overage.				

If the cash count showed $98.50, the entry would be:

Date		Account	Debit		Credit	
1979						
Nov.	30	Cash	98	50		
		Cash Over and Short	1	50		
		Sales			100	00
		To record cash sales and cash shortage.				

Cash Over and Short is classified on the income statement as general expense if a debit or other revenue if a credit.

2 This entry would be made in the cash receipts journal; general journal form is used to simplify this illustration.

Overages and shortages considered unreasonable should be investigated. Unannounced inspections should be held at intervals to determine that the amount of cash in the petty cash fund plus receipted vouchers is equal to the fund amount.

The bank statement

Most major payments are made by check. A check is a written order directing a bank to pay a specified amount of money to the order of a payee. A carbon copy of the check communicates the payment information to the accounting department for recording. Figure 10–2 shows a check and check stub.

It is customary for banks to send depositors a monthly statement together with the cancelled checks and notices of bank charges and credits. The statement shows the activities for the month; it should list:

1. Beginning balance
2. Deposits received
3. Checks paid
4. Other charges and credits to the account
5. Ending balance.

Frederick Hall's bank statement for September, 1979, is shown in Figure 10–3.

The letter combinations listed in the lower section of the bank statement form identify certain entries on the statement.

Certified check (CC) When the depositor requests a check to be certified, the bank immediately deducts the amount of the check from the depositor's balance. This procedure assures the payee that the check will be paid upon presentation.

Figure 10–2
Check and check stub

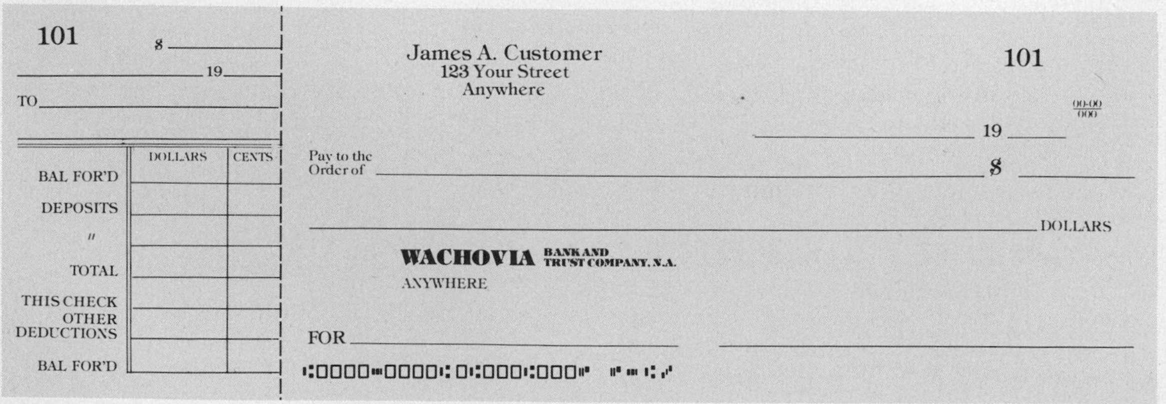

Source: Wachovia Bank and Trust Company, N.A.

Figure 10-3
Bank statement

STATEMENT OF ACCOUNT
WITH
UNITED STATES TRUST COMPANY
BOSTON, MASS.
Acct. No. 037-325079

Frederick Hall
14 Billings Street
Boston, Mass. 02115

Checks and Other Debits			Deposits	Date	Balance
Balance forward from last statement.				Sep. 1, 1979	7,320.00
			450.00	Sep. 3	7,770.00
49.00	1,237.00			Sep. 4	6,484.00
			48.00	Sep. 5	6,532.00
175.00	1,300.00 CC			Sep. 7	5,057.00
14.00			1,650.00	Sep. 11	6,693.00
			762.00	Sep. 15	7.455.00
28.50	27.25	275.00	1,312.00	Sep. 18	8,436.25
2,000.00	367.00	2.00 DM	500.00 CM	Sep. 27	6,567.25
4.00 SC				Sep. 28	6,563.25

CC—Certified Check
NSF—Not Sufficient Funds
SC—Service Charge
DM—Debit Memo
CM—Credit Memo
OD—Overdraft

Not sufficient funds (NSF) Deposits generally include checks received from trade customers. A customer's check that has been deposited may not clear on presentation for payment because the customer's bank balance is less than the amount of the check. If so, the check is charged back against the depositor's balance, the entry is identified by the letters NSF, and the check is returned to the depositor. The legal authority for this deduction is that credit to the depositor's account for checks deposited is conditional on their being honored on presentation.

Service charge (SC) A service charge is a charge by the bank for acting as a depository for funds. The charge is based on the amount of activity of the account in terms of number of items deposited and checks presented for payment.

Debit memo (DM) A debit memo is a deduction from the depositor's account for additional services rendered (or an adjustment of an error); for example, the charge for collecting a note receivable is reported in a debit memo. In effect, the bank's liability to the depositor for the amount on deposit is reduced by the amount of the debit memo.

Credit memo (CM) A credit memo is a credit, usually shown in the Deposits column, for items collected (or an adjustment of an error); for example, the collection of a note receivable left at the bank by a depositor is reported in a credit memo. The bank's liability to the depositor is increased by the amount of the credit memo.

Overdraft (OD) An overdraft is the amount by which withdrawals exceed the depositor's available balance. The overdraft, if permitted, is usually entered in red in the Balance column. Because of automatic bank loan renewal arrangements or for other reasons, a bank may pay checks even when an overdraft results. The amount of the overdraft is a current liability.

Reconciliation procedure

The use of a checking account is essential to the control of cash. It has already been stated that total receipts should be deposited intact daily and that all payments should be made by check. For each entry in the depositor's books there should be a counterpart in the bank's books. All debits to Cash in the depositor's books should be matched by credit entries to the depositor's account in the bank's books; all credit entries to Cash in the depositor's books should be matched by debit entries to the depositor's account. For instance, cash received from a customer is recorded in the company's books by debiting Cash and crediting Accounts Receivable; the bank, on receiving the cash, increases the depositor's account. The company records a payment to a creditor by debiting Accounts Payable and crediting Cash; the bank decreases the depositor's account.

The records of the depositor and of the bank will not normally agree at the end of the month because of items that appear on one record but not on the other. It is necessary, therefore, to reconcile the two balances and to determine the *adjusted,* or true, cash balance. Discrepancies between the balances may be due to the time lag in recording deposits and checks, to special charges and credits of which the depositor or the bank is unaware, or to errors and irregularities. The bank reconciliation is prepared as follows:

1. Deposits shown on the bank statement are compared with those entered in the cash receipts journal. Deposits made too late in the month to be credited by the bank on the current statement are referred to as *deposits in transit*. The bank reconciliation for the previous month should be inspected for any deposits in transit at the end of that period; they should appear as the early deposits of the current period. Any items not on the statement should be investigated.
2. Checks paid and returned by the bank (cancelled checks) are arranged in numerical order and compared with the entries in the cash payments journal. Checks that have not yet been presented to the bank for payment are called *outstanding checks*. The previous bank reconciliation should be inspected for outstanding checks.
3. Special debits and credits made by the bank—usually reported in debit or credit memos—are compared with the depositor's books to see if they have already been recorded.
4. Any errors in the bank's or the depositor's records that become apparent during completion of the prior steps are listed.

NAME
Bank Reconciliation
Date

Per Books

Cash Balance per Ledger, Date		$XXX
Add:		
(1) Any proper increases in cash already recorded by the bank that have not been recorded as yet by the firm		
Example: Collection of note by bank	$XX	
(2) Any error in the firm's books that failed to reveal a proper increase in cash or that improperly decreased cash		
Example: Check from customer for $90 entered as $70	XX	XX
Total		$XXX
Deduct:		
(1) Any proper decreases in cash already recorded by the bank that have not been recorded as yet by the firm		
Example: Bank service charges	$XX	
(2) Any error in the firm's books that failed to reveal a proper decrease in cash or that improperly increased cash		
Example: Check issued in payment to a creditor for $462 entered as $426	XX	XX
Adjusted Cash Balance, Date		$XXX

Per Bank

Cash Balance per Bank Statement, Date		$XXX
Add:		
(1) Any proper increases in cash already recorded by the firm that have not been recorded as yet by the bank		
Example: Deposits in transit	$XX	
(2) Any error by the bank that failed to reveal a proper increase in cash or that improperly decreased cash		
Example: Another depositor's check incorrectly charged to this depositor's account	XX	XX
Total		$XXX
Deduct:		
(1) Any proper decreases in cash already recorded by the firm that have not been recorded as yet by the bank		
Example: Outstanding checks	$XX	
(2) Any error by the bank that failed to reveal a proper decrease in cash or that improperly increased cash		
Example: Firm's deposit of $679 entered by bank as $697	XX	XX
Adjusted Cash Balance, Date		$XXX

Figure 10–4
Format for a bank reconciliation

A format for a bank reconciliation is given in Figure 10–4. Errors and adjustments in the Per Books section require entries in the general journal (or cash journals) to correct the books; adjustments in the Per Bank section do not require entries.

Frederick Hall's August bank reconciliation is shown in Figure 10–5.

Note that the August 31 cash balance per the bank is the same as the beginning balance of the September statement (Figure 10–3).

Figure 10–5
Bank reconciliation

FREDERICK HALL
Bank Reconciliation
August 31, 1979

Cash balance per ledger, August 31, 1979	$6,400.00	Cash balance per bank statement August 31, 1979		$7,320.00
		Add: Deposit in transit, August 31, 1979		450.00
		Total		$7,770.00
		Deduct: Outstanding Checks		
		Check	Amount	
		680	$ 49.00	
		694	1,237.00	
		701	84.00	1,370.00
Adjusted cash balance, August 31, 1979	$6,400.00	Adjusted cash balance, August 31, 1979		$6,400.00

Hall's cash records for September 1979 show the following items:

Cash Deposits

Sept. 4		$ 48.00
11		1,650.00
14		762.00
18		1,312.00
28		1,050.00
Total from cash receipts journal		$4,822.00

Checks Issued

Sept. 3	702	$ 175.00
5	703	1,300.00
7	704	14.00
14	705	82.50
14	706	312.25
18	707	27.25
26	708	2,000.00
26	709	367.00
28	710	103.00
Total from cash payments journal		$4,381.00

The statement received from the bank (Figure 10–3) shows a balance of $6,563.25 as of September 30, 1979. The following items were received from the bank together with the bank statement:

Cancelled checks:	Check	Amount
	680	$ 49.00
	694	1,237.00
	702	175.00
	703	1,300.00
	704	14.00
	705	28.50
	707	27.25
	708	2,000.00
	709	367.00
	Check of Frederick Hale	275.00

Memos:

Credit memo, $500, for a note receivable collected by the bank on September 27.

Debit memo, $2, dated September 27, for collection fee charged by bank.

Notification of a certified check for $1,300 deducted on September 7. (Even if the certified check, No. 703, had not been cancelled by the bank during September, it would not be listed on the bank reconciliation as outstanding, because it has been entered on both Hall's and the bank's records and would therefore not need to be reconciled.)

Service charge notification, $4, dated September 28.

Following receipt of the bank statement, Hall prepares the bank reconciliation statement shown in Figure 10–6 (see Figures 10–3 and 10–5 for supporting data).

FREDERICK HALL
Bank Reconciliation
September 30, 1979

Per Books

Cash balance per ledger, September 30, 1979		$6,841.00
Add: Customer's note collected by bank		500.00
Error in entering check No. 705:		
Entered as . . .	$82.50	
Corrected Amount	28.50	54.00
Total		$7,395.00
Deduct: Bank service charge	$ 4.00	
Collection fee	2.00	6.00
Adjusted cash balance, September 30, 1979		$7,389.00

Per Bank

Cash balance per bank statement, September 30, 1979		$6,563.25
Add: Depost of Sep. 28 in transit to bank		1,050.00
Check of Frederick Hale deducted by bank in error		275.00
Total		$7,888.25
Deduct: Outstanding Checks		
Check	Amount	
701	$ 84.00	
706	312.25	
710	103.00	499.25
Adjusted cash balance, September 30, 1979		$7,389.00

Figure 10–6
Bank reconciliation

The following points should be emphasized:

1. The beginning balance in the Per Books section is taken from the general ledger Cash account; it was determined as follows:

Cash balance per ledger, August 31, 1979 (Figure 10–5) . .	$ 6,400.00
Add deposits	4,822.00
Total	$11,222.00
Deduct checks issued	4,381.00
Cash balance per ledger, September 30, 1979	$ 6,841.00

2. Check no. 705 was incorrectly recorded in Hall's books as $82.50 instead of $28.50. The error overstated cash disbursements and therefore understated the ending cash balance by $54 = ($82.50 − $28.50).
3. The beginning balance in the Per Bank section is the last amount in the Balance column of the bank statement for the month of September (Figure 10–3).
4. The deposit of $1,050 made on September 28 was not credited on the bank statement and is considered to be in transit.
5. While determining the outstanding checks, Hall discovered that the bank had deducted in error a check for $275 signed by another depositor, Frederick Hale. This resulted in an understatement of the bank balance on the bank statement. The bank was notified about this error.
6. Check no. 701 was listed as an outstanding check on the bank reconciliation of August 31 (Figure 10–5). Since it has not yet been presented to the bank for payment, it continues to be listed as an outstanding check.

All the items that appear in the Per Bank section of the bank reconciliation for the previous month must be traced to the current month's bank statement. For example, a deposit not credited in the prior month should appear with the initial deposits for the current month; similarly, improper charges or credits of the preceding month should appear as corrections on the current month's statement.

All additions to, and deductions from, the balance per books must be entered on Hall's books to bring the general ledger Cash account balance into agreement with the adjusted cash balance. The Cash account balance of $6,841 should be increased by $548 = ($500 + $54 − $6) to show the actual cash balance of $7,389 as of September 30, 1979.

The required entries are shown below in general journal form:

Date		Account	Debit	Credit
1979				
Sep.	30	Cash	498 00	
		Bank Service and Collection Charges Expense	2 00	
		Notes Receivable		500 00
		To record collection of notes receivable by bank and related charge.		
	30	Cash	54 00	
		Accounts Payable		54 00
		To record correction of error in entering check no. 705 as $82.50 instead of $28.50.		
	30	Bank Service and Collection Charges Expense	4 00	
		Cash		4 00
		To record bank service charge for the month of September.		

These entries may be made in the cash journals for September if the journals have not been footed and posted, or the following compound entry may be made in the general journal:

Date		Account	Debit	Credit
1979				
Sep.	30	Cash	548 00	
		Bank Service and Collection Charges Expense	6 00	
		Notes Receivable		500 00
		Accounts Payable		54 00
		To adjust the Cash account per bank reconciliation for September.		

After the entry is posted, Hall's Cash account appears as shown below. Note that the beginning balance for the new period (October) agrees with the adjusted cash balance in the bank reconciliation. The explanations would be omitted in an actual account. They are shown here so that the reader may trace the source of each entry.

Cash						Account No. 101
Date		**Explanation**	**F**	**Debit**	**Credit**	**Balance**
1979						
Sep.	1	Beginning balance	√			6,400 00
	30	Cash deposits	CR18	4,822 00		11,222 00
	30	Checks issued	CP20		4,381 00	6,841 00
	30	Adjustment	J31	548 00		7,389 00

Only the items from the reconciliation that either increase or decrease the balance per books need to be entered in the journal. The items that increase or decrease the balance per bank already have been recorded on the depositor's books and, therefore, require no adjusting entry. Any errors made by the bank should be brought to the bank's attention. If a running cash balance is maintained in the checkbook, the necessary adjustments must also be made there.

The form of bank reconciliation shown in Figure 10–4 is commonly used because the adjusted cash balance is a significant figure; it represents the true cash balance, the amount subject to withdrawal. The form also may be prepared in advance and the items entered directly into the appropriate sections as they are determined.

The voucher system

The accounting system must be designed not only to enable the recording of transactions and the preparation of financial statements but also to achieve other managerial objectives: (1) to furnish analyses and reports of past, current, and projected events and (2) to establish internal controls to protect the assets of the business against loss through errors or fraud. The achievement of these objectives goes hand in hand with the achievement of maximum operating efficiency and maximum earnings. A properly functioning voucher system plays a key role in establishing and maintaining effective internal control.

The voucher system is a method of accumulating, verifying, recording, and disbursing all the expenditures of a business. The system covers any transaction (except for payments out of petty cash) that will require the payment of cash, including the purchase of merchandise (Figure 10–7), services, supplies, and plant and equipment, and the payment of expenses. Expenditures are verified, classified, and recorded when they are incurred. All expenditures must be properly authorized and, except for petty cash transactions, are paid by check.

Reference has been made to the importance of having a built-in system to protect the assets of a business against loss through fraud or error. The voucher system is designed to achieve this internal control by distributing the duties of authorizing expenditures, reporting the receipt of goods or services, and signing checks. This division of duties prevents cash being disbursed from the business without proper approval and then only after verifications made by several members of the organization.

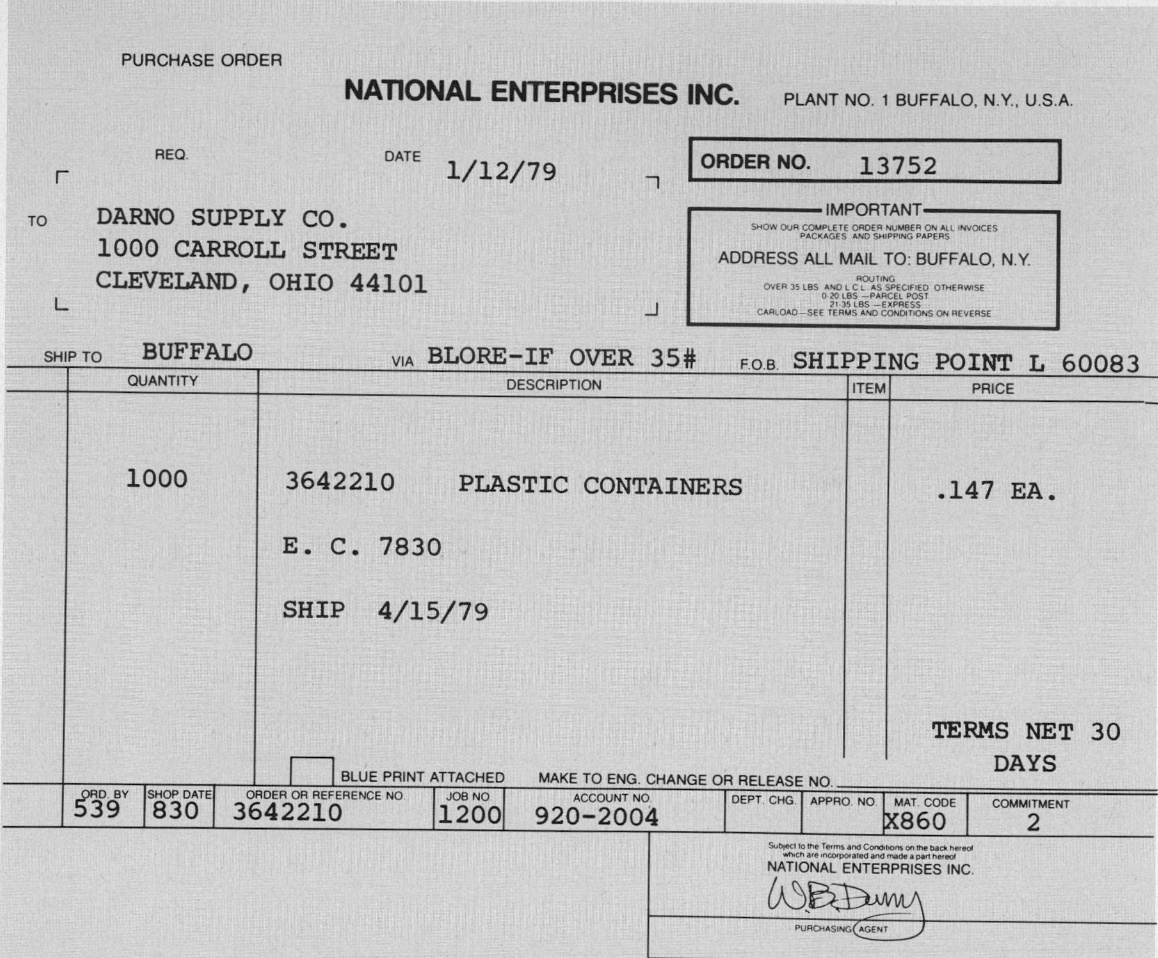

PURCHASE ORDER

NATIONAL ENTERPRISES INC. PLANT NO. 1 BUFFALO, N.Y., U.S.A.

REQ. DATE 1/12/79

ORDER NO. 13752

TO DARNO SUPPLY CO.
1000 CARROLL STREET
CLEVELAND, OHIO 44101

IMPORTANT
SHOW OUR COMPLETE ORDER NUMBER ON ALL INVOICES PACKAGES AND SHIPPING PAPERS
ADDRESS ALL MAIL TO: BUFFALO, N.Y.
ROUTING
OVER 35 LBS AND L C L AS SPECIFIED OTHERWISE
0-20 LBS —PARCEL POST
21-35 LBS —EXPRESS
CARLOAD—SEE TERMS AND CONDITIONS ON REVERSE

SHIP TO BUFFALO VIA BLORE-IF OVER 35# F.O.B. SHIPPING POINT L 60083

QUANTITY	DESCRIPTION	ITEM	PRICE
1000	3642210 PLASTIC CONTAINERS E. C. 7830 SHIP 4/15/79		.147 EA. TERMS NET 30 DAYS

☐ BLUE PRINT ATTACHED MAKE TO ENG. CHANGE OR RELEASE NO.

ORD. BY	SHOP DATE	ORDER OR REFERENCE NO.	JOB NO.	ACCOUNT NO.	DEPT. CHG.	APPRO. NO.	MAT. CODE	COMMITMENT
539	830	3642210	1200	920-2004			X860	2

Subject to the Terms and Conditions on the back hereof which are incorporated and made a part hereof
NATIONAL ENTERPRISES INC.
PURCHASING AGENT

Figure 10–7
Purchase order

Source: IBM

The voucher

The *voucher* is a serially numbered form that is the written authorization for each payment. It is prepared from the seller's invoice or group of invoices or from other documents that serve as evidence of the liability. The voucher form is tailored to meet the needs of the particular business.

The voucher, not the invoice (Figure 10–8), is the basis for the accounting entry. The invoice, together with acknowledgments or approvals of the receipt of goods or services, and other supporting papers are the underlying documents for the voucher. The voucher form should provide space for such things as:

1. Summary of the invoice data
2. Accounts to be debited
3. Details of payment

NIXON GLASS
NIXON, VIRGINIA

SOLD TO: ODIN CHEMICAL CO, BROCKTON, PENNSYLVANIA

DATE: 1/11/79

SHIPPED TO: SAME

VIA THOMAS MOTOR FREIGHT

TERMS	FOB NIXON	CUST. ORDER NO.	OUR ORDER NO.			INVOICE NO.
2-10 NET 30		11472	45981			24027

QUANTITY	ITEM NO.	DESCRIPTION	UNIT	UNIT COST	AMOUNT
144	18716	DEMI JOHN FRAMED	E	1.18	$ 169.92
6	9497	FLASK 5 GAL FIREGLASS	E	8.43	50.58
0010	55843	JAR 1 QT FLINTGLASS	M	26.37	263.70
					$ 484.20*

ACCOUNTS PAYABLE VOUCHER

TRANS. CODE	VENDOR NAME		
	Nixon Glass Company, Nixon Virginia		
VENDOR NUMBER	INVOICE DATE		INVOICE NUMBER
1179	1/11/79		24027
VOUCHER NUMBER	DUE DATE		GENERAL ACCOUNT
326	1/21/79		351
APPROVED BY	INVOICE AMOUNT		484.20
DRJ	DISCOUNT		9.68
	NET AMOUNT		474.52

ACCOUNT NUMBER	SUB-CODE	AMOUNT
351	160	169.92
351	115	50.58
351	210	263.70

Source: IBM (adapted)

Figure 10–8
Voucher and invoice

4. Initials of persons who have checked accuracy of quantities, unit prices, extensions, and discount terms
5. Signature of the person who authorizes the payment
6. Signature of the person who records the voucher.

The voucher register

The *voucher register* is an elaboration of the purchases journal. It is a journal for recording all liabilities approved for payment. The register is ruled in columns for the frequently used accounts to be debited or credited.

The voucher register form must be tailored to meet the needs of the particular enterprise. The register provides columns for each general class of expenditure and an Other General Ledger Accounts column with space for the account number of the specific detail account to be debited or credited. This gives the advantage of almost unlimited flexibility combined with economy of space. The voucher register of the Deacon Company is shown in Figure 10–9.

The function of the Vouchers Payable account is the same as that of the Accounts Payable account. It is a controlling account—its balance represents the total of the unpaid vouchers recorded in the voucher register. Unpaid vouchers may, therefore, be readily determined to be those without entries on the corresponding line of the Paid column or those in the *unpaid voucher* file. At the end of the period, a list of the unpaid vouchers in the file should be prepared for reconciliation with the balance of the Vouchers Payable account in the general ledger.

Vouchers are entered in the voucher register in numerical order. An entry is made in the Credit Vouchers Payable column for the amount due on each vouch-

Date		Voucher Number	Name	Paid Date	Paid Check No.	Credit Vouchers Payable
1979				1979		
Jan.	2	314	Wheaton Company	1/8	709	3,500
	2	315	Dover Furniture Company	1/5	708	800
	6	316	L. Kett			90
	9	317	Palmer Company	1/23	731	1,204
	10	318	Payroll	1/10	711	1,575
	10	319	Petty Cash	1/10	712	80
	31	335	Internal Revenue Service	1/31	732	850
	31	336	State Division of Employment Security	1/31	733	297
	31	337	Internal Revenue Service	1/31	734	315
			Totals			22,324
						(201)

Figure 10–9
Voucher register

er. The account or accounts to be debited are indicated on the voucher, and entries are made in one of the special debit columns or in the Other Accounts column if no special column is available. This column provides space for the name of the account to be debited, a ledger folio (F) column, and an Amount Debit column. Entries in the Other General Ledger Accounts column may be posted to the ledger daily; all the other columns are posted in total only at the end of the month to the general ledger account indicated in the column heading. Ledger folio references are shown beneath the double ruling for the items. The posting procedure is the same as for other special journals.

The check register

The check register replaces the cash payments journal as a book of original entry for all cash payments except petty cash. The check register of the Deacon Company is shown in Figure 10–10.

No payment is made until a specific voucher has been prepared, recorded, and approved. Hence, each entry is a debit to Vouchers Payable, a credit to Cash, and a credit to Purchases Discounts, if any. No other columns are needed, because the transaction already has been classified under an appropriate heading in the voucher register. Checks are entered in the check register in numerical sequence, one line to each check. At the time the check is entered in the check register, a notation must also be made in the Paid column of the voucher register showing the date of payment and the check number.

The check register will include a Purchases Discounts column only if the vouchers are recorded in the voucher register at gross invoice amounts. This register shows not only the serial number of the check but also the number of the voucher being paid.

					Page 8
Debit			Other General Ledger Accounts		
Purchases	Misc. Selling Expense	Misc. General Expense	Other Accounts Debit	F	Amount Debit
3,500					
			Office Equipment	163	800
		90			
			{Notes Payable	203	1,200
			{Interest Expense	851	4
			Accrued Wages and Salaries Payable	201	1,575
30	25	25			
			{FICA Taxes Payable	212	240
			{Income Tax Withholdings Payable	215	610
			State Unempl. Taxes Payable	213	297
			Fed'l Unempl. Taxes Payable	214	315
					11,826
9,780	475	243			(x)
(351)	(600)	(700)			

Some companies that use the net price method (see Chapter 7) prepare each voucher for the net amount due. This means that if payment is not made within the discount period, an additional voucher will be required, underscoring the expense for lost discounts. The entry in the voucher register for the additional voucher is a debit to Purchases Discounts Lost and a credit to Vouchers Payable. One check is made out for the full amount due as shown by the two vouchers. A simpler method is to enter lost discounts in a special column of the check register headed Purchases Discounts Lost Debit.

Control of unpaid vouchers

The unpaid vouchers can be readily determined—they are the ones that have not been marked either "Paid" or "Cancelled" in the Paid column. A schedule of unpaid vouchers is prepared at the end of the month; the total should correspond to the balance of the Vouchers Payable account in the general ledger. Thus, the

CHECK REGISTER

Date		Vou. No.	Name	Check No.	Vouchers Payable Dr.	Purchases Discounts Cr.	Cash Cr.
1979							
Jan.	5	315	Dover Furniture Company .	708	800		800
	8	314	Wheaton Company	709	3,500	70	3,430
	9	302	Johnson and Son	710	305		305
	10	318	Payroll	711	1,575		1,575
	10	319	Petty Cash	712	80		80
	23	317	Palmer Company	731	1,204		1,204
	31	335	Internal Rev. Service . .	732	850		850
	31	336	State Div. of Employ. Sec	733	297		297
	31	337	Internal Rev. Service . .	734	315		315
			Totals		13,154	113	13,041
					(201)	(365)	(101)

Figure 10–10
Check register

unpaid vouchers file is a subsidiary record supporting the Vouchers Payable account.

Recording and paying vouchers

The first entry in the voucher register is for approved voucher 314, payable to the Wheaton Company for $3,500 worth of merchandise received; terms 2/10, n/30. On January 8, check 709 is issued to the Wheaton Company for $3,430. An entry is made in the check register, dated that day, debiting Vouchers Payable for $3,500 and crediting Purchases Discounts and Cash for $70 and $3,430, respectively. The number 314 entered in the Voucher Number column cross-references the check with the paid voucher. After this entry is made, the date of the entry and the check number are entered in the Paid column of the voucher register on the line for voucher 314. The voucher with its supporting documents is removed from the unpaid voucher file and filed in the *vendor's file*.

When a note payable becomes due, a voucher is prepared for the maturity value of the note and entered in the voucher register. In Figure 10–9, voucher 317 was issued to authorize payment of the liability to the Palmer Company. Two lines are required for the amounts debited in the Other Accounts column: Notes Payable ($1,200) and Interest Expense ($4). The payment of the voucher then is recorded in the check register in the usual manner.

Under the voucher system, the payroll for the period is recorded as usual in the payroll records. The liability is entered in the general journal by debiting the payroll expense accounts and crediting Accrued Salaries and Wages Payable and the accounts for the deductions. A voucher is prepared for the amount of the net payroll, and a check is issued to the *paymaster*. In Figure 10–9, the payroll of January 10 is covered by voucher 318 and paid with check 711.

At the end of the month, payment of the tax liabilities is recorded in the voucher register. Assuming that the total taxable December payroll of the Deacon Company was $2,000 and that income taxes of $610 were withheld from employees' earnings, voucher 335 and check 732 (Figure 10–9) are made payable to the Internal Revenue Service for $850 = ($610 + $240 in FICA taxes). The check and the depositary receipts for October and November accompany the report form.

January 31 is also the last day for filing the state unemployment tax form for the last quarter (October through December). Assuming that wages subject to the tax were $14,850, voucher 336 and check 733 were made payable to the State Division of Employment Security for $297 = ($14,850 × 0.02 merit rate).

Assuming that the total payroll subject to the federal unemployment compensation tax was $31,500 in 1978, voucher 337 records the liability for $315 = ($31,500 × 0.01).

Posting from the voucher register and the check register

The voucher register money columns are totaled at the end of the month, and the totals of the debit columns are compared with the totals of the credit columns to determine that they are equal. The totals of all the special columns are posted to the proper accounts in the general ledger; the amounts in the Other General Ledger Accounts Debit column have been posted individually. The posting symbol reference VR8 is entered in the ledger account folio (F) columns to cross-reference postings from the voucher register, page 8.

The check register columns are totaled at the end of the month. The total of the Vouchers Payable Debit column should equal the totals of the two credit columns, Purchases Discounts and Cash. Postings are made at the end of the month to the three general ledger accounts. The symbol CR with the page number is used in the ledgers to cross-reference postings from the check register.

Elimination of the accounts payable ledger

When the voucher system is used, the subsidiary accounts payable ledger can be eliminated. Each numbered voucher is entered on a separate line in the voucher register and may be considered as a credit to a creditor's account. When the liability is settled and a notation is made in the Paid column, it is equivalent to a debit to that same creditor's account. The file of unpaid vouchers replaces the accounts payable ledger. When all posting is up to date, the total of the unpaid vouchers must agree with the total of the Vouchers Payable controlling account.

Advantages and limitations of the voucher system

In a properly functioning voucher system all invoices must be verified and approved for payment. As a result, responsibility is fixed and the possibility of error or fraud is reduced. The recording of all vouchers in a single journal (the voucher register) provides for prompt recognition of liabilities and their proper accounting classification as assets, expenses, or other costs. Economy in recording is effected by elimination of the accounts payable ledger and by grouping invoices under a single voucher. The maintenance of a chronological unpaid voucher file facilitates the payment of invoices without loss of discounts. This file also enables management to determine its future cash needs for the settlement of liabilities. The systematic filing of paid vouchers provides a ready reference source for data and underlying documents for audit of disbursements.

On the other hand, the voucher system has certain limitations. The difficulties in handling special transactions and the need for the preparation of separate vouchers involve extra clerical and accounting work. The elimination of the accounts payable ledger results in a loss of valuable reference data, although this may be overcome by maintaining a file, arranged in alphabetical order by name of vendor, of copies of all vouchers. In addition, a card file could be kept that would provide a cross reference for any purpose desired.

Glossary

Bank reconciliation A statement which shows the specific items that account for the differences between the balance reported by the bank and the amount shown on the depositor's books.

Bank statement A monthly statement sent by a bank to its depositors together with canceled checks and notices of bank charges and credits.

Cash over and short An income statement account showing a discrepancy in the daily count of cash between actual cash receipts and cash disbursements and the cash register readings or from the petty cash fund.

Certified check A depositor's check, payment of which is guaranteed by a bank by endorsement on the face of the check, the bank having previously deducted the amount of the check from the depositor's balance.

Check register A book of original entry for all cash disbursements except petty cash.

Deposits in transit Deposits made too late in the month to be credited by the bank on the current statement.

Internal control A built-in system of self-policing for the effective control and safeguarding of cash and other assets.

NSF check A customer's check that has been deposited but did not clear on presentation for payment because the customer's bank balance was less than the amount of the check.

Outstanding checks Checks sent to payees but not yet presented to the depositor's bank for payment.

Petty cash A separate cash fund for the payment of relatively minor items when payment by check is impracitcal.

Voucher A serially numbered form that is the written authorization for each expenditure prepared from the seller's invoice or group of invoices or from other documents that serve as evidence of the liability.

Voucher register A columnar journal for recording and summarizing all liabilities approved for payment.

Voucher system A method of accumulating, verifying, recording, and disbursing all the expenditures of a business. It covers all payments except those from the petty cash fund.

Questions

Q10–1 Why is it advantageous to deposit total cash receipts intact and to make all disbursements by check?

Q10–2 (a) What is a petty cash fund? (b) How does it operate? (c) Why should the petty cash fund always be replenished at the end of each accounting period?

Q10–3 Explain the matching relationships between the cash records of the bank and those of the depositor.

Q10–4 Explain the following terms:

a. Certified check
b. Total of listed checks
c. Service charge
d. Not sufficient funds
e. Debit memorandum
f. Credit memorandum
g. Overdraft
h. Imprest system

Q10–5 Explain the effect, if any, on the bank statement balance of each of the following bank reconciliation items:

a. Outstanding checks total $323.
b. The bank recorded a $650 deposit as $560.
c. The service charge for the month was $7.
d. Deposits in transit total $800.
e. A note payable of $500 made to the bank by the depositor became due.

Q10–6 (a) What is the voucher system? (b) What is a voucher? (c) What is a voucher register? (d) What are the advantages of the voucher system? (e) What are the disadvantages of the voucher system?

Q10–7 (a) What are some of the basic concepts of internal control of cash? (b) Why must the independent auditor test for the adequacy of the internal controls? (c) What are some of the internal control techniques for safeguarding cash?

Q10–8 (a) How often should bank reconciliations be prepared? (b) What are the steps to be followed when preparing the bank reconciliation? (c) Which items must be entered on the books?

Q10–9 (a) What is a check register? (b) What column headings are needed for the check register?

Q10–10 What procedures should be followed to control unpaid vouchers?

Class exercises

CE10–1 (Recording transactions in voucher register) A section of a voucher register, showing the unpaid vouchers as of April 30, 1979, is given below:

Date		Vou. No.	Name	Paid		Credit Vou. Pay.	Debit Purch.	Other General Ledger Accounts		
				Date	Ck. No.			Account	Debit	Credit
1979										
Apr.	5	270	J. Sims			2,250				
	10	272	W. Mores			2,000				
	21	291	Bea Co.			2,500				
	28	305	N. Gill			1,500				

The following transactions, among others, occurred during May:

1979

May 1 Issued check no. 651 in payment of voucher no. 270, less 2 percent.

1 Issued voucher no. 309 to H. Niles for $3,750 worth of merchandise; terms, n/15.

8 Issued check no. 652 in payment of voucher no. 305, less 1 percent.

15 Issued check no. 653 in payment of voucher no. 291 less 1 percent.

17 By special agreement with H. Niles, the purchase of May 1 is to be paid for in installments: $1,250 immediately and the balance by June 16. Canceled voucher no. 309 and issued vouchers no. 311 and 312. Check no. 654 was issued in payment of voucher no. 311.

Required:

1. Enter the unpaid vouchers in a voucher register similar to the one shown (draw double rules under the last entry to exclude the April amounts from the May totals); record the May transactions in the voucher register and a check register.
2. Enter the total of unpaid vouchers as of April 30, $8,250, as a credit in the Vouchers Payable general ledger account; post to Vouchers Payable from the voucher register and check register.
3. Prepare a schedule of unpaid vouchers.

CE10–2 (Recording transactions in special journals) The Lortz Co. uses a voucher system. During June 1979, the following selected transactions were completed:

1979

June 1 Purchased $5,000 worth of merchandise from the Sea Company; terms, 2/10, n/30.

9 Made a partial payment on the June 1 purchase. The check is made out for $2,094.75, representing a partial payment on which a discount is allowed.

15 Paid a 45-day, 12 percent note for $10,000 due today.

30 Paid $1,250 for June rent.

Required: Record the transactions in general journal form and indicate the journal in which each transaction would be properly recorded.

CE10–3 (Internal control)

a. The manager of a shoe department employing six salesmen has found on a number of occasions that the cash in the register at the end of the day is less than the amounts shown on the record of sales for that day. Each salesman rings up his own sales but the cash register has only one cash drawer. What recommendations would you make to the manager?
b. How do the use of a petty cash system and the regular reconciliation of the bank account protect the company against mistakes and losses?
c. You note that the independent auditor, when making his or her examination, reconciles (1) total deposits shown on the bank statement with total receipts shown in the cash receipts journal and (2) total disbursements shown on the bank statement with total checks drawn as recorded in the cash payments journal. Explain why the auditor makes these reconciliations.
d. It is essential for a business to establish internal controls to prevent the misappropriation of cash. Does management have other responsibilities relating to cash? Explain.

CE10–4 (Recording petty cash transactions) The transactions of the petty cash fund of the Ader Company during the months of July and August 1979 follow:

1979

July 3 Established an imprest petty cash fund in the amount of $350.

10 Replenished the fund and increased it to $750. The following items were in the petty cash box:

Coins and currency	$ 12.50
Vouchers for:	
Telephone and telegraph	124.30
Advances to employees	50.00
Postage stamps	100.00
Miscellaneous office supplies	63.20
Total	$350.00

Aug. 31 Replenished the fund again at the close of the Ader Company's fiscal year. The petty cash box contained the following items:

Coins and currency		$ 48.64
Vouchers for:		
Telephone and telegraph	$ 34.47	
Office supplies	23.10	
Postage	141.18	
Traveling expense	201.76	
Entertainment expense	212.32	
Repairs	85.88	
Hardware supplies	2.65	701.36
Total		$750.00

Required: Journalize the transactions.

CE10–5 (Bank reconciliation) The Cash account of the Baur Company showed a balance of $2,459.17 on March 31, 1979. The bank statement showed a balance of $2,533.23. Other differences between the information in the firm's Cash account and the bank's records are listed below.

1. A deposit of $130.46 made on March 31 was not recorded by the bank before the bank statement was issued.
2. The following items were returned with the bank statement:
   a. A credit memo for $123.53 correcting an erroneous charge made last month by the bank.
   b. A debit memo for $5.28 for rental of a safety deposit box.
   c. A customer's check for $8.25 received on account, which the firm had included in its deposit on March 27, was returned marked NSF.
   d. A canceled check in the amount of $225.50 drawn by the Bower Company and charged by the bank against the account of the Baur Company by mistake.
3. Check no. 298 was made out correctly for $19.44 in payment of office supplies, but was entered in the cash payments journal as $19.54; it was also returned with the statement.
4. Outstanding checks on March 31 totaled $443.45.

Required:

1. Prepare a bank reconciliation as of March 31, 1979.
2. Prepare the journal entries to adjust the Cash account as of March 31, 1979.

Exercises and problems

P10–1 State the underlying reason for each of the following procedures:

a. The ticket taker at the theater tears in half each ticket presented for admission and returns one-half to the theater goer.
b. The clerk in the department store gives the customer a cash register receipt.
c. After the company treasurer signs a batch of checks, she returns the attached supporting documents, but not the checks (which she mails), to the accounting department.

P10–2 The bookkeeper of the Jacobs Company, in need of money to pay off his debts, "borrows" $500 by pocketing some cash and checks mailed in by customers. He enters appropriate credits to each customer's account for payment made. Can this theft be concealed for a short period? indefinitely? What measures should a company take to prevent the misappropriation of cash or other assets?

P10–3 On May 1, 1979, the Meier Company established a petty cash fund of $675. On May 31, 1979, the fund consisted of cash and other items as follows:

Coins and currency	$142.50
Vouchers for postage stamps	141.00
Freight and express invoices	192.00
Salvation Army contribution receipt	75.00
Postdated check from an employee	124.50

Required: Make the entries (a) to establish the fund; (b) to replenish the fund; (c) to increase the fund from $675 to $900 on May 31; (d) to reduce the fund from $675 to $450 on May 31.

P10–4 The Piper Company has an imprest petty cash fund of $1,500. On October 31, 1979, the fund consisted of cash and other items as follows:

Coins and currency		$ 795.00
Vouchers for:		
Transportation in	$337.86	
Telephone	32.25	
Postage expense	324.48	
Stationery	1.50	696.09
Total		$1,491.09

Required: Assuming that the petty cash fund was replenished, make the necessary adjusting entry at October 31, 1979.

P10–5 The Rice Company's Cash account shows a balance of $20,818.47 as of April 30, 1979. The balance on the bank statement on that date is $23,334.27. Checks for $750, $533.46, and $126.54 are outstanding. The bank statement shows a charge for a check made out by the Reece Company for $75. The statement also shows a credit of $1,200 for a customer's note that had been left with the bank for collection. Service charges for the month were $19.20.

Required: What is the true cash balance as of April 30?

P10–6 From the following data prepare a bank reconciliation and entries to adjust the books of the Petrini Company as of March 31, 1979.

Balance on bank statement	$6,153.50
Balance on books	5,704.02
Bank service charge	10.86
Credit for a customer's note collected by the bank (includes interest of $7.28)	169.78
Deposit made on March 31, not credited by the bank	330.33

Check no. 786 for $581 was entered in the cash payments journal as $518

A customer's check for $16.77 was returned marked NSF on March 30

Outstanding checks:

Check No.	*Amount*
817	$ 65.00
818	97.57
825	538.09

P10–7 The Rose Company records all vouchers at the net amount. Record the following transactions in general journal form, indicating the proper book of original entry.

1979

Oct. 2 Issued a voucher payable to the Gray Company for $2,400 worth of merchandise; terms, 2/10, n/30.

5 Issued a voucher payable to Greene, Inc. for $3,000 worth of merchandise; terms, 3/10, n/30.

12 Issued a check to the Gray Company in payment of the October 2 voucher.

Nov. 3 Issued a voucher payable to Greene, Inc., for the discount not taken on the transaction of October 5.

3 Issued a check payable to Greene, Inc. for the amount due.

P10–8 The Ginn Company uses a voucher system. During August 1979, the following selected transactions were completed:

1979

Aug. 1 Issued voucher no. 171 payable to the Piaf Company for $4,500 worth of merchandise; terms, n/10.

11 Gave the Piaf Company a 20-day, 10 percent note in payment of voucher no. 171.

31 Issued voucher no. 189 payable to the Piaf Company for the maturity value of the note of September 11.

31 Issued check no. 97 in payment of voucher no. 189.

Required: Record the transactions in general journal form, indicating the journal in which each transaction would be properly recorded.

P10–9 Grosse, Inc., completed the following transactions, among others, during October 1979.

1979

Oct. 2 Issued voucher no. 45 payable to the York Company for $1,000 worth of merchandise; terms 2/10, n/30.

6 Received a credit memorandum for $100 from the York Company for unsatisfactory merchandise returned. Canceled voucher no. 45 and issued voucher no. 61 for the proper amount.

10 Issued check no. 25 in payment of voucher no. 61, less a 2 percent discount.

Required: Record the transactions in general journal form, indicating the journal in which each transaction would be properly recorded assuming:

a. Invoices are recorded at their gross amount.
b. Invoices are recorded at their net amount.

P10–10 The Babbah Company prepares its vouchers for the net amount due. A section of the voucher register, showing the unpaid vouchers as of June 30, is given below.

Date		Vou. No.	Name	Paid		Credit Vou. Pay.	Debit Purch.	Debit Purch. Disc. Lost	Other General Ledger Accounts		
				Date	Ck. No.				Account	Debit	Credit
1979											
June	1	78	W. Robe			98					
	2	81	Bean Co.			1,960					
	5	82	Sand & Son			392					

Among the company's July transactions are the following:

1979

July 3 Issued check no. 110 in payment of voucher no. 78. No discount was lost.

5 Issued voucher no. 83 payable to Sand & Son for $8 discount lost on the purchase of June 5.

6 Issued check no. 111 in payment of vouchers no. 82 and 83.

10 Issued voucher no. 84 to the George Company for $1,000 worth of merchandise; terms, 2/10, n/30.

14 Issued voucher no. 85 to Wells, Inc. for $1,500 worth of merchandise; terms 1½/10, n/30.

17 By special arrangement with the Bean Company the purchase of June 2 (invoice $2,000; terms, 2/10, n/30) is to be paid for in installments: $800 immediately and the balance on August 16. Issued voucher no. 86 for the purchase discount lost. Canceled vouchers no. 81 and 86 and issued vouchers no. 87 and 88. Issued check no. 112 in payment of voucher no. 87.

20 Issued check no. 113 in payment of voucher no. 84.

Required:

1. Enter the unpaid vouchers as of July 1 in a voucher register similar to the one shown above; record the July transactions in the voucher register and a single-column check register.
2. Enter the total amount of unpaid vouchers as of July 1 ($2,450) as a credit to the Vouchers Payable general ledger account; post to a Vouchers Payable account from the voucher register and the check register.
3. Prepare a schedule of unpaid vouchers.

P10–11 (Integrative) Sacks, Inc., deposits all cash receipts intact daily and reconciles bank statements with cash records each month. Surprise counts of the petty cash fund are made periodically. Checks are issued only if supported by properly authorized vouchers and the person who approves vouchers for payment is not permitted to sign the checks for those payments. The clerks who handle cash are not permitted to make entries in the cash records, sign checks, or authorize cash disbursements.

The following data are taken from the records of Sacks, Inc., and from the monthly bank statement furnished them by the National Trust Company:

a.	Balance per bank statement, June 30, 1979		$134,655.77
b.	Balance per books, June 30, 1979		87,477.74
c.	Outstanding checks, June 30, 1979		51,373.47
d.	Receipts of June 30, 1979, deposited July 3, 1979 ..		8,507.52
e.	Service charge for June, per debit memo		6.16
f.	Proceeds of bank loan, June 15, 1979, discounted for 3 months at 10 percent a year, omitted from the company's books (the face value of the note is $16,000.00)		15,600.00
g.	Deposit of June 30, 1979, omitted from bank statement		4,627.86
h.	Error on bank statement in entering deposit of June 26, 1979:		
	Corrected amount	$5,091.84	
	Entered as	5,090.84	1.00
i.	Check of Saxe, Inc. charged in error		4,304.00
j.	Proceeds of a customer's note collected by bank on June 16, 1979, not entered in the company's books:		
	Principal	$3,200	
	Interest	32	
	Total	$3,232	
	Less collection fee	8	3,224.00
k.	Error on bank statement in entering deposit of June 9, 1979:		
	Entered as	$5,614	
	Correct amount	5,604	10.00
l.	Deposit of Sachs Corporation credited in error		2,880.00
m.	Debit memo for noninterest-bearing note not recorded by the company		8,000.00
n.	A check from Tippett, Inc. was returned marked NSF; no entry has been made on the company's records		462.90

Required:

1. Prepare a bank reconciliation as of June 30, 1979.
2. Prepare the journal entries necessary to adjust the books of Sacks, Inc. as of June 30, 1979. The books are closed annually June 30.
3. What specific safeguards are provided by the company's internal cash control procedures?

P10–12 (Integrative) The Hall Company prepared the following bank reconciliation as of March 31, 1979:

HALL COMPANY
Bank Reconciliation
March 31, 1979

Balance per bank		$24,927.50
Less outstanding checks		
Check	*Amount*	
580	$4,051.00	
599	196.00	
600	6.80	4,253.80
Balance per books		$20,673.70

The bank statement for the month of April was as follows:

SECOND NATIONAL BANK
Statement of account with Hall Company

Checks			Deposits	Date		Balance
				1979		
				April	1	24,927.50
4,051.00					2	20,876.50
196.00	24.00	230.00	1,570.00		6	21,996.50
200.00			390.00		11	22,186.50
124.46	397.00	6.80			16	21,658.24
2,220.00	180.00 NSF				21	19,258.24
1,720.00	30.80		5,000.00		26	22,507.44
5.50 SC			1,521.60		29	24,023.54

Cash receipts for the month:

Date	Amount
April 5	$1,570.00
10	390.00
23	5,000.00
28	1,521.60
30	1,000.00

Cash disbursements for the month:

Check	Amount	Check	Amount
601	$ 24.00	607	$1,364.42
602	1,720.00	608	99.80
603	230.00	609	40.00
604	200.00	610	1,520.00
605	2,220.00	611	124.46
606	287.00	612	397.00

The canceled checks returned by the bank included a check for $30.80 made out by the Hill Company and charged to the Hall Company in error. The NSF check had been received from a customer on account.

Required:

1. Prepare the bank reconciliation as of April 30, 1979.
2. Make the necessary adjusting journal entries.

P10–13 (Integrative) The Novac Company installed the voucher system on April 1, 1979 and prepared its vouchers at gross amounts. The following transactions were completed during April:

1979

April 3 Established a petty cash fund of $50 by the issuance of voucher 362; issued check 357 in payment of this voucher.

3 Purchased a one-year insurance policy from Liberty Insurance Company for $600. Issued voucher 363 and check 358 in payment of the voucher.

4 Issued voucher 364 payable to Kay Realty for $200 for the April rent; issued check 359 in payment of the voucher.

5 Issued voucher 365 payable to R. Kelly, Inc. for $925 worth of merchandise, terms 1/10, n/30.

10 Issued voucher 366 payable to L. Scotch Company for $1,200 worth of merchandise; terms n/10.

11 Issued voucher 367 payable to Danvers Supply Company for $200 worth of office supplies; issued check 360 in payment of the voucher.

17 Issued voucher 368 payable to J. Waitt Company for $1,025 worth of merchandise; terms 2/10, n/30.

18 Recorded the following payroll data in the general journal:

Gross salaries:	Salesmen	$ 750	
	Office	450	
	Executive	$1,000	$2,200
Deductions:	FICA tax	$ 132	
	Federal income tax	400	
	U.S. bonds	75	
	Employee loan	20	
	Community fund	10	637
Net amount due			$1,563

Issued voucher 369 payable to Payroll for the net amount due to employees. Issued check 361 in payment of the voucher.

20 The L. Scotch Company agreed to an extension of time on its invoice due today, as follows: $600 payment due in 20 days and another $600 payment due in 30 days. Canceled voucher 366 and issued vouchers 370 and 371.

24 Purchased two electric typewriters from Atlas Office Company for $1,500. Issued voucher 372 for $500 and check 362 in partial payment. Issued voucher 373 for $1,000 for the balance, payable in 30 days.

25 Issued voucher 374 payable to the S. Furry Company for $800 worth of merchandise; terms 1/10, n/60.

26 Issued check 363 in payment of voucher 370.

28 Issued voucher 375 to the *Salem Sun* for $75 worth of advertising. Issued check 364 in payment of the voucher.

Required:

1. Prepare a voucher register, a check register, and a two-column general journal similar to the illustrations in the text and record the April transactions.
2. Open a Vouchers Payable account and post all entries affecting that account.
3. Prove the end-of-month balance of the Vouchers Payable account by preparing a schedule of unpaid vouchers.

P10–14 (Minicase) The Stenn Company employs an office manager, a cashier, an accounts receivable bookkeeper, two clerk-typists, and ten salesmen. The bookkeeper records all charge sales made to customers; she also opens the mail each day and credits the customers' accounts for remittances, turning the money over to the cashier. The monthly bank statement is received directly by the bookkeeper, who prepares the bank reconciliation.

Collections from cash sales are turned over by the salesmen to the cashier, together with a cash sales invoice. The cashier compares these invoices daily with the cash register tapes. Disbursements for petty cash items are made by the cashier out of cash receipts. The cashier fills out a petty cash slip, which is signed by the person receiving the cash. All other disbursements are by check, signed by either the office manager or the owner of the company. Entries in the cash receipts journal and in the cash payments journal are generally made by the office manager. In his absence, the cashier handles the cash receipts journal and the accounts receivable bookkeeper handles the cash payments journal.

Required:

a. Make a list of practices that are wrong with this system.
b. What basic internal controls are lacking?
c. How can the system be improved without increasing the present staff?

P10–15 (Minicase) Fred Sparrow, a friend of yours, has recently opened a men's and ladies' clothing store in your town and he asks you to help him "with the books." His wife keeps the accounting records but her knowledge of accounting is limited. Mr. Sparrow is especially concerned with the system of recording cash payments. Invoices have not been handled properly and there have been errors in amounts paid and loss of available cash discounts. Furthermore, he wants to be sure that the salaries of his clerks are being properly recorded and reported.

Required:

1. Using sample transactions and columnar accounting paper with appropriate column headings, prepare the entries for Mrs. Sparrow's guidance when she records the actual transactions. Also provide her with some basic do's and don't's for the processing of invoices, vouchers, checks, and other source documents.
2. Explain to both Mr. and Mrs. Sparrow how often and to whom they should make payments of employees and employer's FICA taxes, employees' federal and state income taxes withheld, and unemployment taxes. Finally, explain how these amounts are determined.

Income measurement and asset valuation issues

part three

chapter eleven

Introduction

In periods of high interest rates it is extremely important for a manager to have a good working knowledge of simple interest and short-term financing methods that utilize interest. Making sales and purchases on account has become standard business practice. Individuals and businesses alike buy and sell merchandise, invest in stocks and bonds, and even acquire plant and equipment on credit. The short-term financing device of creating accounts payable has been discussed in previous chapters, particularly Chapter 7. This chapter discusses several other short-term financing devices, such as issuance of notes to trade creditors, borrowing from banks on a company's own notes, and discounting notes receivable from customers.

In addition, this chapter discusses simple interest, accounting for notes receivable, and accounting for drafts.

Short-term financing: notes payable and notes receivable

Learning goals

To compute simple interest.
To label the elements of a promissory note.
To understand the transference of a promissory note and the meaning of the various forms of endorsements.
To determine the maturity dates of promissory notes.
To record transactions dealing with issuance of notes payable.
To record end-of-period adjustments for accrued liabilities.
To understand the apportionment of discount on notes payable to interest expense of the appropriate periods.
To record notes receivable transactions.
To calculate the proceeds of notes receivable discounted at banks and to record the discounting of notes receivable.
To record end-of-period adjustments for accrued interest on notes receivable and the apportionment of interest revenue.

Key terms

accrued interest receivable
accrued interest payable
cash proceeds
contingent liability
discounts
discount on notes payable
dishonored note
draft
- *cashier's check*
- *certified check*
- *sight draft*
- *time draft*
- *trade acceptance*

effective interest
endorsement
- *blank endorsement*
- *full endorsement*
- *qualified endorsement*

maturity date
maturity value
negotiable
noninterest-bearing note
notes payable
notes receivable
notes receivable discounted
promissory note
protest fee
simple interest
tickler file
unearned interest

Simple interest

Interest is the price of credit. Simply stated, interest may be called the rental charge made for the use of money. Because it is similar to the cost of supplies used during operations, interest to the maker of a note is an expense; to the payee of the note it is a revenue.

Simple interest is computed on the original principal (face value) of a note or a time draft. Interest amounts that may have accrued on the principal in past periods are *not* added to the amount on which interest is calculated.

Assume that Joan Rockness gives Thomas Blocher a 9 percent, 60-day note that has a principal amount of $4,000. The interest specified on a note or a draft, unless otherwise indicated, is an annual fraction or rate on the principal, or face amount, of the instrument. Thus, in Joan Rockness' note, the price, or rental charge, for the use of $4,000 for one year is $360 = ($4,000 × 0.09). Since the term of the note, however, is less than one year, the interest must be computed by multiplying the interest amount for one year by a fraction; the numerator is the term of the note in days and the denominator, the number of days in a year. The formula is:

$$\text{Interest} = \text{Principal} \times \text{Rate} \times \text{Time}$$

This is usually stated as I = PRT. In Rockness' note, the interest calculation for the 60-day period is:

$$I = \$4{,}000 \times 0.09 \times \frac{60}{360}$$

$$I = \$60$$

It is a common commercial practice to assume that the year contains 360 days (or 12 months of 30 days each) in computing interest. This practice is followed here, but it should be understood that the amount of bias in the final interest calculation is 1/73, that is:

$$\frac{365 - 360}{365} = \frac{1}{73}$$

Short-cut methods for calculating simple interest

A considerable saving of time is often possible by using various shortcuts for computing interest. Two of these methods are referred to as the 6 percent, 60-day method and the 6 percent, 6-day method. To illustrate the mathematical rationale behind these methods, it is helpful to design a basic formula for each method. For example, using the traditional interest formula, I = PRT, it is possible to state a formula for computing interest at 6 percent for 60 days on any principal by the following process:

$$I_{6\% \text{ for } 60 \text{ days}} = P \times 0.06 \times \frac{60}{360} = \frac{1}{100} P = 0.01 P$$

The new formula for computing interest on any principal at 6 percent for 60 days is $I_{6\% \text{ for } 60 \text{ days}} = 0.01\,P$. For example, the interest on $10,462 for 60 days at 6 percent can be computed as follows:

$$I = 0.01 \times \$10{,}462 = \$104.62$$

From the above example, observe that this formula involves the simple process of moving the decimal point in the principal two places to the left. A rule, therefore, may be stated verbally for these cases, viz.: to compute interest at 6 percent for 60 days, move the decimal point in the principal two places to the left. The following examples illustrate this verbal rule:

The interest at 6% for 60 days on $2,463.24 is $24.63.
The interest at 6% for 60 days on $4,465.00 is $44.65.

A similar formula and rule can be stated for the 6 percent, 6-day method: The formula for computing interest at 6 percent for 6 days on any principal is:

$$I_{6\% \text{ for } 6 \text{ days}} = P \times 0.06 \times \frac{6}{360} = \frac{1}{1000}P = 0.001\,P$$

A verbal rule for computing interest at 6 percent for 6 days on any principal is: to compute interest at 6 percent for 6 days on any principal, move the decimal point in the principal three places to the left. For example:

The interest at 6% for 6 days on $3,416.28 is $3.42.
The interest at 6% for 6 days on $8,960.00 is $8.96.

Either or both of these short-cut methods may be used for terms other than 6 or 60 days. The term of the note can be stated as a fraction or multiple of 6 or 60 days, and the interest may be quickly computed. To illustrate, the interest at 6 percent for 45 days on $4,000 can be computed as follows:

Interest for 60 days at 6% is	$40.00	
Interest for 30 days at 6% is ½ of $40.00, or		$20.00
Interest for 15 days at 6% is ¼ of $40.00, or		10.00
Interest for 45 days at 6% is		$30.00

The interest at 6 percent for 72 days on $4,720 can be computed as follows:

Interest for 60 days at 6% is	$47.20
Interest for 6 days at 6% is	4.72
Interest for 6 days at 6% is	4.72
Interest for 72 days at 6% is	$56.64

These short-cut methods also can be applied when the interest rate is other than 6 percent. If the interest rate is higher or lower than 6 percent, the interest calculation is first made at 6 percent, following which an adjustment is made for the difference between the 6 percent rate and the particular rate. The following two examples will illustrate these adjustments:

1. Interest at 7% on $3,600 for 90 days:

Interest at 6% for 60 days is	$36.00
Interest at 6% for 30 days is ½ of $36.00, or	18.00
Interest at 6% for 90 days is	$54.00
Interest at 1% for 90 days is ⅙ of $54.00, or	9.00
Interest at 7% for 90 days	$63.00

2. Interest at 4½% on $4,800 for 30 days:

Interest at 6% for 60 days is	$48.00
Interest at 6% for 30 days is ½ of $48.00, or	$24.00
Less: Interest at 1½% for 30 days is ¼ of $24.00, or	6.00
Interest at 4½% for 30 days is	$18.00

One advantage of the short-cut methods is that they require relatively simple arithmetical computations, thereby reducing the possibility of error. This observation is true when interest rates and terms are such that the mathematical manipulations are quite evident, but if rates and terms are "odd" and require elaborate adjustments, calculation time may not be reduced. Under these circumstances it might be better to resort to the use of the basic interest formula:

$$I = PRT$$

More about promissory notes

The promissory note was illustrated briefly in Chapter 1 and mentioned in other preceding chapters. Now we need to know details about this credit form.

A *negotiable promissory note* may be defined as an unconditional written promise to pay a specified sum of money to the order of a designated person, or to bearer, at a fixed or determinable future time or on demand. The term *negotiable* indicates that it can be legally transferred by its owner to another person or institution provided that the actions described in the following paragraphs are taken.

A typical note is illustrated in Figure 11–1. Joan Rockness, the *maker* gives Thomas Blocher, the designated *payee,* a 9 percent, 60-day note for $4,000, dated April 19, 1979, in payment for a purchase of merchandise. The outstanding characteristics of a note are the following:

1. The instrument must be in writing, signed by the maker.

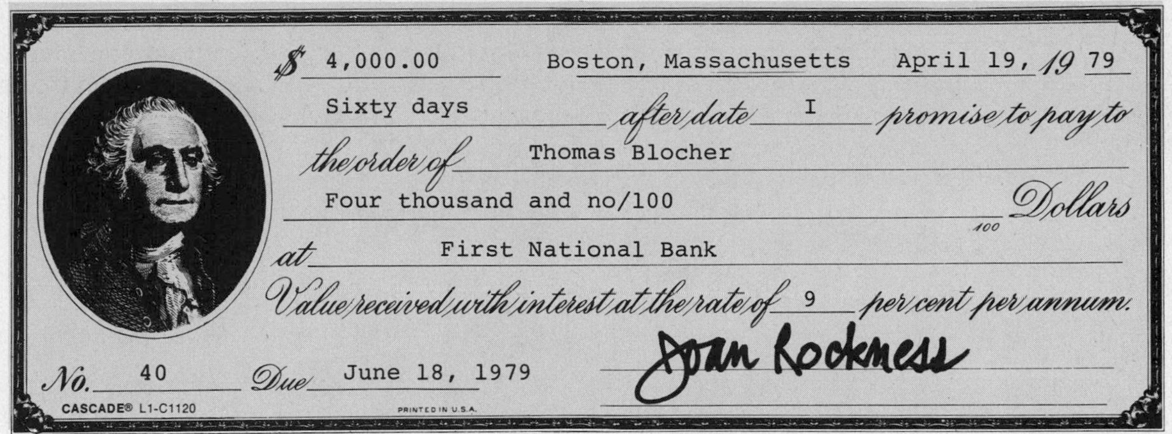

$ 4,000.00 Boston, Massachusetts April 19, 19 79

Sixty days after date I promise to pay to

the order of Thomas Blocher

Four thousand and no/100 /100 Dollars

at First National Bank

Value received with interest at the rate of 9 per cent per annum.

No. 40 Due June 18, 1979 Joan Rockness

CASCADE® L1-C1120 PRINTED IN U.S.A.

Figure 11–1 A promissory note

2. The instrument must contain an unconditional promise to pay a certain sum in money.
3. The instrument may be payable to the order of a designated person, the payee, or it may be payable to bearer (that is, anyone who holds the note).
4. The instrument must be payable either on demand or at a determinable time in the future.
5. The instrument may or may not be interest bearing.

The ownership of a negotiable promissory note is transferred simply by delivery if it is payable to the bearer; otherwise, it is transferred by endorsement and delivery.

A *blank endorsement* consists of a signature of the owner, or the payee, on the back of the instrument. A *full endorsement* consists of a notation on the back of the document, "Pay to the order of (name of person or company)," accompanied by the signature of the owner, say Thomas Blocher. If the endorser—the owner who is transferring the document—wishes to pass title to the instrument and at the same time to relieve himself of any further liability, he places his signature on the back of the note and adds the phrase "without recourse." This form is a *qualified endorsement*.

From the viewpoint of the maker, Joan Rockness, the note illustrated in Figure 11–1 is a liability and is recorded by crediting Notes Payable. From the viewpoint of the payee, Thomas Blocher, the same note is an asset and is recorded by debiting Notes Receivable. At the maturity date, June 18, 1979, Thomas Blocher or his agent, the First National Bank, will expect to receive $4,060 in cash for the note and interest, and Joan Rockness will expect to pay $4,060 in cash.

Maturity dates of notes

The *term* of a note may be expressed in years, months, or days. To determine the *maturity date* of a note expressed in months or years, count the number of months or years from the issuance date. For example, a two-year note dated

April 3, 1979, is due on April 3, 1981, and a two-month note dated April 3, 1979, is due on June 3, 1979. Occasionally, when time is expressed in months, there may be no corresponding date in the maturity month, in which case the last day of the month of maturity is used; a three-month note dated March 31 is due on June 30, and a one-month note dated January 29, 30, or 31 is due on the last day of February. If the term of the note is expressed in days, the maturity date is found by counting forward the specified number of days after the date of the note, excluding the date of the note but including the maturity date. The note of Joan Rockness in Figure 11–1 has an issuance date of April 19; the due date of June 18 is determined as follows:

Total days in April	30
Date of note in April	19
Number of days note runs in April (excluding April 19)	11
Total days in May	31
Total number of days note has run through May 31	42
Due date in June (60 days minus 42 days)	18
Term of the note	60

If the term of a note that is expressed in days includes an entire month, count the actual number of days in that month. The determination of the number of calendar days in a term expressed in months is the same as the calculation for a term expressed in days. Thus, a two-month note dated April 19 is due 61 days later on June 19. Interest may be computed for either 60 or 61 days. Though banks generally compute interest by using the exact number of days—61 days in the example—on their loans made directly to customers, the usual commercial practice is to calculate interest (as in the example) for two months of 30 days each, or 60 days rather than 61 days. The typical commercial practice is followed in this text; that is, the interest computation on a one-month note is based on 30 days; on a two-month note, 60 days; and so on.

Notes payable—short-term financing

The issuance of notes to trade creditors and the borrowing from banks on a company's own notes are two short-term financing devices discussed below. Managers faced with the decision about which method or which alternative to choose must consider for each method both its current and expected future availability and its effective cost. In general, a financial manager should choose the method or methods that will produce and continue to produce the desired short-term funds at the lowest long-run cost. In applying this general rule to specific financial decisions, management must consider such related variables as the availability of collateral, financial institutional connections, and the attendant effect on long-term debt financing.

Recording procedures involving notes payable

All notes payable may be recorded in a single Notes Payable account in the general ledger, disclosing supplementary details including name of payee, the interest rate, and the terms of the note, as shown below.

Notes Payable — Acct. No. 205

Date		Explanation	F	Debit	Credit	Balance
1979						
Nov.	15	B. B. Barker, 9%, 60 days	J62		2,000 00	2,000 00
	24	B. T. Arnold, 8%, 30 days	J65		450 00	2,450 00
Dec.	3	J. L. Jones, 8%, 90 days	J70		800 00	3,250 00
	10	F. T. Merrick, 8%, 60 days	J74		1,000 00	4,250 00
	18	P. O. Paulson, 9%, 90 days	J76		950 00	5,200 00
	24	B. T. Arnold (paid)	CR40	450 00		4,750 00

Issuance of notes for plant and equipment The following examples illustrate the recording of notes payable in the acquisition of plant and equipment.

Assume that on July 10, 1979, the Ace Company buys from the Triangle Machine Company a bookkeeping machine at a cost of $4,000; the creditor agrees to take a 90-day, *noninterest-bearing note* for the purchase price. This transaction is recorded as follows:

1979				
Jul.	10	Office Equipment	4,000 00	
		Notes Payable		4,000 00
		To record the purchase of a bookkeeping machine and the issuance of a 90-day non-interest-bearing note to Triangle Machine Company.		

On the maturity date, 90 days later, the payment of the note is recorded as follows:

1979				
Oct.	8	Notes Payable	4,000 00	
		Cash		4,000 00
		To record payment of a 90-day noninterest-bearing note issued to the Triangle Machine Company.		

Although the transaction of October 8, 1979, should be entered in the Ace Company's cash payments journal, for teaching purposes a general journal entry is shown to illustrate the *effect* of the transaction.

Few creditors, if any, accept noninterest-bearing notes. Therefore, in the second example, assume that the Ace Company purchases the same bookkeeping machine, but gives the Triangle Machine Company a 9 percent, 90-day note. The journal entry is similar to the previous one.

Date		Account	Debit	Credit
1979 Jul.	10	Office Equipment	4,000 00	
		Notes Payable		4,000 00
		To record the purchase of a bookkeeping machine and the issuance of a 9%, 90-day note to the Triangle Machine Company.		

On October 8, 1979, the payment of the note and interest to the Triangle Machine Company is recorded as follows:

Date		Account	Debit	Credit
1979 Oct.	8	Notes Payable	4,000 00	
		Interest Expense	90 00	
		Cash		4,090 00
		To record payment of a 9%, 90-day note and interest to the Triangle Machine Company.		

Issuance of notes for merchandise A business may use notes as a means of postponing payment of merchandise purchased for resale. These transactions may be recorded as were those in the preceding section. However, since the volume of business done with a particular supplier or customer must be known for managerial purposes, such as applying for quantity discounts, it is helpful to have a subsidiary ledger account showing the total history for all transactions with a particular firm. To supply management with this information, the accountant may wish to record all merchandise transactions involving notes through the Accounts Payable account and the individual creditors' accounts in the subsidiary ledger. For example, assume that on October 11, 1979, the Ace Company purchases merchandise costing $3,600 from the Boone Company and issues a 9 percent, 45-day note to the creditor. The note and interest are paid on November 25, 1979. These transactions are recorded as follows:

Date		Account	Debit	Credit
1979 Oct.	11	Purchases	3,600 00	
		Accounts Payable—Boone Company .		3,600 00
		To record merchandise purchased.		
	11	Accounts Payable—Boone Company . .	3,600 00	
		Notes Payable		3,600 00
		To record the issuance of a 9%, 45-day note to the Boone Company.		
Nov.	25	Notes Payable	3,600 00	
		Interest Expense	40 50	
		Cash		3,640 50
		To record payment of a note and interest to the Boone Company.		

Issuance of notes in settlement of open accounts A firm may issue a note to an open-account creditor as a means of further postponing payment, or a creditor may require a debtor to give a note if the account is past due. The entry for the issuance of a note in settlement of an open account payable is similar to the second entry dated October 11 in the previous section.

Issuance of notes to borrow from banks A business faced with the possibility of losing cash discounts may find it advantageous to borrow money from a bank to pay the open accounts within the discount periods. A 2/10, n/30 cash discount, for example, represents an annual cost saving of 36 percent, as was illustrated in Chapter 7. It is a sound financial decision to borrow money at 9 percent, for example, to prevent the loss of a 36 percent cost saving.

Banks and other grantors of credit handle notes in two ways: (1) money may be borrowed on an interest-bearing note signed by the borrower or (2) money may be advanced on a noninterest-bearing note *discounted* by the borrower. In the first case, the borrower receives the face value of the note and pays the face value plus the accumulated interest on the maturity date. In the second case, the note is noninterest bearing because the interest, or *discount,* is deducted in advance, and the borrower receives only the discounted value. At the maturity date, the borrower pays the face value of the note. The element of interest is present in either case; the difference is primarily one of form. There may also be notes that are noninterest bearing because the payee does not want to charge interest for some reason.

Assume that on March 1, 1979, the Ace Company borrows $10,000 from the First National Bank, giving a 9 percent, 60-day note, and that on April 30 it pays the bank for the note and interest. The issuance and payment of the note are recorded in the Ace Company's books as follows:

1979						
Mar.	1	Cash	10,000	00		
		Notes Payable			10,000	00
		To record a 9%, 60-day note issued to the First National Bank.				

Apr.	30	Notes Payable	10,000	00		
		Interest Expense	150	00		
		Cash			10,150	00
		To record payment of a 9%, 60-day note to the First National Bank.				

Assume that on May 1, 1979, the Ace Company borrows money from the City National Bank, discounting its own $10,000, 60-day, noninterest-bearing note at the *discount rate* of 9 percent. The amount of cash received in this case is $9,850, or $10,000 less a discount of $150, computed by applying the discount rate to the face value which is the maturity value for the discount period of 60 days. If the maturity date falls within the current accounting period—the calendar year is assumed—the following entries are made in the Ace Company's books:

Date		Account	Debit	Credit
1979				
May	1	Cash	9,850 00	
		Interest Expense	150 00	
		Notes Payable		10,000 00
		To record a noninterest-bearing note issued to the City National Bank discounted at 9% for 60 days.		
Jun.	30	Notes Payable	10,000 00	
		Cash		10,000 00
		To record payment of a non-interest-bearing note to the City National Bank.		

Assume that the Ace Company had issued the note on December 16, 1979. Since the maturity date falls in the accounting year 1980, under the nonreversing approach the following entry would be made:

Date		Account	Debit	Credit
1979				
Dec.	16	Cash	9,850 00	
		Discount on Notes Payable	150 00	
		Notes Payable		10,000 00
		To record a noninterest-bearing note discounted at 9%, for 60 days.		

The $150 discount is not prepaid and should *not* be debited to Prepaid Interest, as is sometimes done. The interest is not paid until the note matures. At that time, the net amount borrowed of $9,850 plus total interest of $150 is paid; therefore, the balance of Discount on Notes Payable represents a potential interest expense. Accordingly, adjusting entries are required at December 31, 1979, and 1980, to transfer the applicable expense portions of the balance of Discount on Notes Payable to the Interest Expense account of the respective years; the adjusting entries are illustrated later in this chapter.

Discount on Notes Payable should be shown in the balance sheet as a contra account to (subtracted from) Notes Payable under Current Liabilities. On the date of issuance of the note, it causes the carrying value to indicate the net amount of funds received from creditors on note. Later, as adjustments are made to the Discount on Notes Payable account, the difference between the Notes Payable account and the balance of the Discount on Notes Payable account shows the net amount borrowed plus accrued interest on that amount.

In both the March 1 and May 1 bank loans, the amount paid at maturity was $150 more than the amount received from the bank by the borrower. However, the borrower had the use of $10,000, or the full face value of the interest-bearing note (March 1 bank loan), whereas only $9,850 was available from the noninterest-bearing discounted note. The *effective interest rate* (i) on a discounted note may be computed by the following formula:

$$i = \frac{D}{P} \times \frac{12}{T}$$

where D = the amount of the discount
P = the net proceeds
12 = months in the year, and
T = the term of the note in months

The effective interest in the example thus is not 9 percent; rather, it is 9.137 percent, calculated as follows:

$$i = \frac{\$150}{\$9,850} \times \frac{12}{2} = 1.522843\% \times 6 = 9.137\%$$

The accountant should carefully determine the effective interest rate of a loan, since this is relevant to making any short-term financial decision. The amount of the discount on a note is the difference between its value on the date of discount and its value at maturity. *Maturity value* is the amount that will be paid at maturity; it is the principal plus total interest for the life of the note. Since discount and interest are similar in that each represents the charge for the use of money, the Interest Expense account is used in this text to record the incurred portion of expense for each of these items.

Discount

A* discount *may be defined as a deduction made from a gross future sum to arrive at the current present value of that sum.

End-of-period adjustments

Since interest is incurred continuously throughout the life of a note payable, it is necessary to make adjusting entries for the interest expense on those notes payable that mature in a later accounting period. Two kinds of adjustments are considered: the accrual of interest on an interest-bearing note payable and the expense apportionment on a discounted note payable.

Assume that the Adjusto Company has the following accounts in its general ledger as of December 31, 1979:

Notes Payable — Acct. No. 205

Date		Explanation	F	Debit	Credit	Balance
1979						
Dec.	1	Hamm Co., 9%, 90 days	J17		9,300 00	9,300 00
	16	Bank of Rodin, 120 days discounted at 9%	CR12		7,200 00	16,500 00

Discount on Notes Payable — Acct. No. 205A

Date		Explanation	F	Debit	Credit	Balance
1979						
Dec.	16		CR12	216 00		216 00

At December 31, 1979, the following two adjusting entries are made:

1979						
Dec.	31	Interest Expense	69	75		
		Accrued Interest Payable			69	75
		To record accrued interest on the note issued to the Hamm Co.; interest for 30 days at 9% on $9,300 is $69.75.				
	31	Interest Expense	27	00		
		Discount on Notes Payable			27	00
		To record the transfer of $27.00 interest from the Discount on Notes Payable account to the Interest Expense account on the note discounted at the Bank of Rodin: $7,200 x 0.09 x 15/360.				

Comments on these two entries follow:

1. The amount of the accrued interest on a note issued to the Hamm Company is figured at 9 percent for 30 days, the number of days after December 1, including December 31. Of course, no interest for the time period after December 31, 1979, should be recorded as an expense of 1979.
2. The second adjusting entry transfers interest from the Discount on Notes Payable account to the Interest Expense account. There are two methods by which the interest expense of $27.00 for 1979 can be determined: (1) The amount of the discount may be multiplied by a fraction consisting of the age of the note as of the adjustment date divided by the term—in the example, 15/120 × $216 = $27.00. (2) An ordinary interest computation may be made—interest at 9 percent on $7,200 for 15 days is $27.00.

On March 1, 1980, when the Adjusto Company pays the Hamm Company for the note and interest, under the nonreversing approach the following journal entry is made:

1980						
Mar.	1	Notes Payable	9,300	00		
		Accrued Interest Payable	69	75		
		Interest Expense	139	50		
		Cash			9,509	25
		To record payment of a 9%, 90-day note and interest to the Hamm Co.				

The credit to Cash of $9,509.25 includes the payment of two liabilities already on the books, Notes Payable and Accrued Interest Payable. The payment of interest expense of $139.50 = (9% × 60/360 × $9,300) is entirely applicable to 1980.

The April 15, 1980, payment of the $7,200 to the Bank of Rodin is recorded in the following journal entry:

1980				
Apr.	15	Notes Payable	7,200 00	
		Cash		7,200 00
		To record payment of a note to the Bank of Rodin.		

Since the note is noninterest bearing, no interest is recorded at the time of payment. However, the $189 balance in the Discount on Notes Payable account represents an expense of the year 1980. The following adjusting entry is made as of December 31, 1980, to transfer this amount to the Interest Expense account:

1980				
Dec.	31	Interest Expense	189 00	
		Discount on Notes Payable		189 00
		To apportion the amount of interest expense applicable to the year 1980.		

Notes receivable

Many firms accept promissory notes from customers. This will enable them to discount these notes at financial institutions (same as selling to) as a means of obtaining short-term funds. The accounting for notes receivable is similar to that for notes payable. Hence, a pattern similar to that used in the foregoing section to describe notes payable is followed below in the discussion of notes receivable.

Recording procedures—notes receivable

Many businesses make use of promissory notes in sales of merchandise on credit. These businesses include firms selling high-priced durable goods such as furniture, farm machinery, and automobiles. Notes receivable are also received by a financial institution when it lends money.

It is perhaps even more important to keep good accounting records for notes receivable than it is for notes payable. After all, the payee of a note payable will send a statement to the maker that a note is due, so there is little danger that the maker will overlook the due date. The holder of notes receivable must have the records arranged so that he or she can notify the debtor that the note is due. This requires that notes receivable be filed according to maturity dates in a tickler file that is properly safeguarded. A *tickler file* reveals the due date of notes in an obvious manner—by dates or color coding or some other visual display indicating the due date.

All notes receivable are usually recorded in a single general ledger account. The tickler file of notes receivable plus the general ledger account containing such information as the maker, the term, the interest rate, and any property pledged as security (collateral) make it unnecessary for a firm to maintain a subsidiary notes receivable ledger. The Notes Receivable account of the Travis Armour Company is shown here.

Notes Receivable — Acct. No. 111

Date		Explanation	F	Debit		Credit		Balance	
1979									
Nov.	1	C. Anson, 45 days, 8%	J51	775	00			775	00
Dec.	16	C. Anson, paid	CR20			775	00	-0-	
	20	B. Barker, 90 days, 9%	J60	425	00			425	00
	20	L. Watts, 60 days, 8%	J60	500	00			925	00

Each debit posting indicates that an asset, Notes Receivable, has been acquired from a customer; each credit entry indicates that a particular note has been settled by payment or renewal or has been dishonored (not paid). In addition to the dollar amounts in the money columns, the Explanation columns should give the maker's name, the term of the note, the interest rate, and any other relevant information.

If this information is not provided in the Explanation column of the Notes Receivable account, then it must be provided in some other supplementary records in order to make easy later accounting such as adjustments. For example, if the volume of transactions warrants it, a special notes receivable register could be created. Special Debit and Credit money columns could be inserted, along with memorandum columns for supplementary information. This register could serve as both a journal and a subsidiary record of notes receivable.

Receipt of a note for a sale Assume that on March 3, 1979, the Potter Company sells merchandise to John Rawson and receives a 9 percent, 90-day note for $1,300. The following entries are made:

Date		Account	Debit		Credit	
1979						
Mar.	3	Accounts Receivable—John Rawson . .	1,300	00		
		Sales			1,300	00
		To record sales of merchandise.				
	3	Notes Receivable	1,300	00		
		Accounts Receivable—John Rawson .			1,300	00
		To record the receipt of a 9% 90-day note from John Rawson.				

The first entry is made so that the customer's account in the subsidiary ledger will contain a complete record of all credit sales transactions. This information is useful to management in making decisions about collection efforts and further extension of credit.

On June 1, 1979, when the Potter Company receives a payment from John Rawson, the following entry is made:

1979				
Jun.	1	Cash	1,329 25	
		Notes Receivable		1,300 00
		Interest Earned		29 25
		To record receipt of payment from John Rawson for note and interest due today.		

The Interest Earned account is a revenue account. The balance of this account is closed at the end of the accounting period to the Income Summary account.

Receipt of a note in settlement of an open account Assume that Ralph Tanner owes the Potter Company $3,700, due on July 10, 1979. On August 1 the Potter Company agrees to accept a 60-day, noninterest-bearing note with a face value of $3,755.50 (the amount receivable, $3,700, plus interest at 9 percent for 60 days) in settlement of the open account. This procedure is common among retailers who plan to discount their notes to banks for cash. Banks prefer that most, if not all, of their notes be noninterest bearing. The major reason is one of simplicity of accounting in that the maturity value is equal to the principal amount of the note. Since the maturity date of this note falls within the current accounting period—the calendar year is assumed—the following entry is made:

1979				
Aug.	1	Notes Receivable	3,755 50	
		Accounts Receivable—Ralph Tanner.		3,700 00
		Interest Earned		55 50
		To record receipt of a 60-day, noninterest-bearing note, with interest of $55.50 included in the face value, from Ralph Tanner.		

The credit of the entire $55.50 to the revenue account, Interest Earned, is permissible, since that amount will become revenue by the time the books are closed on December 31.

When payment is received on September 30, the following entry is made:

1979				
Sep.	30	Cash	3,755 50	
		Notes Receivable		3,755 00
		To record collection of note from Ralph Tanner.		

If the note of August 1, 1979, had been received on December 1, 1979, all the interest would *not* be earned by December 31, 1979. The following entry is required:

1979				
Dec.	1	Notes Receivable	3,755 50	
		Accounts Receivable—Ralph Tanner.		3,700 00
		Unearned Interest (Included in Face of Notes Receivable) . . .		55 50
		To record receipt of a 60-day, noninterest-bearing note, with interest of $55.50 included in face value, from Ralph Tanner.		

The Unearned Interest account, credited for $55.50, represents the interest that will be partly earned in 1979 and partly earned in 1980. The unearned interest should *not* be classified on the balance sheet as a current liability, as is sometimes done. Rather, it should be shown as a contra account to Notes Receivable, to reduce that account to an estimate of its present value at the present time. This present worth figure, the carrying value, increases as the note approaches maturity date, and represents the approximate amount that could be received by discounting the note at a bank. The Unearned Interest account will require adjusting entries at December 1979 and 1980, to apportion the amount of applicable revenue earned in the respective years to the operations of those years. This procedure is described later in this chapter.

Dishonor of a note receivable by the maker

If a note cannot be collected at maturity, it is said to be *dishonored* by the maker. Another term that is often used is *defaulting* on a note. Once the maturity date of a note passes without the note being collected, an entry should be made transferring the face value of the note plus any uncollected accrued interest to the Accounts Receivable account.

Assume that on June 1, 1979, Ronald Reynolds issued a 9 percent, 90-day note for $4,000 to the Potter Company. At the maturity date, August 30, 1979, Reynolds fails to pay the amount of the note and interest, at which time the following entry is made on the books of the Potter Company:

1979				
Aug.	30	Accounts Receivable—Ronald Reynolds	4,090 00	
		Notes Receivable		4,000 00
		Interest Earned		90 00
		To record the dishonor by Ronald Reynolds of a 9%, 90-day note.		

Two questions arise in connection with this entry: (1) Why should $90 be recognized as revenue and credited to the Interest Earned account? (2) Why should the item be allowed to remain as a valid accounts receivable?

Under the accrual concept, the interest has been earned. It represents a valid claim against the maker of the note; if the face of the note is collectible, then so is the interest. This leads to the answer to the second question. The fact that a note is uncollectible at its maturity is not a definite indication that it will never be collected. In the absence of evidence to the contrary most business firms assume that notes will ultimately be collected. If the amounts involved are material all possible steps including legal action will certainly be taken to collect both accounts and notes receivable, and only after such steps have failed will an account be considered to be written off as a loss.

End-of-period adjusting entries for interest on notes receivable

The adjusting entries for interest on notes receivable parallel the adjusting entries for interest on notes payable. The major problem is accurate measurement of the revenue, Interest Earned, and the asset, Accrued Interest Receivable, or the contra-asset account, Unearned Interest (Included in Face of Notes Receivable). To illustrate the adjusting entries and the effect they have on the accounting for notes and interest in the next accounting period, assume that the Emerson Company has the following accounts in its general ledger as of December 31, 1979:

Notes Receivable — Acct. No. 111

Date		Explanation	F	Debit	Credit	Balance
1979 Nov.	1	Linda Wilson, 9%, 150 days	J71	3,440 00		3,440 00
Dec.	1	George Akins, 90-days noninterest-bearing note, but interest of $108 is in the face.	J79	4,908 00		8,348 00

Unearned Interest (Included in Face of Notes Receivable) — Acct. No. 111A

Date		Explanation	F	Debit	Credit	Balance
1979 Dec.	1	Interest in face of George Akins note	J79		108 00	108 00

At December 31, 1979, the accountant for the Emerson Company makes the following adjusting entries:

Date		Account	Debit	Credit
1979 Dec.	31	Accrued Interest Receivable	51 60	
		Interest Earned		51 60
		To record the accrued interest on the Linda Wilson note at 9% for 60 days.		
	31	Unearned Interest (Included in Face of Notes Receivable)	36 00	
		Interest Earned		36 00
		To record the transfer of 1/3 of $108 interest on the note from George Akins from the Unearned Interest account to the Revenue account.		

Comments on these adjustments follow:

1. The accrued interest receivable on the note from Linda Wilson is figured at 9 percent for 60 days, the number of days after November 1 including December 31. No interest for the period after December 31, 1979, should be recorded as revenue in the year 1979.
2. The second adjustment involves the apportionment of interest revenue earned in a given period, 1979, to that year.

On March 1, 1980, when the Emerson Company collects the George Akins note, the following entry is made:

Date		Account	Debit		Credit	
1980						
Mar.	1	Cash	4,908	00		
		Notes Receivable			4,908	00
		To record collection of a note from George Akins.				

Since the note is noninterest-bearing on the face, no interest is recorded at the time of collection. However, a balance of $72 remains in the Unearned Interest account, representing revenue earned in the year 1980. Thus, an adjusting entry is necessary as of December 31, 1980, to transfer this amount to the Interest Earned account:

Date		Account	Debit		Credit	
1980						
Dec.	31	Unearned Interest (Included in Face of Notes Receivable)	72	00		
		Interest Earned			72	00
		To apportion the amount of interest revenue applicable to the year 1980.				

A slightly different problem is associated with the collection of the note from Linda Wilson. The following entry is made on March 31, 1980, when the note is collected assuming that the adjusting entry was not reversed:

Date		Account	Debit		Credit	
1980						
Mar.	31	Cash	3,569	00		
		Notes Receivable			3,440	00
		Accrued Interest Receivable . . .			51	60
		Interest Earned			77	40
		To record collection of a 9%, 150-day note and interest from Linda Wilson.				

The debit of $3,569 to Cash represents the collection of two receivables already on the books, Notes Receivable and Accrued Interest Receivable, and of a revenue, Interest Earned, of $77.40, which was earned in, and is entirely applicable to, the year 1980.

Discounting customers' notes receivable

For a business that receives a large number of notes from customers and who may need to obtain cash to continue operations, it may be economically advantageous to obtain this cash by *discounting* its *notes receivable* at a bank rather than holding them to maturity. The bank purchases the notes for cash less a discount. If the credit rating of the firm is good, most banks will usually discount customers' notes receivable because, if the maker fails to pay the bank the maturity value when it is due, the firm that has discounted the note—having previously endorsed it—must make payment to the bank.

***A potential obligation on the part of the endorser such as the one described above is referred to as a* contingent liability.**

Contingent liability

Determining the cash proceeds

As far as the bank is concerned, it is making a loan to the borrower, based on the maturity value of the note including any interest, because that is the amount the bank will collect from the maker at the maturity date. The discount the bank deducts is based on a stipulated rate of the maturity value for the period the note has to run. The balance represents *cash proceeds*. To compute the proceeds of a discounted note:

1. The maturity value, or the principal plus the total interest to maturity, is determined.
2. The discount period, or the number of days the note still has to run after the date of the discount, is found.
3. The discount is computed at the stipulated bank rate for the discount period.
4. The discount is deducted from the maturity value to find the cash proceeds.

This sequence may be stated as:

$$P = MV - (MV \times d \times RL)$$

where P = the cash proceeds
MV = the maturity value
d = the rate of discount
RL = the remaining life of the note

Assume that on April 19, 1979, the Fuller Company receives from Edward Grande a 9 percent, 60-day note for $4,000 in settlement of a past-due open account. This transaction is recorded as follows:

1979						
Apr.	19	Notes Receivable	4,000	00		
		Accounts Receivable—Edward Grande			4,000	00
		To record receipt of a 9% 60-day note from Grande in settlement of a past-due open account.				

On May 1, 1979, the Fuller Company, needing short-term funds, decides to discount Grande's note at the bank's rate of 8 percent. Calculation of the proceeds follows:

1.	Maturity value of note (principal of $4,000 plus total interest of $60)		$4,060.00
2.	Due date	June 18	
3.	Period of discount:		
	May 1—May 31 (not counting May 1)	30 days	
	June 1—June 18 (including June 18)	18 days	
		48 days	
4.	Discount at 8% for 48 days on the maturity value: 0.08 x $4,060 x 48/360		43.31
	Net Cash Proceeds		$4,016.69

Recording the proceeds

The entry on the Fuller Company's books is:

1979				
May	1	Cash	4,016.69	
		Notes Receivable Discounted		4,000.00
		Interest Earned		16.69
		To record the discounting of Edward Grande's 9%, 60-day note at the bank at 8%.		

The Notes Receivable Discounted account is used to indicate that the Fuller Company, having endorsed the note before turning it over to the bank, is now obligated to pay the bank if Grande fails to do so; that is, the Fuller Company would have to pay the $4,000 contingent liability plus the $60 interest at 9 percent for 60 days, plus any protest fee charged by the bank. A *protest fee* is a charge made by the bank for notifying the last endorser that the maker has failed to pay the amount of the note and interest. The obligation assumed by the Fuller Company is contingent on Grande's payment, and the account is therefore referred to as a *contingent liability account*. The Notes Receivable Discounted account brings the existence of the contingent liability to the attention of the reader of the balance sheet.

Full disclosure

In preparing financial statements, **full disclosure** *of all essential facts such as contingent liabilities is of paramount importance.*

Grande does not need to be informed that the note has been discounted, and no entry is required on his books; his obligation to pay the maturity value of the note on its presentation by the legal owner remains unchanged.

Presentation on the balance sheet

Assume that on May 31 the Notes Receivable account shows a balance of $7,000 (including the $4,000 note discounted on May 1). The balance sheet prepared on that date may disclose the existence of the contingent liability by a footnote or supplementary note to the balance sheet as follows:

Assets	
Current Assets	
Notes Receivable (see Note 1)	$3,000.00

Note 1: The company is contingently liable for notes receivable discounted in the amount of $4,000.

Disclosure of the contingent liability can also be made by offsetting Notes Receivable Discounted against Notes Receivable in the balance sheet in the following manner:

Assets		
Current Assets		
Notes Receivable	$7,000.00	
Deduct Notes Receivable Discounted	4,000.00	
Net Notes Receivable		$3,000.00

Payment of a discounted note

The bank normally does not notify the discounter of payment by the maker. Therefore, if notification of dishonor is not received from the bank it is assumed that the maker has paid the note at the maturity date, and the discounter is released from the contingent liability. The entry on the Fuller Company's books to eliminate the contingent liability is:

1979						
Jun.	18	Notes Receivable Discounted	4,000	00		
		Notes Receivable			4,000	00
		To eliminate the contingent liability on Grande's note, which was discounted on May 1, 1979.				

The entry on *Edward Grande's books* on the date of payment is:

1979						
Jun.	18	Notes Payable	4,000	00		
		Interest Expense	60	00		
		Cash			4,060	00
		To record payment to the bank for a 9%, 60-day note issued to the Fuller Company on April 19, 1979.				

The debit to Interest Expense is for the full 60-day period. It is assumed that no adjusting entry has been made previously for any interest expense.

Nonpayment of a discounted note

If Edward Grande dishonors the note at the maturity date, the bank must follow a certain formal procedure involving the preparation of notarized protest documents to establish the legal basis for the collection of the full amount from the Fuller Company. Assuming that the bank charges a protest fee of $5, the following entries are made on the Fuller Company's books when the company pays the bank the face value of the note, the interest, and the protest fee.

1979				
Jun.	18	Accounts Receivable—Edward Grande .	4,065 00	
		Cash		4,065 00
		To record payment of Edward Grande's note, which was discounted and is now dishonored by Grande.		
		Protest Fee . . . . . . $ 5		
		Interest 60		
		Face Value 4,000		
		Total $4,065		
	18	Notes Receivable Discounted	4,000 00	
		Notes Receivable		4,000 00
		To record the elimination of the contingent liability and Grande's discounted and dishonored note.		

Observe that *Accounts Receivable,* instead of Notes Receivable Discounted, is debited in the entry recording the cash payment. This procedure avoids the error of treating discounted notes as though they were actual liabilities; since payment is made as soon as the contingency is realized, no book liability needs to be recorded. The second journal entry is necessary to remove the contingent liability after the cash payment for the dishonored note is made.

The fact that a note is dishonored does not mean that it will be definitely uncollectible or that it should be written off as a loss. Grande, in this case, may pay at a later date, either voluntarily or on a court order. The account remains open in the accounts receivable ledger until it is settled or definitely determined to be uncollectible and written off.

Drafts — appendix one

A *draft* is a written order to pay, such as a bank check, with the same negotiability as a note, for which it is often used as a substitute. Commercial drafts, excluding checks, are used to enforce the collection of open accounts, to obtain the advantages of both a written acknowledgment and a negotiable instrument, and for C.O.D. (collect on delivery) shipments.

The person who issues the order and draws the draft is the *drawer;* the person to whom it is addressed and who is to make payment is the *drawee;* and the person to whom payment is to be made is the *payee*. If the drawer names himself or herself as the payee—a common occurrence with commercial drafts—the draft becomes a two-party document similar to a note. The types of drafts used in business are (1) *ordinary checks,* (2) *certified checks,* (3) *cashier's or treasurer's checks,* (4) *sight drafts,* (5) *time drafts,* and (6) *trade acceptances.*

An *ordinary check* is one form of a three-party sight draft; it is accounted for as cash received from a customer or as cash paid when a check is written. A *certified check* is a check that has been stamped *certified* by a bank and for which the bank reduces the drawer's account immediately at the time of certification. A *cashier's* or *treasurer's* check is purchased from a bank; such a check is written by officials of a bank and is guaranteed by the bank; cashiers' checks are treated as cash items.

A *commercial sight draft,* a demand for payment by the person to whom money is owed, may be used to attempt to collect money from a customer who has a past-due account, or may be used to make a C.O.D. sale. The sight draft, attached to the order bill of lading (the document authorizing the passage of title to the goods; this same document is also a receipt given by the common carrier), is mailed to the customer's bank. Since the customer cannot get the merchandise without the order bill of lading, the payment of the draft must precede receipt of the bill of lading and delivery of the goods by the warehouse or the transportation firm. To help account for the shipment of merchandise, a journal entry made at the time the sight draft is drawn would debit Accounts Receivable and credit Sales. No entry would be made for the draft itself at this time, because the drawing of a draft is simply an intent until the draft is accepted. When the draft is honored by payment and the drawer is notified of the fact, Cash and an expense account for any collection fee charged by the bank are debited and Accounts Receivable is credited.

A *time draft* is due after the passage of a specified period. The drawer presents the instrument to the drawee, who indicates his or her agreement to pay the draft at maturity by writing "Accepted" across the face of the draft and signing it properly. The accounting entry usually made on the drawee's books when the drawee accepts a time draft drawn by a creditor for an amount of a past-due open account is a debit to Accounts Payable and a credit to Notes Payable. When he or she receives the accepted draft from the debtor, the drawer debits Notes Receivable and credits Accounts Receivable. The accounting for any interest that the draft bears is similar to that for notes. The interest may accrue from the date of the draft—*60 days from date*—or from the date the draft was accepted by drawee—*60 days from sight*. A *trade acceptance* is a special form of time draft used in connection with a special sales transaction. The document is drawn by the seller of merchandise. Its acceptance by the buyer serves as an acknowledgment of the purchase, and it then assumes the same status as a note. Trade acceptances may be used to ensure prompt payment and to borrow money.

A rough approximation of the cost of borrowing money on installment purchases

appendix two

An essential factor in all short-term financial decisions is the effective cost of the particular means of financing. Even though legislation requires the disclosure of the effective annual interest cost of borrowed funds, debtors should be familiar with the computations involved in the determination of these rates, or at least in approximating these rates. This knowledge is particularly important when individuals are faced with the decision of selecting a single method from among several alternative short-term financing methods.

With installment purchase plans where the effective interest rate is not stated, it is particularly helpful to know a method of quickly approximating this rate. Such an approximation involves making the simplifying assumption that each payment constitutes equal reductions in the principal amount owed; thus the average debt for the interest period is the original principal divided by two. Then the interest for the period can readily be compared with the average outstanding principal. One must be very careful to ''annualize'' any interest rate that is determined. To illustrate this approximation, assume that merchandise costing $1,000 is purchased; this amount is to be paid in twenty-four equal monthly installments of $50 each (which includes interest). The calculation is as follows:

1. Average outstanding principal = $1,000/2 = $500.
2. Annual absolute interest cost:
   Total interest for two years = ($50 x 24) – $1,000 = $200.
   Interest for one year = $200 ÷ 2 = $100.
3. Rough approximation of effective annual interest rate = $100/$500 = 20 percent per year, or 1.67 percent each month.

Glossary

Accrued interest payable A liability representing the interest that has accumulated on notes payable or other interest-bearing liabilities.

Accrued interest receivable An asset representing the interest that has accumulated on notes receivable or other interest-bearing receivables.

Blank endorsement The signature of the owner, the payee, on the back of a negotiable instrument; the endorsement guarantees the validity of the instrument and warrants the payment of the instrument in case of dishonor by the maker at maturity.

Cash proceeds The amount of cash that is received when a firm discounts a note at a bank.

Cashier's check A check drawn by the cashier of a bank on itself; cashier's checks are sold to individuals or businesses for a small fee.

Certified check An ordinary bank check, personal or business, stamped "Certified" and signed by an official of the bank; thus the bank reduces the drawer's account when the check is certified and guarantees the check.

Contingent liability An amount that may become a liability in the future *if* certain events occur.

Discount An amount subtracted from a future sum to determine net cash proceeds as at the present time.

Discount on notes payable A contra to the Notes Payable account representing the interest that was deducted from the face amount of the note; the Discount on Notes Payable amount will be allocated to the applicable periods to which the interest expense belongs.

Dishonored note A note that has not been paid by the maker at the maturity date.

Draft A written order signed by the drawer directing the drawee to pay a specified sum of money to the order of a designated person or to bearer (either is the payee), at a fixed or determinable future time or on demand.

Effective interest The correct interest computed on only the remaining balance of an unpaid debt for the specific time period, usually stated as an annual fraction.

Full endorsement An endorsement consisting of a notation on the back of a negotiable instrument of "Pay to the order of (name of person or company)" accompanied by the signature of the owner; the full endorsement requires the subsequent endorsement of the named endorsee before the instrument can be transferred further.

Interest The price of credit; a rental charge for the use of money.

Maturity date The date on which a negotiable instrument is due and payable.

Maturity value The amount payable (or receivable) on a negotiable instrument at its maturity date; it includes face value plus any stated interest.

Negotiable A characteristic of a document that permits it to be transferred for value received by endorsement to another person.

Noninterest-bearing note A note which does not bear any interest on the face; the principal sum named in the note is the maturity value of the note.

Notes payable Amount payable to creditors supported by formal written promises to pay.

Notes receivable Claims against individuals or companies supported by formal written promises to pay. A note receivable may be either a trade note or a nontrade note.

Notes receivable discounted An account that discloses the contingent liability for customers' notes which have been discounted.

Promissory note An unconditional written promise to pay a specified sum of money to the order of a designated person, or to bearer, at a fixed or determinable future time or on demand.

Protest fee A fee charged by a bank or financial institution for a note which is dishonored (not paid) at maturity.

Qualified endorsement An endorsement accompanied by the phrase "without recourse," that tends to relieve the endorser of any further liability.

Sight draft A demand for immediate payment to oneself (the drawer) or to another person (that is, when draft is presented for payment); an ordinary check is a sight draft.

Simple interest Interest on the original principal only.

Time draft A draft that is due after the passage of a specified period; the time may be measured from the date that the draft is drawn or from the date that the draft is accepted by the drawee.

Trade acceptance A special form of time draft arising out of a specific sales transaction.

Unearned interest An amount included in the face value of a note receivable; it represents future interest revenue, and should be disclosed on the balance sheet as a contra item to Notes Receivable.

Questions

Q11–1 Define the term interest. Assume that a man pays $10 for borrowing $100 for a year and 55 cents for a gallon of gasoline. Discuss the nature —similarities and differences—of each of these figures.

Q11–2 Describe two short-cut methods of calculating simple interest. Discuss the reason that the methods will provide correct answers.

Q11–3 Many firms attempt to disguise the effective simple interest rate charged for funds that are loaned. From personal experience or from research, name three ways that are used to disguise the effective simple interest rate.

Q11–4 Explain the following terms or procedures (a) negotiable instrument, (b) the 6 percent, 60-day method, (c) interest-bearing note, (d) the maker of a note, and (e) the payee of a note.

Q11–5 Discuss the managerial factors that a company must consider in determining what method of short-term financing it should choose.

Q11–6 Describe briefly how a person may calculate the effective interest rate on his own note discounted at a bank.

Q11–7 Under what conditions would a company issue notes? Give four examples where notes are issued very frequently.

Q11–8 Explain the following terms or procedures (a) discounting a note, (b) bank discount rate, (c) contingent liability, (d) proceeds, (e) maturity value, and (f) a dishonored note.

Q11–9 The accountant for the Davis Company recorded the receipt of a note on a sale to Lane Brown as follows:

Notes Receivable	1,150	
Sales		1,150

State how you think the transaction should have been recorded and give your reason.

Q11–10 The following account balances appear in the general ledger of the Carwan Company:

Notes Receivable	
35,000	

Notes Payable	
	20,000

Notes Receivable Discounted	
	15,000

(a) What is the amount of customers' notes outstanding? (b) What amount of customer notes are in the Carwan Company's possession? (c) What amount of customers' notes have been discounted? (d) What is the Carwan Company's contingent liability on discounted notes? (e) How would these accounts be shown in the balance sheet?

Q11–11 Six transactions related to a sale to a customer are recorded in the T accounts. Describe each transaction.

Cash	
(c) 904	(d) 911
(f) 916	

Accounts Receivable	
(a) 900	(b) 900
(d) 911	(f) 911

Notes Receivable	
(b) 900	(e) 900

Notes Receivable Discounted	
(e) 900	(c) 900

Sales	
	(a) 900

Interest Earned	
	(c) 4
	(f) 5

Q11–12 (a) What is a contingent liability? (b) May there be more than one person contingently liable on a particular note? Explain. (c) What amounts must a person who is contingently liable on an interest-bearing note pay if the maker dishonors the note on its due date?

Class exercises

CE11–1 (Journalizing notes payable transactions) The Thompson Company completed the following transaction during 1979 and 1980:

1979

Jan. 2 Purchased $3,680 worth of merchandise from the Nolta Company; issued a 9 percent, 60-day note.

Mar. 3 Paid the Nolta Company the amount due for the note and interest.

3 Issued a 9 percent, 45-day note for $4,000 to Owens, Inc., in settlement of an open account.

Apr. 17 Paid Owens, Inc., $3,000 on the March 3 note plus all the interest; issued a new 10 percent, 30-day note for the balance of the principal.

May 17 Paid Owens, Inc., for the April 17 note.

June 1 Discounted its own 30-day, noninterest-bearing note, made out to the First National Bank in the amount of $8,000, at a discount rate of 9 percent.

July 1 Paid the First National Bank the amount due.

Dec. 1 Issued a 9 percent, 90-day note for $5,680 to the Petersen Company in settlement of an open account.

Dec. 16 Discounted its own 60-day, noninterest-bearing note, made out to the Second National Bank in the amount of $10,000 at a discount rate of 9 percent.

1980

Feb. 14 Paid the Second National Bank the amount due.

Mar. 1 Paid amount due to Petersen Company for the note issued on December 1, 1979.

Required: Journalize the transactions, including any necessary adjusting entries on December 31, 1979 and 1980.

CE11–2 (Effective interest computation) The following transactions took place at the Harrod Company:

a. Discounted its own 90-day, noninterest-bearing note for $5,000 at a bank at 9 percent.
b. Borrowed $4,800 in cash from a bank; interest at 8 percent on $4,800 is added to the note, making the principal amount of the note $5,184; the note is to be paid off in monthly installments over 12 months ($432 each month).

Required: Compute the effective interest cost in each case.

CE11–3 (Journalizing note receivable transactions) The following were among the transactions of the Queens Company for 1979 and 1980:

1979

Jan. 6 Sold merchandise worth $1,860 to I. Rose and received a 9 percent, 45-day note.

Feb. 20 Collected the amount due from I. Rose.

Mar. 1 Received a 9 percent, 75-day note for $3,400 from N. Richards in settlement of an open account.

May 15 N. Richards dishonored his note.

June 1 Sold merchandise worth $2,000 to W. Walters and received a 90-day, noninterest-bearing note for the amount of the sale plus interest at 9 percent.

Aug. 30 Collected the amount due from W. Walters.

Nov. 16 Received a 9 percent, 120-day note for $4,860 from J. Aikens in settlement of an open account.

Dec. 1 Received a 90-day, noninterest-bearing note from H. Barrow in settlement of an open account of $4,400. The note had interest of $66 included in the face value.

1980

Mar. 1 Received the amount due from H. Barrow.

16 Received the amount due from J. Aikens.

Required: Journalize the transactions, including any necessary adjusting entries on December 31, 1979 and 1980.

CE11–4 (Journalizing discounted note transaction) Record in general journal form the following note transactions on the books of S. Young, the maker, and W. Highland, the payee:

a. On July 1, S. Young purchased $4,900 worth of merchandise on account from W. Highland.
b. S. Young gave a 9 percent, 90-day note, dated August 21, to W. Highland in settlement of his account.
c. On August 31, W. Highland discounted S. Young's note at the Second Street Bank at a discount rate of 9 percent.
d. On the maturity date, S. Young paid the bank the maturity value of the note.

Exercises and problems

P11–1 The following were among the transactions of the Baltimore Company for 1979 and 1980:

1979

Jan. 2 Purchased $4,500 worth of merchandise from the Alston Company, and issued a 9 percent, 45-day note.

Feb. 16 Paid note and interest due the Alston Company.

Mar. 15 Issued a 9 percent, 90-day note to the Peters Company in settlement of an open account of $5,000.

June 13 Paid the Peters Company $2,000 on principal and all the interest for the preceding 90 days; issued a new 10 percent, 60-day note for the balance of the principal.

Aug. 12 Paid the remaining amount due the Peters Company.

Nov. 25 Issued a 9 percent, 75-day note to the Milton Company in settlement of an open account of $6,600.

1980

Feb. 8 Paid the amount due the Milton Company.

Required: Journalize the transactions, including any necessary adjusting entries on December 31, 1979.

P11–2 The following were among the transactions of the Dawson Company for 1979 and 1980:

1979

June 10 Discounted its own 90-day, noninterest-bearing note, made out to the Bank of Columbia in the principal amount of $8,000, at a discount rate of 8 percent.

Sept. 8 Paid the Bank of Columbia amount due.

Dec. 1 Discounted its own 90-day, noninteresting-bearing note, made out to the National Bank in the principal amount of $4,000 at a discount rate of 9 percent. (Assume that the books are closed on December 31.)

1980

Mar. 1 Paid the amount due the National Bank.

Required: Journalize the transactions including any necessary adjusting entries on December 31, 1979 and 1980.

P11–3 The Norman Company negotiated a 90-day loan (reference l) with the Durham Bank, which was paid on its due date (reference m). It arranged for another 90-day loan (reference x) with the Burlington Bank, which was also paid when due (reference y).

Cash		Notes Payable to Bank		Interest Expense	
(l) 3,000	(m) 3,045	(m) 3,000	(l) 3,000	(m) 45	
(x) 2,955	(y) 3,000	(y) 3,000	(x) 3,000	(x) 45	

Required: (1) Describe the type of negotiable instrument used by the Durham Bank; (2) the Burlington Bank. (3) Which loan is more favorable to the Norman Company? Why?

P11–4 The Home Appliance Company sells a standard refrigerator for $240 in cash or on terms of $25 down and $40 a month for six months. In order to meet competition, the Company is considering changing its credit terms to a $25 down payment and $20 a month for 12 months.

Required: Compute the approximate effective annual interest rate under (a) the present plan and (b) the proposed plan. Carry your computations to two decimal places. Assume that each installment includes a uniform monthly reduction in the carrying charge.

P11–5 The following notes were received by Allison, Inc.:

Date of Note	*Term of Note*
March 10, 1979	60 days
April 4, 1979	90 days
March 10, 1979	2 months
April 4, 1979	3 months
January 31, 1979	1 month

Required: Determine the maturity date of each note.

P11–6 The following information pertains to five notes:

1. $3,200 at 9 percent for 60 days
2. $4,600 at 9 percent for 30 days
3. $2,400 at 9 percent for 72 days
4. $6,600 at 8 percent for 60 days
5. $9,000 at 8½ percent for 45 days

Required: Using the short-cut methods discussed in this chapter, compute the amount of interest on each note.

P11–7 Information regarding four notes held by the Sampson Company is given below:

Date of Note	*Term of Note*	*Interest Rate*	*Principal*
November 1, 1979	90 days	7%	$4,200
November 16, 1979	120 days	10%	6,400
December 1, 1979	60 days	8%	7,200
December 16, 1979	30 days	9%	3,600

Required: Assume that books are closed on December 31, 1979. Compute the amount of simple interest that will be debited to Accrued Interest Receivable.

P11–8 The following were among the transactions of the Finn Corporation for 1979 and 1980:

1979

Jan. 18 Sold merchandise worth $850 to H. Hawser and received a 9 percent, 70-day note.

Mar. 12 Received a 9 percent, 120-day note from B. Newton in settlement of an open account of $2,400.

Mar. 29 Collected the amount due from H. Hawser.

July 10 B. Newton dishonored his note.

Nov. 15 Received a 9 percent, 90-day note from R. Hoode in settlement of an open account of $3,000.

1980

Feb. 13 Collected the note and interest from R. Hoode.

Required: Journalize the transactions, including any necessary adjusting entries as of December 31, 1979.

P11–9 (Appendix) On September 5, 1979, the Adolph Television Company sold $1,800 worth of merchandise to Milton Company on account and received a 9 percent, 60-day note. This note was discounted at 9 percent on October 20, 1979, at the Toxboro Trust Company. At maturity date the note was dishonored by the Milton Company and the Adolph Television Company paid the maturity value plus a $2.50 protest fee.

Required: Journalize the transactions on the books of the Adolph Television Company.

P11–10 (Appendix) Kaye Sawyer owed the Frix Marta Company $850 for merchandise that she had purchased. Since the debt was past due, Marta drew a sight draft and sent it to Miss Sawyer's bank for collection. Sawyer paid the sight draft. The bank charged $1.50 for its services.

Required: Journalize the transactions on the books of Kaye Sawyer and the Frix Marta Company.

P11–11 The Master's Company accepts trade notes from its customers. As of December 31, 1979, it had accepted only one: a 7 percent, 90-day note on December 1, 1979. At the end of the year, the following adjusting entry was made:

1979			
Dec. 31	Accrued Interest Receivable	210.00	
	Interest Earned		210.00
	To record interest at 7 percent for 30 days on the note received from T. S. Ballentine December 1 in settlement of an open account receivable.		

Required: Reconstruct the entry made on December 1 to record the receipt of the note from T. S. Ballentine. Show all your calculations.

P11–12 On June 30, the Malone Company's trial balance included the following accounts:

Notes Receivable	$12,600
Notes Receivable Discounted (credit)	5,000

The notes receivable register showed the following supporting details:

Note No.	*Face Value*	*Date of Note*	*Term of Note*	*Interest Rate*	*Remarks*
1	$3,000	May 29, 1979	60 days	8%	Discounted at bank on June 30, 1979. Bank discount rate, 8%.
2	2,000	May 1, 1979	120 days	9%	Discounted at bank on June 16, 1979. Bank discount rate, 8%.
3	4,000	June 16, 1979	30 days	6%	
4	3,600	June 21, 1979	90 days	9%	

This disposition of the four notes was:

Note 1: Paid at the bank by the maker on the maturity date.

Note 2: Dishonored by the maker. The Malone Company paid the bank the maturity value of the note plus a $3 protest fee.

Note 3: Paid by the maker on the maturity date.

Note 4: On July 10, 1979, the Malone Company had its own $3,000 non-interest-bearing note due at the bank. Malone Company paid its $3,000 note by discounting Note 4 (the bank discount rate was 6 percent) and received the balance due in cash. The maker of Note 4 paid the bank on the maturity date.

Required: Prepare dated general journal entries to record the disposition of each note.

P11–13 (Integrative) During 1979, the Indeck Manufacturing Company completed the following transactions, among others:

1979

Jan. 4 Sold $3,000 worth of merchandise to S. M. Friedberg on account.

6 Sold $4,500 worth of merchandise to C. D. Burch on account.

8 Sold merchandise to Jay Swan for $390 on invoice 1001.

10 Sold merchandise to Ray Faulk for $2,150 on invoice 1002.

12 Credited Ray Faulk for returned merchandise with an invoice price of $350.

14 Received a check for the amount due from Jay Swan on invoice 1001.

15 Sold merchandise to the Scuppernong Company for $460 on invoice 1003.

17 Received $230 in cash from the Scuppernong Company in partial payment of invoice 1003.

21 Received a check for the amount due from Ray Faulk.

23 C. D. Burch gave an 8 percent, 20-day note, payable at the First National Bank.

23 S. M. Friedberg gave a 9 percent, 30-day note, payable at the National Shawmut Bank.

24 Sold $3,200 worth of merchandise to E. Hazelwood, Inc., on account.

25 Received a 10 percent, 20-day note, payable at the Worcester County Trust Company, from E. Hazelwood, Inc.

27 Sold $7,500 worth of merchandise to Fenn & Company and received an 8 percent, 30-day note, payable at the Second National Bank.

Feb. 13 C. D. Burch's note of January 23 was dishonored.

14 Received a check from E. Hazelwood, Inc., for $1,200 plus interest, and accepted a new 10 percent, 90-day note payable at the Worchester County Trust Company for the balance of the note of January 25.

22 Received payment from S. M. Friedberg in payment of his note due today.

26 Received a check from Fenn & Company for $3,500 plus interest, and accepted a new 8 percent, 30-day note payable at the Second National Bank for the balance of the note of January 27.

28 Discounted Fenn & Company's note of February 26 at the Lynn Bank at 10 percent.

Mar. 15 Sold merchandise to the Albermarle Company for $3,000 on invoice 1004.

23 Received a check for the amount due from the Albermarle Company on invoice 1004.

28 Received notice that Fenn & Company had dishonored its note of February 26. Paid the bank the maturity value of the note plus a $3 protest fee.

30 Sold merchandise to the Paris Company for $2,850 on invoice 1005.

30 Sold merchandise to the Ronson Company for $3,250 on invoice 1006.

Required:

1. Journalize the transactions.
2. Post all entries to the Accounts Receivable controlling and subsidiary accounts.

P11–14 (Minicase) Albert's Home Products Company is a large retail operation that specializes in household appliances such as refrigerators, ranges, water heaters, washing machines, dryers, and air conditioners. It has been in business for a number of years and has developed a good reputation.

The firm uses a different method of financing purchases from each of several dealers; one of these, Servinator, Inc., ships products to the Company C.O.D. Therefore, when shipments are received, Albert's Home Products Company must make immediate payment. The Company issues a promissory note to the Chatham Bank, and the bank increases the checking account balance of the Company. The checking account balance includes a deposit that will later be equal to the check issued to Servinator, Inc. Albert's Home Products Company is required to pay the bank immediately upon sale of the appliance. The bank charges interest at 5 percent.

The firm also uses different financing methods when selling the appliances to its customers, as follows:

1. Some customers pay cash for an appliance at the time of the sale.
2. Some preferred customers are permitted to charge their purchases on open account, at terms of n/30 or n/60.
3. The remaining customers sign promissory notes, which will be paid according to agreed dates. The face amount of these notes include interest at a 6 percent annual rate and carrying charges are a standard amount of $10.

During 1979, the following selected transactions took place:

1979

June 4 Placed an order with Servinator, Inc., for a refrigerator costing $265. On June 14, the appliance was received C.O.D. and a check was issued in payment; on the same day, a note was signed at the bank and the bank made a deposit to the Company's checking account. On July 10, the refrigerator was sold to Lawrence Davis for $350. Davis signed a promissory note for the purchase price plus interest to November 10 and the carrying charge. Both Albert's Home Products Company and Davis paid their creditors on the due dates.

Required:

1. Record the transactions in general journal form.
2. Indicate the net effect of the above transactions on the accounts indicated. Use a plus sign (+) to indicate an increase, a minus sign (−) to indicate a decrease, and a zero (0) to indicate no effect.

Transaction Date	Current Assets	Current Liabilities	Owner's Equity	Net Income
June 4				

3. Describe any problems of disclosure which may arise from these procedures.

chapter twelve

Introduction

Buying and selling on open charge accounts has become standard practice. Individuals and businesses alike buy and sell merchandise, plant and equipment, supplies and other items on credit. Because of this trend toward the extension of credit terms for transactions involving all types of goods and services, there is a great need for the control and analysis of receivables by management.

This chapter stresses the elementary accounting for sources and classification of receivables, accounting for bad debts expense, aging of accounts receivable, comparison of the direct write-off method with the estimating method, and credit card sales.

Accounts receivable and bad debts

Learning goals

To label the sources and classification of receivables.
To understand the nature of bad debts expense.
To determine bad debts expense by the balance sheet and income statement approaches.
To record the bad debts adjustment.
To describe the uses of the aging schedule of accounts receivable.
To distinguish between the direct write-off and the estimating method of accounting for bad debts expense.
To record the recovery of a bad account previously written off.
To explain balance sheet classification of an opposite balance in accounts receivable or accounts payable.
To understand recording and valuation of receivables resulting from credit card sales.
To recognize the importance of the internal control of accounts receivable.

Key terms

aging schedule
bad debts expense
  balance sheet approach
  income statement approach
bad debts recovered
credit balances in customer accounts
nontrade receivables
trade receivables
valuation account
  allowance for doubtful accounts
  allowance for sales discounts
  allowance for sales returns and allowances

Sources and classification of receivables

As has been stated previously, a receivable represents a claim against individuals or companies for cash or other assets. There are two broad groups of receivables:

1. Those arising out of a trade or a sale of goods or services, referred to as trade receivables.
2. All the other receivables arising out of a variety of claims of a source other than trade.

Trade receivables

Trade receivables are of two classes, accounts receivable and notes receivable. *Accounts receivable* are claims against customers for sales made on open account. Generally these are shown in a ledger account entitled, Accounts Receivable. If there is some question about whether the item is a trade receivable or a nontrade receivable, it is theoretically acceptable to entitle the account, Accounts Receivable, Trade. *Notes receivable* are claims supported by written formal promises to pay; that is, promissory notes from customers. Both categories represent the same legal claims against customers. The chief advantage to a firm of holding a note receivable is that it is a written acknowledgment that the debt exists. The note also is a negotiable instrument and permits the firm to discount it for cash or use it as collateral for a loan from a bank. Notes can arise from either a trade or from a nontrade situation. For a note to be a trade receivable, it must arise from a sale of goods or services. The accounting for notes was discussed in Chapter 11.

Nontrade receivables

Other types of receivables arise from nontrade sources. Some types of nontrade receivable accounts are presented here briefly to show the wide variety of receivables: Accounts Receivable, Employees, arises from a loan made to an employee; Accrued Interest Receivable represents the accrual of interest on notes receivable or other interest-bearing instruments; Investment in Bonds, sometimes called Bonds Receivable, represents claims against companies for money loaned to them for interest-yielding bonds; Refundable Deposits are made by companies as good-faith indications for such business events as contract bids with government agencies or others.

Classification of receivables

Receivables that are due and collectible within a year should be shown in the Current Assets section of the balance sheet. To repeat, the terms *Accounts Receivable* and *Notes Receivable,* if unqualified, should be understood to represent trade receivables collectible within one year or one operating cycle. Nontrade receivables that are not due or are not collectible within a year should be shown under Long-Term Investments.

Bad debts expense

Matching revenue and expenses

A basic principle in accounting is that in any accounting period the earned revenue and the actual expense incurred in realizing that revenue should be related.

The cost of the goods sold and all other expenses incurred during the period should be related to or should be deducted from the revenue of that period. Hence, as indicated in Chapters 5 and 6, the cost of a machine is spread over the period during which the machine is used to arrive at a fair measure of the net income for each period. It would be inaccurate to charge the entire cost at the time of purchase or disposal of the machine.

Similarly, since the balance in the Accounts Receivable account represents uncollected amounts included in revenue, losses that may arise through failure to collect any of the receivables should be recognized as an expense of doing business *(bad debts expense)* during the period when the sales were made. Thus, accounts receivable originating from sales made for credit in 1979 and determined to be uncollectible in 1980 represent a bad debts expense of the year 1979. It also follows that the Accounts Receivable account in the balance sheet should be shown at the amount expected to be realized through actual cash collections from customers. If accounts receivable are shown at their gross amount without any accompanying adjustment for the estimated uncollectible portion, the total asset and the total owner's equity would be overstated to the extent of the failure to recognize an expense that arises out of the uncollectible sale of goods on account.

Recording the bad debts adjustment

To illustrate the recording of a bad debts adjustment, assume that on December 31, 1979, the credit department of the Gadson Company, having analyzed sales during 1979 and past-due accounts, determines that out of the current year's sales, $650 will be uncollectible. This amount represents a bad debts expense to be shown in the General and Administrative Expenses section of the income statement as a deduction from revenue. The estimated losses pertain to accounts receivable resulting from sales of the current period; therefore, in accordance with the principle of the periodic matching of expenses and revenues, estimated bad debts losses should be charged against revenue.

The adjusting general journal entry recorded on December 31, 1979, and the posting of the entry to the general ledger are shown below:

1979							
Dec.	31	Bad Debts Expense	609	650	00		
		Allowance for Doubtful					
		Accounts	121A			650	00
		To record estimated loss on uncollectible accounts receivable.					

Bad Debts Expense
(expense)
Acct. No. 609

Date		Explanation	F	Debit		Credit		Balance	
1979 Dec.	31		J65	650	00			650	00

Allowance for Doubtful Accounts
(asset valuation)
Acct. No. 121A

Date		Explanation	F	Debit		Credit		Balance	
1979 Dec.	31		J65			650	00	650	00

A *valuation account* refers to a contra account which is subtracted from another account to arrive at the book value or carrying value. It is assumed that there was no previous balance before adjustments in the valuation account, Allowance for Doubtful Accounts, and that no account receivable had been written off during the year 1979. These complications are discussed in more detail later in this chapter.

Since the amount of $650 is an estimate and is not related to specific customers' accounts, the credit must be made to a contra account or valuation account. If the credit were to be made directly to Accounts Receivable without corresponding credits to subsidiary accounts, the equality of the controlling account and the subsidiary accounts would no longer exist. The use of the valuation account, Allowance for Doubtful Accounts, permits a reduction in the asset account without destroying this essential equality. Allowance for Doubtful Accounts is shown in the balance sheet as a deduction from the related asset account.

Assets

Current Assets		
Cash		$1,210.00
Accounts Receivable	$6,945.00	
Deduct Allowance for Doubtful Accounts	650.00	6,295.00
Notes Receivable		1,000.00

The amount of $6,295 represents the expected net cash to be received when the accounts receivable are collected.

As actual accounts receivable are determined to be uncollectible during subsequent accounting periods, Allowance for Doubtful Accounts is debited instead of Bad Debts Expense, with offsetting credits to the controlling account and the specific customers' accounts involved. This procedure is required because the expense already has been recognized by the bad debts adjusting entry. A debit to Bad Debts Expense at the time of write-off would cause the loss to be recorded twice.

Assume that on May 1, 1979, the Gadson Company decides that a claim of $80 against Thomas Lee for a sale made on March 1, 1979, is uncollectible. The entry is:

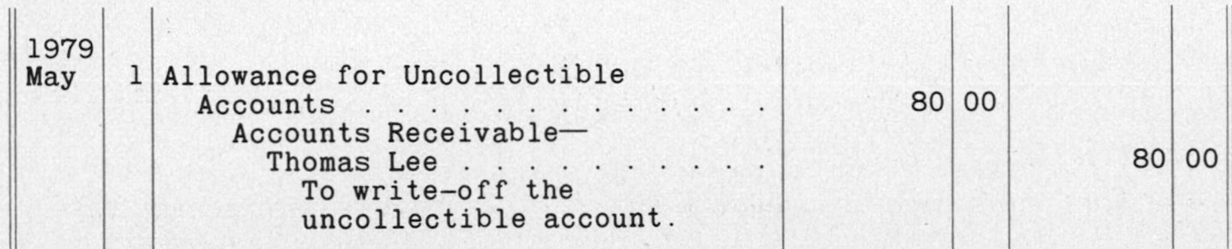

1979				
May	1	Allowance for Uncollectible Accounts	80 00	
		Accounts Receivable— Thomas Lee		80 00
		To write-off the uncollectible account.		

Estimating the amount of bad debts expense

It is necessary for management to make a careful estimate, based on judgment and past experience, of the amount of its uncollectible accounts. Accurate records must be kept and overdue accounts must be carefully analyzed.

Two different approaches are commonly used in estimating bad debts. In this text, these methods are referred to (1) as the *income statement approach,* based on the dollar volume of sales, and (2) as the *balance sheet* approach, based on the amount of receivables.

The income statement approach In the income statement approach, we must answer the question, ''How much bad debt expense is associated with this year's sales?'' Thus in associating the bad debts expense directly with dollar volume of sales, the estimate should be based on a percentage of an income statement item; typically, it is based on a percentage of sales less sales returns and allowances. The percentage is determined from information derived from the company's past experience. Even though it is not usually done, it may be desirable to establish the percentage on the basis of charge sales only, excluding cash sales, particularly if the ratio of cash sales to total sales fluctuates from year to year. The method is simple to apply and furnishes an equitable basis for distributing bad debts losses. Since the computation used in this method yields the amount of the bad debts expense for the year, any existing balance in the Allowance for Doubtful Accounts is ignored. Thus, a small error in the same direction over the years could accumulate to a large amount in the Allowance for Doubtful Accounts, since its balance is usually ignored in the adjustment process.

To illustrate the adjustment by this approach, assume that an examination of the accounts of a given company for the preceding five years shows that approximately one-half of 1 percent of credit sales have proven to be uncollectible. Assume further that credit sales for a particular year are $200,000 and that there is a credit balance of $105 in Allowance for Doubtful Accounts before adjustments are made. The bad debts expense for the year is $1,000 = (0.005 ×

$200,000), and in recording the adjustment, the $105 balance in the Allowance for Doubtful Accounts is ignored. The adjusting entry is:

1979				
Dec.	31	Bad Debts Expense	1,000 00	
		Allowance for Doubtful Accounts		1,000 00
		To record the bad debts expense for year.		

Once the foregoing information is posted, the Allowance for Doubtful Accounts and Bad Debts Expense accounts would appear as indicated below:

GENERAL LEDGER

Allowance for Doubtful Accounts — Acct. No. 121A

Date		Explanation	F	Debit	Credit	Balance
1979						
Dec.	31	Balance	✓			105 00
	31	Adjustment	J64		1,000 00	1,105 00

Bad Debts Expense — Acct. No. 609

Date		Explanation	F	Debit	Credit	Balance
1979						
Dec.	31	Adjustment	J64	1,000 00		1,000 00

After the adjusting entry is posted to the Allowance for Doubtful Accounts, its balance is $1,105. Notice that this amount is different from the $1,000 amount of Bad Debts Expense for the year. This does not represent an error, since the two accounts measure different things:

1. The Allowance for Doubtful Accounts measures the estimated uncollectible accounts receivable regardless of what years' sales gave rise to the receivables.
2. The Bad Debts Expense account measures the losses arising out of only the current year's sales on account.

The balance sheet approach The balance sheet approach requires an adjustment of the existing balance of Allowance for Doubtful Accounts to an amount that, when deducted from Accounts Receivable on the balance sheet, will show accounts receivable at their net realizable value. With this approach, we must seek an answer to the question, "How large a valuation allowance is needed to disclose our receivables at the net cash to be realized from those items?" Thus in the balance sheet approach, the amount of the balance sheet item, Accounts Receivable, rather than the income statement item, sales volume, is used as the base for the adjustment. The necessary adjustment for the balance of Allowance for Doubtful Accounts is determined by either of two procedures: (1) the balance necessary to maintain the Allowance for Doubtful Accounts is established by *aging* the accounts receivable (that is, analyzing them by the amount of time they have remained unpaid) and adjusting the existing balance of Allowance for Doubtful Accounts to the proper amount or (2) the balance of Allowance for Doubtful Accounts is adjusted to an amount equal to an estimated blanket percentage of current accounts receivable.

Aging the accounts receivable Aging the accounts receivable involves consideration of such factors as the date on which payment was due, the number of days that have elapsed since the due date, and any other available data of a financial nature that give some clue to collectibility of the accounts. A columnar work sheet like the one shown in Figure 12–1 is often used to facilitate the analysis of the Accounts Receivable account. It is sometimes referred to as an *aging schedule*. In an electronic data processing (EDP) accounting system, the aging schedule is one of the products of data processing.

All the accounts in the accounts receivable subsidiary ledger with their corresponding account balances are listed in the Customer's Name and Total Balance columns. The age classifications that make up each balance in the Total Balance column are then extended to the appropriate columns. The aging method yields a more satisfactory Allowance for Doubtful Accounts than does any other method, because the estimate is based on a study of individual customer's accounts rather than on a blanket percentage of a single general ledger account balance. Only a detailed analysis will disclose the accounts that are not past due but may be uncollectible, and the long overdue accounts that may give indication of eventual collectibility. However, the bad debts expense of a given year could be greatly distorted by the use of this method. For instance, if recoveries of accounts receivable previously written off or the write-off in the current year of

Figure 12–1
Analysis of accounts receivable by age

FRED ROGERS COMPANY
Analysis of Accounts Receivable by Age
December 31, 1979

			Items Past Due			
Customer's Name	Total Balance	Not Yet Due	1–30 Days	31–60 Days	61–90 Days	Over 90 Days
Walter G. Arnold	$ 880.00	$ 800.00	$ 80.00			
Allan Conlon	1,800.00	1,000.00	500.00	$ 300.00		
Charles Peacock	50.00				$ 50.00	
Richard C. Smith	320.00	100.00	200.00	20.00		
Jerome Werther	960.00				900.00	$ 60.00
[Others]	51,990.00	27,220.00	15,460.00	5,280.00	730.00	3,300.00
Totals	$56,000.00	$29,120.00	$16,240.00	$5,600.00	$1,680.00	$3,360.00
Percent of Total	100	52	29	10	3	6

accounts receivable arising from prior years' sales are run through the Allowance for Doubtful Accounts without any designation of which of these items affect prior years' net income, the bad debts expense of the current year would be distorted.

The analysis of accounts receivable is useful to management not only as an aid to the accomplishment of the accounting for bad debts expense but also for the purpose of making credit-type decisions. In interpreting this information for credit decisions, management should also compare the current analysis of accounts receivable by age with those of earlier periods, especially the age-group percentages. Currently, 52 percent of the total accounts receivable are not yet due, 29 percent are past due from 1 to 30 days, and so on. When compared with earlier years, percentage increases in the lower age classifications with offsetting decreases in the older classes are favorable.

The analysis in Figure 12–1 may be used to determine the proper balance to be established in Allowance for Doubtful Accounts. To make this determination, companies may apply a sliding scale of percentages based on previous experience to the total amount shown in each column. The computation to determine expected losses for the Fred Rogers Company is shown below.

	Amount	Estimated Percentage Uncollectible	Allowance for Doubtful Accounts
Not yet due	$29,120.00	3	$ 873.60
1–30 days past due	16,240.00	4	649.60
31–60 days past due	5,600.00	10	560.00
61–90 days past due	1,680.00	20	336.00
Over 90 days past due	3,360.00	50	1,680.00
Totals	$56,000.00		$4,099.20

On the basis of this summary, $4,099.20 of the outstanding accounts receivable on December 31 may become uncollectible. Consequently, an Allowance for Doubtful Accounts with a balance of $4,099.20 should be established. Before the adjusting entry is made, the existing balance in the account must be considered. The Fred Rogers Company has a present credit balance in Allowance for Doubtful Accounts of $150, a provision remaining from earlier periods. The adjusting entry amount will be for $3,949.20 = ($4,099.20 − $150); when this amount is transferred to the allowance account, it will bring that account up to $4,099.20, the estimated probable uncollectible accounts. The adjusting journal entry is:

			Debit	Credit
1979				
Dec.	31	Bad Debts Expense	3,949.20	
		Allowance for Doubtful Accounts		3,949.20
		To increase the asset valuation account by the estimated loss.		

Assume, however, that the Allowance for Doubtful Accounts had a debit balance of $300 before adjustment, rather than a credit balance of $150. The adjusting entry would be for \$4,399.20 = (\$4,099.20 + \$300); after this entry is posted, the allowance account will contain the desired credit balance of \$4,099.20.

Use of blanket percentage to obtain allowance for doubtful accounts An analysis of accounts receivable by age is time consuming; if there is a reliable pattern, the Allowance for Doubtful Accounts may be based on a single blanket percentage of accounts receivable computed as follows for the Garu Company:

End of Year	Balance of Accounts Receivable	Total Losses from Uncollectible Accounts
1976	\$20,000.00	\$ 800.00
1977	24,000.00	480.00
1978	22,000.00	700.00
Totals	\$66,000.00	\$1,980.00

The average loss of the past three years has been 3 percent = (\$1,980 ÷ \$66,000). Assume that at the end of 1979 total accounts receivable are \$30,000 and a credit balance of \$150 is in the allowance account. Estimated uncollectible accounts at 3 percent of accounts receivable are \$900 = (\$30,000 × 0.03). The following adjusting entry at the end of 1979 on the books of the Garu Company increases the Allowance for Doubtful Accounts to the desired amount of \$900.

Date		Account	Debit	Credit
1979				
Dec.	31	Bad Debts Expense	750 00	
		Allowance for Doubtful Accounts		750 00
		To increase the asset valuation account to the estimated uncollectible account.		

A portion of the information for the following partial balance sheet is taken from the preceding data.

GARU COMPANY
Partial Balance Sheet
December 31, 1979

Assets

Current Assets		
Cash		\$ 3,200.00
Accounts Receivable	\$30,000.00	
Deduct Allowance for Doubtful Accounts	900.00	29,100.00
Notes Receivable		18,000.00

Promissory notes receivable arising from the sale of merchandise may also prove to be uncollectible. As was learned in Chapter 11, the amount due from the customer on a dishonored note is removed from Notes Receivable and transferred to

Accounts Receivable. The amount will remain in the Accounts Receivable account until it either is collected or it is determined to be uncollectible and written off in the usual manner. When notes receivable specifically arise from the sale of merchandise, the current provision for estimated bad debts losses should be adequate to cover outstanding notes receivable and accounts receivable. The following partial balance sheet presentation shows that the allowance covers Notes Receivable and Accounts Receivable jointly.

GARU COMPANY
Partial Balance Sheet
December 31, 1979

Assets

Current Assets		
Cash		$ 3,200.00
Accounts Receivable	$30,000.00	
Notes Receivable	18,000.00	
Total	$48,000.00	
Deduct Allowance for Doubtful Accounts and Notes	900.00	47,100.00

Writing off uncollectible accounts

When it is decided that a customer's account is definitely uncollectible, the amount due should be written off. Assuming that on February 15, 1980, the Garu Company definitely determined that the account of a customer, Joseph Nykerk, is uncollectible, the entry to record the write-off is:

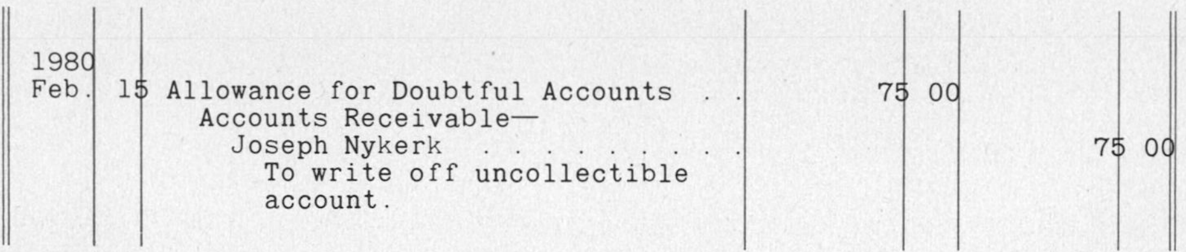

Date		Account	Debit	Credit
1980				
Feb.	15	Allowance for Doubtful Accounts	75 00	
		Accounts Receivable—Joseph Nykerk		75 00
		To write off uncollectible account.		

This entry has no effect on the net realizable value of the receivables; it only adjusts the balances of two accounts. The entry does not affect expenses, because no expense was incurred on February 15, 1980; the expense was recorded by the adjusting entry of December 31, 1979. Assume that immediately before this entry was made, the books of the Garu Company showed the following balances:

Accounts Receivable	$30,000.00
Allowance for Doubtful Accounts (credit)	900.00

When the entry to right of Nykerk's account is posted, the result is:

	Balances Before Write-Off	Write-Off	Balances After Write-Off
Accounts Receivable	$30,000.00	$75.00	$29,925.00
Deduct Allowance for Doubtful Accounts	900.00	75.00	825.00
Estimated Realizable Value	$29,100.00		$29,100.00

This calculation points up the fact that since the loss was recorded in the period when the sale was made, the subsequent write-off does not change assets, liabilities, or owner's equity.

Recovery of bad debts

An account that is written off as uncollectible may later be recovered in part or in full. In that event, the entry that was made to write off the account is reversed to the extent of the amount recovered or expected to be recovered. Assuming that Joseph Nykerk settles with his creditors for 50 cents on the dollar and that a check for $37.50 is received, the required journal entries are:

Date		Account	Debit		Credit	
1980						
Nov.	15	Accounts Receivable—Joseph Nykerk .	37	50		
		Allowance for Doubtful Accounts .			37	50
		To restore the collectible portion of the account previously written off.				
	15	Cash	37	50		
		Accounts Receivable—Joseph Nykerk			37	50
		To record collection.				

The debit and the credit to Accounts Receivable—Joseph Nykerk cancel each other, but they are necessary if a complete record of all transactions with the customer is to be maintained. Such a record may be of considerable aid if further extension of credit to Joseph Nykerk comes up for consideration at some future date.

Direct write-offs in period of discovery

A company that uses the direct write-off method postpones recognition of a bad debts expense until the receivable is definitely thought to be uncollectible. In this case, an Allowance for Doubtful Accounts is *not* used, and no end-of-period adjusting entry for estimated losses is made. The February 15, 1980, entry on the books of the Garu Company to remove Joseph Nykerk's account in full under the direct write-off method is:

			Debit	Credit
1980				
Feb.	15	Bad Debts Expense	75 00	
		Accounts Receivable— Joseph Nykerk		75 00
		To write off uncollectible account.		

By this method, the loss is recognized in the *period of write-off* rather than in the period when the sale is made. The direct write-off method, as well as the allowance method previously illustrated, is acceptable for federal income tax reporting purposes. This method, however, does not assign each accounting period with the losses arising out of sales made in that period and therefore violates the principle of matching expenses and revenue in each accounting period. Thus the error in matching causes the net income shown in the income statement to be in error. It also causes the net receivables to be realized as shown in the balance sheet to be in error.

An account previously written off in the period of discovery may be subsequently collected in part or in full. Assume again that on November 15, 1980, Nykerk makes a settlement of 50 cents on the dollar and issues a check for $3,750. The required journal entries are:

			Debit	Credit
1980				
Nov.	15	Accounts Receivable— Joseph Nykerk	37 50	
		Bad Debts Recovered		37 50
		To restore the collectible portion of the account previously written off.		
	15	Cash	37 50	
		Accounts Receivable— Joseph Nykerk		37 50
		To record payment received.		

Bad Debts Recovered is a revenue account; its balance may be reported in the Other Revenue section of the income statement.

Comparison of the two recording procedures

The two methods of recording bad debts expense are compared in Figure 12–2, assuming the following data:

Allowance for Doubtful Accounts (credit balance, January 1)	$ 4,200
All sales on account	510,000
Cash collections on account	495,000
Sales returns and allowances	4,000
Accounts receivable written off as uncollectible	3,950

Bad Debts Recovered .... $ 250
The basis for estimating bad debt losses is
1 percent × (Sales minus Sales Returns and Allowances).

Valuation accounts for returns and allowances and cash discounts

The net realizable amount of receivables on the balance sheet indicates the amount of collections available to the firm after allowing for bad debts expense. For example, Accounts Receivable of $30,000 and a corresponding Allowance for Doubtful Accounts of $2,000 should result in a company's collecting approximately $28,000. In reality, other deductions may be made that will decrease this amount. Typical deductions are sales returns, sales allowances, cash discounts granted to customers for prompt payments, and collection expenses.

Ideally, all these additional deductions should have corresponding valuation accounts, so that Accounts Receivable in the balance sheet will be stated at an amount closer to the net amount that will be collected. However, such valuation accounts as Allowance for Sales Returns and Allowances and Allowance for Sales Discounts are rarely used because, as a practical matter, the adjusting entry to debit the expense account will have no significant effect on net income because the items carried over from one year and recognized as an expense at the

Figure 12–2
Two methods of accounting for bad debts expense

Transactions (Jan. 1– Dec. 31, 1979)	Estimating Bad Debts Expense			Direct Write-Off		
All sales on account	Accounts Receivable . Sales	510,000 00	 510,000 00	Accounts Receivable . Sales	510,000 00	 510,000 00
Cash received on account	Cash . . . . Accounts Receivable.	495,000 00	 495,000 00	Cash . . . . Accounts Receivable.	495,000 00	 495,000 00
Sales returns and allowances	Sales Returns and Allowances . . . . . Accounts Receivable . . .	4,000 00	 4,000 00	Sales Returns and Allowances . . . . . Accounts Receivable . . .	4,000 00	 4,000 00
Accounts receivable determined to be uncollectible	Allowance for Doubtful Accounts . . . . . . Accounts Receivable . . .	3,950 00	 3,950 00	Bad Debts Expense . . Accounts Receivable.	3,950 00	 3,950 00
Bad debts recovered	Accounts Receivable . Allowance for Doubtful Accounts. Cash . . . . Accounts Receivable.	250 00 250 00	 250 00 250 00	Accounts Receivable . Bad Debts Recovered. Cash . . . . Accounts Receivable.	250 00 250 00	 250 00 250 00
Adjusting entry December 31, 1979 ($510,000 − $4,000 = $506,000; $506,000 x 0.01 = $5,060)	Bad Debts Expense . . . Allowance for Doubtful Accounts.	5,060 00	 5,060 00	(No Entry is made.)		
Closing entry, December 31, 1979	Sales . . . . Sales Returns and Allowances . . Bad Debts Expense . Income Summary . . .	510,000 00	 4,000 00 5,060 00 500,940 00	Sales . . . . Bad Debts Recovered . Bad Debts Expense . Sales Returns and Allowances . . Income Summary . . .	510,000 00 250 00	 3,950 00 4,000 00 502,300 00

beginning of the year will counterbalance the failure to recognize these same items at end of a year. Moreover, these adjustments are not recognizable for income tax purposes.

Credit card fees

Today there is widespread use of credit cards issued by many different credit card companies. These companies charge a fee ranging from 3 to 7 percent for accepting and collecting the receivable. This fee, charged by the credit card companies on credit card sales made to customers, actually represents an expense that combines cash discount, bad debts expense, collection fees, and accounting expense. Since the amount of the fee charged by the credit card company is a known amount, the business making credit card sales should set up the receivable at the net amount to be received and debit an expense for the amount of the credit card fee. Receivables from credit card companies should not be merged with the other trade receivables that require a measurement of bad debts expense, discussed earlier in this chapter.

Opposite balances in accounts receivable and accounts payable

In the accounts receivable ledger, the customers' accounts normally have debit balances. Sometimes an overpayment, a sales return or a sales allowance after a customer has paid an account or an advance payment may convert the balance into a credit.

Assume that there is a net debit balance of $29,600 in an accounts receivable ledger consisting of 100 accounts, as follows:

98 accounts with a debit balance	$30,000.00
2 accounts with a credit balance	400.00
Net debit balance of 100 accounts receivable	$29,600.00

The debit amount of $30,000 and the credit amount of $400 would appear on the balance sheet as follows:

Current Assets		Current Liabilities	
Accounts Receivable	$30,000.00	Credit Balances in Customer Accounts	$400.00

The controlling account balance of $29,600 should not be used in the balance sheet, because it would conceal the current liability of $400. Similarly, if the accounts payable ledger contains creditors' accounts with debit balances, the balance sheet should show the total credit balances and the total debit balances of accounts payable. For example, if a company has a net balance in the Accounts Payable controlling account of $88,600, with certain subsidiary ledger accounts having debit balances that total $1,400, it should disclose this information in its balance sheet as follows:

Current Assets		Current Liabilities	
Debit Balances in Creditor Accounts . .	$1,400.00	Accounts Payable	$90,000.00

Internal control—accounts receivable

As in the case of cash, adequate safeguards must be established for accounts receivable. A general principle of internal control is applicable to the internal control of receivables: there should be a separation of duties so that the work of one employee can be checked and verified by the work of another employee. For example, it is important that persons who maintain the accounts receivable records should not have access to cash. Recording of returns and allowances, discounts, and bad debts write-offs should be authorized by an officer and should be separated from the cash receipt and cash disbursement functions. Statements of account should be checked and mailed to customers by someone other than the accounts receivable bookkeeper. An independent check should be established to see that the statements sent to customers are in agreement with the accounts receivable records. Delinquent accounts should be reviewed periodically by a responsible official. Adequate control over receivables begins with the approved sales order and continues through the remaining stages in the credit sales process: approval of credit terms, recording of shipment, customer billing, recording of the receivable and its collection, and approval of subsequent adjustments.

Glossary

Aging schedule A columnar work sheet showing the individual receivables by age groups according to time elapsed from due date. The individual age groups are also totaled and a percentage analysis is computed to aid in determining the allowance for doubtful accounts.

Allowance for doubtful accounts A valuation account contra to accounts receivable showing the amount of estimated uncollectible accounts as of a given date.

Allowance for sales discounts A valuation account related to accounts receivable showing the amount of estimated sales discounts that will be taken and thus reduce the net amount receivable from the accounts receivable.

Allowance for sales returns A valuation account related to accounts receivable showing the amount of estimated sales returns and allowances that will occur and that will reduce the net amount receivable from accounts receivable.

Bad debts expense An expense account showing the estimated uncollectible credit sales made in a given time period, that is, for one year if the accounting period is a year, or actual write-offs if the direct write-off method is used.

Bad debts recovered A revenue account that is credited for the recovery of an account receivable previously written off under the direct write-off method.

Balance sheet approach A method of estimating the adjusted amount that is needed in the Allowance for Doubtful Accounts; the estimate is based on the balance sheet item, Accounts Receivable.

Credit balances in customer accounts A liability item representing the amounts due customers because of overpayment or a sales return made after payment had been made.

Income statement approach A method of estimating the bad debts expense for a given period; the estimate is based on an income statement item, Sales.

Nontrade receivable A receivable arising from a source other than from sales of merchandise or sales of ordinary services.

Trade receivables Claims against customers arising from sales of merchandise or sales of ordinary services.

Valuation account A contra asset account; an account that is related to and offsets, in whole or in part, one or more other accounts. A contra-asset account should be deducted from the asset to which it is related to determine a carrying or book value.

Questions

Q12–1 List five different categories of receivables and state the probable balance sheet classification of each. The following format is suggested:

Receivable Item	*Probable Balance Sheet Classification*

Q12–2 Discuss the general principle of the valuation of trade receivables.

Q12–3 a. Explain the function of the Allowance for Doubtful Accounts account.
b. What methods may be used to estimate the Allowance for Doubtful Accounts?
c. How is Allowance for Doubtful Accounts shown on the balance sheet?

Q12–4 Distinguish between the income statement approach and the balance sheet approach in estimating the bad debts expense.

Q12–5 A company attempting to state its accounts receivable at their net realizable value may have to establish accounts other than the Allowance for Doubtful Accounts. Name three other possible valuation accounts for Accounts Receivable.

Q12–6 The Slavon Company, which had Accounts Receivable of $56,850 and an Allowance for Doubtful Accounts of $2,610 on January 1, 1979, wrote off in 1979 a past due account of N. Healy for $575.

a. What effect will the write-off have on the total current assets of the company immediately before and after the write-off?
b. On net income for 1979? Explain.

Q12–7 What kind of account (asset, liability, expense, etc.) is Allowance for Doubtful Accounts? Is the normal balance a debit or credit?

Q12–8 John Davok owes a firm $400. This amount is considered to be uncollectible. Give the journal entry to record the write-off (a) assuming the allowance method is used and (b) assuming the direct write-off method is used.

Q12–9 A company has systematically adjusted its Allowance for Doubtful Accounts at the end of the fiscal year by adding a fixed percent of the year's sales less sales returns and allowances. After five years the credit balance on the Allowance for Doubtful Accounts has become disproportionately large in relationship to the balance in Accounts Receivable. Give two possible explanations.

Q12–10 When a company adjusts its Allowance for Doubtful Accounts to a percentage of Accounts Receivable, the balance of the Allowance account will tend to be partially self-correcting provided that there is only a small error in the percentage that is being applied. The Bad Debts Expense for certain years, on the other hand, may contain a sizeable error. Discuss the reason(s) for this situation.

Q12–11 How does the valuation of receivables arising from credit card sales differ from the valuation of other trade receivables?

Class exercises

CE12–1 (Use of Allowance for Doubtful Accounts) The following transactions of the Elvond Company occurred in 1979, 1980, and 1981. The company uses the estimating procedure in accounting for bad debts.

1979
Dec. 31 Recorded bad debts expense of $4,650 for 1979.

1980
Mar. 10 Wrote off O. N. Collier's account of $650 as uncollectible.
Nov. 10 Wrote off various other accounts of $3,150 as uncollectible.
Dec. 31 Recorded bad debts expense of $4,265 for 1980.

1981
Feb. 6 O. N. Collier remitted $450 of the amount he owed the firm and agreed to pay the remainder in 30 days.

Required: Journalize the transactions.

CE12–2 (Direct write-off method) The following transactions of the Darwin Company occurred in 1980 and 1981. The company uses the direct write-off method of accounting for bad debts.

1980		
Jan.	13	Wrote off B. E. Goodson's account of $313 as uncollectible.
Nov.	13	Wrote off O. N. Fair's account of $213 as uncollectible.
	20	Recovered the $313 from B. E. Goodson.
Dec.	13	Wrote off S. P. Santee's account of $613 as uncollectible.
1981		
Mar.	10	Recovered the $213 from O. N. Fair.

Required: Journalize the transactions.

CE12–3 (Adjusting entries for bad debts) The partial trial balance of the Dellur Company at December 31, 1979, before any adjustments are made, is given:

DELLUR COMPANY
Partial Trial Balance
December 31, 1979

	Debit	*Credit*
Accounts Receivable	$80,000	
Notes Receivable	30,000	
Allowance for Doubtful Accounts and Notes	600	
Sales		$112,500
Sales Returns and Allowances	2,500	

Required: Prepare the adjusting entries for the bad debts expense under the following assumptions:

a. Allowance for Doubtful Accounts and Notes is to be increased to 4 percent of trade receivables.
b. The bad debts expense is estimated to be 1.8 percent of net sales.

Exercises and problems

P12–1 The Adam Company, which uses an Allowance for Doubtful Accounts, had the following transactions involving worthless accounts in 1979 and 1980:

1979

Dec. 31 Recorded bad debts expense of $2,200.

1980

Mar. 5 Wrote off N. O. Girard's account of $520 as uncollectible.

Apr. 10 Wrote off A. M. Stanley's account of $560 as uncollectible.

Sept. 6 Recovered $560 from A. M. Stanley.

Required: Journalize the transactions.

P12–2 The accounts receivable ledger of the Valley Distributing Company shows the following data on December 31, 1979. The general ledger showed a $200 credit balance in Allowance for Doubtful Accounts before adjustments.

Name of Customer	*Invoice Date*	*Amount*
Modesto Fruit Company	May 2, 1979	$ 600.00
Neri Brothers	August 15, 1979	335.50
Paley Fruitrees, Inc.	October 2, 1979	719.85
	December 8, 1979	275.00
Temple Grapefruit Company	March 3, 1979	445.00
Royal Fruit Company	November 11, 1979	822.50
Yosemite Produce Company	November 20, 1979	250.00
	September 4, 1979	465.75
	July 10, 1979	922.00
[Others]	December 5, 1979	20,000.00

Terms of sale are n/30.

Required:

1. Prepare an analysis of accounts receivable by age.
2. Compute the estimated loss based on the following fixed percentages:

		Estimated Percentage Uncollectible
Accounts not due		0.5
Accounts past due:	1–30 days	1.0
	31–60 days	3.0
	61–90 days	10.0
	91–120 days	25.0
	121–365 days	50.0

3. Record the bad debts expense.

P12–3 The Cash account page in the general ledger of the Winslow Corporation has been temporarily misplaced. The following data are available:

	December 31		*Year*
	1980	*1979*	*1980*
Accounts Receivable, Trade	$73,000	$59,000	
Allowance for Doubtful Accounts	5,200	3,100	
Sales			$605,000
Sales Discounts			10,350

During 1980 accounts receivable of $4,350 were written off as uncollectible and one account of $600, written off in 1980 was collected and recorded in the following manner:

Accounts Receivable	600	
Allowance for Doubtful Accounts		600
Cash	600	
Accounts Receivable		600

Required: Compute the cash received from customers during 1980.

P12–4 The balance of Allowance for Doubtful Accounts of the Richland Company on January 1, 1979, was $3,200. During 1979 uncollectible accounts totaling $2,900 were written off. The Company collected $300 on one of these accounts after it had been written off. The balance of the Accounts Receivable account on December 31, 1979 was $82,000.

Required: Make the journal entries to (1) charge off the worthless accounts during 1979, (2) record the collection of the $300, and (3) make the adjusting entry on December 31, 1979, for the bad debts expense. Assume that uncollectible accounts average 4 percent of the uncollected accounts.

P12–5 The Allowance for Doubtful Accounts of the Bay State Company showed a credit balance of $200 on December 31, 1979, before adjustments were made. The bad debts expense for 1979 is estimated at 2 percent of the charge sales of $90,000 for the year.
The following transactions occurred during the next two years:

1980

May 1 Wrote off George Shaw's $900 account as uncollectible.

Oct. 15 Wrote off John Foley's $1,200 account as uncollectible.

Nov. 30 Received a check from George Shaw for $100 in final settlement of the account written off on May 1. He had been adjudged bankrupt by the courts.

Dec. 31 An analysis of accounts receivable by age indicated that accounts doubtful of collection totaled $1,900. (Note that the method of estimating bad debts has been changed.)

1981

Aug. 21 Wrote off Joseph Sack's $1,800 account as uncollectible.

Dec. 31 Estimated that uncollectible accounts receivable totaled $2,400.

Required:

1. Record transactions in general journal form.
2. Post to a ledger account for Allowance for Doubtful Accounts.

P12–6 On December 31, 1979, John Delaney's trial balance showed the following:

Accounts Receivable	$72,000
Allowance for Doubtful Accounts (credit)	300

After making an analysis of the accounts receivable, Delaney estimates the accounts doubtful of collection at $3,000.

During the year 1980 the following transactions occurred:

1. Sales on account were $320,000.
2. Accounts written off as uncollectible totaled $3,300.
3. Collections from customers on account were $308,900. This includes a receipt of $100 that had been written off during the year as uncollectible.

On December 31, 1980, the accounts doubtful of collection were estimated at $3,400.

Required:

1. Set up ledger accounts for Accounts Receivable and Allowance for Doubtful Accounts; record the balance as of December 31, 1979 in these accounts; and then make the entries for 1979 and 1980 directly into these accounts.
2. Compute the bad debts expense deduction in the income statement for the year 1980, using (a) the direct write-off method; (b) the Allowance for Doubtful Accounts method.

P12–7 The Catawba Company uses the direct write-off method of accounting for bad debts. It had the following transactions involving worthless accounts in 1979:

1979

Feb. 13 Wrote off Joseph White's account of $400 as uncollectible. The merchandise had been sold in 1978.

Aug. 13 Wrote off Alfred Green's account of $612 as uncollectible.

Dec. 10 Recovered $400 from Joseph White.

Required: Journalize the transactions.

P12–8 The Bowan Trading Company had charge sales of $550,000 during 1979 and Accounts Receivable of $52,500 and a credit balance of $150 in Allowance for Doubtful Accounts at the end of the year.

Required: Record the bad debts expense for the year, using each of the following methods for the estimate: (a) The Allowance for Doubtful Accounts is to be increased to 5 percent of Accounts Receivable. (b) Bad Debts Expense is estimated to be 1/2 of 1 percent of charge sales. (c) The Allowance for Doubtful Accounts is to be increased to $3,100 as indicated by an aging schedule. (d) Which method would you choose and why?

P12–9 The trial balance of the Hathaway Company included the following accounts on August 31, 1979, the end of its fiscal year:

Accounts Receivable	$ 53,000
Allowance for Doubtful Accounts (credit)	300
Sales	383,000

Uncollectible accounts are estimated at 5 percent of Accounts Receivable.

Required:
1. Make the adjusting entry to record the bad debts expense.
2. State the bad debts expense for the year.
3. Show the presentation of Accounts Receivable and Allowance for Doubtful Accounts in the August 31, 1979 balance sheet.
4. Give the entry to write off the account of an insolvent customer, James Whitney, for $800.

P12–10 The balance of the Accounts Receivable account of the Sanderson Company at December 31, 1979 was $173,360. Two customers' accounts in the subsidiary ledger show credit balances of $3,160 and $1,200.

Required:
1. What is the amount that would be shown on the balance sheet as Accounts Receivable under Current Assets?
2. How would the credit balances in the customers' accounts be disclosed?

P12–11 The Accounts Receivable controlling account of the John Slavon Company shows a balance of $690,000 on June 30, 1979. A summary of the analysis of accounts receivable by age shows accounts outstanding from the date of the invoice as follows:

Accounts not due:		$520,000
Accounts past due:	1–30 days	80,000
	31–60 days	50,000
	61–150 days	30,000
	151 days and over	10,000
		$690,000

Allowance for Doubtful Accounts has a debit balance of $420 on June 30, before adjustments. The adjustment of the allowance account is to be based on the following schedule of percentages estimated uncollectible:

Accounts not due:		1/2 of 1%
Accounts past due:	1–30 days	3%
	31–60 days	6%
	61–150 days	20%
	151 days and over	50%

Required:

1. Prepare the necessary adjusting entry as of June 30, 1979.
2. Prepare a partial balance sheet, showing Accounts Receivable and Allowance for Doubtful Accounts.

P12–12 (Integrative) The accounts receivable ledger of the Wombleg Company showed the following information on March 31, 1980:

Fountain Duncan

1979									
Aug.	12		S27	4,250	00			4,250	00
Sept.	10		S33	743	00			4,993	00
	30		CR15			4,250	00	743	00
Oct.	12		S45	1,407	00			2,150	00
Nov.	14		S52	415	00			2,565	00
Dec.	10		CR27			415	00	2,150	00
1980									
Jan.	12		S6	500	00			2,650	00
	13		CR4			1,407	00	1,243	00
	15		S7	1,783	00			3,026	00
	17	Allowance on 1/15 invoice	J2			93	00	2,933	00

Martha Easley

Date		Explanation	Ref.	Debit	Credit	Balance
1979						
Nov.	12		S51	1,000 00		1,000 00
Dec.	12		CR28		500 00	500 00
1980						
Jan.	29		S9	761 00		1,261 00
Mar.	10		S17	1,550 00		2,811 00
	31		CR11		1,550 00	1,261 00

Lloyd London

Date		Explanation	Ref.	Debit	Credit	Balance
1979						
Dec.	12		S56	5,401 00		5,401 00
1980						
Jan.	12	Note	J2		3,000 00	2,401 00
Feb.	26		S14	1,800 00		4,201 00
Mar.	26		S22	3,000 00		7,201 00

Nelson Parker

Date		Explanation	Ref.	Debit	Credit	Balance
1979						
Aug.	1		S24	973 00		973 00
Oct.	12		S45	76 00		1,049 00
1980						
Jan.	2	Return	J2		700 00	349 00
Feb.	3		S10	699 00		1,048 00
	12		S13	300 00		1,348 00
Mar.	30		CR11		899 00	449 00

Required:

1. Prepare an analysis of accounts receivable by age as of March 31, 1980. Assume that the terms of sale are n/30.
2. Make the adjusting entry for the bad debts expense on the basis of the age of the accounts as follows:

Accounts not due		1/2 of 1%
Accounts past due:	1–30 days	2%
	31–60 days	5%
	61–90 days	10%
	91 days and over	33-1/3%

There is a debit balance of $400 in Allowance for Doubtful Accounts on March 31, 1980, before adjustments.

P12–13 The following transactions of the Calvin Swain Company occurred during 1979.

1979

Jan. 2 Sold merchandise with a list price of $10,000 subject to a trade discount of 20 percent, 10 percent, and 10 percent, terms 2/10, n/30, to Samuel Adams.

10 Received a check from Samuel Adams in settlement of his account.

20 Sold merchandise worth $8,000 to Arthur Jefferson on account, terms n/10.

Feb. 1 Received a 9 percent, 120-day note from Jefferson in settlement of account.

19 Discounted Jefferson's note at the Bank of Chapel Hill at 8 percent. Endorsed the note in blank and followed the practice of recording the contingent liability.

June 1 Jefferson dishonored his note. The bank charged for the note and interest plus a protest fee of $6.00.

Required:

1. Journalize the transactions. Use the gross method of recording receivables and handling cash discounts.
2. What is the equivalent lump-sum trade discount to a 20 percent, 10 percent, and 10 percent chain trade discount? Show computations.

P12–14 (Minicase) The Nunnly Company uses a cash receipts journal, a cash payments journal, a single-column purchases journal, a single-column sales journal, and a two-column general journal. The Accounts Receivable account in the general ledger at May 31, 1979, is given (posting references have been omitted).

Accounts Receivable — Acct. No. 102

Date		Explanation	F	Debit	Credit	Balance
1979						
May	1	Balance	✓			23,500
	5				1,500	22,000
	10				125	21,875
	25			1,502		23,377
	28				1,502	21,875
	31			26,200		48,075
	31				19,750	28,325

During the month, the general journal was used to record transactions with only two customers. The subsidiary ledger accounts of these two customers are shown below.

William Ernest

1979						
May	1	Balance	✓			(300)
	6		S2	700		400
	10		J4		125	275

Allen Zonker

1979						
May	1	Balance	✓			1,500
	5	(20-day note)	J4		1,500	–0–
	25		CP6	1,502		1,502
	28		J4		1,502	–0–

Required:

1. Explain the \$300 credit balance on May 1 in Willaim Ernest's account.
2. What would the posting references for the May 31 entries in the Accounts Receivable controlling account be?
3. What should be the total of the schedule of accounts receivable on May 31?
4. Explain the transaction that resulted in the debit of \$1,502 on May 25 in Allen Zonker's account.
5. State in narrative form the transactions that resulted in each of the following credits to the Accounts Receivable controlling account: May 5, \$1,500; May 10, \$125; May 28, \$1,502.

chapter thirteen

Introduction

Inventory in a nonmanufacturing business is generally understood to mean goods owned by the business for sale to customers. Other acceptable terms are merchandise inventory or simply merchandise. Up to this point in the text, the value of the merchandise inventory has been specified. In Chapter 13 the basis for placing a valuation on inventory is explained. This discussion leads to the development of a figure necessary in the income statement, cost of goods sold.

Inventories and cost of goods sold

Learning goals

To name the factors involved in placing a valuation on the inventory.
To distinguish between periodic and perpetual inventory systems.
To be able to use FIFO, LIFO, and average costing assumptions under both the periodic and the perpetual systems.
To record transactions on the inventory record cards.
To compute cost of goods sold under the periodic and perpetual systems.
To explain the effect of various cost flow assumptions on financial statements.
To apply the concept of "lower of cost or market" to the inventory valuation.
To use both the gross margin method and the retail method of estimating inventory values.

Key terms

consistency
cost
cost of goods sold
FIFO
gross margin method
historical cost
LIFO
lower of cost or market (LCM)
moving average
periodic system
perpetual system
replacement cost
retail method
specific-identification method
stock record card
weighted average

Basis of inventory valuation: cost

Inventories are originally recorded at cost. AICPA has defined *cost* to include all expenditures "incurred in bringing an article to its existing condition and location."[1] Cost consists of the invoice price of the merchandise (less purchases discounts) plus transportation in, insurance while in transit, and any other expenditures made by the buyer to get the merchandise to the place of business. The determination of total cost valuation of an inventory is relatively simple when each stock item acquired can be marked and identified permanently with its specific cost. This procedure, the *specific-identification* method, is possible in certain businesses—for example, with automobiles on a dealer's lot. In most businesses—say with gasoline in a service station—specific identification is not possible. Accordingly, three assumptions are used to assign costs. Each is an *assumption* regarding flow of costs through the business. They do *not* represent the actual flow of goods. They are

first-in, first-out (FIFO),
last-in, first-out (LIFO), and
average.

The method used to determine cost should be the one that "most clearly reflects periodic income."[2] Regardless of the method used, the cost standard set by AICPA (also referred to as *historical cost*) restricts the proper uses of the word *valuation* in inventory accounting to the statement of items at cost, or at modifications of cost. Although there are other concepts of value; this chapter concentrates on historical (or prior) cost, which is objective and subject to more exact measurement than other concepts.

Two inventory systems

Two systems for determining inventory quantities on hand are in use: periodic (physical count) and perpetual (continuous record). To illustrate both systems of assigning cost to inventories, the following information about a single inventory item, a stapler (stock number 802A), is given.

1979		
Apr.	1	Inventory on hand consisted of 40 units (or staplers) that were purchased in March at $2.20 each.
	5	Purchased 120 staplers at $2.60 each.
	12	Sold 110 staplers.
	16	Purchased 70 staplers at $2.80 each.
	28	Sold 60 staplers.

1 American Institute of Certified Public Accountants, *Accounting Research Bulletin No. 43,* Chapter 4.

2 *Bulletin No. 43,* Chapter 4.

The number on hand on April 30, 1979, determined by physical count, is 60 staplers. This on-hand amount is verified below. Presented with the calculation is a rearrangement of cost information to be used in later illustrations.

		Units	Unit Cost	Total Cost
Inventory, April 1		40	$2.20	$ 88.00
Purchases:				
April 5		120	2.60	312.00
April 16		70	2.80	196.00
Total Units Available for Sale		230		$596.00
Sales:				
April 12	110			
April 28	60			
Total Sales		170		
Inventory, April 30		60		

Periodic inventory

With the *periodic inventory system,* the value of the inventory, for the balance sheet and for computing the cost of goods sold, can only be determined at the end of each annual accounting period by a complete physical count and pricing of all inventory items. Acquired goods not on hand are assumed to have been sold. This causes losses through theft, breakage, or other causes to be automatically included in the cost of goods sold as a deduction from revenue. Small retail businesses often use the periodic system as a matter of expediency, since it does not require a continuous record of inventory balances.

First-in, first-out (FIFO) costing The periodic *FIFO* method of determining the cost of goods on hand and the cost of goods sold is based on the *assumption* that the units are sold in the order in which they were acquired; that is, the oldest units on hand are sold first, the units acquired next are sold next, and so on. This assumption relates only to the method of accounting and not to the actual physical movement of the goods. It may or may not approximate the actual physical flow. The unsold units on hand at the date of the inventory are assumed to be the units acquired most recently. Consequently, for income measurement, earlier costs are matched with revenue and the most current costs are used for balance sheet valuation.

Under the periodic FIFO assumption the 60 staplers on hand at April 30, 1979 are part of the lot purchased on April 16. Therefore the cost assigned to the inventory is:

60 units at $2.80	$168.00

The cost of goods sold would be computed as:

Total goods available for sale	$596.00
Deduct ending inventory	168.00
Cost of goods sold	$428.00

The assumption that oldest goods are sold first leads to an alternative method of computing cost of goods sold as follows:

Date of Sale	Sales Made From	Units	Unit Cost	Total Cost
Apr. 12	Beginning inventory	40	$2.20	$ 88.00
	Purchase of April 5	70	2.60	182.00
Apr. 28	Purchase of April 5	50	2.60	130.00
	Purchase of April 16	10	2.80	28.00
		170		$428.00

Last-in, first-out (LIFO) costing Periodic *LIFO* costing assumes that the cost of goods sold should be based on prices paid for the most recently acquired units and the inventory consists of the oldest units on hand. During periods of continuously rising prices, the higher prices of the most recent purchases are included in the cost of goods sold, thereby reducing taxable income. Also, it is claimed that the cost of goods sold is more realistic, thereby achieving a closer matching of expired costs with revenue. The application of periodic LIFO costing is illustrated as follows:

Ending inventory (60 units):	
From beginning inventory, 40 units at $2.20	$ 88.00
From purchase of April 5, 20 units at $2.60	52.00
Cost assigned to April 30 inventory	$140.00

The cost of goods sold could be computed as was done under the periodic FIFO method as:

Total goods available for sale	$596.00
Deduct ending inventory	140.00
Cost of goods sold	$456.00

The assumption that newest goods are the first sold leads to the following alternative method of computing cost of goods sold:

Date of Sale	Sales Made From	Units	Unit Cost	Total Cost
Apr. 28	Purchase of April 16	60	$2.80	$168.00
Apr. 12	Purchase of April 16	10	2.80	28.00
	Purchase of April 5	100	2.60	260.00
		170		$456.00

Weighted average costing Under *weighted average* costing the ending inventory is priced at the end of each accounting period at a unit cost computed by dividing the total cost of all goods available for sale by the total physical units available for sale. Similarly, all quantities sold are stated at a uniform price—the computed average price for the period (typically one month). The assignment of costs to goods sold during the month must be delayed until the end of the month so that the weighted average cost computation can be made.

The weighted average cost for the period, the inventory valuation, and the cost of goods sold are computed as follows:

Date		Units	Unit Cost	Total
1979				
Apr.	1 Beginning inventory	40	$2.20	$ 88.00
	5 Purchase	120	2.60	312.00
	16 Purchase	70	2.80	196.00
	Total available for sale	230		$596.00

$$\text{Weighted average unit cost} = \frac{\text{Cost of goods available for sale}}{\text{Units available for sale}} = \frac{\$596}{230}$$
$$= \$2.5913$$

Units on hand, April 30	60
Inventory valuation = (60 x $2.5913)	$155.48
Units sold	170
Cost of goods sold = (170 x $2.5913)	$440.52

Perpetual inventory

The *perpetual inventory system* provides for a continuous book inventory of items on hand. An inventory record card (often called a *stock record card*) or a record in a computer storage device is kept for each inventory item. When units are purchased or sold, the inventory record for the item must be adjusted to show the updated quantity on hand. The maintenance of continuous inventory records does not eliminate the need for a complete annual physical inventory. Companies that use the perpetual inventory system should take physical counts of portions of the inventory during the course of the year to test whether the records are in agreement with quantities actually on hand, or they should take a single end-of-year count. Only by physical count will shrinkage such as evaporation losses, theft, or duplicate shipments be discovered. A perpetual inventory may be costly to maintain, especially when the inventory includes numerous items of small value. A company may desire to maintain continuous records for only certain classifications of its inventory. A hardware supply company, for example, may find it better to use the perpetual inventory system only for items with a high unit selling price and the periodic inventory system for all other items.

First-in, first-out (FIFO) costing A perpetual inventory card using the FIFO costing method is illustrated in Figure 13–1. As each shipment of goods is received, its quantity, unit cost, and total cost are recorded as a separate batch. When goods are sold, the oldest goods on hand are assumed to make up the sale. The balance on hand, unit cost, and total cost *for each batch from which units are assumed to remain* are recorded in the Balance columns.

The cost of the 110 units sold on April 12 is assumed to consist of the 40 units on hand on April 1 and 70 units from the April 5 purchase. The cost of the 60 units sold on April 28 is assumed to consist of the remaining 50 units from the April 5 purchase and 10 units from the April 16 purchase. When a sale or the balance on hand consists of units from more than one batch (see sale of April 12 in Figure 13–1) brackets are used to indicate that the two sets of figures should be combined. Since the 60 units on hand on April 30 are all assumed to be from the batch purchased on April 16, no brackets are required for the balance. The cost of goods sold is the sum of the Total Cost column in the Issued (or Sold) section of the card. For this stapler the cost of goods sold is:

Sale of April 12 ($ 88.00 + $182.00)	$270.00
Sale of April 28 ($130.00 + $ 28.00)	158.00
Cost of goods sold	$428.00

Last-in, first-out (LIFO) costing When LIFO is used with a perpetual system each sale is listed at the unit cost of the latest acquisition, up to the amount assumed to be still on hand. For instance in Figure 13–2 the 110 units sold on April 12 are assumed to have come from the units received on April 5. The balance on hand, unit cost, and total cost for each batch from which units are assumed to be on hand are recorded in the Balance columns.

The inventory on April 30 is assumed to consist of:

40	units at	$2.20 =	$ 88.00
10	units at	2.60 =	26.00
10	units at	2.80 =	28.00
60	units	. . . . .	$142.00

The cost of goods sold is $454. This figure is obtainable by adding the Total Cost column of the Issued (or Sold) section of the inventory card ($286.00 + $168.00 = $454.00).

Figure 13–1 Perpetual inventory card (FIFO)

Item: Stapler, Stock Number 802A, Location L-7

Date	Ref.	Received (or Purchased)			Issued (or Sold)			Balance		
		Quantity	Unit Cost	Total Cost	Quantity	Unit Cost	Total Cost	Quantity	Unit Cost	Total Cost
1979 Apr. 1	Balance							40	2.20	88.00
5	*P.O. 673	120	2.60	312.00				40 120	2.20 2.60	88.00 312.00
12	†S.T. 401				40 70	2.20 2.60	88.00 182.00	50	2.60	130.00
16	P.O. 690	70	2.80	196.00				50 70	2.60 2.80	130.00 196.00
28	S.T. 407				50 10	2.60 2.80	130.00 28.00	60	2.80	168.00

*Purchase Order
†Shipping Ticket

Item: Stapler, Stock Number 802A, Location L-7

Date		Ref.	Received (or Purchased)			Issued (or Sold)			Balance		
			Quantity	Unit Cost	Total Cost	Quantity	Unit Cost	Total Cost	Quantity	Unit Cost	Total Cost
1979 Apr.	1	Balance							40	2.20	88.00
	5	*P.O. 673	120	2.60	312.00				40	2.20	88.00
									120	2.60	312.00
	12	†S.T. 401				110	2.60	286.00	40	2.20	88.00
									10	2.60	26.00
	16	P.O. 690	70	2.80	196.00				70	2.80	196.00
	28	S.T. 409				60	2.80	168.00	40	2.20	88.00
									10	2.60	26.00
									10	2.80	28.00

*Purchase Order
†Shipping Ticket

Figure 13–2
Perpetual inventory card (LIFO)

Moving average costing The moving average method is illustrated in Figure 13–3. Units are priced at the average price—that is, total cost of units on hand divided by quantity on hand. This average unit price is used for sales until additional units are purchased. Then, a new average unit price must be computed. For example, the receipt of 120 units on April 5 required computation (a) following Figure 13–3. Also, the purchase of April 16 required that a new unit price again be computed. It is illustrated in computation (b) following Figure 13–3.

Figure 13–3
Perpetual inventory card (moving average)

Item: Stapler, Stock Number 802A, Location L-7

Date		Ref.	Received (or Purchased)			Issued (or Sold)			Balance			
			Quantity	Unit Cost	Total Cost	Quantity	Unit Cost	Total Cost	Quantity	Unit Cost	Total Cost	
1979 Apr.	1	Balance							40	2.20	88.00	
	5	P.O. 673	120	2.60	312.00				160	2.50	400.00	(a)
	12	S.T. 401				110	2.50	275.00	50	2.50	125.00	
	16	P.O. 690	70	2.80	196.00				120	2.675	321.00	(b)
	28	S.T. 409				60	2.675	160.50	60	2.675	160.50	

Computations:

(a)			(b)		
40	at $2.20 =	$ 88.00	50	at $2.50 =	$125.00
120	at 2.60 =	312.00	70	at 2.80 =	196.00
160	. . . . .	$400.00	120	. . . . .	$321.00
Average = $2.50			Average = $2.675		

As in the other perpetual methods, the cost of goods sold is the sum of the amounts in the Total Cost column of the Issued (or Sold) section; under the moving average method it is $435.50 = ($275.00 + $160.50). However, it is not necessary to separate batches and brackets are not required. Receipts and issues (sales) are added to or deducted from the balance.

Two methods compared and analyzed

The amount of the ending inventory as well as the amount of the cost of goods sold is identical under either the periodic or the perpetual inventory system when FIFO costing is used. This is because in each instance the goods on hand are assumed to consist of the most recently acquired units.

Under LIFO costing, however, the valuations of the cost of goods sold and ending inventory may differ under the two systems. When LIFO costing is used with the perpetual inventory system, prices at the beginning of the period that would be assumed to be in the ending valuation with the periodic inventory system may have been dropped from the running balance as goods are issued. When the inventory is taken only at the end of the period, the dates of sales are ignored. Although the LIFO procedure may be used appropriately with either periodic or perpetual inventories, it is important that the system selected should be followed consistently. The following tabulation illustrates the different results of LIFO costing with the perpetual and the periodic inventory systems:

	Periodic Inventory	Perpetual Inventory
Inventory, April 1	$ 88.00	$ 88.00
Purchases	508.00	508.00
Total goods available for sale	$596.00	$596.00
Inventory, April 30	140.00	142.00
Cost of goods sold	$456.00	$454.00

Similarly, the weighted average (periodic system) and the moving average (perpetual system) yield different results.

With the same example used to illustrate both the results were:

	Periodic Inventory	Perpetual Inventory
Inventory, April 1	$ 88.00	$ 88.00
Purchases	508.00	508.00
Total goods available for sale	$596.00	$596.00
Inventory, April 30	155.48	160.50
Cost of goods sold	$440.52	$435.50

Regardless of whether the periodic or perpetual system is used the method used to determine inventory valuation can have a direct effect on the financial statements. In a period of rising or falling prices—especially if the inventory turnover is rapid—the difference in inventory valuation can be significant. In the example used in this chapter the price of a stapler rose from $2.20 to $2.80 in the month of April. To illustrate the comparative effect of rising prices on the financial statements under perpetual FIFO, moving average, and LIFO costing, the basic data for the preceding discussions are used again. Two additional assumptions are made: (1) The selling price of each unit is $5.50, and (2) the operating expenses for the month are $200. These computations of income are for a single inventory item. The effect of the different methods on net income would be proportionately increased with increasing volume and number of items. The effect of the three methods of allocating inventory cost and cost of goods sold under the stated assumptions is highlighted in Figure 13–4.

During a period of rising prices, FIFO costing results in the highest ending inventory valuation, gross margin on sales, and net income with the lowest cost of goods sold. Given the same rising market conditions, the LIFO inventory method gives the opposite results: lowest ending inventory valuation, gross margin on sales, and net income with highest cost of goods sold. During a period of falling prices, FIFO results in the lowest ending inventory valuation, gross margin on sales, and net income and the highest cost of goods sold; LIFO gives the opposite results.

LIFO's purpose is to match revenue with current cost, rather than with earliest cost, as is done under FIFO costing. The major advantage of LIFO costing is that during a prolonged period of generally rising prices, lower year-to-year earnings are reported resulting in lower income tax. A major disadvantage is that during inflationary periods LIFO costing results in a significant understatement of current assets, which limits the significance and usefulness of the balance sheet.

Figure 13–4 shows that the amounts for the income statement items listed under moving average costing fall between the corresponding amounts for FIFO and LIFO costing. The same position would be maintained in a falling market. Moving average costing reduces the effect of widely fluctuating prices.

The balance sheet classifies the ending inventory as a current asset; consequently, this statement as well as the income statement is affected by the method of inventory valuation used. Because inventory is often the largest single item in the Current Assets section, the method of assigning cost may have a significant effect on statement analysis.

Although historical cost is the primary basis used for inventory valuation, some accountants recommend the use of *replacement cost*.[3] This may be defined

Figure 13–4
Summary tabulation

	FIFO	Moving Average	LIFO
Sales (170 Units x $5.50)	$935.00	$935.00	$935.00
Cost of Goods Sold	428.00	435.50	454.00
Gross Margin on Sales	$507.00	$499.50	$481.00
Deduct Operating Expenses	200.00	200.00	200.00
Net Income	$307.00	$299.50	$281.00

	FIFO	Moving Average	LIFO
Ending Inventory	$168.00	$160.50	$142.00

3 In March 1976, the Securities and Exchange Commission issued a ruling that requires companies with inventories and gross plant aggregating more than $100 million and amounting to more than 10 percent of total assets to disclose the current replacement cost of inventories on their balance sheets. This disclosure may be made by footnote; it is mandatory for financial statements after December 25, 1976.

as the current cost of replacing the inventory items at the inventory date in the ordinary course of business, assuming access to the usual sources of supply and at volumes in which the goods are usually purchased. Others recommend reporting parallel figures showing both historical cost and current cost, thereby providing the user with a better basis for evaluating past performance and for predicting future performance. The use of current cost would eliminate the need for a cost-flow assumption—LIFO, FIFO, average—and would result in a better matching of expired cost and revenue. The balance sheet valuation would also be more significant. To quote an expert's opinion: "Where current value varies obviously and significantly from historical cost, the accountant should feel compelled to modify the recorded amount. Replacement cost may prove to be the most meaningful basis for modification of inventory and plant and equipment under some circumstances."[4]

Lower of cost or market (LCM)

The various methods of inventory valuation discussed thus far in this chapter are methods of arriving at the cost of the inventory. However, a long-standing convention in accounting holds that inventories may be valued at the *lower of cost or market* (LCM). The term market broadly means the cost of replacing the goods as of the balance sheet date. Cost is determined by any of the methods discussed in this chapter.

The process of valuing the inventory at LCM occurs at the end of the accounting period when financial statements are prepared. It may be applied (1) to each item individually, (2) to each major inventory category, or (3) to the entire inventory. On the basis of the inventory tabulations in Figure 13–5 (FIFO costing is assumed), the valuation under each procedure is as follows (Items A and B

Figure 13–5
Application of LCM

Column Numbers	1	2	3	4	5	Basis For Lower of Cost or Market 6	7	8
Item	**Quantity**	**Unit Cost**	**Unit Market Price**	**Total Cost**	**Total Market**	**Unit**	**Major Category**	**Total Inventory**
Category X:								
Item A . . .	100	$10.00	$ 9.00	$1,000.00	$ 900.00	$ 900.00		
Item B . . .	200	4.00	6.00	800.00	1,200.00	800.00		
Subtotal				$1,800.00	$2,100.00		$1,800.00	
Category Y:								
Item C . . .	400	1.00	1.25	$ 400.00	$ 500.00	400.00		
Item D . . .	600	6.00	5.00	3,600.00	3,000.00	3,000.00		
Item E . . .	250	3.00	2.50	750.00	625.00	625.00		
Subtotal				$4,750.00	$4,125.00		4,125.00	
Totals				$6,550.00	$6,225.00			$6,225.00
Inventory at Lower of Cost or Market						$5,725.00	$5,925.00	$6,225.00

4 Arthur Andersen & Co., *Accounting and Reporting Problems of the Profession,* 4th ed., 1973, p. 54.

are assumed to constitute category X and the remaining items constitute category Y):

1. If each item is valued individually, the inventory is reported as $5,725 (column 6).
2. If the inventory is valued by major categories, it is reported as $5,925 (column 7).
3. If the inventory is valued in total, it is reported as $6,225 (column 8).

Estimation of inventory

Gross margin method

Taking a physical inventory or maintaining perpetual inventory records is often costly and time consuming. For some purposes an estimate is needed. To prepare monthly financial statements, check the accuracy of a physical inventory, or estimate inventory valuation when an accurate valuation cannot be made (as in the case of a fire loss) the *gross margin method* of estimating the inventory may be used. This method is a procedure for calculating the inventory value by deducting the estimated cost of goods sold from the total cost of the goods available for sale.

Assume that during the previous three years the Needham Company has averaged a gross margin rate on sales of 30 percent, as shown below ($126,000 ÷ $420,000 = 30%).

	Prior Years			
	1976	1977	1978	Totals
Sales	$124,000.00	$142,000.00	$154,000.00	$420,000.00
Cost of Goods Sold	87,420.00	97,980.00	108,600.00	294,000.00
Gross Margin	$ 36,580.00	$ 44,020.00	$ 45,400.00	$126,000.00
Gross Margin Rate				30%

For the current year, the following data are available from the records of the company:

Inventory—January 1, 1979	$ 20,000.00
Purchases during 1979	110,000.00
Sales during 1979	160,000.00

Under the *gross margin method*, the estimated inventory on December 31, 1979 would be computed as follows:

a. Sales − Gross margin = Cost of goods sold
   $160,000 − (0.30 x $160,000) = $112,000
b. Beginning inventory + Net cost of purchases[5] − Cost of goods sold = Ending inventory
   $20,000 + $110,000 − $112,000 = $18,000

5 In both methods transportation in should be added to purchases and discounts and returns and allowances should be deducted.

On the basis of the foregoing computation, the partial income statement is as follows:

NEEDHAM COMPANY
Partial Income Statement
For the Year Ended December 31, 1979

Sales		$160,000.00
Cost of Goods Sold		
Inventory, January 1, 1979 (given)	$ 20,000.00	
Purchases (given)	110,000.00	
Total goods available for sale	$130,000.00	
Estimated Inventory, December 31, 1979 (item b)	18,000.00	
Cost of Goods Sold (item a)		112,000.00
Gross Margin (Sales – Cost of Goods Sold). .		$ 48,000.00

This method is based on the assumption that the rate of gross margin on sales is substantially the same in every period. It is accurate, therefore, only to the extent that the assumed gross margin rate is accurate. A careful study should be made of possible differences between the past data from which the assumed rate is derived and the corresponding current data. Appropriate adjustments should be made for significant differences.

Retail method

Another method of estimating the ending inventory at cost when its retail valuation is known is the retail inventory method. Its value is twofold: (1) It serves as a means of computing the ending inventory without a physical count and (2) it provides a method of centrally controlling inventories that consist of a variety of items dispersed over several departments or several branch stores. Goods are charged to the departments or branches at their selling price, records of both cost and selling price of goods purchased are kept centrally, and records of sales are kept in the usual manner. From these records, the inventory valuation may be prepared at any time. Under the *retail method* the estimated inventory at retail is derived by deducting the sales during the period from the total goods available for sale priced at retail. This amount is then converted to cost by applying the cost percentage (the ratio of the cost of goods available for sale to the retail price of those goods). This is illustrated in Figure 13–6.

Both the gross margin method and the retail inventory method are based on a calculation of the gross margin rate. The gross margin method uses past experience as a basis; the retail inventory method uses current experience. The gross margin method is therefore less reliable, because past experience may be different from the current experience.

A physical inventory should be taken periodically. This inventory is first computed at the retail selling prices marked on the goods, reduced to cost by using the cost percentage, and then compared with the inventory value computed as shown in Figure 13–6. If there have been losses due to thefts or shrinkage, the

Figure 13–6
Retail inventory method

	Cost	Retail
Inventory at beginning of period	$ 20,000.00	$ 30,000.00
Purchases during period	180,000.00	270,000.00
Total goods available for sale	$200,000.00	$300,000.00
Cost percent (ratio of cost to retail) $\frac{\$200,000.00}{\$300,000.00}$ = 66 2/3%		
Sales during period		258,000.00
Inventory at retail		$ 42,000.00
Estimated inventory at cost . . . . (66 2/3% of $42,000)	$ 28,000.00	

valuation based on the physical inventory will be less than that shown by the records, and an adjustment is made to decrease the account, Merchandise Inventory.

The retail inventory method offers a means of determining a company's inventory at frequent intervals without taking a physical count—a valuable tool for purposes of preparing financial statements or other reports that require an inventory valuation. Its reliability rests on the assumption that the percentage of cost to retail is fairly uniform within the several departments of the company and for all the various items sold, and that the percentage is equally applicable to the goods sold and the goods unsold. If that is not the case, separate records should be maintained for the different departments and for the different items handled. Use of the retail inventory method is permissible for federal income tax purposes.

Consistency in application of inventory valuation procedures

Different procedures may be used to place a valuation on various classes of the inventory. It is most important, therefore, that the selected method should be followed consistently from year to year in each class. Inconsistency in inventory pricing, cost allocations, and financial statement presentation would make year-to-year comparisons of operating results and financial position meaningless. Since such comparisons often serve as the basis for managerial decisions and decisions of external users of accounting information, the importance of consistency becomes evident.

Consistency

Whatever the method chosen, a company should follow it consistently from year to year.

The concept of *consistency* may be applied at several levels. Consistency is important not only in the matter of valuation procedures followed but also with respect to the classification of items in financial statements. Consistency in classification applies to the grouping of items within each statement as well as to year-to-year consistency. The principle of consistency does not preclude required changes properly made and fully disclosed. A change from FIFO to LIFO inventory costing, for example, requires an explanation accompanying the financial statements of the year of change, giving the nature of the change and its effect.

Inventory control

The principle of the separation of duties is equally applicable to merchandise. Internal controls must be established to protect against loss, theft, and misappropriation of inventory. The system for receiving, storing, issuing, and paying for the merchandise must provide for such records and supporting documents and for the assignment of individual responsibility and accountability as will safeguard the assets. Absence of control over inventories can be a serious detriment to the successful management of a business. An excessive inventory is expensive to carry. Studies made indicate that the costs of carrying an inventory—taxes, insurance, warehousing, handling, and inventory taking—may be as high as 25 percent of the original purchase price. This is exclusive of lost potential earnings (interest) on the funds tied up in inventories. On the other hand, sufficient items and quantities must be stocked to provide customers with good service.

Maintaining a proper balance to avoid both shortages and excesses of inventory requires organization and planning. Control plans must provide for day-to-day comparisons of projected inventory acquisitions with current sales volume. A reduction in sales volume will result in excess inventories unless adjustments are made.

A real-life example

STONEY PAINT COMPANY

Inventory Sheet **Sheet No. 37**

Stock Number	Description	Quantity	Unit Price	Amount
17x503	Enamel, Outside, Yellow	108	6.50	702.00
17x519	Enamel, Outside, Green	27	6.25	168.75
	Grand Total			27,602.83

Merchandise Inventory Acct. No. 132

Date		Explanation	F	Debit	Credit	Balance
1979						
Dec.	29	Balance forward	✓			27,601 18
	31		P16	400 00		28,001 18

After the physical count had been completed on December 31, 1979, the inventory supervisor caused recounts to be made on all items in which she suspected there could be errors. All inventory tickets are now considered to be correct and have been listed on 37 inventory sheets. (The end portion of sheet number 37 is shown above.) Each item has been priced and extended.

The general ledger account, Merchandise Inventory, shows a balance that does not agree with the value of the physical count. An entry to adjust the account will be made as follows:

Dec.	31	Loss From Inventory Shrinkage . . .	398	35		
		Merchandise Inventory			398	35
		To adjust account for merchandise evaporated, lost, stolen or otherwise missing.				

Glossary

Consistency The concept that uniformity—with full disclosure for any departures—from year to year, especially in inventory pricing, cost allocation, and financial statement presentation, is essential to make comparisons meaningful.

Cost of an inventory item The expenditures incurred in bringing an inventory item to its existing condition and location.

Cost of goods sold The amount of total cost of merchandise allocated to items sold during the period.

FIFO A method of determining the cost of goods on hand and the cost of goods sold based on the assumption that the units are sold in the order in which they were acquired.

Gross margin method A method of estimating inventory value by deducting the cost of goods sold from the total cost of goods available for sale. The cost of goods sold is the product of the average gross margin percentage for prior periods applied to sales for the current period.

Historical cost See cost above.

LIFO A costing method based on the assumption that the cost of goods sold should be calculated on prices paid for the most recently acquired units and that the units on hand consist of the oldest units acquired.

Lower of cost or market (LCM) An inventory valuation method by which units are valued at the lower of either original acquisition cost or at replacement cost (market) for those units in inventory whose replacement cost has fallen below original acquisition cost.

Moving average An inventory costing method by which the cost of each purchase is added to the cost of units on hand, and the total cost is divided by the total quantity on hand to find the average unit price.

Periodic inventory An inventory system by which the valuation of the inventory for balance sheet presentation is determined at the end of each annual period by a complete physical count and pricing of all inventory items. Cost of goods sold must be computed.

Perpetual inventory An inventory system of record keeping that provides for a continuous book inventory of items on hand.

Replacement cost The current cost of replacing inventory items using the usual sources of supply and in quantities usually bought.

Retail method A method of estimating inventory value. The ratio of the cost of goods to the selling price is used to convert the inventory valued at retail to cost.

Specific identification An inventory costing method by which the unit cost is identified specifically with the related supporting acquisition document.

Stock record card A perpetual record kept for each item of inventory.

Weighted average A costing method by which the ending inventory and the cost of goods sold are priced at the end of each accounting period at a unit cost computed by dividing the total cost of goods available for sale by the physical units available for sale.

Questions

Q13–1 What specific elements are included in the cost of an item of inventory?

Q13–2 Why is it important that the selected system of inventory valuation be applied consistently from year to year? Does strict compliance with the principle of consistency preclude a change from FIFO to LIFO?

Q13–3 Distinguish between the perpetual and the periodic inventory systems. Does the perpetual inventory system eliminate the need for a physical inventory count?

Q13–4 How do overstatements or understatements of inventory affect net income in the period when the error is made? In the following period?

Q13–5 What effect do the different methods of inventory valuation have on the financial statements?

Q13–6 Compare the gross margin method with the retail inventory method.

Q13–7 An audit of the records of the Bates Company showed that the ending inventory on December 31, 1978, was overstated by $7,600 and that on December 31, 1979, the inventory was understated by $9,300. What was the effect of the errors on the income statement for each year? What was the overall effect for the two-year period assuming no further errors were made in inventories?

Q13–8 Explain the effect on the balance sheet valuation and on the income determination of the use of LIFO as compared with FIFO (a) if prices have risen during the year; (b) if prices have fallen during the year.

Q13–9 Define the term market as used in LCM inventory valuation.

Q13–10 (a) What is the relationship between the actual physical flow of goods in and out of inventory and the method used for inventory valuation? (b) What inventory valuation method should a company use if, as new shipments of inventory items are received, they are commingled with identical items on hand in storage bins?

Class exercises

CE13–1 The records of Yvonne Byers show the following data as of December 31, 1979:

a. Cost of merchandise on hand, based on a physical count $50,000
b. Merchandise sold to a customer, but held pending receipt of shipping instructions (included in item a) 1,800
c. Merchandise shipped out on December 30; invoice mailed and debited to Accounts Receivable (not included in item a) ... 2,200
d. Unrecorded bill for transportation in on some goods included in item a 750
e. Cost of spoiled merchandise (to be given away); not included in item a 200

Required: What is the cost of the inventory on December 31, 1979 for financial statement reporting purposes?

CE13–2 The following items were included in the income statements of the Troxler Company for the years ended December 31, 1979, and 1978:

	1979	*1978*
Cost of goods sold	$ 69,000	$ 76,000
Gross margin	142,000	135,000
Net income	35,000	20,000

An audit of the records revealed that the merchandise inventory at December 31, 1978, was understated by $4,000.

Required: What was the effect of the error on the amounts given? What happens if the $4,000 error is not detected in the audit?

CE13–3 The inventory of the Beskov Company on January 1, and December 31, 1979 consisted of 21,250 and 31,250 units, respectively, of Commodity X-1. The beginning inventory was priced at $1,700. The following purchases were made during the year:

Date	*Quantity*	*Cost*
January 3	12,500	$1,125
April 16	21,250	1,800
July 5	30,000	2,850
October 2	7,500	750
December 15	20,000	1,600

Required: Determine the cost of the December 31, 1979 inventory by each of the following methods: (a) LIFO; (b) FIFO; (c) weighted average. Assume that the periodic inventory system is used.

CE13–4 The beginning inventory, purchases, and sales of an item by the Engleman Company for the month of July 1979 were as follows:

1979		
July	1	Inventory on hand consisted of 100 units at $3.15 each.
	12	Sold 50 units.
	15	Purchased 40 units at $3.00 each.
	17	Purchased 60 units at $2.70 each.
	19	Sold 30 units.
	26	Purchased 50 units at $3.45 each.
	29	Sold 40 units.

Required: What was the cost of the units on hand on July 31 (a) under the perpetual inventory moving average method and (b) under the periodic inventory weighted average method?

CE13–5 The entire stock of the Pearl Company was destroyed by fire on June 22, 1979. The books of the company (kept in a fireproof vault) showed the value of goods on hand on June 1 to be $40,000. Transactions for the period June 1 through June 22 resulted in the following amounts:

Sales	$98,780
Sales Returns	2,105
Purchases	79,800
Purchases Returns	1,815
Transportation In	1,475

The rate of gross margin on sales for the previous three years averaged 35 percent.

Required: Determine the cost of the inventory destroyed by the fire.

CE13–6 The books of Hill Street Department Store show the following data for the leather goods department for the year 1979, its first year of operations:

Purchases (at cost)	$4,900
Purchases (at selling price)	8,650
Sales	8,175

Required: Estimate the inventory on December 31, 1979, by the retail method.

CE13–7 James Henry, Jr. had the following items in stock on December 31, 1979:

Item	*Quantity*	*Unit Cost*	*Unit Market Price*
Class A:			
Item M	50	$5.00	$4.00
Item N	100	2.00	3.00
Item O	200	7.00	6.50
Class B:			
Item X	200	1.00	1.25
Item Y	300	3.00	2.50
Item Z	125	1.50	1.25

Required: Compute the inventory valuations that could be used in financial statements if Henry uses lower of cost or market.

Exercises and problems

P13–1 Purchases and sales data for the first three years of operation of the Colby Company for a single item were as follows (purchases are listed in order of acquisition):

	1977	*1978*	*1979*
Sales	19,200 units at $52	24,000 units at $62	29,000 units at $68
Purchases	6,500 units at 25	9,000 units at 35	11,000 units at 43
	10,000 units at 27	10,000 units at 37	7,500 units at 46
	8,000 units at 33	6,500 units at 40	8,000 units at 48

Required:

1. Prepare a schedule showing the number of units on hand at the end of each year.
2. Compute the year-end inventories under the periodic inventory system for each of the three years, using (a) FIFO and (b) LIFO.
3. Prepare income statements for each of the three years through gross margin on sales on the basis (a) of FIFO, (b) of LIFO, and (c) of weighted average. Use the periodic system.

P13–2 The following data are from the inventory records of a single item of the Nottingham Company for June, 1979:

Date		Purchases	Sales	Balance
June	1			100 units at $1.10
	5	200 units at $1.30		
	8	100 units at 1.40		
	12		120 units	
	16	40 units at 1.50		
	19		60 units	
	23		40 units	
	27	100 units at 1.60		

Required: Determine the ending inventory and the cost of goods sold using:

1. FIFO and (a) the periodic inventory system, (b) the perpetual inventory system.
2. LIFO and (a) the periodic inventory system, (b) the perpetual inventory system.
3. Weighted average and the periodic inventory system.
4. Moving average and the perpetual inventory system.

P13–3 The Maryland Machine Company buys and sells planers. Purchases and sales during March, 1979 are shown below.

		Purchases	Sales
March	2	88 units at $300	
	3		160 units
	9	84 units at 375	
	15	92 units at 340	
	20		60 units
	25	88 units at 360	
	30		172 units

The inventory on March 1 consisted of 100 units at $350 each.

Required:

1. Compute the cost of goods sold during March, using LIFO and the periodic inventory system.
2. Compute the cost of goods sold during March, using FIFO and the perpetual inventory system.

P13–4 The following information pertains to a stock item of Estes Drive Publishers:

1979		
January 1	On hand	10,000 units at $9.00
February 14	Purchase	12,000 units at 9.75
June 12	Purchase	14,000 units at 9.00
November 13	Purchase	10,000 units at 9.50
December 31	On hand	12,000 units

The periodic inventory system is used.

Required: Compute the cost of the inventory on December 31, 1979, (a) under FIFO and (b) under LIFO.

P13–5 The Northeastern Company calculates its inventory by the gross margin method for interim statement purposes. The inventory on January 1 was $53,200, net purchases during January were $139,650, and net sales for the month were $199,500. The gross margin rate is estimated at 35 percent of net sales.

Required: What was the estimated inventory on January 31?

P13–6 The inventory of the Isaacs Upholstering Company on December 31, 1979, consisted of the following items:

		Unit	
	Quantity	*Cost*	*Market*
Frames			
Type F–1	100	$14.25	$15.50
Type F–12	200	26.00	22.50
Type F–15	10	21.50	21.00
Spring (sets)			
Type S–1	500	7.28	8.50
Type S–12	1,000	10.50	11.50
Type S–15	300	8.60	6.00

Required:

1. Compute the ending inventory at the lower of cost or market, applied (a) to each item, (b) to each category, and (c) to the entire inventory.
2. What is the effect of each application of LCM on the gross margin in the current year? in the following year?

P13–7 The records of the Stereo Sound Shop show the following information for the month of June 1979:

Sales	$100,000
Transportation In	1,500
Purchases at cost	71,250
Purchases at retail	105,000
Inventory—June 1, at cost	26,250
Inventory—June 1, at retail	37,500

Required: Estimate the June 30 inventory at cost using the retail inventory method.

P13–8 The Pulaski Company estimates its merchandise inventory when preparing monthly financial statements. The following information is available on April 30:

	Cost	*Retail*
Merchandise Inventory, April 1	$120,000	$ 195,000
Purchases during April (net)	975,000	1,650,000
Transportation In during April	6,000	
Sales during April (net)		960,000

Required:

1. Compute the estimated inventory on April 30, using the gross margin method. On the basis of past experience Pulaski estimates a rate of gross margin of 40 percent for the current year.
2. Compute the estimated inventory on April 30, using the retail inventory method.

P13–9 The Washington Company closes its books annually on December 31, at which time the merchandise inventory is determined by a physical count. For its monthly interim statements, however, inventory estimates based on the gross margin method are used. Condensed partial income statements for the years 1976, 1977, and 1978 follows:

	1976	*1977*	*1978*
Sales	$437,500	$500,000	$550,000
Cost of Goods Sold	262,500	295,000	319,000
Gross Margin	$175,000	$205,000	$231,000

The merchandise inventory on December 31, 1978 was $87,500. During January, 1979 sales were $55,000 and purchases were $50,000.

Required:

1. Compute the inventory on January 31, 1979, based (a) on the gross margin rate for the prior three years and (b) on the 1978 gross margin rate.
2. Which gross margin rate should be used? Why?

P13–10 On July 1, 1979 Ester Golden established the Golden Company with an investment of $20,000 in cash. Purchases and sales of an item during the month are shown below.

1979

July	1	Purchased 2,880 units at $19.20.
	10	Sold 1,680 units at $32.
	13	Purchased 2,400 units at $20.40.
	17	Sold 2,640 units at $32.
	22	Purchased 3,600 units at $21.20.
	28	Sold 2,160 units at $32.

Operating expenses were $22,400. Cash settlements on all transactions were completed by the end of the month.

Required:

1. Prepare perpetual inventory schedules, using (a) FIFO, (b) LIFO, and (c) moving average.
2. Prepare income statements and balance sheets based on each of the foregoing methods of inventory valuation.
3. Explain why the different methods yield different results. Which method is correct?
4. What factors should Golden consider in her choice of method of inventory valuation?
5. Which method would you recommend? Explain.
6. FIFO reflects price increases of goods on hand in net income but these are not real profits because, as the inventory is depleted, replacement costs will be higher. Do you agree? Explain.

P13–11 (Integrative) In October, 1979 the Nykerk Company began buying and selling a recently patented stamping machine. Transactions for the month follow:

1979

Oct. 2 Purchased a machine at $9,900.

6 Purchased a machine at $10,500.

13 Sold a machine at $21,000.

20 Purchased a machine at $12,000.

27 Sold a machine at $21,000.
Operating expenses for October were $12,000.

Required:

1. Record the information on perpetual inventory records, using each of the following methods: (a) FIFO, (b) moving average, and (c) LIFO.
2. Prepare an income statement based on each of these three methods of inventory valuation.
3. Give reasons for the variations in the cost of goods sold and the net income in the three statements.
4. What factors should be considered when choosing a method of inventory valuation?
5. Assume that Nykerk is about to purchase another machine before the end of the month but asks you first (a) how the purchase will affect the net income for the month, and (b) whether to defer the purchase until early in November. The price will not change. What would you recommend?

P13–12 (Minicase) Ralph Myers Wholesale Supply maintains perpetual inventory cards for all merchandise items. An inventory is taken annually. Serially numbered perforated tags are placed in each bin in the storeroom. The physical count is made by teams of two employees each. One employee fills in the stock number, description, and quantity on each half of the perforated tag. The other team member follows behind; checks the stock number, the description, and the count; removes one half of the perforated tag, and sends it to the office. In the office the quantity from the tags is entered on inventory sheets that already have the stock number and descriptions listed. The quantities on the inventory sheets are compared with the stock record cards and are then priced at the lower of cost or market.

Required: Explain the purpose of each step of this procedure. What should be done if the count quantity and stock record quantity of an item are not the same? What precautionary steps must be taken immediately before, during, and after the count?

chapter fourteen

Introduction

Industrial expansion often requires large expenditures for land, buildings, machinery, and equipment. This chapter deals with determination of and accounting for cost of plant assets, the allocation of these asset costs to the appropriate accounting periods, the disposal or retirement of plant assets, and related problems of management planning and control. It also deals with accounting for other long-lived assets such as natural resources, land, and for intangible assets.

Plant and equipment

Learning goals

To know which cost elements are included in the original cost of plant and equipment.
To understand the nature of depreciation, depletion, and amortization.
To know the acceptable methods of computing depreciation and to make the necessary accounting entries.
To differentiate between capital and revenue expenditures.
To account for disposal of plant and equipment items including trade-in transactions.
To record depletion of natural resources and to understand the accounting for depletion costs as part of cost of goods sold or as inventory.
To identify, define, and account for intangible assets.
To state plant and equipment items on the balance sheet.
To be familiar with valuation concepts other than historical cost.

Key terms

accelerated (declining-amount) methods
declining balance method
sum-of-the-years' digits method
amortization
book value (carrying value)
capital expenditure
capitalization
depletion
depreciation
estimated useful life (EUL)
intangible assets
copyright
franchise
goodwill
patent
leasehold
organization costs
production methods (for depreciation)
production-unit method
working-hours method
purchasing power
gains
losses
replacement cost
revenue expenditures
salvage value
straight-line method
tangible assets

The term plant and equipment denotes all assets of a tangible and relatively permanent nature, acquired for use in the regular operations of the business, not for resale, and whose use or consumption will cover more than one accounting period. This classification includes land, buildings, machinery, trucks, fixtures, tools, office machines, furniture and furnishings, patterns, and dies. The terms plant assets, capital assets, fixed assets, tangible assets, long-lived assets, and operational assets are often used as synonyms for plant and equipment. *Wasting assets,* such as timber, oil and gas, or minerals, are accounted for in a manner similar to plant and equipment. The term *intangible assets* denotes nonphysical rights and expected benefits that come from ownership. Their use and value is dependent on and limited by the degree of legal protection they provide (patents, copyrights, franchises, trademarks), economic factors (goodwill), the prevailing technology in the industry (secret formulas and processes), and the passage of time (leaseholds). These terms will be defined more fully later in this chapter.

Cost of plant and equipment

The cost of plant and equipment includes the purchase price (less any cash discount) plus all other expenditures required to secure title and to get the asset ready for operating use. The cost of buildings includes permit fees, excavation and grading, architectural and engineering fees, and remodeling costs. The cost of machinery includes transportation, installation, and all other costs incurred in preparing the machinery for operations.

Assume that a company purchases a machine for $5,000 at terms of 2/10, n/60, with freight to be paid by the buyer. Installation of the machine requires specialized electrical wiring and the construction of a cement foundation. All these expenditures are debited to the asset account. The total asset cost includes the following:

Purchase price	$5,000.00
Deduct 2 percent cash discount	100.00
Net purchase price	$4,900.00
Transportation	125.00
Cost of wiring	75.00
Construction of a special foundation	110.00
Total asset cost	$5,210.00

The cost price of the machine is the net cash paid on the purchase; the entry to record this purchase is:

1979						
Jun.	1	Machinery	4,900	00		
		Cash			4,900	00
		Purchased a machine.				

The entry for the freight payment is:

1979						
Jun.	11	Machinery	125	00		
		Cash			125	00
		Paid freight on delivery of machine.				

The entry to record the payment for installation of the machine is:

1979 Jun.	12	Machinery	185 00	
		Cash		185 00
		Paid for installation of machine.		

When these entries are posted, the Machinery account shows a total cost for the machine of $5,210. If the discount of $100 is not taken, it should still be deducted from the purchase price of $5,000 and debited to Discounts Lost—Nonmerchandise Items. An asset acquired in some manner other than by cash payment—for example, by gift or issuance of securities—is valued on the basis of the amount of cash that would be required for its acquisition *(fair market value)*. When a used plant asset is acquired, all expenditures incurred in getting the asset ready for use—paint, replacement parts, and so on—are debited to the asset account.

The cost of land includes brokers' fees, legal fees, transfer taxes, as well as costs incurred in preparing the land for use, such as grading, clearing, and the removal of unwanted existing structures less amounts received for scrap and salvage. Land is shown separately on the balance sheet because it is not subject to depreciation. However, improvements to land—landscaping, lighting, parking areas, fencing—which deteriorate through usage, are subject to depreciation and should be classified in a separate account, such as Land Improvements. A typical plant and equipment record form is shown in Figure 14–1.

Figure 14–1 Equipment record

EQUIPMENT RECORD

NAME OF ASSET **ASSET NO.** **CLASS NO.** **ACCT. NO.**

Made by

Manufacturer's Serial No.

Location

Purchased From

Purchase Guarantee

Year Type Model Size

H. P. Generated or Required

Estimated Life Years Depreciation Rate % or $ Per

Estimated Residual Value $

Insurance Carried

Appraised by When Appraised 19 Appraised Value $ Appraisal Report Reference

ACCUMULATED DEPRECIATION			NET ASSET VALUE	DATE	DESCRIPTION	POSTING REF.	COST		
YEAR	ANNUAL AMT.	TO DATE					DEBIT	CREDIT	BALANCE

Depreciation of plant and equipment

Several factors limit the serviceability of plant assets, chiefly wear and tear through ordinary use, accidental damage, inadequacy, level of repairs or maintenance, and obsolescence. Inadequacy may be due to changes in the nature of the business—method of manufacture, location, or type or design of product—that necessitate the disposition or replacement of plant assets. Obsolescence is due to technological advances that necessitate replacement of an existing asset with a new model. Although the serviceable life of the asset cannot be definitely known at the time of its acquisition, the cost of the asset cannot be considered as an expense chargeable entirely either to the period of acquisition or to the period of disposal. It is better to make an estimation of the useful life of the asset for purposes of making the periodic debit to expense than to omit the charge on the grounds that there is no strictly scientific way of making such an estimation.

Depreciation is an estimate of lost or expired usefulness. It recognizes that depreciable assets used in the business have a predictable and limited service life, over which asset costs should be allocated for the purpose of income measurement. The emphasis is on the systematic periodic debit to expense rather than the resulting balance sheet valuation.

Purpose of depreciation

Since most plant and equipment assets have a limited useful life, their cost is properly allocable as an expense to the accounting period in which the assets are used. The* purpose of depreciation *is to recognize the expiration of asset cost through use. Its primary purpose is cost allocation.

Estimated useful life (EUL)

It is often difficult to predict the useful service life of an asset. The estimate is important, because the amount of cost assigned to each period (depreciation for a period) is deducted from current revenue, thereby affecting net income for the period. Past experience, standard operating policies, and equipment replacement policies may be used in estimating the period during which the asset can or will be used by the business. A machine may be able to withstand wear and tear for perhaps twenty years, but it may be used for only ten years because it has become too slow or too small for current requirements; or it may have to be replaced because the particular model has become obsolete. In any case, the cost is allocated over the *estimated useful life* (EUL) of the asset.

Estimated salvage value

Salvage value (or residual value) is the amount that is expected to be recovered when the asset is ultimately scrapped, sold, or traded in. If an expenditure will be required in dismantling or removing the asset, the estimated gross salvage value is reduced by the anticipated removal cost. It is frequently assumed that the salvage value will be offset by the removal cost; in this case, depreciation is computed on the total cost of the asset. Also, total cost may be depreciated when the salvage value is known to be negligible. A company may trade in any assets that have a market value. For example, some businesses trade in cars, trucks, and office equipment for new models after a period of use. In such instances, the estimated cash market value at the date of trade-in should be deducted in arriving at the depreciable amount. Experience will enable the company to arrive at a salvage value factor.

Methods of computing depreciation

A number of methods are used to calculate periodic depreciation charges; each may give a significantly different result. The method selected in any specific instance should be based on a careful evaluation of all the factors involved, including estimated useful life, intensity of use, rapidity of changes in the technology of the industry and of the equipment, and revenue-generating potential. The objective is to charge each period in proportion to the benefits received during that period from the total pool of expected benefits over the asset's useful life. Procedures for allocating the cost of the asset to each accounting period within its service life are based on either uniform or varying charges. By the use of certain methods, the amounts charged to each period may be irregular, or they may follow a regularly increasing or decreasing pattern.

The method selected for computing depreciation is crucial, because the amount of the charge affects the income measurement for current and future periods and the carrying value of the asset in the balance sheet.

Straight-line method Under the straight-line method depreciation is considered a function of time, and a uniform portion of the cost is allocated to each accounting period. Degrees of use, age, or efficiency factors are not considered in determining the amount of depreciation to be assigned to each period. The straight-line method may be expressed as follows:

$$\frac{\text{Cost less salvage value}}{\text{Number of accounting periods in estimated useful life of asset}} = \text{Depreciation for each accounting period}$$

Assume that a machine costing \$5,210, with an estimated service life of five years and an estimated net salvage value of \$210, is purchased on January 2, 1979. The annual depreciation charge is:

$$\frac{\$5{,}210 - \$210}{5} = \$1{,}000 \text{ per year}$$

The straight-line method is popular primarily because it is simple to use. It assumes, however, level operating efficiency, repair and maintenance, and revenue contributions. Straight-line depreciation can also be computed by use of a straight-line rate. The annual rate is calculated by dividing 100 percent by the number of years in EUL (or alternatively, 1/n, where n = EUL).

Production methods Production methods relate depreciation to usage or to results rather than time, recognizing either working hours or units of output *(production units)* with each unit being charged with an equal amount regardless of decline in service effectiveness, decline in revenue generated, or level of repair and maintenance requirements.

The *working-hours method* requires an estimate of useful life in service hours instead of years. The charge to depreciation for an accounting period is determined as follows:

$$\frac{\text{Cost less salvage value}}{\text{Total estimated working hours}} = \text{Depreciation expense per hour}$$

$$\begin{matrix}\text{Depreciation} \\ \text{expense} \\ \text{per hour}\end{matrix} \times \begin{matrix}\text{Working hours} \\ \text{for the} \\ \text{period}\end{matrix} = \begin{matrix}\text{Depreciation} \\ \text{expense for} \\ \text{the period}\end{matrix}$$

An alternative computation procedure is:

$$\text{Cost less salvage value} \times \frac{\begin{matrix}\text{Working hours} \\ \text{for the period}\end{matrix}}{\begin{matrix}\text{Total estimated} \\ \text{working hours}\end{matrix}} = \begin{matrix}\text{Depreciation} \\ \text{expense for} \\ \text{the period}\end{matrix}$$

Assume, for example, that a truck costing $35,000 with a salvage value of $5,000 is expected to be driven 150,000 miles. If it is driven 10,000 miles during an accounting period, the computation for the period would be:

$$\frac{\$35{,}000 - \$5{,}000}{150{,}000 \text{ miles}} = \$0.20 \text{ per mile}$$

$$\$0.20 \times 10{,}000 \text{ miles} = \$2{,}000 \text{ depreciation expense for the period}$$

Under the *production-unit method,* depreciation is computed on units of output, and therefore an estimate of total units of output is required. Assume, for example, that a machine costing $21,000 with a salvage value of $1,000 had an estimated productive life of 10,000 units. If 1,500 units were processed during the current period, the charge to depreciation for the period would be:

$$\frac{\$21{,}000 - \$1{,}000}{10{,}000 \text{ units}} = \$2 \text{ per unit produced}$$

$$\$2 \times 1{,}500 \text{ units} = \$3{,}000 \text{ depreciation expense for the period}$$

The production methods allocate cost in proportion to the use that is made of the asset, the assumption being that there is a correlation between units of use and revenue generated. The straight-line method ignores use, emphasizing the fact that the asset is available; depreciation expense is regarded as a measure of such availability, irrespective of the extent of use.

Accelerated methods The use of accelerated methods results in larger depreciation charges during the early years of asset life with gradually decreasing charges in later years. Some commonly used forms are the declining-balance method and the sum-of-the-years'digits method.

Under the *declining-balance method,* a uniform depreciation rate is applied in each period to the remaining carrying value (cost less accumulated depreciation). For federal income tax purposes, the rate may not exceed twice the straight-line rate, termed double-rate declining balance (DDB), for most new assets. Another commonly used rate is 150 percent declining balance, which is one and one-half times the straight-line rate. Salvage value is ignored under this method although the asset cannot be depreciated below a reasonable salvage value, presumably because the arithmetic of this method is such that it will never reduce the asset balance to zero. At the end of the EUL, therefore, the remaining balance (less salvage) may be depreciated under the straight-line method over a period determined at that time or by an adjustment in the amount of the depreciation for the final period, or it may continue to be reduced at the fixed percentage of the book value until it is retired from use.

Assume that a machine costing $15,300 is purchased on January 2, 1978; the estimated useful life is five years; and the estimated salvage value is $300. Use of the double-rate declining balance method (DDB) results in a 40 percent depreciation rate—twice the straight-line rate of 20 percent—which is applied to the remaining book value unadjusted for salvage value. The amounts, rounded to the nearest dollar, are as follows:

Year	Computation	Annual Depreciation	Accumulated Depreciation	Book Value
1978	40% of $15,300	$6,120	$ 6,120	$9,180
1979	40% of 9,180	3,672	9,792	5,508
1980	40% of 5,508	2,203	11,995	3,305
1981	40% of 3,305	1,322	13,317	1,983
1982	40% of 1,983	793	14,110	1,190

The entry to record the depreciation charge for 1980 and the balance sheet presentation of the machine at the end of that year are as follows:

Date		Account	Debit		Credit	
1980						
Dec.	31	Depreciation Expense—Machinery and Equipment	2,203	00		
		Accumulated Depreciation—Machinery and Equipment . . .			2,203	00
		To record depreciation for the year.				

Assets		
Plant and Equipment		
Machinery and Equipment	$15,300.00	
Deduct Accumulated Depreciation . .	11,995.00	$3,305.00

Under the *sum-of-the-years'-digits method,* depreciation for any year is determined by multiplying the cost less salvage of the asset by a fraction: the denominator is the sum of the numbers of the years of estimated useful life of the asset; the numerator is the number of the specific period applied in reverse order, or the number of years remaining, including the current year. The following steps may be followed in sequence in making the calculations:

1. Calculate the sum of the series represented by the life of the asset starting with 1 up to the life of asset (assume EUL of 5 years):
   $1 + 2 + 3 + 4 + 5 = 15.$
2. The denominator is: The sum-of-the-years' digits from step 1.
3. The numerator is: The number of years left as of the end of each period plus 1.
4. The numerators are:
   End of year 1 $5 = (4 + 1)$
   2 $4 = (3 + 1)$
   3 $3 = (2 + 1)$
   4 $2 = (1 + 1)$
   5 $1 = (0 + 1)$.
5. The annual depreciation charges are: cost of asset (less salvage) × fraction for that year.

On the basis of the same facts as above, the annual depreciation is computed as follows:

Year	Years' Digits	Fraction	Annual Depreciation
1978	5	5/15 x $15,000.00	$ 5,000.00
1979	4	4/15 x 15,000.00	4,000.00
1980	3	3/15 x 15,000.00	3,000.00
1981	2	2/15 x 15,000.00	2,000.00
1982	1	1/15 x 15,000.00	1,000.00
Total	15		
Total depreciation for 5 years			$15,000.00

For long-lived assets, the sum-of-the-years'-digits can be found by using the formula for a simple arithmetic progression, $s = n/2\ (a + l)$, where n = EUL, $a = 1$, and l = the last year. In the previous example, the computation would be:

$$\text{Number of years in series} = n/2\ (a + l) = 5/2\ (1 + 5) = 15$$

A comparison of three methods shows the following depreciation under each:

Year	Straight Line	Double-Rate Declining Balance (40%)	Sum of the Years' Digits
1978	$ 3,000.00	$ 6,120.00	$ 5,000.00
1979	3,000.00	3,672.00	4,000.00
1980	3,000.00	2,203.00	3,000.00
1981	3,000.00	1,322.00	2,000.00
1982	3,000.00	793.00	1,000.00
Totals	$15,000.00	$14,110.00	$15,000.00

The double-rate declining-balance method results in the highest depreciation in the first year because of the higher rate and the higher base ($15,300 as compared with $15,000). However, an undepreciated amount of $1,190 = ($15,300 − $14,110) remains at the end of the fifth year. If the machine is to be kept in service, $890 = ($1,190 − $300) may be written off on a straight-line basis over the remaining period of use.

Depreciation for partial accounting periods

A consistent method should be followed for recording depreciation on assets acquired or retired during the accounting period. Since depreciation is an estimate, exact methods, such as counting the number of days of use, are immaterial and not commonly used. One method that is commonly used because it is simple and relevant is to consider that a plant asset is purchased as of the beginning of the month of acquisition if it is purchased on or before the fifteenth of the month. We then consider that a plant asset is purchased on the first day of the following month if it is purchased on or after the sixteenth of the month. The minimum measurable unit of time for the depreciation expense charge is one month.

Assume that a machine costing $6,500 with an estimated life of ten years and salvage value of $500 was purchased on November 10, 1979. Depreciation on the machine for the calendar year 1979, using straight line, is:

$$\frac{\$6{,}500 - \$500}{10} \times \frac{2}{12} = \$100$$

The year-end entry to record depreciation on the machine for two months is:

1979				
Dec.	31	Depreciation Expense—Machinery and Equipment . .	100 00	
		Accumulated Depreciation—Machinery and Equipment		100 00
		To record depreciation on machine.		

If the machine had been acquired on or after November 16, the amount in the entry would be $50. Depreciation may have to be recorded for a partial accounting period when an asset is sold, discarded, or exchanged for another asset. In these situations, depreciation must be recorded to the date of the event, assuming that the asset has not already been fully depreciated. The amount of depreciation to be charged for the month of disposal is based on the method followed for acquisitions.

Guidelines for depreciation methods

The method that is most practical and meaningful for the user should be selected. Since the amount of the depreciation deduction has a direct effect on net income and since the alternative methods of calculating depreciation result in different amounts, the method chosen may significantly affect the income tax liability. Any tax savings become available for investment in new plant and equipment or for any other use management chooses. *Minimization of income taxes by choice of depreciation method is a good management practice*. It is acceptable practice to use one depreciation method for income tax reporting and a different method for financial reporting.

The straight-line method is simple to apply and is satisfactory under conditions of fairly uniform usage. The production methods allocate depreciation in proportion to usage or output. This is important if usage is the dominant cause of loss in usefulness of the asset. The accelerated methods are based on the hypothesis that the service rendered by a plant asset is greatest in the early years of use; hence, that depreciation charged under these methods results in a more accurate matching of expense and revenue. Another reason is that as an asset gets older, it requires more maintenance. The increasing maintenance expenses in later years are offset by the diminishing depreciation expense, thus equalizing, to some extent, the total expense of the asset and thereby achieving a better matching of expense with revenue. There is also a financial (tax) reason. The timing of the depreciation deductions under the accelerated methods so that larger amounts are deducted in the earlier years of use results in proportionately reduced income and income taxes payable during those years. The same total tax is paid over the life of the asset's use regardless of the depreciation method used. But the difference in the timing creates a definite financial advantage equal to the interest-free use of cash from the reduced tax payments by the owner during the earlier years.

The process of recording depreciation does not provide or segregate funds for the replacement of property at the end of its EUL. The amount of the tax saving is not necessarily reinvested in the business as cash available for the replacement of equipment. It is possible for a business to segregate an amount of cash equal to the periodic depreciation charges, but such funds, if available, probably would result in a greater return when used in the regular operations of the business.

Capital and revenue expenditures

Capital versus revenue expenditures

The term **expenditure** *refers to a payment or a promise to make a future payment for benefits received—that is, for assets or services. Expenditures made on plant and equipment assets during the period of ownership may be classified either as capital expenditures or as revenue expenditures. A* **capital expenditure** *results in an increase in the book value of an asset account; a* **revenue expenditure** *results in an addition to an expense account.*

Capital expenditures are significant payments benefiting two or more periods. They include asset alterations, additions to existing assets, improvements to plant assets (betterments), and replacements. Through the depreciation process, these expenditures become expenses of future accounting periods. They prolong the useful life of the asset, make it more valuable, or make it more adaptable. Most commonly they are recorded as increases in plant and equipment; the expenditure is said to have been *capitalized*. Original purchases of land, buildings, machinery, and office equipment are also capital expenditures.

Expenditures for extraordinary repairs made to equipment during its life are also classified as capital expenditures if they extend the useful life or capacity of the asset or otherwise make the asset more serviceable (for example, overhaul of an aircraft engine). Some accountants view an extraordinary repair as restoring the effects of previous wear, that is, as a recovery of previous asset services. They record the increase in the asset by debiting Accumulated Depreciation, thereby canceling past depreciation charges.

Revenue expenditures benefit a current period and are made for the purpose of maintaining the asset in satisfactory operating condition. A routine repair or the replacement of a minor part that has worn out is an expense of the current accounting period, to be deducted from the revenue for the period. These expenditures do not increase the serviceability of the asset beyond the original estimate, but rather represent normal maintenance costs.

Careful distinction between capital and revenue expenditures is one of the fundamental problems of accounting; it is essential for the matching of expenses and revenue and, therefore, for the proper measurement of net income. A capital expenditure recorded as a revenue expenditure—as, for example, a purchase of office equipment debited to Office Expense—causes an understatement of net income in that year. If the error is not corrected, net income for the following years will be overstated by the amount of depreciation expense that would otherwise have been recognized. Conversely, a revenue expenditure recorded as a capital expenditure—as, for example, an office expense debited to Office Equipment—overstates net income for that year. If the error is not corrected, net income for the following years will be understated by the depreciation charge on the overstated portion of the Office Equipment account.

Disposal of plant and equipment

An asset may be disposed of by sale, by being traded in as part of the purchase price of a replacement, or by simply being discarded. The accounting treatment of sales and of discards is similar; the treatment of trade-ins is somewhat different.

An asset may still be in use after it is fully depreciated—that is, when the balance of the Accumulated Depreciation account, assuming that the salvage value is zero, is equal to the cost of the asset. In this case, no further depreciation is taken and no further entries are required until the asset is disposed of. In the balance sheet, the Plant and Equipment amount may be followed by a notation of the portion that represents fully depreciated assets still in use.

Sale or discard of plant and equipment

When an asset is sold or discarded, the entry for the transaction must remove the appropriate amounts from the asset and the accumulated depreciation accounts. Assume, for example, that a company acquires a truck on January 2, 1978, at a cost of $5,000. Depreciation is recorded on a straight-line basis at the rate of $1,000 annually (salvage value is assumed to be zero). Three situations, together with the methods of accounting for the disposal of the truck, are illustrated.

Example 1. Sale of asset at a price equal to book value. The truck is sold on July 1, 1982, for $500. The first entry is to record the depreciation for the current year, up to the date of the sale.

Date		Account	Debit		Credit	
1982						
Jul.	1	Depreciation Expense—Trucks	500	00		
		Accumulated Depreciation—Trucks .			500	00
		To record depreciation on trucks for the six-month period 1/1/82 to 7/1/82.				

The Accumulated Depreciation account now has a credit balance of $4,500, as shown below.

Accumulated Depreciation—Trucks

Date		Explanation	F	Debit		Credit		Balance	
1978									
Dec.	31					1,000	00	1,000	00
1979									
Dec.	31					1,000	00	2,000	00
1980									
Dec.	31					1,000	00	3,000	00
1981									
Dec.	31					1,000	00	4,000	00
1982									
Jul.	1					500	00	4,500	00

The book value of the truck is $500 as follows:

Cost at acquisition	$5,000.00
Accumulated depreciation	4,500.00
Book value	$ 500.00

As shown above, the book value of an asset—as distinguished from market value and replacement value—is its cost at acquisition reduced by the portion of the accumulated depreciation account applicable to that asset. Other terms commonly used are carrying value and undepreciated cost.

The entry to record the sale is:

1982				
Jul.	1	Cash	500 00	
		Accumulated Depreciation—Trucks . .	4,500 00	
		Trucks		5,000 00
		To record sale of truck.		

The purpose of this entry is to record the receipt of cash, eliminate the accumulated charges from the Accumulated Depreciation account, and reduce the asset account by the original cost of the truck.

Example 2. Sale of asset at a price above book value. The truck is sold on July 1, 1982, for $600. The entry to record the depreciation for the current year, up to the date of the sale, is the same as in Example 1 and is assumed to have been made. The following entry is made to record the sale:

1982					
Jul.	1	Cash		600 00	
		Accumulated Depreciation—Trucks		4,500 00	
		Trucks			5,000 00
		Gain on Disposal of Equipment			100 00
		To record sale of truck at a gain computed as follows:			
		Cost of truck	$5,000.00		
		Deduct accumulated depreciation	4,500.00		
		Book value of truck	$ 500.00		
		Amount received	600.00		
		Gain on disposal	$ 100.00		

Gains and losses on disposal of plant assets are measured by the difference between the book value of an asset and the proceeds from its disposal: a gain results when the proceeds are greater than the book value; a loss results when the proceeds are less than the book value. If the asset is fully depreciated, the book value is zero and the gain is the full amount realized from the sale. A gain or loss may be indicative of error in estimating the asset's useful life, salvage value, or both. Also, the book value of the asset and, therefore, the gain or loss on disposal are affected by the depreciation procedure used. Gain on Disposal of Equipment is shown in the income statement under Other Revenue.

Example 3. Sale of asset at a price below book value. The truck is sold on July 1, 1982, for $400 in cash. Again, the entry to record the depreciation applicable to the year of sale is the same as in Example 1 and is assumed to have been made.

The entry to record the disposal is:

1982				
Jul.	1	Cash	400 00	
		Accumulated Depreciation—Trucks	4,500 00	
		Loss on Disposal of Equipment	100 00	
		Trucks		5,000 00
		To record sale of truck at a loss computed as follows:		
		Cost of truck . . . $5,000.00		
		Deduct accumulated depreciation . . . 4,500.00		
		Book value of truck . . . $ 500.00		
		Amount received . . . 400.00		
		Loss on disposal . . . $ 100.00		

Loss on Disposal of Equipment is shown in the income statement under Other Expenses.

√Trade-in of plant and equipment—dissimilar assets

It is common practice to exchange, or trade in, used property when new property is acquired. If the trade-in allowance is not arbitrarily excessive (as a partial offset to an unrealistic list price of the new asset), it may be considered to be its fair market value and, therefore, the proper selling price of the old asset. The new asset is recorded at its list price. If the trade-in allowance is excessive, the list price is ignored and the fair market value of the asset traded in is used in arriving at the cost of the new asset. After the accumulated depreciation up to the date of the trade-in is recorded, the book value of the old asset is compared with its trade-in allowance. A gain is recognized if the trade-in allowance is greater than the book value, and a loss is recognized when the trade-in allowance is less than the book value. When the book value and the trade-in allowance are equal, however, there is no recognized gain or loss.

Example 1. Trade-in allowance the same as book value. A lathe that cost $5,000 with accumulated depreciation of $4,500 up to the date of the trade-in is exchanged for a compressor listed at $4,000; the trade-in allowance is $500. The list price has not been inflated (as is sometimes the practice) for bargaining purposes. Consequently, the trade-in allowance also represents fair market value. The new asset is recorded at its cash market price—the cash payment plus the fair market value of the old asset. The transaction is recorded as follows:

1979				
Sep.	1	Equipment (new compressor)	4,000 00	
		Accumulated Depreciation (old lathe)	4,500 00	
		Cash		3,500 00
		Equipment (old lathe)		5,000 00
		To record trade-in of old lathe for a new compressor.		

The cash payment of $3,500 is calculated as follows:

Selling price—new asset	$4,000.00
Trade-in allowance—old asset	500.00
Cash payment	$3,500.00

There is no gain or loss in this example because the trade-in allowance is the same as the book value.

Example 2. Trade-in allowance less than book value. The old asset in Example 1 is traded in for an allowance (the fair market value) of $400.

Date		Account		Debit	Credit
1979					
Sep.	1	Equipment (new compressor)		4,000 00	
		Accumulated Depreciation (old lathe)		4,500 00	
		Loss on Disposal of Equipment		100 00	
		Cash			3,600 00
		Equipment (old lathe)			5,000 00
		To record trade-in of equipment at a loss computed as follows:			
		Cost of old asset	$5,000.00		
		Accumulated depreciation to date of trade-in	4,500.00		
		Book value—unrecovered cost	$ 500.00		
		Trade-in allowance	400.00		
		Loss on trade-in	$ 100.00		

A loss is recorded because the book value of $500 is greater than the fair market value of $400. Furthermore, the new dissimilar asset received cannot be recorded at more than its fair market value of $4,000.

Example 3. Trade-in allowance greater than book value. The old asset in Example 1 is exchanged for a new one listed at $4,000; the trade-in allowance (the fair market value) is $800.

Date		Account		Debit	Credit
1979					
Sep.	1	Equipment (new compressor)		4,000 00	
		Accumulated Depreciation (old lathe)		4,500 00	
		Cash			3,200 00
		Equipment (old lathe)			5,000 00
		Gain on Disposal of Equipment			300 00
		To record trade-in of old lathe for new compressor at a gain computed as follows:			
		Cost (lathe)	$5,000.00		
		Accumulated depreciation to date . . .	4,500.00		
		Book value	$ 500.00		
		Trade-in allowance	800.00		
		Gain on trade-in	$ 300.00		

A gain is recorded because the fair market value of $800 is greater than the book value of $500.

√Trade-in of plant and equipment—similar assets

An Accounting Principles Board opinion requires a different procedure for recording exchanges of *similar* productive assets, defined as those "that are of the same general type, that perform the same function or that are employed in the same line of business."[1] The cost of the new asset is measured by the book value of the old asset plus the required additional expenditure (cash paid or its equivalent) or:

Cost of new asset = Book value of old asset + Expenditure

The excess of trade-in allowance over book value is viewed not as a gain but as a reduction from an inflated list price. However, an excess of book value over trade-in value is viewed as a loss, and is recognized immediately. List prices and trade-in values are not recognized in the accounts. They enter only into the computation of the required cash outlay. Under this rule, the unrecognized gain on the exchange is absorbed in the cost valuation of the new asset. To illustrate, assume that in the above examples, the old lathe was traded for a new but similar lathe, the numbers remaining unchanged. Using the numbers from the foregoing Example 3, the exchange for a similar asset would be recorded as follows:

Date		Account		Debit	Credit
1979					
Sep.	1	Equipment (new asset)		3,700 00	
		Accumulated Depreciation (old asset)		4,500 00	
		Cash			3,200 00
		Equipment (old asset)			5,000 00
		To record trade-in.			
		Cost of new equipment computed as follows:			
		Cost of old equipment	$5,000.00		
		Accumulated depreciation	4,500.00		
		Book value	$ 500.00		
		Cash paid ($4000–$800)	3,200.00		
		Cost of new equipment	$3,700.00		

The exchange in the foregoing Example 2, however, would be recorded as shown previously:

Date		Account		Debit	Credit
1979					
Sep.	1	Equipment (new compressor)		4,000 00	
		Accumulated Depreciation (old lathe)		4,500 00	
		Loss on Disposal of Equipment		100 00	
		Cash			3,600 00
		Equipment (old lathe)			5,000 00
		To record trade-in of equipment at a loss computed as follows:			
		Cost of old asset	$5,000.00		
		Accumulated depreciation to date of trade-in	4,500.00		
		Book value—unrecovered cost	$ 500.00		
		Trade-in allowance	400.00		
		Loss on trade-in	$ 100.00		

1 APB *Opinion No. 29,* "Accounting for Nonmonetary Transactions," par. 3.

The theory underlying the accounting for similar assets is that, unlike exchanges of dissimilar assets, the exchange of one piece of equipment for another similar piece of equipment does not change revenue. It does not represent the completion of a cycle involving the old asset. The substitution of one productive asset for a similar productive asset is normally not the occasion for the recognition of a gain.

Changing depreciation charges

The periodic depreciation charge may require revision under two circumstances: as the result of (1) an additional capital expenditure made on an original asset or (2) errors in the original EUL. In either case, the new depreciable cost is typically allocated over the remaining life of the property on which the expenditure was made. Assume, for example, that an additional wing costing $8,000 is added to a five-year-old factory building. The original cost of the building was $33,000, the estimated salvage value was $3,000, and the estimated useful life was twenty-five years. The straight-line method of depreciation has been used. The calculation of the revised annual depreciation charge is:

Original cost	$33,000.00
Deduct five years' accumulated depreciation ($30,000 x 0.04 = $1,200 per year x 5 years)	6,000.00
Book value	$27,000.00
Additional cost	8,000.00
New book value	$35,000.00
Deduct estimated salvage value	3,000.00
New depreciable cost	$32,000.00
New annual depreciation charge, based on a remaining useful life of 20 years ($32,000 x 0.05)	$ 1,600.00

If the improvement prolongs the life of the asset or increases its salvage value, the calculations must be altered to give effect to such changes. For example, if after the addition of the wing the remaining useful life were estimated to be twenty-four years and the estimated salvage value were $3,800, the revised annual depreciation charge would be determined as follows:

New carrying value	$35,000.00
Deduct estimated salvage value	3,800.00
New depreciable cost	$31,200.00
New annual depreciation charge, based on a remaining useful life of 24 years ($31,200 x 0.04167)	$ 1,300.00

When it is discovered that an error has been made in the EUL, a new depreciation schedule is prepared. From that point on, the new depreciation amount will be recorded.

Depletion of natural resources

Natural resources, or wasting assets, such as oil wells, mines, or timber tracts, should be recorded in the asset account at cost. As the resource is extracted, its asset value is reduced. The process of estimating and recording the periodic charges due to the exhaustion or expiration of a natural resource is called *depletion*. It is recorded on the books by a debit to the Depletion Cost account and a credit to the Accumulated Depletion account. In the balance sheet, accumulated depletion is classified as a contra account to be deducted from the cost of the resource.

The periodic depletion charge is usually calculated on an output basis similar to the production-unit method of recording depreciation. The cost of the wasting asset is divided by the estimated available units of output, to arrive at a per unit depletion charge. The number of units removed during the accounting period multiplied by the per unit depletion charge represents depletion for that period. For example, if the asset is a mineral measured in tons:

$$\frac{\text{Cost} - \text{Salvage}}{\text{Estimated tons to be mined}} = \text{Depletion per ton}$$

Assume that a mine costs $180,000 and contains an estimated 400,000 tons of ore. It is estimated that the net salvage value will be $20,000. The per unit depletion charge is:

$$\frac{\$180{,}000.00 - \$20{,}000.00}{400{,}000} = \$0.40 \text{ per ton}$$

If 10,000 tons are mined during an accounting period and 8,000 tons were sold, the cost of goods sold would be calculated as follows:

Cost of goods sold:	
Depletion (10,000 units x $0.40)	$ 4,000.00
Other costs of production (assumed to be $1 per unit)	10,000.00
Total cost of production	$14,000.00
($14,000 ÷ 10,000 units = $1.40 per unit)	
Deduct ending inventory (2,000 units x $1.40 per unit)	2,800.00
Cost of goods sold (8,000 units x $1.40)	$11,200.00

The Depletion Cost Account and other accounts representing the wages of the miners and production costs associated with mining activities are closed into the Ore Inventory Account. Using the perpetual inventory system, the cost of ore sold is transferred from the Ore Inventory account to an account called Cost of Goods Sold.

The Cost of Goods Sold is deducted in the income statement from the revenue realized from the sale of 8,000 tons of ore. The balance of the Ore Inventory account includes the allocated portion of mine depletion cost and the proportionate amount of the other costs of production. This is illustrated in the following T account flow chart:

Ore Inventory			Cost of Goods Sold	
14,000	11,200	→	11,200	

The balance of the T accounts consist of the following costs:

	Ore Inventory	Cost of Goods Sold
Depletion:		
2,000 units x $0.40	$ 800.00	
8,000 units x 0.40		$ 3,200.00
All other costs of production (assumed):		
2,000 units x $1.00	2,000.00	
8,000 units x 1.00		8,000.00
Totals	$2,800.00	$11,200.00

Intangible assets

Intangible assets are nonphysical rights that are of future value to the business because they shelter the firm from competition or provide other similar advantage to the owner. Some intangibles, whether purchased or self-developed, such as patents, copyrights, franchises, and leaseholds, can be readily identified and their cost measured. Others, such as goodwill, are not specifically identifiable or measurable.

The process of estimating and recording the periodic charges to operations due to the expiration of an intangible asset is called *amortization*. It is similar to computing and recording depreciation on a plant and equipment item by the straight-line method. The amount to be amortized annually is computed by dividing the asset cost by the legal life or the EUL whichever is shorter. The entry is a debit to an amortization expense account and a credit directly to the asset account. The straight-line method is generally used in view of the difficulties and uncertainties in estimating useful economic life and future benefits. But other methods are acceptable if they better match revenues and expenses.

Difficulties and uncertainties arise from the uniqueness of intangibles. The estimated useful life may be limited by law (copyright), by contract, by legislation (franchise), or by the economic factors of demand and competition (patents). Other intangibles (goodwill, trademarks) have an unlimited or indefinite life. Furthermore, some can be separately identified (franchise), whereas others cannot be, because they relate to the total entity (goodwill); finally, some intangibles are purchased, while others are developed within the firm.

The AICPA Accounting Principles Board concluded: ". . . that a company should record as assets the costs of intangible assets acquired from others, including goodwill acquired in a business combination. A company should record as expenses the costs to develop intangible assets which are not specifically identifiable. The Board also concludes that the cost of each type of intangible asset should be amortized by systematic charges to income over the period estimated to be benefited. The period of amortization should not, however, exceed forty years."[2]

Patents

The United States Patent Office grants *patents:* exclusive rights to the owners to produce and sell their inventions or discoveries for a period of seventeen years. All the costs involved in developing and acquiring a patent are included in the intangible asset account, Patents. The cost of a patent may be large and should be capitalized and amortized over the economic useful life of the asset or seventeen years, whichever is shorter. The Patents account may be credited directly (simply as a matter of custom) for the amortized portion; the account debited is called Amortization of Patent Cost or Patent Amortization Expense.

1979				
Dec.	31	Patent Amortization Expense	1,000 00	
		Patents		1,000 00
		To record amortization of patents for 1979.		

Goodwill

Goodwill is a general term combining a variety of intangible factors relating to the reputation of a firm and its ability to realize above-normal net income returns on an investment. Such factors as favorable customer relations; loyal and competent employees; possession of valuable patents, franchises, or copyrights; a high-quality product; and efficient management all aid in the development of goodwill. The goodwill that is built up over the years as the result of efficient management is not recorded on the books since there is no measurable cost of acquisition. Furthermore, those disbursements which may have contributed indirectly to the build-up of the goodwill, have been recorded as deductions from revenue (example: goodwill created through advertising expenditures). However, if the assets and goodwill of one company are purchased by another, the purchased goodwill should be recorded as an asset at cost.

The amount to be paid for goodwill is usually a result of a bargaining process between the buyer and the seller. The debit to Goodwill is the excess of the cost (purchase price) over the amounts allocable to assets other than Goodwill. APB Opinion No. 17 requires that goodwill be amortized, using the straight-line method, over a period not to exceed forty years. The amortization expense is not an allowable deduction on the owner's income tax return. (For estimating goodwill, see Appendix two).

2 APB *Opinion No. 17*, "Intangible Assets", par. 9.

Copyrights

A *copyright* is an exclusive right to publish a literary or an artistic work, granted by the federal government. The copyright is recorded at cost and is subject to amortization either over its legal life—twenty-eight years—or its useful economic life. If the copyright is obtained directly, the cost is small and is usually written off entirely in the first year. If it is purchased, the cost may be large enough to warrant periodic amortization. In practice, however, since revenues from copyrighted material are uncertain and are often limited to a relatively brief period, the cost of a copyright is added to the other costs of the first printing and enters into the inventory cost of the books or other printed materials.

Franchises

A *franchise* is a monopolistic right granted by a government or an entity in the private sector to render a service or to produce a good. A right to operate a bus line or a railroad or the exclusive use of a television transmitting channel is a valuable asset to the owner. The cost of obtaining the franchise is amortized over its life. Franchises are also used in industry whereby a manufacturer grants a dealer the exclusive privilege to sell the manufacturer's product within a defined geographical area.

Leaseholds and leasehold improvements

Leaseholds are rights to the use of land, buildings, or other property. If they are paid for in advance, they should be classified as capital expenditures. Leasehold improvements, such as buildings, are sometimes constructed on leased property. Leaseholds and leasehold improvements should be amortized over the life of the lease or over the estimated useful life of the asset, whichever is shorter. With respect to lease commitments that have not been classified as capital leases (or capital expenditures), a recent FASB statement states that the lessee should disclose: "Future minimum rental payments required as of the date of the latest balance sheet presented, in the aggregate and for each of the five succeeding fiscal years."[3]

Research and development

In theory, current expenditures for research and development should be capitalized to the extent that they will benefit future periods whether in the form of new or better products, reduced costs, or other benefits; when future benefits are uncertain, research and development costs should be expensed. Prior to FASB Statement No. 2,[4] a number of alternatives were used, varying from charging all expenditures to income when incurred to deferring all expenditures and amortizing them over the years of benefit.

3 FASB *Statement No. 13*, "Accounting for Leases." par. 7.
4 FASB *Statement No. 2*, "Accounting For Research and Development Costs."

Since future benefits from research are difficult to estimate—especially pure research, although less so for new or better product development—current practice favors expensing research and development costs when incurred. The FASB Statement requires that most research and development costs be treated as expenses when incurred.

Organization costs

This is an intangible asset resulting from expenditures made incidental to incorporation and is defined and discussed further in Chapter 16.

Valuation concepts — appendix one

The historical cost convention—that is, that assets should be carried in accounting records at the cost to acquire them—has been the basic valuation rule for many years. It has the advantage of being a measure of value that can be "proved" by actual evidence. Because of inflation and deflation, however, entities find themselves with a mixture of assets that were acquired at many different price levels. Comparison within entities and between entities becomes less useful; not only asset values, but also net income figures become distorted. Two basic approaches to the solution of this problem have been proposed. One would use the historical (actual) cost adjusted for price-level change; the other would use replacement cost.

Price-level adjusted data

In December 1974, the FASB issued a proposed statement of accounting standards that would require supplemental reports showing historical cost adjusted for price-level change. Some of the figures in the financial statements would be adjusted by a factor derived from index numbers representing the amount of inflation (or deflation) for each year. The proposed index, derived from Gross National Product figures by the U.S. Department of Commerce, is the GNP Implicit Price Deflator Index. It is an index of the level of prices of all goods and services.

The factor used to adjust items not classified as monetary items (described below) is:

$$\frac{\text{Index Number at End of Current Year}}{\text{Index Number at Date of Acquisition}} = \text{Adjustment Factor}$$

For example, assume that a machine is acquired for $20,000 at a date when the index is 120. It is being reported in a financial statement in a later year when the index at the end of the year is 150. The adjustment factor, or conversion ratio, would be:

$$\frac{150}{120} = 1.25$$

The adjustment would be $20,000 × 1.25 = $25,000. A similar adjustment would be required for depreciation expense, accumulated depreciation, and other non-monetary items.

Adjustments like these simply restate the historical cost figures in terms of current dollars. In other words, the adjusted cost is simply the number of today's dollars required for the amount of purchasing power invested when the item was bought. Price-level adjustments made with a general price level index ignore all other factors that might change the valuation. A tract of land bought at the same time as the $20,000 machine would also be adjusted by the factor 1.25. But it may have been purchased in an undeveloped area that now has become an industrial park. Its fair market value could now be three or four times its original cost.

The procedures described in the FASB proposal would require computation of what is known as purchasing power gains and losses. A purchasing power gain is realized when one holds a monetary liability—that is, a liability (such as accounts payable) which must be paid off in a fixed amount of dollars—during a period of inflation (rising prices). A purchasing power loss is realized when one holds a monetary asset—cash, accounts receivable, notes receivable and such—during a period of inflation. These gains and losses are real. If, for example, you hold $100 in cash over the period when the price level index rises from 120 to 150, you would need $125 = ($100 × 1.25) to buy the same amount of goods and services. Therefore, you have actually lost $25 in terms of goods you could buy today.

The net monetary gain or loss from price level changes is measured by the difference between the monetary items based on historical cost and the same items adjusted for changes in price level. To illustrate, *assume* the following price indexes:

1978—end of year	120*
1979—average	150
1979—end of year	165

*These are not the actual indexes for these years.

Using these indexes, the historical and price-level adjusted monetary assets and liabilities for the Andover Company are as follows:

	Historical Cost	Conversion Ratio	Restated to 12/31/79 Dollars	Itemized Gain (Loss)
Monetary assets and liabilities on 1/1/79:				
Cash	$ 412,000	165/120	$ 566,500	$(154,500)
Accounts receivable	300,000	165/120	412,500	(112,500)
Accounts payable	(209,000)	165/120	(287,375)	78,375
Bonds payable	(300,000)	165/120	(412,500)	112,500
Net monetary items, 1/1/79	$ 203,000		$ 279,125	$ (76,125)
Add: Monetary receipts during the year:				
Sales	750,000	165/150*	825,000	(75,000)
Deduct: Monetary payments during the year:				
Purchases	(450,000)	165/150*	(495,000)	45,000
Other expenses	(125,000)	165/150*	(137,500)	12,500
Net monetary items, 12/31/79	$ 378,000		$ 471,625	
Net purchasing power loss ($471,625 – $378,000)				$ (93,625)

*Average index is used for items acquired or paid evenly during the year.

The net purchasing power loss of $93,625 measures the purchasing power loss incurred by the Andover Company because the losses from holding monetary assets exceeded the gains from holding monetary liabilities during a period of rapidly rising prices. Under the FASB proposal the loss would be reported in the supplemental income statement in arriving at net income for the period.

Replacement cost

The general price level adjustments discussed above are for the purpose of reporting the impact of general inflation on the purchasing power of the dollar common to all goods and services. Such adjustments must be distinguished from changes in price levels of specific goods or services that are influenced by specific factors not common to all goods and services.

Replacement cost is the cost of replacing an asset with another asset of equivalent capacity. For inventories, replacement cost is the amount that would be required to buy the same items in the quantities that an entity normally purchases. For plant and equipment, replacement cost is the amount that would be required to buy the same productive capacity. This does not necessarily mean buying the same model of a machine; in fact, one would probably buy a more modern design. But it does mean the amount required to replace the present productive capacity, and is considered, in most cases, to approximate current economic value.

In March, 1976 the Securities and Exchange Commission (SEC) issued Accounting Series Release 190 (ASR 190) requiring that financial statements of large businesses show replacement cost information, as a supplement to historical cost, for inventories; plant and equipment; depreciation, depletion and amortization; and cost of goods sold. The purpose was to aid investors in developing an understanding of the impact of inflation on the current operations of the firm. The SEC did not require the presentation of data restated for changes in the general purchasing power of the dollar. It noted, however, that general price level adjustment might be applied either to historical cost or to current replacement cost financial data. ASR 190 did not require the disclosure of the effect on net income of calculating cost of goods sold and depreciation on a current replacement cost basis. The SEC recognized the theoretical and practical difficulties involved in a current replacement-cost-based measure of net income as well as the limitations of figures based on the arbitrary assumptions and judgment involved in estimating current replacement cost. The SEC indicated that several methods of estimating current replacement cost were acceptable including the use of published indexes adjusted for changes in technology, engineering estimates, vendor quotations, and published price lists.

After the issuance of ASR 190 by the SEC, the FASB deferred consideration of its price-level adjustment proposal. The Board concluded that more study is needed. Although it appears certain that more information about the effects of inflation on valuation will appear in financial statements, a commonly-accepted method of reporting it is not available at this writing. "An accounting model that will truly measure an entity's net worth and earning power is the dream of every accountant. But neither economics nor accounting will ever reach the state of precision or perfection necessary to do that job."[5]

Some real-life examples

The Shell Oil Company is a major U.S. corporation that has made price-level-adjusted data available. Figure A14–1 contains some selected information from Shell's reports for 1975. When historical costs are adjusted for general price level changes, the sales figure is increased by about 2 percent. Shell's plant and equipment, however, is increased by 33 percent; depreciation and depletion increased by 24 percent.

5 Jack C. Robertson, "Business Income Determination Through Use of Current Cost Accounting" (A Study Made under the Auspices of Coopers and Lybrand, November, 1976).

Figure A14–1 Shell Oil Company—1975 annual report extracts

	Amounts in Millions of Dollars	
	Historical dollars	*Dollars of current purchasing power**
Revenues	$8,224	$8,414
Purchasing power gain (loss) on:		
Long-term debt	—	68
Other monetary items	—	(16)
Net income	515	438
Property, plant and equipment (net)	4,389	5,828
Depreciation, depletion, etc.	597	739
Net income (per share)	7.59	6.46

*Based on purchasing power dollars at December 31, 1975.
Source: *Business Week,* May 5, 1975.

Barber-Ellis of Canada, Limited has used replacement-cost accounting. Some extracts from its 1974 reports are shown in Figure A14–2. While this does not result in an adjustment to the sales figure, there is an increase of 37.5 percent in depreciation and depletion. There is also a decrease of almost 40 percent in net income in Barber-Ellis' supplemental replacement-cost figures.

Figure A14–2 Barber-Ellis of Canada, Ltd.—1974 report extracts

	Amounts in Millions of Dollars	
	Replacement-cost accounting	*Historical-cost accounting*
Sales	$69.1	$69.1
Net Income	2.0	3.3
Property, plant and equipment	7.1	5.4
Depreciation and depletion	1.1	0.8

Source: *Business Week,* May 5, 1975.

The Western Union Corporation reported to the SEC that "its plant and equipment would cost $1.61 billion to replace as of the end of 1976, compared with the $1.11 billion carried on its books on a historical cost basis . . . its 1976 earnings of $34 million would be erased if it had based its depreciation charges on current cost of replacing its entire physical plant."[6]

Although it is generally agreed that a method of accounting that does not adequately reflect the impact of inflation will materially overstate real net income, "the business rationale in this country appeared to be that there was no

6 *The New York Times,* Jan. 31, 1977.

point in reporting smaller profits unless tax advantages were available at the same time.''[7] It does not seem likely that tax laws will be changed to permit replacement cost accounting for federal income tax purposes.

Estimating goodwill

appendix two

Since goodwill is related to excess earning power, the accountant is often called upon to prepare analyses and projections of earning capacity for the negotiators engaged in the purchase and sale of a business.

The emphasis in such analyses is on future earnings. Several of the techniques used for estimating goodwill are based on the company's earnings in excess of what may be normally expected by similar businesses. For example, the Sills Company with net assets of $300,000 expects to earn about $45,000 annually or a return of 15 percent on net assets during the next five years. Other companies in the same line of business are expected to earn about 10 percent annually on their net assets.

Three methods that may be used in measuring goodwill are illustrated below.

1. *Capitalization of earnings.*

Expected earnings	$ 45,000
Normal rate of return on net assets	10 percent
Net asset base required to generate expected earnings using the normal rate of return ($45,000 ÷ 10 percent) .	$450,000
Sills Company net assets	300,000
Estimated goodwill based on capitalization of expected earnings	$150,000

2. *Capitalization of excess earnings.* A variation of method 1 is to capitalize excess earnings at a rate above the normal rate of return. The assumption is that although earnings at a normal rate may be expected to continue indefinitely, the prospect of excess earnings is less certain. This uncertainty is built in to the calculation through the use of a higher than normal rate.

   Assuming a normal rate of 10 percent and a higher than normal rate of 25 percent are used, the calculation of goodwill for the Sills Company is:

Estimated excess earnings above normal	$ 15,000*
Goodwill—excess earnings capitalized at 25 percent ($15,000 ÷ 0.25)	$ 60,000
Total valuation:	
Net assets	$300,000
Goodwill	60,000
Total	$360,000

*Expected earnings of $45,000 − (10% of $300,000).

7 *The New York Times,* Jan. 31, 1977.

3. *Years' purchase of excess earnings.* This method measures goodwill in terms of a limited number of years during which the earnings are expected to continue or the length of time it will take for the goodwill to be recovered from excess earnings. The goodwill for the Sills Company, assuming that the excess earnings will continue for five years, is:

Estimated excess earnings as calculated above	$15,000
Years of purchase	5
Goodwill	$75,000

Glossary

Accelerated methods Depreciation methods that result in larger depreciation charges during the early years of asset life with gradually decreasing charges in later years.

Amortization Often used as a general term to cover write-down of assets; it is most commonly used to describe periodic allocation of costs of intangible assets.

Book value The net amount at which an asset is carried on the books or reported in the financial statements.

Capital and revenue expenditures Capital expenditures are payments or promises to make a future payment for assets that will benefit more than one accounting period. Revenue expenditures are those that benefit the current period only and are debited to appropriate expense accounts.

Capitalized An expenditure made that will benefit one or more future periods and is, therefore, carried forward (capitalized) as an asset.

Carrying value See book value.

Copyright An exclusive right granted by the federal government to publish a literary or an artistic work.

Declining-amount methods Depreciation methods that result in larger depreciation charges during the early years of the asset life with gradually decreasing charges in later years.

Depletion The process of estimating and recording the periodic charges to operations because of the exhaustion of a natural resource.

Franchise A monopolistic right granted by a government or other entity to produce goods or render services.

Goodwill A general term embodying a variety of intangible factors relating to the reputation of a firm and its ability to generate above-normal earnings.

Intangible assets Nonphysical rights and expected benefits that come from the ownership of such assets.

Leasehold Rights to the use of land, buildings, or other property.

Monetary assets and liabilities For purposes of price level accounting, those assets and liabilities whose amounts are fixed in terms of the number of dollars regardless of changes in the general price level.

Price-level-adjusted cost The number of current dollars required for the amount of general purchasing power invested when the item was bought.

Production methods Charges for depreciation based on usage or results rather than time (mileage, units of output).

Purchasing power gains and losses The difference between the monetary items based on historical cost and the same items adjusted for changes in price levels.

Replacement cost The current cost of replacing one specific asset with another asset of equivalent capacity.

Salvage value The amount of asset cost that is expected to be recovered when the asset is ultimately scrapped, sold, or traded in.

Straight line method A depreciation method that allocates a uniform portion of the depreciable asset cost to each accounting period.

Sum-of-the-years'-digits method A declining amount method of depreciation.

Tangible assets (long-term) Land, structures, and equipment of a tangible and long-lived nature, acquired for use in the regular operations of the business.

Questions

Q14–1 (a) List some expenditures other than the purchase price that make up the cost of plant and equipment. (b) Why are cash discounts excluded from the cost of plant and equipment? (c) What problems in cost determination arise when used plant assets are acquired? (d) What does the term *plant and equipment* encompass?

Q14–2 (a) What distinguishes a capital expenditure from a revenue expenditure? (b) What is the effect on the financial statements if this distinction is not properly drawn?

Q14–3 Student A maintains that if a plant asset has a fair market value greater than its cost after one year of use, no depreciation need be recorded for the year. Student B insists that the fair market value is irrelevant in this context. Indicate which position you support and give your reasons.

Q14–4 What are some of the factors that must be considered (a) when the depreciation method to be used is chosen? (b) when depreciation is recorded?

Q14–5 The basis for depreciation is generally original (historical) cost. Is there any other basis that could logically be used?

Q14–6 Since the total amount to be depreciated cannot exceed the cost of the asset, does it make any difference which method is used in calculating the periodic depreciation charges? Explain.

Q14–7 Describe the conditions that might require the use of each of the following methods of depreciation: (a) straight line, (b) production, (c) accelerated.

Q14–8 What procedures may be followed in recording depreciation on assets acquired during the accounting period?

Q14–9 What is the relationship, if any, between the amount of the annual depreciation charges on plant assets and the amount of money available for the new plant assets?

Q14–10 What accounting problems result (a) from the trade-in of one like plant asset for another? (b) from the sale of a plant asset?

Q14–11 (a) Distinguish between the terms *depreciation, depletion,* and *amortization.* (b) How is the periodic depletion charge determined?

Q14–12 (a) What are intangible assets? What factors must be considered when the acquisition of intangibles is (b) recorded? (c) amortized?

Q14–13 It has been argued that with proper maintenance certain equipment will last almost indefinitely, in which case depreciation is not necessary. Do you agree? Explain.

Q14–14 (Appendix one) What is the position of the SEC regarding disclosure requirement for property, plant, and equipment? What is your position?

Q14–15 Cutler-Hammer explains in its report to its shareholders that depreciation provisions were generally computed by the sum-of-the-years' digits method, "which distributes the greatest cost of the assets to the early years of their estimated lives." Do you agree with the apparent rationale for using this method of depreciation? Explain fully.

Q14–16 Assume that Cutler-Hammer had been using the straight-line method. Would its adoption of the sum-of-the-years' digits method be more likely to ensure the availability of funds that will be needed to replace assets when they are no longer useful?

Q14–17 What is the relationship between the balance in the Accumulated Depreciation—Machinery account and the availability of funds for replacing machinery? What is the relationship between the quantity and the quality of a company's repair and maintenance programs and the amount and rate of the provisions for depreciation?

Q14–18 The Seashore Company reported a change, for financial reporting purposes, from an accelerated method to the straight-line method of computing depreciation. Indicate (a) the probable reason for the changeover, (b) which accounts are affected, and (c) the effect on the financial statements.

Class exercises

CE14–1 (Computing depreciation expense) The Frongillo Company began business on July 1, 1979, with three new machines. Data for the machines are as follows:

Machine	*Cost*	*Estimated Salvage Value*	*EUL (years)*
A	$ 93,000	$ 9,000	12
B	126,000	14,000	10
C	34,000	6,000	7

Required: Compute the depreciation expense for the first two years by each of the following methods: (a) straight line, (b) sum-of-the-years' digits, and (c) double-rate declining balance.

CE14–2 (Capital and revenue expenditures) On January 2, 1979 the Tello Company purchased a machine for $30,000. Its estimated useful life was 8 years with no salvage value. Additional expenditures were made for transportation, $500, and installation costs, $900. On June 30, 1986, repairs costing $8,000 were made, increasing the efficiency of the machine and extending its useful life to 4 years beyond the original estimate. On December 1, 1987, some minor worn-out parts were replaced for $300. On October 2, 1989, the machine was sold for $5,000.

Required: Give the journal entries to record (a) the purchase, (b) annual depreciation for 1979, (c) the extraordinary repair on June 30, 1986, (d) annual depreciation for 1986, (e) the ordinary repair on December 1, 1987 and (f) the disposal on October 2, 1989. The company uses the straight-line method.

CE14–3 (Asset sale; trade-in) On January 2, 1979 the Da-Laur Company purchased a machine costing $20,000 with a useful life of 10 years and salvage value of $2,000. Assume that the sum-of-the-years' digits method is used to record depreciation.

Required: Give the journal entries to record the sale or trade-in of the machine, on the basis of each of the following assumptions:

1. Sale of the machine for $3,000 at the end of the sixth year.
2. Sale of the machine for $4,000 at the end of the fourth year.
3. Trade-in of the machine at the end of the sixth year for a new dissimilar machine listed at $25,000. The corporation paid $15,000 in cash to acquire the new machine.
4. Assuming the same facts as in (3), record the trade-in for a new similar machine.

CE14–4 (Accounting policy decision problem) The Guthrie Company has acquired depreciable plant and equipment items totaling $100,000. (1) Using a 10-year life and no salvage value, calculate the effect on net income for the first three years for each of the following methods of depreciation:

a. Straight line
b. Sum-of-the-years' digits
c. Double-rate declining balance

(2) Which method should be chosen? Why?

CE14–5 (Computing depreciation expense) The Middlesex Company acquired a compressor on July 2, 1979, at a cost of $25,000. The compressor had an estimated useful life of eight years and a salvage value of $2,500. Two years later the compressor was completely overhauled and rebuilt at a cost of $5,000. These improvements were expected to increase the estimated useful life of the compressor by four years from July 1, 1981.

Required: Prepare all entries through December 31, 1981. The company reports on a calendar-year basis and uses straight-line depreciation.

CE14–6 (Appendix one, computing monetary purchasing power gain or loss) The balance sheet of the Lois Company as of December 31, 1978, included the following:

Cash	$275,000
Notes and Accounts Receivable	200,000
Notes and Accounts Payable	112,500
9 percent Mortgage Bonds Payable	125,000

The income statement for the year 1979 included the following:

Sales	$850,000
Purchases	425,000
Other expenses (exclusive of depreciation)	125,000

Price levels for 1979 were:

Beginning of year	120
Average for the year	135
End of year	150

Required: Prepare a schedule showing the monetary purchasing power gain or loss during 1979.

CE14–7 (Appendix two, estimating goodwill) The Boston Company with net assets of $60,000 is expected to earn about 20 percent annually on its net assets during the next three years. Competing companies in the industry are expected to earn about 15 percent annually on their net assets.

The New York Company is negotiating for the purchase of the Boston Company.

Required: What amount will the New York Company have to pay for goodwill if the method used for measuring goodwill is based on (1) capitalization of earnings? (2) capitalization of excess earnings? (3) three years' purchase of excess earnings?

Exercises and problems

P14–1 For each of the following items, indicate the account to be debited:

a. Expenditure for installing machinery.
b. Expenditure for trial run of new machinery.
c. Expenditure for conveyor system for machinery.
d. Payment of delinquent taxes on land (taxes were delinquent at the date of purchase of the land).
e. Expenditure for extensive plumbing repairs on a building just purchased.
f. Sales tax paid on new machinery just purchased.
g. Payment of incorporation fees to the state.
h. Expenditure for a major overhaul that restores a piece of machinery to its original condition and extends its useful life.
i. Expenditure for an addition to a building leased for 20 years.
j. Amount paid for a purchased business in excess of the appraised value of the net assets.

P14–2 The Saganey Company made the following expenditures on the acquisition of a new machine:

Invoice cost ($19,000) less 2 percent cash discount	$18,620
Transportation charges	570
Installation charges	950
Property insurance—premiums for three years	570
Materials and labor used during test runs	285

Required: What is the cost of the machine?

P14–3 The DiMaggio Company purchased a machine for $10,000; terms, 1/10, n/60.

Required: Record (a) the acquisition of the machine and (b) payment of the invoice within the discount period.

P14–4 The Furbush Company solicited bids for a new wing for its factory building. The lowest bid received was $25,000. The company decided to do the work with its own staff, and the wing was completed for a total cost of $22,000.

Required: Record the expenditure.

P14–5 On April 1, 1979, a calculating machine used in the office of the Kelly Company was sold for $400. The sale was recorded by a debit to Cash and a credit to Office Equipment for $400. The machine had been purchased on October 1, 1976, for $1,200 and had been depreciated at the rate of 10 percent annually (no salvage value) through June 30, 1978. The Kelly Company closes its books annually on June 30.

Required: Make an entry to correct the accounts as a result of the transaction.

P14–6 On February 1, 1976, the Wirsen Company acquired a press costing $15,000 with an estimated useful life of five years and a salvage value of $1,000. On August 1, 1979, the press was traded in for a new one with a cash market price of $20,000. The dealer allowed $4,200 on the old press, and the balance was paid in cash.

Required: Record the trade-in on the books of the Wirsen Company, on the basis (a) of recognition of gain or loss and (b) of nonrecognition of gain or loss. (c) Contrast the entries in (a) and (b) and state how the nonrecognition of the gain or loss in (b) is compensated for.

P14–7 The Provincetown Company purchased a truck on January 2, 1979, for $12,500. It had an estimated useful life of six years and a trade-in value of $500.

Required: Compute the depreciation charge for the year 1979 under the following methods: (a) straight line, (b) sum-of-the-years' digits, (c) double-rate declining balance, and (d) production, assuming an operating life of 100,000 miles and 18,000 miles of actual use the first year.

P14–8 The Seviyah Company reported a net income of $150,000 for the year 1979. The owner noted that the beginning and ending inventories were $600,000 and $750,000, respectively, although the physical quantities on hand were relatively stable. She also noted that deductions for depreciation averaged 10 percent on plant and equipment costing $1,350,000, although the current dollar value of the assets is estimated at $1,800,000. The owner suggests that the reported net income is erroneous. Comment.

P14–9 The Cape Company purchased a mine for $336,000. It was estimated that the land contained 1,120,000 tons of a recoverable mineral deposit, and that after recovery of the deposits the land would have a salvage value of $16,000. During the first year, 96,000 tons were recovered and 80,000 tons were sold. Labor and overhead costs were $160,000.

Required: Determine (a) the cost of goods sold and (b) the ending inventory valuation.

P14–10 On January 2, 1979 the City Company purchased land and an old building for $200,000. The land is appraised at $20,000; the building is estimated to have a useful life of 20 years and a salvage value of $10,000. After three years' use, the building was remodeled at a cost of $75,000. At this time, it was estimated that the remaining useful life of the building would be 25 years with a salvage value of $20,000.

Required: Using the straight-line method of depreciation, give the entries (a) for the purchase of the land and building, (b) for depreciation for 1979 (c) for remodeling costs, and (d) for depreciation for 1982.

P14–11 The condensed income statement of the Bluebell Company for the year ended March 31, 1979, was as follows:

Sales	$500,000
Cost of Goods Sold	300,000
Gross Margin	$200,000
Operating Expenses	
(includes depreciation expense of $20,000)	125,000
Net income	$ 75,000

Required: (a) Assuming that beginning and ending Accounts Receivable, Accounts Payable, and Merchandise Inventory balances were approximately the same, how much cash was generated by operations? (b) Did the depreciation expense deduction result in a direct cash increase of $20,000? Explain.

P14–12 (a) "The government gave away $2.7 billion in tax revenue." (b) "An unwarranted windfall." (c) "A bonanza." These are some of the statements made by some public officials and economists following an announcement by the U.S. Treasury Department reducing the depreciation EUL guidelines by about 20 percent.

Required:

1. Do you agree with the above quotations? Explain.
2. What is the Treasury Department's motive in permitting faster write-offs?
3. What is the effect of the Treasury Department's action on net income?

P14–13 The G & G Company purchased land and buildings for $450,000; the buildings were demolished at a cost of $17,000, salvaged materials were sold for $4,000, and a new building was constructed on the site for $4,000,000. The following additional expenditures were incurred during construction:

Fees for permits and licenses	$ 1,500
Interest on money borrowed for payment of construction costs	2,000
Architectural fees	25,000
Insurance	1,500
Real estate taxes	2,000
Land grading and leveling	10,000
Promotional literature describing the new facility	1,000
Trees, shrubs, and other landscaping costs	7,500

Required: Open T accounts for (a) Land, (b) Buildings, and (c) Operating Expenses. Post the transactions to the accounts.

P14–14 On January 2, 1979, the Crisway Company purchased a new machine for $75,000 with an estimated salvage value of $5,000 and an estimated useful life of six years, or 9,000 machine-hours. The plant manager expects to use the machine for 2,200 hours during 1979, and 1,500 hours during 1980.

Required:

1. Compute the depreciation expense for each of the first two years by the following methods: (a) straight line, (b) production, (c) sum-of-the-years' digits, and (d) double-rate declining balance.
2. Assume that the Crisway Company is in an industry in which rapid changes in technology have, in the past, made existing equipment obsolete. How does this affect the estimate of the asset's useful life?

P14–15 The following information was taken from the books of the Matthew Herson Company.

	Machine A	*Machine B*	*Machine C*
Date acquired	January 2, 1979	January 2, 1980	January 2, 1981
Cash payment	$30,800	$8,800	$39,600
Estimated salvage value	2,000	2,400	4,400
Estimated useful life in years	5	6	7
Method of depreciation	Sum-of-the-years' digits	Straight line	Double-rate declining balance

On January 2, 1980 machine A, with a value of $18,800, was traded for a dissimilar machine B, which listed for $28,000.

Required:

1. Give all the necessary entries to record the transactions through December 31, 1981. The books are closed annually on December 31.
2. What is the entry for the trade-in of machine A for machine B if B is a similar machine?

P14–16 The Shakespar Company purchased a tract of land at a cost of $200,000. It was estimated that the land contained 1,000,000 tons of a recoverable ore deposit and that after recovery of the deposits, the land would have a resale value of $25,000. Costs of clearing the area and drilling mine shafts were $300,000. During 1979, the first year of operations, 90,000 tons were recovered and 70,000 tons were sold for $8 a ton. Labor and overhead costs were $200,000, and general and administrative expenses were $50,000.

Required:

1. Prepare the income statement for the year.
2. Prepare a partial balance sheet showing how the foregoing would be reported as at December 31, 1979.

P14–17 (Integrative) Following are certain selected transactions and events of the Behr Company relating to its plant and equipment accounts.

a. Purchased a machine on January 2, 1979 at a cost of $8,000 with an estimated life of 10 years and no salvage value. On July 1, 1981, the machine was traded in for a new but similar model with a cash market price of $10,000. The trade-in allowance was $5,000. The fair market price of the old machine was $4,000.
b. On April 1, 1979 acquired patent rights to a new product at a cost of $25,000. The patent was approved by the U.S. Patent Office one year ago. The Behr Company expects to earn well above normal profits on the patented product for about five years, at which time competing products will reduce earnings to normal levels.
c. On July 1, 1979 the company purchased equipment for $40,000 plus a 3 percent sales tax, terms, 2/10, n/60. The invoice was paid within the discount period. The estimated useful life of the equipment was 15 years with no salvage value. Additional expenditures were made for freight, $750; installation costs, $1,500; and costs of a trial run, $250. On April 1, 1980 the company built an adapter to the equipment in its own plant at a cost of $2,000. The adapter increased the speed and output of the equipment by 10 percent. The bid price for the work by an outside contractor was $2,500.
d. The general manager suggests to her controller that depreciation on some of the equipment should be accelerated to increase funds that will be needed for their early replacement, because she expects some of the specialized machines to become technically obsolete within a few years. She also wants to capitalize the cost of an extensive advertising campaign on several new products that was con-

ducted during 1979 at a cost of $25,000 and which, she expects, will help to generate sales of the products for at least three years.

Required:

1. (Item a) Make all necessary entries through December 31, 1981. The company uses straight-line depreciation and reports on a calendar-year basis.
2. (Item b) Make all necessary entries through December 31, 1980.
3. (Item c) Make all necessary entries through December 31, 1980.
4. (Item d) How should the controller respond to the suggestions?

P14–18 (Minicase) The following accounting practices and procedures were reported on the financial statements submitted to the Cape Cod Trust Company by applicants for bank loans:

a. Trade names and goodwill acquired through purchases prior to 1968 are being amortized over a 25-year period; subsequent purchases aggregating $1,530,000 will be amortized when it becomes evident that the value of the asset has diminished.
b. Television and feature film costs are amortized in the proportion of rentals earned to date to management's estimate of ultimate rentals. If management's estimate indicates a loss, the full amount of the loss is charged against income.
c. Franchises consist of contracts to import whiskeys, liquors, and other distilled spirits which, in the opinion of the management, have continuing value and accordingly are not amortized. Other intangibles of $3,670,363 are being amortized over periods not exceeding 20 years.
d. The company follows the practice of accumulating costs applicable to immature fruit crops including care-taking expenses and depreciation. Costs during the year are capitalized and charged to earnings when the fruit crop is sold.

Required:

1. Comment critically on each of the foregoing practices and state your suggestions.
2. Do any of the methods used violate the proper matching of revenue and expense?
3. What alternative methods might have been used in each instance?
4. Do the methods used indicate an explicit attempt to influence reported net income? If so, in what way?
5. What are some specific circumstances underlying the choice of accounting method in each case?

P14–19 (Appendix one) The following data relate to the Kornfeldt Company.

Net monetary assets, December 31, 1978	$121,800
Monetary receipts and payments during 1979:	
Sales	450,000
Purchases	270,000
Other expenses (exclusive of depreciation)	75,000

Required: Calculate the monetary purchasing power gain or loss for the year. Apply the following price indexes:

1979—beginning of year	125
1979—average for the year	140
1979—end of year	150

P14–20 (Appendix one) Harper Industries owns buildings in various parts of the United States and Canada. The first building was acquired at $10,000 when the general price-level index was 80. The latest building was purchased for $150,000 in 1979 when the price-level index was 160. Many buildings were acquired in the years between. All buildings are carried on the balance sheet at cost less accumulated depreciation which is computed on a straight-line basis.

In 1979 the balance sheet showed

Buildings (at cost)	$2,170,000.00
Deduct Accumulated Depreciation	680,000.00
	$1,490,000.00

Depreciation charges in 1979 were $168,000. The general manager of Harper Industries knows that the company has turned down opportunities to sell the buildings at twice their cost. He also feels that the depreciation expense being charged each year is too small and is causing nct incomc to bc overstated. He is concerned that the owner and potential creditors are not receiving a true picture of the condition of Harper Industries even though their statements are audited each year.

Required: Briefly discuss:

a. Ways in which Harper's financial statements may be misleading and why.
b. Some possible approaches that Harper might take to make more meaningful disclosure of assets and income.

P14–21 (Appendix two, estimating goodwill) The Flores Company is negotiating for the purchase of the Groom Company with assets (exclusive of goodwill) of $90,000 and liabilities of $30,000. Average annual earnings for the Groom Company are expected to be $15,000.

Required: Estimate the goodwill under each of the following independent methods:

1. Goodwill equal to earnings capitalized at 15 percent, the normal rate for the industry.
2. Goodwill equal to capitalization of the excess earnings above 12 percent, the normal rate for the industry.
3. Goodwill equal to five years of excess earnings. The normal rate for the industry is 16 percent.

Accounting objectives and standards

part four

chapter fifteen

Introduction

In the last ten to fifteen years studies have been made to identify the goals of accounting. It is generally agreed that the basic goal of financial statements is to provide information that is useful for economic decisions. Users of accounting information will be more effective in decision making if they understand the accounting standards that were used in preparation of the financial statements on which they rely. The chapter begins with a brief description of some of the authoritative bodies influential in creating these standards. There is a discussion of generally accepted accounting principles (GAAP), and some of the more common of these are illustrated by application to a typical set of financial statements.

Accounting objectives and standards

Learning goals

To recognize the major sources of guidance for accounting methods.
To know the history and functions of principal authoritative bodies in accounting.
To recognize the basic goals of accounting.
To know the major guidelines that govern accounting methods and practices.
To achieve more complete interpretation of financial statements.

Key terms

AAA
accounting objective
accounting practice
accounting principle
accounting standard
accrual basis
APB
APB Opinions
ARBs
attest function
CASB
CIA
CMA
conservatism
consistency
CPA
entity concept
FASB
FASB Statement
full disclosure
generally accepted accounting principles (GAAP)
going concern concept
historical cost
matching of expenses and revenue
materiality
NAA
objective evidence principle
periodicity
SEC
stable dollar concept

In previous chapters emphasis has been placed on accounting methods or practices. It has been necessary to concentrate on the techniques of operating the basic accounting model. However, recording and reporting of financial data are not done for their own sake. It is appropriate at this point to reconsider the reasons for some of the accounting rules and practices. It is also appropriate to consider from an overall viewpoint the authority upon which those accounting practices are built.

This chapter begins with a brief description of some of the authoritative bodies that have been influential in developing what have come to be known as *generally accepted accounting principles (GAAP)*. These authoritative bodies have worked on a national scale to enable the accounting profession to adapt to changes as businesses have grown larger and more complex. They continue to function actively.

In the last ten to fifteen years studies have been made to identify the goals of accounting. It is generally agreed that the basic goal of financial statements is to provide information that is useful for economic decisions. Starting with this basic assumption, study groups have identified other broad goals called *accounting objectives*. Some of these are discussed in this chapter as a background for specific standards.

Within the scope of the accounting objectives, certain fundamental guidelines serve to determine whether or not specific practices or methods are acceptable. These fall under the term of generally accepted accounting principles, but more recently are becoming known as *accounting standards*. Users of accounting information will be more effective in decision making if they understand the accounting standards that were used in preparation of the financial statements they rely on. Some of the more common standards are discussed in this chapter and are illustrated by application to a typical set of financial statements.

Authoritative bodies

American Institute of Certified Public Accountants (AICPA)

The AICPA (formerly named the American Institute of Accountants, AIA) was created in 1936 by the merger of the two then-existing national accounting organizations. Since January 1, 1936, it has been the basic authoritative body for the certified public accountants in the United States. It requires that members possess the CPA certificate. The CPA certificate, issued by the states (under provisions of law of individual states), has the common basis that each holder must pass a two-and-one-half day examination in accounting theory, accounting practice, business law, and auditing.

In 1937 the Institute created a Committee on Accounting Procedure, which issued a series of Accounting Research Bulletins (ARBs). These bulletins set forth the opinions of the Committee on specific controversial methods of accounting procedure. After the Committee had researched a problem and published its opinion in an ARB, members of the Institute were required, in general, to comply. The last such bulletins were published in 1959. AICPA also had a Committee on Terminology, which issued a series of *Accounting Terminology Bulletins* (ATBs). These bulletins, the last of which was issued in 1957, were issued in the interest of standardizing descriptive terms used in accounting. On September 1, 1959, these two committees were merged to form the Accounting Principles Board (APB). The APB continued both of the series of bulletins in effect, but decided to publish a new set of pronouncements from 1959 on. The most important of these are the *Opinions of the Accounting Principles Board* (APB *Opinions*). They are in a numbered series, starting with number 1 in 1962. When the APB was replaced in 1973 it had issued 31 opinions. Each of these opinions provides guidance in a specific area—for example, accounting for the cost of pension plans. They carry authority because they are widely accepted. In the rare instance that a CPA finds circumstances under which he or she cannot follow an APB Opinion, he or she must be able to justify such actions. There are more than 100,000 CPAs in the United States, 80,000 of whom belong to the AICPA. Because these are the professionals whose certifications attest to the fairness of the accounting statements of most businesses, it is obvious that the AICPA is a powerful authoritative body.

Financial Accounting Standards Board (FASB)

In 1972 the Financial Accounting Standards Board was established. The FASB is now the independent nongovernmental body in the United States to develop and issue standards of financial accounting.

The seven members of the FASB serve full time and are paid for their services. At least four of the members must be CPAs drawn from public practice. To assist FASB members in their work on a continuing agenda of projects, there is a technical staff. When the FASB assumed responsibility for issuing accounting guidelines, it left the numbered series of APB Opinions in effect. As it began to issue FASB Statements of Financial Accounting Standards, its form of basic accounting guidelines, some APB Opinions were replaced or modified. By mid-1977 the FASB had issued 16 *Statements,* so that today accountants must look to a mixture of APB *Opinions* and FASB *Statements* for authoritative guidance. As time passes it is expected that FASB *Statements* will be the primary nongovernmental source of authority. However, several other bodies are important in shaping accounting practices.

Cost Accounting Standards Board (CASB)

The Defense Production Act Amendments of 1970 included a provision that provided for a five-member Cost Accounting Standards Board. The CASB is an agent of Congress. It is headed by the Comptroller General of the United States. The other four members are appointed by the Comptroller General for four-year terms. Originally the CASB was created to issue standards to bring uniformity to cost accounting by defense contractors. Its authority has now been extended to nondefense negotiated federal government contracts in excess of $100,000. By January 1, 1976, the CASB had issued eleven standards dealing with a variety of topics such as depreciation of plant assets; use of FIFO, LIFO, or average inventory costing; and assignment of pension costs to accounting periods. Because they are likely to seek government business or to be subcontractors under federal contracts at some time, CASB standards are important to accountants in most industrial concerns. Unlike the FASB, the standards issued by the CASB have the authority of the law behind them.

Securities and Exchange Commission (SEC)

The SEC was created by the Securities Exchange Act of 1934. It has the legal authority to prescribe accounting methods for firms whose shares of stock and whose bonds are sold to the investing public on the stock exchanges. The law requires that such companies make annual reports to the SEC with information in great detail about their operations. The SEC has broad powers as to the amount and type of information to be included in these annual reports and the methods used to develop the information that they contain. Since its creation in 1934 the SEC has concentrated on protection of investors. It has given high priority to the public disclosure of financial information in a fair and accurate manner. In its first forty years the SEC issued relatively few detailed accounting rules. It preferred to leave this task for the accounting profession to perform.

In recent years the SEC has become much more active in exercise of its legal power to prescribe accounting practices. In March, 1976 the SEC announced that, commencing on December 25, 1976, large companies must show in financial statements their inventories; cost of goods sold; productive capacities; and depreciation, depletion, and amortization on a "replacement cost" basis.[1] Also, in early 1976, the SEC established an advisory committee to make a thorough study of practices and policies of corporations with regard to disclosure of information important to the investment process. According to the chairman of that study, the trend seems to be toward providing to the public more "forward-looking" information.[2]

American Accounting Association (AAA)

Beginning in 1916 as an association of accounting instructors, the organization now called the AAA has grown to a large organization today oriented toward accounting research, education research, and matters of academic interest. An example of the work of AAA is the 1966 publication, *A Statement of Basic Accounting Theory,* often referred to as "ASOBAT." This book represents two years of work by a committee of nine members—all leaders in the accounting field. AAA publishes a quarterly journal, *The Accounting Review,* in which cur-

1 Replacement cost was defined in Chapter 14.

2 Commissioner A. A. Sommer, Jr. Address before the 1976 Southeast Regional Group, American Accounting Association at Tampa, Florida, April 12, 1976.

rent accounting topics are discussed. The AAA exerts considerable influence on accounting practices through the work of its standing committees such as the Committee on Financial Accounting Standards and the Committee on Professional Examinations.

National Association of Accountants (NAA)

The National Association of Cost Accountants was formed in 1919. As its interests broadened to include all aspects of managerial accounting (oriented toward internal users of information), its name was changed to National Association of Accountants (NAA). In addition to its research and publication activities, NAA is the sponsor of the Institute of Management Accounting, which prepares and administers the national examination for the Certificate in Management Accounting (CMA). The CMA examination is also a two-and-one-half day test covering five major managerial accounting areas.

Other bodies

While these groups probably exert the strongest influence on accounting practice, several others are part of the total group of authoritative bodies in accounting. The Institute of Internal Auditors sponsors the Certified Internal Auditor (CIA) examination. The Financial Executives Institute publishes a monthly journal and has sponsored studies on accounting problems.

It is obvious that there is no single source of authority for accounting rules; the accountant must be responsive to many bodies. Fortunately, there is a great deal of interaction and cooperation among them.

Accounting objectives

Before proceeding to a discussion of some specific accounting standards, brief attention will be given to accounting objectives. Figure 15–1, reprinted from a publication of the FASB, indicates the importance of accounting objectives by placing them at the top position. *Accounting objectives* are the basic goals of accounting. Figure 15–1 indicates that attention should be turned to matters such as accounting and reporting standards, interpretations of standards, and practices only after objectives have been determined. To determine what accounting objectives are, studies should be made to understand the qualitative characteristics of accounting information and what information is needed. Some work has already been done along these lines.

Three major studies have led to the defining of accounting objectives. The 1966 *Statement* (referred to as ASOBAT in the discussion of AAA) by the American Accounting Association listed four basic factors for judging the usefulness of accounting information. In 1971, APB Statement No. 4 established seven standards of quality for accounting data, and then, in its 1973 report, *Objectives of Financial Statements,* an AICPA Study Group listed a set of qualita-

Figure 15–1
Hierarchy of elements in a conceptual framework for financial accounting and reporting

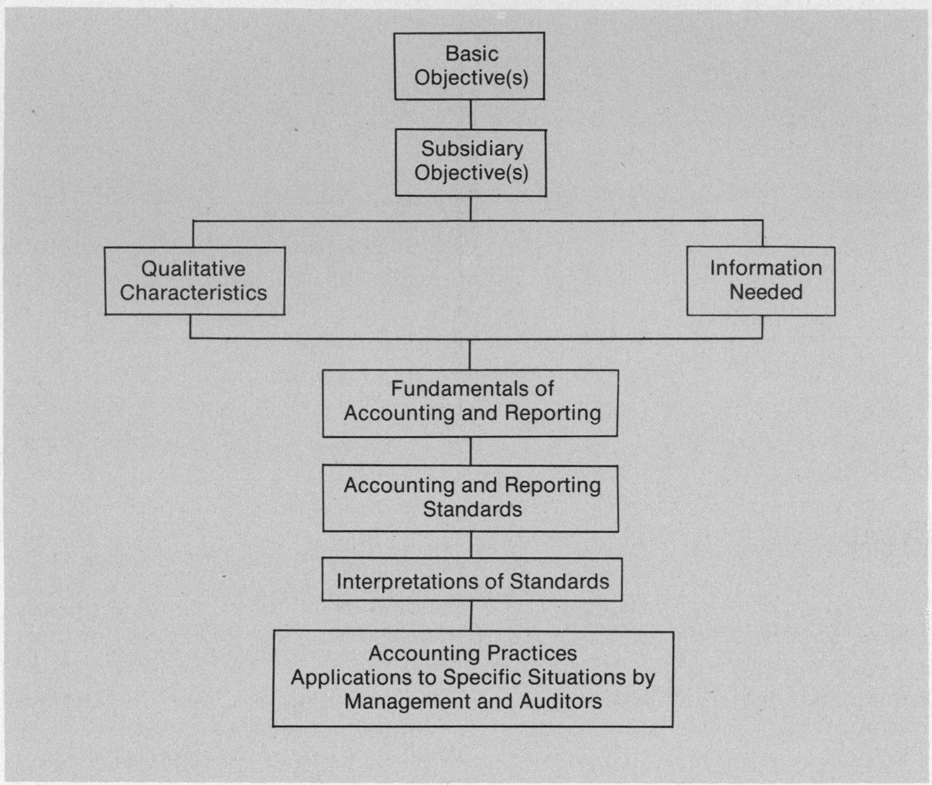

Source: © *Financial Accounting Standards Board.* Reprinted by permission.

tive characteristics of reporting. These are integrated in Figure 15–2. In most of these criteria, there is close agreement in definitions of the terms; all studies give top priority to *relevance*. Relevance means that the information should be directly essential to the decision need. Otherwise it is not useful.

In its 1973 report, *Objectives of Financial Statements,* the AICPA Study Group described twelve objectives of financial statements. The basic objective of financial statements according to this study group is to provide information that is useful in making economic decisions. Other objectives the study group identified include:

> To provide information useful in making investment decisions and loan decisions,
> To provide information that will enable users to form opinions of the earning power of business enterprises, to make earning power comparisons and to make predictions about the future of a business,
> To provide information about governmental and not-for-profit entities so that the effectiveness of the management of such entities can be judged, and
> To report on activities of the enterprise that affect society as a whole.

AAA ASOBAT Criteria (1966)	APB Statement No. 4 Standards (1971)	AICPA Study Group Characteristics (1973)
1. Relevance	0-1 Relevance	Relevance and materiality
2. Verifiability	0-2 Understandability	Form and substance
3. Freedom from bias	0-3 Verifiability	Reliability
4. Quantifiability	0-4 Neutrality	Freedom from bias
	0-5 Timeliness	Comparability
	0-6 Comparability	Consistency
	0-7 Completeness	Understandability

Figure 15-2
Comparison of qualitative criteria for accounting reports

Because the group was headed by Robert M. Trueblood the study is sometimes referred to as the Trueblood Report. [3]

Accounting standards

Within the conceptual framework elements in Figure 15-1 are fundamentals of accounting and reporting including accounting standards. A *standard* (formerly called an accounting principle) is a fundamental guideline that serves as a yardstick to determine whether or not a specific accounting method is an acceptable practice.

Although it is not considered necessary to provide here an organized list of generally accepted accounting principles (standards), some of the more important generally accepted concepts are discussed.

Entity concept

The accountant must maintain separate sets of records for each business enterprise of an owner, and must guard against intermingling of transactions of the enterprise and personal transactions of the owner. This concept was discussed thoroughly in Chapter 1.

Going concern

It is assumed that the entity will continue in operation indefinitely unless there is evidence to the contrary. For example, the accountant in a going concern does not record assets at liquidation value; instead, the basis chosen for valuation will be one consistent with the idea that the business will continue in existence over the expected useful life of any asset. Because of the going concern assumption, the accountant records prepaid insurance at the value of its unexpired fraction of cost and not at its cash surrender value. Long-term debts are reported at their face value and not at the amount it is estimated that creditors would receive if the

3 *Objectives of Financial Statements* (New York: AICPA, 1973).

company were to go out of business. This concept also supports reporting of plant items at historical cost. As mentioned earlier, the SEC now requires that this information for certain large companies be supplemented by replacement cost.

Consistency

In some instances acceptable alternative methods can be used in accounting records. For example, inventories can be costed at FIFO, LIFO, or average. Once a choice has been made, the principle of consistency requires that the same procedure should be followed in all future entries so that statements covering different time periods will be comparable. This principle is not applied blindly; if there is sufficient reason to change an accounting method the accountant may do so. However, APB Opinion No. 20 requires that the financial statements for a period in which such a change is made must disclose (1) the nature of the change, (2) the reasons for the change, and (3) the cumulative effect of changing to a new method.

Conservatism

Where acceptable alternatives exist, the one normally chosen would be that which produces the least favorable immediate result. The principle of conservatism aims to avoid favorable exaggeration in accounting reports. Reporting inventories at lower of cost or market is an example of this standard.

Periodicity

Financial statements will be prepared at regular specified time periods before the end of the lifetime of the firm. This principle holds that items of expense and revenue can be allocated to such time periods. Such an assignment to periods is necessary for proper matching of expenses and revenue for income determination. It is for this reason that adjusting entries are made. The accrual concept is essential to this standard. Items of expense and revenue should be recognized at the time of the occurrence of the economic events that produced them without regard to the timing of the related collection or payment of cash.

Objective evidence principle

To the greatest extent possible, the amounts used in recording events will be based upon objective evidence as compared to subjective judgment. Sales invoices, receiver's reports, and other source documents provide such evidence. It should follow that two separate accountants, independently recording transactions from such documents, would arrive at the same result. (Without the objective evidence principle, the attest function of CPAs could not hold the high degree of confidence which it enjoys today.) This does not mean that certain items are not to be estimated. Under the allowance method, for example, bad debts expense is an estimated amount. Another example is the use of the gross margin or retail methods of estimating inventories. When such estimates are necessary, however, they should be based upon past experience or upon some other logical base that is used consistently from year to year.

Materiality

An item small enough (in dollar amount or in proportion to other items) such that it would not influence a decision based upon the statement in which it is used is immaterial. The accounting treatment thereof need not follow prescribed accounting principles. (For example, the inventory value of unused stationery in the typing pool or paper clips in the office would not be counted as part of the supplies inventory at the end of a period.) Materiality depends upon the size and the nature of the item relative to the size of the business. In a very small business an inventory error of $300 may definitely be large enough to influence the decision of the user of the financial statement in which it is made. On the other hand an error of $300 in valuation of inventories of a multimillion-dollar company would be unlikely to be considered material.

An example of the nature of an item affecting the materiality is found in the SEC attitude toward payments by companies to foreign governments in order to secure business. The SEC did not direct its concern toward legality or morality. However, the SEC was concerned that failure to report them violated the materiality standard because

> . . . the amounts of money involved in overseas payments were in most cases clearly not material in terms of the assets of the corporation, its revenues, its profits or its net worth. But the Commission quickly concluded that . . . the relevant issue was . . . the amount of the business that might be adversely affected in some way because of the payments.[4]

Full disclosure

Financial statements should report all significant financial and economic information relating to an entity. If the accounting system does not automatically capture some specific item of significance, it should be included in a footnote to the accounting statements. An example is shown in the financial statement illustrations that follow this section.

As indicated earlier in this chapter, the SEC has placed primary emphasis on disclosure. The primary function of accounting is to provide information needed to make resource allocation decisions. Accounting should, in an objective manner, make available the unfavorable as well as the favorable aspects of an enterprise—business, government, or not-for-profit. Information that is not part of recorded historical data in the accounting records should be reported if it is material. In recent years some accountants are advocating the publication of

4 *The Week in Review*, (Haskins and Sells, April 9, 1976).

forecasts by management in annual reports to disclose management's predictions for the coming year.

Stable dollar concept

This principle assumes that the dollar is sufficiently stable in value to be used as the basic unit of measure in accounting without adjustment for price-level fluctuations. Many accountants challenge the general use of this principle on the grounds that it simply is not true. In 1975 the FASB began studies of price-level-adjustments techniques that would make statements more comparable across a span of years. In 1976, the SEC issued its replacement cost edict. Some foreign countries—for example, Brazil—have adopted accounting systems that recognize that the monetary unit is not stable.

Historical cost concept

The cost principle holds that actual cost—arrived at through arm's-length bargaining—is the appropriate amount to be used to record the value of a newly acquired asset. There is little argument that historical cost is the only objective value at which to record an asset at the time it is acquired. However, there are strong reasons to believe that the historical cost of some assets becomes less useful as they grow older. Actually, our present accounting methods use a form of modified historical cost. An example is the reporting on the balance sheet of plant and equipment at cost less accumulated depreciation.

Other concepts

Many other concepts and assumptions might be included in the list. As research and study continue, certain standards will be revised and new ones can be expected. Accounting systems are designed to meet users' needs. These needs continue to increase in scope and complexity as changes occur in the environment in which users make economic decisions. It is the ongoing task of the FASB to develop and publish new and revised accounting standards that will enable accounting methods to keep pace with these changes.

Financial statements illustrated

To illustrate the results of application of certain accounting standards, the financial statements for a typical large single proprietorship are presented. Several examples of the effects of accounting standards on these statements will be pointed out. The Tarrant Trading Company is the *entity* on which these statements focus. It is a *going concern* that has had a profitable year in 1979. Its assets are stated on the balance sheet at *historical cost* modified by offsets such as the allowance for doubtful accounts and notes and by accumulated depreciation.

Notice the footnotes that are a part of the statements. Significant accounting policies are revealed in Note A as required by APB Opinion No. 22. Two facts are significant: that inventory cost is determined by the LIFO method and that inventory is valued on the balance sheet at lower of cost or market (LCM). The statement user may conclude from this information that cost of goods sold more nearly reflects current cost than if some other inventory method were used. The method of depreciation and the estimated useful lives of plant assets are disclosed. Since the straight-line method is being used, we may predict that 1980 depreciation charges will be about the same as 1979 if there is no significant change in amount of plant and equipment. Although Tarrant Trading Company would be exempt from the SEC requirement that replacement cost of certain assets be disclosed, the company has chosen to make full disclosure of replacement costs in Note A.

Notes B and C provide another example of the principle of *full disclosure*. The information as to payment dates on the mortgage enables the reader to make a judgment as to when above-normal cash needs will arise. Note C about a contingent liability provides information not found elsewhere in the statements.

Of importance to readers of financial statements is the auditors' opinion. As indicated in Chapter 1, the opinion by the independent auditors that these statements "present [information] fairly" is called the *attest function*. Because the statements are audited external users have more confidence in them. Note that the auditors also are of the opinion that the standard of *consistency* has been followed by Tarrant Trading Company.

Examples of several other accounting standards can be found in these statements. The presence of prepaid items among the assets and of accrued items among the liabilities indicate that the *accrual basis* of accounting is being followed. The use of lower of cost or market in inventory valuation follows the principle of *conservatism*. The *stable-dollar* concept is being followed in reporting assets at historical cost, but is offset to some degree by use of the LIFO inventory method and the reporting of replacement costs in Note A.

With any system of measurement one must understand the basic units of measure. Accounting is no exception. The best decision maker is the person who can apply and interpret the basic objectives and standards of accounting.

TARRANT TRADING COMPANY — Exhibit A
Income Statement
For the Year Ended December 31, 1979

Net Sales		$7,222,000.00
Cost of Goods Sold		5,032,251.00
Gross Margin		$2,189,749.00
Operating Expenses		
Selling Expenses	$776,389.00	
General and Administrative Expenses	708,638.00	1,485,027.00
Net Income from Operations		$ 704,722.00
Other Revenues and Expenses		
Interest Expense	$ 74,080.00	
Gain on Disposal of Land	21,200.00	52,880.00
Net Income		$ 651,842.00

TARRANT TRADING COMPANY
Statement of Owner's Equity
For the Year Ended December 31, 1979

Exhibit B

S. D. Bennett, Capital, January 1, 1979	$3,616,551.00
Add Net Income per Income Statement	651,842.00
Total	$4,268,393.00
Deduct Withdrawals	600,000.00
S. D. Bennett, Capital, December 31, 1979	$3,668,393.00

TARRANT TRADING COMPANY
Balance Sheet
December 31, 1979

Exhibit C

Assets

Current Assets			
Cash		$ 76,000.00	
Trade Accounts Receivable	$736,000.00		
Notes Receivable	100,000.00		
Total	$836,000.00		
Deduct Allowance for Doubtful Accounts and Notes	12,540.00	823,460.00	
Merchandise Inventory		3,705,570.00	
Prepaid Insurance and Other Prepaid Items		38,300.00	
Total Current Assets			$4,643,330.00
Property, Plant and Equipment (at cost)			
Land		$ 300,000.00	
Buildings	$ 682,000.00		
Machinery and Equipment	839,660.00		
Furniture and Fixtures	216,208,00		
Leasehold Improvements	56,327.00		
Total	$1,794,195.00		
Deduct Accumulated Depreciation and Amortization	527,132.00	1,267,063.00	
Total Plant and Equipment			1,567,063.00
Total Assets			$6,210,393.00

Liabilities and Owner's Equity		
Current Liabilities		
Notes Payable	$370,000.00	
Accounts Payable	825,000.00	
Accrued Payroll and Other Accrued Items	421,000.00	
Total Current Liabilities		$1,616,000.00
Long-Term Debt		
Mortgage Payable		926,000.00
Total Liabilities		$2,542,000.00
Owner's Equity		
S. D. Bennett, Capital		3,668,393.00
Total Liabilities and Owner's Equity		$6,210,393.00

Notes to financial statements

Note A. Summary of significant accounting policies

Inventory The inventory is stated at the lower of cost, determined on the last-in, first-out basis, or market. The replacement cost is $4,100,000.00; the difference between replacement cost and LIFO carrying cost is $394,430.00.

Depreciation and amortization Depreciation of plant and equipment and leasehold improvement amortization is provided on the straight-line method based upon the following useful lives:

Item	*Years*
Buildings	33
Machinery and Equipment	5 to 10
Furniture and Fixtures	10
Leasehold Improvements	5

The replacement cost of plant and equipment is estimated to be $2,500,000.00.

Note B. Long-term debt

The mortgage payable, secured by buildings and by plant and equipment, is due in four payments of $231,500.00 commencing in 1989 and annually thereafter.

Note C. Litigation

The company is defending a product liability suit in amount of $250,000.00. Management and legal counsel are of the opinion that the outcome will not have a material effect on the balance sheet or results of operations.

AUDITORS' REPORT[5]

S. D. Bennett, Proprietor
TARRANT TRADING COMPANY

We have examined the balance sheet of Tarrant Trading Company as of December 31, 1979 and the related statements of income and owner's equity for the year then ended. Our examination was made in accordance with generally accepted auditing standards and included such tests of the accounting records and such other auditing procedures as we considered necessary under the circumstances.

In our opinion the aforementioned financial statements present fairly the financial position of Tarrant Trading Company at December 31, 1979 and the results of operations for the year then ended in conformity with generally accepted accounting principles applied on a consistent basis.

Corelli, Mason, and Hicks

Corelli, Mason, and Hicks
Certified Public Accountants

Glossary

AAA American Accounting Association.

Accounting objective A basic statement identifying a goal or purpose of accounting.

Accounting practice A specific method for recording of an economic event.

Accounting principle See Accounting standard.

Accounting standard A fundamental guideline that serves as a basis for acceptance or rejection of an accounting method. (Formerly called an accounting principle.)

APB Accounting Principles Board of the AICPA.

APB Opinion Formally promulgated guidelines from the APB.

ARB Accounting Research Bulletin.

Attest function The certification by CPAs as to fairness of the representations made by an entity's financial statements.

CASB Cost Accounting Standards Board.

CIA Certified Internal Auditor

5 The typical auditors' report would express an opinion on the fairness of reporting of a fourth major statement entitled the statement of changes in financial position. This statement is discussed in Chapter 21.

CMA An accountant who has passed the national examination and has met the requirements of the Institute of Management Accounting for the Certificate in Management Accounting.

Conservatism Choosing the alternative that produces the least favorable statement results.

Consistency Adhering to a selected method period after period.

CPA (Certified Public Accountant) An accountant who has passed the national examination and has met the requirements of state law for independent practice in accounting.

Entity concept The focus of accounting is on a specific individual organization.

FASB (Financial Accounting Standards Board) Successor to the APB.

FASB Statement Formally promulgated accounting guidelines from the FASB.

Generally accepted accounting principles (GAAP) The set of accounting standards (see above) that are currently generally accepted as valid.

Going concern concept An assumption that the accounting entity will continue to exist.

Historical cost Actual cost outlay in dollars at the time of acquisition.

Matching concept See periodicity.

Materiality An item large enough to influence decisions should be recorded in accordance with generally accepted accounting principles.

NAA National Association of Accountants.

Objective evidence principle Amounts recorded should be based upon evidence that can be verified.

Periodicity The idea that expense and revenue can be allocated to and matched in periods that are shorter than the life of a business.

SEC Securities and Exchange Commission.

Stable dollar concept Assumption that the value of the dollar is steady enough to compare different years without adjustment.

Questions

Q15–1 What is the distinction between (1) an accounting objective, (2) an accounting standard, and (3) an accounting practice?

Q15–2 Describe the AICPA. Who are its members?

Q15–3 What is the SEC? What is its basic purpose and authority? What is the legal basis for the SEC?

Q15–4 Student A says, "Despite the fact that the SEC has not actively prescribed a set of accounting principles, it has strongly influenced those that have been developed over the last forty years." Do you agree or disagree? Why?

Q15–5 (a) What is an APB Opinion? (b) Are any of them still effective? (c) If any are still effective, how do they affect the practices of accountants in corporations?

Q15–6 What is the major purpose of the FASB? How does it affect the work of accountants?

Q15–7 Distinguish between the CASB and the FASB as to (1) scope and coverage of the work of each and (2) power to enforce the standards they promulgate.

Q15–8 What is the work of a CPA? How does one become a CPA? Describe the attest function.

Q15–9 The accountant for a business does not count the paper clips in office desk drawers as part of the inventory of office supplies. What accounting standard is being followed?

Q15–10 At the end of each accounting period an adjustment to the Prepaid Insurance account is made to recognize the amount of expired insurance applicable to that period. What standard is involved?

Q15–11 Before issuing an FASB Statement, the FASB issues a Discussion Memorandum, with arguments and alternative solutions of the accounting problem. In a Discussion Memorandum on price-level reporting, could you show that the stable-dollar assumption is not valid? What are some arguments that you would use?

Class exercises

CE15–1 Identify the authoritative body described by each of the following:

1. Replaced the APB as the issuer of accounting standards.
2. A body oriented toward accounting research and matters of academic interest.
3. Has legal authority to overrule FASB.
4. Issues statements promulgating standards that are binding upon CPAs performing the attest function.
5. Issues standards that must be followed in accounting for U.S. Government contracts.
6. Issued opinions and statements providing accounting standards 1959–1973.
7. Sponsors the CMA examination.

CE15–2 Identify each of the following as an accounting objective, standard or practice.

1. Providing to users of financial statements information useful for predicting, comparing, and evaluating enterprise earning power.
2. Choosing the alternative that produces the least favorable immediate result when more than one acceptable alternative exists.
3. Choosing the gross price method of recording purchases discounts.

CE15–3 You have been asked to correct the following income statement. In addition to a corrected statement, provide comments on accounting standards that have not been followed.

BETTY PARKER'S DRESS SHOPPE
Income Statement
For the Year Ended December 31, 1979

Sales	$500,000
Deduct Amounts Uncollected	100,000
Net Sales	$400,000
Payments for Purchases	220,000
Gross Margin on Sales	$180,000
Operating Expenses	160,000
Net Income From Operations	$ 20,000
Gain from Adjustment of Inventory to Current Price Level	20,000
Net Income	$ 40,000

Your review of business papers reveals the following information:

a. The payment for purchases includes a $20,000 carryover from 1978 invoices while $30,000 of the 1979 invoices were unpaid at December 31.
b. Included in the operating expenses are:
   (1) a 1978 bonus to employees in the amount of $4,000 which was actually paid in January 1979.
   (2) $300 a month for payments on Ms. Parker's new compact car.
   (3) Depreciation of $1,000. The 20-year life building cost $80,000 in 1977, but Ms. Parker felt that it deteriorated only about $1,000 in 1979. In prior years her accountant used the straight-line method with no salvage value.
c. The inventory at December 31, 1978 was $36,000; at December 31, 1979 it was $50,000.
d. You also find in the files a notice from local tax authorities that the state legislature had enacted a 10 percent tax on all high-fashion clothing effective January 1, 1980. Ms. Parker does not know how this will affect her 1980 sales, but her attorney has told her that there is a chance the law may be declared unconstitutional.

Exercises and problems

P15–1 Mason Company is housed in a building that was purchased in 1979 for $37,500. Mr. Mason, the proprietor, has just refused an offer of $50,000 for the building. It is carried on the city tax records at an assessed valuation of $42,000. Show how this building should appear in Mason Company's balance sheet.

P15–2 Blumenthals, on December 31, 1979, has completed the physical inventory count. Using LIFO (as they have done for years) the total cost valuation has been determined to be $2,186,000. The following items have come to the attention of the accountant:

a. Lower of cost or market valuation is
   1. $2,000,000 on a unit basis,
   2. $2,062,000 on a class basis, and
   3. $2,103,000 on a total inventory basis.
b. An error in count on one item has been made; it would increase the cost valuation by $12.
c. Repricing the entire inventory at FIFO would increase its valuation (and increase net income) by $300,000.

Required:

1. The dollar amount that should be shown in the Current Assets section of the balance sheet.
2. A footnote that will make proper disclosure of inventory valuation methods and alternative valuations.
3. An opinion as to (a) whether the $12 error is material and (b) whether the FIFO figure should show anywhere in the statements.

P15–3 Mr. Syed Basheer, the owner of a business, collected an overdue account of $250 while on a vacation trip. He used the money to pay some of his vacation expenses and reported the matter to his accountant upon return from vacation.

Required:

1. In general journal form, a journal entry to record this transaction.
2. What accounting concept requires that an entry be made?

P15–4 Empire State Products began in 1978 to provide a six-month warranty on every item it sells. In 1978, with sales of $1,000,000, the costs to repair or replace items under warranty amounted to $18,500. In 1979, sales were $1,500,000 and warranty costs were $24,000. The accountant feels that the 1979 warranty expense reported in the income statement should be $24,000. The sales manager estimates that an additional $4,000 of expense will be incurred in 1980 to repair or to replace items sold in 1979 on which the warranty period has not yet expired.

Required:

1. What amount of expense should be reported for 1979?
2. What accounting standards provide guidance for the foregoing decision?

P15–5 Fill in the blanks in the following crossword puzzle entitled "Accounting Standards."

ACROSS

2. Recording assets at actual price paid is the ____________ cost concept.
3. Choosing an alternative that gives the least favorable immediate result.
7. Separation of business transactions from those of the owner.
8. ____________ concern standard assumes that a business will continue in operation.
9. Reporting of all significant financial and economic information (two words).
10. Recognition of revenue from sales before receiving of payment for them.

DOWN

1. Adhering to a chosen alternative method.
4. The ____________ evidence standard should cause two accountants to arrive at same result given the same data.
5. The basic unit of measurement does not change (two words).
6. Stationery in the typing pool is not counted in the supplies inventory.

P15–6 Identify each of the following as (1) an accounting objective, (2) an accounting standard, or (3) an accounting practice.

a. Revenues should be recorded when a sale is made even if collection is not made until a later period.
b. Charise Cole Stores has an accounting system in which cash discounts are recognized only when actually taken.
c. Long-lived assets (such as delivery trucks) should be depreciated periodically to allocate their cost among periods of use.
d. Financial statements should provide information that is useful in making decisions about allocation of economic resources.
e. Charise Cole's apartment rent should not be recorded as an expense of the business, Charise Cole Stores.
f. In an annual report of a large corporation, comparative sales for the past five years are shown without any adjustment to dollar figures for inflation.
g. Financial statements should report on activities that affect society as a whole.

P15–7 Identify each of the following organizations by its full name.

a. AAA
b. AICPA
c. APB
d. CASB
e. FASB
f. NAA
g. SEC
h. CIA
i. FEI

P15–8 As accountant for ERISA Company, you have included the following footnote as part of the balance sheet:

"Note 1. Although not included in the liabilities above, a damage suit has been instituted against the company by the Environmental Protection Agency. Although management is defending this suit, it is estimated that damages up to $100,000 could be levied against the company."

Mr. John Erisa, proprietor of the company, objects to this information being made public. In a short memorandum to Mr. Erisa, explain the accounting standard which makes it necessary to include this footnote on the balance sheet.

P15–9 The periodicity principle (or standard) requires allocation of portions of expense and revenue to specific time periods. Show, in general journal form, the adjusting entries for correct matching of expenses and revenue for the year ended December 31, 1979 in each of the following situations:

a. An insurance policy covering the building for one year was purchased on May 1, 1979 at a cost of $600. The asset, Prepaid Insurance, was debited with $600 at the time of purchase.
b. Three months rent collected in advance on December 1, 1979 was credited to Rent Earned in the amount of $450.
c. Unpaid salaries on December 31, 1979 amounted to $2,475. They will be paid along with the additional amounts due on the next regular payday which falls in January, 1980.
d. The store equipment, which was purchased in 1975 at a cost of $8,000, is estimated to have a 10-year useful life with no salvage value at the end of 10 years. No depreciation has been recorded for 1979.

P15–10 (Minicase) Following is a balance sheet for the Dreyfous Company.

DREYFOUS COMPANY
Balance Sheet
December 31, 1979

Assets			*Liabilities and Owner's Equity*		
Current Assets			Current Liabilities		
Cash	$119,000		Accounts Payable	$ 20,000	
			Mortgage Note Payable		
Inventory (at cost)	300,000	$419,000	(due May 1, 1980)	150,000	$170,000
Plant and Equipment			Owner's Equity		
Land	$ 60,000				
Building	260,000	320,000	Lewis Dreyfous, Capital		569,000
Total Assets		$739,000	Total Liabilities and Owner's Equity		$739,000

Mr. Dreyfous has requested that you prepare a memorandum for him explaining some aspects of his accounting practices. Some of his specific concerns are:

1. Should Dreyfous submit financial reports to the FASB? If so, when? If not, to what agency and how often?
2. The inventory cost is determined by the FIFO method. Many items carried therein are no longer useful and have little (if any) market value. Is the company violating any accounting standards in its balance sheet presentation of inventory? If so, what would be the correct reporting procedure?

3. Both the land and building are revalued annually by an accounting department committee. The value used is their best judgment of the amount that could be realized in cash if the company were to liquidate. Mr. Dreyfous wonders if accounting standards support this practice.
4. The administrative offices carry supplies of postage stamps that are debited to an expense account when purchased. Sometimes these amount to as much as $150. It is wondered if these should be shown as an asset. Why or why not?

Required: Prepare a memorandom to Mr. Dreyfous explaining the accounting standards that apply to the areas in which he has raised questions. Include specific recommendations.

Organizational forms and reporting issues

part five

chapter sixteen

Introduction

The great majority of business enterprises in the United States are owned and operated by a single individual or by groups of individuals. Depending upon their form of organization, these privately-owned businesses fall into three categories: single proprietorships, partnerships, and corporations. Distinctive features of each along with some of their advantages and disadvantages are explained in this chapter.

The entries for *operating transactions* are the same for all forms of business. It is the entries for formation of the business, withdrawal of funds, and the closing process that are different. This chapter first compares accounting for single proprietorships and partnerships. It then goes into detail about some of the accounting methods for partnerships and brings corporations into the comparison.

Organizational forms: proprietorships, partnerships, and corporations

Learning goals

To understand the forms of business organizations, their distinctive features and advantages.
To review accounting methods for owner's equity of proprietorships.
To understand the nature and origin of owners' equity.
To record transactions affecting the owners' equity of partnerships and the flow of closing entries.
To understand different methods of computing the division of partnership profits.
To become familiar with methods of recording the admission of a partner and the liquidation of a partnership.
To identify the characteristics of a corporation and its advantages and disadvantages.
To be aware of how corporations raise capital.

Key terms

agreed ratio
bonds
capital stock
corporation
dividends
drawing
general partner
goodwill
limited liability
limited partner
liquidation
mutual agency
organization costs
par value
partnership
proprietor
realization
retained earnings
shareholder
single proprietorship
stock certificate
stockholder
unlimited liability

In its long history, accounting has served a variety of organizational entities. The forms of these entities changed as the centers of power and wealth changed. In early economic history, the entity was the central bureaucracy, the temple or the household of the nobleman. During the Middle Ages the partnership form was popular; later came the corporations. An outgrowth of the early household organization is the small individual proprietorship which still exists in large numbers.

The owner's, partners', or stockholders' equity of a business results from assets contributed by the proprietor, partners, or stockholders and from earnings retained in the business. The characteristics of each of these three forms of business are introduced in this chapter.

Single proprietorships

Characteristics

Size Usually smaller than the other two forms of business, proprietorships are often found in retail sales and service businesses. Enterprises such as restaurants, laundries, specialty clothing stores, and hardware stores fall into this category.

Ease of formation No formal procedures are required to form a single proprietorship. A person need only comply with state and local licensing laws to go into business offering a product or a service to the public.

Legal liability The owner is entitled to all the income of a single proprietorship; he or she is responsible for all of the losses and is legally liable for all debts of the business. Known as *unlimited liability,* this feature means that the personal assets of the owner (including assets outside the business entity) are legally available to satisfy claims of creditors.

Unlimited liability

In a proprietorship, the personal and business assets of the owner are legally available to satisfy creditors' claims on the business.

Raising of capital The capital with which to establish the business is provided by the owner. It comes from the personal wealth of the owner, sometimes supplemented by borrowing.

Taxation of income Because the single proprietor is a self-employed person, all income or loss of the business is considered to be a part of his or her taxable income. The federal and state income tax returns of the owner must, therefore, include income from the business.

Advantages and disadvantages

Its small size often works to the disadvantage of a single proprietorship. The total amount of assets is limited to the amount that the owner can provide from personal wealth or from borrowing. In most cases the owner is also the manager. This is sometimes an advantage because of the freedom to make decisions without having to consult with other owners. It is also a disadvantage because so few individuals have managerial skills in marketing, finance, inventory management, and the many other functional areas in which managers perform. Multiple ownership is more likely to bring a range of business skills into the management of an enterprise. Unlimited liability is a clear disadvantage to the proprietor, who runs the risk of losing not only the assets committed to the business but other personal wealth as well.

Another disadvantage is the lack of provisions for continuity of the business. Upon death or retirement of the owner the present business must be dissolved. Even though it may be sold, the existing firm has disappeared and a new one has been formed.

Because capital is provided by the owner, all gains of the business belong to the owner. They do not have to be shared with partners or other stockholders. Since income of a single proprietorship is a part of the personal income of the owner, it is subject to tax at individual income tax rates.

Accounting methods

The methods of accounting for owner's equity of a single proprietorship have been illustrated in the opening chapters of this book. Since there are no legal requirements to segregrate owner's equity, and since there is only one owner, the entire owner's equity can be shown on the balance sheet opposite a single caption such as Mary Jolly, Capital. In order to show the amounts of routine withdrawals by the owner, a contra account to the proprietor's capital account such as Mary Jolly, Drawing, is used during the business year and closed into the Capital account at the end of the period.

To illustrate the accounts used for recording paid-in capital and other owner's equity items of a single proprietorship, assume that on January 2, 1979, Mary Jolly formed the Jolly Appliance Company with a cash investment of $20,000. On June 15, she withdrew $6,000 in anticipation of earnings; a summary of the accounts on December 31 showed the net income for the year to be $10,000. The entries to record these events are:

1979						
Jan.	2	Cash	20,000	00		
		Mary Jolly, Capital			20,000	00
		To record investment by proprietor to form a retail appliance business to be called the Jolly Appliance Company.				
Jun.	15	Mary Jolly, Drawing	6,000	00		
		Cash			6,000	00
		To record withdrawal by proprietor in anticipation of earned income.				

1979				
Dec.	31	Income Summary	10,000 00	
		Mary Jolly, Capital		10,000 00
		To close net income to the Capital account.		
	31	Mary Jolly, Capital	6,000 00	
		Mary Jolly, Drawing		6,000 00
		To close the balance of the Drawing account.		

The statement of owner's equity for 1979 would appear as shown below.

JOLLY APPLIANCE COMPANY
Statement of Owner's Equity
For the Year Ended December 31, 1979

Mary Jolly, Capital (Investment, January 2, 1979)	$20,000.00
Add Net Income for the Year	10,000.00
Total	$30,000.00
Deduct Withdrawals	6,000.00
Mary Jolly, Capital, December 31, 1979	$24,000.00

The Owner's Equity section of the balance sheet as of December 31, 1979, would appear as follows:

Owner's Equity	
Mary Jolly, Capital	$24,000.00

Up to this point in this text, the single proprietorship form of business has been used to illustrate the workings of the basic accounting model. With the few changes to owners' equity accounts explained later in this chapter, the same model can now be extended to the other two forms of business organization—partnerships and corporations.

Partnerships

"A partnership is an association of two or more persons to carry on as co-owners a business for profit."[1] The association described in this definition may be based upon an oral or a written agreement. Although many partnerships have only two partners, some have many. For example, some of the nationally-known certified public accounting firms have 100 or more partners. Of the three basic forms of business in the United States, the partnership is the least used.

Characteristics

Unlike a single proprietorship, the name of a partnership is likely to give a clue to the type of business organization. It is obvious that the firm of Ahern, Allen, and Arnold has more than one owner, and one would suspect that it is a partnership.

1 *Uniform Partnership Act,* Part II, Section 6.

Other characteristics of a partnership tend to be similar to those of a single proprietorship.

Size Because of additional owners to serve as a source of capital, partnerships tend to be somewhat larger than single proprietorships. However, their original capital investment must come from the personal wealth and borrowing power of the partners. Since many partnerships have only two or three partners, this form of business is not generally found among the larger firms in the United States.

Ease of formation Like single proprietorships, partnerships are relatively easy to form. Although it is desirable that a written agreement form the basis of the association, partnerships may be formed on the basis of a verbal agreement.

With a few exceptions, the states have incorporated the Uniform Partnership Act into their statutes. The Act contains no special provisions for the formation of a partnership, but does contain provisions that regulate the relations of partners with each other and relations of partners with persons outside the partnership.

Legal liability All partners are usually liable jointly and individually for the debts of the partnership. Under certain circumstances the liability of a partner may be limited to the amount of that partner's investment. Such a partner, known as a *limited partner,* has restrictions placed upon the business activities in which that limited partner can engage. Partners who are active in the business are known as *general partners* and are subject to unlimited liability. Every partnership must have at least one general partner. Like single proprietors, their assets outside the business entity are available to satisfy creditor claims. An aspect of liability peculiar to a partnership is the concept of *mutual agency*. Every partner is an agent of the partnership when performing acts to carry on the business. Thus the act of a single partner is binding on the partnership and upon each of the other partners.

In a partnership the acts of each partner are binding on all other partners. **Mutual agency**

Raising of capital The initial capital of a partnership must be raised from the personal wealth (or borrowing) of the partners. While the additional persons involved would normally provide more capital than a single proprietorship, the partnership form of business does not provide for any special or unique method of bringing additional assets into the business.

Taxation of income A partnership must file an income tax return, but it is for information only. The various forms of revenue, expenses, and other tax-deductible items are identified with each individual partner on the partnership return. In the federal income tax return, Form 1065, Schedule K shows each partner's share of the taxable items; each partner is then required to include those items in his or her personal income tax return.

Advantages and disadvantages

Partnerships, while restricted in amounts of original capital by the personal wealth and borrowing power of the partners, can raise larger amounts of money than single proprietorships. They also tend to have a better credit rating because each partner is personally liable for debts of the business.

Partnerships, while easy to form, have a definite legal status under the Uniform Partnership Act. Their relationships with the public—for example, rules pertaining to conveyance of real property—are provided for in specific sections of the Act. Thus, both the partners and the public can carry on business with greater certainty than do single proprietorships. The Act contains provisions that may have been omitted in the partnership agreement. If, for example, there was no agreement made as to distribution of partnership profits or losses, the Act provides that they shall be shared equally.

By bringing more than one person into the operation of a business, there is greater opportunity to provide a variety of management skills. One partner may have expert knowledge in finance, another in marketing, and so on. Multiple management, however, has its disadvantages. Already mentioned is the mutual agency concept whereby the act of one partner is binding upon the others. Another disadvantage is the need to secure agreement among existing partners upon the admission of a new partner. Thus, transfer of ownership may be difficult to accomplish.

Partnerships suffer from the same lack of continuity that affects single proprietorships. Upon the death or retirement of a partner, the business is dissolved. Dissolution of a partnership does not necessarily require that all assets be sold and that the business must cease operations. It does, however, mean that technically the former partnership has ceased to exist and that a new one has taken its place.

Accounting methods

Two aspects of accounting are unique to partnerships. Both focus upon the owners' equity accounts. First, it is necessary when preparing financial statements to divide the net income (or loss) among the partners. Second, it is necessary to maintain a separate Capital account and a separate Drawing account for each partner. For a simple illustration of these requirements, assume that Teresa Mann and Gary Core are partners in the public accounting firm of Mann and Core. The partners' equity section of the balance sheet at December 31, 1978 appeared as follows:

Partners' Equity		
Teresa Mann, Capital	$62,500.00	
Gary Core, Capital	47,500.00	$110,000.00

If Mann and Core share profits and losses equally, the entry to close out a net income of $72,300 in 1979 would be:

			Debit		Credit	
1979						
Dec.	31	Income Summary	72,300	00		
		Teresa Mann, Capital			36,150	00
		Gary Core, Capital			36,150	00
		To transfer net income to Capital accounts.				

Assuming that each had withdrawn $1,000 per month in anticipation of profits in 1979, their Drawing accounts would each have a balance of $12,000. The following entry would close the Drawing accounts into the respective Capital accounts.

			Debit		Credit	
1979						
Dec.	31	Teresa Mann, Capital	12,000	00		
		Gary Core, Capital	12,000	00		
		Teresa Mann, Drawing			12,000	00
		Gary Core, Drawing			12,000	00
		To close the Drawing accounts.				

The allocation of profits and losses to the partners is based on mutual agreement. If no articles or other evidence of agreement exist, the law assumes that profits and losses are to be divided equally even when the factors of investment, ability, or time are unequal. Since allocation is based on mutual agreement, there are many ways to distribute profits and losses.

Interest and agreed ratio The partners may agree to allow for differences in capital investments as well as for differences in services rendered by allowing interest on capital balances and distributing the remainder in an *agreed ratio. Interest, as it is used here, is not an expense but rather a mechanism for dividing a portion of earnings in the ratio of contributed capitals,* with the remainder divided in some other ratio. If 6 percent interest is allowed on opening capital balances, the division is as follows:

	Mann	Core	Total
Interest on opening capital			
6% of $62,500.00	$ 3,750.00		
6% of $47,500.00		$ 2,850.00	
Total interest			$ 6,600.00
Remainder: 2/3 and 1/3	43,800.00	21,900.00	65,700.00
Totals	$47,550.00	$24,750.00	$72,300.00

The entry to record this allocation of net income is:

			Debit		Credit	
1979						
Dec.	31	Income Summary	72,300	00		
		Teresa Mann, Capital			47,550	00
		Gary Core, Capital			24,750	00
		To allocate the net income for the year divided 2:1 after allowing for 6 percent interest on opening capital balances.				

Salaries, interest, and agreed ratio A part of the net income may be divided to recognize differences in capital balances, another part to recognize differences in the value of services rendered, and the remainder in an agreed ratio. Although entitled "salary allowances," these are not an expense but, as with interest on capital balances, they are a mechanism for dividing a portion of the earnings. Computation is as follows:

	Mann	Core	Total
Salary allowances	$10,000.00	$ 8,000.00	$18,000.00
Interest on opening capital			
6% of $62,500.00	3,750.00		
6% of $47,500.00		2,850.00	
Total interest			6,600.00
Remainder divided equally	23,850.00	23,850.00	47,700.00
Totals	$37,600.00	$34,700.00	$72,300.00

The entry to record the allocation is:

			Debit	Credit
1979				
Dec.	31	Income Summary	72,300 00	
		Teresa Mann, Capital		37,600 00
		Gary Core, Capital		34,700 00
		To allocate the net income for the year equally after allowing for salaries and interest on capital balances.		

If there is an agreement for a salary allowance and interest allowance, the salary and interest allocations must be made even though the net income is less than the total of such allocations. The shortage is divided in the same ratio used for dividing an excess of net income over total salaries and interest. To illustrate, assume the same facts as in the previous example except that the net income for the year is $21,000. The computation is:

		Mann	Core	Total
Salary allowances		$10,000.00	$ 8,000.00	$18,000.00
Interest on opening capital				
6% of $62,500.00		3,750.00		
6% of $47,500.00			2,850.00	
Total interest allowances				6,600.00
Total allowances		$13,750.00	$10,850.00	$24,600.00
Deduct excess of allowances over net income				
Total allowances	$24,600.00			
Net income	21,000.00			
Excess divided equally		(1,800.00)	(1,800.00)	(3,600.00)
Allocation of net income		$11,950.00	$ 9,050.00	$21,000.00

The entry to record the allocation is:

1979				
Dec.	31	Income Summary	21,000 00	
		Teresa Mann, Capital		11,950 00
		Gary Core, Capital		9,050 00
		To allocate the net income for the year.		

Partnership financial statements The changes in partners' equity accounts during the year are shown in a statement of partners' equity. Its form is similar to the statement of owner's equity for a single proprietorship and the statement of retained earnings for a corporation (Figure 18–2). It is a supporting statement for the total partners' equities reported in the balance sheet. Assume the same facts as in the preceding example except that each partner made additional investments during the year as shown. The statement of partners' equity for Mann and Core is shown as:

Figure 16–1
Statement of partners' equity

MANN AND CORE
Statement of Partners' Equity
For the Year Ended December 31, 1979

	Mann	Core	Total
Partners' capital balances, January 2, 1979	$62,500.00	$47,500.00	$110,000.00
Add additional investments	10,000.00	8,000.00	18,000.00
Net income	11,950.00	9,050.00	21,000.00
Totals	$84,450.00	$64,550.00	$149,000.00
Deduct withdrawals	12,000.00	12,000.00	24,000.00
Partners' capital balances, December 31, 1979	$72,450.00	$52,550.00	$125,000.00

The statement of partners' equity provides an explanation of the changes in partners' capital balances over a period of time. The basic format flows from old balance to new balance in the same manner as a statement of owner's equity for a proprietorship. Note, however, in Figure 16–1 a separate column is provided for each partner. Thus Gary Core can trace the change in his capital from $47,500 on December 31, 1978 to its new total of $52,550 on December 31, 1979.

On December 31, 1979, the balance sheet would disclose the new equity balances as follows:

Partners' Equity		
Teresa Mann, Capital	$72,450.00	
Gary Core, Capital	52,550.00	$125,000.00

Proof of these new balances may be found in Figure 16–1.

The entries to close the partners' Drawing accounts are as follows:

1979						
Dec.	31	Teresa Mann, Capital	12,000	00		
		Teresa Mann, Drawing			12,000	00
		To close partner's Drawing account.				
	31	Gary Core, Capital	12,000	00		
		Gary Core, Drawing			12,000	00
		To close partner's Drawing account.				

The financial statements of a partnership are similar to those of a single proprietorship. The allocations of net income to the partners may be shown below the Net Income line of the income statement or, if they are too numerous, in a supplementary statement. The balance sheet shows the individual capital account balances as of the end of the period and their total; or, if they are too numerous, the individual balances are shown in the supplementary statement of partners' equities.

Admission of a new partner

The admission of a new partner technically dissolves the old partnership although, in the absence of complete dissolution or winding up, the business continues as before. A new partner may either (1) *purchase* an interest from one or more of the other partners or (2) be admitted as a partner by making an *investment* in the partnership.

If the new partner buys an interest from one of the original partners, partnership assets are unchanged, because the transfer of assets is directly between the persons involved. The only entry on the partnership books is a transfer of the agreed share from the old partner's capital account to a capital account opened for the new partner. Assume that A and B are partners, each with capital balances of $60,000 and that A, with B's consent, sells one-half of his interest to C for $35,000. The entry required to record C's admission is:

1979						
Mar.	1	A, Capital	30,000	00		
		C, Capital			30,000	00
		To record C's admission to partnership.				

The amount paid by C to A has no effect on this entry, since there is no change in partnership assets or total capital. The $5,000 gain is a personal profit to A, which occurs outside the entity.

C may be admitted by making an investment of cash or other assets directly to the firm, thereby increasing partnership assets and total capital. The amount credited to the incoming partner's Capital account may be measured by the value of his investment. Admission of a new partner, however, is often the occasion for recognizing *goodwill*—an intangible asset attributable to either the new partner or the old partnership—or a bonus may be allowed the old partners or the incoming partner.

Goodwill

Goodwill *is an intangible asset that represents an expected greater than normal level of earnings of a business in its industry.*

If the old partnership has been successful, the new partner may agree, as a condition, that part of his investment be considered a bonus from him to the old partners. On the other hand, if the old partners need additional resources—funds, skills, or both—that the new partner will contribute, they may agree to credit the new partner with an amount greater than his investment in the form of either a bonus or goodwill.

Assume that A and B are partners, sharing gains and losses equally, with capital account balances of $30,000 and $42,000. Some conditions under which C, a new partner, may be admitted, and the resulting journal entries, are illustrated below.

1. C is admitted to a one-third interest equal to his investment of $40,000, total capital to be $120,000. Since net assets will equal $112,000 after C's $40,000 investment is added to present capital of $72,000, then goodwill is $8,000:

Agreed total capital after C's admission		$120,000.00
Present capital ($30,000 + $42,000)	$72,000	
C's investment	40,000	112,000.00
Goodwill		$ 8,000.00

Date		Account	Debit	Credit
1979				
May	1	Cash	40,000 00	
		Goodwill	8,000 00	
		A, Capital		4,000 00
		B, Capital		4,000 00
		C, Capital		40,000 00
		To record C's admission to partnership.		

Goodwill is recognized and is credited to the old partners in their profit-and-loss-sharing ratios. If it is determined that the increase of $8,000 is attributable to a specific asset (or assets), then the specific asset account (or accounts) should be debited rather than the Goodwill account.

2. C is admitted to a one-third interest by investing $48,000, total capital to be $120,000, of which C is to be credited with $40,000. Since assets equal $120,000 after C's investment is added, and total capital is to be $120,000, there is no goodwill. However, since C invests $48,000, but is credited with $40,000 (1/3 of $120,000), the difference of $8,000 is a bonus paid by C to be credited to the old partners in their profit-and-loss-sharing ratio.

1979				
May	1	Cash	48,000 00	
		A, Capital		4,000 00
		B, Capital		4,000 00
		C, Capital		40,000 00
		To record C's admission to partnership.		

3. C invests $30,000 for a one-third interest, total capital to be $102,000.

1979				
May	1	Cash	30,000 00	
		A, Capital	2,000 00	
		B, Capital	2,000 00	
		C, Capital		34,000 00
		To record C's admission to the partnership.		

Since assets equal $102,000 after C's investment is added, there is no goodwill. However, since C invests $30,000 but is credited with $34,000 (1/3 of $102,000), the old partners are providing a special inducement to C by crediting him with $4,000 more than his actual investment. To give this extra credit to C, the old partners must accept a reduction in their capital accounts for the amount of the bonus in their profit-and-loss-sharing ratio.

Liquidation of a partnership

A partnership may be terminated by selling the assets, paying the creditors, and distributing the remaining cash to the partners. This total process is called *liquidation* of a partnership; conversion of assets to cash is called *realization*. Gains and losses resulting from the sale of assets must first be distributed to the capital accounts in profit-and-loss-sharing ratios before making any distribution of cash to the partners. If, after all gains and losses are distributed, a partner's capital account shows a debit balance, that partner must pay in the deficiency from his personal resources. If that partner has no personal resources, his deficiency must be absorbed by the other partners.

To illustrate, assume that A, B, and C (a partnership different from the preceding one), whose balance sheet is shown below, decide to sell their noncash assets, pay their creditors, and distribute the remaining cash to themselves.

A, B, and C
Balance Sheet
May 31, 1979

Assets	
Cash	$ 50,000.00
Other Assets	250,000.00
	$300,000.00
Liabilities and Partners' Equities	
Liabilities	$100,000.00
A, Capital	100,000.00
B, Capital	60,000.00
C, Capital	40,000.00
	$300,000.00

The noncash assets are sold for $280,000; profits and losses are shared equally. The summary below shows the liquidation sequence.

	Cash	Other Assets	Liabilities	Capital A	Capital B	Capital C
Balances before realization	$ 50,000.00	$250,000.00	$100,000.00	$100,000.00	$60,000.00	$40,000.00
1 Sale of assets at a gain	280,000.00	(250,000.00)		10,000.00	10,000.00	10,000.00
Balances	$330,000.00		$100,000.00	$110,000.00	$70,000.00	$50,000.00
2 Payment of creditors	(100,000.00)		(100,000.00)			
Balances	$230,000.00			$110,000.00	$70,000.00	$50,000.00
3 Cash distribution to partners	(230,000.00)			(110,000.00)	(70,000.00)	(50,000.00)

Amounts to be distributed to the partners **3** are the balances in their capital accounts after each partner is credited with her share of the gain on the sale of the assets **1**.

The journal entries to record the liquidation of the partnership are as follows:

Date		Account	Debit	Credit
1979				
Jun.	7	Cash	280,000 00	
		Other Assets		250,000 00
		A, Capital		10,000 00
		B, Capital		10,000 00
		C, Capital		10,000 00
		To record the sale of other assets and to allocate the gain to the partners' Capital accounts in their profit-and-loss-sharing ratio.		
	15	Liabilities	100,000 00	
		Cash		100,000 00
		To record payment to creditors.		
	20	A, Capital	110,000 00	
		B, Capital	70,000 00	
		C, Capital	50,000 00	
		Cash		230,000 00
		To record the cash distribution to the partners and to close the Capital accounts.		

Sale of assets at a loss in the process of liquidation may result in a capital deficiency in a partner's capital account. If the partner cannot cover the deficiency from her personal assets, it is allocated to the other partners is an additional loss in the profit-and-loss-sharing ratio that exists between themselves. If, for example, the assets in the foregoing illustration are sold for $100,000, C's one-third share of the resulting loss of $150,000 = ($250,000 – $100,000) is $50,000, or $10,000 more than the balance in her capital account. The payments to A and B must be such as to leave credit balances in their accounts that will exactly absorb each partner's share of C's $10,000 deficiency if C is unable to cover it. This is accomplished by treating C's deficiency as an additional loss and distributing it to A and B in their profit-and-loss-sharing ratio (which is now 1 to 1), or $5,000 to each partner.

A summary statement follows:

	Cash	Other Assets	Liabilities	Capital A	Capital B	Capital C
Balances before realization ...	$ 50,000.00	$250,000.00	$100,000.00	$100,000.00	$60,000.00	$ 40,000.00
Sale of assets at a loss	100,000.00	(250,000.00)		(50,000.00)	(50,000.00)	(50,000.00)
Balances	$150,000.00		$100,000.00	$ 50,000.00	$10,000.00	$(10,000.00)
Payment to creditors	(100,000.00)		(100,000.00)			
Balances	$ 50,000.00			$ 50,000.00	$10,000.00	$(10,000.00)
Cash distribution to partners ..	(50,000.00)			(45,000.00)	(5,000.00)	
Balances				$ 5,000.00	$ 5,000.00	$(10,000.00)

If C subsequently pays the $10,000 to the partnership, the amount will be distributed equally to A and B and all the accounts will be reduced to zero balances. Failing that, the $10,000 debit balance in C's account will be distributed to A and B and all accounts reduced to zero balances.

The journal entries to record the liquidation are as follows:

Date		Account	Debit	Credit
1979 Jun.	7	Cash	100,000 00	
		A, Capital	50,000 00	
		B, Capital	50,000 00	
		C, Capital	50,000 00	
		Other Assets		250,000 00
		To record the sale of other assets and to allocate the loss to the partners' Capital accounts in their profit-and-loss-sharing ratio.		
	15	Liabilities	100,000 00	
		Cash		100,000 00
		To record payment to creditors.		
	20	A, Capital	45,000 00	
		B, Capital	5,000 00	
		Cash		50,000 00
		To record the cash distribution to the partners.		
	20	A, Capital	5,000 00	
		B, Capital	5,000 00	
		C, Capital		10,000 00
		To close the Capital accounts.		

The entry to reduce the Capital accounts to zero balances would be the same whether or not C subsequently pays her deficiency since payment, if any, would be made by C to A and B directly. Of course, A and B have a legal claim against C for any remaining deficiency in her Capital account.

Corporations

A corporation is a legal entity as well as an accounting entity. This means that, in the eyes of the law, a corporation is an artificial being. As such it has the powers and rights of and may act as a single individual. Although it acts through its officers and directors, a corporation may enter into contracts, sue or be sued in court, and carry on other activities of an individual in the business world.

Characteristics

Size In general, the corporate form of business is sizeable in terms of wealth, income, and number of employees. In its third quarter report in 1975, for example, the Ford Motor Company listed total assets of more than 14 billion dollars, worldwide sales of more than 6 billion dollars for the quarter, with a quarterly net income of 56 million dollars. Although there are many more single proprietorships than corporations in this country, the largest share of the dollar volume of business is done by corporations.

Ease of formation Of the three types of business, the corporate form is the most difficult to establish. A corporation is established upon the issuance of a charter. The charter is the copy of the articles of incorporation prepared by the incorporators, which is returned by the Secretary of State (or another designated state official) together with a certificate of incorporation. Although state laws vary, most states require that at least three persons apply for a charter to form a corporation. Among the items usually specified in a corporate charter are:

The name of the corporation
The type of business in which it is authorized to engage
The duration of existence (usually perpetual unless specified otherwise)
The location of its principal office or place of business
The classes (or types) of shares of capital stock, and the number of shares of each type that the corporation will be authorized to issue.

In addition to legal fees incurred in preparation of an application for a corporate charter, some states charge incorporation fees. These and other initial costs of formation of a corporation are considered to be intangible assets of the business and are carried on the balance sheet under the title, Organization Costs.

Legal liability The corporation is a separate and distinct legal entity. It alone is liable to creditors; stockholders or shareholders are not personally liable for debts the corporation is unable to pay. If a corporation gets into serious financial difficulties its shares of stock may become worthless. Even so, the assets of the owners who hold those shares are not legally available for satisfaction of corporate debts. This feature is called *limited liability*.

Limited liability

In the corporate form of organization, the personal assets of the owners (shareholders) are not legally available to satisfy creditors' claims on the corporation.

Raising of capital A corporation can raise much larger amounts of capital than a single proprietorship. Its ownership is broken up into small elements called *shares* of capital stock which can be offered for sale to the public. A person, called a *stockholder* or *shareholder,* can own a single share of stock in a corporation or may own hundreds of shares. A corporation may have a few shareholders or millions of shareholders.

Ownership in a corporation is evidenced by a stock certificate (Figure 16–2). A *stock certificate* is a printed or engraved, serially numbered document issued to the stock purchaser as evidence of ownership of the stated number of shares of *capital stock* of the issuing corporation. These shares are issued to individuals or organizations who have obtained their shares of capital stock in exchange for funds invested in the company or for services rendered, or who have acquired shares from previous investors. Transfer of the shares from one person to another is accomplished by filling in the assignment section on the reverse of the stock certificate (Figure 16–3). The buyer sends the assigned stock certificate to the corporation or to its transfer agent, who records the transfer on the corporation's capital stock records, cancels the old certificate, and issues a new one to the new owner. Stock certificates are often bound with attached stubs in the same manner as checkbooks. The perforated stock certificate is removed, and the stub is filled in and retained by the corporation as a permanent record.

The stock certificate pictured in Figure 16–2 represents shares of stock having a par value of $5 per share. *Par value* per share is an arbitrary amount placed

Figure 16–2 Stock certificate

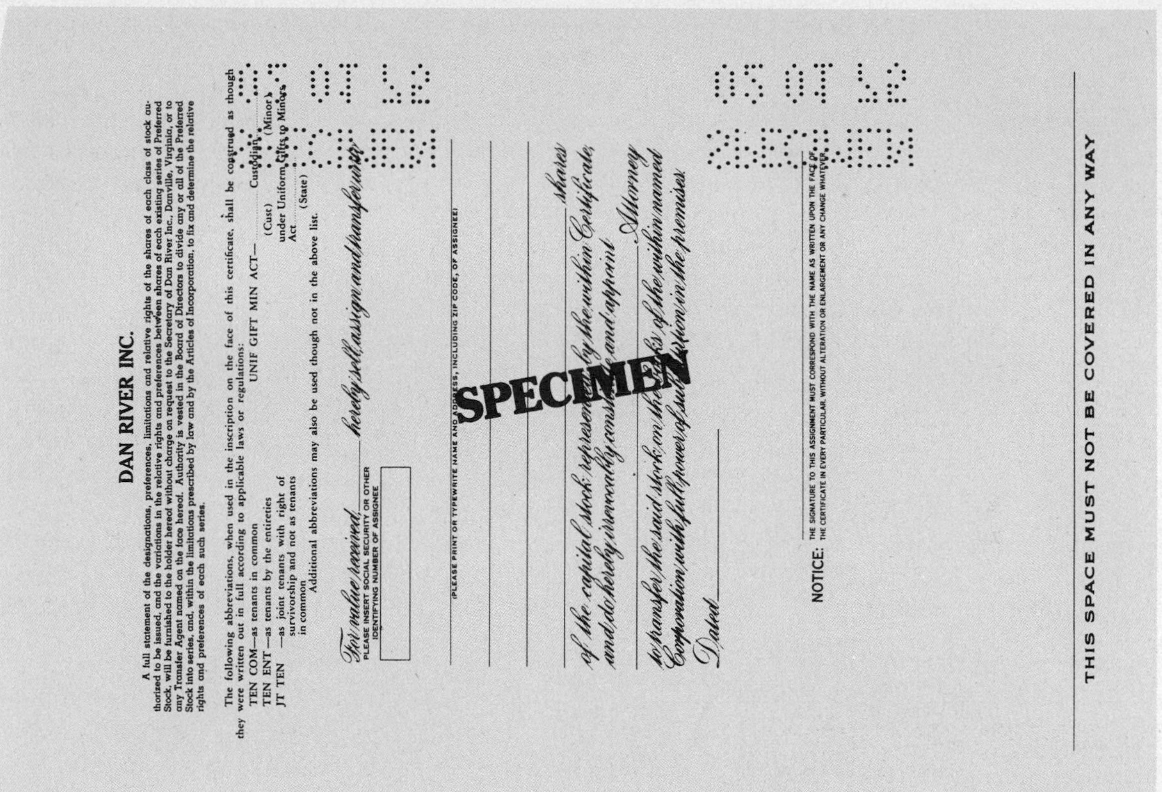

DAN RIVER INC.

A full statement of the designations, preferences, limitations and relative rights of the shares of each class of stock authorized to be issued, and the variations in the relative rights and preferences between shares of each existing series of Preferred Stock, will be furnished to the holder hereof without charge on request to the Secretary of Dan River Inc., Danville, Virginia, or to any Transfer Agent named on the face hereof. Authority is vested in the Board of Directors to divide any or all of the Preferred Stock into series, and, within the limitations prescribed by law and by the Articles of Incorporation, to fix and determine the relative rights and preferences of each such series.

The following abbreviations, when used in the inscription on the face of this certificate, shall be construed as though they were written out in full according to applicable laws or regulations:

TEN COM—as tenants in common
TEN ENT—as tenants by the entireties
JT TEN —as joint tenants with right of survivorship and not as tenants in common

UNIF GIFT MIN ACT— .... Custodian ....
(Cust) (Minor)
under Uniform Gifts to Minors
Act ....
(State)

Additional abbreviations may also be used though not in the above list.

For value received, ______ *hereby sell, assign and transfer unto*

PLEASE INSERT SOCIAL SECURITY OR OTHER IDENTIFYING NUMBER OF ASSIGNEE

______

(PLEASE PRINT OR TYPEWRITE NAME AND ADDRESS, INCLUDING ZIP CODE, OF ASSIGNEE)

______

______

______ *shares*

of the capital stock represented by the within Certificate, and do hereby irrevocably constitute and appoint

______ *Attorney*

to transfer the said stock on the books of the within named Corporation with full power of substitution in the premises.

Dated ______

SPECIMEN

NOTICE: THE SIGNATURE TO THIS ASSIGNMENT MUST CORRESPOND WITH THE NAME AS WRITTEN UPON THE FACE OF THE CERTIFICATE IN EVERY PARTICULAR, WITHOUT ALTERATION OR ENLARGEMENT OR ANY CHANGE WHATEVER.

THIS SPACE MUST NOT BE COVERED IN ANY WAY

Figure 16–3
Reverse side of stock certificate

upon each class of stock in the charter. The significance of par value is discussed on page 550. Each original investor who transfers cash or other assets to the corporation in exchange for shares of stock must invest an amount at least as great as par value. For example, a person who obtains 50 shares of stock of Dan River, Inc. by original investment, must pay in to the corporation at least $250. The journal entry on the books of the corporation to record issuance of stock at par value would be:

1979 Sep.	7	Cash	250	00		
		Capital Stock			250	00
		To record the issuance of 50 shares at par.				

The account entitled Capital Stock represents stockholders' equity. It is similar in nature to the accounts Mary Jolly, Capital (proprietorship), or Gary Core, Capital (partnership). After stock has been issued to an investor, shares may be sold and resold over and over to subsequent owners. These transfers are private transactions between the buyers and sellers, and do not bring additional capital into the corporation. Easy transferability is one of the advantages of stock ownership, and makes it possible for corporations to raise large amounts of capital from investment by thousands of individuals.

Taxation of income Because the corporation is treated as a legal entity separate and distinct from its stockholders, it is taxed as a business entity. The tax is based on corporate net income before taxes and is recorded by an entry such as:

1979						
Dec.	31	Income Tax Expense	xxx	xx		
		Income Taxes Payable			xxx	xx
		To record taxes due.				

The Income Tax Expense account is deducted in the income statement from income before taxes to arrive at net income after taxes. Income Taxes Payable is classified as a current liability in the balance sheet.

The end-of-period closing of revenue and expense accounts into the Income Summary is the same for all forms of business organizations. For corporations, however, income tax is one of the expense items. At the end of each accounting period, the after-tax net income is transferred to an account called Retained Earnings. For example, if a corporation had earnings of $18,120 in 1979, the entry would be:

1979						
Dec.	31	Income Summary	18,120	00		
		Retained Earnings			18,120	00
		To close the Income Summary account.				

U.S. corporations paid 1977 federal income taxes at the rate of 20 percent on the first $25,000 of taxable income; 22 percent on the second $25,000; and 48 percent on all taxable income over $50,000. An individual stockholder of a corporation may exclude from his or her taxable income the first $100 of dividends received each year on shares of stock held. All dividends received by individuals in excess of $100, however, must be included in taxable income in the stockholder's individual tax return.

Advantages and disadvantages

The ability to develop into a business with assets worth billions of dollars is an advantage of the corporate form. It allows for mass production of a diversified line of products and services and their distribution on a national and international basis. A business of this size can afford and can attract the most talented and experienced professional managers that are available. Other advantages include the ability to raise large sums of capital and the limited liability feature that protects the shareholders of the business from a disastrous loss. In case of a business failure the most that any shareholder stands to lose is the amount paid for the number of shares of stock held. The ease of transfer of ownership and the potential for permanent existence are also advantages of the corporate form of organization.

As with the other types of business, there are disadvantages. One of them is the difficulty and cost of formation. Although limited liability is an advantage in attracting investors, it is sometimes a disadvantage if the corporation desires to borrow money. Since only the assets of the corporation (not the total wealth of its shareholders) are available as security, potential lenders may tend to be more cautious and may demand higher interest rates when dealing with corporations. Finally, the requirement for inclusion of all but the first $100 of corporate dividends in the taxable income of individuals is a disadvantage of the corporate form of business. It may be argued that this amounts to double taxation of the same income.

A portion of the earnings of corporations may be paid out to the shareholders. Such distributions of earnings to stockholders are *dividends,* usually made quarterly by check. The amount of dividends a stockholder receives is based upon the number of shares held. Ford Motor Company's *Third Quarter Report* for the year 1975 was mailed on December 1, 1975, to each stockholder. Enclosed with the report was a check for a quarterly dividend payment of 60 cents a share. A stockholder who owned fifteen shares received a check for $9. A corporation is not required by law to pay any or all of its earnings to owners as dividends. Another source of capital for corporations, therefore, is the amount of earnings that are retained for use in the business. Such amounts are reflected in a stockholders' equity account called Retained Earnings. At September 30, 1975, Ford had more than 5 billion dollars in retained earnings.

As legal entities, corporations have the right within the scope of their charters, to enter into contracts and to engage in long-term and short-term borrowing to raise capital. Short-term borrowing is often based on the general credit of the corporation by negotiating loans with banks. These loans are usually due in one year or less. Long-term borrowing by corporations extends over periods as long as twenty or thirty years. To borrow money for such long periods of time, corporations issue certificates of indebtedness called *bonds*. On October 9, 1975, for example, the Savannah Electric and Power Company announced a new issue of $20 million of first mortgage bonds paying interest at 12½ percent per year due 1981. Simply stated, the company is borrowing money from the public to be repaid in six years and is offering certain of its properties as security.

In summary then, corporations can raise large amounts of capital in three major ways: from investors by issuance of transferable shares of stock to individuals, by retaining a portion of corporate assets earned through profitable operations for use in the business, and from borrowing.

Glossary

Agreed ratio The fixed proportions agreed upon in advance by the partners for the division of partnership earnings.

Bonds Certificates of long-term indebtedness in writing.

Capital stock Shares representing fractional elements of ownership of a corporation; also the title of an account in which is recorded the par value of stock issued.

Corporation A form of business authorized by a state as a legal entity; in the eyes of the law it is an artificial being with the rights and responsibilities of an individual.

Dividends Cash or other asset distributions of retained earnings made by a corporation to its stockholders.

Drawing Reduction in the equity of a proprietor or of a partner resulting from cash or other assets withdrawn from the business in anticipation of income earned.

General partner A partner who has unlimited liability for the debts of a partnership.

Goodwill An intangible asset that represents an expected greater than normal level of earnings of a business in its industry.

Limited liability A liability restricted by law. A characteristic of a corporation whereby the stockholders have no personal liability for debts of the business.

Limited partner A characteristic of a limited partnership whereby a partner has no personal responsibility for debts of the partnership.

Liquidation The process of terminating a business by selling the assets, paying the creditors, and distributing the remaining cash to the partners.

Mutual agency The acts of one partner are binding on the others; each partner is the agent of the other partners.

Organization costs An intangible asset account that is debited for the initial cost of forming a corporation. These costs include incorporation fees, legal costs, and other similar costs.

Par value The nominal or face value printed on a stock certificate representing the minimum amount to be paid to the issuing corporation by the original investor.

Partnership An association of two or more persons to carry on, as co-owners, a business for profit.

Proprietor The sole owner of a business enterprise.

Realization The conversion of the assets of a business to cash.

Retained earnings Undistributed earnings that have been retained for use in a corporation.

Shareholders Persons who own shares of capital stock in a corporation.

Single proprietorship A business that is owned entirely by one individual.

Stock certificate A printed or an engraved serially numbered document issued to the stock purchaser as evidence of ownership of shares of stock in a corporation.

Stockholders Same as shareholders.

Unlimited liability A characteristic of single proprietorships and partnerships; an owner has personal liability for the debts of the business.

Questions

Q16–1 What are at least four unique characteristics of each of the forms of business organization?

Q16–2 What is the extent of the responsibility of the owner of a majority of the shares of stock of a corporation to pay its debts if it gets into financial difficulties?

Q16–3 What is the meaning of the term "legal entity"? How does it differ from an "accounting entity"?

Q16–4 Can a partnership exist without any general partners? Explain.

Q16–5 What are some methods by which a corporation can raise capital that are not available to a single proprietorship?

Q16–6 What is the meaning of par value?

Q16–7 Since it represents earnings retained for use in the business, is the Retained Earnings account an asset? Explain.

Q16–8 Does each state have a different set of laws to regulate partnerships? Explain.

Q16–9 What is the basis of the argument that earnings of a corporation are subject to income tax more than once?

Q16–10 Does the dissolution of a partnership terminate the business? Explain.

Q16–11 In which form of business organization is ownership most readily transferable? Explain why.

Q16–12 Can a partnership business continue after the death or retirement of one of the partners? Explain.

Q16–13 Thomas Duffy and Yvon Kay formed a partnership. Duffy invested $10,000 in cash, Kay invested land and a building with cash market value of $25,000. Five years later they agree to terminate the partnership, and Kay demands the return to her of the land and building. Is she justified in her demand? Explain.

Q16–14 D. Gold and W. Golay agreed orally to form a partnership as of January 10, 1979. They postponed formalization of their agreement pending the return of their attorney, who was out of town. D. Gold invested $40,000 in cash; W. Golay invested land and buildings worth $20,000 and $80,000, respectively. On January 11, the building was completely destroyed by an accidental explosion, and they terminated their partnership. W. Golay claims that both the land and the $40,000 belong to him. Is he right? Explain.

Q16–15 F. Hahn and G. Root are partners with capital account balances of $40,000 each. They share profits one-third and two-thirds, respectively. (a) Is this an equitable arrangement? (b) Assume that 10 percent interest on capital balances is agreed on. How will profits of $12,000 be distributed? (c) What account should be charged for the interest on the capital balances?

Q16–16 M. Nadja and E. Pevay form a partnership by oral agreement. The matter of profit distribution is not discussed. Nadja invests $15,000 and Pevay $10,000. At the end of the first year Nadja contends that he should be credited with 60 percent of the profits of $10,000. Pevay disagrees. (a) Is Nadja right? (b) How could this disagreement have been avoided?

Class exercises

CE16–1 (Balance sheet) These December 31, 1979 figures have been taken from the records of Shelby Bennett, Management Consultant:

Accounts Payable	$12,500
Accounts Receivable	13,800
Building	40,000
Cash	25,000
Delivery Equipment	14,000
Land	11,500
Mortgage payable (due July 1, 1985)	28,000
Notes Payable (due July 1, 1980)	11,000
Notes Receivable	1,800
Prepaid Insurance	1,200
Wages Payable	1,400

Required: Prepare a balance sheet at December 31, 1979.

CE16–2 (Closing entries) Refer to CE16–1 and add the following assumptions:

a. Additional accounts are contained in the ledgers as follows:

Income Summary		Shelby Bennett, Capital		Shelby Bennett, Drawing	
176,200	225,000		20,000	14,400	

b. All expense and revenue accounts have been closed.

c. The figure in the Capital account is the balance at January 1, 1979; the figure in the Drawing account represents withdrawals of $1,200 per month during 1979.

Required: Complete the closing entries.

CE16–3 (Owners' equity) Refer to CE16–1 and substitute the following set of assumptions:

a. The figures came from the partnership of Davis and Ratchford.
b. The January 1, 1979 Capital account balances were as follows:

Jerrine Davis, Capital	$ 8,000
Charles Ratchford, Capital	12,000

c. The December 31, 1979 Drawing account balances were:

Jerrine Davis, Drawing	$ 9,600
Charles Ratchford, Drawing	10,800

d. Net income for 1979 was $48,800.

Required:

1. Make the journal entry to allocate net income. (The partners share income and losses equally.)
2. Complete the closing entries.
3. Show how the Owners' Equity section of the balance sheet would appear on December 31, 1979.

CE16–4 (Journal entries) On February 6, 1979, C. Madison, R. Deal, and E. Serrano received a charter establishing the MDS Corporation and authorizing it to issue 10,000 shares of $15 par value capital stock.

Required: Journalize the following transactions on the books of the corporation:

a. 100 shares of stock were issued on February 7, 1979 to each incorporator for expenses they had incurred in connection with organizing the corporation.
b. A local lawyer agreed to accept capital stock at par value in payment of her fee of $2,025 for services rendered in obtaining the charter. The stock was issued on February 10, 1979.
c. 3,000 additional shares of stock were issued to each of the incorporators for cash at par value on February 15, 1979.
d. During 1979, the corporation's after-tax income amounted to $37,500. (Show in a single journal entry dated December 31, 1979; debit "Various Debits.").
e. On December 28, 1979 the directors voted to declare a dividend of $1.00 per share to be paid on January 10, 1980. (Hint: Credit "Dividends Payable.")

CE16–5 (Stockholders' equity) Assuming that the proper closing entries had been completed, show the Stockholders' Equity section of the balance sheet for MDS Corporation (CE16–4) at December 31, 1979.

CE16–6 (Recording partnership transactions) The following selected transactions occurred in the partnership of Scalia and Edes:

1979

Jan. 2 Allan Scalia and Otto Edes formed a partnership on this date, making the following investments:

Scalia invested $55,000 in cash. Edes contributed his equity in a building and lot. The partners agreed that the building was worth $90,000 and the land, $15,000. There was a mortgage on the land and building with a face value of $27,000; the mortgage carried an interest rate of 9 percent, and the interest was last paid on October 2, 1978. The partnership assumed all liabilities relating to the mortgage.

Mar. 1 Scalia withdrew $800 cash in anticipation of income to be earned.

Apr. 1 Edes withdrew merchandise from the business. The merchandise cost $600 and had a selling price of $800. The firm uses the periodic inventory system.

Oct. 2 Scalia was allowed to withdraw $12,000 in cash to pay a personal debt. The amount exceeds any anticipated income to be earned.

Required: Record the transactions.

CE16–7 (Distribution of partnership profits and losses) V. Edry and Andrew Sibley formed a partnership on January 1, 1979, with investments of $25,000 and $40,000, respectively.

On July 1, 1979, Sibley invested an additional $10,000.

Required: Make the appropriate journal entries to record the distribution of profits and losses on the basis of each of the following assumptions:

1. Net income is $12,000, profits and losses are shared equally.
2. Net loss is $5,000; the partnership agreement provides that profits are to be distributed 55 percent to Edry and 45 percent to Sibley; the method of distributing losses was not specified.
3. Net income is $10,000, to be distributed in the ratio of capital balances as of December 31, 1979.
4. Net income is $20,000, to be distributed as follows: salaries of $10,000 to Edry and $12,000 to Sibley; interest of 8 percent on ending capital balances; remainder to be distributed equally.

CE16–8 (Statement of partners' equity) B. Reyes, J. Arre, and T. Reuben formed a partnership on May 1, 1978, with investments of $15,000, $11,000, and $13,000, respectively. Profits and losses were to be shared equally. During the next twelve months, Reyes and Arre made additional investments of $5,000 each; Reuben invested an additional $6,000 and withdrew $2,500. Net income for the period was $30,000.

Required: Prepare (a) a statement of partners' equity for the year ended April 30, 1979, and (b) entries to close the partners' Drawing accounts.

Exercises and problems

P16–1 Joseph Capelli, owner of Capelli's Grocery, asks you to determine the value of his equity in the business as of December 31, 1979. In your computations you determine that net income of the business in 1979 was $17,800. In addition, you find that the following transactions occurred during 1979:

Original investment	$ 9,000
Additional investment	10,000
Personal withdrawals	12,000

Required:

a. Establish T accounts for Joseph Capelli, Capital and Joseph Capelli, Drawing. Post all available data to those T accounts.
b. Prepare a statement of owner's equity.

P16–2 Agnes Price and Ralph Maggio formed a partnership on May 10, 1979. Price contributed $15,000 in cash, land worth $9,000, a building appraised at $60,000, and a truck valued at $3,000. The land and building are encumbered by a mortgage of $12,000 which is assumed by the partnership. Maggio contributed $15,000 in cash.

Required:

a. Make the general journal entries on the books of the new partnership to record its formation.
b. Prepare, in report form, a balance sheet for the partnership which will do business under the name, Magpri Consultants.

P16–3 Ron Crawford and Jim Larocio form a partnership during their senior year in college to provide tutoring service to new students. After graduation they continue the business, hiring other students to help with much of the actual tutoring. Their trial balance on December 31, 1979, is as follows:

Accounts Receivable	$ 1,250
Cash	3,000
Jim Larocio, Drawing	6,000
Jim Larocio, Capital	7,775
Ron Crawford, Drawing	6,000
Ron Crawford, Capital	2,000
Salaries Expense	11,250
Supplies on Hand	1,625
Supplies Used	2,520
Tutoring Revenue	21,870

Required:

a. Prepare the December 31, 1979 closing entries.
b. Prepare a statement of partners' equity using three money columns headed, Crawford, Larocio, and Total.
c. Explain why the equity of each partner declined in a profitable year.

P16–4 In their partnership agreement, Charles Panos and Bea Roth agreed to divide profits and losses as follows: (a) 10 percent interest on average capital balances, (b) salaries of $10,800 each, and (c) the remainder shared equally.

Required: Prepare a schedule showing the allocation of net income of $35,100, assuming average capital balances of $18,000 and $36,000 for Panos and Roth, respectively.

P16–5 P. Woods and J. Zebal formed a partnership on June 8, 1979. Woods contributed $10,000 in cash, land worth $6,000, a building appraised at $40,000 (the land and the building are encumbered by a mortgage of $8,000, which is assumed by the partnership), and a truck valued at $2,000. Zebal contributed $10,000 in cash.

Required: (a) Make the entries to record the formation of the partnership. (b) Why may Woods be willing to enter into a partnership in which he contributes five times as much as his partner?

P16–6 C. Poe, and R. Resh form a partnership.

Required: Journalize their investments based on each of the following independent assumptions:

1. Each partner invests $6,000 in cash.
2. Poe invests $7,000 in cash, and Resh invests $9,000 in cash.
3. Poe invests $2,000 in cash, land worth $8,000, a building worth $20,000, and merchandise worth $3,000. Resh invests $25,000 in cash.
4. Poe invests $3,000 in cash, land worth $5,000, and a building worth $20,000. The partnership agrees to assume a mortgage payable of $10,000 on the land and building. Resh invests $3,000 in cash, store equipment worth $6,000, and merchandise worth $2,000.
5. Before the formation of the partnership, Poe and Resh were competitors. They decide to form the partnership for their mutual advantage; the partnership assumes their existing assets and liabilities at book values as follows:

	Poe	*Resh*
Cash	$ 6,000	$ 7,000
Accounts Receivable	13,000	16,000
Merchandise Inventory	30,400	22,200
Delivery Equipment (net)	7,000	10,400
Store Equipment (net)	12,000	20,000
Totals	$68,400	$75,600
Accounts Payable	$26,800	$24,400
Notes Payable	10,000	12,000
Poe, Capital	31,600	
Resh, Capital		39,200
Totals	$68,400	$75,600

6. Assume the same facts as in 5 above, except that the merchandise and equipment are to be recorded at their fair market valuations as follows:

	Poe	*Resh*
Merchandise Inventory	$28,000	$22,000
Delivery Equipment (net)	8,000	10,000
Store Equipment (net)	10,000	14,000

P16–7 J. Retik and G. Poal form a partnership to operate a food brokerage business.

Required: Record their initial investments, on the basis of each of the following assumptions:

1. Retik and Poal each invest $10,000 in cash.
2. Retik and Poal invest $4,000 and $2,500 in cash, respectively.
3. Retik invests $4,000 in cash, merchandise worth $7,500, a building worth $30,000, and land worth $9,000; Poal invests $10,000 in cash, office equipment worth $6,000, and store equipment worth $10,000.
4. Retik and Poal transfer the following assets and liabilities to the partnership as their initial investments:

	Retik	*Poal*
Cash	$ 6,000	$ 4,500
Accounts Receivable	10,000	12,000
Merchandise Inventory	20,000	17,000
Delivery Equipment (net)	12,000	–0–
Store Equipment (net)	–0–	11,000
Accounts Payable	15,000	16,000
Notes Payable to Bank	13,000	15,000

P16–8 A, B, and C, whose balance sheet information is shown below, have decided to liquidate their partnership. Their general ledger shows the following balances on March 31, 1979:

Cash	$10,000
Accounts Receivable	12,500
Inventories	50,000
Machinery	62,500
Accounts Payable	10,000
A, Capital	25,000
B, Capital	37,500
C, Capital	62,500

Proceeds from the sale of noncash assets were as follows:

Accounts Receivable	$ 7,500
Inventories	22,500
Machinery	12,500

Required: Prepare a schedule in good form showing the final distribution of the remaining cash following the sale of the assets and the payment of creditors.

P16–9 Peter Kerr and Tom Stevens formed a partnership on January 2, 1979. Certain relevant accounts are given as of December 31, 1979.

Peter Kerr, Capital

Date		Explanation	Debit		Credit		Balance	
1979								
Jan.	2				80,000	00	80,000	00
Jul.	1				20,000	00	100,000	00
Aug.	1		10,000	00			90,000	00

Peter Kerr, Drawing

Date		Explanation	Debit		Credit		Balance	
1979								
Dec.	31		6,000	00			6,000	00

Tom Stevens, Capital

Date		Explanation	Debit		Credit		Balance	
1979								
Jan.	2				100,000	00	100,000	00
Dec.	1				12,000	00	112,000	00

Tom Stevens, Drawing

Date		Explanation	Debit		Credit		Balance	
1979								
Dec.	31		8,000	00			8,000	00

The net income for 1979 was $10,000. The following provisions appeared in the articles of copartnership:

Net income shall be divided as follows:

Salary allowances: Kerr, $6,000; Stevens, $8,000.
Interest allowances: 9 percent on beginning-of-year capital balances.
Remainder: divided 55 percent to Kerr and 45 percent to Stevens.

Required: Prepare the journal entries to allocate the net income to the partners' accounts and to complete the closing process.

P16–10 Assume that A and B are equal partners, each with a capital balance of $39,000.

Required: Record the admission of C under each of the following assumptions:

a. A sells her interest to C for $42,000.
b. C invests $39,000 for a one-fourth interest (two possible solutions).
c. C invests $39,000 for a one-fourth interest, total capital to be $130,000.
d. C invests $39,000 for a one-third interest, total capital to be $117,000.
e. C invests $45,500 for a one-third interest, total capital to be $136,500.
f. C invests $26,000 for a one-third interest, total capital to be $117,000.
g. C invests $46,800 for a one-fourth interest, total capital to be $124,800.
h. C invests $46,800 for a one-half interest, total capital to be $124,800.

P16–11 (Integrative) The accountant for Lindsay and Limon, interior decorators, prepared the following adjusted trial balance at December 31, 1979.

Cash	$ 4,850	
Accounts Receivable	12,600	
Supplies	3,800	
Prepaid Insurance	2,750	
Office Equipment	12,000	
Accumulated Depreciation—Office Equipment		$ 3,500
Building	80,000	
Accumulated Depreciation—Building		10,000
Accounts Payable		4,500
Accrued Salaries Payable		500
Mortgage Payable		20,000
David Lindsay, Capital		25,000
David Lindsay, Drawing	15,000	
Howard Limon, Capital		20,000
Howard Limon, Drawing	12,000	
Professional Fees		85,000
Supplies Used	3,000	
Depreciation Expense—Office Equipment	1,200	
Depreciation Expense—Building	4,000	
Utilities Expense	1,200	
General Expense	1,500	
Property Tax Expense	1,000	
Interest Expense	1,600	
Salaries Expense	12,000	
	$168,500	$168,500

Required:

1. Prepare an income statement for the year showing the allocation of net income to each partner. The partners have agreed to divide profits and losses as follows: (a) 10 percent interest on capital balances at the beginning of the year, (b) salaries of $15,000 each, and (c) the remainder equally. Each partner made an additional investment of $3,000 on July 1, 1979.
2. Prepare a statement of partners' equity for the year.
3. Prepare a balance sheet as of December 31, 1979.

P16–12 A group of incorporators received a charter establishing Drag and Stag, Inc., for the purpose of opening a series of night spots. The corporation was authorized to issue 50,000 shares of $20 par value capital stock. Record in general journal form the following transactions in 1979:

1979	
Mar. 6	Issued 100 shares to a law firm in payment of $2,000 in legal fees in connection with incorporation.
Mar. 8	Issued, for cash, 25,000 shares at par.
Mar. 10	Purchased the building and equipment of an existing night spot for $32,000. Issued 1,000 shares of stock and paid $12,000 in cash for this purchase. ($8,000 of the cost was allocated to equipment.)
Apr. 12	Purchased a second building for $40,000 and equipment for $10,000. Paid for both by issuance of stock at par.
Jun. 7	The directors of Drag and Stag, Inc. declared dividend number one of 50 cents a share to be paid on June 30. (Hint: Credit Dividends Payable.)
Jun. 30	Paid dividend number one to the stockholders.
Jun. 30	Closed the Dividends account into Retained Earnings.

P16–13 (Integrative) The post-closing trial balance for the Jones, Smith, and Scott Partnership at June 30, 1979 contains the following items:

Cash	$10,800
Accounts Receivable	16,200
Notes Receivable	3,200
Merchandise Inventory	21,600
Prepaid Insurance	2,200
Equipment	35,200
Accumulated Depreciation—Equipment	8,200
Accounts Payable	10,260
Notes Payable	8,640
Accrued Wages Payable	2,700
Jones, Capital	23,760
Smith, Capital	23,760
Scott, Capital	11,880

On July 1, 1979, the state issued a charter establishing the Jones, Smith, and Scott Corporation authorized to issue 100,000 shares of capital stock with a par value of $20 a share.

Required:

1. Record on the books of the new corporation the following transactions:

   1979

   Jul. 2 The corporation took over all assets and liabilities of the Jones, Smith, and Scott Partnership issuing an appropriate number of shares of stock at par to Jones, Smith, and Scott in exchange for their interests in the partnership.

   Jul. 3 Jones, Smith, and Scott invested additional cash in the corporation and were issued (at par) 10,000, 10,000 and 5,000 shares respectively.

   Jul. 5 An additional 25,000 shares were issued to numerous individuals at par for cash.

   Dec. 20 Jones, Smith, and Scott Corporation paid a $0.60 per share cash dividend.
2. Record the July 2, 1979, transaction on the books of the Jones, Smith, and Scott Partnership.
3. Assume that in addition to the transactions in (1) above, Jones, Smith, and Scott Corporation had after-tax earnings of $262,180 in the fiscal year ended June 30, 1980. No additional stock had been issued and no additional dividends were declared. Show the Stockholders' Equity section of the balance sheet at June 30, 1980.

P16–14 (Minicase) Joseph, Michael, and Sarah Litzberg have owned and operated as partners a business known as Litzberg's Daredevils. Along with ten employees and equipment valued at about $200,000, they travel the carnival and state fair circuit each summer with a crowd-thrilling automobile stunt show. Business is seasonal, and each of the three partners owns a home in the southwest where the families are located permanently. The partners feel that they could double the amount of annual revenue with the addition of more equipment and the hiring and training of two or three more drivers. Sarah and Michael Litzberg are in favor of such action, but Joseph is hesitant. He points out that twice during the past season, a car ran into a section of bleachers with damages amounting to thousands of dollars; it was fortunate that the costs did not run into the hundreds of thousands. He has heard something about limited liability of the corporate form of business, but really doesn't understand what it would mean to Litzberg's Daredevils. All three partners agree to seek your advice. Prepare for them a brief discussion that will outline and explain the advantages and disadvantages of changing from the partnership to the corporate form of business.

chapter seventeen

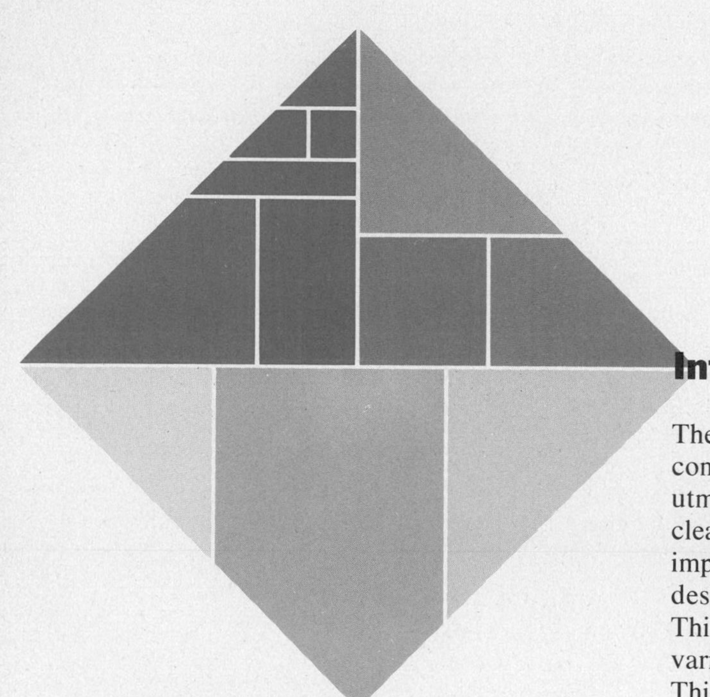

Introduction

The stockholders' equity in a corporation comes from a number of sources. It is of the utmost importance that these sources be clearly distinguished and stated. It is equally important that the terminology used to designate them be precise and meaningful. This chapter begins with a discussion of the various sources of stockholders' equity. This is followed by a description of the different classes of stock and the meaning and significance of the different "value" terms used to measure capital stock. The recording of transactions involving capital stock is then described. The chapter concludes with an illustration in T-account form of the functions of the owners' equity accounts for the three forms of business organization.

Corporations: paid-in capital

Learning goals

To know the sources of paid-in capital of corporations.

To recognize and differentiate between various classes of capital stock and their various value classifications.

To record the issuance of stock.

To account for stock subscriptions.

To understand the classifications of paid-in capital other than capital stock.

To be familiar with the functions of the equity accounts of the three forms of business organizations.

Key terms

common stock
donated capital
excess over par or stated value
legal capital
liquidation value
market value
no-par stock
paid-in capital
preferred stock
premium on capital stock
stated value
stock subscription

Sources of capital

Operating transactions of corporations are recorded in the same manner as those of proprietorships and partnerships. The chart of accounts must be designed, however, to distinguish between the two primary sources of corporate capital: investments by stockholders and earnings reinvested. This distinction is essential because state laws provide that earnings may be distributed to the stockholders but that, both for the protection of corporate creditors and for the continued operation of the business, amounts exceeding invested assets cannot be legally distributed to the shareholders. Hence, separate accounts designating the several sources of stockholders' equity should be kept and clearly set forth in the Stockholders' Equity section of the corporate balance sheet. The various sources of stockholders' equity are outlined in Figure 17–1 and are described in this and the next chapter.

Figure 17–1
Sources of stockholders' equity

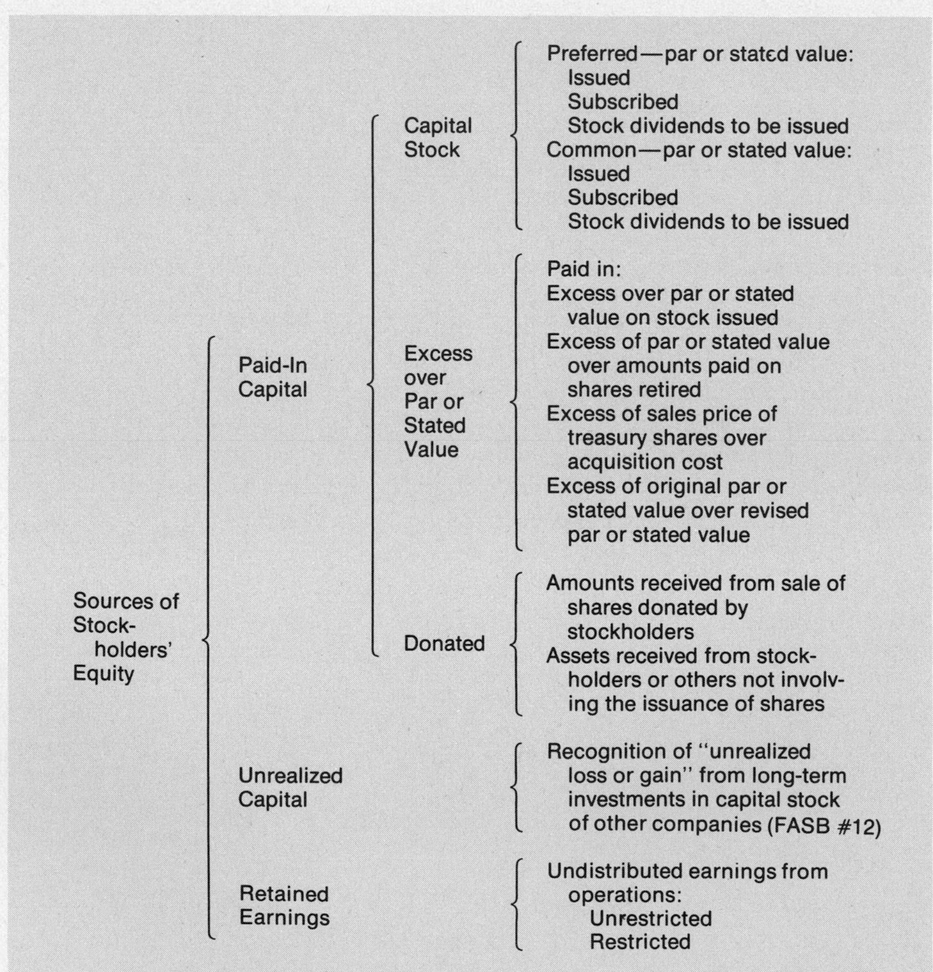

Capital stock

The charter granted by the state of incorporation authorizes the newly formed corporation to issue a designated number of shares of capital stock. The corporation usually secures authorization to issue more shares than it anticipates issuing at the outset. This allows for additional sales in the future without seeking further authorization by the state. The total number of shares issued cannot exceed the number of shares authorized.

General ledger accounts for authorized but unissued stock need not be opened. Detail with respect to the number of shares authorized is customarily included as part of the description in the Stockholders' Equity section of the balance sheet. The balance sheet presentation may be as shown below.

```
Stockholders' Equity
  Paid-in Capital
    Common Stock, $100 par value, authorized 1,000 shares,
    issued 500 shares . . . . . . . . . . . . . . . . . . . $50,000.00
```

Classes of stock

Stock is usually issued in two classes, common and preferred.

Preferred stock One of the reasons for issuing two or more classes of stock is to endow one class with certain features that will make it more salable. The attractive feature of *preferred stock* is that, when a dividend declaration is made by the board of directors, the preferred stockholders must be paid at the stated rate and amount for the class of stock before payments are made to other stockholders. The same preference applies when a corporation is dissolved: assets remaining after satisfaction of creditor claims are used first to redeem the claims of preferred stockholders; the remainder of the assets, if any, are paid to the other stockholders. Preferred stockholders, on the other hand, are often restricted to a specific dividend rate and do not, therefore, benefit from extra earnings. A preferred stockholder is usually denied the right to vote.

Common stock If a corporation issues only one class of stock, then all shares are treated alike, and, there being no preferences, that class of stock is called *common stock*. If there is more than one class, the class that does not have preferences and that shares only in the remainder of earnings or assets distribution is known as common stock. This class of stock does have voting privileges.

"Value" of stock

Frequently used "value" concepts include par value and no-par value, stated value, market value, redemption value, and liquidation value. Only the term "market value" gives a direct indication of the worth of the stock.

Par value of stock The term *par value* refers to a specific dollar amount per share, which is printed on the stock certificate, and generally *represents the minimum amount that must be paid to the issuing corporation* by the original purchaser of the stock. Par value may be any amount set forth in the corporation's charter and is rarely an indication of what the stock is actually worth. Par value is used as the basis for recording the stock on the corporate books. It is often established at a nominal value (referred to as low par value) and may have little or no economic significance.

Par value *The face value of a stock as set forth in the charter of the issuing corporation; it is the amount credited to the capital stock account by the corporation to record the issue.*

Stated value of stock When stock is issued as no-par value, the directors often assign a *stated,* or uniform, value to each share. This value becomes the basis for recording the stock on the corporate books, and the accounting is the same as for par value stock.

We will compare three alternative entries for the issuance of the same stock. Assume that the King Corporation issues 1,000 shares of common stock for $110,000.

First, assuming that the par value of the stock is $100:

1979				
Dec.	5	Cash	110,000 00	
		Common Stock		100,000 00
		Premium on Common Stock		10,000 00
		Issued 1,000 shares of stock for cash at $110 per share.		

Next, assuming that the stock is no-par value with a $75 stated value:

1979				
Dec.	5	Cash	110,000 00	
		Common Stock		75,000 00
		Paid-in Capital—Excess Over Stated Value		35,000 00
		Issued 1,000 shares of stock for cash at $110 per share.		

When no-par stock is issued, many accountants prefer to use an account entitled, Paid-in Capital—Excess Over Stated Value, thus restricting the use of Premium on Capital Stock to par value stock only.

Stated value *For a stock without par value the corporate directors assign a value to each share. For accounting purposes this value is essentially the same as par value.*

The premium on stock, or excess over stated value, is that part of the capital paid in by stockholders that is not credited to the capital stock accounts for each class of stock. Separate paid-in accounts are kept so that the balance sheet shows the specific sources of capital. Such precise source accounts are also desirable to establish their availability as a source for dividends or other distributions to stockholders, in states that permit such distributions.

The third alternative assumes that the stock is no-par value and has no stated value:

1979						
Dec.	5	Cash	110,000	00		
		Common Stock			110,000	00
		Issued 1,000 shares of stock for cash at $110 per share.				

Market value of stock The market value of stock is not determined by its par value. The term *market value* is used to indicate the amount that a share will bring the seller if the stock is offered for sale. Market prices change daily and can be determined readily for many stocks by reference to the stock market quotations carried in daily newspapers or to a financial magazine or financial service publication. Market value reflects price level changes; available investment funds; economic and political factors; and the feelings, hopes, and expectations of investors.

The actual price in dollars a share of stock will bring at the time the owner offers it for sale. **Market value**

Legal, or stated, capital The term *legal capital,* or *stated capital,* incorporated in the laws of a number of states, places certain restrictions on the return of capital to the stockholders in order to protect creditors. The restriction limits the amount of investment that can be withdrawn by stockholders either as dividends or by the corporation buying back capital stock to the point where there may be insufficient funds left to satisfy creditors' claims. The creditors of a corporation do not have access to the personal resources of the stockholders; their only investment protection is in the corporate assets.

Legal capital ***is the minimum amount of capital that must be left in the corporation. Consequently, creditors are assured that in the event of corporate losses the investors as a group will absorb the losses up to the amount of the capital.*** **Legal capital**

State laws vary considerably as to the method of determining and applying such restriction provisions. The accountant may require the assistance of an attorney on questions involving legal capital. In some states, for example, legal capital is considered to be the total proceeds from the sale of stock. In other states the directors of a corporation that has issued no-par value stock may, by resolution, designate a portion of the paid-in capital as the legal capital, or the state may designate a minimum amount. On par value stock, the legal capital is the par value of all the shares issued. When, as is often the case, the par value is low in relation to the issue price, the legal capital will be much less than the total paid in by shareholders. In such a situation legal capital is not a significant constraint on amounts to be distributed to stockholders, and the security of the creditors depends rather on the firm's operating and financial policies and resources.

Redemption value and liquidation value Two other "value" terms commonly used are redemption value and liquidation value. *Redemption value* is the specified price to be paid when redeemable preferred stock is repurchased by the issuing company or when turned in by the shareholder under specified conditions. *Liquidation value* is the specified price per share to be paid to preferred shareholders upon the voluntary or involuntary liquidation of a corporation.

Recording capital stock transactions

Great care needs to be taken to record stock transactions in strict compliance with the corporate laws of the state of incorporation, keeping in mind the interests of the stockholders and the creditors. Enough accounts should be created, especially those arising from invested capital, so that the Stockholders' Equity section shows in adequate detail the sources of the corporate capital.

Authorization and issuance of stock

The initial entry on a corporate set of books may be a simple narrative statement setting forth certain basic data taken from the corporate charter, including the name of the corporation, the date of incorporation, the nature of the business, and the number and classes of shares authorized to be issued. After the initial narrative entry has been made, assume that the following three transactions took place at the Crown Corporation, which is organized as a wholesale hardware supply business authorized to issue 2,000 shares carrying $100 par value. Explanations to journal entries have been omitted in these obvious cases.

Transaction 1 One-half the stock is issued at par value for cash.

1979						
Feb.	1	Cash	100,000	00		
		Common Stock			100,000	00

Transaction 2 A total of 900 shares is issued for $40,000 in cash plus land and buildings having a fair cash value of $10,000 and $40,000 respectively.

1979				
Feb.	10	Cash	40,000 00	
		Land	10,000 00	
		Buildings	40,000 00	
		Common Stock		90,000 00

Transaction 3 A total of 100 shares is issued to the organizers of the corporation in payment for their services.

1979				
Mar.	1	Organization Costs	10,000 00	
		Common Stock		10,000 00

The Stockholders' Equity section of the Crown Corporation balance sheet after these three transactions shows the following:

Stockholders' Equity	
Paid-in Capital	
Common Stock, $100 par value; authorized and issued 2,000 shares	$200,000.00

Issuance of stock at a premium

Assume that a corporation is organized with an authorized capital of $100,000, consisting of 1,000 shares of $100 par value stock, which are issued for $108,000. The entry is:

1979				
Nov.	1	Cash	108,000 00	
		Common Stock		100,000 00
		Premium on Common Stock		8,000 00

When capital stock is offered for sale, the price it will bring depends not only on the condition and reputation of the corporation, but also on the availability of funds for investment and other external factors. When stock is issued above its par value, the difference is credited to Premium on Common Stock. An alternative title is Paid-in Capital—Excess Over Par Value. The account represents the excess of the issue price per share over the par value per share. Although the premium appears in a separate account, it is part of the total capital paid in by investors. By use of a separate account for the excess over par value paid in on the stock, the par value may be shown readily in the balance sheet. If more than one class of stock has been issued at a premium, separate premium accounts should be kept. Issuance of stock in excess of par or stated value does not constitute earnings, and premiums therefrom should never be recorded in accounts showing corporate earnings.

Immediately following the issuance of the 1,000 shares for $108,000, the Stockholders' Equity section appears as shown below.

Stockholders' Equity		
Paid-in Capital		
Common Stock, $100 par value; authorized and issued 1,000 shares	$100,000.00	
Premium on Common Stock	8,000.00	
Total Paid-in Capital		$108,000.00

Issuance of stock at a discount

In most states, par value stock may not be issued at a discount. Since low par values are quite common, issuance at a discount seldom occurs. If and when a stock issue is for less than par, the difference between the par value and the issue price of the stock is debited to Discount on Common Stock. The account appears as a deduction in the Stockholders' Equity section of the balance sheet.

Capital stock subscriptions

The descriptions of stock issuance transactions in the previous sections were based on the assumption that full payment for the stock was received and the stock certificates were issued at once. This condition normally exists for small or closely held corporations. In the following transactions, *subscriptions,* or pledges to buy the stock, are taken first, and payment is made later in single lump sums or in installments. The purchaser signs a formal, legally enforceable *subscription contract* in which he or she agrees to buy a certain number of shares of stock and to make certain specified payments. The stock certificates are not issued until completion of the payment.

The Subscriptions Receivable account is similar in nature and function to the Accounts Receivable account. It is a current asset and shows the amount due on stock that has been subscribed but has not been fully paid for. It is debited for the issue price, not necessarily the par or stated value, of the stock and is credited for collections as they are received. Like the Accounts Receivable account, it is a controlling account with supporting detail kept in a subsidiary *subscribers ledger,* which contains the accounts of the individual subscribers. When more than one class of stock is issued, separate Subscriptions Receivable accounts should be kept for each class.

The Capital Stock Subscribed account is a temporary capital stock account. It shows the par or stated value amount of stock that has been subscribed, but the stock certificates for the amount in the account have not been issued pending receipt of the payments still due on the stock as shown in the Subscriptions Receivable account. The account is credited for the par or stated value of the subscribed stock then debited for the par or stated value when the stock is issued, with the permanent Capital Stock account being credited. If no-par value shares without a stated value are issued, the Capital Stock Subscribed account is debited or credited for the full subscription price.

The subscriber to stock normally acquires the full status of a stockholder with all rights and privileges even though he or she is not in possession of the stock certificate. The stock subscription agreement, however, may restrict such rights until full payment is received.

Issuance by subscription at a premium The Green Corporation is authorized to issue 6,000 shares of $100 par value common stock. On July 1, 5,000 shares are issued at a price of $105 a share for cash and subscriptions are received for 1,000 shares. A 60 percent down payment is received; the remaining 40 percent is payable in two installments of $21,000 each on August 2 and September 1. The journal entries are:

Date		Account	Debit		Credit	
1979						
Jul.	1	Cash	525,000	00		
		Common Stock			500,000	00
		Premium on Common Stock			25,000	00
		To record the issuance of 5,000 shares of $100 par value stock for cash at $105 a share.				
	1	Subscriptions Receivable—Common Stock	105,000	00		
		Common Stock Subscribed			100,000	00
		Premium on Common Stock			5,000	00
		To record the receipt of subscriptions for 1,000 shares of $100 par value stock at $105 a share.				
	1	Cash	63,000	00		
		Subscriptions Receivable—Common Stock			63,000	00
		To record the receipt of a 60 percent down payment on the stock subscription of July 1.				
Aug.	2	Cash	21,000	00		
		Subscriptions Receivable—Common Stock			21,000	00
		To record the receipt of the first 20 percent installment on the stock subscription of July 1.				
Sep.	1	Cash	21,000	00		
		Subscriptions Receivable—Common Stock			21,000	00
		To record the receipt of the second and final installment on the stock subscription of July 1.				
	1	Common Stock Subscribed	100,000	00		
		Common Stock			100,000	00
		To record the issuance of stock certificates for 1,000 shares of stock.				

When stock is subscribed at a premium, the entire excess over par or stated value is credited to the Premium on Stock account at the time the stock is subscribed (see the second entry of July 1). As a matter of practical convenience, the premium is recognized at the time of subscription—not proportionately as installments are collected. The amount of the entry for the issuance of the stock certificates is the par or stated value of the stock; the existence of a premium does not affect the amount recorded.

Partial balance sheets as of July 1 and September 1 are shown below.

July 1, 1979

Assets

Current Assets	
Subscriptions Receivable—Common Stock	$ 42,000.00

Stockholders' Equity

Paid-in Capital	
Common Stock, $100 par value; authorized 6,000 shares, issued 5,000 shares	$500,000.00
Common Stock, subscribed but not issued, 1,000 shares	100,000.00
Premium on Common Stock	30,000.00

September 1, 1979

Stockholders' Equity

Paid-in Capital	
Common Stock, $100 par value; authorized and issued 6,000 shares	$600,000.00
Premium on Common Stock	30,000.00

If preferred stock is issued in addition to common stock, special accounts would be opened as required for Subscriptions Receivable—Preferred Stock, Preferred Stock Subscribed, and Premium on Preferred Stock.

Depending on the statutes of the state of incorporation, a defaulting subscriber may (1) forfeit the amounts paid in, (2) forfeit only the loss resulting from the resale of the shares, or (3) receive the number of shares that could have been purchased for the amounts paid in.

Donations

Cities and towns will often make tax concessions and local organizations will donate land, buildings, or other facilities to entice a corporation to establish itself in the area. Sometimes donations of assets or stock are made by the stockholders of a company in financial difficulties to enable it to raise funds. A gift or donation to a corporation increases the assets and the stockholders' equity and is credited to Paid-In Capital—Donations. A contribution of land and buildings by a town to a newly established firm is recorded by the receiving corporation at the fair market value of the assets contributed as shown below (the fair market values are assumed).

1979						
Oct.	4	Land	80,000	00		
		Buildings	20,000	00		
		Paid-in Capital-Donations			100,000	00
		To record, at fair market value, the land and buildings contributed by the Town of Lee.				

Accounts for recording capital—summary

Figures 17–2 and 17–3 present a summary of the accounts for recording capital in each of the three major forms of business. The basic concept of total ownership equity is the same in all forms; the difference is in detail provided. A single proprietorship needs only a single capital account for the owner, but a partnership requires a separate capital account for each owner. In a corporation, the total ownership equity is divided into accounts that show where the capital came from —a requirement of law in most states.

Figure 17–2 Accounts for recording capital

Proprietorship-Accounting for Owner's Equity

Name of Proprietor, Capital	
1. Withdrawals of permanent capital are recorded as debits. 2. A Drawing account debit balance is closed into this account at the end of the period. 3. Any loss for the period is recorded as a debit.	1. The original investment is recorded as a credit. 2. Additional permanent investments are also credited to this account. 3. The net income for the period is recorded as a credit.

Name of Proprietor, Drawing	
Withdrawals in anticipation of profits earned during the period are debited to this account.	Drawing account balance is closed to the proprietor's capital account.

Partnership-Accounting for Partners' Equity

Name of Partner, Capital (separate account for each partner)	
1. Withdrawals of permanent capital are recorded as debits. 2. A Drawing account debit balance is closed into this account at the end of the period. 3. Each partner's share of any loss for the period is recorded as a debit.	1. The original investment is recorded as a credit. 2. Additional permanent investments are also credited to this account. 3. Each partner's share of income is recorded as a credit.

Name of Partner, Drawing (separate account for each partner)	
Withdrawals in anticipation of profits earned during the period are debited to this account.	Drawing account balance is closed to partner's capital account.

After the partnership closing entries have been posted, each Capital account normally has a credit balance showing the partner's equity in the net assets of the firm. A debit balance indicates a deficiency. An additional investment must be made by the partner to provide for the cumulative excess of withdrawals and losses over investments and profits.

Capital Stock	
	Credited with the par or stated value of the stock issued.

Premium on Capital Stock	
	Credited for the excess of the issuing price over the par value of stock.

Dividends	
Debited when dividends are declared.	Credited when this account is closed annually into Retained Earnings.

Retained Earnings	
1. Debited when the Dividends account is closed. 2. Debited with total amount of net losses.	Credited with total amounts or after-tax net income.

Figure 17–3 Corporation— equity accounts

Glossary

Common stock If a corporation issues only one class of stock, then all shares are treated alike, and, there being no preferences, that class of stock is called common stock. If more than one class of stock is issued, common stock represents the residual and proportionate class of ownership.

Donated capital Increases in stockholders' equity resulting from gifts of assets or stock made to the corporation.

Excess over par or stated value That part of the capital paid in by stockholders that is not credited to the capital stock accounts.

Legal capital The minimum amount of capital that must be left in the corporation for the protection of creditors, and which cannot be withdrawn by the stockholders.

Liquidation value The specified price per share to be paid to preferred shareholders upon voluntary or involuntary liquidation of a corporation.

Market value The amount that a share of stock will bring the seller if the stock is offered for sale.

No-par value stock Stock without an indicated par value.

Paid-in capital Amounts invested by stockholders and gifts by donors.

Par-value The nominal or face value printed on a stock certificate representing the minimum amount to be paid to the issuing corporation by the original purchaser.

Preferred stock A class of capital stock having preferences as to dividends and as to assets upon liquidation.

Premium on capital stock The amount in excess of par value received by the issuing corporation for its stock.

Stated capital See legal capital.

Stated value The value assigned to each share of no-par stock by the directors of the corporation.

Stock certificate A printed or engraved serially numbered document issued to the stock purchaser as evidence of ownership of the stated number of shares of capital stock of the issuing corporation.

Stock subscription A pledge to buy capital stock with payment to be made later in a single lump sum or in installments.

Unrealized capital The difference between the aggregate market value and the aggregate cost of the investment in long-term securities recognized at the end of the accounting period.

Questions

Q17–1 (a) What books and records do corporations have that are not necessary for single proprietorships or partnerships? (b) What is meant by the following terms: authorized capital stock, stock certificate, share of stock, par value stock, no-par value stock?

Q17–2 What is meant by (a) preferred stock? (b) common stock? (c) stockholders' equity? (d) retained earnings?

Q17–3 Distinguish between authorized and unissued stock and issued and outstanding stock.

Q17–4 Student A says that if he were buying stock, he would purchase only stock having a par value. Student B takes the opposite viewpoint. Discuss.

Q17–5 What is legal capital? How is it determined? How does it differ from paid-in capital? retained earnings? stockholders' equity? Why should the state of incorporation regulate the amount that may be distributed to stockholders in the form of dividends?

Q17–6 Student A says that Subscriptions Receivable is a current asset; student B argues that the account belongs in the Stockholders' Equity section. Discuss.

Q17–7 Define and give the significance of each of the following terms: (a) par value of stock; (b) market value of stock; (c) preferred stock; (d) corporation.

Class exercises

CE17–1 (Recording capital stock issuance; stockholders' equity) The Eduardo Company was organized on July 1, 1979, with authority to issue 50,000 shares of $50 par value preferred stock and 30,000 shares of no-par value, $15 stated-value common stock. The following transactions occurred during the year.

1979

July 2 Issued for cash 24,000 shares of preferred stock at $51 a share.

10 Issued for cash 16,000 shares of common stock at $20 a share.

16 Issued for cash 4,000 shares of preferred stock at $50 a share.

20 Received subscriptions for 8,000 shares of common stock at $17 a share with a down payment of 50 percent and the balance due on September 30.

31 Received subscriptions for 12,000 shares of preferred stock at $51 a share; one-half the price was received on subscription, with the remainder due on September 30.

Aug. 2 Issued 100 shares of preferred stock to an attorney in payment for services, valued at $5,000, rendered in organizing the corporation.

Sept. 15 Issued 2,000 shares of common stock in exchange for land and a building appraised at $12,000 and $35,000 respectively.

30 Collected the installment due on the subscriptions of July 20 and July 31.

30 Net income from operations, after income taxes, for the period July 1 to September 30 was $50,000 (debit Other Assets).

Required:

1. Record the transactions in appropriate ledger accounts.
2. Prepare the Stockholders' Equity section of the balance sheet as of September 30, 1979.

CE17–2 (Recording stock subscriptions) The Lincoln Corporation was authorized to issue 20,000 shares of no-par value common stock and 20,000 shares of $20 par value preferred stock. Organizers of the corporation received 3,000 shares of the no-par value common stock for services valued at $8,500. A total of 3,000 shares of the preferred stock was issued for cash at $20 a share, and 3,000 shares of common stock were issued for cash at $5 a share. A total of 4,000 shares of preferred stock was subscribed at $22 a share. One-half the subscribers paid in full.

Required: (a) Record the transactions in ledger accounts. (b) Prepare a balance sheet.

CE17–3 (Recording stock issuance) The China Corporation was authorized to issue 5,000 shares of common stock.

Required: Record the issue of 4,000 shares at $7.25 a share assuming (a) that the shares have a $5 par value; (b) that the shares have no-par and no stated value; (c) that the shares have a stated value of $3.

CE17–4 (Stockholders' equity section) On December 31, 1979 the ledger of the Ryder Company included the following accounts:

Notes Receivable	$ 15,000
Merchandise Inventory	75,000
Marketable Securities—U.S. Government Bonds	8,000
Common Stock ($100 par value)	300,000
Retained Earnings	100,000
Subscriptions Receivable—Common Stock	40,000
Preferred Stock ($10 par value)	150,000
Goodwill	30,000
Common Stock Subscribed	150,000
Organization Costs	20,000
Premium on Preferred Stock	12,000
Building	225,000
Premium on Common Stock	30,000
Notes Receivable Discounted (*Hint:* A contra to Notes Receivable)	7,000
Cash	90,000
Research and Development Costs	110,000

Required: Prepare the Stockholders' Equity section of the balance sheet as of December 31, 1979.

Exercises and problems

P17–1 The following selected transactions occurred at the newly formed Lev Corporation:

1979

July	2	Received a charter authorizing the issuance of 5,000 shares of $50 par value preferred stock and 50,000 shares of no-par value common stock with a stated value of $5 per share.
	3	Issued 25,000 shares of common stock at $10 per share for cash.
	3	Issued 500 shares of common stock to an incorporator for a patent that had been perfected.
	5	Received subscriptions from four investors for 250 shares each of preferred stock at $52.50.
	5	Received 60 percent down payments on the subscriptions from all four subscribers.
	20	Received payment in full from all of the preferred subscribers, and issued the stock.
Aug.	10	Received a subscription from Ralph Leahy for 500 shares of the preferred stock at $50 a share.
	10	Collected 60 percent of Leahy's subscription total. The balance is due on September 1, 1979.

Required: Record the transactions in general journal form.

P17–2 The Lexington Corporation acquired the plant and equipment of the Mayo Company in exchange for 20,000 shares of its $25 par value common stock.

Required: Record the acquisition, assuming that if the assets had been acquired for cash, the purchase price would have been (a) $525,000; (b) $500,000.

P17–3 The Peck Corporation is authorized to issue 15,000 shares of $50 par value common stock. The following transactions occurred:

1. Issued for cash 3,000 shares at par value.
2. Issued 100 shares to the promotors for services valued at $5,000.
3. Issued 100 shares to attorneys for services, valued at $5,000, in organizing the corporation and securing the corporate charter.
4. Issued 1,800 shares in exchange for a factory building and land valued at $85,000 and $12,000 respectively.
5. Issued for cash 1,500 shares at $50 a share.
6. Issued for cash 3,000 shares at $60 a share.

Required: Record the transactions in general journal form.

P17–4 The Zavod Corporation was authorized to issue 30,000 shares of no-par value common stock with a $20 stated value and 10,000 shares of 10 percent preferred stock, $100 par value. At the end of one year of operations, the Zavod Corporation's trial balance included the following account balances:

Preferred Stock	$660,000
Common Stock	440,000
Subscriptions Receivable—Common	106,000
Subscriptions Receivable—Preferred	275,000
Preferred Stock Subscribed	330,000
Common Stock Subscribed	165,000
Premium on Common Stock	77,000

Required: How much cash has been collected from the stock transactions?

P17–5 The 1979 annual report of Polaris Company includes the following note to its financial statements:

During the year the stockholders approved a change in the authorized capital stock of the company from 15,000 shares, $100 par value preferred stock to 500,000 shares, no-par value, and from 2,000,000 shares, $1 par value common stock to 3,000,000 shares, $1 par value common stock.

Required: (a) What was the effect of these changes on the company's financial statements? (b) What was the purpose of the changes?

P17–6 (Integrative) The Isaacs Corporation was organized on January 2, 1979, with authority to issue 10,000 shares of $100 par value common stock. The following transactions occurred during the year:

1979		
Jan.	10	Issued for cash 150 shares at $102 per share.
Feb.	19	Issued for cash 150 shares at $100 per share.
Mar.	1	Issued 2,000 shares for land and a building with a fair market value of $200,000. One-eighth the total valuation was allocable to the land.
June	1	Received subscriptions for 1,000 shares at $104 per share, payable 40 percent down and the balance in two equal installments due on August 2 and October 2.
	11	Paid $5,000 for legal fees incurred in organizing the corporation.
July	5	Purchased equipment for $60,000 in cash.
Aug.	2	Received the installment due on the subscription of June 1.
Oct.	2	Received the installment due on the subscription of June 1.

Dec. 15 Received subscriptions for 1,000 shares at $100 a share payable 40 percent down and the balance in two equal installments due on February 15, 1980, and April 15, 1980.

31 Recorded the following entry, summarizing the net effects of the results of operations before income taxes for the year:

1979				
Dec.	31	Cash	35,000 00	
		Accumulated Depreciation—Building		6,000 00
		Accumulated Depreciation—Equipment		3,000 00
		Income Summary		26,000 00

31 Recorded the income tax liability of $4,500.

31 Closed the Income Summary account.

Required:

1. Record the transactions in appropriate ledger accounts.
2. Prepare a balance sheet as of December 31, 1979.

P17–7 (Minicase) James Irwin and Enid Joel, equal partners in a plastics manufacturing company, wish to expand their production facilities. They plan to dissolve the partnership and to transfer all partnership assets and liabilities to a newly formed corporation authorized to issue 100,000 shares of $5 par value voting common stock and 1,000 shares of $100 par value, 8 percent nonvoting preferred stock.

The accounts of the partnership at the time of the transfer to the corporation, to be called Irnid Corp., Inc. are:

Cash	$ 5,500	
Accounts Receivable	12,400	
Allowance for Doubtful Accounts		$ 860
Merchandise Inventory	20,000	
Prepaid Expenses	1,000	
Land	10,000	
Building (net)	58,000	
Equipment (net)	30,000	
Accounts Payable		20,000
Accrued Liabilities		1,040
James Irwin, Capital		57,500
Enid Joel, Capital		57,500
	$136,900	$136,900

The following transactions occurred immediately following incorporation:

1. Each partner was issued common stock at par in amounts equal to his partnership interests.
2. Issued 40 shares of preferred stock at $103 a share for cash.
3. Issued 15,000 shares of common at $5.50 a share for cash.
4. Cash payments were made for incorporation fees, $500, legal services in forming the corporation, $750, and printing costs for the stock certificates, $250.

Required:

1. Record the transactions on the books of the corporation (the partnership books are used).
2. Prepare a balance sheet.
3. What did Irwin and Joel gain by incorporating their partnership? What did they sacrifice?

chapter eighteen

Introduction

In this chapter the discussion of the various sources of stockholders' equity is continued. Emphasis is placed on the importance of retained earnings, dividends, and treasury stock and on the methods used to record them. The meaning and computation of book value is discussed. At the end of the chapter there is a complete illustration of the stockholders' equity section of the balance sheet with an explanation of each major item.

Corporations: retained earnings, dividends, and treasury stock

Learning goals

To increase the depth of knowledge of paid-in capital.
To understand in detail the total owners' (stockholders') equity section of a corporation.
To understand the nature of retained earnings and dividends.
To record transactions involving cash dividends and stock dividends.
To understand and account for stock splits.
To record treasury stock transactions.
To compute book value.
To prepare *in good form* the stockholders' equity section of the balance sheet.

Key terms

arrearage
book value
cumulative, noncumulative
deficit
dividend
participating, nonparticipating
retained earnings
retained earnings, restricted
stock dividend
stock split
treasury stock

Retained earnings

Undistributed earnings arising from profitable operations are known as *retained earnings*. These are sources of stockholders' equity other than transactions involving the company's own stock. Such terms as *earned surplus, retained income, accumulated earnings,* and *earnings retained for use in the business* are also used to designate the earnings that have not been distributed to the stockholders as dividends. If cumulative losses and dividend distributions exceed earnings, the Retained Earnings account will have a debit balance and will be shown in the balance sheet as a deduction from stockholders' equity under the caption *Deficit*.

Retained earnings—restricted

The creation of special Restricted Retained Earnings accounts indicates that a portion of the earnings of the corporation is not available for dividends. This does not mean that a special cash fund has been set up, nor does the restriction provide cash funds. The restrictions do not in any way alter the total retained earnings or the total stockholders' equity. The segregation of retained earnings is an accounting device by which a corporation, following a resolution of the board of directors, intentionally reduces the amount of earnings available for dividend distributions, thus indicating its intention to conserve corporate assets for other purposes. The restriction of retained earnings does not reduce the overall retained earnings but merely earmarks a portion of the earnings in an account specifically designated to indicate its purpose. The same information can be communicated by a footnote or by a parenthetical notation.

Each restricted account, although separated from the parent Retained Earnings account, is nevertheless a part of retained earnings and is so classified in the Stockholders' Equity section of the balance sheet. When the special account has served its purpose and the requirement for which it was set up no longer exists, the amount in the restricted account is transferred back into the Retained Earnings account.

Restrictions may be either voluntary or involuntary. A restriction for plant expansion, for example, may be set up by voluntary action of the board of directors. The purpose of this restriction is to show management's intention to retain cash or other assets for use in connection with a projected plant expansion program rather than to distribute them in the form of dividends. When cash dividends are paid, the assets of the corporation are depleted. To the degree, then, that dividend declarations are restricted, assets are retained for other business purposes such as plant expansion. Involuntary restrictions may be required either by state statute, covered later in this chapter, or by contract. When a corporation enters into an agreement for a long-term loan, the terms of the contract may require periodic restrictions of retained earnings, accumulating over the term of the loan to an amount equal to the loan. The purpose of the restriction is to reduce the amount of cash earnings that might otherwise be distributed to the stockholders as dividends, and to improve the corporation's ability to make periodic interest payments and any other payments required under the terms of the loan. The journal entry to record this type of restriction is a debit to Retained Earnings and a credit to Retained Earnings—Restricted for Long-Term Loan Retirement. This entry is reversed whenever its intended purpose has been accomplished and continuance of the restriction is no longer necessary.

Dividends

The term *dividend* refers to the distribution of cash, stock, or other corporate property by a corporation to the stockholders. A dividend must be declared formally by the board of directors, a record of which should be entered in the *minute book* (a record of the minutes of meetings of the board of directors); the entry should indicate the date the dividend was declared, the record date to determine the eligibility of stockholders of record on that date, and the date of the payment. For a cash dividend distribution to be made, there must be accumulated unrestricted retained earnings and there must be assets available for distribution. If there are no accumulated earnings, the dividend becomes a reduction in paid-in capital, which may be illegal. There may be adequate earnings but insufficient cash or other readily distributable type of assets. A corporation may have a good earnings record but no cash available for dividends because the cash may have been used to acquire other assets (land, buildings, machinery, or inventory), or funds are being accumulated for an anticipated expansion program or other corporate needs. Only the board of directors has the authority to determine whether a dividend is to be paid, to which classes of stock it is to be paid, and the time, manner, and form of payment. This applies to all classes of stockholders, preferred and common.

There have been court cases in which stockholders have attempted to force a dividend declaration that they felt was being deliberately withheld by the board of directors. Except in rare instances, courts have been reluctant to interpose and order dividend payments. Once formal action has been taken by the board, however, the declaration immediately becomes a current liability of the corporation. The state corporation laws contain dividend provisions that must be observed by the board of directors. It is customary, for example, particularly for larger corporations with numerous stockholders, to make a public announcement of the dividend declaration in newspapers or magazines.

The term dividend is most often used to designate a cash distribution. A dividend may be paid in property other than cash; a company may, for example, distribute marketable securities or merchandise. A well-known distillery once declared a dividend and made a pro rata distribution of whiskey late in December. The term stock dividend is used to designate the distribution of additional shares of stock to existing stockholders. The term *liquidating dividend* refers to a distribution of assets by a company being liquidated, or a distribution whose effect is to reduce the stockholders' equity from paid-in capital. Thus, a liquidating dividend is a distribution of paid-in capital when there are no accumulated retained earnings or when a deficit exists. The term ex-dividend indicates that the quoted price of the shares does not include a dividend declared and payable on a specified future date to shareholders of record as of a specified date prior to the payment date.

Declaration of a dividend

The dividend may be stated as a percent of par or as a specified amount per share. Following is a typical dividend note:

National Ore Company

60 Rockefeller Plaza, New York, N.Y.

Dividend No. 310

The Board of Directors has today declared a regular quarterly dividend at the rate of forty seven and one-half cents ($47\frac{1}{2}$¢) per share on the Common Stock of this Company, payable January 15, 1980 to stockholders of record at the close of business December 31, 1979.

J. V. Couches
Secretary

December 14, 1979

The holder of 100 shares of common stock of the National Ore Company will be mailed a check for $47.50 on January 15, 1980. An investor who buys the stock in time to be recorded as its owner by December 31, 1979, the record date, will receive the dividend. An investor who buys stock of this company too late to be recorded as owner by the record date is said to buy the stock ex-dividend—that is, without the right to receive the latest declared dividend. Stock traded on the stock exchanges is quoted ex-dividend typically three days prior to the record date to allow time for the recording and delivery of the securities. During the interval between December 31, 1979 and January 15, 1980 the company prepares the list of eligible stockholders and performs all other tasks incident to the mailing of the dividend checks.

The Dividends account is debited each time a dividend is declared. If the Foxx Corporation had 10,000 shares of stock outstanding and declared its regular quarterly dividend of 30 cents a share on January 7, payable on January 28, this quarter would be recorded as follows:

Date		Account	Debit		Credit	
1979						
Jan.	7	Dividends	3,000	00		
		Dividends Payable			3,000	00
		To record the declaration of a 30 cents a share cash dividend on 10,000 shares of common stock outstanding.				
	28	Dividends Payable	3,000	00		
		Cash			3,000	00
		To record payment of the dividend declaration on January 7.				

At the end of the year the Dividends account would contain a debit balance of $12,000 (four quarterly entries). Since it is a temporary account that serves the purpose of reducing stockholders' equity similar to the Drawing accounts in single proprietorships and partnerships, it is closed into a permanent stockholders' equity account at the end of the year. For the Foxx Company such an entry would be:

1979						
Dec.	31	Retained Earnings	12,000	00		
		Dividends			12,000	00
		To close the Dividends account.				

Although some prefer to debit Retained Earnings to record a dividend declaration, the use of a Dividends account has the advantage of segregating dividends declared during the year; it also keeps Retained Earnings clear of charges that would require analysis at the end of the year when the statement of retained earnings is prepared. The Dividends account is a temporary stockholders' equity account; it has a debit balance and represents a reduction in the stockholders' equity. It is shown on the statement of retained earnings as a deduction from the total of the beginning balance of Retained Earnings plus net income and other credits to Retained Earnings. Dividends Payable, on either common or preferred stock, is a current liability.

Dividends on preferred stock

As mentioned in Chapter 17, preferred stock enjoys certain dividend preferences. The right to a dividend of a preferred stockholder must await a formal declaration by the board of directors. On declaration, the preferred stockholders are entitled to a stated amount per share before any dividend distribution is made to holders of common stock.

If the preferred stock is *cumulative,* undeclared dividends are accumulated and must be paid and the current dividend on preferred must be paid before any dividend payment is made on common stock. These dividends not declared in past periods on cumulative preferred stock are referred to as a *dividend arrearage*. If the preferred stock is *noncumulative,* a dividend passed (not formally declared by the board of directors) in any one year is lost. Preferred stock, whether cumulative or noncumulative, may be either *participating* or *nonparticipating*.

If the preferred stock is participating, it receives its specified dividend and a share of any additional dividends declared. The manner of determining the amount of the additional dividend depends on the terms of the stock contract. If the preferred stock is *fully participating,* it participates on a pro rata basis at the same rate based on par value with the common stock in dividend distributions after the common stock has received an amount equal to the stipulated preference rate on the preferred stock. *The participation may be limited* in the stock contract to a specified rate or amount per share. If the preferred stock is nonparticipating, it receives the stipulated rate only, and the balance of the dividend distribution, irrespective of amount, is paid to the common stockholders. Most preferred stock issues are cumulative and nonparticipating.

The following example illustrates the application of the dividend preference of cumulative and nonparticipating preferred stock.

A corporation has outstanding 1,000 shares of 5 percent cumulative nonparticipating preferred stock and 2,000 shares of common stock, each with a par value of $100. Undistributed earnings are $75,000, there is a dividend arrearage of $5,000, and a $32,000 dividend is declared. The required journal entry for the dividend declaration is:

Date		Account		Debit	Credit
1979					
May	10	Dividends—Preferred Stock		10,000 00	
		Dividends—Common Stock		22,000 00	
		Dividends Payable—Preferred Stock			10,000 00
		Dividends Payable—Common Stock			22,000 00
		To record dividend declaration distributed as follows:			
		To preferred stock:			
		Arrearage	$ 5,000.00		
		Current year's preference dividend	5,000.00		
		To preferred	$10,000.00		
		To common stock:			
		Remainder	22,000.00		
		Total distribution	$32,000.00		

If we assume the same facts except that the preferred stock is cumulative and fully participating—that is, the preferred stock shares at an equal rate with the common stock in the amount distributed in excess of the 5 percent preferred dividend and a comparable dividend on the common stock, the distribution of the $32,000 would be:

	To Preferred	*To Common*
Arrearage	$ 5,000.00	
Current rate at 5%, or $5 per share:		
To preferred stock: 1,000 shares × $5	5,000.00	
To common stock: 2,000 shares × $5		$10,000.00
Participation at 4%*, or $4 per share:		
To preferred stock: 1,000 shares × $4	4,000.00	
To common stock: 2,000 shares × $4		8,000.00
Total distribution	$14,000.00	$18,000.00

$$* \quad \frac{\$32{,}000.00 - \$20{,}000.00}{\text{Total par value of preferred and common of } \$300{,}000.00} = 4\%$$

If we now assume that the preferred is cumulative except that it participates to a maximum of 2 percent, or $2 a share above its preference rate, the distribution is:

	To Preferred	To Common
Arrearage	$ 5,000.00	
Current rate to preferred and common	5,000.00	$10,000.00
Participation:		
Preferred stock: 1,000 shares × $2	2,000.00	
Common stock: remainder		10,000.00
Total distribution	$12,000.00	$20,000.00

Preferred stock may also be preferred in distributing assets; this means that if the corporation is liquidated, the preferred stockholders must be paid before any liquidating payments are made to the common stockholders. The manner of the preference application depends on the wording in the stock contract. The preference may be for the par value of the preferred stock, the par value and accumulated dividends, or some other stipulated amount. If the preferred stock is not preferred as to assets, then the assets are usually distributed to all classes of stockholders on an equal basis proportionate to the respective par values.

Stock dividends

The term *stock dividend* refers to the issuance by a corporation of additional shares of its authorized stock without additional payment of any kind by the stockholders. There are various occasions for the declaration of a stock dividend, such as:

A large unappropriated retained earnings balance
A desire by the directors to reduce the market price of the stock
A desire to increase the permanent capitalization of the company by converting a portion of the retained earnings into capital stock
A need to conserve available cash.

A stock dividend does not change the total stockholders' equity in the corporation; it simply transfers some retained earnings to paid-in capital. A cash dividend, on the other hand, decreases both the assets and the stockholders' equity. A stock dividend has no effect on either total assets or total stockholders' equity; the change is entirely within the Stockholders' Equity section (Retained Earnings decreases and Paid-In Capital increases). To illustrate, assume that the Truro Corporation, with $500,000 common stock, $100 par value, outstanding, and retained earnings of $80,000 declares a $50,000 stock dividend. The effect of the declaration on the stockholders' equity is shown below.

	Stockholders' Equity		
	Immediately before Declaration	*Immediately after Declaration*	*Immediately after Stock Issuance*
Stockholders' equity:			
Common stock,			
$100 par value	$500,000.00	$500,000.00	$550,000.00
Stock dividends			
to be issued		50,000.00	
Retained earnings	80,000.00	30,000.00	30,000.00
Total stockholders'			
equity	$580,000.00	$580,000.00	$580,000.00

The Stock Dividends to be Issued account is part of the stockholders' equity. It is not a liability, because its reduction will result not in a reduction of a current asset but rather in an increase in capital stock. The account should therefore be shown after Capital Stock in the Stockholders' Equity section of the balance sheet.

It is evident that a stock dividend has no effect on the total stockholders' equity; the relative interest of each stockholder is, therefore, unchanged. For example, John Green, a stockholder with 100 shares before the stock dividend, will have 110 shares after the stock dividend. His proportionate holdings remain unchanged at 2 percent of the total stock outstanding. Hence, all his rights and privileges are unaltered, as shown below.

	Line	*Before Declaration*	*After Declaration*
Total stockholders' equity	1	$580,000.00	$580,000.00
Number of shares outstanding	2	5,000	5,500
Stockholders' equity per share			
(line 1 ÷ line 2)	3	$ 116.00	$ 105.45
Shares owned by John Green	4	100	110
Green's equity (line 4 × line 3)	5	$ 11,600.00	$ 11,600.00

A stock dividend, nevertheless, is significant to the stockholder. The dividend does not alter the recipient's equity in the company and is not, therefore, considered income. There is no income tax on a stock dividend. If the stock dividend does not cause a significant decline in the price of stock, the stockholder's gain is equal to the market value of the new shares received. If, in addition, the corporation does not reduce the amount of its cash dividends per share, the stockholder gains the dividends on the additional shares. It is this aspect—the expectation of greater dividends as well as the availability of more shares for possible ultimate profitable resale—that creates a favorable reception for a stock dividend.

A stock dividend provides certain advantages to the corporation. Its earnings are capitalized (that is, retained earnings are transferred to capital stock accounts), there is no reduction in assets, and the corporation may plow back its earnings for expansion or other purposes. The corporation also may wish to reduce the market price of its shares in order to attract more buyers; by issuance of more shares, the price per share will decrease. At the same time, a stock dividend makes possible larger total dividend distributions without a change in the regular dividend rate.

When there are two classes of stockholders, the stock dividend normally applies only to the common stockholders. Payment, however, may be in either preferred or common stock. The various court rulings are not consistent with respect to the rights of preferred stockholders to participate in a stock dividend, although generally preferred stockholders have no such rights.

Recording small stock dividends The AICPA has recommended that for *small dividends*—those involving the issuance of less than 20 or 25 percent of the number of shares previously outstanding—the corporation should transfer from retained earnings to capital stock and other paid-in capital accounts "an amount equal to the fair value of the additional shares issued."[1]

To illustrate, assume that the market value of the stock dividend shares issued by the Truro Corporation in the previous example was $60,000 = (500 shares at $120 a share) and that the board of directors, in authorizing the stock dividend, directed that the dividend be recorded at market value. The entries to record the declaration and stock issuance are:

			Debit	Credit
1979				
May	1	Stock Dividends		
		(or Retained Earnings)	60,000 00	
		Stock Dividends To Be Issued . .		50,000 00
		Paid-in Capital-Excess of Par		
		Value on Stock Dividends . . .		10,000 00
		To record declaration of stock dividend.		
	15	Stock Dividends To Be Issued	50,000 00	
		Common Stock		50,000 00
		To record issuance of stock dividend.		

If the account Stock Dividends is used, it would be closed to Retained Earnings at the end of the year.

The rationale with respect to small stock dividends is that since the market value of the shares previously held remains substantially unchanged and since "many recipients of stock dividends look upon them as distributions of corporate earnings and usually in an amount equivalent to the fair value of the additional shares issued"[2]—that is, as a cash dividend—the accounting should be such as to show the amount of retained earnings available for future dividend distribution.

1 "Restatement and Revision of Accounting Research Bulletins," *Accounting Research Bulletin* No. 43, Chapter 7, Section B, par. 10.

2 *Accounting Research Bulletin* No. 43, Chapter 7, Section B, par 10.

Recording large stock dividends For *large stock dividends*—those involving the issuance of more than 25 percent of the number of shares previously outstanding—the AICPA recommends that "there is no need to capitalize retained earnings other than to the extent occasioned by legal requirements."[3] This means that for large stock dividends, the amount of retained earnings capitalized (transferred to paid-in capital) is represented by the par or stated value of the shares issued. To illustrate, assume that the Truro Corporation has sufficient retained earnings and declares a stock dividend of 2,500 shares, or 50 percent of the 5,000 shares previously outstanding. The entry to record the stock issuance is shown below.

Date		Account	Debit		Credit	
1979						
May	1	Stock Dividends				
		(or Retained Earnings)	250,000	00		
		Common Stock			250,000	00
		To record the issuance of 2,500 shares of additional common stock as a stock dividend.				

The rationale with respect to large stock dividends is that the effect is to reduce materially the share market value, and the transaction is "a split-up effected in the form of a dividend." There is, therefore, no need to capitalize retained earnings beyond the legal requirements.

Stock split

A corporation may wish to reduce the par value of its stock, or it may desire to reduce the price at which the stock is being issued to make it more salable. This is accomplished by a *stock split,* whereby the shares outstanding are increased and the par or stated value per share is reduced. The total par or stated value of the outstanding shares remains the same. No journal entries are required, and there is no change in retained earnings. The capital stock ledger account headings are changed to show the new par or stated value per share and the subsidiary stockholders' ledger is revised to show the new distribution of shares.

Assume, for example, that a corporation has outstanding 100,000 shares of $50 par value common stock. The current market price of the stock is $175 a share. The corporation, wishing to reduce this high market price to create a broader market for a forthcoming additional stock issue, reduces the par value from $50 to $25 and increases the number of shares from 100,000 to 200,000. This is called a "2-for-1 split-up," because the number of shares owned by each shareholder is doubled. The split in shares may be accomplished by calling in all the old shares and issuing certificates for new shares on a 2-for-1 basis or by issuing an additional share for each old share previously owned. This action is

3 *Accounting Research Bulletin* No. 43, Chapter 7, Section B, par. 11.

recorded either by a memorandum notation in the capital stock account or by the following journal entry:

1979				
Dec.	1	Common Stock, $50 par value	5,000,000 00	
		Common Stock, $25 par value		5,000,000 00
		To record a 2-for-1 split-up, increasing the number of outstanding shares from 100,000 to 200,000 and reducing par value from $50 to $25.		

It may be assumed that the market price of the shares will now be reduced sufficiently to enhance the marketability of the new issue.

Both stock dividends and stock splits change the number of shares outstanding without changing the pro rata share of ownership of each stockholder or total stockholders' equity. A stock dividend, unlike a stock split, requires a transfer from Retained Earnings to Paid-in Capital, and increases the capital stock account by the par or stated value of the dividend shares. A stock split, unlike a stock dividend, changes the par or stated value of the capital stock without changing the dollar balances of any accounts.

Treasury stock

A corporation may repurchase some of its own stock, preferred or common, or receive it as a donation, exchange, or settlement of a debt. Such stock is known as *treasury stock*. Treasury stock, if it has been fully paid for originally, may be issued at a price below par or stated value without the assumption of a contingent discount liability by the purchaser of discount stock to the corporation's creditors for the amount of the discount. Treasury stock does not fall into the category of new issues; it is the corporation's own stock that has been issued and later reacquired. While being held in the treasury, it is issued but not outstanding stock and therefore does not have voting or dividend rights.

A corporation may purchase some of its own stock, at or below the market price, to bolster a sagging market or to meet the needs under a plan whereby the company's own stock is distributed to its employees in place of other compensation. Sometimes the stock is purchased because it is available at a favorable price. Acquisition of treasury stock has the effect of reducing the assets and the stockholders' equity. The Treasury Stock account, therefore, should appear in the Stockholders' Equity section as a deduction from total stockholders' equity. Since the acquisition of treasury stock results in a distribution of corporate assets to stockholders, some states have enacted restrictive provisions pertaining to this kind of acquisition to protect the corporate creditors. The restrictive provisions vary widely. Some require a restriction of retained earnings to the extent of the disbursement for the treasury stock. If a corporation faces financial difficulties, certain influential stockholders could have the corporation buy back their shares, thereby reducing the amount available for the creditors and other stockholders.

Recording the purchase of treasury stock

When a corporation reacquires by purchase shares of its own stock, the Treasury Stock account is debited for the cost of shares acquired—not at par value as some theorists prefer—because it is simple and is the method used most frequently in practice. To illustrate, assume that the Lee Corporation reacquires twenty shares of its own stock at $55 a share. The entry is as shown below.

Date		Account	Debit		Credit	
1979						
Aug.	1	Treasury Stock—Common	1,100	00		
		Cash			1,100	00
		Purchased 20 shares of own stock at $55 a share.				

The purchase of the twenty shares of stock reduces cash by $1,100 and the stockholders' equity by $1,100. It also reduces the number of shares outstanding. It does not reduce the amount of issued stock, because the purchase of the shares is recorded not by a debit to Common Stock but by a debit to a special Treasury Stock account, which is shown in the Stockholders' Equity section as a deduction from Total Paid-In Capital and Retained Earnings.

Recording issuance of treasury stock—above cost

The reissuance of treasury stock is recorded by a credit to Treasury Stock for the cost of the shares. The difference between the cost and the issue price of treasury stock when it is issued above cost is credited to Paid-In Capital from Treasury Stock Transactions. To illustrate, assume that the Lee Corporation reissues five shares for $65 a share. The entry is shown below.

Date		Account	Debit		Credit	
1979						
Oct.	2	Cash	325	00		
		Treasury Stock—Common			275	00
		Paid-In Capital from Treasury Stock Transactions—Common . . .			50	00
		Reissued 5 shares of treasury stock at $65 a share.				

The Stockholders' Equity section of the Lee Corporation's balance sheet after the reissuance of the five shares is shown below (other amounts are assumed).

Stockholders' Equity	
Paid-in Capital	
Common Stock, $50 par value; authorized and issued 1,000 shares of which fifteen shares are held in treasury	$50,000.00
Premium on Common Stock	2,500.00
From Treasury Stock Transactions	50.00
Total Paid-In Capital	$52,550.00
Retained Earnings	20,000.00
Total Paid-In Capital and Retained Earnings	$72,550.00
Deduct Cost of Treasury Stock—Common	825.00
Total Stockholders' Equity	$71,725.00

Recording issuance of treasury stock below cost

The entry to record the issuance of treasury stock below cost depends on the existence of capital accounts that are not considered to be part of the stated capital. To illustrate, assume that the Lee Corporation issues another five shares of treasury stock (which cost $275) for $225. The difference of $50 is debited to Paid-In Capital from Treasury Stock Transactions, as follows:

1979				
Nov.	1	Cash	225 00	
		Paid-in Capital from Treasury Stock Transactions—Common	50 00	
		Treasury Stock—Common		275 00
		Reissued 5 shares of treasury stock at $45 each.		

If the negative difference on the issue of the shares exceeds the amount in Paid-in Capital from Treasury Stock Transactions—Common, the excess is debited to any other Paid-in Capital account arising from the original issuance of the same class of stock that is not a part of the stated capital (Excess over Par or Stated Value, for example). In the absence of such accounts, the difference between the cost and the selling price of the treasury stock is debited to Retained Earnings. To illustrate, assume that the Lee Corporation reissues the remaining ten shares at $50 per share. The entry to record the transaction is:

1979				
Nov.	30	Cash	500 00	
		Premium on Common Stock*	50 00	
		Treasury Stock		550 00
		Reissued the remaining ten shares of treasury stock at $50 per share.		

*If there had not been any paid-in capital in excess of stated capital, the debit would have been to Retained Earnings.

Recording treasury stock donations

One or more shareholders may donate a portion of their shares to the corporation for reissuance to raise needed cash. Shares acquired by donation do not affect the balance sheet, as there is no change in the assets, liabilities, or stockholders' equity. On acquisition, a memorandum is made in the Treasury Stock account indicating the date and the number of shares donated. When the shares are reissued, the proceeds are credited to Paid-in Capital—Donations.

Book value of capital stock

Book value represents the net assets per common share outstanding. The book value of a share of stock (or the stockholders' equity per share, assuming there is only one class of stock outstanding) is computed as follows:

	Line	Amount
Total stockholders' equity	1	$750,000.00
Number of shares outstanding	2	6,000
Book value per share (line 1 ÷ line 2)	3	$ 125.00

Book value

The term* book value *or book amount is used to indicate the equity per share based on net assets (assets minus liabilities), or stockholders' equity of the issuing corporation. The book value of a share of stock of any class is derived by dividing the total stockholders' equity applicable to that class by the number of shares of stock of that class issued and outstanding.

The stockholders' equity applicable to a given class of stock depends upon their respective claims against the assets in liquidation, not upon the amounts invested by each class of shareholders. The book value per share is the amount each stockholder would receive for each share held in the theoretical event of liquidation after the assets are sold without gain or loss. Since the valuations on the books—especially for inventories and plant equipment—do not necessarily reflect market conditions, the book value of a share of stock may be of little significance as an indicator of the resale value of the stock. When more than one class of stock is outstanding, it becomes necessary to determine the liquidation claims of each class against the net assets of the corporation. If, for example, the preferred stock is cumulative and nonparticipating and there are dividends in arrears, the stockholders' equity is divided between the two classes on the basis of the preferences accorded to the preferred stock in liquidation. Assume that a corporation has the following capital structure:

Common stock, $100 par value; issued 1,000 shares	$100,000.00
Preferred stock, 6%, $100 par value; cumulative, nonparticipating; issued 1,000 shares	100,000.00
Excess over stated value of no-par common stock	5,000.00
Retained earnings	45,000.00
Retained earnings—restricted for plant addition	10,000.00
Total stockholders' equity	$260,000.00

Dividends are in arrears for two years. The preferred shareholders have a claim on the assets in liquidation of an amount equal to par value plus any dividends in arrears.

The book value of a share of preferred stock at the end of the year is computed as follows:

Preferred stock, $100 par value; issued 1,000 shares	$100,000.00
Dividends in arrears (2 years × $6,000)	12,000.00
Total equity of preferred stockholders	$112,000.00
Number of shares outstanding	1,000
Book value per preferred share	$ 112.00

The book value of a share of common stock is computed as shown:

Total stockholders' equity	$260,000.00
Deduct equity of preferred stockholders	112,000.00
Total equity of common stockholders	$148,000.00
Number of shares outstanding	1,000
Book value per common share	$ 148.00

Earnings per share

For a company with a simple capital structure (the Dixon Corporation in Figure 18–3), earnings per share is derived by dividing net income by the weighted average of the number of common shares of stock outstanding during the year. Dividends payable to preferred stock shareholders must first be deducted from net income to get the earnings allocable to the common stock shareholders. For a company with a complex capital structure—one with bonds and preferred stock that are convertible into common stock—the calculation is quite complicated and is beyond the scope of this text.

Stockholders' equity

The Stockholders' Equity section of the Dixon Corporation's balance sheet as of December 31, 1979, and the income statement and statement of retained earnings for 1979 are shown in Figures 18–1, 18–2, and 18–3. Each item in the stockholders' equity statement is numbered and is discussed in the following paragraphs. Duplicate numbers are used for related items. Brief technical account titles may be used, for convenience, in journals and ledgers, because these records are for internal use only and the functions of the accounts are understood by the users. However, for external reporting, these account titles should be either replaced or supplemented by descriptive language to minimize possible misunderstanding by nontechnical readers of the statement. The nature and significance of the items should not be obscured by the use of jargon nor the absence of supporting detail.

1 On the date of its organization, the Dixon Corporation issued 2,000 shares of preferred stock at $105 per share. The total par value of these shares (2,000 × $100 = $200,000) is labeled Preferred Stock. This amount represents part of the legal, or stated, capital. The excess ($5 × 2,000) over the par value of the preferred stock is reported separately as Premium on Preferred Stock.

2 The Dixon Corporation also issued 5,000 shares of no-par value common stock at $60 per share. The stated value of the shares—originally $50 per share but reduced to $40 per share on December 31—multiplied by the number of shares issued ($40 × 5,000) is shown as Common Stock. The excess of the issue price ($60) over the original stated value ($50) multiplied by the number of shares issued ($10 × 5,000), not being part of the stated capital, is shown separately as

Figure 18–1
Income statement

DIXON CORPORATION
Income Statement
For the Year Ended December 31, 1979

Exhibit A

Sales		$1,300,000.00
Net Income		120,000.00
Earnings Per Share		$ 22.92

Earnings per share on common stock is calculated as follows:

Net income for 1979		$120,000.00
Deduct: Preferred dividend requirement—2,000 shares at $5 a share		10,000.00
Net income allocable to common stock		$110,000.00
Common Shares:		
Issued and outstanding (5,000–500)	4,500	
To be issued on stock subscribed	300	4,800
Earnings per share—Common Stock ($110,000/4,800)		$ 22.92

Paid-In Capital—Excess over Stated Value on Common Stock. The excess of the original stated value ($50) over the revised stated value ($40), multiplied by the number of shares issued ($10 × 5,000), is also entered separately, for the same reason; it is labeled Paid-In Capital—Excess from Reduction of Stated Value of 5,000 Shares of Common Stock from $50 to $40 per Share.

3 On July 10, the Dixon Corporation acquired 1,000 shares of its own common stock for $55 per share. On August 2, it sold 500 shares for $60 per share. The excess of the issue price over the cost is shown as Paid-In Capital from Treasury Stock Transactions—Common.

4 On July 10, the Dixon Corporation reacquired 1,000 shares of its own common stock for $55,000. The laws of the state in which it is incorporated limit the payment of dividends to the extent of the amount in the unrestricted Retained Earnings account. Since both the purchase of treasury stock and the declaration of a cash dividend reduce corporate assets and the stockholders' equity, the limitation applies equally to dividend payments and to treasury stock acquisitions. A company with free retained earnings of $25,000, for example, may either reacquire treasury stock or declare cash dividends, or do both, pro-

Figure 18–2
Statement of retained earnings

DIXON CORPORATION
Statement of Retained Earnings
For the Year Ended December 31, 1979

Exhibit B

Retained Earnings, January 1, 1979	$130,000.00
Net Income for 1979	120,000.00
Total	$250,000.00
Dividends	50,000.00
Retained Earnings, December 31, 1979	$200,000.00

Figure 18-3
Partial balance sheet—stockholders' equity

DIXON CORPORATION
Partial Balance Sheet
December 31, 1979

Exhibit C

	Stockholders' Equity		
	Paid-In Capital		
1	Preferred Stock, 5 percent cumulative, nonparticipating, $100 par value, authorized 2,500 shares; issued 2,000 shares	$200,000.00	
1	Premium on Preferred Stock	10,000.00	
	Total Paid in by Preferred Stockholders		$210,000.00
2	Common Stock, no par value, $40 stated value; authorized 7,000 shares, issued 5,000 shares of which 500 shares are held in treasury	$200,000.00	
2	Excess over Stated Value on Common Stock	50,000.00	
	Excess from Reduction of Stated Value of 5,000 Shares of Common Stock from $50 to $40 per share	50,000.00	
3	From Treasury Stock Transactions—Common	2,500.00	
5	Common Stock Subscribed but not Issued	12,000.00	
	Total Paid In by Common Stockholders		314,500.00
	Other Paid-In Capital		
7	Donation of Land by Town of Needham		50,000.00
	Total Paid-In Capital		$574,500.00
6	Retained Earnings:		
	Restricted:		
	For Treasury Stock Acquisitions	$ 27,500.00	
	For Anticipated Plant Expansion	45,000.00	
	Total Restricted	$ 72,500.00	
	Unrestricted	127,500.00	
	Total Retained Earnings		200,000.00
	Total		$774,500.00
4	Deduct Cost of Treasury Stock—Common		27,500.00
	Total Stockholders' Equity		$747,000.00

vided the total disbursement is not over $25,000. Such a restriction improves the protection of the corporate creditors. The treasury stock amount of $27,500 ($55,000 from the transaction of July 10 less $27,500 from the transaction of August 2) appears twice in the Stockholders' Equity section: (1) as a restriction of retained earnings and (2) as a reduction in the stockholders' equity resulting from a distribution of $27,500 in cash to the stockholders from whom the stock was acquired.

5 Subscriptions have been received from key employees under a stock option plan for 300 shares of common stock. Stock certificates will be issued on receipt of the uncollected portion of the subscription price as shown in the asset account Common Stock Subscriptions Receivable.

6 The Retained Earnings balance represents undistributed earnings from current and from prior years. $72,500 was restricted for specific purposes; and the remainder, $127,500, is unrestricted.
7 A building site with an estimated cash market value of $50,000 was donated by the town of Needham as an inducement to the Dixon Corporation to establish itself there. This gift increased the assets and the paid-in capital.

Glossary

Arrearage The amount of dividends on preferred stock passed or in arrears for any year or number of years.

Book value per share For capital stock, it represents the portion of the stockholders' equity assigned to a class of stock divided by the number of shares of that class of stock issued and outstanding.

Cumulative preferred stock The class of preferred stock on which undeclared dividends are accumulated and must be paid together with the current dividend before any dividend payment can be made on common stock.

Deficit The caption used in the balance sheet to designate a Retained Earnings account which has a debit balance.

Dividend A distribution of cash, stock, or other corporate property by a corporation to stockholders.

Noncumulative preferred stock The class of preferred stock on which a dividend not declared (passed) in any one year is lost.

Nonparticipating preferred stock A class of preferred stock that receives its specified dividend rate but that does not participate in any additional dividends declared.

Participating preferred stock A class of preferred stock that receives its specified dividend and shares in further dividends after common receives an amount equal to the basic preferred rate.

Retained earnings Undistributed earnings from regular operations and gains from sale of assets.

Retained earnings—restricted The portion of retained earnings not available for dividends.

Stock dividend The issuance by a corporation of additional shares of its authorized stock without additional payment by the stockholders.

Stock split An increase in the number of shares of stock outstanding without a change in the total par or stated value of the outstanding shares.

Treasury stock A company's own stock previously issued and outstanding but reacquired either by purchase or gift or in settlement of a debt.

Questions

Q18–1 (a) What are the major subdivisions of the Stockholders' Equity section of the balance sheet? (b) Why must particular care be taken in subdividing the Stockholders' Equity section?

Q18–2 (a) What is the purpose of restricting retained earnings? (b) Is the restriction of retained earnings the same as the establishment of a special cash fund?

Q18–3 The following quotation is adapted from the notes to the financial statements of a large company, "Retained earnings of $28,500,000 are restricted from payment of cash dividends on common stock because of a promissory note agreement. Further restrictions of $1,700,000 are made to cover the cost of the company's own common stock reacquired." What is the significance of this note (a) to a short-term creditor, (b) to a long-term creditor, (c) to a stockholder?

Q18–4 What is meant by the term *book value?* How is book value computed? Has it any real significance as a financial measure of the worth of stock?

Q18–5 Preferred stock enjoys certain preferences. (a) What are these preferences? (b) How do they affect dividend distributions?

Q18–6 (a) What is a stock dividend? (b) What conditions prompt the declaration of a stock dividend? (c) How does a stock dividend affect (1) the total stockholders' equity, (2) the total assets, (3) the book value per share, (4) the taxable income of the recipient, (5) the market price per share?

Q18–7 (a) What is accomplished by a stock split? (b) How is it recorded? (c) How does it affect (1) the total stockholders' equity, (2) the book value per share, (3) the market price per share?

Q18–8 (a) What is treasury stock? (b) Why do corporations buy back their own shares? (c) How does the reacquisition of a company's own shares affect its financial position? (d) Why do some states place certain restrictions on treasury stock acquisitions? (e) How is the purchase of treasury stock recorded? (f) How is the issuance of treasury stock recorded? (g) How does the issuance of treasury stock affect the financial statements?

Class exercises

CE18–1 (Recording corporate transactions; stockholders' equity) Following is the Stockholders' Equity section of the balance sheet of the Janus Corporation as of December 31, 1978.

Common Stock, no-par value; issued and outstanding 50,000 shares		$ 600,000
Retained Earnings		
Restricted		
For Lawsuit Damages	$ 50,000	
For Plant Expansion	250,000	
Unrestricted	150,000	450,000
Total Stockholders' Equity		$1,050,000

The following transactions occurred during the year 1979 (restriction of retained earnings is required):

1. Acquired 7,500 shares of its own common stock at $12 a share.
2. Paid $6,000 in settlement of the lawsuit for injuries.
3. Issued 4,000 shares of treasury stock at $17 a share.
4. One of the stockholders donated land and a building worth $25,000 and $75,000 respectively.
5. Paid a cash dividend of $1.50 a share.
6. Reduced the retained earnings restriction for plant expansion by $50,000.
7. Net income for the year after income taxes was $60,000 (make the closing entry).

Required:

1. Enter the December 31, 1978 balances in ledger accounts.
2. Journalize the transactions and post to the appropriate accounts.
3. Prepare the Stockholders' Equity section of the balance sheet as of December 31, 1979.
4. What is the effect of the retained earnings restrictions (a) on the financial statements and (b) on the individual shareholders?

CE18–2 (Effect of cash and stock dividends) The Stockholders' Equity section of the Maio Corporation's balance sheet consists of the following accounts:

Common Stock, $100 par value; issued 500 shares	$50,000
Retained Earnings	35,000
Total Stockholders' Equity	$85,000

Required:

1. (a) Prepare the journal entries to record the declaration and the payment of an $8-per-share cash dividend. (b) Compute the book value per share of the common stock immediately before the declaration of the dividend and immediately after the payment of the dividend.
2. Assume that the corporation declares a stock dividend instead of a cash dividend, each stockholder to receive one dividend share for each 5 shares now held. Complete requirements 1a and 1b on the basis of this assumption.
3. John Berwick owns 50 shares of Maio Corporation stock. What was his equity (a) before the stock dividend and (b) after the stock dividend?
4. Discuss the purpose, advantages, and disadvantages of a stock dividend from the viewpoint (a) of the stockholder and (b) of the issuing corporation.
5. Suppose the board of directors declared a 2-for-1 stock split, which the stockholders approved. How would this affect John Berwick? the company's balance sheet? the earnings per share?

CE18–3 (Recording corporate transactions) The Berylco Corporation was organized on April 1, 1979, with authority to issue 15,000 shares of no-par value common stock and 7,500 shares of 9 percent preferred stock, $50 par value. During 1979, the following transactions occurred:

1. Issued 750 shares of preferred stock at $56 a share.
2. Issued 6,000 shares of common stock for cash at $15 a share. A stated value of $12 a share is set by the board of directors for the common stock.
3. Issued 150 shares of common stock, in lieu of a $2,000 fee, to the corporation's attorneys for their services in drafting the articles of incorporation and a set of bylaws.
4. Acquired 300 shares of common stock for $3,500 from the estate of a deceased stockholder.
5. Reissued the 300 shares of the treasury stock at $15 a share.
6. Declared a 9 percent dividend on preferred stock and a 30 cents-per-share dividend on common stock. The dividends are payable on January 10, 1980, to stockholders of record on December 31, 1979. The board also authorized the restriction of retained earnings of $15,000 for plant expansion.

Required: Prepare the journal entries to record the transactions.

CE18–4 (Effect on retained earnings) Indicate the effect, if any, of each of the following transactions on total retained earnings of the Story-Tell Company.

1. The board of directors declared a stock dividend to be issued one month from the current date.
2. Issued the stock dividend declared in transaction 1.
3. Wrote off Accounts Receivable against the Allowance for Doubtful Accounts.
4. Paid accounts payable.
5. Collected accounts receivable.
6. Issued $50 par value common stock at $57 a share.
7. Restricted retained earnings for contingencies.
8. Issued $50 par value preferred stock at $55 a share.
9. Purchased machinery on open account.
10. Issued long-term notes and received cash in return.

CE18–5 (Book value per share) The condensed balance sheet of the Boode Corporation as of December 31, 1979 was as follows:

Total Assets	$1,450,000
Liabilities	$ 400,000
Preferred Stock, 9 percent, $50 par value; cumulative	200,000
Common Stock, no-par value; stated value $5	600,000
Premium on Preferred Stock	20,000
Excess over Stated Value of Common Stock	30,000
Retained Earnings—Restricted for Plant Expansion .	100,000
Retained Earnings	100,000
Total Liabilities and Stockholders' Equity	$1,450,000

Required:

1. Find the book value per share of common stock, assuming that there are no dividend arrearages. The liquidating value of the preferred stock is equal to the par value plus any dividends in arrears.
2. Find the book value per share of common stock, assuming that dividends on the preferred stock are in arrears for the years 1977 and 1978.
3. What is the significance of the book value per share?
4. What is the interrelationship between book value per share and market value per share?

Exercises and problems

P18–1 The Stockholders' Equity section of the Fisch Company's balance sheet shows the following:

Common Stock, no-par value, issued 15,000 shares	$270,000
Retained Earnings	90,000
Total	$360,000

Required: What is the cumulative effect on stockholders' equity of each of the following events, occurring in sequence: (a) the declaration of a 5 percent stock dividend; (b) the distribution of the dividend; (c) the acquisition of 200 shares of the company's own stock for $18 a share; (d) the issuance of these shares for $20 a share; (e) the declaration of a $1-per-share cash dividend; (f) the payment of the dividend.

P18–2 The Glasgow Company restricted retained earnings of $30,000 to cover a lawsuit by a customer. The lawsuit was ultimately settled for $15,000.

Required: Make all the necessary journal entries.

P18–3 The 1979 annual report of LaBrie Corporation states in a note to its financial statements that "The terms of certain note agreements restrict the payment of cash dividends on common stock. The amount of retained earnings not so restricted on December 31, 1979, was approximately $122,000."

Required:

1. Of what usefulness is the statement regarding the amount of restricted retained earnings? the amount not restricted?
2. The cash dividend distributions during 1979 were $14,908; net income for the year was $84,010. Do the stockholders have the right to dividends up to $84,010? up to $122,000?
3. Total shareholders' equity at December 31, 1979 was $860,703. Does this indicate what the shareholders would receive in the event of liquidation? of sale? Explain.

P18–4 The Mill Brook Corporation entered into an agreement with the town of Brewster to build a plant there. The town donated land and buildings valued at $40,000 and $100,000, respectively.

Required: Record the transaction.

P18–5 The capital stock of the Rez Corporation consists of no-par value common stock with a $5 stated value.

Required: Record: (a) the issuance of 750 shares at $10 a share, (b) the reacquisition of 200 shares at $9 a share (restriction of retained earnings is not required), (c) the reissuance of the treasury stock at $12 a share, (d) a reduction in the stated value to $3 a share, (e) a 2-for-1 stock split.

P18–6 The Tel-Guard Company's balance sheet shows the following:

Common stock, par value $50; 10,000 shares	$500,000
Retained Earnings	250,000

Required: Give the effect on these accounts of each of the following independent situations: (a) All the stock is called in and 20,000 shares of no-par value stock are issued, the entire proceeds constituting legal capital. (b) The old shares are replaced by 20,000 shares of no-par value, $25 stated-value common stock. (c) Each stockholder receives a stock dividend of one additional share for every three shares now held.

P18–7 On March 1, 1979, the Merk Corporation was authorized to issue 25,000 shares of $25 par value common stock and 2,000 shares of 9 percent preferred stock, $100 par value. The following transactions occurred between March 1 and December 31, 1979:

1. Issued 6,000 shares of common stock at $25 a share and 1,500 shares of preferred stock at $102 a share.
2. Purchased the assets of the Leib Company at their fair cash value: the assets consisted of land worth $20,000, buildings worth $150,000, and plant and equipment worth $200,000. Issued 14,000 shares of common stock in payment.
3. Purchased 1,000 shares of its own common stock at $22.50 a share. (The laws of the state of incorporation require a restriction of retained earnings equal to the cost of treasury stock.)
4. Established a restriction on retained earnings for contingencies of $20,000.
5. Issued 400 shares of treasury stock for $23 a share.
6. Earnings through December 31 after federal income taxes were $90,000 (make the closing entry).
7. Declared a 75 cents-per-share dividend on the common stock and a $4.50 dividend on the preferred stock.

Required:

1. Record transactions in appropriate ledger accounts.
2. Prepare the Stockholders' Equity section of the balance sheet as of December 31, 1979.

P18–8 The Stockholders' Equity section of the Goldberg Corporation's balance sheet as of June 30, 1978, is shown below.

Stockholders' Equity	
Common Stock, $50 par value; issued 2,000 shares ..	$100,000
Retained Earnings	65,000
Total Stockholders' Equity	$165,000

The following transactions occurred during the next twelve months:

1. Established a retained earnings restriction of $10,000 for a pending lawsuit.
2. Received, as a donation from the town of Taunton, land and a building worth $20,000 and $115,000 respectively.
3. Declared a 2 percent stock dividend. The shares to be issued are currently quoted at $55 a share.
4. Purchased 100 shares of its own stock for $54 a share.
5. Issued the stock certificates for the stock dividend.
6. Received 200 shares of stock as a gift from one of the stockholders of the corporation.
7. Issued 100 of the donated shares for $5,600.
8. Issued 50 shares of treasury stock for $3,000.
9. Net income for the year after income taxes was $35,000 (make the closing entry).

Required:

1. Enter the balances as of June 30, 1978, in ledger accounts.
2. Open other ledger accounts as needed and record the transactions directly into the accounts.
3. Prepare the Stockholders' Equity section of the balance sheet as of June 30, 1979.

P18–9 The following information is taken from the Stockholders' Equity section of the Chia Corporation's balance sheet as of December 31, 1979:

Preferred Stock, 10 percent cumulative and nonparticipating, $100 par value; authorized and issued 3,000 shares	$ 300,000
Common Stock, no-par value; stated value $20; authorized 40,000 shares; issued 20,000 shares	400,000
Excess over Stated Value of Common Stock	840,000
Retained Earnings—Restricted for Plant Expansion	80,000
Retained Earnings—Restricted for Bond Redemption	40,000
Retained Earnings—Unrestricted	300,000
Total Stockholders' Equity	$1,960,000

Dividends on the preferred stock are in arrears for 1977 and 1978.

Required:

1. Compute the book value per share of the common stock. The liquidating value of the preferred is equal to par value plus any dividends in arrears.
2. Assume that the market value of the Chia Corporation common stock was one-half the book value per share. Does this indicate that faulty accounting principles or procedures were used? Give some reasons for the difference in book and market values per share.

P18–10 The Stockholders' Equity section of the All-Type Corporation's balance sheet as of December 31, 1978 was as follows:

Stockholders' Equity	
Capital Stock	
Preferred Stock, 10 percent, $50 par value; authorized and issued 5,000 shares	$ 250,000
Common Stock, $40 par value; authorized and issued 15,000 shares	600,000
Premium on Common Stock	75,000
Retained Earnings	300,000
Total Stockholders' Equity	$1,225,000

Transactions for the year 1979:

1. Declared a $70,000 cash dividend for 1979. (The preferred stock is cumulative and nonparticipating; there are no dividends in arrears.)
2. Paid the dividend declared in transaction 1.
3. Purchased 1,000 shares of its own preferred stock for $75 a share (a restriction of retained earnings is not required).
4. Established a restriction on retained earnings of $15,000 for contingencies.
5. Issued 400 shares of treasury stock for $80 a share.
6. Earnings from operations for the year after income taxes were $225,000 (make the closing entry).
7. Issued 300 shares of treasury stock for $95 a share.
8. The principal stockholder donated to the corporation a warehouse valued at $40,000.

Required:

1. Prepare journal entries to record the transactions.
2. Post to accounts.
3. Prepare the Stockholders' Equity section of the balance sheet as of December 31, 1979.
4. Why do you think the principal stockholder donated his warehouse to the corporation?

P18–11 An analysis of the Treasury Stock account of Teddy, Inc., shows the following debit entries during 1979:

Date	*Lot No.*	*Description*	*No. of Shares*	*Class of Stock*	*Amount*
1979					
Jan. 10	1	Purchase	192	Common	$7,680
Feb. 16	2	Purchase	128	Preferred	2,560
Apr. 20	3	Purchase	80	Common	3,360
May 3	4	Gift	40	Preferred	1,000
3	5	Gift	40	Common	1,280

The following credit entries were made:

1979					
Feb. 6	1	Sale	80	Common	$3,520
12	1	Sale	32	Common	1,380
16	1	Sale	32	Common	1,250
Mar. 1	2	Sale	112	Preferred	2,800
Apr. 20	3	Sale	64	Common	2,950
23	1	Sale	32	Common	1,100
July 20	4	Sale	40	Preferred	800
26	5	Sale	32	Common	650

The bookkeeper has followed the policy of debiting the account at cost for purchases and at the prevailing market price for gifts; all credits to the accounts are for the net proceeds from sales. The common stock was originally issued at a substantial premium; the preferred stock was originally issued at par value.

Required:

1. Give the journal entries to correct the Treasury Stock account (compute costs by specific identification).
2. Give the journal entry to restrict an amount of retained earnings equal to the cost of the shares on hand.
3. Is it appropriate for a company to trade in its own stock?
4. Give some reasons why a company may want to reacquire its own shares.

P18–12 (Integrative) The following account balances were taken from the ledger of the McEachern Company as of December 31, 1979:

Premium on Preferred Stock	$ 60,000
Paid-In Capital—Donated	144,000
Paid-In Capital from Treasury Stock Transactions—Common	12,000
Preferred Stock, 9 percent cumulative, $100 par value; issued 9,600 shares	960,000
Retained Earnings—Restricted for Plant Additions	192,000
Retained Earnings—Restricted for Contingencies	24,000
Paid-In Capital—Excess of Original Stated Value over Revised Stated Value of Common Stock	180,000
Common Stock, no-par value; stated value $20; issued 24,000 shares	480,000
Retained Earnings	396,000
Treasury Stock—Common (600 shares)	18,000
Paid-In Capital—Excess over Stated Value of Common Stock	48,000
Estimated Income Taxes Payable	115,000
Organization Costs	24,000

Required:

1. Prepare the Stockholders' Equity section of the balance sheet as of December 31, 1979.
2. Give a brief statement of the origin and function of each account.
3. Compute (a) the amount contributed by the preferred stockholders, (b) the amount contributed by the common stockholders, (c) the book value per share of common stock, (d) the book value per share of preferred stock, assuming that the current year's preferred dividends are in arrears.
4. How does the reacquisition by a company of its own shares affect (a) the financial statements? (b) the individual shareholders?

P18–13 (Minicase) The 1979 annual report of the OJC Corporation included an explanatory note, a portion of which is shown below:

Shareholders' Equity
The Board of Directors on June 6, 1979, declared a 100 percent common stock distribution on common shares, payable July 18, 1979.

Series preference stock, no par value, amounting to 1,000,000 shares have been authorized. The initial series of such series preference stock is the $3.20 preference stock of which 215,000 shares are authorized and 76,654 are outstanding. The preference stock ranks junior as to dividends and in liquidation to the $3 preferred stock of which 112,254 shares are authorized and 47,088 are outstanding.

The $3 preferred and the $3.20 preference shares are each convertible into 3.6 common shares, have liquidating preferences of $65 and $100 per share, respectively, redeemable beginning in 1984 at $68 and $103 per share, respectively, and are entitled to one vote per share. The company has been advised by counsel that there are no restrictions on retained earnings as a result of the excess of liquidating preferences over stated value of the preferred stocks.

In January 1979, the company increased the number of authorized shares of common stock from 7,000,000 to 45,000,000 shares. Of the common shares authorized but unissued at December 31, 1979, a total of 15,949,307 was reserved for the conversion of preferred stocks and convertible subordinated debentures and for exercise of stock options and warrants.

Required:

1. What was achieved by the 100 percent common stock distribution (a) from the corporation's viewpoint? (b) from the stockholders' viewpoint?
2. How did the stock distribution affect the balance sheet?
3. What is the significance of the advice by counsel regarding retained earnings restrictions?
4. Give some reasons for the large increase in the number of authorized shares of common stock.

chapter nineteen

Introduction

The acquisition of both short-term and long-term capital as well as the accounting for these transactions are issues facing management of modern corporations. Earlier we discussed various sources of this capital: investment of the owners (Chapter 17), retention of earnings (Chapter 18), and obtaining of short-term funds (Chapter 11 and others). To promote a more complete understanding of the subject of capital, this chapter will present an overview of current liabilities, introduce some new current liabilities, discuss bonds payable in some depth, and introduce certain other long-term liabilities.

Bonds payable and other liabilities

Learning goals

To review current liabilities.
To introduce additional current liabilities.
To understand the nature and classification of bonds payable.
To compare bonds with capital stock.
To understand the reason for issuing bonds instead of capital stock.
To record transactions for (a) bond issuance, (b) bond retirement and refunding, and (c) conversion of bonds into capital stock.
To record an early retirement of bonds payable.
To understand the nature of underwriting bonds.
To make the accounting entries for bond sinking funds.
To understand the nature of and account for mortgages payable and long-term unsecured notes payable.

Key terms

amortization of premium or discount
bearer bond
bond, bond certificate
bondholder
callable bond
carrying value
contract interest rate
convertible bond
coupon bond
current liability
debenture or debenture bond
discount on bonds payable
effective-yield rate
income bond
indenture
leverage
long-term liabilities
long-term unsecured notes payable
mortgage payable
operating cycle
premium on bonds payable
refunding
registered bonds
retirement
secured bonds, unsecured bonds
serial bonds
sinking fund
trading on the bondholders' equity

Current liabilities: a review

Definition of current liabilities

Current liabilities represent obligations, the payment or settlement of which requires the use of current assets or the creation of other current liabilities within a year or operating cycle, whichever is the longer period. The *operating cycle* is the length of time, on the average, that it takes a company to acquire an inventory, sell it and to collect the receivable. If this period of time is longer than a year, this longer period of time will be used to determine whether an obligation is current. If the period of time is shorter than a year, the *year* will be the length of time used to determine whether an obligation is current.

Current liabilities we have discussed in earlier chapters include:

Bank overdrafts
Accounts payable (trade)
Vouchers payable
Notes payable (trade)
Notes payable, bank
Maturing bonds payable
Current installments of serial bonds payable
Credit balances in customer accounts
Accrued interest payable
Property taxes payable
Sales taxes payable
FICA taxes payable
State unemployment compensation taxes payable
Federal unemployment compensation taxes payable
Federal income taxes payable
Employees' income tax withholdings payable
Unearned subscriptions.

Valuation of current liabilities

An ideal method of valuation of current liabilities is to present them on the balance sheet at their present value, removing from the face the implied interest element. This ideal method is not usually followed, however, for short-term items arising from normal trade transactions. Current liabilities are generally presented on the balance sheet at their full maturity value. However, when certain contra valuation items such as *Discounts on Note Payable* (discussed in Chapter 11) are recorded, they should be shown on the balance sheet as an offset to the Notes Payable, thus reducing the particular item to an approximation of its present liquidation value.

Current liabilities: a brief overview

A *bank overdraft,* represented by a credit balance in the Cash account, arises when a firm writes checks for more than it has deposited in the bank and the bank pays these checks (see Chapter 10). *Accounts and vouchers payable* result from the purchase of merchandise, supplies, and equipment on 30-, 60-, or 90-day open charge accounts. So-called ''cash terms''—no carrying charges are assigned—are often extended for a period of ninety days or more. During this period, cash may be obtained from new sales and used to pay for the merchandise obtained on the open charge account (see Chapters 7 and 10). *Bonds payable* (formal written promises to pay), though they may have been originally issued with lives as long as fifty years or more, are classified as a current liability on the balance sheet prepared at the end of the fiscal year immediately preceding the year they mature. *Serial bonds* are bonds that are paid off in installments. The installment payable within the next year or operating cycle would be classified as a current liability on the balance sheet. Customers sometimes unintentionally overpay a company; or they may buy an item on credit, pay the amount, and then return the item to receive credit rather than a refund. In this way a credit balance arises in these customers' accounts. The customers' accounts with credit balances should not be offset against other accounts receivable; rather, they should be shown as a current liability in the balance sheet with the title, *Credit Balances in Customer Accounts*. Certain current liabilities are the results of payroll deductions. For example, *FICA Taxes Payable* and *Employees' Income Tax Withholdings Payable* are current liabilities created when a firm withholds certain amounts from periodic salary payments. Other similar current liabilities are recorded because of taxes assessed against the payroll of a company: *State Unemployment Compensation Taxes Payable, Federal Unemployment Compensation Taxes Payable, FICA Taxes Payable* (see Chapter 9). The liability for federal income taxes is recorded when a company records its own federal income tax expense. *Unearned Subscriptions* are not liquidated by payment but are earned within the next year or the operating cycle; current assets are consumed in the earning process.

Two other current liability accounts covered in more detail below are *Property Taxes Payable* and *Sales Taxes Payable*.

Property taxes payable

Property taxes are assessed by municipal, county, and some state governments on the value of certain property as of a given date; a legal liability arises on this date. If annual financial statements are prepared, however, and if the tax is paid within the fiscal year, an entry can be made debiting Property Taxes Expense and crediting Cash. Under these circumstances no liability needs to be created at the date of the assessment of the tax. On the other hand, if monthly financial statements are prepared, it is possible and even legally proper to place the entire liability for property taxes on the books. The usual accounting treatment, however, is to accrue on a month-by-month basis the proportionate amount of the year's property tax expense and the corresponding property tax liability in the form of an end-of-month adjusting entry. Consider the example of the Bigdome Company that has an annual property tax assessment of $1,200 as of January 1, 1979, for the year 1979. Assume that it desires to prepare monthly financial statements and also assume that the property tax will not be paid until November or December, 1979. The following entry could be made to record the monthly accrual on the taxpayer's books for January 31, 1979:

1979						
Jan.	31	Property Taxes Expense	100	00		
		Property Taxes Payable			100	00
		To record the monthly accrual of property taxes: 1/12 x $1,200 = $100.				

Similar entries would be made at end of each month to record the property tax expense.

Sales taxes payable

Most states have a law, which levies a sales tax on the purchase of certain types of merchandise by customers. The typical law levies a tax on the customer buying the merchandise but requires the seller to collect the tax and to remit it to the appropriate governmental unit. To illustrate, assume that a retail sales tax of 4 percent is levied on all sales in a given state. If Saleo Company sells merchandise for cash with a retail sales price of $10,000, it would have to collect $10,400. This transaction is recorded as follows:

1979						
Jun.	30	Cash	10,400	00		
		Sales			10,000	00
		Sales Taxes Payable			400	00
		To record cash sales with a 4 percent sales tax.				

Comments on this entry follow:

1. As indicated on similar previous occasions, this entry should be recorded in the cash receipts journal.
2. Although Saleo Company collects the sales taxes, the amount belongs to the state government, hence a liability must be created for the amount payable to the state government. It is a current liability. A sales tax return must be filed—usually on a monthly basis—by the Saleo Company. At the time the return is filed, the sales tax is paid. Then an entry is made debiting Sales Taxes Payable and crediting Cash.

Some small businesses absorb the sales taxes or lump the collection of the tax into the Sales account. Suppose, for example, that the Lightweight Company collected sales tax but credited both the proceeds of sales and the collection of sales taxes into the Sales account; at the end of June, the Sales account showed a credit balance of $124,800. With a 4 percent sales tax, on *all* goods sold, then an adjusting entry would have to be made as follows:

1979						
Jun.	30	Sales	4,800	00		
		Sales Taxes Payable			4,800	00
		To remove the sales taxes from the Sales account.				

The calculation of the sales taxes payable is as follows:

Let x = Sales only
0.04 x = Sales taxes
1.04 x = Sales plus the sales taxes, the amount which is in the Sales account before adjustment.

Then 1.04 x = $124,800
x = $124,800 ÷ 1.04
x = $120,000

The sales tax could be proved thus:

$$4\% \times \$120{,}000 = \$4{,}800$$

Sales taxes charged to credit customers may require some alteration of the sales journal. One way to handle this issue is to place extra columns in the sales journal as indicated below. Consider one illustration to be recorded in the journal: Assume that on June 10, 1979, the Saleo Company sold merchandise on credit to Taxim Company, sales amount, $400; sales taxes, $16, terms n/30. This could be recorded as follows:

SALES JOURNAL

Date		Sales Invoice Number	Account Debited	Terms	Debit		Credit			
					Accounts Receivable		Sales Taxes Payable		Sales	
1979 Jun.	10	1016	Taxim Company	n/30	416	00	16	00	400	00

Long-term liabilities: definitions and types

Obligations that have maturity dates beyond the year or operating cycle are classified on the balance sheet as *long-term liabilities* or long-term debt. The maturity dates of some of the long-term debt items cover 50 or more years. Often these obligations are paid off from the proceeds derived from the issuance of other long-term debt instruments. Under these circumstances long-term debt has an effect that is similar to certain types of capital stock.

Typical kinds of long-term liabilities are bonds payable; mortgages payable; and long-term notes payable, unsecured. These liabilities are discussed more fully here.

Bonds payable

One of the means by which businesses and governments acquire funds that will not be repaid for many years is the issuance of bonds. A *bond,* or bond certificate, is a written promise under the corporate seal to pay a specific sum of money on a specified or determinable future date to the order of a person named in the certificate or to the order of the bearer. An example of a corporate bond is the 9 percent sinking fund debentures, due 1995, issued by the Burlington Industries, Inc.

Bonds are usually issued in denominations of $100, $500, $1,000, or $5,000 each. This variation enables the issuing company to obtain funds from many different investors or groups of investors. Denominations smaller than $100 have been used by the U.S. government in its Series E Savings Bond issues. On the other hand, municipal bonds issued in $5,000 denominations are also common.

Bonds may be issued directly to buyers by the borrowing corporation or they may be marketed through agents such as banks, brokers, or other underwriting syndicates. These agents, in turn, sell these bonds through their own channels and charge a fee to the issuing company for the selling of the bonds. *Bondholders* are creditors of the corporation. Except for currently maturing amounts, the Bonds Payable account is a long-term liability. Bonds contain provisions for interest to be paid at regularly stated intervals. Interest is usually paid semiannually on industrial bonds.

A bond, like a promissory note, represents a corporate debt to the borrower, which must be satisfied from the assets of the corporation in preference to stockholders' equity claims. The contract or covenant between the corporation and its bondholders is called a bond *indenture*.

Classification of bonds

A corporation may issue several kinds of bonds that are tailored to meet the particular financial needs of the issuing corporation. Bonds may be registered to an individual or unregistered (bearer) bonds. They may be secured by assets or unsecured.

Registered bonds Registered bonds are issued in the name of the bondholder. They require proper endorsement on the bond certificate to effect a transfer from one owner to another. The debtor corporation or its transfer agent, usually a bank or trust company appointed by the corporation, maintains complete ownership records. Bonds may be registered both as to principal and interest, in which case interest checks are issued only to bondholders of record. It is possible, however, to register the principal only. One popular form of these is coupon bonds. The owner of *coupon bonds* detaches interest coupons from the bond certificate and deposits them at the stated interest dates at the owner's bank or at a designated bank.

Bearer bonds Bonds may be issued without being registered in the name of the buyer; title to them is held by the bearer. These bonds may also be coupon bonds. This method is least burdensome to the issuing corporation because it does not have to write the semiannual interest checks. The owner must take particular care against loss or theft of the certificates, or unauthorized removal of the coupons attached to the bonds.

Secured bonds A secured bond is one that pledges some part of the corporate assets as security for the bond. The asset pledged may consist of land and buildings (referred to as *real estate mortgage* bonds), machinery (*chattel mortgage* bonds), negotiable securities (*collateral trust* bonds), or other corporate assets. Several loans may use the same assets for collateral; this gives rise to *first mortgage* bonds and *second mortgage* bonds. The numbers indicate the order to be followed in satisfying the mortgageholders' claims if the corporation fails to meet its obligations under the bond indenture. The *bond indenture* is the contract between the corporation and the bondholder. In the event of default (failure to pay the bonds by the issuer) the property may be sold and the proceeds used to pay creditors. Second and third mortgage bonds necessarily carry a higher interest rate than first mortgage bonds because of the order of priority of payment in the event of a default; thus, they are not as marketable as first mortgage bonds and are more costly to the borrowing company. It is, therefore, desirable for the borrower to raise the required funds through a single, large first mortgage bond issue.

Unsecured bonds Unsecured bondholders rank as general, or ordinary, creditors of the corporation and rely upon the corporation's general credit. Such bonds are commonly referred to as *debenture bonds,* or often simply as *debentures*. Sometimes debenture bonds are issued with a provision that interest payments will depend on earnings; these are called *income bonds*.

Bonds may have other special features; for instance, the bonds may mature serially (*serial* bonds); specified portions of the outstanding bonds will mature in installments and be paid at stated intervals. Sometimes the issuing corporation retains an option to call in the bonds before maturity (*callable* bonds); in other cases the bondholder may be given an option to exchange the bonds for capital stock (*convertible* bonds). The bond indenture may require the issuing corporation to make deposits to a *sinking fund,* often in the name of a trustee for the bondholders, at regular intervals. This ensures the availability of adequate funds for the redemption of the bonds at maturity.

Bonds compared to capital stock

A better knowledge of bonds may be gained by referring to the following chart, in which bonds are compared to capital stock.

Comparison of Bonds to Capital Stock

Bonds	*Capital Stock*
Bondholders are creditors.	Stockholders are owners.
Bonds Payable is a long-term liability account.	Capital Stock is a stockholders' equity account.

Bondholders, along with other creditors, have primary claims on assets in liquidation.	Stockholders have residual claims on assets in liquidation.
Interest is typically a fixed charge; it must be paid or the creditors can institute bankruptcy proceedings against the debtor corporation.	Dividends are not fixed charges; even preferred dividends are at best only *contingent charges;* these are paid if income is sufficient and if declared by the corporate board of directors.
Interest is an expense.	Dividends are not expenses; they are distributions of net income.
Interest is deductible in arriving at both taxable and business income.	Dividends are not deductible in arriving at taxable and business income. (See Chapter 28.)
Bonds do not carry voting rights.	All stock carries voting rights unless they are expressly denied by contract, as is usually the case with preferred stock.

It is important for an accountant to understand the variety of factors that cause managers to issue bonds rather than capital stock. One factor influencing this decision is that management, by issuing bonds, has access to an important market source of funds it would not have through a stock issue. Many banks and other financial institutions are restricted by law in the amount of stock they can buy. They then look for an alternative investment—often an investment in bonds.

A second factor, *leverage,* involves *trading on the bondholder's equity.* Leverage can be described simply: If funds borrowed at 8 percent can be used in the business enterprise to earn 19 percent after taxes, additional earnings of 11 percent (19% − 8%) accrue to the common stockholders. However, the opposite effect is always possible: the borrowed funds may earn less than the cost of borrowing. This is an instance of unfavorable leverage.

A third reason why corporations decide to issue bonds instead of capital stock is the high rate of income tax on corporate net income. If a corporation pays at least half its net income in federal and state income taxes, it naturally considers the issuance of bonds as a means of effecting a considerable tax saving.

To illustrate how leverage and heavy income taxes affect the choice of alternative methods of fund raising, assume that the Levirite Corporation, which has $100 par value common stock outstanding in the amount of $1,000,000, needs $500,000 to purchase additional plant and equipment. Three plans are under consideration: Plan 1 is to issue additional common stock at $100 par value; Plan 2 is to issue 8 percent preferred stock at $100 par value, cumulative and nonparticipating; Plan 3 is to issue 7 percent bonds.

	Plan 1	Plan 2	Plan 3
Common stock	$1,000,000.00	$1,000,000.00	$1,000,000.00
Additional funds	500,000.00	500,000.00	500,000.00
Total	$1,500,000.00	$1,500,000.00	$1,500,000.00
Net income before bond interest and income taxes	$ 350,000.00	$ 350,000.00	$ 350,000.00
Deduct bond interest expense	–0–	–0–	35,000.00
Net income after bond interest expense	$ 350,000.00	$ 350,000.00	$ 315,000.00
Deduct income taxes (assumed rate of 50%)	175,000.00	175,000.00	157,500.00
Net income after income taxes	$ 175,000.00	$ 175,000.00	$ 157,500.00
Deduct dividends on preferred stock	–0–	40,000.00	–0–
Available for common stock dividends or reinvestment in Levirite Corporation	$ 175,000.00	$ 135,000.00	$ 157,500.00
Projected earnings per share on common stock (15,000 shares outstanding under Plan 1; 10,000 shares under Plans 2 and 3)	$ 11.67	$ 13.50	$ 15.75

All three plans assume that the securities will be issued at face or par value, that earnings of $350,000 annually before the bond interest expense is deducted will be maintained, and that an income tax rate of 50 percent will prevail.

Assuming that earnings per share on common stock is the best basis for making the decision, Plan 3 is desirable for the common stockholders, particularly if the net income exceeds $350,000, because the bond interest rate is fixed. If the annual net income falls below $350,000, one of the other plans may become more advantageous. Since the securities market and corporate net earnings remain uncertain, there is no exact mathematical formula to solve this financial problem. The decision requires sound judgment based on past experience and projected future needs.

A fourth reason for management to issue bonds instead of common stock is that bonds, and to a lesser extent preferred stock, aid in offsetting losses due to shrinkage in the purchasing power of the funds invested in assets. Bonds, for example, carry fixed contract maturity values in terms of the monetary unit at the maturity date. If the value of the dollar decreases before the bonds are paid, a gain resulting from the use of the more valuable money received at the time of borrowing accrues to the owners of the business.

A fifth factor is control. The issuance of additional common stock may result in a loss of management control, because the ownership of the corporation is distributed over a larger number of stockholders. Bondholders, on the other hand, are creditors and do not participate in managerial decisions, except in the rare instances when this is a specific provision of the bond indenture.

Other reasons may influence the decision of management to issue bonds; but these five factors indicate the scope of the problem.

Authorizing the bond issue

Even after management decides that bonds should be issued, it is faced with months of preliminary work before the bonds can actually be floated, or sold. For example, the exact amount to be borrowed, the *nominal* or *contract interest rate* (the rate on the bond certificate that applies to the face value), the maturity date, and the assets, if any, to be pledged must be determined. The provisions of the bond indenture must be chosen with extreme care. For instance, should the bonds be callable, and should they be convertible into some other form of security? Careful long-range financial planning helps to reduce the cost of securing the long-term funds. For example, if there is any chance that the company will need additional funds in the near future, management should not close the door on the possibility of marketing additional bonds by pledging the company's total mortgageable assets. In this case, management probably should seek authority for a bond issue large enough to meet all foreseeable needs.

The financial vice-president, working with other corporate officers, is responsible for finding answers to these and other questions. This officer prepares a written report for the board of directors, summarizing the proposed features of the bond financing and stating why the funds are needed, how they are to be used, and the means of ultimately retiring the bond issue. Various alternative methods of raising funds, such as those shown in the example of the Levirite Corporation, are presented to point up the financial advantage of issuing the bonds.

The board of directors studies this written report, along with the laws of the state in which the company is incorporated, the corporate charter, and the corporate bylaws, before passing a resolution recommending to the stockholders that bonds be issued; a record of the resolution is entered in the minute book of the corporation. Next, the proposal is presented to the stockholders for their approval. Once this approval has been gained, the board of directors prepares a resolution instructing the proper corporate officers to issue the bonds and sign the necessary documents. The final step is the issuance of a formal certified statement that the approval of the board of directors and the stockholders has been obtained. Approval by the stockholders is required because the bondholders have a preferred position; as creditors they have a prior claim to the assets of the corporation in the event of liquidation.

Accounting for issuance of bonds payable

No formal journal entry is required to record the authorization of the bond issue by the stockholders, but a memorandum should be made in the Bonds Payable account indicating the total amount authorized. This information is needed when the balance sheet is prepared, since it should disclose the total authorization as well as the amount issued.

The issue price, usually stated as a percentage of the face value, is affected primarily by the prevailing market interest rate on bonds of the same grade. Bonds are graded by various financial institutions; the grade depends on the financial condition of the issuing corporation. The highest grade is AAA; the next, AA; and in descending order: A, BBB, and down to a grade that is simply referred to as "unrated." If on the issue date the average effective market interest rate on bonds of any particular grade exceeds the contract interest rate on bonds of the same grade being issued, investors will offer less than the face value of the bonds. They will do this so that interest checks received plus the extra amount (the amount of the discount) that is received at maturity will yield to the investors the rate they could have received on other similar grade bonds. Also, if the stated nominal interest rate is higher than the current market rate, investors will tend to offer more than the face value. This concept is developed more fully in the section entitled, **Why bonds sell at a premium or discount.**

Bonds issued at face value

To show the essential similarity between the accounting for notes payable (see Chapter 11) and the accounting for bonds payable, the first illustration is a simple situation in which a corporation issues bonds at face (sometimes called issuance at *par*) on an interest date. Suppose that the Adden Corporation needs funds and that the best alternative is to issue bonds. The stockholders approve a bond issue of $200,000. Ten-year, 9 percent, first mortgage bonds are to be issued. The interest will be paid semiannually on April 1 and October 1. Adden Corporation closes its books each December 31. Assume that the corporation issues all of the authorized bonds on April 1, 1979, at 100, or at face value—the 100 means 100 percent of face. The entries to record the issue, to pay the first interest payment, and to make the adjusting entry on December 31 are presented below.

1979						
Apr.	1	Cash	200,000	00		
		First Mortgage Bonds Payable . . .			200,000	00
		To record the issuance of 9 percent bonds due April 1, 1989.				
Oct.	1	Bond Interest Expense	9,000	00		
		Cash			9,000	00
		To record the payment of interest on the first mortgage bonds.				
Dec.	31	Bond Interest Expense	4,500	00		
		Accrued Bond Interest Payable . .			4,500	00
		To record the accrual of bond interest for three months.				

Comments on these three entries follow:

1. The First Mortgage Bonds Payable account is a long-term liability since it will not be repaid for 10 years. On the balance sheet, the particular real property that is pledged as security should be disclosed in a footnote.
2. The entries to record the Bond Interest Expense are very similar to those recording Interest Expense on notes payable discussed in Chapter 11.
3. The adjusting entry for accrued bond interest is similar to the recording of accrued interest on notes payable. Accrued Bond Interest Payable is a current liability since it must be liquidated in three months—on April 1, 1980.

Why bonds sell at a premium or discount

If the average market interest rate on bonds of any particular grade is higher than the contract interest rate on bonds of the same grade being issued, investors will offer less than the face value of the bonds in order to make up the difference between the rates. The difference *(discount)* between the issue price and the maturity values plus receipts of the semiannual interest will give the investors a return on their investments approximating the return on similar amounts invested at the prevailing market interest rate. By the same token, if the stated interest rate is higher than the current market rate, investors will tend to offer a *premium* (an amount greater than the face value) because they know that this premium will be returned to them to the extent that the periodic interest payments exceed the amount that they would receive on other investments made at the current market rate.

Two examples are presented to emphasize the reasons for bonds selling at a premium or a discount. First, assume that the Heavy Company has an AAA financial rating and is planning to issue debenture bonds. Assume also that all the AAA debenture bonds on the market have an effective average market interest rate of 8 percent. If the Heavy Company issues debenture bonds with an 8 percent contract interest rate, it will receive the face value of the bonds. If, however, the Heavy Company issues bonds with a 9 percent contract rate, it will receive an amount in excess of the face value; that is, the bonds will sell at a *premium*. On the other hand, even with its excellent credit rating, if the Heavy Company issues bonds with a 7 percent contract rate, it will receive an amount less than face value; that is, the bonds will sell at a *discount*.

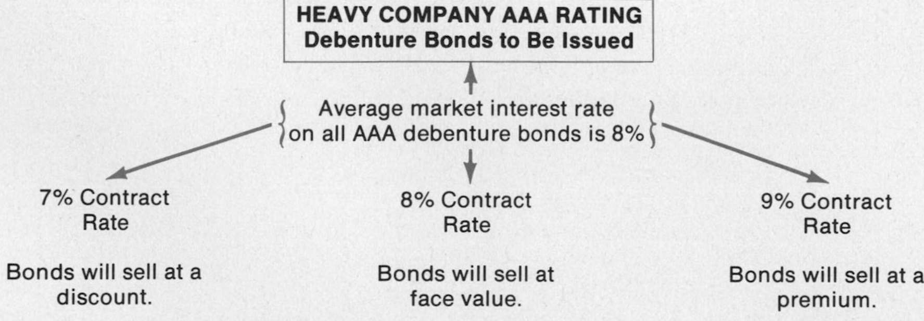

The second example will help to show that the financial condition of a company is not the basic determinant of the issue price of the company's bonds. Assume that the Light Company, with a BB financial rating, intends to issue first mortgage bonds. Further assume that the average effective market interest rate on BB first mortgage bonds is 10 percent. If the Light Company issues its bonds with a 10 percent contract interest rate, it will receive the face value of the bonds. Even with its relatively poor credit rating, if it issues bonds with an 11 percent contract, the Light Company will receive an amount in excess of the face value; but if the Light Company issues bonds with a 9 percent contract interest rate, it will receive an amount less than the face value.

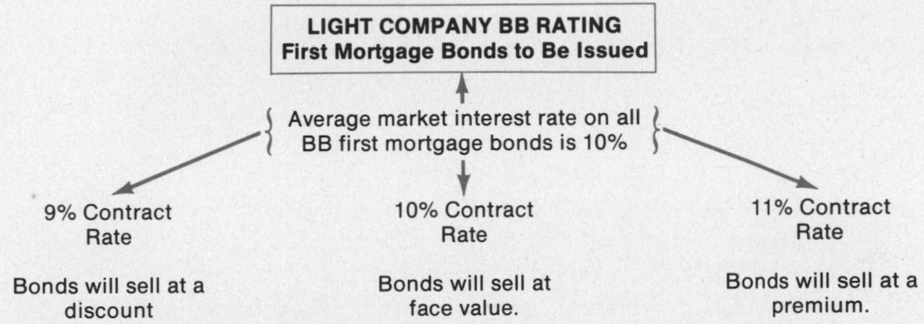

From the information presented above, observe that the premium and the discount arise as a result of differences in the average market rate of interest on a given grade of bond and the particular contract rate on these bonds. A knowledge of this fact suggests the approach to the accounting for the amortization of the premium and discount elements given in the illustrations which follow.

Bonds issued at a premium on an interest date

The next illustration relates to the issue of bonds at a premium on an interest date. The recording sequence is the same in each of the next two examples. First, an entry is made to record the bond issue; next, any peculiarity of financial statement presentation is discussed; after this, the accounting procedure for interest payments is described; finally, the recording of the *retirement* of the bonds at the maturity date is shown. Assume that on July 1, 1979, the Levirite Corporation is authorized to issue 8 percent first mortgage bonds with a face value of $600,000 and a maturity date of June 30, 1994. Interest is paid semiannually on June 30 and December 31. All the bonds are issued on July 1, 1979, at 103; that is, at 103 percent of their face value; and the following entry is made:

1979						
Jul.	1	Cash	618,000	00		
		First Mortgage Bonds Payable . . .			600,000	00
		Premium on Bonds Payable			18,000	00
		To record the issuance of 8 percent first mortgage bonds due June 30, 1994.				

A balance sheet prepared on July 1, 1979, would show Bonds Payable and Premium on Bonds Payable as follows:

Long-Term Liabilities		
8% First Mortgage Bonds Payable, due June 30, 1994	$600,000.00	
Premium on Bonds Payable	18,000.00	
Total Long-Term Liabilities		$618,000.00

The assets pledged as security for the bonds payable would be disclosed in the following footnote:

Land and Buildings costing $1,200,000 (market value $1,400,000) are pledged as security for the bonds payable.

This method of disclosure is consistent with the concept that the right side of the balance sheet describes the sources of business funds.

Amortization of premium: straight-line The Premium account will be reduced by periodic amortization and thus will be smaller on each subsequent statement. Again, this procedure is consistent with the concept that when bonds are issued at a premium, each interest payment contains, in effect, a payment of the interest earned on the investment and also a partial return of the amount borrowed from the investor. If part of the $618,000 borrowed is repaid, a balance sheet prepared at a later date would naturally show a smaller amount. The footnote describing the assets pledged as security for the long-term debt is a disclosure of important information that may influence the decision of an investor to buy or not to buy the company's bonds.

The amount received from the issuance of the bonds is $18,000 greater than the amount that must be repaid at maturity. This amount is not a gain, for it does not seem logical to assume that revenue can result directly from the borrowing process. The premium arose because the contract rate of interest on the bonds issued was higher than the prevailing market rate on similar grade bonds; therefore, it is sound accounting practice to allocate part of the premium on bonds payable to each period as a reduction of the periodic bond interest expense. The straight-line method of allocation is most commonly used, and will be emphasized in this text. In summary, under the straight-line amortization method, the total bond interest expense over the life of a bond issue is equal to the total amount of cash paid for interest reduced by the amount of the premium.

The bond interest expense of the Levirite Corporation is recorded on December 31, 1979, as follows:

1979				
Dec.	31	Bond Interest Expense	23,400 00	
		Premium on Bonds Payable	600 00	
		Cash		24,000 00
		To record the semiannual bond interest payment and amortization; the amount of the amortization is $18,000 ÷ 30 semiannual periods = $600.		

If the $18,000 premium on the bonds payable represents a reduction in interest over the entire 15-year life of the bonds, it is evident that by the straight-line amortization method the reduction in interest for the six months ended December 31, 1979, is $18,000 divided by 30 semiannual periods, or $600.

This compound entry emphasizes that the $24,000 constitutes the payment of effective bond interest expense of $23,400 and a partial return of the amount borrowed, the $600 amortized. (It is suggested that, for the problems in this text, premiums or discounts on bonds payable be amortized each time the bond interest expense is recorded to emphasize that this amortization is an adjustment of the bond interest expense.) Even though the compound entry is acceptable, two separate entries may be made: (1) one entry to record the payment of the semiannual bond interest, and (2) a separate entry to record the semiannual amortization of the premium.

Assuming the use of straight-line amortization of the premium on bonds payable, the proof of the $23,400 semiannual bond interest figure can be calculated by another means as follows:

Cash payments to be made:	
Face value of bonds at maturity	$ 600,000.00
Total interest—8% x 15 years x $600,000	720,000.00
Total cash payments	$1,320,000.00
Cash receipts:	
Bonds with face value of $600,000 issued at 103 . . .	618,000.00
Net interest expense for 15 years	$ 702,000.00
Net semiannual interest expense:	
$\frac{\$702,000}{30 \text{ semiannual periods}}$	$ 23,400.00

In borrowing money, it is essential to know the effective cost of the particular credit, thus a formula for the approximation of effective interest rate (i) or *effective-yield rate* on bonds issued at a premium can be stated as follows:

$$i = I \div \left(F + \frac{P}{2}\right)$$

where I = annual absolute interest, adjusted for amortization of premium
F = face value of bonds
P = total premium (so that $\frac{P}{2}$ = average premium)

The effective interest rate on the Levirite Corporation bonds is approximately 7.68 percent = [$46,800 ÷ ($600,000 + $18,000/2)]. This is calculated by dividing the annual absolute effective amount of interest by the average carrying value (face value plus unamortized premium) of the bonds issued. The effective interest rate computation emphasizes the fact that the premium on the bonds results in a downward adjustment of the 8 percent contract rate to the effective rate.

Assume that the 8 percent first mortgage bonds payable are paid *(retired)* on June 30, 1994. After the June 30, 1994 (the first entry below) semiannual interest payment entry is made, the Premium on Bonds Payable account has a zero balance. The second entry records the retirement of the bonds at maturity.

			Debit		Credit	
1994						
Jun.	30	Bond Interest Expense	23,400	00		
		Premium on Bonds Payable	600	00		
		Cash			24,000	00
		To record the last semiannual interest payment on the 8 percent bonds payable and the last semiannual amortization of bond premium.				
	30	First Mortgage Bonds Payable	600,000	00		
		Cash			600,000	00
		To record the retirement of the 8 percent bonds payable at maturity.				

Bonds issued at a discount on an interest date

For the third illustration, assume that on July 1, 1979, the Beta Company is authorized to issue 7 percent debenture bonds with a face value of $200,000 and a maturity date of June 30, 1989. Interest is paid semiannually on June 30 and December 31. All the bonds are issued on July 1, 1979, at 97. The discount is caused by the difference in the prevailing market interest rate on similar grades of debenture bonds and the contract rate of interest on the bonds issued. In the case of the Beta Company's debenture bonds, their contract interest rate is lower than the prevailing market rate on a similar grade of securities. The issuance of these bonds may be recorded as follows:

			Debit		Credit	
1979						
Jul.	1	Cash	194,000	00		
		Discount on Bonds Payable	6,000	00		
		Debenture Bonds Payable			200,000	00
		To record the issuance of 7 percent debenture bonds due June 30, 1989.				

A balance sheet prepared on July 1, 1979, would disclose Bonds Payable and Discount on Bonds Payable as follows:

Long-Term Liabilities		
7% Debenture Bonds Payable, due June 30, 1989	$200,000.00	
Deduct Discount on Bonds Payable	6,000.00	
Total Long-Term Liabilities		$194,000.00

Note the similarity of this method to the disclosure of a premium on bonds payable.

Amortization of discount: straight-line The following compound entry records the first semiannual interest payment by the Beta Company and semiannual amortization of the Discount on Bonds Payable account.

1979				
Dec.	31	Bond Interest Expense	7,300 00	
		Cash		7,000 00
		Discount on Bonds Payable		300 00
		To record semiannual bond interest payment and amortization; the amount of amortization is $6,000 ÷ 20 semiannual periods = $300.		

This entry indicates that the effective semiannual interest expense is $7,300, not $7,000. Assuming the straight-line method of amortization, the effective interest is equal to the cash interest payment plus a pro rata share of the discount: in effect, a part of the total interest cost over the entire life of the bonds. This accounting procedure, therefore, recognizes the reason for the discount on the bonds—that the contract rate of interest was lower than the prevailing market interest rate on similar grades of securities.

Assuming the use of straight-line amortization of the discount on bonds payable, the proof of this semiannual bond interest expense can be seen by the following calculation.

Cash payments:	
Face value of bonds at maturity	$200,000.00
Total interest—7% x 10 years x $200,000	140,000.00
Total cash payments	$340,000.00
Cash receipts:	
Bonds with face value of $200,000 issued at 97	194,000.00
Net interest expense for 10 years	$146,000.00
Net semiannual interest expense:	
$\frac{\$146,000}{20 \text{ semiannual periods}}$	$ 7,300.00

A formula for the approximation of effective interest rate *(i)* on bonds issued at a discount can be stated as follows:

$$i = I \div \left(F - \frac{D}{2}\right)$$

where I = annual absolute interest, adjusted for amortization of discount

F = face value of bonds

D = total discount (so that $\frac{D}{2}$ = average discount)

The effective interest rate is approximately 7.41 percent = [$14,600 ÷ ($200,000 − $6,000/2)]. The bond discount results in an upward adjustment of the 7 percent contract rate to its effective yield rate of 7.41 percent.

Retirement of bonds at maturity On June 30, 1989, the 7 percent debenture bonds payable are retired. After the June 30, 1989, semiannual interest payment entry is made (the first entry below), the Discount on Bonds Payable account has a zero balance. The second entry records the retirement of the bonds at maturity.

Date		Account	Debit	Credit
1989				
Jun.	30	Bond Interest Expense	7,300 00	
		Cash		7,000 00
		Discount on Bonds Payable		300 00
		To record the last semiannual interest payment and final amortization of bond discount on the 7 percent bonds payable.		
	30	Debenture Bonds Payable	200,000 00	
		Cash		200,000 00
		To record the retirement of 7 percent bonds payable at maturity.		

Bonds issued between interest dates

The preceding three examples emphasized the basic accounting procedures and the reasons for amortizing bond premiums and discounts. A more complex problem involving the issuance of bonds between interest dates is presented below.

Bonds may be authorized by the stockholders but not issued for several months or even years because market conditions are not favorable. Some of the bonds may be issued and the rest held until a specific need for the additional funds arises. Often, the time needed for clerical work delays issuance past an interest date. The interest on bonds issued between interest dates will have accrued from the last interest date to the date of issuance. Since the bonds carry an inherent promise to pay not only the face value at maturity but six months' interest at each interest date, it is customary in these cases for the investor to pay the issue price of the bonds plus an amount equal to the accrued interest. In turn, the first interest payment will be for one full interest period—six months' interest—thereby returning to the purchaser the accrued interest paid plus the interest earned from the date of purchase to the current interest date.

Assume that on October 1, 1977, the Allen Company is authorized to issue 9 percent debenture bonds with a face value of $1,000,000 and a maturity date of October 1, 1987. The semiannual interest dates are April 1 and October 1. The bonds are held until *June 1, 1979,* when bonds with a face value of only $400,000 are floated at 105 plus accrued interest. The amount of cash that the Allen Company receives is $426,000: $420,000 for the bonds plus $6,000 for accrued interest. Note that the promise to pay six months' interest is not retroactive beyond April 1, 1979, the interest date preceding the date of issuance. On October 1, 1979, the purchaser of the bonds receives an interest payment of $18,000, although the interest on $400,000 at 9 percent from June 1 to October 1 is only $12,000. The payment includes a return of the $6,000 that the investor paid for accrued interest on June 1, as illustrated in Figure 19–1.

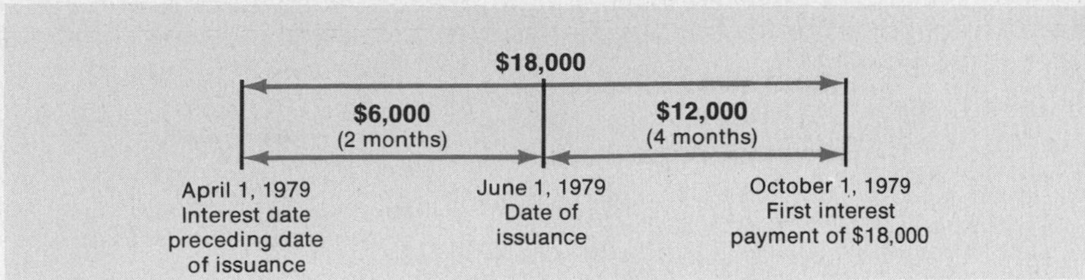

Figure 19–1
Accumulation of interest

The Allen Company records the bond issuance as shown below:

1979				
Jun.	1	Cash	426,000 00	
		Debenture Bonds Payable		400,000 00
		Premium on Bonds Payable		20,000 00
		Accrued Bond Interest Payable . .		6,000 00
		To record the issuance of bonds at 105 plus accrued interest.		

The accrued interest is credited to a current liability account, since it must be repaid on the next interest date.

The entries to record the payment of semiannual interest and the amortization of bond premium are shown below.

1979				
Oct.	1	Bond Interest Expense	12,000 00	
		Accrued Bond Interest Payable . . .	6,000 00	
		Cash		18,000 00
		To record the payment of semiannual interest at 9 percent on bonds payable.		
	1	Premium on Bonds Payable	800 00	
		Bond Interest Expense		800 00
		To record the amortization of the bond premium for four months: $20,000 ÷ 100 mos. x 4 = $800.		

The entry for the interest payment reflects the amounts shown in Figure 19–1; that is, the semiannual cash payment includes a return of $6,000 for the accrued interest that was sold to the investor plus $12,000 for interest actually earned by the investor for the four months' use of the money.

Amortization period

Amortization covers only the period from the date of issuance to the maturity date.

The date of authorization and even the preceding interest date are not relevant to the start of the amortization period. For the bonds of the Allen Company, the amortization period begins on June 1, 1979, and ends on October 1, 1987, a total of 100 months. The amount of bond premium to be amortized each month is $200 = ($20,000 ÷ 100 months); the amount for four months is $800 = ($200 × 4).

End-of-period adjustments Assuming that the Allen Company closes its books on a calendar-year basis, the following adjusting entries are made on December 31, 1979:

			Debit	Credit
1979				
Dec.	31	Bond Interest Expense	9,000 00	
		Accrued Bond Interest Payable . .		9,000 00
		To record the accrual of bond interest for three months computed as follows: ($400,000 x 0.09 x 3/12 = $9,000).		
	31	Premium on Bonds Payable	600 00	
		Bond Interest Expense		600 00
		To record the accrual of bond premium for three months: 3 x $200 = $600.		

The effect of the end-of-year adjustments is that the Bond Interest Expense account reflects the correct interest expense ($19,600) incurred for the seven months during which the bonds were outstanding (June 1 to December 31).

On April 1, 1980, the next regular interest date, the following entries are made to record the payment of interest and the amortization of the bond premium:

			Debit	Credit
1980				
Apr.	1	Bond Interest Expense	9,000 00	
		Accrued Bond Interest Payable . . .	9,000 00	
		Cash		18,000 00
		To record the payment of semiannual bond interest.		
	1	Premium on Bonds Payable	600 00	
		Bond Interest Expense		600 00
		To record the amortization of bond premium for three months: 3 x $200 = $600.		

Note that only three months' amortization of the bond premium is recorded. This coincides with the three months' bond interest expense incurred and recorded to April 1, 1980.

Underwriting bond issues

Brokers, banks, or investment syndicates often act as agents for the issuing corporation or they *underwrite* the flotation of a bond issue, just as they do in the issuance of capital stock. The entire authorized bond issue of a corporation may be turned over to the underwriter at a specified price, say 103½. The underwriter then offers the bonds to the public at a slightly higher market price, say 104. This arrangement ensures that the issuing corporation will receive the full specified amount of funds on a given date. The amount of premium or discount is based on the net amount that the issuing corporation receives from the underwriter, not on the market price paid by the investors for the bonds.

Consider, for example, the case of a company that plans to issue 9 percent bonds with a face value of $1,000,000. The company turns the bonds over to the underwriter at 103½, for a total price of $1,035,000. The underwriter, according to the underwriting agreement, plans to sell the bonds at 104. Even though the investors pay $1,040,000 for the bonds, the issuing company receives only $1,035,000 and hence considers that the bonds are issued at a premium of $35,000.

Retirement and refunding of bonds payable

The borrowing company may retire its outstanding bonds at the maturity date by paying the contract face value in cash. Even if the bonds were originally issued at a premium or a discount, the entry to record the retirement is a debit to Bonds Payable and a credit to Cash for the face value. Serial bonds are retired in serial installments. Assume, for example, a $500,000, 10-year serial bond issue, $50,000 to be retired at face value at the end of each year. The annual retirement entry is again a debit to Bonds Payable and a credit to Cash for $50,000. The retirement schedule is established by the issuing corporation and may provide for several retirement dates beginning a fixed number of years after the date of issue.

Other methods of retiring bonds include (1) the retirement of all or part of a bond issue by call (the exercise of the issuer's right to redeem), or purchase on the open market before the bonds are actually due; (2) the retirement of bonds by *refunding* (refinancing by issuing new bonds on new terms); (3) the conversion of bonds payable into capital stock, and (4) the retirement of bonds with sinking fund assets and the attendant problem of accumulating the sinking fund.

Retirement of bonds before maturity

A corporation that has issued bonds may find itself with more cash than it expects to need for operations, thus permitting it to retire all or part of its outstanding bonded indebtedness prior to maturity date. Management may decide to retire the bonds immediately if the cash is available, if there appears to be no better alternative use now or in the future for the excess cash, and if it wishes to decrease the fixed charges for the bond interest. For bonds to be retired by a corporation before maturity—that is, to be *callable*—the indenture must contain a *call provision* permitting the issuing corporation to redeem the bonds by paying a specified price, usually slightly above face value; or if the bonds are not callable, the issuing company may redeem them before the maturity date by purchasing them on the open market. Retirement of bonds at a price less than the *carrying value* (face plus unamortized premium or face minus unamortized discount) adjusted to the date of retirement results in a gain; a loss is incurred if the purchase price exceeds the adjusted carrying value. Material gains and losses on the early retirement of bonds payable are classified in the income statement as extraordinary items and are shown in the income statement in a section (at the bottom of the statement) entitled Extraordinary Items.

To illustrate the early retirement of bonds payable, suppose that the Allen Company (see illustration on pages 615–616) found itself with excess cash on October 1, 1980. It decided to retire all of the debenture bonds which had been issued on June 1, 1979. These bonds were retired at 104½ on the October 1, 1980, interest date. The liability accounts as of this date are illustrated below.

Debenture Bonds Payable — Acct. No. 251

Date		Explanation	F	Debit	Credit	Balance
1979 Jun.	1		CR62		400,000 00	400,000 00

Premium on Bonds Payable — Acct. No. 252

Date		Explanation	F	Debit	Credit	Balance
1979 Jun.	1		CR62		20,000 00	20,000 00
Oct.	1		J75	800 00		19,200 00
Dec.	31		J79	600 00		18,600 00
1980 Apr.	1		J91	600 00		18,000 00
Oct.	1		J98	1,200 00		16,800 00

As can be observed, the carrying value of the liability (face plus unamortized premium) is $416,800. Thus if the Allen Company pays $418,000 = (1.045 × $400,000) for the bonds, there is a loss on retirement of $1,200 = ($418,000 − $416,800). This information is recorded in the journal as follows:

Date		Account	Debit	Credit
1980 Oct.	1	Debenture Bonds Payable	400,000 00	
		Premium on Bonds Payable	16,800 00	
		Loss on Retirement of Bonds Payable	1,200 00	
		Cash		418,000 00
		To record the retirement of the debenture bonds at 104½.		

Once the foregoing is posted, the two liability accounts will be reduced to zero. As stated above the Loss on Retirement of Bonds Payable, if material, is shown in the income statement as an extraordinary loss.

Refunding

Bonds also may be retired by refunding; that is, by refinancing them through issuing of new bonds on new terms. The proceeds from the new issue are specifically designated for the retirement of the old bond issue. The old bondholders may be given the option of exchanging their bonds for the new bonds at the call price. This procedure helps reduce the refinancing costs of the issuing corporation because it would eliminate a possible brokerage fee. A refunding decision may be called for if it is possible to redeem bonds with a relatively high interest rate and to substitute bonds with a lower interest rate. Other reasons for refunding are to replace an issue about to mature with a new issue, thus extending the maturity date, or to retire outstanding bonds containing a requirement that funds be accumulated to retire the bonds.

In the accounting procedure for refunding, the retirement should be recorded in entries similar to those described for the retirement of the Allen Company bonds (see pages 617–618). Accounting for the new issue is the same as described earlier in this chapter for the Beta Company (see pages 612–613).

Conversion of bonds into common stock

To make certain bonds more attractive to investors, and thus to increase their marketability, the bond agreement may give investors the option of exchanging bonds on a given interest date, or dates, for a certain number of shares of stock, usually common, of the issuing company. These securities, referred to as convertible bonds, have the advantage of offering the investor an initial fixed return on investment combined with an opportunity to share in profitable operations of the issuing company by later conversion of the bonds to stock. The terms and conditions for conversion are designated in the bond indenture. Conversion is at the option of the bondholder, so that if earnings are unfavorable he or she does not need to exercise the conversion privilege and may retain the fixed return and greater security of the bonds. The conversion of bonds into stock changes the legal and accounting status of the security holder from creditor to owner. When conversion occurs, the generally accepted accounting procedure is to transfer the *carrying value of the convertible bonds payable* to *paid-in capital accounts,* which probably will include both Common Stock and Premium on Common Stock.

Bond sinking fund

The borrowing corporation may agree in the bond indenture to accumulate funds to retire the bonds at maturity. Periodic cash payments are made to a sinking fund trustee, usually a bank or a trust company. These payments are ordinarily invested in revenue-producing securities. When the bonds mature, the sinking fund trustee sells the securities, and the proceeds are used to pay the bondholders. In some instances the corporation itself may act as trustee, thereby retaining control over the activities of the sinking fund.

To illustrate the operation of a simple sinking fund managed by a trustee, assume that on the authorization date, January 1, 1979, the Fundo Corporation issues 10-year sinking fund bonds with a face value of $600,000. The bond indenture provides that at the end of each year a deposit of $60,000—reduced by any net earnings of the funds from its investments—be made to the trustee. The entry to record the initial deposit with the trustee is shown below.

1979				
Dec.	31	Bond Sinking Fund	60,000 00	
		Cash		60,000 00
		To record the initial sinking fund deposit with the trustee.		

The Bond Sinking Fund account is a controlling account. The trustee must invest all the available cash in the fund in revenue-producing securities. As a practical matter, it would not always be possible for the trustee to invest odd amounts of cash or to purchase securities immediately on the receipt of cash. Hence, the bond sinking fund is composed of a number of individual items, such as cash, securities, and accrued interest receivable. It is unnecessary for Fundo Corporation to maintain a separate general ledger account for each asset contained in the bond sinking fund. This is true because the trustee will keep detailed records.

If, at the end of the second year, the trustee reports net earnings of $2,000 from investments in bonds, the following entries record the second deposit:

1980				
Dec.	31	Bond Sinking Fund	2,000 00	
		Bond Interest Earned		2,000 00
		To record net earnings of the bond sinking fund per report of the trustee.		
	31	Bond Sinking Fund	58,000 00	
		Cash		58,000 00
		To record the second sinking fund deposit with the trustee; the amount is $60,000 less the earnings of $2,000 or $58,000.		

The following entry is made to record the retirement of the bonds at maturity by the payment of assets in the bond sinking fund:

1989				
Jan.	1	Sinking Fund Bonds Payable	600,000 00	
		Bond Sinking Fund		600,000 00
		To record the retirement of the bonds at maturity date with the sinking fund.		

The Bond Sinking Fund account is classified in the Assets section as a long-term investment on each balance sheet except the one prepared at the end of the year preceding the date of the retirement of the bonds. On this statement, Bond Sinking Fund should be shown as a current asset and Sinking Fund Bonds Payable should be disclosed as a current liability.

Restriction of retained earnings for bond redemption

In addition to the requirement for sinking fund deposits, the bond indenture may require a restriction of retained earnings up to the amount in the sinking fund. The bondholders thus are provided with twofold protection: the sinking fund insures the availability of adequate cash for the redemption of the bonds, and the restriction of retained earnings for bond redemption reduces the amount available for distribution as dividends to the stockholders. This restriction enhances the company's cash position and its ability to meet its regular needs as well as its requirements for bond interest and bond sinking fund payments. An improved cash position also is advantageous in enabling the company to meet its regular operational cash requirements and to maintain a favorable credit standing.

To illustrate, assume that the bond indenture of Fundo Corporation, provides for a restriction of retained earnings. The entry at the end of each year is:

1979 – 1988				
Dec.	31	Retained Earnings	60,000 00	
		Retained Earnings—Restricted for Bond Redemption		60,000 00
		To record the restriction of retained earnings equal to the annual increase in the bond sinking fund.		

Retained Earnings—Restricted for Bond Redemption is shown in the Stockholders' Equity section of the balance sheet under Retained Earnings. It should be noted that the provisions of the bond indenture may require (1) the creation of the bond sinking fund only, (2) a restriction on retained earnings until the bonds are redeemed only, or (3) both a bond sinking fund and a restriction on retained earnings. When the bonds are redeemed at maturity, the contractual restriction on retained earnings is removed. The journal entry to record the removal of the restriction is:

1989				
Jan.	1	Retained Earnings—Restricted for Bond Redemption	600,000 00	
		Retained Earnings		600,000 00
		To remove the restriction on retained earnings on retirement of the bonds.		

The unrestricted balance of Retained Earnings now has been increased by an amount equal to the maturity value of the bonds. We should bear in mind, however, that the reversal of the restriction on retained earnings does not create any assets that would be available for distribution to the stockholders. Assets may have been permanently committed to the enlargement of the business in the form of plant expansion. Thus, the earnings of the corporation may have been reinvested rather than being paid out as cash dividends. Sometimes corporations use this occasion to declare a stock dividend. The declaration and issue of a stock dividend would produce the net effect of a debit to Retained Earnings and a credit to Common Stock.

Mortgage payable

Another long-term liability is a mortgage payable. A *mortgage payable* arises from the purchase on credit of land and building where the purchaser gives to the seller a long-term note with a mortgage attached. A *mortgage* is an assignment of an interest in property to the seller as collateral in case the purchaser defaults on the payment of the long-term obligation. Should the purchaser default on payments, the seller could petition the court to sell the property at public auction. The proceeds derived from the sale would go first to pay the seller (mortgagee) in full. Any other proceeds would go to the buyer (mortgagor). Interest on a mortgage payable is usually payable either monthly or semiannually, although it could be paid in other ways depending upon the terms of the particular mortgage contract.

Assume that on July 1, 1979, the Jones Company purchased land and building for $100,000: the cost of the land is determined to be $20,000 and buildings, $80,000. Also assume that Jones Company made a down payment of $10,000 and gave the seller a 9 percent, 20-year mortgage for $90,000. The interest on the mortgage is to be paid on June 30 and December 31. The initial purchase entry and the payment of the first interest are recorded as follows:

Date		Account	Debit		Credit	
1979						
Jul.	1	Land	20,000	00		
		Buildings	80,000	00		
		Cash			10,000	00
		Mortgage Payable			90,000	00
		To record the purchase of land and building by paying cash of $10,000 and issuance of a 9 percent, 20-year mortgage for the balance.				
Dec.	31	Interest Expense	4,050	00		
		Cash			4,050	00
		To record the payment of semiannual interest on the mortgage.				

Long-term unsecured notes payable

Money may be borrowed on a long-term basis by the issuance of an *unsecured long-term note payable*. Firms or individuals with a good credit rating are able to borrow significant amounts for long periods of time and to issue to the credit grantor an unsecured long-term note. The credit grantor will require that annual financial statements be filed with it. A balance sheet and income statement are the statements which are usually filed with the grantor of credit. If interest is payable semiannually, the accounting for the issuance of long-term notes is essentially the same as the accounting for a mortgage payable. The typical transaction would involve a debit to Cash and a credit to Long-Term Unsecured Notes Payable. The accounting for interest payment is exactly the same as that for a mortgage payable.

Glossary

Amortization of premium or discount on bonds payable The periodic writing off of the premium or discount on bonds payable as a decrease or an increase to interest expense; amortization is usually accomplished by the straight-line method.

Bearer bond A bond issued without the owner's name being registered; the title to this kind of bond is deemed to be vested in the holder of the bond.

Bond A written promise under the corporate seal to pay a specified sum of money on a specified or determinable future date to the order of a person named in the bond certificate or to the order of bearer.

Bond certificate Evidence that a loan has been made to a corporation; it contains the written promise under the corporate seal to pay a specific sum of money on a specified or determinable future date to the order of a person named in the certificate or to the order of bearer.

Bondholder A creditor who has lent money to a corporation or government and has received a bond certificate as evidence of the loan.

Bond indenture A contract between the corporation issuing bonds and the bondholder; it will contain all privileges, restrictions, covenants, and other provisions of the contract.

Bond sinking fund Segregation of assets for the purpose of retiring bonds usually at maturity.

Callable bond A bond for which the issuing corporation retains an option to retire the bonds before maturity at a specified price on specific dates.

Carrying value of bonds payable The face or principal amount of the bonds payable plus the unamortized premium, or face minus the unamortized discount on bonds payable.

Contract or nominal interest rate The rate of interest that is written in a bond indenture; it is the rate based on face or principal amount that will be paid on the stated periodic interest dates.

Convertible bond A bond that contains a provision entitling the bondholder to exchange the bond for capital stock at the bondholder's option.

Coupon bond A bond that has the periodic interest coupon attached to the bond certificate.

Current liability An obligation the payment or settlement of which requires the use of current assets or the creation of other current liabilities within a year or operating cycle, whichever is the longer period of time.

Debenture bond Often referred to as a debenture; it is an unsecured bond—one that carries no specific pledge of collateral.

Discount on bonds payable The amount by which the face value of bonds exceeds the price received for the bonds on issuance; it arises because the nominal (contract) rate of interest is lower than the going market rate of interest on similar grade bonds.

Effective-yield rate The actual rate of interest incurred on a liability after adjustment for premium or discount.

Income bond A bond with a provision that interest payments will depend upon earnings.

Leverage The practice of trading on the bondholders' equity; that is, borrowing money at a given rate of interest and utilizing the borrowed funds in the business to earn a higher rate of return than the borrowing rate.

Long-term liabilities Obligations that are due to be paid after the coming year or the operating cycle.

Long-term unsecured notes payable Long-term notes issued to grantors of credit that do not have a specific pledge or collateral; they are long-term liabilities.

Mortgage payable Long-term notes issued with a pledge of specified plant and equipment for the loan granted.

Operating cycle The length of time it takes a business to sell, on the average, its entire inventory and then to collect the resulting receivables.

Premium on bonds payable The excess of the price received for bonds payable above face value; it arises because the nominal (contract) rate of interest is higher than the going market rate of interest on similar grade bonds.

Refunding Refinancing by the issuance of new bonds on new terms.

Registered bond A bond whose owner's name is recorded by the issuing corporation; for this bond to be transferred to another individual, it must be endorsed and a request must be filed to have the owner's name changed on the records of the issuing corporation.

Retirement The payment of the principal amount at maturity or at an earlier date.

Secured bond A bond for which the issuing corporation pledges some part of the firm's property as security in case of financial difficulty.

Serial bonds Bonds that mature in periodic installments and will be paid at stated intervals of time.

Trading on the bondholders' equity A practice of borrowing money at a given rate of interest and utilizing the borrowed funds in the business to earn a higher rate of return than the borrowing rate.

Unsecured bond A bond for which there is no specific pledge of assets for security; these are also called debenture bonds.

Questions

Q19–1 (a) Define current liability. (b) Give five examples of current liabilities. (c) Define operating cycle.

Q19–2 In light of the definition of a current liability, justify the classification of Unearned Magazine Subscriptions as a current liability.

Q19–3 What is the basis for distinguishing between a current and long-term liability?

Q19–4 What problems arise in the valuation of liabilities?

Q19–5 What are the usual current liabilities that arise in connection with payroll transactions?

Q19–6 When should the liability for property taxes be recognized in the accounting records? Over what period should property taxes be charged to expense? Explain.

Q19–7 Where would you normally report the following items on the balance sheet?

a. Bank overdraft
b. Cash dividends payable
c. Estimated income taxes payable
d. Insurance premiums received in advance for a five-year period by an insurance company
e. Notes receivable discounted
f. Current maturities of a serial bond payable
g. Customer accounts with credit balances
h. Stock dividend to be issued
i. Accrued vacation pay
j. Interest on notes payable, deducted from the face of the note in determining the net proceeds
k. Mortgage payable.

Q19–8 Distinguish between nominal and cffcctive interest rates on bonds.

Q19–9 On January 1, 1979, the Knox-Mix Company issued 20-year, 8 percent bonds with a face value of $2,000,000. Interest is payable semiannually on June 30 and December 31. The proceeds to the company were $1,900,000; that is, on January 1, 1979, the bonds had a market price of 95 percent of face value. Explain the nature of the $100,000 difference between the face value and the market value of the bonds.

Q19–10 Identify the following terms: (a) registered bonds; (b) bearer bonds; (c) secured bonds; (d) unsecured bonds; (e) serial bonds; (f) convertible bonds; (g) coupon bonds; (h) income bonds.

Q19–11 A corporation needs cash for the acquisition of plant and equipment. It is considering three alternative sources; additional common stock, 9 percent preferred stock, and 7 percent bonds. (a) What are some of the factors involved in this decision? (b) Will the decision affect the present common stockholders? Discuss.

Q19–12 (a) What are the general requirements for the approval of a bond issue? (b) Should the stockholders always approve a bond issue? Why?

Q19–13 (a) Why does the buyer of a bond purchased between interest dates pay the seller for accrued interest on the bond? (b) Is the accrued interest included in the stated purchase price of the bond?

Q19–14 (a) What is the difference to the issuing corporation between common stock issued at a premium and bonds issued at a premium? (b) Does revenue result from either?

Q19–15 Before its bonds mature, a corporation may retire them by: (a) paying cash; (b) refunding; or (c) conversion. Explain each of these methods.

Q19–16 Under what circumstances may refunding of a bond issue be advisable?

Q19–17 On December 31, 1979, a corporation has serial bonds with a face value of $500,000 outstanding. These bonds mature annually in $100,000 amounts, beginning June 30, 1980. How will the bonds be shown on the balance sheet as of (a) December 31, 1979, (b) December 31, 1980, and (c) December 31, 1981?

Q19–18 Why does not a firm issue bonds with a contract rate of interest equal to the prevailing market rate of interest and thus not have to worry about a premium or discount on the bonds?

Q19–19 Differentiate between mortgage payable and long-term unsecured notes payable.

Class exercises

CE19–1 (Recording of sales taxes) The Sour Cream Company made the following sales during the month of December.

1979

Dec. 10 Cash sales to customers with an invoice price, excluding sales taxes, of $1,500.

Dec. 18 Credit sales to customers with an invoice price, excluding sales taxes, of $2,500, terms n/30.

1980

Jan. 15 Paid sales taxes for December, 1979.

Required: Assume that there is 4 percent tax levied on all sales and that sales tax is payable on January 15 of next year, journalize the above transactions and make adjusting entries if any.

CE19–2 (Recording mortgage payable and interest) The Foothills Airfreight Company purchased land and buildings on May 1, 1979, for $700,000. Land is valued at $150,000 and buildings at $550,000. The company made a down payment of 20 percent and gave the seller an 8 percent, 30-year mortgage for the remaining amount. The interest on the mortgage is to be paid at the end of every 3 months; that is, the first payment is to be made on July 31.

Required:

1. Record the initial purchase.
2. Record the first interest payment on the mortgage.
3. Record the second interest payment on the mortgage.
4. Make adjusting entry assuming the company closes its books on December 31.

CE19–3 (Accounting for the issuance of bonds) In each of the following cases assume: (a) 9 percent bonds with a face value of $400,000; (b) date of authorization, January 1, 1979; (c) interest payable each January 1 and July 1; (d) maturity date of bonds, January 1, 1989; and (e) year ends December 31.

	Case A	*Case B*	*Case C*	*Case D*
Date of issuance	Jan. 1, 1979	Jan. 1, 1979	Jan. 1, 1979	Mar. 1, 1979
Issue price	100	102	97	101 plus accrued interest

Required:

1. Prepare all the journal entries for 1979 relating to each case.
2. For Cases B and C prepare a schedule proving the interest cost for 1979.
3. For Cases B and C calculate the approximate effective interest rate.

CE19–4 (Retirement of bonds before maturity) On April 1, 1979, the Rintab Company issued 9 percent bonds with a face value of $300,000 at 106 plus accrued interest. The bonds have a maturity date of August 1, 1987, and interest is paid each February 1 and August 1.

On August 1, 1980, the Rintab Company purchased its own bonds with a face value of $100,000 on the open market at 102.

Required: Assuming that the books of the Rintab Company are closed each December 31, prepare all the entries relevant to the bonds for the years 1979 and 1980.

CE19–5 (Accounting for bond sinking fund) On the date of authorization, January 1, 1979, the Funder Corporation issued four-year sinking fund bonds with a face value of $200,000 at 100. The sinking fund indenture requires an annual contribution at the end of each of the four years to provide for the retirement of the bonds at maturity. As an added protection, the terms of the bond indenture require that retained earnings be restricted in an annual amount equal to the total addition to the sinking fund. The Funder Corporation is to make a deposit to the Rex Bank, which has been named trustee of the sinking fund, of amounts that when added to the sinking fund earnings will total $50,000 each year. The Rex Bank guaranteed the Funder Corporation a return of 6 percent annually. The bank will credit the sinking fund account with this return each December 31.

Required:

1. Record the issuance of the sinking fund bonds.
2. Give all the entries for the four years to record the deposits to the sinking fund and the related restrictions on retained earnings.
3. Record the retirement of the sinking fund bonds by the trustee on the maturity date and the removal of the retained earnings restriction.

Exercises and problems

P19–1 Listed below are selected transactions from the Romanski Faucet Company during the current fiscal year. Assume a 3 percent sales tax is levied on all goods sold and that the sales price in the transactions does not include the sales tax.

1979

Jan. 15 Sold merchandise for cash to Monty-Foome Company with a retail sales price of $20,000.

23 Collected $309 (sales price $300, tax $9) from Lower Company for sales made on December 15 of last year, on terms n/60.

31 Paid sales taxes collected.

Mar. 31 The total of the annual property taxes amounts to $1,200 for 1979. Quarterly property taxes of $300 for the quarter ending March 31 of current year are to be recognized on the books for quarterly financial statements.

Apr. 15 Sold merchandise on credit to Upper Company; sales amount, $7,000, terms n/30.

30 Paid sales taxes.

May 14 Received check number 781 from Upper Company for $7,000 plus sales taxes.

Nov. 10 Paid the annual property taxes of $1,200 assuming that proper entries have been made for the preceding three quarters.

Required: Journalize the above selected transactions.

P19–2 The Fine Webb Paper Company Mill produces a product called linear board in jumbo reels having a standard width of 34 inches and a fixed length of 100 yards. The customers can order reels of smaller widths, but they would have to pay a higher price for it. The company follows a policy of crediting to the Sales account all sales and collection of 5 percent sales tax levied on all goods sold. The following sales were made by the paper company during the month of April:

1979

Apr. 4 Sold for cash 15 reels of 34 inches width to Bayview Company at a price (excluding sales taxes) of $200 per reel.

12 Sold for cash 10 reels of 22 inches width and 20 reels of 11 inches width to DeMara Company at a price (excluding sales taxes) of $150 and $75 per reel, respectively.

25 Sold for cash 34 reels of 15 inches width to Glen Raven Company at a price (excluding sales taxes) of $125 per reel.

Required:
1. Make journal entries to record all sales transactions.
2. Make the necessary adjusting entries that the company would have to make at the end of April to remove the sales tax from the Sales account.

P19–3 On the date of authorization, January 1, 1979 the Walters Corporation issued 10-year, 8 percent bonds with a face value of $500,000 at 100. Interest is payable each January 1 and July 1.

Required:
1. Record the issuance of the bonds.
2. Record the first interest payment.
3. Record the accrued interest expense on December 31, 1979.

P19–4 The Collins Company purchased land and buildings on June 1, 1979, for $200,000. Land is valued at $50,000 and buildings at $150,000. The company made a 25 percent down payment and gave the seller a 12 percent, 30-year mortgage for the remaining amount. The interest on the mortgage is to be paid at the end of each month; that is, the first interest payment is to be made on June 30.

Required:

1. Record the initial purchase.
2. Record the first interest payment on mortgage on June 30.
3. Record the interest payment for December, 1979.

P19–5 The Calico Mills makes the majority of its sales on credit. The following were the sales made by the mill during the first week in February. Assume a 4 percent sales tax on all goods sold is levied on retail sales. The sales amount given below does not include the sales taxes.

1979

Feb. 2 Sold merchandise on credit to "Famous Maker Dresses"; sales amount $10,000, terms n/30.

3 Sold merchandise on credit to "Handsome Men"; sales amount $15,865, terms n/45.

6 Sold merchandise on credit to "Pretty Women"; sales amount $20,219, terms n/60.

6 Sold merchandise on credit to "Laymen's Suits"; sales amount $5,687, terms n/15.

Required:

1. Record the above transactions in the Sales Journal. Use a Sales Journal with amount columns for Sales, Sales Taxes Payable and Accounts Receivable.
2. Post these accounts at the end of the week to the Accounts Receivable ledger.

P19–6 The Jimson Company maintains a controlling account entitled Payables, the balance of which at December 31, 1979, was $48,650. Subsidiary ledger and other information reveal the following:

a. 306 trade accounts (credit balances)	$36,000
b. 4 trade accounts (debit balances)	650
c. 5 trade notes	8,000
d. 2 loans from the president and vice president	5,300

Required: Show how this information should be reported on the balance sheet.

P19–7 The following are the account balances and other data, some of which relate to liabilities and obligations of the Fine Webb Paper Company at December 31, 1979:

Accounts Payable	$ 20,500
Notes Payable	10,000
Discount on Notes Payable	2,000
Accounts Receivable	100,000
Bonds Payable, $20,000 due at March 31 of each year	160,000
Accrued Salaries Payable	1,500
Employees' Income Taxes Withheld Payable	300
FICA Taxes Withheld Payable	750
Property Taxes Payable	1,000
Cash Dividends Payable	2,000
Income Taxes Payable	12,000
Unearned Service Contract Revenue (contracts are for one year)	1,500
Loans from Officers (reviewed annually)	20,000

Required: Prepare the current liability section of the balance sheet at December 31, 1979.

P19–8 On the date of authorization, January 1, 1979, the White Corporation issued 10-year, 8 percent bonds with a face value of $600,000 at 104½. Interest is payable each January 1 and July 1.

Required:

1. Record the issuance of the bonds.
2. Record the first interest payment.
3. Record the accrued interest expense on December 31, 1979.
4. State how the bonds payable should be shown on the balance sheet prepared as of December 31, 1979, assuming that (a) the bonds are unsecured debenture bonds and (b) the bonds are secured by a first mortgage on land and buildings.
5. Record the retirement of the bonds on January 1, 1989, by the payment of cash.

P19–9 On the date of authorization, January 1, 1979, the Jensen Corporation issued 20-year, 9 percent bonds with a face value of $500,000 at 102. Interest is payable each January 1 and July 1.

Required:

1. Record the issuance of the bonds.
2. Record the first interest payment and amortization of the premium.
3. Record the accrued interest expense and amortization of the premium on December 31, 1979.
4. Open a Bond Interest Expense account and post the transactions.
5. Prepare a schedule proving the interest cost for 1979.
6. Compute the approximate effective interest rate.
7. State how bonds payable and premium on bonds payable should be shown on the balance sheet prepared as of December 31, 1979, assuming that the bonds are unsecured debenture bonds.

P19–10 On the date of authorization, January 1, 1979, the Dastor Corporation issued 10-year, 8 percent bonds with a face value of $200,000 at 97. Interest is payable each January 1 and July 1.

Required:

1. Record the issuance of the bonds.
2. Record the first interest payment and amortization of the discount.
3. Record the accrued interest expense and amortization of the discount on December 31, 1979.
4. Open a Bond Interest Expense account and post the transactions.
5. Prepare a schedule proving the interest cost for 1979.
6. Compute the approximate effective interest rate.
7. State how the bonds payable and discount on bonds payable should be shown on the balance sheet prepared as of December 31, 1979, assuming that the bonds are first mortgage bonds with land and buildings pledged as security.

P19–11 On October 1, 1979, the Western Corporation issued 9 percent bonds with a face value of $800,000 at 103 plus accrued interest. The bonds mature on June 1, 1987 and interest is paid each June 1 and December 1. The amortization of premium is recorded each time Bond Interest Expense is recorded. The bonds are retired by the payment of cash on June 1, 1987.

Required: Prepare all the entries relating to the bond issue during 1979 and 1987.

P19–12 On April 1, 1979, the stockholders of the Nathan Corporation authorized the issuance of 10-year, 8 percent first mortgage bonds with a face value of $600,000. The bonds mature on April 1, 1989, and interest is payable each April 1 and October 1.

Required: Make journal entries to record the following transactions:

1979

Jun. 1 Issued the bonds at 104 plus accrued interest.

Oct. 1 Paid the semiannual interest. (Assume that Premium on Bonds Payable is amortized by the straight-line method each time Bond Interest Expense is recorded.)

Dec. 31 Accrued the bond interest.

31 Closed the Bond Interest Expense account.

1980

Apr. 1 Paid the semiannual interest.

Oct. 1 Paid the semiannual interest.

Dec. 31 Accrued the bond interest.

P19–13 Use the data stated in P19–12, except assume that (a) On June 1, 1979, the bonds were issued at 98 plus accrued interest and (b) Discount on Bonds Payable is amortized by the straight-line method each time Bond Interest Expense is recorded.

Required: Prepare the entries for the period June 1, 1979 to December 31, 1980.

P19–14 On March 1, 1979, the authorization date, the Millsboro Company issued 10-year, 8 percent debenture bonds with a face value of $500,000 at $101\frac{1}{2}$. Interest is payable each March 1 and September 1. The company closes its books on December 31. The following selected transactions and adjustments were made:

1979

Mar. 1 Issued all the bonds for cash.

Sept. 1 Paid the semiannual interest.

Dec. 31 Accrued the bond interest.

1980

Mar. 1 Paid the semiannual interest.

Sept. 1 Paid the semiannual interest.

Dec. 31 Accrued the bond interest.

1989

Mar. 1 Paid the semiannual interest.

1 Paid the bonds outstanding at maturity.

Required:

1. Record the transactions. (Assume that the premium is amortized by the straight-line method each time Bond Interest Expense is recorded.)
2. Set up a Premium on Bonds Payable ledger account and post all entries to that account for the entire 10-year period.

P19–15 (a) On the authorization date, January 1, 1979, the Welbourne Corporation issued 10-year bonds with a face value of $1,000,000. Under the terms of the bond indenture, a sinking fund is to be maintained to provide for the retirement of the bonds at maturity. Deposits are to be made with a trustee at the end of each year in amounts that, when added to the sinking fund earnings, will total $100,000. Assume that the fund will earn 6 percent a year.

Required:

1. Record the deposit with the trustee on December 31, 1979.
2. Record the deposit with the trustee on December 31, 1980.

(b) Assume that the bond indenture (see Part a) requires a restriction on retained earnings equal to the amount of the sinking fund.

Required:

1. Record the restriction at the end of 1979 and 1980.
2. Record the removal of the restriction at the maturity date.

P19–16 Selected accounts for the three trial balances of the Leder Corporation are presented:

	Adjusted		*Unadjusted*
	12/31/78	*12/31/79*	*12/31/80*
Debits			
Bond Interest Expense	$ 7,100	$ 42,600	$ 31,950
Credits			
Accrued Bond Interest Payable	11,250	11,250	–0–
9% Bonds Payable—issued 11/1/78	500,000	500,000	500,000
Premium on Bonds Payable	23,400	21,000	19,200

The data from the adjusted trial balances are correct. The bonds were issued between interest-payment dates.

Required:

1. Compute the following:
   a. Original issue price as of November 1, 1978.
   b. Maturity date.
   c. Semiannual interest payment dates.
2. Reconstruct the journal entry to record the issuance of the bonds on November 1, 1978.
3. Prepare any required adjusting or correcting entries as of December 31, 1980.

P19–17 The Bridgeman Company issued 8 percent bonds on September 1, 1979, at a certain price plus accrued interest. The bonds mature on June 1, 1989. Interest is paid each June 1 and December 1. The accountant for the Company recorded the first semiannual bond interest payment as follows:

1979				
Dec.	1	Bond Interest Expense	5,554 00	
		Accrued Bond Interest Payable	5,314 00	
		Discount on Bonds Payable		240 00
		Cash		10,628 00
		To record the payment of semiannual bond interest and amortization of the discount for three months.		

Required:

1. Compute the following:
   a. Face value of bonds issued.
   b. Original issue price and discount.
2. Reconstruct the journal entry to record the issuance of the bonds on September 1, 1979.

P19–18 (Integrative) On April 1, 1979, the stockholders of the Union Airline Corporation authorized the issuance of 20-year, 8 percent, first mortgage bonds with a face value of $600,000. The bonds mature on April 1, 1999, and interest is payable each April 1 and October 1.

Required: Under each of the conditions stated below, record (a) the issuance of bonds, (b) the first interest payment, (c) the accrued interest expense and amortization of the premium or discount, if any, on December 31, 1979, (d) the retirement of the bonds and any other necessary entries on April 1, 1999, by the payment of cash.

1. On April 1, 1979, issued the bonds at 100.
2. On April 1, 1979, issued the bonds at 103.
3. On July 1, 1979, issued the bonds at 97 plus accrued interest.

P19–19 (Minicase) The directors of Casco Bay Appliance Company are studying the following figures as of December 31, 1979:

Current assets	$ 3 million	Current liabilities	$ 2 million
Equipment	80 million	Long-term 8% notes	10 million
Other assets	17 million	Common stock	80 million
		Retained earnings	8 million
Total	$100 million	Total	$100 million

Net income in 1979 before income taxes was $18 million; after taxes $10 million. The best planning estimate indicates that another $50 million invested in equipment now will increase 1980 income before interest, taxes, and dividends by $10 million. They have narrowed down to two methods of raising funds:

1. Issuance of $50 million of 8 percent rolling equipment bonds at par to mature in 10 years.
2. Issuance of $50 million of 7 percent preferred stock at par.

Required: What are some important points the directors should consider in deciding upon a recommendation to stockholders? If any analyses are used, assume a tax rate of 50 percent.

chapter twenty

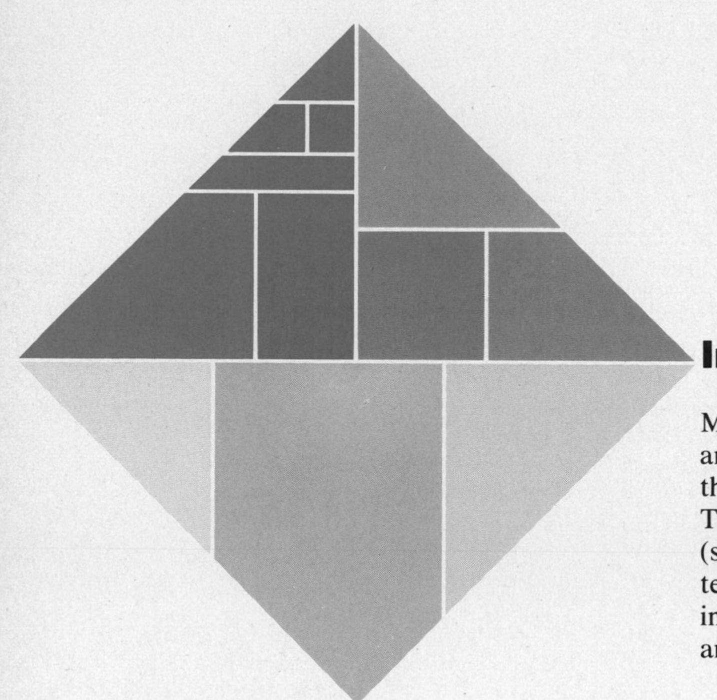

Introduction

Most companies at times have excess funds and invest these funds in various ways other than buying plant and equipment items. These companies often buy securities (stocks and bonds) of other companies as temporary or long-term investments. These investments, their differences, similarities, and values, are the subject of this chapter.

Investments: temporary investments in marketable securities and long-term investments

Learning goals

To differentiate between long-term and temporary investments.
To understand and record temporary investments in marketable securities.
To understand and record transactions using the cost and equity methods of accounting for long-term stock investments.
To be acquainted with the valuation methods of long-term investments in stock.
To understand why an investor would acquire bonds at a premium or a discount.
To record some transactions pertaining to long-term investments in bonds.
To compute the approximate effective interest rate on bond investments acquired at a premium or discount.
To determine and record appropriate end-of-period adjustments for accrued interest on bond investments.
To understand the nature of other long-term investment items.

Key terms

accrued bond interest receivable
amortization of discount
amortization of premium
amortization period
blue-chip stocks or bonds
bond
bond interest earned
cash surrender value
contract (or nominal) interest rate
cost method
dividends earned
effective-interest rate
equity method
face value
long-term investments
lower of cost or market
marketable securities
nominal (or contract) interest rate
parent company
realizable cost
subsidiary company
subsidiary income
subsidiary loss
temporary investments in marketable securities

Temporary investments in marketable securities

Nature of temporary investments in marketable securities

A firm should give serious consideration to the investment of any seasonal excess of cash as it becomes available. In this way, it hopes to maximize its income by putting idle, nonrevenue-producing funds to work when they are not needed in the operations of the business. If it is expected that the funds will be needed in the near future, they can be invested in readily saleable securities. In order to be readily saleable, the securities should be listed on a stock exchange or have another accepted medium through which they could be and normally are sold. These securities should be high-grade bonds, other debt instruments, or *blue-chip stocks* listed on a stock exchange by a financially strong corporation. If blue-chip stocks are to be purchased, the ones to be considered should be those that are not likely to fluctuate widely in price and, when sold, will return as much or more than the amount that was originally invested. That is to say, the primary emphasis with temporary investments is the preservation of the amount originally invested. Because of the low risk involved this kind of security yields a relatively low rate of return, a common characteristic of readily saleable, high-grade securities. Such temporary investments are classified as current assets because the intent of management is to convert them back into cash as soon as a seasonal shortage of cash is experienced. The accounting examples that follow illustrate the recording of the purchase of bonds accompanied by the receipt of interest and the purchase of stock accompanied by the receipt of dividends.

Bonds as temporary investments

Assume that on July 1, 1979, Hoffman Company purchases as temporary investments 6 percent, AAA bonds of the Terrell Company with a face value of $30,000, at 102 plus accrued interest. Interest is paid on January 1 and July 1. The brokerage fee and other costs incident to the purchase are $60. This information is recorded as follows:

1979						
Jul.	1	Temporary Investments in Marketable				
		Securities—Bonds of Terrell Company	30,660	00		
		Cash			30,660	00
		To record the purchase of bonds of the				
		Terrell Company as temporary investments.				

Recording assets at cost

As are all assets, Temporary Investments in Marketable Securities are recorded at full cost. Cost includes brokerage fee as well as other incidental costs.

The following points deserve emphasis:

1. In accordance with the generally accepted principle of recording all assets at

cost, Temporary Investments in Marketable Securities are recorded at full cost, including the brokerage fee and other incidental costs.

2. The account title, Temporary Investments in Marketable Securities—Bonds of Terrell Company, includes the general ledger control account Temporary Investments in Marketable Securities and the name of the individual bond for posting to a subsidiary record, referred to as an *investment register*.

Assuming that books are closed on December 31, 1979, the accountant for the Hoffman Company would accrue the semiannual bond interest as follows:

Date		Account	Debit	Credit
1979				
Dec.	31	Accrued Bond Interest Receivable	900 00	
		Bond Interest Earned		900 00
		To accrue the semiannual interest on the Terrell Company bonds.		

Then the receipt of semiannual interest on January 1, 1980, is recorded as follows:

Date		Account	Debit	Credit
1980				
Jan.	1	Cash	900 00	
		Accrued Bond Interest Receivable		900 00
		To record receipt of semiannual bond interest on bonds of the Terrell Company.		

To complete the cycle, assume that on February 1, 1980, Hoffman Company found that it needed cash and decided to sell the bonds of the Terrell Company. They were sold at 101¾ (net of brokerage fees and other costs) plus accrued interest; the transaction is recorded as follows:

Date		Account	Debit	Credit
1980				
Feb.	1	Cash	30,675 00	
		Realized Loss on Disposal of Temporary Investments	135 00	
		Bond Interest Earned		150 00
		Temporary Investments in Marketable Securities—Bonds of Terrell Company		30,660 00
		To record sale of temporary investment securities.		

1. The computation of the gain on disposal of temporary investments is:

Original full cost of bonds	$30,660.00
Less: Selling price of bonds ($30,000 × 101.75%)	30,525.00
Realized loss on disposal of temporary investments	$ 135.00

2. The cash received comes from two sources: the sale of the bonds, $30,525, and the sale of the earned interest, $150.
3. The Temporary Investments in Marketable Securities account must be credited with the same amount for which it was originally debited; that is, the cost.

Realized Loss on Disposal of Temporary Investments is shown in the income statement under Other Expense. Management must consider this loss, along with the Bond Interest Earned, in evaluating the success of its decision to invest in the bonds of Terrell Company.

Stocks as temporary investments

To illustrate the recording of a purchase of stock as a temporary investment, assume that on April 1, 1979, Bowan Company purchases 200 shares of Byrd Corporation preferred stock at $105 per share. Brokerage fees are $108. The entry to record the purchase is:

1979						
Apr.	1	Temporary Investments in Marketable Securities—Preferred Stock of Byrd Corporation	21,108	00		
		Cash			21,108	00
		To record the purchase of 200 shares of Byrd Corporation preferred stock at $105 a share.				

The amount of the debit to the asset is the full cost including brokerage fees.

Assume that on July 1, 1979, a quarterly dividend of $1.50 per share is received on the 200 shares of the Byrd Corporation stock. The entry to record the dividend is:

1979						
Jul.	1	Cash	300	00		
		Dividends Earned			300	00
		To record the receipt of a quarterly dividend from the Byrd Corporation.				

Dividends Earned is classified under Other Revenue on the income statement.

Again, to meet a seasonal cash shortage, on September 15, 1979, the preferred stock of Byrd Corporation is sold for $106.50 per share (net of brokerage fees and other costs). The sale is recorded as follows:

1979						
Sep.	15	Cash	21,300	00		
		Temporary Investments in Marketable Securities—Preferred Stock of Byrd Corporation			21,108	00
		Realized Gain on Disposal of Temporary Investments			192	00
		To record sale of preferred stock of Byrd Corporation at $106.50 a share.				

Realized gain on disposal of temporary investments is determined as follows:

Selling price of preferred stock (200 × $106.50)	$21,300.00
Less: Original full cost	21,108.00
Realized gain on disposal of temporary investments	$ 192.00

To repeat, Realized Gain on Disposal of Temporary Investments is shown on the income statement under Other Revenue. Management must consider this amount, along with Dividends Earned, in evaluating the success of its decision to buy the preferred stock as a temporary investment.

Valuation of temporary investments in marketable securities

Ideally, all current assets should be shown at current market price on the balance sheet since this statement should reflect the financial position as of a given time. Certain companies, such as insurance companies, disclose their temporary investments at current market price. Most companies, however, value these securities at either cost or lower of total cost or total market (LCM) calculated as in the method indicated in Chapter 13 for inventory items.

At cost Temporary investments in debt instruments of other entities may be valued at either cost or lower of cost or market. Cost is certainly the simplest of all valuation methods to apply to these securities since they are initially recorded at cost. If they are valued at cost, the current market value of the securities, obtainable from the financial page of any daily newspaper, should also be disclosed in the balance sheet by a parenthetical notation as shown below to enable the reader to evaluate the item for purposes of financial position analysis.

Assets

Current Assets		
Cash		$ 562,000.00
Temporary Investments in Marketable Securities—		
Bonds; (current market price, $175,000),		
shown at cost		158,000.00
Accounts Receivable	$200,000.00	
Deduct Allowance for Doubtful		
Accounts	8,000.00	192,000.00
Merchandise Inventory		300,000.00
Prepaid Insurance		2,000.00
Total Current Assets		$1,214,000.00

Note that even though the current market value is disclosed parenthetically, the securities are valued at cost; that is, only the original cost is added into the figures that are totaled. The cost method is consistent with the fundamental principle of matching expired costs (or expenses) and revenues as well as with income tax requirements.

At lower of cost or market Because of a substantial decline in the value of many ownership securities (common and some preferred stocks) during 1973 and 1974, the Financial Accounting Standards Board concluded in 1975 that temporary investments in ownership securities should be valued at the lower of total market or total cost of all security items.[1] Their pronouncement makes the LCM method the current acceptable standard for valuation of these securities. Although the accounting is somewhat complex, the authors feel that students should be acquainted with the basic accounting for this method of valuation. Hence an illustration and more detailed discussion are presented in an appendix to this chapter.

Long-term investments in stocks and bonds

Stocks and bonds are the two major items in which firms make investments to be held for a long period of time. Other long-term investments include: accounts receivable and notes receivable (long-term), land held for future use, cash surrender value of life insurance on key officers, special funds such as that to retire bonded indebtedness or that to buy plant and equipment items, and other similar items.

In this discussion we will emphasize stocks and bonds. Only brief consideration is given to the remaining items.

Although a company may buy stock in another company specifically for the dividend revenue, it may also buy the stock in order to control that company. It may buy a substantial percentage of the stock of another company—which then becomes its *subsidiary*—for the purpose of expanding and diversifying its operations and gaining a more prominent competitive position, possibly accompanied by a steady supply of merchandise or the creation of sales outlets. The company acquiring a majority of the voting stock of another company is referred to as a *parent company*. The acquisition of a controlling interest in one or more subsidiary corporations frequently leads to the combining of the financial statements of the affiliated companies into a set of consolidated statements. An example of these is presented in the Appendix to this book.

Shares of stock may be purchased directly from the issuing company, but they are more likely to be acquired through a broker on the New York Stock Exchange, the American Stock Exchange, or other exchanges. If shares of stocks are not listed on an exchange, they are said to be sold *over the counter*—that is, sold through other securities dealers.

1 FASB *Statement* No. 12, December 1975.

Accounting for investment in stock

The cost method of recording and valuation

Companies that make long-term investment in stocks as well as temporary investments should initially record the items at full cost including brokerage fees and postage. *APB Opinion No. 18* recommends that an investing company that buys less than 20 percent of the common stock of a domestic company and an investing company that buys certain other common stock should account for these investments by the *cost method,* which is described in this section. If cash is paid for the purchase of stock, there is no problem in establishing cost. Where cash payment is not paid problems of valuation may arise. A sound accounting rule is to record the investment asset at the most objective measurement of the *cash-equivalent* cost of the securities. To illustrate, assume first that on July 1, 1979, the Sutton Company purchases 1,000 shares of $100 par value common stock of Earl Corporation at 105 with a broker's fee of $440. The investor's total cost is $105,440, and the following entry is made.

1979						
Jul.	1	Investment in Stocks—Common Stock				
		of Earl Corporation	105,440	00		
		Cash			105,440	00
		To record the purchase of 1,000 shares of $100 par value common stock of Earl Corporation; the cost is computed as follows: (1,000 shares x $105 = $105,000) + $440 = $105,440.				

Observe that the asset, Investment in Stocks, is debited for *the cost,* not the par value, of the stock. The account title shows the general ledger controlling account, Investment in Stocks, and the subsidiary account title, Common Stock of Earl Corporation. The information about the specific stock is transferred to a supplementary or subsidiary record, often called the investment register.

To illustrate the accounting for receipt of declared dividends, assume that the board of directors of Earl Corporation declared a quarterly divident of $0.60 per share at the end of September. As a general rule, for convenience, a cash dividend is not recorded until it is actually received. If Sutton Company received the dividend check from Earl Corporation on November 10, 1979, it records this information as follows:

1979						
Nov.	10	Cash	600	00		
		Dividends Earned			600	00
		To record the receipt of a $0.60 per share dividend from the Earl Corporation.				

A necessary exception to the foregoing cash-basis rule is the case of a dividend declared in one year and payable in another year.

Recognizing declared dividends

Sound accrual accounting theory dictates that the dividend revenue be recognized in the year in which the dividend is declared, not in the year in which it is paid.

Instead of cash dividends a corporation may issue additional shares of stock to stockholders without requiring additional cash. Two different devices may be used to accomplish this objective: (1) additional shares of common stock may be issued to the common stockholders as a stock dividend, or (2) additional shares of stock may be issued to the stockholders in exchange for the stock held by them. This latter device is referred to as a stock split. Financial managers of modern corporations make frequent use of both stock dividends and stock splits to reduce the market price per share and thus to put the stock in a more favorable price range. The additional shares received by an investing company are not revenue to it. Only a memorandum entry is necessary to record the increase in the number of shares owned. The unit cost is decreased, however, because of the larger number of shares held after the stock dividend is issued. For example, assume that Earl Corporation declares a 100 percent stock dividend (a 2-for-1 split would be treated in the same way). Receipt of the additional 1,000 shares on December 12, 1979, by Sutton Company is noted in the journal as follows (the original 1,000 shares had cost $105,440):

1979				
Dec.	12	Memorandum Entry—Today there were received 1,000 shares of stock of Earl Corporation, representing a 100 percent stock dividend. The cost per share of the stock is recomputed as follows:		
		Old Number of Shares: 1,000 — New number of shares: 2,000		
		Total cost: $105,440 — New cost per share: $52.72		

The realized gain or loss per share on any subsequent sale of Earl Corporation stock is determined by comparing the selling price with the adjusted cost of $52.72 per share.

Financial statement disclosure The Dividends Earned balance is disclosed in the income statement under Other Revenue, whereas the Investment in Stocks account is reported in the balance sheet under Long-Term Investments, a noncurrent caption appearing between Current Assets and Plant and Equipment.

Valuation of long-term investments in stocks

At cost If the investment in stocks is considered to be a permanent, nonmarketable item and if the percentage of ownership is less than 20 percent, then the cost method is the generally accepted method of balance sheet valuation. As with temporary investments, long-term investments are initially recorded at cost; therefore, there would be no valuation problems. These items would be disclosed on the balance sheet at the figures which appear in the ledger accounts.

At lower of cost or market On the other hand, if the investment in these ownership securities is considered to be an investment in long-term *marketable* securities, FASB *Statement* No. 12 requires that these equity securities be valued at the lower of total cost (of all such securities) and total market. At this stage of learning, the reader should be aware of this fact, but the accounting process for accomplishing this valuation is not an elementary topic and is not presented here.

Accounting for investment in subsidiary

In the illustrations thus far, investments in other corporations have been carried at cost, and revenue from these investments has been recognized only as dividends were declared. The Accounting Principles Board has ruled that, when a corporation's investment in a domestic or foreign subsidiary is large enough to presume ability to control it, the *equity method* should be used to account for the investment.[2] In its *Opinion* No. 18, the Board concluded that ownership of 20 percent or more of the voting stock of another company is evidence of ability to exercise control.

The equity method

Under the equity method, the initial purchase is recorded at cost. After the initial acquisition, however, the investment account of the parent company is debited or credited to give recognition to income or losses and dividend declarations of the subsidiary. The following transactions of the Parenter and Sunner Corporations are used to illustrate the equity method:

1979
Jan. 2 Parenter Corporation purchased 40 percent of the stock of the Sunner Corporation at *book value* for $400,000.
Aug. 8 Sunner Corporation declared and paid a total dividend of $20,000.
Dec. 31 Sunner Corporation earned a net income of $80,000 for 1979.
1980
Dec. 31 Sunner Corporation suffered a net loss of $3,000 in 1980.

2 APB *Opinion* No. 18, "The Equity Method of Accounting for Investments in Stock," March, 1971, p. 355.

Transactions affecting the Parenter Corporation are recorded by the equity method as follows:

			Debit		Credit	
1979						
Jan.	2	Investment in Stocks—Common Stock of Sunner Corporation	400,000	00		
		Cash			400,000	00
		To record purchase of 40 percent of the stock of Sunner Corporation.				
Aug.	8	Cash	8,000	00		
		Investment in Stocks—Common Stock of Sunner Corporation			8,000	00
		To record receipt of dividend from the Sunner Corporation.				
Dec.	31	Investment in Stocks—Common Stock of Sunner Corporation	32,000	00		
		Subsidiary Income			32,000	00
		To record parent's share of reported net income.				
1980						
Dec.	31	Subsidiary Loss	1,200	00		
		Investment in Stocks—Common Stock of Sunner Corporation			1,200	00
		To record parent's share of reported net loss.				

When the foregoing information is posted, the Investment in Stocks account will appear as presented below. (The posting references have been omitted.)

Investment in Stocks — Acct. No. 152

Date		Explanation	F	Debit		Credit		Balance	
1979									
Jan.	2	Initial cost of 40% of stock of Sunner		400,000	00			400,000	00
Aug.	8	Receipt of dividend (40% of total) .				8,000	00	392,000	00
Dec.	31	Share of Sunner's net income for 1979		32,000	00			424,000	00
1980									
Dec.	31	Share of Sunner's net loss for 1980				1,200	00	422,800	00

Using the equity method, a parent corporation recognizes an economic reality: income and losses of its subsidiary are also part of the parent corporation's own income and losses. The two accounts, Subsidiary Income and Subsidiary Loss would be closed to Income Summary and shown on Parenter's income statement under Other Revenues and Other Expenses. Since the parent's share of net income is included in revenue by the entry made at the end of the year, the receipt of dividends would be considered a return of a portion of the parent's investment —not revenue. APB *Opinion* No. 18 became effective December 31, 1971; therefore many long-term investments in common stock are now accounted for under the equity method.

In the foregoing illustration, it is assumed that the Parenter Corporation purchased the stock of Sunner Corporation at book value. If the stock had been purchased at a figure over or below book value, additional entries *amortizing* the excess or deficiency may be required under some circumstances. These additional complexities are discussed in detail in most intermediate and advanced textbooks.

Accounting for investment in bonds

A number of institutional investors are prohibited by law from buying common stock; others are restricted in the amount of common stock they may buy. Organizations such as banks, insurance companies, some trusts, and pension funds may acquire bonds as sound investments. Industrial companies also frequently buy bonds, either for the interest revenue to be received or for reasons of business connection.

Accounting for the purchase of long-term bonds is practically the mirror image of accounting for the issuance of bonds and notes. Both of these instruments are written promises to pay sums in the future. Bonds are issued in formal certificates with specified denomination, usually $1,000 each. Various kinds of bonds are issued: some secured by mortgage, some unsecured (referred to as debentures), and some convertible into common stock. (A description of the different bonds is provided in Chapter 19.) Bonds are graded according to quality (AAA to ungraded) by various financial institutions. The grade depends on the financial condition of the issuing corporation. The decision to buy a given kind or grade of bond will depend upon: (1) security desired, (2) amount of risk that is acceptable (with higher net interest rates as risk increases), (3) safety of both principal and interest, and (4) other factors. If, on the issue date, the stated interest applicable to the face value of the bonds issued—also called *contract* or *nominal* rate—is the same as the prevailing market interest rate for the particular grade of bonds, the investor can buy these bonds at face value. On the other hand, if there is a difference between the contract bond interest rate and the prevailing market rate for the particular grade of bonds, the investor will pay a price for the bonds which is above or is below face value; that is, the investor will buy the bonds at a *premium* or a *discount*.

The accounting for four different bond investments are discussed:

Bonds purchased at face value on an interest date
Bonds purchased at a premium on an interest date
Bonds purchased at a discount on an interest date
Bonds purchased between interest dates.

Bonds purchased at face value on an interest date

The first example is a simple situation in which a company purchases bonds at face value on an interest date. The same sequence is followed in each of the first three examples. First, an entry is made to record the purchase of the bonds; next, any peculiarity of financial statement presentation is discussed; after this, the accounting procedure for the receipt of interest is described.

Assume that on July 1, 1979, the Cane Bank purchases Rockness Corporation 8 percent debenture bonds with a face value of $200,000 and a maturity date of June 30, 1999. Interest is paid twice a year on June 30 and December 31. All the bonds are purchased on July 1, 1979, at a total cost of 100. This means that the cost is 100 percent of face. Thus, in this case, the bonds are purchased at face value. (In this and the next four examples, we will assume that all costs—for bonds, brokerage fees and any transfer taxes are included in the stated price of the bonds.) The following entry is made to record the purchase of these bonds as long-term investments:

1979						
Jul.	1	Investment in Bonds—Rockness Corporation Debenture Bonds . . .	200,000	00		
		Cash			200,000	00
		To record the purchase of Rockness Corporation Debenture bonds, 8 percent maturity date, June 30, 1999.				

Two comments should be made about the entry:

1. The similarity between this entry and the receipt of short-term notes, discussed in Chapter 11, is clear.
2. The debit entry shows the controlling account, Investment in Bonds, and the subsidiary ledger information (the individual bond issue which is purchased). The particular subsidiary ledger could be in the form of an investment register rather than a formal separate ledger, as is maintained for Accounts Receivable.

A balance sheet prepared after this transaction would report the bond investment as follows:

Long-Term Investments:	
Investment in Bonds, valued at cost	$200,000.00

The Long-Term Investment caption appears on the balance sheet between Current Assets and Plant and Equipment. Long-Term Investments in Bonds are shown on the balance sheet at cost or cost adjusted for amortization of any premium or discount; this valuation procedure is discussed in the next two illustrations.

The Cane Bank records the receipt of the first semiannual interest payment on December 31, 1979, as follows (the purchase of the bonds and the receipt of interest are normally recorded in the cash payments and cash receipts journals):

1979				
Dec.	31	Cash	8,000 00	
		Bond Interest Earned		8,000 00
		To record the receipt of the semiannual interest on the Rockness Corporation bonds.		

A similar entry is made each June 30 and December 31 until the bonds are retired and the principal amount is paid to the Cane Bank. It is possible for all the interest received to be credited to a single Interest Earned (revenue) account. In the present case, however, the interest received on bonds is considered to be material enough to suggest a separate general ledger revenue account called Bond Interest Earned.

On June 30, 1999, when the principal amount of the bonds is paid to the Cane Bank, Cane's accountant would make the following entry to record the receipt of the *last* interest amount and the principal amount of the bonds:

1999				
Jun.	30	Cash	208,000 00	
		Investment in Bonds—Rockness Corporation Debenture Bonds . .		200,000 00
		Bond Interest Earned		8,000 00
		To record receipt of the final interest payment and the principal amount of the Rockness bonds.		

Why bonds sell at a premium or discount

As stated in Chapter 19, if the average effective market interest rate on bonds of any particular grade is higher than the contract interest rate of bonds of the same grade being issued, investors will offer less than the face value of the bonds in order to make up the difference between the rates. The difference between the issue price and the maturity value, plus receipts of the semiannual interest, will give the investors a return on their investments approximating the yield of similar amounts invested at the prevailing market interest rate. By the same token, if the stated interest rate is higher than the current market rate, investors will tend to offer more than the face value amount of the bonds. The reason for this is that the investors know that the premium paid will, in effect, be returned to them to the extent that the periodic interest payments exceed the amount that they would otherwise receive on investments made at the current market rate.

To repeat, the premium and discount arise as a result of differences in the average market rate of interest on a given grade of bond and the particular contract rate on these bonds. A knowledge of this fact suggests the approach to the accounting for the amortization of the premium and discount elements given in the two illustrations which follow.

Bonds purchased at a premium on an interest date

Assume that on July 1, 1979, the Premo Corporation purchases 8 percent first mortgage bonds of the Blocher Corporation. The bonds were authorized on July 1, 1979, and have a face value of $300,000 with a maturity date of June 30, 1994. Interest is paid semiannually on June 30 and December 31. Premo Corporation pays 103 for the bonds and records the purchase in the following manner:

1979						
Jul.	1	Investment in Bonds—Blocher				
		Corporation First Mortgage Bonds .	309,000	00		
		Cash			309,000	00
		To record the purchase of Blocher 8 percent bonds which mature on June 30, 1994.				

Observe that the asset account is debited for the *full cost* of the bonds just as a Machinery account would be. On the books of the investor, no separate premium or discount account is set up when bonds are purchased at a premium or discount.

A balance sheet prepared on July 1, 1979, would show the Investment in Bonds under Long-Term Investments as follows:

Assets	
Long-Term Investments	
Investment in Bonds, valued at cost	$309,000.00

Accounting for interest receipts and straight-line amortization of premium element The amount paid for the Blocher Corporation Bonds is $9,000 more than will be received when the bonds are collected at maturity. This amount is *not* a loss to the investor. It arose because the contract rate of interest on the bonds was higher than the prevailing average market rate on similar grade bonds. It, therefore, appears to be logical and is sound accounting practice to allocate part of the premium element to each period as a reduction of the periodic bond interest revenue. The straight-line method of assigning the appropriate part of this premium element to the bond interest revenue is the most commonly used method and the one we use in this text. In summary, we can say that the total bond interest revenue over the life of the bond issue is equal to the total amount of cash received for interest reduced by the amount of the premium element.

Using this general principle and straight-line amortization, the Premo Corporation would record the receipt of the first interest payment as follows:

1979						
Dec.	31	Cash	12,000	00		
		Bond Interest Earned			11,700	00
		Investment in Bonds—Blocher Corporation First Mortgage Bonds			300	00
		To record the receipt of semiannual bond interest and the amortization of the premium element: $9,000 ÷ 30 semiannual periods = $300.				

Note that, since no separate premium account was set up, amortization of the premium element is credited directly to the Investment in Bonds account. If the $9,000 premium element represents a reduction in bond interest revenue over the entire 15-year life of the bonds, it is evident that by the straight-line amortization method, the reduction in bond interest revenue for the six months ended December 31, 1979, is $9,000 divided by 30 semiannual periods or $300.

This compound entry shows that the $12,000 interest receipt is composed of receipt of net interest revenue of only $11,700 and a partial repayment of the original amount which was paid for the bonds, the $300 which is amortized. (It is suggested that, for the problems in this book, the premium and discount elements of the Investment in Bonds be amortized each time the bond interest revenue is recorded to emphasize that this amortization is an adjustment of the bond interest revenue.) Even though the compound entry is acceptable, two separate entries may be, and in practice probably will be, made: (1) one entry to record the receipt of the semiannual interest, which *will be* made in the cash receipts journal, and (2) a separate entry to record the semiannual amortization of the premium element which may be made in the general journal, and it often may be made at the end of the year as an adjusting entry. (These two separate entries are illustrated with the more complex examples where bonds are purchased between interest dates; see page 657.)

The validity of the $11,700 semiannual bond interest revenue figure can be checked and proved by the following calculation.

Total cash receipts for the 15 years:	
Collection of face value at maturity	$300,000.00
Total interest at contract rate:	
8% × $300,000 × 15 years	360,000.00
Total cash collections	$660,000.00
Total cash payment to purchase bonds:	
Bonds with face of $300,000 purchased at 103	309,000.00
Net interest revenue for 15 years	$351,000.00
If Premo Corporation recognizes the earning of this revenue equally (the straight-line approach) over the 30 semiannual periods, then the Bond Interest Earned for a six-month period is:	
$351,000 ÷ 30 semiannual periods	$ 11,700.00

As indicated in Chapters 11 and 19, the effective rate of interest that is earned on a given investment is an excellent way of determining relative profitability of various investments. An approximation of the effective interest (i) on bond investment can be determined by the use of the following formula:

$$i = I \div \left(F + \frac{P}{2} \right)$$

where I = annual absolute interest, adjusted for amortization of premium element

F = face value of bonds

P = original premium element

$\frac{P}{2}$ = average premium

The approximate effective interest rate on the investment in Blocher Corporation bonds is 7.68 percent = [$23,400 ÷ ($300,000 + $9,000/2)]; that is, the absolute effective annual bond interest revenue divided by the average book value of the Investment in Bonds. The effective interest rate computation emphasizes the fact that the premium element of the Investment in Bonds results in a downward adjustment of the 8 percent contract rate to the approximation of the effective rate of 7.68 percent.

Bonds purchased at a discount on an interest date

Assume that on July 1, 1979, the Discus Corporation purchases Caidell Company's 7 percent debenture bonds with a face of $400,000 and a maturity date of June 30, 1989. Assume, further, that the bonds are purchased on date of authorization at a total price of 97. Interest dates are June 30 and December 31. The discount is caused by the difference in the existing average market rate on similar grades of debenture bonds and the contract rate of interest on the Caidell bonds being purchased. The Caidell Company's debenture bonds have a contract interest rate that is lower than the prevailing market rate on similar grade securities. The purchase of the bonds may be recorded as follows:

1979						
Jul.	1	Investment in Bonds—Caidell Company Debenture Bonds	388,000	00		
		Cash			388,000	00
		To record purchase of 7 percent debenture bonds due June 30, 1989; the cost is determined as follows: $400,000 x 0.97 = $388,000.				

A balance sheet prepared on July 1, 1979, would disclose the Investment in Bonds as follows:

Assets

Long-Term Investments
Investment in Bonds, valued at cost $388,000.00

Note the similarity of disclosure with that of the premium case. After the first amortization entry is made, the Investment in Bonds will be valued at cost plus the adjustment for amortization.

The following compound entry records the receipt of the first semiannual interest from the Caidell Company and the semiannual amortization of the discount element of the Investment in Bonds:

			Debit	Credit
1979				
Dec.	31	Cash	14,000 00	
		Investment in Bonds—Caidell Company Debenture Bonds	600 00	
		Bond Interest Earned		14,600 00
		To record the receipt of semiannual bond interest and the amortization of the discount element: $12,000 ÷ 20 semiannual periods = $600.		

Observe that the amount of the amortization of the discount is debited, which increases the Investment in Bonds account. This entry indicates that the effective semiannual bond interest revenue is $14,600 despite the fact that the company received only $14,000 in cash. With the use of the straight-line method of amortization, the net effective interest amount is equal to the semiannual cash collection plus a prorata share of the discount element that will be received at the maturity date of the bonds. This accounting procedure, therefore, recognizes the reason for the discount on the bonds—the fact that the contract rate of interest on the Caidell bonds was lower than the existing average market interest rate on similar grades of debenture bonds.

The amount of the net semiannual bond interest revenue can be proved in a different manner by the following calculation:

Total cash receipts for the 10 years:	
Collection of face value at maturity	$400,000.00
Total interest at contract rate:	
7% × $400,000 × 10 years	280,000.00
Total cash collections	$680,000.00
Total cash payment to purchase bonds:	
Bonds with a face of $400,000 purchased at 97	388,000.00
Net bond interest revenue for 10 years	$292,000.00

If the Discus Corporation recognizes the earning of this revenue equally (the straight-line approach) over the 20 semiannual periods, the Bond Interest Earned for a six-month period is:

$292,000 ÷ 20 semiannual periods	$ 14,600.00

A formula for the approximation of the effective interest rate on average book value of a bond investment purchased at a discount may be stated as follows:

$$i = I \div \left(F - \frac{D}{2}\right)$$

where I = annual absolute interest, adjusted for amortization of the discount element of the bond investment
F = face value of the bonds
D = original discount element
$\frac{D}{2}$ = average discount element

The effective interest earned on the Caidell bonds is 7.41 percent = [\$29,200 ÷ (\$400,000 − \$12,000/2)]. Note that the discount element on the Investment in Bonds results in an upward adjustment of the 7 percent contract rate to its approximate effective yield of 7.41 percent.

Bonds purchased between interest dates

The preceding examples emphasized the basic accounting procedures and the reasons for amortizing the premium and discount elements on the Investment in Bonds. A more complex problem involving the purchase of bonds between interest dates with the required end-of-period adjustments is presented below.

Recording the purchase Bonds may be authorized by the stockholders but not issued for several months or even years because market conditions are not favorable. The interest on bonds issued between interest dates will have accrued from the last interest date to the date of issuance. Since the bonds carry a promise to pay not only the face value at maturity but six months' interest at each interest date, it is customary in these cases for the investor to pay the issue price of the bonds plus an amount equal to the accrued interest. In turn, the first interest payment (as promised in writing by the bond indenture) will be for one full interest period—six months' interest—thereby returning to the purchaser the accrued interest that was paid plus the interest earned from the date of purchase to the current interest date.

Assume that on June 1, 1979, Intro Company purchases Nikolai Company 9 percent debenture bonds with a face value of \$400,000 and a maturity date of October 1, 1987. Assume that the interest is paid semiannually on April 1 and October 1 and that the bonds had been authorized way back on October 1, 1977, but had not been issued until June 1, 1979. Intro Company pays 105 plus accrued interest. The total amount of cash that the Intro Company would have to pay for these bonds is \$426,000: \$420,000 for the bonds plus \$6,000 for the accrued interest purchased. Note that the promise to pay six months' interest is not retroactive beyond April 1, 1979, the interest date immediately preceding the date of purchase. On October 1, 1979, Intro Company receives an interest check in the amount of $18,000, although the interest on $400,000 at 9 percent from June 1 to October 1 is only $12,000. The semiannual interest check includes a collection of the $6,000 the Intro Company paid for the accrued bond interest receivable purchased on June 1, as illustrated in Figure 20–1.

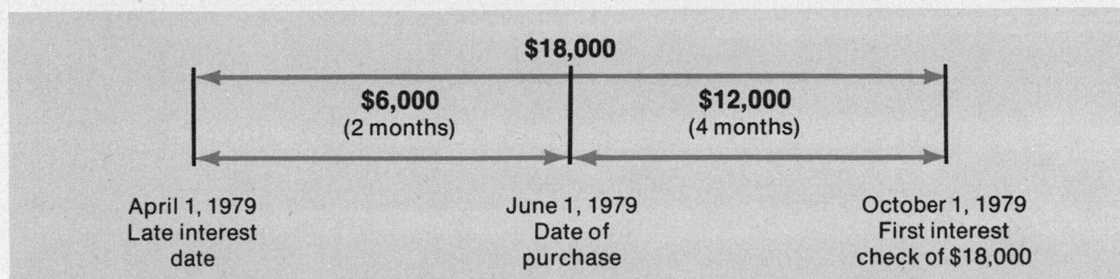

Figure 20–1
Accumulation of interest

The Intro Company records the purchase of the bonds as shown below:

1979				
Jun.	1	Investment in Bonds—Nikolai Company Debenture Bonds	420,000 00	
		Accrued Bond Interest Receivable . .	6,000 00	
		Cash		426,000 00
		To record the purchase of Nikolai Company debenture bonds at 105 plus accrued interest.		

The accrued bond interest receivable is debited to a current asset account, since it will be collected on the next interest date.

The entries to record the collection of the semiannual interest and the amortization of the premium element of the bond investment are shown below:

1979				
Oct.	1	Cash	18,000 00	
		Accrued Bond Interest Receivable		6,000 00
		Bond Interest Earned		12,000 00
		To record the collection of semiannual interest on 9 percent bonds of the Nikolai Company.		
	1	Bond Interest Earned	800 00	
		Investment in Bonds—Nikolai Company Debenture Bonds		800 00
		To record the amortization of the premium element for 4 months: $20,000 x 4/100 = $800.		

Instead of merging the foregoing information in one compound entry, two recording entries are made since it is somewhat easier to handle the more complex information one step at a time. The entry for the interest collection reflects the amounts shown in Figure 20–1, that is, the semiannual interest check includes a collection of $6,000 for Accrued Bond Interest Receivable purchased plus $12,000 for interest actually earned by the investor for the four months' use of its money.

Amortization period

The amortization of the premium element is for only the period from the date of purchase to the maturity date.

Neither the date of authorization nor the preceding interest date is relevant to the start of the amortization period. For the investment in Nikolai Company bonds, the amortization period begins on the *date of purchase,* June 1, 1979, and ends at the *maturity date,* October 1, 1987, a total amortization period of 100 months. The amount of the premium element to be amortized each month is $200 = ($20,000 ÷ 100 months); the amount for four months is $800 = (4 × $200) or, as stated in the foregoing journal entry, $800 = ($20,000 × 4/100).

End-of-period adjustments Assuming that the Intro Company closes its books on a calendar-year-basis, the following entries are made on December 31, 1979:

Date		Accounts and Explanation	Debit	Credit
1979				
Dec.	31	Accrued Bond Interest Receivable . .	9,000 00	
		Bond Interest Earned		9,000 00
		To record the accrual of bond interest earned for three months.		
	31	Bond Interest Earned	600 00	
		Investment in Bonds—Nikolai Company Debenture Bonds		600 00
		To record the amortization of premium element on bond investment for three months: 3/100 x $20,000 = $600.		

The effect of the end-of-year adjustment is that the Bond Interest Earned account reflects the correct interest revenue ($19,600) earned during the seven months which the bonds were held by the investor (June 1 to December 31). The Bond Interest Earned account is closed to Income Summary. The Accrued Bond Interest Receivable account is shown as a current asset on the balance sheet and under the nonreversing approach remains on the books until the next regular interest date.

Recording interest collection in following year On April 1, 1980, the next regular interest date, the following entries are made to record the collection of interest and the amortization of the premium element of the bond investment:

Date		Accounts and Explanation	Debit	Credit
1980				
Apr.	1	Cash	18,000 00	
		Bond Interest Earned		9,000 00
		Accrued Bond Interest Receivable .		9,000 00
		To record the collection of semiannual interest on the Nikolai Company bonds.		
	1	Bond Interest Earned	600 00	
		Investment in Bonds—Nikolai Company Debenture Bonds		600 00
		To record the amortization of premium element for three months: 3/100 x $20,000 = $600.		

Note that only three months' amortization of the premium element of the bond investment is recorded. The reason for this is that only three months' bond interest revenue is earned and recorded on April 1, 1980.

Other long-term investment items

Other long-term investment items are briefly discussed below.

Long-term accounts receivable

For these accounts receivable to be classified as Long-Term Investments, they should be nontrade items resulting, say, from loans to officers or to other employees. Observe that trade installment accounts receivable of three-years length are *still classified as current assets* since the operating cycle would now be three years not one year.

Long-term notes

Often both secured or unsecured notes may be acquired for long-term purposes. Much of the accounting for Investment in Bonds would apply to the accounting for Investment in Long-Term Notes.

Land held for future plant expansion

Only land actually used in operations should be classified as plant and equipment. Land purchased for a future plant building site should be classified as a Long-Term Investment.

Cash surrender value of life insurance

Many companies will insure the lives of their key officers and will take out life insurance policies which after a certain period of time have a cash value that can be obtained upon the cancellation of the insurance policies. This cash value reduces the effective Life Insurance Expense and should be set up as a Long-Term Investment on the company which has taken out the policies.

Long-term funds

Companies create long-term funds for various purposes such as to retire a long-term debt, to buy plant and equipment, and for other purposes. The start of a long-term fund is to segregate cash; but this cash should not remain idle. It should be invested. When investments occur, they should be accounted for as other investments are. The only difference: the investment item should have as a part of its title the name of the particular fund, as, Plant and Equipment Acquisition Fund—Investments in Bonds.

In this chapter, only the elementary topics involving Long-Term Investments have been presented. Other complex topics such as sales of investments, conversion of one type of investment into another type, and other complexities are covered in most intermediate and advanced accounting texts.

Valuation of temporary investments in equity marketable securities at lower of cost or market

appendix

Learning goal

To be acquainted with the valuation process of temporary investments in marketable equity securities at lower of cost or market.

Key terms

equity securities
net unrealized gain-temporary investments in marketable securities
net unrealized loss-temporary investments in marketable securities
valuation allowance-net unrealized loss in value of temporary investments in marketable securities

Until 1976, the typical method of valuing all temporary investments was cost. The Financial Accounting Standards Board, because of the substantial declines in market value of equity securities during 1973 and 1974, concluded that *all* temporary investment in equity marketable securities should be treated as a single asset item and should be shown on the balance sheet at the lower of total cost or total market of these temporary investments. In its *Statement* No. 12, the FASB has defined *equity securities* as including ownership shares or the right to acquire or dispose of ownership shares in a company at fixed or determinable prices. The term does not include preferred stock that by its terms either *must* be redeemed by the issuing company or is redeemable at the option of the investor. It also does not include treasury stock or convertible bonds.[3]

3 FASB *Statement* No. 12, December 1975.

Both the *realized* gains and losses on sales of these temporary investments in these equity securities and those *unrealized* gains and losses (recognized before a sale of the securities) arising from changes in the valuation allowance should be included in the determination of net income of the period in which they *occur*. The *valuation allowance* is the amount by which the total cost of the securities exceeds the total market value.

To illustrate the method recommended by the FASB, suppose that the Brummet Company purchased the following three common stocks as a temporary investment during 1979:

Common Stock	*Cost*
A	$10,000.00
B	5,000.00
C	7,000.00

Suppose further that the Brummet Company held all these securities through 1980; and then on January 15, 1981, it sold Common Stock A for $9,500. The accounting for the valuation at December 31, 1979, and 1980 and the sale on January 15, 1981, are presented in the following paragraphs. Value information concerning the portfolio as of December 31, 1979, is presented below:

Common Stock	*Cost When Purchased*	*Market Value as of December 31, 1979*
A	$10,000.00	$12,000.00
B	5,000.00	3,000.00
C	7,000.00	2,000.00
Total	$22,000.00	$17,000.00

The difference between the total cost of $22,000 and the total market of $17,000 is a $5,000 loss. This loss is said to be an *unrealized* one since *no* sale has been made. The recommended title of this loss is Net Unrealized Loss—Temporary Investment in Marketable Securities and, as stated previously it should be shown on the 1979 income statement.

The adjusting entry necessary to give recognition to the valuation at December 31, 1979, is:

Date		Account	Debit	Credit
1979				
Dec.	31	Net Unrealized Loss—Temporary Investment in Marketable Securities	5,000 00	
		Valuation Allowance—Net Unrealized Loss in Value of Temporary Investment in Marketable Securities		5,000 00
		To give recognition to lower of cost or market method of valuation of temporary investments.		

The balance sheet at December 31, 1979, shows the following:

Assets	
Current Assets	
Temporary Investment in Marketable Securities (at cost)	$22,000.00
Deduct Valuation Allowance—Net Unrealized Loss	5,000.00
Temporary Investments at Lower of Cost or Market	$17,000.00

If the Brummet Company does not sell any of these securities during 1980, it will have to go through the same valuation process again on December 31, 1980. Assume that the price of Common Stock A goes down in 1980 and the price of the other securities goes up. This value information is shown below:

Common Stock	*Cost When Purchased in 1979*	*Market Value as of December 31, 1980*
A	$10,000.00	$ 9,000.00
B	5,000.00	6,000.00
C	7,000.00	5,000.00
Total	$22,000.00	$20,000.00

There is still an *unrealized loss* difference of $2,000 between the total cost and the total market, but since there was a $5,000 unrealized loss recognized during 1979, there has been a *net recovery* of $3,000 during 1980. Thus, the Valuation Allowance must be decreased and an *unrealized* gain must be recorded by the following adjusting entry at December 31, 1980:

Date		Account	Debit	Credit
1980 Dec.	31	Valuation Allowance—Net Unrealized Loss in Value of Temporary Investments in Marketable Securities	3,000 00	
		Net Unrealized Gain—Temporary Investment in Marketable Securities		3,000 00
		To give recognition to lower of cost or market method of valuation of temporary investments.		

The account, Net Unrealized Gain—Temporary Investments in Marketable Securities, arises because there is a net increase in the total market value during 1980 as shown below:

	Market Value as of December 31, 1979	Market Value as of December 31, 1980	Net Increase in Total Value
Total	$17,000	$20,000	$3,000

The gain is *unrealized* since *no sale* has been made. Despite the fact that it is unrealized, it is still closed to the Income Summary and is shown on the income statement under Other Income.

The balance sheet at December 31, 1980, shows the following:

Assets		
Current Assets:		
Temporary Investments in Marketable Securities (at cost)	$22,000.00	
Deduct Valuation Allowance—Net Unrealized Loss	2,000.00	
Temporary Investments in Marketable Securities at Lower of Cost or Market . . .		$20,000.00

To illustrate the accounting for a subsequent sale of a security, consider the sale of Common Stock A as of January 15, 1981. As stated above, assume that this security is sold for $9,500. Remember that only the original cost of the common stock of $10,000 and the selling price of $9,500 now need to be considered to determine the realized loss or gain. Thus the sales transaction is recorded as follows:

Date		Account	Debit		Credit	
1981						
Jan.	15	Cash	9,500	00		
		Realized Loss on Sale of Temporary Investments	500	00		
		Temporary Investments in Marketable Securities—Common Stock A			10,000	00
		To record sale of Marketable Security A.				

The Realized Loss on Sale of Temporary Investments is calculated in the typical manner by comparing only the original cost with the selling price, thus:

Cost of Common Stock A, When Purchased	$10,000
Less: Selling Price as of January 15, 1981	9,500
Realized Loss on Sale of Temporary Investments	$ 500

The loss is shown in the income statement under Other Expenses. It is said to be *realized* since the sale has *now* taken place.

In the adjusting entry at December 31, 1981, any change in the Valuation Allowance, say a decrease because of the sale of Common Stock A, would be recorded as an unrealized gain. Remember, however, that the amount of the unrealized gain which is recognized *must not and cannot reduce the Valuation Allowance below zero*.

Book and tax accounting differ when it comes to recognizing gains and losses on temporary investments in marketable securities. For tax purposes, no gain or loss would be recognized, during 1979 or 1980. The difference between cost of $10,000 and selling price of $9,500 would result in a tax loss of $500 in 1981.

Glossary

Accrued bond interest receivable A current asset account which shows the amount of interest that has accumulated and is receivable at any given time.

Amortization of premium or discount elements of bond investment The process of writing off these elements with a corresponding adjustment to Bond Interest Earned.

Amortization period The period over which the premium or discount elements are written off; it starts with date of purchase and ends with the maturity date.

Blue-chip stocks or bonds High-grade stocks and bonds that are listed on one of the stock exchanges.

Bond A written promise under the corporate seal to pay a certain sum in the future to the named payee or to bearer.

Bond interest earned An Other Revenue account which shows the net interest earned on bonds—the gross amount received adjusted for amortization of premium or discount element of bond investment.

Cash surrender value of life insurance The cash value that can be received if an insurance policy is cancelled.

Contract interest rate The interest rate that is stated on the bonds themselves; sometimes called nominal rate.

Cost method of accounting for investment in stocks An accounting method whereby stock is recorded at cost and dividends received are recorded as revenue—no other income or loss from the subsidiary is recognized.

Dividends earned An Other Revenue account representing the amount received as dividends on investments in stock.

Face value of bonds The principal amount which will be paid at the maturity date of bonds.

Effective rate of interest The relationship of the net bond interest revenue earned to the average book value of the Investment in Bonds.

Equity method of accounting for investment in stocks A method of accounting for investment in stocks, which adjusts the cost of the investment by the parent's share of the net income or net loss of the subsidiary and treats receipts of dividends as a return of the Investment in Stock.

Equity securities Ownership shares in common stock and certain preferred stock.

Long-term investments Investments in stocks, bonds, other securities, and certain other kinds of property that management intends to hold for a long period.

Lower of cost or market A method of valuation of temporary investments in marketable equity securities or inventory items. In the lower of cost or market method of valuation of temporary investments, the total cost of the securities is compared to the total market; the total which is lower is chosen as the value to be presented on the balance sheet.

Net unrealized gain—temporary investments in marketable securities This item is unrealized since the securities have not yet been sold; it arises when securities recover some previously-lost market value.

Net unrealized loss—temporary investments in marketable securities This Other Expense income statement loss item is unrealized since the securities have not yet been sold; it arises out of the lower of cost or market valuation process when the market value is lower than cost.

Marketable securities High-grade, securities purchased by a firm *usually* to be held for a short period; they are usually classified as current assets on the balance sheet; certain long-term securities could be considered as marketable securities.

Nominal interest rate The interest rate that is stated on the bonds—sometimes called contract interest rate.

Parent company An investing company that acquires a controlling interest in the voting stock of another company.

Realizable cost The amount which could be obtained if the investment securities were to be sold.

Subsidiary A company, the majority of whose voting capital stock is held by another company, referred to as the parent company.

Subsidiary income An Other Revenue account representing the parent's share of the net income of a subsidiary irrespective of whether it is received as a dividend or not.

Subsidiary loss An Other Expense representing the parent's share of the net loss of a subsidiary.

Temporary investments in marketable securities Investments in high-grade, blue-chip securities that management intends to hold for a relatively short period; these are always classified as current assets on the balance sheet.

Valuation allowance—net unrealizable loss in value of temporary investments in marketable securities A valuation offset to Temporary Investments in Marketable Securities reflecting the excess of total cost of the securities over the total market value of the temporary investments.

Questions

Q20–1 What are temporary investments in marketable securities? How are they classified on the balance sheet?

Q20–2 List four types of investments that may qualify as temporary investments in marketable securities.

Q20–3 Name and discuss the methods of valuation of temporary investments in marketable securities.

Q20–4 Why does a firm buy securities as temporary investments?

Q20–5 Why do firms acquire stock as a long-term investment?

Q20–6 Describe the two methods of recording and valuation of long-term investments in common stock.

Q20–7 Do dividends legally accrue? Explain and contrast with interest on bonds.

Q20–8 How does a firm account for recognition of declared dividends?

Q20–9 What is a stock split-up? Discuss the accounting for a stock split-up from the point of view of the investor. Would there be any difference in the accounting for a stock dividend as compared to the accounting for a stock split from the point of view of the investor?

Q20–10 Generally speaking, the accounting for long-term investment in bonds is the mirror image of the accounting for the issuance of bonds and notes. Discuss. Describe the accounting for the investment in bonds.

Q20–11 Name the various groups of investors who typically buy bonds as a long-term investment.

Q20–12 Why do bonds sell at a premium or discount?

Q20–13 Why is premium or discount amortized over the holding period of the bond and not over its life?

Q20–14 State the balance sheet classifications of (a) Bond Sinking Fund; (b) Accrued Bond Interest Receivable; (c) Accrued Bond Interest Payable; (d) Cash Surrender Value of Life Insurance; (e) Long-Term Secured Notes Receivable.

Class exercises

CE20–1 (Accounting for temporary investments in marketable securities) The Carlin Company had the following transactions in temporary investments during 1979.

1979

May 1 Purchased 8 percent bonds of Gauld Company with a face value of $300,000 at 109. Interest is paid each May 1 and November 1. Brokerage fees and other costs incident to the purchase were $180. The bonds have a maturity date of November 1, 1999.

15 Purchased 500 shares of preferred stock of Day Corporation at $104 a share. Dividends of $8 a year are paid semiannually on May 15 and November 15. Brokerage fees and other costs incident to the purchase were $102.

Oct. 2 Sold bonds of Gauld Company with a face value of $150,000 at 112 plus accrued interest.

Nov. 1 Received semiannual interest on the remaining bonds of Gauld Company.

20 Received the semiannual dividends on the preferred stock of Day Corporation.

Dec. 31 Accrued the interest on the bonds of Gauld Company.

Required: Journalize the transactions.

CE20–2 (Valuation of temporary investments in marketable securities) The Cox Company had the following temporary investments as of December 31, 1979, all acquired during the year.

	Cost	Market Price at December 31, 1979
Bonds of Dunn Company	$31,480	$32,050
Bonds of Eaton Company	15,000	14,700
Bonds of Fedel Company	32,100	30,500

On February 1, 1980, the Cox Company sold the bonds of Eaton Company for $14,500. On March 1, 1980, the company sold the bonds of Fedel Company for $31,000. Ignore the interest on these bonds.

Required:

1. Show how the investments should be shown on the balance sheet for December 31, 1979.
2. Record the sales of temporary investments in marketable securities in 1980 (the temporary investments are carried at cost).

CE20–3 (Accounting for long-term investment in stocks at cost) The Pater Company had the following transactions involving long-term investment in stocks in 1979.

1979

Jan. 6 Purchased 2,000 of the 50,000 shares outstanding of $100 par value common stock of Sun Company at 120.

May 1 Received a $2 per share cash dividend from the Sun Company.

June 1 Purchased 1,000 shares of $100 par value common stock of Sun Company at 128.

Sept. 1 The Sun Company split up its stock four for one. The Pater Company exchanged 3,000 shares of $100 par value stock for 12,000 shares of no-par value stock.

Oct. 10 The Pater Company sold 1,000 shares of the stock of Sun Company for $40 per share. On October 1, the Sun Company had declared a $1 per share cash dividend payable on October 25 to stockholders of record on October 20.

25 Received the cash dividend on the remaining shares of stock of Sun Company.

Required:

1. Journalize the transactions.
2. Show how the long-term investment in stocks (they are nonmarketable) should be shown on the balance sheet at December 31, 1979.

CE20–4 (Accounting for long-term investment—equity method) The Late Company acquired 400,000 shares of Middleton Company in 1979 at a total cost of $1,600,000. Middleton Company has 600,000 shares outstanding.

Required: What entries would be made by the Late Company in 1980 for the following data, assuming the investment account is carried on the equity basis?

a. Middleton Company announces net income of $60,000 for the first six months and pays a cash dividend of 20 cents per share.
b. Middleton Company announces a net loss of $18,000 for the second six months and distributes a 5 percent stock dividend.
c. The Late Company acquires an additional 26,250 shares of Middleton Company stock at $4 per share.

CE20–5 (Accounting for the purchase of bonds as a long-term investment) Assume that Adams, Inc., purchased 9 percent bonds of Pearl Corporation under each of the following conditions (the authorization date is January 1, 1979.)

	Case A	*Case B*	*Case C*
Face value of each bond	$500	$1,000	$10,000
Term of bond issue (years)	10	20	20
Interest payable on	Jan. 1 & July 1	Jan. 1 & July 1	Jan. 1 & July 1
Date of purchase	Jan. 1, 1979	Jan. 1, 1979	Mar. 1, 1979
Number of bonds purchased	40	20	20
Purchase price	100	98½	102 (plus accrued interest)

Required: For each case, record (a) the purchase of the bonds; (b) the receipt of the first interest payment, accompanied by the entry to record proper amortization, and (c) the adjusting entry for interest accrual on December 31, 1979, accompanied by the entry to record proper amortization.

Exercises and problems

P20–1 On July 1, 1979, the Relich Company purchased 8 percent, AAA first mortgage bonds of the Pacific Company with a face value of $100,000 at 102½ plus $68 brokerage fees. Interest is payable on July 1 and January 1.

Required: If these bonds were purchased as a temporary investment, what account title(s) would be debited and what amount(s).

P20–2 The Hayes Company had the following transactions in temporary investments during 1979.

1979

Jan. 2 Purchased 8 percent, AAA bonds of Dunn Company with a face value of $100,000 at 102. Interest is paid on January 1 and July 1. Brokerage fees and other costs incident to the purchase were $65. The bonds have a maturity date of July 1, 1999.

Apr. 10 Purchased 400 shares of $100 par value preferred stock of Foster Company at $105 a share. Dividends of $8 per year are paid semiannually on January 1 and July 1. Brokerage fees and other costs incident to the purchase were $125.

July 1 Received the semiannual interest from the Dunn Company.

5 Received the semiannual dividends from the Foster Company.

Aug. 1 Sold the bonds of Dunn Company at 102½ plus accrued interest.

Required: Journalize the transactions.

P20–3 (Appendix) The Key Company had the following temporary investments as of December 31, 1979.

	Cost	*Market Price at December 31, 1979*
Common Stock of Berry Co.	$21,000	$21,200
Common Stock of Clayton Co.	18,500	18,100
Common Stock of Bragdon Co.	27,000	26,500

The following transactions involving the investments occurred in 1980:

1980

Jan. 16 Sold the common stock of Clayton Company for $18,200.

Feb. 15 Sold the common stock of Bragdon Company for $26,450.

Required:

1. Assuming the use of a valuation offset account, record the necessary adjusting entry under the lower of cost or market method.
2. Show how the temporary investments should be shown on the balance sheet at December 31, 1979.
3. Record the sales of the temporary investments during 1980.

P20–4 The Winston Company had the following transactions involving temporary investments during 1979.

1979

Mar. 1 Purchased 7 percent, AAA bonds of Larson Company with a face value of $150,000 at 101. Interest is paid each March 1 and September 1. Brokerage fees and other costs incident to the purchase were $140. The bonds have a maturity date of September 1, 1988.

15 Purchased 500 shares of preferred stock of Krager Company at $60 a share. The annual dividend amount of $4 per share is paid semiannually on February 15 and August 15. Brokerage fees and other costs incident to the purchase were $104.

Aug. 15 Sold 100 shares of preferred stock of Krager Company at $65 a share. On August 10, the board of directors of the Krager Company declared the regular semiannual dividend on this stock payable on August 25 to stockholders of record on August 20. (Hint: The selling price to be allocated to each share of stock is $63; the $2 difference represents dividends earned sold with the stock and this amount should be credited to Dividends Earned.)

25 Received the dividend on the remaining preferred stock of Krager Company.

Sept. 1 Received semiannual interest on the bonds of Larson Company.

Oct. 2 Sold the bonds of Larson Company at 102 plus accrued interest.

Required: Journalize the transactions.

P20–5 (Appendix) The Scott Company had the following temporary investments as of December 31, 1979.

	Cost	*Market Price at December 31, 1979*
Common stock of Remson Co.	$40,000	$38,400
Common stock of Page Co.	20,000	29,200

On February 1, 1980, immediately after receiving and recording the semiannual dividend the Scott Company sold the common stock of Remson Company for $38,000.

Required: Record the sale on February 1, 1980. The investments were purchased during 1979. They are carried at the lower of cost or market and a valuation offset account is used.

P20–6 The Parento Company had the following transactions in long-term investment in stocks during 1979.

1979

Jan. 5 Purchased 1,000 of the 1,000,000 outstanding shares of $100 par value common stock of Sunno Company at 107.

Feb. 20 Received a cash dividend of $1 per share from the Sunno Company.

Mar. 10 Purchased 2,000 shares of $100 par value common stock of Sunno Company at 112.

July 1 Received a $1.10 per share cash dividend from the Sunno Company.

Dec. 1 The Sunno Company split up its stock two for one. The Parento Company exchanged 3,000 shares of $100 par value stock for 6,000 shares of no-par value stock.

31 The Sunno Company declared a $1 per share cash dividend payable January 18, 1980, to stockholders of record on December 31, 1979.

Required: Journalize the transactions using the cost method.

P20–7 On January 1, 1979, the Elderdee Corporation purchased as a long-term investment 9 percent bonds of Charles Corporation with a face value of $300,000 at 102½. The bonds have a maturity date of January 1, 1989. Interest is payable each January 1 and July 1.

Required: Record (a) the purchase of the bonds by the Elderdee Corporation, and (b) all the necessary remaining entries for 1979.

P20–8 Assume that the Elderdee Corporation (see P20–7) purchased the Charles Corporation bonds at 99 instead of 102½.

Required: Prepare all the required entries for 1979.

P20–9 On May 1, 1979, the Gudderson Company purchased as a long-term investment 9 percent bonds of Celler Company. Interest is paid semiannually on May 1 and November 1. The bonds mature on May 1, 1991. On November 1, 1979, the accountant for the Gudderson Company prepared the following entry to record the receipt of bond interest and the amortization of the discount.

1979				
Nov.	1	Cash	5,647 50	
		Investment in Bonds—Celler Company Bonds	90 00	
		Bond Interest Earned		5,737 50
		To record the receipt of bond interest from the Cellar Company and to amortize the discount for six months.		

Required: From this information, reconstruct the journal entry that was made to record the purchase of bonds. Show all your calculations.

P20–10 The Peters Company had the following transactions involving long-term investment in stocks in 1979.

1979

Jan. 2 Purchased 15,000 of the 25,000 outstanding shares of $50 par value common stock of Sunner Company at 60. The book value of the common stock is $60 per share.

Mar. 26 Received a cash dividend of $1 per share on the stock of Sunner Company.

Sept. 10 The Sunner Company declared a 100 percent stock dividend. The Peters Company received 15,000 additional shares of $50 par value common stock from the Sunner Company.

Dec. 31 The Sunner Company declared a 75 cent per share cash dividend payable January 16, 1980, to stockholders of record on December 31 1979. The Sunner Company reported a net income of $100,000.

Required:

1. Journalize the transactions using the equity method.
2. Show how the long-term investment in stocks should be shown on the balance sheet of the Peters Company as of December 31, 1979.

P20–11 On May 1, 1979, the Isaacs Company purchased 8 percent bonds of Barley Company with a face value of $160,000 at 103. The bonds mature on May 1, 1989, and interest is paid each May 1 and November 1. The books are closed each December 31.

Required: Journalize all necessary entries on the books of the Isaacs Company for 1979 and 1980 assuming that proper straight-line amortization is recorded each time bond interest is recorded.

P20–12 On April 1, 1979, the Roughton Company purchased 8 percent bonds of Sparrow Company with a face value of $400,000 at 98 plus accrued interest. The bonds mature on August 1, 1987, and interest is paid each February 1 and August 1. On August 1, 1987, the Roughton Company received the face amount of the Sparrow Company bonds at maturity and the last interest payment. The books are closed each December 31.

Required:

1. Journalize all necessary entries on the books of the Roughton Company for 1979, assuming that proper straight-line amortization is recorded each time bond interest is recorded.
2. Assuming that proper accounting is carried out in the years 1980 through 1987, prepare all the entries for the year 1987 including the receipt of interest on February 1 and August 1, the proper discount amortization, the receipt of the face amount of the bonds at maturity, and any other necessary adjusting and closing entries at December 31.

P20–13 On June 1, 1979, the Eton Company purchased as a long-term investment 9 percent bonds of Hamilton Company at a certain price plus accrued interest. Interest is payable semiannually on April 1 and October 1. The bonds mature on October 1, 1998. On October 1, 1979, the accountant for the Eton Company prepared the following entry to record the receipt of bond interest and the amortization of the premium:

1979						
Oct.	1	Cash	8,325	00		
		Investment in Bonds—Hamilton Company			60	00
		Accrued Bond Interest Receivable			2,775	00
		Bond Interest Earned			5,490	00
		To record the receipt of semiannual bond interest from the Hamilton Company and to amortize the premium for four months by the straight-line method.				

Required:

1. Compute and state separately (a) the face value of the bonds, (b) the original purchase price of bonds.
2. From the information given, reconstruct the journal entry to record the purchase of the bonds by the Eton Company.

P20–14 Jaye Davis received an inheritance of $400,000. He plans to invest this amount in bonds which he contemplates holding for several years. After consulting with his broker and other advisers, he has narrowed his decision to the following four bonds:

1. 10 percent, 10-year, grade A debenture bonds of Alpha Company, which are selling at 104.
2. 8 percent, 10-year, grade AAA first mortgage bonds of Beta, which are selling at 99.
3. 6 percent, 10-year, grade A debenture bonds of Kappa Company, which are selling at 80.
4. 9 percent, 10-year, grade AAA debenture bonds of Delta Company, which are selling at 100.

Required:

1. Compute the approximate effective interest yield on each bond, and prepare a list indicating the order of yield from the highest to the lowest.
2. Which bond would be the safest? What criteria should you use? What additional information would be helpful in determining safety of principal and safety of interest? Discuss the method of rating bonds.
3. Which bond would you recommend that Jaye Davis buy? Give reasons for your answer.

P20–15 The Western and Eastern Corporations each have 60,000 shares of no-par stock outstanding. Adams, Inc. acquired 51,000 shares of Western stock and 57,000 shares of Eastern stock in 1976. Changes in retained earnings for Western and Eastern for 1979 and 1980 are as follows:

	Western Corporation	*Eastern Corporation*
Retained earnings (deficit), Jan. 1, 1979	$ 25,000	$ (5,000)
Cash dividends, 1979	(15,000)	
	$ 10,000	$ (5,000)
Net Income, 1979	25,000	40,000
	$ 35,000	$ 35,000
Cash dividends, 1980	–0–	(7,500)
	$ 35,000	$ 27,500
Net income (loss), 1980	(7,500)	(10,000)
Retained earnings, Dec. 31, 1980	$ 27,500	$ 17,500

Required:

1. Give any entries required on the books of Adams, Inc. for 1979 and 1980, assuming that investments in subsidiaries are carried at cost.
2. Give any entries required on the books of the parent for 1979 and 1980, assuming that investments in subsidiaries are carried on the equity basis.
3. State which method would conform to current generally accepted accounting standards and explain why.

P20–16 (Integrative) The following transactions relate to the long-term investments of Bellview Airline Corporation.

1979

Jan. 2 Purchased 15,000 of 50,000 outstanding shares of Costa Mesa Television, Inc. common stock for $14 per share. Book value was $14 per share. The acquisition gave the Bellview Airline Corporation a significant degree of control of Costa Mesa Television, Inc.

Feb. 1 Purchased $1,000,000 of Lower Company first mortgage 8 percent bonds at face value plus accrued interest. Interest is payable semiannually on December 1 and June 1 with maturity 10 years from this past December 1, 1978.

15 Purchased 10,000 of 200,000 outstanding shares of San Jacinto Company, $100 par value, common stock at $650 per share.

May 5 Received cash dividend on San Jacinto Company common stock of $5 per share.

June 1 Received semiannual interest on Lower Company Bonds.

Aug. 5 Received cash dividend on San Jacinto Company common stock of $5 per share and a 4 percent stock dividend.

Sept. 15 Sold the shares of San Jacinto Company common stock received as a stock dividend for $625 per share and purchased 250 of $1,000, 7 percent debenture bonds of Donald's Inc. at 94 (94 percent of par value) with interest payable semiannually, on September 15 and March 15 with maturity 16 years from date of purchase.

30 Received a cash dividend of 75 cents per share from Costa Mesa Television, Inc.

Nov. 5 Received cash dividend on San Jacinto Company common stock of $5 per share.

Dec. 1 Received semiannual interest on Lower Company Bonds.

31 Costa Mesa Television, Inc. reported net income for the year of $82,000.

Required:

1. Record the above transactions in general journal form and record any adjustments required at December 31. Amortize all premiums and discounts to the nearest half month, using the straight-line method.
2. Prepare a schedule of investments as they would appear on the balance sheet at the end of the year.

P20–17 (Minicase) The Goodwin Corporation has three stockholders who own the following common shares (the Corporation has only common shares outstanding):

R. A. Goodwin	3,000 shares
B. E. Dealer	3,000 shares
I. M. Inman	4,000 shares

Inman has agreed to sell his shares at book value (based on generally accepted accounting standards) to the Nucorp Corporation, provided past profits have been recorded with reasonable accuracy. A review of past records of the Goodwin Corporation indicates the following:

The bad debts expense of the Corporation has been estimated to be 1 percent of credit sales. The Allowance for Doubtful Accounts appears as follows since the Corporation was formed:

Allowance for Doubtful Accounts

Date		Explanation	F	Debit		Credit		Balance	
1975									
Dec.	31	Adjustment	J17			1,500	00	1,500	00
1976									
July	10	Write off	J26	760	00			740	00
Dec.	31	Adjustment	J29			1,800	00	2,540	00
1977									
Nov.	18	Write off	J36	1,000	00			1,540	00
Dec.	31	Adjustment	J41			2,400	00	3,940	00
1978									
Sept.	2	Write off	J47	1,400	00			2,540	00
Dec.	31	Adjustment	J54			2,300	00	4,840	00
1979									
Aug.	8	Write off	J61	1,360	00			3,480	00
Dec.	31	Adjustment	J67			2,600	00	6,080	00

In addition, the Goodwin Corporation made an investment in Renug Corporation bonds with a face value of $20,000 five years ago. The bonds cost $16,400 and had 18 years of life remaining at the time of purchase. The discount was never amortized because the Corporation had always intended to sell the bonds in the following year, but for one reason or another had not done so.

The Corporation had also made an investment in the stock of Rumson Corporation four years before, and it appears on the books at its original cost of $47,400. The stock has increased in market value steadily each year and is presently worth approximately $64,000.

The Goodwin Corporation's net income has averaged $80,000 during the past five years, and average stockholder's equity has been $400,000. Goodwill of $12,000 appears on the Corporation's books.

Required:

1. As an accounting consultant for the Nucorp Corporation, would you feel that the determination of past net income has been reasonably accurate?
2. If you were adjusting the assets of the Goodwin Corporation preparatory to the sale of Inman's stock, how much would the adjustment be? Discuss.
3. If you believe that the income has been incorrectly computed, state how you would change the Corporation's accounting policies.

chapter twenty-one

Introduction

The income statement and the statement of retained earnings (or statement of owner's equity) disclose the causes of part—but not all—of the changes that take place in balance sheet items during an accounting period. Several types of financial transactions are not reflected in the income statement; an example is the purchase of a plant asset. Such transactions do, however, cause changes in working capital, cash, and other financial resources—that is they cause changes in the company's financial position.

A fourth major accounting statement is prepared to disclose the causes of changes in resources of a firm. It is called the *Statement of Changes in Financial Position*. This chapter describes this statement and explains how to prepare the statement based on two major concepts.

Statement of changes in financial position

Learning goals

To understand the meaning of the statement of changes in financial position.
To understand the various definitions of *funds*.
To know the effect on working capital of increases or decreases in each type of current asset or current liability.
To prepare a schedule of changes in working capital.
To compute the amount of working capital provided by operations.
To use the T-account method to develop sources and uses of working capital based on the working capital concept of funds.
To use the T-account method to develop sources and uses of funds based on the all-financial resources concept of funds.
To use the T accounts to prepare a statement of changes in financial position on either a working capital basis or an all-financial resources basis.

Key terms

all financial resources
changes in working capital
comparative balance sheet
current account
direct T-account method
financial resources summary
funds
noncurrent account
operating summary
schedule of changes in working capital
sources of funds
statement of changes in financial position
uses of funds
working capital
working capital summary

Evolution of content of the statement

Prior to 1971, some but not all annual reports presented various statements of sources and uses of funds (the typical name given at that time to the present statement of changes in financial position). These older statements defined funds in several different ways: working capital, cash only, cash and securities, current assets, or all financial resources. The definition of funds most often used was *working capital,* which consists of all current assets not needed to liquidate current liabilities. Therefore, *working capital* is a dollar amount; mathematically it is equal to total current assets minus total liabilities. Thus, a statement of sources and uses of working capital was frequently included in many annual reports.

In 1971 the Accounting Principles Board, in *APB Opinion No. 19,* recommended that the broader concept of "all financial resources" be used. It also recommended (1) that the title of the statement be Statement of Changes in Financial Position and (2) that this statement be a basic financial statement for each period for which an income statement is presented.[1] This latter requirement means that the statement of changes in financial position is mandatory in financial reports and is equal in status to the other three end-of-period financial statements.

APB Opinion No. 19 requires a business to disclose in the statement of changes in financial position the sources and uses of all financial resources, that is "all important aspects of its financing and investing activities regardless of whether cash or other elements of working capital are directly affected."[2] The terms *sources* and *uses* respectively refer to the inflows and outflows of financial resources of the business. As previously stated financial resources may be viewed as total resources, working capital, and in other ways. The *Opinion* specifically permits flexibility in form, content, and terminology in the statement. It strongly suggests, however, that information about *sources* and *uses of working capital* or *cash* be appropriately described, in addition to the inclusion of other financial information such as the issuance of bonds payable in exchange for land, the issuance of common stock to acquire plant and equipment items, the conversion of bonds into common stock, and other financial transactions that *do not affect* working capital.

The statement of changes in financial position has two broad purposes:

1. To strengthen financial planning by providing historical information on sources and uses of financial resources
2. To help explain to financial statement users the causes of changes in financial position from the balance sheet (statement of financial position) prepared as of a given date to the one prepared as of the end of the next period.

Typically, in the preparation of a statement of changes in financial position, attention is *usually* focused first on working capital and then on financing and

1 *APB Opinion No. 19,* "Reporting Changes in Financial Position," March, 1971, p. 374.
2 *APB Opinion No. 19,* p. 374.

investing activities that do not affect working capital. It is therefore appropriate that we turn first to a careful consideration of working capital—specifically the preparation of a statement of changes in financial position showing only sources and uses of working capital. This will be referred to as the working capital basis. After this narrower concept is carefully identified, the broader concept of "all financial resources" will be illustrated.

Working capital basis

The chief *sources of working capital* are operations, additional investments by owners, long-term borrowing, and the sale of assets. The chief *uses of working capital* are purchases of noncurrent assets, payment of long-term debt, and reduction of the owner's or the stockholders' equity, by drawings or dividends. The statement of changes in financial position on a working capital basis emphasizes the interrelationship of the sources (inflows) and uses (outflows) of working capital. A chart of working capital inflows and outflows based on an analogy between the flow of working capital through a business and the flow of water into and out of a container is shown in Figure 21–1.

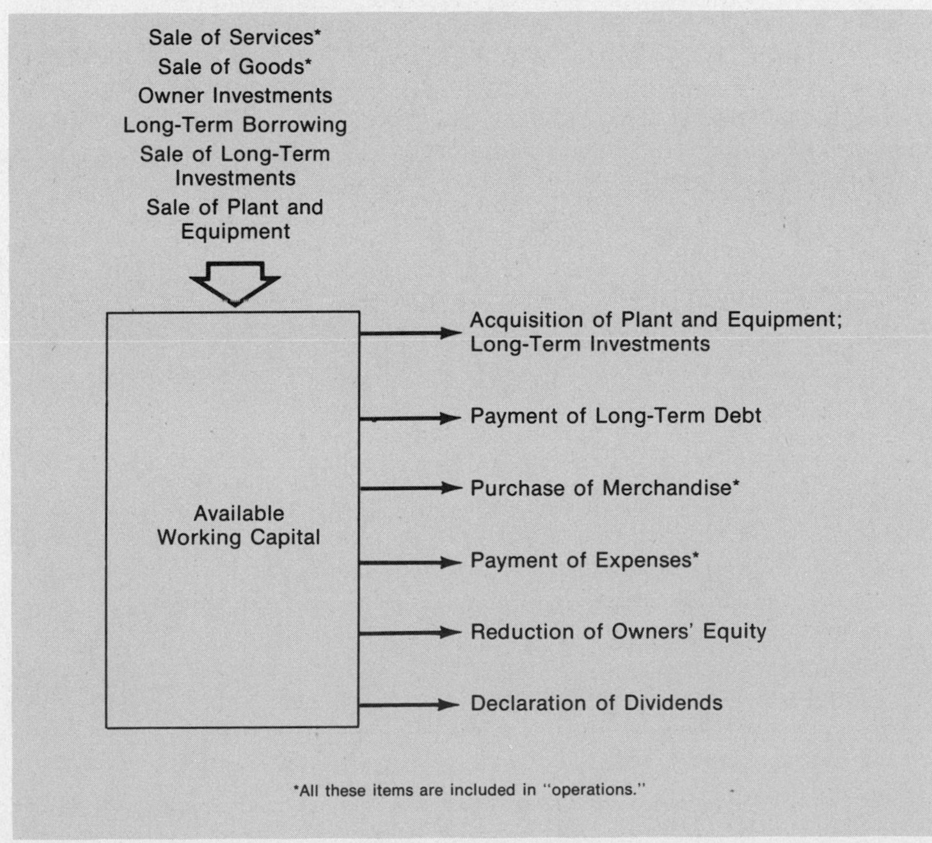

Figure 21–1
Working capital inflows and outflows

Purpose of the statement

It is often difficult for management and others to understand how the net income for a period was used and what effect the flow of working capital had throughout the business. Readers of the conventional financial statements often ask such questions as: Where did the working capital come from? What was done with it? What happened to the various asset items during the period? Why did working capital decrease although earnings were favorable? Why were dividends not larger? Is the company solvent? Where did the working capital for replacement or expansion come from? What kind of financial decisions were made during the period? The statement of changes in financial position helps to answer these questions.

The smooth flow of working capital into and out of a business is the result of a continuing series of managerial decisions, often requiring a high level of skill and judgment. The statement helps the reader to understand not only the financial well-being of the company but also the effectiveness of the financial policies of its management.

Sources and uses of working capital

A source of working capital; that is, a cause of increase in working capital must result in:

1. An increase in total current assets without a corresponding increase in total current liabilities, or
2. A decrease in total current liabilities without a corresponding decrease in total current assets.

A use of working capital; that is, a cause of decrease in working capital, must result in:

1. A decrease in total current assets without a corresponding decrease in total current liabilities, or
2. An increase in total current liabilities without a corresponding increase in total current assets.

Since these *changes in working capital;* that is, sources and uses, are compiled for a specific period, a month or a year, there are two possible alternative approaches to determining the sources and uses of working capital.

1. Analyze every transaction occurring during the period that affects a current asset or a current liability to determine the causes of changes in working capital. This method would require considerable effort, because many changes in both current assets and current liabilities *do not* change working capital—for example, the collection of accounts receivable.
2. Analyze every transaction occurring during the period that affects a *noncurrent account*—long-term investments, plant and equipment, intangible assets, long-term liabilities, and stockholders' equity, to determine the causes of change in working capital. This approach is a shorter one. It can be used

because every change in working capital must result in a change in one or more of the noncurrent accounts.[3]

The second approach is used in the following pages to determine the sources and uses of working capital that will be incorporated in the statement of changes in financial position—working capital basis.

Three kinds of business transactions

Since there is great variety in the transactions that enter into the inflow and outflow of working capital, it is helpful to classify transactions in distinctive categories on the basis of whether or not they have an effect on working capital.

1. *Transactions that change a current and a noncurrent account.* An example is the acquisition of a tract of land for cash. This transaction changes working capital and is therefore reported in the statement of changes in financial position—working capital basis.
2. *Transactions that change current asset or current liability accounts but have no effect on working capital.* The purchase of merchandise on account and the settlement of an account receivable both change the current accounts but do not change the amount of working capital. These transactions are not reported in the statement of changes in financial position prepared on a rigid working capital basis. On the other hand, note that the purchases of merchandise and sales of merchandise are automatically included in the statement by being included in the overall category of "changes caused by operations" as illustrated in the following pages.
3. *Transactions that change noncurrent accounts only.* For example, the acquisition of a tract of land by a company in exchange for its own stock does not change working capital and is, therefore, not reported in the statement prepared on a working capital basis. Other transactions in this category include conversion of bonds payable into common stock and changes in valuation of plant and equipment. It is apparent, however, that information about the acquisition of assets of a material amount by the use of nonworking capital items should be shown on the statement of changes in financial position. Omission of this information is a definite weakness of the statement prepared on a rigid working capital basis.

Working capital provided by operations

Recall that in Chapter 6 for cross-referencing purposes it was suggested that the statements be marked

Exhibit A—the income statement
Exhibit B—the statement of owner's equity
Exhibit C—the balance sheet.

3 For a mathematical proof of this statement, see Ching-Wen Kwang and Albert Slavin, "The Mathematical Unity of Funds-Flow Analyses," *NAA Bulletin*, Section 1, January 1965, pp. 49–56.

We will now mark the statement of changes in financial position as Exhibit D.

A primary source of working capital is the regular operating activities of the business. The determination of working capital from this source is complicated by the fact that the change in working capital may be greater than, or less than, the net income shown in the income statement. To illustrate the calculation of the working capital provided by operations, assume that the Donlee Company's income statement for the year ended December 31, 1979, is as follows:

DONLEE COMPANY
Income Statement
For the Year Ended December 31, 1979

Exhibit A

Sales		$11,000.00
Cost of Goods Sold		7,000.00
Gross Margin on Sales		$ 4,000.00
Operating Expenses		
Depreciation—Plant and Equipment	$ 400.00	
Other	2,100.00	2,500.00
Net Income		$ 1,500.00

An analysis of this statement in terms of the change in working capital resulting from operations shows the following:

DONLEE COMPANY
Income Statement
(converted from accrual basis to a working capital basis)
For the Year Ended December 31, 1979

	Income Statement	Working Capital Increase or (Decrease)	Explanation
Sales	$11,000.00	$11,000.00	Increase in cash or accounts receivable
Cost of Goods Sold	7,000.00	(7,000.00)	Decrease in inventories
Gross Margin on Sales	$ 4,000.00	$ 4,000.00	
Operating Expenses			
Depreciation—Plant and Equipment	$ 400.00	-0-	Decrease in net income and the carrying value of plant and equipment
Other	2,100.00	(2,100.00)	Decrease in cash or increase in accounts payable
Total Operating Expenses	$ 2,500.00		
Total Outflow of Working Capital		$(2,100.00)	
Net Income	$ 1,500.00		
Working Capital Provided by Operations		$ 1,900.00	

For brevity, the required adjustment to net income to compute working capital from operations may be determined by working backward as follows:

Working capital provided by operations
Net income (before extraordinary items) $1,500.00

Add nonworking capital charges to Income Summary:	
Depreciation Expense—Plant and Equipment	400.00
Working capital provided by operations exclusive of extraordinary items	$1,900.00

The second, shorter method of calculating the working capital provided by operations is the typical method in general use. Accountants feel that if the income statement were converted to a statement of working capital provided by operations, many of the operating items on that statement would be duplicated on this one. The typical approach to the calculation of working capital provided by operations, the approach recommended by *APB Opinion No. 19,* may be generalized as follows:

Net income before extraordinary items	$XX
Add: Nonworking capital charges to operations (expenses, losses, adjuncts (additions) to expenses or contra (offsets to) items to revenue, which do not affect working capital)	XX
	$XX
Less: Nonworking capital credits to operations (revenues, gains, adjuncts to revenue or contra items to expense which do not affect working capital)	XX
Working capital provided by operations	$XX

Or being a bit more specific, we can show the calculation of working capital provided by operations in the following manner:

COMPUTATION OF WORKING CAPITAL PROVIDED BY OPERATIONS

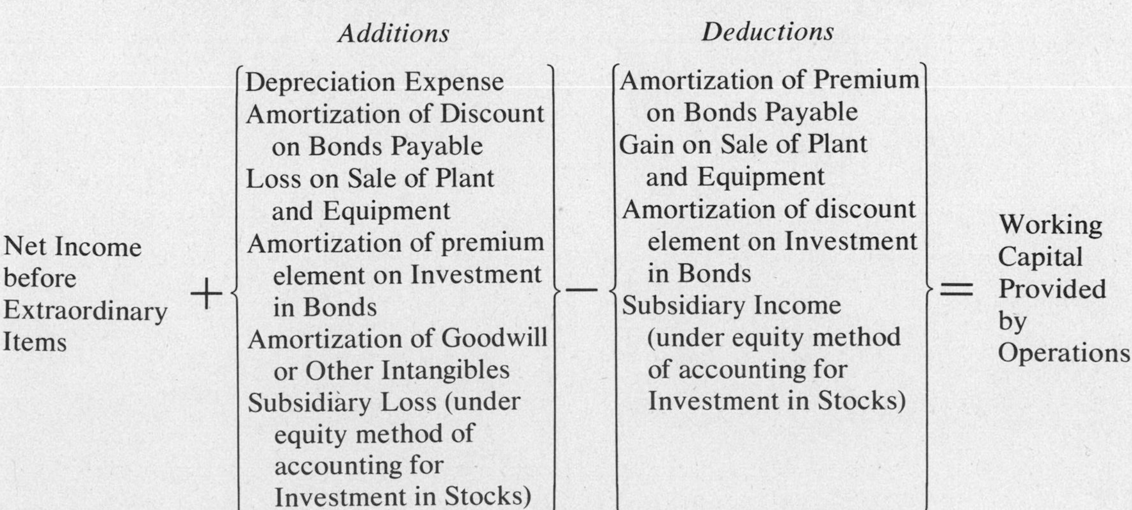

All of the additions and deductions included in the computation are reflected in the income statement. They represent costs and expenses or gains and losses that enter into the determination of net income but do not affect working capital in the current period. The relevant expenditures either were made in a prior period or will be made in a future period. The recognition of depreciation, for example, while essential to income measurement, does not change the amount of working capital. Recall that *APB Opinion No. 19* requires that the calculation of working capital from operations start with net income before extraordinary items. In *Opinion No. 30* the APB tightened up on what can qualify as an extraordinary item (see Chapter 22); therefore the final net income figure *will typically be* the net income before extraordinary items.

To illustrate the preparation of a simple form of the statement of changes in financial position on the working capital basis, the balance sheet of the Columbia Company, Inc., is given.

COLUMBIA COMPANY, INC.
Comparative Balance Sheet
December 31, 1979 and 1978

Exhibit C

	December 31 1979	December 31 1978	Increase or (Decrease)
Assets			
Current Assets			
Cash	$ 30,000.00	$ 32,000.00	$ (2,000.00)
Accounts Receivable (net)	65,000.00	52,000.00	13,000.00
Merchandise Inventory	112,000.00	92,000.00	20,000.00
Unexpired Insurance	3,000.00	4,000.00	(1,000.00)
Total Current Assets	$210,000.00	$180,000.00	$ 30,000.00
Plant and Equipment	$470,000.00	$438,000.00	$ 32,000.00
Deduct Accumulated Depreciation	105,000.00	98,000.00	7,000.00
Net Plant and Equipment	$365,000.00	$340,000.00	$ 25,000.00
Total Assets	$575,000.00	$520,000.00	$ 55,000.00
Liabilities and Stockholders' Equity			
Current Liabilities			
Accounts Payable	$ 60,000.00	$ 81,000.00	$(21,000.00)
Bank Loans Payable (short term)	31,500.00	26,500.00	5,000.00
Accrued Payables	3,500.00	2,500.00	1,000.00
Total Current Liabilities	$ 95,000.00	$110,000.00	$(15,000.00)
Stockholders' Equity			
Capital Stock	$410,000.00	$350,000.00	$ 60,000.00
Retained Earnings	70,000.00	60,000.00	10,000.00
Total Stockholders' Equity	$480,000.00	$410,000.00	$ 70,000.00
Total Liabilities and Stockholders' Equity	$575,000.00	$520,000.00	$ 55,000.00

Additional information:
Net earnings for 1979, $35,000
Dividend declared in 1979, $25,000

Step 1 in preparing the statement of changes in financial position on a working capital basis is to determine the changes in working capital. Such an analysis is easily made in Schedule D-1 shown below.

COLUMBIA COMPANY, INC.
Schedule of Changes in Working Capital
For the Year Ended December 31, 1979

Schedule D-1

	December 31		Changes in Working Capital	
	1979	1978	Increase	Decrease
Current Assets				
Cash	$ 30,000.00	$ 32,000.00		$ 2,000.00
Accounts Receivable (net)	65,000.00	52,000.00	$13,000.00	
Merchandise Inventory	112,000.00	92,000.00	20,000.00	
Unexpired Insurance	3,000.00	4,000.00		1,000.00
Total Current Assets	$210,000.00	$180,000.00		
Current Liabilities				
Accounts Payable	$ 60,000.00	$ 81,000.00	21,000.00	
Bank Loans Payable (short-term)	31,500.00	26,500.00		5,000.00
Accrued Payables	3,500.00	2,500.00		1,000.00
Total Current Liabilities	$ 95,000.00	$110,000.00		
Working Capital	$115,000.00	$ 70,000.00	$54,000.00	$ 9,000.00
Net Increase in Working Capital				45,000.00
			$54,000.00	$54,000.00

Step 2 is to analyze the changes in all the noncurrent accounts.

COLUMBIA COMPANY, INC.
Analysis of Changes in Noncurrent Accounts
For the Year Ended December 31, 1979

		Effect on Working Capital	
		Increase	Decrease
Plant and Equipment			
Balance, 12/31/78	$438,000.00		
Acquisitions during 1979 . . .	32,000.00		$ 32,000.00
Balance, 12/31/79	$470,000.00		
Accumulated Depreciation—Plant and Equipment			
Balance, 12/31/78	$ 98,000.00		
Depreciation for 1979	7,000.00	$ 7,000.00*	
Balance 12/31/79	$105,000.00		
Capital Stock			
Balance, 12/31/78	$350,000.00		
Stock Issued	60,000.00	60,000.00	
Balance, 12/31/79	$410,000.00		
Retained Earnings			
Balance, 12/31/78	$ 60,000.00		
Net Income for 1979	35,000.00	35,000.00	
Dividends declared	(25,000.00)		25,000.00
Balance, 12/31/79	$ 70,000.00		
		$102,000.00	$ 57,000.00
Net Increase in Working Capital			45,000.00
		$102,000.00	$102,000.00

*Nonworking capital charge to Income Summary.

Step 3 is to prepare a statement of changes of financial position—working capital basis for 1979 (Exhibit D), which follows.

COLUMBIA COMPANY, INC. — Exhibit D

Statement of Changes in Financial Position—Working Capital Basis

For the Year Ended December 31, 1979

Working Capital Was Provided by		
Operations		
Net Income (before extraordinary items) . .		$ 35,000.00
Add Nonworking Capital Charges against Operations		
Depreciation of Plant and Equipment . .		7,000.00
Working Capital Provided by Operations Exclusive of Extraordinary Items		$ 42,000.00
Issuance of Capital Stock		60,000.00
Total Working Capital Provided		$102,000.00
Working Capital Was Used for		
Purchase of Equipment	$32,000.00	
Declaration of Dividends	25,000.00	
Total Working Capital Used		57,000.00
Net Increase in Working Capital (See Schedule D-1)		$ 45,000.00

Preparing the statement using the T-account method

Although a statement of changes in financial position on a working capital basis can be prepared directly from analysis of the accounts reflected in a comparative balance sheet as in the preceding example, it becomes more difficult to prepare as the number of transactions and accounts to be analyzed increases. Some systematic method is needed to facilitate the analysis of the transactions required for the preparation of the formal statement. Several techniques may be used for this purpose, all of which lead to the same result. The technique known as the *direct*, or *T-account*, method is often used because of its relative simplicity and clarity. The basic steps are as follows:

Step 1. A schedule of changes in working capital is prepared.

Step 2. A T account is opened for each *noncurrent* balance sheet item and the amount of the net increase or decrease, obtained from the comparative balance sheet is entered in each account. Increases in assets and decreases in liabilities and stockholders' equity accounts are debit changes and are entered on the debit side; decreases in assets and increases in liabilities and stockholders' equity accounts are credit changes and are entered on the credit side. A single horizontal line is then drawn under each amount, across the account.

Step 3. Two additional T accounts, Working Capital Summary and Operating Summary, are opened. The Working Capital Summary account represents a condensation of all the current asset and current liability accounts; the amount entered in this account is, therefore, the net change in working capital as determined in step 1: it is a debit if there is a net increase; a credit if there is a net decrease. A single horizontal line is drawn under this figure, also. The Operating Summary account is used to determine the amount of working capital provided by operations: no amount is found in this account at this point. The amounts entered above the horizontal lines in the T accounts are added to make sure that total debits equal total credits.

Step 4. The net changes entered above the horizontal lines in the T accounts in steps 2 and 3 represent, in summary form, all the transactions that occurred during the period. These transactions are now reconstructed by separate entries below the horizontal lines in the appropriate T accounts. The aim is to ''match'' or ''account for'' each above-the-line balance. An offsetting debit or credit to a noncurrent account may be made to:

1. *Another noncurrent account.* Although such a transaction does not affect working capital, the entry is made so that all changes may be explained.
2. *Working Capital Summary.* This account is debited or credited for transactions other than revenue and expense that affect working capital and noncurrent accounts.
3. *Operating Summary.* This account is debited or credited for transactions affecting revenue, expense, nonworking capital charges to operations, and nonworking capital credits to operations. It adjusts the net income figure to a figure representing working capital provided by operations.

Step 4 is completed only when the balance of the amounts below the horizontal line in each account is equal to the net change entered above the horizontal line in steps 2 and 3. This insures that all the transactions that affect working capital have been accounted for. Each entry should be identified by a letter or number (together with a brief notation in the two summary accounts), giving the source of the entry to facilitate the preparation of the formal statement.

Step 5. The balance of Operating Summary is closed into Working Capital Summary.

Step 6. The formal statement of changes in financial position on a working capital basis is prepared. Operating Summary shows the details of working capital provided by operations. Working Capital Summary contains details of sources and uses of working capital; the debit entries represent sources, the credit entries are uses.

Illustration of the working capital basis

The comparative balance sheet of the Rock Corporation and related supplementary data are used to illustrate the step-by-step T-account method for the preparation of a statement of changes in financial position—working capital basis.

ROCK CORPORATION
Comparative Balance Sheet
December 31, 1979 and 1978

Exhibit C

	December 31 1979	December 31 1978	Increase or (Decrease)
Assets			
Current Assets			
Cash	$ 16,000.00	$ 21,000.00	$(5,000.00)
Accounts Receivable (net)	19,600.00	16,600.00	3,000.00
Merchandise Inventory	31,000.00	21,000.00	10,000.00
Total Current Assets	$ 66,600.00	$ 58,600.00	$ 8,000.00
Long-Term Investments (at cost)	$ 22,000.00	$ 19,000.00	$ 3,000.00
Plant and Equipment			
Land	$ 18,000.00	$ 18,000.00	$ -0-
Buildings	126,000.00	110,000.00	16,000.00
Accumulated Depreciation—Buildings	(38,000.00)	(35,000.00)	(3,000.00)*
Machinery	152,000.00	125,000.00	27,000.00
Accumulated Depreciation—Machinery	(37,000.00)	(25,000.00)	(12,000.00)*
Total Plant and Equipment	$221,000.00	$193,000.00	$28,000.00
Intangible Assets	$ 9,000.00	$ 10,000.00	$(1,000.00)
Total Assets	$318,600.00	$280,600.00	$38,000.00
Liabilities and Stockholders' Equity			
Current Liabilities			
Accounts Payable	$ 23,000.00	$ 19,000.00	$ 4,000.00
Notes Payable	3,500.00	4,000.00	(500.00)
Total Current Liabilities	$ 26,500.00	$ 23,000.00	$ 3,500.00
Long-Term Liabilities			
Mortgage Payable	32,000.00	35,000.00	(3,000.00)
Total Liabilities	$ 58,500.00	$ 58,000.00	$ 500.00
Stockholders' Equity			
5% Preferred Stock, $100 par value	$ 55,000.00	$ 50,000.00	$ 5,000.00
Common Stock, no-par value $10 stated value	125,000.00	110,000.00	15,000.00
Premium on Common Stock	13,000.00	10,000.00	3,000.00
Retained Earnings	67,100.00	52,600.00	14,500.00
Total Stockholders' Equity	$260,100.00	$222,600.00	$37,500.00
Total Liabilities and Stockholders' Equity	$318,600.00	$280,600.00	$38,000.00

*These items represent increases to contra asset accounts, which in turn represent decreases in assets.

ROCK CORPORATION Income Statement For the Year Ended December 31, 1979		Exhibit A
Sales		$125,000.00
Cost of Goods Sold		70,000.00
Gross Margin on Sales		$ 55,000.00
Operating Expenses		
Depreciation—Machinery	$12,000.00	
Depreciation—Building	3,000.00	
Amortization of Intangibles	1,000.00	
Other	20,675.00	36,675.00
Operating Margin		$ 18,325.00
Gain on Sale of Investments		1,000.00
Net Income		$ 19,325.00

An analysis of the income statement, the statement of retained earnings, and the changes in the noncurrent items discloses the following supplementary information:

1. Net income per statement (this is the net income before extraordinary items) $19,325.00
2. Depreciation
   a. Machinery 12,000.00
   b. Building 3,000.00
3. Amortization of intangible assets 1,000.00
4. Dividends declared and paid 4,825.00
5. Payment on mortgage payable 3,000.00
6. Investments costing $4,000 were sold for $5,000 (the gain of $1,000 was included in net income). Since investments increased by $3,000, additional investments costing $7,000 = ($4,000 + $3,000) must have been acquired.
7. Plant and Equipment
   a. No machinery was sold during the period. Acquisitions, therefore, must have cost $27,000.
   b. No buildings were disposed of during the period. Acquisitions, therefore, must have cost $16,000.
8. Issuance of Stock
   a. Preferred—50 shares at par value
   b. Common—1,500 shares at $12 per share

Step 1. A schedule of changes in working capital is prepared.

ROCK CORPORATION
Schedule of Changes in Working Capital
For the Year Ended December 31, 1979

Schedule D-1

	December 31		Changes in Working Capital	
	1979	1978	Increase	Decrease
Current Assets				
Cash	$16,000.00	$21,000.00		$ 5,000.00
Accounts Receivable (net)	19,600.00	16,600.00	$ 3,000.00	
Merchandise Inventory	31,000.00	21,000.00	10,000.00	
Total Current Assets	$66,600.00	$58,600.00		
Current Liabilities				
Accounts Payable	$23,000.00	$19,000.00		4,000.00
Notes Payable	3,500.00	4,000.00	500.00	
Total Current Liabilities	$26,500.00	$23,000.00		
Working Capital	$40,100.00	$35,600.00	$13,500.00	$ 9,000.00
Net Increase in Working Capital				4,500.00
			$13,500.00	$13,500.00

Step 2. A T account is opened for each noncurrent balance sheet item and the amount of change during the year is entered. A single horizontal line is drawn under each amount as shown below.

Long-Term Investments	
3,000	

Mortgage Payable	
3,000	

Buildings	
16,000	

5% Preferred Stock	
	5,000

Accumulated Depreciation —Buildings	
	3,000

Common Stock	
	15,000

Machinery	
27,000	

Premium on Common Stock	
	3,000

Accumulated Depreciation —Machinery	
	12,000

Retained Earnings	
	14,500

Intangible Assets	
	1,000

Step 3. Two additional T accounts are opened—Working Capital Summary and Operating Summary. The net change in working capital is entered in the

Working Capital Summary account, and a line is drawn. Before proceeding to step 4 the accountant should test the accuracy of the debit and credit changes in the T accounts including the net change in working capital: the sum of the debit changes must equal the sum of the credit changes.

Operating Summary	
Net income + nonworking capital charges to operations	Nonworking capital credits to operations

Working Capital Summary	
4,500	
Increases in working capital (sources)	Decreases in working capital (uses)

Step 4. The transactions for the year are reconstructed in separate summary entries and reflected below the horizontal rules of each account. The entries indicated by the changes in the comparative balance sheet and the supplementary data are made directly to the T accounts. They are shown in general journal form only to facilitate the explanation. They are posted to the T accounts only—*not to the regular general ledger accounts.*

		Debit	Credit
(a)	Operating Summary—Net Income	19,325 00	
	Retained Earnings		19,325 00

The amount of $19,325, the net income for the period, was originally recorded as a closing entry by a debit to Income Summary and a credit to Retained Earnings. In this entry, Operating Summary is debited in place of Income Summary, since the balance of the Operating Summary account will show the increase in funds of $19,325 resulting from the revenue and expense transactions for the period.

		Debit	Credit
(b)	Operating Summary—Depreciation of Machinery	12,000 00	
	Accumulated Depreciation—Machinery		12,000 00

This entry represents the annual depreciation charge. The original debit was to Depreciation Expense—Machinery, an expense account. It is evident that the assumption made in entry (a), that all expenses decrease working capital, is not valid. Working capital is used to acquire machinery, but the periodic depreciation (allocation of this cost as a deduction from revenue) does not affect working capital. The debit in this entry will, therefore, be added to the debit from entry (a) in determining the amount of working capital provided by operations.

		Debit	Credit
(c)	Operating Summary—Depreciation of Buildings	3,000 00	
	Accumulated Depreciation—Buildings		3,000 00

The reason for this entry is the same as for entry (b). All depreciation charges decrease net income without decreasing working capital provided by operations.

(d)	Operating Summary—Amortization of Intangibles	1,000	00		
	Intangible Assets			1,000	00

This entry represents the amortization of a cost paid for in a prior period. The reason for the entry is the same as for entry (b): amortization also decreases net income without decreasing working capital.

(e)	Retained Earnings	4,825	00		
	Working Capital Summary—Cash Dividends Declared			4,825	00

Dividends were declared and paid, resulting in a decrease in working capital. If the dividends were declared but not paid, the credit to Dividends Payable would increase current liabilities and decrease working capital. Entry (e) would, therefore, be the same.

(f)	Working Capital Summary—Sale of Investments	5,000	00		
	Long-Term Investments			4,000	00
	Operating Summary—Gain on Sale of Investments			1,000	00

Securities that cost $4,000 were sold for $5,000. The gain on the sale is an ordinary item and is included in the reported net income of $19,325, and in Operating Summary through entry (a). But the effect of the sale was to increase working capital by a total of $5,000; hence, the debit to Working Capital Summary for $5,000 in entry (f). Furthermore, the increase in working capital resulting from the gain ($1,000) should be reported as an integral part of the *total* increase in working capital from sale of investments ($5,000) and not as a part of working capital provided by operations. The credit of $1,000 to Operating Summary, therefore, cancels a like amount included in Operating Summary through entry (a).

The T account for Long-Term Investments now appears as shown.

Long-Term Investments

Debit	Credit
3,000	
	(f) 4,000

Since the balance below the horizontal line must be the same as the balance above the line, a debit entry of $7,000 must be made. It may be assumed that securities costing $7,000 were acquired. In practice, reference would be made to the records to confirm this assumption.

		Debit	Credit
(g)	Long-Term Investments	7,000 00	
	Working Capital Summary—Purchase of Investments		7,000 00
(h)	Machinery	27,000 00	
	Working Capital Summary—Purchase of Machinery		27,000 00

The explanation for entry (h) is the same as for entry (g). Since no machinery was sold during the period, it may be assumed that the net change represents acquisitions.

Entry (i) is based on an assumption similar to that used in entries (g) and (h).

		Debit	Credit
(i)	Buildings	16,000 00	
	Working Capital Summary—Purchase of Buildings		16,000 00
(j)	Working Capital Summary—Issuance of Preferred Stock at Par Value	5,000 00	
	5% Preferred Stock		5,000 00

Fifty shares of preferred stock were issued at par value and provided working capital.

		Debit	Credit
(k)	Working Capital Summary—Issuance of Common Stock at Premium	18,000 00	
	Common Stock		15,000 00
	Premium on Common Stock		3,000 00

Fifteen hundred shares of common stock were issued at $12 a share and provided $18,000 of working capital.

		Debit	Credit
(l)	Mortgage Payable	3,000 00	
	Working Capital Summary—Payment on Mortgage		3,000 00

The decrease in Mortgage Payable is assumed to be due to a cash payment.

At this point, the balance below the horizontal line in each noncurrent account is equal to the net change above the line. All the transactions affecting funds have been reproduced and the change in each account has been "accounted for."

Step 5. The balance in the Operating Summary account is now $34,325, representing the working capital provided by operations. This balance is transferred to Working Capital Summary.

		Debit	Credit
(m)	Working Capital Summary—Working Capital Provided by Operations	34,325 00	
	Operating Summary		34,325 00

The completeness and accuracy of the work is verified by the equality of the balances above and below the rule of the Working Capital Summary account. The original $4,500 is "matched" or "accounted for" by the debit balance of $4,500 in entries below the horizontal line.

Long-Term Investments

	Debit		Credit
	3,000		
(g)	7,000	(f)	4,000
bal. 3,000			

Mortgage Payable

	Debit		Credit
	3,000		
(l)	3,000		

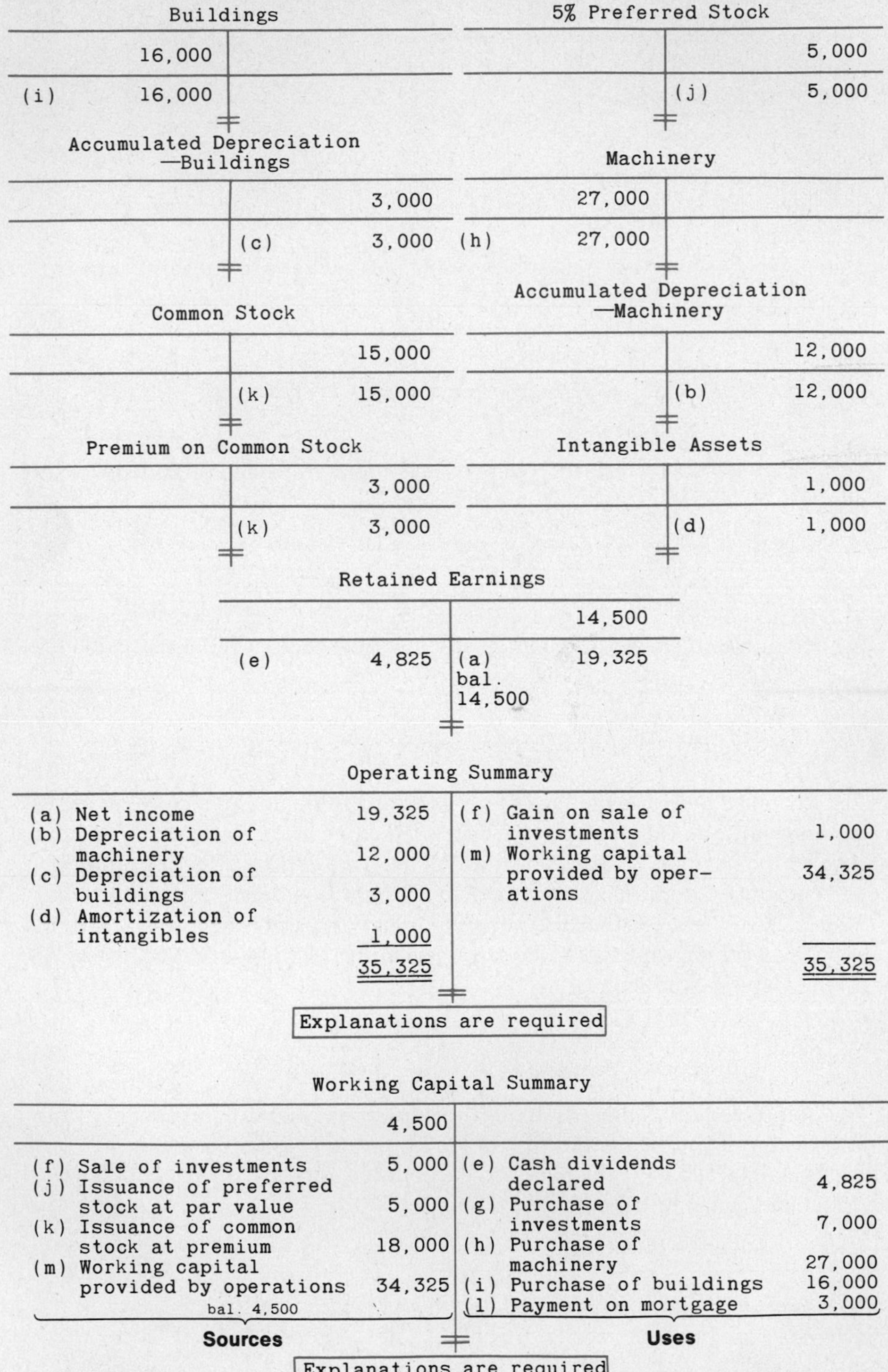

Buildings

16,000	
(i) 16,000	

5% Preferred Stock

	5,000
	(j) 5,000

Accumulated Depreciation—Buildings

	3,000
	(c) 3,000

Machinery

27,000	
(h) 27,000	

Common Stock

	15,000
	(k) 15,000

Accumulated Depreciation—Machinery

	12,000
	(b) 12,000

Premium on Common Stock

	3,000
	(k) 3,000

Intangible Assets

	1,000
	(d) 1,000

Retained Earnings

	14,500
(e) 4,825	(a) 19,325
	bal. 14,500

Operating Summary

(a) Net income	19,325	(f) Gain on sale of investments	1,000
(b) Depreciation of machinery	12,000	(m) Working capital provided by operations	34,325
(c) Depreciation of buildings	3,000		
(d) Amortization of intangibles	1,000		
	35,325		35,325

Explanations are required

Working Capital Summary

	4,500		
(f) Sale of investments	5,000	(e) Cash dividends declared	4,825
(j) Issuance of preferred stock at par value	5,000	(g) Purchase of investments	7,000
(k) Issuance of common stock at premium	18,000	(h) Purchase of machinery	27,000
(m) Working capital provided by operations	34,325	(i) Purchase of buildings	16,000
bal. 4,500		(l) Payment on mortgage	3,000
Sources		**Uses**	

Explanations are required

Note that explanations are required for the last two summary accounts so that the formal statements can be prepared from these two accounts.

It is suggested that the accountant place some symbol in the T accounts to indicate that he or she has explained all the changes that have occurred in these accounts during the year. An equals sign (=) written across the vertical line of the T account is an excellent symbol to describe that the accountant has completed the task. When each T account has an equals sign (=) written across the vertical line of the T, the accountant can quickly ascertain that he or she has completed the total work requirement of the T accounts. The individual can then proceed to step 6, the preparation of the formal statement.

Step 6. The formal statement of changes in financial position on the working capital basis can now be prepared directly from the Working Capital Summary and Operating Summary accounts: the debits represent sources of working capital; the credits represent uses of working capital. Supporting figures for working capital received from operations must be taken from the Operating Summary account. The completed statement follows.

ROCK CORPORATION — Exhibit D
Statement of Changes in Financial Position—Working Capital Basis
For the Year Ended December 31, 1979

Working Capital Was Provided by		
Operations		
Net Income (before extraordinary items)		$19,325.00
Add Nonworking Capital Charges against Operations		
Depreciation of Machinery		12,000.00
Depreciation of Buildings		3,000.00
Amortization of Intangibles		1,000.00
Total		$35,325.00
Deduct Nonworking Capital Credits to Operations		
Gain on Sale of Investments		1,000.00
Working Capital Provided by Operations Exclusive of Extraordinary Items		$34,325.00
Sale of Investments		5,000.00
Issuance of Preferred Stock		5,000.00
Issuance of Common Stock		18,000.00
Total Working Capital Provided		$62,325.00
Working Capital Was Used for		
Declaration of Dividends	$ 4,825.00	
Purchase of Investments	7,000.00	
Purchase of Machinery	27,000.00	
Purchase of Buildings	16,000.00	
Payment on Mortgage Payable	3,000.00	
Total Working Capital Used		57,825.00
Net Increase in Working Capital (see Schedule D-1)		$ 4,500.00

All-financial resources concept of funds

As early as 1963, *APB Opinion No. 3* encouraged *but did not require* firms to present a statement of changes in financial position broadened to include "all financial resources" as the concept of funds.[4] As stated previously, when *APB Opinion No. 19* was issued in 1971, it made this statement a basic statement and also made mandatory the use of the all-financial resources concept rather than a concept limited to working capital or cash.

Comparison of two concepts

An interpretation of the information contained in *APB Opinion No. 19* indicates that the *all-financial resources concept* would include the following:

1. Sources and uses of working capital (or cash in some cases), plus
2. Sources and uses of other financial resources not affecting working capital, such as:
   a. Issuance of bonds payable or other long-term debt instrument in exchange for plant and equipment items.
   b. Issuance of capital stock in exchange for plant and equipment items.
   c. Conversion of bonds payable into common stock.
   d. Conversion of preferred stock into common stock.
   e. The exchange of one plant and equipment item for another plant and equipment item.

Each item listed in 2 above would be shown both as a source of financial resources and as a use of financial resources. Consider, for example, the issuance of bonds payable for land:

1. The issuance of bonds payable would be listed as a source of financial resources.
2. The acquisition of land would be listed as a use of financial resources.

Not all changes in balance sheet items are to be listed as sources and uses of financial resources. Specifically excluded by *APB Opinion No. 19* are the following:

1. Stock dividends
2. Restrictions on retained earnings.

These items are considered primarily to be accounting changes that do not alter the basic nature of financial resources.

4 *APB Opinion No. 3,* The Statement of Source and Application of Funds," October, 1963, p. 12.

Illustration of the all-financial resources concept

The following unclassified balance sheet and additional information are given for the Allresourco Company.

ALLRESOURCO COMPANY
Comparative Balance Sheet
December 31, 1979 and 1978

Exhibit C

	December 31 1979	December 31 1978	Change Increase (Decrease)
Assets			
Cash	$ 525,000.00	$ 415,000.00	$110,000.00
Accounts Receivable (net)	90,000.00	80,000.00	10,000.00
Merchandise Inventory	593,000.00	400,000.00	193,000.00
Prepaid Insurance	6,000.00	5,000.00	1,000.00
Land	100,000.00	-0-	100,000.00
Machinery	450,000.00	400,000.00	50,000.00
Accumulated Depreciation—Machinery	(30,000.00)	(20,000.00)	10,000.00
	$1,734,000.00	$1,280,000.00	
Liabilities and Stockholders' Equity			
Accounts Payable	$ 25,000.00	$ 20,000.00	5,000.00
Dividends Payable	50,000.00	10,000.00	40,000.00
9% Bonds Payable	300,000.00	-0-	300,000.00
Premium on 9% Bonds Payable	9,000.00	-0-	9,000.00
Convertible Preferred Stock	-0-	150,000.00	(150,000.00)
Common Stock, $10 par	900,000.00	800,000.00	100,000.00
Premium on Common Stock	50,000.00	-0-	50,000.00
Retained Earnings	400,000.00	300,000.00	100,000.00
	$1,734,000.00	$1,280,000.00	

Additional information

a. Net income for 1979 was $150,000 (this is net income before extraordinary items).
b. A dividend of $50,000 was declared on December 15, 1979, payable on January 12, 1980.
c. On December 28, 1979, the company traded in a machine, which had cost $100,000 and had an accumulated depreciation of $10,000, for new machinery costing $150,000; the trade-in allowance, which was equal to fair market value of the old machine, was $80,000. The balance was paid in cash. The loss of $10,000 is an ordinary loss.
d. The annual depreciation expense on machinery was $20,000.
e. On January 1, 1979, the company issued at 105 for cash 9 percent bonds with a face value of $200,000. The maturity date of the bonds is January 1, 1989.

f. On December 31, 1979, the company issued directly to Hall Realty Company 9 percent bonds with a face value of $100,000 at 100 for land valued at $100,000.
g. The convertible preferred stock was converted during 1979 into 10,000 shares of $10 par value common stock.
h. The annual amortization of premium on 9 percent bonds payable was $1,000.

Solution to the problem follows:

ALLRESOURCO COMPANY
Schedule of Changes in Working Capital
For the Year Ended December 31, 1979

Schedule D-1

	December 31		Changes in Working Capital	
	1979	1978	Increase	Decrease
Current Assets				
Cash	$ 525,000.00	$415,000.00	$110,000.00	
Accounts Receivable (net)	90,000.00	80,000.00	10,000.00	
Merchandise Inventory	593,000.00	400,000.00	193,000.00	
Prepaid Insurance	6,000.00	5,000.00	1,000.00	
Total Current Assets	$1,214,000.00	$900,000.00		
Current Liabilities				
Accounts Payable	$ 25,000.00	$ 20,000.00		$ 5,000.00
Dividends Payable	50,000.00	10,000.00		40,000.00
Total Current Liabilities	$ 75,000.00	$ 30,000.00		
Working Capital	$1,139,000.00	$870,000.00	$314,000.00	$ 45,000.00
Net Increase in Working Capital				269,000.00
			$314,000.00	$314,000.00

Even when the all-financial resources basis is used, *APB Opinion No. 19* requires the details of the changes in individual working capital items to be presented. One method is to prepare a schedule of changes in working capital as indicated in the foregoing illustrations.

For the purpose of clarity the entries to the T accounts are presented in general journal form. The entries will be lettered to correspond to the letters preceding the additional information. Since the all-financial resources concept is being followed, the account equivalent to working capital summary has been renamed Financial Resources Summary. This change of name seems to be indicated because the new summary account will be used not only to record sources and uses of working capital, but also to record those sources and uses of financial resources that do not affect working capital.

(a)	Operating Summary—Net Income	150,000 00	
	Retained Earnings		150,000 00
(b)	Retained Earnings	50,000 00	
	Financial Resources Summary—Declaration of Dividends		50,000 00

The foregoing transaction (b) represents a use of financial resources, since it decreases working capital even though it will not be paid until 1980.

(c)	Financial Resources Summary				
	—Disposal of Machinery	80,000	00		
	Machinery	150,000	00		
	Operating Summary—Loss on Disposal				
	of Machinery	10,000	00		
	Accumulated Depreciation				
	—Machinery	10,000	00		
	Machinery			100,000	00
	Financial Resources Summary				
	—Purchase of Machinery . . .			150,000	00
(d)	Operating Summary—Depreciation				
	of Machinery	20,000	00		
	Accumulated Depreciation				
	—Machinery			20,000	00
(e)	Financial Resources Summary				
	—Issuance of 9% Bonds Payable				
	at 105	210,000	00		
	9% Bonds Payable			200,000	00
	Premium on 9% Bonds				
	Payable			10,000	00
(f)	Financial Resources Summary				
	—Issuance of 9% Bonds Payable				
	at 100	100,000	00		
	9% Bonds Payable			100,000	00
	Land	100,000	00		
	Financial Resources Summary				
	—Purchase of Land			100,000	00

Even though the bonds in transaction (f) are issued directly to the realtor for the land, the transaction must be disclosed both as a source of financial resources and as a use of financial resources. The two entries are suggested as a means of more carefully delineating this problem.

(g)	Financial Resources Summary				
	—Issuance of Common Stock	150,000	00		
	Common Stock			100,000	00
	Premium on Common Stock			50,000	00
	Convertible Preferred Stock	150,000	00		
	Financial Resources Summary				
	—Retirement of Convertible				
	Preferred Stock			150,000	00

This transaction is similar to entry (f)—it must be shown as both a source and a use of financial resources. The paid-in capital in excess of the $10 par value was credited to Premium on Common Stock.

(h)	Premium on 9% Bonds Payable	1,000	00		
	Operating Summary—Amortization				
	of Premium on 9% Bonds				
	Payable			1,000	00

The amount of the amortization of premium on 9 percent bonds payable is a nonworking capital credit against operations; that is, it resulted in an increase in net income, by way of decreasing bond interest expense, without increasing working capital.

(i)	Financial Resources Summary—Operations	179,000 00	
	Operating Summary—Transfer of Operating Amount to Financial Resources Summary		179,000 00

The T accounts with the foregoing entries posted to them appear below:

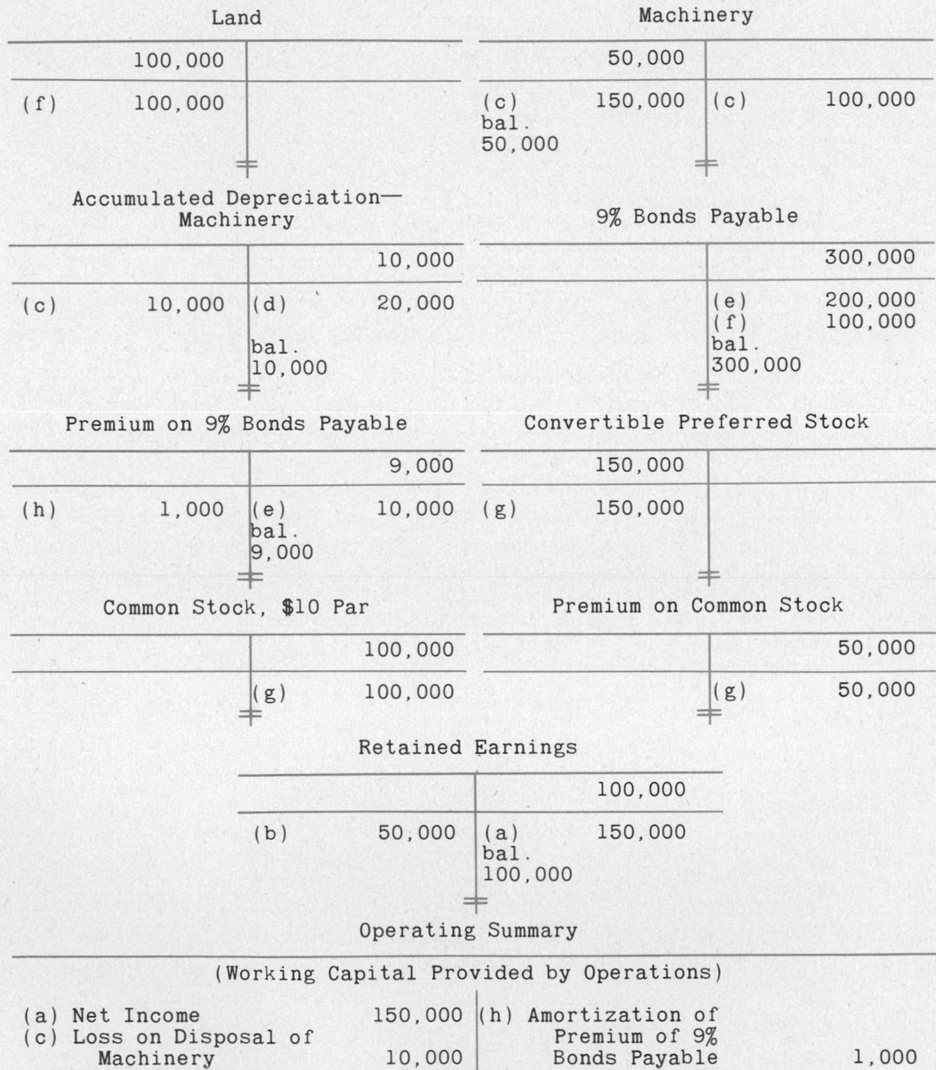

Land

	100,000		
(f)	100,000		

Machinery

	50,000		
(c)	150,000	(c)	100,000
bal. 50,000			

Accumulated Depreciation—Machinery

			10,000
(c)	10,000	(d)	20,000
		bal. 10,000	

9% Bonds Payable

			300,000
		(e)	200,000
		(f)	100,000
		bal. 300,000	

Premium on 9% Bonds Payable

			9,000
(h)	1,000	(e)	10,000
		bal. 9,000	

Convertible Preferred Stock

	150,000		
(g)	150,000		

Common Stock, $10 Par

			100,000
		(g)	100,000

Premium on Common Stock

			50,000
		(g)	50,000

Retained Earnings

			100,000
(b)	50,000	(a)	150,000
		bal. 100,000	

Operating Summary

(Working Capital Provided by Operations)

(a) Net Income	150,000	(h) Amortization of Premium of 9% Bonds Payable	1,000
(c) Loss on Disposal of Machinery	10,000	(i) To Financial Res. Summary	179,000
(d) Depr. of Machinery	20,000		

Financial Resources Summary

Sources		Uses	
Net Increase in Working Capital	269,000		
(c) Disposal of Machinery	80,000	(b) Declaration of Dividends	50,000
(e) Issuance of 9% Bonds Payable at 105	210,000	(c) Purchase of Machinery	150,000
(f) Issuance of 9% Bonds Payable at 100	100,000	(f) Purchase of Land	100,000
(g) Issuance of Common Stock	150,000	(g) Retirement of Convertible Preferred Stock	150,000
(i) Operations	179,000		450,000
	719,000		
bal. 269,000			

The formal statement of changes in financial position is shown in Exhibit D.

ALLRESOURCO COMPANY
Statement of Changes in Financial Position
For the Year Ended December 31, 1979

Exhibit D

Financial Resources Were Provided by		
Operations		
Net Income (before extraordinary items)		$150,000.00
Add Nonworking Capital Charges to Operations		
Loss on Disposal of Machinery		10,000.00
Depreciation of Machinery		20,000.00
Total		$180,000.00
Deduct Nonworking Capital Credits to Operations		
Amortization of Premium on 9% Bonds Payable		1,000.00
Working Capital Provided by Operations Exclusive of Extraordinary Items		$179,000.00
Disposal of Machinery		80,000.00
Issuance of 9% Bonds Payable at 105		210,000.00
Issuance of 9% Bonds Payable at 100		100,000.00
Issuance of Common Stock		150,000.00
Total Financial Resources Provided		$719,000.00
Financial Resources Were Used for		
Declaration of Dividends	$ 50,000.00	
Purchase of Machinery	150,000.00	
Purchase of Land	100,000.00	
Retirement of Convertible Preferred Stock	150,000.00	
Total Financial Resources Used		450,000.00
Net Increase in Working Capital (See Schedule D-1)		$269,000.00

Other concepts of funds

There are many useful concepts of funds other than working capital and all financial resources. Two of these are: cash and cash and temporary investments. The specific concept that is used in the preparation of the statement of changes in financial position will depend upon the purpose and objectives of the particular statement. For example, for many short-run financial purposes, a statement based on cash is definitely of more importance than perhaps any other fund concept; such a statement is quite useful to management for analysis in budgeting and forecasting cash requirements. With the extremely high interest rates in effect today, the administration of cash is of paramount importance.

The basic logic of the analysis for a cash-basis statement of changes in financial position is the same as for a working-capital basis statement: an analysis of the relationships of the items in the financial statements. The causes of the changes in cash—the source and uses of cash—are determined by analyzing the changes in all accounts other than Cash. Figures from the income statement are used to determine the changes in cash as a result of operations, and figures from the balance sheet together with supplementary data reveal the remaining causes for the changes in cash.

As with working capital provided by operations, a major problem is the determination of the cash generated by operations; this problem is complicated by the fact that the revenue and expense figures used for income measurement are different from cash receipts and cash disbursements. The time lag in the settlement of accounts with customers and creditors and the prepayment of certain expenses, for example, necessitate the conversion of accrual-basis revenue and expense amounts to the cash equivalent.

Thus in applying the T-account procedure for purposes of preparing a statement of changes in financial position on a cash basis, it is necessary to open a T account for every balance sheet account for which a periodic change is recorded, including an Operating Summary account and the Cash Summary account. The transactions causing changes in cash are reconstructed in summary form through a process of analyzing the changes in all accounts other than Cash and by reference to supplementary information. Since the procedural approach is similar to the two preceding illustrations, an expanded example is not shown here.

Glossary

All financial resources A concept of funds that includes the disclosure of not only the sources and uses of working capital or cash, but also other financial and investment information that does not affect working capital.

Changes in working capital Transactions that involve a current account and a noncurrent account, thereby causing an increase or decrease in working capital.

Comparative balance sheets The balance sheet as of a given date compared with one or more immediately preceding balance sheets.

Current account Any current asset or current liability account.

Direct T-account method A method of determining the sources and uses of funds by analyzing changes in a set of T accounts.

Financial resources summary A T account in the direct T-account method used to record on the debit side the sources of all financial resources and on the credit side the uses of all financial resources.

Funds In the context of the statement of changes in financial position, funds may mean cash, working capital, cash and temporary investments in marketable securities, current assets, or all financial resources, depending upon the needs of the user.

Noncurrent account Any account on the balance sheet *other than* current assets and current liabilities; specifically, a noncurrent account is any one of the long-term investments, plant and equipment, intangibles, long-term liabilities, or stockholders' equity accounts.

Operating summary A T account in the direct T-account method used to record the working capital provided by or used in operations.

Schedule of changes in working capital A schedule of comparative balances in current assets and current liabilities that shows how each account balance change affected working capital.

Sources of funds Inflows of financial resources.

Statement of changes in financial position A statement showing sources and uses of funds prepared either (1) on all-financial resources basis (recommended by *APB Opinion No. 19*), (2) on working-capital basis, (3) on cash basis, or (4) on some other concept of funds.

Uses of funds Outflows of financial resources

Working capital Current assets less current liabilities, or amount of current assets not required to liquidate current liabilities.

Working capital summary A T account in the direct T-account method used to record on the debit side all sources of working capital and on the credit side all uses of working capital.

Questions

Q21–1 What is meant by the term *funds?* Discuss three popular concepts of funds.

Q21–2 In its *Opinion No. 19* the APB recommended what concept of funds for typical presentation in annual reports?

Q21–3 The statement of changes in financial position is now a fourth major financial statement subject to the independent auditor's opinion. Secure an annual report (from your library) dated prior to 1971 and one dated after 1971 and compare the difference in location of the statement in the annual report and the dfference in the title and content of the statement. Check to see whether the statement of changes in financial position prepared after 1971 conforms to the criteria stated in *APB Opinion 19*.

Q21–4 What is the purpose of the statement of changes in financial position?

Q21–5 How may working capital provided by operations be determined?

Q21–6 What are the chief sources of working capital from operations? the chief uses of working capital for operations?

Q21–7 Certain transactions are eliminated from the statement of changes in financial position—working capital basis. Why? Give some examples.

Q21–8 How may the statement of changes in financial position—working capital basis be used to advantage by management? by investors? by others?

Q21–9 How may the statement of changes in financial position—cash basis be used to advantage by management? by investors? by others?

Q21–10 What are some of the sources of information for the preparation of the statement of changes in financial position—working capital basis?

Q21–11 What is the effect of a dividend declaration on working capital? of the payment of a dividend?

Q21–12 What is the effect of depreciation of plant and equipment (a) on working capital? (b) on cash?

Q21–13 The net income as shown on the income statement and the working capital provided by operations are different amounts. Why?

Q21–14 Which items are included in a statement of changes in financial position prepared under all-financial resources concept that are not included on a statement prepared under the working capital concept?

Q21–15 Does the statement of changes in financial position eliminate the need for the balance sheet? for the income statement? Discuss.

Q21–16 What is the effect on working capital of a change to an accelerated method of depreciation?

Q21–17 In arriving at working capital provided by operations, certain items are added to net income and other items are deducted. Illustrate and explain.

Q21–18 The accounts receivable of a business totaled $30,000 at the beginning of the year and $24,000 at the end of the year. Accounts receivable written off as uncollectible during the year amounted to $2,600 and cash discounts allowed to customers amounted to $1,200. The sales for the year were $70,000. What were the cash receipts during the year from sales of the current and prior periods?

Q21–19 The purchases of merchandise of a business amounted to $100,000 during 1979. Accounts payable at the beginning and end of the year were $33,000 and $29,600, respectively; notes payable given to trade creditors in settlement of open accounts were $8,000 at the beginning of the year and $8,800 at the end of the year. Returns and allowances on purchases were $870. What were the cash payments during 1979 for purchases of 1979 and prior periods?

Class exercises

CE21–1 (Statement of changes in financial position—working capital basis) The December 31, 1979, and 1978 balance sheets of the Rockwell Company carried the following debit and credit amounts:

	December 31	
	1979	*1978*
Debits		
Cash	$ 20,400	$ 25,200
Accounts Receivable (net)	70,200	65,800
Merchandise Inventory	170,400	172,800
Prepaid Expenses	3,000	3,600
Office Equipment	10,000	11,200
Store Equipment	59,600	56,600
Totals	$333,600	$335,200
Credits		
Accumulated Depreciation—Office Equipment	$ 5,000	$ 4,800
Accumulated Depreciation—Store Equipment	15,000	13,000
Accounts Payable	44,800	47,000
Notes Payable (Short-Term)	20,000	10,000
Common Stock, $10 par value	220,000	200,000
Premium on Common Stock	13,000	11,000
Retained Earnings	15,800	49,400
Totals	$333,600	$335,200

Additional information:

a. The net loss for 1979 was $3,800.
b. Depreciation expense on office equipment was $1,000; on store equipment, $3,400.
c. Office equipment that was carried at its cost of $1,200 with accumulated depreciation of $800 was sold for $600. The gain was credited directly to Retained Earnings.
d. Store equipment costing $4,400 was purchased.
e. Fully depreciated store equipment that cost $1,400 was discarded and its cost and accumulated depreciation were removed from the accounts.
f. Cash dividends of $8,000 were declared during the year.
g. A 2,000-share stock dividend was declared and issued. On the date of declaration, the common stock of the company had a fair market value of $11 a share.

Required: Prepare a statement of changes in financial position for 1979 using the *working capital basis*. Use the direct T-account approach.

CE21–2 (Statement of changes in financial position—all financial resources) The Welt Corporation reported the following information in regard to changes in financial position during 1979.

WELT CORPORATION
Comparative Balance Sheet
December 31, 1979 and 1978

Exhibit C

	December 31 *1979*	*1978*	*Change Increase (Decrease)*
Cash	$ 787,500	$ 622,500	$165,000
Accounts Receivable (net)	135,000	120,000	15,000
Merchandise Inventory	889,500	600,000	289,500
Prepaid Insurance	9,000	7,500	1,500
Land	150,000	–0–	150,000
Machinery	675,000	600,000	75,000
Accumulated Depreciation on Machinery	(45,000)	(30,000)	15,000*
	$2,601,000	$1,920,000	
Accounts Payable	$ 37,500	$ 30,000	7,500
Dividends Payable	75,000	15,000	60,000
9% Bonds Payable	450,000	–0–	450,000
Premium on 9% Bonds Payable	13,500	–0–	13,500
Convertible Preferred Stock	–0–	225,000	(225,000)
Common Stock, $10 Par	1,350,000	1,200,000	150,000
Premium on Common Stock	75,000	–0–	75,000
Retained Earnings	600,000	450,000	150,000
	$2,601,000	$1,920,000	

*This is an increase to a contra asset, which in turn represents a decrease in the asset, Machinery.

Additional information:

a. Net income for 1979, $225,000.
b. A dividend of $75,000 was declared on December 12, 1979, payable on January 16, 1980.
c. On December 29, 1979, the company traded in a machine which had cost $150,000 and had an accumulated depreciation of $15,000 for new machinery costing $225,000; the trade-in allowance was equal to fair market value of $120,000. The balance was paid in cash. The loss of $15,000 is an ordinary loss.
d. The annual depreciation expense on machinery was $30,000.
e. On January 1, 1979, the company issued 9 percent bonds with a face value of $300,000 at 105 for cash. The maturity date of the bonds is January 1, 1989.

f. On December 31, 1979, the company issued directly to Orange Realty Company 9 percent bonds with a face value of $150,000 at 100 for land valued at $150,000.
g. The convertible preferred stock was converted during 1979, into 15,000 shares of $10 par value common stock.
h. The annual amortization of premium on 9 percent bonds payable was $1,500.

Required:
1. Prepare a separate schedule of changes in working capital.
2. Prepare a statement of changes in financial position for 1979 using the *all-financial resources basis*. Use the direct T-account approach.

CE21–3 (Statement of changes in financial position—working capital and cash basis) The following data are taken from the books of the Walpole Corp. (amounts are in thousands of dollars):

Debits	*December 31* 1979	1978
Cash	$ 630	$ 570
Temporary Investments in Marketable Securities	212	100
Receivables (net)	290	250
Inventories	190	140
Long-Term Investments	140	220
Machinery	1,000	700
Buildings	1,200	400
Land	70	70
Totals	$3,732	$2,450

Credits	1979	1978
Accumulated Depreciation	$ 550	$ 300
Accounts Payable	200	150
Notes Payable (Short-Term)	100	50
Mortgage Bonds Payable	1,000	500
Common Stock	1,100	800
Premium on Common Stock	110	–0–
Retained Earnings	672	650
Totals	$3,732	$2,450

WALPOLE CORPORATION **Exhibit A**
Income Statement
For the Year Ended December 31, 1979

Sales		$1,200
Cost of Goods Sold		674
Gross Margin on Sales		$ 526
Operating Expenses		
Depreciation—Machinery	$100	
Depreciation—Buildings	160	
Other Expenses	200	460
Net Income from Operations		$ 66
Gain on Sale of Long-Term Investments—Ordinary		24
Total		$ 90
Loss on Sale of Machinery—Ordinary (proceeds were $30)		10
Net Income		$ 80

Required:

1. Prepare a statement of changes in financial position—working capital basis for 1979.
2. Prepare a statement of changes in financial position—cash basis for 1979.

CE21-4 (Working capital generated by operations) You are given the following combined statement:

FULTON COMPANY — Exhibit A
Statement of Income and Retained Earnings
For the Year Ended December 31, 1979

Revenue and Other Credits		
Sales		$300,000
Interest Earned		5,250
Correction of Prior Year's Income— Overstatement of 1977 Depreciation of Machinery		2,500
Total		$307,750
Expenses, Losses and Other Charges		
Cost of Goods Sold	$235,000	
Salaries and Wages Expense	20,000	
Bad Debts Expense	2,000	
Advertising Expense	5,000	
Depreciation Expense	30,000	
Office Expense	10,000	
Unrealized Loss on Reduction of Marketable Securities to Market	2,500	
Loss on Sale of Machinery	4,000	
Interest Expense	2,000	
Total		310,500
Net Loss for the Year		$ (2,750)
Retained Earnings, December 31, 1978		505,250
Total		$502,500
Deduct Dividends declared June 2, 1979, and paid July 2, 1979	$ 50,000	
Dividends declared December 2, 1979, to be paid January 2, 1980	75,000	
Stock dividends declared and issued in 1979	100,000	
Total		225,000
Retained Earnings, December 31, 1979		$277,500

Interest Earned represents a receipt of $5,025 in cash and the amortization of discount on bonds purchased for investments (long term) of $225. The Interest Expense figure was increased by $175 for amortization of discount on bonds payable and was decreased by $100 for amortization of a premium on bonds payable.

Required:

1. Starting with the net loss for the year, compute, in schedule or T-account form, the working capital provided (or used) by operations during 1979.
2. Compute the amount of working capital provided or used in connection with the dividend policy of the company.

Exercises and problems

P21–1 The following transactions occurred in a given company:

1. Purchased U.S. Treasury notes maturing in six months.
2. Declared and issued a stock dividend to common stockholders.
3. Restricted retained earnings for anticipated plant expansion.
4. Issued common stock in exchange for a building.
5. Acquired machinery for $50,000; paid $20,000 in cash and issued a long-term note for the balance.
6. Reacquired some outstanding preferred stock for retirement.
7. Issued additional common stock at a premium for cash.
8. Issued bonds directly to preferred shareholders.

Required: For each of the foregoing transactions, state whether it (1) was a source of working capital, (2) was a use of working capital, or (3) had no effect on working capital.

P21–2 Refer to P21–1 and state which of the transactions are a source or use of all financial resources, yet are not a source or use of working capital.

P21–3 The Plant and Equipment section of the Ward Company's comparative balance sheet shows the following amounts:

	December 31	
	1979	*1978*
Plant and Equipment		
Machinery	$550,000	$500,000
Deduct Accumulated Depreciation	250,000	240,000
Total Plant and Equipment	$300,000	$260,000

Acquisitions of new machinery during 1979 totaled $140,000. The income statement shows depreciation charges for the year of $70,000 and a loss from machinery disposals of $24,000.

Required: Determine the original cost and accumulated depreciation of machinery sold during 1979 and the proceeds of the sale; prepare a partial statement of changes in financial position—working capital basis.

P21–4 For each of the following cases, compute the working capital generated by operations.

	A	*B*	*C*	*D*	*E*
Net income (loss) per income statement	$15,000	$(15,000)	$55,000	$45,000	$(20,000)
Depreciation of plant and equipment	2,000	2,000	4,500	3,000	1,000
Ordinary gain (loss) on sale of long-term investment			(1,000)	2,000	(500)
Periodic amortization of discount on bonds payable			1,000	500	250
Periodic amortization of patents				500	300

P21–5 The comparative balance sheet of the Wayland Company, as of December 31, 1979, and 1978 disclosed the following:

	December 31 1979	1978
Debits		
Cash	$ 96,000	$ 126,000
Accounts Receivable (net)	117,600	99,600
Merchandise Inventory	170,000	130,000
Long-Term Investments	136,000	120,000
Machinery	700,000	600,000
Buildings	540,000	450,000
Land	100,000	100,000
Patents	36,000	40,000
Totals	$1,895,600	$1,665,600
Credits		
Accumulated Depreciation—Machinery	$ 80,000	$ 60,000
Accumulated Depreciation—Buildings	70,000	40,000
Accounts Payable—Trade	110,000	100,000
Notes Payable—Trade	16,000	20,000
Mortgage Payable	100,000	120,000
Common Stock	1,100,000	1,000,000
Retained Earnings	419,600	325,600
Totals	$1,895,600	$1,665,600

Additional information:

a. Net income for the year was $94,000.
b. There were no sales or disposals of plant or equipment during the year.

Required: Prepare a statement of changes in financial position using the *working capital basis* for 1979.

P21–6 You are given the following information about certain items for two companies during a year.

	1	*2*
Accounts Receivable—Beginning of Year ..	$ 54,000	$ 80,000
Accounts Receivable—End of Year	70,000	76,000
Sales	210,000	300,000
Uncollectible Accounts Written Off	1,000	1,500
Cash Discounts on Sales	2,000	5,000

Required: For each company determine the amount of cash received from customers.

P21–7 You are given the following information about certain items for two companies during a year:

	1	*2*
Beginning Inventory	$ 24,000	$ 30,000
Ending Inventory	20,000	36,000
Purchases	150,000	170,000
Beginning Accounts Payable	20,000	28,000
Ending Accounts Payable	24,000	20,000
Discounts on Purchases	2,000	3,000

Required: For each company determine the amount of cash disbursements for merchandise.

P21–8 Comparative financial statement of the Framison Corporation showed the following balances:

	December 31	
	1979	*1978*
Cash	$ 50,000	$ 52,000
Other Current Assets	110,000	115,000
Plant and Equipment (net)	140,000	110,000
Current Liabilities	110,000	115,000
Stockholders' Equity	190,000	162,000

There were no disposals of plant and equipment during the year. Depreciation expense for 1979 was $8,000. Dividend payments totaled $10,000.

Required: Prepare a schedule explaining the cause of the decrease in cash in spite of reported net income of $38,000.

P21–9 Following is the comparative postclosing trial balance of the Marks Company:

MARKS COMPANY
Comparative Postclosing Trial Balance
December 31, 1979 and 1978

	December 31 1979	1978
Debits		
Cash	$ 17,500	$ 25,000
Accounts Receivable (net)	47,500	40,000
Merchandise Inventory	130,000	97,500
Marketable Securities (Temporary)	–0–	55,000
Prepaid Expenses	2,000	1,250
Plant and Equipment	250,000	150,000
Patents	32,000	34,000
Totals	$479,000	$402,750
Credits		
Accumulated Depreciation—Plant and Equipment	$ 67,500	$ 50,000
Accounts Payable	50,000	30,000
Common Stock	250,000	250,000
Retained Earnings	111,500	72,750
Totals	$479,000	$402,750

Additional data:

a. Net income for the period was $62,500.
b. Dividends declared were $23,750.
c. The temporary investment in marketable securities was sold at a gain (included in a) of $7,500.
d. Equipment with an original cost of $10,000 and accumulated depreciation of $5,000 was sold at an ordinary loss (included in a) of $1,000.
e. Patents are being amortized over their legal life of 17 years.

Required: Prepare a statement of changes in financial position for 1979 using the *working capital basis*.

P21–10 (Integrative) The following information regarding the changes in financial position is indicated for the year 1979 for the Dalton Company.

DALTON COMPANY
Comparative Balance Sheet
December 31, 1979 and 1978

Exhibit C

	December 31		*Change*
	1979	*1978*	*Increase (Decrease)*
Cash	$262,500	$207,500	$ 55,000
Accounts Receivable (net)	45,000	40,000	5,000
Merchandise Inventory	296,500	200,000	96,500
Prepaid Insurance	3,000	2,500	500
Land	50,000	–0–	50,000
Machinery	225,000	200,000	25,000
Accumulated Depreciation—Machinery	(15,000)	(10,000)	5,000*
	$867,000	$640,000	
Accounts Payable	$ 12,500	$ 10,000	2,500
Dividends Payable	25,000	5,000	20,000
9% Bonds Payable	150,000	–0–	150,000
Premium on 9% Bonds Payable	4,500	–0–	4,500
Convertible Preferred Stock	–0–	75,000	(75,000)
Common Stock, $10 par	450,000	400,000	50,000
Premium on Common Stock	25,000	–0–	25,000
Retained Earnings	200,000	150,000	50,000
	$867,000	$640,000	

*This is an increase in a contra asset.

Additional information:

a. Net income for 1979, $75,000.
b. A dividend of $25,000 was declared on December 16, 1979, payable on January 14, 1980.
c. On December 27, 1979, the company traded in a machine which cost $50,000 and had accumulated depreciation of $5,000 for new machinery costing $75,000; the trade-in allowance, which was equal to fair market value of the old machine, was $40,000; the balance was paid in cash. The loss of $5,000 is an ordinary loss.
d. The annual depreciation expense on machinery was $10,000.
e. On January 1, 1979, the company issued 9 percent bonds with a face value of $100,000 at 105 for cash. The maturity date of the bonds is January 1, 1989.

f. On December 31, 1979, the company issued directly to Biltmore Realty Company 9 percent bonds with a face value of $50,000 at 100 for land valued at $50,000.

g. The convertible preferred stock was converted during 1979 into 5,000 shares of $10 par value common stock.

Required:

1. Prepare a schedule of changes in working capital.
2. Prepare a statement of changes in financial position using the all-financial resources concept for 1979. Use the direct T-account approach.

P21–11 (Integrative) You are given the following information from the books of the Broad Corporation.

BROAD CORPORATION
Balance Sheet Accounts
December 31, 1979 and 1978

Exhibit C

	December 31		*Change*
	1979	*1978*	*Increase (Decrease)*
Debits			
Cash	$ 26,400	$ 31,200	$ (4,800)
Accounts Receivable	95,200	64,800	30,400
Merchandise Inventory	44,000	56,000	(12,000)
Machinery	164,800	174,800	(10,000)
Sinking Fund Cash	20,000	–0–	20,000
Totals	$350,400	$326,800	$ 23,600
Credits			
Allowance for Doubtful Accounts	$ 5,600	$ 5,000	$ 600
Accumulated Depreciation—Machinery	32,400	36,400	(4,000)
Accounts Payable	42,000	48,400	(6,400)
Dividends Payable	4,000	–0–	4,000
Bonds Payable	40,000	–0–	40,000
Premium on Bonds Payable	1,900	–0–	1,900
Capital Stock	200,000	200,000	–0–
Retained Earnings	4,500	37,000	(32,500)
Retained Earnings—Restricted for Sinking Fund	20,000	–0–	20,000
Totals	$350,400	$326,800	$ 23,600

BROAD CORPORATION
Statement of Retained Earnings
For the Year Ended December 31, 1979

Exhibit B

Balance, December 31, 1978		$37,000
Add Net Income for year ended December 31, 1979		1,500
Total		$38,500
Deduct Dividends Declared and Paid in Cash	$10,000	
Dividend Declared Payable January 15, 1980	4,000	
Appropriation for Sinking Fund	20,000	34,000
Balance, December 31, 1979		$ 4,500

BROAD CORPORATION
Income Statement
For the Year Ended December 31, 1979

Exhibit A

Sales		$170,900
Cost of Goods Sold		130,000
Gross Margin on Sales		$ 40,900
Operating Expenses		
Salaries Expense	$29,400	
Bad Debts Expense	600	
Depreciation of Machinery	7,000	
Taxes Expense	800	
Insurance Expense	600	38,400
Net Income from Operations		$ 2,500
Other Ordinary Expenses		
Bond Interest Expense	$ 2,100	
Deduct Amortization of Bond Premium	100	
Net Bond Interest Expense	$ 2,000	
Other Ordinary Revenue		
Gain on Sale of Machinery	1,000	1,000
Net Income to Retained Earnings		$ 1,500

Additional data:

a. Bonds payable in the amount of $40,000 were issued on April 30, 1979, at 105.

b. Machinery that cost $14,000 and had accumulated depreciation of $11,000 was sold for $4,000 in cash.

Required: Prepare a schedule of working capital changes and a statement of changes in financial position—working capital basis for 1979 by the T-account approach. Submit all supporting computations, including the T accounts.

P21–12 (Integrative) The Western Company revealed the following information regarding its changes in the comparative balance sheet during 1979:

THE WESTERN COMPANY
Comparative Balance Sheet
December 31, 1979 and 1978

Exhibit C

	December 31 1979	1978	*Change Increase (Decrease)*
Cash	$ 918,750	$ 726,250	$192,500
Accounts Receivable (net)	157,500	140,000	17,500
Merchandise Inventory	1,037,750	700,000	337,750
Prepaid Insurance	10,500	8,750	1,750
Land	175,000	–0–	175,000
Machinery	787,500	700,000	87,500
Accumulated Depreciation—Machinery	(52,500)	(35,000)	17,500*
	$3,034,500	$2,240,000	
Accounts Payable	$ 43,750	$ 35,000	8,750
Dividends Payable	87,500	17,500	70,000
9% Bonds Payable	525,000	–0–	525,000
Premium on 9% Bonds Payable	15,750	–0–	15,750
Convertible Preferred Stock	–0–	262,500	(262,500)
Common Stock, $10 par	1,575,000	1,400,000	175,000
Premium on Common Stock	87,500	–0–	87,500
Retained Earnings	700,000	525,000	175,000
	$3,034,500	$2,240,000	

*This is an increase in a contra asset.

Additional information:

a. Net income for 1979, $262,500.
b. A dividend of $87,500 was declared on December 19, 1979, payable on January 14, 1980.
c. On December 30, 1979, the company traded in a machine which cost $175,000 and had an accumulated depreciation of $17,500 for new machinery costing $262,500; the trade-in allowance, which was equal to fair market value of the old machine, was $140,000; the balance was paid in cash. The loss of $17,500 is an ordinary loss.
d. The annual depreciation expense on machinery was $35,000.
e. On January 1, 1979, the company issued 9 percent bonds with a face value of $350,000 at 105 for cash. The maturity date of the bonds is January 1, 1989.
f. On December 31, 1979, the company issued directly to Lynch Realty Company 9 percent bonds with a face value of $175,000 at 100 for land valued at $175,000.

g. The convertible preferred stock was converted during 1979 into 17,500 shares of $10 par value common stock.
h. The annual amortization of premium on 9 percent bonds payable is recorded by the straight-line method.

Required:
1. Prepare a separate schedule of changes in working capital.
2. Prepare a statement of changes in financial position for 1979 using the all-financial resources concept. Use the direct T-account approach.
3. Prepare a statement of changes in financial position for 1979 using the working capital basis. Use the direct T-account approach.

P21–13 (Integrative) The comparative balance sheet of the Thoreson Company as of December 31, 1979 and 1978 and related supplementary data are as follows:

THORESON COMPANY
Comparative Balance Sheet
December 31, 1979 and 1978

Exhibit C

Assets	*December 31* 1979	1978
Current Assets		
Cash	$ 50,000	$ 46,000
Marketable Securities	80,000	70,000
Accounts Receivable (net)	130,000	124,000
Merchandise Inventory	120,000	100,000
Total Current Assets	$ 380,000	$ 340,000
Investments (at cost)	$ 160,000	$ 20,000
Plant and Equipment		
Land	$ 100,000	$ 100,000
Buildings (net)	450,000	350,000
Machinery (net)	400,000	280,000
Total Plant and Equipment	$ 950,000	$ 730,000
Total Assets	$1,490,000	$1,090,000

Liabilities and Stockholders' Equity

Current Liabilities		
Accounts Payable—Trade	$ 190,000	$ 180,000
Notes Payable—Trade	20,000	50,000
Total Current Liabilities	$ 210,000	$ 230,000
Long-Term Liabilities		
Mortgage Bonds Payable	150,000	50,000
Total Liabilities	$ 360,000	$ 280,000
Stockholders' Equity		
8% Preferred Stock, $100 par value	$ 200,000	$ –0–
Common Stock, $10 par value	700,000	700,000
Retained Earnings	230,000	110,000
Total Stockholders' Equity	$1,130,000	$ 810,000
Total Liabilities and Stockholders' Equity	$1,490,000	$1,090,000

Additional data:

a. Net income for the year 1979 was $140,000.
b. Dividends declared during year were $20,000.
c. Depreciation was: Machinery, $40,000; Buildings, $20,000.
d. There were no plant and equipment disposals during the year.
e. The company issued 2,000 shares of 8 percent preferred stock at par value.
f. Investments (long-term) costing $20,000 were sold for $28,000. The gain is an ordinary one and is included in Item a.

Required:

1. Prepare a separate schedule of changes in working capital.
2. Prepare a separate schedule of working capital provided by operations.
3. Prepare a statement of changes in financial position for 1979 using the working capital basis. Use the direct T-account approach.

P21–14 (Minicase) The following information is presented in the annual reports of the Woodbury Corporation.

WOODBURY CORPORATION — Exhibit A
Income Statement
For the Year Ended December 31, 1979

Sales		$3,550,000
Cost of Goods Sold		2,110,000
Gross Margin on Sales		$1,440,000
Operating Expenses		
Depreciation—Plant and Equipment	$ 55,000	
Other Expenses	110,000	165,000
Net Income before Taxes		$1,275,000
Income Taxes @ 48%		612,000
Net Income		$ 663,000

WOODBURY CORPORATION — Exhibit D
Statement of Changes in Financial Position—Working Capital Basis
For the Year Ended December 31, 1979

Working Capital was Provided by		
Operations		
Net Income (before extraordinary items)		$663,000
Add Nonworking Capital Charges to Operations		
Depreciation of Plant and Equipment		55,000
Working Capital Provided by Operations Exclusive of Extraordinary Items		$718,000
Working Capital was Used for		
Purchase of Equipment	$450,000	
Early Retirement of Bonds Payable in Current Year	300,000	
Total Working Capital Used		$750,000
Net Increase (Decrease) in Working Capital		$ (32,000)

WOODBURY CORPORATION
Schedule of Changes in Working Capital
For the Year Ended December 31, 1979

Exhibit D-1

	December 31		Changes in Working Capital	
	1979	*1978*	*Increase*	*Decrease*
Current Assets				
Cash	$ 30,000	$ 35,000		$ 5,000
Accounts Receivable (net)	65,000	50,000	$15,000	
Merchandise Inventory	100,000	95,000	5,000	
Prepaid Insurance	2,000	3,000		1,000
Total Current Assets	$197,000	$183,000		
Current Liabilities				
Accounts Payable	$110,000	$ 85,000		25,000
Bank Loans Payable (short term)	48,000	30,000		18,000
Accrued Payables	8,000	5,000		3,000
Total Current Liabilities	$166,000	$120,000		
Working Capital	$ 31,000	$ 63,000	$20,000	$52,000
Net Decrease in Working Capital			32,000	
			$52,000	$52,000

Walter Davis and his wife own 10,000 shares of stock in the Woodbury Corporation and would like to know why no dividends were declared in 1979 even though net income for the year was $663,000.

Required: Using the information given above, justify the corporation's decision not to declare a dividend to Mr. and Mrs. Walter Davis.

chapter twenty-two

Introduction

The accounting department of a business organization prepares a number of different kinds of reports. Some are for external users, who must make decisions such as whether to invest or extend credit to the business. These may be in the form of annual reports with historical data for the past two or more years. Or they may be special credit reports requested by a bank. Reports are also prepared for internal users—those persons who must make managerial decisions.

This chapter discusses some of these reports in terms of their history and function. It also explains some techniques for interpretation and analysis of the data they contain.

Financial statement analysis, interpretation, and disclosure

Learning goals

To understand how outside groups use financial reports to make decisions about investment or granting of credit.
To understand the use of financial reports for managerial decisions within the organization.
To use comparative financial statements to draw conclusions about the organization from year-to-year changes.
To compute and interpret trend percentages.
To prepare and interpret common-size statements.
To compute and interpret commonly-used ratios.
To develop the ability to use ratio analysis in evaluating solvency and profitability of an organization.

Key terms

accounting conventions
common-size statements
comparative statements
current assets
current liabilities
current ratio
earning-power measurements
horizontal analysis
long-term liabilities
multiple-step income statement
prior period adjustment
ratio analysis
return on stockholders' equity
revenue-dollar statements
single-step income statement
solvency measurements
stockholders' equity
trend percentages
turnover
vertical analysis

Guidelines for financial reporting

Reporting to external users

The importance of financial reporting to outside groups has paralleled the growth of the corporate form of enterprise. Early American corporations revealed very little financial information to anyone outside the internal management. Annual financial reports to stockholders were meager and consisted usually of condensed and unaudited financial statements.

With the growth of corporations, the New York Stock Exchange became interested in information that was being furnished to stockholders. In 1898, for example, the Exchange, in reviewing the application of a particular company for a listing of a stock, requested that the applicant present detailed statements to the stockholders prior to each annual meeting. This was the birth of the detailed annual corporate reports made available today to the stockholders. These reports, in addition to a summary letter from the president or the chairman of the board of directors, contain a detailed audited comparative balance sheet and income statement and other descriptive and analytical information about the present and future outlook of the corporation.

Corporate financial reports may take a slightly different form when a corporation requests a loan from a bank or establishes a line of credit. The grantor of credit under these circumstances will dictate the kind and form of reports. Often, only a balance sheet is required. In other cases, additional reports, such as an income statement, a statement of changes in financial position (discussed in Chapter 21), and other statistical and financial reports may be required.

Reporting to management

If users of financial statements are to make intelligent decisions based on accounting data, they must understand these data. A major function of the accounting department of a corporation, therefore, is to supply the necessary financial reports to management in meaningful form. The accounting department records the data, prepares the financial statements, and also may prepare ratio, trend, and percentage analyses. The financial data are used by the corporate executives, who are responsible for the conduct of the business, to measure past performance in terms of costs and revenue, to determine the efficiency and effectiveness of the various departments, to determine future business policies, and to report to the stockholders.

The form of managerial reports often cannot be predetermined. The particular form depends on the decision that is to be made. If these reports are to be most beneficial, however, they should (1) be current, (2) contain sufficient details regarding the particular problem to be solved, and (3) present acceptable alternatives.

There is a constantly increasing reliance by business executives on information systems. Large-scale production; wide geographical distribution; the increasing trend toward corporate business expansion and delegation of authority, complex income tax legislation, and increasing government regulation of business are some of the factors requiring greater management reliance on corporate financial reports.

Purpose of financial reports

Financial statements, whether in an annual report to stockholders, a prospectus for investors, or a report to grantors of credit or to management, should be prepared carefully. They should furnish the least-informed reader with enough information to permit an intelligent decision concerning some aspect of the entity.

More than forty years ago the purpose of financial statements appearing in annual corporate reports was stated rather well by a group of very forward-thinking accountants as follows:

> Financial statements are prepared for the purpose of presenting a periodical review or report on progress by the management and deal with the status of the investment in the business and the results achieved during the period under review. They reflect a combination of recorded facts, accounting conventions, and personal judgments; and the judgments and conventions applied affect them materially. The soundness of the judgments necessarily depends on the competence and integrity of those who make them and on their adherence to generally accepted accounting principles and conventions.[1]

Recorded facts in the above statement refers to the data in financial statements as taken from the accounting records. The amounts of cash, accounts receivable, and plant and equipment, for example, represent recorded facts. *Accounting conventions* are basic assumptions or conditions accepted by common consent. These conventions are concerned with the problems of asset valuation, allocation of expenditures between asset and expense classifications in the accounting period, and the proper measurement of income.

Basic financial reporting concepts

Accounting statements are prepared on the assumption that each enterprise is a separate entity, that all business transactions can be expressed in dollars, that the enterprise will continue in business indefinitely, and that reports will be prepared at regular intervals.

Importance of personal judgment

Accounting is ultimately an art and not an exact science, and financial statements must therefore reflect the opinion and judgment of the accountant and of management.

For example, the estimated life and the method of depreciation to be used in the valuation of plant and equipment, the method of inventory valuation, and the valuation of intangibles (patents, goodwill, and so on) are some areas that require

1 "Examination of Financial Statements by Independent Public Accountants," *Bulletin of American Institute of Certified Public Accountants,* (January, 1936), p. 1.

opinion and judgment. Equally competent accountants, given the same set of facts, may arrive at different results. Thus, the element of personal judgment and preference affects the financial statements.

Basic purpose of financial statements

In short, the basic purpose of financial statements is to transmit to interested groups, both external and internal, information that is useful in making economic decisions.

Reporting net income—a controversy

Extraordinary items *APB Opinion No. 9,* modified later by *Opinion No. 30,* was issued in an effort to resolve a long-standing controversy regarding the reporting of *extraordinary items*—that is, items unrelated to the regular operations of the firm: items that are unusual in nature *and* that occur infrequently. Involved were the twin problems of (1) what constitutes net income for a period and (2) what items were to be classified as extraordinary. Some held the view that all items affecting net income, including such items as losses from fires or natural hazards and nonrecurring gains or losses from the disposal of assets, should be reported in the income statement. Others argued that only operating revenue and expenses should be included in measuring net income, and that the inclusion of nonoperating items such as the foregoing would distort net income. *APB Opinion No. 9* attempted to resolve the two issues by stating that "net income should reflect all items of profit and loss recognized during the period with the sole exception of prior period adjustments."[2] Extraordinary items, described carefully in terms of nature and amount, should be "segregated from the results of ordinary operations and shown separately in the income statement."[3]

In actual practice, however, the classification of items as "extraordinary" or "ordinary" was unreliable. It could be slanted in whatever direction best served the client's perceived needs to manage the amounts reported as net income before extraordinary items and net income after extraordinary items. As a consequence, *Opinion No. 30* was issued to further define and restrict the classification of items as extraordinary. The Board stated that "extraordinary items are events and transactions that are distinguished by their unusual nature *and* by the infrequency of their occurrence,"[4] taking into consideration the environment in which the business operates. The following items were cited as examples of gains and losses that should *not* be reported as extraordinary.[5]

Write-down or write-off of receivables, inventories, equipment leased to others, or intangible assets
Gains or losses from exchange or translation of foreign currencies, including those relating to major devaluations and revaluations
Gains or losses on disposal of a segment of a business

2 *APB Opinion No. 9,* "Reporting the Results of Operations," (1966), par. 2.

3 *APB Opinion No. 9,* "Reporting the Results of Operations," (1966), par. 17.

4 *APB Opinion No. 30,* "Reporting the Results of Operations," (1973), par. 20.

5 *APB Opinion No. 30,* "Reporting the Results of Operations," (1973), par. 23.

Other gains or losses from sale or abandonment of property, plant, or equipment used in the business
Effects of a strike, including those against competitors and major suppliers
Adjustment of accruals on long-term contracts.

Prior-period adjustments Charges or credits to beginning retained earnings are excluded from the determination of net income for the current period. The APB's position was to restrict such prior period adjustments as to exclude all but those that "are rare in modern financial accounting." In *Statement No. 16* (June, 1977) the FASB virtually eliminated the prior period adjustment category entirely. It prohibits prior period adjustments for all items of profit or loss, including provisions for settlement of litigation and income tax assessments. Only a correction of an error in the financial statements of a prior period that is discovered subsequent to their issuance is accounted for and reported as a prior period adjustment.[6]

Intraperiod tax allocation The APB has ruled that the total income tax expense for a period should be related to income before extraordinary items, and adjustments of prior periods. In the income statement for the period, each of these items is reported along with its related tax consequence of transactions involving the items. The application of intraperiod tax allocation is illustrated in Figures 22–1, 22–2, 22–3, and 22–4.

Two types of income statement

Multiple-step income statement The multiple-step income statement is illustrated in Figure 22–2. The groupings in this statement furnish the following essential data: gross margin on sales, net income before income taxes, and

Figure 22–1 Single-step income statement

NEVANS CORPORATION
Income Statement
For the Year Ended December 31, 1979
Exhibit A

Sales		$390,000.00
Revenue Deductions		
Cost of Goods Sold	$200,000.00	
Selling and General Expenses	60,000.00	
Income Taxes	65,000.00	325,000.00
Net Income Before Extraordinary Item		$ 65,000.00
Extraordinary Loss (net of applicable income tax reduction of $6,000)		
Loss from Riot Damages		6,000.00
Net Income		$ 59,000.00
Earnings Per Share		$ 1.18

6 The only other exception dealt with in FASB *Statement No. 16* is an income tax benefit adjustment that is too narrow and technical for further discussion here.

Figure 22-2
Multiple-step income statement

NEVANS CORPORATION Condensed Income Statement For the Year Ended December 31, 1979		Exhibit A
Sales		$390,000.00
Cost of Goods Sold		200,000.00
Gross Margin on Sales		$190,000.00
Selling and General Expenses		60,000.00
Net Income Before Income Taxes		$130,000.00
Income Taxes		65,000.00
Net Income Before Extraordinary Items		$ 65,000.00
Loss from Riot Damages	$12,000.00	
Less Tax Reduction	6,000.00	
Extraordinary Loss (net of applicable income tax saving)		6,000.00
Net Income		$ 59,000.00
Earnings Per Share		$ 1.18

extraordinary items. These figures are valuable in making statistical analyses, in comparing current data with prior periods of the company and with data of the industry, and in financial planning. The usefulness of this form of statement to management justifies its popularity. Note that the deduction for income taxes is proportionate to net income before income taxes and that the extraordinary loss is on a net after tax credit basis (loss of $12,000 reduced by a tax credit of $6,000).

Figure 22–3 illustrates the reporting of a prior-period adjustment. Figure 22–4 is a combined statement of income and retained earnings (some items are omitted to avoid duplication of material in Figure 22–1). This form is favored by

Figure 22-3
Statement of retained earnings

NEVANS CORPORATION Statement of Retained Earnings For the Year Ended December 31, 1979		Exhibit B
Retained Earnings, December 31, 1978 (as previously reported)		$220,000.00
Adjustment of Prior-Years' Income:		
Correction of accounting error:		
1977 depreciation expense overstated . .	$15,000.00	
Less additional tax assessment	7,500.00	
Prior years' adjustment (net of applicable income tax)		$ 7,500.00
Retained Earnings, December 31, 1978 (restated)		$227,500.00
Net Income per Income Statement (Fig. 22-1 or Fig. 22-2)		59,000.00
Total		$286,500.00
Dividends Declared		25,000.00
Retained Earnings, December 31, 1979		$261,500.00

Figure 22-4 Combined statement of income and retained earnings

NEVANS CORPORATION Combined Statement of Income and Retained Earnings For the Year Ended December 31, 1979			Exhibit A
Sales			$390,000.00
Net Income (Fig. 22-1 or Fig. 22-2)			$ 59,000.00
Retained Earnings, December 31, 1978 (as previously reported)		$220,000.00	
Adjustment of Prior Year's Income:			
Correction of accounting error:			
1977 depreciation expense overstated	$15,000.00		
Less additional tax assessment	7,500.00		
Prior year's adjustment (net of applicable income tax)		7,500.00	
Retained Earnings, December 31, 1978 (restated)			227,500.00
Total			$286,500.00
Dividends Declared			25,000.00
Retained Earnings, December 31, 1979			$261,500.00
Earnings Per Share			$ 1.18

those who wish to report within one statement all changes in retained earnings during the year. A disadvantage of this form is that it does not end with the amount of net income.

Single-step income statement The single-step income statement shows all the revenue items and the amount of total revenues, followed by a listing of all expenses and losses the total of which is deducted from total revenue to determine net income. This form of statement has the advantage of easy readability. There are no intermediate additions and deductions, with accompanying labeled subtotals, that may confuse the untrained reader. It is primarily for this reason that this form has become increasingly popular in recent years. The single-step statement is best adapted for annual reports to stockholders, since they are not vitally interested in operating details.

Certain intermediate figures that are important for management purposes, such as the cost of goods sold, the gross margin on sales, and the net income before income taxes, are not shown. Furthermore, only a skilled reader is able to determine operating income, because extraordinary items are intermingled with ordinary items. The income statement of the Nevans Corporation is illustrated in single-step form in Figure 22-1 but is modified so as to report the extraordinary loss in accordance with the disclosure requirements of APB Opinion No. 9.

Guidelines for accounting changes

In another effort to limit the number of alternative reporting practices, the APB in *Opinion No. 20* issued guidelines dealing with situations where changes must be made in accounting methods, in estimates, and in correcting errors. With respect to changes in accounting principle (example: a change in depreciation method), the Board stated that an accounting principle, once adopted, should be changed "only if the enterprise justifies the use of an alternative acceptable accounting principle on the basis that it is preferable."[7]

APB Opinion No. 20 states further that the reason why the newly adopted accounting principle is preferable should be clearly explained. It also requires that the cumulative effect of the change should be shown. The intent of the opinion was to restrict the opportunities for changing net income by switching back and forth between alternative accounting methods. The arbitrary "management" of operating results, whether it be to smooth out peaks and valleys in periodic net income, or for any other management purpose, impairs the reports. Even when income fluctuates, the effort should be to achieve the truth in reporting as closely as it can be perceived.

With respect to a change in an accounting estimate (example: a change in the estimated useful life of a depreciable asset), the Board concluded "that the effect of a change in accounting estimate should be accounted for in (a) the period of change if the change affects that period only or (b) the period of change and future periods if the change affects both."[8] The *Opinion* also deals with changes in reporting entity, a discussion of which is beyond the scope of this text. With respect to the *disclosure* of accounting errors, the Board concluded that "the nature of an error in previously-issued financial statements and the effect of its correction on income before extraordinary items, net income, and the related per share amounts should be disclosed in the period in which the error was discovered and corrected."[9]

Interpretation of financial data

The figures in financial statements may be said to have significance in the following respects:

1. In themselves, they are measures of absolute quantity. When an analyst sees that a company has $50,000 in cash, he or she understands that figure in terms of current purchasing power. However, the absolute amount does not tell whether it is adequate for the current needs of the particular company. Some other means of determining its significance is required.
2. A degree of significance is indicated when figures are compared with similar amounts for other years and other companies. If $50,000 in cash was shown on the balance sheet at the end of the previous year, if that amount was suffi-

7 APB Opinion No. 20, *Accounting Changes,* par. 16 (1971).

8 Ibid, par. 31.

9 Ibid, par. 37.

cient at that time, and if no changes in needs are foreseen, then it may be assumed that a cash balance of $50,000 is adequate now.

3. The consideration of financial data in conjunction with related figures is also significant. When current assets are compared with current liabilities, the dollars of current assets behind each dollar of current liabilities can be determined. This comparison is often accomplished by what is termed a ratio. More specifically, a *ratio* is one amount in direct relationship to another amount.

Four tools of financial statement analysis are available to the user of the data. Each is related to the ways in which financial data have significance. These tools will be discussed in the remainder of this chapter. They are:

Comparative statements
Percentage analyses (horizontal and vertical)
Ratio analyses
Combinations of the above.

The central theme of any analysis is the evaluation of financial data through comparisons and measurement by some consistent standard to determine performance. Standards for comparison include a company's past performance, performance of companies in the same field, and industry comparisons.

In using each of these standards, the analyst should be aware of certain basic limitations. For example, if a company earned only $100 last year and earns $200 during the current year it has improved 100 percent, yet it may not be a growth company. Performance of other companies and the industry standards have similar pitfalls. Even with these difficulties, these standards of comparison can be extremely beneficial as a means of revealing improvements and declines, and thus can be helpful in the interpretation of statement data.

It should be emphasized that financial statement analysis involves more than just numbers. It requires an understanding of the nature and limitations of accounting and some knowledge of the business and the people operating the business. Discussions with the *people* involved may yield valuable insights that are not apparent from the application of the other financial analysis tools.

Comparative financial statements

A study of the balance sheet of a company and the results of its operations for a period is more meaningful if the analyst has available the balance sheets and the income statements for several periods. Trends can be better ascertained when three or more financial statements are compared. It is not uncommon to find *comparative statements* for ten years in annual reports. One large corporation in its recent annual report showed comparative financial statements covering a period of fifteen years.

Comparability of data on statements

For effective analysis, the company statements being compared must be based on the consistent application of generally accepted accounting principles over the period covered by the comparison. If there is an absence of comparability, it should be made known in the accountant's report.

If a comparison is to be made of one company with one or more other companies or with an entire industry, it must also first be carefully established that the data in the comparison are based on reasonably uniform and consistent accounting methods and principles.

The effect on net income, for example, of a changeover from FIFO to LIFO in valuing inventories must be clearly disclosed in the report.

The AICPA makes the following recommendations regarding comparative financial statements:

> The presentation of comparative financial statements in annual and other reports enhances the usefulness of such reports and brings out more clearly the nature and trends of current changes affecting the enterprise. Such presentation emphasizes the fact that statements for a series of periods are far more significant than those for a single period and that the accounts for one period are but an installment of what is essentially a continuous history.[10]

The use of comparative information in annual corporate reports to stockholders is nearly universal. Other devices are also used to present the entire financial story as clearly and attractively as possible. Although there is no uniformity in the kind of visual and statistical aids used, some of the more common are:

Comparative statements with accompanying *trend percentages*
Common-size statements, which present individual figures as percentages of a base total or some other established norm
Pictorial statements using bar or line graphs to emphasize particular trends, ratios, or relationships
Pie charts showing the allocation of each company sales dollar.

Any of these methods of presentation can make an interesting and informative report, aimed at perhaps the largest audience in the history of corporate reporting. Some of these devices are illustrated in this chapter.

Comparative balance sheets—horizontal analysis

Successive balance sheets of a company may be given side by side. These statements can be made more meaningful if the dollar amount of increase or decrease and the percentage of increase or decrease are also shown. This percentage analysis is often referred to as *horizontal analysis* (the comparisons are on a

10 Accounting Research Bulletin No. 43, *Restatement and Revision of Accounting Research Bulletins,* Chap. 2, Sec. A, par. 1.

horizontal plane from left to right). In a two-year comparison, the earlier year is the *base* year.

This form of statement is illustrated in Figure 22–5, the comparative balance sheet of the Belvin Company. In this illustration, the year 1978 is the base year and represents 100 percent. Accounts Receivable increased by 30.8 percent ($8,000 ÷ $26,000) during 1979; Notes Payable decreased by 5 percent ($1,000 ÷ $20,000); and Cash increased by $16,000, or 100 percent. The December 31, 1979, cash balance is twice the December 31, 1978, balance; Retained Earnings as of December 31, 1979, are almost twice the amount shown on December 31, 1978. No additional plant and equipment assets were acquired; the decreases reflect the annual depreciation deductions.

The change that occurred during 1979 for the Belvin Company is apparently favorable. Current assets increased by 42.3 percent, whereas current liabilities increased by only 18.5 percent. The total stockholders' equity increased by 20

Figure 22–5 Comparative balance sheet—horizontal analysis

BELVIN COMPANY
Comparative Balance Sheet
December 31, 1979 and 1978

Exhibit C

	December 31		Amount of Increase or (Decrease) during 1979	Percent of Increase or (Decrease) during 1979
	1979	1978		
Assets				
Current Assets				
Cash	$ 32,000	$ 16,000	$16,000	100.0
Accounts Receivable (net)	34,000	26,000	8,000	30.8
Inventories	45,000	36,000	9,000	25.0
Total Current Assets	$111,000	$ 78,000	$33,000	42.3
Plant and Equipment				
Land	$ 7,000	$ 7,000	$ -0-	-0-
Building (net)	116,000	119,000	(3,000)	(2.5)
Store Equipment (net)	23,000	25,000	(2,000)	(8.0)
Total Plant and Equipment	$146,000	$151,000	$(5,000)	(3.3)
Total Assets	$257,000	$229,000	$28,000	12.2
Liabilities and Stockholders' Equity				
Current Liabilities				
Accounts Payable	$ 34,000	$ 26,000	$ 8,000	30.8
Notes Payable	19,000	20,000	(1,000)	(5.0)
Accrued Payables	11,000	8,000	3,000	37.5
Total Current Liabilities	$ 64,000	$ 54,000	$10,000	18.5
Long-Term Liabilities				
Mortgage Payable	55,000	60,000	(5,000)	(8.3)
Total Liabilities	$119,000	$114,000	$ 5,000	4.4
Stockholders' Equity				
Capital Stock	$109,000	$100,000	$ 9,000	9.0
Retained Earnings	29,000	15,000	14,000	93.3
Total Stockholders' Equity	$138,000	$115,000	$23,000	20.0
Total Liabilities and Stockholders' Equity	$257,000	$229,000	$28,000	12.2

percent; this is reflected by an increase in all the current assets. The favorable position of Retained Earnings, accompanied by an increase in working capital, was accomplished without resort to long-term borrowing, because Mortgage Payable and Notes Payable have decreased during the period. Additional working capital was acquired by the issuance of stock.

Comparative Income Statement. A single income statement is just one link in a continuous chain reporting the operating results of the business. Comparative income statements are required for an analysis of trends and for making decisions regarding possible future developments. An income statement showing the results of operations for a single year is inadequate for purposes of analyzing the significance of the changes that have occurred.

The comparative statement of income and retained earnings of the Belvin Company is shown in Figure 22–6. The year 1978 is again used as the base year. Gross Margin on Sales increased by 25.4 percent, Net Income before Income Taxes increased by 67.2 percent; and Total Operating Expenses decreased by 0.6 percent. These favorable changes resulted primarily from an increase in sales. Income taxes increased by 106.4 percent.

There is a close relationship between the cost of goods sold, the volume of sales, and net income before income taxes. In periods of exceptionally high sales volume, net income before income taxes tends to rise (percentage of increase, 67.2) at a faster rate than do sales (percentage of increase, 30.5). In periods of declining sales volume, earnings fall more sharply than sales. This is because a significant part of the operating expenses are constant (or fixed)—they are not affected by the current sales volume. Such fluctuations in net income can be eliminated if unit sales prices are increased in periods of low sales volume and reduced in periods of high sales volume. Such a pricing policy, however, would be undesirable from the customers' viewpoint and impracticable from the company's viewpoint. It becomes important, therefore, that management know the volume at which profits begin. This figure, the *break-even point,* is that volume of sales at which the business will neither make a profit nor incur a loss. Break-even analysis is discussed and illustrated in Chapter 27.

Percentage increases or decreases are calculated only when the base figure is positive. When there is no figure for the base year or when base year amounts are negative, there is no extension into the Percent of Increase or (Decrease) column. When there is a positive amount in the base year and none in the following year, the percent of decrease is 100, as shown below.

	1979	*1978 (Base Year)*	*Amount of Increase or (Decrease) During 1979*	*Percent of Increase or (Decrease) During 1979*
Notes Receivable	$3,000.00	–0–	$3,000.00	
Notes Payable	–0–	$2,000.00	(2,000.00)	(100.00)
Net Income or (Loss)	4,000.00	(1,000.00)	5,000.00	

Exhibit A

BELVIN COMPANY
Comparative Statement of Income and Retained Earnings
For the Years Ended December 31, 1979 and 1978

	Years Ended December 31		Amount of Increase or (Decrease) during 1979	Percent of Increase or (Decrease) during 1979
	1979	1978		
Sales (net)	$197,000	$151,000	$46,000	30.5
Cost of Goods Sold	123,000	92,000	31,000	33.7
Gross Margin on Sales	$ 74,000	$ 59,000	$15,000	25.4
Operating Expenses				
Selling Expenses				
Advertising Expense	$ 1,200	$ 1,100	$ 100	9.1
Sales Salaries Expense	18,300	17,900	400	2.2
Depreciation Expense—Store Equipment	2,000	2,000	-0-	-0-
Total Selling Expenses	$ 21,500	$ 21,000	$ 500	2.4
General Expenses				
Depreciation Expense—Building	$ 3,000	$ 3,000	$ -0-	-0-
Insurance Expense	675	650	25	3.8
Miscellaneous General Expense	425	350	75	21.4
General Salaries Expense	7,200	8,000	(800)	(10.0)
Total General Expenses	$ 11,300	$ 12,000	$ (700)	(5.8)
Total Operating Expenses	$ 32,800	$ 33,000	$ (200)	(0.6)
Operating Income	$ 41,200	$ 26,000	$15,200	58.5
Other Expenses				
Interest Expense	2,750	3,000	(250)	(8.3)
Net Income Before Income Taxes	$ 38,450	$ 23,000	$15,450	67.2
Income Taxes	14,450	7,000	7,450	106.4
Net Income After Income Taxes	$ 24,000	$ 16,000	$ 8,000	50.0
Retained Earnings, January 1	15,000	9,000	6,000	66.7
Total	$ 39,000	$ 25,000	$14,000	56.0
Dividends Declared	10,000	10,000	-0-	-0-
Retained Earnings, December 31	$ 29,000	$ 15,000	$14,000	93.3
Earnings Per Share	$ 1.20	$ 0.80	$ 0.40	50.0

Figure 22–6 Comparative statement of income and retained earnings—horizontal analysis

Trend percentages—horizontal analysis

Comparative financial statements for several years may be expressed in terms of trend percentages for horizontal analysis.

Trend percentages

Management can more readily study changes in financial statements between periods by establishing a base year and expressing the other years in terms of the base year. The base year, may be any typical year in the comparison—the first, the last, or any of the other years.

To illustrate, a partial comparative income statement is presented in Figure 22–7. The amounts in Figure 22–7 are converted into trend percentages with 1978 as the base year, as shown in Figure 22–8.

Each item in the 1978 column of Figure 22–7 is assigned a weight of 100 percent. All the amounts in other years are expressed as trend percentages, or percentages of the figures for the base year. Each base year amount is divided into the same item for the other years. Trend percentages for sales, for example, are calculated as follows: 1979: $95,000 ÷ $100,000 = 95; 1980: $120,000 ÷ $100,000 = 120; and 1981: $130,000 ÷ $100,000 = 130. When the base year amount is larger than the corresponding amount in another year, the trend percentage is less than 100 percent; conversely, when the base year amount is the lesser of the two, the trend percentage is more than 100 percent.

The trend percentage statement is an analytical device for condensing the absolute dollar data of comparative statements. The device is especially valuable to management because readability and brevity are achieved by substituting percentages for large dollar amounts, which in themselves are difficult to compare. Trend percentages are generally computed for the major items in the statements; minor amounts are omitted, the objective being to highlight the significant changes.

An evaluation of the trend percentages requires a careful analysis of the interrelated items. Sales, for example, may show increases over a four-year period leading up to a trend percentage of 150 percent for the fourth year. This is unfavorable if it is accompanied by trend percentages of 200 percent for cost of goods sold, 175 percent for selling expenses, and 95 percent for net income before income taxes. Other unfavorable trends include an upward trend in receivables and inventories accompanied by a downward trend in sales, and a downward trend in sales accompanied by an upward trend in plant and equipment. Favorable trends would be an increase in sales accompanied by a decrease in cost of goods sold and selling expenses or an increase in current assets accompanied by a decrease in current liabilities.

Trend percentages show the degree of increase and decrease; they do not indicate the causes of the changes. They do, however, single out unfavorable developments for further analysis and investigation by management. A marked change may have been caused by inconsistency in the application of accounting principles, by fluctuating price levels, or by controllable internal factors (for example, an unnecessary increase in merchandise inventory or a decrease in operating efficiency).

Figure 22–7 Partial comparative income statements for four years*

	1978	*1979*	*1980*	*1981*
Sales (net)	$100,000	$95,000	$120,000	$130,000
Cost of Goods Sold	60,000	58,900	69,600	72,800
Gross Margin on Sales	$ 40,000	$36,100	$ 50,400	$ 57,200
Total Selling Expenses	$ 10,000	$ 9,700	$ 11,000	$ 12,000
Net Income before Income Taxes	$ 5,000	$ 3,800	$ 8,400	$ 10,400

*The years are listed in ascending order to facilitate analysis when data for three or more years are given. The reverse (descending order) is usually found in corporate annual reports.

	1978	1979	1980	1981
Sales (net)	100%	95%	120%	130%
Cost of Goods Sold	100	98	116	121
Gross Margin on Sales	100	90	126	143
Total Selling Expenses	100%	97%	110%	120%
Net Income before Income Taxes	100%	76%	168%	208%

*The years are listed in ascending order to facilitate analysis when data for three or more years are given. The reverse (descending order) is usually found in corporate annual reports.

Figure 22–8 Comparative trend percentages for four years*

Common-size statements—vertical analysis

Comparative statements with percentages of increase or decrease and trend percentages provide for horizontal analysis. Similarly, common-size statements provide for *vertical analysis*. In this form, the comparisons are made vertically from top to bottom for an analysis of the component changes that occur from period to period with certain base totals within those periods.

Common-size statements

***Thus total assets, total liabilities and stockholders' equity, and net sales are each converted to a base of 100 percent. Each item within each classification is expressed as a percentage of the base; each asset, for example, is expressed as a percentage of total assets. Since these bases represent 100 percent in all the statements in the comparison, there is a common basis for analysis; therefore, the statements are referred to as* common-size statements.**

Comparisons can be made within the company, with other companies in the same industry, or with entire industry figures. Thus, important relationships can be spotted even when comparisons are made with companies of unlike size; and any significant differences may indicate that a decision should be made. The common-size statements supplemented by additional analytical financial data are effective tools for a historical financial study of a business or industry.

The comparative common-size balance sheet and the comparative common-size income statement are shown in Figure 22–9 and 22–10.

Common-size balance sheets The method of converting dollar amounts into common-size percentages, using data from Figure 22–9, is shown below.

$$\frac{\text{Accounts receivable (1979)}}{\text{Total assets (1979)}} = \frac{\$34{,}000}{\$257{,}000} = 13.2\%$$

Accounts Receivable in 1979 represent 13.2 percent of the total assets. For each dollar of total assets there were 13.2 cents of accounts receivable.

$$\frac{\text{Accounts payable (1978)}}{\text{Total liabilities and stockholders' equity (1978)}} = \frac{\$26{,}000}{\$229{,}000} = 11.4\%$$

Figure 22–9
Comparative common-size balance sheet—vertical analysis

BELVIN COMPANY
Comparative Common-Size Balance Sheet
December 31, 1979 and 1978

Exhibit C

	December 31		Common-Size Percentages December 31	
	1979	1978	1979	1978
Assets				
Current Assets				
Cash	$ 32,000	$ 16,000	12.5	7.0
Accounts Receivable (net)	34,000	26,000	13.2	11.4
Inventories	45,000	36,000	17.5	15.7
Total Current Assets	$111,000	$ 78,000	43.2	34.1
Plant and Equipment				
Land	$ 7,000	$ 7,000	2.8	3.0
Building (net)	116,000	119,000	45.1	52.0
Store Equipment (net)	23,000	25,000	8.9	10.9
Total Plant and Equipment	$146,000	$151,000	56.8	65.9
Total Assets	$257,000	$229,000	100.0	100.0
Liabilities and Stockholders' Equity				
Current Liabilities				
Accounts Payable	$ 34,000	$ 26,000	13.2	11.4
Notes Payable	19,000	20,000	7.4	8.7
Accrued Payables	11,000	8,000	4.3	3.5
Total Current Liabilities	$ 64,000	$ 54,000	24.9	23.6
Long-Term Liabilities				
Mortgage Payable	55,000	60,000	21.4	26.2
Total Liabilities	$119,000	$114,000	46.3	49.8
Stockholders' Equity				
Capital Stock	$109,000	$100,000	42.4	43.7
Retained Earnings	29,000	15,000	11.3	6.5
Total Stockholders' Equity	$138,000	$115,000	53.7	50.2
Total Liabilities and Stockholder's Equity	$257,000	$229,000	100.0	100.0

Accounts Payable for 1978 represents 11.4 percent of total liabilities and stockholders' equity. For each dollar of total liabilities and stockholders' equity there were 11.4 cents of accounts payable.

Each current asset item has increased both in dollar amount and as a percentage of the total assets. Total current assets for 1979 have increased by 9.1 percent (43.2% − 34.1%) over 1978; total current liabilities for 1979 have increased by only 1.3 percent. Thus, the working capital position has been strengthened. Increases in net income and proceeds from the sale of stock appear to have caused increases in each current asset item. The company did not invest in plant and equipment; the decreases in Store Equipment and Building are due to deductions for annual depreciation charges.

Figure 22–10 Comparative commom-size income statement—vertical analysis

BELVIN COMPANY
Comparative Common-Size Income Statement
For the Years Ended December 31, 1979 and 1978

Exhibit A

	Year Ended December 31		Common-Size Percentages Year Ended December 31	
	1979	1978	1979	1978
Sales (net)	$197,000	$151,000	100.0	100.0
Cost of Goods Sold	123,000	92,000	62.4	60.9
Gross Margin on Sales	$ 74,000	$ 59,000	37.6	39.1
Operating Expenses				
Selling Expenses				
Advertising Expense	$ 1,200	$ 1,100	0.6	0.7
Sales Salaries Expense	18,300	17,900	9.3	11.9
Depreciation Expense—Store Equipment	2,000	2,000	1.0	1.3
Total Selling Expenses	$ 21,500	$ 21,000	10.9	13.9
General Expenses				
Depreciation Expense—Building	$ 3,000	$ 3,000	1.5	1.9
Insurance Expense	675	650	0.4	0.4
Miscellaneous General Expenses	425	350	0.2	0.2
General Salaries Expense	7,200	8,000	3.7	5.4
Total General Expenses	$ 11,300	$ 12,000	5.8	7.9
Total Operating Expenses	$ 32,800	$ 33,000	16.7	21.8
Net Operating Margin	$ 41,200	$ 26,000	20.9	17.3
Other Expenses				
Interest Expense	2,750	3,000	1.4	2.0
Net Income before Income Taxes	$ 38,450	$ 23,000	19.5	15.3
Income Taxes	14,450	7,000	7.3	4.7
Net Income	$ 24,000	$ 16,000	12.2	10.6
Earnings Per Share	$ 1.20	$ 0.80		

The ratio of stockholders' equity to total assets has increased, with corresponding decreases in the ratio of total liabilities to total assets. On December 31, 1978, the ratio of total liabilities to total assets was 49.8 percent; a year later this decreased to 46.3 percent. The overall financial position of the Belvin Company has improved.

Common-size income statement The common-size income statement of the Belvin Company is shown in Figure 22–10. Examples of the conversion of income statement dollar amounts into common-size percentages are shown below.

$$\frac{\text{Gross margin on sales (1979)}}{\text{Net sales (1979)}} = \frac{\$74{,}000}{\$197{,}000} = 37.6\%$$

Gross margin on sales for 1979 represents 37.6 percent of net sales; for each dollar of net sales there was a margin of 37.6 cents.

$$\frac{\text{Total operating expenses (1978)}}{\text{Net sales (1978)}} = \frac{\$33,000}{\$151,000} = 21.9\%$$

Total operating expenses for 1978 represent 21.9 percent of net sales; for each dollar of net sales there were 21.9 cents of total operating expenses.

A comparison of the cost of goods sold for the two years shows an increase of 1.5 percent (62.4% − 60.9%) and a corresponding decrease in the gross margin. This relatively modest change may result from reductions of original sales prices. Increases in amounts and percentages of inventories accompanied by a decrease in gross margin may indicate an overinvestment in inventories.

The change in total operating expenses is favorable. Sales increased by $46,000 = ($197,000 − $151,000), whereas dollar volume of total operating expenses remained approximately the same. The Belvin Company has increased the efficiency of its operations by increasing dollar sales without increasing its operating costs—a favorable development. The amount of increase in income taxes is at best a partially uncontrollable factor.

In addition to the analyses already illustrated, other ratios such as sales returns and allowances to sales revenue, sales discounts to sales revenue, purchases returns and allowances to purchases, and purchases discounts to purchases furnish information useful to management for controlling various activities, especially when they are compared from period to period.

Disposition of each sales dollar

Annual reports often include graphic presentations of the disposition of each revenue dollar. These may take the form of a pie chart, bar graph, or simple statement. Such a presentation is often more meaningful to the reader than a detailed income statement and is popular for its simplicity and effectiveness.

A revenue-dollar statement for Belvin Company is shown below.

	1979	*1978*
Each sales dollar was allocated as follows:		
Cost of Goods Sold	$0.624	$0.609
Selling Expenses	0.109	0.139
General Expenses	0.058	0.079
Interest Expense	0.014	0.020
Income Taxes	0.073	0.047
Net Income	0.122	0.106
Total Sales Dollar	$1.000	$1.000

The disposition of each sales dollar from the foregoing statement is shown in these pie charts:

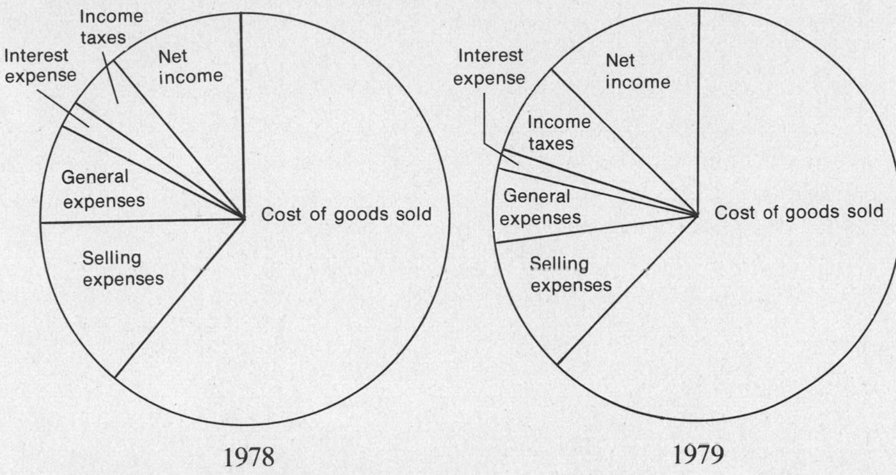

Basis for evaluation—ratio analysis

To provide information that will be of maximum assistance in decision making, the financial data should be in a form and manner that make them understandable, meaningful, and useful. The absolute amounts contained in the balance sheet for the Belvin Company are quite useful to management but they tell only part of the story. For example, a total current asset amount of $111,000 indicates a certain purchasing-power command over goods and services, but how adequate is this amount for the Belvin Company? The data become more meaningful when they are compared with other related information of current or past years. A financial decision should not be based on any one ratio. The ratios are effective only when used in combination with related ratios and with other relevant financial information.

Three types of measurements based on the financial statements are central to certain financial management decisions. They are discussed below under the following headings:

Short-run solvency measurements
Long-run solvency measurements
Earning power measurements.

Short-run solvency measurements

Three basic indicators of ability to pay short-term debts are the current ratio, the acid-test ratio, and working capital ratios.

Current ratio The relationship of current assets to current liabilities gives some indication of the firm's ability to pay its current debts as they mature. This relationship is called the *current ratio;* it is computed by dividing the current assets by the current liabilities. The computation for the Belvin Company is shown below:

		December 31	
		1979	1978
1.	Total current assets	$111,000.00	$78,000.00
2.	Total current liabilities	64,000.00	54,000.00
3.	Current ratio (line 1 ÷ line 2)	1.73	1.44

The Belvin Company has approximately $1.73 of current assets for every $1 of current liabilities.

In the past, as a rule of thumb, a current ratio of 2 to 1 was considered satisfactory. Analysts generally agree, however, that no one ratio is sufficient; other factors to be considered, include the nature of the business, the season of the year, the composition of the specific items in the current assets category, and the quality of the management of the company.

Grantors of credit emphasize the relative convertibility of the current assets into cash. To illustrate, assume that the A Company and the B Company have the following current ratios:

	A Company	B Company
Current Assets		
Cash	$ 500	$10,000
Accounts Receivable	700	14,000
Merchandise Inventory	28,800	6,000
Total Current Assets	$30,000	$30,000
Current Liabilities		
Accounts Payable	$15,000	$15,000
Current ratio	2:1	2:1

Although each company has a current ratio of 2 to 1, the B Company is apparently in a far better position to meet its obligations. The A Company first must sell its $28,800 merchandise inventory and then convert the resulting receivables into cash; or it can sell its inventory for cash as a single lot, probably for less than the stated value. The B Company has $24,000 in cash and receivables and only $6,000 in merchandise inventory to be converted. The A Company thus may have a favorable current ratio but may be unable to pay its current liabilities because of an unfavorable distribution of the current assets.

Acid-test ratio A supplementary test of the ability of a business to meet its current obligations is the acid-test ratio, which is expressed as follows:

$$\text{Acid-Test Ratio} = \frac{\text{Quick Current Assets}}{\text{Current Liabilities}}$$

If the analyst is not satisfied with the current ratio as an indicator of liquidity, he may use the acid-test ratio, which excludes merchandise inventory and prepaid items and is, therefore, a more rigorous test of short-run solvency than is the current ratio. *Quick current assets* include only cash, readily marketable securities, and receivables. If the quick current assets are larger than the current liabilities (that is, if the acid-test ratio is better than 1 to 1), there is evidence of a strong short-term credit position and indication that the company is able to meet its currently maturing obligations.

The acid test ratio for the Belvin Company is computed as follows:

	December 31	
	1979	1978
Quick current assets:		
Cash	$32,000.00	$16,000.00
Accounts receivable	34,000.00	26,000.00
1. Total quick current assets	$66,000.00	$42,000.00
2. Current liabilities	64,000.00	54,000.00
Acid-test ratio (line 1 ÷ line 2)	1.03 to 1	0.78 to 1

The Belvin Company had, on December 31, 1979, $1.03 in quick current assets for each dollar of current liabilities. This means that, unlike the previous year-end, the company does not have to rely on the liquidation of inventories as a source of funds for the payment of current liabilities.

Working capital ratios

Four types of working capital ratios are the working capital turnover, the receivables turnover, and two inventory ratios.

Working capital turnover The relationship between working capital and sales (the *working capital turnover*) tests the efficiency with which the working capital is used. The computation is shown below.

	December 31	
	1979	1978
Working capital:		
Current assets	$111,000	$78,000
Current liabilities	64,000	54,000
Working capital	$ 47,000	$24,000
Average working capital ($24,000 + $47,000 = $71,000) ÷ 2	$ 35,500	
Net sales for 1979	197,000	
Working capital turnover for 1979 ($197,000 ÷ $35,500)	5.55	

The Belvin Company sold $5.55 worth of merchandise for each dollar of working capital. Another viewpoint is that each dollar invested in working capital was recovered, reinvested, and recovered again 5.55 times. The degree of financial strength indicated by this ratio is best determined by comparison with other businesses in the same line.

Receivables turnover and average collection period Two guides to the overall condition of the accounts receivable are the average collection period and the annual *receivables turnover*. If goods are sold on terms of 2/10, n/30, the amount of accounts receivable outstanding at any time should be less than the credit sales for the last 30 days, because many of the sales will have been paid within the discount period. If allowance is made for slow-paying accounts, the receivables may represent 30 to 35 days' sales. If the receivables exceed this limitation, a careful analysis of all the accounts should be made.

Average collection periods vary with the industry and with the firm's credit policy. Wholesalers of shoes may average 45 days, compared with grocery wholesalers, whose average is about 15 days. For a standard of comparison, the preceding year's rate or the industry rate may be used. The increase in the turnover rate for the Belvin Company indicates an improvement and reflects a decreasing relative amount of working capital tied up in receivables.

	1979	1978
1. Net credit sales	$197,000	$151,000
2. Days in year	365	365
3. Net credit sales per day (line 1 ÷ line 2)	$ 540	$ 414
4. Average trade receivables (balance at beginning of year + balance at end of year) ÷ 2	$ 30,000	$ 28,000 (assumed)*
Average collection period (line 4 ÷ line 3)	56 days	68 days
Receivables turnover per year (line 1 ÷ line 4)	6.6 times	5.4 times

*It is necessary to make an assumption here because the January 1, 1978, trade receivables balance is not given.

If line 1 covered sales for a period of less than one year, then line 2 would be changed accordingly. Thus, if the sales were for a three-month period, line 2 would show 91 days (one-fourth of 365 days).

Turnover of merchandise inventory The quantity of goods to be kept on hand is a major business decision. It is considered good management to carry as little inventory as possible and to turn it over as rapidly as possible. Good management must guard against excessive inventories, the consequences of which could be an abnormal drain on working capital that could lead to financial difficulties. The greater the inventory, the greater the amount of money tied up, extra space required, and extra handling costs, as well as an increased possibility of loss through shrinkage, style changes, or other factors. Inadequate inventories, on the other hand, may result in higher costs due to buying in smaller quantities and the possible loss of business if the item the customer wants is out of stock. Good management, therefore, requires a careful evaluation of all these factors in establishing inventory levels.

One of the ratios used in inventory analysis is the *inventory turnover*—the relationship between inventory and the cost of goods sold. It is computed by dividing the cost of goods sold rather than net sales by the average inventory. The figure used may be the average of the beginning and ending inventories of the period or, preferably, the average of the end-of-month inventories involved, to minimize the effect of seasonal fluctuations. Although high turnover is usually a sign of good management, this ratio varies widely from one industry to another. A wholesaler of automobile parts and accessories may average five inventory turnovers per year as compared with thirty-five or more for a wholesaler of perishables such as meat and poultry. Also, a high-volume, low-margin business such as a fast-food chain would have to turn over its inventory more often than a business having a low-volume, high-margin policy, such as an art gallery.

The 1979 inventory turnover is computed as shown:

1.	Cost of goods sold for 1979	$123,000
	Average merchandise inventory:	
2.	January 1, 1979	$ 36,000
3.	December 31, 1979	45,000
4.	Total	$ 81,000
5.	Average (line 4 ÷ 2)	$ 40,500
	Turnover of inventory (line 1 ÷ line 5)	3.0

The Belvin Company sold and replaced its merchandise inventory three times during the year 1979; that is, the cost of merchandise sold was three times greater than the average cost of merchandise on hand. The rate may be computed for individual items or for major categories in order to establish item-by-item control.

Ratio of inventory to working capital The *ratio of inventory to working capital* is an indication of the amount of working capital represented by inventory.

$$\frac{\text{Ending inventory}}{\text{Working capital}} = \frac{\$45{,}000}{\$47{,}000} = 95.7\%$$

For the Belvin Company, this 1979 ratio, being less than 100 percent, indicates that the current debt can be paid in full from quick current assets (those other than inventory), assuming that all receivables can be collected. For this ratio to be less than 100 percent, the quick current assets must be greater than current liabilities.

Long-run solvency measurements

Ratios for investment in plant and equipment The investment by a company in plant and equipment assets may vary considerably, depending on the nature of the business. Manufacturing concerns require a greater investment in machinery and equipment than do retail or wholesale firms. The relationship of the plant and equipment to total assets and to sales should be in proper proportion for the industry. If the amount invested in plant and equipment is too high, fewer funds are available for working capital purposes. Depreciation charges will also be high, resulting in either higher sales prices or lower profits. Finally, the long-term liabilities will be greater, resulting in greater interest costs and the need for funds to pay off debts as they mature.

The following three ratios, used to determine whether there has been an overinvestment in plant and equipment, will be discussed below: plant and equipment to long-term liabilities; plant and equipment to stockholders' equity; and net sales to plant and equipment.

The *ratio of plant and equipment to long-term liabilities* is obtained by dividing the total carrying value of the plant and equipment by the long-term liabilities. This comparison is important to the long-term creditors if any of the plant and equipment has been mortgaged as security for loans. The smaller the ratio, the greater is the dependence on long-term borrowing to finance plant and equipment acquisitions.

The *ratio of plant and equipment to stockholders' equity* is obtained by dividing the total carrying value of the plant and equipment by the stockholders' equity. An investment in plant and equipment that is less than stockholders' equity (a ratio of less than 1.0) indicates that the entire amount of plant and equipment could have been bought by the capital obtained from the owners.

The *ratio of net sales to plant and equipment,* or plant and equipment turnover, is found by dividing net sales by the total carrying value of the plant and equipment. A decreasing ratio over a time period shows a possible overinvestment in plant and equipment. For example, an investment in plant and equipment that exceeds sales (ratio less than 1.0) indicates an overinvestment in plant and equipment, thus resulting in higher interest, taxes, maintenance expenses, and depreciation charges, and lower working capital. A heavy investment in land, buildings, and machinery greatly restricts the mobility of a company if a change in plant location or type of product manufactured is desirable.

These analyses, when based on historical cost of plant and equipment, do not reflect the effect of changing economic and technological conditions and market price fluctuations. The Accounting Objectives Study Group of the AICPA concluded that different valuation bases are preferable for different assets and liabilities and that "financial statements might contain data based on a combination of valuation bases."[11] The SEC requires disclosure of replacement cost information; others have proposed the use of current value accounting.

Number of times bond interest earned In addition to the effective interest rate computations discussed in Chapter 19, another important ratio is used by investors in bonds. The number of times bond interest expense is earned is of special interest to bond investors as a measure of the safety of their investment; it is an indication of a firm's ability to meet its annual bond interest requirement. To illustrate, assume that Anne Corporation has bonds outstanding with a face value of $500,000 and that in 1979 it reports bond interest expense of $40,000, income taxes of $60,000, and net income (after income taxes) of

11 *Objectives of Financial Statements* (New York: AICPA, 1973), p. 41.

$80,000. Since bond interest expense is deductible in determining taxable income, the following formula seems appropriate:

$$\text{Number of times bond interest expense is earned} = \frac{\text{Net income} + \text{Income tax expense} + \text{Annual bond interest expense}}{\text{Annual bond interest expense}}$$

Substituting the amounts given for the Anne Corporation,

$$\text{Number of times bond interest earned} = \frac{\$80,000 + \$60,000 + \$40,000}{\$40,000} = 4.5 \text{ times}$$

A ratio of 4.5 times appears to be relatively safe for the investors holding bonds of Anne Corporation, although there are no established universal standards of safety. The safety margin depends in part on the type of collateral used, the type of business in which the firm is engaged, and the liquidity of the firm. Investors in a privately-owned public utility with mortgageable plant assets, for example, may feel secure with a ratio of 2.5 times; whereas investors in other businesses without mortgageable assets may feel insecure with a ratio smaller than 5 times.

Number of times preferred dividends earned A similar investor-oriented ratio is the *number of times preferred dividends is earned.* This ratio is of particular interest to investors in preferred stock. To illustrate, assume that Anne Corporation has 7 percent preferred stock outstanding with a par value of $1,000,000. Since preferred dividends are *not* deductible in determining taxable income, the following formula is appropriate:

$$\text{Number of times preferred dividends is earned} = \frac{\text{Net income (after taxes)}}{\text{Annual preferred dividends}}$$

Substituting the amounts given for Anne Corporation,

$$\text{Number of times preferred dividends is earned} = \$80,000 \div \$70,000 = 1.14 \text{ times}$$

The adequacy of this ratio must be interpreted in a similar manner as that described for the number of times bond interest expense is earned; that is, the safety margin that is acceptable will depend in part on the type of business in which the firm is engaged, the liquidity of the firm, and other factors.

Equity ratios A significant measure of the stability of a business is the percentage relationship of the equities of the creditors and the owners in the total assets. The equity ratios for the Belvin Company at the end of 1979 are computed as follows:

a. Creditors' interest in assets:

$$\frac{\text{Total liabilities}}{\text{Total assets}} = \frac{\$119{,}000}{\$257{,}000} = 46.3\%$$

b. Stockholders' interest in assets:

$$\frac{\text{Total stockholders' equity}}{\text{Total assets}} = \frac{\$138{,}000}{\$257{,}000} = 53.7\%$$

The creditors have an equity of 46.3 cents, and the stockholders have an equity of 53.7 cents, of each asset dollar. Many analysts consider the equity ratios equal in importance to the current ratio as indicators of credit strength and sound management. There are no universally accepted percentage relationships to serve as guides for the equity ratios, but it is generally felt that the larger the stockholders' equity ratio, the stronger the financial condition of the business. A company may, for example, borrow money on a long-term note for working capital purposes. The loan increases the current assets and creates a more favorable current ratio; but it also reduces the stockholders' equity ratio, signaling a possible over-dependence on outside sources for financial needs.

Earning power measurements

Per-share profitability Of considerable significance and usefulness to the investor are the ratios of earnings and dividends to the market value of the shares, because it is the cash represented by the market value of the shares that can be put to other uses. Three such ratios are:

$$\text{Earnings yield rate} = \frac{\text{Earnings per share}}{\text{Market value per share}}$$

$$\text{Dividends yield rate} = \frac{\text{Dividends per share}}{\text{Market value per share}}$$

$$\text{Price-earnings ratio} = \frac{\text{Market value per share}}{\text{Earnings per share}}$$

A careful analysis of the relationship and trend of these ratios indicates the profitability of the firm as related to the market value of its shares, its ability to pay dividends, and its growth prospects. Sometimes known by the term "times earnings" the price-earnings ratio (P/E ratio) is watched carefully by investors.

Rate of return on total investment The relationship of the earnings of a business to its total resources is an important indicator of the effectiveness of management in generating a return to suppliers of capital, as well as a method of predicting future earnings. The rate of return on total investment is:

$$\begin{matrix}\text{Net income for year} \\ + \\ \text{Interest expense}\end{matrix} \div \begin{matrix}\text{Average total} \\ \text{assets}\end{matrix} = \begin{matrix}\text{Rate of return} \\ \text{on total investment}\end{matrix}$$

For the Belvin Company, for 1979, the computation is:

$$(\$24{,}000 + \$2{,}750) \div \frac{(\$257{,}000 + \$229{,}000)}{2} - 11.0\%$$

The Belvin Company earned 11.0 cents for each dollar of assets used in the business. Since total assets equals total equities, it may also be said that the company earned 11.0 cents for each dollar invested in the company—whether by outside creditors or by stockholders.

Rate of return on stockholders' equity The relationship between earnings and the average stockholders' investment is a significant measure of the profitability of a business and is of particular interest to the corporate shareholders. The rate of the Belvin Company for 1979 is:

$$\frac{\text{Net income}}{\text{Average stockholders equity}} = \frac{\$24{,}000}{(\$138{,}000 + \$115{,}000)/2} = 19.0\%$$

The rate of return on the stockholders' equity is 73 percent higher than the rate of return on total investments. This means that the return to stockholders is well above the fixed rates on the mortgage payable. The difference of 8.0% = (19% − 11.0%) between the two rates is called the *capital leverage factor*. The Belvin Company is favorably "trading on the equity" of its creditors by using that portion of total equities as a cushion or base from which to borrow from outside sources at rates below those earned on stockholders' equity.

Other influences on profitability

The techniques and procedures for the analysis of financial statements are useful tools for gaining an insight into the financial affairs of a business. The analyst must also evaluate many other influences that, although not specifically reflected in the statements, may nevertheless influence the future of the company. The analyst should look for sudden changes in key management personnel; shifts in employee or customer loyalty; development of new competing products; and broad shifts in the social, political, or economic environment. Another factor that must be evaluated with care is the impact of changing price levels on the statements (this topic is covered in Chapter 14). Differences in financial statements may also be due to the wide variations that exist within the framework of generally accepted accounting principles and procedures—in the valuation of inventories, the selection of depreciation bases, the treatment of intangibles, and the method of disclosing extraordinary and nonrecurring items, for example.

Limitations of ratio analysis

A particular ratio may be satisfactory under one set of circumstances and entirely unsatisfactory under another set. Ratios are generalizations and reflect conditions that exist only at a particular time. The ratios change continually with the continuing operations of the business. Sole reliance on ratio analysis may at times give a misleading indication of financial condition. The ability to understand and interpret ratios correctly, however, reduces the area over which subjective judgment must be exercised and thus aids the analyst in making sound decisions.

The ratios and comparisons discussed in this chapter are valuable managerial aids, provided the user is aware of their limitations. The current ratio of 1.73 to 1 for the Belvin Company at the end of 1979 shows the relationship between two groups of items as of a given moment of time only. The ratio may fluctuate considerably during the course of the year. Furthermore, the ratio may have little meaning unless it is related to the entire business unit.

Tabulation of major ratios

A tabulation of significant ratios arranged in an outline of their primary measurements is shown in Figure 22–11, indicating the range of possibilities in the analysis of financial statements.

Figure 22–11
Major ratios

Ratio	Computation of Ratio	Indicates
Short-Run Solvency Measurements		
1. Current Ratio	$\frac{\text{Current Assets}}{\text{Current Liabilities}}$	The ability of a business to meet its current obligations
2. Acid-Test Ratio (quick ratio)	$\frac{\text{Quick Current Assets}}{\text{Current Liabilities}}$	The ability of a business to meet quickly from assets readily convertible into cash unexpected demands for working capital
3. Average Number of Days' Sales Uncollected (Collection Period)	$\frac{\text{Average Accounts Receivable}}{\text{Net Credit Sales}} \times 365$ OR (1) Net Credit Sales ÷ 365 = Net Credit Sales Per Day (2) $\frac{\text{Average Accounts Receivable}}{\text{Net Credit Sales Per Day}}$	The rapidity with which the accounts receivable are collected; the average number of days elapsing from the time of sale to the time of payment

Ratio	Computation of Ratio	Indicates
4. Merchandise Inventory Turnover	Cost of Goods Sold / Average Inventory	The number of times the merchandise inventory was replenished during the period, or the number of dollars in the cost of goods sold for each dollar of inventory
Long-Run Solvency Measurements		
5. Plant and Equipment to Long-Term Liabilities	Plant and Equipment (net) / Long-Term Debt	The adequacy of protection to long-term creditors
6. Plant and Equipment to Stockholders' Equity	Plant and Equipment (net) / Stockholders' Equity	The extent to which owner sources are being used to finance plant and equipment acquisitions
7. Sales to Plant and Equipment (Plant Turnover)	Net Sales / Average Plant and Equipment (net)	Dollar of sales per dollar of investment in plant and equipment assets
8. Number of Times Bond Interest Earned	(Net Income + Income Taxes + Annual Bond Interest Expense) / Annual Bond Interest Expense	The primary measure of the safety of an investment in bonds—the ability of a firm to meet its bond interest requirement
9. Number of Times Preferred Dividends Earned	Net Income / Annual Preferred Dividends	The primary measure of the safety of an investment in preferred stock—the ability of a firm to meet its preferred dividend requirement
10. Creditors' Equity Ratio	Total Liabilities / Total Assets	The percent of creditor sources of total assets
11. Stockholders' Equity Ratio	Stockholders' Equity / Total Assets	The percent of owner sources of total assets
Earning Power and Growth Potential Measurements		
12. Earnings Yield Rate	Earnings per Share / Market Value per Share	Earnings as related to market value of the shares
13. Dividends Yield Rate	Dividends per Share / Market Value per Share	Dividend payout as related to market value of the shares
14. Earnings Per Share of Common Stock	(Net Income minus Annual Preferred Dividend) / Outstanding Common Shares	The company's earning power as related to common stockholders' equity
15. Price-Earnings Ratio	Market Price per Share / Earnings per Share	Market value per share as related to profitability of the firm.

Ratio	Computation of Ratio	Indicates
16. Rate of Return on Total Investment	$\frac{\text{Net Income + Interest Expense}}{\text{Average Total Assets}}$	The profitableness of the business expressed as a rate of return on total investments by both owners and creditors.
17. Rate of Return on Stockholders' Equity	$\frac{\text{Net Income}}{\text{Average Stockholders' Equity}}$	The profitableness of the business expressed as a rate of return on the stockholders' equity

Other Measurements

Financial Structure Measurements: These measurements can be determined from a common-size balance sheet which shows the composition of items on the balance sheet.

Asset Utilization Ratios: These are measures of asset turnover or the dollars of sales generated by each dollar of investment in total assets or in each individual asset.

Operating Performance Ratios: These are measures which show the relationship of each income statement item or groups of items to sales.

Disclosure in financial statements — appendix

Recent actions taken by the SEC have been aimed at helping financial statement users in their analysis and interpretation of the statements and in their assessment of the enterprise's past performance and future prospects. They relate to:

- Expanded requirements for interim (quarterly) reporting
- Explanations of quarter-to-quarter changes by management
- Inclusion of data on replacement cost (see Chapter 14)
- Better recognition of business uncertainties (for example, disclosure regarding uncertainty in loan portfolios of banks)
- Increased responsibility on the part of public accountants.

Line-of-business or segment reporting

For some years, the SEC, the New York Stock Exchange, the Federal Trade Commission, and private groups such as security analysts have urged that financial reports carry a more detailed breakdown of results from various divisions of diversified companies. They think that investors can make better investment decisions if profits and losses in each segment of a company are disclosed separately rather than being buried in a single set of consolidated statements. A *con-*

solidated statement shows the combined financial information of several separate corporations.

The FASB issued *Statement No. 14* (December 1976) requiring that those doing business in more than one industry report revenue, income, and identifiable asset data of the enterprise's operations in different industries, its foreign operations and export sales, and its major customers. This information is reported as part of the financial statements or the footnotes. The Board, concluding that such information is useful for an analysis and understanding of the statements, stated: "In analyzing an enterprise, a financial statement user often compares information about the enterprise with information about other enterprises, with industry-wide information, and with national or international economic information in general. Those comparisons are helpful in determining whether a given enterprise's operations may be expected to move with, against, or independently of developments in its industry and in the economy within which it operates.[12]

The Newhall Land and Farming Company of Valencia, California (see statements in Appendix), in its 1976 *Annual Report,* disclosed line-of-business information for a five-year-period as shown in Figure A22–1. This information is in addition to the reporting of line of business amounts for revenues and expenditures in the income statement. From the data one can determine that all lines were profitable. Operating income as a percent of sales in 1976 appears to range from a low of about 16 percent in residential real estate to a high of about 82 percent in the real estate category called land. These figures are much more useful than simply to know that overall net income before interest, general and administrative expenses and taxes was about 22 percent.

Figure A22–1
Line of business disclosure

(in thousands)

Year ended February 28/29	1976	1975	1974	1973	1972
Revenues					
Agriculture	$41,297	$43,984	$31,307	$25,668	$20,912
Recreation	26,364	21,703	15,777	9,957	1,247
Energy	5,151	4,483	3,309	3,115	3,309
Real Estate					
Commercial	4,280	3,456	3,051	2,787	2,166
Land	2,586	2,407	2,835	3,029	2,795
Residential	6,477	5,363	4,445	1,918	—
Interest and other	986	740	1,002	1,073	2,996
Total	$87,141	$82,136	$61,726	$47,547	$33,425
Operating income (before general and administrative, interest and income taxes)					
Agriculture	$ 7,440	$ 9,670	$ 5,730	$ 1,248	$ 1,665
Recreation	5,016	3,954	1,606	(2,513)	139
Energy	1,587	2,046	1,800	1,893	2,200
Real Estate					
Commercial	1,975	1,449	1,339	1,139	820
Land	2,128	1,204	2,205	2,609	2,253
Residential	1,057	640	586	219	—

12 FASB Statement No. 14, *Financial Reporting for Segments of a Business Enterprise,* par. 58 (1976).

Glossary

Accounting conventions Basic assumptions or conditions accepted by common consent.

Common-size statements Statements in which each element is shown as a percentage of some major total.

Comparative statements Successive financial statements of a company given side by side.

Current assets Cash and other assets that are reasonably expected to be realized in cash or sold or consumed during the normal operating cycle of the business or one year, whichever is longer.

Current liabilities Obligations whose liquidation will require the use of current assets, or the creation of other current liabilities, within a year or operating cycle, whichever is longer.

Earning power measurements Ratios that measure the ability of a firm to earn adequate income. The ratios that relate to income.

Earnings per share of common stock The company's earning power as related to common stockholders' equity.

Extraordinary items Events and transactions that are of an unusual nature and that recur infrequently.

Horizontal analysis Successive balance sheets of a company presented side by side with the dollar amount of increase or decrease together with the percentage or proportionate increase or decrease.

Long-run solvency measurements The measure of the ability of a firm to meet its long-term obligations; the adequacy of the protection to long-term creditors.

Long-term liabilities Obligations that will not be liquidated until after the current year or the operating cycle.

Multiple-step income statement A form of income statement that groups revenue and deductions so as to arrive at a series of intermediate subtotals culminating in net income after extraordinary items.

Prior period adjustments Transactions of a previous period that are handled as direct adjustments of retained earnings and, therefore, excluded from net income of the current period.

Rate of return on stockholders' equity Net income divided by average stockholders' equity (called Net Income to Stockholders' Equity).

Rate of return on total investment Net income plus interest expense divided by the average total assets.

Ratio analysis The analysis of the proportionate changes of financial items from period to period by converting the dollar amount of change to a percentage, a decimal, or a fraction.

Revenue dollar statement The conversion of the dollar amount of each item in the income statement to a ratio with net sales representing the base or $1.00.

Short-run solvency measurements Ratios that test the ability of a company to meet its current obligations from all or part of its current assets.

Single-step income statement A form of income statement in which all revenues appear in one section, and all deductions from revenue in another section, without any intermediate subtotals.

Stockholders' equity The excess of assets over liabilities; the section of the balance sheet that shows the amounts and sources of assets from investors and from earnings.

Trend percentages An analytical device for condensing the absolute dollar data of comparative statements.

Turnover A form of analysis, for example, inventory turnover and receivables turnover.

Vertical analysis Successive financial statements of a company presented side by side with comparisons made of the period to period proportionate changes of the components with certain base totals within those periods (see common-size statements).

Questions

Q22–1 (a) What are some limitations of financial statements? (b) List and discuss some factors contributing to the development of financial reporting to outside groups.

Q22–2 (a) Discuss the characteristics of a good managerial report. (b) Discuss the purposes of financial statements.

Q22–3 Discuss four basic devices that are commonly used to achieve interpretative statement presentation.

Q22–4 "The financial statement analyst should have available comparative statements, showing changes in absolute amounts and percentage changes." Explain.

Q22–5 Comment on the significance of each of the following factors to the financial statement analyst:

1. A steadily increasing price level
2. An increase in inventory
3. An increase in plant and equipment
4. An increase in sales
5. An increase in sales and a decrease in accounts receivable
6. An increase in liabilities

Q22–6 Trend percentages are of limited usefulness (a) because they do not indicate whether the change is favorable or unfavorable, (b) because the change may be in relation to a year that is not typical or normal, and (c) because they do not measure the effectiveness of management. Discuss.

Q22–7 What are the advantages and limitations to the analyst of the following: (a) comparative statements, (b) trend percentages, and (c) common-size percentages?

Q22–8 Explain how each of the following would be determined:

1. A company's earning power
2. The extent to which owner sources have been used to finance plant and equipment acquisitions
3. The adequacy of protection to long-term creditors
4. The rapidity with which the accounts receivable are collected
5. The ability of a business to meet quickly the unexpected demands for working capital

Q22–9 What ratios or other analytical devices will help to answer the following questions?

1. Is there an overinvestment in plant and equipment?
2. Are the assets distributed satisfactorily?
3. Is there adequate protection for creditors?
4. How is the business being financed?
5. Are earnings adequate?
6. Is there a satisfactory relationship between creditor and owner financing?
7. Are costs and expenses too high? Are sales adequate?

Q22–10 (a) What knowledge must an analyst possess to evaluate financial statement data successfully? (b) What are some of the influences that are not specifically reflected in financial statements but which an analyst must evaluate to draw correct inferences from analysis of financial statements?

Class exercises

CE22–1 (Financial statements; prior period adjustments) The following information is taken from the books of the Prague Company on December 31, 1979 (100,000 shares of common stock are outstanding).

Retained Earnings (credit), December 31, 1978	$ 65,000
Sales	560,000
Cost of Goods Sold	280,000
Adjustment for Cost of Machinery Charged to Equipment Repairs in 1978	7,000
Income Taxes	85,000
Understatement of Depreciation in Prior Years	12,000
Selling, General, and Administrative Expenses	90,000
Dividends Declared and Paid	50,000

Required:

1. Prepare a multiple-step income statement and a statement of retained earnings.

2. Prepare a combined statement of income and retained earnings.
3. Prepare a single-step income statement.

CE22–2 (Comparative statements: amount and percentage of increase or decrease) The condensed comparative statements of Snow, Inc., are given:

SNOW, INC. — Exhibit C
Comparative Balance Sheet
December 31, 1979 and 1978

	December 31	
	1979	*1978*
Current Assets	$180,000	$155,000
Plant and Equipment	190,000	205,000
Total Assets	$370,000	$360,000
Current Liabilities	$ 69,000	$ 54,500
Long-Term Liabilities	70,000	75,000
Total Liabilities	$139,000	$129,500
Capital Stock	$200,000	$200,000
Retained Earnings	31,000	30,500
Total Stockholders' Equity	$231,000	$230,500
Total Liabilities and Stockholders' Equity	$370,000	$360,000

SNOW, INC. — Exhibit A
Comparative Statement of Income and Retained Earnings
For the Years Ended December 31, 1979 and 1978

	Years Ended December 31	
	1979	*1978*
Sales (net)	$495,000	$550,000
Cost of Goods Sold	376,000	410,000
Gross Margin on Sales	$119,000	$140,000
Operating Expenses	82,000	95,000
Net Income before Income Taxes	$ 37,000	$ 45,000
Income Taxes	18,500	22,500
Net Income	$ 18,500	$ 22,500
Retained Earnings, January 1	30,500	30,000
Total Net Income and Retained Earnings	$ 49,000	$ 52,500
Dividends Paid	18,000	22,000
Retained Earnings, December 31	$ 31,000	$ 30,500
Earnings Per Share	$ 1.39	$ 1.69

Required:

1. Prepare a comparative statement of income and retained earnings, showing the amount and percentage of increase or decrease during 1979.
2. Prepare a comparative balance sheet, showing the amount and percentage of increase or decrease during 1979.
3. Write a report indicating whether the financial condition and operating results are favorable or unfavorable and stating your reasons.

CE22–3 (Comparative statements—trend percentages) The following information is taken from the books of the Beatrice Company:

	1978	*1979*	*1980*	*1981*
Sales (net)	$135,000	$147,500	$156,250	$168,750
Cost of Goods Sold	78,000	86,840	91,600	98,400
Accounts Receivable	20,000	23,000	24,400	26,800
Merchandise Inventory	35,000	40,600	43,050	45,850
Net Income	12,000	12,240	12,600	12,960

Required:

1. Calculate the trend percentages (1978 is the base year).
2. Point out the favorable and unfavorable tendencies.

CE22–4 (Common-size statements: revenue-dollar statements) The comparative condensed financial statements of the Gary Company are given:

GARY COMPANY — Exhibit C
Comparative Balance Sheet
December 31, 1979 and 1978

	December 31	
	1979	*1978*
Current Assets	$ 80,000	$ 97,500
Plant and Equipment	210,000	162,500
Total Assets	$290,000	$260,000
Current Liabilities	$ 52,000	$115,000
Long-Term Liabilities	126,000	60,000
Total Liabilities	$178,000	$175,000
Capital Stock	$ 98,000	$ 75,000
Retained Earnings	14,000	10,000
Total Stockholders' Equity	$112,000	$ 85,000
Total Liabilities and Stockholders' Equity	$290,000	$260,000

GARY COMPANY Exhibit A
Comparative Income Statement
For the Years Ended December 31, 1979 and 1978

	Years Ended December 31	
	1979	*1978*
Sales (net)	$320,000	$285,000
Cost of Goods Sold	183,600	161,250
Gross Margin on Sales	$136,400	$123,750
Operating Expenses		
Selling Expenses	$ 68,200	55,000
General Expenses	40,300	27,500
Total Operating Expenses	$108,500	$ 82,500
Net Income	$ 27,900	$ 41,250

Required:

1. Prepare:
   a. A comparative common-size balance sheet.
   b. A comparative common-size income statement.
   c. A comparative revenue-dollar statement.
2. Discuss the financial condition and operating results of the company, emphasizing favorable and unfavorable trends.
3. Compute some of the major ratios and indicate their significance to the Gary Company.

Exercises and problems

P22–1 The following groups of items are presented for various companies as of December 31, 1979 and 1978, or for the years then ended:

	1979	*1978*
1. Sales	$ 620,000	$ 480,000
Cost of Goods Sold	400,000	320,000
Operating Expenses	100,000	80,000
Net Income	90,000	60,000
2. Current Liabilities	300,000	200,000
Mortgage Bonds Payable	450,000	500,000
3. Common Stock	1,200,000	1,000,000
Preferred Stock	300,000	400,000
Retained Earnings (deficit)	(10,000)	100,000

4. Cash	$142,000	$ 212,000
Accounts Receivable	130,000	140,000
Inventories	60,000	80,000
Other Current Assets	3,000	2,000
Land	20,000	20,000
Buildings	500,000	420,000
Accumulated Depreciation—Buildings	72,000	60,000

Required: Compute the percentage increase or decrease for each item, and indicate possible reasons for the changes.

P22–2 The following information is given:

	1979	*1978*
Net Sales	$635,000	$510,000
Cost of Goods Sold	425,000	370,000
Selling Expenses	70,000	55,000
General Expenses	40,000	35,000
Other Revenue	2,000	3,500
Other Expenses	1,000	4,000
Income Taxes	61,000	30,000

Required:

1. Prepare a comparative income statement with common-size percentages.
2. Indicate the favorable and unfavorable changes.

P22–3 The following condensed information is taken from the balance sheet of the Marjorie Company:

	December 31	
	1979	*1978*
Current Assets	$228,000	$170,000
Plant and Equipment (net)	290,000	300,000
Current Liabilities	130,000	122,000
Long-Term Liabilities	100,000	120,000
Capital Stock	225,000	200,000
Retained Earnings	63,000	28,000

Required: Prepare a condensed balance sheet showing the dollar amounts and the percentages of increase or decrease during 1979.

P22–4 The following balances were taken from the books of the Hekimian Corporation as of June 30, 1979 and 1978:

	June 30	
	1979	*1978*
Current Assets	$230,000	$170,000
Plant and Equipment	290,000	305,000
Current Liabilities	130,000	110,000
Long-Term Liabilities	115,000	130,000
Common Stock	225,000	200,000
Retained Earnings	50,000	35,000

Required: Prepare a comparative balance sheet showing common-size percentages.

P22–5 The following revenue and expense data of the Crotty Company for the year 1979 are given:

Sales	$210,000
Cost of Goods Sold	130,000
Selling Expenses	18,000
General Expenses	12,000
Interest Expense	2,500
Income Taxes	23,750
Net Income	23,750

Required: Prepare a revenue-dollar statement.

P22–6 In the left-hand column a series of transactions is listed; in the right-hand column, a series of ratios:

Transaction	*Ratio*
1. Declaration of a cash dividend	Current ratio
2. Write-off of an uncollectible account receivable to Allowance for Doubtful Accounts	Receivables turnover
3. Purchase of inventory on open account	Acid-test ratio
4. Issuance of 10-year mortgage bonds	Rate of return on total assets
5. Issuance of additional shares of stock for cash	Creditors' equity ratio
6. Issue of stock dividend on common stock	Earnings per share
7. Appropriation of retained earnings	Rate of return on stockholders' equity

8. Purchase of supplies on open account	Current ratio
9. Payment to short-term creditor in full	Acid-test ratio
10. Payment of accounts payable (no discount involved)	Inventory turnover

Required:
State whether each transaction will cause the indicated ratio to increase, decrease, or remain unchanged. For the current ratio, receivables turnover, acid-test ratio, and inventory turnover, assume that the ratio is greater than 1 before each transaction occurred.

P22–7 The following information is taken from the books of the Hutton Company on December 31, 1979 (50,000 shares of common stock are outstanding):

Retained Earnings (credit), December 31, 1978	$ 85,000
Sales	750,000
Dividends Declared	65,000
Selling, General, and Administrative Expenses	280,000
Income Taxes	33,000
Cost of Goods Sold	390,000
Overstatement of Depreciation in Prior Years (net of tax)	8,000
Extraordinary Loss (net of income tax reduction of $10,000)	10,000

Required:
1. Prepare a multiple-step income statement and a statement of retained earnings.
2. Prepare a combined statement of income and retained earnings.
3. Prepare a single-step income statement.

P22–8 The postclosing trial balance of the Oriot Corporation is given:

ORIOT CORPORATION
Postclosing Trial Balance
December 31, 1979

Cash	$ 80,000	
Marketable Securities (at cost; market value is $56,000)	50,000	
Accounts Receivable	144,000	
Allowance for Doubtful Accounts		$ 6,000
Merchandise Inventory	450,000	
Accrued Bond Interest Receivable	12,000	
Prepaid Insurance	6,000	
Bond Sinking Fund	20,000	
Investment in Bonds—Excel Company Bonds	200,000	
Delivery Equipment	16,000	
Accumulated Depreciation—Delivery Equipment		4,000
Machinery and Equipment	900,000	
Accumulated Depreciation—Machinery and Equipment		100,000
Accounts Payable		144,000
Estimated Income Taxes Payable		100,000
Accrued Bond Interest Payable		12,000
First Mortgage 8% Bonds Payable		200,000
Discount on First Mortgage Bonds Payable	2,400	
Second Mortgage 10% Bonds Payable		100,000
Premium on Second Mortgage Bonds Payable		2,000
Preferred Stock, 10%, $100 par value		400,000
Common Stock, $25 par value		600,000
Retained Earnings		116,400
Prepaid Rent	4,000	
Retained Earnings—Restricted for Plant Addition		80,000
Retained Earnings—Restricted for First Mortgage Bond Redemption		20,000
Totals	$1,884,400	$1,884,400

Required: Prepare the balance sheet for the Oriot Corporation as of December 31, 1979, showing working capital and net assets on the left-hand side balanced by stockholders' equity on the right-hand side.

P22–9 (Minicase) Statements for the Gloria Company as of December 31, 1979 follow:

GLORIA COMPANY — Exhibit A
Income Statement
For the Year Ended December 31, 1979

Gross Sales	$295,800
Sales Returns and Allowances	4,500
Net Sales	$291,300
Cost of Goods Sold	208,000
Gross Margin on Sales	$ 83,300
Operating Expenses	65,300
Net Income from Operations	$ 18,000
Interest on Bonds Payable	800
Net Income before Income Taxes	$ 17,200
Federal Income Taxes	6,200
Net Income	$ 11,000
Earnings Per Share	$ 12.25

GLORIA COMPANY — Exhibit C
Balance Sheet
December 31, 1979

Assets

Current Assets			
Cash		$12,000	
Accounts Receivable	$95,000		
Deduct Allowance for Doubtful Accounts	6,000	89,000	
Inventory		80,000	
Total Current Assets			$181,000
Plant and Equipment			
Land		$20,000	
Building	$60,000		
Deduct Accumulated Depreciation	12,000	48,000	
Store Equipment	$15,000		
Deduct Accumulated Depreciation	7,000	8,000	
Total Plant and Equipment			76,000
Total Assets			$257,000

Liabilities and Stockholders' Equity

Current Liabilities		
Accounts Payable	$86,600	
Accrued Expenses Payable	29,000	
Total Current Liabilities		$115,600
Long-Term Liabilities		
Bonds Payable		20,000
Total Liabilities		$135,600
Stockholders' Equity		
Preferred Stock, 6%, $100 Par Value	$20,000	
Common Stock, $100 Par Value	80,000	
Retained Earnings	21,400	
Total Stockholders' Equity		121,400
Total Liabilities and Stockholders' Equity		$257,000

On December 31, 1978, the inventory was $100,000 and the total stockholders' equity was $115,000.

Required: Compute the following ratios (carry to two decimal places) and interpret their significance.

Current ratio
Acid-test ratio
Inventory turnover
Ratio of stockholders' equity to total assets
Rate of return on stockholders' equity
Ratio of plant and equipment assets to long-term debt
Number of times preferred dividends earned
Number of times bond interest earned

P22–10 (Integrative) The Levi Corporation has issued convertible bonds under an agreement to maintain net assets, defined in the agreement as assets minus all liabilities except the convertible bonds, at an amount not less than 230 percent of the convertible bonds outstanding; to maintain current assets at not less than 200 percent of the current liabilities; and to maintain working capital at not less than 100 percent of the convertible bonds outstanding.

On December 31, 1979, the corporation's adjusted trial balance was as follows:

LEVI CORPORATION
Adjusted Trial Balance
December 31, 1979

	Debit	*Credit*
Cash	$ 10,000	
Marketable Securities (temporary)	75,000	
Accounts Receivable	74,000	
Allowance for Doubtful Accounts		$ 3,000
Inventory	113,000	
Prepaid Expenses	6,000	
Land	18,000	
Building	156,000	
Accumulated Depreciation—Building		21,000
Equipment	224,000	
Accumulated Depreciation—Equipment		42,000
Accounts Payable		69,000
Notes Payable, 4-year (due 12/20/82)		75,000
Accrued Expenses Payable		6,000
Convertible Bonds Payable		200,000
Common Stock		150,000
Retained Earnings		110,000
Totals	$676,000	$676,000

In January 1980, it was discovered that title had passed as of December 31, 1979 on incoming merchandise costing $100,000. Since the merchandise was not on hand, it was not included in the inventory. The corporation had recorded $50,000 of collections from customers received on January 2, 1980, under the date of December 31, 1979, on the theory that such collections in all probability were in the mail before midnight, December 31, 1979. In the afternoon of January 2, 1980, the corporation wrote and mailed checks to creditors, dating and recording the checks as of December 31, 1979; the checks amounted to $50,000, equal to the collections in transit.

Required:

1. Contrast, by means of comparative ratios, the reported conditions with those you believe more fairly indicate the status of the corporation. Limit your comparison to the ratios mentioned in the agreement with the bondholders.
2. Comment briefly on your findings.

P22–11 (Appendix) Shepherd, Inc. is a diversified company engaged in the sale of electronic parts, processed foods, and household appliances. The company has always published a single set of consolidated statements showing revenue, deductions from revenue, and net income, in totals only. The Controller of the company believes that the usefulness of the company's statements would be considerably improved if the income statement items were reported by product line.

Required:

1. Should the company adopt the Controller's recommendation? Why?
2. Identify some of the reporting problems involved in making the changeover.

P22–12 (Appendix) Refer to Problem 22–11. Assume that Shepherd, Inc. sells its products to four major groups of customers: (1) Department of Defense, (2) certain foreign countries, (3) unaffiliated domestic customers, and (4) affiliated company-wide customers.

Required:

Prepare a possible format for reporting the company's revenue from sales.

Cost accumulation and control

part six

chapter twenty-three

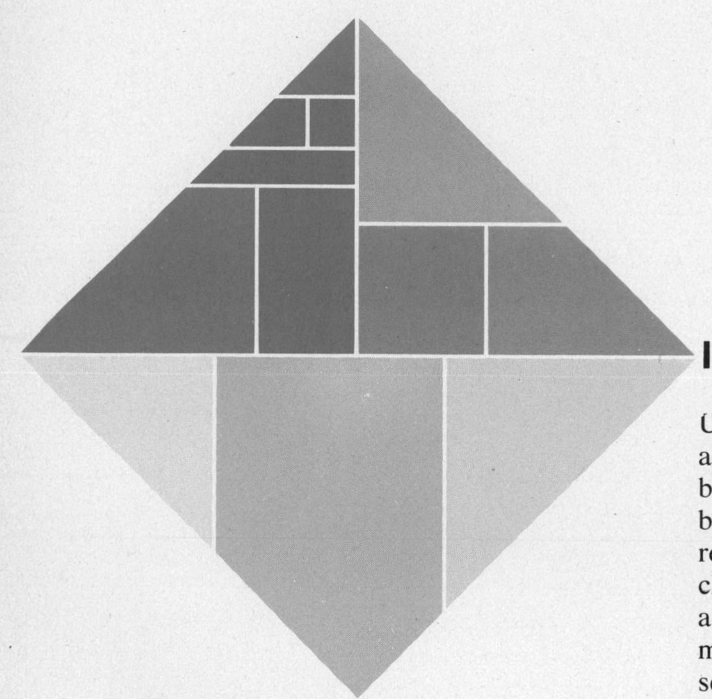

Introduction

Up to this point in the text only the accounting for service or trading businesses has been considered. A trading business buys goods in finished form and resells those goods in the same form. This chapter begins the study of accounting for a manufacturing business, which buys materials and uses labor and other factory services to convert those materials into finished goods for sale.

Accounting for a manufacturing firm

Learning goals

To understand that the cost of goods manufactured by a manufacturing firm represents the same concept as purchases by a merchandising firm.
To know the nature of the three types of inventories in a manufacturing concern.
To compute cost of materials used under a periodic inventory system.
To develop an understanding of manufacturing overhead and to identify specific overhead cost items.
To distinguish between inventoriable costs and period expenses.
To prepare schedules of cost of goods manufactured and cost of goods sold.
To add to knowledge of work sheet techniques by addition of the manufacturing columns.
To understand the concepts of allocation of expenditures between manufacturing costs and period expenses.

Key terms

allocation basis
amortization of patents
cost of goods manufactured
cost of goods sold
direct labor
finished goods
indirect labor
inventoriable costs
manufacturing overhead
manufacturing summary
materials inventory
materials used
work in process inventory

Inventories

A merchandising firm has a single inventory account; it represents goods purchased for resale and is usually called *Merchandise Inventory*. A manufacturing firm has three major inventory accounts:

1. *Materials Inventory* consists of the items of materials and parts used to make the company's product or products. Some of the items may be raw materials such as ore or crude petroleum products. Others may be finished products of a supplying manufacturer—say gaskets, cement, or sheet steel. They have the common characteristic that they are intended to be used in the manufacturing process and become part of the final product.
2. *Work in Process Inventory* represents the sum to date of costs invested in those items that are partly completed in the manufacturing process. At the end of any period a firm will have some items on the workbenches and assembly lines in the factory that are incomplete. They will probably be completed in the next accounting period, and their cost is carried on the end-of-period balance sheet as Work in Process Inventory.
3. *Finished Goods Inventory* comprises the stock of the firm's products that have been completed in the manufacturing process and are ready for sale. The cost to manufacture those goods that are transferred to the Finished Goods Inventory during an accounting period is usually shown in a supporting accounting schedule. This schedule is very important to management; it gives details of the *cost of goods manufactured.* As can be seen in Figure 23–1, *cost of goods manufactured represents to a manufacturing firm the same concept that purchases represent to a trading firm.* Figure 23–1 compares the Cost of Goods Sold section of the income statements of two firms. The same dollar amounts have been used to make the point that the only real difference is the source of the input of goods into the stock of resale merchandise. In the merchandising firm there is the problem (explained in chapter 7) of accounting for the net cost of purchases. The major accounting problem in a manufacturing firm is the determination of cost of goods manufactured.

Figure 23–1
Comparison of cost of goods sold sections

Merchandising Firm		Manufacturing Firm	
Merchandise Inventory, January 1, 1979	$ 23,200.00	Finished Goods Inventory, January 1, 1979	$ 23,200.00
		Add Cost of Goods Manufactured (Schedule A-1)	229,845.00
Add Purchases (Net)	229,845.00	Cost of Finished Goods Available for Sale	$253,045.00
Cost of Merchandise Available for Sale	$253,045.00	Deduct Finished Goods Inventory, December 31, 1979	19,600.00
Deduct Merchandise Inventory, December 31, 1979	19,600.00		
Cost of Goods Sold	$233,445.00	Cost of Goods Sold	$233,445.00

Cost of goods manufactured

The three basic classifications of manufacturing costs are (1) materials used, (2) direct labor, and (3) manufacturing overhead. Each is described in detail in the sections that follow. First, however, to present a broad picture of how they contribute to the stock of goods for resale, a summary schedule of cost of goods manufactured is shown in figure 23–2. The dollar amounts used in Figure 23–1 and Figure 23–2, as in all illustrations in this chapter, are from the records of a manufacturing firm, the Cola Manufacturing Company. This illustration will be carried throughout so that the interrelationship of the various cost elements can be understood more clearly.

As the next three sections are studied, the reader should come to understand the concept of *inventoriable costs*. Several items of cost that have heretofore been recorded as period expenses are not so treated in a manufacturing firm. Instead, they become a part of inventory of goods for resale. They finally appear in the income statement as cost of goods sold.

Figure 23–2
Summary schedule of cost of goods manufactured

COLA MANUFACTURING COMPANY
Schedule of Cost of Goods Manufactured
For the Year Ended December 31, 1979

Schedule A-1

Work in Process Inventory, January 1, 1979 . .		$ 31,725.00
Add:		
Materials Used	$ 92,350.00	
Direct Labor	102,030.00	
Manufacturing Overhead	50,740.00	245,120.00
Total		$276,845.00
Deduct Work in Process Inventory, December 31, 1979		47,000.00
Cost of Goods Manufactured		$229,845.00

Materials used

All materials that can be feasibly identified as becoming a part of the finished product are known as *direct materials*. The cloth used in the manufacture of a suit, for example, is obviously direct materials. Some items may be incorporated into the finished product, but it may not be economical to measure and record them. An example would be the thread used to manufacture the same garment. Although it is incorporated into the suit, it is considered too expensive to trace the thread to the specific product being manufactured. Accordingly such items of materials are known as *indirect materials*. Another form of indirect materials are those items necessary to the production process but not used in the product—oil for the machinery or cleaning compound for the floor are examples. Indirect materials are accounted for as an element of manufacturing overhead (to be discussed in more detail later in this chapter).

The cost of direct materials used in the manufacture of a product may be determined by the periodic inventory method in exactly the same manner as is the cost of goods sold in a trading business. Figure 23–3 shows the computation of materials used by the Cola Manufacturing Company in 1979. In order to simplify the illustration it will be assumed that all materials used in the Cola Manufacturing Company are direct materials. The treatment of indirect materials will be taken up in Chapters 24 and 25.

Figure 23–3
Computation of materials used

Materials Used

Materials Inventory, January 1, 1979			$ 58,300.00
Add Materials Purchases		$91,000.00	
Deduct:			
Purchases Returns And Allowances	$2,800.00		
Purchases Discounts	2,650.00	5,450.00	
Net Cost of Materials Purchases			85,550.00
Cost of Materials Available for Use			$143,850.00
Deduct Materials Inventory, December 31, 1979			51,500.00
Cost of Materials Used			$ 92,350.00

Direct labor and indirect labor

The wages paid to factory employees performing operations directly on the product are referred to as *direct labor*. Other factory employees perform tasks in support of production operations but do not work directly in the construction, composition, or fabrication of the finished goods. Wages and salaries of the foremen, repair personnel and stockroom storekeepers fall into this category; they are classified as *indirect labor*. Indirect labor is an element of manufacturing overhead. It is the function of the timekeeping personnel to identify labor charges as direct or indirect when the payroll is prepared. In a general manufacturing accounting system, the gross pay of factory personnel is debited to either the Direct Labor or Indirect Labor accounts.

During 1979 Cola Manufacturing Company incurred (including both paid and accrued) total wages and salaries of $266,230. This figure was made up of the following:

Direct Labor	$102,030.00
Indirect Labor	22,600.00
Salesmen's Salaries	55,100.00
Executive Salaries	60,500.00
Office Salaries	26,000.00
Total	$266,230.00

Two of the above items, direct labor and indirect labor, are *inventoriable costs*. The others are *period expenses*.

Manufacturing overhead

All factory costs incurred in the manufacturing process other than the cost of materials used and direct labor are classified as *manufacturing overhead*. Other terms used for this group of costs are *indirect manufacturing costs* and *manufacturing burden*. Selling expenses and general and administrative expenses are not considered to be manufacturing overhead. They reflect the costs of distribution of the product and of administration of the overall firm and are not part of the manufacturing function; they are period expenses. In accounting for a general manufacturing operation, nominal (temporary) accounts are carried in the general ledger for each of the elements of manufacturing overhead. Separate nominal accounts are carried for period expenses.

Two manufacturing overhead accounts that have already been explained are Indirect Materials and Indirect Labor. Some other typical examples are:

Small tools used. This represents the cost of small hand tools that are lost or broken during the year. Because of the great variety of such tools, their low cost, and the difficulty of predicting an estimated useful life, it is not economical to carry small tools in a plant and equipment account and depreciate them. It is much simpler to debit all acquisitions to an asset account, Small Tools. At the end of each accounting period a physical count is made; the difference between the asset account balance and the value of tools on hand as shown by the physical count is the cost of small tools used—an element of manufacturing overhead.

Amortization of patents. Most patents are for manufacturing processes. The cost of patents is amortized over their economically useful life or their legal life, whichever is shorter. The periodic amortization charge is an element of manufacturing overhead.

Factory rent. The amount of rent charged for the buildings that house the factory is a part of manufacturing overhead. In some cases the same building may contain production operations along with activities related to selling and administration. If so, the total cost must be allocated among manufacturing overhead, selling expense, and general and administrative expense. Procedures for allocation of costs and expenses are discussed later in this chapter.

Heat, light, and power. This manufacturing overhead item is either the cost of purchasing or of producing in one's own power plant the energy to operate production equipment and to provide heat and light to the factory. Like factory rent, it is sometimes necessary to allocate cost between manufacturing overhead and period expenses.

Factory insurance. Insurance that covers factory equipment or materials and work in process inventories is a cost of manufacturing. Insurance on the finished goods inventory is usually a selling expense. As in the case of rent, if insurance covers a building used both for production and nonproduction activities, its cost must be allocated between manufacturing overhead and period expenses.

Depreciation—machinery and equipment. In a trading business, depreciation charges were all treated as expenses of the accounting period in which recorded. In a manufacturing firm, depreciation of all items of plant and equipment that are used in production is a part of manufacturing cost and a part of the manufacturing overhead. Depreciation of delivery equipment continues to be a selling expense; depreciation of office equipment is a general and administrative expense.

Others. Brief descriptions have been given only of manufacturing overhead items that had been previously mentioned or will be encountered in the Cola

Manufacturing Company illustration. It is important to recognize that any cost of manufacturing a firm's product that is not direct materials or direct labor is classified as manufacturing overhead. Some other typical factory costs that are overhead items are:

Overtime premium pay	Repairs and maintenance
Employer's FICA taxes	Hospitalization insurance
Unemployment compensation taxes	Group insurance
Vacation pay	Property taxes
Pension plan contributions	Factory supplies used.

In Figure 23–2, the total manufacturing overhead cost for Cola Manufacturing Company was shown in a single amount, $50,740. Figure 23–4 provides information in detail by element of factory overhead cost incurred. This information and the materials used (Figure 23–3) can be combined with direct labor cost and the work in process inventories to provide a more complete schedule of cost of goods manufactured in 1979. Such a schedule is included with the statements that follow the explanation of the work sheet.

Figure 23–4
Computation of manufacturing overhead cost

Manufacturing Overhead	
Indirect Labor	$22,600.00
Factory Rent	9,600.00
Heat, Light, and Power	7,290.00
Factory Insurance	1,050.00
Depreciation—Machinery and Equipment	10,200.00
Total Manufacturing Overhead	$50,740.00

Cost of goods sold

The cost of goods sold in a manufacturing firm that uses the periodic inventory system is computed in a manner similar to a merchandising firm. The ending inventory is determined by physical count of finished goods. The computation of cost of goods sold in Figure 23–1 uses figures from the Cola Manufacturing Company.

Work sheet for a manufacturing firm

Aside from the fact that there are three inventories instead of one, there is another important difference between the work sheets of a manufacturing firm and a merchandising firm. In the work sheet for a manufacturing firm, a pair of columns headed *Manufacturing* is added. Into these columns are extended all the debit and credit balances representing elements that enter into the cost of manufacturing the product. These include materials inventory, direct labor, manufacturing overhead items, and the work in process inventory. The debits in this pair of columns should always be larger than the credits; the difference is *cost of goods manufactured*. The cost of goods manufactured is transferred to the Income Statement Debit column as illustrated in Figure 23–5 at the bottom of the work sheet.

Adjusting entries on the manufacturing work sheet

The entries in the Adjustments columns of the work sheet are based on the information that follows. The letters correspond to those used on the work sheet.

Figure 23–5 Work sheet for a manufacturing company

COLA MANUFACTURING COMPANY
Work Sheet
For the Year Ended December 31, 1979

Account Title	Trial Balance		Adjustments		Manufacturing		Income Statement		Balance Sheet	
	Dr.	Cr.	Dr.	Cr.	Dr.	Cr.	Dr.	Cr.	Dr.	Cr.
Cash	12,000								12,000	
Accounts Receivable	78,350								78,350	
Allowance for Doubtful Accounts		650		(a) 1,037						1,687
Materials Inventory	58,300				58,300	51,500			51,500	
Work in Process Inventory	31,725				31,725	47,000			47,000	
Finished Goods Inventory	23,200						23,200	19,600	19,600	
Prepaid Insurance	2,100			(b) 1,500					600	
Office Equipment	6,050								6,050	
Accumulated Depreciation—Office Equipment		2,000		(d) 605						2,605
Store Equipment	10.000								10,000	
Accumulated Depreciation—Store Equipment		4,000		(d) 1,000						5,000
Machinery and Equipment	51,000								51,000	
Accumulated Depreciation—Machinery and Equipment		10,000		(c)10,200						20,200
Accounts Payable		29,200								29,200
Capital Stock		180,000								180,000
Retained Earnings		12,855								12,855
Dividends	10,000								10,000	
Sales		420,000						420,000		
Sales Returns and Allowances	5,200						5,200			
Sales Discounts	2,400						2,400			
Materials Purchases	91,000				91,000					
Materials—Purchases Returns and Allowances		2,800				2,800				
Materials—Purchases Discounts		2,650				2,650				
Direct Labor	98,530		(e) 3,500		102,030					
Indirect Labor	21,200		(e) 1,400		22,600					
Rent	12,000				9,600		1,800S 600G			
Heat, Light, and Power	8,100				7,290		405S 405G			
Advertising Expense	6,500						6,500			
Salesmen's Salaries Expense	50,000		(e) 5,100				55,100			
Executive Salaries Expense	60,500						60,500			
Office Salaries Expense	26,000						26,000			
	664,155	664,155								
Bad Debts Expense			(a) 1,037				1,037			
Insurance			(b) 1,500		1,050		300S 150G			
Depreciation—Machinery and Equipment			(c)10,200		10,200					
Depreciation Expense—Office Equipment			(d) 605				605			
Depreciation Expense—Store Equipment			(d) 1,000				1,000			
Accrued Wages and Salaries Payable				(e)10,000						10,000
Income Tax Expense			(f) 7,368				7,368			
Income Taxes Payable				(f) 7,368						7,368
			31,710	31,710	333,795	103,950				
Cost of Goods Manufactured						229,845	229,845			
					333,795	333,795	422,415	439,600	286,100	268,915
Net Income							17,185			17,185
							439,600	439,600	286,100	286,100

S = Selling Expenses
G = General and administrative expenses

Entry a. The bad debts expense was estimated at 1/4 of 1 percent of gross sales less sales returns and allowances. The amount of the adjustment was computed as:

Gross sales	$420,000.00
Deduct sales returns and allowances	5,200.00
Net sales	$414,800.00
Bad debts expense percentage	x 0.0025
Bad debts expense	$ 1,037.00

The debit records the estimated bad debts charge; the credit increases Allowance for Doubtful Accounts to $1,687 = ($650 + $1,037). This adjustment debits an expense, not a manufacturing, account. Accordingly, the expense is extended into the Income Statement columns.

Entry b. Insurance of $1,500 has expired. The debit records the cost of the expired insurance; the credit decreases the asset account. Note that a portion of insurance is classified as manufacturing overhead. The remainder is a period expense. The procedure for allocating the $1,500 total is explained in the next section. $1,050 is extended to manufacturing: the remaining $450 is divided between selling expense (indicated by S) and general and administrative expense (indicated by G) in the Income Statement columns.

Entry c. The annual depreciation rate for factory machinery and equipment is 20 percent. Since all the equipment was acquired prior to 1979 a full year's depreciation is taken, based on the amount shown in the trial balance. The computation is as follows:

Cost of machinery and equipment	$51,000
Annual depreciation rate	x 0.20
Depreciation for 1979	$10,200

The debit records the depreciation of the machinery and equipment as a manufacturing overhead item—not as an expense; the credit increases the Accumulated Depreciation—Machinery and Equipment account.

Entry d. The annual depreciation rate for both office equipment and store equipment is 10 percent. All the office and store equipment was acquired prior to 1979. Consequently, a full year's depreciation expense is taken based on the amount of each account shown in the trial balance. The computations are as follows:

	Office equipment	Store equipment
Cost	$6,050	$10,000
Annual depreciation rate	x0.10	x 0.10
Depreciation for 1979	$ 605	$ 1,000

The debits record the depreciation expense for the office and store equipment;

the credits increase the corresponding Accumulated Depreciation accounts.

Entry e. The accrued wages and salaries payable as of December 31, 1979, were

Direct labor	$ 3,500.00
Indirect labor	1,400.00
Salesmen's salaries	5,100.00
Total	$10,000.00

The debits record all the wages and salaries incurred but not paid; the credit records the accrued liability. Here is an example of debits both to manufacturing accounts and to a period expense.

Entry f. The estimated income tax liability is $7,368. The debit records the estimated income tax; the credit records the estimated income tax liability.

Allocation of costs and expenses on the work sheet

In the Trial Balance and Adjustments columns, certain accounts represent cost incurred partly in the manufacturing processes and partly in the selling and general and administrative functions. Assume that a study was made late in 1978 to find an equitable method for allocating these items. As a result of this study, the following bases for allocation were decided on:

Rent	Square footage of building space used.
Heat, light, and power	Actual readings from meters in the factory, in the sales rooms, and in the general and administrative areas.
Insurance	Cost of comprehensive policies covering the buildings allocated on the basis of square footage; other insurance costs on basis of value of items insured.

From these bases, converted to percentages, the following allocations were made:

		Allocation					
		Manufacturing		Selling		General	
Item	Total	%	Amount	%	Amount	%	Amount
Rent	$12,000.00	80	$9,600.00	15	$1,800.00	5	$600.00
Heat, light, and power	8,100.00	90	7,290.00	5	405.00	5	405.00
Insurance	1,500.00	70	1,050.00	20	300.00	10	150.00

On the line of the work sheet for each of these items, the total of the Trial Balance and Adjustments columns is extended to the appropriate column. The Rent debit balance of $12,000, for example, is distributed as follows: $9,600 = ($12,000 × 0.80) is extended to the Manufacturing Debit column; $1,800 = ($12,000 × 0.15) and $600 = ($12,000 × 0.05) are extended to the Income Statement Debit column. Note that the $9,600 is classified as manufacturing overhead (Factory Rent), $600 as a general and administrative expense, and $1,800 as selling expense.

The letters S and G after the expense figures identify the specific income statement classifications of selling or general and administrative expenses. These letters may be further used for amounts extended as a lump sum in a single column to facilitate the precise classification of the accounts if the formal income statement is prepared directly from the work sheet.

Ending inventories on the manufacturing work sheet

The ending inventories at December 31, 1979, are as follows:

Materials	$51,500.00
Work in Process	47,000.00
Finished Goods	19,600.00

All three amounts are entered as debits in the Balance Sheet columns. The two that affect manufacturing cost—Materials and Work in Process—are entered as credits in the Manufacturing columns. The Finished Goods is a part of the cost of goods sold computation and is entered as a credit in the Income Statement columns.

Entering the three inventories as debits in the Balance Sheet columns establishes them as the new end-of-year current asset value of inventories. Entering these same amounts as credits serves to reduce the cost of goods manufactured and the cost of goods sold because they offset the debits (including beginning inventory figures) that are extended to the Manufacturing columns and the Income Statement columns.

Financial statements

The Manufacturing columns of the work sheet contain all the amounts required for the preparation of the schedule of cost of goods manufactured; each amount is used once. Similarly, the Income Statement and Balance Sheet columns contain the figures needed for the preparation of the income statement, statement of retained earnings, and balance sheet. The financial statements and the schedule of cost of goods manufactured are illustrated in Figures 23–6, 23–7, 23–8, and 23–9.

As indicated in Chapter 21, a *statement of changes in financial position* must also be prepared. Because the format of this statement for a manufacturing firm

COLA MANUFACTURING COMPANY Schedule of Cost of Goods Manufactured For the Year Ended December 31, 1979				Schedule A-1
Work in Process Inventory, January 1, 1979				$ 31,725.00
Materials Used:				
Materials Inventory, January 1, 1979			$ 58,300.00	
Materials Purchases		$91,000.00		
Deduct: Purchases Returns and Allowances	$2,800.00			
Purchases Discounts	2,650.00	5,450.00		
Net Cost of Materials Purchases			85,550.00	
Cost of Materials Available for Use			$143,850.00	
Deduct Materials Inventory, December 31, 1979			51,500.00	
Cost of Materials Used			$ 92,350.00	
Direct Labor			102,030.00	
Manufacturing Overhead:				
Indirect Labor		$22,600.00		
Factory Rent		9,600.00		
Heat, Light, and Power		7,290.00		
Factory Insurance		1,050.00		
Depreciation—Machinery and Equipment		10,200.00		
Total Manufacturing Overhead			50,740.00	
Total Period Manufacturing Costs				245,120.00
Total				$276,845.00
Deduct Work in Process Inventory, December 31, 1979				47,000.00
Cost of Goods Manufactured (to Exhibit A)				$229,845.00

Figure 23-6
Schedule of cost of goods manufactured

is essentially the same as that indicated in Chapter 21, the statement is not repeated here.

Accounting entries

After the work sheet has been completed and the statements prepared, the adjustments are recorded in the general journal and posted to the appropriate accounts. This process has been illustrated in earlier chapters for nonmanufacturing firms. There is no difference in journalizing and posting adjusting entries for a manufacturing firm.

In the closing process for a manufacturing firm a new account, *Manufacturing Summary,* is opened at the end of each accounting period. All account balances that enter into the computation of cost of goods manufactured are closed into the general ledger account, Manufacturing Summary. These account balances are the same figures that are found in the Manufacturing columns of the work sheet.

Figure 23–7
Income statement

COLA MANUFACTURING COMPANY
Income Statement
For the Year Ended December 31, 1979

Exhibit A

Sales			$420,000.00
Deduct: Sales Returns and Allowances		$ 5,200.00	
Sales Discounts		2,400.00	7,600.00
Net Sales Revenue			$412,400.00
Cost of Goods Sold:			
Finished Goods Inventory, January 1, 1979		$ 23,200.00	
Add Cost of Goods Manufactured (Schedule A-1)		229,845.00	
Cost of Finished Goods Available for Sale		$253,045.00	
Deduct Finished Goods Inventory, December 31, 1979		19,600.00	
Cost of Goods Sold			233,445.00
Gross Margin on Sales			$178,955.00
Operating Expenses:			
Selling:			
Rent Expense	$ 1,800.00		
Heat, Light, and Power Expense	405.00		
Advertising Expense	6,500.00		
Salesmen's Salaries Expense . .	55,100.00		
Insurance Expense	300.00		
Depreciation Expense— Store Equipment	1,000.00		
Total Selling Expenses . . .		$ 65,105.00	
General and Administrative:			
Rent Expense	$ 600.00		
Heat, Light, and Power Expense	405.00		
Executive Salaries Expense . .	60,500.00		
Office Salaries Expense	26,000.00		
Bad Debts Expense	1,037.00		
Insurance Expense	150.00		
Depreciation Expense— Office Equipment	605.00		
Total General and Administrative Expenses . .		89,297.00	
Total Operating Expenses . .			154,402.00
Net income before Income Taxes . .			$ 24,553.00
Income Tax Expense			7,368.00
Net Income After Income Taxes (To Exhibit B)			$ 17,185.00

Earnings per Share: $0.95

Figure 23–8
Balance sheet

COLA MANUFACTURING COMPANY
Balance Sheet
December 31, 1979

Exhibit C

Assets

Current Assets			
Cash		$ 12,000.00	
Accounts Receivable	$78,350.00		
Deduct Allowance for Doubtful Accounts	1,687.00	76,663.00	
Materials Inventory		51,500.00	
Work in Process Inventory		47,000.00	
Finished Goods Inventory		19,600.00	
Prepaid Insurance		600.00	
Total Current Assets			$207,363.00
Plant and Equipment			
Office Equipment	$ 6,050.00		
Deduct Accumulated Depreciation .	2,605.00	$ 3,445.00	
Store Equipment	$10,000.00		
Deduct Accumulated Depreciation .	5,000.00	5,000.00	
Machinery and Equipment	$51,000.00		
Deduct Accumulated Depreciation .	20,200.00	30,800.00	
Total Plant and Equipment . . .			39,245.00
Total Assets			$246,608.00

Liabilities and Stockholders' Equity

Current Liabilities		
Accounts Payable	$ 29,200.00	
Accrued Wages and Salaries Payable	10,000.00	
Income Taxes Payable	7,368.00	
Total Current Liabilities . . .		$ 46,568.00
Stockholders' Equity		
Capital Stock, $10 Par Value . .	$180,000.00	
Retained Earnings (Exhibit B) . .	20,040.00	
Total Stockholders' Equity . .		200,040.00
Total Liabilities and Stockholders' Equity		$246,608.00

The final balance of the Manufacturing Summary account is the cost of goods manufactured. It is closed into the Income Summary account. The remaining closing entries are the same as for a merchandising business.

The closing journal entries for Cola Manufacturing Company are as follows:

GENERAL JOURNAL　　Page 18

Date		Account	Debit	Credit
1979 Dec.	31	Manufacturing Summary	333,795 00	
		Materials Inventory		58,300 00
		Work in Process Inventory		31,725 00
		Materials Purchases		91,000 00
		Direct Labor		102,030 00
		Indirect Labor		22,600 00
		Rent		9,600 00
		Heat, Light, and Power		7,290 00
		Insurance		1,050 00
		Depreciation—Machinery and Equipment		10,200 00
		To close beginning inventories and the debit-balance manufacturing accounts.		
	31	Materials Inventory	51,500 00	
		Work in Process Inventory	47,000 00	
		Materials Purchases Returns and Allowances	2,800 00	
		Materials Purchases Discounts	2,650 00	
		Manufacturing Summary		103,950 00
		To enter ending inventories and to close the credit-balance manufacturing accounts.		
	31	Income Summary	229,845 00	
		Manufacturing Summary		229,845 00
		To close the Manufacturing Summary account.		

GENERAL JOURNAL　　Page 19

Date		Account	Debit	Credit
1979 Dec.	31	Income Summary	192,570 00	
		Finished Goods Inventory		23,200 00
		Sales Returns and Allowances		5,200 00
		Sales Discounts		2,400 00
		Rent		2,400 00
		Heat, Light, and Power		810 00
		Advertising Expense		6,500 00
		Salesmen's Salaries Expense		55,100 00
		Executive Salaries Expense		60,500 00
		Office Salaries Expense		26,000 00
		Bad Debts Expense		1,037 00
		Insurance		450 00
		Depreciation Expense—Office Equipment		605 00
		Depreciation Expense—Store Equipment		1,000 00
		Income Tax Expense		7,368 00
		To close beginning inventory of Finished Goods and the debit-balance income accounts.		
	31	Finished Goods Inventory	19,600 00	
		Sales	420,000 00	
		Income Summary		439,600 00
		To enter the ending finished goods inventory and to close the credit-balance revenue accounts.		
	31	Income Summary	17,185 00	
		Retained Earnings		17,185 00
		To close net income into Retained Earnings.		
	31	Retained Earnings	10,000 00	
		Dividends		10,000 00
		To close the Dividends account.		

Figure 23–9
Statement of retained earnings

COLA MANUFACTURING COMPANY Statement of Retained Earnings For the Year Ended December 31, 1979	Exhibit B
Retained Earnings, January 1, 1979	$12,855.00
Net Income for the Year (Exhibit A)	17,185.00
Total	$30,040.00
Deduct Dividends	10,000.00
Retained Earnings, December 31, 1979 (To Exhibit C)	$20,040.00

The posting of closing entries and the preparation of a postclosing trial balance for a manufacturing firm do not differ from procedures illustrated for other businesses in earlier chapters. Upon completion of posting, all nominal (temporary) accounts have a zero balance.

As mentioned in the introduction to this chapter, these procedures using a periodic inventory system are adequate to determine net income of a general manufacturing firm. They do not, however, provide the information needed for effective managerial control. If a manufacturing firm is to continue in business it should establish a cost accounting system using a manufacturing budget and a perpetual inventory system. These topics will be covered in Chapters 24 and 25.

Glossary

Allocation basis See Manufacturing Overhead Allocation Basis.

Amortization of patents The amount of patent cost applicable to a given time period; it is an element of manufacturing overhead for a manufacturing firm.

Cost of goods manufactured The cost of the units of finished products completed during a given period; it is calculated by adding the beginning work in process inventory to the three period manufacturing cost elements and deducting the ending work in process inventory.

Cost of goods sold for manufacturing firm Often referred to as cost of sales; it is computed by adding the beginning finished goods inventory to the cost of goods manufactured for the period and subtracting the ending finished goods inventory.

Direct labor The wages paid to employees performing operations directly on the product being manufactured.

Finished goods The inventory of finished products of a manufacturing firm.

Indirect labor The labor cost of those workers whose efforts are not directly identified with the conversion of specific material into specific finished products; for example, the factory janitor's salary is an indirect labor cost.

Inventoriable costs Costs that will become part of the finished goods inventory. Such costs do not appear as period expenses in the income statement. Ultimately they become part of cost of goods sold.

Manufacturing firm A firm that makes finished products out of basic materials by applying direct labor costs and other manufacturing costs to convert the basic materials into finished goods.

Manufacturing overhead All factory costs incurred in the manufacturing process other than the cost of direct materials used and direct labor; examples are indirect labor, small tools used, and factory insurance.

Manufacturing overhead allocation basis Certain costs are joint costs incurred in several company functions, including the manufacturing function. These costs must be allocated to the respective functions by some equitable method; hence an allocation base is selected. For example, rent may be allocated on the basis of square footage of building space used by each function.

Manufacturing summary A summary account used in the closing process for a manufacturing firm to which all items used in the calculation of cost of goods manufactured are closed.

Materials The inventory, at cost, of material held for consumption in fabricating the finished product of a manufacturing firm; other terms are raw materials or materials inventory.

Materials used The cost of the materials used in manufacturing during a given period. Under the periodic inventory method the amount is the sum of beginning materials inventory plus net cost of materials purchases less ending materials inventory.

Work in process The inventory of partly finished products in various stages of completion at any given time.

Questions

Q23–1 What is an inventoriable cost? A periodic expense?

Q23–2 A manufacturing firm has three inventory accounts. Name each of these accounts and describe briefly what the balance in each at the end of any accounting period represents.

Q23–3 Explain each of the following terms: (a) materials used, (b) direct labor, and (c) manufacturing overhead.

Q23–4 What are the criteria that differentiate between direct labor and indirect labor, direct material and indirect material?

Q23–5 What is the difference between cost of goods manufactured and cost of goods sold?

Q23–6 Describe the purpose and function of the Manufacturing columns in the work sheet.

Q23–7 During a given period the cost of materials used by a manufacturing firm was $50,000. The materials inventory increased by $5,000 during the period. What was the cost of materials purchased?

Q23–8 The books of the Glenville State Corporation showed the following information:

Inventories	*12/31/79*	*12/31/78*
Finished Goods	$24,000.00	$18,000.00
Work in Process	17,250.00	10,500.00
Materials	15,900.00	19,050.00

Explain how each amount will be shown in (a) the work sheet, (b) the schedule of cost of goods manufactured, (c) the income statement, and (d) the balance sheet.

Q23–9 When a given cost is applicable partly to manufacturing and partly to the administrative or selling function, how is the amount divided between the two?

Q23–10 Identify some of the problems involved in the measurement of the periodic inventories of work in process and finished goods.

Q23–11 Would the accounting system explained in Chapter 23 be acceptable for a major automobile manufacturer? Why or why not?

Q23–12 What financial statement is prepared from the information in the Manufacturing columns of the work sheet?

Class exercises

CE23–1 (Computation of materials used) The following information is available from the records of the Barth Manufacturing Company.

Materials inventory, December 31, 1978	$ 38,250.00
Materials inventory, December 31, 1979	30,000.00
Materials purchases, 1979	600,000.00
Transportation in on materials purchases, 1979	12,000.00
Materials purchases returns and allowances, 1979	15,000.00
Materials purchases discounts, 1979	10,500.00

Required: In schedule form, compute the cost of materials used in 1979.

CE23–2 (Computation of cost of goods sold) The following information is available from the records of the Keene Company:

Finished goods inventory, December 31, 1978	$ 75,000.00
Cost of goods manufactured in 1979	900,000.00
Finished goods inventory, December 31, 1979	90,000.00
Work in process inventory, December 31, 1978	31,500.00
Work in process inventory, December 31, 1979	37,950.00

Required: In schedule form compute the cost of goods sold in 1979.

CE23–3 (Journal entries; schedule of cost of goods manufactured) The Lees/McRae Manufacturing Company uses a regular accounts payable system of recording liabilities for materials purchases. During 1979, the firm completed certain transactions as follows:

1. Purchased materials on account for $62,750.
2. Paid transportation charges amounting to $2,050 on materials.
3. Received $2,750 credit for materials returned.
4. Issued checks for $50,250 in payment of liability for materials purchased.
5. Paid direct labor wages of $37,500 (ignore payroll taxes).
6. Paid the following items: factory rent, $2,750; heat, light, and power, $3,400; indirect labor, $2,600; and miscellaneous factory cost, $600.
7. Made year-end adjusting entries to record expired factory insurance of $1,250, small tools cost of $750, and depreciation on machinery and equipment of $3,750.

Required:

1. Journalize the transactions and post to ledger accounts.
2. Prepare a schedule of cost of goods manufactured. Inventories were are follows:

	Beginning	*Ending*
Materials	$5,250.00	$4,250.00
Work in process	2,000.00	2,300.00

   Beginning balance in selected accounts are: Cash, $120,000; Prepaid Insurance, $2,500; Small Tools, $1,000; Accumulated Depreciation—Machinery and Equipment, $10,000.
3. Journalize the entries to close the nominal manufacturing accounts.

CE23–4 (Work sheet, statements, and closing entries) The condensed adjusted trial balance of the Hanke Corporation on December 31, 1979, after adjustment, consisted of the following:

Cash	$150,000.00
Accounts Receivable	105,000.00
Finished Goods, December 31, 1978	90,000.00
Work in Process, December 31, 1978	60,000.00
Materials, December 31, 1978	75,000.00
Plant and Equipment	375,000.00
Accumulated Depreciation—Plant and Equipment	75,000.00
Accounts Payable	180,000.00
Common Stock ($100 par value)	375,000.00
Retained Earnings	135,000.00
Sales	630,000.00

Materials Purchases	225,000.00
Direct Labor	150,000.00
Manufacturing Overhead	120,000.00
Selling Expenses	30,000.00
General Expenses	15,000.00

Inventories on December 31, 1979.

Finished goods	$ 75,000.00
Work in process	90,000.00
Materials	105,000.00

Required: Prepare (a) a manufacturing work sheet, (b) a schedule of cost of goods manufactured, (c) an income statement, (d) a balance sheet, and (e) the closing entries.

Exercises and problems

P23–1 The following data are taken from the books of the Ghesing Company for the year 1979:

Materials purchases	$ 50,000.00
Direct labor	100,000.00
Manufacturing overhead	100,000.00
Materials inventory change (amount of increase of ending inventory over beginning inventory)	15,000.00
Work in process inventory (decrease)	10,000.00
Finished goods inventory (increase)	5,000.00

Required: Determine (a) the cost of goods manufactured and (b) the cost of goods sold.

P23–2 Manufacturing overhead is 20 percent of cost of goods manufactured. Direct labor is 30 percent of sales and 60 percent of cost of goods manufactured. Ending materials inventory is $8,000 more than beginning materials inventory. Sales totaled $200,000 for the year.

Required: Compute the net cost of materials purchased during the year. This company never has any work in process inventory at the end of each period.

P23–3 Compute the missing amounts in the following tabulation:

	Beginning Inventory of Materials	*Materials Purchases*	*Transportation In on Materials*	*Materials Purchases Returns and Allowances*
1.	$2,250	$12,900	$?	$450
2.	?	3,750	450	300
3.	5,250	?	1,050	300

(continued below)

	Materials Purchases Discounts	*Net Cost of Materials Purchases*	*Cost of Materials Available for Use*	*Ending Inventory of Materials*	*Cost of Materials Used*
1.	$225	$14,250	$?	$?	$12,750
2.	?	3,750	8,250	?	5,400
3.	600	?	29,850	7,500	?

P23–4 Compute the missing amounts in the following tabulation:

	Net Sales	*Beginning Inventory of Finished Goods*	*Cost of Goods Manufactured*	*Cost of Finished Goods Available for Sale*	*Ending Inventory of Finished Goods*	*Cost of Goods Sold*	*Gross Margin on Sales*
1.	$61,500	$?	$45,000	$60,000	$?	$ 38,250	$?
2.	?	37,500	?	?	15,000	121,500	30,000
3.	90,000	?	60,000	90,000	?	?	15,750

P23–5 The Bunker Corporation acquired certain patent rights for $100,000 and spent an additional $46,000 in further developing them.

Required:

1. Record the acquisition and development of the patents.
2. Record the patent amortization for one year on the basis of a full legal life of 17 years.
3. Record the patent amortization on the basis of an assumed useful economic life of eight years.

P23–6 The following Small Tools account is from the books of the Huyett Corporation:

Small Tools

Date		Explanation	Debit	Credit	Balance
1979					
Jan.	1	Balance			20,800 00
Aug.	3	(Purchase)	5,200 00		26,000 00

The inventory of small tools on hand on December 31, 1979, was priced at $13,500 based on physical count.

Required:

1. What part of the Small Tools account is allocated to 1979?
2. Prepare the entry to adjust the Small Tools account.

P23–7 The adjusted trial balance of the Rupert Corporation included the following items:

Rent	$14,000.00
Heat, Light, and Power	8,400.00
Insurance	4,800.00
Taxes	4,000.00
Depreciation	8,000.00

The accountant for the Rupert Corporation determined the following allocation percentages:

	Manufacturing	*Selling*	*General*
Rent	80%	15%	5%
Heat, light, and power	90	3	7
Insurance (plant and equipment)	60	20	20
Taxes	70	20	10
Depreciation	75	10	15

Required: Enter the account balances in the Adjusted Trial Balance columns of a manufacturing work sheet and using the allocation percentages given, extend the items to the appropriate columns of the work sheet.

P23–8 The following information is from the books of the Hacking Company.

	June 30, 1978	*June 30, 1979*	*Year Ended June 30, 1979*
Materials	$ 30,000.00	$ 34,500.00	
Work in Process	44,700.00	43,050.00	
Finished Goods	110,250.00	106,350.00	
Materials Purchases			$ 413,250.00
Transportation in—Materials			20,550.00
Direct Labor			465,000.00
Manufacturing Overhead			394,500.00
Sales			$1,750,000.00

Required:

1. Compute the cost of goods manufactured.
2. Compute the cost of goods sold.
3. Compute the gross margin on sales.

P23–9 Following are the Manufacturing columns of the work sheet of the Fall Corporation for the year ended December 31, 1979:

	Manufacturing	
	Debits	*Credits*
Materials Inventory	$ 45,000	$ 43,500
Work in Process Inventory	30,000	37,500
Materials Purchases	105,000	
Direct Labor	52,500	
Indirect Labor	11,250	
Rent	4,800	
Heat, Light, and Power	3,600	
Depreciation—Plant and Equipment	4,500	
Miscellaneous Factory Costs	3,750	
	$260,400	$ 81,000
Cost of Goods Manufactured		179,400
	$260,400	$260,400

Required:

1. Prepare a schedule of cost of goods manufactured for 1979.
2. Journalize the closing entries pertaining to the manufacturing functions.

P23–10 The following accounts and amounts, arranged in alphabetical order, were taken from the completed work sheet of the Home Manufacturing Corporation:

Accounts Receivable	$ 427,500.00
Accumulated Depreciation—Machinery and Equipment	147,000.00
Advertising Expense	21,750.00
Allowance for Doubtful Accounts	9,000.00
Bad Debts Expense	8,250.00
Cash	38,250.00
Depreciation—Machinery and Equipment	16,500.00
Direct Labor	232,500.00
Factory Insurance	22,500.00
Factory Rent	45,000.00
Finished Goods Inventory, December 31, 1978	352,500.00
Finished Goods Inventory, December 31, 1979	318,000.00
Heat, Light, and Power—Factory	21,750.00
Indirect Labor	64,500.00
Machinery and Equipment	345,000.00
Materials Inventory, December 31, 1978	277,500.00
Materials Inventory, December 31, 1979	281,250.00
Miscellaneous Factory Costs	29,550.00
Prepaid Insurance	16,500.00
Purchases—Materials	692,250.00
Purchases Discounts—Materials	22,500.00
Purchases Returns and Allowances—Materials	18,000.00
Sales	2,227,500.00
Sales Discounts	31,500.00
Sales Returns and Allowances	21,000.00
Salesmen's Salaries Expense	202,500.00
Small Tools	93,000.00
Small Tools Used	9,750.00
Transportation In—Materials	11,250.00
Work in Process Inventory, December 31, 1978	225,000.00
Work in Process Inventory, December 31, 1979	180,000.00

Required:

1. Prepare the schedule of cost of goods manufactured for 1979.
2. Prepare a partial income statement through Gross Margin on Sales for 1979.
3. Prepare the Current Assets section of the balance sheet.

P23–11 (Integrative) The postclosing trial balance of the Free Manufacturing Company on December 31, 1978, is shown below.

FREE MANUFACTURING COMPANY
Postclosing Trial Balance
December 31, 1978

	Debits	*Credits*
Cash	$ 378,750.00	
Accounts Receivable	195,000.00	
Allowance for Doubtful Accounts		$ 9,750.00
Materials Inventory	270,000.00	
Work in Process Inventory	360,000.00	
Finished Goods Inventory	330,000.00	
Prepaid Insurance	18,000.00	
Supplies Inventory	6,400.00	
Patents	15,000.00	
Small Tools	10,100.00	
Machinery and Equipment	375,000.00	
Accumulated Depreciation		120,000.00
Accounts Payable		420,000.00
Accrued Wages and Salaries Payable		90,000.00
Dividends Payable		300,000.00
Income Taxes Payable		202,500.00
Common Stock, $100 par value; issued 6,000 shares		600,000.00
Retained Earnings		216,000.00
Totals	$1,958,250.00	$1,958,250.00

Condensed transactions for 1979:

1. The accrued wages and salaries payable as of December 31, 1978, consisted of the items listed below. Under the nonreversing approach no entry is required; this detailed information is needed for a later entry.

Direct labor	$30,000.00
Indirect labor	22,500.00
Salesmen's salaries	18,000.00
Executive salaries	19,500.00

2. Sales on account for the year were $2,250,000.00.
3. Collections from customers were:

Accounts receivable	$1,950.000.00
Deduct discounts allowed	19,500.00
Amount collected	$1,930,500.00

4. Purchased materials on account for $540,000.00.
5. Dividends due stockholders were paid in the amount of $300,000.00.
6. Freight and other transportation charges on materials were paid in the amount of $9,000.00.
7. Credit received for materials returned totaled $16,500.00.
8. Accounts payable for materials were paid as follows:

Accounts payable	$592,500.00
Deduct discounts taken	11,850.00
Amount paid	$580,650.00

9. Payrolls paid during year were (ignore the payroll taxes):

Direct labor	$240,000.00
Indirect labor	109,500.00
Salesmen's salaries	142,500.00
Executive salaries	154,500.00

10. The following items were also paid:

Small tools	$ 4,500.00
Insurance (debit Prepaid Insurance)	18,000.00
Supplies	10,800.00
Rent	90,000.00
Repairs and maintenance	37,500.00
Miscellaneous general expenses	18,000.00
Miscellaneous selling expenses	6,300.00
Heat, light, and power	27,000.00

11. Dividends declared by the board of directors were $120,000.00.
12. Accounts receivable written off during year amounted to $13,500.00.
13. Merchandise returned by customers and credit granted totaled $34,500.00.
14. Paid income taxes of $202,500.00.

Inventory and adjustment data:

a. Depreciation of machinery and equipment is 10 percent of original cost.
b. All patents had an economic life of 10 years as of the beginning of the year.
c. Prepaid insurance as of December 31, 1979, was $14,250.00.
d. The bad debts expense is estimated at 1/2 of 1 percent of net sales.
e. The small tools inventory as of December 31, 1979, was $12,150.00.
f. Supplies on hand as of December 31, 1979, amounted to $5,250.00

g. Estimated income taxes were $397,500.00.
h. December 31, 1979, inventories were:

Materials	$285,000.00
Work in process	315,000.00
Finished goods	300,000.00

i. Allocation percentages are as follows:

Item	*Manufacturing*	*Selling*	*General*
Insurance	80	10	10
Supplies	70	20	10
Rent	80	15	5
Repairs and maintenance	90	5	5
Heat, light, and power	80	15	5

Required:

1. Enter the December 31, 1978, postclosing trial balance amounts in appropriate ledger accounts.
2. Record the condensed transactions for 1979 and post to accounts (omit dates and posting references). Add new accounts as needed.
3. Prepare (a) a work sheet, (b) a schedule of cost of goods manufactured, (c) an income statement, (d) a statement of retained earnings, and (e) a balance sheet.

P23–12 (Minicase) The Crewel Manufacturing Company produces a single commodity. A summary of its activities for 1979 follows.

	Units	*Amount*
Sales	90,000	$900,000.00
Materials inventory, 12/31/1978		48,000.00
Work in process inventory, 12/31/1978		60,000.00
Finished goods inventory, 12/31/1978 ...	18,000	72,000.00
Materials inventory, 12/31/1979		36,000.00
Work in process inventory, 12/31/1979 ...		75,000.00
Finished goods inventory, 12/31/1979 ...	24,000	?
Materials purchases		192,000.00
Direct labor		135,000.00
Manufacturing overhead costs		108,000.00

Required:

1. Prepare a schedule of cost of goods manufactured for 1979. Indicate on the schedule the number of units completed for the year and the cost per unit of finished goods.
2. Determine the gross margin on sales for the year, assuming that the transfer of the cost of finished goods to cost of goods sold is on the LIFO basis. Show all your computations.
3. Discuss the accounting concepts underlying the selection of the LIFO basis versus the FIFO basis. Which of these two methods should be chosen if sound accounting concepts are followed? Why?

chapter twenty-four

Introduction

As explained in Chapter 23, a company that makes the product it sells needs to use some additional accounts in its ledger to gather information for calculating the cost of goods manufactured. The type of accounting for general manufacturing operations described in Chapter 23 is often not adequate to meet the needs of management. The additional records needed to provide this information are known as a *cost accounting system*. This chapter explains the nature and purpose of one type of cost accounting system, *job order cost accounting,* and also introduces the concept of the *budget*.

Job order cost accounting

Learning goals

To understand the concept of cost accounting systems.
To increase knowledge of the perpetual inventory concept.
To compute and use a predetermined overhead rate.
To understand the use of cost sheets as a subsidiary Work in Process Inventory ledger.
To journalize the entries involved in using a job order cost accounting system.

Key terms

applied manufacturing overhead
budget
cost of goods sold
cost sheet
factory payroll
indirect labor
indirect materials
job order cost system
manufacturing overhead control
materials requisition
predetermined overhead rate
producing department
product cost
time ticket
unit cost

Cost accounting makes managers more effective in several ways. With information on cost to manufacture a single unit of product (instead of overall cost of goods manufactured), they do a better job of setting selling prices. Managers, with information on specific costs made available as a job progresses, can do a better job of controlling those costs. The periodic inventory system used in the illustration of accounting for general manufacturing operations in Chapter 23 is not adequate for a cost accounting system. Accordingly, in this chapter a *perpetual inventory* system will be used for Materials Inventory and for Finished Goods Inventory.

Perpetual inventories—a review

When the perpetual system is used a separate record is maintained for each item in the inventory. In Chapter 13 this record was illustrated in the form of inventory record cards. Many companies keep the inventory records on computer files, but the principles are the same. Figure 24–1 illustrates the relationship between the Materials Inventory account in the general ledger and the subsidiary ledger composed of the inventory record cards. Assuming that the October 3 entry represents a purchase of 400 units of stock number 22B at $2 each and that Whittier Company makes the entry in the general journal, it would appear as follows:

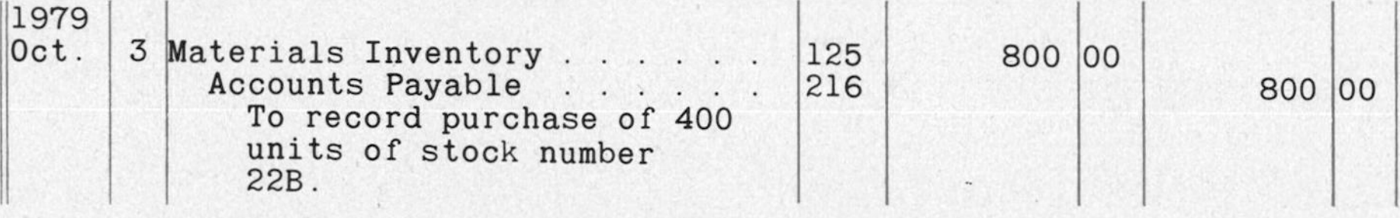

1979							
Oct.	3	Materials Inventory	125	800	00		
		Accounts Payable	216			800	00
		To record purchase of 400 units of stock number 22B.					

Figure 24–1 Materials inventory and subsidiary ledger

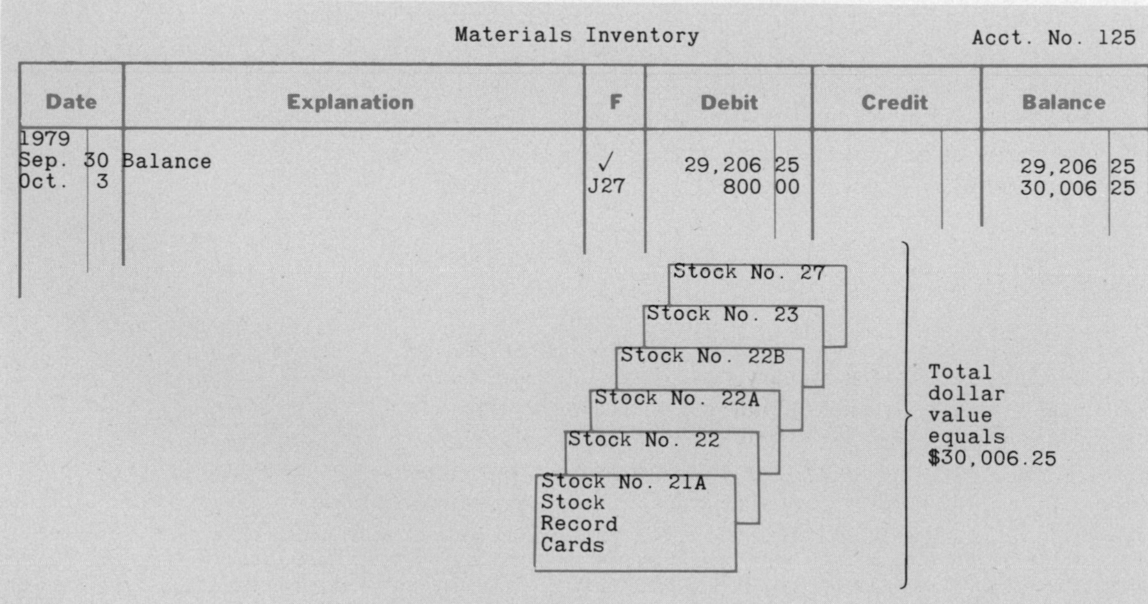

Materials Inventory — Acct. No. 125

Date		Explanation	F	Debit		Credit		Balance	
1979									
Sep.	30	Balance	✓	29,206	25			29,206	25
Oct.	3		J27	800	00			30,006	25

MATERIALS REQUISITION

No. 00326

Date 10-4-79 Issue to Dept 2 Charge to Job No. 62

Stock Number	Description	Qty.	Unit Cost	Amount
21A	Gaskets	50	1.00	50.00
22B	Couplings	100	2.00	200.00
	Total			250.00

Approved by J. Seibert Received by O. Haines

Figure 24–2
Materials requisition

The receipts into and issues out of the materials storeroom are posted daily to the stock record cards. Receipts are posted from copies of *receiving reports* illustrated and explained in Chapter 8 (Figure 8–2). Issues are posted to the stock record cards daily from a source document called a *materials requisition*. A typical materials requisition is illustrated in Figure 24–2. If it is possible to identify the job on which issued materials are to be used, it is an issue of *direct materials*. Issues of material for general use (for example, lubricating oil for factory machinery) are called issues of *indirect materials*. In most manufacturing firms, materials requisitions are not posted to the general ledger account daily, but are summarized and posted at the end of a period—say monthly. Of course, the equality of total dollar value of the account, Materials Inventory, in the general ledger and the total dollar value of the stock record cards (as shown in Figure 24–1) is true only when all postings are up to date.

Similar procedures are used for the Finished Goods Inventory account. There is a set of inventory records (stock record cards) with a separate card for each item of product manufactured. Increases are posted to the stock record cards as manufacturing jobs are completed and transferred to the finished goods storeroom. Decreases are posted as sales are made. When postings to both the general ledger and subsidiary ledger are up to date, the balance in the Finished Goods Inventory account is equal to the total dollar value of balances in the subsidiary ledger.

Cost sheets

In a job order cost accounting system there is a subsidiary record for each job that is in process. This subsidiary record is called a *cost sheet*. (Figure 24–4 illustrates a typical cost sheet.) Materials, direct labor, and manufacturing overhead costs are recorded separately on the cost sheet. Materials costs are recorded from copies of materials requisitions. Direct labor costs are recorded from individuals' *time tickets* prepared in each production department.[1] A typical time ticket is pictured in Figure 24–3. A separate time ticket is made for each

1 Direct labor can be identified to a specific job. Indirect labor (for example, stockroom personnel) cannot.

Figure 24–3
Time ticket

Time Ticket

Ticket No.	Employee Name	Clock No.	Job No.	Hours	Rate
976	John Seibert	3890	62	8	$10.00

Date 10-4-79 Foreman Angie Smith

person each time that person works on a job. John Seibert worked a full day on job number 62 on October 4. On October 5 at least two persons worked on job number 62 because the cost sheet shows two time tickets for a total of 16 hours. Manufacturing overhead costs are allocated to jobs at a rate that was determined at the beginning of the year. The rate in this firm is $4 per direct-labor hour. The method of determining an overhead rate will be explained in the next section of this chapter.

Figure 24–4
Job order cost sheet

WHITTIER COMPANY

Cost Sheet

Quantity and Description: 2 Power Brake Assemblies   Job No. 62

Date Started: Oct. 4, 1979   Date Completed: Oct. 10, 1979

For: Stock

Direct Materials			Direct Labor			
Date	Requisition Number	Amount	Date	Time Ticket Number	Hours	Amount
10/4	00326	250.00	10/4	976	8	80.00
10/6	00418	151.00	10/5	1021 & 1022	16	136.00
10/10	00672	450.00	10/6	1101 & 1102	12	131.00
			10/9	1135 & 1140	10	116.00
			10/10	1200	4	60.00
	Total	851.00		Totals	50	523.00

Summary

	Amount	Per Unit
Materials	$ 851.00	$425.50
Labor	523.00	261.50
Overhead (50 hours at $4.00)	200.00	100.00
	$1,574.00	$787.00

When a job is completed the total direct materials cost and total direct labor hours and cost are determined. Using a base for allocation (in this case, direct labor hours) and the predetermined overhead rate, the amount of manufacturing overhead is allocated and recorded on the cost sheet. Overhead allocated and recorded in this manner is said to be *applied*. Total cost of the job is the sum of the three elements of cost—materials, labor, and overhead. The *unit cost* of $787 is determined by dividing the total cost by the number of units produced.

During the period a job is in the production process or *producing department* its cost sheet is being posted daily with direct materials and direct labor charges. The total file of cost sheets representing all jobs being worked on at any time is a subsidiary ledger to the Work in Process account. At the end of an accounting period the incomplete job cost sheets would be footed, and the amount of overhead allocated to date noted on them. Their total cost would then be equal to the general ledger account, Work in Process.

The manufacturing overhead budget and rate

The specific identification of the direct material and labor costs incurred on a given job order can be determined readily. Manufacturing overhead, however, cannot be economically identified with a specific job order. Some manufacturing overhead items—depreciation, insurance, rent, and property taxes, for example—are related to the passage of time and are not affected by production volume, whereas other manufacturing overhead costs—power, cutting oil, and small tools, for example—vary with the volume of production. If completed product costs are to be currently available to management, it becomes necessary to apply manufacturing overhead to job order cost sheets on a predetermined, or estimated, basis. Management must prepare an estimate of manufacturing overhead costs for the coming year. This estimate (or financial plan), called a *budget*, provides for management a tool for control of manufacturing overhead.

Overhead rate

The calculation of a **predetermined overhead rate** *is based (1) on budgeted manufacturing overhead cost for the planned production and (2) on an estimated volume factor that reflects planned future production.*

Calculation of overhead rate

A cause and effect relationship should exist between the factor selected and the manufacturing overhead cost. To illustrate, assume that the Whittier Company budget plans for manufacturing overhead costs of $800,000 and a production level of 200,000 direct labor hours during 1979. In this plant, there is a close relationship between direct labor hours and manufacturing overhead. The predetermined overhead rate for 1979 is calculated as follows:

$$\frac{\text{Budgeted manufacturing overhead}}{\text{Planned direct labor hours}} = \frac{\$800{,}000}{200{,}000} = \$4 \text{ per direct labor hour.}$$

Since job number 62 required 50 labor hours (see Figure 24–4), a charge of $200 = (50 hours × $4) is recorded on that job order cost sheet for overhead.

If actual direct labor hours during 1979 are 200,000, as estimated, the Whittier Company will have applied $800,000 = (200,000 hours × $4) in manufacturing overhead costs to the various job order cost sheets. If, as is likely, a variance exists between the actual costs and the estimated amounts, there will be a balance in the Manufacturing Overhead Control account. A debit balance indicates overhead *underapplied* (overhead applied is less than actual overhead) and a credit balance indicates overhead *overapplied* (overhead applied is more than actual overhead). Although the under- or overapplied manufacturing overhead affects work in process, finished goods, and cost of goods sold, in general practice it is treated as an adjustment to the largest of these items, the cost of goods sold, and is closed into that account at the end of the year.

Other bases (volume factors) for applying manufacturing overhead are (1) direct labor dollars, (2) machine hours, (3) units of production, and (4) material cost. The method of computation of a predetermined overhead rate using any of these bases is the same as for direct labor hours. Assume that the Whittier Company selects the material cost basis and budgets the direct material cost to be $3,200,000 for planned production in 1979. The computation of the predetermined overhead rate based on material cost is as follows:

$$\frac{\text{Budgeted manufacturing overhead}}{\text{Budgeted material cost}} = \frac{\$800{,}000}{\$3{,}200{,}000} = 25\% \text{ of material cost}$$

The overhead to be applied to job order 62 (Figure 24–4) would be $212.75 = (direct material cost of $851.00 × 0.25 predetermined overhead rate).

Selecting the basis of allocation

An important management decision is the selection of the proper basis for allocating overhead. The basis that should be selected is one that charges the job with an amount of manufacturing overhead most nearly corresponding to the actual manufacturing overhead costs incurred on the job. A detailed analysis should be made of all cost and production factors involved prior to the selection of a base, and should be continously reconsidered. The direct labor hours method is used widely because it recognizes the relationship of time and overhead cost; that is, an increase in direct labor hours on a job will normally result in a corresponding increase in the factory overhead costs caused by that job.

Journal entries and flow of costs

The costs in a cost accounting system flow through various accounts on their way to becoming part of the cost of goods sold. Although selling expenses and general and administrative expenses exist in manufacturing firms, the emphasis here is on product costs. *Product costs* are those costs that become part of the product made. In Figure 24–5 it can be seen that costs are first captured in the Materials Inventory, Factory Payroll, and Manufacturing Overhead Control accounts. As materials are used, labor is performed, and overhead is applied, the costs move into Work in Process. Upon completion of specific jobs the costs that have been gathered in Work in Process are transferred to Finished Goods Inventory. Then as goods are sold, the costs move into the Cost of Goods Sold account, later to be closed into the Income Summary.

Figure 24–5 Flow chart for job order cost system

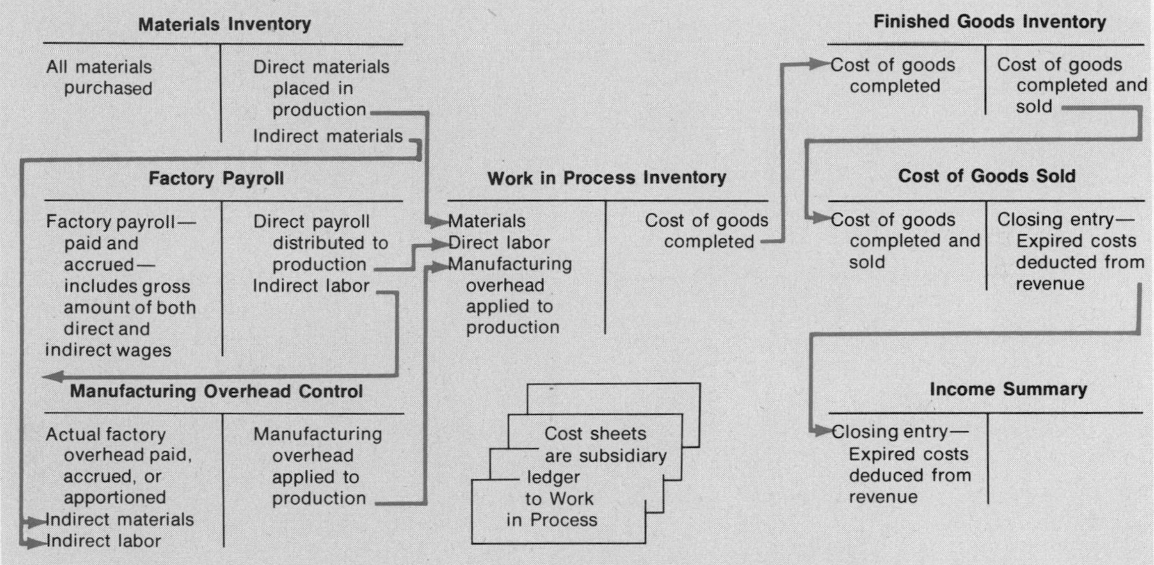

Journal entries are of course required to record this flow of costs. Although special journals can be used in a cost accounting system, the entries for the Whittier Company are made in general journal form. Some of these entries are accumulated until the end of a month and made in summary form. The illustration for the Whittier Company will focus upon job number 62; we will assume for simplicity that no other work was done in October. (This is, of course, not a realistic assumption.) The following journal entries would be made:

1979				
Oct.	3	Materials Inventory	800 00	
		Accounts Payable		800 00
		To record purchase of materials and supplies to be used in the manufacturing process.		
	31	Work in Process Inventory	851 00	
		Manufacturing Overhead Control	100 00	
		Materials Inventory		951 00
		To record the issuance of direct and indirect materials to production. (It is assumed that $100 of indirect materials were issued.)		
	31	Factory Payroll	600 00	
		Cash or Accrued Factory Wages Payable		600 00
		(And liabilities for all payroll deductions)		
		To record the factory payroll for the period.		

Date		Accounts and explanation	Debit	Credit
1979 Oct.	31	Work in Process Inventory	523 00	
		Manufacturing Overhead Control	77 00	
		Factory Payroll		600 00
		To record the distribution of all factory wages—direct wages to production and indirect wages assumed to be $77.00 to manufacturing overhead.		
	31	Manufacturing Overhead Control	100 00	
		Various Accounts		100 00
		(Cash, Accumulated Depreciation, and so on) To record actual factory overhead paid, accrued, or apportioned.		
	31	Work in Process Inventory	200 00	
		Manufacturing Overhead Control		200 00
		To record the overhead applied to production by the use of a predetermined rate.		
	31	Finished Goods Inventory	1,574 00	
		Work in Process Inventory		1,574 00
		To record the cost of goods completed in the current period.		
	31	Cost of Goods Sold	787 00	
		Finished Goods Inventory		787 00
		To record the expired cost of goods sold during the period (assume the sale of one of the two power brakes).		
Dec.	31	Income Summary	787 00	
		Cost of Goods Sold		787 00
		To close the Cost of Goods Sold account at the end of the period.		

Two additional journal entries are needed to complete this illustration. Assume that the sales price of the power brake is $1,200.

Date		Accounts and explanation	Debit	Credit
1979 Oct.	31	Accounts Receivable	1,200 00	
		Sales		1,200 00
		To record the sale of one power brake.		
Dec.	31	Sales	1,200 00	
		Income Summary		1,200 00
		To close the Sales account into Income Summary at the end of the period.		

Under- and overapplied manufacturing overhead

In the simplified illustration for the Whittier Company overhead incurred is $277 = (indirect materials of $100, indirect labor of $77, and miscellaneous cost of $100). Only $200 was applied to job 62 leaving an underapplied balance of $77. Actual overhead costs tend to fluctuate because of seasonal and other factors. Therefore, under- and overapplied balances are carried forward from month to month. In the final month of the accounting year such balances are closed—usually to Cost of Goods Sold.

Evaluation of the job order cost system

In some industries such as shipbuilding, where direct materials and direct labor can readily be traced to a specific unit of product, job order costing is almost a necessity. In low-volume or high-unit-cost situations where the product is produced on a special ''made-to-order'' basis, job order systems are appropriate. But job order systems are expensive to maintain. The need to trace carefully the time of individual direct labor personnel to a product requires extra effort. Separate materials requisitions must be made for each job number even though a number of jobs may be under way in the same department.

Some companies use job order procedures for part of their operations and process cost accounting procedures for other parts. Chapter 25 covers process cost accounting procedures.

Glossary

Applied manufacturing overhead The amount of overhead cost allocated (debited) to Work in Process using a predetermined rate.

Budget A financial plan for future operations.

Cost of goods sold An account used to accumulate the cost of goods that have been sold when a perpetual inventory system is used.

Cost sheet A record of costs of each job in a job order cost accounting system. The file of cost sheets is a subsidiary ledger to the account, Work in Process Inventory.

Direct labor Costs of labor that can be identified directly with a job.

Direct materials Materials issued that can be identified with a specific job.

Factory payroll An account used in cost accounting as a clearing account for factory labor costs. It is debited with the gross amount of factory labor. It is credited as direct labor is transferred into Work in Process and indirect labor is transferred into Manufacturing Overhead Control.

Indirect labor Cost of factory labor that cannot be identified with a specific job.

Indirect materials Materials used in production operations that cannot be identified to a specific job.

Job order cost system A cost accounting system that accumulates cost information by specific jobs. It is used in low-volume or high-unit-cost situations. It is needed when the product is custom made.

Manufacturing overhead control The account that accumulates actual charges to manufacturing other than direct materials and direct labor.

Materials requisition A source document used to withdraw materials from the storeroom for use in the production departments.

Predetermined overhead rate A rate, based upon budgeted overhead costs and planned production, used to apply (allocate) overhead charges to Work in Process Inventory.

Producing departments A department engaged directly in the production of goods for sale.

Product cost A cost incorporated in the inventories instead of being charged as an expense of the period (an inventoriable cost).

Time ticket A record of hours and rate that is prepared each time a person works on a job.

Unit cost The cost to produce one unit. When a job order calls for more than one unit, the unit cost is found by dividing total cost by the number of units.

Questions

Q24–1 What factors should be taken into account in deciding when to use a job order cost accounting system?

Q24–2 What subsidiary ledgers are controlled by (a) Work in Process Inventory, (b) Materials Inventory and (c) Finished Goods Inventory?

Q24–3 What is the function of a job order cost sheet?

Q24–4 What documents provide information for direct materials and direct labor costs on a job order cost sheet?

Q24–5 Under a job order cost accounting system does indirect labor ever become a part of Work in Process Inventory? Explain.

Q24–6 What is a manufacturing overhead rate? Explain how it is computed and some possible bases for establishing an overhead rate.

Q24–7 If the base used to determine the manufacturing overhead rate is direct labor cost, is the rate expressed in dollars or as a percent? Explain.

Q24–8 What is a budget? Why is the manufacturing overhead budget necessary to computation of the overhead rate?

Q24–9 What is the meaning of the term "applied" when it is used in connection with manufacturing overhead cost?

Q24–10 Diagram the flow of materials, labor and overhead costs from the time they are originally incurred until they become part of cost of goods sold. Use T accounts to do this.

Class exercises

CE24–1 (Use of cost sheet) Glen Ellyn Works uses a job order cost accounting system. For job number 0862 the following information is available:

DIRECT MATERIALS			DIRECT LABOR			
	Requisition			*Time Ticket*		
Date	*Number*	*Amount*	*Date*	*Number*	*Hours*	*Rate*
5-2-79	136	$201.50	5-2-79	3260	6	$7.00
5-4-79	182	60.00	5-3-79	3310	8	7.50
5-8-79	205	118.25	5-4-79	3331	8	7.50

The manufacturing overhead rate is $5 per direct labor hour.

Required:

1. Record the above data in a cost sheet similar to the one pictured in Figure 24–4.
2. If job number 0862 calls for production of 25 lawn sprinklers, what is the unit cost?

CE24–2 (Journal entry for completion of job) Following is the general ledger Work in Process account for a company for which posting is up to date in all ledgers.

Work In Process *Acct. No. 130*

Date		Explanation	F	Debit	Credit	Balance
1979						
May	30	(Materials)	J16	13,216 50		13,216 50
	30	(Labor)	J16	26,000 00		39,216 50
	30	(Manufacturing Overhead)	J16	39,000 00		78,216 50

Manufacturing overhead is applied on the basis of *direct labor cost.*

Required:

1. Compute the manufacturing overhead rate.
2. Job number 317 is completed on June 5, 1979, and transferred to the finished goods storeroom. Its total cost is $28,580. Prepare the journal entry to record the transfer.

CE24–3 (Computation of overhead rate) The Slager Boat Builders manufacturing overhead budget for 1979 is $1,000,000. Production plans call for 200,000 direct labor hours and a total direct labor cost of $1,250,000. Planned direct materials cost is $600,000.

Required: Compute the rate at which manufacturing overhead is to be applied to Work in Process Inventory if the base is:

1. Direct labor hours
2. Direct labor cost
3. Direct materials cost.

CE24–4 (Job order cost system) John Fletcher Ware Manufacturers completed the following transactions during the month of April 1979:

1. Purchased materials for $75,000.
2. Requisitioned materials for production as follows:

Job 101	$18,000
Job 102	12,000
Job 103	7,500
Job 104	4,500
	$42,000

3. Requisitioned materials for general factory use, $6,000 (debit Manufacturing Overhead Control).
4. Paid the factory payroll totaling $72,000 (ignore payroll taxes). The direct factory labor cost was distributed as follows.

	Hours	*Amount*
Job 101	7,500	$15,000
Job 102	4,500	9,000
Job 103	10,500	23,625
Job 104	9,000	20,250
		$67,875

Indirect labor used cost $4,125.

5. Incurred additional overhead costs of $64,125 (credit Accounts Payable).
6. Applied manufacturing overhead to job order cost sheets at the rate of $2.25 per direct labor hour.
7. Completed Jobs 101, 102, and 103 and transferred them to finished goods.
8. Sold Jobs 101 and 102 on account for $135,000.
9. Transferred the balance of Manufacturing Overhead Control to Cost of Goods Sold.

Required:

1. Prepare journal entries to record the transactions.
2. Post to a Work in Process Inventory account.
3. Post to a cost sheet for each of the four jobs.

Exercises and problems

P24–1 The cost sheet shown below was taken from the files of Dade Manufacturing Company.

Description 10 H.D. Dryers Job No. 820
Date Started 4-4-79 Date Completed 4-12-79
For Special Order

Direct Materials			Direct Labor			
Date	Requisition	Amount	Date	Time Ticket	Hours	Amount
4/4	028	38.50	4/4	1036	8	72.00
4/5	047	100.00	4/11	1213	8	80.00
4/6	049	20.00	4/12	1272	6	54.00

Summary

Direct Materials	$158.50
Direct Labor	206.00
Manufacturing Overhead . .	?
Total	$?

Overhead is applied at the rate of 150 percent of direct labor cost. The dryers were delivered to the finished goods storeroom on April 12, 1979, and to the customer for whom they were made on April 13, 1979. The contract price for this order was $90 per dryer.

Required:

1. Provide the missing figures on the cost sheet.
2. Prepare the journal entry for transfer of the job to the finished goods storeroom.
3. Prepare the journal entries for delivery to the customer.

P24–2 The information shown below was taken from the job order cost sheets in the files of DeKalb Company. All items manufactured prior to August 21, 1979, had been sold.

Job Order No.	*Balance September 1*	*Production Cost in September*	*Remarks*
531	$2,500.00	$ 0	Completed 8/21
532	3,000.00	0	Completed 8/30
533	840.00	2,340.00	Completed 9/6
534	540.00	2,460.00	Completed 9/13
535	420.00	2,520.00	Completed 9/21
536	0	2,088.00	Incomplete 9/30
537	0	1,092.00	Incomplete 9/30

Jobs 531, 532, and 533 were sold to customers in September.

Required: Compute balances of:
1. Work in Process Inventory at September 1.
2. Finished Goods Inventory at September 1.
3. Cost of Goods Sold in September.
4. Work in Process Inventory at September 30.
5. Finished Goods Inventory at September 30.

P24–3 The Work in Process Inventory account at the end of November 1979 is as follows:

Work In Process Inventory

Date		Explanation	F	Debit		Credit		Balance	
1979									
Nov.	30	(Direct Materials)	J60	30,000	00			30,000	00
	30	(Direct Labor)	J60	42,000	00			72,000	00
	30	(Manufacturing Overhead)	J61	21,000	00			93,000	00
	30	(To Finished Goods)	J62			87,000	00	6,000	00

Only job number 137 is in process after November 30, 1979. Direct materials charged to job number 137 total $1,500. Manufacturing overhead is applied to Work in Process Inventory on the basis of direct labor cost.

Required: Determine the amount charged to job number 137 for direct labor and the amount of manufacturing overhead applied to job 137.

P24–4 DeAnza Fabricators uses a job order cost accounting system in accounting for construction and sale of special design drilling equipment. During August 1979 the following summary transactions occurred:
1. Issued $40,000 of materials for use in jobs and $3,000 for general factory use.
2. Paid a factory payroll consisting of $50,000 of direct labor and $4,000 of indirect labor. There were no accrued wages at the beginning or the end of August. (Ignore payroll taxes.)
3. Applied manufacturing overhead at 75 percent of direct labor cost.
4. Completed jobs that cost $48,000.

Required: Prepare journal entries to record the transactions.

P24–5 Pharr Company has prepared its manufacturing overhead budget for 1979 at a total estimated cost of $840,000. Production schedules indicate usage of direct materials will be $1,050,000 and that 120,000 direct labor hours will be used at a cost of $700,000.

Required: Compute the manufacturing overhead rate for 1979 based on:
1. Direct labor hours
2. Direct labor cost
3. Direct materials cost.

P24–6 Walnut Construction Company completed construction of a special order snow removal machine on November 7, 1979. Total costs on the cost sheet at the time of completion were:

Direct materials	$21,200.35
Direct labor	12,327.62
Total	$33,527.97

Manufacturing overhead is applied at the rate of 80 percent of direct labor cost. The machine was delivered to the city maintenance department on November 9 at a contract price of $50,000.

Required:

1. The general journal entry to apply manufacturing overhead.
2. The general journal entry to record the completion of the job.
3. The general journal entries to record delivery to the city.
4. Assuming that this was the only job completed and sold in 1979, the entries to close accounts affecting this machine into Income Summary.

P24–7 (Integrative) The following were among the transactions completed by the Fruitvale Avenue Manufacturing Company during December 1979. There was no work in process on December 1, 1979.

1. Purchased materials on account for $54,000.
2. Requisitioned materials for production as follows:

Job 90	$12,000.00
Job 91	10,500.00
Job 92	13,500.00
Job 93	7,500.00
Total	$43,500.00

3. Requisitioned materials for general factory use, $4,500.
4. Paid the factory payroll for December amounting to $63,000. (Ignore payroll taxes.) Direct labor was distributed as follows:

Job 90	$15,000.00
Job 91	13,500.00
Job 92	17,250.00
Job 93	11,250.00
Total	$57,000.00

Indirect labor was $6,000. There were no accrued wages at the beginning or end of the month.

5. Recorded additional actual overhead costs for the month of $64,000. (Credit Various Accounts.)
6. Total direct labor hours worked on jobs were as follows:

Job 90	2,000
Job 91	1,800
Job 92	2,300
Job 93	1,500
Total	7,600 hours

   Manufacturing overhead is applied to jobs at the rate of $3 per direct labor hour.
7. Completed jobs 90, 91 and 93 and transferred them to finished goods inventory.
8. Sold jobs 90 and 93 on account for $105,000.

Required:
1. Journalize the transactions.
2. Post to a Work in Process Inventory account.
3. Prepare a cost sheet for each job and post the required cost data to them.
4. Verify the ending work-in-process inventory.

P24–8 (Minicase) Harper Constructors, Incorporated is a builder of mobile homes. Their output is about 10 homes per day. Although Harper produces several standard models for sale to dealers, about half of the company's work is done on a special-order basis. In such cases there are modifications to the basic design to suit the special needs of the buyer.

Harper Constructors carries an inventory of parts and supplies of about 1,500 different stock items. Orders for stock replenishment are placed each Thursday when the foreman makes a tour through the stockroom and makes a note of items that appear to be low in stock. It is frequently necessary to place long-distance telephone calls and pay air freight charges when an item runs out of stock. The cost of materials used is determined by computation after a monthly physical count has been made.

Each month the company accountant prepares a schedule of cost of goods manufactured. She cannot distinguish between direct and indirect materials or labor so she allocates 75 percent of each as direct and 25 percent as indirect. The allocation is not based on any type of study, but she feels it is fairly realistic. In order to determine the unit cost of a mobile home, she divides the number completed each month into total cost of goods manufactured.

The company's board of directors is interested in applying for listing of their stock on a national stock exchange, but feels that it would not be accepted by the exchange because of its poor accounting system.

Required: Prepare a proposal for an accounting system for Harper Constructors, Incorporated that would best suit their needs. Include recommendations in detail for a system, the general ledger accounts needed, and specific source documents that should be used.

chapter twenty-five

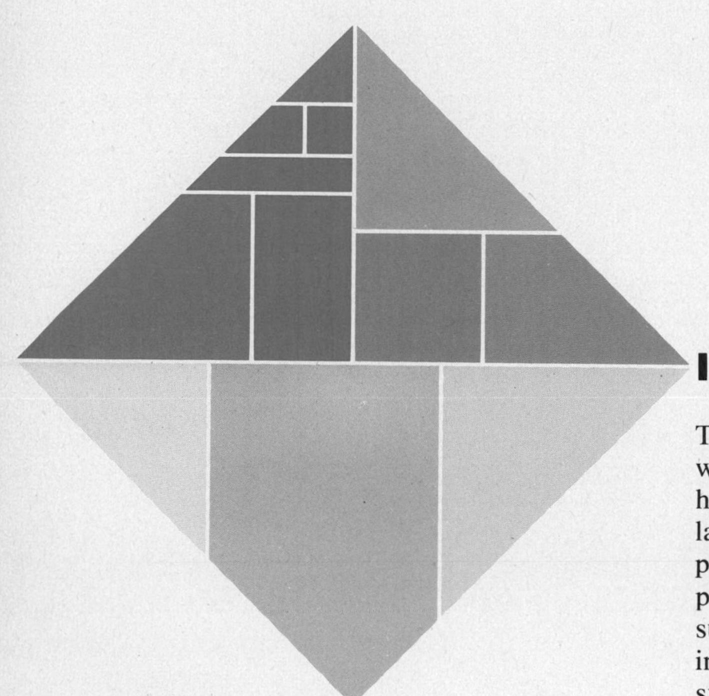

Introduction

Thus far, only job order cost accounting, where costs are identified with specific jobs, has been considered. In many companies large quantities of identical units of product—for example, aspirin tablets—are produced in a continuous flow through successive departments. This chapter introduces the process cost accounting system used by such companies in which the manufacturing process is continuous and uniform.

Process cost accounting

Learning goals

To apply the concept of cost accumulation by departments or cost centers.
To describe the flow of costs in a process cost accounting system.
To define the *concept* of equivalent units.
To compute equivalent units and unit costs for materials, labor, and overhead.
To understand a *cost of production report*.
To record the journal entries for the flow of costs in a process cost accounting system.

Key terms

cost center
cost of production report
cost schedule
equivalent production units
prior department costs
process cost system
quantity schedule
unit cost

In a process cost accounting system, costs are identified with each department. A record is maintained of the work done in each department in terms of units of product. Unit cost is then determined by dividing total units produced into total departmental costs. The focus, then, is on units of the organization, rather than on specific jobs. Accordingly, there will be a change in the Work in Process Inventory account from a single account for all jobs in process to a separate account for each department. In place of a set of cost sheets to serve as a subsidiary ledger for Work in Process Inventory, a monthly departmental *cost of production report* is produced. This report is useful not only in determining unit costs but also in managerial control in the company.

The cost center

Process cost accounting systems do more than enable the determination of cost per unit of product. They also make it possible to accumulate costs by departments or *cost centers*.

Cost center

A **cost center** *is the lowest level organizational unit in the company to which management has decided that specific costs will be directly identified as the responsibility of the supervisor of that unit.*

A production department—for example, the Finishing Department—may be a cost center. However, a department may contain two or more cost centers. Suppose finishing is made up of two distinct operations, polishing and packaging. If costs can be identified directly with each operation, the Finishing Department could have two cost centers if it serves management's purpose best to accumulate costs for each of these two units of the company. For each cost center, there is a separate Work in Process Inventory account. If the Finishing Department is considered to be the cost center, its account would be Work in Process—Finishing. Management may want to identify separately costs that are the responsibility of the two supervisors of polishing and packaging. If so, two accounts, Work in Process—Polishing and Work in Process—Packaging, would be used. Each of those two units is designated as a cost center. In the illustration of process cost accounting in this chapter each cost center will be a production department.

Flow of costs in a process cost system

The distinction between direct and indirect materials and labor in a process cost system is different from a job order cost system. Costs are *direct costs* whenever they can be identified with a specific production department (or cost center). Only materials and labor that cannot be traced to a single department are *indirect*. As in a job order system, if the cost cannot be traced directly it becomes a part of manufacturing overhead.

The flow of costs in a process cost system is illustrated in Figure 25–1. As in a job order system, the costs begin with charges to Materials Inventory, Factory Payroll, and Manufacturing Overhead accounts. As work goes on, the costs move into the Work In Process accounts. There is a separate Work in Process account for each cost center. In Figure 25–1 the flow is first into Work in Process—Cooking Department then into Work in Process—Finishing Department and finally into Finished Goods Inventory.

The accounting system—especially in the Work in Process Inventory accounts—follows the actual flow of resources through the production process. Figure 25–2 diagrams the flow of resources. Materials, labor, and overhead arc used in a succession of departments in a continuous flow until the completed

Figure 25–1
Flow chart for process cost system

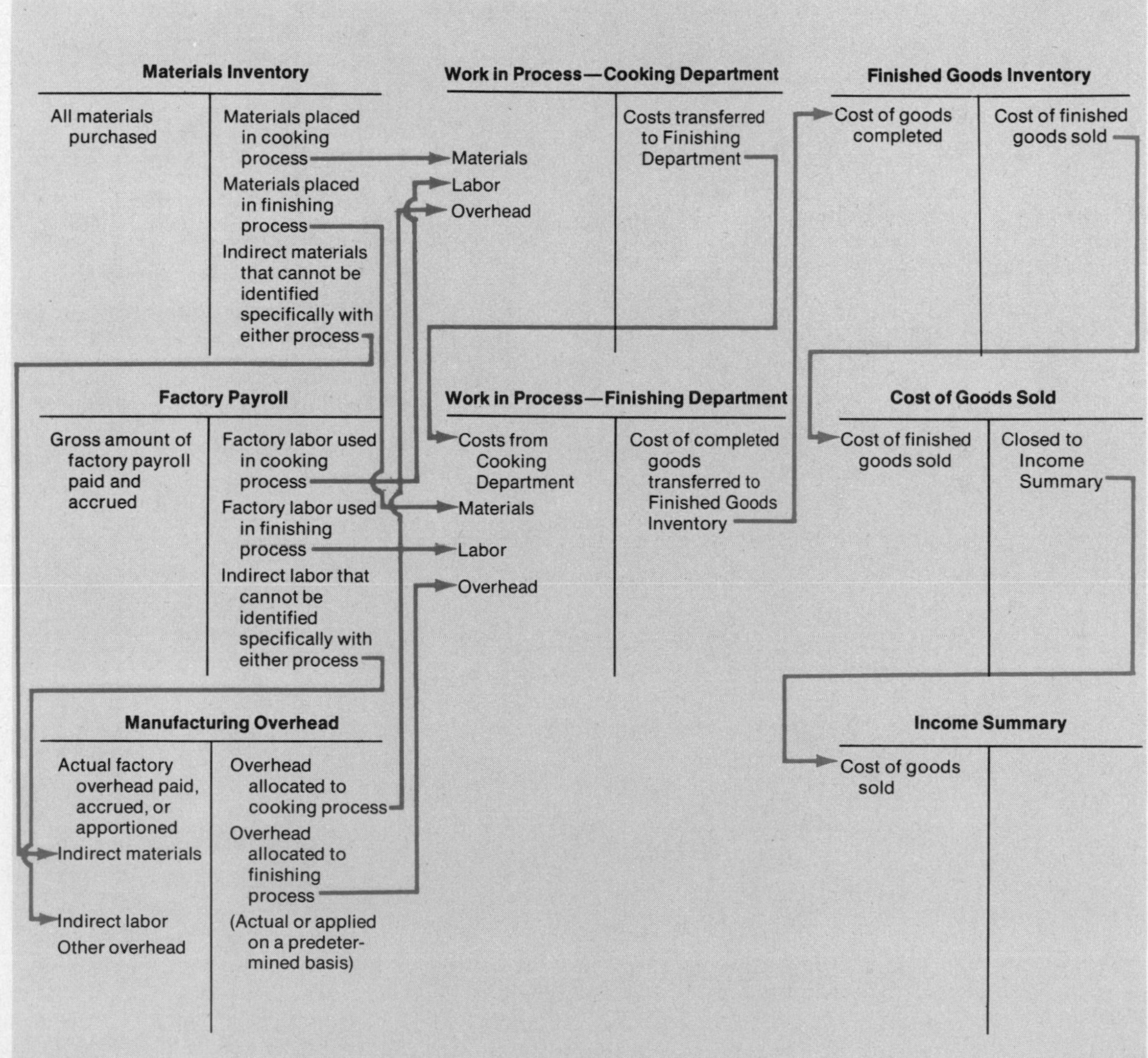

Figure 25–2
Flow of resources in a process system

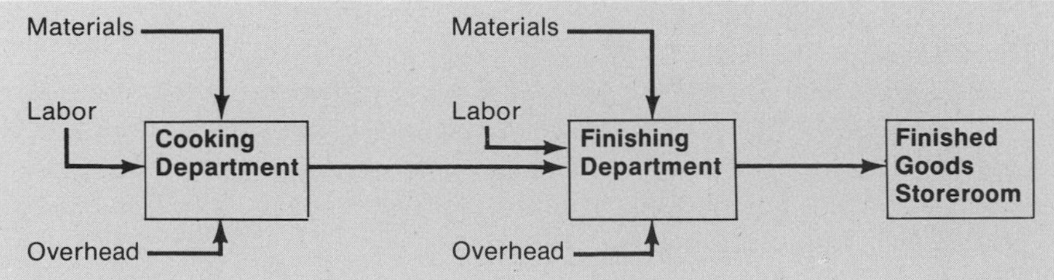

product finally ends up in the finished goods inventory. In a process cost accounting system we capture the costs in each department or cost center *and add them to get the total cost* of making the product. For the production process diagrammed in Figure 25–2 unit costs are determined as the product leaves the Cooking Department. To that cost is added the costs incurred in the finishing department. The cumulative amount is the cost to be debited to Finished Goods Inventory.

Process cost accounting illustration

The Pompano Chemical Company produces a single product named Browardmint that is processed in two departments, Cooking and Finishing. On July 1, 1979, there is no beginning work in process inventory in the Cooking Department. During July 50,000 units of Browardmint are started in the Cooking Department; of this amount 40,000 units are completely processed and transferred to the Finishing Department. As of July 31, 10,000 units are still in the cooking process—these 10,000 units are 100 percent complete as to materials and 50 percent complete as to labor and overhead. The July costs in the Cooking Department are:

Direct materials	$10,000.00
Direct labor	13,500.00
Manufacturing overhead	11,250.00

In the Finishing Department, there is a beginning (July 1) work in process inventory of 4,000 units. These units are 75 percent complete as to labor and overhead; no materials are added in the Finishing Department. During July 40,000 units are received from the Cooking Department. Of the 44,000 units of Browardmint to be accounted for in the Finishing Department, 38,000 are finished and transferred to Finished Goods Inventory leaving, on July 31, 6,000 units still in process in Finishing. These 6,000 units in the Finishing Department's ending work in process inventory are 33⅓ percent complete as to labor and overhead. The dollar figures for July in the Finishing Department are:

July 1 Work In Process Inventory	$ 5,300.00
July costs:	
Direct materials	–0–
Direct labor	14,800.00
Manufacturing overhead	13,320.00

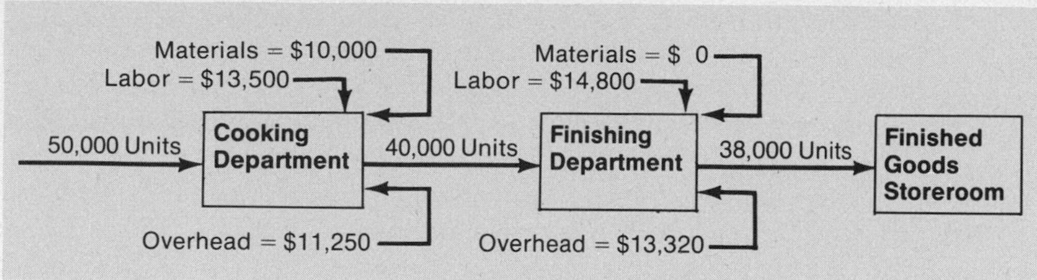

Figure 25–3
Pompano Chemical Company—July production

The situation just described is diagrammed in Figure 25–3. The beginning and ending work in process inventories are not shown in the diagram, but are an important part of computation of the unit costs in each department.

Allocation of costs in cooking department

Quantity schedule A *quantity schedule* is prepared for each department, showing the number of units of the product processed during a given period. Such a schedule for the Cooking Department is illustrated in Figure 25–4. The stage of completion for the July 31 work in process inventory is an average estimate; in other words, the Browardmint that has just entered the Cooking Department has material added but no labor or overhead; the Browardmint that is almost ready to leave Cooking has almost all the labor and overhead absorbed; thus, the average work in process *in this case* has all the material cost and one-half the labor and overhead costs.

Figure 25–4
Quantity schedule, cooking department

	Units	
Quantity to be accounted for		
Units in process at beginning of period	-0-	
Units started in process	50,000	
Total	50,000	
Quantity accounted for		
Transferred to Finishing Department	40,000	
Units still in process at end of period	10,000	(all material, 1/2 L and O)
Total	50,000	

Schedule of equivalent production Equivalent production is the finished unit equivalent of the units completely and partially processed in a given period. In other words, *it is the number of whole units that could have been completed if all the effort and costs for the period had been applied only to wholly finished units*. The changing of work in process units to the equivalent of whole units is necessary when computing unit costs. Also, there may be a different number of units—called *equivalent production units*—for material, for labor and for overhead. The schedule of equivalent production for the Cooking Department is illustrated in Figure 25–5.

In the Cooking Department, there is no beginning work in process inventory to complete; hence zeros are entered in the Materials column and in the Labor and Overhead column (Figure 25–5). Units started and finished in this period (July) totaled 40,000 and are shown in both the Materials column and the Labor and Overhead column. Units *started and finished* are those units that were begun this period with no prior period work in them and completely finished in the department in this period. The amount of such units is computed by subtracting the number of units in beginning work in process from units transferred out. The ending work in process inventory consists of 10,000 units. Its stage of completion is such that all the materials have been received (10,000 is entered in the Materials column), and one-half labor and overhead has been done (5,000 is entered in the Labor and Overhead column). It is assumed that the costs expended in completing one-half the work on 10,000 units are the same as the cost of completing 5,000 units.

Figure 25–5
Schedule of equivalent production, cooking department

	Materials		Labor and Overhead	
Beginning work in process inventory (to complete)	-0-		-0-	
Units started and finished (this period)	40,000		40,000	
Equivalent whole units contained in ending work in process inventory (stage of completion)	10,000	= (10,000 × 100%)	5,000	= (10,000 × 1/2)
Equivalent production units	50,000		45,000	

Unit cost computation Unit costs are computed for each element—materials, labor, and overhead. Each cost element in the Total Cost column is divided by the corresponding equivalent units produced to determine the *unit costs* as indicated in Figure 25–6.

Figure 25–6
Unit cost computation, cooking department

	A	÷	B	=	C
Element	Total Cost		Equivalent Units		Unit Cost
Materials	$10,000.00		50,000		$0.20
Labor	13,500.00		45,000		0.30
Overhead	11,250.00		45,000		0.25
Totals	$34,750.00				$0.75

Accumulated cost distribution The total accumulated cost of the Cooking Department ($34,750) is divided between the ending work in process inventory and the 40,000 units transferred to the next department. The ending work in process inventory is valued as follows:

Materials	10,000 units × $0.20	$2,000.00
Labor	10,000 units × 1/2 × $0.30	1,500.00
Overhead	10,000 units × 1/2 × $0.25	1,250.00
Work in Process Inventory—Cooking Department, July 31, 1979		$4,750.00

The cost of the 40,000 units transferred to the Finishing Department is computed as follows:

Cost in the beginning work in process inventory	$ –0–
Cost to complete the beginning work in process inventory	–0–
Cost of units started and completed in July (40,000 × $0.75)	30,000.00
Total cost of goods transferred to next department	$30,000.00

The section of the cost of production report (Figure 25–7) that displays the accumulated cost distribution is called the *cost schedule*.

Cost of production report At the end of each month the accountant prepares for each department a *cost of production report*. The parts of the cost of production report for Pompano Chemical Company's Cooking Department have been developed in this illustration. Figure 25–7 combines all of these elements to provide to management an overview of production activity for July 1979.

POMPANO CHEMICAL COMPANY—COOKING DEPARTMENT
Cost of Production Report
For The Month Ended July 31, 1979

Quantity Schedule	Units	
Quantity to be accounted for		
Units in process, July 1	–0–	
Units started in process	50,000	50,000
Quantity accounted for		
Transferred to next department	40,000	
Units in process, July 31	10,000	50,000
Cost Schedule	Total Costs	Unit Costs
Work in process, July 1	$ –0–	--
Costs added in July		
Materials	10,000.00	$0.20
Labor	13,500.00	0.30
Overhead	11,250.00	0.25
Total to be accounted for	$34,750.00	
Transferred to next department	$30,000.00	$0.75
Work in process, July 31	4,750.00	
Total accounted for	$34,750.00	

Computation of Unit Costs

$$\text{Materials} = \frac{\$10{,}000 \text{ July costs}}{50{,}000 \text{ equivalent units}} = \$0.20$$

$$\text{Labor} = \frac{\$13{,}500 \text{ July costs}}{45{,}000 \text{ equivalent units}} = \$0.30$$

$$\text{Overhead} = \frac{\$11{,}250 \text{ July costs}}{45{,}000 \text{ equivalent units}} = \$0.25$$

Figure 25–7 Cooking department cost of production report

Allocation of costs in finishing department

Quantity schedule The quantity schedule for the Finishing Department is shown in Figure 25–8.

Figure 25–8 Quantity schedule, finishing department

	Units*	
Quantity to be accounted for		
Units in process at beginning of period	4,000	(3/4 L and O)
Units received from Cooking Department	40,000	
Total	44,000	
Quantity accounted for		
Transferred to Finished Goods Inventory	38,000	
Units still in process at end of period	6,000	(1/3 L and O)
Total	44,000	

*No materials are added in the Finishing Department.

Schedule of equivalent units The 4,000 units in the beginning work in process inventory were three-fourths complete as to the elements of labor and overhead on July 1. Therefore, these 4,000 units receive the last one-fourth of their labor and overhead during this cost period (July). Each should be equated with one-fourth of a unit of labor and of overhead. Consequently, 1,000 units = (4,000 units × 1/4) are entered in the L and O column, as shown in Figure 25–9. The number of units started and finished during this period is determined as follows:

[Units transferred to finished goods inventory (38,000)] − [Units in beginning work in process inventory (4,000)] = [Units started and finished (34,000)]

These 34,000 units are recorded in the L and O column. Each unit in the ending work in process inventory of 6,000 units received one-third of its labor and overhead this month. The stage of completion of the ending work in process inventory, expressed in terms of whole units, is 2,000 = (6,000 units × 1/3). This figure is recorded in the L and O column. The total of the L and O column (37,000 units) represents equivalent production units for the month of July.

Figure 25–9 Schedule of equivalent production, finishing department

	Materials	L and O	
Beginning work in process inventory (to complete)	–0–	1,000	= (4,000 units × 1/4)
Units started and finished	–0–	34,000	
Equivalent whole units contained in ending work in process inventory (stage of completion)	–0–	2,000	= (6,000 units × 1/3)
Equivalent production units	–0–	37,000	

Unit cost computation Since no materials are added in the Finishing Department, the departmental unit cost is computed by dividing the cost of labor and overhead added in July by the equivalent production for July. This computation is shown in Figure 25-10.

Figure 25-10 Unit cost computation, finishing department

Element	A Total Cost	÷	B Equivalent Production	=	C Unit Cost
Labor	$14,800.00		37,000		$0.40
Overhead	13,320.00		37,000		0.36
Totals	$28,120.00				$0.76

Accumulated cost distribution The total cost to be accounted for in the Finishing Department is shown as follows:

Work in Process Inventory (July 1) beginning	$ 5,300.00
Cost from the preceding department, the Cooking Department, transferred to the Finishing Department during July :	
40,000 units (unit cost $0.75)	30,000.00
Cost added to the foregoing units by the Finishing Department during July (labor and overhead only)	28,120.00
Total cost for which an accounting must be made	$63,420.00

This cost is accounted for by the amount assigned to the 38,000 units finished and transferred to the storeroom and the amount assigned to the July 31 work in process inventory. The beginning work in process inventory and the new July production (started and finished) are typically recorded separately and are costed on the FIFO basis; that is, the beginning work in process inventory is assumed to be completed before the new production is completed and costed. The cost of the completed 4,000 units which were in the July 1 (beginning) work in process inventory, the cost of the new production of 34,000 units which were started and finished during July, and the cost of the 6,000 units in the July 31 (ending) work in process inventory are shown as follows:

Accumulated Cost Distribution (Finishing Department)			
The completed cost of the 4,000 units in the beginning work in process inventory:			
Cost of the July 1 Work in Process Inventory, from June		$5,300.00	
Added July cost to complete these 4,000 units:			
Labor added 4,000 × 1/4 × $0.40	$400.00		
Overhead added 4,000 × 1/4 × $0.36	360.00	760.00	
Total cost of the 4,000 completed (unit cost, $1.515 = $6,060 ÷ 4,000)			$ 6,060.00

The completed cost of the new production, the units started and finished during July:		
34,000 × $1.51		51,340.00
Total cost of the 38,000 units completed		$57,400.00
The cost of the Work in Process Inventory, July 31:		
Cost from the Cooking Department		
6,000 × $0.75	$4,500.00	
Labor added during July		
6,000 × 1/3 × $0.40	800.00	
Overhead added during July		
6,000 × 1/3 × $0.36	720.00	
The cost of the Work in Process Inventory, July 31		6,020.00
Total accumulated cost distribution		$63,420.00

It should be observed that the total cost of the first 4,000 units finished and transferred to finished goods is $6,060, or $1.515 per unit. The 34,000 new units that were started and completed in July have a cost of $0.75 carried forward from the Cooking Department plus $0.76 added in Finishing. The $0.75 per unit cost carried from cooking to finishing is known in the Finishing Department as *prior department cost*. Thus, a cumulative unit cost of $1.51 applies to those 34,000 units. The overall unit cost is $1.5105 = ($57,400 ÷ 38,000).

Cost of production report

The schedule of equivalent production, the quantity schedule, the accumulated costs, and the distribution of these for the Finishing Department are combined into a cost of production report in Figure 25–11.

Flow of process costs—summary journal entries

Summary entries to record the flow of costs for the Pompano Chemical Company follow Figure 25–11 (assuming that the same units manufactured were sold).

When the finished goods are sold, the costs are transferred to Cost of Goods Sold, entry (f), and the customers are billed for the sales. The entry to record the billing of customers would be a debit to Accounts Receivable and a credit to Sales at the selling price. It should be noted that the accountant of the Pompano Chemical Company was able to assign all materials and labor costs to the applicable department; hence, none of these costs had to be considered as manufacturing overhead.

Figure 25–11 Finishing department cost of production report

POMPANO CHEMICAL COMPANY—FINISHING DEPARTMENT
Cost of Production Report
For the Month Ended July 31, 1979

Quantity Schedule	Units	
Quantity to be accounted for		
Units in process, July 1	4,000	
Received from prior department	40,000	44,000
Quantity accounted for		
Transferred to finished goods	38,000	
Units in process, July 31	6,000	44,000
Cost Schedule	**Total Cost**	**Unit Cost**
Work in process, July 1	$ 5,300.00	--
Cost added in July:		
Prior department costs	30,000.00	$0.75
Labor	14,800.00	0.40
Overhead	13,320.00	0.36
Total to be accounted for	$63,420.00	
Transferred to Finished Goods	$57,400.00	$1.5105
Work in process, July 31	6,020.00	
Total accounted for	$63,420.00	

Computation of Unit Costs
Prior department costs (see Figure 25-7) = $0.75

$$\text{Labor} = \frac{\$14{,}800 \text{ July costs}}{37{,}000 \text{ equivalent units}} = \$0.40$$

$$\text{Overhead} = \frac{\$13{,}320 \text{ July costs}}{37{,}000 \text{ equivalent units}} = \$0.36$$

Date		Account	Debit	Credit
		(a)		
1979 Jul.	31	Work in Process—Cooking Department	10,000 00	
		Materials Inventory		10,000 00
		To record issuance of direct materials in July.		
		(b)		
	31	Work in Process—Cooking Department	13,500 00	
		Work in Process—Finishing Department	14,800 00	
		Factory Payroll		28,300 00
		To record direct labor costs in July.		
		(c)		
	31	Work in Process—Cooking Department	11,250 00	
		Work in Process—Finishing Department	13,320 00	
		Manufacturing Overhead		24,570 00
		To record manufacturing overhead applied in July.		
		(d)		
	31	Work in Process-Finishing Department	30,000 00	
		Work in Process-Cooking Department		30,000 00
		To record transfer of 40,000 units to Finishing Department.		
		(e)		
	31	Finished Goods Inventory	57,400 00	
		Work in Process—Finishing Department		57,400 00
		To record transfer of 38,000 units of Browardmint to finished goods storeroom.		
		(f)		
	31	Cost of Goods Sold	57,400 00	
		Finished Goods Inventory		57,400 00
		To record cost of sale of 38,000 units of Browardmint.		

Despite their value to managers in the planning and control process, job order and process cost accounting systems are limited to recording historical costs. The next chapter will take up a modification of these systems that allows the accountant to record what costs ought to be as well as what costs actually are. That system is called a *standard cost accounting* system.

Glossary

Cost center An organizational unit for which costs are accumulated within a firm. The commonly-used cost center in this chapter is a producing department.

Cost of production report A report combining the quantity schedule, equivalent units of production, the accumulated costs, the distribution of cost, and the calculation of unit costs for each department.

Cost schedule A segment of a cost of production report. It shows total and unit costs.

Equivalent units The total work done in a department expressed in terms of whole units even though some are only partly completed.

Prior department costs Costs attaching to units of product received from a prior department. These are costs already invested in the product in one or more departments before it is received to be worked on in the present department.

Process cost system A cost accounting system appropriate for production operations that make large quantities of identical product in a continuous process. Costs are traced to and identified with producing segments (departments or other cost centers) rather than to jobs.

Producing department A department engaged directly in the production of the product being manufactured.

Quantity schedule A schedule accounting for the number of units of product worked on in a given time period.

Unit cost The cost per unit of product of the work done in a production department. It is computed by dividing equivalent units into current period costs for materials, labor, and overhead.

Questions

Q25–1 What type of industry is likely to use a process cost system? Give some examples.

Q25–2 What are the major differences between a process cost system and a job order cost system? What are the major similarities?

Q25–3 What is the function of a quantity schedule?

Q25–4 What are equivalent units of work done? Are they concerned with percentage of completion?

Q25–5 Distinguish between a quantity schedule and a schedule of equivalent units.

Q25–6 Do costs incurred in a prior department show on the cost schedule for the present department? Why or why not?

Q25–7 Student A says that it should only be necessary to prepare a production cost report for the last department that works on a product because it contains cumulative cost. Do you agree? Explain.

Q25–8 What help would it be to management to compare production cost reports for a department for consecutive months? What specific bits of information might be studied and why?

Q25–9 Is it necessary to prepare a time ticket in Department A each time a person changes jobs? Explain.

Q25–10 Does a process cost system eliminate the need for materials requisitions? Explain.

Class exercises

CE25–1 (Quantity schedule) Western Company began August 1979 with 17,000 units in process in Department A. During the month 33,000 units were added. 32,000 units were completed and transferred to Department B. No units were lost or spoiled in process.

Required: Prepare a quantity schedule for August.

CE25–2 (Equivalent units) Seacoast Manufacturers began February 1979 with 1,000 units in process in the Mixing Department. These 1,000 units were 100 percent complete as to materials and 70 percent complete as to labor and overhead. 5,000 units were completed and transferred to the Forming Department. At the end of February there were 500 units in process in Mixing that were 100 percent complete as to materials and 50 percent complete as to labor and overhead.

Required: Compute equivalent units of work done in the Mixing Department in February.

CE25–3 (Cost computation) The following information is taken from the books of the Clouse Company in August 1979:

Schedule of Equivalent Production

	Materials	*L and O*
Equivalent production of Clousite	15,000	12,000

The beginning work in process inventory consisted of 1,500 units, 70 percent complete as to materials and 40 percent complete as to direct labor and overhead. The August 1979 cost to manufacture was:

Materials	$ 45,000.00
Direct labor	36,000.00
Manufacturing overhead	30,000.00
Total	$111,000.00

Cost of the beginning work in process inventory was $8,400. There were 7,500 units of Clousite started and finished during August.

Required: Compute the total cost of only the 7,500 units that were started and finished during August 1979.

Exercises and problems

P25–1 The following information is taken from the records of a firm that produces one standardized product in a single process:

a. Beginning work in process inventory: 3,000 units 75 percent complete as to materials and 40 percent complete as to direct labor and manufacturing overhead.
b. Finished and transferred to finished goods inventory: 90,000 units during the period.
c. Ending work in process inventory: 1,500 units, 60 percent complete as to materials and 20 percent complete as to direct labor and manufacturing overhead.

Required: Compute the equivalent production for each element of cost for the period.

P25–2 Cost information for Department 3 of the Crisp Company for June is shown below (there was no beginning work in process inventory).

	Total Cost	*Unit Cost*
Production costs		
Costs from preceding department	$270,000.00	$1.80
Costs added during June within department:		
Materials	$ 60,000.00	
Direct labor	82,800.00	
Manufacturing overhead	27,600.00	
Total costs added	$170,400.00	
Total costs	$440,400.00	

The quantity schedule is:

	Units
Quantity to be accounted for	
Units transferred from Department 2	150,000
Quantity accounted for	
Units completed and transferred to storeroom	132,000
Units unfinished at end of month	18,000
Total	150,000

The work in process in Department 3 at the end of June is complete as to materials and one-third complete as to direct labor and manufacturing overhead.

Required:

1. Compute the equivalent units of work in June in Department 3.
2. Compute the unit cost of production in Department 3 for materials, labor, and manufacturing overhead added in Department 3.
3. Compute the total cost and unit cost of goods transferred to finished goods inventory.
4. Compute the cost of the work in process inventory in Department 3 at the end of June.

Show computations in good form.

P25–3 The Merrimack Company had production costs for 1979 as follows:

Materials	$280,000.00
Labor	296,000.00
Overhead	206,000.00

On January 1, 1979, the Finished Goods Inventory account appeared as follows:

Finished Goods Inventory

Date		Explanation	F	Debit		Credit		Balance	
1979 Jan.	1	Balance (12,000 units)		120,000	00			120,000	00

There was no beginning or ending work in process. During 1979, 78,990 units of product were completed and transferred into the finished goods storeroom. On December 31, 1979, there were 8,500 finished units on hand.

Required:

1. Cost of goods sold assuming that the Finished Goods Inventory is costed on a FIFO assumption.
2. Value of Finished Goods Inventory on December 31, 1979.

P25–4 The Fruitvale Manufacturing Company began operations on January 1, 1979. It plans to manufacture a single standardized product called Enzo, which requires a single process.

During January it started and finished 12,000 units of Enzo. There was no January 31 work in process inventory. The company's costs for January were:

Materials	$ 78,000.00
Direct labor	102,000.00
Manufacturing overhead	122,400.00
Total	$302,400.00

During February, the company started and finished 13,500 units of Enzo; it had 600 units in process as of February 28, 1979, in the following stage of completion:

Materials	75%
Direct labor and manufacturing overhead	50%

Costs for February were:

Materials	$ 86,490.00
Direct labor	113,160.00
Manufacturing overhead	135,792.00
Total	$335,442.00

During March, the company completed 15,000 units, including the beginning work in process inventory. It had 750 units in process as of March 31 in the following stage of completion:

Materials	100%
Direct labor and manufacturing overhead	60%

Costs for March were:

Materials	$ 91,800.00
Direct labor	121,200.00
Manufacturing overhead	145,440.00
Total	$358,440.00

Required: For each month, where applicable (a) prepare a schedule of equivalent production; (b) compute the unit of cost of materials, direct labor, and manufacturing overhead; (c) compute the total cost to be accounted for; (d) compute the cost of completed units; and (e) compute the cost of the ending work in process inventory.

P25–5 The Chula Vista Company makes a product in two processes. In both processes all materials are added when the units of the product are started in the processing. During July 1979, the company started 12,000 units in Process 1; 9,000 units were completed and sent to Process 2. The remaining 3,000 were one-half complete in Process 1. There were 1,500 units three-quarters complete in Process 2 at the beginning of the month; at the end of the month 2,700 were on hand, two-thirds complete. The following costs were incurred:

	Process 1	*Process 2*
Beginning work in process inventory	$ –0–	$13,005.00
Materials	36,000.00	3,900.00
Labor	16,800.00	8,475.00
Manufacturing overhead	23,100.00	6,780.00

Required: (For each process separately)

1. Calculate the equivalent units produced.
2. Calculate the unit cost of material, direct labor, and overhead for July.
3. Calculate the cost of the units completed and transferred.
4. Calculate the cost of the ending work in process inventory in each process.

P25–6 (Integrative) The Seattle Chemical Company manufactures a product in two processes: grinding and blending. All materials go into process at the beginning in the Grinding Department, but are added continuously in the Blending Department. During September, the company started 36,000 units in the Grinding Department; at the end of the month 6,000 of them remained in the work in process inventory, one-quarter complete. The others went to the Blending Department, where there were 9,000 units, one-third complete, at the start of the month, and 12,000 units, three-quarters complete, at the end. Costs were as follows:

	Department	
	Grinding	*Blending*
Work in process, August 31	$ –0–	$27,360.00
Direct materials	39,600.00	16,500.00
Direct labor	22,050.00	26,400.00
Manufacturing overhead	15,750.00	21,450.00

Required: Prepare a cost of production report for each department.

P25–7 (Minicase) In the first six months of 1979, unit costs of the Miranda Company's single product were as follows:

January	$4.98	April	$5.01
February	6.02	May	6.30
March	3.80	June	3.95

Mr. Miranda had the accounting department install a process cost accounting system on January 1, 1979. His plant has only one producing department, and he feels that these variations in reported unit costs are too significant to ignore.

As an independent accountant, you have been asked to look over his cost accounting methods to determine the reasons for the differences in unit costs.

Required: Draw up a check list of practices and methods that you would investigate before making a report to Mr. Miranda.

chapter twenty-six

Introduction

In the first chapter of this book two functions of management, *planning* and *controlling,* were described as examples of internal uses of accounting information. This chapter is about planning and controlling. It contains a discussion of profit planning and an example of the budget formulation process. The concept of responsibility accounting is introduced along with the use of flexible budgets and the use of standards in a cost accounting system is shown in an illustration.

Forecasting, budgeting, and standard cost accounting

Learning goals

To differentiate between fixed and variable costs.

To know the basic concepts of budget preparation and profit planning.

To describe a typical budget structure.

To formulate specific budget schedules beginning with a sales forecast.

To know how to use specific budget schedules to prepare a projected income statement.

To define the concept of a flexible budget.

To discuss the control function and the concepts of responsibility accounting.

To understand the concept of standards applied to a cost accounting system.

Key terms

budget
cash forecast
controlling
fixed costs
flexible budget
labor efficiency variance
labor rate variance
materials price variance
materials quantity variance
performance report
planning
profit planning
projected statements
relevant volume range
responsibility accounting
standards
standard cost card
standard costs
standard cost system
variable costs
variance

Budget: the basic planning tool

Profit planning is carried out by the use of budgets. As defined in Chapter 1, a *budget* is a financial plan for a future period. Budgets are usually prepared on a short-term basis; the most common time period used is one year. All individuals and groups perform budgeting to some degree. John Smith, before leaving school for a weekend at the beach, gives some thought to the expenses he will have and to how he plans to meet them. Families tend to budget on a month-to-month basis. Most do not prepare a formal written budget, but they do have knowledge of upcoming expenditures such as house payments, utility bills, food bills, and other items that tend to recur each month. They also have a fairly good idea of the amount of take-home pay that can be expected to meet expenses. Unfortunately, most families—and many businesses—never get beyond this informal stage. For a business, the failure to establish and use a formal budget structure often results in (1) lost sales due to underproduction, (2) excess inventory costs due to overproduction, (3) excessive personnel turnover, and (4) general lack of control over the outcome of business operations in terms of profits. The result for many firms is a business failure that might have been avoided by profit planning.

The nature of costs

Fundamental to budgeting and profit planning is a knowledge of the patterns of cost (cost behavior) within the various cost elements. Costs can generally be classified as fixed or variable. A *fixed cost* remains the same *in total* regardless of changes in volume of production. Total *variable cost* changes directly in proportion to changes in volume. If volume in the second quarter is 120 percent of volume in the first quarter of the year, we would expect building rent, depreciation, or property taxes to remain the same. They are examples of fixed cost. However, we would expect direct labor or direct materials usage to increase by 20 percent, because they are examples of variable cost.

Some costs are neither fixed nor variable, but tend to be *semifixed* or *semivariable*. We may need one inspector if output is between zero and 500 units per day; at 501 units a second inspector must be added. Within a limited volume range, however, all costs can be separated into fixed and variable components. This volume range over which cost behavior can be predicted is called the *relevant volume range* or *relevant range*.[1]

The budget structure

The budget planning process must begin with a forecast of sales known as the *sales budget*. The sales budget is usually prepared in detail by product and by

1 Obviously, cost behavior patterns are not stable over the entire range of production possibilities from zero to 100 percent of capacity. Somewhere between those two extremes is a range—different for each firm—over which costs can be predicted to follow a pattern. It is this range that is relevant to production planning.

territory. Several techniques are used to develop a sales forecast. One method is to ask salespersons to submit an estimate of the quantities they expect to sell in the next year. Another approach is to study sales from the customers' point of view by conducting a market survey in which customers are asked what they plan to buy. A third method in common use is to project trends by using historical data from the accounting records and adjust the trends by a factor which reflects the amount of price competition in the particular industry, the state of the economy and the effect it is estimated these factors will have on sales of specific products in the coming year.

Figure 26–1 pictures a typical budget structure for a manufacturing business. With the sales budget prepared a company can then develop supporting budget schedules. For a manufacturer, the major supporting schedule is the *production budget*. After production requirements are known, schedules can be developed for labor costs, materials costs, and manufacturing overhead costs. Each of these is a separate budget and, as shown in Figure 26–1, flows from information contained in the production budget.

Figure 26–1
Budget structure

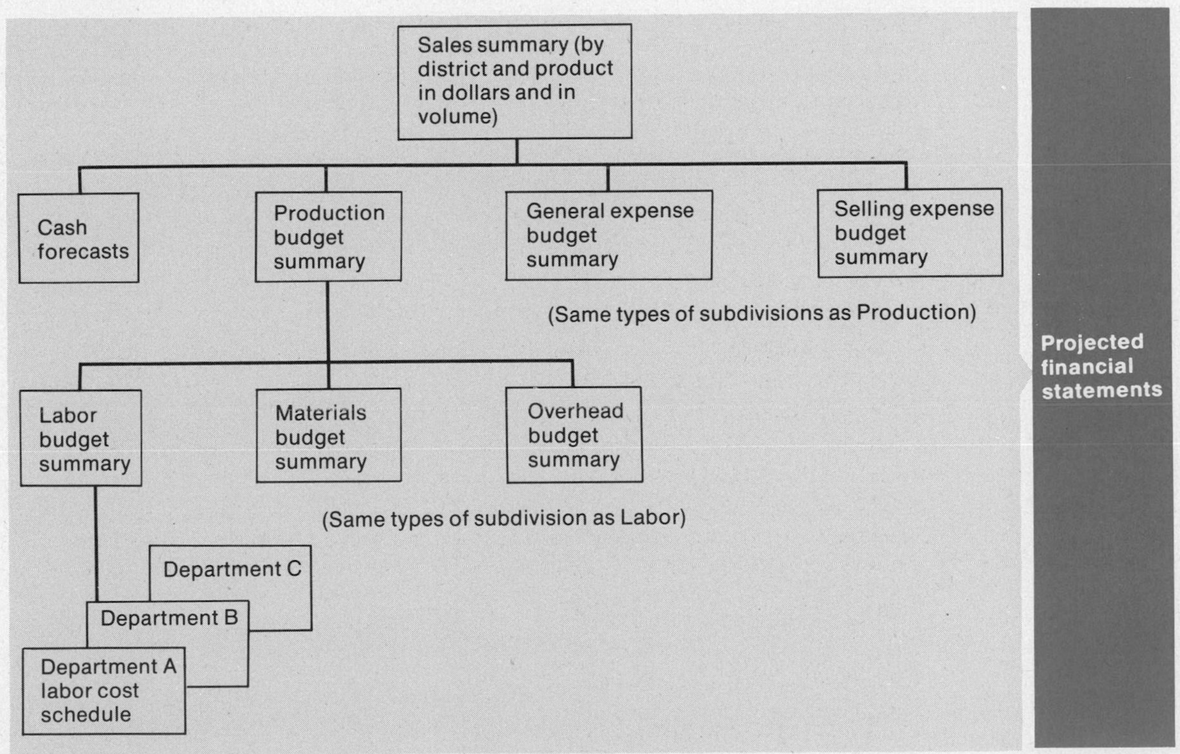

From the sales budget (and studies of economic conditions) we can forecast the amounts of expenses and prepare a *general expense budget* and a *selling expense budget*. Along with the schedules of labor, materials, and overhead costs, these provide information on cash outflows. The sales budget provides information on expected cash inflows. Based upon these schedules we can now prepare a *cash forecast* for the year. The cash forecast, like the other schedules, is broken into quarterly (or monthly) receipts and payments and allows management to arrange in advance for any necessary borrowing of money or for temporary investment of excess cash.

At the right-hand side of Figure 26–1 the ultimate goal of the total budget process is indicated. With information from the individual schedules, it is possible to develop a *projected income statement* and a *projected balance sheet* for the budget period. If the indicated profit is not in line with management's target, it may be necessary to adjust some of the plans; intensified sales efforts or cost reductions, for example. When the indicated profit and the balance sheet relationships are in line with management's target, it is then the task of supervisory personnel to exercise control over sales and costs to attain the profit goals that were set in the budget process.

The budget process: an illustration

As an example of the development of projected financial statements, consider the case of Upstate Manufacturing Company, which produces two styles of leather hats. Figure 26–2 provides cost information on the two styles. From past experience and special cost studies the variable costs per unit of production (per hat) have been determined.

Figure 26–2 Variable costs for Upstate Manufacturing Company

Requirements for One Hat

	Style I	Style II
Materials:		
2 feet @ $0.30	$0.60	
5 feet @ $0.30		$1.50
Direct Labor:		
1/10 hour @ $8.00	0.80	
1/4 hour @ $8.00		2.00
Variable Factory Overhead:		
100% of Direct Labor Cost	0.80	2.00
Variable Manufacturing Costs per Hat	$2.20	$5.50
Variable Selling Expenses per Hat	0.20	0.20
Variable General Expenses per Hat	0.10	0.30
Total Variable Costs per Hat	$2.50	$6.00

Past experience taken from Upstate's accounting records indicate that they expect to operate within the relevant range in 1979 and that fixed costs will be:

Fixed factory overhead	$ 50,000.00
Fixed selling expenses	45,000.00
Fixed general expenses	75,000.00
Total	$170,000.00

UPSTATE MANUFACTURING COMPANY Sales Budget For the Year Ending December 31, 1979				
	Product			
	Style I		Style II	
	Units	Amount	Units	Amount
First Quarter	2,000	$15,000.00	3,000	$ 45,000.00
Second Quarter	1,800	13,500.00	2,500	37,500.00
Third Quarter	3,200	24,000.00	5,000	75,000.00
Fourth Quarter	4,000	30,000.00	7,000	105,000.00
Total	11,000	$82,500.00	17,500	$262,500.00

Figure 26-3
Sales summary

Upstate's management considers that a before-taxes profit of about 12 percent of sales is an appropriate figure for their company. Accordingly, their profit planning will use 12 percent as a target figure.

Sales budget

The sales force has prepared estimates of sales and, after consideration of the economic outlook, management has approved the sales budget shown in Figure 26–3. Style I sells for $7.50 and Style II sells for $15.00. To make the illustration less complex, we assume that both Style I and Style II are sold in only one territory. In actual practice a company would further divide its sales budget by districts or by territories.

Production budget

In order to protect against loss of sales from being out of stock, Upstate has a policy of requiring that the inventory of finished goods at the end of each quarter be equal to 20 percent of the anticipated sales of the next quarter. From the sales budget and the application of this inventory policy a production budget in units has been developed and is shown in Figure 26–4.

It should be noted that the required ending inventory of each quarter (the 20 percent of anticipated sales policy) becomes a beginning inventory of the next quarter, thus reducing production requirements in that period.

Labor, materials, and overhead budgets

With the production requirements for each quarter of 1979 known, Upstate can now develop estimates of labor, materials, and overhead costs.

These would normally be presented as separate schedules. They are gathered together in one summary in Figure 26–5. Another simplifying assumption has

Figure 26–4
Production summary

UPSTATE MANUFACTURING COMPANY
Production Budget (in units)
For the Year Ending December 31, 1979

	Style I			
	1st Quarter	2nd Quarter	3rd Quarter	4th Quarter
Required for Sales	2,000	1,800	3,200	4,000
Required for Ending Inventory	360	640	800	440*
Total	2,360	2,440	4,000	4,440
Less Beginning Inventory	400	360	640	800
Production Requirements	1,960	2,080	3,360	3,640
	Style II			
Required for Sales	3,000	2,500	5,000	7,000
Required for Ending Inventory	500	1,000	1,400	640*
Total	3,500	3,500	6,400	7,640
Less Beginning Inventory	600	500	1,000	1,400
Production Requirements	2,900	3,000	5,400	6,240

*Based on estimate of sales for first quarter of 1980.

been made in Figure 26–5: there are no beginning or ending inventories of raw materials. Although this is not a realistic assumption it does allow us to assume that all materials used in a quarter are purchased in that same quarter. An actual materials purchases budget would recognize beginning and ending inventories to determine purchase requirements in the same way they were used in Figure 26–4.

Figure 26–5
Labor, materials and variable overhead summary

UPSTATE MANUFACTURING COMPANY
Labor, Materials, and Variable Overhead Budget
For the Year Ending December 31, 1979

	1st Quarter		2nd Quarter		3rd Quarter		4th Quarter	
	Units	Amount	Units	Amount	Units	Amount	Units	Amount
Labor Hours:								
Style I @ $8	196	$ 1,568.00	208	$ 1,664.00	336	$ 2,688.00	364	$ 2,912.00
Style II @ $8	725	5,800.00	750	6,000.00	1,350	10,800.00	1,560	12,480.00
Total Labor	921	$ 7,368.00	958	$ 7,664.00	1,686	$13,488.00	1,924	$15,392.00
Material in Feet:								
Style I @ $0.30	3,920	$ 1,176.00	4,160	$ 1,248.00	6,720	$ 2,016.00	7,280	$ 2,184.00
Style II @ $0.30	14,500	4,350.00	15,000	4,500.00	27,000	8,100.00	31,200	9,360.00
Total Materials	18,420	$ 5,526.00	19,160	$ 5,748.00	33,720	$10,116.00	38,480	$11,544.00
Variable Factory Overhead		$ 7,368.00		$ 7,664.00		$13,488.00		$15,392.00
Total Variable Manufacturing Cost		$20,262.00		$21,076.00		$37,092.00		$42,328.00

UPSTATE MANUFACTURING COMPANY
Variable Nonmanufacturing Expense Budget
For the Year Ending December 31, 1979

	1st Quarter	2nd Quarter	3rd Quarter	4th Quarter
Variable Selling Expenses:				
Style I @ $0.20	$ 400.00	$ 360.00	$ 640.00	$ 800.00
Style II @ $0.20	600.00	500.00	1,000.00	1,400.00
Variable General Expenses:				
Style I @ $0.10	200.00	180.00	320.00	400.00
Style II @ $0.30	900.00	750.00	1,500.00	2,100.00
Totals	$2,100.00	$1,790.00	$3,460.00	$4,700.00

Figure 26–6
Summary of variable nonmanufacturing expenses

Other cost budgets

Separate schedules would be made for variable selling expenses, variable general expenses, fixed manufacturing overhead costs, fixed selling expenses, and fixed general expenses. They would be presented in detail by line item such as indirect labor, indirect materials, advertising, or office salaries. To keep this illustration simple they are presented in summary form only in Figures 26–6 and 26–7.

Cash forecast

In order to concentrate on the main theme of this chapter—the development of budget schedules—we will assume that all of Upstate's transactions are in cash. Again, this is not a realistic assumption but it allows us to illustrate the cash forecast without the complexities caused by varying collection periods. The cash forecast is presented in Figure 26–8. Individual line items in this budget schedule are keyed in parenthesis to the Figure from which they were taken. Some comments need to be made about Upstate's cash forecast. First, it should be noted that noncash items such as depreciation are probably part of the fixed expenses. Expenses such as depreciation do not belong in the cash forecast; in this case it is

Figure 26–7
Summary of fixed costs

UPSTATE MANUFACTURING COMPANY
Fixed Costs Budget
For the Year Ending December 31, 1979

	Period*			
	1st Quarter	2nd Quarter	3rd Quarter	4th Quarter
Factory Overhead . . .	$12,500.00	$12,500.00	$12,500.00	$12,500.00
Selling Expenses . . .	11,250.00	11,250.00	11,250.00	11,250.00
General Expenses . . .	18,750.00	18,750.00	18,750.00	18,750.00
Totals	$42,500.00	$42,500.00	$42,500.00	$42,500.00

*Assumed to be incurred evenly over the year

UPSTATE MANUFACTURING COMPANY
Cash Forecast
For the Year Ending December 31, 1979

	Period			
	1st Quarter	2nd Quarter	3rd Quarter	4th Quarter
Receipts				
Beginning balance	$15,000.00*	$10,138.00	($ 4,228.00)	$ 11,720.00
Collections from Sales (26-3) . . .	60,000.00	51,000.00	99,000.00	135,000.00
Total Cash Available	$75,000.00	$61,138.00	$94,772.00	$146,720.00
Expenditures:				
Materials, Labor and Variable Overhead (26-5)	$20,262.00	$21,076.00	$37,092.00	$ 42,328.00
Other Variable Costs (26-6)	2,100.00	1,790.00	3,460.00	4,700.00
Fixed Expenses (26-7)	42,500.00	42,500.00	42,500.00	42,500.00
Total Expenditures	$64,862.00	$65,366.00	$83,052.00	$ 89,528.00
Balance forward	$10,138.00	($ 4,228.00)	$11,720.00	$ 57,192.00

*Assumed

Figure 26-8
Cash forecast

assumed that all of the company's fixed expenses were cash payments. Second, management is alerted to the fact that a shortage of cash will develop in the second quarter and carry over into the third quarter of 1979. An advantage of budgeting is that, being forewarned of this need, management can make advance arrangements to borrow funds on a short-term basis. Repayment can be made in the third or fourth quarter. When such arrangements are made the cash forecast can be revised to show the effect of the borrowing and repayment.

Projected financial statements

Using the data from the budget structure, the projected income statement in Figure 26–9 has been prepared. The net income before taxes of $42,192 is 12.2 percent of sales, which is in line with management's profit-planning goal of 12 percent. Since there is not enough information available about Upstate Manufacturing Company to develop a projected balance sheet, it is not illustrated here.

Figure 26-9
Projected income statement

UPSTATE MANUFACTURING COMPANY
Projected Marginal Income Statement
For the Year Ending December 31, 1979

Sales (26-3)		$345,000.00
Variable Manufacturing Costs (26-5)	$120,758.00	
Other Variable Costs (26-6)	12,050.00	132,808.00
Marginal Income		$212,192.00
Fixed Costs and Expenses (26-7)		170,000.00
Net Income Before Taxes		$ 42,192.00

Responsibility accounting: control through budgeting

Although the Upstate Manufacturing Company illustration was not developed to that depth, Figure 26–1 shows that the labor, materials, overhead, general expense, and selling expense budgets should be developed for each department that is involved in such costs. The labor budget is a summary of three labor cost schedules—those for Department A, Department B, and Department C. The supervisor of Department A is responsible for control of labor costs for that department and for all other Department A cost schedules. To measure the performance of the departmental supervisors in carrying out this task, companies practice responsibility accounting.

Responsibility accounting

Responsibility accounting ***traces cost, expense, and revenue measurements to specific segments of the organization (usually a department, division, or section thereof). Periodic comparisons of actual figures with budgeted (planned) figures can then provide a basis for the evaluation of performance of each such organizational element and for corrective action where needed (controlling).***

Responsibility accounting does not require a separate set of accounting records. However, the accounts described in Chapters 24 and 25 for developing product costs must be classified and subdivided to the same organizational level as the budget. When this is done, reports such as the one illustrated in Figure 26–10 can be prepared.

Similar reports are issued for each department for each schedule in the budget structure. This includes reports on sales as well as costs. Managers at all levels are responsible for explaining the variances from planned results and for taking action for correction when necessary. Note, for example, that indirect labor in Upstate's Department A has exceeded the budget by more than 40 percent. The weakness in the type of performance report shown in Figure 26–10 is that it makes no allowance for change in production volume. Thus, a factor that is beyond the control of the supervisor of Department A may be affecting this unfavorable report. This weakness can be overcome by the use of a flexible budget.

Figure 26–10 Budget performance report

UPSTATE MANUFACTURING COMPANY
Department A—Manufacturing Overhead
For the Quarter Ended June 30, 1979

Budget Item	Expenditures		
	Budget	Actual	Variance*
Factory Supplies	$ 300.00	$ 295.00	$ 5.00 F
Light and Power	400.00	410.00	10.00 U
Indirect Labor	350.00	500.00	150.00 U
Other Costs	1,000.00	975.00	25.00 F
Totals	$2,050.00	$2,180.00	$130.00 U

*F indicates a favorable variance; U indicates an unfavorable variance.

A flexible manufacturing overhead budget

A budget that gives recognition to varying levels of production and to the costs that change with these levels is called the *flexible budget*. It provides management with a basis for analyzing—and, therefore, controlling—the variances between budgeted and actual costs. This is accomplished by comparing actual expenditures with previously established budgeted amounts, *adjusted for varying levels of production*. A series of budgets is prepared, showing estimated or standard costs at various levels of production. Since it is not practical to set up budgets for every possible level of operation, adjustment may be necessary if, for example, the flexible budgets are at 100-unit intervals and actual production falls at a point between the intervals. The preparation of a flexible budget involves an analysis of the degree and extent to which each item of cost is affected by changes in volume of production. The flexible budget, therefore, is essentially a series of fixed budgets.

Assume that Department A of the Upstate Manufacturing Company had the following schedule of overhead costs in support of its work in the planned production of 2,080 Style I hats and 3,000 Style II hats in the second quarter of 1979:

Variable Costs	
Factory Supplies	$ 300.00
Light and Power	400.00
Indirect Labor	350.00
Total Variable Costs	$1,050.00
Fixed Costs	$1,000.00
Total Budgeted Costs	$2,050.00

If Upstate produces at a volume other than planned, the budget for Department A should be adjusted accordingly. Figure 26–11 shows a flexible manufacturing overhead budget for various possible levels of production.

Figure 26–11 Department A flexible manufacturing budget

UPSTATE MANUFACTURING COMPANY
Department A—Manufacturing Overhead
For the Quarter Ending June 30, 1979

	Level of Production as Percent of Plan			
	85%	90%	95%	100%
Variable Costs:				
Factory Supplies	$ 255.00	$ 270.00	$ 285.00	$ 300.00
Light and Power	340.00	360.00	380.00	400.00
Indirect Labor	297.50	315.00	332.50	350.00
Total Variable Costs	$ 892.50	$ 945.00	$ 997.50	$1,050.00
Fixed Costs	1,000.00	1,000.00	1,000.00	1,000.00
Total Budgeted Costs	$1,892.50	$1,945.00	$1,997.50	$2,050.00

Assume that Upstate's actual production in the second quarter is at 93 percent of the plan. Figure 26–11 shows that Department A should incur manufacturing overhead costs somewhere between $1,945.00 and $1,997.50. The variable costs should be 93 percent of the original production plan while the fixed costs should remain the same as originally budgeted. Accordingly, a new performance report can be prepared as shown in Figure 26–12. In this report the variable costs are adjusted to 93 percent of the original budget, but fixed costs are kept at the original figure. This gives an adjusted budget for the level of production actually attained. Now we can see that the total variance is significantly greater after the volume reduction is taken into consideration. The supervisor of Department A needs to review carefully the causes of excess usage of variable items. There may be valid explanations for the differences; or the use of manpower and other resources may be inefficient. Reports such as the one in Figure 26–12 bring the exceptions to the attention of management; efforts can then be concentrated on these exceptions.

Standard cost accounting

Either historical costs or standard costs can be used under both job order and process cost accounting systems. Therefore, a *standard cost system* is not a third type of cost accounting system; it is simply the application of predetermined costs in recording data in the accounts of either a job order or process system. Even though this is true, we will illustrate standard cost accounting with only a process system.

Standard costs are based upon engineering studies of (1) the kind and quality of material requirements; (2) the operating time, qualifications, and methods of production workers; and (3) the judgment of management as to what overhead costs should be. For each product there is developed a *standard cost card* (sometimes called a specification) showing what the product's costs should be. Standards are developed for (1) materials, (2) labor, and (3) overhead. When actual

Figure 26–12
Budget performance report

UPSTATE MANUFACTURING COMPANY
Department A—Manufacturing Overhead
For the Quarter Ended June 30, 1979

Budget Item	Expenditures		
	Adjusted Budget	Actual	Variance
Variable Costs:			
Factory Supplies	$ 279.00	$ 295.00	$ 16.00 U
Light and Power	372.00	410.00	38.00 U
Indirect Labor	325.50	500.00	174.50 U
Totals	$ 976.50	$1,205.00	
Fixed Costs	1,000.00	975.00	25.00 F
Totals	$1,976.50	$2,180.00	$203.50 U

costs are compared with standard costs the *variances* (or differences) are determined. A variance caused by actual costs being greater than standard is an *unfavorable* variance. A variance caused by actual costs less than standard is a *favorable* variance.

A company could develop standards and use them only for comparison with actual costs at the end of the period. Stronger managerial control will result, however, when the standards are incorporated into the accounting system. The latter method will be illustrated and explained here.

Illustration of a standard cost system

A standard cost has already been determined for the products of the Upstate Manufacturing Company. The standard cost card would be as follows:

	Standard Cost Per Hat	
	Style I	*Style II*
Materials:		
2 feet @ \$0.30	\$0.60	
5 feet @ \$0.30		\$1.50
Labor		
1/10 hour @ \$8.00	0.80	
1/4 hour @ \$8.00		2.00
Overhead:		
214% of direct labor cost	1.712	4.28
Total	\$3.112	\$7.78

When the standard cost card is compared with the data in Figure 26–2 it will be noted that the materials and labor costs per hat are the same. This is because both are pure variable costs; only variable costs are shown in Figure 26–2. There is \$50,000 of fixed manufacturing overhead in the 1979 budget in addition to variable overhead of \$43,912 = (100 percent of direct labor cost). Accordingly, total budgeted overhead cost is \$93,912 = (\$50,000 fixed + \$43,912 variable). The standard overhead rate is computed in the same manner as any overhead rate. Upstate uses direct labor cost as the base, so that the overhead rate is

$$\frac{\text{Total overhead budget}}{\text{Total direct labor budget}} = \frac{\$93{,}912}{\$43{,}912} = 2.1386 \doteq 214\%$$

Variances

In a standard cost system variances arise in connection with materials, labor, and overhead. To explain and illustrate them along with the flow of costs the following assumptions are made about the first quarter of 1979:

1. Actual production was 1,950 Style I hats and 2,950 Style II hats.
2. 18,500 feet of leather was purchased at $0.31 per foot; all was used in production.
3. 960 direct labor hours were used at a cost of $7.95 per hour.
4. Actual overhead costs incurred were $16,100.

Costs are recorded in the inventory accounts at standard; variances are recorded in separate general ledger accounts where they are highlighted for management attention. Using the assumption that Upstate Manufacturing Company has only one department, journal entries for the first quarter are illustrated.

Materials The two variances that arise with respect to material are *materials price variance* and *materials quantity variance*. The price variance is computed as follows:

18,500 feet × $0.31 =	$5,735.00	actual cost of material purchased.
18,500 feet × $0.30 =	5,550.00	standard cost of material purchased.
Difference	$ 185.00	unfavorable.

The journal entry to record the purchase of materials is

Account	Debit	Credit
Materials Inventory	5,550 00	
Materials Price Variance	185 00	
Accounts Payable		5,735 00

Another way to compute this variance is 18,500 feet × $0.01 (excess unit cost) = $185.00.

The *quantity variance* is the difference between the standard cost of material that should have been used and material that was actually used. To determine this we need to know how much should have been used. It is called standard material for production attained.

1,950 Style I hats at 2 feet	=	3,900 feet
2,950 Style II hats at 5 feet	=	14,750
Standard material	=	18,650 feet
Actual material used	=	18,500
Savings (less than standard)	=	150 feet (favorable)

The variance is favorable; 150 feet × $0.30 = $45.00. The journal entry for issuance of materials is:

Account	Debit	Credit
Work in Process Inventory	5,595 00	
Materials Inventory		5,550 00
Materials Quantity Variance		45 00

The inventory account, Work in Process, is debited with the standard material cost for production attained. Comparing this entry with the materials purchase entry one notes that a debit in a variance account is unfavorable while a credit in a variance account represents a favorable variance. In the first quarter of 1979 Upstate paid more than standard price for materials, but made up for some of the excess cost by saving on usage.

Labor The two variances that arise with respect to labor are similar to materials. They are the labor rate variance and the labor efficiency variance. The *labor rate variance* is caused by paying a rate that differs from standard. For Upstate it is:

960 hours worked × $8.00 (standard)	=	$7,680.00
960 hours worked × $7.95 (actual)	=	7,632.00
Difference	=	$ 48.00 (favorable)

This variance is favorable; another way to compute it is 960 hours worked × (the saving of $0.05) = $48.00.

The *labor efficiency variance* is based upon the amount of labor that should have been used compared with actual labor used. Upstate's labor efficiency variance is:

1,950 Style I hats × 1/10 hour × $8.00	=	$1,560.00
2,950 Style II hats × 1/4 hour × $8.00	=	5,900.00
Standard labor (932½ hours)	=	$7,460.00
Actual labor = (960 hours × $8.00)	=	7,680.00
Excess labor cost	=	($ 220.00) (unfavorable)

Another way to compute this unfavorable variance is 27½ excess hours × $8.00 = $220.00. The journal entry to record direct labor is

Work in Process Inventory	7,460 00	
Labor Efficiency Variance	220 00	
Labor Rate Variance		48 00
Factory Payroll		7,632 00

Management can see that more labor hours were used than allowed by the standard for production attained. This unfavorable development was partly offset by an average labor cost that was $0.05 per hour less than standard.

Overhead In a standard cost system, overhead is applied on the basis of standard for the production actually produced. Upstate would apply 214 percent of the standard direct labor cost of $7,460—an amount of $15,964.40. Actual overhead incurred was $16,100.00, which is $135.60 greater than standard. There are several ways to analyze the unfavorable (underapplied) total overhead variance. The variance stems from two sources: (1) a spending difference and (2) a volume difference. Actual overhead costs may be greater or smaller than the budget would allow for the amount of production attained. This part of the total variance is usually controllable in the department concerned. The volume difference is caused by applying overhead costs to work in process on a base that is greater or smaller than the budget. The volume difference is often beyond the control of the department supervisor.

Evaluation of standard costing

The use of standard costs provides management with a powerful control tool. In addition to information on costs being incurred, supervisors know what costs *ought to be*. Deviations from amounts that costs ought to be appear as variances in the several variance accounts. Any significant variance can be studied to determine the cause and to correct the deficiency if necessary.

Standard costs, if they are carefully established, allow for accurate estimates of the cost of new orders. With knowledge of expected costs, a much better job of establishing selling prices can be performed.

On the other hand, a standard cost system is expensive to maintain. Each time a production method changes, a new standard must be established. In large companies several employees are engaged in the full-time task of keeping standards up to date.

Glossary

Budget A subdivided plan (sales, production, and so on) for a future period's operations. It is usually expressed in financial terms.

Cash forecast A subdivision of the budget structure, this schedule sets forth a prediction of monthly cash inflows and outflows.

Controlling The management function that consists of monitoring variances in business activity: comparing actual with planned activity, and taking action to bring performance into line with forecasts.

Fixed costs Costs that remain the same when levels of activity or volume change.

Flexible budget A budget that gives recognition to varying levels of production and the costs that change with these levels. A series of fixed budgets for various levels of production.

Labor efficiency variance The difference between actual and standard labor hours multiplied by the standard rate.

Labor rate variance The difference between actual and standard rate of direct labor multiplied by the actual hours of direct labor.

Materials price variance The difference between the actual and standard unit price of materials multiplied by the quantity purchased.

Materials quantity variance The difference between the actual and standard quantity of materials used multiplied by the standard price.

Performance report A report of actual versus planned performance. An example is a report showing factory overhead budget by line item, actual costs for the same items, and the variances.

Planning The management function that defines the goals and objectives of an organization.

Profit planning Budgeting of sales and costs with a specific profit percentage as a target. Adjustments are made to the budget to attain the planned profit.

Projected statements Estimated financial statements for a future period based upon budget data.

Relevant volume range The volume range over which cost behavior is somewhat stable and can be reasonably predicted.

Responsibility accounting Tracing of costs, expense, and revenue identified with specific persons or segments of the organization. Periodic comparisons are made of actual versus planned performance.

Standards A philosophy or concept as to what things ought to be.

Standard cost card The specification that describes the standard materials, labor, and overhead cost for a product.

Standard costs Predetermined costs based upon the concept of a standard and upon engineering studies.

Standard cost system A cost accounting system devised to collect both historical and standard costs. The standard costs end up in the inventory accounts; any differences between standard and actual appear in variance accounts.

Variable costs Costs that are affected in total in direct proportion to change in the volume of output.

Variance The difference—favorable or unfavorable—between actual and planned performance.

Questions

Q26–1 What are some of the advantages of budgeting in a business organization?

Q26–2 Are budgets and profit planning related? How?

Q26–3 List eight different budget schedules and explain the purpose of each.

Q26–4 In a profit-making organization, which budget schedule is usually prepared first? Why?

Q26–5 Production planning must consider inventory quantities. Which inventories affect production schedules? How?

Q26–6 What are the reasons for making a cash forecast?

Q26–7 What are some techniques for preparing a sales budget? Describe each technique that you list.

Q26–8 If a company uses a standard cost system, is the need for budgeting and profit planning eliminated? Explain.

Q26–9 Should a not-for-profit organization such as a local community fund have a budget? Why or why not?

Q26–10 What is responsibility accounting?

Q26–11 Does responsibility accounting require a separate accounting system? Explain.

Q26–12 Upon completion of the budgeting process, management finds that the projected profit is short of the planned profit target. What actions can be taken?

Q26–13 Identify and explain the materials and labor variances.

Q26–14 What is meant by "standard for production attained"?

Class exercises

CE26–1 (Sales budget) Council Enterprises produces three products. Sales information for 1978 taken from the accounting records shows the following:

Product	*Unit Selling Price*	*Total Sales*
X	$15	$144,000
Y	$12	120,000
Z	$20	170,000

The general economic outlook is for a 10 percent increase in consumer purchases of products of this nature. In addition, the sales manager feels certain that the company can obtain in the first quarter of 1979 a one-time order for 1,000 units of product Z that will be in addition to expected sales of Z. Normal sales occur 20 percent, 30 percent, 25 percent, and 25 percent respectively in the four quarters of the year.

Required: Prepare, in good form, a sales budget for 1979 that will contain both units and dollar amounts of forecast sales by quarters.

CE26–2 (Manufacturing budgets) Expected sales of the Longhorn Company for 1979 are as follows:

	Units of Product			
	1st Quarter	*2nd Quarter*	*3rd Quarter*	*4th Quarter*
Product A	20,000	22,000	18,000	30,000
Product B	16,000	11,000	14,000	18,000
Product C	11,000	15,000	12,000	13,000

It is company policy to have on hand at the end of each quarter an inventory of finished goods equal to 10 percent of planned sales for the next quarter. (In the first quarter of 1980 it is estimated that 15,000 of each product will be sold.)

The standard costs of products are as follows:

	Product		
	A	*B*	*C*
Materials @ $0.60 per lb	$6.00	$3.00	$4.80
Labor @ $7.50 per hour	3.75	2.50	1.50
Variable Overhead	100% of direct labor		

Materials are produced by a firm located next door; it is never necessary for Longhorn to carry an inventory.

Required:

1. A production budget by units of product
2. A materials purchases budget
3. A direct labor budget
4. A schedule showing a summary of total variable manufacturing costs per quarter.

CE26–3 (Cash forecast) Clary and Beck, Incorporated makes all sales on credit. Their accounts receivable records show that 50 percent of their sales are paid for in the month of sale with a 2 percent cash discount taken; the remaining 50 percent are paid in the month following sale without discount. Payments for purchases are made 2/3 in the month of purchase and 1/3 in the month following. No discounts are offered by their vendors. Payrolls and other expenses are paid as incurred.

The following estimates apply to the year 1979:

	March	*April*	*May*	*June*
Sales	$50,000	$72,000	$60,000	$80,000
Payrolls	10,000	10,500	10,500	11,000
Purchases	24,000	27,000	30,000	36,000
Other Expenses	8,000	20,000	10,000	10,000

Cash balance on hand April 1, 1979, is expected to be $4,800.

Required:

1. Prepare a cash forecast for the second quarter of 1979.
2. Will the company need to arrange for borrowing funds? If so, in what month can they plan to make repayment?

CE26–4 (Responsibility accounting) The manufacturing overhead budget for the Blending Department of the Arapahoe Company for 1979 is as follows:

ARAPAHOE COMPANY
Blending Department
Overhead Budget for the Year 1979
Based on Production of 50,000 Units

Variable Costs:	
Indirect Labor	$150,000
Indirect Materials	75,000
Other Items	300,000
Total Variable Costs	$525,000
Fixed Costs:	
Superintendence	$ 50,000
Depreciation of Building	25,000
Other Fixed Costs	150,000
Total Fixed Costs	$225,000
Total Costs	$750,000

The company works 50 weeks each year, closing for two weeks for vacations. Fixed costs are expected to be incurred evenly over the year.

In the second week of April 1979 the Blending Department produced 1,000 units and incurred costs as follows:

Indirect labor	$3,130
Indirect materials	1,490
Other variable items	6,135
Superintendence	1,000
Depreciation of building	500
Other fixed costs	3,000

Required:

1. Prepare a report for the week ended April 14, 1979, showing for the Blending Department budgeted costs, actual costs, and variances.
2. Indicate which variances, if any, are the responsibility of the supervisor of the Blending Department.

CE26–5 (Standard cost accounting with a flexible budget) The Maple Objects Company used a standard cost system and a fixed manufacturing overhead budget in 1978 as follows:

Direct labor hours	80,000
Fixed costs:	
Depreciation—factory building	$ 32,000.00
Factory taxes	2,400.00
Depreciation—machinery and equipment	64,000.00
Other costs (item data omitted)	141,600.00
Total fixed costs	$240,000.00
Variable costs:	
Light and power	$ 8,000.00
Factory supplies	4,000.00
Other costs (item data omitted)	68,000.00
Total variable costs	$ 80,000.00
Total manufacturing overhead	$320,000.00

In 1979, the management decided to prepare a flexible overhead budget at 80, 90, 100, and 110 percent of capacity levels of production. The 1978 budget represents 100 percent; at 100 percent 1979 costs are expected to be the same as they were in 1978. The standard unit cost of the product is as follows:

Materials: 1 piece of Material 1B35	$ 6
Direct labor: 2 hours at $5	10
Manufacturing overhead: 2 hours at $4	8
Total	$24

Production data for 1979.

1. There was no beginning work in process inventory.
2. 38,800 units started in production.
3. 38,000 units completed.
4. 800 units in process (all materials added and one-quarter labor and overhead) at the end of 1979.

Condensed transactions for 1979.

1. Materials purchased totaled 40,000 pieces at $6.04.
2. Materials requisitioned for production were 39,620 pieces.
3. Direct labor was 77,000 hours at $4.96 an hour.
4. Manufacturing overhead totaled $308,800.
5. Manufacturing overhead was applied to production on the basis stated.
6. Units finished were 38,000.
7. Units sold were 37,600 at $44 each.

Required:

1. Construct the flexible budget.
2. Record the transactions for 1979.
3. Post to a Work in Process Inventory account and prove the ending balance.

Exercises and problems

P26–1 Nelson and Kapoor, Incorporated produces three products and forecasts sales for the quarter ended March 31, 1979 as follows:

Product	*Sales in Units*
Standard	108,000
Premium	90,000
Supreme	116,000

Management feels that ending inventories for each quarter must be equal to one-fifth of sales in that quarter just ended. Beginning inventories are:

Standard	20,000
Premium	12,000
Supreme	20,000

Required: Prepare a production budget in units.

P26–2 Brevard Electronics is preparing the sales budget for a new model citizens band radio—Model CB2X1—to be introduced in 1979. It is planned to accept orders for deliveries commencing October 2, 1979, to take advantage of year-end holiday sales opportunities. The sales department has learned that a competitor sold an average of 20,000 units per month in 1978 of a similar model and it feels it can do as well. The economic forecast predicts a general increase in all sales of 10 percent in 1979 over 1978. The new model will sell for $120 per set. Management plans to end the year with 15,000 units in inventory.

Required:

1. A monthly sales forecast in units and dollars for the fourth quarter of 1979.
2. A monthly production budget in units.

P26–3 Richland Company has prepared the following production budget:

RICHLAND COMPANY
Production Budget
For the Quarter Ending September 30, 1979

Product	*Production in Units* *July*	*August*	*September*
X	10,200	12,000	11,800
Y	13,500	16,000	18,000
Z	6,000	5,500	7,000

The standard cost cards for these products show the following materials requirements per unit:

Material	*Unit Cost*	*Product X*	*Product Y*	*Product Z*
A31	$0.20	2 lbs.	0	3 lbs.
B46	0.15	0	3 lbs.	0
C 17	0.30	0	1 lb.	2 lbs.

Inventories on July 1, 1979, are:

A31	500 lbs.
B46	1,000 lbs.
C17	600 lbs.

It is Richland's policy to end each month with a materials inventory equal to the figures shown for July 1.

Required: Prepare a monthly materials purchases budget for the quarter in units and dollars.

P26–4 Richland Company (see P26–3) shows the following standard labor costs per unit of product:

Product	*Labor Required*
X	1/2 hour @ $8
Y	1/5 hour @ 10
Z	1 hour @ 7

Required: Prepare a labor budget projecting labor costs per month for each product for the quarter ending September 30, 1979.

P26–5 Suffolk Shops manufactures a line of containers using a process system through several departments. The budget for the Packing Department for August 1979 was based upon packing of 8,000 cases of containers. Summarized budgeted costs were:

Variable costs	$36,000
Fixed costs	40,000
Total	$76,000

Actual output of the Packing Department was 9,600 cases in August with costs as follows:

Variable costs	$42,432
Fixed costs	40,000
Totals	$82,432

Management thinks that the supervisor of the Packing Department has not performed very well because August costs exceeded the budget by $6,432.

Required: Present a computation to show whether the Packing Department has actually performed below or above the standard set by the budget.

P26–6 Ferrum, Incorporated has the following balances on December 31, 1978:

Cash	$22,000
Accounts Receivable	25,000
Accounts Payable	35,000

The sales budget projects sales as follows:

	January	*February*	*March*
Cash sales	$12,000	$17,000	$13,000
Sales on account	30,000	20,000	22,000

Based upon the production budget, other schedules indicate that costs will be:

	January	*February*	*March*
Materials purchases on account	$39,000	$23,000	$27,000
Cash payments for labor and overhead	15,000	12,000	9,000
Depreciation	4,000	4,000	4,000

Terms of sales and purchases on account are n/30 (assume collections and payments are made in the following month).

Required: Prepare a cash forecast for the quarter ended March 31, 1979.

P26–7 Multinational Company sold Product A at $300 and Product B at $250 in 1978. Total 1978 sales were:

	Units of Product	
	A	*B*
United States sales	10,000	15,000
European sales	5,000	8,000
Asian sales	9,000	3,000
Rest-of-the-World sales	8,000	8,000
Total	32,000	34,000

After studying data pertaining to operating costs, management has decided upon a sales price increase of 10 percent for each model in 1979. With the new selling price a sales increase (in units) of 5 percent is expected in all sales territories except the Rest-of-the-World, where sales in newly-developing countries are expected to cause an increase of 10 percent over 1978.

Required: Prepare a forecast of sales in units and in dollars by territory for 1979.

P26–8 Ten pounds of sugar at $0.30 a pound are standard for production of a given product by the Manatee Company. During August, 28,000 pounds of sugar were purchased at $0.32 a pound. 25,000 pounds of sugar were put into process; 2,470 equivalent units of product were produced.

Required: Compute the materials price and quantity variances.

P26–9 The Palmetto Company's standard cost card for production of 100 gallons of orange juice showed the following direct labor cost:

7 hours at $6 per hour

Production for the month was 120,000 gallons; 8,320 direct labor hours were used at a total labor cost of $50,752.

Required: Compute the labor rate variance and the labor efficiency variance.

P26–10 (Integrative) The standard cost card for the Cedar Rapids Company showed the following information on its commodity, Martelle:

Materials: 4 gallons of syrup at $4 each	$16
Direct labor: 6 hours at $6	36
Total materials and direct labor cost	$52

Production data for 1979.

1. Beginning work in process inventory: 200 units, 60 percent complete as to materials and 40 percent complete as to direct labor and manufacturing overhead.
2. Completed during 1979, 40,000 units.
3. Ending work in process inventory: 4,000 units, 80 percent complete as to materials and 50 percent complete as to direct labor and manufacturing overhead.

Transactions involving materials and labor during 1979.

1. Purchased 192,000 gallons of syrup at $4.04 a gallon.
2. Requisitioned 172,480 gallons of syrup for production.
3. Factory payroll incurred during the period was 247,680 hours at a total cost of $1,491,033.60 (ignore payroll taxes).
4. A standard direct labor cost was assigned to production on the basis of the standard cost card.

Required: Record the transactions establishing the materials and labor variances in appropriate accounts.

P26–11 (Minicase) The management of Iranson Products has determined that a before-tax net income of 10 percent of sales is a proper target figure for the company. As the last step in the budget process, the accountant has prepared the following statement:

IRANSON PRODUCTS
Projected Income Statement
For the Year Ending December 31, 1979

Sales	$420,000
Total Variable Costs	300,000
Marginal Income	$120,000
Total Fixed Costs	100,000
Net Income Before Taxes	$ 20,000

Since the projected net income does not meet Iranson's profit-planning target, a meeting has been called to review the entire budget structure. You, as the company's accountant, have been asked to be prepared to make recommendations for possible courses of action at the budget-review meeting. You have determined three options to be possible:

1. Increase sales by 33⅓ percent by a special campaign that would add $25,000 to fixed costs.
2. Decrease fixed costs by $35,000 by accepting a 16⅔ percent decrease in sales.
3. Decrease variable costs by 20 percent with an accompanying increase in fixed costs of 38 percent. Sales would remain the same.

Required: Explain the effect on the company's profit-planning target of each of the three feasible options, the reasons for this effect, and your recommendation as to which (if any) the company should adopt.

Chapter 26
Forecasting, budgeting, and standard cost accounting

chapter twenty-seven

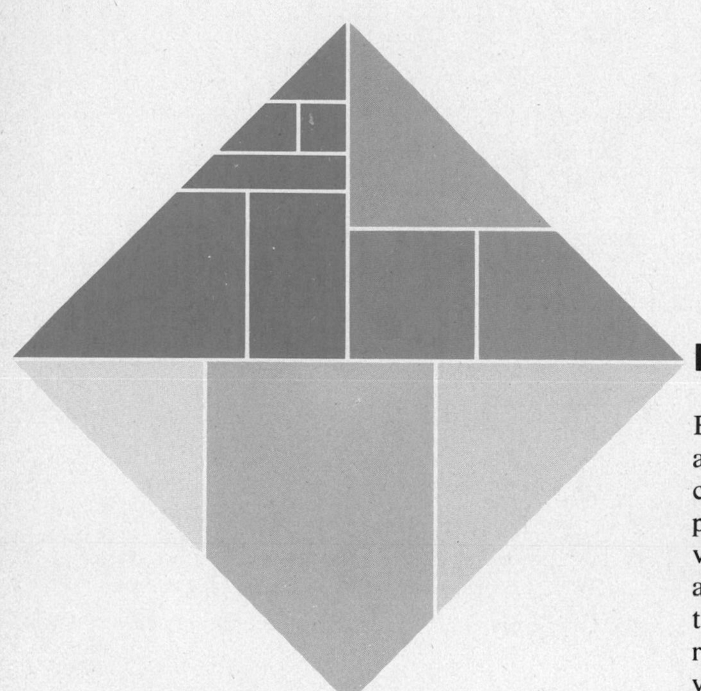

Introduction

Business decisions are made only after alternative courses of action have been considered. But the mere act of considering possible courses of action is not of much value to the manager unless information is also available as to the consequences of those choices. In this chapter the relationships between three factors—costs, volume of business activity, and income—are discussed. Some ways that knowledge of these relationships can be used to make better decisions are illustrated and explained. Before costs can be analyzed and interpreted for managerial use, however, the content and behavior of various costs must be known. Therefore, certain basic cost concepts are reviewed and discussed in the following section.

Using cost information for management decisions

Learning goals

To define the various views of costs.
To be able to use cost, volume, and income relationships in break-even analysis.
To understand the application of knowledge of cost behavior to specific management decisions such as special order pricing, make or buy, or discontinuance of a department.
To describe how capital budgeting decisions affect each other and how they affect income.
To introduce compound interest concepts.

Key terms

break-even point
capital budgeting
compound interest
contribution margin
contribution-margin percentage
excess present value
fixed costs
make-or-buy decisions
marginal cost
marginal income
margin of safety
opportunity cost
out-of-pocket costs
payback
percentage of safety
present value method
profit-volume ratio
profitability index
rate of return
semifixed costs
semivariable costs
sunk costs
time value of money
variable costs

Concepts of cost: a review

Fixed costs are the costs that, without change in present productive capacity, are not affected by changes in volume of output. For instance, rent on a factory building is a fixed cost because it does not change when productive volume increases or decreases.

Variable costs are those that are affected in total by changes in the volume of output. The cost of materials, for example, is a variable cost because it increases in direct proportion to the increase in the number of units produced.

Semifixed costs are costs that vary in steps; they are not affected by changes in volume of output within a given range of output. For example, one inspector may be required for an output of 0 to 10,000 units; two may be required for outputs of 10,001 to 20,000 units; and so on. *Semivariable* costs are costs that include both a fixed and a variable component. An example is a foreman who receives a base salary plus a bonus determined by amount of production.

Marginal costs (or differential costs) are the differences in cost between two levels of output. This may be the additional cost necessary to produce an additional unit, or for example, it may be the additional cost to move from 90 percent of capacity to 95 percent of capacity.

Opportunity costs are costs of forgoing one thing to get an acceptable alternative. For example, a company may make a large investment in plant and equipment, thereby giving up an opportunity to invest the same money in bonds. The lost bond interest is an opportunity cost.

Out-of-pocket costs are costs that require direct expenditures, such as wages. These are costs that may be saved if a specific project or plan is not carried out.

Sunk costs are costs that have already been incurred. They cannot be recovered if the project in which they were invested is dropped. Accordingly, they are usually not a factor to consider in decisions affecting the future. An example is the purchase of a machine that stamps the company's brand label on boxes, and would have no resale value.

Break-even analysis

The *break-even point* is the volume of sales at which the business will neither earn income nor incur a loss. It is the point at which total costs, or expenses, and total revenue are exactly equal. At this volume of sales, net income is equal to zero. The break-even point can be expressed in terms of dollars of total sales or in terms of total units of a product sold. In either event it is the level of business at which total revenues will recover the exact amount of total costs and, therefore, the business will "break even."

Computation of break-even point

In discussion of the flexible budget it was noted that management can divide semifixed and semivariable costs into their fixed and variable elements so that all costs can be classed as either fixed or variable. The techniques for doing this are beyond the scope of this text and will not be explained here. However, in the discussions in this chapter, it will be assumed that the cost accounting department has already identified all costs and expenses as either fixed or variable. Because this has been done, total cost is the sum of total fixed costs (TFC) and total variable costs (TVC). Since the break-even point is the dollar volume of sales at which the business will neither earn income nor incur a loss, the following equation can be used to describe it:

$$S_{bep} = TFC + TVC$$

where S_{bep} = dollar volume of sales at the break-even point. S_{bep} is unknown in the foregoing equation. Management is asking the basic question: What is the dollar volume of sales needed to recover total cost and begin to make a profit?

Assume that the Chetney Manufacturing Company has total variable costs of $240,000 at its 100 percent capacity level. Also assume that Chetney produces 20,000 units at the normal 100 percent level. Accordingly, the variable cost per unit is $12. If the selling price per unit is $30, each unit manufactured and sold will bring in $18 of revenue in excess of variable cost. This $18 is known as the *unit contribution margin*. Now management's question is: How many times must we generate the unit contribution margin before total fixed costs are paid off? The answer is found by dividing total fixed costs by the unit contribution margin. This is the number of units that must be made and sold to break even.

Budget data for Chetney Corporation are shown in Figure 27–1. Total fixed costs are expected to be $210,006. Since $210,006 ÷ $18 = 11,667, the company must generate the unit contribution margin 11,667 times to break even. The sale of 11,667 units brings total revenue of $350,010. This is the break-even point (S_{bep}). Proof of this calculation is as follows:

Sales		$350,010
TFC	$210,006	
TVC (11,667 × $12)	140,004	
Total Costs		350,010
Profit		$ –0–

Another approach to the break-even point computation

Variable costs per unit divided by selling price per unit is a fraction representing the percentage of variable costs in each sales dollar. Let VC = variable cost per unit and SP = sales price per unit. Then, since 1 = 1.0 = 100 percent, the term, 1 − VC/SP, represents the percent of contribution that each sales dollar makes toward paying off fixed costs. This term is sometimes known as the *profit-volume ratio* or the *P/V ratio*. We will call it the *contribution margin percentage*.

To illustrate, use the budgeted data of Chetney Manufacturing Company in Figure 27–1.

Figure 27–1
Data for break-even computation

	Fixed	Variable	Budgeted Net Income Calculation
Budgeted sales:			
20,000 units @ $30 each			$600,000.00
Budgeted costs			
Direct materials		$ 50,000.00	
Direct labor		70,000.00	
Factory overhead	$100,006.00	80,000.00	
Selling expenses	60,000.00	30,000.00	
Administrative expenses	50,000.00	10,000.00	
Totals	$210,006.00	$240,000.00	450,006.00
Budgeted net income			$149,994.00

From Chetney's budget figures we calculated variable cost per unit as $12 = ($240,000 variable cost ÷ 20,000 units). Selling price is $30 per unit, so that the ratio of variable costs to sales is

$$\frac{VC}{SP} = \frac{\$12}{\$30} = 0.40$$

The break-even point in dollars can be computed by dividing total fixed costs by the contribution margin percentage. It is the following:

$$S_{bep} = \frac{TFC}{1 - VC/SP} = \frac{\$210{,}006}{1 - 0.40} = \frac{\$210{,}006}{0.60} = \$350{,}010$$

If unit costs are unknown the variable cost percentage could have been computed by using total figures as follows:

$$\text{Variable cost percentage} = \frac{\text{Total budgeted variable costs}}{\text{Total budgeted sales}} = \frac{\$240{,}000}{\$600{,}000} = 0.40$$

With 40 percent of sales required to cover variable costs then 60 percent of sales—or 60 cents from each sales dollar—is available to apply toward fixed costs. Chetney Company's contribution margin percentage (or P/V ratio) can be interpreted another way. If 60 cents of each sales dollar is available to pay fixed costs, the total amount of fixed costs will have been recovered at the break-even point. Proof of this result can be seen as follows:

$$350{,}010 \text{ sales dollars} \times \$0.60 = \$210{,}006 = \text{TFC}.$$

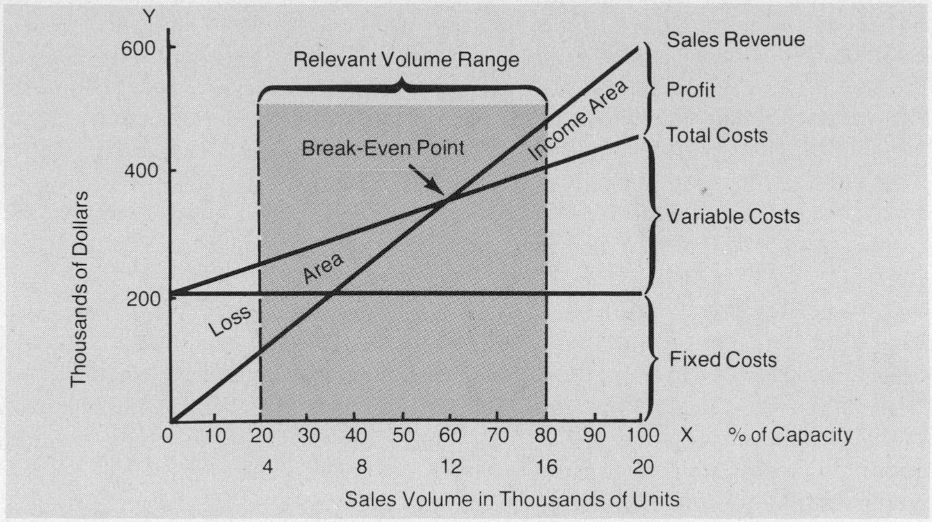

Figure 27–2 Typical break-even chart

The break-even chart

One effective way of presenting the relationship of fixed and variable costs to sales at different volume levels is the break-even chart. Two variations of a break-even chart for Chetney Manufacturing Company are shown in Figures 27–2 and 27–3. On both charts the vertical (Y axis) line measures dollars. Both cost dollars and sales dollars are measured on the Y axis. The horizontal base line (X axis) measures volume. On both charts the volume (or output) is measured in two ways—(1) percent of capacity and (2) units of product. It is assumed for purposes of illustration that total output can be sold and that costs include all costs of producing and selling the product.

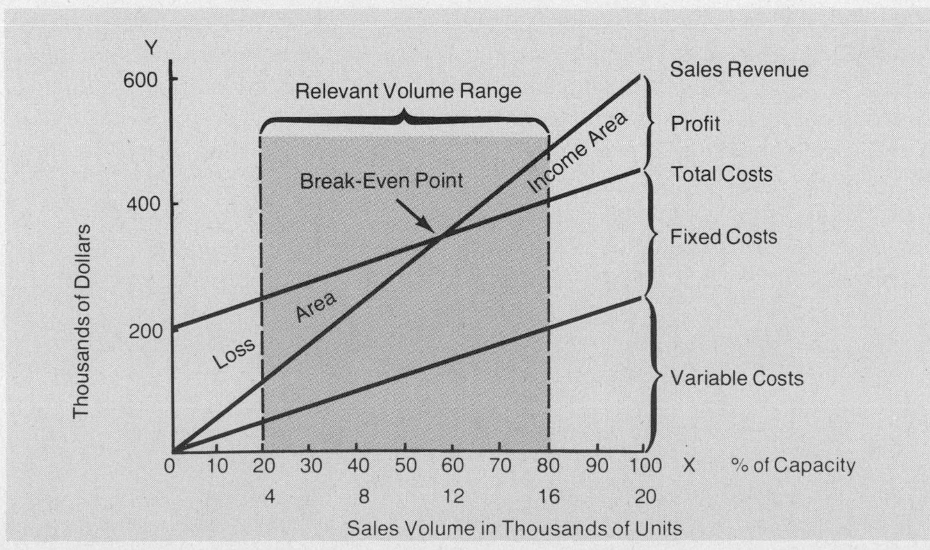

Figure 27–3 Inverted break-even chart

Figure 27–2 is the conventional form of break-even chart. The fixed costs, assumed to be unaffected by volume changes, are represented by a horizontal line that starts at $210,006 on the Y axis and runs parallel to the base line out to 100 percent capacity of 20,000 units. The variable costs represent the distance between the total costs line and the fixed costs line. Because variable costs increase directly in relation to volume they cause the total costs line to slope upward showing greater total costs as volume increases. This cost increase is caused entirely by increase in total variable costs—the fixed costs remain the same.

The sales are measured on a 45-degree line rising upward from zero or the origin. The intersection of the sales line and the total costs line is the point where total sales equal total costs—the definition of the breakeven point. The distance between the sales line and the total costs line (measured vertically on the Y axis at any given volume) is income or loss. To the left of the break-even point the amount is a loss; the loss area is indicated on the chart. To the right of the break-even point the amount is a profit; the income area is also indicated on the chart.

In Figure 27–3 the fixed costs are shown above the variable costs. This form of inverted break-even chart shows the amount of unrecovered fixed costs as we move upward on the sales line toward the break-even point.

Both charts show by broken lines the *relevant volume range* as a distance measured horizontally on the X axis. For Chetney Manufacturing Company this area runs from 20 percent to 80 percent capacity, but there is no specific area that can be designated for all businesses.

Marginal income

Marginal income statements

Marginal income, or *contribution margin,* is the excess of revenue over related variable costs and variable expenses. It is the amount of revenue that is available to pay fixed costs and then generate a profit. The marginal income statement, therefore, separates costs and expenses into their fixed and variable elements. It is a convenient means of presenting data to management when charts or other forms might not be as serviceable. The break-even sales volume can be calculated readily from such a statement. A marginal income statement for the Chetney Manufacturing Company is shown in Figure 27–4 (see Figure 27–1 for supporting data).

Figure 27–4 Marginal income statement

Sales (net): 20,000 units x $30 each	$600,000.00
Variable Costs and Expenses	240,000.00
Marginal Income	$360,000.00
Fixed Costs and Expenses	210,006.00
Net Income	$149,994.00

A marginal income statement emphasizes the contribution of each sales dollar toward the recovery of fixed costs and toward net income. Marginal income must equal fixed costs if the firm is to break even; marginal income must exceed fixed costs if a net income is to be realized. Thus, in Figure 27–4, 60 cents out of each sales dollar contributes toward the recovery of fixed costs until $210,006 is recovered at the break-even point of $350,010. After that point, 60 cents of each dollar contributes to net income.

Margin of safety

The *margin of safety* is the dollar volume of sales above the break-even point, or the amount by which sales may decrease before losses are incurred. The margin of safety for the Chetney Company is computed as follows:

Sales	$600,000.00
Deduct break-even sales	350,010.00
Margin of safety	$249,990.00

A loss will not be incurred unless budgeted sales decrease by more than $249,990. The *percentage of safety* is computed as follows:

$$\frac{\text{Margin of safety}}{\text{Net sales}} = \frac{\$249,990}{\$600,000} = 0.4167$$

Any decreases in budgeted sales up to 41.67 percent can be absorbed before a loss is incurred.

There is a relationship between the contribution margin percentage and the percentage of safety. It is

$$\text{Contribution margin percentage} \times \text{Percentage of safety} = \text{Profit as a percentage of sales.}$$

For the Chetney Manufacturing Company at a sales level of $600,000:

$$0.60 \times 0.4167 = 0.25, \text{ or } 25\%$$

Note that 25 percent of $600,000 = $150,000. The net income shown in Figure 27–4 is $149,994. The difference of $6 is due to rounding to four decimal places.

Marginal income planning

The effect of any prospective changes in operations can be determined rapidly when data on costs are divided between the fixed and variable elements. This kind of evaluation and analysis is demonstrated in the following case.

The York Manufacturing Company is considering expanding its present plant facilities at a time when the plant is operating at full capacity. Two important factors that must be considered before the decision is made are (1) the sales volume required with the planned expansion to earn the current income and (2) an appraisal from the marketing department of whether this figure can be reached and exceeded.

Assume the following data for the York Manufacturing Company:

	Under Present Plant Facilities		Under Proposed Plant Facilities	
Sales		$300,000.00		$400,000.00
Variable costs	$ 90,000.00		$120,000.00	
Fixed cost	175,000.00	265,000.00	231,000.00	351,000.00
Net income		$ 35,000.00		$ 49,000.00

The following basic formula (expanded from the break-even formula) is appropriate to determine the sales volume required with the planned expansion to earn a specified amount of income:

$$S = \frac{TFC + I}{1 - \dfrac{TVC}{TS}}$$

In this version of the formula, I = the specified amount of income. All that has been done is to add that amount to total fixed costs before dividing by the contribution margin percentage. The data for the York Company may be substituted in the above formula to determine the volume of sales needed to maintain current net income of $35,000.

$$S = \frac{\$231{,}000 + \$35{,}000}{1 - (\$120{,}000/\$400{,}000)} = \$380{,}000$$

This is verified as follows:

YORK MANUFACTURING COMPANY
Income Statement
Projected For Plant Expansion to Earn Present Income

Sales (S)		$380,000.00
Variable Costs (0.30S)	$114,000.00	
Fixed Costs	231,000.00	345,000.00
Net Income (currently being earned)		$ 35,000.00

It is assumed in this illustration that the variable cost rate will continue to be 30 percent of sales. It is possible that the additional facilities may permit an increase in the productivity of labor or purchasing economies, thus causing a decrease in the variable cost rate. Other factors must be considered in determining whether the proposed expansion is warranted. The acquisition of additional plant and equipment involves long-term investments, possible long-term financing, and increased taxes, insurance, maintenance, and other costs. Management should be reasonably assured that it will be able to make sustained use of the added facilities.

Among other considerations for York's management is the fact that the expansion program will raise the break-even point as indicated in the computation below:

	Present Facilities	Proposed Facilities
Fixed costs	$175,000.00	$231,000.00
Contribution margin percentage	0.70	0.70
B/E point (FC ÷ 0.70)	$250,000.00	$330,000.00

This means that York will commence to incur a net loss if management makes the proposed expansion and sales fall below $330,000. Under present facilities a drop in sales down to $250,000 can be experienced before losses start.

On the other hand, the proposed expansion would increase York's percentage of safety if the marketing department is confident that it can reach the proposed sales figure of $400,000. This would be calculated as follows:

	Present Facilities	Proposed Facilities
1 Budgeted sales	$300,000.00	$400,000.00
2 Break-even sales volume . . .	250,000.00	330,000.00
3 Margin of safety	$ 50,000.00	$ 70,000.00
4 Percentage of safety (**3** ÷ **1**).	16 2/3%	17 1/2%

Since the contribution percentage remains the same, a higher profit as a percent of sales can be expected. Using the relationship

Contribution percentage × Percentage of safety = Profit as a percent of sales, we can calculate the following:

	Profit as a Percent of Sales	
	Present Facilities	Proposed Facilities
0.70 x 0.167.	11 7/10%	
0.70 x 0.175.		12 1/4%

Decision making is not an automatic process. Given information as to possible outcomes and consequences of the proposed expansion plan, management of York Corporation must now exercise human judgment and decide which course to take. However, with the use of these cost, volume, and income relationship tools, they are in a much better position to make the decision.

Decisions based on cost analysis

Pricing of special orders

A decision management often confronts is whether or not to accept a special order involving the production of additional units beyond outstanding commitments. An analysis of preexisting cost patterns will not necessarily furnish the required data for such a decision. Each new situation requires a new cost analysis, and the concept of marginal cost must be considered. On a unit basis, *marginal cost* is the cost that must be incurred to produce one more unit than is currently being produced. If the price of the special order exceeds its marginal costs (which will equal variable costs if unused capacity is available and if there are no alternative uses for this available capacity) the offer should be accepted.

To illustrate, assume the following unit cost data for the Platte Company, based on a budgeted annual production of 60,000 units which is 75 percent of capacity. For Platte Company to increase production from 60,000 to 60,001 units an increase in cost of $6.00 would be incurred.

Manufacturing costs	
Direct materials	$2.00
Direct labor	2.50
Variable overhead costs	1.50
Total variable costs	$6.00
Fixed overhead costs ($180,000 ÷ 60,000 units)	3.00
Total unit cost	$9.00
Fixed selling and administrative expenses	$100,000.00

The Platte Company has been offered a long-term contract for 20,000 additional units annually at a unit price of $8.50. Since the purchaser is to attach his own label to the product, the Platte Company's normal sales price of $15 each will not be affected. Because fixed costs are not affected by the volume of production, fixed manufacturing overhead will remain at $180,000. The special offer price of $8.50 exceeds the marginal cost (unit variable cost) of $6. The regular sales are not affected, and a gain of $50,000 is realized on the additional order; the offer should be accepted. The comparative budget data verify this conclusion as follows:

PLATTE COMPANY
Budgeted Comparative Income Statement
For the Year Ending December 31, 1979

	Present Production	Additional Order	Totals
Sales			
60,000 units at $15.00	$900,000.00		
20,000 units at 8.50		$170,000.00	$1,070,000.00
Variable Manufacturing Costs			
60,000 units at $ 6.00	360,000.00		
20,000 units at 6.00		120,000.00	480,000.00
Marginal Income	$540,000.00	$ 50,000.00	$ 590,000.00
Fixed Costs*	280,000.00		280,000.00
Net Income	$260,000.00	$ 50,000.00	$ 310,000.00

*Includes fixed manufacturing overhead cost of $180,000 and selling and administrative expenses of $100,000, which are fixed costs.

Deciding to make or buy

If adequate plant facilities and the ability to assure proper quality exist, management may have the option of making a particular part or buying it from an outside supplier. The decision depends upon a comparison of cost to make with cost to buy. In making such a comparison, opportunity cost may be a consideration.

Assume that the Nivals Company manufactures a part at a total unit cost of $20.40. The cost to make consists of the following:

Direct materials	$ 4.50
Direct labor	7.50
Variable overhead costs	3.60
Total variable costs	$15.60
Fixed overhead costs	4.80
Total unit cost	$20.40

The Nivals Company can purchase this part from a reliable supplier for $18.15. If the available plant facilities represent sunk costs that cannot be recovered by some other use of the facilities, than the firm should continue to make the part. The total cost of $20.40 is greater than the quoted purchase price of $18.15, but the difference would defray only a part of fixed overhead costs.

If, however, Nivals Company can make an alternative use of these facilities, it may save money by purchasing the part. *Opportunity cost,* the amount of revenue forgone by not making the alternative use of the facilities, becomes relevant to the decision. Assume that Nivals makes 10,000 parts per year, and that the company could rent these facilities to Catherine Dorsam if they stopped manufacture of the part and bought it instead. The amount of rent to be received becomes an opportunity cost. Consider these possible situations:

	No Alternative Use	*Rent to Catherine Dorsam for $20,000*	*$40,000*
Variable cost to make	$156,000.00	$156,000.00	$156,000.00
Opportunity cost to make	–0–	20,000.00	40,000.00
Subtotal	$156,000.00	$176,000.00	$196,000.00
Cost to buy	181,500.00	181,500.00	181,500.00
Saving from buying	($ 25,500.00)	($ 5,500.00)	$ 14,500.00

If there is no alternative use of the facilities, management should continue to make the part. Also, if the rent that could be earned is only $20,000, Nivals Company would save by making the part. However, when the rent that can be earned is $40,000, the cost to buy is less than the cost to make, and Nivals should purchase the part.

Nivals Company's decision was whether to continue making a part or to buy it.

The parallel problem—whether to commence to make a part that is now being bought—involves essentially the same factors for consideration.

Abandonment of a department, territory, or product

The decision whether or not to abandon a supposedly unprofitable department, territory, or product involves a careful analysis of the effect of the abandonment on the fixed and variable cost and the marginal contribution. If a department, territory, or product produces any marginal contribution, it should not be abandoned unless the newly created capacity—that is a substituted new department, territory, or product—could be committed to a more profitable use.

A departmental income statement of the Muskegon Clothing Company is shown in Figure 27–5. The accountant has been asked by management for the probable effect on total costs if the children's department is eliminated. To make this effect clear, the accountant has separated fixed costs and variable costs in the income statement. Management knows that closing the department will entirely eliminate sales, cost of goods sold, and gross margin of the children's department, but fixed costs now being allocated to it will continue, and must be reallocated to other departments.

A summary analysis reveals the cost tabulation shown in Figure 27–6.

Figure 27–5
Departmental income statement

MUSKEGON CLOTHING COMPANY
Income Statement
For the Month Ended December 31, 1979

	Men's Department	Women's Department	Children's Department	Total All Departments
Sales (Net)	$39,455.00	$64,000.00	$17,200.00	$120,655.00
Cost of Goods Sold	26,828.00	45,222.00	13,315.00	85,365.00
Gross Margin on Sales	$12,627.00	$18,778.00	$ 3,885.00	$ 35,290.00
Deduct Operating Expenses				
Fixed Expenses:				
Rent	$ 1,080.00	$ 1,800.00	$ 720.00	$ 3,600.00
Depreciation of Store Equipment	200.00	250.00	50.00	500.00
Executive Salaries	1,301.50	2,598.00	650.50	4,550.00
Office Salaries	579.00	1,156.50	289.50	2,025.00
Heat and Light	225.00	375.00	150.00	750.00
Totals	$ 3,385.50	$ 6,179.50	$ 1,860.00	$ 11,425.00
Variable Expenses:				
Advertising	$ 490.50	$ 795.00	$ 214.50	$ 1,500.00
Sales Salaries	4,525.00	6,015.00	1,757.50	12,297.50
Sales Commissions	375.00	550.00	120.00	1,045.00
Insurance	240.00	300.00	60.00	600.00
Bad Debts Expense	37.50	87.50	25.00	150.00
Miscellaneous General Expense	200.00	250.00	50.00	500.00
Totals	$ 5,868.00	$ 7,997.50	$ 2,227.00	$ 16,092.50
Total Operating Expense	$ 9,253.50	$14,177.00	$ 4,087.00	$ 27,517.50
Net Income or (Loss)	$ 3,373.50	$ 4,601.00	$(202.00)	$ 7,772.50

As a result of this study, the effect of discontinuing the children's department can be reasonably forecast as follows:

Net operating income of all departments (Figure 27–5)		$7,772.50
Reduction in gross margin on sales (Figure 27–5)	$3,885.00	
Reduction in expenses (Figure 27–6)	2,227.00	
Reduction in net operating income		1,658.00
Combined net operating income with children's department eliminated		$6,114.50

On the basis of this calculation, the children's department should not be eliminated even though it shows a net loss. The marginal contribution of this department ($3,885 − $2,227) was absorbing $1,658 of the fixed expenses.

If the children's department is discontinued, the $1,860 fixed cost now being allocated to it would continue. Since the children's department is making a marginal contribution of $1,658 = ($1,860 − $202) toward this fixed cost, its elimination would result in a comparable loss in monthly net income as has already been demonstrated. Note carefully, however, that the Muskegon Clothing Company has no other profitable use for the space now being occupied by the children's department.

Budgeting capital expenditures

Capital budgeting refers to the allocation and commitment of funds to long-term capital investment projects. The amount of such investments or expenditures is usually large, and they are made expecting benefits to be received over a number of years. Capital budgeting concerns itself with the development, selection, and evaluation of proposals for plant expansion and modernization, equipment replacement, product development, and so on. The nature of these investments and their effect on the long-range welfare of a company make it very important that they be analyzed and evaluated with the utmost care.

Types of capital expenditure

The types of capital expenditure can perhaps best be illustrated by questions involving capital investment decisions, such as the following:

Expansion. Shall we buy additional equipment to supply the actual or anticipated increase in demand for our product? Shall we expand our facilities to produce new products? Shall we acquire the necessary facilities to make parts that we are now buying from outside sources?

Figure 27–6
Effect on costs of elimination of children's department

	Cost of Operation Charged Directly or Allocated to Children's Department	Effect of Elimination of Children's Department	
		Costs Eliminated	Costs Not Eliminated
Fixed expenses	$1,860.00		$1,860.00
Variable expenses . . .	2,227.00	$2,227.00	
Totals	$4,087.00	$2,227.00	$1,860.00

Replacement. Shall we replace present equipment with new and more efficient equipment? Shall we automate our production lines? Shall we buy machine A or machine B? Shall we lease the new equipment or shall we buy it?

Other. Some investments are made on noneconomic grounds. Will more recreational facilities for use by employees—even though they may not directly reduce costs or increase revenue—improve employer-employee relations? Must an investment to eliminate sound nuisances or smoke hazards be made in compliance with Environmental Protection Agency requirements? Even if it is not mandatory, should the company choose to make such an investment in acknowledgement of corporate social responsibility?

Rate of return

Business people make investments to get a satisfactory return. The definition of a satisfactory rate of return depends on a number of factors in the economy. In the long run, the rate of return must be adequate to attract new capital. The selection of an appropriate rate of return is central to the capital expenditure decision, since it has a direct influence on the decision.

The selected *rate of return* is the rate that the funds could earn if they were invested in the best available alternative project. Since funds used on project A, for example, are not available for use on project B, the amount that could have been earned on project B is sacrificed. The amount or rate so sacrificed constitutes an *opportunity cost*—the minimum that must be earned on the chosen project.

Determining the cash flows

A capital investment generates flows of cash into and out of the business over a period. A comparison of several investment projects from which the best choice is to be made requires a comparison of the expected cash flows that the projects will bring. The concern is with future, not past, amounts. It is also with the items that will be different. Clearly, a cost or a revenue amount that will be the same under all the alternatives from which a choice is to be made does not have an effect upon the decision. The *investment cost* is an immediate outflow. After-tax *increases in revenue* or *reductions in costs* represent inflows. Management must use cost accounting and budget data to predict the amounts of inflows. After management has determined expected cash flows a method is needed to compare projects and determine the most desirable. Some methods of measuring the desirability of investment projects follow.

Payback

Desirability of a project can be measured by a single criterion, *payback* or payout. That is, how soon will the cash invested in the project be returned? Payback is a measure of the time required for the accumulated cash earnings from a project to equal the cash investment.

$$\frac{\text{Investment}}{\text{Annual net cash inflows}} = \text{Payback}$$

In theory, the shorter the payback time, the less the risk. The popularity of payback is due to its simplicity and to its effectiveness as an initial screening measure, especially for high-risk investments in which the useful life is difficult to project. It is also useful in evaluating projects of such obvious merit that refined analysis is not needed, and in evaluating projects showing no financial merit. The factors it ignores are (1) the useful life, (2) the amount and pattern of cash flows beyond the payback point, (3) disposal values, (4) the time value of money, and (5) the profitability of the investment. To illustrate, assume the following figures:

Project	*Net investment*	*Annual net cash savings**
A	$10,000.00	$2,500.00
B	20,000.00	5,000.00

*After taxes

The payback on both projects is four years; on this basis they are equally desirable. However, if it is further assumed that Project A has a four-year life and Project B a five-year life, it becomes obvious that these proposals are not equally desirable. B provides a $5,000 inflow in its fifth year that is not considered in the payback computation.

Accounting rate of return

To overcome one of the limitations of the payback method, some companies use the *accounting rate of return*. The formula for this model is

$$\frac{\text{Annual after-tax cash inflows} - \text{annual depreciation}}{\text{Original investment}} = \begin{array}{l}\text{Rate of return on}\\ \text{original investment.}\end{array}$$

To illustrate, assume the purchase of a machine for $30,000 that will provide after-tax cash savings of $6,000 per year for an estimated useful life of ten years.

If the straight-line method of depreciation is used, the depreciation charge is $3,000 per year. Then

$$\frac{\$6,000 - \$3,000}{\$30,000} = 10 \text{ percent return on original investment.}$$

Some accountants compute the rate of return on average investment. In the above example, this rate would be

$$\frac{\$6,000 - \$3,000}{\$30,000 \div 2} = 20 \text{ percent return on average investment.}$$

Whichever rate of return is used, the emphasis is placed on profitability of the investment, thus overcoming one of the limitations of the payback method. The accounting rate of return still shares a major weakness of the payback method; it ignores the time value of money.

To recognize the compound interest aspect (or time value of money), we may use one of the discounted cash flow methods such as the present value method.

Time value of money

Money placed on deposit earns interest. The interest earned may be paid to the investor periodically as in the case of bond interest. An alternative treatment is to allow the interest to accumulate and earn further interest on itself. This alternative is called compound interest.

Compound amount Compound interest is added to the principal amount at the end of each period. Therefore, the interest for the next period is computed at the same rate, but on a greater amount. For example, if $1,000 is deposited at 5 percent compounded annually, the amount grows as follows:

Year	*Amount at beginning of year*	*Interest for year*	*Amount at end of year*
First	$1,000.00	$50.00	$1,050.00
Second	1,050.00	52.50	1,102.50
Third	1,102.50	55.13	1,157.63
Fourth	1,157.63	57.88	1,215.51

The amount of interest for each period is greater than the period before it because the 5 percent rate is being applied to a larger base each time. The example above could be pictured as follows:

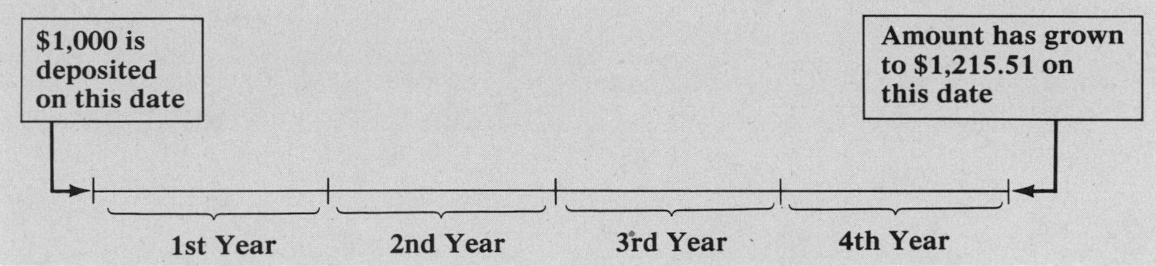

Present value When a single deposit or investment (as in the above example) is involved, the original deposit is known as the *present value of an amount*. The future value is known as the *amount of a single sum*. Thus, $1,215.51 is the amount to which $1,000 will grow at the end of four years when it is compounded at 5 percent annually. Viewed from the other side, $1,000 is the present value of $1,215.51 under the same circumstances.

Amount of an ordinary annuity When more than one deposit is made the series of deposits is called an *annuity*. Using the foregoing example, suppose that $1,000 is deposited *at the end of each year* with interest at 5 percent compounded annually. The amount would grow as follows:

Year	*Amount at Beginning of Year*	*Interest for Year*	*Additional Deposit*	*Amount at End of Year*
First	$ –0–	$ –0–	$1,000.00	$1,000.00
Second	1,000.00	50.00	1,000.00	2,050.00
Third	2,050.00	102.50	1,000.00	3,152.50
Fourth	3,152.50	157.63	1,000.00	4,310.13

This example could be pictured as

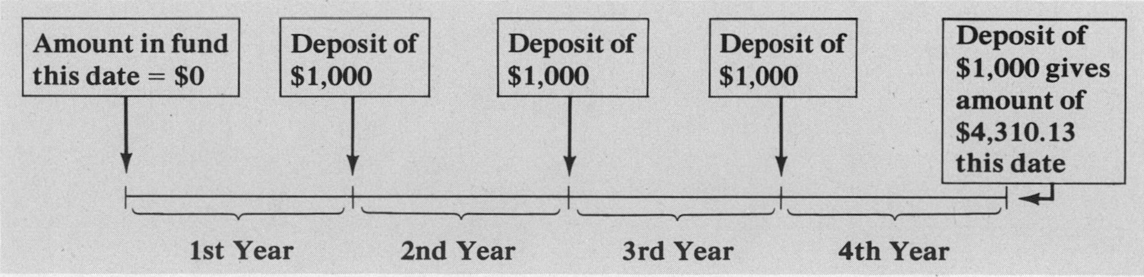

Because deposits are made at the end of each year, this is called an *ordinary annuity*. The annual deposits are called *rents*. The *amount of an ordinary annuity* of four rents of $1,000 each is $4,310.13 at 5 percent.

Present value of an ordinary annuity Sometimes we wish to deposit a single sum at the beginning of a time period and make periodic withdrawals. Suppose it is desired to withdraw $1,000 at the end of each year for 4 years with money worth 5 percent compounded annually. The amount to be deposited at the beginning is known as the *present value of an ordinary annuity*. The present value in the foregoing situation is $3,545.95, demonstrated as follows:

Year	*Amount at Beginning of Year*	*Interest for Year*	*Withdrawal*	*Amount at End of Year*
First	$3,545.95	$177.30	$1,000.00	$2,723.25
Second	2,723.25	136.16	1,000.00	1,859.41
Third	1,859.41	92.97	1,000.00	952.38
Fourth	952.38	47.62	1,000.00	–0–

This example could be pictured as:

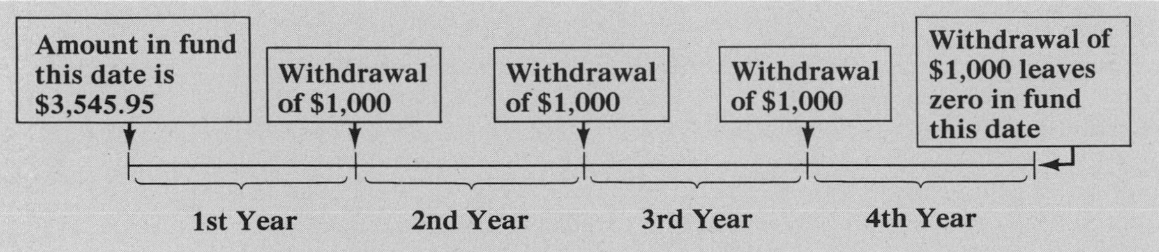

The periodic cash inflows from a capital investment are the same as withdrawals from an ordinary annuity. Any salvage value to be received upon disposition of a piece of capital equipment is the same as the present value of an amount. Formulas and tables are available to compute or to look up the present values of inflows. These present values can be compared with the outflow (cost of the investment) to determine desirability of an investment. The difference between the present value of inflows and the investment needed to get them is called *excess present value* if the inflows are greater.

Present value method

Assume that the East Company is planning to buy a new press for $25,000, with an estimated useful life of 10 years. Freight and installation costs will be $1,500. The press being replaced originally cost $20,000, has a carrying value of $8,000 and a remaining life of 10 years, and can be sold for $4,000. The new press is not expected to change revenue but is expected to reduce annual labor costs, including fringe benefits, by $5,500, and to increase yearly power costs by $1,000. Maintenance, taxes, and insurance will be unchanged. The advisability of the replacement is being questioned. Money is worth 14 percent compounded annually.

Step 1. *Net cash investment.* The first step is to determine the net amount of initial cash investment required. For East Company this amounts to:

Purchase price of new press	$25,000.00
Freight and installation	1,500.00
Total	$26,500.00
Deduct proceeds from sale of old press	4,000.00
Net investment	$22,500.00

The carrying value of the old press is irrelevant because it represents a past (or sunk) cost, not a future cost. Whatever the carrying value, the net investment is $22,500. The selling price of the old machine is relevant because it represents a reduction of the cash investment.

Step 2. *Net cash inflows.* The East Company proposal falls into the cost reduction category. The relevant cash inflows are the costs that will be different—the differential costs—if the proposal is adopted. The expected change in annual operating cash flows will be as follows:

Cost decreases (labor)	$5,500.00
Deduct cost increases (power)	1,000.00
Net annual savings	$4,500.00

This step involves a careful analysis of all operating costs to determine which costs will be increased and which decreased. Only those cost changes that will change cash flows should be considered.

Step 3. *Estimated useful life.* This step is necessary for any long-lived asset. The question to be answered is: How long will the new press contribute to the earnings of the firm? The East Company has estimated this to be 10 years.

Step 4. *Excess present value.* The net annual savings is $4,500. By using compound interest tables, the East Company can determine the present value of a cash inflow of $4,500 per year for the next 10 years. With money worth 14 percent compounded annually that amount is $23,472.52. In other words, East should be willing to invest $23,472.52 to receive a cash inflow of $4,500 per year. The present value of the cash inflows (savings) is then compared with the present value of the outflow (actual net cash investment) as follows:

Present value of inflows	$23,472.52
Net cash investment (actual)	22,500.00
Excess present value	$ 972.52

Since the present value of the cash inflows is in excess of the present outflows, this investment is better than the return of 14 percent that East could obtain elsewhere. If the present value of cash inflows were less than the net investment, East Company should look for another use of its available funds.

Profitability index The greater the excess present value, the more desirable the investment. This leads to a device or index that allows a company to rank several proposals in order of desirability. The *profitability index* is

$$\frac{\text{Present value of inflows}}{\text{Net investment}} = \text{Profitability index.}$$

For the East Company, this is

$$\frac{\$23{,}472.52}{\$22{,}500.00} = 1.043.$$

Any alternative investment with a profitability index greater than 1.043 would be ranked above this proposed new press in order of desirability.

Limitations of present value The primary objective is to find a way to compare and choose the best from several proposed capital expenditures. The concept of present value has theoretical validity and practicability in the capital budgeting process. It provides the basis for a systematic analysis of available alternative investment proposals. But sophistication and refinement of procedure cannot insure a best choice if the data are wrong. The data used are projections of expectations—often long range—involving revenue, cost, equipment life, human and material performance, and so on. Under such conditions of uncertainty, skillful managerial judgment is imperative. Finally, some factors cannot be quantified. An investment may have a direct or indirect effect on morale or on relations with the community, which, if not carefully judged, could cause harm. There is usually no single right answer. Sophisticated analytical procedures will not cancel the effects of poor judgment as to market potential, available resources, and environmental factors—economic, political, and social.

Summary of methods

The discussions in this chapter have omitted many important quantitative decision making techniques that require accounting data. Topics such as linear programming, use of probabilities and expected value have been left for more advanced courses in accounting. Figure 27–7 summarizes the formulas that have been explained in this chapter.

Figure 27–7
Formulas used for decision making

1. $$\frac{\text{Total fixed cost}}{\text{Unit contribution margin}} = \text{Break-even sales in units}$$
2. $$\frac{\text{Unit (or total) variable costs}}{\text{Unit (or total) sales price}} = \text{Variable cost percentage}$$
3. 1 − variable cost percentage = Contribution margin percentage or P/V ratio
4. $$\frac{\text{Total fixed costs}}{\text{Contribution margin percentage}} = \text{Break-even sales in dollars}$$
5. $$\frac{\text{Margin of safety}}{\text{Net sales}} = \text{Percentage of safety}$$

6. **Contribution margin percentage × Percentage of safety = Profit as a percent of sales**

7. $$\frac{\textbf{Original investment}}{\textbf{Annual net cash inflows}} = \textbf{Payback period in years}$$

8. $$\frac{\textbf{After-tax cash inflows} - \textbf{annual depreciation}}{\textbf{Original investment}} = \textbf{Rate of return on original investment}$$

9. $$\frac{\textbf{After-tax cash inflows} - \textbf{annual depreciation}}{\textbf{Original investment} \div 2} = \textbf{Rate of return on average investment}$$

10. **Present value of cash inflows − Present value of investment = Excess present value**

11. $$\frac{\textbf{Present value of cash inflows}}{\textbf{Present value of investment}} = \textbf{Profitability index}$$

A real-life example

Jacksonville Service Company (called Jaxco) has developed a method of converting an inexpensive model of transistor radio into a citizens band radio that sells for $40 each. Jaxco's production department has developed a proposal to add computerized controls to the process which would decrease variable costs by $4 per unit and would increase production from 15,200 units to 23,500 units per year. The sales manager feels that the additional units can be sold only if the $4 per unit cost saving is passed on to the customer. But the new computer equipment must be rented at a cost of $100,000 per year.

Jaxco's accounting department develops the following data:

	Present Method	*New Method*
Sales (15,200 @ $40)	$608,000.00	
(23,500 @ $36)		$846,000.00
VC (15,200 @ $25)	$380,000.00	
(23,500 @ $21)		$493,500.00
FC	160,000.00	260,000.00
Total cost	$540,000.00	$753,500.00
Net income	$ 68,000.00	$ 92,500.00
P/V ratio	0.375	0.4167
Break-even point	$426,666.67	$624,000.00
Margin of safety	181,333.33	222,000.00
Percentage of safety	0.2982	0.2624
Profit as percent of sales	0.111825	0.109342

After studying the above data it is clear to management that the important question is: How sure is the sales manager of the sales increase? The break-even point has increased sharply; if sales fall below 17,333 units, Jaxco will lose money. However, if the prediction is correct, there will be a profit increase of

$24,400 even though total profits as a percent of sales will drop slightly. The degree of accuracy of the sales forecast is critical to the decision. But now management knows what to focus on. It will make a thorough market survey to test the sales prediction of 23,500 units.

Glossary

Accounting rate of return A method of evaluating capital investments; it equals (after-tax inflows − depreciation) ÷ cost of original investment.

Amount of an ordinary annuity The future sum of a series of deposits and their compound interest.

Break-even point The volume of sales at which the business will neither earn income nor incur a loss.

Capital budgeting The allocation and commitment of funds to long-term capital investment projects.

Compound amount The future sum of a single deposit and its compound interest.

Compound interest Interest earned not only on the original deposit but also on interest earned in the past but not yet paid. This term also refers to the difference between the future sum and the original deposit(s) made.

Contribution margin Selling price minus variable cost.

Contribution margin percentage Marginal income divided by sales; same as 1 − (variable costs as a percentage of sales).

Excess present value The difference, at a common point of time, between the cost of the investment and the present value of the expected earnings from the investment.

Fixed costs Costs that, without a change in present productive capacity, are not affected by changes in volume of output.

Make-or-buy decision The decision whether to make a product or to buy it outside.

Marginal cost On a unit basis, the additional cost required to produce one more unit of product than is currently being produced.

Marginal income The excess of revenue over related variable costs and variable expenses.

Margin of safety The dollar volume of sales above the break-even point.

Opportunity costs The cost of forgoing one thing—investment, operation, material, process, and so on—to get an acceptable alternative.

Out-of-pocket costs Costs that give rise to direct expenditures.

Payback A method of measuring the desirability of a project in terms of how soon the cash invested in a project will be recovered.

Percentage of safety The margin of safety divided by net sales.

Present value method The conversion of cash inflows and outflows over time to the present, using an estimated discounting rate, for purposes of comparing capital expenditures.

Present value of an amount The future sum reduced by the compound interest in it.

Present value of an ordinary annuity The single sum at the beginning of a time period that, at compound interest, will provide specific periodic withdrawals.
Profitability index Present value of inflows in ratio to net investment.
P/V ratio Same as contribution margin percentage.
Semifixed costs Costs that are not affected by changes in volume of output, but only within a short volume range.
Semivariable costs Costs that include both a fixed and a variable component.
Sunk costs Already incurred costs that cannot be recovered by abandonment of the project.
Time value of money The idea that a dollar in the future is not equal to a dollar in present time, because it could earn interest when placed on deposit.
Variable costs Costs that are affected in total by changes in the volume of output.

Questions

Q27–1 Define the following terms: (a) fixed costs, (b) variable costs, (c) out-of-pocket costs, and (d) sunk costs.

Q27–2 (a) What is meant by the term break-even point? (b) How is it computed? (c) What are its practical applications? (d) What are its limitations?

Q27–3 Define the following terms: (a) marginal income, (b) margin of safety, and (c) marginal income statement.

Q27–4 Under what circumstances would it be advantageous for a manufacturer in the United States to accept a one-time order for a product from a foreign buyer?

Q27–5 (a) What use does management make of cost data in deciding to make or buy a certain part? (b) Should fixed costs enter into the decision?

Q27–6 (a) Is it possible for one of three departments in a retail store to show a net loss even though its elimination would decrease the total net income of the entire store? (b) What intangible factors must be considered when deciding whether or not a certain department should be eliminated?

Q27–7 Cost-volume-earnings analysis (break-even analysis) is used to determine and express the interrelationships of different volumes of activity (sales, costs, and sales prices) to earnings. More specifically, the analysis is concerned with what will be the effect on earnings of changes in sales volume, sales prices, sales mix, and costs.

1. Certain terms are fundamental to cost-volume-earnings analysis. Explain the meaning of each of the following terms:
   a. Fixed costs
   b. Variable costs
   c. Relevant volume range
   d. Break-even point
   e. Margin of safety.
2. Several assumptions are implicit in cost-volume-earnings analysis. What are these assumptions?

Q27–8 What is capital budgeting? Why are the principles of compound interest useful in capital budgeting?

Q27–9 What consitutes a satisfactory rate of return? How is a rate selected?

Q27–10 Why is it appropriate in making capital budgeting decisions to emphasize the relevant cash flows rather than net income changes with valuations based on generally accepted accounting principles?

Q27–11 What is meant (a) by excess present value? (b) by profitability index?

Q27–12 What are the steps to be taken in measuring the excess present value of a proposed capital expenditure?

Q27–13 (a) Define payback (b) What are its advantages? (c) its disadvantages?

Q27–14 What limitations are inherent in applying present value procedures to capital budgeting decisions?

Class exercises

CE27–1 (Break-even sales; income planning in conjunction with expansion of plant facilities) The Dade Manufacturing Company is operating at full capacity. It has under consideration a plan for the expansion of its plant facilities. Current and projected income statement data are shown below.

	Under Present Plant Facilities		*Under Proposed Plant Facilities*	
Sales		$750,000.00		$1,125,000.00
Variable costs	$300,000.00		$450,000.00	
Fixed costs	360,000.00	660,000.00	540,000.00	990,000.00
Net income		$ 90,000.00		$ 135,000.00

Required:

1. What is the present break-even point?
2. What is the break-even point under the proposed plan?
3. What will be the amount of sales necessary to realize the current net income of $90,000 under the proposed plan?
4. Prepare an income statement to prove your answer to requirement 3.

CE27–2 (Acceptance or rejection of an offer) The El Cajon Shop is operating at 65 percent capacity, producing 225,000 pairs of men's boots annually. Actual unit cost and selling price data for the year 1979 are as follows:

Direct materials	$15.00
Direct labor	9.00
Variable overhead costs	4.50
Total variable costs	$28.50
Fixed overhead costs ($2,700,000 ÷ 225,000)	12.00
Total unit cost	$40.50
Selling price	$76.50

The company has been offered a long-term contract to sell 80,000 pairs of men's boots annually to a Mexican importing firm at $34.50 a pair. This will not affect domestic sales. Fixed overhead costs of $2,700,000 as well as fixed selling and administrative costs of $2,400,000 will not be affected by the new order.

Required: Prepare comparative statements for management indicating whether or not this long-term contract should be accepted.

CE27–3 (Make-or-buy decision) The New London Company can produce a part at the following costs:

Direct materials	$14.40
Direct labor	19.20
Variable overhead costs	8.00
Subtotal	$41.60
Fixed overhead costs	12.80
Total unit costs	$54.40

The company can purchase the part for $44.80. It makes 1,000 per year.

Required: Should the part be purchased: (a) if fixed overhead unit cost of $12.80 is a sunk cost? (b) if Michelle Nykerk will pay $5,000 per year to rent those plant facilities now devoted to making the part?

CE27–4 (Department abandonment) The following condensed marginal income statement is available for Dubuque Department Store for 1979.

	Departments			
	A	*B*	*C*	*Total*
Sales (net)	$28,000.00	$24,000.00	$20,000.00	$72,000.00
Variable Costs	14,400.00	21,600.00	9,600.00	45,600.00
Marginal Income	$13,600.00	$ 2,400.00	$10,400.00	$26,400.00
Fixed Costs	8,000.00	6,400.00	5,450.00	19,850.00
Net Income or (Loss)	$ 5,600.00	($4,000.00)	$ 4,950.00	$ 6,550.00

Required:
1. Should Department B be eliminated? Explain.
2. Assume that none of the fixed costs can be eliminated if Department B is abandoned, and that the 1980 operational results for Departments A and C are the same as in 1979. Prepare a condensed marginal income statement for 1980 assuming that Department B is eliminated.

CE27–5 (Payback; accounting rate of return; excess present value) Hampshire, Inc. plans to invest $200,000 in certain improved metal fabrication equipment that is expected to save $50,000 (net after taxes) annually for ten years. Assume straight-line depreciation with no salvage value.

Required:
1. Compute the payback period.
2. Compute the accounting rate of return on original investment.
3. Compute the accounting rate of return on average investment.
4. Compute excess present value if the value of money is 20 percent. (The present value of $50,000 per year for 10 years at 20% = $209,624.)
5. Compute the profitability index.

Exercises and problems

P27–1 For the year 1979, the Parliament Company estimates fixed costs at $440,000 and variable costs at $3.15 a unit.

Required:

1. How many units must be sold to break even, assuming a unit sales price of $7.00?
2. Prepare an income statement to prove your answer.

P27–2 The Murphy Company has fixed costs of $704,000 a year. Its variable costs are $10.60 a unit and its sales price is $17.60 a unit. It is considering the purchase of machinery that will increase the fixed costs to $810,000 a year, but will enable the company to reduce variable costs to $7.75 a unit.

Required:

1. Compute the break-even point before and after the acquisition of the new machinery, giving it in both sales dollars and units of product.
2. If net income before the acquisition is $140,000, how many units will have to be sold after the machinery is acquired to maintain the net income?
3. Do you recommend purchase of this machinery? Why?

P27–3 The fixed costs in the Pacific Company are now $1,175,000 a year. They are expected to increase to $1,224,000 next year. Variable costs will also go up from $7.05 to $7.70 a unit. Its product sells for $15.50 a unit.

Required: How much sales revenue must be obtained to have a net income (before taxes) of $115,000 next year?

P27–4 A new machine costing $510,000 is under consideration. The product it makes sells for $16 a unit and requires materials costing $3.50, direct labor of $5.10 and other variable costs of $0.50 a unit. Sales of 65,000 units a year are assumed. Applicable annual fixed costs other than depreciation amount to $195,000. The company pays income tax on all earnings at the rate of 50 percent.

Required: Compute the payback period.

P27–5 The Strum Company manufactures and sells 2,500,000 units of its product in the United States annually. The selling price per unit is $48; variable costs are $19.50 a unit, and fixed costs are $24 a unit. It is now operating at 60 percent capacity.

Required: Should the company accept an additional order to sell 800,000 units abroad (a) at $18 a unit? (b) at $19 a unit? (c) at $21.60 a unit? (d) at $16.80 a unit? Explain your answer to each question.

P27–6 The Clouse Company was organized early in 1979. During 1979, it produced and sold 9,600 units; costs for the year were:

Variable costs:	
Direct materials	$ 69,120.00
Direct labor	92,160.00
Manufacturing overhead	110,400.00
Selling and administrative expenses	28,800.00
Fixed costs:	
Manufacturing overhead	43,200.00
Selling and administrative expenses	19,200.00

The selling price per unit is $70.

Required:

1. Calculate the break-even point.
2. Prepare a marginal income statement for 1979.
3. Compute the margin of safety, expressed as a dollar amount.

P27–7 The McEwen Company estimates its costs at full capacity as follows:

Fixed	$840,000.00
Variable	480,000.00

Fixed costs are constant at all levels of operation; variable costs vary in direct proportion to sales. Sales at full capacity are estimated at $1,600,000.

Required:

1. Calculate the break-even point.
2. Determine the break-even percentage of operating capacity.
3. Compute the margin of safety, expressed as a dollar amount.
4. Compute the percentage of safety.
5. Compute the net income as a percent of sales by the formula: Contribution margin percentage × Percentage of safety.
6. Prove the computation in 5 with a marginal income statement assuming full capacity sales.

P27–8 Motors, Incorporated manufactures an assembly; unit costs are as follows:

Direct materials	$ 4.80
Direct labor	3.20
Variable overhead costs	1.60
Subtotal	$ 9.60
Fixed overhead costs	2.40
Total	$12.00

The company can purchase this part for $10.75. The company uses 10,000 assemblies per year.

Required: Should the assembly be purchased: (a) if fixed overhead unit cost of $2.40 is a sunk cost? (b) if an alternative use that will bring in revenue of $10,000 per year can be made of the plant facilities now devoted to making the assembly?

P27–9 The following operational information is available for Pinnix Department Store for 1979.

	Department 1	2	3
Net operating income (loss)	$ 50,000.00	$100,000.00	($25,400.00)
Marginal income	110,000.00	187,500.00	10,000.00

Required:

1. Should department 3 be eliminated?
2. If department 3 is eliminated and the 1980 operating results for department 1 and 2 are the same as in 1979, how much higher (or lower) will the 1980 net operating income be?

P27–10 What is the payback period on an investment with an initial cash outlay of $20,000 and after-tax cash inflows of $6,000 a year for an estimated useful life of five years? What is the accounting rate of return on original investment? Use the straight-line method of depreciation.

P27–11 (Integrative) A machine that costs $20,000 will reduce present operating costs by $4,000 a year after taxes. Money is worth 16 percent.

Required:

1. Compute the payback period.
2. Compute the accounting rate of return on original investment with an estimated useful life of 20 years.
3. Is the rate of return on original investment acceptable in view of apparent alternative investment opportunities (that is, with money worth 16 percent)?
4. The present value of an annual cash inflow of $4,000 for 20 years at 16 percent is $23,715. Under the present-value method is this an acceptable investment?
5. Using the information in 4, compute the profitability index.
6. What are some weaknesses of using (a) payback, (b) accounting rate of return, and (c) present value method in this decision?

P27–12 (Minicase) Suzanne, Inc. manufactures and distributes throughout southern Florida a cosmetic called Miami Holiday. At normal capacity of 100 percent the company produces and sells 50,000 cases per year at a sales price of $240 per case. At this level, costs per case are:

Direct materials	$ 25.00
Direct labor	50.00
Variable factory overhead	40.00
Variable selling and administrative expenses	10.00
Fixed factory overhead	40.00
Fixed selling and administrative expenses	35.00
Cost per case	$200.00

The company's sales force is confident that it can sell an additional 10,000 cases per year at the same price. To produce this additional quantity would require expansion of plant capacity that would increase annual fixed costs by $1,000,000. The only cost savings would be a decrease in direct labor amounting to $15 per case and a decrease in variable factory overhead amounting to $10 per case.

Before making a decision on the expansion proposal the president has ordered a study of its effect on the break-even point, the margin of safety, the percentage of safety, and net income as a percent of sales. Calculate these figures for present business and the proposed expansion. Present comparative marginal income statements to support your computations.

Income taxes

part seven

chapter twenty-eight

Introduction

An introduction to federal income taxes is included in an elementary accounting text to emphasize the difference between business income and taxable income. Accordingly, in this chapter the basic structure of the federal income tax system as amended by the Tax Reduction and Simplification Act of 1977 is explained. Consideration is also given to topics such as tax planning and the impact of income tax on business decisions. A brief introduction to some financial reporting problems caused by income taxes is included.

Federal income taxes: basic formula and tax planning

Learning goals

To explain the difference between net income and final taxable income.
To know the basic structure of the federal income tax system.
To recognize the nature of tax planning.
To recognize the impact of income taxes on business decisions.
To introduce the idea of income tax allocation.

Key terms

adjusted gross income
avoidance of taxes
capital assets
capital gains and losses
deductions
evasion of taxes
excess itemized deductions
exemption
final tax table income
flat standard deduction
gross income
head of household
interperiod income tax allocation
itemized personal deductions
itemizer taxpayer
nonitemizer taxpayer
tax credit
taxable income
tax rate schedule
tax table
tax table income
tentative taxable income
tentative tax table income
unused zero bracket amount
zero bracket amount

Classes of taxpayers

Four kinds of separate entities are subject to the federal income tax: individuals, corporations, estates, and trusts. Two of these entities, estates and trusts, need a brief description. Estates come into existence when an individual dies and leaves income-producing assets in an estate. Even if these assets are to be distributed to the heirs, they will remain in the estate for a certain period of time. A trust, created by a contract or by a will, transfers assets to a trustee to be managed for the specific purpose named in the trust document.

Each of these entities must submit a calculation of the income tax on a specific type of tax return to the federal governmental organization named to handle the collection of taxes, the Internal Revenue Service. This submission is referred to as the *filing* of the tax return. In addition to the filing of a return, each must pay a tax, if applicable, on its taxable income.[1] Single business proprietorships and partnerships are not taxed as separate business entities. Rather, the single proprietor reports business income along with all personal income on Form 1040, the U.S. Individual Income Tax Return. The partnership files a separate informational return, Form 1065, but each partner reports his or her share of net income, together with the personal nonpartnership income on Form 1040.

Tax accounting methods

The Internal Revenue Code enacted by the United States Congress sets forth rules and the Internal Revenue Service establishes regulations regarding the inclusion and exclusion of certain revenue and expense items and the use of certain methods and procedures in computing taxable income. The Internal Revenue Code, however, permits taxpayers to select certain options, among them the alternative of choosing the cash or the accrual basis of computing net income under certain circumstances. The taxpayer should choose the method permissible under the law that will postpone and avoid (not evade) taxes, thereby conserving working capital and achieving the taxpayer's goal of the lowest long-run tax cost.

Cash basis

When the *cash basis* is used income is recognized when cash is received and expenses are considered to be incurred when the cash payment is made. The cash basis usually is *not* a satisfactory method of measuring net business income. For tax purposes, however, it is well suited for individuals not engaged in business and also, to a lesser extent, for businesses in which inventories, payables,

1 Some trusts, all of whose income goes to beneficiaries, file tax returns for information purposes only. The income received from these trusts should be reported by the individual beneficiaries on their individual tax returns. Under these circumstances, the trust would not pay any income taxes.

and receivables are *not* a major factor. In this latter case, the calculation of net income by the cash method may approximate that calculated by the accrual basis method. An individual whose only income is salary is required to use the cash basis.

The cash basis for income tax purposes is modified in two ways. First, the cost of long-lived assets, such as machinery or a truck, cannot be deducted in the year of purchase when cash is paid. The taxpayer must treat these items as assets and apportion their cost over their useful service lives. Second, revenue is recognized when it is constructively received, that is, when the revenue is in the control of the taxpayer. For example, interest credited to a savings and loan account is deemed to be constructively received even though the cash is not yet in the hands of the taxpayer.

Accrual basis

The *accrual basis* of measuring income has been discussed in preceding chapters of this text. Under this method revenue is recognized in the period when a sale is made or a service is rendered, irrespective of when cash is received; expenses are recognized in the period when services or goods are utilized in the production of revenue. The accrual basis is required of those businesses in which production, purchases, and sales of merchandise are significant factors. Under these circumstances, the Internal Revenue Code requirement that the accrual basis be used follows generally accepted accounting principles. The sales and cost-of-goods-sold figures are typically calculated by the accrual basis. Thus, since a significant difference could result from the use of the cash basis as compared with the accrual basis under the circumstances described above, the Internal Revenue Code specifies the use of the accrual basis as the generally accepted basis. Any taxpayer (other than a person whose only income is salary) who maintains a set of accounting records may elect to use the accrual basis.

Individual income tax

The individual taxpayer computes federal income tax by following the outline provided on the U.S. Individual Income Tax Return, Form 1040. Figure 28–1 presents the basic tax formula for individuals who are required to compute their tax by the use of income tax tables and also for individuals who must use the tax rate schedules. Regardless of which alternative a taxpayer must follow the calculation is identical down through adjusted gross income. Each of the steps in the tax formula is discussed below.[2]

2 The information in this chapter is based on the 1977 Tax Reduction and Simplification Act applicable to 1977 and 1978. All references in the chapter will be to the year of 1978. The reader should be aware that the tax law has been altered by Congress annually for the last several years.

Sources of gross income

Legal gross income All income not specifically excluded by law is includable in gross income. In addition to the items mentioned in Figure 28–1, gam-

Figure 28–1 Individual income tax chart

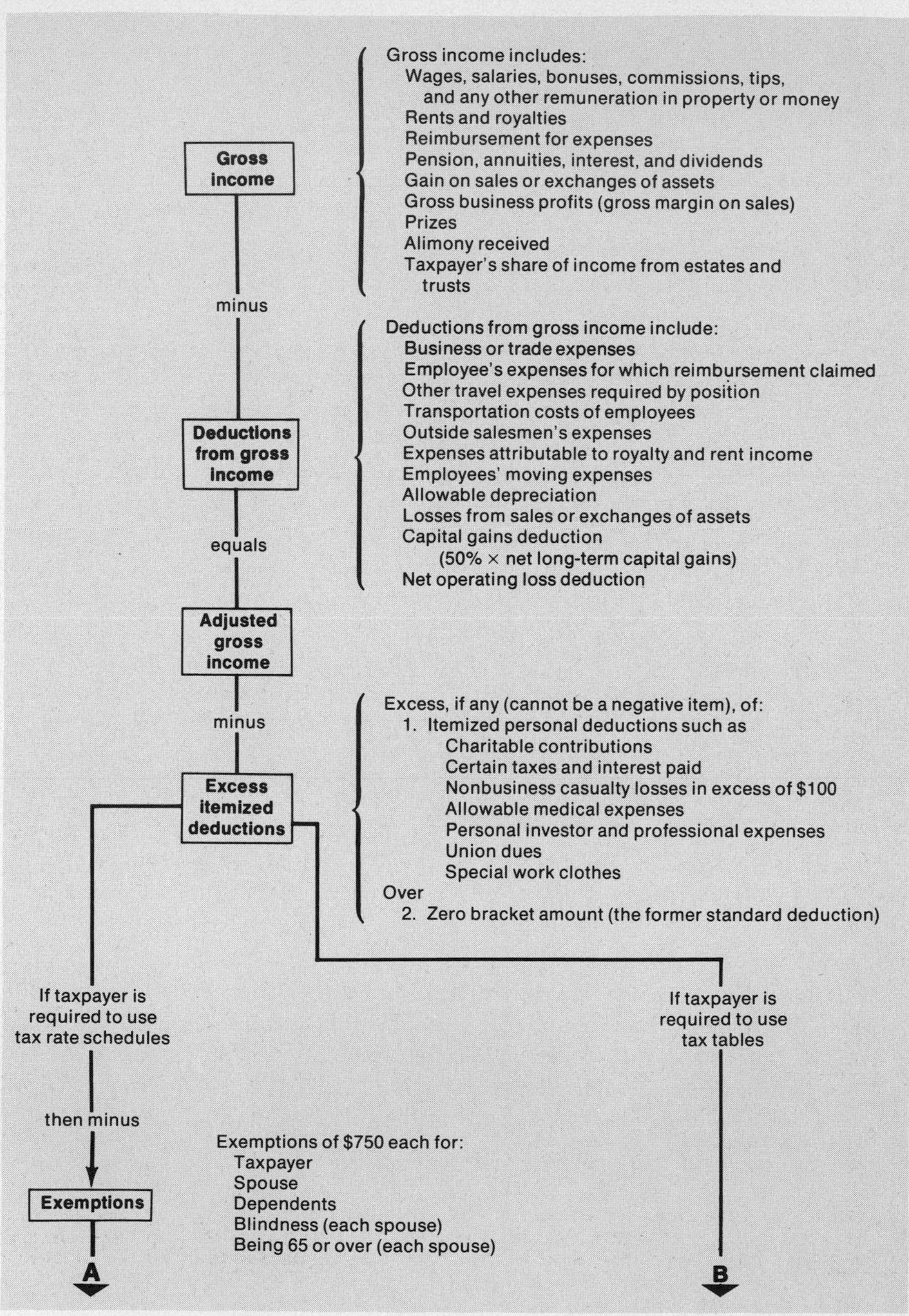

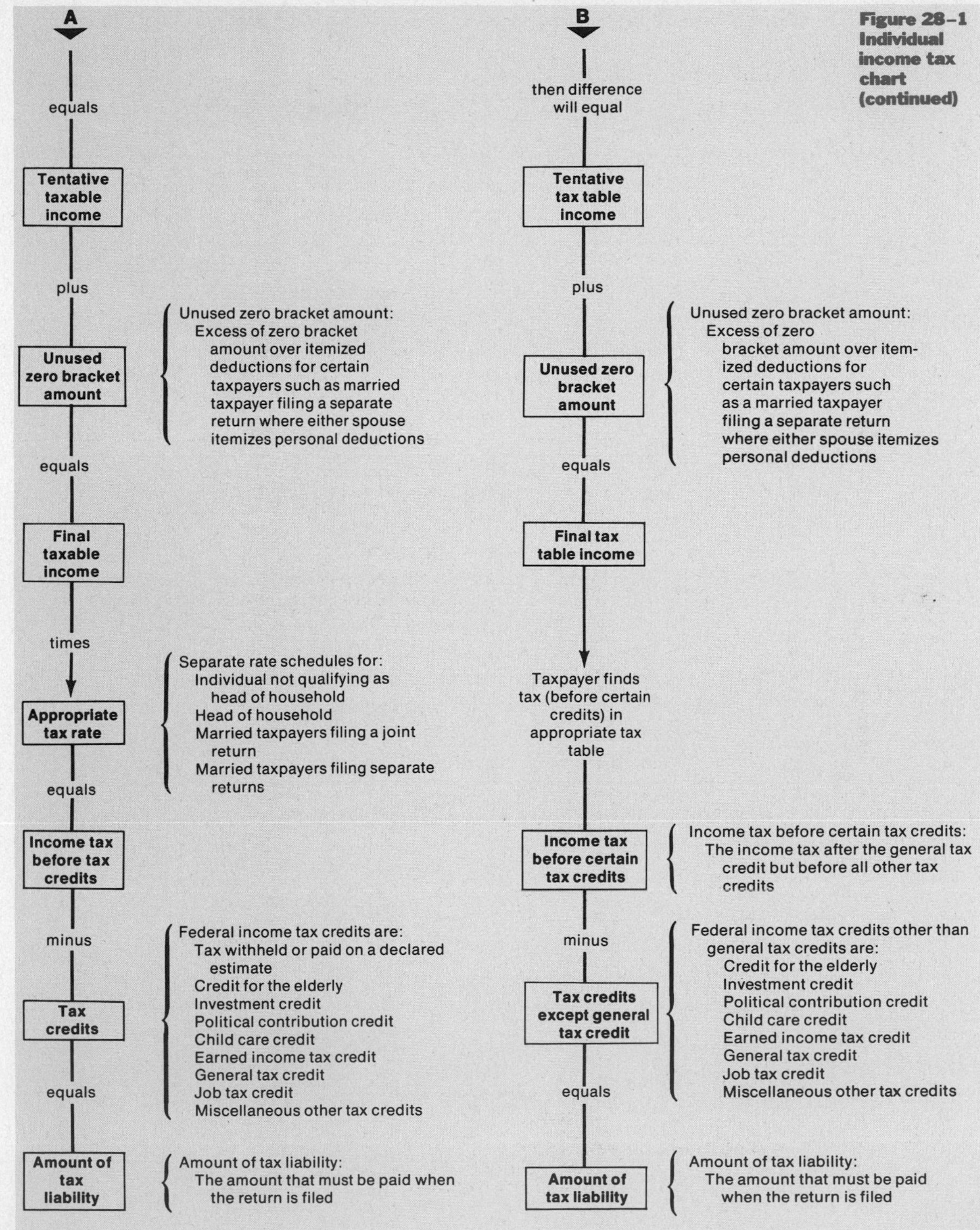

Figure 28–1 Individual income tax chart (continued)

bling winnings and income from illegal activities must be included in gross income. Al Capone, for example, is only one of several gangsters who have been jailed for *tax evasion,* the failure to properly report all legal gross income including the amounts gained from illegal activities. Capone was never convicted for performing any of those illegal activities, only for the tax evasion and failure to pay the appropriate tax.

One additional item deserves to be commented on briefly here. The gain on sale of certain types of assets that are legally designated as capital assets (mainly stocks and bonds) is a *capital gain.* This gain may be a short-term capital gain (treated as ordinary income); it results from the sale of a capital asset held for one year or less. Or, the gain may be a long-term capital gain; it results from the sale of a capital asset held for more than a year. The long-term capital gains receive favorable tax treatment and are discussed in more detail after all the steps in the tax formula have been considered.

Items not qualifying as gross income The following items specifically excluded by law, Treasury regulations, or court decisions need not be reported as gross income:

- Interest on state and municipal bonds and notes
- Qualified dividends received by each spouse who actually owns stock, not to exceed $100 for each owner
- Gifts, inheritances, and bequests received
- Life insurance proceeds received on the death of the insured
- Amounts received from workmen's compensation, unemployment compensation, and other kinds of insurance, with a limit of usually $100 a week, under certain conditions
- Social Security receipts
- Return of investment portion of annuity receipts and other returns of capital investments
- GI benefits and certain veteran's payments.

Deductions from gross income for adjusted gross income

The various classes of deductions from gross income are indicated in Figure 28–1. In general, they are self-explanatory. A brief word about a few should suffice.

Business expenses are the ordinary and typical expenses of carrying on a trade, business, or profession. In actual practice, business expenses are deducted from business revenue on a separate Schedule C to Form 1040 (Figure 28–9), and only the net income from business is included in adjusted gross income.

Allowable employee expenses are required for the performance of a job or position in connection with employment. *Losses from sales or exchanges* of capital assets qualify as capital losses and hence would follow the rules stated in Figure 28–6. *The capital gains deduction* is 50 percent of the net long-term capital gains. Computation of the net long-term capital gains is covered in a later section of this chapter.

Excess itemized deductions

A taxpayer may itemize allowable personal deductions only if they exceed the flat standard deduction now referred to as the *zero bracket amount*. A taxpayer who itemizes personal deductions is referred to as an *itemizer taxpayer*. One who does not itemize is called a *nonitemizer taxpayer*.

Zero bracket amount (flat standard deduction) The Tax Reduction and Simplification Act of 1977 created a new flat standard deduction applicable to 1977 and later years as follows:

Zero Bracket Amount (Flat Standard Deduction)	*Applicable to Following Taxpayer*
$3,200	Married persons filing joint returns and for certain qualifying surviving spouses who are allowed to file joint returns
1,600	Married persons filing separate return
2,200	Single persons and heads of household

The term "standard deduction" no longer appears in the tax law. The new flat standard deduction amounts given above, are called *zero bracket amounts*. These amounts appear as the lowest tax brackets in the tax rate schedules (see Figure 28–5) and are incorporated in the tax tables.[3] These lowest brackets in the tax schedules bear a tax rate of zero. This is the reason that the flat standard amounts are called the *zero bracket amounts*. Since these flat amounts are built into the tax tables and the tax rate schedules as zero tax rate brackets, they benefit both itemizer and nonitemizer taxpayers. However, taxpayers whose itemized deductions exceed the zero bracket amount (flat standard deduction) may deduct only their *excess itemized deductions;* that is, the excess of the itemized allowable personal deductions over the zero bracket amount.

3 Tax tables have been prepared and labeled A for single taxpayers, B for married taxpayers filing jointly and qualifying widows and widowers, C for married taxpayers filing separately, and D for heads of household. These tables apply only to tax table income up to $20,000 ($40,000 for married taxpayers filing joint returns and for qualifying widows and widowers); they are illustrated later in this chapter.

Itemized personal deductions As indicated above, if a taxpayer would benefit by itemizing the personal deductions, he or she may still itemize the allowed personal deductions. Some of the main allowable personal deduction items are:

Contributions
Certain taxes expense
Nonbusiness casualty losses in excess of $100
Allowable medical expenses
Personal investor and professional expenses
Union dues
Special work clothes
Interest on most personal loans including mortgage interest

Many of these personal deductions have restrictions and limits that need to be examined in more detail.

Contributions to recognized charitable, religious, and educational organizations are limited to a percentage that may vary from 20 to 50 percent of adjusted gross income. The limitation depends upon two factors: whether the qualifying organization is *publicly supported* or is a certain type of private foundation; and whether the contribution is made in the form of a cash or in the form of certain noncash items, such as stocks and bonds. Publicly supported organizations include religious, educational, Community Chest, and other charitable organizations that derive the majority of their funds from the general public. The nonpublicly supported charities that have a limitation of 20 percent include private foundations that do not distribute all their revenue within two and one-half months following the close of the year to qualifying charities. Taxpayers who contribute stocks and bonds to qualifying organizations have a maximum limit for these contributions of 30 percent of adjusted gross income.

The contributions are presented on Schedules A and B of Form 1040 in the segment as shown in Figure 28–2.

Gross medical expenses include doctor, hospital, and dental fees; the cost of medicines and drugs in excess of one percent of adjusted gross income; travel to receive medical treatment; and medical and hospital insurance.

Deductible medical expenses consist of one-half the medical and hospital insurance, not to exceed $150, plus the amount of medical and dental expenses and remaining medical and hospital insurance in excess of three percent of adjusted gross income, with no maximum limit. To illustrate the computation of the itemized deductible medical expenses, assume that a taxpayer has an adjusted gross income of $20,000; medical and hospital insurance premium cost of $360; drugs of $310; and other medical, dental, and hospital expenses of $1,800. The amount of the deductible medical expense that would be permitted is calculated on a segment of the Schedules A and B of Form 1040 as shown in Figure 28–3.

Schedule A Itemized Deductions (Schedule B is on back)

Medical and Dental Expenses (not compensated by insurance or otherwise) (See page 14 of Instructions.)

Line	Amount	Cents
1 One-half (but not more than $150) of insurance premiums for medical care. (Be sure to include in line 10 below) . . .	150	00
2 Medicine and drugs	310	00
3 Enter 1% of line 31, Form 1040 . . .	200	00
4 Subtract line 3 from line 2. Enter difference (if less than zero, enter zero) . .	110	00
5 Enter balance of insurance premiums for medical care not entered on line 1 . .	210	00
6 Enter other medical and dental expenses:		
a Doctors, dentists, nurses, etc. . . .	1,800	00
b Hospitals		
c Other (itemize—include hearing aids, dentures, eyeglasses, transportation, etc.) ▶		

Contributions (See page 16 of Instructions for examples.)

Line	Amount	Cents
21 a Cash contributions for which you have receipts, cancelled checks or other written evidence		
b Other cash contributions. List donees and amounts. ▶		
22 Other than cash (see page 16 of instructions for required statement)		
23 Carryover from prior years		
24 **Total contributions (add lines 21a through 23).** Enter here and on line 36 . . ▶		

Casualty or Theft Loss(es) (See page 16 of Instructions.)

Line	Amount	Cents
25 Loss before insurance reimbursement .		
26 Insurance reimbursement		

Figure 28–2 Deductible contributions on schedules A & B, form 1040

Deductible taxes fall into six general categories. The taxes that may be deducted in calculating the federal income tax are indicated on the segment of Schedules A and B of Form 1040, as shown in Figure 28–4.

Nonbusiness casualty losses may also be itemized on form 1040. A portion of the casualty losses not compensated by insurance, such as damage done by storms or wrecks, are deductible as itemized. The amount allowable is that amount in excess of $100 for each casualty.

Taxpayers required to use tax rate schedules

The 1977 Act provides tax rate schedules that are based on final taxable income. Taxpayers who have taxable income above a certain amount[4] designated by the Internal Revenue Service must calculate their income tax by applying the appropriate tax rate to taxable income. In discussing the calculation of taxable income, however, let's return to the tax formula (Figure 28–1). In addition to the excess itemized deductions, the amount of the exemptions must be deducted from adjusted gross income to first calculate tentative taxable income.

Exemptions

A personal *exemption* of $750 is allowed for the taxpayer, for the spouse if a joint return is filed, and for each person who qualifies as a dependent of the taxpayer.

4 This amount is the amount in excess of $20,000; for a single taxpayer and the amount in excess of $40,000 for married taxpayers filing joint returns.

Schedule A Itemized Deductions (Schedule B is on back)

Medical and Dental Expenses (not compensated by insurance or otherwise) (See page 14 of Instructions.)

1 One-half (but not more than $150) of insurance premiums for medical care. (Be sure to include in line 10 below) . . .	150	00
2 Medicine and drugs	310	00
3 Enter 1% of line 31, Form 1040 . . .	200	00
4 Subtract line 3 from line 2. Enter difference (if less than zero, enter zero) . .	110	00
5 Enter balance of insurance premiums for medical care not entered on line 1 . .	210	00
6 Enter other medical and dental expenses:		
a Doctors, dentists, nurses, etc. . . .	1,800	00
b Hospitals		
c Other (itemize—include hearing aids, dentures, eyeglasses, transportation, etc.) ▶		
7 Total (add lines 4 through 6c) . . .	2,120	00
8 Enter 3% of line 31, Form 1040 . . .	600	00
9 Subtract line 8 from line 7 (if less than zero, enter zero)	1,520	00
10 Total (add lines 1 and 9). Enter here and on line 33 . . . . ▶	1,670	00

Taxes (See page 14 of Instructions.)

11 State and local income		
12 Real estate		
13 State and local gasoline (see gas tax tables)		
14 General sales (see sales tax tables) . .		
15 Personal property		
16 Other (itemize) ▶		
17 Total (add lines 11 through 16). Enter here and on line 34 . . . . . ▶		

Interest Expense (See page 16 of Instructions.)

18 Home mortgage		
19 Other (itemize) ▶		

Contributions (See page 16 of Instructions for examples.)

21 a Cash contributions for which you have receipts, cancelled checks or other written evidence		
b Other cash contributions. List donees and amounts. ▶		
22 Other than cash (see page 16 of instructions for required statement)		
23 Carryover from prior years		
24 Total contributions (add lines 21a through 23). Enter here and on line 36 . . ▶		

Casualty or Theft Loss(es) (See page 16 of Instructions.)

25 Loss before insurance reimbursement .		
26 Insurance reimbursement		
27 Subtract line 26 from line 25. Enter difference (if less than zero, enter zero) .		
28 Enter $100 or amount on line 27, whichever is smaller		
29 Casualty or theft loss (subtract line 28 from line 27). Enter here and on line 37 . ▶		

Miscellaneous Deductions (See page 16 of Instructions.)

30 Union dues		
31 Other (itemize) ▶		
32 Total (add lines 30 and 31). Enter here and on line 38 . . . . ▶		

Summary of Itemized Deductions (See page 17 of Instructions.) **A**

33 Total medical and dental—line 10 . .		
34 Total taxes—line 17		
35 Total interest—line 20		
36 Total contributions—line 24		
37 Casualty or theft loss(es)—line 29 . .		
38 Total miscellaneous—line 32		
39 Total deductions (add lines 33 through 38). ▶		
40 If you checked Form 1040, box: 2 or 5, enter $3,200; 1 or 4, enter $2,200; 3, enter $1,600		

Figure 28–3 Calculation of deductible medical expense

Additional exemptions may be claimed if the taxpayer or spouse is blind and or if either is 65 years or over.

Under the law, a dependent is a person who: receives over one-half support from the taxpayer; is closely related to the taxpayer or lives in the home; has received less than $750 in gross income during the year (unless the dependent is a child of the taxpayer under 19 years old or a full-time student); and has not filed a joint return.

9 Subtract line 8 from line 7 (if less than zero, enter zero) . . . . | 1,520 | 00
10 Total (add lines 1 and 9). Enter here and on line 33 . . . . ▶ | 1,670 | 00

Taxes (See page 14 of Instructions.)

11 State and local income . . . . . .
12 Real estate . . . .
13 State and local gasoline (see gas tax tables)
14 General sales (see sales tax tables) . .
15 Personal property . . . .
16 Other (itemize) ▶
17 Total (add lines 11 through 16). Enter here and on line 34 . . . . . . ▶

Interest Expense (See page 16 of Instructions.)

18 Home mortgage . . . .

29 Casualty or theft loss (subtract line 28 from line 27). Enter here and on line 37 . ▶

Miscellaneous Deductions (See page 16 of Instructions.)

30 Union dues . . . .
31 Other (itemize) ▶
32 Total (add lines 30 and 31). Enter here and on line 38 . . . . ▶

Summary of Itemized Deductions (See page 17 of Instructions.) **A**

33 Total medical and dental—line 10 . .
34 Total taxes—line 17 . . . .
35 Total interest—line 20 . . . . . .
36 Total contributions—line 24 . . . .
37 Casualty or theft loss(es)—line 29 . .

Figure 28–4 Deductible taxes on Schedules A and B, Form 1040

Taxable income figures

Tentative taxable income is adjusted gross income minus the sum of the excess itemized deductions and exemptions. In the majority of the cases tentative taxable income also will be final taxable income.

To illustrate a typical kind of situation, assume that David Bowen, an unmarried taxpayer with no dependents, has an adjusted gross income of $24,000 for 1978. His itemized deductions total $3,000. The allowable zero bracket amount (flat standard deduction) is $2,200. Final taxable income for David Bowen is calculated below.

Final Taxable Income:

Adjusted gross income			$24,000
Deduct sum of:			
1. Excess itemized deductions:			
Itemized deductions	$3,000		
Minus: Zero bracket amount	2,200		
Excess itemized deductions		$800	
2. Personal exemption: 1 x $750		750	1,550
Tentative taxable income			$22,450
Plus: Unused zero bracket amount (this normally will be zero; the exceptions are described below)			0
Final taxable income			$22,450

The federal income tax would be calculated by applying the appropriate rates from the tax rate schedules (see Figure 28–5) to the taxable income of $22,450.

Unused zero bracket amount In determining final taxable income, certain taxpayers who receive various other tax benefits are required to add back to tentative taxable income *any* excess of the allowed zero bracket amount (flat standard deduction) over the actual itemized personal deductions. This excess is referred to as the *unused zero bracket amount*. The following individuals are

Figure 28–5 Individual income tax rate schedules

1977 Tax Rate Schedules

If you cannot use one of the Tax Tables, figure your tax on the amount on Schedule TC, Part I, line 3, by using the appropriate Tax Rate Schedule on this page. Enter tax on Schedule TC, Part I, line 4.
Note: *Your zero bracket amount has been built into these Tax Rate Schedules.*

SCHEDULE X—Single Taxpayers Not Qualifying for Rates in Schedule Y or Z

Use this schedule if you checked **Box 1** on Form 1040—

If the amount on Schedule TC, Part I, line 3, is: / Enter on Schedule TC, Part I, line 4:

Not over $2,200 .... —0—

Over—	But not over—		of the amount over—
$2,200	$2,700	14%	$2,200
$2,700	$3,200	$70+15%	$2,700
$3,200	$3,700	$145+16%	$3,200
$3,700	$4,200	$225+17%	$3,700
$4,200	$6,200	$310+19%	$4,200
$6,200	$8,200	$690+21%	$6,200
$8,200	$10,200	$1,110+24%	$8,200
$10,200	$12,200	$1,590+25%	$10,200
$12,200	$14,200	$2,090+27%	$12,200
$14,200	$16,200	$2,630+29%	$14,200
$16,200	$18,200	$3,210+31%	$16,200
$18,200	$20,200	$3,830+34%	$18,200
$20,200	$22,200	$4,510+36%	$20,200
$22,200	$24,200	$5,230+38%	$22,200
$24,200	$28,200	$5,990+40%	$24,200
$28,200	$34,200	$7,590+45%	$28,200
$34,200	$40,200	$10,290+50%	$34,200
$40,200	$46,200	$13,290+55%	$40,200
$46,200	$52,200	$16,590+60%	$46,200
$52,200	$62,200	$20,190+62%	$52,200
$62,200	$72,200	$26,390+64%	$62,200
$72,200	$82,200	$32,790+66%	$72,200
$82,200	$92,200	$39,390+68%	$82,200
$92,200	$102,200	$46,190+69%	$92,200
$102,200	....	$53,090+70%	$102,200

Tax Rate Schedule 1

SCHEDULE Y—Married Taxpayers and Qualifying Widows and Widowers
If you are a married person living apart from your spouse, see page 7 of the instructions to see if you can be considered to be "unmarried" for purposes of using Schedule X or Z.

Married Filing Joint Returns and Qualifying Widows and Widowers

Use this schedule if you checked **Box 2 or Box 5** on Form 1040—

If the amount on Schedule TC, Part I, line 3, is: / Enter on Schedule TC, Part I, line 4:

Not over $3,200 .... —0—

Over—	But not over—		of the amount over—
$3,200	$4,200	14%	$3,200
$4,200	$5,200	$140+15%	$4,200
$5,200	$6,200	$290+16%	$5,200
$6,200	$7,200	$450+17%	$6,200
$7,200	$11,200	$620+19%	$7,200
$11,200	$15,200	$1,380+22%	$11,200
$15,200	$19,200	$2,260+25%	$15,200
$19,200	$23,200	$3,260+28%	$19,200
$23,200	$27,200	$4,380+32%	$23,200
$27,200	$31,200	$5,660+36%	$27,200
$31,200	$35,200	$7,100+39%	$31,200
$35,200	$39,200	$8,660+42%	$35,200
$39,200	$43,200	$10,340+45%	$39,200
$43,200	$47,200	$12,140+48%	$43,200
$47,200	$55,200	$14,060+50%	$47,200
$55,200	$67,200	$18,060+53%	$55,200
$67,200	$79,200	$24,420+55%	$67,200
$79,200	$91,200	$31,020+58%	$79,200
$91,200	$103,200	$37,980+60%	$91,200
$103,200	$123,200	$45,180+62%	$103,200
$123,200	$143,200	$57,580+64%	$123,200
$143,200	$163,200	$70,380+66%	$143,200
$163,200	$183,200	$83,580+68%	$163,200
$183,200	$203,200	$97,180+69%	$183,200
$203,200	....	$110,980+70%	$203,200

Tax Rate Schedule 2

Married Filing Separate Returns

Use this schedule if you checked **Box 3** on Form 1040—

If the amount on Schedule TC, Part I, line 3, is: / Enter on Schedule TC, Part I, line 4:

Not over $1,600 .... —0—

Over—	But not over—		of the amount over—
$1,600	$2,100	14%	$1,600
$2,100	$2,600	$70+15%	$2,100
$2,600	$3,100	$145+16%	$2,600
$3,100	$3,600	$225+17%	$3,100
$3,600	$5,600	$310+19%	$3,600
$5,600	$7,600	$690+22%	$5,600
$7,600	$9,600	$1,130+25%	$7,600
$9,600	$11,600	$1,630+28%	$9,600
$11,600	$13,600	$2,190+32%	$11,600
$13,600	$15,600	$2,830+36%	$13,600
$15,600	$17,600	$3,550+39%	$15,600
$17,600	$19,600	$4,330+42%	$17,600
$19,600	$21,600	$5,170+45%	$19,600
$21,600	$23,600	$6,070+48%	$21,600
$23,600	$27,600	$7,030+50%	$23,600
$27,600	$33,600	$9,030+53%	$27,600
$33,600	$39,600	$12,210+55%	$33,600
$39,600	$45,600	$15,510+58%	$39,600
$45,600	$51,600	$18,990+60%	$45,600
$51,600	$61,600	$22,590+62%	$51,600
$61,600	$71,600	$28,790+64%	$61,600
$71,600	$81,600	$35,190+66%	$71,600
$81,600	$91,600	$41,790+68%	$81,600
$91,600	$101,600	$48,590+69%	$91,600
$101,600	....	$55,490+70%	$101,600

Tax Rate Schedule 4

SCHEDULE Z—Unmarried or legally separated taxpayers Who Qualify as Heads of Household

Use this schedule if you checked **Box 4** on Form 1040—

If the amount on Schedule TC, Part I, line 3, is: / Enter on Schedule TC, Part I, line 4:

Not over $2,200 .... —0—

Over—	But not over—		of the amount over—
$2,200	$3,200	14%	$2,200
$3,200	$4,200	$140+16%	$3,200
$4,200	$6,200	$300+18%	$4,200
$6,200	$8,200	$660+19%	$6,200
$8,200	$10,200	$1,040+22%	$8,200
$10,200	$12,200	$1,480+23%	$10,200
$12,200	$14,200	$1,940+25%	$12,200
$14,200	$16,200	$2,440+27%	$14,200
$16,200	$18,200	$2,980+28%	$16,200
$18,200	$20,200	$3,540+31%	$18,200
$20,200	$22,200	$4,160+32%	$20,200
$22,200	$24,200	$4,800+35%	$22,200
$24,200	$26,200	$5,500+36%	$24,200
$26,200	$28,200	$6,220+38%	$26,200
$28,200	$30,200	$6,980+41%	$28,200
$30,200	$34,200	$7,800+42%	$30,200
$34,200	$38,200	$9,480+45%	$34,200
$38,200	$40,200	$11,280+48%	$38,200
$40,200	$42,200	$12,240+51%	$40,200
$42,200	$46,200	$13,260+52%	$42,200
$46,200	$52,200	$15,340+55%	$46,200
$52,200	$54,200	$18,640+56%	$52,200
$54,200	$66,200	$19,760+58%	$54,200
$66,200	$72,200	$26,720+59%	$66,200
$72,200	$78,200	$30,260+61%	$72,200
$78,200	$82,200	$33,920+62%	$78,200
$82,200	$90,200	$36,400+63%	$82,200
$90,200	$102,200	$41,440+64%	$90,200
$102,200	$122,200	$49,120+66%	$102,200
$122,200	$142,200	$62,320+67%	$122,200
$142,200	$162,200	$75,720+68%	$142,200
$162,200	$182,200	$89,320+69%	$162,200
$182,200	....	$103,120+70%	$182,200

Tax Rate Schedule 3

required to add back the unused zero bracket amount:

A married individual filing a separate return where either spouse itemizes deductions;

A nonresident alien;

A U.S. citizen who is entitled to exemption under the Internal Revenue Code for income from the U.S. possessions; and

An individual who meets all of the following three conditions: (a) is either under 19 years of age or is a full-time student in an educational institution for some part of five calendar months during the year, (b) may be claimed as a dependent on the parents' return, and (c) has any unearned income (dividends, interest, or other) for the year.

In calculating final taxable income, the above individuals follow the same steps as those outlined in the David Bowen example, but then they must take an extra step. They must calculate the amount of the unused zero bracket amount, which is then added to the tentative taxable income to arrive at the *final taxable income*. To illustrate, assume that Linda Hoffman is a married woman entitled to file a joint return with her husband. Her spouse also files a separate return on which his personal deductions are itemized. In 1978, Hoffman has an adjusted gross income of $43,000, itemized deductions of $1,200, and one personal exemption. She would compute her final taxable income for 1978 as follows:

Final Taxable Income:			
Adjusted gross income			$43,000
Step One			
Deduct sum of:			
1. Excess itemized deductions:			
Itemized deductions	$1,200		
Minus: Zero bracket amount	1,600	$ 0	
2. Personal exemption: 1 x $750		750	750
Tentative taxable income			$42,250
Step Two			
Plus: Unused zero bracket amount:			
Zero bracket amount (flat standard deduction)		$1,600	
Minus: Total itemized personal deductions		1,200	
Unused zero bracket amount			400
Final taxable income			$42,650

Then to calculate the federal income tax before any tax credits, Hoffman would apply the rates for a married taxpayer filing separately (see Rate Schedule 4, Figure 28–5) to the final taxable income of $42,650.

Individual income tax rates

Once the final taxable income is properly determined, the income tax before any tax credits is computed by multiplying the appropriate tax rates by the net final taxable income. The tax rates that are applied depend upon the rate qualification of the taxpayer. There is a separate tax schedule for a single person who does not qualify as head of household, a schedule for an individual who *does* qualify as head of household, a schedule for a married couple filing a joint return, another schedule for married taxpayers filing separate returns, and still another schedule for estates and trusts. All these rates are *progressive;* that is, those with the lowest taxable incomes are taxed at the lowest rate and those with the largest taxable incomes are taxed at progressively higher rates. The progressive character of the individual tax rate can be observed from each of the schedules in Figure 28–5, which shows the individual income tax rates starting at 14 percent and rising gradually to 70 percent. (The taxpayer must consult the latest Internal Revenue Service rates before preparing a federal income tax return.)

The separate tax schedule for married taxpayers is designed to eliminate tax inequity for married couples in states having community property laws that permit them to divide gross income and in states that do not have such laws. Married couples filing a joint return determine final income tax before credits by applying the rates indicated in Rate Schedule 2 of Figure 28–5, the tax rates that are specifically applicable to married taxpayers filing joint returns.

It should be noted that marital status is determined as of December 31 of a given taxable year. For example, a couple that married on December 31, 1978, would qualify to file a joint return for the entire taxable year of 1978.

The special tax schedule for head of household (Rate Schedule #3 of Figure 28–5) provides an element of relief for widows or widowers and others who qualify as head of household to compensate them partially for the additional family burden that they must carry. Only two categories of persons may qualify as head of household: one who is unmarried (or separated) at the end of the taxable year and one who is married at the end of the year to an individual who was a nonresident alien at any time during the taxable year. Moreover, the individual must have furnished over one-half the cost of maintaining as the taxpayer's home a household that during the entire year, except for temporary absences, was occupied as the principal place of abode and as a member of such household (1) by any related person, other than the taxpayer's unmarried child, grandchild, or stepchild for whom the taxpayer is entitled to a deduction for an exemption, unless the deduction arises from a multiple support agreement, or (2) by the taxpayer's unmarried child, grandchild, or stepchild, even though such child is not a dependent. The rates, as shown in Rate Schedule 3 of Figure 28–5, are lower than for nonhead-of-household unmarried individuals but are higher than those for married couples filing joint returns.

It should be noted that the 1977 Act changed the tax rate structure for estates and trusts. They used to be subject to the income tax rates applicable to a single individual who did not qualify as head of household. Now, the taxable income of an estate or of a trust is taxed at different rates—the rate schedule for estates and trusts is not shown in this book. The tax rates for the other taxable entity, the corporation, are presented in connection with the discussion of the corporate income tax.

Maximum marginal tax on earned income The tax law provides a maximum marginal tax rate of 50 percent on *personal services income*. Personal services income includes income that is earned by the result of personal effort such as salary income and commissions and amounts received from pensions and annuities. *Unearned income* results from investments in stocks and bonds; it includes dividends and interest.

Examples of calculations of income tax before tax credits To illustrate how a taxpayer would use the tax rate schedules shown in Figure 28–5, let us consider two different examples.

Example 1. Allastair Weyman, a single unmarried individual, has final taxable income of $42,200.* His income tax before any credits would be calculated as follows:

Tax on first $40,200 (from rate schedule)	$13,290.00
Tax on the next $2,000 at 55 percent	1,100.00
Income tax before any tax credits	$14,390.00

*A major part of the income is from dividends and interest.

Example 2. Harold and Rose Brooks, a married couple filing a joint return, have final taxable income of $82,200.* Their income tax before any credits would be calculated as follows:

Tax on first $79,200 (from rate schedule)	$31,020.00
Tax on the next $3,000 at 58 percent	1,740.00
Income tax before any tax credits	$32,760.00

*A major part of the income is from dividends and interest.

Tax credits

After the income tax has been computed, certain special credits may be deducted from this amount in computing the amount of the tax liability currently outstanding. Tax credits are typically allowed for the following:[5]

Income tax withheld or paid on declared estimate A taxpayer takes credit for all salary withholding income taxes and for advance payments made on the basis of the Declaration of Estimated Income Tax, Form 1040–ES.

Credit for the elderly This credit was previously called retirement income credit. Persons who have worked for at least 10 years, in which at least $600 was earned in each year, who are now receiving qualifying retirement pay, and individuals over 65 who meet the same earnings test and who receive primarily

5 The credits against the income tax are changed frequently by Congress. The ones listed here are the ones applicable to 1978 income taxes.

rents, interest, and dividends are entitled to a tax credit. The amount of this tax credit has been changed frequently by Congress. It also depends upon the amount of adjusted gross income a taxpayer has and the amount of Social Security income a taxpayer receives.

Investment credit The allowable investment tax credit is 10 percent of the cost of qualifying business equipment purchased in a given year. This credit is granted to encourage businesses to keep their plants modern and up to date.

Political contribution credit or deduction The 1971 Revenue Act provides a credit directly against tax due amounting to one-half a taxpayer's actual political contribution with a maximum credit of $12.50, or $25 for a couple filing a joint return; alternatively the taxpayer could elect to take an itemized personal deduction for such actual contribution, up to a maximum $50, or $100 for a couple filing a joint return.

Child care credit An annual nonrefundable tax credit of 20 percent of actual qualifying child care cost up to $2,000 for one dependent (and $4,000 for two or more dependents) is allowed. The person cared for must be under the age of 15, or a disabled dependent or spouse. The child care expenses must be incurred to enable the taxpayer(s) to be gainfully employed.

Earned income credit This credit has been extended by the 1977 Act for two more years. It is applicable to low-income workers who have an *earned income* —wages, salaries, and earnings from self-employment. The credit is figured on the adjusted gross income (or earned income, if greater) of amounts between $0 and $7,999. The maximum credit is 10 percent of a worker's first $4,000, or $400. The credit is reduced by an amount equal to 10 percent of the taxpayer's adjusted gross income (or earned income, if greater) above $4,000. Thus a taxpayer who has earned income of $5,000 would receive a credit of only $300 = [(10% × $4,000) − (10% × $1,000)]. This credit, scheduled to expire on December 31, 1978, is intended to encourage those who receive Social Security payments to seek employment. Observe that this credit has a negative income tax element included in it. A taxpayer with $4,000 earned income and six exemptions would pay no tax but yet would receive a "refund" check for $400 from the federal government.

General tax credit Under the general tax credit provision (scheduled to expire on December 31, 1978), an individual is entitled to take a tax credit in an amount equal to the larger of two amounts: 2 percent of the first $9,000 of final taxable income or $35 for *each* personal exemption including the exemption for dependents, age, and blindness.

To illustrate, assume that Samuel and Esther Johnston file a joint return and have five exemptions. They have a 1978 income tax of $31,020 before any tax credits. Assume that they have paid $28,000 of estimated taxes for the year.

Their general tax credit and amount of remaining tax liability is calculated below.

Income tax before any credits		$31,020.00
Deduct tax credits:		
Estimated income tax paid with declared estimate	$28,000.00	
General tax credit—larger of		
1. 2% x 9,000 = $180, or		
2. $35 x 5 = 175	180.00	28,180.00
Amount of remaining tax liability (to be paid when Form 1040 is filed)		$ 2,840.00

Job tax credit The 1977 Act allows both corporations and other businesses (individuals and partnerships running a business) to take a credit against their income tax of an amount up to $100,000 annually for 1977 and 1978 for wages paid to additional new employees. The maximum credit for *each new* employee is $2,100 = (50 percent of the first $4,200 of new wages paid). Also provided in the Act was a 10 percent bonus credit for hiring handicapped individuals referred through vocational rehabilitation programs. This 10 percent also applies to the first $4,200 of new wages paid to handicapped individuals subject to a limitation that requires a percentage calculation that is not discussed here.

Miscellaneous tax credits A few other rather infrequent tax credits are allowed. For example, a credit is allowed for taxes paid to foreign countries on income that is also taxed by the United States.

Taxpayers required to use tax tables

Let us now look at the second track of our income tax formula (see Figure 28–1): the tax calculation for those taxpayers who are required to use tax tables to calculate their income tax. The Internal Revenue Service was directed by the Tax Reduction and Simplification Act of 1977 to prescribe tax tables in which the zero bracket amount (the flat standard deduction), personal exemptions, and the general tax credit are to be incorporated. Use of these tax tables is required by applicable individual taxpayers whether or not they itemized their personal deductions.

These tax tables were prepared immediately prior to the publication of this book. They encompass eleven pages of tables. They are labeled A for single taxpayers, B for married taxpayers filing jointly and qualifying widows and widowers, C for married taxpayers filing separately, and D for heads of household. The tables apply only to tax table income up to $20,000 ($40,000 for those filing joint returns). Because of the sheer volume of these tables, only one selection is presented here. Illustrated on page 918 is part of Table B for married taxpayers filing jointly with tax table incomes of $33,200 to $40,000.

It should be noted that since all these tables are not presented in this book that the end-of-chapter exercises and problems contain instructions requiring the use of tax rate schedules rather than the use of tax tables.

1977 Tax Table B—MARRIED FILING JOINTLY (Box 2) and QUALIFYING WIDOW(ER)S (Box 5)

(Continued)

(If your income or exemptions are not covered, use Schedule TC (Form 1040), Part I to figure your tax)

If line 34, Form 1040 is— Over	But not over	And the total number of exemptions claimed on line 7 is— 2	3	4	5	6	7	8	9
		Your tax is—							
33,200	33,250	7,125	6,839	6,569	6,299	5,999	5,694	5,389	5,113
33,250	33,300	7,144	6,857	6,587	6,317	6,017	5,712	5,407	5,129
33,300	33,350	7,164	6,875	6,605	6,335	6,035	5,730	5,425	5,145
33,350	33,400	7,183	6,893	6,623	6,353	6,053	5,748	5,443	5,161
33,400	33,450	7,203	6,911	6,641	6,371	6,071	5,766	5,461	5,177
33,450	33,500	7,222	6,930	6,659	6,389	6,089	5,784	5,479	5,193
33,500	33,550	7,242	6,949	6,677	6,407	6,107	5,802	5,497	5,209
33,550	33,600	7,261	6,969	6,695	6,425	6,125	5,820	5,515	5,225
33,600	33,650	7,281	6,988	6,713	6,443	6,143	5,838	5,533	5,241
33,650	33,700	7,300	7,008	6,731	6,461	6,161	5,856	5,551	5,257
33,700	33,750	7,320	7,027	6,749	6,479	6,179	5,874	5,569	5,273
33,750	33,800	7,339	7,047	6,767	6,497	6,197	5,892	5,587	5,289
33,800	33,850	7,359	7,066	6,785	6,515	6,215	5,910	5,605	5,305
33,850	33,900	7,378	7,086	6,803	6,533	6,233	5,928	5,623	5,321
33,900	33,950	7,398	7,105	6,821	6,551	6,251	5,946	5,641	5,337
33,950	34,000	7,417	7,125	6,839	6,569	6,269	5,964	5,659	5,354
34,000	34,050	7,437	7,144	6,857	6,587	6,287	5,982	5,677	5,372
34,050	34,100	7,456	7,164	6,875	6,605	6,305	6,000	5,695	5,390
34,100	34,150	7,476	7,183	6,893	6,623	6,323	6,018	5,713	5,408
34,150	34,200	7,495	7,203	6,911	6,641	6,341	6,036	5,731	5,426
34,200	34,250	7,515	7,222	6,930	6,659	6,359	6,054	5,749	5,444
34,250	34,300	7,534	7,242	6,949	6,677	6,377	6,072	5,767	5,462
34,300	34,350	7,554	7,261	6,969	6,695	6,395	6,090	5,785	5,480
34,350	34,400	7,573	7,281	6,988	6,713	6,413	6,108	5,803	5,498
34,400	34,450	7,593	7,300	7,008	6,731	6,431	6,126	5,821	5,516
34,450	34,500	7,612	7,320	7,027	6,749	6,449	6,144	5,839	5,534
34,500	34,550	7,632	7,339	7,047	6,767	6,467	6,162	5,857	5,552
34,550	34,600	7,651	7,359	7,066	6,785	6,485	6,180	5,875	5,570
34,600	34,650	7,671	7,378	7,086	6,803	6,503	6,198	5,893	5,588
34,650	34,700	7,690	7,398	7,105	6,821	6,521	6,216	5,911	5,606
34,700	34,750	7,710	7,417	7,125	6,839	6,539	6,234	5,929	5,624
34,750	34,800	7,729	7,437	7,144	6,857	6,557	6,252	5,947	5,642
34,800	34,850	7,749	7,456	7,164	6,875	6,575	6,270	5,965	5,660
34,850	34,900	7,768	7,476	7,183	6,893	6,593	6,288	5,983	5,678
34,900	34,950	7,788	7,495	7,203	6,911	6,611	6,306	6,001	5,696
34,950	35,000	7,807	7,515	7,222	6,930	6,629	6,324	6,019	5,714
35,000	35,050	7,827	7,534	7,242	6,949	6,647	6,342	6,037	5,732
35,050	35,100	7,846	7,554	7,261	6,969	6,665	6,360	6,055	5,750
35,100	35,150	7,866	7,573	7,281	6,988	6,683	6,378	6,073	5,768
35,150	35,200	7,885	7,593	7,300	7,008	6,701	6,396	6,091	5,786
35,200	35,250	7,905	7,612	7,320	7,027	6,719	6,414	6,109	5,804
35,250	35,300	7,924	7,632	7,339	7,047	6,737	6,432	6,127	5,822
35,300	35,350	7,944	7,651	7,359	7,066	6,755	6,450	6,145	5,840
35,350	35,400	7,963	7,671	7,378	7,086	6,773	6,468	6,163	5,858
35,400	35,450	7,983	7,690	7,398	7,105	6,791	6,486	6,181	5,876
35,450	35,500	8,002	7,710	7,417	7,125	6,809	6,504	6,199	5,894
35,500	35,550	8,022	7,729	7,437	7,144	6,827	6,522	6,217	5,912
35,550	35,600	8,041	7,749	7,456	7,164	6,845	6,540	6,235	5,930
35,600	35,650	8,061	7,768	7,476	7,183	6,863	6,558	6,253	5,948
35,650	35,700	8,080	7,788	7,495	7,203	6,881	6,576	6,271	5,966
35,700	35,750	8,100	7,807	7,515	7,222	6,900	6,594	6,289	5,984
35,750	35,800	8,119	7,827	7,534	7,242	6,919	6,612	6,307	6,002
35,800	35,850	8,139	7,846	7,554	7,261	6,939	6,630	6,325	6,020
35,850	35,900	8,158	7,866	7,573	7,281	6,958	6,648	6,343	6,038
35,900	35,950	8,178	7,885	7,593	7,300	6,978	6,666	6,361	6,056
35,950	36,000	8,197	7,905	7,612	7,320	6,997	6,684	6,379	6,074
36,000	36,050	8,217	7,924	7,632	7,339	7,017	6,702	6,397	6,092
36,050	36,100	8,236	7,944	7,651	7,359	7,036	6,720	6,415	6,110
36,100	36,150	8,256	7,963	7,671	7,378	7,056	6,738	6,433	6,128
36,150	36,200	8,275	7,983	7,690	7,398	7,075	6,756	6,451	6,146
36,200	36,250	8,295	8,002	7,710	7,417	7,095	6,774	6,469	6,164
36,250	36,300	8,314	8,022	7,729	7,437	7,114	6,792	6,487	6,182
36,300	36,350	8,334	8,041	7,749	7,456	7,134	6,810	6,505	6,200
36,350	36,400	8,353	8,061	7,768	7,476	7,153	6,828	6,523	6,218
36,400	36,450	8,373	8,080	7,788	7,495	7,173	6,846	6,541	6,236
36,450	36,500	8,392	8,100	7,807	7,515	7,192	6,865	6,559	6,254
36,500	36,550	8,412	8,119	7,827	7,534	7,212	6,884	6,577	6,272
36,550	36,600	8,431	8,139	7,846	7,554	7,231	6,904	6,595	6,290

Continued next column

If line 34, Form 1040 is— Over	But not over	And the total number of exemptions claimed on line 7 is— 2	3	4	5	6	7	8	9
		Your tax is—							
36,600	36,650	8,451	8,158	7,866	7,573	7,251	6,923	6,613	6,308
36,650	36,700	8,470	8,178	7,885	7,593	7,270	6,943	6,631	6,326
36,700	36,750	8,491	8,197	7,905	7,612	7,290	6,962	6,649	6,344
36,750	36,800	8,512	8,217	7,924	7,632	7,309	6,982	6,667	6,362
36,800	36,850	8,533	8,236	7,944	7,651	7,329	7,001	6,685	6,380
36,850	36,900	8,554	8,256	7,963	7,671	7,348	7,021	6,703	6,398
36,900	36,950	8,575	8,275	7,983	7,690	7,368	7,040	6,721	6,416
36,950	37,000	8,596	8,295	8,002	7,710	7,387	7,060	6,739	6,434
37,000	37,050	8,617	8,314	8,022	7,729	7,407	7,079	6,757	6,452
37,050	37,100	8,638	8,334	8,041	7,749	7,426	7,099	6,775	6,470
37,100	37,150	8,659	8,353	8,061	7,768	7,446	7,118	6,793	6,488
37,150	37,200	8,680	8,373	8,080	7,788	7,465	7,138	6,811	6,506
37,200	37,250	8,701	8,392	8,100	7,807	7,485	7,157	6,830	6,524
37,250	37,300	8,722	8,412	8,119	7,827	7,504	7,177	6,849	6,542
37,300	37,350	8,743	8,431	8,139	7,846	7,524	7,196	6,869	6,560
37,350	37,400	8,764	8,451	8,158	7,866	7,543	7,216	6,888	6,578
37,400	37,450	8,785	8,470	8,178	7,885	7,563	7,235	6,908	6,596
37,450	37,500	8,806	8,491	8,197	7,905	7,582	7,255	6,927	6,614
37,500	37,550	8,827	8,512	8,217	7,924	7,602	7,274	6,947	6,632
37,550	37,600	8,848	8,533	8,236	7,944	7,621	7,294	6,966	6,650
37,600	37,650	8,869	8,554	8,256	7,963	7,641	7,313	6,986	6,668
37,650	37,700	8,890	8,575	8,275	7,983	7,660	7,333	7,005	6,686
37,700	37,750	8,911	8,596	8,295	8,002	7,680	7,352	7,025	6,704
37,750	37,800	8,932	8,617	8,314	8,022	7,699	7,372	7,044	6,722
37,800	37,850	8,953	8,638	8,334	8,041	7,719	7,391	7,064	6,740
37,850	37,900	8,974	8,659	8,353	8,061	7,738	7,411	7,083	6,758
37,900	37,950	8,995	8,680	8,373	8,080	7,758	7,430	7,103	6,776
37,950	38,000	9,016	8,701	8,392	8,100	7,777	7,450	7,122	6,795
38,000	38,050	9,037	8,722	8,412	8,119	7,797	7,469	7,142	6,814
38,050	38,100	9,058	8,743	8,431	8,139	7,816	7,489	7,161	6,834
38,100	38,150	9,079	8,764	8,451	8,158	7,836	7,508	7,181	6,853
38,150	38,200	9,100	8,785	8,470	8,178	7,855	7,528	7,200	6,873
38,200	38,250	9,121	8,806	8,491	8,197	7,875	7,547	7,220	6,892
38,250	38,300	9,142	8,827	8,512	8,217	7,894	7,567	7,239	6,912
38,300	38,350	9,163	8,848	8,533	8,236	7,914	7,586	7,259	6,931
38,350	38,400	9,184	8,869	8,554	8,256	7,933	7,606	7,278	6,951
38,400	38,450	9,205	8,890	8,575	8,275	7,953	7,625	7,298	6,970
38,450	38,500	9,226	8,911	8,596	8,295	7,972	7,645	7,317	6,990
38,500	38,550	9,247	8,932	8,617	8,314	7,992	7,664	7,337	7,009
38,550	38,600	9,268	8,953	8,638	8,334	8,011	7,684	7,356	7,029
38,600	38,650	9,289	8,974	8,659	8,353	8,031	7,703	7,376	7,048
38,650	38,700	9,310	8,995	8,680	8,373	8,050	7,723	7,395	7,068
38,700	38,750	9,331	9,016	8,701	8,392	8,070	7,742	7,415	7,087
38,750	38,800	9,352	9,037	8,722	8,412	8,089	7,762	7,434	7,107
38,800	38,850	9,373	9,058	8,743	8,431	8,109	7,781	7,454	7,126
38,850	38,900	9,394	9,079	8,764	8,451	8,128	7,801	7,473	7,146
38,900	38,950	9,415	9,100	8,785	8,470	8,148	7,820	7,493	7,165
38,950	39,000	9,436	9,121	8,806	8,491	8,167	7,840	7,512	7,185
39,000	39,050	9,457	9,142	8,827	8,512	8,187	7,859	7,532	7,204
39,050	39,100	9,478	9,163	8,848	8,533	8,206	7,879	7,551	7,224
39,100	39,150	9,499	9,184	8,869	8,554	8,226	7,898	7,571	7,243
39,150	39,200	9,520	9,205	8,890	8,575	8,245	7,918	7,590	7,263
39,200	39,250	9,541	9,226	8,911	8,596	8,265	7,937	7,610	7,282
39,250	39,300	9,562	9,247	8,932	8,617	8,284	7,957	7,629	7,302
39,300	39,350	9,583	9,268	8,953	8,638	8,304	7,976	7,649	7,321
39,350	39,400	9,604	9,289	8,974	8,659	8,323	7,996	7,668	7,341
39,400	39,450	9,625	9,310	8,995	8,680	8,343	8,015	7,688	7,360
39,450	39,500	9,646	9,331	9,016	8,701	8,362	8,035	7,707	7,380
39,500	39,550	9,667	9,352	9,037	8,722	8,382	8,054	7,727	7,399
39,550	39,600	9,688	9,373	9,058	8,743	8,401	8,074	7,746	7,419
39,600	39,650	9,709	9,394	9,079	8,764	8,421	8,093	7,766	7,438
39,650	39,700	9,730	9,415	9,100	8,785	8,440	8,113	7,785	7,458
39,700	39,750	9,751	9,436	9,121	8,806	8,461	8,132	7,805	7,477
39,750	39,800	9,772	9,457	9,142	8,827	8,482	8,152	7,824	7,497
39,800	39,850	9,793	9,478	9,163	8,848	8,503	8,171	7,844	7,516
39,850	39,900	9,814	9,499	9,184	8,869	8,524	8,191	7,863	7,536
39,900	39,950	9,835	9,520	9,205	8,890	8,545	8,210	7,883	7,555
39,950	40,000	9,856	9,541	9,226	8,911	8,566	8,230	7,902	7,575

The tax tables *cannot* be used by a certain group of taxpayers; for example, an estate or trust, any individual who claims the exclusion for foreign earned income and other individuals who are entitled to certain tax privileges such as those who use income averaging.

Tax table income figures

Broadly speaking, the term *tax table income* relates to the income brackets appearing in the tax tables for 1977 and later years. The meaning of the term will vary with certain situations. *Tentative tax table income* is adjusted gross income less excess itemized deductions. In *most* cases the tentative tax table income and final tax table income will be the *same* figure since the unused zero bracket amount will be zero for most taxpayers. Three examples are given to illustrate the calculation of the final tax table income.

Example 1.—A nonitemizer taxpayer Edward Brummet, an unmarried taxpayer, has an adjusted gross income of $18,000 for 1978. His itemized deductions total $2,000 for the year. They are less than his $2,200 zero bracket amount (flat standard deduction). He, therefore, would not itemize his deductions for the year. Brummet's tax table income is the same as his adjusted gross income of $18,000. To determine his income tax before all credits except the general tax credit, he would simply consult the tax table income bracket for $18,000 in the tax table governing unmarried individuals (not heads of household). It should be pointed out that in the calculation of final tax table income for a nonitemizer taxpayer, no computation of the zero bracket amount, personal exemption, or the general tax credit is necessary because these items have already been built into the tax tables.

Example 2.—An itemizer taxpayer Nancy Bowen, who qualifies as a head of household, has an adjusted gross income of $20,000 for 1978. Her itemized deductions for the year total $4,000. She would compute her final tax table income as follows:

Final Tax Table Income:		
Adjusted gross income		$20,000.00
Deduct excess itemized deductions:		
Total itemized deductions	$4,000.00	
Minus: Zero bracket amount	2,200.00	1,800.00
Final Tax table income		$18,200.00

In the above calculation it should be noted that because the zero bracket amount, the flat standard deduction, is built into the tax tables, a taxpayer whose itemized deductions exceed the zero bracket amount is entitled to deduct the itemized deductions only to the extent that these deductions exceed the zero bracket amount. Thus a taxpayer must reduce the total amount of the itemized deductions by the amount of the applicable zero bracket amount and then subtract the remaining excess itemized deductions from the adjusted gross income. The result in this case is final tax table income.

Example 3.—A taxpayer with an unused zero bracket amount As mentioned in the above section dealing with those taxpayers who are required to use tax rate schedules, four categories of taxpayers who receive certain tax benefits are required to add back to the tentative tax table income any unused zero bracket amount. These four are: a married taxpayer filing a separate return where either spouse itemizes deductions, a nonresident alien, a U.S. citizen who is entitled to exemption under the Internal Revenue Code for income from U.S. possessions, and a youth who is attending college under certain circumstances. *Illustration:* June Smith, a married woman entitled to file a joint return with her husband, has an adjusted gross income of $19,250 for 1978. Her husband, Robert Smith, files a separate return for 1978 on which he itemizes his deductions. June also files a separate return for 1978 and her itemized deductions total $1,000. She would determine her final tax table income as follows.

Final Tax Table Income:		
Step One		
Adjusted gross income		$19,250.00
Deduct excess itemized deductions:		
Total itemized deductions	$1,000.00	
Minus: Zero bracket amount	1,600.00	-0-
Tentative tax table income		$19,250.00
Step Two		
Plus: Unused zero bracket amount:		
Zero bracket amount	$1,600.00	
Minus: Total Itemized deductions	1,000.00	$ 600.00
Final tax table income		$19,850.00

The calculation in Step Two is necessary because the zero bracket amount, the flat standard deduction, is built into the tax table and, as required by law, a married person filing separately must itemize deductions if her or his spouse itemizes deductions. The effect of Step Two is to prevent a married taxpayer filing a separate return from receiving the benefit of the full built-in zero bracket amount (flat standard deduction) when her or his itemized deductions are lower than the applicable zero bracket amount.

Tax credits applicable to those taxpayers required to use tax tables

The income tax figure determined from the tax tables is the income tax before all credits except the general tax credit. In other words, the tax figure from the tax table is *after* the general tax credit but *before* any of the other tax credits have been deducted. Thus the tax credits that may be offset against the tax figure derived from tax tables are: income tax withheld or paid on declared estimate; credit for the elderly; investment credit; political contribution credit; child care credit; earned income credit; new job credit; and a few other miscellaneous credits (but *not* the general tax credit).

Other tax considerations

Before we consider a rather extended illustration of the individual income tax, let us look briefly at three other tax issues: capital gains and losses, an additional tax on tax preference items, and income averaging.

Capital gains and losses

As indicated earlier in this chapter, gains and losses on the sale of assets legally designated as capital assets (the majority of these are stocks and bonds) are classified as capital gains and losses. Recall that gains and losses on the sale of capital assets held for one year or less are *short-term capital gains and losses*. Gains and losses on the sale of capital assets held for more than one year are *long-term capital gains and losses*.

The income tax treatment of gains and losses on sale of capital assets is extremely important, because *net long-term capital* gains receive favorable tax treatment as is discussed below. The amount of gain or loss is the difference between the selling price and the tax basis. The tax basis is cost when the asset was acquired by purchase. The tax basis in certain cases, however, may be fair market value or some other basis. For example, it may be the basis in the hands of the donor when the property was acquired by gift.

Short-term capital gains are 100 percent included in adjusted gross income and are taxed as are *ordinary income* items. On the other hand, only one-half of net long-term gains are included in adjusted gross income. In addition, the *maximum* rate of tax applicable to the gross (before the 50 percent reduction) gains is 25 percent on the first $50,000 of gross gain plus 35 percent of the excess above $50,000.

In computing deductible capital losses, the sum of 100 percent of the short-term losses plus 50 percent of long-term losses may be deducted from other gross income up to a maximum of $3,000, or the taxable income, whichever is smaller. The unused portion of the capital loss, however, may be carried over to future years, without any limitation on the number of years, and offset against the ordinary income of these years, not to exceed the maximum limitations for each year as stated. When losses are carried forward to future years, they maintain their short-term or long-term character.

Net capital gains and losses The income tax law requires that long-term and short-term transactions be combined in a certain way in computing adjusted gross income. First, all long-term gains must be combined with long-term losses in order to determine the *net* long-term gain or loss. Short-term gains and losses must also be combined. This netting of long-term and short-term items produces a number of situations that require further explanation. For example, a taxpayer may have both a net long-term gain and a net short-term gain. In this case, he or she would treat the two items separately: the entire short-term gain would be included in gross income and treated as ordinary income. Similarly, the taxpayer who has both net short-term losses and net long-term losses would combine 100 percent of the short-term capital loss plus 50 percent of the long-term capital loss into one figure. Then the taxpayer would deduct up to $3,000 in the computation of adjusted gross income. On the other hand, a taxpayer may have short-term gains greater than short-term losses, or long-term gains greater than long-term losses. These must be combined to arrive at a net figure for short-term gain or long-term gain. These rules are illustrated in Figure 28–6.

Alternative tax on long-term capital gains As mentioned above there is an alternative tax on certain long-term capital gains of taxpayers, depending upon whether the taxpayer will benefit from its application. As previously stated, long-term capital gains are subject to a maximum tax of 25 percent on the first $50,000 of gross gain (before the 50 percent reduction) plus 35 percent of the excess above $50,000 of gross long-term gain. To illustrate, assume that in 1978

Figure 28–6 Capital gain and loss rules

CASE A

Net LTCG	$5,000
Net STCG	1,000

Includable in AGI:

All the STCG is included, but only one-half LTCG; the total included in AGI is $3,500. Note that the entire gain of $6,000 is included in gross income and that a deduction of $2,500 from gross income is allowed to calculate the amount to be included in AGI of $3,500.

CASE B

Net LTCL	$2,000
Net STCL	2,000
Total Capital Loss	$4,000
Less: 50 percent of net LTCL	1,000
Deductible Capital Loss	3,000

Deductible from Gross Income:

Only $3,000 is deductible in 1978 to arrive at AGI. Losses carried forward (none here) maintain their short-term or long-term character. Losses carried forward may *always* be offset against later *capital gains* without limit.

CASE C

Net LTCG	$4,000
Net STCL	2,500
Net Capital gain (long-term)	$1,500

Includable in AGI:

50 percent of the $1,500, or $750, is included.

CASE D

Net LTCL	$4,200
Net STCG	5,600
Net Capital Gain (short-term)	$1,400

Includable in AGI:

The entire $1,400 would be included and taxed as is ordinary income.

Abbreviations used in this illustration are:

Net LTCG—Net long-term capital gain
Net STCG—Net short-term capital gain
Net LTCL—Net long-term capital loss
Net STCL—Net short-term capital loss
AGI—Adjusted gross income

Mr. and Mrs. John Fox have the following taxable income indicated on a joint return:

Net final taxable income excluding net long-term capital gains	$79,200.00
Net long-term capital gains before 50 percent reduction . .	25,000.00

By including $12,500 of net long-term capital gains in final taxable income, there would be $91,700 of final taxable income and an indicated tax of $38,280, computed as follows:

Tax on first $91,200	$37,980.00
Add tax on remaining $500: 60% x $500	300.00
Indicated Tax	$38,280.00

Yet, since long-term capital gains are subject to a maximum tax of 25 percent on the first $50,000 and 35 percent on the excess of the amount above $50,000, without giving consideration to the 50 percent reduction, the actual alternative tax would be $37,270, computed as follows:

Tax on ordinary taxable income of $79,200	$31,020.00
Tax on capital gains of $25,000 (25% x $25,000)	6,250.00
Total income tax for 1978	$37,270.00

An additional tax

There is a tax in addition to that resulting from applying the rates as published in Figure 28–5. The Revenue Act of 1969 imposed a minimum tax on high-income taxpayers who have certain "tax preference items" such as accelerated depreciation, stock options, long-term capital gains, and others. Form 4625, Computation of Minimum Tax, must be filed if a taxpayer has tax preference items in excess of $10,000, even though there may be no minimum tax due.

Income averaging for individuals

Those taxpayers who have unusual fluctuations in income can use the allowable averaging device to ease the tax bite in peak income years. For incoming averaging to apply, the taxpayer must have at least $3,000 of "averagable income" that can be made up of almost any kind of ordinary or capital gains income. Schedule G of Form 1040 provides the instructions and formula required for income averaging. The basic logic back of the taxing of fluctuating peak income is to tax the excess amount above an average base period income at a lower bracket rate than it would be taxed if the gross amount were included in taxable income.

Individual income tax: an illustration

The following hypothetical case illustrates the major features of the individual federal income tax computation:

Thomas Brown, 44 years old, is married to Mary Brown, 40 years old. They have two children: a son, Thomas, Jr., 15; and Katherine Kay, a 20-year-old college student. The Browns furnish over one-half the support of both their children, although Katherine Kay works as a summer camp counselor and earned $900 in 1978. Brown owns and operates a grocery store under the name of Brown Groceries. Mrs. Brown did not earn any income in 1978. Relevant business and personal information for the family is shown in Figure 28–7.

The computation of the tax liability on a joint return filed by the Browns appears in summary form in Figure 28–8. Supporting information is shown in Schedules 1 through 5.

Before leaving the tax calculation for Thomas and Mary Brown, it should be of interest to the readers to see a segment of Schedule C, Form 1040, on which the net income of a business similar to the Brown Groceries would be calculated. As can be seen in Figure 28–9, the Schedule C is nothing more than a regular income statement.

Figure 28–7
Tax information—Thomas and Mary Brown

Income

Net income from Brown Groceries (gross margin on sales of $90,000 less operating expenses of $40,000)	$50,000.00
Interest on U.S. Bonds	1,000.00
Interest on State of Massachusetts Bonds	1,800.00
Dividends on stock jointly owned	3,200.00

Net long-term capital gain from sale of 100 shares of National Carbon Company Stock:

Date Acquired	Date Sold	Tax Basis (Cost)	Selling Price	Gain
1/10/76	4/1/78	$4,000.00	$5,000.00	$ 1,000.00

Net short-term capital gain from sale of 200 shares of United Electric Company Stock:

Date Acquired	Date Sold	Tax Basis (Cost)	Selling Price	
1/10/78	4/1/78	$2,000.00	$2,500.00	500.00

Expenditures

Contribution to church and university	$ 3,800.00
Contribution to United Fund	400.00
Interest paid on personal loans	300.00
Personal property taxes paid to town and county	692.00
State taxes paid	
Sales tax	158.00
Automobile license tags	24.00
Gasoline tax	100.00
Family medical expenses	
Doctor and hospital fees	400.00
Drugs and medicine	140.00
Amount paid in 1978 as a result of filing Form 1040-ES, Declaration of Estimated Income Tax	15,000.00

Figure 28–8 Computation of the tax liability

THOMAS AND MARY BROWN
Computation of Amount of Income Tax Liability
Taxable Year 1978

Gross income (Schedule 1)		$95,500.00
Deductions from gross income		
Operating expenses of the grocery store (from Figure 28-7)	$40,000.00	
Capital gains deduction 50% x Net LTCG of $1,000	500.00	
Total deductions from gross income		40,500.00
Adjusted gross income		$55,000.00
Deduct excess itemized deductions		
Itemized deductions (Schedule 2)	$ 5,450.00	
Minus zero bracket amount	3,200.00	
Excess itemized deductions	$ 2,250.00	
Personal exemptions (Schedule 3)	3,000.00	5,250.00
Tentative taxable income		$49,750.00
Add unused zero bracket amount		.00
Final taxable income		$49,750.00
Federal income tax before tax credits (Schedule 4)		$15,335.00
Tax credits (Schedule 5)		15,180.00
Amount of tax liability		$ 155.00

Schedule 1—Gross Income

Gross margin on sales of Brown Groceries	$90,000.00
Interest on U.S. Bonds	1,000.00
Dividends received ($100 per owner-spouse is excluded)	3,000.00
Net long-term capital gains before any deductions	1,000.00
Net short-term capital gains (100% included) . .	500.00
(Interest on State of Massachusetts Bonds is 100% excludable)	
Total gross income	$95,500.00

Schedule 2—Personal Deductions

Contributions (both apply since they do not exceed allowable limitation—all are qualifying special contributions)	$ 4,200.00
Interest paid on personal loans	300.00
Property taxes	692.00
Sales taxes	158.00
Gasoline tax	100.00
(The $24 paid for license tags is not deductible as a tax, and the medical expenses are not large enough to be included.)	
Total personal deductions	$ 5,450.00

Schedule 3—Personal Exemptions

Thomas Brown	1
Mary Brown	1
Katherine Kay (Under a special relief provision of the tax law, she qualifies as an exemption for Brown—even though she earned over $750 income—she would have to file a return and could claim an exemption for herself; but Brown may also claim her as an excemption) . .	1
Thomas, Jr.	1
Total	4

Value of personal exemption: 4 x $750 = $3,000

Schedule 4—Computation of Federal Income tax

Referring to Rate Schedule No. 2, Figure 28-5 for married couples filing joint returns:*	
Income tax on first $47,200	$14,060.00
Plus 50% x 2,550	1,275.00
Total federal income tax for 1978	$15,335.00

*The calculation of the tax by applying the alternative capital gains tax to net long-term capital gains will not produce a lower total tax figure.

Schedule 5—Tax Credits

Amount paid in 1978 as a result of filing Form 1040-ES, Declaration of Estimated Income Tax for Individuals	$15,000.00
General tax credit: larger of (2% x $9,000) or (4 x $35)	180.00
Total tax credits	$15,180.00

Reporting partnership income

Partnerships are not taxed as separate entities. Rather, the relevant revenues and expenses of the partnership are reported on an informational return, Form 1065, and the individual partners report their respective shares of operating income, net long-term and short-term capital gains, dividends received, contributions, tax-exempt income, and any other items that require special treatment on their own U.S. Individual Income Tax Returns.

Consider the partnership firm of O'Koren and O'Casey, which has an ordinary taxable income of $100,000 after salaries of $8,000 to George O'Koren and $10,000 to Philip O'Casey. Relevant items belonging to each partner are indicated in Figure 28–10.

On his U.S. Individual Income Tax Return, O'Koren, for example, would consolidate the following items with his own personal income and deductions: salary received from partnership, $8,000; ordinary income from partnership, $70,000; net long-term capital gains (only 50 percent included, but subject to special tax on net long-term capital gains), $700; net short-term capital gains,

Figure 28–9 Schedule C (Form 1040) profit or (loss) from business or profession

SCHEDULE C (Form 1040)
Department of the Treasury Internal Revenue Service

Profit or (Loss) From Business or Profession

(Sole Proprietorship)
Partnerships, Joint Ventures, etc., Must File Form 1065.
► Attach to Form 1040. ► See Instructions for Schedule C (Form 1040).

1977

Name of proprietor | Social security number

A Principal business activity (see Schedule C Instructions) ►..........; product ►..........
B Business name ►..........
C Employer identification number ►..........
D Business address (number and street) ►..........
City, State and ZIP code ►..........

C

	Yes	No
E Indicate method of accounting: (1) ☐ Cash (2) ☐ Accrual (3) ☐ Other ►..........		
F Was an Employer's Quarterly Federal Tax Return, Form 941, filed for this business for any quarter in 1977?		
G Did you own the business at the end of 1977?		
H How many months in 1977 did you own this business? ►..........		
I Check valuation method(s) used for total closing inventory: ☐ cost, ☐ lower of cost or market, ☐ other (if "other," attach explanation).		
Was there any substantial change in determining quantities, costs, or valuations between opening and closing inventory? If "Yes," attach explanation.		

Income

	Line	Amount
1 Gross receipts or sales $.......... Less: returns and allowances $.......... Balance ►	1	
2 Less: Cost of goods sold and/or operations (Schedule C–1, line 8)	2	
3 Gross profit	3	
4 Other income (attach schedule)	4	
5 **Total income** (add lines 3 and 4)	5	

Deductions

	Line	Amount
6 Depreciation (explain in Schedule C–2)	6	
7 Taxes on business and business property	7	
8 Rent on business property	8	
9 Repairs	9	
10 Salaries and wages not included on line 3, Schedule C–1 (exclude any paid to yourself)	10	
11 Insurance	11	
12 Legal and professional fees	12	
13 Commissions	13	
14 Amortization (attach statement)	14	
15 a Pension and profit-sharing plans (see Schedule C Instructions)	15a	
b Employee benefit programs (see Schedule C Instructions)	b	
16 Interest on business indebtedness	16	
17 Bad debts arising from sales or services	17	
18 Depletion	18	
19 Other business expenses (specify):		
a		
b		
c		
d		
e		
f		
g		
h		
i		
j		
k		
l		
m		
n		
o		
p Total other business expenses (add lines 19a through 19o)	19p	
20 Total deductions (add lines 6 through 19p)	20	
21 Net profit or (loss) (subtract line 20 from line 5). Enter here and on Form 1040, line 13. **ALSO** enter on Schedule SE, line 5a ►	21	

Did you claim a deduction for expenses of an office in your home? ☐ Yes ☐ No

235–060–1

Figure 28–10
Partnership tax information

O'KOREN AND O'CASEY PARTNERSHIP
Tax Information—Taxable Year 1978

	Total	O'Koren's Share	O'Casey's Share
Partnership ordinary income . . .	$100,000.00	$70,000.00	$30,000.00
Net long-term capital gains . . .	2,000.00	1,400.00	600.00
Net short-term capital gains . .	1,000.00	700.00	300.00
Dividends received	10,000.00	7,000.00	3,000.00
Contributions*.	(2,200.00)	(1,540.00)	(660.00)
Interest received on municipal bonds	1,100.00	770.00	330.00
Total partnership income per books	$111,900.00	$78,330.00	$33,570.00

*These are debits and are deducted in arriving at book partnership income

$700; dividends received (net of $100 exclusion, assuming that O'Koren is single and does not own any stocks personally), $6,900; and contributions, $1,540. The interest received on municipal bonds is tax exempt and hence would be excluded from O'Koren's gross income. O'Koren's individual federal income tax would then be computed in the manner described in Figure 28–8.

Corporate income taxes

The income of a business corporation is subject to a separate income tax. The owners, the stockholders, are *also partially taxed* on any income from dividends received from the corporation. Yet the corporation is not allowed to deduct any of these dividends paid to stockholders. The corporate tax rate schedule for 1978 is a simple three-step progressive structure.

Taxable Income	*Tax Rate*
$0 to $25,000	20%
$25,000 to $50,000	22%
over $50,000	48%

In general, the taxable income of a corporation is computed in the same manner as the taxable income of an individual. Among the exceptions is the fact that a corporation may not take certain personal deductions allowed to individuals. For example, a corporation is not entitled to personal exemptions, the zero bracket amount, or such personal deductions as medical expenses. Since personal deductions are not allowed, the concept of adjusted gross income would be meaningless and, therefore, is not applicable to the corporation.

The $100 dividend exclusion is not applicable to corporations. Normally, they may deduct from gross income 85 percent of dividends received from domestic corporations. Under certain conditions, when a consolidated return is filed for a parent and those companies that are owned by the parent, the consolidated group may, in effect, deduct 100 percent of dividends received by members of the group from each other, that is, the intercompany dividend amount.

Capital losses of a corporation can be deducted *only* against capital gains. Capital losses may be carried back three years and forward five years (1976 law) and may be offset against any capital gains earned during those years, not counting the year of the loss. The unlimited carryover of capital losses is applicable only to *individuals;* carryovers by corporations are limited to *five* years, except for banks which have *ten years.*

Net long-term capital gains are 100 percent includable in taxable income of corporations but are subject to a maximum tax rate of 30 percent. For example, if the Kupchak Corporation reported a taxable income in 1978 of $100,000 composed entirely of net long-term capital gains, its tax would be only $30,000; but if it reported an ordinary business income of $100,000, its tax would be $34,000.

A maximum limit of 5 percent of net income, figured without regard to the contribution deduction, for corporate contributions is imposed on corporations. Any contribution in excess of this limit may be carried over to the five succeeding years and deducted, provided the total contributions including the carried-over amounts are within the 5 percent limit of the appropriate years.

The Corporate Income Tax Return, Form 1120, must be filed two and one-half months after the end of the taxable fiscal year. Corporations are generally required to prepay their income tax.

The major features of the corporate income tax are illustrated by the tax computation for the LaGarde Corporation, shown in Figures 28–11 and 28–12.

Income tax planning

Since 1913 the weight of the income tax has become heavier and heavier on individuals, estates, trusts, and corporations. Today a large part of the income dollar of all taxpayers goes to various government agencies in the form of taxes, with the income tax taking one of the largest bites. Therefore, it seems that the

Figure 28–11
Book income statement

LAGARDE CORPORATION
Income Statement—Per the Books
For the Year Ended December 31, 1978

Revenues		
Net Sales		$500,000.00
Expenses		
Cost of Goods Sold	$250,000.00	
Operating Expenses other than Capital Losses and Charitable Contributions	80,000.00	
Capital Losses	8,000.00	
Charitable Contributions	12,000.00	
Total Expenses		350,000.00
Net Income before Income Taxes		$150,000.00
Less Federal Income Taxes (see Figure 28–10)		64,020.00
Net Income		$ 85,980.00

Figure 28–12
Corporate income tax computation

LAGARDE CORPORATION
Tax Computation—Taxable Year 1978

Revenues		$500,000.00
Expenses		
Cost of Goods Sold	$250,000.00	
Operating Expenses other than Capital Losses and Charitable Contributions	80,000.00	
Capital Losses (none allowed)	.00	
Charitable Contributions (the smaller of actual of $12,000, or 5% x $170,000 = $8,500.00)	8,500.00	338,500.00
Net Final Taxable Income		$161,500.00
Tax Computation		
Tax on first $25,000 of taxable income at 20%: 20% x 25,000		$ 5,000.00
Tax on next 25,000: 22% x $25,000		5,500.00
Tax on final taxable income in excess of $50,000: 48% x $111,500		53,520.00
Total 1978 corporate income tax		$ 64,020.00

management of taxpaying entities should plan certain controllable transactions in a manner that will minimize the tax cost in the long run. In other words, management should avoid all income taxes possible by the legal method of preventing a tax liability from coming into existence, referred to as *tax avoidance;* but it should never evade taxes by failure to report income, by illegal reporting, or by nonpayment of taxes.

The essence of tax planning is determining in advance what the income tax effect of transactions are; with the effect thus determined, the taxpayer can make those transactions that will result in the minimization of the income tax. For example, the timing of revenue receipts and expense is an excellent way of controlling taxable income. A few general rules illustrate this point. A taxpayer should avoid bunching taxable revenue in one year with related expenses falling in another. If he or she anticipates high revenue in a succeeding year, the taxpayer should hold off discretionary expenses and make these in the high-revenue year in order to minimize taxable income. If a change in income tax rates is anticipated, the taxpayer should accelerate or postpone revenue and expenses accordingly. He or she should avoid, if possible, the offsetting of short-term capital losses against long-term capital gains in the same year, because only 50 percent of net long-term capital gains are includable in taxable income.

Many relief provisions are present in the income tax law, and should be used by taxpayers to the fullest extent possible. Some examples follow:

> The use of LIFO in inventory valuation when prices are rising (permission must be obtained from the Internal Revenue Service for a company to switch inventory pricing methods).

The use of allowable accelerated depreciation methods and the use of the shorter average estimated useful lives allowed under the Asset Depreciation Range provision of the Internal Revenue Code.

In summary, these guidelines should be observed:

All controllable transactions should be planned in light of the tax consequences. Although a taxpayer may be able to do something about the tax effect before a transaction occurs, he or she can legally do nothing except follow the tax law after the transaction has already taken place.

Evidence of transactions should be preserved; in other words, a set of books should be maintained. Even a cash-basis salaried individual taxpayer should establish as a minimum a simple columnar journal of cash receipts and cash expenditures. In case of an audit by a representative of the Internal Revenue Service, this kind of record would be very valuable.

Impact of income taxes on business decisions

With the present extremely high income tax rates, it is essential for prudent business managers to consider carefully the effect of income taxes on the various alternatives under review. There is a saying among businessmen that a tax dollar saved, with a tax rate of approximately 50 percent, is as profitable as two dollars of net operating income earned. In the preceding section, certain suggestions were made regarding how to plan transactions so as to minimize the amount of income tax; this planning is one aspect of decision making. In this section, however, the focus is on the impact of taxes on the choice of form of business organization, effect on financial arrangements, effect on adoption of accounting procedures, and the effect on hold- or sell decisions.

When one or more individuals decide to establish a business, one of the first decisions that must be made is the selection of the legal form of organization—sole proprietorship, partnership, or corporation. Income taxes, along with many other factors, may help to influence the choice. Three tax provisions must be kept in mind: A sole proprietor must pay a tax on the entire taxable income of the business. A partner must pay a tax on his or her proportionate share of the taxable partnership income, whether distributed or not. A corporation (unless it exercises its option in the law to file its return as a partnership) must report and pay a tax on its income, and the stockholders must include their dividend income on their individual returns.

From the viewpoint of one individual who is to be involved in the formation of a new business, a calculation must be made to estimate how he or she would fare from a tax standpoint under the alternative business forms. This calculation would require a determination of anticipated after-tax net income of the corporation, the salary to be received by the major stockholder, the net income of the sole proprietorship, and a calculation of the available disposable income for the proprietor. If the calculation shows one form to yield a larger disposable net income, that business form, holding all other items constant, may be the one that should be used.

As indicated in Chapter 19, income taxes may influence the particular financing arrangement that a firm uses to obtain new long-term capital. The main thrust of this problem results from the fact that dividends are not deductible in arriving at taxable income, whereas interest expense is deductible. Thus, if a decision has to be made in regard to whether or not to issue bonds as compared to common or preferred stock, the calculation of taxable income and the resultant income taxes may be a deciding factor.

Certain accounting procedures may be adopted because of tax factors. For example, the LIFO inventory method may be chosen for tax purposes because of anticipation that it may yield a lower taxable income than would other inventory pricing methods. The tax law requires that LIFO be used for book purposes if it is used for tax purposes. This tax requirement thus forces firms to adopt a procedure that may not, in most cases, produce the best income figure for business decisions. Another example of possible unsound accounting procedures involves the nonrecognition of gains and losses on trade-in of plant and equipment items, discussed in Chapter 14.

Because of a difference between tax rates on ordinary income and on long-term capital gains, the income tax may influence an owner's decision to hold or to sell an income-producing asset. If the present value of the future after-tax income is higher than the after-tax income resulting from a sale, then the income-producing property should be held. On the other hand, if the after-tax gain resulting from the possible sale is greater than the present value of the after-tax income, then the property should be sold.

Differences between financial accounting income and taxable income

Taxable income must be computed in accordance with statutes and administrative regulations of the federal government. Computation of business income for financial reporting purposes, however, should be based on accepted accounting standards. Using two methods of computation will lead to apparent discrepancies between the two net income figures. Any feature of the tax law that increases taxable income also increases the amount of tax; likewise, any feature of the law that decreases the amount of taxable income decreases the amount of tax. A summary of the four major differences between traditional business income and taxable income follows:

Some items not considered to be revenue by generally accepted accounting principles are taxed as revenue by the law.

Some items considered as business expenses are not deductible for tax purposes.

Some items generally considered to be business revenue are exempt from tax by law.

Some items not generally considered to be business expenses are deductible for tax purposes.

Taxable nonbusiness revenues

The most important taxable receipts that are not generally considered to be business revenues are certain unearned revenue items such as advance receipts of rent, interest, or royalties. The federal government levies the tax in the year of receipt, when the cash for payment is presumably available. Sound accounting, on the other hand, recognizes these items as revenue in the year in which they are earned. An exception to the general tax rule stated is the unearned subscriptions revenue received by publishing companies. These particular entities are permitted to report taxable revenue on the basis of the accrual earning process as opposed to the time of the cash receipt.

Nondeductible business expenses

Several kinds of items would normally be considered business expenses but are not allowed for tax purposes. Five representative examples are listed below:

As indicated in the discussion of corporate income tax, charitable contributions in excess of 5 percent of net income, figured without regard to the contribution deduction, are not deductible even when they are made for an ostensible business purpose.

Interest on money borrowed to purchase tax-exempt securities is not deductible.

Premiums paid on life insurance policies carried by the corporation on the lives of its key personnel are not deductible if the corporation names itself as beneficiary—sound accounting requires that the amount of the premium in excess of increases in cash surrender value (the investment in the policies) should be considered an expense.

The federal income tax itself is not an expense for tax purposes.

Any amortization of an indefinite-life intangible fixed asset, particularly goodwill, is not deductible.

Tax-exempt business revenue

Several revenue items are exempt from taxation because of various reasons ranging from social desirability to administrative expediency. Three representative examples of items specifically exempted by the Internal Revenue Code are listed here:

Interest received on state and municipal bonds and notes is specifically exempt from taxation.

A portion of net long-term capital gains, in effect, is exempt, since usually there is a maximum tax rate on such gains.

Life insurance proceeds received on the death of the insured are not taxed.

Deductions allowed by tax law not generally considered to be business expenses

The tax law provides special relief provisions and investment incentives that are not generally deducted from business revenue to measure net income. Among these are the following:

The part of allowable accelerated depreciation that is in excess of sound depreciation expense

The net operating loss deduction—a special feature of the tax law designed to give taxpayers who suffer a loss in a given bad year some relief from taxes paid in the three years immediately preceding, or the five years following, the year of the loss.

Additional questions regarding the differences between income figures are raised in the Appendix to this chapter, in which the impact of these differences on financial reporting is considered.

Financial reporting problems—interperiod income tax allocation

appendix

The differences between taxable income and business income fall into two classes: (1) those that tend to result in a near-permanent difference between taxable and business income and (2) those for which the difference between taxable income and business income is washed out in time. Financial reporting problems caused by the latter class are magnified by the size of the current income tax. The controversy centers around the proper measurement of the federal income tax expense. If the income tax is a business expense, the matching concept seems to dictate that it be computed on the basis of reported business income, taking into consideration the timing differences in class 2 above.

Because the above assumption seems to be valid for those companies that have material timing differences between taxable income and reported business book income, the Accounting Principles Board in its *Opinion No. 11* has concluded that the income tax expense must be allocated among the relevant periods and that the deferred method of tax allocation should be followed.

Interperiod income tax allocation: two illustrations

The income tax expense for the current year under the matching concept is based on book net income. When differences exist between book net income and taxable net income, the accepted practice is to allocate income taxes between the relevant periods. The practice is referred to as interperiod income tax allocation. This procedure is made necessary because of two types of timing differences that wash out over time. One type of timing difference arises when revenue is recognized in one accounting period for book purposes but is not taxed until later periods, or when an expense is recognized on the tax return but is not recognized in the accounting records until a later period. A second type of timing difference arises when revenue is recognized on the tax return before it is recognized in the books, or when expenses are recognized for book accounting purposes before they are deducted on the tax return. The first difference will give rise to a postponed income tax liability, which will be paid at a later date. The second will create prepaid income tax items, which will be postponed and allocated as income tax expense of future periods. Specific examples of the cause of these two timing differences are given in the preceding section of this chapter.

Two illustrations are given to introduce the accounting procedures involved in the deferred method of interperiod income tax allocation. First, consider an example that would create a postponed income tax liability referred to as deferred income tax liability; the classic example is the difference between book depreciation and tax depreciation. Assume, for example, that the Calgary Corporation deems that the straight-line depreciation method is appropriate for its books and hence adopts this method, but uses the sum-of-the-years'-digits method for its tax return. Assume that the company acquired a major machine that costs $300,000 and has an estimated five-year life with no salvage value; also assume that the income tax rate is 50 percent. If the company earns $500,000 each year (before depreciation expense and income tax expense), the effect of these procedures on pretax book accounting income and taxable income is shown below:

Year	*Accounting Income Before Depreciation and Income Taxes*	*Accounting Depreciation (Straight Line)*	*Tax Return Depreciation (SYD)*	*Pretax Book Accounting Income*	*Taxable Income*
1	$ 500,000	$ 60,000	$100,000	$ 440,000	$ 400,000
2	500,000	60,000	80,000	440,000	420,000
3	500,000	60,000	60,000	440,000	440,000
4	500,000	60,000	40,000	440,000	460,000
5	500,000	60,000	20,000	440,000	480,000
Totals	$2,500,000	$300,000	$300,000	$2,200,000	$2,200,000

Note that *total* pretax accounting income and taxable income are the same for the five-year period. The journal entries to record the income tax liability and the income tax expense at the assumed rate of 50 percent are presented below:

		Debit	Credit
Year 1	Income Tax Expense	220,000	
	Income Taxes Payable		200,000
	Deferred Income Tax Liability		20,000
	To record tax expense on reported net income of $440,000 at assumed rate of 50 percent.		
Year 2	Income Tax Expense	220,000	
	Income Taxes Payable		210,000
	Deferred Income Tax Liability		10,000
	(The explanations for years 2 to 5 are omitted, since they are essentially the same as those for year 1.)		
Year 3	Income Tax Expense	220,000	
	Income Taxes Payable		220,000
Year 4	Income Tax Expense	220,000	
	Deferred Income Tax Liability	10,000	
	Income Taxes Payable		230,000
Year 5	Income Tax Expense	220,000	
	Deferred Income Tax Liability	20,000	
	Income Taxes Payable		240,000

Under the inferred assumptions that the tax law has not changed and that the Deferred Income Tax Liability account refers only to the machinery purchased in year 1, the five-year history of this account is shown below:

Deferred Income Tax Liability — Acct. No. 251

Date		Explanation	F	Debit	Credit	Balance
Year	1		J176		20,000 00	20,000 00
	2		J276		10,000 00	30,000 00
	4		J376	10,000 00		20,000 00
	5		J476	20,000 00		-0-

The typical balance sheet classification of this account is as a long-term liability.

The above example of a firm using one depreciation method for book purposes and another for tax purposes in only one of the many available alternative practices that cause differences between tax accounting and book accounting, resulting in a temporary difference between taxable income and business income—a difference that washes out in time. Other cases must be considered carefully to see whether they warrant the allocation of the income tax between periods. Although it appears theoretically sound to make use of this practice in all relevant cases, the deciding factors, of course, are the size of the amounts involved and the complexity of the procedure in regard to a particular case. A company may use a depreciation method for tax purposes different from the theoretically appropriate book method because it has interest-free use of the funds resulting from the postponement of the tax payments.

The second illustration involves a temporary difference that creates a prepaid income tax item. Consider, for example, the advanced receipt of a three-year rental revenue of $600,000 by the Guelph Company. Other book net income before taxes is $100,000 each year. The advanced receipt of rent is fully taxable in the year of receipt; for book purposes, however, $200,000 would be recognized in each of the three years. The book income and taxable income are summarized below:

Year	*Book Accounting Income Other Than Rental Income*	*Additions to Book Accounting for Rental Revenue*	*Pretax Book Accounting Income*	*Taxable Income*
1	$100,000	$200,000	$300,000	$700,000
2	100,000	200,000	300,000	100,000
3	100,000	200,000	300,000	100,000
Totals	$300,000	$600,000	$900,000	$900,000

Using the interperiod income tax allocation procedures, the Guelph Company would determine the income tax expense for each period on the basis of accounting income and would record the difference between the current income tax liability and income tax expense as prepaid income taxes. Journal entries to record income taxes at the assumed rate of 50 percent for the three years are shown below.

Year 1	Income Tax Expense (50% × $300,000)	150,000	
	Prepaid Income Taxes	200,000	
	Income Taxes Payable		350,000
Year 2	Income Tax Expense	150,000	
	Prepaid Income Taxes		100,000
	Income Taxes Payable		50,000
Year 3	Income Tax Expense	150,000	
	Prepaid Income Taxes		100,000
	Income Taxes Payable		50,000

The income tax expense of $150,000 would be shown on the income statement, but the statement should include a footnote disclosing the fact that the income tax liability is different each year.

Some accountants oppose the recognition of interperiod income tax allocation. They state that the income tax is a distribution of income, not an expense, and that the matching concept is therefore not involved. They also argue that the timing differences are not temporary, especially when a firm continues to replace and to add plant items each year. Where the amounts are material and the differences are expected to be reversed, it is the authors' opinion that the interperiod income tax allocation is a theoretically sound procedure and should be recorded in the accounts of the corporation.

Glossary

Adjusted gross income Gross income less deductions from gross for adjusted gross income; these include business-related and revenue-producing expenses.

Avoidance of taxes A legal method of postponing taxes or preventing a tax liability from coming into existence.

Capital assets Stocks, bonds, and other property that by law specifically are identified as capital assets.

Capital gains and losses Any excess or deficiency of cash receipts above or below the bases (usually cost) of capital assets sold.

Evasion of taxes Illegal tax reporting, failure to report taxes, or the nonpayment of taxes.

Excess itemized deductions The excess of the total itemized personal deductions over the zero bracket amount.

Exemption Deduction allowed by law, valued at $750 each for taxpayer, spouse, dependents and other.

Final taxable income Adjusted gross income less excess itemized deductions and total value of exemptions plus usual zero bracket amount, if any.

Final tax table income Adjusted gross income less excess itemized deductions plus unused zero bracket amount.

Flat standard deductions See zero bracket amount.

Gross income All revenue items and gross margin on sales that are legally includable in the total figure, which is the starting point for the calculation of taxable income.

Head of household A single individual who heads a household that contains dependent persons; special tax schedules are provided for heads of household to provide an element of relief to compensate them for the additional family burden they must carry.

Interperiod income tax allocation The allocation of the income tax expense among periods caused by a temporary timing difference between reported book income and taxable income.

Itemized personal deductions Personal items that are allowed by law to be deducted from adjusted gross income; these include contributions, allowable medical expenses, union dues, and others.

Itemizer taxpayer A taxpayer who elects to itemize personal deductions.

Nonitemizer taxpayer A taxpayer who elects not to itemize personal deductions; then he or she will have included in final tax table income or final taxable income the zero bracket amount.

Tax credit A credit that is allowed to be subtracted from the income tax itself; tax credits are allowed for income tax withheld or paid on a declared estimate, credit for elderly, investment credits, child care credit, earned income credits, and others.

Taxable income See final taxable income and tentative taxable income.

Tax rate schedule Any one of five tax schedules for: single individuals, married taxpayers filing separate returns, married taxpayers and surviving spouses filing joint returns, heads of household, and estates and trusts.

Tax table A table showing the amount of the income tax for those taxpayers with a taxable income of a given amount specified by the Internal Revenue Service.

Tentative taxable income Adjusted gross income less the sum of excess itemized deductions and personal exemption.

Tentative tax table income Adjusted gross income less excess itemized deductions.

Unused zero bracket amount The excess of the zero bracket amount over the itemized deduction; certain taxpayers must consider this item.

Zero bracket amount This amount was formerly called the standard deduction; it is $2,200 for a single taxpayer and head of household, $3,200 for married taxpayers filing a joint return; and $1,600 for married taxpayers filing separate returns.

Questions

Q28–1 (a) Distinguish between the cash and accrual bases of accounting. (b) What is a modified cash basis?

Q28–2 (a) Define the term *gross income* from an individual income tax point of view. (b) List six items that must be reported as gross income. (c) List four items that are excludable from gross income.

Q28–3 (a) What is the individual income tax zero bracket amount? (b) State the amount applicable for all kinds of individual taxpayers.

Q28–4 Smith, a bachelor, earned $20,000 in final taxable income in 1978. What amount of federal income tax would be saved if he were to marry on December 31, 1978, a woman who had no taxable income in 1978? (Use tax rate schedules to calculate tax.)[6]

6 Many of these tax calculations would have to be made by the use of tax tables, but since all of the tax tables are not included in this chapter, the student is asked to make all calculations by applying the applicable rates found in the tax rate schedules.

Q28–5 (a) For tax purposes, what are capital assets? (b) Distinguish between short-term and long-term capital gains. (c) The timing of capital gains and losses is important in tax planning. Discuss.

Q28–6 John Allen, aged 21, is attending the State University. During the summer of 1978, he worked as a construction laborer and earned $850. His parents contributed $1,850 toward his support in 1978. Can Allen's parents claim him as an exemption?

Q28–7 Samuel Sawyer elected to use the cash basis for tax purposes. During 1978 he collected $12,000 from clients for services rendered in prior years, and billed clients for $30,000 for services rendered in 1978. His accounts receivable as of December 31, 1978, totaled $8,700, all arising out of services rendered in 1978. What is the amount of gross income he should report on his Form 1040 for 1978?

Q28–8 John and Susan Adams owned some shares of stock. During 1978, they received $700 in dividends. Dividends of $610 were received on stock owned by John Adams only. The remainder was received on stock owned by Susan Adams. What would be the dividends included in gross income on a joint return?

Q28–9 List and briefly discuss the computational differences between the individual income tax and the corporation income tax.

Q28–10 Compare the income tax treatment of capital losses for the individual income taxpayer and for the corporate taxpayer.

Q28–11 (a) State the objective of tax planning. (b) Discuss ways and means of accomplishing tax planning.

Q28–12 In outline form, state four ways that traditional business income may differ from taxable income; give two specific illustrations for each way.

Q28–13 List some tax factors that should be considered in deciding whether to organize a new business as a corporation, a partnership, or a proprietorship.

Class exercises

CE28–1 (Individual income tax computation) Adam Kennedy, 66 years old, is married to Sara Kennedy, who is 63. They have two children: John, 16, and Susan, 21, who is attending a university. The Kennedys furnish over one-half the support for both their children, although Susan works as a salesclerk in the summer and earned $950 in 1978. Kennedy owns and operates a service station under the name of Kennedy Service Station. Mrs. Kennedy did not have any earned income in 1978.

Relevant business and personal information for the family is shown:

Cash Receipts	
Gross revenue from Kennedy Service Station	$100,000
Interest on bonds	1,000
Interest on State of Virginia bonds	3,450
Dividends on stock jointly owned	4,200
Cash proceeds from insurance policy for fire damage on nonbusiness property that had an original cost of $1,800	1,800

Capital gains

Sale of 200 shares of National Fruit Company common stock:

Date Acquired	*Date Sold*	*Cost*	*Selling Price*
3/4/71	5/2/78	$24,000	$28,000

Sale of 100 shares of United Fusbits Company common stock:

Date Acquired	*Date Sold*	*Cost*	*Selling Price*
4/2/78	8/10/78	$10,000	$10,600

Expenditures	
Cost of goods sold ($55,000) and operating expenses ($15,000) of Kennedy Service Station	$70,000
Contributions to church and university	2,000
Contribution to Community Chest	800
Interest paid on personal loans	600
Property taxes paid to town and county	800
State taxes paid	
Sales tax	160
Automobile license tags	24
Gasoline tax	100
Family medical expenses	
Doctor and hospital fees	800
Drugs and medicine	120
Blue Cross-Blue Shield Hospital Insurance	280
Amount paid in 1978 on declared estimated tax for 1978	7,000

Required: In an orderly schedule form, compute the income tax liability remaining to be paid for 1978 assuming that a joint return is filed. (Use tax rate schedules to calculate tax.)

CE28–2 (Information to be reported on partnership informational return) Hanners and Newton are partners sharing profits 2:1, respectively. The following information has been taken from the partnership records for the year 1978:

Taxable ordinary income (less partners' salaries)	$60,000
Long-term capital gains	9,000
Short-term capital gains	3,600
Short-term capital losses	3,000
Dividends received	1.800
Charitable contributions	2,100
Interest on Orange County bonds	900
Salaries to partners ($5,000 to Hanners and $4,000 to Newton)	9,000
Net income per books before partner's salaries	79,200

Assume that Hanners is 40 years old and single, and that he has the following tax information from sources other than the partnership:

Dividends received	$8,000
Long-term capital losses	3,000
Itemized deductions	1,500

Required:

1. Prepare a schedule showing the information that should be presented on the partnership informational return.
2. Compute the 1978 income tax for Hanners. (Use tax rate schedules to compute tax.)

CE28–3 (Corporate income tax computation) The Lundee Corporation reported the following information for 1978:

Sales	$2,000,000
Cost of goods sold	1,100,000
Operating expenses other than capital losses and charitable contributions	500,000
Capital losses	20,000
Charitable contributions	25,000
(There were no capital gains)	

Required: Compute the corporate income tax for 1978.

CE28–4 (Appendix: Interperiod income allocation) In 1978, 1979, and 1980 the taxable income reported by the Mabel Corporation for income tax purposes has differed from the book net income before taxes reported on its income statement. The record is as follows:

Net Income Before Taxes

Year	*Income Statement*	*Tax Return*
1978	$112,500	$82,500
1979	67,500	78,750
1980	63,750	75,000

Included in book net income as reported on the income statement in 1978 was $11,250 of interest earned on municipal bonds that is not subject to income tax at any time. Also during 1978, $18,750 of deductions were taken for income tax purposes that will not be reported as book expenses until later years. In 1980, the company incurred a book accounting loss of $6,000, $2,250 of which was deductible. In all other respects income reported on the income statement is ultimately subject to income taxes. Assume that the company is subject to a combined state and federal income tax rate of 60 percent on all taxable income.

Required:

1. Prepare journal entries necessary to record income taxes in each of the three years and to make an interperiod allocation of income taxes on the basis of the information provided. Show supporting calculations.
2. Assuming that all income taxes due (as reported on the company's tax returns) were paid during the year following their accrual, what are the balances at the end of 1980 in the company's two tax liability accounts?

Exercises and problems

P28–1 Saul Allison, a bachelor, had the following cash receipts during the year:

Salary earned as a professor	$14,000
Receipt of insurance proceeds for fire damages to personal car	500
Dividends from domestic companies	2,000
Interest on U.S. Government bonds	600
Interest on North Carolina State bonds	700
Total Cash Receipts	$17,800

Required: Compute the amount of gross income subject to the individual income tax.

P28–2 Dunn and Pauline Carson filed a joint return in 1978. They had the following taxable income after deductions and exemptions:

Ordinary taxable income	$100,000
Long-term capital gains (before reduction)	30,000
Total	$130,000

Required: Compute the 1978 federal income tax. Remember that the income tax on net long-term capital gains cannot exceed a certain percentage of the long-term gain. (Use tax rate schedules to compute the amount of tax.)

P28–3 Answer the following items:

1. Which of the following outlays is *not* a potential deduction from income for the computation of taxable income?
   a. Contribution to the Boy Scouts
   b. Payment of property taxes
   c. Payment of federal income taxes
   d. Payment of bond interest charges
   e. Payment of building rental charge.
2. Justice Corporation was formed late last year and started operations on January 1 of the current year. In forming the corporation, organizational expenditures of $120,000 were incurred and paid. If Justice elects to amortize these expenses, its maximum deduction for tax purposes in the current year is (a) $120,000, (b) $24,000, (c) $12,000, (d) $–0–, (e) none of the preceding. (Hint: A corporation may amortize organizational cost over 5 years or more.)

(IMA adapted)

P28–4 Answer the following items.

1. Chambers Corporation bought a machine in 1972 for $30,000. The corporation used this machine in its manufacturing operation until November 1978 when it was exchanged for a similar, but larger, machine having a list price of $65,000 and which could be bought at a cash price of $60,000. At the date of exchange, the adjusted basis of the original machine was $12,000, and Chambers paid $35,000 on the exchange. The gain or loss recognized for tax purposes on the exchange by Chambers Corporation and its tax basis of the new machine immediately after the exchange, are:
   a. Gain recognized $13,000; basis $60,000
   b. No gain or loss recognized; basis $60,000
   c. No gain or loss recognized; basis $47,000
   d. Gain recognized $18,000; basis $65,000
   e. Loss recognized $5,000; basis $60,000.

2. An *improper* tax accounting method for a manufacturing corporation is: (a) cash method, (b) accrual method, (c) hybrid method [a combination method], (d) installment method, (e) LIFO for inventories.

(IMA adapted)

P28–5 Answer the following items:

1. Sigma Corporation carried a $500,000 insurance policy on the life of its president with itself as the beneficiary. On August 1 of the current year, the president died. On September 1, Sigma received a check from the insurance company for $500,000. The current year's premium for this policy, up to the date of the president's death, was $15,000. In computing Sigma's taxable income for the current year:
   a. The $15,000 should be deducted as an expense and the $500,000 should be included in gross income.
   b. The $15,000 should not be deducted as an expense, but the $500,000 should be included in gross income.
   c. The $15,000 should be deducted as an expense, but the $500,000 should not be included in gross income.
   d. The $15,000 and the $500,000 should be ignored.
   e. None of the above.
2. The income tax treatment of individual and corporate taxpayers agrees in the following respect:
   a. Excess capital losses may be carried forward five years.
   b. Excess capital losses may *not* be carried back.
   c. Excess capital losses may be offset against income from other sources, but only to a limited extent.
   d. Excess capital losses retain their identity as either long-term or short-term losses in the year to which they are carried.
   e. None of the above.

3. For the taxable year ended December 31, 1978, Davis Corporation had taxable income of $100,000 before taking into account any gains or losses on the sale of assets. Information concerning its sales of assets follows:

	Type of Asset	
	Operating Equipment	*Land Held as Investment*
Date acquired	1/1/77	7/7/70
Date sold	12/31/78	5/4/78
Useful life	10 yrs.	n/a
Accumulated depreciation (straight line)	$10,000	n/a
Cost	50,000	$80,000
Selling price	20,000	30,000

Davis Corporation's taxable income after taking into account these two sales of property would be: (a) $100,000, (b) $99,000, (c) $80,000, (d) $30,000, (e) none of the preceding.

4. Vacconey Corporation's taxable income for 1978 was $120,000. All taxable income resulted from regular operations of the corporation. Vacconey's tax liability before credits for 1978 would be: (a) $57,600, (b) $60,000, (c) $44,100, (d) $51,100, (e) none of the preceding. (Use actual tax rates.)

(AICPA adapted)

P28–6 Roy and Abigall Butts had the following income and related information for 1978:

Salary to Roy Butts	$10,000
Dividends on stock owned by Roy Butts	2,000
Dividends on stock owned by Abigail Butts	1,000
Abigail Butts sold some stock she had acquired on April 1, 1968 on March 15, 1978, at a gain of	4,000
Roy Butts sold some stock he had acquired on July 1, 1978 on November 15, 1978, at a loss of	1,500

Required: Compute the adjusted gross income subject to tax on a joint return filed by Roy and Abigail Butts.

P28–7 Randolph Peters, who is 45 years old, is married to Alice Peters, who is 41 years old. They have two children: Duncan, 9 years old, and Sue, 14. Peters owns and operates a hardware store under the name of the Peters Hardware Company.

Tax and other information for 1978 are as follows:

Cash Receipts	
Gross sales of Peters Hardware Company (all sales are for cash)	$200,000
Interest on Dare County bonds	2,000
Dividends on stock owned by Alice Peters	6,000
Cash inherited by Alice Peters	20,000
Capital gains on stock sold by Alice Peters	
Long-term gains	10,000
Short-term gains	1,200
Expenditures	
Cost of goods sold of Peters Hardware Company	100,000
Operating expenses of Peters Hardware Company	40,000
Contribution to church	8,000
Contribution to Community Chest	1,000
Interest paid on personal loans	800
Personal property taxes	1,000
State taxes paid	
Sales taxes	175
Automobile license tags	30
Gasoline tax	120
Family medical expenses	
Doctor and hospital fees	1,200
Hospital insurance—Blue Cross/Blue Shield	320
Drugs and medicine	500
Amount paid in 1978 on declared estimated tax for 1978	20,000

Required: Compute the income tax liability remaining to be paid for 1978 assuming that a joint return is filed. (Use tax rate schedules to compute the tax.)

P28–8 Each of the following five cases represents a possible situation with respect to capital gains and losses. Assume that Allen Sims, a bachelor, has a salary income of $10,000 in addition to the items shown:

1. Long-term capital gains of $8,000; long-term capital losses of $4,000; short-term capital gains of $6,000; short-term capital losses of $3,000
2. Long-term capital gains of $8,000; short-term capital losses of $16,000
3. Long-term capital gains of $4,000; long-term capital losses of $8,000; short-term capital gains of $2,000; short-term capital losses of $7,000
4. Long-term capital gains of $10,000; short-term capital losses of $6,000
5. Long-term capital gains of $1,000; long-term capital losses of $500; short-term capital loss of $1,200.

Required: Compute Allen Sims' adjusted gross income in each case for the year 1978.

P28–9 The following information relates to a taxpayer:

Gross revenue (including $1,000 in interest received on South Carolina bonds and $1,000 in dividends)	$13,900
Deductions to arrive at adjusted gross income	800
Payments made on declaration of estimated tax for 1978 .	1,200
Long-term capital gains	1,500
Short-term capital losses	2,900
Itemized deductions	1,060

Required:

1. Compute the remaining income tax liability, assuming that the taxpayer is married, that both he and his wife are under 65, that they have three dependent children, and that the wife did not receive any separate income. (Use tax rate schedules to compute the tax.)
2. Compute the remaining income tax liability, assuming that the taxpayer is single and under 65.

P28–10 King and Johnson are partners; they share profits 3:1, respectively. The following information has been taken from the partnership records for the year 1978:

Taxable ordinary income (less partners' salaries)	$24,000
Long-term capital gains	10,000
Short-term capital losses	4,000
Dividends received	2,000
Charitable contributions	800
Interest on Florida State bonds	1,000
Salaries to partners ($6,000 to King; $4,000 to Johnson) .	10,000
Net income per books before partners' salaries	42,200

Assume that King is 68 years old and single, and has the following tax information from sources other than the partnership:

Dividends received	$6,000
Long-term capital losses	1,600
Itemized deductions	2,000

Required:

1. Prepare a schedule showing the information that should be presented on the partnership informational return.
2. Compute King's 1978 income tax. (Use tax rate schedules to compute the tax.)

P28–11 The Heller Corporation reported the following information for 1978.

Sales	$1,890,000
Cost of goods sold	920,000
Operating expenses, other than capital losses and charitable contributions	380,000
Capital losses	18,000
Charitable contributions	21,000

Required: Compute the corporate income tax for 1978.

P28–12 (Integrative) Parm Quarles, who is 67 years old, and his wife Mimie Quarles, who is 64 years old, file a joint return. They have two children: Parm, Jr., is 30 years old; Vera, 21 years old, is attending Harper Community College full time. Mr. and Mrs. Quarles furnish over one half the support for Vera although she earned $1,150 on a summer job in 1978. Various receipts and expenditures of Mr. and Mrs. Quarles are listed below.

Mr. Quarles

Cash receipts	
Withdrawal by proprietor from business (sales $270,000; cost of goods sold, $154,000; operating expenses, $52,000)	$30,000
Cash dividends received	2,600
Gain on sale of stock purchased five years ago	4,000
Interest received on school district bonds	2,000
Expenditures	
Contribution to church and university	6,000
Contribution to United Fund	200
Personal property taxes	1,000
Insurance on residence	200
Automobile license plates	24
State sales taxes	150
State gasoline tax	100
Medical expenses	
Drugs and medicines	380
Hospital insurance	280
Doctor and hospital bills	1,050
Interest on personal loans	700
Payment on declaration of estimated tax	21,500

Mrs. Quarles

Cash receipts	
Rental of apartment building	$10,000
Dividends received on stock	850
Received from sale of stock purchased for $3,600 four months previously	2,900
Expenditures	
Apartment building (original cost on January 1, 1970 was $63,000. Sum-of-the-years'-digits depreciation is used for tax purposes, with an assumed life of 20 years and no salvage value)	
Interest on business indebtedness	900
Property taxes	1,600
Insurance for 1978	210
Repairs and maintenance	1,800
Contribution to church	300

Required: Compute the remaining tax liability for 1978 for Mimie and Parm Quarles on a joint return. (Use tax rate schedules to compute tax.)

P28–13 (Integrative) (a) Information for a business operation under two different forms of business organization is given below.

		Corporation	*Partnership*
Sales		$1,000,000	$1,000,000
Expenses			
Salary to John T. Adams	$ 30,000		
Other	870,000	900,000	870,000
Net operating income		$ 100,000	$ 130,000
Dividends		$ 40,000	
Drawings			$ 30,000

Required: For both forms of business organization state the amount of gross income that John T. Adams will have to report on his individual tax return. Under the corporate form of organization, Adams will own 60 percent of the outstanding stock. Under the partnership form of organization, he will have a 60 percent interest in the partnership. Assume that there are no contributions nor capital losses included in the corporate expenses.

(b) Assume the facts set forth in (a) and that the business is organized as a corporation. Assume further that the corporation can earn 12 percent before corporate income tax on an additional investment of $100,000.

Adams is willing to make an additional investment of $100,000 in the business and is considering the following alternative arrangements:

1. A long-term loan of $100,000 at 8 percent interest.
2. An investment of $100,000 for an additional 1,000 shares of stock. After the issuance of the additional 1,000 shares, 5,000 shares will be outstanding.

Required: Assuming that the corporation will distribute as additional dividends all incremental after-tax income from its use of the $100,000, estimate the increase in Adam's taxable income under each alternative.

(c) From the information given in part (a):

Required: Compute income tax expense of the corporation.

(d) Assume that John T. Adams is married, has two young children, and his dependent parents living with him, and his wife has no taxable income.

Required: From the income that you get from part (a), with the business formed as a corporation, calculate John T. Adams income tax liability for 1978, assuming he files a joint return. (Use the tax rate schedules to compute the tax.)

P28–14 (Appendix) The Intergrove Company began business on January 1, 1978. Anticipating a growth in its delivery business over the next few years, the company has developed plans for the purchase of delivery equipment as shown below:

Date of Acquisition (beginning of year)	*Cost of New Equipment*	*Salvage Value*	*Estimated Service Life (in years)*
1978	$100,000	$10,000	5
1979	480,000	30,000	5
1980	690,000	60,000	5
1981	200,000	70,000	5
1982	150,000	30,000	5
1983	166,000	16,000	5

The head accountant of the company is studying the question of depreciation policies on the delivery equipment. The accountant feels that the company should adopt the sum-of-the-years'-digits method of depreciation for income tax purposes but still continue to use the straight-line method for normal accounting and reporting purposes. If this policy is adopted, book net income would differ from taxable income; and this difference would require, in the head accountant's opinion, the use of interperiod income tax allocation procedures in the company's accounting records.

Required:

1. Prepare a schedule showing the difference between taxable income and book income that will result in each year of the six-year period if the head accountant adopts the policy described.
2. Determine the balance that would appear in the Deferred Income Tax Liability account at the close of 1983 if interperiod income tax allocation procedures were followed, and assuming that an income tax rate of 45 percent were applicable.

P28–15 (Minicase) The Cannady Production Company, a textile manufacturer, has recently had a change in ownership and top management. Robert James, the new president, is a retired military officer and is noted for being an excellent organizer and administrator. James is gaining a reputation around the office for asking hard questions and for requiring complete and logical answers.

During one of the mornings that James is devoting to familiarizing himself with the workings of the accounting department, he reviews the latest federal corporate tax return and the latest income statement in the corporate annual report. He immediately notices that the taxable income of $136,495 on the tax return and the net income before income taxes of $219,400 on the income statement are not the same amount. On closer examination he observes that the following items are not the same on each report.

1. Depreciation expense is $92,510 on the income statement and $147,250 on the tax return.
2. Cost of goods sold is $929,180 on the income statement and $951,200 on the tax return.
3. Interest earned is $1,200 on the income statement and $880 on the tax return.
4. Gain on disposal of machinery is $5,790 on the income statement and does not appear on the tax return.
5. Bad debt expense is $6,400 on the income statement and $6,350 on the tax return.
6. Amortization of organization costs does not appear on the income statement and is $85 on the tax return.

He also notes that the income tax expense on the income statement is not the same as the income tax on the tax report.

By this time he is confused and bewildered. He approaches you, an assistant accountant in the tax division, and questions the discrepancies. (He has a dual purpose in asking you questions. He wishes answers to his questions and wishes to evaluate your knowledge of tax accounting.)

Required:

1. Reconcile the two different income amounts. (Hint: A corporation may amortize organization costs over 5 years or more.)
2. Identify what might be a complete and logical reason for each of the six differences. (Remember that you wish to convince the new president of your competence.)
3. (a) Why does income tax expense on the income statement differ from the income tax on the tax report? (b) What is the basis for each calculation? (c) Which would you expect to be the larger? Why?

Business combinations and consolidated financial statements

appendix

Consolidated statements

When a company acquires a controlling portion of the voting shares of another company, unified managerial control is achieved just as if the two companies were a single larger unit, even though each company retains its separate legal and individual identity. The corporation that holds the voting stock and controls the operations of other companies is known as the parent company; the companies controlled by the parent are called subsidiaries. The portion of the stock of the controlled companies held by persons outside the parent company is referred to as the minority interest.

When financial and managerial control exists, the parent company should prepare **consolidated financial statements.**

Consolidated statements

Consolidated statements present the financial affairs of the parent company and its subsidiaries as if they were a single economic unit. The major published financial reports for such families of corporations are in consolidated form. The terms "consolidation" and "consolidated" are commonly used not in their legal sense, denoting a form of business combination, but rather to describe the accounting process of combining the accounts of a controlling parent company with the accounts of its subsidiary companies.

Consolidated statements should be prepared (1) when the parent company owns over 50 percent of the voting stock of the subsidiaries; (2) when the business activities of the companies are related or similar; and (3) when the financial condition of the group as a single economic unit is a valid representation of the operating results and condition of the individual companies.

Membership in a consolidated group does not eliminate the legal responsibilities of each company to its own creditors and stockholders. Each corporation, as a separate legal entity, is responsible for its own decisions and its own obligations. Hence, even when consolidated statements are made each separate entity prepares its own financial statements.

Typical of a corporation that prepares consolidated statements is The Newhall

Land and Farming Company of Valencia, California. With its subsidiaries responsible for manufacture of various products, its 1976 annual report gives a picture of the total economic entity. In its income statement, Newhall shows both revenues and operating expenses by line of business—agriculture, recreation, energy, and three categories of real estate operations.

Note 1 to the consolidated financial statements summarizes significant accounting policies as required by APB *Opinion No. 22.* In Note 1 the Basis of Consolidation indicates that all subsidiaries are wholly owned. It also states that all significant intercompany transactions were *eliminated* in the process of preparing consolidated statements. Such eliminations prevent the overstatement of revenues, expenses, assets and liabilities when all the legal entities are reported on as a single economic unit. An account owed to the parent company by Valencia Corporation, one of Newhall's subsidiaries, would be eliminated from total receivables and total payables in the consolidated balance sheet.

The Newhall Land and Farming Company's fiscal year ends annually on February 28. During the fiscal year ended February 28, 1976, Newhall made a change in allocating expenses. As required by APB *Opinion No. 20,* that change is explained (Note 10) and the independent accountants concurred in the change in their auditor's report.

The Newhall Land and Farming Company and Subsidiaries

Consolidated Statement of Income and Retained Earnings

Years Ended February 29, 1976 and February 28, 1975

(in thousands)

	1976	1975
Revenues		
Agriculture	$ 41,297	$ 43,984
Recreation	26,364	21,703
Energy	5,151	4,483
Real Estate		
Commercial	4,280	3,456
Land	2,586	2,407
Residential	6,477	5,363
Interest and other	986	740
	87,141	82,136
Operating Expenses		
Agriculture	33,857	34,314
Recreation	21,348	17,749
Energy	3,564	2,437
Real Estate		
Commercial	2,305	2,007
Land	458	1,203
Residential	5,420	4,723
All other	1,412	1,551
	68,364	63,984
Interest	2,569	2,845
General and administrative	2,203	1,909
	73,136	68,738
Income before taxes and effect of accounting change	14,005	13,398
Taxes on income (note 2)	5,900	6,163
Income before effect of accounting change	8,105	7,235
Effect of accounting change, net (note 10)	—	(597)
Net Income	8,105	6,638
Retained earnings at beginning of year:		
As previously reported	43,525	39,195
Adjustment for cumulative effect on prior years of tax settlement (note 2)	(1,002)	(1,002)
As adjusted	42,523	38,193
Net loss of certain subsidiaries for the two months ended February 28, 1974 (note 9)	—	(340)
Dividends paid or declared ($.40 and $.36 per share)	(2,186)	(1,968)
Retained earnings at end of year	$ 48,442	$ 42,523
Per share of common stock (note 1):		
Income before effect of change in accounting	$1.48	$1.32
Effect of accounting change	—	(.11)
Net income	$1.48	$1.21

See notes to consolidated financial statements

The Newhall Land and Farming Company and Subsidiaries

Consolidated Balance Sheet

February 29, 1976 and February 28, 1975

	1976	1975
	(in thousands)	
ASSETS		
Current assets		
Cash	$ 2,421	$ 2,184
Marketable securities (note 8)	3,878	435
Accounts and notes receivable (note 8)	5,675	7,439
Inventories (note 8)	14,015	13,274
Prepaid expenses	2,653	2,352
Total current assets	28,642	25,684
Property and equipment (note 8)	100,560	93,019
Investments in and advances to farm cooperatives	1,964	1,660
Deposits on leased agricultural equipment	2,270	2,102
Other assets	2,097	1,965
	$135,533	$124,430
LIABILITIES AND STOCKHOLDERS' EQUITY		
Current liabilities		
Notes payable to banks (note 3)	$ 835	$ 770
Current maturities of long-term liabilities	308	307
Accounts payable	9,265	8,275
Dividends payable	546	492
Income taxes (note 2)		
Currently payable	3,136	1,763
Deferred	6,045	4,476
Total current liabilities	20,135	16,083
Convertible subordinated debentures (note 4)	33,778	33,778
Other long-term liabilities (note 5)	5,603	6,375
Deferred income taxes (note 2)	8,773	6,869
Commitments and contingencies (note 11)		
Stockholders' equity (notes 4 and 7)		
Common stock without par value, authorized 10,000,000 shares, outstanding—5,466,206 shares, excluding 6,902 in treasury	16,437	16,437
Capital surplus	2,365	2,365
Retained earnings (notes 2 and 9)	48,442	42,523
Total stockholders' equity	67,244	61,325
	$135,533	$124,430

See notes to consolidated financial statements

The Newhall Land and Farming Company and Subsidiaries

Consolidated Statement of Changes in Financial Position

Years Ended February 29, 1976 and February 28, 1975

(in thousands)

	1976	1975
Sources of Working Capital		
Operations		
Income before effect of accounting change	$ 8,105	$ 7,235
Add—Depreciation and amortization	5,212	4,775
—Deferred income taxes	1,904	1,714
—Other	61	187
Working capital provided from operations	15,282	13,911
Effect of accounting change, net	—	(597)
Proceeds (payments)—Federal Land Bank loan	(240)	3,394
Proceeds from sales of property and equipment, net	765	1,279
Marketable securities reclassified to current assets	—	435
Receipts/payments on current portion of long-term receivables and liabilities	386	486
Sales of investments	56	128
	16,249	19,036
Uses of Working Capital		
Purchase of property and equipment	13,445	11,655
Investments in and advances to farm co-operatives	304	207
Dividends paid or declared	2,186	1,968
Deposits on leased agricultural equipment, net	168	1,407
Increases in long-term receivables and payments on long-term liabilities	680	605
Repurchase of debentures	—	293
Other, net	560	391
	17,343	16,526
Increase (decrease) in working capital for the year	(1,094)	2,510
Working capital provided from change in year-ends of certain subsidiaries	—	954
Increase (decrease) in working capital	$ (1,094)	$ 3,464
Changes in Components of Working Capital		
Increase (decrease)		
Cash	$ 237	$ 469
Marketable securities	3,443	435
Accounts and notes receivable	(1,764)	2,629
Inventories	741	(262)
Prepaid expenses	301	277
	2,958	3,548
Notes payable to banks	65	(4,200)
Current maturities of long-term liabilities	1	203
Accounts payable	990	1,890
Dividends payable	54	82
Income taxes—Currently payable	1,373	235
—Deferred	1,569	1,874
	4,052	84
Increase (decrease) in working capital	$ (1,094)	$ 3,464

See notes to consolidated financial statements

Notes to Consolidated Financial Statements

Note 1. Summary of Significant Accounting Policies

Accounting policies related to each of the Company's lines of business are:

AGRICULTURE/FARMING Revenue is recognized as crops are sold. Most of the crops are sold to farmers cooperatives (or to food processors), which market the crops throughout a period approximately one year after harvest. Upon harvest, the Company estimates the proceeds to be received from sales of the current year's crop and records these amounts as unbilled receivables. In the year following harvest, the Company records any final adjustments of such estimated amounts resulting from changing market conditions. Net income for the years ended February 29, 1976 and February 28, 1975 increased approximately $936,000 and $700,000, respectively, resulting from such adjustments.

Costs directly related to crops are included in inventory until a sale is recognized. Costs incurred during the development stage of vineyard and orchard crops (ranging from three to ten years) are capitalized and amortized over the productive life of the vines or trees. Costs which cannot be readily identified with a specific harvested crop or other revenue producing activity are expensed as incurred.

Agricultural inventories include materials and supplies, crops in process and processed crops (primarily dehydrated alfalfa and sugar beet products) and are valued at the lower of cost or market, determined on the first-in, first-out method.

AGRICULTURE/CATTLE Revenue is recognized upon sale. Cattle inventory is valued at the lower of cost or market determined on an average cost basis.

RECREATION Food and merchandise revenues at the amusement park and other activities are recorded as cash sales. Revenues from ticket sales are recognized as the tickets are presented for admission.

ENERGY Oil royalties (and the Company's share of the revenues from refined products derived from royalties paid in kind) are recognized as the oil is produced and sold. Gas is sold under a long-term contract with a major utility and revenue is recognized as the gas is produced. Drilling and development costs of producing gas wells are capitalized and amortized over a period which approximates the period of recovery of the mineral reserves. Costs relating to non-productive drilling are charged against income as incurred. Acquisition costs of unproven oil or gas properties are deferred and expensed as the leases are abandoned.

REAL ESTATE/COMMERCIAL Revenue from leasing commercial, industrial and multi-family housing properties is recognized in accordance with the provisions of the leases.

REAL ESTATE/LAND Land sale transactions are generally under agreements which require release of the land sold from the lien securing the related notes receivable approximately in proportion to the amount of cash received. Revenues and related costs are recognized as if each release was a separate sale.

REAL ESTATE/RESIDENTIAL Revenue from sale of single family and condominium living units is recognized at the close of escrow. Inventory, including property taxes and interest on construction borrowings, is relieved based on the ratio of the sales value of each unit to the estimated total sales value of the project.

Other general accounting policies are:

BASIS OF CONSOLIDATION The consolidated financial statements include the accounts of the Company and its subsidiaries, all of which are wholly owned. All significant intercompany transactions are eliminated.

MARKETABLE SECURITIES The cost of securities sold is based on the average cost of all shares of each security held at the time of sale. During fiscal 1976, the Company realized gains of $364,000 on the sale of marketable equity securities.

PROPERTY AND EQUIPMENT Property is stated at cost (or, if on hand as of March 13, 1913, at appraised value as of that date), less proceeds from sales of easements and rights of way.

Depreciation of property and equipment is provided on a straight-line basis over the estimated useful lives of the various assets. Lives used for calculating depreciation are as follows: buildings—25 to 40 years; entertainment park facilities—15 years; equipment—4 to 10 years; water supply systems, orchards, roads and other land improvements—10 to 60 years.

Expenditures for maintenance, repairs and minor renewals are charged to income as incurred; expenditures for improvements, replacements and major renewals are capitalized. Assets retired, or otherwise disposed of, are eliminated from the asset accounts along with related amounts of accumulated depreciation. Any gains or losses from disposals are included in income.

INCOME TAXES Taxes are provided on all revenue and expense items included in income, regardless of the period in which such items are recognized for tax purposes, except for items representing a permanent difference between pre-tax accounting income and taxable income. Investment tax credits are recognized in the period in which the qualifying assets are placed in service.

PER SHARE AMOUNTS Income per share is computed by dividing the applicable income by the weighted average number of shares outstanding during each year increased by the effect of dilutive stock options. Such average shares were 5,477,000 in 1976 and 5,466,000 in 1975. The conversion provisions of the debentures do not have a dilutive effect.

RETIREMENT PLANS The Company has a retirement plan covering substantially all of its employees. Pension expense is based on actuarially computed normal service costs.

Note 2. Income Taxes

The components of income tax expense are as follows (in thousands):

	1976	1975
Currently payable		
Federal	$1,913	$2,025
State	514	550
	2,427	2,575
Deferred		
Federal	2,812	3,037
State	661	551
	3,473	3,588
Taxes on income	$5,900	$6,163

The difference between the effective tax rates for fiscal 1976 and 1975 and the 48% federal income tax statutory rate can be attributed to the following (in thousands):

	1976 Amount	1976 %	1975 Amount	1975 %
Federal income tax statutory rate	$6,722	48.0	$6,431	48.0
State income taxes, net of federal income tax benefit	611	4.3	571	4.3
Investment tax credits	(556)	(4.0)	(362)	(2.7)
Excess of statutory depletion over cost depletion	(343)	(2.4)	(310)	(2.3)
Benefit of capital gains rate	(518)	(3.7)	(188)	(1.4)
Other, net	(16)	(.1)	21	.1
Income tax rate reflected in the Company's financial statements	$5,900	42.1	$6,163	46.0

The above amounts do not include a $663,000 tax benefit, attributable to the change in accounting in 1975, which reduced taxes currently payable in that year.

The provision for deferred income tax results from timing differences between the recognition of revenue and expense for pre-tax accounting income on the one hand and taxable income on the other as follows (in thousands):

	1976	1975
Excess of tax depreciation over financial statement depreciation	$ 456	$ 571
Different annual reporting period for tax and financial statement purposes	1,304	654
Cash basis accounting used for tax purposes	318	1,190
Other, net	1,395	1,173
	$3,473	$3,588

The Internal Revenue Service (IRS) has examined the federal income tax returns for the tax years 1968 through 1972 and the examination of the tax years 1973 and 1974 is currently in progress. As a result of these examinations, the IRS proposed tax deficiencies based on the tax treatment accorded gains on land sales which could have resulted in additional taxes through fiscal 1975 of approximately $2,350,000. On December 3, 1974, the Company petitioned the United States Tax Court for a redetermination of the additional tax deficiency for the years 1968 through 1970. The Company recently reached agreement with the government on the land sale issue for the years 1968 through 1970, subject to final approval by the Tax Court. In addition, the Company entered into closing agreements with the IRS with respect to this issue for all years through 1974. These agreements resulted in a total tax deficiency of approximately $1,002,000 relating to the Company's fiscal years ending February 28, 1974 and prior, which amount has been included in income taxes currently payable and charged to retained earnings as a prior period adjustment.

Note 3. Notes Payable to Banks

The Company has borrowings outstanding of $835,000 at February 29, 1976 against short-term lines of credit aggregating $17,500,000. Compensating balance requirements under the lines of credit are not material. Generally, the lines of credit are reaffirmed annually but can be withdrawn at any time at the option of the banks. Weighted average borrowings and interest rates during the fiscal year, based on amounts outstanding at each month-end, were $1,805,000 and 7.5% in 1976 and $6,285,000 and 11.1% in 1975. The maximum short-term borrowings outstanding at any month-end were $3,135,000 and $8,820,000, respectively. The interest rate applicable to the $835,000 loan outstanding at February 29, 1976 was 7.25%.

Note 4. Convertible Subordinated Debentures

The 6% subordinated debentures, payable in 1995, are convertible into common stock at $41 per share (853,659 shares are reserved for conversion). The Company has the option to redeem the debentures at premiums which decrease ratably from 104.2% in 1976 to 100% in 1990. The Company is required to make sinking fund payments beginning in 1981 of not less than 5% nor more than 10% of the aggregate principal amount of debentures outstanding on January 1, 1980. At February 29, 1976, $20,574,000 of retained earnings were free of dividend restrictions required by the terms of the debentures. During fiscal 1975, the Company recorded a gain of $177,000 arising from the purchase of debentures with a face value of $470,000. As of February 29, 1976, the Company was holding $1,222,000 face value of debentures which are available to meet future sinking fund requirements.

Note 5. Other Long-Term Liabilities

	(in thousands)	
	1976	1975
Federal Land Bank note payable	$3,154	$3,394
6% note payable	938	983
Advances from land developers for construction of water mains	611	712
Accrued retirement liability	443	476
Other	765	1,117
	5,911	6,682
Less current maturities	308	307
	$5,603	$6,375

The Federal Land Bank note provides for a variable interest rate (9% at February 29, 1976), is payable in annual instalments of $240,000 and is secured by a deed of trust on property with a book value of $2,833,000. An additional $3,800,000 line of credit from the Federal Land Bank is available to the Company.

The 6% note is payable in annual instalments of $45,000 and is secured by a deed of trust on property with a book value of $2,058,000.

The Company has entered into deferred compensation agreements with certain of its present and former officers; prior service costs of $443,000 relating to these agreements were recorded as expense in prior years.

Annual maturities of long-term liabilities for the five years ending subsequent to February 29, 1976 are as follows: 1977—$428,000; 1978—$409,000; 1979—$388,000; 1980—$393,000; 1981—$393,000.

Note 6. Retirement Plans

Retirement plan expense was $325,000 and $229,000 for 1976 and 1975, respectively. The plan is fully funded for prior and current service costs.

The Company amended certain provisions of its retirement plan during fiscal 1976 to conform to the requirements of the Employee Retirement Income Security Act of 1974. The amendments are not expected to have a material effect on the Company's results of operations.

Note 7. Stock Option and Incentive Compensation Plans

Under the terms of Newhall's Executive Incentive Plan, the Board of Directors may provide for incentive compensation awards to certain key management personnel of up to five percent of each fiscal year's income before taxes on income after reduction for the aggregate amount of dividends declared during such year. The Board of Directors authorized awards of $489,000 and $508,000 as incentive compensation under the Plan for fiscal 1976 and 1975, respectively.

Under the Stock Option Plan, adopted in fiscal 1975, qualified and nonqualified stock options may be granted at prices not less than fair market value at date of grant. The options are not exercisable for at least one year from date of grant and the term of the options may not exceed five years from date of grant for qualified options and ten years for nonqualified options. A total of 250,000 shares of common stock are reserved for grant under the Plan.

During fiscal 1975, the Company granted qualified stock options on 76,700 shares exercisable at $9.875 per share (aggregate of $757,412); 18,475 of these shares became exercisable during 1976. The market price at the date the 18,475 shares became exercisable was $12.625. During fiscal 1976, stock options on 2,800 shares were cancelled and the Company granted additional qualified stock options on 35,000 shares and nonqualified stock options on 54,200 shares at $12.375 per share (aggregate of $1,103,850). No options have been exercised to date and at February 29, 1976, an additional 86,900 shares were available for future grant.

Note 8. Composition of Certain Financial Statement Captions

	(in thousands)	
	1976	1975
MARKETABLE SECURITIES		
Commercial paper	$ 3,700	
Marketable equity securities at cost (market value $806,000 and $1,255,000; the difference between cost and market is all unrealized gains)	178	$ 435
	$ 3,878	$ 435
ACCOUNTS AND NOTES RECEIVABLE		
Trade receivables, less allowance for doubtful accounts of $379,000 and $223,000	$ 1,657	$ 2,761
Unbilled accounts receivable		
Agriculture products	2,614	3,489
Oil and gas revenues	591	539
Current receivables on land sold under land release agreements, net of deferred income of $279,000 and $976,000	56	202
Other	757	448
	$ 5,675	$ 7,439
INVENTORIES		
Agriculture inventories		
Materials and supplies	$ 918	$ 1,067
Crops in process	3,193	2,845
Harvested and processed crops	3,245	3,930
	7,356	7,842
Cattle	1,360	465
Residential construction costs	2,714	2,703
Entertainment park		
Materials and supplies	1,359	859
Retail merchandise	726	686
Other	500	719
	$ 14,015	$ 13,274

Note 8 (continued)

	(in thousands)	
	1976	1975
PROPERTY AND EQUIPMENT		
Land	$ 29,839	$ 29,471
Buildings	16,728	15,973
Entertainment park facilities	41,092	35,432
Equipment	16,440	14,384
Water supply systems, orchards, roads, etc.	21,206	18,560
Work in progress	5,225	4,294
	130,530	118,114
Accumulated depreciation	29,970	25,095
	$100,560	$ 93,019

Depreciation expense applicable to operations is as follows:

Agriculture	$1,698	$1,635
Recreation	2,582	2,313
Energy	255	175
Real Estate	518	516
Other	86	92
	$5,139	$4,731

Note 9. Conforming Fiscal Years of Subsidiaries

In fiscal 1975, management changed the fiscal year-ends of several of the Company's subsidiaries from December 31, to February 28/29. A net loss of $340,000 ($.06 per share) from the results of operations of these subsidiaries for the two months ended February 28, 1974 was charged directly to retained earnings. The change did not have a significant effect on net income for the year ended February 28, 1975 since that period included a similar loss.

Note 10. Change in Accounting Principles

In years prior to 1975, costs incurred subsequent to the end of natural cattle and farming years were deferred and charged to operations in the following period. During fiscal 1975, management determined that it would be more appropriate to expense those costs which could not be readily identified with a specific harvested crop or other revenue producing activity. The aggregate amount of such costs included in inventory at February 28, 1974, of $1,260,000, less tax benefits of $663,000, resulted in a $597,000 charge, "change in accounting", in fiscal 1975. The change had the effect of decreasing income before effect of accounting change for fiscal 1975 by approximately $240,000 ($.04 per share).

Note 11. Commitments and Contingent Liabilities

The Company is involved in litigation relating to various matters. Management is of the opinion that no material loss will result from these lawsuits.

Total rental expense for the years ended February 29, 1976 and February 28, 1975 was $3,139,000 and $1,456,000, including $1,953,000 and $828,000 for equipment rental, respectively. At February 29, 1976, the aggregate minimum rental commitments under non-cancelable leases are as follows (in thousands):

Year Ending	Equipment Rental	Other
1977	$1,250	$291
1978	736	184
1979	320	72
1980	267	12
1981	80	—

The Company has estimated construction commitments aggregating $1,181,000 at February 29, 1976.

Report of Independent Accountants

To the Board of Directors and Shareholders of The Newhall Land and Farming Company

We have examined the consolidated balance sheet of The Newhall Land and Farming Company and its subsidiaries as of February 29, 1976 and February 28, 1975, and the related consolidated statements of income and retained earnings and of changes in financial position for the years then ended. Our examinations were made in accordance with generally accepted auditing standards and accordingly included such tests of the accounting records and such other auditing procedures as we considered necessary in the circumstances.

As more fully described in Note 10 to the consolidated financial statements, the Company changed its method of accounting during fiscal 1975 for certain costs previously deferred in connection with its cattle and farming operations.

In our opinion, the consolidated financial statements examined by us present fairly the financial position of The Newhall Land and Farming Company and its subsidiaries at February 29, 1976 and February 28, 1975, and the results of their operations and the changes in their financial position for the years then ended, in conformity with generally accepted accounting principles consistently applied during the period subsequent to the change, with which we concur, made as of March 1, 1974, referred to in the preceding paragraph.

Price Waterhouse & Co.

Los Angeles, California *April 16, 1976*

Index

D

E

F

G

H

I

M

N

Q

R

S

Check list of key figures for class exercises and problems

Chapter one

CE1–1 Three
CE1–2 Total assets, $19,000
CE1–3 Plant and equipment, $22,000
CE1–5 Current assets, $43,840
CE1–6 Total assets, $75,358
P1–1 (1) Total assets, $106,500
P1–5 Total current liabilities, $26,000
P1–6 Mary Halfpenny, Capital, $115,680
P1–7 Total assets, $111,687

Chapter two

CE2–1 (1) Total assets as of March 1, 1979, $75,000
Total assets as of March 2, 1979, $105,000
Total assets as of March 3, 1979, $112,500
Total assets as of March 15, 1979, $110,000
Total assets as of March 20, 1979, $110,000
Total assets as of March 31, 1979, $110,000
CE2–2 Total assets, $1,143,000
P2–1 Total assets, $546,500
P2–3 Total assets as of May 1, 1979, $100,000
Total assets as of May 3, 1979, $104,000
Total assets as of May 5, 1979, $119,000
P2–4 (4) Total assets, $174,000
P2–5 (1) Trial balance totals, $113,900
(2) Total current assets, $45,900; total plant and equipment, $68,000
P2–6 (1) Trial balance totals, $145,000; total liabilities, $50,000; total owner's equity, $95,000
P2–8 (3) Trial balance totals, $121,200
P2–9 (A) Current liabilities, $100,000
(B) Long-term liabilities, $100,000
(C) Current assets, $50,000
(D) Owner's equity, $140,000
P2–10 (1) Trial balance totals, $115,010
(2) Total current assets, $11,360; total plant and equipment, $103,650
P2–11 Trial balance totals, $164,320; total current assets, $41,110; total plant and equipment, $123,210
P2–12 (1) Total assets, $16,950
P2–13 (2) Trial balance totals, $123,900
(3) Total current assets, $55,900

Chapter three

P3–1 The trial balance would be out of balance for each of the errors
P3–2 a, 5; b, 3; c, 1; d, 4; e, 7
P3–5 (1) Debit balance of cash, $800
P3–7 (3) Total accounts receivable, $150
P3–8 (3) Total accounts payable, $180

Chapter four

CE4–1 (3) Trial balance totals, $3,965
(4) Total accounts receivable, $360
CE4–2 (3) Trial balance totals, $7,570
(5) Net income, $820
(7) Postclosing trial balance totals, $7,070
CE4–3 (3) Postclosing trial balance totals, $75,800
P4–1 (3) Total accounts receivable, $150
P4–2 (3) Total accounts payable, $610
P4–3 Net income closed to John Duncan, Capital, $4,000
P4–4 (a) Owner's equity at beginning of year, $53,500
(b) Net income for 1979, $4,200
(c) Withdrawal by owner during 1979, $2,400
P4–5 H. Hobson, Capital, January 1, 1979, $3,950
P4–6 Commissions earned, $186,500
P4–7 Trial balance totals, $14,900
P4–8 (6) Trial balance totals, $25,375
(7) Total accounts receivable, $50
(8) Total accounts payable, $875
P4–9 (1) Net loss, $2,250
(2) Chipper Garnella, Capital, January 31, 1979, $2,750

Chapter five

CE5–1 Adjustment 6: Debit Advertising supplies, $70
Adjustment 11: Debit Accrued rent receivable, $125
P5–1 (C) Net income: cash basis, $110; accrual basis, $440
P5–2 (1) Depreciation expense, $1,200
(2) Accumulated depreciation as of December 31, 1979, $1,200; as of December 31, 1980, $2,400
(3) Book value as of December 31, 1979, $4,000; as of December 31, 1980, $2,800
P5–3 Adjustment (a): Insurance expense, $50
Adjustment (b): Advertising supplies expense, $500
Adjustment (c): Rent expense, $400
Adjustment (d): Office supplies expense, $780
Adjustment (e): Depreciation expense, $150
P5–5 (a) Office supplies expense for 1980, $2,050
(b) Expenditure for insurance premiums during 1980, $690
P5–6 Adjustment (c): Debit Office supplies expense for $150
Adjustment (g): Debit Unearned Rent for $2,400
P5–7 Adjustment (a): Debit Depreciation Expense for $3,050
Adjustment (d): Debit Prepaid Insurance for $425
P5–8 (5) Trial balance totals, $2,255.50

Chapter six

CE6–1 Net income for 1979, $12,730
CE6–2 (1) Net income, $2,615
(2) Total assets, $12,000
(3) Loren Boerner, capital, July 31, 1979, $4,330
CE6–4 (1) Net income is overstated by $124,125
P6–1 (2) Net income for 1979, $10,000
(3) Total assets, $48,000
P6–2 (2) Net income for May, $270
(3) Net loss under cash basis, $750
P6–3 Trial balance totals before adjustments, $42,150;
Adjusted trial balance totals, $44,220
P6–4 (2) Revised net income, $33,600;
Revised total assets, $119,700
P6–5 (1) Net income, $7,050
(2) Tyson Fulton, Capital, December 31, 1979, $20,050
P6–6 (7) Net income, $2,623.83
Total assets, $6,323.83
(8) Total accounts receivable, $732
Total accounts payable, $300
(13) Postclosing trial balance totals, $6,328
P6–7 The following adjustment is unusual:
(f) Debit Unearned Advertising $750
Credit Advertising Revenue $750
P6–11 (1) Optional; (3) Optional; (5) Reversing; (6) Reversing
P6–14 (1) a, b, f, and g are reversing entries.

P6–15 Balance in certain accounts before closing:
Accrued Interest Receivable, $110
Discount on Notes Payable, $160
Accrued Wages Payable, $800

P6–16 (2) The following adjusting entries should be reversed: a, d, e, f, g

P6–17 (2) The following adjustments would have an (r) in date column: Accrued Interest Receivable, Accrued Wages Payable, Accrued Interest Payable, and Unearned Rent

P6–18 (2) Revised net income, $11,975
Revised total assets, $40,900
(3) Newton Ikerd, Capital, December 31, 1979, $31,675

Chapter seven

CE7–1 (1) Cost of goods sold, $1,413
(2) Cost of goods sold, $1,398

CE7–2 (1) Adjusted Trial balance totals, $2,116,200; net income, $129,500
(2) Gross margin on sales, $389,400; net income, $129,500
(3) Capital, December 31, 1979, $788,000
(4) Total assets, $982,300

P7–1 Case (1), $10,900; Case (3), $22,900

P7–2 Gross margin on sales, $6,500

P7–3 Cash remittance, $4,282

P7–4 (a) Purchases Discounts Lost, $100

P7–6 Net income, $7,600

P7–7 Credit for payment of May 15, $2,577.32

P7–8 (1) Trial balance totals, $209,090; net income, $15,005
(2) Cost of goods sold, $78,760
(3) Capital, June 30, 1979, $77,805
(4) Total assets, $90,180

P7–9 (1) Trial balance totals, $1,005,200; net income, $50,446
(2) Cost of goods sold, $411,400; Capital, December 31, 1979, $205,146; total assets, $364,812

Chapter eight

CE8–1 Balances: Cash, $44,669; Accounts Receivable, $480; Accounts Payable, $1,790

CE8–2 Total Others Accounts Debits, $50,300

P8–1 Total sales journal, $1,555

P8–2 Total purchases journal, $2,585

P8–3 Total cash receipts, $51,204

P8–4 Total cash payments, $52,725

P8–6 Total sales journal, $5,590; cash receipts, $13,793.60

P8–7 Total cash receipts, $55,361; cash payments, $37,926

Chapter nine

CE9–1 (1) Net amount total, $962.90

CE9–2 (a) $4,000

CE9–3 (a) Accrued Salaries and Wages Payable, $2,780
(b) Payroll Tax Expense, $242.50

P9–1 (a) Accrued Wages and Salaries Payable, $4,245

P9–2 Employer's payroll tax expense, $6,400

P9–3 Total expenditure, $22,700

P9–4 (b) Payroll Tax Expense, $231

P9–6 (1) Net pay, $1,082.65

P9–7 (1) Accrued Salaries Payable, $788
(2) Payroll Tax Expense, $95.50

Chapter ten

CE10–1 (1) Column totals: Vouchers Payable, $7,500; Purchases, $3,750; Other, $3,750. Check register: Cash, $7,415
(3) Vouchers Payable, May 31, 1979, $4,500

CE10–2 Voucher #301, $2,137.50

CE10–4 July 10, Cash, $737.50; August 31, Cash, $701.36

CE10–5 (1) Adjusted cash balance, March 31, 1979, $2,445.74

P10–3 (b) Credit to Cash, $532.50

P10–4 Credit to Cash, $705

P10–5 True cash balance, April 30, 1979, $21,999.27

P10–6 Adjusted cash balance, March 31, 1979, $5,783.17

P10–7 October 2, voucher register; November 3, check register

P10–8 August 1, voucher register; August 11, general journal

P10–9 (a) October 10, Purchases Discounts, $18

P10–10 (1) Column totals: Vouchers Payable, $4,505.50; Purchases, $2,457.50; Purchases Discounts Lost, $48; Other, $2,000. Check register: Cash, $2,278
(2) Balance, $2,677.50

P10–11 Adjusted cash balance, June 30, 1979, $97,832.68

P10–12 Adjusted cash balance, April 30, 1979, $21,743.12

P10–13 (1) Column totals: Vouchers Payable, $9,338; Purchases, $3,950; Miscellaneous Selling Expenses, $75; Other, $5,313. Check register, $3,788
(3) $4,350

Chapter eleven

CE11–1 Interest expense for transactions on March 3, 1979, $55.20; April 17, 1979, $45; May 17, 1979, $8.33; June 1, 1979, $60
Adjusting entries at December 31, 1979 contain a credit to Accrued Interest Payable for $42.60 and a credit to Discount on Notes Payable for $37.50
CE11–2 (a) Effective interest, 9.21%
(b) Effective interest, 16%
CE11–3 Interest earned for transactions on February 20, 1979, $20.93; May 15, 1979, $63.75; June 1, 1979, $45
The December 31, 1979 adjusting entries contain a debit to Accrued Interest Receivable for $54.68 and a debit to Unearned Interest (included in) Face of Notes Receivable) for $22
CE11–4 Cash proceeds, $4,910.04
P11–1 The December 31, 1979 adjusting entry includes a debit to Interest Expense for $59.40
P11–2 The December 31, 1979 adjusting entry includes a credit to Discount on Notes Payable for $30
P11–3 (1) Interest-bearing note
(2) Noninterest-bearing note discounted
P11–4 (a) Effective interest, 46.5%
(b) Effective interest, 23.3%
P11–5 Maturity date for first note dated March 10, 1979 is May 9, 1979; second note dated April 4, 1979 is July 3, 1979
P11–6 (1) $48; (2) $34.50; (3) $43.20; (4) $88; (5) $95.63
P11–7 (1) $49; (3) $48
P11–8 The December 31, 1979 adjusting entry will include a debit to Accrued Interest Receivable for $34.50
P11–9 Cash proceeds for October 20, 1979 discounting is $1,820.15
P11–11 Face of note, $36,000
P11–12 Cash proceeds for Note 1, $3,021.08; Note 2, $2,026.12
P11–13 (1) Cash proceeds February 28, 1979, $3,995.35
(2) Accounts Receivable, March 31, 1979, $14,879.67
P11–14 The July 10 note will have interest of $17 in the face of the note

Chapter twelve

CE12–1 The write-off of uncollectible accounts on March 10 and November 10, 1980 is to Allowance for Doubtful Accounts
CE12–2 The write-off of uncollectible accounts on January 13, November 13, and December 13, 1980 is to Bad Debts Expense
CE12–3 (a) Bad debts expense, $5,000
(b) Bad debts expense, $1,980
P12–1 The write-off of uncollectible accounts on March 5 and April 10, 1980 is to Allowance for Doubtful Accounts
P12–2 (3) Bad Debts Expense, $1,047.66
P12–3 Cash received from customers during 1980, $576,900
P12–4 (3) Bad Debts Expense, $2,680
P12–5 (2) Allowance for Doubtful Accounts, December 31, 1981, $2,400
P12–6 December 31, 1980, Accounts Receivable, $79,900; Allowance for Doubtful Accounts, $3,400
P12–7 The write-off of uncollectible accounts on February 13 and August 13, 1979 is to Bad Debts Expense
P12–8 (a) Bad Debts Expense, $2,475
(b) Bad Debts Expense, $2,750
(c) Bad Debts Expense, $2,950
P12–9 (1) Bad Debts Expense, $2,350
P12–10 (1) Accounts Receivable under Current Assets, $177,720
(2) The credit balances in customers' accounts would be a current liability
P12–11 (1) Bad Debts Expense, $19,420
P12–12 (2) Bad Debts Expense, $1,371.32
P12–13 (1) The cash proceeds for the February 19, 1979 discounting is $8,053.23
(2) Equivalent lump-sum trade discount, 35.2%
P12–14 (2) Debit-S; Credit-CR
(3) $28,325

Chapter thirteen

CE13–1 Merchandise inventory, $48,950
CE13–2 Net income 1979, $31,000
CE13–3 LIFO periodic, $2,600; weighted average, $9,825
CE13–4 Moving average, $400.78
CE13–5 Inventory destroyed by fire, $56,621.25
CE13–6 Inventory at cost, $268.85
CE13–7 Unit basis, $2,806.25

P13–1 (2) 1978 FIFO, $271,100; (3) 1978 gross margin LIFO, $595,500; 1979 gross margin weighted average, $714,548.40
P13–2 (1) FIFO periodic inventory, $464; (2) LIFO perpetual cost of goods sold, $304; (3) weighted average periodic inventory, $432.59
P13–3 (1) LIFO periodic, $134,860; (2) FIFO perpetual cost of goods sold, $134,260
P13–4 (b) LIFO periodic, $109,500
P13–5 Estimated inventory, January 31, $63,175
P13–6 Unit basis, $22,075
P13–7 Estimated inventory at cost, $29,524.75
P13–8 (1) Estimated inventory, April 30, $525,000; (2) Estimated inventory at cost, $528,079.50
P13–9 (a) Estimated inventory, January 31, $105,094
(b) Estimated inventory, January 31, $105,600
P13–10 (1) (a) FIFO inventory, $50,880; (b) LIFO inventory, $48,960; (2) Net income, moving average, $54,657.62
P13–11 (1) (b) Moving average inventory, $11,100;
(2) Net income, FIFO, $9,600

Chapter fourteen

CE14–1 Two-year totals: (a) $44,400; (b) $76,460; (c) $90,495
CE14–2 (d) Depreciation Expense, $3,070
CE14–3 (1) Loss on Disposal, $2,273
CE14–4 Net income reductions: SL, $15,000; SYD, $24,546; DDB, $24,400
CE14–5 Depreciation Expense debits: 1979, $1,406; 1980, $2,182; 1981, $2,570
P14–2 Total cost, $20,425
P14–5 Loss on sale, $500
P14–6 (a) Loss on sale, $1,000; (b) Cost of new press, $21,000
P14–7 (b) $3,428.57
P14–9 Cost of units sold, $156,189
P14–10 (d) Depreciation Expense-Building, $8,380
P14–11 Cash increase from operations, $95,000
P14–13 Land Improvements, $7,500
P14–14 (1) (b) 1979, $17,116; (1) (d) 1980, $16,666.67
P14–15 (1) Depreciation Expense, 1981, $15,514
P14–16 (1) Net income, $321,194
P14–17 (3) Depreciation Expense, 1980, $2,965.26

Chapter fifteen

CE15–1 (3) SEC; (5) CASB
CE15–3 Net income, $128,600
P15–1 Building should be shown at $37,500 minus accumulated depreciation
P15–2 Market is less than cost
P15–3 Debit drawing account
P15–4 Warranty expense, $28,000
P15–5 (5) Stable dollar; (9) Full disclosure
P15–9 (c) Accrued Salaries and Wages Payable, $2,475

Chapter sixteen

CE16–1 Total assets, $107,300
CE16–3 (3) Total partners' equity, $48,400
CE16–5 Total stockholders' equity, $169,590
CE16–7 (4) Credit A. Sibley, Capital, $12,000
P16–1 Capital, December 31, 1979, $24,800
P16–2 Total assets, $102,000
P16–3 (b) Capital balances, December 31, 1979, $5,825 and $50
P16–4 Roth's share, $18,450
P16–5 (a) P. Woods, Capital, $50,000
P16–6 (3) Resh, Capital, $33,000
P16–7 (3) Retik, Capital, $50,500
P16–8 Cash distribution: B, $8,750; C, $33,750
P16–9 Kerr's share, $2,090
P16–11 (1) Net income, $59,500
(3) Total assets, $102,500
P16–12 June 7, Dividends, $14,300
P16–13 (3) Total stockholders' equity, $1,289,798

Chapter seventeen

CE17–1 (2) Total stockholders' equity, $2,594,000
CE17–2 (b) Total stockholders' equity, $171,500
CE17–3 (c) Premium on Common Stock, $17,000
CE17–4 Total stockholders' equity, $742,000
P17–1 July 3, Common Stock is credited, $125,000; July 3, Common Stock is credited, $2,500
P17–2 (a) Credit Common Stock, $500,000
P17–3 (4) Premium on Common Stock, $7,000
P17–4 Total cash collected, $1,291,000
P17–6 (2) Total assets, $460,300
P17–7 (2) Total assets, $222,660

Chapter eighteen

CE18–1 (3) Total stockholders' equity, $1,118,250

CE18–2 1 (b) Stockholders' equity: Before, $85,000; after, $81,000

2 (b) Stockholders' equity: Before, $85,000; after, $85,000

CE18–3 (6) Dividends—Preferred Stock, $3,375; Dividends—Common Stock, $1,845

CE18–5 (1) Book value per share of common, $7.08

(2) Book value per share of common, $6.63

P18–1 (c) Stockholders' equity before, $360,000; after, $356,400

(e) Retained earnings before, $76,500; after, $60,750

P18–4 Credit Donated Capital for $140,000

P18–5 (d) Paid-in Capital—Excess from Reduction of Stated Value, $1,500

(e) Memorandum entry; new stated value, $1.50 per share

P18–6 (a) No effect

P18–7 (2) Total stockholders' equity, $728,400

P18–8 (3) Total stockholders' equity, $338,200

P18–9 (1) Book value per share of common, $78.50

P18–10 (3) Total stockholders' equity, $1,405,500

P18–11 (1) Net adjustment, $202

P18–12 (1) Total stockholders' equity, $2,478,000

(3) Book value, common, $61.18 a share; book value, preferred, $109 a share

Chapter nineteen

CE19–1 Sales taxes paid on January 15, 1980, $160

CE19–2 (4) The debit to Interest Expense on December 31, 1979 is $7,466.67

CE19–3 (1) The debit to Bond Interest Expense on December 31, 1979 for each Case: (A) $18,000; (B) $17,600; (C) $18,600; (D) $17,796.61

(3) Effective interest: Case B, 8.7%; Case C, 9.4%

CE19–4 The total bond interest expense for the year 1979, $18,630; 1980, $21,390. The gain on retirement of bonds, $3,040

CE19–5 (2) The credit to Interest Earned on:
December 31, 1980, $3,000
December 31, 1981, $6,000
December 31, 1982, $9,000

P19–1 The April 30, 1979 sales taxes payable, $210

P19–2 (2) The adjustment to Sales, $512.50

P19–3 (3) The December 31, 1979 adjustment would include a debit to Bond Interest Expense for $20,000

P19–4 (2 & 3) Monthly interest expense, $1,500

P19–5 The weekly total of the debit to Accounts Receivable, $53,841.84

P19–6 The debit balances in creditors' accounts would be shown under current assets; the accounts payable amount of $36,000 would be a current liability

P19–7 Total current liabilities, $67,550

P19–8 (3) The December 31, 1979 adjusting entry would include a debit to Bond Interest Expense, $22,650

P19–9 (4) Bond Interest Expense account balance as of December 31, 1979, $44,500

(6) Effective interest, 8.8%

P19–10 (4) Bond Interest Expense account balance as of December 31, 1979, $16,600

(6) Effective interest, 8.4%

P19–11 The total bond interest expense for 1979, $17,217.39; 1987, $28,695.65

P19–12 The total bond interest expense for 1979, $26,576.27; 1980, $45,559.33

P19–13 The total bond interest expense for 1979, $28,711.86; 1980, $49,220.33

P19–14 (2) The balance in the Premium on Bonds Payable at:
December 31, 1979, $6,875
December 31, 1981, $5,375
December 31, 1986, $1,625

P19–15 (a) (1 & 2) Debit Bond Sinking Fund for $100,000 and $94,000

(b) (1) Debit Retained Earnings at end of each year for $100,000

P19–16 (1) Original issue price, $523,800 plus accrued interest

P19–17 (1) Face of bonds, $265,700
Original issue price, $256,340 plus accrued interest

P19–18 Bond interest expense for 1979 under each case:
(1) $36,000
(2) $35,325
(3) $24,455.70

P19–19 Plan 1 probably should be used; it would have $12,000,000 of income available to common shareholders

Chapter twenty

CE20–1 The realized gain on disposal of marketable securities on the October 2 sales was $4,410.
The debit to Accrued Interest Receivable on December 31, 1979 was $2,000

CE20–2 (1) The bonds could be valued either: at cost, $78,580, or at lower of cost or market, $77,250
(2) The realized loss on February 1, 1980 sale, $500; March 1, 1980 sale, $1,100

CE20–3 (1) The total dividends earned amount for 1979, $16,000

CE20–4 (a) Subsidiary Income for first six months, $40,000
(b) Subsidiary Loss for last six months, $12,000

CE20–5 The total bond interest earned for 1979 under each Case: (A) $1,800; (B) $1,815; (C) $14,831.93

P20–1 Temporary Investment in Marketable Securities, $102,568

P20–2 The realized gain on disposal of temporary investments on August 1, $435

P20–3 (2) The lower of cost market value of temporary investments, $65,800
(3) The realized loss on sales in 1980:
January 16, 1980 sale, $300
February 15, 1980 sale, $550

P20–4 The revenue amounts earned in 1979:
Dividends earned, $1,000
Bond Interest Earned, $6,125

P20–5 The realized loss on the sale of the temporary investments on February 1, 1980, $2,000

P20–6 The total dividends earned for 1979, $10,300

P20–7 The total bond interest earned for 1979, $26,250

P20–8 The total bond interest earned for 1979, $27,300

P20–9 Face value of bonds, $123,340

P20–10 The credit to Subsidiary Income on December 31, 1979, $60,000

P20–11 The total bond interest earned for 1979; $8,213.33; 1980, $12,320

P20–12 The total bond interest earned for 1979, $24,720; 1987, $19,226.67

P20–13 (1) Original face value of bonds, $185,000
Original purchase price, $188,480 plus accrued interest

P20–14 Effective yield on each of the four bonds: (1) 9.4%; (2) 8.1%; (3) 8.9%; (4) 9%

P20–15 (1) Total dividends earned recognized in 1979, $12,750
(2) Total subsidiary income recognized in 1979, $59,250
(3) Equity method follows current GAAP

P20–16 The total revenue recognized during 1979:
Bond Interest Earned, $77,981.78
Dividends Earned, $150,000
Subsidiary Income, $24,600

P20–17 (3) Bad debts expense should be based on 0.5% of credit sales instead of 1%

Chapter twenty-one

CE21–1 Decrease in working capital, $11,200
Working capital provided by operations, $600

CE21–2 Increase in working capital, $403,500
Working capital provided by operations, $268,500

CE21–3 (1) Increase in working capital, $162
Working capital provided by operations, $326
(2) Cash provided by operations, $336

CE21–4 (1) Working capital provided by operations, $28,600

P21–1 Items, 1, 2, 3, 4, and 8-no effect; 5 and 6-use; 7-source

P21–2 Items 4, 8 would be both a source and use; Item 5 would be a mixture

P21–3 Original cost of machinery sold, $90,000
Proceeds from sale of machinery, $6,000

P21–4 Funds provided or (used) for: (a) 17,000; (b) ($13,000); (c) $61,500; (d) $47,000; (e) ($17,950)

P21–5 Increase in working capital, $22,000
Working capital provided by operations, $148,000

P21–6 Cash received from customers for Company 1, $191,000; Company 2, $297,500

P21–7 Cash paid to suppliers for Company 1, $144,000; Company 2, $175,000

P21–8 Cash provided by operations, $46,000

P21–9 Decrease in working capital, $41,750
Working capital provided by operations, $88,000

P21–10 Increase in working capital, $134,500
Working capital provided by operations, $89,500

P21–11 Increase in working capital, $15,400
Working capital provided by operations, $7,400

P21–12 Increase in working capital, $470,750
Working capital provided by operations, $313,250

P21–13 Increase in working capital, $60,000
Working capital provided by operations, $192,000

Chapter twenty-two

CE22–1 (1) Net income, $105,000; retained earnings, December 31, 1979, $115,000

CE22–2 (1) Net sales, (10.0%); Net income, (17.8%)

CE22–3 (1) Sales (net) 1979, 109.3%; 1980, 115.7%; 1981, 125.0%

CE22–4 (1) (a) Common-size percentages for current assets, December 31, 1978, 37.5%; December 31, 1979, 27.6%
(b) Common-size percentages for net income for 1978, 14.47%; for 1979, 8.72%
(c) Net income: 1978, $0.14; 1979, $0.09

P22–1 Sales increase, 29%; Cash increase, 33%

P22–2 Common-size percentages: Net income for 1978, 3.8%; for 1979, 6.3%

P22–3 Percent of increase for total assets, 10.2%

P22–4 Common-size percentages: current assets, December 31, 1978, 35.8%; December 31, 1979, 44.2%

P22–5 Net income, $0.113

P22–7 (1) Net income, $37,000; retained earnings, December 31, 1979, $65,000
(2) Net income after extraordinary items, $37,000

P22–8 Net assets, $1,216,400

P22–9 Acid-test ratio, 0.87 to 1; inventory turnover, 2.31; number of times bond interest earned, 22.50

P22–10 Adjusted Trial Balance totals, $744,000

Chapter twenty-three

CE23–1 Materials used, $594,750

CE23–2 Cost of goods sold, $885,000

CE23–3 Balances: Cash, $20,850; Accounts Payable, $9,750;
(2) Cost of goods manufactured, $115,350

CE23–4 (a) Totals manufacturing columns, $630,000; (b) Cost of goods manufactured, $435,000; (c) Net income, $135,000; (d) Total assets, $825,000

P23–1 (a) Cost of goods manufactured, $245,000;
(b) Cost of goods sold, $240,000

P23–2 Materials used, $20,000; net cost of materials purchased, $28,000

P23–3 (1) Transportation In-Materials, $2,025;
(2) Materials purchases discounts, $150;
(3) Cost of materials used, $22,350

P23–4 (1) Beginning inventory of finished goods, $15,000;
(2) Net sales, $151,500;
(3) Ending inventory of finished goods, $15,750

P23–6 Small tools used, $12,500

P23–8 (1) Cost of goods manufactured, $1,290,450;
(2) Cost of goods sold, $1,294,350;
(3) Gross margin, $455,650

P23–9 (1) Cost of goods manufactured, $179,400

P23–10 (1) Cost of goods manufactured, $1,146,300;
(2) Gross margin, $994,200;
(3) Total current assets, $1,345,500

P23–11 (1) Cash, $358,500, Accounts receivable, $447,000;
(3a) Cost of goods manufactured, $1,042,215; net income, $396,420;
(3e) Total assets, $1,960,920

P23–12 (1) Cost of goods manufactured, $432,000;
(2) Gross margin, $495,000

Chapter twenty-four

CE24–1 Cost per unit, $26.07

CE24–2 (2) Debit amount, $28,580

CE24–3 (1) $5; (2) 80%; (3) 166⅔%

CE24–4 (2) Work in Process Inventory, $45,000; (3) Job 101, $49,875

P24–1 (1) Total cost, $673.50

P24–2 (1) $1,800; (3) $8,680; (5) $5,940

P24–3 Manufacturing overhead, $1,500
P24–5 (1) $7 per direct labor hour; (3) 80% of materials cost
P24–6 (4) Income Summary (debit), $43,390.07
P24–7 (1) Finished Goods Inventory (debit), $85,650;
(2) Work in Process Inventory, $37,650

Chapter twenty-five

CE25–1 Total accounted for, 50,000 units
CE25–2 Materials, 4,500 units; labor and overhead, 4,550 units
CE25–3 Cost of 7,500 units, $63,750
P25–1 Materials, 88,650 units; labor and overhead, 89,100 units
P25–2 (3) Cost transferred to finished goods, $396,000;
(4) Work in Process, $44,400
P25–3 (1) Cost of goods sold, $817,850.10;
(2) Cost of finished goods, $84,149.89
P25–4 (a) Equivalent units, February, 13,950 units;
(b) Materials cost, January, $6.50; labor cost, February, $8.20; overhead cost, March, $9.60;
(c) Cost to be accounted for, March, $366,642;
(d) Completed units, March, $354,222;
(e) Work in Process, March 31, $12,420
P25–5 (1) Process 1, materials, 12,000 units; labor and overhead, 10,500 units;
(2) Unit costs, Process 2, materials, $0.43\frac{1}{3}$; labor, $1.00; overhead, $0.80; (3) Completed and transferred, Process 2, $27,750;
(4) Work in Process, Process 1, $14,700
P25–6 Grinding, transferred out, $69,000; Blending, transferred out, $115,560; Work in Process, $45,150

Chapter twenty-six

CE26–1 Fourth quarter: Product X, 2,640 units, $39,600; Product Y, 2,750 units, $33,000; Product Z, 2,338 units, $46,760
CE26–2 (1) Product A: First quarter, 20,200 units; second quarter, 21,600 units; third quarter, 19,200 units; fourth quarter, 28,500 units;
(2) Total materials for Product B, 294,500 lb., $176,700;
(3) Total labor for Product C, 10,280 hours, $77,100;
(4) Total variable manufacturing cost, $2,080,380
CE26–3 (1) Cash balance forecast for June 30, $38,680
CE26–4 (1) Total variance, $255 U
CE26–5 (1) At 80%, $304,000; at 90%, $312,000; at 110%, $328,000;
(2) Materials Quantity Variance, $4,920 U; Labor Efficiency Variance, $3,000 U; (3) Work in Process Inventory, $8,400
P26–1 Production required, Standard, 109,600 units; Premium, 96,000 units; Supreme, 119,200 units
P26–2 (1) Total sales, 66,000 units, $7,920,000;
(2) Production required, December, 37,000 units
P26–3 Material A-31: July, 38,400 units, $7,680; August, 40,500 units, $8,100; September, 44,600 units, $8,920
P26–4 Labor for September, $132,200
P26–5 Adjusted budget, $83,200; total variance, $768 F
P26–6 Cash balance forecast for March 31, $6,000
P26–7 Total sales, Product B, 36,100 units, $9,927,500
P26–8 Purchase price variance, $560 U; materials quantity variance, $90 U
P26–9 Wage rate variance, $832 U; labor efficiency variance, $480 F
P26–10 Materials Price Variance, $7,680 U; Wage Rate Variance, $4,953.60 U

Chapter twenty-seven

CE27–1 (1) S_{bep}, $600,000; (2) S_{bep}, $900,000; (3) S_{bep}, + $90,000, $1,050,000; (4) Net income, $90,000
CE27–2 Additional income, $480,000
CE27–3 (2) Savings from buying, $1,800
CE27–4 (2) Net income without B, $4,150
CE27–5 (1) Payback, 4 years; (3) 30%; (4) excess present value, $9,624;
(5) profitability index, 1.048
P27–1 (1) Break-even point, 114,286 units (rounded)
P27–2 (1) Break-even point before acquisition, 100,572 units (rounded); after, 82,234 units (rounded); (2) break-even point, 96,447 units (rounded)
P27–3 S_{bep}, $2,660,832.80
P27–4 Annual cash flow, $126,750; payback period, 4.02 years
P27–5 Reject offers (a), (b) and (d)

P27–6 (1) S_{bep}, \$112,868.20; (2) net income, \$309,120; (3) margin of safety, \$559,132 (rounded)

P27–7 (1) S_{bep}, \$1,200,000; (2) 75%; (3) margin of safety, \$400,000; (4) percentage of safety, 25%; (5) 17½%; (6) net income, \$280,000

P27–8 (b) Savings to buy, (\$1,500)

P27–9 (2) Projected 1980 income, \$115,000

P27–10 Payback, 3⅓ years; return on original investment, 10%

P27–11 (1) Payback, 5 years; (2) return on original investment, 15%; (4) excess present value, \$3,715; (5) profitability index, 1.186

P27–12 At 50,000 cases: S_{bep}, \$7,826,086, profit as % of sales, 16.7%, net income, \$2,000,000; at 60,000 cases: S_{bep}, \$8,142,856, profit as % of sales, 25.4% net income, \$3,650,000

Chapter twenty-eight

CE28–1 Tax liability outstanding, \$407.50

CE28–2 (2) Federal income tax after general tax credit, \$21,287

CE28–3 Corporate income tax, \$168,900

CE28–4 (2) The December 31, 1980 balance in Deferred Income Tax Liability, \$0; Income Taxes Payable, \$45,000

P28–1 Gross Income, \$16,500

P28–2 Federal income tax, \$50,760

P28–3 (1) c; (2) b

P28–4 (1) c; (2) a

P28–5 (1) d; (2) e; (3) a; (4) c

P28–6 Adjusted gross income, \$14,050

P28–7 Tax liability outstanding, \$833.15

P28–8 Adjusted gross income: (1) \$15,000; (2) \$7,000; (3) \$7,000; (4) \$12,000; (5) \$9,300

P28–9 (1) Refund due, \$450.50
(2) Tax liability outstanding, \$222.50

P28–10 (2) Federal income tax after general tax credit, \$8,647.50

P28–11 The federal income tax, \$259,620

P28–12 Remaining tax liability, \$147

P28–13 (a) Estimated gross income for corporation, \$53,900; for partnership (share), \$78,000
(b) (2) After issuance of stock, Adams owns 68%
(c) Corporation tax, \$34,500
(d) Income tax after general tax credit, \$14,950

P28–14 December 31, 1981 balance in Deferred Income Tax Liability, \$69,300

P28–15 (1) Net income before income tax on income statement, \$219,400